PENGUIN BOOKS

THE PENGUIN INDIA REFERENCE YEARBOOK 2007

Derek O'Brien is Asia's best-known knowledge game show host. The host of *The Cadbury Bournvita Quiz Contest*, Derek is also the quizmaster for *The Brand Equity Quiz*. Besides quizzing, Derek and his team of more than seventy associates have been working closely with teachers and students for more than a decade now to make knowledge available in a fun and interesting way. In addition to *The Penguin India Reference Yearbook*, Derek compiles and edits *The Penguin–CNBC-TV18 Business Yearbook* for Penguin Books.

Content for *The Penguin India Reference Yearbook 2007* was provided by Amit Ghosh, Nayan Chaudhury, Shalini Chaudhury, Anik Ghosal, Anushtup Haldar, Indrani Bhattacharya, Sreevalsa Menon, Sarbajit Ghosh and Debkumar Mitra at Derek O'Brien and Associates Pvt Ltd, and supplemented by inputs from the editorial team at Penguin Books India.

The Penguin India
REFERENCE YEARBOOK 2007

Compiled and Edited by
Derek O'Brien

PENGUIN BOOKS

PENGUIN BOOKS
Published by the Penguin Group
Penguin Books India Pvt Ltd, 11 Community Centre, Panchsheel Park, New Delhi 110 017, India
Penguin Group (USA) Inc., 375 Hudson Street, New York, NY 10014, USA
Penguin Group (Canada), 90 Eglinton Avenue East, Suite 700, Toronto, Ontario, M4P 2Y3, Canada (a division of Pearson Penguin Canada Inc.)
Penguin Books Ltd, 80 Strand, London WC2R 0RL, England
Penguin Ireland, 25 St Stephen's Green, Dublin 2, Ireland (a division of Penguin Books Ltd)
Penguin Group (Australia), 250 Camberwell Road, Camberwell, Victoria 3124, Australia (a division of Pearson Australia Group Pty Ltd)
Penguin Group (NZ), cnr Airborne and Rosedale Roads, Albany, Auckland 1310, New Zealand (a division of Pearson New Zealand Ltd)
Penguin Group (South Africa) (Pty) Ltd, 24 Sturdee Avenue, Rosebank, Johannesburg 2196, South Africa

Penguin Books Ltd, Registered Offices: 80 Strand, London WC2R 0RL, England

First published by Penguin Books India 2006

10 9 8 7 6 5 4 3 2 1

ISBN 10: 0-14310-087-4
ISBN 13: 978-0-14310-087-4

Typeset in Humanst521 BT by InoSoft Systems, Noida
Printed at Sanat Printers, Kundli, Haryana

Cover design by Hatch Design

Publisher's Note

We are proud to present the third edition of the phenomenally successful *Penguin India Reference Yearbook*, and we hope that you will find this year's Yearbook to be even better than before. The 2007 edition of the Yearbook is a special issue with 'Sixty Years of Indian Independence' as its theme. There are 80 more pages to this year's edition, and the total of 1056 pages are packed with useful information of every kind.

The cover story for this year's edition, on the theme of 'Sixty Years of Indian Independence', examines various areas of the country's development and achievements. This section features pieces by A.P.J. Abdul Kalam, Edward Luce, John Wright, Mani Shankar Aiyar, Manoj Joshi, Namrata Joshi, Pratap Bhanu Mehta, Prem Shankar Jha, Rajmohan Gandhi, Sanjay Suri, Sitaram Yechuri, Urvashi Butalia, Usha Albuquerque and William Dalrymple. A number of these feature articles were written exclusively for this publication.

This year's Yearbook introduces a section titled '100 Indians Who Are Changing India'. This section includes profiles of a hundred people, from A.P.J. Abdul Kalam and A.R. Rahman to Vir Sanghvi and Yogi Deveshwar, who are making a difference in India today and changing the way we look at ourselves as Indians. The 'Newsmakers' segment of this year's special edition is also significantly enhanced, to include and comment on every major happening that has taken place in India and the world over the past twelve months.

Another special feature of this year's Yearbook is its quizzes. In 2007, Penguin India celebrates its twentieth anniversary, and to mark this occasion, this year's Yearbook carries a special 20/20 quiz, featuring 400 questions (20 questions each in 20 sets) on various topics related to India. In addition, there is a collection of 500 all-new quiz questions on India's post-Independence history and current affairs in the GK section.

The sections on Politics, Economy, Science, Career, Sports, Arts and General Knowledge have been completely revised and updated for this year's edition, and feature substantial new information along with easy-to-refer-to news segments. In addition, of course, *The Penguin India Reference Yearbook 2007* retains all the popular features of its first two editions, including India and world datelines, historical timelines, colour maps and flags, and a comprehensive index. The India and World sections add up to some 500 pages, and have been thoroughly updated for this year's edition, and over 200 small maps have been included for easy reference.

As always, *The Penguin India Reference Yearbook* prides itself on the authenticity, currency and comprehensiveness of the information that it contains. All information is fully updated till 1 November 2006.

We hope that you will find this year's Yearbook to be useful through the year as a desk reference and ready reckoner. Please do keep writing in to us with your comments and suggestions on the Yearbook. You can reach us at editorial@in.penguingroup.com. For bulk purchases and institutional orders, please contact sales@in.penguingroup.com.

Contents

The Penguin 20/20 Quiz

Festivals of India

1. Which sixteenth century Vaishnava saint-poet's birth anniversary is celebrated on *Dol Purnima*?
2. What does the Sikh community celebrate just a day after Holi?
3. The Sindhi festival *Cheti Chand* is celebrated in honour of which deity?
4. In which temple in Tamil Nadu is the *Cittirai* Festival held?
5. In which festival in Bihar is the rising sun and the setting sun worshipped?
6. In the honour of which god is *Ananta Chaturdashi* celebrated?
7. According to the Malayalam calendar, in which month is Onam celebrated?
8. Which festival was known as *Bhratri-dvitiya* in Vedic times?
9. Along the banks of which river is the Sonepur Mela held?
10. In honour of which sage is *Guru Purnima* celebrated?
11. Which festival is known as *Saluno* in Haryana?
12. In which month of the Jewish calendar is Purim celebrated?
13. In which state is *Shigmoutsav* celebrated?
14. Which festival were the Sikhs celebrating at the Jallianwala Bagh, when the massacre happened in 1919?
15. Which festival means 'dedication' in Hebrew?
16. The people of which religion celebrate *Tu bi-shevat*, a New Year for trees which is symbolized by planting of trees?
17. *Dhanteras*, held before the main festival of *Deepavali*, is celebrated in honour of Dhanvantari. What is Dhanvantari the god of?
18. Which Sikh guru organized the Khalsa?
19. The Guruvayur Temple Festival, celebrated on the ekadashi day of Karttika, commemorates the installation of the image of which deity?
20. In which state is the Jwalamukhi Festival celebrated?

Answers

1. Chaitanya Mahaprabhu 2. Holla Mohalla 3. Udero Lal 4. The Meenakshi temple in Madurai 5. Chhath Festival 6. Vishnu 7. Chingam 8. *Bhaiya Duj* 9. Gandak 10. Veda Vyasa 11. *Raksha Bandhan* 12. Adar 13. Goa 14. *Baisakhi* 15. *Hanukka* 16. Jews 17. Medicine 18. Guru Gobind Singh 19. Krishna 20. Himachal Pradesh

The Penguin 20/20 Quiz

India and the Asian Games

1. In which Asian Games was kabaddi introduced as a medal sport?
2. Which is the only Asian city to have hosted the Asian Games on four occasions between 1951 and 2002?
3. In the history of the Asian Games, when has India achieved its best standing in the overall medals tally?
4. Who scored the winning goal to bag the football gold in the inaugural Asiad?
5. The 2002 Asian Games were held in which Korean city?
6. In the 10th Asian Games held at Seoul in 1986, who won 4 gold medals and 1 silver medal in the track and field events?
7. Which Indian won two golds and a silver at the 1998 Bangkok Asiad?
8. At which Asiad was kho-kho introduced as a demonstration sport?
9. Who was the Indian captain when India won the Asian Games gold medal in hockey for the second time?
10. Which Indian sprinter won four gold medals, two in each Asian Games, held in 1958 and 1962 respectively?
11. Whose long jump effort of 8.07 m at the Teheran Asiad is ranked among the highest in the annals of Indian sport?
12. What was the name of the mascot of the 1982 Asian Games?
13. In which year did the Indian women's hockey team win gold for the first time in the Asian Games?
14. In which country were the 2006 Asian Games held?
15. When India won the football gold in 1951, they beat Iran. Which team did they beat to win the gold in 1962?
16. In the 1998 Asian Games, the men's finals standings were India (gold), Pakistan (silver) and Bangladesh (bronze). Which sport is being referred to?
17. Which female athlete took an oath on behalf of all competitors at the opening ceremony function of the 1982 Asiad?
18. Name the bantamweight boxer who won a gold medal for India at the 1998 Asian Games held at Bangkok.
19. Who won the 800 m run in the 1982 Asiad with a timing of 1 minute, 46.81 seconds?
20. Who won two gold medals in tennis at the 1994 Hiroshima Asiad?

Answers

1. Beijing Asiad, 1990 2. Bangkok 3. First Asiad, New Delhi, 34 medals 4. Sahu Mewalal 5. Busan 6. P. T. Usha 7. Jyotirmoyee Sikdar 8. 1982 9. Dhanraj Pillay, 1998 10. Milkha Singh 11. T. C. Yohannan 12. Appu 13. 1982 14. Qatar 15. South Korea 16. Kabaddi 17. Geeta Zutshi 18. Dingko Singh 19. Charles Borromeo 20. Leander Paes

The Penguin 20/20 Quiz

Indian Railways

1. Who designed the Victoria Terminus?
2. In 1863, who formally opened the extension of the GIP Railway over the Bhor Ghat section into the Deccan Plateau?
3. In 1852, what was the name given to the locomotive that was used to carry material for the construction of railway services in Mumbai?
4. The 'Great Indian Rover' was launched on 10 February 1983. This train was built so that people could visit the sites associated with which religion?
5. Fill in the blank to complete the following statement: 'In 1886, W. Newman & Co. published the first Newman's Indian _______ for train timetables.'
6. Darjeeling Himalayan Railway is the second in the world to be conferred the World Heritage status by UNESCO. Which is the first?
7. Apart from Miraj in Maharashtra and New Jalpaiguri in West Bengal, which other station in India is served by all the three gauges namely - broad, metre and narrow?
8. Delhi Main station holds the record for being equipped with the largest Route Relay Interlocking system. Which company completed the changeover in a record time of 44 hours?
9. What were the names of the three locomotives that hauled the fourteen railway carriages of the first train?
10. In association with which company did Indian Railways introduce the rail credit cards in June 1999?
11. In 1997, Indian Railways ran two exhibition trains. The first one started from Kanyakumari. From where did the second start?
12. To which zone does the Calcutta Metro Rail belong?
13. What is the name of the mascot of the Indian Railways?
14. Who blamed the Railways for carrying 'the pest of westernization'?
15. Which train passes through the most number of Indian states?
16. In which state is the longest platform of the world located?
17. At which railway station in Bihar was L. N. Mishra, the then Railway Minister, assassinated on 2 January 1975?
18. Which is the southernmost station of India?
19. Which railway station serves Lucknow?
20. Who was the Railway minister at the time of the Gaisal train accident?

Answers

1. Fredrick William Stevens 2. Sir Bartle Frere 3. Steam Iron Horse 4. Buddhism 5. Bradshaw 6. Semmering Railway of Austria 7. Yelahanka in Karnataka 8. Siemens Ltd 9. Sultan, Sindh, Sahib 10. Standard Chartered Bank 11. Porbandar 12. None 13. Bholu 14. Mahatma Gandhi 15. Himsagar Express 16. West Bengal. 17. Samastipur 18. Kanyakumari 19. Charbagh 20. Ram Vilas Paswan

The Year in Review

India Dateline

October 2005

1: Vice-Admiral Sureesh Mehta assumes command of the Eastern Naval Command of the Indian Navy. The Jammu and Kashmir Assembly introduces a Bill seeking to make provisions for the application of the Muslim Personal Law (Shariat) to Muslims in the state.

2: The Indian delegation at the World Trade Organization submits a revised offer in August 2005 in the ongoing negotiations under the General Agreement on Trade in Services (GATS) of the WTO. The revised offer is conditional on other WTO members.

3: India and Pakistan sign an agreement making it obligatory for either country to notify the other at least seventy-two hours before testing ballistic missiles within a 40-km radius of the International Boundary and the Line of Control (LoC). The Union Health and Family Welfare Ministry suggests an increase in the retirement age of doctors, with a compulsory stint in rural areas and the last posting preferably near their home towns. The Supreme Court declares that until further orders, the rules framed by the Centre empowering states to relax the ban on use of loudspeakers till midnight during festivals and religious activities for fifteen days in a year would remain in force.

5: The Union ministries of tourism and health and family welfare decide to start a website and create a database to promote health tourism in India.

6: The Union Cabinet approves the creation of the 'Prarambhik Shiksha Kosh' (PSK) with the money collected from the education cess since the last fiscal year. India signs a deal to construct six French submarines in the country at a cost of over Rs 15,000 crore.

7: The Supreme Court declares the 23 May Presidential Proclamation, dissolving the Bihar Assembly, unconstitutional.

8: In a major earthquake, over 300 people are killed and more than 700 injured in Jammu and Kashmir. The Centre offers an assistance of Rs100 crore to Jammu and Kashmir for relief operations in quake-affected areas of the border state. Mittal Steel Company (MSC) NV signs three MoUs with the Jharkhand government for setting up a mining and steel-making facility and for improving the technical skills and education facilities in the state.

9: The Ratnagiri Gas and Power Private Ltd, the new entity of the defunct Dabhol Power Project, starts operations. The Board of Control for Cricket in India (BCCI) serves a cautionary reminder to the seventeen contracted players and those selected for

The Penguin 20/20 Quiz

Chandigarh

1. Which is the highest building in Chandigarh?
2. What was Rock Garden creator Nek Chand's original occupation?
3. Which flower garden is supposedly Asia's largest?
4. What popular epithet does Chandigarh enjoy?
5. Which two states have their government offices in Chandigarh?
6. Near the foothills of which famous range does Chandigarh lie?
7. In Chandigarh, what does 'SCO' stand for?
8. Who were originally appointed by the Punjab government to plan Chandigarh?
9. In Chandigarh, what is known as the system of 7V's?
10. Name the artificial lake that lies to the south-west of the Rock Garden.
11. Le Corbusier designed Chandigarh. What was his original name?
12. How did Chandigarh get its name?
13. Chandigarh is made up of how many numbered sectors?
14. It was initially called the Rose Festival. By what name is it known today in Chandigarh?
15. What in Sector 17 was designed by Le Corbusier as the 'Pedestrian's Paradise'?
16. Which Chandigarh-born Indian cricketer's father represented India in a Test match against New Zealand in 1981?
17. Which section of the Leisure Valley has been set aside to allow the people to plant trees in memory of the deceased?
18. Who was Chandigarh's first Chief Commissioner?
19. Le Corbusier's edict on the city of Chandigarh says that: 'No personal statues shall be erected in the city or parks of Chandigarh'. Therefore, where, according to the edict, will the commemoration of persons take place?
20. Which Indian personality said this about Chandigarh: 'Let this be a new town symbolic of the freedom of India... Chandigarh is rightly associated with the name of Goddess Chandi—Shakti, or power'?

Answers

1. The Secretariat 2. Road Inspector 3. The Rose Garden 4. 'City Beautiful' 5. Punjab and Haryana 6. Shivalik Hills 7. Shop-Cum-Office 8. American town planner Albert Mayer and Polish architect Matthew Nowicki 9. The Roads of Chandigarh 10. Sukhna Lake 11. Charles Edouard Jeanneret 12. From the Chandi Mandir located in the village Mani Majra 13. 47 (There is no Sector 13 as 13 is considered an unlucky number) 14. Festival of Gardens 15. The central plaza 16. Yuvraj Singh 17. Smriti Upavana 18. Dr M.S. Randhawa 19. Bronze plaques 20. Jawaharlal Nehru

the tour of Zimbabwe to refrain from going public on the contentious episode involving Sourav Ganguly and coach Greg Chappell.

10: The death toll in the Jammu and Kashmir earthquake rises to 927, including 619 in Baramulla and 301 in Kupwara, the worst-affected frontier districts. Former Lok Sabha Speaker and All-India Trinamool Congress leader P.A. Sangma resigns from the fourteenth Lok Sabha.

11: The Election Commission issues notice to Rajya Sabha member Jaya Bachchan on a complaint that she is holding an office of profit and that she should be disqualified.

12: N.R. Narayana Murthy, chairman and chief mentor, Infosys Technologies, declares his retirement as executive chairman of the company in August 2006.

13: The ministry for petroleum and natural gas announces a bio-diesel policy. It will come into force from 1 January 2006. The national selection committee appoints Rahul Dravid as captain for the forthcoming one-day series against Sri Lanka and South Africa. Dravid replaces Sourav Ganguly, who led India in a record 49 Tests and 147 one-day internationals.

14: The Centre turns down the G.T. Nanavati and K.G. Shah Commission's request to furnish a copy of the correspondence between the former President, K.R. Narayanan, and the then prime minister, Atal Bihari Vajpayee, on the Gujarat riots. The ministry of consumer affairs, food and public distribution prepares a national building code, which can help to minimize disasters due to natural calamities such as earthquakes.

15: A unit of women 'Black Cat' commandos is created in the elite National Security Guards (NSG) for the first time in the country.

16: The draft paper on National Strategy for Manufacturing is brought out by the National Manufacturing Competitiveness Council (NMCC).

17: The architect of the 'white revolution,' Verghese Kurien, is re-elected as the chairman of the Gujarat Co-operative Milk Marketing Federation (GCMMF) for another three years.

18: An estimated 43 per cent of the 1.23-crore electorate exercise their franchise in the first phase of polling for the fifty-seven Assembly seats in Bihar. A total of 541 candidates, including thirty-seven women, are in the fray. The President appoints Justice Yogesh Kumar Sabharwal, the seniormost judge of the Supreme Court, as the thirty-sixth Chief Justice of India, with effect from 1 November. Ratan Tata is announced chairman of the group's privately held company, Tata Teleservices Ltd.

20: The Union Cabinet announces the increasing of the limit of foreign direct investment (FDI) in telecom from 49 to 74 per cent. It addresses the clarifications sought by the stakeholders, including cellular companies and equipment manufacturers. The Board of Control for Cricket in India's (BCCI) marketing committee awards the telecast rights of the two one-day series of twelve matches, involving India–Sri Lanka and India–South Africa, to Prasar Bharati at a cost of Rs 90 crore and the production right to Trans World International (TWI) at a cost of Rs 6.93 crore. Infosys chairman and chief mentor N.R. Narayana Murthy resigns as chairman of Bangalore International Airport Ltd (BIAL) following remarks made by former prime minister H.D. Deve Gowda questioning his contribution to the idea of the greenfield airport coming up at Devanahalli.

21: The India–Mexico Joint Commission signs five agreements in foreign service training, culture, scientific cooperation, education and diplomatic and official visa exemptions.

22: The Union ministry of civil aviation approves an integrated modernization package for Tiruchi airport.

The Penguin 20/20 Quiz

Bhimsen Joshi

1. Which was the first National Award to be conferred upon Pandit Bhimsen Joshi?
2. Name the album that Pandit Bhimsen Joshi cut with Pandit Hariprasad Chaurasia.
3. Which 'raag' did Pandit Bhimsen Joshi perform at the concert where he announced his retirement?
4. Which immediate family member of Pandit Bhimsen Joshi was a well-known 'kirtankar'?
5. Which famous musician from the Scindia's 'darbar' first took Pandit Bhimsen Joshi under his wings?
6. Who taught Pandit Bhimsen Joshi the basics of 'Khayal-gayaki'?
7. Who jokingly remarked that Pandit Bhimsen Joshi should be called 'Hawai Gandharva'?
8. In the early 1970, in which four-hour concert of devotional music did Pandit Bhimsen Joshi display a fine blend of Purandardasa with Kabir?
9. Which well-known singer is Panditji's 'guru bhai'?
10. Where did Panditji announce his plans of retirement from live concerts?
11. Which gharana does Pandit Bhimsen Joshi represent?
12. Name the book authored by Panditji's father chronicling the life-story of his illustrious son.
13. What is Panditji's middle name?
14. In which village of Karnataka was Pandit Bhimsen Joshi born?
15. Why was Panditji often referred to as the 'flying musician of India'?
16. Which famous director, writer and lyricist made a documentary film on Pandit Bhimsen Joshi in 1992?
17. With which musician did Pandit Bhimsen Joshi cut the album *Basant Bahar*?
18. Who has composed the music for the bhajan, titled *Ye Tanu Mundana be Mundna*, sung by Pandit Bhimsen Joshi?
19. What was the profession of Panditji's father?
20. His first public concert in Pune was to mark the shashtyabdipoorti (sixtieth anniversary) of which musician?

Answers

1. Padma Shri, 1972 2. *Megh Malhar* 3. *Raag Puriya Dhanashri* 4. His grandfather, Bhimashankar 5. Ustad Hafiz Ali Khan 6. Sawai Gandharva 7. Noted writer and humourist Pu La Deshpande 8. Sant Vaani 9. Pandit Pheroze Dastur 10. Dnyaneshwar Hall, Pune University 11. Kirana 12. *Naad Putra* 13. Gururaj 14. Gadag 15. He was always travelling (the pilots of Indian Airlines and airport officials called him thus) 16. Gulzar 17. Pandit Ravi Shankar 18. Srinivas Khale 19. He was a schoolteacher 20. Sawai Gandharva

25: The Reserve Bank of India raises the interest rate at which the Central bank borrows from commercial banks (called the reverse repo rate) by one-fourth of one per cent (or 25 basis points). The Supreme Court appoints former chief election commissioner T.S. Krishnamurthy as observer for conducting the BCCI elections scheduled to be held at Kolkata before 30 November.

26: About 41 per cent of the 1.3-crore voters exercise their franchise in the second phase of the Bihar Assembly elections in sixty-two constituencies.

27: India offers Rs 112.45 crore in assistance to Pakistan for relief and rehabilitation of the 8 October earthquake victims. The Cabinet Committee on Economic Affairs (CCEA) approves the setting up of a committee to appraise projects involving public–private partnership, where the capital cost or the cost of the underlying assets of the projects exceeds Rs 100 crore.

28: The Volcker report names Natwar Singh, India's external affairs minister, as 'non-contractual beneficiaries' of Iraqi oil sales in 2001 under the United Nations Oil-for-Food programme. At least sixty persons are killed as serial blasts rock two market places and a bus in New Delhi. In an all-cash deal worth Rs 6,700 crore ($1.5 billion), Vodafone, the world's largest mobile service provider with a presence in thirty nations, acquires ten per cent stake in India's biggest mobile operator, Bharti Tele-Ventures Limited (BTVL).

30: H.K.L. Bhagat, former Union minister, passes away.

31: Mahasweta Devi, eminent author and social activist, is presented with the twentieth Indira Gandhi Award for National Integration. Vice-Admiral Venkat Bharathan assumes charge as the vice-chief of Naval Staff. The Sensex rallies back ending a month-long bear phase during which it had lost 949 points. The Madras High Court clears the sale of assets of the Standard Motors Limited that was wound up in October 1996 for Rs 154.10 crore. R.C. Lahoti lays down office as the Chief Justice of India.

November 2005

2: Congress leader Ghulam Nabi Azad is sworn in as the tenth chief minister of Jammu and Kashmir. People's Democratic Party leader Muzaffar Hussain Baig becomes deputy chief minister.

3: The Union Cabinet gives its nod for setting up a special purpose vehicle to be known as India Infrastructure Finance Company to fund mega-projects. The Union Cabinet approves the setting up of the National Investment Fund (NIF) and making it operational so as to clear the decks for ploughing of 75 per cent of its income derived through the disinvestment proceeds of Central public-sector enterprises (CPSEs) for funding social sector projects.

4: The CBSE directs affiliated schools to provide free education to all students who are 'single child' in their family. The former Delhi chief minister, Madan Lal Khurana, retires from active politics.

5: The Union minister of state for water resources, Jaiprakash Narayan Yadav, quits the Cabinet as a fallout of the issuance of a non-bailable arrest warrant against him.

6: The Centre appoints former diplomat Virendra Dayal as 'special envoy' to liaise with the UN on the Volcker report references.

7: Natwar Singh is relieved of the external affairs ministry portfolio. India and Pakistan open the first post of the LoC Chaka da Bagh for quake relief in Kashmir, marking a new chapter in bilateral ties. The Centre notifies increased foreign direct investment ceiling of 74 per cent in the telecom sector. The Sensex touches a three-week high of 8206.83 after foreign institutional investors turn bullish.

The Penguin 20/20 Quiz

Bombay Talkies

1. On the site of whose summer mansion was Bombay Talkies built?
2. In the 1930s, which eminent film personality directed all of the Bombay Talkies films?
3. Which old-time colleague of Himanshu Rai was selected as the in-house writer for all Bombay Talkies' productions?
4. Name the production company that S. Mukherjee and Ashok Kumar started after they temporarily left Bombay Talkies.
5. Which all-time film legend came to Mumbai in 1944 and joined Bombay Talkies as a clapper boy under Amiya Chakravarty?
6. Which was the last film produced under the Bombay Talkies banner?
7. Which 1939 hit revived the falling fortunes of Bombay Talkies after a series of flops?
8. After Rai's death, which was the first hit film produced by S. Mukherjee who became the new head of Bombay Talkies?
9. Which film icon did Devika Rani recruit into Bombay Talkies after she spotted him while working at a canteen for the British Army?
10. The film *Achhut Kanya* was based on which story?
11. Which was the first film of Bombay Talkies'?
12. With which film did Franz Osten make his debut in India?
13. Which Bombay Talkies film had the nationalist song *Jai Jai Janani Janmabhoomi*?
14. Who were the scenarists of Bombay Talkies?
15. In which capacity did Ashok Kumar join Bombay Talkies?
16. What was the original name of Saraswati Devi, a music director mainly associated with Bombay Talkies?
17. Which Peshwar-born actor director started as a clapper-boy in Bombay Talkies?
18. Which was the first Bombay Talkies' film in which Dev Anand acted?
19. Who was the resident star of Bombay Talkies?
20. Who played the male lead in the Aparna Sen starrer film *Bombay Talkies*?

Answers

1. F. E. Dinshaw 2. Franz Osten 3. Niranjan Pal 4. Filmistan 5. Raj Kapoor 6. *Tamasha*, 1952 7. *Kangan* 8. *Punar Milan* 9. Dilip Kumar 10. The Level Crossing 11. *Jawani Ki Hawa* 12. *Prem Sanyas* 13. *Janmabhoomi* 14. Niranjan Pal and J.S. Casshyap 15. Laboratory Assistant 16. Khursheed Manchershah Minocher-Homji 17. Raj Kapoor 18. *Baazi* 19. Devika Rani 20. Shashi Kapoor

9: Former President Kocheril Raman Narayanan (85) passes away. Indian and Pakistani authorities open the second point along the Line of Control at Aman Setu for exchange of relief material. The government allows 49 per cent foreign direct investment in asset reconstruction companies, in contribution of banking sector reforms. The Vishwa Bharati University confers Deshikottama award on Czech Republic President, Vaclav Klaus. The government decides to permit FDI up to a maximum of 49 per cent in the equity capital of asset reconstruction companies (ARCs).

10: The Union communications and information technology minister, Dayanidhi Maran, launches the national portal of India—India.gov.in.

11: The Sensex zooms 162 points to end at a month's high of 8471.04. Underworld don Abu Salem, one of the prime accused in the 1993 Bombay serial blasts, and his companion, Monica Bedi, are extradited and brought home by the CBI after a three-year legal battle with Portugal.

12: Justice Ajit Prakash Shah is sworn in as the twenty-second chief justice of the Madras High Court. Madhu Dandavate (81), former Union finance minister and scholar-politician, passes away.

13: The third phase of polling for the Bihar Assembly passes off peacefully with 47 per cent turnout.

14: The fourth relief centre along the LoC is opened at Tatapani. This is the first time in fifty-eight years that a link on this side has been set up with southern PoK.

15: The SEBI announces the creation of a separate window in both the Bombay Stock Exchange and the National Stock Exchange for executing huge block deals.

16: The fifth and last relief point along the LoC is opened at Hajipeer (PoK) and Silikot (Uri). Bharat Hotels (BHL), controlled by Lalit Suri, gets the 90 per cent stake in Asia's oldest operating hotel—the 165-year-old Great Eastern Hotel (GEH). Air Sahara becomes the first private Indian airline to offer direct flights to the US in code-share agreement with American Airlines (AA).

17: The government decides to divest 15 per cent of its stake in Shipping Corporation of India.

18: The prime minister shifts Jaipal Reddy to the urban development ministry and Priyaranjan Dasmunshi gets information and broadcasting.

19: 48 per cent polling is recorded in the final phase of Bihar Assembly elections. President A.P.J. Abdul Kalam presents the 2004 Indira Gandhi Prize for Peace, Disarmament and Development to Thai princess, Maha Chakri Sirindhorn. Afghanistan President, Hamid Karzai, is chosen for the 2005 prize.

21: Goa triumphs in the Santosh Trophy football tournament in Kochi.

22: The Janata Dal (United) leader Nitish Kumar wins a resounding victory in the Bihar Assembly polls, bringing the fifteen-year rule of the Rashtriya Janata Dal to an end. The Maharashtra revenue minister Narayan Rane wins the Malvan–Kankavali Assembly by-elections by a massive margin of 63,372 votes. Congress candidate Priya Dutt wins the north-west Mumbai Lok Sabha seat by 1.72 lakh votes.

23: India and Indonesia agree to establish a 'strategic partnership'.

24: The JD(U) leader Nitish Kumar is sworn in Bihar chief minister. The Geological Survey of India announces the discovery of 'the world's oldest fossil of a rodent' in Jaisalmer district of Rajasthan. The find was the result of a three-month exploration early this year. India signs MoU with Turkey for oil exploration.

26: The Madhya Pradesh chief minister, Babulal Gaur, resigns and Shivraj Singh Chouhan is chosen to succeed

The Penguin 20/20 Quiz

Gwalior

1. According to legend, after which sage was Gwalior named?
2. Which music maestro did Javed Akhtar collaborate with to create the album *Sangam*?
3. Which palace is the residence of the present Maharaja of Gwalior?
4. Which city houses the cenotaph of the Rani of Jhansi?
5. Which actor has rendered the introduction to *Samvedna*, an album of songs written by Atal Bihari Vajpayee?
6. Located at about 122 kms from Gwalior, which fort city was the capital of Raja Nal?
7. Which Gwalior born musician has said: 'Music should be felt and experienced. Music satisfies the soul. It can be appreciated without knowing it'?
8. Which temple was originally called the Sahasrabahu temple?
9. Who built the Man Mandir Palace in Gwalior?
10. Which Mughal emperor jailed Guru Hargobind, the sixth Sikh guru, in the fortress of Gwalior?
11. In Scindia School for Boys, what do the students do at 'Astachal'?
12. Which deity is the 'Teli ka Mandir' dedicated to?
13. In 1971, which constituency was Madhav Rao Scindia first elected from?
14. The 'Gwalior Gharana' started in the reign of which emperor?
15. Who is the cricket stadium at Gwalior named after?
16. Who was the Gujari Mahal in Gwalior made by the Tomar king Raja Mansingh built for?
17. Which disease did Saint Gwalipa save the local chieftain Suraj Sen from?
18. How do we know musician Tanna Mishra better?
19. Which political leader from Gwalior has authored the book *Lok Path se Raj Path*?
20. Whose CD titled *Bhairav* has been voted among the best 50 classical albums of the world for the year 1995 announced in the BBC magazine?

Answers

1. Gwalipa 2. Nusrat Fateh Ali Khan 3. Jai Vilas Palace 4. Lashkar 5. Amitabh Bachchan 6. Narwar 7. Amjad Ali Khan 8. Sas Bahu ka Mandir 9. Raja Man Singh 10. Jahangir 11. They sit together in silence for a while and watch the sun go down. 12. Pratihara Vishnu 13. Guna 14. Akbar 15. Captain Roop Singh 16. The Gujar queen Mrignayani 17. Leprosy 18. Tansen 19. Vijaya Raje Scindia 20. Amjad Ali Khan

tions scam. The Central government indicates revision of the rates of fringe benefit tax under some heads and simplification of the rules for the convenience of taxpayers.

29: The Centre clears the SAFTA pact.

31: Lal Krishna Advani resigns as BJP president.

January 2006

3: Union science and technology minister Kapil Sibal unveils a seven-point action plan proposed to be implemented during the next twelve months. It includes the setting up of a one-million-a-day plant for conversion of seawater into drinking water off the Tamil Nadu coast by the middle of the year and an autonomous board of science and engineering research, which will create a pool of 1,000 scientific positions for young researchers in India and abroad. C.N.R. Rao, the chairman of the scientific advisory council to the prime minister and eminent scientist, becomes the first recipient of the India Science Award 2004 instituted by the Government of India. The Sensex hits the 9,500 mark.

5: The Andaman and Nicobar Islands administration declares that it will provide at least one daily-wage job for a year to each family affected by the tsunami. About 6,313 families have been identified for the scheme after a door-to-door survey was conducted. Prime Minister Manmohan Singh announces lifting the ban on recruitment in the Union territory to fill 650 vacant government posts.

6: The Union Cabinet approves the inclusion and modification of certain castes and communities in the Central list of Other Backward Classes (OBCs). The government increases the issue price of foodgrains for both Above Poverty Line (APL) and Below Poverty Line (BPL) families, while simultaneously reducing their offtake quantity to 20 kg and 30 kg. It is expected to provide a saving of over Rs 4,500 crore in food subsidy.

7: The Union finance minister P. Chidambaram launches an easy-to-use electronic remittance gateway, 'insta remit,' for overseas Indians, developed by the ministry of overseas Indians affairs, in partnership with the UTI Bank. The health ministry and the American Association of Physicians of Indian Origin (AAPI) sign a memorandum of understanding (MoU) to improve the primary health sector in the country.

9: Abdool Raoof Bundhun, vice-president, Republic of Mauritius, is among eleven persons of Indian origin (PIO), who receive the Pravasi Bharatiya Samman Award from President A.P.J. Abdul Kalam. The Centre decides to introduce 'smart cards' for emigrant workers, containing all information regarding their employment and insurance.

10: The government notifies the interest rate on Employees Provident Fund (EPF) for the current fiscal at 8.5 per cent. As part of its advanced technology initiative in air-breathing propulsion, the Thiruvananthapuram-based Vikram Sarabhai Space Centre of the Indian Space Research Organization (ISRO) designs and develops a Supersonic Combustion Ramjet, recording a major technological breakthrough.

11: Kumar Mangalam Birla is appointed as chairman of the Advisory Committee constituted by the ministry of company affairs.

12: Telecom Regulatory Authority of India (TRAI) asks all operators, who have announced lifetime validity scheme, to provide data relating to traffic, cost and revenue.

13: The Supreme Court issues notice to the Centre, all the states and union territories to examine the scope and powers of the states to allot houses to former chief ministers, ministers and other functionaries. The Supreme

The Penguin 20/20 Quiz

Indian Hockey

1. Who led the first Indian hockey team to the 1928 Amsterdam Olympics?
2. In which Asiad did India win its first hockey gold?
3. Whose penalty stroke against Pakistan helped India regain the Olympic gold at the 1964 Tokyo Olympics?
4. Which team did India defeat to win a fifth Olympic hockey gold at the 1952 Helsinki Games?
5. At the1960 Olympics, to whom did India lose in an Olympic final for the first time?
6. Whose goal in the dying minutes helped India defeat Spain in the 1980 Olympic finals?
7. Which brother duo produced 19 goals between them in India's 24-1 carnage against USA at the 1932 Olympic Games?
8. In the 1998 Asian Games hockey finals against South Korea, this goalkeeper's saves under the bar helped India win the 1998 Asian hockey gold. Name this custodian.
9. When did India and Pakistan meet for the first time in an Olympic hockey final?
10. Which Indian was the highest goal scorer at the 2001 Junior World Cup?
11. How many goals did the Indian custodian of yesteryears, Richard Allen, concede during the 1928 Olympic Games?
12. Who featured in this 1996 footwear ad with the words: 'See the sweat on my face, it's oil for rusty dreams...this is my planet'?
13. At the Asian Games, Pakistan has won the most gold medals and India, the most silver medals. Which country has won the most bronze medals?
14. *To Hell with Hockey* is the autobiography of which hockey player?
15. Who scored 13 goals for India in the 1982 Asian Games?
16. How many matches did India lose in the first three World Cups?
17. Name the only player to have captained India in two World Cups.
18. Which player represented India a maximum of 4 times in the World Cup, but never once as a captain? (Hint: he shares his name with a famous actor)
19. 29 August is observed as National Sports Day. It is the birthday of which hockey great?
20. Prithipal Singh got it in 1961, Ajitpal Singh in 1970, Pargat Singh in 1989 and Ramandeep Singh in 1999. What is being referred to?

Answers

1. Jasdev Singh 2. 1966, Bangkok 3. Mohinder Lal 4. Holland 5. Pakistan 6. Merwyn Fernandes 7. Roop Singh-11 and Dhyan Chand-8 8. Ashish Ballal 9. 1956 Melbourne Olympics 10. Deepak Thakur 11. None 12. Dhanraj Pillai 13. Malaysia 14. Aslam Sher Khan 15. Zafar Iqbal 16. Only one 17. Ajitpal Singh 18. Ashok Kumar 19. Dhyan Chand 20. The Arjuna Award for hockey

their Memoranda of Associations (MoAs).

2: Prime Minister Manmohan Singh launches the National Rural Employment Guarantee Act.

3: Janata Dal (S) leader H.D. Kumaraswamy and Bharatiya Janata Party (BJP) leader B.S. Yediyurappa are sworn in as chief minister and deputy chief minister of Karnataka by Governor T.N. Chaturvedi.

4: The Airports Authority of India (AAI) employees end their four-day strike following a written assurance by the government that there would be no job loss due to modernization of the Delhi and Mumbai airports.

6: The Sensex touches 10,000.

7: Reliance Industries Ltd (RIL) group formally hands over the control of the four demerged companies to the Reliance-Anil Dhirubhai Ambani Group (Reliance-ADAG). The Samajwadi Party suspends its two-time member of parliament from Agra, Raj Babbar, from the Parliamentary Party on charges of 'indiscipline'. India and Serbia and Montenegro conclude a 'Trade and Economic Cooperation Agreement' which includes grant of Most Favoured Nation treatment.

8: The Bharatiya Janata Party–Janata Dal (Secular) government in Karnataka wins a vote of confidence in the Assembly. The motion was supported by 138 members, while sixty-six opposed it. The government issues fresh guidelines for tightening phone-tapping norms.

9: Veteran actress Nadira passes away.

10: The 'India-specific' rules and legislation for setting up special economic zones come into effect.

13: The Union government issues the guidelines on the 'single brand' concept of retail.

14: The Supreme Court orders compulsory registration of marriages irrespective of religion. It direct the Centre and all the states and union territories to amend the rules to this effect within three months.

15: Railway minister Lalu Prasad Yadav flags off the country's fastest Shatabdi Express between New Delhi and Agra.

17: The Board of Control for Cricket in India (BCCI) awards the cable, broadband and direct-to-home telecast rights to Nimbus Communications Ltd for four years. State Bank of India becomes the first Indian bank in China to get approval to start normal banking operations.

18: Bird flu hits India. The Janata Dal (Secular), headed by former prime minister H.D. Deve Gowda, suspends Karnataka chief minister H.D. Kumaraswamy and thirty-nine other MLAs from the party.

20: India, France sign accords. France ready to give nuclear power plants, fuel.

21: Railways ban chicken dishes and eggs.

23: TRAI issues changes in interconnect charges. Long distance call tariffs to come down. The Union Cabinet clears plan to set up technical varsity. Institutions and courses directly run by the universities to remain under respective varsities.

27: Railways withdraws ban on serving chicken, egg. Economic Survey 2005-06 calls for tax and labour reforms.

28: Presenting the budget for 2006-07, Finance Minister P. Chidambaram does not make any change in the corporate and personal IT rates. He widenes the service tax net to include fifteen more services such as credit cards, luxury class air travel and ATM operations to mop up Rs 34,500 crore during the new fiscal.

March 2006

1: Prabhakaran Paleri becomes the new Coast Guard Director-General. The Sensex crosses the 10,500 mark for the first time.

2: India accepts the US government's invitation to take part in the billion dol-

The Penguin 20/20 Quiz

Arundhati Roy

1. What was the name of Esthappan's twin sister in the Booker Prize-winning novel *The God of Small Things*?
2. What was the title of Arundhati Roy's critique on nuclear tests?
3. In which 1988 offbeat Indian film did Arundhati Roy play the role of Radha?
4. Which idyllic river is used as the backdrop in *The God of Small Things*?
5. Which village was the backdrop of her Booker Prize-winning novel?
6. What was the name of Arundhati Roy's critique that was published following the immediate American response to the events that followed the World Trade Center attacks?
7. What was the title of the 26-episode television epic that Arundhati Roy planned with present husband Pradeep Krishen for Doordarshan?
8. Which film does the article, *The Great Indian Rape Trick*, authored by Arundhati Roy, talk about?
9. Which was Arundhati Roy's first non-fiction work?
10. What was the name of the Harper Collins editor (India) who helped Arundhati Roy in getting her award-winning novel published?
11. In which 1986 film did Arundhati Roy play the part of what she prefers to call 'a tribal bimbo'?
12. Which river does her essay *The Greater Common Good* essentially deal with?
13. What is the name of Arundhati Roy's younger brother?
14. What was the slogan of 'Paradise Pickles' in *The God of Small Things*?
15. What is the name of the village in Kerala where Arundhati Roy grew up?
16. What is the full name of Arundhati Roy?
17. When Arundhati Roy won the Booker Prize, which famous Indian author said: 'I feel that she is our own girl... I feel so proud of her'?
18. What was the profession of Arundhati Roy's father?
19. Of which 1992 Pradeep Krishen film did Arundhati Roy write the script?
20. In which year did Arundhati Roy win the Booker Prize for her novel *The God Of Small Things*?

Answers

1. Rahel 2. *The End of Imagination* 3. *In Which Annie Gives It Those Ones* 4. The Meenachil River in Kerala 5. Ayemenem in Kottayam district 6. *The Algebra of Infinite Justice* 7.. *The Banyan Tree* 8. *Bandit Queen* 9. *The Cost of Living* 10. Pankaj Mishra 11. *Massey Sahib* 12. Narmada 13. Lalit 14. Emperor in the realm of taste 15. Aymanam 16. Suzanna Arundhati Roy 17. Kamala Das 18. Tea planter 19. *Electric Moon* 20. 1997

lar FutureGen project, aimed at creating the world's first zero-emissions fossil fuel plant. The Sensex crosses the 10,700-mark for the first time.

8: The Supreme Court sentences Zahira Sheikh, key witness in the Best Bakery case, to one-year imprisonment, and imposes a fine of Rs 50,000 for contempt of court by making a false statement on oath and filing false affidavits.

9: Raj Thackeray launches his new party, the Maharashtra Navnirman Sena. Parliament approves the Railway Budget 2006-07, with the Rajya Sabha passing by voice vote the Appropriation (Railways) Vote on Account Bill, 2006, for Rs 18,662 crore.

10: Parliament passes a Bill which would enable those wanting to set up minority educational institutions to get early clearance from the states as also affiliation to universities.

13: India signs a memorandum of understanding (MoU) with Mauritius to explore for hydrocarbons off the coast of the island nation.

14: The Cabinet accepts the recommendations of the Group of Ministers (GoM), fixing an annual income ceiling of Rs 4 lakhs to identify the creamy layer among backward classes for excluding them from the purview of reservations.

16: Prime Minister Manmohan Singh approves the setting up of a task force on planning for human resource in health services.

17: President A.P.J. Abdul Kalam disqualifies Jaya Bachchan of the Samajwadi Party from Rajya Sabha membership with retrospective effect from 14 July 2004 for holding an 'office of profit' as chairperson of the Uttar Pradesh Film Development Council (UPFDC). India and Russia sign seven agreements, including one between the Indian Space Research Organization (ISRO) and the Russian Federal Space Agency (ROSCOSMOS) on the joint development of Glonass-K navigation satellites.

19: Bharatiya Janata Party suspends former Delhi chief minister Madan Lal Khurana from the primary membership of the party.

20: Union ministers Arjun Singh, Sushil Kumar Shinde, Praful Patel, Hansraj Bhardwaj and Dasari Narayan Rao are elected unopposed to the Rajya Sabha. President A.P.J. Abdul Kalam presents the country's highest civilian awards—Padma Vibhushan, Padma Bhushan and Padma Shri.

21: The Parliament passes the Petroleum and Natural Gas Regulatory Board Bill. The Sensex crosses the 11,000 mark for the first time.

23: The Union Cabinet hikes the dearness allowance of Central government employees and dearness relief for pensioners by three per cent.

25: Anil Ambani resigns from Rajya Sabha.

26: West Bengal Communist Party of India (Marxist) secretary and member of the party's Polit Bureau Anil Biswas (61) passes away. To help the poultry industry, the Union government announces a one-time reduction of four percentage points in interest payment on bank loans taken by poultry units. Samaresh Jung is given the 'David Dixon Award' after being adjudged the Best Athlete of the eighteenth Commonwealth Games.

30: The Union Cabinet decides to double the financial powers of the defence minister from Rs 50 crore to Rs 100 crore and that of the finance minister from Rs 100 crore to Rs 200 crore, to avoid delays in the acquisition of defence equipment and spares.

April 2006

1: Five BJP-ruled states (Chhattisgarh, Gujarat, Jharkhand, Madhya Pradesh and Rajasthan) switch over to the value-added tax (VAT) regime from the sales tax system.

2: The board of governors of the Indian Institute of Management,

The Penguin 20/20 Quiz

Gujarat

1. In 1960, Gujarat was formed as a result of the splitting of which state?
2. Who is Menkan Dada, the saint who served the community with great love and dedication, considered the incarnation of?
3. What kind of animals are traded at the Vautha Mela in Gujarat?
4. After the names of which king's sons in Hindu mythology is the Chitra-Vichitra Mela, the all-adivasi fair held in Gujarat, named?
5. In Gujarat, what is *Bhavai* a type of?
6. What is the small coat, a part of the typical folk costume for the performance of Ras, called?
7. In Kathiawad cuisine, what is a 'chhundo'?
8. Before Gandhinagar, what was the capital of Gujarat?
9. Which great Gujarati scholar started the Gujarat Vernacular Society at Ahmedabad in 1848?
10. Who is the author of the famous bhajan *Vaishnavajan*?
11. In which city in Gujarat was one of the mathas set up by Adi Shankaracharya?
12. Which small place isolated in the Rann of Kutch was ruled by the Khengarji Family from 1548 to 1947? (Hint: made news when the earthquake rocked Gujarat in January 2001)
13. Which place in Gujarat is renowned as the birthplace of Mahatma Gandhi?
14. Which former Chief Minister served as Director, Rajkot Nagrik Sahakari Bank between 1969 and 1974?
15. Who is the International Airport in Ahmedabad named after?
16. According to the *Limca Book of Records 2002*, who was the highest paid CEO in India?
17. Who designed the building of the Indian Institute of Management, Ahmedabad?
18. Along which river is Vadodara located?
19. Who is the author of *Gujaratno Nath*?
20. By what name did the 2nd century AD Greek geographer Ptolemy refer to river Narmada as?

Answers

1. Bombay 2. Lakshman 3. Donkeys 4. Shantanu 5. Folk drama 6. Kedia 7. Pickle 8. Ahmedabad 9. Alexander Kinloch Forbes 10. Narsinh Mehta 11. Dwarka 12. Bhuj 13. Porbandar 14. Keshubhai Patel 15. Vallabhbhai Patel 16. Dhirubhai Ambani 17. Louis Kahn 18. Vishwamitra River 19. K.M Munshi 20. Narmade

Celebrating 20 Years of Penguin Books India

Ahmedabad, decides to increase the fees of the post-graduate management courses by 12 per cent from Rs 1.58 lakh a year to Rs 1.77 lakh a year.

3: An estimated 68 per cent of the 92 lakh electorate exercise their franchise in the first phase of the Assembly elections in Assam. The Sensex crosses the 11,500 mark. India and the US enter into an agreement for collaboration in the $950 million FutureGen project, a public–private initiative to build a coal based power plant without any carbon emissions.

4: The government signs two agreements to set up joint-venture companies involving the public sector Airports Authority of India and the GMR and GVK groups for handing over the Delhi and Mumbai airports for modernization.

5: The Union Cabinet approves the implementation of the 2004 Supreme Court order for disbursement of prorata additional compensation on one-on-one basis to victims of the Bhopal gas tragedy.

6: India creates the record for most consecutive successful ODI chases (15) and clinches the seven-match series against England.

8: The ministry of railways announces reduced fares for advance bookings. The ministry of commerce and industry constitutes a committee, headed by a member of the Planning Commission, to examine the inverted import duty structure in manufacturing.

9: The management of State Bank of India declares a settlement which gives higher pension to 2.10 lakh staff of the country's largest commercial bank. According to the settlement, employees getting up to Rs 21,040 salary would get 50 per cent of their last drawn pay as pension and above that, 40 per cent.

10: Over 70 per cent of a total of 82.27 lakh voters exercise their franchise in the second and final phase of polling in Assam.

12: Rajkumar, doyen of Kannada cinema, passes away.

14: NRI industrialist Lord Swraj Paul and his wife, Lady Aruna Paul, acquire the Overseas Citizenship of India.

16: The health and family welfare ministry issues guidelines to make primary health centres (PHCs) twenty-four-hour delivery and newborn care units.

17: In the first phase of the Assembly elections in West Bengal more than 70 per cent of 68 lakh voters in forty-five constituencies across three districts in the south-western part of the state cast their votes.

18: The Union Cabinet decides to reconfigure the Kishanganga hydro-electric project in Jammu and Kashmir to overcome Pakistani objections.

19: Union science and technology minister, Kapil Sibal, launches a weather portal, which can be accessed at www.indiaweatherwatch.org, and will disseminate information on about 200 locations and five-day forecasts for twenty of them, covering the metros and major cities, apart from giving a general nationwide forecast and zone-wise forecasts.

20: The Sensex crosses the 12,000 mark. India and Pakistan agree not to levy import duties of more than 5 per cent on products traded within the South Asia Free Trade Area (SAFTA).

22: Bharatiya Janata Party general secretary Pramod Mahajan is shot by his younger brother, Pravin Mahajan, at his house in Worli. Polling in sixty-six constituencies in four districts of West Bengal in the second round of the five-phase Assembly elections passes off peacefully. The voter turnout was 74 per cent.

23: The former prime minister, V.P. Singh, announces the formation of a new outfit 'Jan Morcha' headed by suspended Samajwadi Party (SP) Lok Sabha member Raj Babbar.

24: Prime Minister Manmohan Singh constitutes a three-member commit-

The Penguin 20/20 Quiz

Lagaan

1. Name the costume designer for *Lagaan* who had earlier won an Oscar in 1982 in the 'Best Costume Design' category.
2. In *Lagaan*, what was the name of the lower-class villager who became the trump-card spinner for the local team?
3. Who sang the English interlude in Alka Yagnik's *O Re Chhore*?
4. Why was the period of the film shifted from 1885 to 1893?
5. Fill in the blank to complete the line that appeared on the poster of Lagaan: 'Once Upon a Time in ____.'
6. At which film festival did *Lagaan* win the People's Choice Award?
7. Who composed the music for *Lagaan*?
8. Near which real village was the fictional setting of Champaner created for *Lagaan*?
9. Who was the executive producer for *Lagaan*?
10. Who has authored the book *The Spirit of Lagaan: The Extraordinary Story of the Creators of a Classic*, chronicling the events of the making of the film?
11. Who wrote the story of *Lagaan*?
12. While shooting for *Lagaan*, for which two members of the cast did Aamir do kanyadaan when they decided to get married?
13. Which actor went through an emergency appendicitis operation during the shooting of *Lagaan*?
14. The language used in *Lagaan* was a mixture of Awadhi, Brijbhasha and which other language?
15. Which Indian Test cricketer, apart from Sourav Ganguly, officiated as umpire in the Britannia XIII versus Lagaan XIII match held in Mumbai?
16. Which six-letter name, broadly speaking, connects Aamir Khan in *Lagaan* and Aishwarya Rai in *Devdas*?
17. In the film *Lagaan*, which actress played the role of Gauri, Bhuvan's (Aamir Khan's) love?
18. Where was Captain Russell transferred to as a punishment for his behaviour?
19. Which actor plays the role of Captain Andrew Russell in the film?
20. The background of the film is set in which former princely state?

Answers

1. Bhanu Athaiya 2. Kachra 3. Vasundhara Das 4. Because the cuts for the women's clothes were matronly and that too in the shades of blacks and browns 5. India 6. Locarno, Switzerland 7. A.R. Rahman 8. Kunariya 9. Aamir Khan's wife, Reena 10. Satyajit Bhatkal 11. Ashutosh Gowariker 12. British artistes Katkin and Jamie 13. Raghuvir Yadav 14. Bhojpuri 15. Virendra Sehwag 16. Bhuvan (Aamir was Bhuvan in the film *Lagaan* and Aishwarya Rai as Paro had to marry Zaminder Bhuvan in the film *Devdas*) 17. Gracy Singh 18. Central Africa 19. Paul Blackthorne 20. Awadh

Celebrating 20 Years of Penguin Books India

tee, headed by the former comptroller and auditor-general of India, V.K. Shunglu, to go into the relief and rehabilitation of the people affected by the Sardar Sarovar Project.

25: The Forward Markets Commission (FMC) states that real time trading in a commodity by opening the terminals of foreign commodity exchanges in India without the prior approval of the Central government or the FMC would be considered illegal.

26: Parthi Bhatol, chief of the Banaskantha Milk Producers' Union, is elected as the chairman of Gujarat Cooperative Milk Marketing Federation (GCMMF).

27: More than 70 per cent votes are cast in the third round of the five-phase Assembly elections in West Bengal. The Union Cabinet permits the start of Bangalore Metro Rail project. The project is estimated to cost Rs 6,395 crore, inclusive of an escalation of 5 per cent per annum in the cost during the five years it would take to complete its construction. The project would be on the pattern of the Delhi metro rail.

29: The second phase of Assembly elections in Kerala go off peacefully and the polling percentage averages around 70 per cent.

May 2006

1: The Board for Reconstruction of Public Sector Enterprises (BRPSE) clears a Rs 835-crore package for the revival of five machine tool manufacturing units of Bangalore-based HMT Ltd.

2: Bombay Stock Exchange announces that the Anil Ambani-controlled Reliance Communication Ventures Ltd. (RCoVL) will replace Tata Power in the Sensex.

3: Bharatiya Janata Party general secretary Pramod Mahajan passes away. Uma Bharti quits the Madhya Pradesh Assembly seat she had won as a BJP candidate in the last elections. More than 76 per cent of the voters exercise their franchise in fifty-seven Assembly constituencies in Burdwan, Murshidabad and Birbhum districts in West Bengal.

5: Music composer Naushad Ali passes away. For the first time, gold prices crosses the Rs 10,000 mark.

8: The Sensex touches the 12,500 mark. The Reserve Bank of India revises the rate of agency commission on 'other payments' in conduct of government business to nine paise per Rs 100 turnover from Rs 50 per transaction.

9: NASA and ISRO sign an MoU. India's unmanned moon mission Chandrayaan-1 will have on board two US payloads. The mission is slated for launch by early 2008. India is elected to the newly established Human Rights Council with 173 out of 191 votes in the United Nations General Assembly. The Union Cabinet decides to amend the Wildlife (Protection) Act to facilitate the recommendations of the Tiger Task Force and strengthen Project Tiger by giving it statutory and administrative powers.

10: The Sensex crosses the 12,600 mark.

11: The Left Democratic Front (LDF), led by the Communist Party of India (Marxist), acquires two-thirds majority in the Kerala Assembly elections. It secured ninety-eight seats in the 140-member House. In the fourteenth West Bengal Assembly elections, the Left Front acquires more than a two-thirds majority. Sonia Gandhi wins the Rae Bareli Lok Sabha by-election with a margin of over 4.17 lakh votes. The ruling Congress emerges as the single largest party in Assam. India and Israel sign a three-year work plan for cooperation in agriculture.

12: The Lok Sabha unanimously passes the Delhi Laws (Special Provisions) Bill, 2006, which seeks to put a year long moratorium on the ongoing demolitions and sealing of illegal buildings in the capital. The sea version of

The Penguin 20/20 Quiz

Lal Bahadur Shastri

1. Which Poland-born scientist's biography did Lal Bahadur Shastri translate into Hindi?
2. Lal Bahadur Shastri resigned from the post of Minister of Railways and Transport in the Central Cabinet in 1956 as he felt he was responsible for the railway accident at which place?
3. In the presence of which Soviet Premier did Lal Bahadur Shastri sign the Tashkent agreement with Ayub Khan?
4. Who did Lal Bahadur Shastri succeed as the Home Minister in 1961?
5. Which prime minister added the words *Jai Vigyan* to Lal Bahadur Shastri's *Jai Jawan -Jai Kisan* to highlight the aim of all-round progress?
6. In which Indian city is the Lal Bahadur Shastri Stadium located?
7. Who became the acting prime minister after Lal Bahadur Shastri died?
8. Mahtama Gandhi's samadhi is called Raj Ghat. What is Lal Bahadur Shastri's samadhi called?
9. In his childhood, how was Lal Bahadur Shastri lovingly referred to as?
10. Apart from a few yards of cloth, what was the only other thing he accepted as dowry?
11. In which railway town of Uttar Pradesh was Lal Bahadur Shastri born?
12. People jokingly used to call him the 'homeless Home Minister'. Why?
13. Who succeeded Lal Bahadur Shastri as the Prime Minister of India?
14. What did Lal Bahadur Shastri die of?
15. With regard to the Bharat Ratna, what is common to Satyajit Ray, Aruna Asaf Ali and Lal Bahadur Shastri?
16. Sunil Shastri, the son of Lal Bahadur Shastri represents BJP. Which party does Anil Shastri, his other son, represent?
17. In which educational institution did Lal Bahadur Shastri receive the title of 'Shastri'?
18. What was the profession of Lal Bahadur Shastri's father?
19. Lal Bahadur Shastri created the National Dairy Development Board in 1965 to help market milk directly to the consumers. Whom did he choose as president?
20. In which country's capital did Lal Bahadur Shastri pass away?

Answers

1. Marie Curie 2. Aliyalur in Tamil Nadu 3. Aleksey Kosygin 4. Govind Vallabh Pant 5. Atal Bihari Vajpayee 6. Hyderabad 7. Gulzari Lal Nanda 8. Vijay Ghat 9. Nanhe (meaning 'tiny') 10. A spinning wheel 11. Mughalsarai 12. He was so called as he did not have a house of his own. 13. Indira Gandhi 14. A heart attack 15. The award was conferred upon them posthumously 16. Congress 17. Kashi Vidyapeth School 18. He was a teacher 19. Dr Verghese Kurien 20. Uzbekistan

the pilotless target aircraft Lakshya is successfully test-fired over the Bay of Bengal from a range at Gopalpur.

13: Dravida Munnetra Kazhagam president M. Karunanidhi is sworn is as the chief minister of Tamil Nadu by the governor S.S. Barnala.

16: The Lok Sabha passes by voice vote the Parliament (Prevention of Disqualification) Amendment Bill, 2006, which seeks to address the office-of-profit controversy.

17: Parliament approves a Bill seeking to exempt fifty-six posts, including the chairpersonship of the National Advisory Council, from being considered as offices of profit and attracting disqualification for parliamentarians, with the Rajya Sabha approving it through a division.

18: Buddhadeb Bhattacharjee is sworn as the chief minister of West Bengal by Governor Gopalkrishna Gandhi. N. Rangasamy is sworn in as the sixteenth chief minister of Pondicherry. The nineteen-member Kerala Cabinet is sworn in by the governor R.L. Bhatia.

19: Eighteen ministers of the Tarun Gogoi-led Congress–Bodoland People's Progressive Front (Hagrama) coalition in Assam is sworn in by Governor Ajai Singh.

20: The Group of Ministers on the Food Safety and Standards Bill, 2005, finalizes the Bill.

22: The Indian stock market records its sharpest-ever fall in prices on a single day on as the index falls by 1,111.7 points in the course of the day. The Union commerce ministry, to revive the tea industry, announces the launching of a Rs 4,700-crore special purpose tea fund in the current fiscal.

23: The United Progressive Alliance and the Left parties announce that 27 per cent of the seats in Central educational institutions would be available to the Other Backward Classes (OBCs) from June 2007.

25: Prime Minister Manmohan Singh announces the setting up of five working groups to resolve the issues confronting Jammu and Kashmir.

26: The Union Cabinet approves a proposal to rename the Union territory of Pondicherry as Puducherry, in keeping with the resolution passed by the Legislative Assembly of the Union territory for such a change. A Bill to give effect to the decision would be introduced during the monsoon session.

29: The first-ever memorandum of understanding (MoU) is signed between the defence ministries of India and China. The Union government constitutes a thirteen-member Oversight Committee to monitor the implementation of reservation for Other Backward Classes (OBCs) in institutions of higher education.

June 2006

1: The Union government exempts from service tax taxable services provided by the Reserve Bank of India and some taxable services provided to the RBI.

2: Jindal Steel and Power Ltd sign a $2.3 billion iron and steel project in Bolivia. This is the biggest project ever awarded to an Indian company in Latin America. In place of the existing one-page 'Saral' form for filing income-tax (I-T) returns, the Union government introduces a new four-page form ('Form 2F') which seeks to capture the assessee's income as well as expenditure for the entire financial year.

3: Geet Sethi regains the world professional billiards title, defeating England's Lee Lagan by over 1,000 points.

5: Verghese Kurien announces his decision to resign from the chairmanship of the Institute of Rural Management, Anand (IRMA).

6: M. Damodaran, chairman, Securities and Exchange Board of India is elected chairman of the Emerging Mar-

The Penguin 20/20 Quiz

Pune

1. Which car manufacturer is headquartered in Pune?
2. Which famous political leader authored *Bhagawadgita-Rahasya,* an exposition of the sacred book of the Hindus?
3. Which sport's winter season is held in Mumbai, its monsoon season being held in Pune?
4. Dehu, near Pune, was the birthplace of which poet-saint?
5. Which famous person died in pre-independence India in what was earlier known as The Aga Khan's Palace while being imprisoned there?
6. Which institution imparts basic training for officer cadets and is situated 17 kms from Pune?
7. Where would you find a priceless collection of nutcrackers among other things in Pune?
8. Bollywood could recruit from this well-known institution. Name it.
9. Shivneri fort, about 94 kms away from Pune, is the birthplace of which famous Maratha?
10. Where would you find the famous Ganapati temple built by Madhav Rao Peshwa?
11. Which former Indian prime minister described Pune as the ' Oxford and Cambridge of India'?
12. Which spiritual leader's headquarter is located at Koregaon Park, Pune?
13. Which airport serves the city of Pune?
14. Which two rivers border Pune on the north and west respectively?
15. In Pune, what are Alka, Rahul and West End different types of?
16. The Shaniwarwada Palace in Pune was founded by which ruler?
17. What name did the Mughal emperor Aurangzeb give to the city of Pune after the death of his son?
18. Which political leader, the author of the book titled *Atmavritta*, received the Bharat Ratna on his 100th birthday?
19. Who, along with Pandit Vishnushastri Chiplunkar, Principal Gopal Ganesh Agarkar and Madhavrao Namjoshi, founded the Fergusson College in Pune?
20. Who constructed the Bund Gardens in Pune for providing water to the poor?

Answers

1. Mercedes Benz 2. Bal Gangadhar Tilak 3. Horse racing 4. Tukaram 5. Kasturba Gandhi 6. National Defence Academy 7. Raja Dinkar Kelkar Museum 8. The Film and Television Institute of India (FTII) 9. Chhatrapati Shivaji 10. Saras Baug 11. Jawaharlal Nehru 12. Osho Rajneesh, it is named Osho Commune International 13. Lohegaon Airport 14. River Mula and River Mutha 15. Cinemas 16. Baji Rao I 17. Muhiyabad 18. Dhondo Keshav Karve 19. Lokmanya Balgangadhar Tilak 20. Sir Jamshedji Jeejeebhoy

kets Committee of the International Organization of Securities Commissions.

8: Jaya Bachchan and Amir Alam Khan of the Samajwadi Party are declared elected unopposed in the by-elections to the Rajya Sabha from Uttar Pradesh. The Union government exempts from levy of additional duty of customs thirteen categories of products of wholly Nepalese origin.

9: The second Administrative Reforms Commission recommends that the Official Secrets Act, 1923, be repealed. India announces a Rs 1,000 crore package to help Nepal tide over its immediate economic difficulties.

10: In a landmark ruling, the Supreme Court declares that courts, while interpreting a statute, must adopt a construction, which suppresses mischief and advances remedy. Sikkim passes Bill protecting MLAs from disqualification. N.R. Narayana Murthy, chairman and chief mentor of India's second-largest software exporter, Infosys, announces his retirement from the company in August.

11: The Supreme Court rules that timely payment of wages to workers is a must to maintain peace and tranquility in an industry and an employer cannot deliberately delay salaries to employees.

12: Surjit Singh Barnala is appointed governor of Tamil Nadu for a five-year term.

13: The Empowered Sub-Committee of the National Development Council (NDC) on Financial and Administrative Empowerment of the Panchayati Raj Institutions (PRIs) adopts a roadmap on how to move forward in empowering the PRIs financially and administratively.

14: Maharashtra cuts VAT on petrol, diesel.

15: Rahul Bajaj, industrialist, is elected to the Rajya Sabha from Maharashtra. President A.P.J. Abdul Kalam appoints R.S. Gavai to be the governor of Bihar with effect from the date he assumes charge of his office.

16: The Union Cabinet gives its approval for signing the International Convention for the Suppression of Acts of Nuclear Terrorism. The Union Cabinet approves the setting up of a National Fisheries Development Board (NFDB) with an estimated budget of Rs 2,100 crore over the next six years. The Union Cabinet approves a policy for allotting land to political parties for construction of their offices in Delhi. The land will be provided at institutional rates and the extent will depend on the strength of the parties in Parliament.

19: The Union government constitutes a committee to look into the functioning of the All-India Institute of Medical Sciences (AIIMS). The National Wildlife Board allows final clearance to the creation of a Wildlife Crime Control Bureau (WCCB) armed with investigative powers to curb poaching of endangered animals and illegal trade in their parts. It is also decided to provide legal powers under the Wildlife (Protection) Act, 1972, to Army Commanders for containing poaching in the border areas of Jammu and Kashmir and the North-East.

21: Jet Airways fails to get clearance for joining the Sahara Board. Jet's takeover bid falls through.

22: Union rural development minister Raghuvansh Prasad Singh announces Rs 2,000 crore for rural roads connectivity in Jammu and Kashmir under the Pradhan Mantri Gram Sadak Yojana (PMGSY). The amount will be used for connecting 1,820 villages having a population of more than 500. The government clears the sale of 10 per cent equity stake in the public sector National Aluminium Company Limited (NALCO) and Neyveli Lignite Corporation (NLC). The exercise will raise Rs 2,500 crore.

25: Luxembourg-based Arcelor, the world's second largest steel maker, based in Rotterdam, the Netherlands, accepts a merger offer from Mittal

The Penguin 20/20 Quiz

Netaji Subhash Chandra Bose

1. In 1922, of which paper started by Deshbandhu Chittaranjan Das did Netaji become the editor?
2. At which Congress session was Netaji chosen President?
3. In 1936, on Netaji's return to India, where was he arrested?
4. Who was the Commander of Netaji's Rani Jhansi Regiment—the women's wing of the Indian National army?
5. In 1943, while in Tokyo, which historic meeting did Netaji convene?
6. Which neighbouring country was used as passage for Netaji's forces to enter India in 1944?
7. What clarion call did Netaji give to his colleagues in the Indian National Army?
8. Where did Netaji give this call for the first time?
9. Where were the captured soldiers of Netaji's army tried?
10. In 1945, where did Netaji lay the foundation stone for a Martyr's Square?
11. Which famous author wrote about Netaji in his book *Thy Hand, Great Anarch*?
12. In which city did Subhas Chandra Bose first meet his wife Emilie Schenkl?
13. Why was the book *The India Struggle* banned in India?
14. By what name did Subhas Chandra Bose refer to Japan as in the famous speech 'Give Me Blood! I Promise You Freedom!'?
15. What was the name of the hospital in which Netaji supposedly breathed his last?
16. What was mentioned as the cause of Subhas Chandra Bose's death at the hospital where he supposedly died?
17. Where in Tokyo are the ashes of Netaji preserved?
18. Apart from Subhas Chandra Bose, who was the other person to take the ICS exam in 1920?
19. What name did Subhas Chandra Bose acquire at Peshawar?
20. Netaji was born in which city in Orissa?

Answers

1. *Forward* 2. Haripura, 1938 3. Mumbai 4. Colonel Lakshmi Sehgal 5. South East Asian Indian Independence League 6. Myanmar 7. 'Chalo Delhi' 8. Padang, Sinagpore 9. Red Fort, New Delhi 10. Sonan 11. Nirad C. Chaudhuri 12. Vienna 13. The book tended to encourage terrorism and direct action 14. Nippon 15. Nanmon Military Hospital, Taihoku, Taipei 16. 'Burns of third degree' 17. Renkoji Temple 18. K.P.S. Menon 19. Maulvi Ziauddin 20. Cuttack

Steel, the world's number one steel producer.

28: Prime Minister Manmohan Singh launches a quality mark for handloom products on the lines of the wool mark and the silk mark. The Empowered Committee for Pradhan Mantri Gram Sadak Yojana (PMGSY) under the Union Rural Development Ministry approves 134 rural road projects for Bihar, costing Rs 494.87 crore.

29: The Union Cabinet's Committee on Economic Affairs (CCEA) issues in-principle approval to the Indian Council for Agricultural Research (ICAR) for regulation of higher agricultural education. It approves an additional fund of Rs 200 crore for strengthening agricultural education for the remaining period of the current five-year plan, over and above the regular provisions of Rs 720 crore. The government clears the construction of 608 km of roads along the Sino–Indian border at a cost of Rs 992 crore. The Union Cabinet gives private phone companies another three months to comply with the new norms incorporated after the increase in the ceiling on foreign direct investment in the telecom sector from 49 to 74 per cent.

30: The government announces the seat sharing arrangement and the fee structure for professional courses for 2006-07. The government has made an understanding with private colleges on a 50:50 seat-sharing ratio for medical and dental courses and 60:40 for engineering courses. In the case of minority institutions, the seat-sharing ratio between the government and private colleges is 40:60 for medical and dental courses and 50:50 for engineering courses.

July 2006

1: To enhance the quality of customer service and strengthen the grievance redressal mechanism, the Reserve Bank of India constitutes a new department—Customer Service Department (CSD). Thirteen-year-old Parimarjan Negi becomes the youngest chess grandmaster in the world and second youngest in the history of the game.

2: Rahul Dravid becomes the fastest batsman in the history of Test cricket to make 9,000 runs.

3: The parliaments of India and China signs the first-ever agreement to regularize bilateral exchanges. The Union social justice and empowerment ministry prints the Right to Information Act, 2005, in Braille. India clinches the Test series against West Indies; the only previous Test series win in West Indies came in 1971.

4: India and Italy signs a memorandum of understanding (MoU) to pave the way for forming a joint working group that will identify railway projects of mutual interest.

6: India and China inaugurates trade through the Nathu La Pass, linking Sikkim and the Tibet Autonomous Region (TAR). The 4,310-metre-high pass was closed forty-four years ago after the 1962 conflict. The Cabinet Committee on Security approves the purchase of three warships and twenty-eight submarine-fired cruise missiles from Russia. The Cabinet Committee on Economic Affairs decides to retain 100 per cent compulsory packing for foodgrains and sugar in jute bags for the jute year 2006-07 (July to June).

7: India's foreign exchange reserves increase by $952 million to $162.912 billion. Inflation rate slips below the 5 per cent mark.

8: Celebrated author Raja Rao passes away. International Cricket Council (ICC) announces India as the host of the 2011 World Cup final.

11: Terror strikes at Mumbai; over 147 killed in seven serial blasts in Mumbai's suburban railway network.

12: National Statistical Commission comes into operation.

13: The Union government announces increased duty drawback rates

The Penguin 20/20 Quiz

Agra

1. What is the name of the sole entry point to the Agra Fort?
2. The famous Itimad-ud-Daulah tomb was the tomb of which courtier?
3. What is Nai Ki Mandi near the Jama Masjid in Agra famous for?
4. Chini Ka Rauza in Agra is the mausoleum of which high official of the court of Shah Jahan?
5. The Agra area is the only place in India to have three UNESCO World Heritage Monuments. Agra Fort and Taj Mahal are two of them. Which is the third?
6. Which airport serves Agra?
7. Buland Darwaza was built to commemorate the victory of Akbar over which state?
8. About Birbal Bhawan in Agra, which famous French author commented that it was either a very small palace or a very large jewellery box?
9. What was the name of the Goan wife of Akbar who lived at the Golden House?
10. Who was the first person to refer to Agra by its modern name?
11. How do we know Mirza Asadullah Khan better?
12. Which Mughal emperor built the Ram Bagh?
13. Which district borders Agra district on the north?
14. In Agra, where did Prime Minister A. B. Vajpayee meet with General Musharraf?
15. By what name is Agra mentioned in the *Mahabharata*?
16. In the first ever first-class match played at Agra's Sadar Bazar Stadium, which team did Delhi defeat?
17. The tradition of giving a silver key (of the city) to dignitaries visiting Agra was forfeited in the case of General Musharraf's visit. What was he given instead?
18. Which foreign dignitary called Agra 'the city of ghosts'?
19. The tomb of which noble of Jahangir and Shah Jahan's court is popularly known as Chausath-Khambha?
20. Who founded the Battis Khambah, a garden on the left bank of the River Yamuna?

Answers

1. Amar Singh Gate 2. Mirza Ghiyas Beg (Begum Nur Jahan's father) 3. Textiles 4. Afzal Khan 5. Fatehpur Sikri 6. Kheria Airport 7. Gujarat 8. Victor Hugo 9. Maryam 10. Ptolemy 11. Mirza Ghalib 12. Babur 13. Mathura 14. Jaypee Palace Hotel 15. Agraban 16. United Provinces 17. A carpet with a design of the Taj Mahal. 18. Bill Clinton 19. Salabat Khan 20. Buland Khan Khwajasara

that would take into account service tax and bring in eighty-four new items that would be entitled to refund of taxes paid while producing the goods for exports. The Centre approves extension of the 'flexible complementing scheme (FCS)' in force in the Council of Scientific and Industrial Research (CSIR) laboratories to the scientists of the coffee, rubber and spices boards. The Securities and Exchange Board of India asks all stock exchanges to make permanent account number (PAN) mandatory for all the entities/persons trading in the cash market with effect from October.

14: With nine directives failing to curb customer complaints about misleading tariff plans and levying of charges without consent, the Telecom Regulatory Authority of India (TRAI) decides to seek compliance reports on six parameters from all telecom-service providers every year. The Taxation Laws (Amendment) Act that among other things makes it mandatory for charitable institutions and scientific associations with annual receipts of over Rs 1 crore to file tax returns, comes into force.

15: The Supreme Court declares that 'an employer is not liable to pay compensation under the Workmen Compensation Act if his employee dies after a heart attack at the work spot'.

16: The Indian Council of Agricultural Research (ICAR) develops a vaccine against bird flu.

18: The Centre notifies the rules making mandatory carrying of pictorial health warning signs on all packs of tobacco products.

20: The Union Cabinet gives its nod for setting up the Sixth Pay Commission with an eighteen-month tenure to submit its recommendations on wage revision. The Union Cabinet gives its approval for the introduction of a Bill amending the Right to Information Act, 2005. The Union Cabinet approves further amendments to the Wildlife (Protection) Amendment Bill, 2005, to facilitate implementation of the Tiger Task Force recommendations.

21: The Reserve Bank of India allows banks to augment their capital funds through the issue of Innovative Perpetual Debit Instruments (IPDI) in foreign currency up to 49 per cent of the eligible amount (i.e., 15 per cent of Tier I capital) without seeking the prior approval of the RBI subject to compliance with certain specified conditions.

23: The Centre constitutes a commission for economically backward classes.

24: Abhinav Bindra clinches the World Championship gold, the first ever for the country in shooting.

25: Department of Biotechnology under the Union ministry of science and technology releases the 'Jeeva Sampada,' the first-ever digitized inventory of India's vast bio-resource. The Reserve Bank of India (RBI) hikes the short-term indicative interest rates by 25 basis points (0.25 percentage point).

27: The Rajya Sabha passes the Parliament (Prevention of Disqualification) Amendment Bill, 2006, which was returned by President A.P.J. Abdul Kalam on May 25 for reconsideration. The Reserve Bank of India raises the ceiling on investments that can be made by registered domestic mutual funds in overseas markets, besides expanding the investment options available to them. The aggregate ceiling for overseas investment by the funds is increased from $1 billion to $2 billion with immediate effect.

29: India and Bhutan enter into an agreement for long-term cooperation in the field of hydel power and also ink another protocol document for the purchase of power generated by the 1,020 MW Tala hydel project.

31: Delhi High Court declares that the Conditional Access System (CAS) will be implemented in Delhi, Mumbai and Kolkata from 1 January 2007.

The Penguin 20/20 Quiz

Rath Yatra

1. What are the cloth paintings representing the deities during Rath Yatra called?
2. Who is the presiding deity of the Jagannatha temple?
3. According to the Hindu calendar, in which month does the Rath Yatra of Jagannatha takes place?
4. According to legend, which king commissioned the divine architect Vishwakarma to carve the statue of Krishna at the Jagannatha temple?
5. What is the festival during which the new images are installed at the Jagannatha temple called?
6. Whose chariot is also known as Nandighosha?
7. Ananta Barma Chodaganga Dev started the building of the Jagannatha temple? Who completed it?
8. What is the name of Subhadra's chariot?
9. Which temple is the destination of the Rath during the Rath Yatra in Puri?
10. What is the name of the ceremonial sweeping of the floor by the King of Puri ?
11. Who is the guardian deity of the chariot of Jagannatha?
12. Who is the charioteer of Subhadra's chariot?
13. What is the name of the rope that pulls the chariot of Balarama?
14. Who apart from 'Tibra', 'Ghora' and 'Dirghashran' pulls the chariot of Balabhadra?
15. What is the colour of cloth wrappings of the chariot of Subhadra?
16. What is the name of Balarama's chariot?
17. What marks the beginning of the construction of the Raths (chariots) for the ceremonial journey?
18. After bathing the deities, they are kept from public view for treatment and rest for fourteen days. What is this period called?
19. The Jagannath temple is bounded by two enclosures. If the outer enclosure is called Meghanad Prachir, what is the inner enclosure called?
20. What is the return journey of the Rath Yatra called?

Answers

1. Anasara Pati 2. Krishna 3. Ashadha 4. Indradhumna 5. Nav-kalebara 6. Jagannatha 7. Ananga Bhima Dev 8. Deviratha or Darpadalana 9. Gundicha Temple 10. Chhera Pahanra 11. Garuda 12. Arjuna 13. Basuki 14. Swarnanva 15. Red and black 16. Taladhwaj 17. Akshaya Tritiyatithi 18. Anasara 19. Kurma Bedha 20. Bahuda Yatra

August 2006

1: The government bans employment of children as domestic servants or workers, and as helpers in dhabas, restaurants, hotels, motels, teashops, resorts, spas and other recreational centres. The ban, effective from 10 October this year, is imposed under the Child Labour (Prohibition & Regulation) Act, 1986. Infosys Technologies Ltd becomes the first company from India to ring the remote opening bell—only the third time in the thirty-five-year history of NASDAQ.

2: The Centre for Science and Environment (CSE) brings out a new report on the levels of pesticides in soft drinks available in the market. The report indicates the presence of an average of three to five different pesticides in all the samples, twenty-four times higher than the Bureau of Indian Standards (BIS) norms. The Rajya Sabha passes a Bill seeking to consolidate laws relating to food and establish a regulatory body for the food-processing sector. The Lok Sabha approves a bill to regulate and develop the profession of actuaries.

3: The Justice R.S. Pathak Inquiry Authority, which investigated the Iraqi oil-for-food scam, reports that the former external affairs minister K. Natwar Singh, and his son Jagat Singh, an MLA from Rajasthan, misused their positions in getting contracts. The directorate-general of civil aviation (DGCA) devises a computerized written test for aspirants to streamline the procedure of granting Commercial Pilot Licence (CPL). The Sensex touches the 11,000 mark.

4: Veteran Congress leader and former Orissa chief minister Nandini Satpathy passes away. The Central government launches the certified filing centres (CFCs) scheme across the country as part of the e-governance project of the ministry of company affairs to facilitate faster online registration of companies.

8: The Congress suspends the former external affairs minister, K. Natwar Singh, from primary membership of the party and decides to serve a show-cause notice asking him to explain why he should not be expelled. The parliament passes the Juvenile Justice (Care and Protection of Children) Amendment Bill, 2006. Prime Minister Manmohan Singh approves proposals for a thorough restructuring of the organizational configuration of the country's external intelligence establishment, the Research and Analysis Wing.

9: The State Bank of India (SBI) becomes the first Indian bank to begin full-fledged operations in China by opening a branch there.

10: Noted Marathi writer Vinda Karandikar receives the Jnanpith Award for 2003.

11: Prime Minister Manmohan Singh announces Central assistance of Rs 350 crore for flood relief operations in Gujarat. India's forex reserves increase by $1.77 billion to $165.795 billion.

12: The government reconstitutes the National Security Advisory Board (NSAB) with former foreign secretary M.K. Rasgotra named convener for a second term.

15: Prime Minister Manmohan Singh launches Doordarshan's Urdu channel. The Board of Control for Cricket in India (BCCI) Marketing Committee approves sponsorship bids concerning Team India's formal wear and accessories, BCCI Ratings and Awards, and the Board's web portal.

17: The Insurance Regulatory and Development Authority (IRDA) constitutes an Expert Committee under the chairmanship of G.K. Raman to review the regulations governing the licensing of brokers, particularly in the context of the de-tariffing of non-life insurance from next year.

18: President A.P.J. Abdul Kalam gives his assent to the amended Parlia-

The Penguin 20/20 Quiz

Indira Gandhi

1. Indira Gandhi was elected to the seventh Lok Sabha from two places. One was Rae Bareli. What was the other?
2. Who wrote the biography which came into a controversy when Maneka Gandhi decided to sue the author?
3. On which date was Indira Gandhi assassinated?
4. In 1977, Indira Gandhi became the first prime minister to lose an election. She later won a by-election from which constituency in Karnataka?
5. Who played the female lead in *Aandhi*, a film which created a controversy as it bore a resemblance to the life of Indira Gandhi?
6. What was the name of Indira Gandhi's aunt, Jawaharlal Nehru's sister, who was married to the industrialist G.P. Hutheesing?
7. With which Pakistani president did Indira Gandhi sign the Simla Agreement?
8. In which Indian city was Indira Gandhi born?
9. For her contribution to which field was Indira Gandhi conferred the Diploma of Honour by the Argentine Society in 1971?
10. Which jail was she in from 11 September 1942 until 13 May 1943?
11. Which portfolio did Indira Gandhi hold in Lal Bahadur Shastri's cabinet?
12. During Indira Gandhi's rule, which socialist leader began the 'Citizens for Democracy' movement?
13. During which two Lok Sabha sessions was Indira Gandhi expelled from Parliament?
14. On 26 June 1975, which Indian President declared a State of Emergency?
15. Who was the last woman to be elected president of the Congress Party before Indira Gandhi?
16. In 1969, who led the anti-Indira Gandhi faction that resulted in the split of the Congress Party?
17. In the General Elections of 1980, which Karnataka heavyweight did Indira Gandhi defeat?
18. What is Indira Gandhi's middle name?
19. Following Indira Gandhi's victory in the 1980 elections, whom did she appoint as Congress Party General Secretary?
20. What is Indira Gandhi's samadhi in Delhi called?

Answers

1. Medak 2. Katherine Frank 3. 31 October 1984 4. Chikmagalur 5. Suchitra Sen 6. Krishna 7. Z. A. Bhutto 8. Allahabad 9. Protection of animals 10. The Naini Central Jail in Allahabad 11. Minister for Information and Broadcasting 12. Jayaprakash Narayan 13. 5th and 6th sessions 14. Fakhruddin Ali Ahmed 15. Nellie Sengupta, 1933 16. S. Nijalingappa 17. Veerandra Patil 18. Priyadarshini 19. Sanjay Gandhi 20. Shakti sthal

ment (Prevention of Disqualification) Act, 1959, popularly known as the office of profit bill.

19: Parliament adopts the Cantonment Bill, 2006, with the Lok Sabha passing it with a voice vote. The Supreme Court declares that employment in nationalized banks to family members of deceased persons on compassionate grounds is not automatic and will be granted in rare necessitous circumstances.

20: IT major Infosys chairman N.R. Narayana Murthy retires from the service of the company which he had launched as a small firm in the city in 1981.

21: Ustad Bismillah Khan passes away. Viswanathan Anand wins the Chess Classic at Mainz for the sixth time. The Rajya Sabha passes a Bill to rename the Union territory (UT) of Pondicherry as Puducherry.

22: To help publishers across the country, the registrar of newspapers for India (RNI) starts issuing on-line title verification letters by which applications can be submitted on-line and their status known on the RNI website.

24: The Lok Sabha approves the Bill to rename Pondicherry Puducherry. The Lok Sabha passes the Protection of Human Rights (Amendment) Bill.

31: TRAI fixes the maximum retail price for a channel at Rs 5 per month. Broadcasters will have to offer pay channels on an a la carte basis. The maximum price of FTA for thirty channels is fixed at Rs 77 plus taxes. The Seventeenth Law Commission suggests comprehensive 'Witness Identity Protection' (WIP) and 'Witness Protection' (WP) programmes to prevent witnesses from turning hostile under threat from the accused and to ensure that criminal trials do not end in acquittals. The Board of Control for Cricket in India (BCCI) launches the 'BCCI Official Ratings and Awards' for the 2006-07 season.

September 2006

1: Vice-Admiral Rustom Faramroze Contractor is appointed as the new director general (DG) of the Coast Guard.

4: The Telecom Regulatory Authority of India issues an amendment to the Interconnection Regulation to streamline arrangements among service providers for interconnection and revenue-sharing for all broadcasting and cable services. It stipulates, among other things, a notice period of three weeks for disconnection of TV channel signals by a broadcaster to any distributor of TV channels.

5: Jagat Singh, son of former external affairs minister K. Natwar Singh, and MLA, is expelled from the primary membership of the Congress.

7: The Union government announces a grant of 5 per cent additional dearness allowance for its employees with retrospective effect from 1 July.

8: Inflation rate crosses 5 per cent mark.

10: Leander Paes and Martin Damm wins the men's doubles title at the US Open.

12: TADA court in Mumbai holds four of the eight members of the Memon family guilty in the 1993 Mumbai bomb blasts case.

13: The Securities and Exchange Board of India (SEBI) constitutes a new committee—SEBI Committee on Disclosures and Accounting Standards (SCODA).

14: The revised National Building Code 2005, formulated by the Bureau of Indian Standards, is released. The Union government, in consultation with the Reserve Bank of India (RBI), constitutes a Committee on Financial Sector Assessment with reference to the Handbook on the theme brought out in 1995 by the World Bank and the International Monetary Fund.

15: The Sensex closes above the 12,000 mark.

The Penguin 20/20 Quiz

Sachin Tendulkar

1. Which Pakistani player made his debut in the same Test match as Sachin?
2. Sachin was named after which legendary music director?
3. Sachin was born on 24 April 1973. What is his middle name?
4. Who gave Sachin the nickname 'Sten'?
5. In 1992, Sachin became the first overseas player to play for which county?
6. According to Sachin, which is his favourite cricket ground?
7. Sachin did his schooling from which school in Dadar?
8. Who was his famous school coach then?
9. Name the Indian cricketer who was Sachin's teammate and close friend with whom he shared a massive 664 run partnership in school cricket.
10. Sachin has been called Master Blaster. But, which West Indian batsman was also nicknamed Master Blaster?
11. Who was the bowler when Sachin scored his 10,000th ODI run?
12. During the 1999 World Cup, Tendulkar flew back home after his father died. He returned to score 140 against which team?
13. How many runs did Sachin score in the innings in which he equalled Bradman's record of 29 centuries?
14. Sachin scored his first Test double century against which team?
15. Sachin scored a century against which team on his Ranji debut for Bombay?
16. Tendulkar scored his first international century in the second Test against England in 1990. On which cricket ground did he achieve this milestone?
17. Which former English all-rounder paid this compliment to Sachin: 'Everytime I see him he gets better, his concentration reminds me of Sunny'?
18. In 1992, Sachin was the first cricketer to be given out by a third umpire. Who were the two umpires on video duty at that time?
19. Sachin made his one day international debut in 1989-90 at Gujranwala. How many runs did he score then?
20. In which year was he one of the Wisden Cricketers of the Year?

Answers

1. Waqar Younis 2. Sachin Dev Burman. 3. Ramesh 4. Sunil Gavaskar 5. Yorkshire 6. The Sydney Cricket Ground 7. Shardashram High School 8. Ramakant Achrekar 9. Vinod Kambli 10. Vivian Richards 11. Shane Warne 12. Kenya 13. 117 14. New Zealand 15. Gujarat 16. Old Trafford in Manchester 17. Ian Botham. 18. Karl Liebenberg and Cyril Mitchley 19. Zero 20. 1997

Celebrating 20 Years of Penguin Books India

16: Prime Minister Manmohan Singh and Pakistani President Pervez Musharraf decide to put in place an institutional mechanism to counter terrorism.

18: Famous industrialist and philanthropist M.C. Muthiah passes away. Former India football captain Sudip Chatterjee passes away.

19: Yaws, a chronic infectious disease, is declared eliminated from India.

20: The Central Board of Direct Taxes fixes the Cost Inflation Index at 519 for 2006-07.

21: The Union Cabinet approves a Rs 5,742-crore scheme to set up 1 lakh common service centres (CSCs) in rural areas across the country that would offer a basket of government to citizens and business to customer services.

25: *Rang De Basanti* is declared India's entry to the Oscars in the Best Foreign Film category.

27: Former India cricket captain Dilip Vengsarkar is elected chairman of the National Selection Committee for two years. The Sensex touches the 12,400 mark.

29: The Union Cabinet, chaired by Prime Minister Manmohan Singh, approves a Rs 16,978.69-crore rehabilitation package for farmers in the districts of Andhra Pradesh, Karnataka, Kerala and Maharashtra. The Indian Institute of Management, Ahmedabad, agrees to implement the 27 per cent quota for the socially and economically backward classes from the next academic year.

October 2006

3: The Supreme Court directs the Centre and all state governments to prevent unreasonable delay in disposal of criminal cases.

4: The Reserve Bank of India asks banks to 'invariably' offer passbook facilities to individual savings account holders without charging them for the same.

5: 673 dengue cases are reported in Delhi and nearby areas. The Cabinet Committee on Economic Affairs (CCEA) clears a Rs 41,210 crore programme for converting 6,500 km of national highways from four to six lanes through public-private partnership based on the build-operate-transfer model.

6: The Central government approves twenty-five more special economic zones (SEZs), including Indonesia's Salim Group's proposal for setting up two SEZs in West Bengal at an investment of Rs 12,500 crore. Inflation rate rises to 4.77 per cent. The Telecom Regulatory Authority of India (TRAI) issues regulations on the quality of service of broadband services.

8: The Union Health Ministry releases nationwide data on the dengue outbreak.

9: Bahujan Samaj Party (BSP) founder Kanshi Ram passes away.

10: Number of dengue cases crosses 1,000 in Delhi. The ban on the employment of children below the age of fourteen as domestic help and in dhabas, restaurants, hotels and the hospitality sectors comes into effect under the provisions of the Child Labour (Prohibition and Regulation) Act, 1986. Kiran Desai wins the prestigious Man Booker Prize for Fiction 2006 for her novel *The Inheritance of Loss*.

11: The French government confers its highest civilian award the Legion d'Honneur on Bollywood legend Amitabh Bachchan.

13: The Sensex records a new all-time high of 12,690, surpassing the previous high of 12,671 recorded on 11 May. Inflation rate rises to 5.16 per cent.

14: IOL Broadband rolls out India's first IPTV (Internet Protocol Television) service, enabling subscriber access to digital television services through Internet Protocol, in association with the Mahanagar Telephone Nigam Ltd (MTNL).

16: The Union Cabinet approves the process of new wage settlements for employees in Central public sector enterprises (CPSE). The new wage structures are due to come into effect from 1 January 2007. The Sensex records a new all-time high of 12,953.

17: The Union Human Resource Development Ministry revises the guidelines of the Mid-Day Meal Scheme to increase calorie and protein content, and introduce micronutrients in food served under the largest school meal programme in the world.

20: India's forex reserves decline by $324 million to $164.951 billion. Tata Steel acquires Corus—an 18.2 million ton Anglo-Dutch steelmaker—for US$ 8.1 billion. Corus is the ninth biggest steel producer in the world. The deal will catapult the combined entity to a global rank of the fifth among the largest steelmakers in the world.

24: The Union Cabinet is reshuffled. The External Affairs portfolio, which had been with Prime Minister Manmohan Singh since the resignation of K. Natwar Singh, goes to Pranab Mukherjee, while the Labour ministry, which had fallen vacant after TRS chief K. Chandrasekhar Rao quit the cabinet, goes to Oscar Fernandes. A.K. Antony becomes the new Defence Minister.

25: A fire breaks out in a vacuum gas oil hydrotreater unit in Reliance Industries' Jamnagar refinery, resulting in losses estimated at several hundred crore. The Supreme Court directs that relaxation of age limit for general categories or even for SC and ST candidates or retrenched Central government employees, including defence personnel, is not automatic. Punjab beats Bengal 5-3 in penalties to win the Santosh Trophy final played in Gurgaon.

26: The Domestic Violence Act comes into effect. India signs a contract with Russia to buy 330 T-90S main battle tanks (MBTs). HRD Minister Arjun Singh launches phase two of his plans for reservations in education, involving private colleges. A terrorist plot to attack Karnataka's assembly is foiled by the state police. Mumbai police releases full list of terrorists wanted in the 7/11 case. Actor and social activist Shabana Azmi is awarded the International Gandhi Peace Prize in London for her work amongst the disadvantaged women of India, particularly in Mumbai slums. She is the first Indian to get this award.

27: The Union government approves foty-four special economic zones (SEZs), including those of Wockhardt, Ansals, Parsvnath Developers and Sun City, involving an investment of over Rs 40,000 crore.

28: Traders in Delhi meet UPA chairperson Sonia Gandhi in an attempt to stop the sealing of their commercial establishments in residential areas. The deadline for the sealing drive is 31 October. India becomes the sixth member of the exclusive club to have developed a cryogenic stage in rocketry when it successfully tests a full-fledged cryogenic stage for 50 seconds at the Liquid Propulsion Systems Centre (LPSC) at Mahendragiri, Tamil Nadu.

30: The Sensex crosses the 13,000 mark for the very first time, reaches 13,005. Traders go on strike in Delhi; the anti-sealing drive turns ugly when traders clash with police. The Delhi High Court sentences Santosh Kumar Singh to death in the much-publicized case of the rape and murder of law student Priyadarshini Mattoo.

31: Reserve Bank of India hikes repo rate by 0.25 per cent to 7.25 per cent. Admiral Sureesh Mehta takes over as Chief of Naval Staff from Admiral Arun Prakash. Metropolitan Corporation of Delhi (MCD) petitions the Supreme Court to stop the sealing drive.

World Dateline

October 2005

1: A Russian rocket lifts a Soyuz spacecraft towards the International Space Station, carrying the third fare-paying space tourist, American Gregory Olsen.

2: The astronomers who discovered 2003 UB313, referred to as 'the tenth planet' by NASA, announce that it has a moon, S/2005 (2003 UB313) 1, which is being nicknamed Gabrielle.

3: Australians Barry J. Marshall and Robin Warren are named as the recipients of the 2005 Nobel Prize in Physiology or Medicine 'for their discovery of the bacterium Helicobacter pylori and its role in gastritis and peptic ulcer disease'.

4: One million French transportation workers and teachers hold a nationwide strike in opposition to the Prime Minister Dominique de Villepin's economic and labour policies, forcing the closure of schools and airports. Roy J. Glauber, John L. Hall and Theodor W. Hänsch share the 2005 Nobel Prize in Physics. Google and Sun Microsystems announce an alliance to promote each other's products.

5: England international football player Wayne Rooney is named FIFA SOS Ambassador for England, in support of the official World Cup charity. The Royal Swedish Academy of Sciences awards Yves Chauvin, Robert H. Grubbs, and Richard R. Schrock the 2005 Nobel Prize in Chemistry, 'for the development of the metathesis method in organic synthesis'.

7: The UN International Atomic Energy Agency and its Director-General Mohamed ElBaradei share the 2005 Nobel Peace Prize for their efforts to limit the spread of atomic weapons.

10: The Japan Aerospace Exploration Agency successfully tests a $10 million jet that travels at twice the speed of sound. The Royal Swedish Academy of Sciences awards Thomas Schelling and Robert Aumann the 2005 Bank of Sweden Prize in Economic Sciences in Memory of Alfred Nobel, 'for having enhanced our understanding of conflict and cooperation through game-theory analysis'. The former President of Uganda, Milton Obote, passes away.

12: The People's Republic of China launches the manned Shenzhou 6 spacecraft.

13: The presence of the dangerous H5N1 avian influenza virus is confirmed in dead birds found in Turkey, marking the first cases of the disease in Europe. In Stockholm, it is announced that British playwright Harold Pinter is the 2005 winner of the Nobel Prize for Literature.

15: The Iraqi people go to the polls to vote on whether to approve the proposed constitution.

16: Chinese manned spacecraft Shenzhou 6 lands safely in Inner Mongolia, China.

17: Israel bans Palestinians from travelling throughout the West Bank and cuts off contact with the Palestinian Authority. Jens Stoltenberg takes over as the Prime Minister of Norway after Kjell Magne Bondevik. Bill and Melinda Gates Foundation pledges $15 million for the Computer History Museum in Silicon Valley, the world's largest institution dedicated to preserving Information Age artefacts.

19: Saddam Hussein goes on trial in Baghdad for crimes against humanity.

20: Ontario announces its becoming the first Canadian province to extend daylight-saving time.

22: The first case of avian influenza (bird flu) is discovered in the United Kingdom from a South American parrot.

24: Rosa Parks, whose famous refusal in 1955 to surrender her bus seat to a white man in Montgomery, Alabama, triggered a bus-boycott and the beginning of the modern US civil rights movement, passes away. US President George W. Bush nominates Ben Bernanke to succeed Alan Greenspan as chair of the Federal Reserve Board.

25: The United Nations Children's Fund (Unicef), UNAIDS and other partners launch a global campaign, known as 'Unite for Children, Unite Against AIDS'. The Swedish telecom manufacturer Ericsson buys the troubled British telecom manufacturer Marconi.

28: Sinah-1, the first Iranian satellite built jointly with Russia, is launched from Plesetsk Cosmodrome in Murmansk Oblast in north-western Russia.

November 2005

1: The discovery of two additional moons of Pluto is announced.

2: Eighty of the world's top radio astronomers meet in Pune, India, to decide how and where to set up the world's biggest radio telescope, the Square Kilometre Array. Deutsche Telekom AG, Europe's biggest phone company, announces its plan to cut 32,000 jobs from its payroll in Germany in the next three years, 25,000 at its main operations and 7,000 from a staffing agency subsidiary.

7: China closes all Beijing poultry markets because of avian influenza. India opens the first of three frontier checkpoints at Chakan da Bagh in Poonch on the Kashmir Line of Control (LoC) between India and Pakistan, for 2005 Kashmir earthquake relief work.

8: French President Jacques Chirac declares a state of emergency on the twelfth day of the civil unrest.

9: Amir Peretz is elected leader of the Labour Party in Israel, narrowly defeating the incumbent, Shimon Peres. In Israel, archaeologists discover two lines of a Phoenician or Hebrew alphabet on a stone dating to the tenth century BC, suggesting that literacy existed in ancient Israel earlier than had been thought. Venus Express, the first mission to Venus in over a decade, lifts off from the Baikonur Cosmodrome in Kazakhstan.

10: Ellen Johnson-Sirleaf defeats George Weah in the Liberian presidential elections to become the first-ever female president on the continent of Africa. The US House of Representatives drops a provision in the Deficit Reduction Bill that would permit the drilling of the Arctic National Wildlife Refuge. A Boeing 777-200LR Worldliner jet aircraft breaks the record for the longest non-stop passenger airline flight. The 20,000-km (12,500 mile) flight from Hong Kong to London lasted twenty-three hours.

11: Albania suffers its worst ever electric power shortage. Due to low water levels, hydroelectric power is reduced to the minimum and there are blackouts in all the country. The deadly H5N1 bird flu is found in Kuwait, the first case of the virus in the Middle East. Saudi Arabia becomes a member of the World Trade Organization after twelve years of talks. Peter Drucker, Austria-born management visionary, dies in California.

13: Thailand confirms its fourth H5N1 bird flu case this year. The South Asian Association for Regional Cooperation agrees at its summit to admit Afghanistan as a member, and to accord China and Japan observer status.

14: The US government issues warning after receiving credible information that a terrorist threat may exist against official US government facilities in Guangzhou, China.

15: One hundred and seventy three prisoners are found in an Iraqi government bunker in Baghdad, having been starved, beaten and tortured. Sayako, Princess Nori of Japan, marries a commoner and thereby leaves the imperial family, taking the surname of her husband. The French parliament permits President Jacques Chirac's government to extend emergency powers for three months to quell civil unrest. Sony BMG recalls all unsold CDs that are equipped with XCP, a controversial copyright protection software.

16: The health ministry of the People's Republic of China announces the country's first confirmed, and one suspected, cases of avian flu in humans in Hunan province. Australia qualifies for the FIFA World Cup for the first time since 1974 following a victory over Uruguay. Members of the European Parliament pass an item of controversial chemical safety testing legislation, known as the Registration, Evaluation and Authorization of Chemicals (REACH) law.

19: After negotiations, Maoist rebels in Nepal agree to work with opposition politicians in a common front against the rule of King Gyanendra. Prince Albert of Monaco is formally enthroned.

20: *Harry Potter and the Goblet of Fire*, the latest of the film based on the books by J.K. Rowling, earns US$101.4 million in its first three days of release across North America, making it the fourth-largest opening ever.

21: The prime minister of Israel, Ariel Sharon, announces his resignation from Likud.

22: After two months of negotiations, Angela Merkel is elected the first female chancellor of Germany by a coalition of the CDU/CSU and SPD delegates in the Bundestag.

24: Japan finalizes an agreement to forgive $6.1 billion of Iraqi debt, or about 80 per cent of the total owed by Baghdad.

25: Polish defence minister Radek Sikorski opens Warsaw Pact archives to historians. Maps of possible nuclear strikes against western Europe, as well as the possible nuclear annihilation of forty-three Polish cities and 2 million of its citizens by Soviet-controlled forces, are released.

26: Vijaypat Singhania of India sets a world record for the highest hot-air balloon flight, reaching 69,852 feet (20.29 km).

28: The twenty-third South-east Asian Games formally open in Manila, Philippines.

29: Canada's prime minister Paul Martin's minority government is defeated in a confidence motion by a vote of 171–33. The tribunal trying Saddam Hussein and seven co-defendants is adjourned for a second time after hearing posthumous evidence. The United Nations Climate Change Conference opens in Montreal.

30: New policy document on American involvement in Iraq, 'National Strategy for Victory in Iraq', is published by the White House. Surgeons in France carry out the first human face transplant.

December 2005

1: South Africa's Constitutional Court declares that current marriage laws restricting marriage to opposite-sex couples are unconstitutional and must be changed within a year.

3: Adobe Systems merges with Macromedia.

4: Israel launches a series of air strikes as reprisals after the Palestinians fired Qassam rockets.

5: The twenty-third South-east Asian Games officially close with the Philippines gaining the top medal-ranking for the first time. The UK begins registration of civil unions for same-sex couples.

7: The third President of Singapore, Chengara Veetil Devan Nair, passes away. Microsoft loses a South Korean antitrust case, and is fined US$ 32 million.

8: The International Red Cross and Red Crescent Movement adopt a Red

Crystal design, allowing Israel to join as a fully-participating member. In Australia, the voluntary student unionism (VSU) legislation is passed in the Senate.

9: Viacom's Paramount Pictures agrees to buy Dreamworks SKG company, founded by Steven Spielberg, Jeffrey Katzenberg and David Geffen for $1.6 billion. The groups for the 2006 FIFA World Cup to be held in Germany are finalized.

10: The International Atomic Energy Agency and its Director-General Mohamed El Baradei receive the Nobel Peace Prize in Oslo. The other 2005 Nobel Prizes are handed out in Stockholm to Barry J. Marshall and Robin Warren (Physiology or Medicine), Roy J. Glauber and John L. Hall and Theodor W. Hänsch (Physics), Robert H. Grubbs, Richard R. Schrock and Yves Chauvin (Chemistry), Robert J. Aumann and Thomas C. Schelling (Economics), and Harold Pinter (Literature).

12: ASEAN Summit begins in Kuala Lumpur, Malaysia.

13: The Sixth Ministerial Conference of the World Trade Organization opens in Hong Kong. The President of the United States, George W. Bush, acknowledges the deaths of approximately 30,000 Iraqi civilians since the commencement of the Iraq War.

14: The European Parliament adopts the directive on Telecommunications data retention.

15: The European Council meets to discuss the next seven-year budget for the European Union. Voting starts in Iraq to elect the first permanent 275-member Iraqi National Assembly under the new Constitution of Iraq.

16: Bulgaria starts withdrawing its troops from Iraq. The United States Senate rejects the extension of the PATRIOT Act.

17: EU leaders agree on a seven-year spending plan for the twenty-five-nation bloc.

18: Extinct mammoth mitochondrial DNA decoded. Bono, Melinda Gates and Bill Gates are named *Time*'s Persons of the Year.

21: The former President of Iraq, Saddam Hussein, claims in court that American officials tortured him. The US Senate blocks oil drilling in the Arctic National Wildlife Refuge.

22: India's most advanced INSAT-4A telecommunication satellite is successfully launched by the EADS SPACE Transportation generic rocket, Ariane 5, from the spaceport of Kourou in French Guiana. Acetylene and hydrogen cyanide, precursors to life's basic ingredients (DNA and proteins), are found around a star in the constellation Ophiuchus.

23: Astronomers discover new moons and rings around Uranus using the Hubble Space Telescope. Lech Kaczyñski is sworn in as President of the republic of Poland. British private equity group Apax Partners acquires US fashion company Tommy Hilfiger Corp. for $1.6 billion.

28: Europe's 'sat-nav' technology satellite, Giove-A, is launched as part of the Galileo positioning system with the goal of providing access to timing and location information independent of the United States' prevalent GPS system.

29: Chinese state media announces that the country's government will abolish its national agricultural tax, starting 1 January 2006.

January 2006

1: Russian natural gas supplier Gazprom cuts gas supplies to Ukraine, following Ukraine's rejection of a 460 per cent price increase.

3: The Russian and Ukrainian natural gas companies agree to end their dispute and resume gas supply to Ukraine under a complex price scheme in which OAO Gazprom will sell gas to the Rosukrenergo trading company and Ukraine will buy gas from the company for US$ 95. Four years after defaulting on its external debt, Argentina pays its US$ 9.57 billion debt with the IMF.

4: Turkey announces two confirmed human cases of the avian influenza. Intel replaces the old sign, Intel Inside, with a new sign, Intel.

8: An estimated 2 million Muslims officially begin the annual pilgrimage, or hajj, in Mecca, Saudi Arabia. Singapore holds its largest civil counter-terrorism exercise, codenamed Exercise Northstar V, simulating bombing and chemical attacks at four Mass Rapid Transit stations and a bus interchange.

9: *The Phantom of the Opera* surpasses *Cats* as the longest running Broadway musical with its 7,486th performance.

11: The first ministerial meeting of the Asia–Pacific Partnership for Clean Development and Climate begins in Sydney, Australia.

12: The foreign ministers of Britain, France and Germany declare that negotiations with Iran over its nuclear programme have reached a 'dead end'. They recommend that Iran be referred to the United Nations Security Council, where the nation may face sanctions. A stampede during the Stoning the Devil ritual on the last day at the hajj in Mina, Saudi Arabia, kills at least 362 Muslim pilgrims.

15: Michelle Bachelet is elected the first female President of Chile. The Stardust spacecraft successfully lands in the Dugway Proving Ground after collecting dust samples from the comet Wild 2. For the first time, extra-terrestrial samples other than of the moon are collected and the Stardust spacecraft is the fastest man-made object to re-enter the Earth's atmosphere. The ruling emir of Kuwait, Sheikh Jaber Al-Ahmad Al-Jaber Al-Sabah, passes away.

16: Rizgar Mohammed Amin, the chief judge in the Saddam Hussein trial, tenders his resignation, following criticism of his handling of the trial. The UN appeals for US$240 million of food aid for West Africa to feed at least 10 million people affected by the food crisis, with Niger being the worst-affected country.

19: NASA Pluto probe New Horizons is successfully launched.

22: Evo Morales is inaugurated as President of Bolivia, becoming the country's first indigenous American President.

23: In the Canadian federal election, the Conservatives win a plurality of seats in the House of Commons to form a minority government. Ford Motor Company announces plans to close fourteen plants and cut up to 30,000 jobs by 2012.

24: Miyeegombo Enkhbold is chosen as the new prime minister of Mongolia by the State Great Khural. Disney and Pixar Animation Studios announce to merge in a US$ 7.4 billion deal. Opera web browser releases free 'mini' mobile phone browser.

25: Microsoft, in an effort to resolve a controversy with the antitrust authorities of the European Community, announces that it will license some of its source code to rivals. *Deus Caritas Est* (Latin: 'God is love'), the first encyclical of Pope Benedict XVI, is published. Google launches a new, self-censored search engine in China.

26: Palestinian Islamist party Hamas's landslide victory in Palestinian elections ends four decades of rule by the Fatah party. Interpol issues red notices against Pakistan ex-prime minister Benazir Bhutto and her husband, Asif Ali Zardari.

29: Tarja Halonen is re-elected in the second round of the Finnish presidential election with 51.8 per cent of the votes, defeating Sauli Niinistö. Sabah Al-Ahmad Al-Jaber Al-Sabah is confirmed as the new emir of Kuwait, ending a two-week leadership crisis.

30: China and Russia agree to refer Iran to the UN Security Council for its nuclear programme in March of 2006.

31: US oil company ExxonMobil announces profits of $36.1 billion for

2005, a record amount in US corporate history.

February 2006

2: Royal Dutch Shell breaks the record for the highest-ever annual profit for a British company with a total of £13.12bn.

4: Twenty-seven out of thirty-five countries on the IAEA's board of governors vote to refer the nuclear programme of Iran to the United Nations Security Council out of concern over Iran's plans to enrich nuclear materials and to refuse IAEA inspection of the process.

5: Iran resumes most of its nuclear programme after it was voted to be referred to the UN Security Council. However it says that it is still open to renegotiation.

6: Stephen Harper is sworn in as Canada's twenty-second prime minister. German car company BMW is banned from the Google index after attempting to deliberately deceive Google users.

7: The WTO announces that the EU broke international trade rules by stopping imports of genetically modified foods.

8: Chad and Sudan sign the Tripoli Agreement, ending the Chadian–Sudanese conflict.

9: The House of Keys, the lower house of the Isle of Man, a crown dependency of the United Kingdom, votes to lower the voting age to sixteen.

10: The 2006 Winter Olympics open in Turin, Italy. These are the twentieth winter games and the second hosted by an Italian city. Commerce Department reports US trade deficit soars to all-time high of $725.8 billion.

11: US Vice-President Dick Cheney accidentally shoots and injures Harry Whittington while hunting in Corpus Christi, Texas. Steve Fossett completes the world record for the longest non-stop, unrefuelled flight when the Virgin Atlantic Global Flyer lands at Bournemouth airport in southern England after a flight lasting 76 hours and 45 minutes and covering a distance of 26,389.3 miles (42,469.46 km).

14: The British House of Commons votes by 384 to 184 on a conscience vote to implement a full smoking ban in all enclosed public places in England from summer 2007. Syria switches the primary hard currency it uses for foreign goods and services from the US dollar to the euro.

16: After allegations of fraud, officials in Haiti reach an agreement to declare René Préval the winner of the country's election. Tokelau decides to remain a New Zealand territory after a referendum on self-governance. A 60 per cent majority voted in favor of self-governance, but a two-thirds majority was required for the referendum to succeed.

18: Egypt records the presence of avian influenza for the first time.

24: Venezuela orders US airlines to reduce the number of flights into the country by up to 70 per cent in a dispute over safety regulations.

25: Yoweri Museveni, President of Uganda since 1986, is re-elected in the first multiparty election in twenty-five years.

28: For the first time in Europe, a domesticated cat is found infected with the H5N1 bird flu virus. The dead cat was found on the island of Rügen in Mecklenburg-Western Pomerania, Germany.

March 2006

2: The US signs a historic civilian nuclear pact with India, which promises to bolster India's rapidly growing economy.

3: Research In Motion (RIM), a Waterloo, Ontario, Canadian-based company, agrees to pay NTP Inc. $612.5 million to settle NTP's patent-infringement suit against RIM. NTP had argued

RIM's Blackberry wireless-communication devices use technology patented by NTP.

5: Seventy-eighth Academy Awards are announced. *Crash* wins Best Picture, Ang Lee (*Brokeback Mountain*) wins Best Director, Reese Witherspoon (*Walk the Line*) wins Best Actress, and Philip Seymour Hoffman (*Capote*) wins Best Actor.

8: The European Union announces that it has lifted a worldwide ban on the export of British beef introduced in 1996 to prevent the spread of BSE (Mad Cow Disease).

9: UN Secretary-General Kofi Annan launches the Central Emergency Response Fund to provide aid to regions of Africa currently facing starvation.

10: John Profumo, the man famous for Britain's most talked about political scandal of the twentieth century, passes away.

11: The former Yugoslav President Slobodan Miloševic is found dead in his prison cell in The Hague, Netherlands. Michelle Bachelet takes office as the first female President of Chile.

12: Venezuela introduces its new national flag with eight, instead of seven, stars and a slightly altered coat of arms.

13: German drug and chemical manufacturer Merck KGaA announces plans to buy Schering in a merger of 14.6 billion euros. Merck and Schering would become Germany's largest pharmaceutical company.

15: Queen Elizabeth II, head of the Commonwealth, opens the 2006 Commonwealth Games in Melbourne, Australia.

17: Following an outbreak of bird flu in Israel, Europe bans imports of Israeli chicken. The fourth global World Water Forum meets in Mexico City to address problems of water shortages and conflicts.

20: Alexander Lukashenko is reelected as the President of Belarus with 82.6 per cent of all votes.

22: Basque separatist group ETA announces a permanent ceasefire to their thirty-eight-year campaign for independence from Spain, which cost over 800 lives.

24: President Roh Moo-hyun nominates Han Myung-Sook to become South Korea's first woman prime minister.

26: Scotland becomes the first part of the UK to introduce a full smoking ban in enclosed public places and workplaces.

27: The European Union agrees to introduce a standardized European driving licence.

30: Portia Simpson Miller is sworn in as prime minister of Jamaica, becoming the first woman to lead the Commonwealth of Jamaica. NASA and the Russian Federal Space Agency launch the thirteenth mission to the International Space Station when Expedition 13 takes off. On board is Marcos Pontes, the first Brazilian in space.

31: Viktor Yanukovych's Party of Regions wins a plurality in the 2006 parliamentary election in Ukraine.

April 2006

1: Marcos Pontes, Brazil's first astronaut, reaches the International Space Station.

4: Three million people march against the First Employment Contract (CPE) law, in Paris. Thaksin Shinawatra resigns as prime minister of Thailand.

5: Gold prices hit a twenty-five-year high. Procter and Gamble Co. settles a lawsuit against Coca-Cola Co. that claimed the beverage maker was using P&G's patented technology that adds calcium to fruit juices.

6: The World Meteorological Organization announces the retirement of a record five storm names from the 2005 Atlantic hurricane season. Retired names include Dennis, Katrina, Rita, Stan and Wilma.

7: *The Da Vinci Code* author, Dan

Brown, and his publisher, Random House, win the lawsuit that claimed that Brown committed copyright infringement by using ideas similar to those in *The Holy Blood and the Holy Grail*. Germany's trade surplus widens to 12.5 billion euros.

10: The government of France announces the withdrawal of its youth employment law.

12: The UK's Terrorism Act 2006 comes into force, making illegal the act of glorifying terrorism.

16: Pakistan's main stock market index in Karachi set a historic record when it crossed 12,000 points for the first time.

20: The President of Singapore, Sellapan Ramanathan, on the advice of the prime minister (Lee Hsien Loong), dissolves parliament to prepare for the 2006 general election, to be held on 6 May.

21: The African Development Bank (AfDB), which gives loans for infrastructure and poverty reduction projects, cancels $8.5 billion (R51 billion) in debt owed by thirty-three countries.

23: The Hungarian Socialist Party becomes the first re-elected government of Hungary since the end of the Cold War.

24: Iranian President Mahmoud Ahmadinejad unexpectedly lifts a twenty-seven-year ban on female attendance of public sporting events in Iran.

27: Construction begins on the Freedom Tower in New York City.

30: Gulf Air and Philippine Airlines (PAL) sign a code-sharing arrangement on selected routes to the Middle East.

May 2006

1: King Gyanendra of Nepal swears in Girija Prasad Koirala as the new prime minister. Spain, Portugal, Finland and Greece join the UK, Republic of Ireland and Sweden in allowing workers from the ten countries which joined the European Union two years ago free access to their labour markets.

2: Italian prime minister Silvio Berlusconi officially hands in his resignation to President Carlo Azeglio Ciampi.

3: The Nepalese cabinet declares a cease-fire with Maoist rebels and announces that they will no longer consider them a terrorist group.

4: In Israel, a new Cabinet under Prime Minister Ehud Olmert is sworn in. British prime minister Tony Blair's Labour Party suffers one of its worst electoral defeats, losing more than 200 councillors in the 2006 UK local elections, and coming in third place in vote totals. Philippines stock market reaches to highest level in seven years.

8: Judgement is given in London for Apple Computer in a high-profile trademark suit brought by the Beatles' company, Apple Corps.

9: The Estonian parliament ratifies the European constitution, making Estonia the fifteenth EU country to do so.

12: Yoweri Museveni takes his oath of office for a third consecutive term as President of Uganda. Justin Gatlin breaks the world record in the 100-metre dash with a time of 9.76 seconds.

13: Pakistan suffers the highest trade deficit of US$ 9.427 billion US dollars.

14: Incumbent President of Chad, Idriss Déby, wins the 2006 Chadian presidential election held on 3 May with 77.5 per cent of the vote. Prime Minister of the UK, Tony Blair, signs a petition in support of animal testing and condemns the acts of animal-rights extremists.

15: The US State Department announces it will re-establish diplomatic ties with Libya and remove it from its list of states that sponsor terrorism. Giorgio Napolitano is sworn in as President of the Italian Republic, following his election held on 10 May.

17: Barcelona wins the UEFA Champions League, defeating Arsenal 2-1 in the final.

18: Nepali legislators vote unanimously to strip the king (currently Gyanendra) of his powers, effectively turning the Hindu kingdom into a secular constitutional monarchy. Prime Minister Laisenia Qarase of Fiji is sworn in for a second term after winning the 2006 general election.

20: The construction of the Three Gorges Dam wall, the largest dam in the world, is completed in the People's Republic of China.

21: The Republic of Montenegro votes to secede from the State Union of Serbia and Montenegro.

22: Prime Minister Tony Blair declares that British troops should be out of Iraq within four years.

24: The UK government announces plans to overhaul the pension system.

25: Former Enron executives Kenneth Lay and Jeffrey Skilling are found criminally guilty for their role in the demise of the now-defunct energy-trading firm.

28: President Alvaro Uribe gets reelected in the Colombian presidential election, 2006, winning 62.2 per cent of the votes.

30: British mobile phone operator Vodafone posts the largest annual loss in British corporate history—£21.8 billion. The European Court of Justice rules illegal an EU–US agreement to pass airline passenger data to the US authorities, as it does not ensure privacy protection for European passengers. Former Daewoo boss Kim Woo-jung is sentenced to ten years in prison for fraud.

June 2006

1: The sixteenth World Economic Forum on Africa is convened in Cape Town, South Africa. China, France, Germany, Russia, the UK and the US agree on a package of incentives and sanctions for Iran.

3: Pakistan bans *The Da Vinci Code* film because it is said to contain blasphemous material about Jesus. In a special session of parliament, Montenegro declares its independence from Serbia. Czech parliament election leaves the Czech Republic with an even split between party blocs.

5: Alan García of the APRA is reelected President of Peru after winning a runoff with the Union for Peru's Ollanta Humala. Serbia confirms the dissolution of Serbia and Montenegro and declares independence.

6: BAA plc, the owners of London's Heathrow, Gatwick and Stansted Airports, accept a £10 billion takeover bid from a consortium led by Spain's Grupo Ferrovial. Iceland's prime minister Halldór Ásgrímsson resigns after poor showings in local elections. Foreign minister, Geir Haarde, takes over.

8: Microsoft makes Windows Vista beta 2 available for general download. The US House of Representatives definitively rejects the concept of Net neutrality.

9: The 2006 FIFA World Cup begins at Munich.

15: Coalition forces in Afghanistan launch and execute Operation Mountain Thrust to drive Taliban forces out of the southern provinces of Afghanistan. The operation is the largest operation since the start of the Afghanistan war. Bill Gates, Chairman of the Microsoft Corporation, announces that he will step down from his daily duties in 2008.

16: The US House of Representatives passes a resolution supporting President Bush's policy on Iraq.

17: The upper house of the French parliament passes a tough new immigration bill weeks after the lower chamber adopted it. The bill makes it harder for unskilled migrants to settle in France and abolishes the rights of illegal immigrants to remain after ten years.

20: Japanese Prime Minister Junichiro Koizumi announces plans to withdraw his country's troops from Iraq. The 600 soldiers had been deployed to Iraq in 2004 to aid in reconstruction and sparked controversy in Japan, as it was the most ambitious overseas deployment by Japan since World War II.

21: Saddam Hussein's principal defence lawyer, Khamis al-Obeidi, is assassinated in Baghdad.

22: The International Astronomical Union officially names Pluto's recently discovered moons, S/2005 P2 and S/2005 P1, Nix and Hydra.

24: President Gloria Macapagal-Arroyo of Philippines signs a law that repeals the death penalty.

25: Arcelor declares its merger with Mittal Steel. The new company will be called Arcelor–Mittal. Italians vote in a referendum on whether to approve the modification of fifty-three articles in the constitution. Approval would give more power to the prime minister and to the regions, making Italy a federal state. The world's second richest man, Warren Buffett, pledges to donate approximately $37 billion in shares to the Bill and Melinda Gates Foundation, effectively making it the largest charitable organization in history.

27: Nguyen Minh Triet becomes President of Vietnam. Ronaldo breaks the all-time World Cup finals goal-scoring record of fourteen goals set by Gerd Müller of Germany, scoring his fifteenth World Cup goal against Ghana in his eighteenth World Cup match.

29: The US House of Representatives votes to end a twenty-five-year ban on off-shore drilling. Kuwait holds a parliamentary election, the country's first with universal suffrage.

30: With the election of Trish Law in a by-election, the National Assembly for Wales becomes the first legislature in the world to have a majority of female members.

July 2006

1: The UN Security Council votes unanimously to withdraw the 3,500 peacekeeping troops who are currently in Burundi.

2: Israeli prime minister approves a military operation in the northern Gaza Strip aimed at halting Qassam rocket attacks.

3: Greece is suspended from international football competition by FIFA due to Greek government interference in the sport.

4: The space shuttle Discovery takes off from Cape Canaveral for the International Space Station.

6: The Nathu La Pass between India and China, sealed during the Sino–Indian War in 1962, reopens after forty-four years.

7: Polish Prime Minister Kazimierz Marcinkiewicz resigns. Syd Barrett, founder of Pink Floyd, passes away.

8: Israel rejects Hamas's terms for a ceasefire. Israeli forces withdraw from the northern Gaza Strip after an intensive two-day operation aimed at creating a buffer zone to stop Hamas militants from firing rockets at Israel.

9: Italy defeats France in the final of the FIFA World Cup 2006.

10: The UK unveils a new terror alert status system, similar to the United States' Homeland Security Advisory System.

11: Liu Xiang of China sets a new world record for the 110 metres hurdles at the Super Grand Prix in Lausanne with a time of 12.88 seconds. The US government agrees to apply parts of the Geneva Convention to detainees held at the Guantanamo Bay detainment camp.

12: Israeli forces attack installations and Hezbollah positions in Lebanon. Israel files a complaint with the UN Security Council and UN Secretary General Kofi Annan, urging the international community to enforce resolutions calling on the Lebanese government to disarm all militias within its borders and to extend its authority throughout its territory. The Japanese national government announces it will introduce a satellite system that will warn residents of incoming missiles, earthquakes, and other disasters in a 200 million yen program named 'J-ALERT'.

13: Israel imposes an air and sea blockade on Lebanon.

14: Jaroslaw Kaczyñski is sworn in as the new prime minister of Poland by President Lech Kaczyñski, his twin brother.

15: The thirty-second G8 summit begins in St. Petersburg, Russia. The UN Security Council unanimously adopts a resolution calling for weapons-related sanctions against North Korea. The 2006 Central American and Caribbean Games begin in the city of Cartagena, Colombia.

17: Space Shuttle Discovery lands successfully on Runway 33 at the Shuttle Landing Facility of the Kennedy Space Center, ending a thirteen-day mission to the International Space Station. A 7.7 magnitude earthquake off the coast of Indonesia causes a tsunami to crash into Java, causing significant property damage and killing over 100 people.

21: The Supreme Court of Japan rules that foreign governments are no longer immune from lawsuits filed in Japan. The Cassini spacecraft takes pictures of Saturn's moon Titan that appear to show the presence of hydrocarbon lakes.

23: Miss Puerto Rico, Zuleyka Rivera Mendoza, is crowned Miss Universe 2006 in Los Angeles, California.

25: The Interstate Abortion Bill is passed by the United States Senate.

28: The UN Security Council approves a resolution to give Iran until the end of August to suspend uranium enrichment or face the threat of sanctions.

29: Israel rejects a UN call for a truce.

31: Fidel Castro temporarily transfers the duties of the Cuban presidency to brother Raúl before he undergoes a surgical operation.

August 2006

1: Israel's Security Council approves expansion of the ground offensive in Lebanon and rejects a cease-fire until an international peacekeeping force is in place.

2: Israeli prime minister Ehud Olmert declares that there will be no ceasefire in Lebanon until an international force is deployed in the south of the country.

3: North Korea refuses aid after being devastated by flooding. As many as 1.5 million people have been displaced, and over 100 are dead. Ukrainian President Viktor Yushchenko nominates his political rival Viktor Yanukovich to become prime minister. Israel resumes bombing in Beirut.

4: *The Domesday Book*, the 920-year-old census record of England under William the Conqueror, goes online. Viktor Yanukovych became prime minister of Ukraine. Thirty-eight ministers and assistant ministers quit in protest against the Somalia government's failure to make a deal with the Supreme Islamic Courts Council.

5: The Republic of China (Taiwan) severs diplomatic relations with Chad reducing the number of countries maintaining official relations with it to twenty-four. Iran bans Nobel Peace Prize laureate Shirin Ebadi's Defenders of Human Rights Centre on the grounds that the human rights organization did not have a permit from the interior ministry. US and France agree on the wording of a UN resolution to end fighting between Israel and Hezbollah. Cyclist Floyd Landis, winner of the 2006 Tour de France, returns a positive B sample for excess testosterone.

6: The Dechatu river in Ethiopia floods, killing over 200 people. Lebanon rejects a draft UN resolution calling for an end to the conflict between Israel and Hezbollah, insisting it must include an explicit demand for a full Israeli pull-out from south Lebanon.

7: Oil price futures hit a record high for one blend of crude oil (Brent crude).

8: Chadian President Idriss Déby is sworn in to his third term in office. The Arab League makes a formal bid at the UN to secure changes to a draft Israel–Hezbollah ceasefire resolution.

9: Chad and Sudan resume diplomatic relations as part of the Dakar accord.

10: A terrorist plot to blow up planes in mid-flight from the UK to the US is disrupted. More than 1.5 million Chinese evacuate while Super Typhoon Saomai, the strongest to land in China in fifty years, makes landfall in Wenzhou, Zhejiang.

11: The UN Security Council adopts a resolution 15–0, calling for a ceasefire in the 2006 Israel–Lebanon conflict.

13: Israeli government endorses the UN Security Council resolution calling for an end to fighting in southern Lebanon.

14: Thousands of displaced Lebanese and Israelis begin returning home hours after a UN ceasefire to end fighting between Israel and Hezbollah came into force.

16: The International Astronomical Union proposes a new definition for a planet to be voted on 24 August that will include Pluto, Charon, 2003 UB313, and Ceres as planets.

18: Hezbollah hands out cash to war victims in Lebanon. The Israel government sets up a commission to investigate how the military campaign in Lebanon was conducted.

20: Controversy arises at the fourth Test between Pakistan and England at The Oval, London, when umpires rule that ball-tampering has occurred and award the game to England.

22: Russian mathematician Grigori Perelman refuses the Fields Medal. US sprinter Justin Gatlin agrees to an eight-year ban from track and field for a positive drug test. He forfeits the world record he equalled in May. NASA confirms that its new manned space exploration vehicle, expected to succeed the STS (or Space Shuttle) by 2014, will be named *Orion*.

24: Syria decides to cut electric power supplies to Lebanon after Israel bombed power stations during the war. The International Astronomical Union, meeting in Prague, Czech Republic, votes to strip Pluto of its status as a planet.

25: The United Nations Security Council approves a new peacekeeping mission in East Timor.

26: The Ugandan government and rebel group Lord's Resistance Army sign a truce, in efforts to end the twenty-year conflict.

28: Mexico's Federal Electoral Tribunal rules unanimously that results in contested polling stations only marginally affected the lead of Felipe Calderón of the ruling National Action Party over Andrés Manuel López Obrador in July's disputed presidential election.

29: Vivendi Universal, the world's biggest music group, signs a deal to make its music catalogue available on a free legal download service.

31: US contractor Lockheed Martin is chosen over an alliance of Northrop Grumman and Boeing to build the new spacecraft *Orion*. The United Nations Security Council approves resolution 1706, which is meant to resolve the Darfur conflict. Sudan has rejected the resolution.

September 2006

1: Spain approves plans to deploy 1,100 troops to Lebanon as part of a UN peacekeeping force.

2: Italian troops arrive in Lebanon as part of the United Nations Interim Force in Lebanon. Indonesia announces plans to contribute 1,000 troops to the force.

3: Steve Irwin, 'the Crocodile Hunter', is killed by a sting ray while filming a documentary on Australia's Great Barrier Reef.

5: Felipe Calderón of the PAN is declared the winner of Mexico's presidential election. Bill Ford steps down from his position as CEO of Ford Motor Company. He is replaced by Alan Mulally, the former executive vice-president and CEO of Boeing Commercial Airlines. Pakistan signs a truce with pro-Taliban militants on the Afghanistan border and agrees to withdraw most Pakistani troops in exchange for the militants' promise not to support cross-border violence.

6: The Singaporean economy tops a list of 175 economies as the most business-friendly economy in the world in a survey conducted by the World Bank's International Finance Corporation. Côte d'Ivoire prime minister Charles Konan Banny dissolves his Cabinet.

7: The National Liberation Forces (FNL) signs a ceasefire with Burundi, the last rebel group to enter the peace process to end the Burundi civil war. Tony Blair announces that he will step down as prime minister of the United Kingdom within twelve months but declines to give an exact date for his departure.

8: Shuji Nakamura is awarded the Second Millennium Technology Prize for his work on blue and white LEDs. The first recipient of the award was Tim Berners-Lee, developer of the World Wide Web.

9: Space Shuttle *Atlantis* lifts off from John F. Kennedy Space Center in Florida to begin STS-115.

10: Roger Federer wins the US Open, defeating Andy Roddick. The most successful driver in Formula One history, Michael Schumacher, announces his retirement from the sport at the end of the 2006 season.

11: The fourteenth Summit of the Non-Aligned Movement begins in Havana, Cuba.

13: The solar system's largest dwarf planet, designated until now as 2003 UB313, is officially named Eris.

14: US Senate committee approves a bill to give more rights to 'terrorism' detainees.

17: In the 2006 Swedish General election, Alliance for Sweden declares victory after nearly complete official election results showed it narrowly defeating the governing Swedish Social Democratic Party. The prime minister of Sweden, Göran Persson, concedes defeat. Germany defeats Australia and retains their World Cup title in the eleventh edition of the Hockey World Cup.

19: A coup d'état occurs in Thailand, with tanks seen moving into place around government buildings in Bangkok. Prime Minister Thaksin Shinawatra declares a state of emergency.

20: Shinzo Abe is elected as party leader of the Liberal Democratic Party in Japan, replacing the current prime minister Junichiro Koizumi.

21: The leaders of Thailand's coup ban all meetings and other activities by political parties, two days after taking power.

22: Patricia Dunn announces her resignation as Hewlett-Packard's chairman and board member.

23: Ali Abdullah Saleh, in office since 1978, is re-elected as President of Yemen with 77.2 per cent of the votes. Toomas Hendrik Ilves is elected the new President of Estonia, defeating incumbent Arnold Rüütel. Japan's Solar-B mission is launched from the Uchinoura Space Center. With its successful launch, it is rechristened 'Hinode'.

24: Europe retains golf's Ryder Cup to score a third consecutive win, beating the United States by a score of 18.5 to 9.5.

26: Former WorldCom chief Bernard Ebbers reports to a federal prison in the US state of Louisiana to begin a twenty-five-year prison term. The Diet of Japan confirms Shinzo Abe as the prime minister of Japan. At fifty-two, he is the youngest prime minister since World War II. The European Commission confirms that Bulgaria and Romania are set to join the European Union on 1 January 2007.

30: Eighteen-year old Tatiana Kuchaoova from the Czech Republic is crowned Miss World 2006.

October 2006

1: General elections are held in Bosnia and Herzegovina. The Social Democratic Party of Austria wins election in Austria. General Surayud Chulanont is appointed interim prime minister of Thailand by the ruling military regime, following the recent coup. New laws against age discrimination in the workplace—officially titled the Employment Equality (Age) Regulations 2006—come into force in the United Kingdom.

2: Zambia's President, Levy Mwanawasa, is re-elected. □eljko Komšiæ, Nebojša Radmanoviæ and Haris Silajd□iæ are elected new members of the Presidency of Bosnia and Herzegovina, the country's collective head of state. Russia suspends all transport and postal links with Georgia. Andrew Z. Fire and Craig C. Mello win the Nobel Prize in Physiology or Medicine for their work in controlling the activity of genes.

3: United States scientists John C. Mather and George F. Smoot win the Nobel Prize in Physics for research into cosmic microwave background radiation that helps explain the origins of galaxies and stars.

4: The Dow Jones Industrial Average reaches another record high close, rising above 11,850 for the first time. American Roger D. Kornberg wins the 2006 Nobel Prize in Chemistry for describing the essential process of gene copying in cells, research that can give insight into illnesses such as cancer and heart disease.

6: The new Swedish prime minister, Fredrik Reinfeldt, presents his new cabinet.

7: In Latvia, the governing coalition led by Prime Minister Aigars Kalvîtis wins re-election, the first Latvian administration to be re-elected since independence from the Soviet Union in 1991.

9: South Korean Ban Ki-moon is nominated to succeed Kofi Annan as the United Nations Secretary-General in an affirmation vote by the Security Council. North Korea conducts its first nuclear weapon test in an underground facility at Gilju in North Hamgyong province. American Edmund S. Phelps wins the 2006 Nobel Memorial Prize in Economic Sciences for work on the trade-offs between inflation and unemployment.

10: Kiran Desai's novel *The Inheritance of Loss* wins the prestigious Man Booker Prize for Fiction 2006.

12: Turkish writer Orhan Pamuk wins the 2006 Nobel Prize in Literature.

13: Bangladesh's Muhammad Yunus and the Grameen Bank win the Nobel Peace Prize for working to advance economic and social development among the poor.

14: The United Nations Security Council adopts Resolution 1718, imposing sanctions on North Korea in response to its recent nuclear test.

16: The United Nations General Assembly elects Belgium, Indonesia, Italy and South Africa to two-year terms on the Security Council, commencing 1 January 2007.

19: The Dow Jones Industrial Average index closes above 12,000 points.

22: Michael Schumacher, seven times Formula One World Champion, retires from the sport at the end of the 2006 season.

23: Jeffrey Skilling is sentenced to twenty-four years and four months in prison for his role in the collapse of Enron, concluding the trial of Kenneth Lay and Jeffrey Skilling.

28: Street clashes break out in Dhaka between government and opposition supporters as Prime Minister Khaleda Zia's term expires.

29: President Ijazuddin Ahmed is sworn is as head of an interim government in Bangladesh. Final round of elections are conducted in Democratic Republic of Congo. Brazil re-elects President Luiz Inacio Lula da Silva.

31: Former South Africa President Pieter Botha dies. China and ASEAN countries commit themselves to setting up free trade zone by 2010.

Newsmakers

The Reservations Debate

In 2006, anti-reservation protests took place in various parts of India in opposition to the decision of the multiparty coalition United Progressive Alliance (UPA) to implement reservations for Other Backward Classes (OBC) in central and private institutes of higher education.

On 5 April 2006, the human resource development minister Arjun Singh promised to implement a 27 per cent reservation for OBCs in institutes of higher education (twenty central universities, the IITs, NITs, IIMs and AIIMS) after the 2006 state assembly elections, in accordance with the ninety-third Constitutional Amendment of the Constitution which was passed unanimously by both Houses of Parliament. The amendment allows the government to make special provisions for 'advancement of any socially and educationally backward classes of citizens', including their admission in aided or unaided private educational institutions. Gradually this reservation policy is to be implemented in private sector institutions and companies as well. Students protested against this reservation, as the proposal, if implemented, would reduce seats for the general category from the existing 77.5 per cent to less than 50.5 per cent (since members of OBCs are also allowed to contest in the general category). Others also protested claiming that the government's proposal was discriminatory and driven by 'vote-bank' politics. The students against reservation formed a group 'Youth for Equality' and demanded through peaceful protests that the government should roll back its decision.

After Independence, to give a fair representation to weaker sections of society the Indian Constitution introduced provisions for continuing and increasing reservations for the scheduled castes and tribes in government institutions in the 1950s. The original idea was to continue this reservation for ten years but the system continues, with 22.5 per cent of the seats in higher education institutes currently set aside for Scheduled Castes (SCs) and Scheduled Tribes (STs). In 1989, the then Prime Minister V.P. Singh accepted and implemented the proposals of the Mandal Commission which recommended reservations for Other Backward Classes. Many Indian states implemented the OBC reservations in their higher educational institutions. However, a select few higher educational institutions—the IITs, IIMs, AIIMS, etc.—were kept out of the purview of the OBC reservations until now.

On 13 May 2006, medical students protesting in Mumbai were lathi-charged by the police. The nationwide strike by medical students protesting against the lathi-charge was later joined by resident doctors from all over India, thus crippling the health infrastructure of a number of cities. The government took measures to counter the protesting doctors by serving them with suspension letters and asking them to vacate the hostels to make way for newly recruited doctors. Meanwhile, the National Knowledge Commission, a body of eminent persons, dominated by the anti-reservation groups, requested the government to maintain 'status-quo' on the issue until alternative policies to reservation were explored. Students of IIT, Delhi, with the support of PAN IIT, organized a human chain rally on 20 May. Nearly 150 students went on a month long 'relay' hunger strike in AIIMS. After the government reaffirmed its commitment to implementing reservations, the protesters called for a 'civil disobedience movement'. The AIIMS Faculty Association went on a mass casual leave from 25 May to support the anti-quota stir, but made it clear that basic healthcare services would not be disrupted. On 27 May, a huge rally was organized in Delhi. Almost 1 lakh participants from all over India attended the rally and it was declared that the strike by students and junior doctors would continue. On 31 May, in deference to the Supreme Court directive, resident doctors agreed to resume hospital work from 1 June, as the health service was affected seriously due to the strike. However, student protest (both medical and other streams) has continued and a national coordination committee, comprising representatives of medical colleges, IITs and other educational institutions, has been proposed to be formed to lead the agitation. The Supreme Court has also asked the government to clarify the basis on which the reservation policy was being implemented.

Mumbai 7/11

On 11 July 2006, Mumbai experienced a major terror blow that brought back memories of the 1993 serial blasts and the London Underground bombings. The financial capital of India was hit by a series of seven bomb blasts, targeted at the suburban trains of the Western Railways, the backbone of Mumbai's transportation system. The first blast took place at 6.24 p.m., and the explosions continued for approximately eleven minutes, until 6.35, during the after-work rush hour. About 200 people died and over 700 were injured in the attacks. Police said the coordinated blasts took place at Matunga, Khar, Mahim, Jogeshwari, Borivali and Bhayandar; most were on moving trains while two were at stations. The force of the blasts ripped doors and windows off carriages, and scattered luggage. Rescue workers, in monsoon rain, helped survivors from rail cars that were mangled by the quick succession of blasts. The dead and the injured were taken to hospitals in the vicinity.

India's rail systems and airports were put on high alert after the explosions in Mumbai. Mumbai's entire rail network was shut down, stranding hundreds of thousands of commuters. Phone lines to Mumbai from New Delhi were jammed. Prime Minister Manmohan Singh called an emergency meeting with his national security advisers. There was no immediate assertion of responsibility for the attacks, which ostensibly focused on first-class train cars. The blasts came hours after a series of grenade attacks killed at least eight Indian tourists and injured more than thirty other people in Srinagar.

Some 350 people were detained in Maharashtra thirty-six hours after the incident for investigations. On 14 July, Lashkar-e-Qahhar, a terrorist organization possibly linked to Lashkar-e-Taiba (LeT), claimed responsibility for the bombings. In an e-mail to an Indian TV channel, it said that it organized the bombings using sixteen people. According to the e-mail, the main motive was retaliation to the situation in Gujarat and Kashmir and to the alleged oppression of Muslims in certain parts. It also said that the blasts were part of a series of attacks aimed at other sites such as the Mumbai international airport, the Gateway of India, Taj Mahal and the Red Fort in New Delhi.

On 17 July, the forensic science laboratory in Mumbai confirmed the use of a mixture of the highly explosive RDX and ammonium nitrate for the bombings. The presence of these explosives in the post-explosive debris was confirmed by techniques such as liquid chromatography with mass detector (LCMS), gas chromatography with mass detector (GCMS) and ion scan chromatography. They indicated a strong possibility of all the explosives being planted at the Churchgate railway station, the starting point for all affected trains.

On 14 July, following the bomb attacks, minister of state for external affairs, E. Ahamed, announced that India would suspend talks with Pakistan until President Pervez Musharraf abided by his 2004 promise of ending all support to cross-border terrorism, Prime Minister Manmohan Singh however, conveyed India's willingness to be flexible with Pakistan, following Pakistan President Pervez Musharraf's statements that ending the three-year-long peace process would signal a victory for the terrorists.

On 26 October, Mumbai police released the full list of terrorists wanted for the 7/11 blasts; most of them are Pakistan nationals.

India–USA Nuclear Deal

USA and India finalized a nuclear deal after talks between President George W. Bush and Prime Minister Manmohan Singh in Delhi when the former visited India in February–March 2006. For India, which has not signed the Nuclear Non-Proliferation Treaty (NPT), this nuclear deal will end years of international isolation over its nuclear policy and will give access to US civil nuclear technology and open its nuclear facilities to inspection. The deal requires approval from US Congress, which will be asked to pass legislation allowing civil nuclear cooperation to go ahead, as well as from other countries that form a part of the nuclear suppliers' group.

Allowing India to import foreign technology for its civilian nuclear programme will boost global efforts to develop new sources of energy, particularly sources that won't increase the level of climate-warming gases. In exchange for the opportunity to import nuclear know-how, India will disentangle its civilian nuclear programme from its weapons-building facilities, subjecting the civilian side to multilateral inspections designed to ensure that technology or fissile material isn't diverted for military purposes.

Under the agreement, India will classify fourteen of its twenty-two nuclear facilities as being for civilian use, and thus open to inspection. But these exclude its two fast-breeder reactors, the main sources of bomb-making material. Currently, India has fourteen reactors in commercial operation and nine under construction. Nuclear power supplies about 3 per cent of India's electricity and by 2050, nuclear power is expected to provide 25 per cent of the country's electricity. India has limited coal and uranium reserves but its huge thorium reserves—about 25 per cent of the world's total—are expected to fuel its nuclear power programme in future.

France, which signed a similar deal of its own with India earlier, said the accord would help fight climate change and non-proliferation efforts. However, those opposed to the deal, in the US Congress and elsewhere, disagree.

The Volcker Report and Natwar Singh

UN Secretary-General Kofi Annan appointed the Volcker Committee on 21 April 2004, to investigate allegations of corruption in the Oil-for-Food Programme. The Oil-for-Food Programme, established by the United Nations in 1995 (under UN Security Council Resolution 986) and terminated in late 2003, was intended to allow Iraq to sell oil on the world market in exchange for food, medicine, and other humanitarian needs for ordinary Iraqi citizens without allowing Iraq to rebuild its military. The programme was introduced by the Clinton administration in 1995, as a response to arguments that ordinary Iraqi citizens were severely affected by the international economic sanctions aimed at the demilitarization of Saddam Hussein's Iraq, imposed in the wake of the first Gulf War. The sanctions were discontinued in 2003 after the US invasion of Iraq, and the humanitarian functions turned over to the Coalition Provisional Authority. Shortly before US and British forces invaded Iraq, UN Secretary-General Kofi Annan suspended the programme and evacuated more than 300 workers monitoring the distribution of supplies. On 22 May 2003, UN Security Council Resolution 1483 granted authority to the Coalition Provisional Authority to use Iraq's oil revenue. The programme's remaining funds of $10 billion were transferred over a six month winding-up period to the Development Fund for Iraq under the Coalition Provisional Authority's control, representing 14 per cent of the programme's total income over five years. The programme was formally terminated on 21 November 2003 and its major functions were turned over to the Coalition Provisional Authority.

The Independent Inquiry Committee (IIC) into the United Nations Oil-for-Food Programme released its interim report in February 2005. The three-member inquiry was chaired by former Federal Reserve chairman and United Nations Association of the United States of America director Paul Volcker and included South African Justice Richard Goldstone and Swiss Professor of Criminal Law, Mark Pieth. The committee's sixty-member staff, which included three support personnel on loan from the UN, operated on a $30 million budget drawn from the UN Oil-for-Food escrow account. The report made public a list of corporations and politicians across the world who benefited from 'an elaborate scam devised' by now deposed Iraqi dictator Saddam Hussein to make money for his regime. Allegations had sprung up in various publications, including Baghdad's *al-Mada* newspaper, which published names of 270 individuals and a large number of Indian firms/companies. The committee asked all the companies in the list to explain the payments. Virtually none of the Indian firms replied. The Volcker Report said that some companies that were dealing through agents and middlemen might not have known they were bribing the Saddam regime. Jammu and Kashmir Panther's Party leader Bhim Singh, the Congress party, Reliance and K. Natwar Singh are the four 'non-contractual beneficiaries' from India named in the Volcker Report. The report says former external affairs minister K. Natwar Singh and the Congress party sold their oil vouchers to a Swiss oil trading company, Masefield AG. Natwar Singh is shown in Table 3 of the report as the non-contractual 'beneficiary' in connection with 4 million barrels of oil allotted to Masefield AG, the contracting company, which actually lifted only 1.936 million barrels out of this. The Volcker Committee Report said that under the programme, the government of Iraq sold $64.2 billion of oil to 248 companies. In turn, 3,614 companies sold $34.5 billion of humanitarian goods to Iraq. This controversy got murkier when Aneil Mathrani, then Indian ambassador to Croatia and a close aide of Natwar Singh's, alleged that Natwar Singh had used an official visit to Iraq to procure oil coupons for Jagat Singh from Saddam's regime. On 6 December 2005, K. Natwar Singh resigned from the Union cabinet.

The Rise and Fall and Rise Again of the Sensex

In 2005, according to SEBI, foreign investors bought a record $10.7 billion more stocks than they sold. Stocks gained 37 per cent in 2005, the third best in fifteen years. The mutual fund industry supported the market with purchases close to Rs 16,000 crore in 2005. During the past three years, the Sensex almost tripled. The benchmark was Asia's second-best performer in the period, behind only Pakistan's Karachi Stock Exchange 100 Index. International investors have been drawn to India as the country delivered the second-fastest pace of growth among the world's twenty biggest economies. Foreign investors bought a net $521.5 million in shares during the first week of 2006, over double the $206.3 million bought in the same period last year. Robust portfolio investments and heavy fund buying lifted the Bombay Stock Exchange's benchmark 30-share Sensex past the magical 12,000 mark on 20 April 2006. On 11 May, it reached an all-time high of 12, 671. On 18 May, the Sensex registered a fall of 826 points to close at 11,391, leading to suspension of trading for the first time since 17 May 2004. This was the largest ever intraday crash in the history of the Sensex. It figured among the top eight losers in the thirty-three most prominent stock-market indices in the world. The downward slide of the Sensex continued in June. On 6 June, the Sensex closed below 10,000 for the first time since 17 February. On 14 June, it closed below 9,000 for first time since December 2005. According to experts, the flow of foreign funds out of the economy was a major factor in the decline. However, the market managed to bounce back from its lower levels. By the end of June, the Sensex rallied to cross the 10,000 mark again. On 15 September, it crossed the 12,000 mark. On 13 October, the Sensex registered a new all-time high of 12,690, which it surpassed on 16 October, reaching 12,953. On 30 October, the Sensex crossed the 13,000 mark for the very first time.

Pluto is No Longer a Planet

Pluto was discovered in 1930 as a result of an extensive search by astronomer Clyde Tombaugh. Some astronomers have long argued that Pluto's small size, less than one-fifth the diameter of Earth, and a weird tilted orbit that takes it inside Neptune every couple of hundred years, make Pluto more like a Kuiper Belt body than a full-fledged planet. On 24 August 2006, the International Astronomical Union passed a new definition of planet that excludes Pluto and puts it in a new category of 'dwarf planet'.

The definition of 'planet' has for some time been the subject of intense debate. Despite the term having existed for thousands of years, no scientifically accepted definition of 'planet' existed before 24 August 2006. The issue of a clear definition for planet arose in 2005 with the discovery of the trans-Neptunian object 2003 UB313 (now renamed Eris), a body larger than the smallest accepted planet, Pluto. In response, the International Astronomical Union, or IAU, which is internationally recognized by astronomers as the body responsible for resolving issues of astronomical nomenclature, released its final decision on the matter. Amid dramatic scenes in the Czech capital Prague, that saw astronomers waving yellow ballot papers in the air, the IAU took the historic decision to relegate Pluto from a planet to a dwarf planet.

Scientists agreed that for a celestial body to qualify as a planet:

- it must be in orbit around the Sun

- it must be large enough that it takes on a nearly round shape
- it must have cleared its orbit of other objects.

Pluto was automatically disqualified because its highly elliptical orbit overlaps with that of Neptune. It will now join a new category of dwarf planets. A non-satellite body fulfilling only the first two of these criteria is classified as a dwarf planet, while a non-satellite body fulfilling only the first criterion is termed a 'small solar system body' (SSSB). According to the definition, there are currently eight planets and three dwarf planets known in the solar system. The definition does not apply outside the solar system, and so does not include provision for extrasolar planets. Exoplanets are covered separately under a 2003 draft guideline for the definition of planets. The IAU has officially identified Ceres, Pluto and 2003 UB313 (Eris) as dwarf planets.

The redefinition of planet has been criticized and remains controversial. The final vote has come under criticism because of the relatively small percentage of the 9000-strong membership who participated. Of over 2,700 astronomers attending the conference, probably over a thousand voted on the significant resolutions.

Rise of Oil Prices

The price of standard crude oil on NYMEX was under \$25/barrel in September 2003. By 11 August 2005, the price had been above \$60/barrel for over a week and a half. In July 2006, crude oil for August delivery traded over \$79/barrel, an all-time record, and \$4.00/gallon gasoline was being sold in Hawaii. The early and mid-summer 2006 run-up is attributable to increasing gasoline consumption, up 1.9 per cent year over year in the US, and geopolitical tensions as North Korea launched missiles, the on-going Iran nuclear standoff, and the Israel–Lebanon war. 'Rationing by price' is a reality because near-stagnant world crude supply is not meeting ever-increasing demand, as witnessed by oil shortages in Africa, India, and China.

In India the administered price mechanism in the oil sector ensured that the impact of any sharp increase in international oil prices were dissipated by spreading over the price increase through smaller incremental hikes spread over a period of time. The oil pool account even then ran substantial deficits, which were partially recharged when the international oil prices went into a trough phase. Thus the Indian economy was generally protected against sharp spurt in oil prices. Often the administered price mechanism was dismantled in 2002; the retail prices of oil products continues to be regulated by the government. There are only three instances when domestic oil prices registered double-digit growth for two or more consecutive years over the last twenty-two year period: in the early eighties (1983-84 to 1984-85), early nineties (1991-92 to 1993-94) and the early part of current decade (2000-01 to 2001-02). Double-digit oil price increase in 2005-06 will mean another high intensity increase in oil prices that extends into the second year.

However, the results also show that the lagged impact of oil prices explain only around one-third of the fluctuations in manufacturing sector output over the last twenty years. With two-third of the trends in manufacturing sector output remaining outside the purview of oil prices, there is considerable scope for propping up the growth prospects of this sector through other appropriate policy packages. If oil prices remain at \$80/barrel for a full year the growth in the manufacturing sector would go down by 24.5 percentage point which would pull down the GDP by 4.9 percentage points and raise the wholesale prices index by 7.9

percentage points over the current levels. Even in January–March 2006, the average price of the Indian basket of crude varieties was 30 per cent higher than it was a year ago. The overall impact of the high oil prices on the Indian economy is also restrained by other factors like a comfortable balance of payment position, the large foreign exchange reserves and the access to international capital. Despite high international oil prices, India's economy is expected to remain buoyant, underpinned primarily by growing investment and strong consumption, says the Asian Development Bank's Asian Development Outlook.

Mittal Steel and Arcelor Deal

In January 2006, the Netherland-based Mittal Steel made a $22.3-billion bid for Luxembourg-based Arcelor to create a mega-steel company with an output three times bigger than its three nearest rivals combined. Mittal Steel and Arcelor are the world's largest and second-largest steel manufacturers, respectively. Mittal's bid led to objections from the governments of France, Luxembourg and Spain and labour unions that were worried about job losses even though the bidder assured that no worker would lose his job. On March 2006, the Luxembourg government which holds 5.6 per cent of shares of Arcelor ruled out the possibility of selling its shares to Mittal Steel. Finally Mittal Steel and Arcelor of Luxembourg agreed a 26.9 billion euros ($33.6 billion) merger to create a steel group. The deal was completed after a long Arcelor board meeting which agreed to an improved offer of 40.4 euros a share by Mittal, 43 per cent higher than its original offer unveiled in January. The new business will be called Arcelor Mittal. Agreement by Arcelor to recommend the deal to investors came after an epic tussle between the two businesses in which Arcelor, which had called Mittal's original offer '150 per cent hostile', announced a series of defensive measures, including a 6.5bn euros share buy-back and a rival merger with Severstal of Russia. Under the deal, which still has to be put to shareholders, for every Arcelor share they will receive 12.55 euros in cash and 1.084 Mittal shares. Of the total 26.9 billion euros equity value, 31 per cent will be accounted for by a cash payment, the rest in Mittal shares. L.N. Mittal will be the president, while John Kinsch will be the chairman of the merged entity.

Thirty-three Indian Companies in the Forbes Global 2000 List

The Forbes Global 2000 is an annual ranking of the top 2000 corporations in the world by *Forbes* magazine. The ranking is based on a mix of four metrics: sales, profit, assets and market value. With combined sales of $24 trillion; profits, $1.7 billion; assets $88 trillion; market value $31 trillion; and worldwide employees sixty-eight million, the Forbes Global 2000 accounts for a significant chunk of the global economy. The 2006 rankings, which span fifty-five countries, show the gains of emerging economic dynamos such as China and India. It included thirty-six companies based in Hong Kong/China, a gain of eight over the previous list; twenty-eight in mainland China, up three; and thirty-three in India, up three. Here are the Indian companies that featured in the list, along with their ranks:

Name	Rank
ONGC	256
Reliance Industries	298
State Bank of India Group	310
Indian Oil	311
NTPC	463
ICICI Bank	656
Steel Authority of India	764
Bharat Petroleum	1087
Tata Steel	1142

Tata Consultancy Services	1163
ITC	1171
Infosys Technologies	1177
Hindustan Petroleum	1189
HDFC	1206
Tata Motors	1215
Wipro	1225
Punjab National Bank	1243
GAIL (India)	1270
Canara Bank	1299
Bharti Tele-Ventures	1336
Larsen and Toubro	1440
Bharat Heavy Electricals	1524
HDFC Bank	1530
Bank of Baroda	1601
Union Bank of India	1709
Bank of India	1736
IDBI	1759
Oriental Bank of Commerce	1794
Hindalco Industries	1821
National Aluminium	1885
Bajaj Auto	1946
UCO Bank	1976
Indian Overseas Bank	1978

FIFA World Cup 2006

The 2006 World Cup was the eighteenth staging of the FIFA World Cup, held from 9 June to 9 July in Germany. Italy won its fourth world championship title, defeating France in a penalty shootout in the final. Germany defeated Portugal to finish third.

Teams representing 198 national football associations from all six continents participated in the qualification process that began in December 2003. Thirty-two teams qualified from this process for the final tournament. Seven nations qualified for the finals for the first time: Angola, Côte d'Ivoire, Czech Republic, Ghana, Togo, Trinidad and Tobago and Ukraine. Czech Republic and Ukraine were making their first appearance as independent nations.

The finals of the 2006 World Cup were played in twelve German cities and in total, sixty-four games were played. It began on 9 June with the opening ceremony in Munich followed by the Germany–Costa Rica match. In the group stage the thirty-two teams were divided into eight groups of four teams each. Within each group, the teams competed in a round-robin tournament to determine which two of the four teams would advance to the sixteen-team knockout stage, which started on 24 June.

All the expected teams from each group qualified for the knockout stage with the possible exceptions of Poland and Czech Republic. The two big matches in the round of 16 were Spain–France and Netherlands–Portugal in which France and Portugal prevailed respectively. In the rest of the matches, all the favourites advanced to the next round. The quarter-final line up witnessed an unprecedented six previous winners with Ukraine being the only underdog. Germany beat Argentina and Portugal beat England in the penalty shootout while France defeated Brazil by a solitary goal from Thiery Henry. The other team to qualify for the last four was Italy who defeated Ukraine.

In the semi-finals Italy beat Germany in extra time while France beat Portugal 1–0. Germany defeated Portugal 3–1 to finish third at Stuttgart and Miroslav Klose, with five goals under his belt, finished as the highest scorer of the tournament.

France overcame a slow start in the group stage and reached the final, galvanized in part by the performance of captain Zinedine Zidane while Italy progressed with a stellar defence and a balanced attack—they only conceded two goals (an own goal and a penalty) in the tournament. An unusual incident in the final match was Zidane's angry reaction to comments made by Italian defender Marco Materazzi. Near the end of extra time, Zidane head-butted Materazzi in the chest in an off-the-ball incident and was sent off by the referee. After extra time the teams finished in a 1–1 draw and Italy won 5–3 in the penalty shootout.

Zinedine Zidane won the Golden Ball, Italians Fabio Cannavaro and Andrea Pirlo were awarded the Silver and Bronze Balls, with teammate Buffon winning the Lev Yashin award for best goalkeeper. German striker Miroslav Klose won the Golden Boot award as the tournament's top goal scorer, with fellow German striker Lukas Podolski winning the Best Young Player award.

In comparison to earlier World Cups, the tournament was notable for the number of yellow and red cards given out. Players received a record-breaking 345 yellow cards and 28 red cards, with the match between Portugal and the Netherlands accounting for sixteen yellows and four reds.

2007 Cricket World Cup

The 2007 Cricket World Cup will be hosted by the West Indies from 11 March to 28 April 2007. The ten Test match playing countries—Australia, Bangladesh, England, India, New Zealand, Pakistan, South Africa, Sri Lanka, West Indies and Zimbabwe—and Kenya, which has one-day international status, qualified for the World Cup automatically, and five further teams qualified through the 2005 ICC Trophy. They are Bermuda, Canada, Ireland, Netherlands and Scotland. The field of sixteen teams is the largest ever for the Cricket World Cup. These sixteen nations will be divided into four groups of four teams each. The tournament will begin with a league stage and each team will play each of the other teams in its group once. Australia, India, England and West Indies have been placed in separate pools for logistical reasons—they are expected to have the most supporters in attendance, and transport and accommodation capacity in the West Indies is limited. The top two teams from each group will then compete in a 'Super 8' format. This will also use a league system. Each team will carry forward its result against the qualifying team from its own preliminary stage group, and will play the other six qualifying teams once each. The top four teams in the league will qualify for the semi-finals. This system has been modified since the last World Cup, which had a 'Super 6' stage rather than a Super 8. There will be fifty-one matches in all, which is less than the 2003 World Cup, despite the two extra teams taking part. The day after each match is a scheduled reserve day, to allow for weather and other interruptions. Eight venues across the West Indies have been selected to host the tournament. Jamaica will host the opening ceremony on 11 March 2007. The final will be played at Kensington Oval, Bridgetown, Barbados. There will be four additional venues that will host warm-up matches. The Jamaican government is spending over US$80.8 million for 'on the pitch' expenses. This includes refurbishing Sabina Park and constructing the new multi-purpose facility in Trelawny (through a soft loan from China). Another US$20 million is budgeted for 'off-the-pitch' expenses, putting the tally at more than US$100 million or some $7 billion (Jamaican). The total amount of money being spent on stadiums is at least US$300 million. In the search for a character to become the event mascot many options were explored. The extensive research and development sessions generated a common theme across the region. It was named Mello: he is in his teens—cheeky and curious and socially aware. The event identity, a logo that expresses the joy and exuberance of cricketers and cricket fans worldwide, in a Caribbean setting, was developed by the ICC-retained design agency in consultation with Howzat, a Caribbean consortium of agencies.

Bombay Stock Exchange becomes BSE Ltd

In August 2005 the Bombay Stock Exchange (BSE), an association of broker members, transformed itself into a corporate entity, BSE Ltd. The demutualization or corporatization of the BSE was the culmination of a long interactive process between broker members, the Exchange, and the Securities and Exchange Board of India (SEBI). Set up as the Native Share and Stock Brokers Association in 1875, the Exchange has around 725 members and, as on March 2005, Rs 412 crore as reserves, which is now available for business operations. The shares of BSE Ltd would be listed on the BSE itself and the exchange will offer 51 per cent of its equity to its investors.

Pre-Diwali Blasts in Delhi

Terrorists struck Delhi on the eve of Diwali on 29 October 2005, triggering three explosions in two busy markets that ripped through the heart of the city, killing sixty-two people and injuring 200 more. The first explosion took place at around 5.40 pm in the busy Paharganj market. Minutes later, another explosion rocked Sarojini Nagar market in south Delhi, where the maximum casualties were reported. Another blast took place 10 km further south in the Govindpuri area. A hitherto unknown militant outfit, Inquilab, claimed responsibility for the blasts, although Delhi Police claimed that the Lashkar-e-Tayiba were responsible.

Kashmir Earthquake

On 8 October 2005 at 8.50 a.m., an earthquake with a magnitude of 7.6 on the Richter scale shook the Kashmir valley. Its epicentre was in the Kishanganga (Neelam) valley, north of Muzaffarabad, about 125 km from Srinagar and 80 km north-east of Islamabad, but tremors were felt up to 1,000 km from the epicenter and the damage extended to a radius of about 140 km. The official death toll was nearly 50,000. The UN reported that more than 4 million people were directly affected and it left an estimated 3.3 million homeless in Pakistan. It is estimated that damages incurred are well over Rs 30 billion.

Right to Information Act

The Parliament of India enacted the Right to Information Act 2005 which came into force on 12 October 2005. The Act is designed to enable Indian citizens to have access to information that is under the control of organizations defined to be public authorities under the Act. The Act mandates that from 12 October 2005, the general public of India may approach public authorities, including departments of the federal and state governments, government bodies, public sector companies and public sector banks, to make available the information as requested. The Act further mandates that all public authorities be expected to publish the information under Sec. 4 (1) (b) of the Act on various issues relating to the institution through its computerized network. A proposal to amend the Right to Information Act in 2006—whereby file notings could be exempted from the information made available to the general public—met with severe resistance from right to information activists, and the government refrained from modifying the Act in any way.

Saddam Hussein on Trial

Saddam Hussein, former President of Iraq, and seven different defendants have been put on trial for the killing of 148 Shias in Dujail in 1982. They are being tried for allegations of crimes against humanity with regard to events that took place after a failed assassination attempt in Dujail. The first trial of

Saddam Hussein began before the Iraqi Special Tribunal on 19 October 2005. A verdict is due soon. The international community has repeatedly accused Saddam Hussein of war crimes, genocide, and atrocities during his reign in Iraq. Some of the allegations include using poison gas against Iranians during the Iran–Iraq war in the 1980s, dropping chemical weapons on Halabja which killed up to 5,000 people, and committing crimes against humanity and possibly genocide against the Marsh Arabs and Shi'a Arabs in southern Iraq, as well as against Iraqi Kurds in northern Iraq. Throughout the 1990s Saddam Hussein repeatedly violated the sixteen United Nations Security Council resolutions, which are described on the White House's website.

Abu Salem Extradited and Put on Trial

On 20 September 2002, Portugal Interpol arrested Abu Salem and Monica Bedi in Lisbon. Salem was held for entering Portugal using forged documents. An accused in the 1993 bomb blasts and in the killings of Bollywood producer Gulshan Kumar, actress Manisha Koirala's secretary, and a builder along with over fifty other cases, he was cleared for extradition to India by a Portuguese court in February 2004, to face trial in the 1993 Mumbai bomb blasts case. Abu Salem is also accused of ferrying and distributing weapons. In November 2005, Portuguese authorities handed both Salem and Monica Bedi over to the Central Bureau of Investigation on the assurance that the death penalty would not be meted out to either of them (since Portugal does not impose the death penalty). In March 2006, a special TADA court framed charges against Salem and his alleged associate Riaz Siddiqui; eight charges were finally filed. Salem will face trial in the ongoing Mumbai bomb blasts case.

Y.K. Sabharwal Becomes Chief Justice of India

President A.P.J. Abdul Kalam swore in Justice Yogesh Kumar Sabharwal as the Chief Justice of India on 1 November 2005. Sixty-three-year-old Justice Sabharwal succeeded Justice R.C. Lahoti as the thirty-sixth Chief Justice of India. His tenure is fourteen months and will end on 14 January 2007.

NDA Forms Government in Bihar

In November 2005, Janata Dal (United) leader, Nitish Kumar, led the National Democratic Alliance to a resounding victory in the Bihar Assembly elections. The electorate of Bihar created history by bringing fifteen years of political domination by Lalu Prasad Yadav's Rashtriya Janata Dal (RJD) to an end. The clear mandate ended the political uncertainty that had prevailed since the February 2005 elections threw up a hung Assembly in Bihar. The National Democratic Alliance won 143 seats in the 243-member Assembly, with the JD(U) bagging eighty-eight seats and the Bharatiya Janata Party fifty-five; the RJD managed just fifty-four seats. On 24 November 2005 Nitish Kumar was sworn in as the thirty-third chief minister of Bihar.

New Governments in Jammu and Kashmir, Madhya Pradesh and Karnataka

In 2005, Mufti Mohammad Sayeed completed his three-year term as chief minister of Jammu and Kashmir, as per the power-sharing agreement between the PDP–Congress alliance reached in late 2002. Congress leader Ghulam Nabi Azad replaced Mufti Sayeed on 2 November 2005. Azad led the Congress in the assembly elections in 2002, which saw the Congress winning twenty seats. In a post-poll tie-up with the PDP, which got sixteen seats, Congress leadership gave it the first go at power enabling Mufti to become the chief minister.

In Madhya Pradesh, Babulal Gaur stepped down as chief minister in November 2005, after the members of the legislative assembly elected Shivraj Singh Chouhan to the post. On 28 November, Shivraj Singh Chouhan was elected leader of the BJP Legislature Party.

On 28 January 2006, the governor of Karnataka, T.N. Chaturvedi, invited the leader of the Janata Dal (Secular), H.D. Kumaraswamy, to form the government in the state after Chief Minister Dharam Singh's resignation. He was sworn in on 3 February 2006. Although the BJP is the single largest party in the state assembly with seventy-nine MLAs, almost twice the number of MLAs of the JD(S), it conceded the chief minister's post.

Reliance Demerger

Reliance Industries Ltd's (RIL) demerger scheme became effective on December 2005. This became possible when a certified copy of the Bombay High Court order, dated 9 December 2005, sanctioning the scheme of arrangement between RIL and the 'resulting companies', Reliance Energy Ventures Ltd, Global Fuel Management Services Ltd, Reliance Capital Ventures Ltd and Reliance Communication Ventures Ltd, and their respective shareholders and creditors was filed with the Registrar of Companies on 21 December. Dhirubhai Ambani died intestate in July 2002, leaving his sons, Mukesh and Anil, to battle for control of a massive conglomerate that spanned numerous industrial sectors. The Ambanis own about one-third of Reliance, worth about 12 per cent of shares listed on the Bombay Stock Exchange. They settled the ownership issue under the guidance of their mother Kokilaben Ambani and on the basis of the settlement plan drafted by ICICI Bank CEO K.V. Kamath.

Sachin Tendulkar Scores Thirty-fifth Ton in Tests, Fortieth in ODIs

On 10 December 2005, during the first innings of the second Test against Sri Lanka at the Feroz Shah Kotla Ground, Delhi, Sachin Tendulkar scored his thirty-fifth Test hundred and thereby became the highest scorer of centuries in the history of Test cricket, breaking fellow Indian Sunil Gavaskar's twenty-two-year-old record. Gavaskar became the scorer of the highest number of Test centuries in 1983, and scored his last century in 1986, also against Sri Lanka. Tendulkar scored the record-breaking 35th hundred in his 124th Test and 199th innings reaching the landmark in fewer innings than Gavaskar. Tendulkar scored his first Test century as a seventeen-year-old at Manchester against England in 1990. Sachin Tendulkar also holds the record of most centuries scored in the shorter version of the game. His latest one-day ton, his fortieth, came in the DLF Cup in Kuala Lumpur against the West Indies on 14 September 2006.

Sourav Ganguly Dropped from the Indian Team

During India's tour of Zimbabwe in 2005, new coach Greg Chappell suggested that India would be better served if Sourav Ganguly focused on getting his batting organized and stepped down from captaincy. Ganguly revealed this during an interview and also said that he was not ready to do what Chappell had suggested. Chappell then wrote a confidential e-mail to the BCCI president and secretary, complaining about Ganguly's behaviour and about his future plans for Indian cricket. The e-mail leaked to the media on the eve of the BCCI elections, and after the team returned from Zimbabwe, the BCCI had a discussion with both parties in an attempt to settle the issue. Ganguly was subsequently relieved of the captaincy and also dropped from the team. Later, during the Cricket Association of Bengal (CAB) elections in July 2006, Ganguly alleged that someone from the 'Jagmohan Dalmiya camp' had leaked the confidential e-mail sent by Chappell, a statement that was dismissed by the accused faction. Ganguly made a brief comeback in the Tests against Sri Lanka and Pakistan in the 2005-06 season but, since then, has been overlooked. His poor form and his ordinary showing in domestic cricket have doubtless contributed to his being left out of a stellar Indian team, but Ganguly has refused to hang up his boots just yet.

Indian Airlines Becomes Indian

In December 2005 Indian Airlines gave itself a new name and logo, and inducted its first new aircraft in eleven years. The state-run carrier also dropped the word 'Airlines' from its name and would hereafter be known simply as 'Indian'. The name 'Indian' would appear on both sides of the body in English and Devanagari script. The makeover was long overdue, the last change at Indian Airlines Limited (IAL) being in 1967 when it changed its name from Indian Airlines Corporation to Indian Airlines and a slanting IA painted in white on an orange background replaced the green, winged logo. R.K. Swamy BBDO created the new logo of Indian. The wheel in the Konark temple was the inspiration for the new logo.

Terrorists Strike in Bangalore

On 28 December 2005, suspected terrorists barged into the Indian Institute of Science (IIS) in Bangalore and fired indiscriminately, killing M.C. Puri, a retired sixty-four-year-old Professor Emeritus in the Mathematics department of the Indian Institute of Technology, Delhi, and injuring three others. According to police officials, four or five persons entered the IIS campus at around 7 p.m. in a white Ambassador car and opened fire with automatic weapons outside the J.N. Tata auditorium, when delegates of the annual convention of the Operational Research Society of India came out for dinner at the end of the day's proceedings. There were 250 Indian and thirty-six foreign delegates at the convention. An AK-47-like weapon, eleven empty cartridges, two live magazines and a live grenade packed in a cotton pouch were recovered from the scene of the firing.

Modernization of Delhi and Mumbai Airports

The GMR Group and Fraport consortium won the bid for the modernization of Delhi airport, while GVK Industries and South Africa Airports combined to bag the Mumbai airport modernization project in January 2006. Even though GMR–Fraport was the second highest financial bidder for the modernization of the two metro airports, with an investment of about Rs 5,400 crore, it opted for Delhi by matching the top bidder, Reliance-ASA in terms of revenue share to the government. According to the civil aviation minister Praful Patel, GMR–Fraport was given the option to match the top bidder at either of the airports, as it was the sole technically qualified bidder among the five aspirants for Delhi and six for Mumbai airports. For Mumbai, the GVK–South Africa combine emerged as the top bidder offering a revenue share of 38 per cent, followed by GMR's 33 per cent, DS group's 28.12 per cent and Reliance's 21.33 per cent. Reliance Airport Developers filed a petition in the Delhi High Court on the sale of stakes in the New Delhi and Mumbai airports to private companies, seeking 'fairness and transparency in the award of contracts'. Airports Authority of India employees went on strike following the sealing of the modernization bids, fearing that their jobs would be lost if the airports were privatized.

Air-India Purchases Boeings in Bulk

In January 2006, Boeing Commercial Airplanes and Air-India formally announced an order agreement for sixty-eight aircraft. The order is valued at more than $ 11 billion at list prices. It is the single largest commercial airplane order in India's civil aviation history. Of the sixty-eight airplanes, fifty will be inducted into Air-India and eighteen into its low budget airline, Air-India Express. The fifty aircraft ordered for Air-India include eight B777-200LR Medium Capacity Ultra Long-Range aircraft; fifteen B777-300ER Medium Capacity Long-Range aircraft; and twenty-seven B787 Medium-Capacity Long-Range aircraft. For Air-India Express, eighteen 181-seater B737-800W aircraft have been ordered. The phased induction of these aircraft into the Air-India fleet, commencing November 2006, will be completed by 2011.

Disney–Pixar Deal

On 24 January 2006, Disney announced that it had agreed to buy Pixar for approximately $7.4 billion in an all-stock deal. Following Pixar shareholder approval, the acquisition was completed on 5 May 2006. The transaction catapulted Steve Jobs, who was the majority shareholder of Pixar with 50.1 per cent, to Disney's largest individual shareholder with 7 per cent and a new seat on its board of directors. Jobs' new Disney holdings outpace holdings belonging to ex-CEO Eisner, the previous top shareholder who still holds 1.7 per cent, and Disney director emeritus Roy E. Disney, who holds almost 1 per cent of the corporation's shares, and whose criticisms of Eisner included the soured Pixar relationship and accelerated his ouster. As part of the deal, John Lasseter, Pixar executive vice-president and founder, became chief creative officer of the Disney and Pixar animation studios and principal creative adviser at Walt Disney Imagineering which designs and builds the company's theme parks. Pixar President Ed Catmull became president of the Disney and Pixar animation studios.

'Dual Citizenship'

Based on the recommendations of the High Level Committee on Indian Diaspora, the Government of India decided to grant Overseas Citizenship of India (OCI), which most people mistakenly refer to as 'dual citizenship'. Persons of Indian Origin (PIOs) of certain categories who migrated from India and acquired citizenship of a foreign country other than Pakistan and Bangladesh, are eligible for the grant of OCI as long as their home countries allow dual citizenship in some form or the other under their local laws. The OCI scheme has become operational from 2 December 2005, and the prime minister formally launched it on 7 January 2006 at the Pravasi Bharatiya Divas in Hyderabad by symbolically handing over the first OCI certificate to a person of Indian origin. Under the scheme, a foreign national who was eligible to become a citizen of India after 26 January 1950 is eligible for registration as an OCI. NRI industrialist Swraj Paul and his wife Aruna Paul have acquired the Overseas Citizenship of India.

The Phantom of the Opera Breaks *Cats*' Broadway Record

The Phantom of the Opera, a musical composed by Andrew Lloyd Webber, based on the novel by Gaston Leroux, became the highest-grossing entertainment event of all time, with total worldwide box office takings of over $3.2 bn. Having premiered in 1988, it is currently the longest running show on Broadway, achieving the feat on 9 January 2006 with its 7,486th performance, surpassing another Andrew Lloyd Webber musical, *Cats*. The musical was produced by Cameron Mackintosh and Lloyd Webber's Really Useful Group and opened at Her Majesty's Theatre in London on 9 October 1986, where it still runs. It was taken to Broadway in 1987 and officially opened at the Majestic Theatre on 26 January 1988 where it still runs. In London, *Phantom* was highly successful at the 1986 Olivier Awards, where it won prizes for Best Musical and Best Actor in a Musical. At the 1988 Tony Awards, the Broadway production was nominated for eleven awards and won seven, including the coveted Best Musical award. *Phantom* also did well at the 1988 Drama Desk Awards, where it won seven awards and it came second in a BBC Radio 2 listener poll of the 'Nation's Number One Essential Musicals'.

Nimbus Acquires BCCI TV Rights

In February 2006, Nimbus Communications bagged the global media rights for all international and domestic cricket matches owned or controlled by the BCCI, to be played in India. The media rights include all television, Internet and radio rights but exclude mobile telephony. The coverage obtained will require all Test matches and one-day internationals (ODIs) to be telecast in India, the visiting team's nation and the world over. The Board of Control for Cricket in India (BCCI) has signed contracts worth $ 754 million for the next four years, marking an almost ten-fold jump in revenue from the previous four years. The television deal would cover telecast rights for roughly 23 Tests and 55 ODIs.

Delhi–Bhopal Shatabdi Becomes India's Fastest Train

On 15 February 2006, Railway Minister Lalu Prasad Yadav flagged off the subcontinent's fastest train—the Delhi–Bhopal Shatabdi Express. This superfast train runs at a maximum speed of 150 km per hour, significantly faster than the earlier top speed of 120 km per hour for a train on the same route, and decreases travel time between Delhi and Agra from over two-and-a-half hours to less than two hours. The train has a special engine and powerful brakes that ensure safety even at high speeds. This is also the first train in India to have an interlocking anti-climbing device, meaning that in the eventuality of collision with another train, carriages will not climb on each other, drastically reducing casualty figures. Running six days a week, excluding Fridays, the eleven-coach locomotive is pulled by a super-fast WAP-5 engine. The coaches were specially made at the Kapurthala Coach Factory.

Bird Flu Scare

Avian influenza epidemics have struck different parts of the world over the last couple of years. The first reports of bird flu inIndia came from Nawapur in the Nandurbar district of Maharashtra on 19 February 2006. 53,000 birds were culled and 587,000 eggs were destroyed within five days. Another outbreak was reported in the Jalgaon district of Maharashtra, and spilled over into adjoining areas of Madhya Pradesh. The governments of the states that border Maharashtra and others like Jammu and Kashmir and Tamil Nadu banned the import of Maharashtran poultry. The Government of India asked pharmaceutical companies like Cipla to manufacture anti-flu medication and alerted the Indian Army to aid in evacuation operations and drug-distribution measures if the situation worsened. Prices of chicken products across India plummeted resulting in a steep rise in the prices of mutton and fish. Several airlines in India struck chicken off their in-flight menus, and chicken also went off the menu on Indian Railways and in the majority of government office canteens. The country suffered losses estimated at Rs 700 crore with 1.043 million birds, 1.475 million eggs and several thousand tons of feed destroyed. The government paid compensation to the poultry owners whose birds were killed.

Sonia Gandhi Steps Down and Is Re-elected

On 23 March 2006 Congress president and member of parliament Sonia Gandhi announced her resignation from the Lok Sabha and as chairperson of the National Advisory Council. She resigned from the seat in March after she was accused of holding an office of profit, which under the Constitution, was barred for elected public representatives. She was re-elected from her constituency, Rae Bareli, in May 2006, winning the by-election with a huge margin of over 400,000 votes.

Office of Profit Controversy

The office of profit controversy erupted after Samajwadi Party MP Jaya Bachchan was disqualified from the Rajya Sabha for holding an official post (chairperson of the Uttar Pradesh Film Development Corporation) simultaneous to her membership of the Rajya Sabha. The Election Commission recommended disqualification of Bachchan following a complaint by an Uttar Pradesh Congress leader who had lost the election to the Upper House against her. This was followed by Sonia Gandhi's resignation from the Lok Sabha over charges that she was holding the additional post of chairperson of the National Advisory Council, construed as an 'office of profit'. On 17 May 2006, Parliament approved the Parliament Amendment Bill 2006 (for Prevention of Disqualification) that provided exemption of fifty-six posts, including the chairpersonship of the National Advisory Council (NAC), from being considered an office of profit. President Kalam returned the 'office of profit' bill to the Parliament unsigned on 25 May. It was amended and re-sent to the President on 9 August for his approval. Prime Minister Manmohan Singh called on the President twice and the issue was reported to have figured in the discussions. The controversy also saw speculative debates in political circles on presidential powers. On 18 August, President A.P.J. Abdul Kalam gave his approval to the amended Parliament (Prevention of Disqualification) Act, 1959, popularly known as the Office of Profit bill.

Terror Strikes Varanasi

On 7 March 2006, terrorists planted four explosive devices in Varanasi, killing around twenty people and injuring many more. One of the bombs was planted in the Sankat Mochan Temple, a shrine dedicated to Lord Hanuman, while another was planted on a platform of the Varanasi Cantonment Railway Station, the main railway station in the city. At least twelve people were killed in the blasts for which the Islamic group Lashkar-e-Kahab claimed responsibility. The explosions came days after Hindus and Muslims clashed in Lucknow and Hindus looted Muslim shops and burned vehicles in Goa.

Verghese Kurien Calls It a Day

In March 2006 the doyen of India's cooperative movement and the 'white revolution'. Verghese Kurien resigned as member and chairman of the Gujarat Cooperative Milk Marketing Federation (GCMMF) of which he has been chairman since its inception in 1973. GCMMF markets the Amul brand milk and milk products. Only three months earlier, Kurien was unanimously re-elected for three years. He was also the chairman of the National Dairy Development Board since its inception in 1965 until he voluntarily resigned in favour of Dr Amrita Patel in 1999. However, Kurien continues to be the chairman at the Institute of Rural Management, Anand.

Australia–South Africa Set Record ODI Score, Broken by Sri Lanka

On 12 March 2006 at Wanderers Stadium, Johannesburg, one-day cricket was at its best. In an ODI played that day, Australia batted first and scored a staggering 434 runs for 4 wickets in 50 overs, setting the highest team score in an ODI by surpassing Sri Lanka's 398, set in 1996. Several Australian batsmen were in destructive moods with captain Ricky Ponting leading the way with a 105-ball 164. But it was a record that lasted only a few hours. South Africa came out to bat and made their intentions clear from the start and, aided by a 111-ball 175 from Herschelle Gibbs, reached the target with one ball and one wicket to spare. Their unbelievable score of 438 for 9 was the new highest ODI score ever. What they did not know was that Sri Lanka were waiting for an opportunity to regain their record once more. They accomplished this against the Netherlands in Amsteelveen on 4 July 2006 by scoring 443 for 9 in 50 overs, setting the world record for the highest one-day international total afresh. The total number of runs scored in a single day in the Wanderers match (872) is, however, a record that is likely to stand for some time to come.

Aamir Khan Supports the Narmada Bachao Andolan

In April 2006, Aamir Khan participated in demonstrations put up by the Narmada Bachao Andolan committee in New Delhi. In a press conference, he stated that as a concerned Indian citizen, he should lend his support to the poor Adivasis who faced displacement from their homes if the height of the dam were raised. He interacted with protestors at a dharna in Delhi, and appealed to the Government of India to give justice to its people. Aamir's support for the Narmada Bachao Andolan led the Gujarat government and Chief Minister Narendra Modi to prevent his film *Fanaa* from being screened in that state. Subsequently, on 7 August 2006, the Gujarat Forest Department sent a notice to Aamir Khan for allegedly violating the Wildlife Act during the making of *Lagaan* by filming a chinkara, an endangered species of deer, without permission, in the Kutch district.

Death of Pramod Mahajan

On the morning of 22 April 2006, Pramod Mahajan, former Union minister and a master strategist, fundraiser and election manager of the Bharatiya Janata Party, was shot by his youngest brother Pravin Mahajan who fired four bullets from a licensed .32 Belgian pistol at him inside the former's apartment in Mumbai. The first bullet missed Mahajan, but the other three struck him, damaging several internal organs. He was taken to the Hinduja hospital where he underwent an operation and an emergency surgical procedure on 23 April to remove the excess fluid from his body. After struggling for his life for twelve days, Mahajan suffered from a cardiac arrest and died on 3 May 2006. He was fifty-six. Pravin Mahajan surrendered at the Worli police station after the shooting and told the police that he had shot Pramod Mahajan to avenge the frequent humiliation he had suffered at his brother's hands. Police said that Pravin failed to use all nine bullets in the weapon because the gun jammed after the fourth shot. Pramod Mahajan was given a state funeral in Mumbai on 4 May 2006. Pravin Mahajan has been charged with murder under Sec. 302 of the Indian Penal Code. Soon after, on 1 June, grief struck the Mahajan family again when

Pramod Mahajan's son Rahul was admitted to hospital, suffering from a suspected drug overdose; Rahul's aide Vivek Moitra, who was with him, died in the incident. On 6 June Rahul Mahajan was arrested by the Delhi police for sale/purchase and consumption of illegal drugs.

Crisis in Nepal

On 1 February 2005, King Gyanendra of Nepal appointed a government, led by him, and simultaneously enforced martial law in the country. He argued that civil politicians were unfit to handle the Maoist insurgency. A broad alliance against the royal takeover, called the Seven Party Alliance (SPA), was organized, encompassing about 90 per cent of the seats in the dissolved parliament. In December, the SPA signed a twelve-point understanding with the Maoists within whose framework the Maoists committed themselves to multi-party democracy and freedom of speech and called for a cease-fire in the Kathmandu valley. The SPA accepted the Maoist demand for elections to a Constituent Assembly but called for a four-day nationwide general strike between 5 and 9 April. A curfew was announced by the government on 8 April, with reported orders to shoot protestors on sight. Despite this, small, disorganized protests continued in the following days. On 21 April, opposition sources claim, about half a million people took part in the protests in Kathmandu. More conservative estimates talk about 300,000 participants. Later, in the evening, King Gyanendra announced that he would return political power to the people and called for elections to be held as soon as possible. He called on the SPA to nominate a new prime minister of Nepal. King Gyanendra reinstated the old Nepal House of Representatives on 24 April 2006. The reinstitution of parliament was accepted by the SPA. It declared that Girija Prasad Koirala would lead the new government. The SPA stated that the new parliament would hold elections to a body that would frame a new Constitution.

Ban on *The Da Vinci Code*

The Da Vinci Code, one of the biggest Hollywood films of the year, stirred up much controversy worldwide, linked largely to its controversial interpretation of accepted Christian history. The film became a target for criticism by the Roman Catholic Church. At a conference on 28 April 2006, the secretary of the Congregation for the Doctrine of the Faith, a Vatican curial department, specifically called for a boycott of the film. Religious leaders from Beijing to Washington said the film both violated ethics and offended believers with its central premises about the personal life of Jesus Christ. Christian groups in many countries protested against the film and called for it to be banned. The film was also savaged by professional critics upon its premier at the Cannes Film Festival. Its release in India was delayed by a week from its worldwide release date of 19 May following opposition by religious groups. Special screenings for Catholic leaders and the Information and Broadcasting minister Priya Ranjan Dasmunshi were organized prior to its release for public viewing. The Censor Board of India subsequently cleared the film for release without cuts, but demanded a disclaimer at the beginning and the end to stress its 'fictitious' nature. Indian states that banned the film include Andhra Pradesh, Nagaland, Punjab, Goa and Tamil Nadu.

The Rise of the Gold Market

India, the biggest importer and consumer of gold and gold jewellery and the largest scrap market for old gold jewellery, is experiencing a continuing rise in gold prices. In April 1981, the gold price was Rs 1670 per 10 grams. In 1991, Indian gold demand was only

8 per cent of world offtake. The deregulation of the market during the 1990s brought about a dramatic change. Jewellery demand increased from 208 tonnes in 1991 to peak at 658 tonnes in 1998, while demand for investment bars grew from 10 tonnes in 1991 to 116 tonnes in 1998, and registered 85 tonnes in 2002. Though the World Gold Council report showed India's gold demand fell by 27 per cent to 145 tonnes in the January to March 2006 quarter, gold prices crossed the Rs 10,000 level (per 10 grams) in May 2006.

2006 Assembly Elections

In 2006, the state assembly elections in India took place between 3 April and 8 May. The states that went to the polls were Assam, Kerala, Tamil Nadu, West Bengal and Pondicherry. On 14 May 2006, Tarun Gogoi was sworn in for his second consecutive term as the chief minister of Assam in what is Assam's first coalition government headed by the Congress. In Kerala, a Marxist-led Left Democratic Front beat the incumbent Indian National Congress-led United Democratic Front by a margin of fifty-six seats. On 18 May 2006 V.S. Achuthanandan was sworn-in as the chief minister of Kerala as head of a nineteen-member ministry. In Tamil Nadu, the ruling party AIADMK was voted out of power with the DMK alliance regaining power after losing out in the previous elections. M. Karunanidhi took over as the chief minister on 13 May 2006. He heads a minority government, with the DMK's allies—Congress, PMK and the Left parties—extending support from the outside. The Communist Party of India (Marxist)-led Left Front won the 2006 West Bengal Assembly Elections. On 18 May 2006, Buddhadeb Bhattacharya was sworn in as the chief minister of the Left Front government, which returned to power for a historic seventh term. The DPA won twenty-one out of the thirty available seats in the legislative assembly of Pondicherry, thereby securing a majority over the AIDMK, which managed to get only six seats. N. Rangaswamy was sworn in as chief minister in Pondicherry for the second time in succession on 18 May 2006.

The Loneliness of the Long Distance Runner

Four-year-old Budhia Singh is the world's youngest marathon runner. Considered an athletic phenomenon, Budhia, born in Bhubaneshwar, has participated in races of up to 60 km (37.3 miles) which he ran in roughly six hours and thirty minutes. His judo coach Biranchi Das first spotted him after learning that he possessed the ability to run improbable distances for a boy his age. Budhia's ability has brought him fame and he has appeared in a number of television commercials, which have allegedly led to significant financial gains to Das. Controversy over the nature of these gains have led to accusations of exploitation against Biranchi Das and an official inquiry by Indian child-welfare officials was launched on 4 January 2006. Meanwhile, on 1 May 2006, Budhia completed a 65 km run from Puri to Bhubaneswar in just over six hours. In an attempt to break Budhia's record, eight-year-old Mrityunjay Mandal, also from Orissa, set out on an 80 km run from Kalian to Colaba on 24 September, but collapsed 11 km short of the finishing line from sheer exhaustion.

Montenegro Separates from Serbia

The country Serbia and Montenegro was a confederated union of two republics which existed between 2003 and 2006. The two republics, both of which are former republics of socialist Yugoslavia, initially formed the Federal Republic of Yugoslavia (FRY) in 1992. In 2003, the FRY was reconstituted as the State Union of Serbia and Montenegro. On 21 May 2006, Montenegro held a referendum to seek full independence. Final official results indicated on 31 May that 55.5 per cent of voters had elected to become independent.

The subsequent Montenegrin proclamation of independence on 3 June 2006 and the Serbian proclamation of independence on 5 June ended the existence of the State Union of Serbia and Montenegro.

India's Largest SEZ in Haryana

On 19 June 2006 Reliance Ventures Ltd (RVL) and the Haryana State Industrial and Infrastructure Development Corporation (HSIIDC) signed a joint venture agreement to set up the country's largest Special Economic Zone (SEZ) in Haryana, spread across 25,000 acres, at an overall investment of Rs 40,000 crore. RVL also proposes to set up a 2,000 MW power plant to meet the requirements of the SEZ and is contemplating a cargo airport, subject to necessary approvals. Under the agreement, a joint venture company called Reliance Haryana SEZ Ltd has been formed, with Reliance holding a 90 per cent stake and the HSIIDC the remaining 10 per cent. The zone will be located in Gurgaon and Jhajjar districts, flanking the proposed Kundli–Manesar–Palwal expressway on both sides. Mukesh Ambani has stated that the SEZ would focus on emerging industries like nanotechnology and biotechnology. Overall, the SEZ expects to catalyze an investment of over Rs 100,000 crore and generate direct and indirect employment for over 5 lakh people.

Jet Airways–Air Sahara Deal Falls Through

On 21 June 2006, Jet Airways' deal to buy rival carrier Air Sahara fell through after a deadline to complete it passed without an agreement. The $500 million (£284 million) deal would have been the biggest in India's aviation, creating the country's largest airline. According to industry reports, Jet Airways pulled out of the deal on a 'technicality' that it did not receive the necessary regulatory approvals before the final date of closure of the deal. Jet Airways, founded by London-based former travel agent Naresh Goyal, controls about 35 per cent of the Indian domestic airline market. Air Sahara, owned by the Subrata Roy, controls about 9 per cent of India's market. The parties now appear headed for a legal wrangle over the deposit money of $330 million as advance for the acquisition.

Bill Gates to Retire

Microsoft Corporation announced that with effect from July 2008, Bill Gates, its chairman, would transition out of a day-to-day role in the company to spend more time on his global health and education work at the Bill and Melinda Gates Foundation. The company announced a two-year transition process to ensure that there is a smooth and orderly transfer of Gates' daily responsibilities, and said that after July 2008 Gates would continue to serve as the company's chairman and an advisor on key development projects. The company also announced that Chief Technical Officer, Ray Ozzie, would immediately assume the title of chief software architect and begin working side by side with Gates on all technical architecture and product-oversight responsibilities.

Warren Buffett Donates $37 billion to Charity

On 25 June 2006, Warren Buffett announced a donation of about $ 37 billion to Bill Gates' charitable foundation. The donation is thought to be the largest-ever charitable gift in the US. He will hand over 10 million shares in his Berkshire Hathaway firm to the Bill and Melinda Gates Foundation. As well as donating to the Gates foundation, Buffett also pledged 1 million shares to a foundation established for his late wife (Susan Thompson), and 350,000 shares each to foundations for his three children. All the gifts would be awarded annually, with 5 per cent of each donation passed on each year. He confirmed his decision in letters to the recipients, and said he would write a new will to ensure the money continues to be distributed after his death. Warren Buffett is worth an estimated $ 44 billion. The donation doubles the value of the Gates foundation, already one of the world's richest charities.

Tibet–China Rail Link Opened

In June 2006, China opened the world's highest railway, an 1,100-km line that crosses the Tibetan Plateau. President Hu Jintao officially inaugurated the railway. The first section of the railway, from Beijing to Golmud in Qinghai Province, was completed in 1984. But the section connecting Golmud to Lhasa was delayed. The plan was revived in 2001. At its highest point, the railway hits an altitude of 5,072 metres (16,604ft), higher than the peak of any mountain in Europe and more than 200 metres higher than the Peruvian railway in the Andes, which was previously the world's highest track.

N. Gopalaswami is the New Chief Election Commissioner

On 30 June 2006, N. Gopalaswami assumed charge as the fifteenth Chief Election Commissioner (CEC) of India, succeeding B.B. Tandon. His term will end in April 2009. Prior to his appointment as the Chief Election Commissioner of India, Gopalaswami was Election Commissioner concerned with the conduct of elections in both the centre and the states, apart from the elections for the offices of the President and Vice-President of India. He will conduct the next presidential and vice-presidential elections and the crucial Assembly polls in some states, including Uttar Pradesh, next year. Before becoming an Election Commissioner in 2004, Gopalaswami was Union Home Secretary. He served in Gujarat in various capacities, worked as Culture Secretary, Secretary General in the National Human Rights Commission (NHRC) and various other Central departments.

G8 Summit in St Petersburg

The twenty-second summit of the G8 group of industrialized nations took place from 15 to 17 July 2006 outside Saint Petersburg, Russia in the Constantine Palace, in Strelna on the Gulf of Finland. Energy security, education, and the fight against infectious diseases were the main issues, with the conflict between Israel and Lebanon also attracting the attention of world leaders. Because the Group of Eight is primarily an economic forum between the global economic powerhouses, the focus of the G8 summit is the discussion of economic issues. Some of the issues on the agenda were: open trade between Russia and the US, including discussion of Russian entry into the World Trade Organization; multibillion-dollar aircraft manufacturing contracts; free energy markets, especially regarding Russia and former Soviet republics, as well as petroleum from the Middle East; rights for exploration and exploitation of natural gas in Russia and the North Atlantic Ocean / Baltic Sea; alternative energy forms, especially relaxing nuclear power regulations, and development of hydrogen as an economically viable energy platform; discussion of economic impacts of global instability, drugs, and terrorism; education priorities for developed nations, especially encouraging businesses to support education; and a global system to monitor and contain infectious diseases.

Closure of Disinvestment

On 6 July 2006, the United Progressive Alliance (UPA) government announced the temporary suspension of its disinvestments/privatization programme, after a member of the Congress Party-led coalition threatened to quit the government if it proceeded with the sale of a 10 per cent interest in the Neyveli Lignite Corporation (NLC). The Tamil Nadu-based Dravida Munnetra Kazhagam (DMK) had made the threat on the third day of an indefinite strike by 19,000 NLC workers. The strike had forced the NLC to halt its lignite mining operations and to almost halve its power generation. Buoyed by the government's decision to put off the privatization of NLC, the CPI(M) congratulated the DMK for taking a forthright stand in defence of the public sector and asserted that the divestment of profit-making PSUs had now become a 'national issue'. The stock market continued to slide with the shares of public sector undertakings becoming the major casualty, on the back of investors' concern over a possible slowdown in the reform process triggered by the government's decision to hold back all disinvestment proposals. Inspired by this success, NALCO workers at Angul, Damanjodi and Bhuvaneshwar also went on one-day strikes on 23, 24 and 26 June respectively. The working class in Orissa decided to take to the streets in support of the NALCO workers' struggle. Central Trade Unions gave a call for an all-India Protest Day on 5 July with protest marches in Delhi and other places. This united nationwide working-class protest forced the UPA government to roll back its disinvestment proposal. The successful workers' struggles dealt a determined blow to the Central Government's disinvestment plans, not only in the NLC and NALCO, but also in NMDC (National Metropolitan Development Corporation), PFC (Power Finance Corporation), MUL (Maruti Udyog Limited), and HZL (Hindustan Zinc Limited). The government had sought to legitimize disinvestment in these PSUs as a move to generate resources for the social sector and benefit unorganized sector workers.

A Mole in the PMO?

Former external affairs minister and BJP leader Jaswant Singh's memoir *A Call To Honour* sparked off a controversy by alleging that someone in the PMO during P.V. Narasimha Rao's Congress government had been leaking nuclear secrets to the US. Jaswant Singh did not name the mole but sources claimed the allusion was to a bureaucrat who has passed away. Jaswant Singh, currently the leader of the Opposition in the Rajya Sabha, said he had learnt of this a decade ago but remained silent until now as he did not want to sensationalize the issue. In response to a demand from Prime Minister Manmohan Singh that he produce concrete evidence supporting his allegations, Jaswant Singh was only able to come up with a letter that named no one and had already been published in the media.

Prince Makes Headlines

Prince, a six-year-old boy who fell into a borewell in Kurukshetra, topped media headlines for the weekend of 21-23 July 2006, till he was rescued by the army on Sunday. The boy's plight was captured on television cameras and transmitted live across the nation, and the incident was considered important enough to solicit personal assurances for the boy's safety from Haryana chief minister Ranvir Singh Hooda and prime minister Manmohan Singh.

Rains Lash Maharashtra, Gujarat, Andhra Pradesh and Rajasthan

2006 saw heavy monsoon rains in several Indian states including

Maharashtra, Gujarat, Andhra Pradesh and Rajasthan. The death toll in Maharashtra, Gujarat and Andhra Pradesh was 230. Over 3.5 lakh people were evacuated from flood-hit areas in Maharashtra. Torrential rains lashed Nasik, Jalgaon, Amravati and Pune districts for five consecutive days. The Godavari, Krishna and Koyna rivers were in spate and 300 people were marooned in different parts of Nasik. Mumbai was severely flooded for the second year in succession. Surat was inundated following the release of more waters from the Ukai dam on the swollen Tapti river. The Centre announced an aid package of Rs 200 crore for Andhra Pradesh where the flood situation continued to be grim with over 350 villages in the Konaseema region cut off from the rest of the state. At least 106 people are said to have died in the floods that affected close to 11 lakh people across the state. Rains and floods affected twelve districts in Rajasthan killing eighty-five people, including fifty in the Barmer district alone. Thousands of cattle perished, and property and kharif crop damage amounted to Rs 1300 crore.

WTO Negotiations End in Failure

On 24 July 2006, the World Trade Organization's Doha round of free-trade talks was suspended for an indefinite period. Although negotiations may re-start in the future, any immediate possibility of a global reduction in tariffs ended. WTO Director-General Pascal Lamy suspended the World Trade Organization's Doha round of trade talks, which were launched in 2001. The talks aimed at bringing about global agreement among the WTO's 149 members to reduce tariffs on farm, industrial and service sectors. A major point of argument had been whether textiles and clothing should have been separated from other industrial products. Fourteen hours of talks between the so-called G6—the US, European Union, Brazil, Australia, Japan and India—yielded no breakthrough on the question. The European Union and India firmly pointed the finger at the United States for the final breakdown, saying that Washington had been demanding too high a price for cutting into the $20 billion it spends annually on farm subsidies. But the United States maintained that neither the EU nor India was prepared to offer the sort of access to their markets that Washington needed to make a deal on subsidies worthwhile.

Stem-Cell Controversy

On 19 July 2006 US President George W. Bush vetoed a controversial bill, which would have lifted a ban on federal funding for new embryonic stem-cell research, marking the first time in his presidency that he refused to sign into law a bill approved by Congress. The House of Representatives later failed to achieve the necessary two-thirds vote needed to overturn Bush's veto. Bush has said that he is against the use of public funds for research involving the destruction of human embryos. Bush used his first veto to block increased federal spending for such research, despite strong public support for the effort to combat diseases like Alzheimer's, Parkinson's and diabetes. The Stem-Cell Foundation said that the veto is the single biggest setback to the advance of stem-cell research. The news disheartened the great number of US campaigners who have fought hard to introduce the Stem-Cell Enhancement Act, including Republican leader of the Senate, Bill Frist, Nancy Reagan and Arnold Schwarzenegger. The controversial Stem-Cell Research Enhancement Act would lift rules set by Bush in 2001 that make federal funds available only to research on a small number of embryonic stem-cell lines, which existed at that time. A strong and vocal minority of social conservatives back Bush's position.

INSAT-4C, Agni-III Launches Fail

India's maiden attempt to launch a two-tonne communication satellite, INSAT-4C, from home soil failed after the indigenous Geo-synchronous Satellite Launch Vehicle (GSLV) plunged into the sea within a minute of takeoff on 10 July 2006. The launch vehicle, carrying the 2,168 kg satellite to boost Direct-to-Home (DTH) television service and digital newsgathering, deviated from its chartered path soon after lift-off from the Satish Dhawan Space Centre in Sriharikota and disintegrated into a ball of fire. The INSAT-4C launch debacle came a day after the Agni-III nuclear-capable ballistic missile, with a range upto 3,500 km, failed to hit its target off the coast of Orissa and splashed into the sea. The INSAT-4C satellite was the heaviest in its class and this was the first launch of a GSLV from the Rs 350-crore sophisticated launch pad, commissioned in May 2005. The INSAT-4C, the second satellite in the INSAT-4 series, was aimed at strengthening video picture transmission besides providing space for National Informatics Centre's VSAT connectivity. The lifespan of the satellite was expected to be ten years.

Tsunami in Indonesia

A earthquake with a magnitude of 7.7 on the Richter scale rocked the Indian Ocean seabed, 350 km (220 miles) south of Jakarta, on 17 July 2006. The earthquake triggered a tsunami, which hit the south coast of the island of Java, Indonesia. Its height varied from between 2 to 6 metres, damaging houses, boats and hotels on or near the Pangandaran beach and flattening buildings even 400 metres from the coastline. More than 600 people were reported killed, with around 150 others missing. At least 23,000 people fled their homes, either because they were destroyed or for fear of another tsunami.

Israel–Lebanon Conflict

On 12 July 2006, the Israel–Lebanon conflict erupted when a Hezbollah unit crossed into Israel, killed three Israeli soldiers and kidnapped two others in a bid to negotiate a prisoner exchange, a demand that was rebuffed by the Israelis. Israel responded with a naval blockade and bombing attacks on hundreds of targets in Lebanon, including Beirut's airport and the Hezbollah's headquarters in southern Beirut. The Hezbollah rejoinder included rocket attacks targeting northern Israeli cities. Fighting killed thousands of Lebanese civilians and coincided with a two-week-old Israeli military campaign in Gaza in response to the kidnapping of an Israeli soldier by Palestinian militants. The conflict displaced about a million Lebanese and 500,000 Israelis, and disrupted normal life across all of Lebanon and northern Israel. On 11 August, the United Nations Security Council unanimously approved United Nations Security Council Resolution 1701, in an effort to end the hostilities. On 12 August, it was approved by the Lebanese government, and by the Israeli government the following day. A United Nations-brokered ceasefire went into effect on 14 August 2006. On 17 August the Lebanese army began deploying its forces in southern Lebanon as part of the agreement, and Israel began to withdraw some of its forces from the country. A full withdrawal is not expected until the enlarged UNIFIL force has arrived.

Salim Group Invests in West Bengal

On 31 July 2006, the West Bengal government signed India's biggest foreign direct investment (FDI) deal to date with the Salim Group, an Indonesian conglomerate. The deal is for investments of up to Rs 200 billion ($ 4.2 billion) in infrastructure development. Under the agreement, the 'New Kolkata International Development' project promises to change the face of the region with expressways, flyovers, bridges, townships, health cities and economic zones. The deal marks a new beginning in the development of West Bengal—a one-time industrial leader that has fallen behind other states because of the flight of capital caused by militant trade unionism. The agreement was signed between the West Bengal Industrial Development Corporation (WBIDC) and New Kolkata International Development; a Special Purpose Vehicle (SPV) floated by a consortium of the Salim Group, its collaborator Prasun Mukherjee's Universal Success and the Gurgaon-based construction company Unitech. As the state government wants to ensure control over the infrastructure projects, particularly the chemical hub in Haldia, the WBIDC has been granted a stake in the company.

New ICC Chief

On 7 July 2006, Percy Sonn of South Africa took charge as the new president of the International Cricket Council (ICC), replacing Ehsan Mani of Pakistan. The fifty-six-year-old lawyer is the sixth man to fill the seniormost position at cricket's world governing body, and the first from Africa. He will be president for a minimum of two years and a maximum of three. Sonn played a crucial role when South Africa returned to world cricket after the fall of apartheid in 1991 and was the president of the United Cricket Board of South Africa for three years until 2003.

Twenty20 World Cup

The International Cricket Council has decided to organize a Twenty20 World Championship in South Africa in 2007. The tournament will involve not only the ten full ICC members but also the two leading associate sides. Twenty20 cricket has been a huge success wherever it has been played and its popularity has directly led to the staging of a world championship so that the winning team can truly call itself the best in the world in this exciting new form of the game.

Jayawardene and Sangakkara Record Highest Partnership in Tests

In the first Test against South Africa at Colombo, the Sri Lankan pair, Kumara Sangakkara and Mahela Jayawardene, set the highest partnership record for any wicket in a Test match on 29 July 2006, scoring 624 runs together for the third wicket. Sangakkara scored 287 and Jayawardene finished at 374, the highest individual score for a Sri Lankan in Tests (beating Sanath Jayasuriya's 340 scored against India in 1997). They broke the record of 576 runs set by Sanath Jayasuriya and Roshan Mahanama for the second wicket against India at Colombo in 1997. Jayawardene's 374 is the fourth highest individual score in a Test match, and the highest by a right-handed batsman and by a batsman from the subcontinent.

Gatlin and Landis Fail Drug Tests

American cyclist Floyd Landis was fired from the Phonak team on 5 August 2006 when he tested positive for the steroid testosterone after winning the seventeenth stage of the Tour de France. He is still listed as the winner of the 2006 Tour de France but is not considered the champion by Tour officials. Because of a failed drug test, indicating a much higher-than-allowed ratio of testosterone to epitestosterone and the presence of synthetic testosterone during one stage of the race, he is expected to have to forfeit his title. Tour director Christian Prudhomme no longer considers Landis the winner, but ultimately the decision of whether to strip him of his title will be made by the International Cycling Union (UCI).

American sprinter Justin Gatlin is an Olympic gold medalist who shares the world record in the 100 m sprint with Asafa Powell, with a time of 9.77 seconds. However, his record is likely to be revoked after a positive doping test and its resulting eight-year competitive ban. The substance that Gatlin supposedly tested positive for was 'testosterone or its precursor'. The failed test was made public after a relay race on 22 April 2006 and on 29 July 2006. Gatlin told the media that he had been informed by the USADA that he had given a positive doping test.

Narayana Murthy Steps Down as Infosys Head

On his sixtieth birthday on 20 August 2006, N.R. Narayana Murthy stepped down as the executive chairman of Infosys, as per his company's retirement policy. Narayana Murthy had launched Infosys as a small firm in Bangalore in 1981 and took it to enviable heights. However, he is still a member of the Infosys board and continues as the company's non-executive chairman and chief mentor. Nandan M. Nilekani, who was the CEO and MD, took over as the head of Infosys Technologies.

Perelman Refuses Fields Medal

The Fields Medal is awarded every four years on the occasion of the International Congress of Mathematicians to recognize outstanding mathematical achievement for existing work and the promise of future achievement. It is the rough equivalent of the Nobel Prize in prestige: the Fields Medal is widely viewed as the top honour a mathematician can receive. It comes with a monetary award, which in 2006, was US$ 13,400 or 10,550 euros.The Fields Medal Committee is chosen by the Executive Committee of the International Mathematical Union and is normally chaired by the IMU president. It is asked to choose at least two (preferably three or four) Fields medallists, and to have regard in its choice to representing a diversity of mathematical fields. A candidate's fortieth birthday must not occur before 1 January of the year of the Congress at which the Fields Medals are awarded. In 2006, Andrei Okounkov (Russia), Grigori Perelman (Russia), Terence Tao (Australia) and Wendelin Werner (France) were nominated for the award. However, Grigori Perelman, credited with proving the Poincaré conjecture, refused his Fields Medal and did not attend the Congress.

Arvind Kejriwal Wins Ramon Magsaysay Emergent Leadership Award

Arvind Kejriwal, head of the Delhi-based NGO Parivartan, was presented the 2006 Ramon Magsaysay Award for Emergent Leadership in Manila on 31 August 2006. Kejriwal was selected for the honour for leading the Right to Information movement in India. The movement created awareness on fighting corruption and making the government more accountable. Kejriwal was previously with the Income Tax department and recently resigned from government service. He has been a Right to Information campaigner for over four years.

1993 Mumbai Blasts Verdict

Thirteen years after the serial bomb blasts in Mumbai, the TADA court started delivering verdicts in the case from August 2006. About 13,000 pages of evidence have been recorded and more than 600 witnesses have deposed. The examination of the accused ended in November 2001. Till date, only fifty-five people have been found guilty. As many as twenty-four accused, including Dawood Ibrahim, Anees Ibrahim and Tiger Memon, are believed to be outside India. In the first batch of the judgment of the serial blasts that killed 257 people, four members of the Memon family—Yakub, Essa, Yusuf and Rubina—were found guilty.

Pervez Musharraf Publishes Memoirs

In the Line of Fire: A Memoir, written by the president of Pakistan, Pervez Musharraf, was published on 25 September 2006 and launched in New York. Musharraf says in his memoir that he had no choice after the September 11 attacks but to switch from supporting the Taliban to backing the US-led war on terror groups. The book also criticizes the US-led invasion of Iraq, saying it has made the world 'more dangerous', and accuses India of starting the Kargil conflict.

North Korea Conducts Nuclear Test

On 9 October 2006 the Democratic People's Republic of Korea carried out the detonation of a nuclear device. The blast is estimated to have had an explosive force of less than one kiloton. The test was carried out at a mountain in Musadan-ri in Hwadae-ri, near the city of Kilchu, in North HamgyOng province on the northeast coast of North Korea. After the tests were conducted, France, Japan, the United Kingdom and the United States expressed support for implementing sanctions against North Korea under Chapter VII of the United Nations Charter. On 14 October, the United Nations Security Council voted unanimously to impose sanctions on North Korea under Resolution 1718.

Ban Ki-moon Named Next UN Secretary-General

Ban Ki-moon, the current foreign minister of the Republic of Korea, was appointed by the UN General Assembly on 9 October 2006 to succeed Kofi Annan as the next UN Secretary-General from 1 January 2007. This is the first time a South Korean has run in the election for Secretary-General. In February 2006, Ban Ki-moon declared his candidacy to replace Kofi Annan as UN Secretary-General at the end of 2006. He topped each of the four straw polls conducted by the UN Security Council. He was the only one to escape a veto, while each of the five other candidates—including India's Shashi Tharoor—received at least one 'no' vote from the five permanent members of the council—People's Republic of China, France, Russia, the United Kingdom, and the United States.

2006 Nobel Prizes Announced

The Nobel Prizes for 2006 were announced in October. John C. Mather and George F. Smoot won the Physics Nobel for research into cosmic microwave background radiation that helps explain the origin of galaxies and stars. Roger D. Kornberg won the Chemistry Nobel for describing the essential process of gene copying in cells, research that can give insight into illnesses such as cancer and heart disease. Andrew Z. Fire and Craig C. Mello were awarded the Nobel Prize in Physiology or Medicine for their work in controlling the activity of genes. Edmund S. Phelps won the Nobel Memorial Prize in Economic Sciences for work on the trade-offs between inflation and unemployment. Bangladesh's Muhammad Yunus and the Grameen Bank won the Nobel Peace Prize for working to advance economic and social development among the poor with micro-credit. Turkish writer Orahn Pamuk won the Nobel Prize for Literature.

Kiran Desai's *The Inheritance of Loss* wins the 2006 Man Booker Prize for Fiction

On 10 October 2006, Kiran Desai's novel *The Inheritance of Loss* won the very prestigious Man Booker Prize for Fiction for 2006. Harvey McGrath, Chairman of the Man Group plc, presented Kiran Desai with a cheque for £50,000. Kiran Desai is the first Indian-born writer to win the prestigious literary award since Arundhati Roy, whose *The God of Small Things* won in 1997. At thirty-five, Kiran Desai is also the youngest woman ever to win the Booker in its thirty-eight-year history. Kiran Desai is the daughter of renowned writer Anita Desai, who has been shortlisted thrice for the Booker Prize, but has never won. *The Inheritance of Loss* was announced the winner from a shortlist comprising six books.

Shoaib Akhtar, Mohammed Asif Test Positive for Steroids

On 16 October 2006, Pakistan cricketers Shoaib Akhtar and Mohammed Asif were suspended by the Pakistan Cricket Board (PCB) and pulled out of the Champions Trophy team after the pair failed drug tests for the performance-enhancing substance nandrolone. However Shoaib Akhtar declared his innocence and was quoted as saying that he had not knowingly taken any performance-enhancing drugs. The Pakistan Cricket Board-appointed drug tribunal formally chargesheeted the bowlers after conducting its first hearing in Lahore. Noted lawyer Shahid Hamid, another member of the committee and former Pakistan captain and coach Intikhab Alam heard the players separately before handing over the charge sheets. The next hearing has been scheduled on 26 October. During the hearing, the two players reportedly pleaded their innocence and requested the PCB to get their B samples tested.

Racing Legend Michael Schumacher Retires

Seven-time world champion Michael Schumacher retired from Formula One after the Brazilian Grand Prix on 22 October 2006. He ended his career with a record ninety-one F1 titles including seven in his final season—two more than the next most successful champion, Argentine Juan Manuel Fangio. Schumacher also holds the record for the most Grand Prix starts (250) and most pole positions (68). Schumacher won the drivers' world championship in 1994, 1995, 2000, 2001, 2002, 2003 and 2004. He is statistically the greatest driver the sport has ever seen, and the most successful Formula One driver in history. He was the first racing driver to win the F1 World championship under the German flag and the world's first billionaire athlete, with an annual salary reported to be around $80 million in 2004. Kimi Raikonen will replace Schumacher in the Ferrari team in 2007 and would be partnered by Felipe Massa.

Controversy Surrounds Mohammad Afzal's Death Sentence

Mohammad Afzal is accused and convicted of conspiracy to storm the Indian parliament in December 2001. In 2004, the Supreme Court of India sentenced him to death. The sentence was to be carried out on 20 October 2006 but is now stayed, after Afzal's family filed a mercy petition to the President. There is a lot of pressure to issue clemency to Afzal from poltical parties in Kashmir, who believe hanging Afzal would have negative effects on the peace process in Kashmir. During the attack on the Parliament believed to have been conducted by the Lashkar-e-Toiba (LET) and the Jaish-e-Mohammad (JEM), seven members of the security forces were killed.

Dengue and Chikungunya Outbreaks

An outbreak of mosquito-borne diseases dengue and chikungunya across India has left scores of people dead and hospitalized. Dengue fever is an infectious disease, transmitted by mosquitoes found in hot and humid climates. It is characterized by nosebleeds, headaches, high fever, joint and muscle pain and can lead to vomiting and nausea. The incubation period is usually two weeks. A total number of 7,488 cases and 124 deaths resulting from dengue have been reported in India as a whole, the majority of which are from Delhi. Apart from Delhi, the maximum number of dengue cases have been reported from Rajasthan (909) followed by Kerala (834), Gujarat (456), West Bengal (627),Uttar Pradesh (513),Tamil Nadu (308), Punjab (586), Maharashtra (582), Haryana (305), Karnataka (92) and Andhra Pradesh (79). Along with dengue, chikungunya fever has infected as many as 45 per cent of people in some areas of India. The disease, which is rarely life-threatening and causes severe joint pain and high fever, has spread to 151 districts in eight Indian states. A total number of 1,653 confirmed cases and no deaths have been reported as a whole, from Maharashtra, Karnataka, Andhra Pradesh, Gujarat, Tamil Nadu, Madhya Pradesh, Kerala, Rajasthan, Pondicherry and Delhi.

Amitabh Bachchan Awarded Legion d'Honneur

On 11 October 2006, Amitabh Bachchan's sixty-fourth birthday, the French government announced that it is conferring its highest honour, the Legion d'Honneur, on the Bollywood legend. French President Jacques Chirac bestowed the honour on Bachchan as a tribute to his 'exceptional career in the world of cinema and beyond'. The Legion d'Honneur is the highest distinction that can be conferred on a French citizen or foreigner.

Union Cabinet Reshuffled: Pranab Mukherjee Becomes External Affairs Minister, A.K. Antony Gets Defence

The much-awaited Union Cabinet reshuffle took place on 24 October 2006. Pranab Mukherjee takes over as the new foreign minister. The post had been lying vacant since K. Natwar Singh was removed following the oil-for-food scandal. RJD's Jayprakash Narayan Yadav and Karnataka actor-turned-politician M.H. Ambareesh were inducted as Ministers of State (MoS). Senior Congress leader A.K. Antony was inducted as a Union cabinet minister. He replaces Pranab Mukherjee as defence minister. Oscar Fernandes, formerly a minister without portfolio, will take over the Ministry of Labour as Minister of State with independent charge. The Labour Ministry had been without a full-fledged minister since the departure of Telangana Rashtriya Samiti (TRS) leader K. Chandrashekhar Rao. In a minor reshuffle of portfolios, Mani Shankar Aiyar gets additional charge of 'development of the north-eastern region'.

Pondicherry is Renamed Puducherry, Bangalore to Become Bengaluru

In August 2006, Parliament passed a Bill renaming the union territory of Pondicherry as Puducherry. The people of the union territory had been demanding that its name revert to Puducherry, which was what it was called before it was colonized by the French, since the name reflects its ancient culture. The Karnataka government has announced that the name of the city of Bangalore would revert to its pre-colonial name of Bengaluru from 1 November 2006. Mangalore is similarly renamed Mangaluru and Mysore, Mysoru.

Obituaries

Harold Leventhal, 86, renowned folk music promoter who worked with Woody Guthrie, introduced Bob Dylan in his first major concerts hall show, and introduced sitar maestro Ravi Shankar to American audiences, died on 4 October 2005. He was stationed in India during World War II while serving in the Army Signal Corps, and produced several films about the folk music world, including *Alice's Restaurant, Bound for Glory* (which received two Academy Awards) and *Wasn't That a Time!*

Milton Obote, 80, Uganda's first prime minister and a two-time president whose initial term ended with a coup led by Idi Amin and whose second was known for its harsh repression, died on 10 October 2005 at a South African hospital.

Rosa Parks, 92, a black seamstress whose refusal to relinquish her seat to a white man on a city bus in Montgomery in 1955 grew into a mythic event that helped touch off the civil rights movement of the 1950s and 1960s, died on 24 October 2005 at her home in Detroit. She worked as an aide to Congressman John Conyers, and founded the Rosa and Raymond Parks Institute for Self Development to develop leadership among Detroit's young people.

Nirmal Verma, 76, noted Hindi writer and Jnanpith Award winner, passed away in New Delhi on 25 October 2005 after suffering a prolonged illness. He was a pioneer of a new short story genre (New Story Movement in Hindi Literature). His popular novels include *Raat Ka Reporter* and *Lal Tin Ka Chhatt*.

Richard Errett Smalley, 62, Nobel laureate, one of the best-known and respected scientists in nanotechnology, died on 28 October 2005 at M.D. Anderson Cancer Center in Houston after a long battle with cancer. Smalley joined Rice University in 1976, and received the 1996 Nobel Prize in Chemistry for the discovery of buckminsterfullerene molecules, or buckyballs, together with Robert Curl and Harold Kroto.

H.K.L. Bhagat, 83, former Union minister and a powerful figure in India's ruling Congress Party in the 1970s and 1980s, died in New Delhi on 29 October 2005 after prolonged illness. Bhagat served as mayor of Delhi and as the chief whip of Delhi Pradesh Congress Committee (DPCC).

Amrita Pritam, 86, well-known Punjabi female fiction writer and poet, died on 31 October 2005 in New Delhi after a long illness. She entered politics as a member of the Rajya Sabha, and until 1961 worked for state-owned All India Radio. She was a recipient of the Padma Vibhushan award, and several works of hers have been translated into English, including the autobiographical works *Black Rose* and *Revenue Stamp* (*Raseedi Tikkat* in Punjabi). Her novel *Pinjar* was made into a Hindi film.

V.K. Madhavan Kutty, 71, former editor of the Malayalam daily, *Mathrubhumi*, died on 1 November 2005. He was a founder director of the satellite channel Asianet, a Padma Bhushan awardee, was conferred the Kerala Sahitya Akademi award in 1991 and the 'Swadeshabhimani Puraskaram' in 2002 by the Kerala government.

Kocheril Raman Narayanan, 85, tenth President of India from 1997 to 2002, died on 9 November 2005. He held key positions as India's Ambassador to China and the US and vice-chancellor of Jawaharlal Nehru University, won three successive Lok Sabha elections from Ottapalam in Kerala on a Congress ticket, and was a member of the Union Council of ministers in the Rajiv Gandhi government. He became India's vice-president in 1992 and was elected President in 1997.

Peter Ferdinand Drucker, 95, Austrian-born management theorist and the creator of corporate society, passed away on 11 November 2005. Author of *The Practice of Management* and *Concept of Corporation*, Drucker was awarded the Presidential Medal of Freedom by US President George W. Bush in 2002.

Madhu Dandavate, 81, former Union finance minister, passed away on 12 November 2005. Dandavate was finance minister in the cabinet of V.P. Singh, and also the deputy chairman of the Planning Commission in 1990 and again from 1996 to 1998.

George Best, 59, football player for Manchester United between 1963 and 1974, passed away on 25 November 2005. He won the prestigious European Footballer of the Year and Football Writers' Association Player of the Year in 1968, and in the same year helped Manchester United to European Cup glory. He represented Northern Ireland and therefore never played in a World Cup.

Chengara Veetil Devan Nair, 82, former president of Singapore, died on 7 December 2005 in Hamilton, Canada. A lawmaker and leader of a trade union movement, he served from 1981 to 1985 as the third Singaporean President.

A.K. Rao, 76, an award-winning aerospace scientist, passed away on 10 December 2005 in Hyderabad after a heart attack. He was the youngest professor and dean of Engineering at the Indian Institute of Science (IIS), Bangalore. Also credited with setting up the Lockheed International Research Institute at the IIS in the early 1980s, he was consultant to NASA and to the world's top aircraft companies Lockheed Martin and Boeing.

Ramanand Sagar, 87, veteran filmmaker, writer and producer, died of natural causes at his Juhu residence on 12 December 2005. For the first ten years of his professional career he was a journalist and in 1950 established his own film production company Sagar Art Corporation with *Mehmaan*, his first film. He produced fifty films including successes like *Insaniyat*, *Kohinoor*, *Pegaam*, *Ghunghat*, *Zindagi*, *Aankhen*, *Lalkar*, *Aarzoo*, *Geet* and *Bhagavat*, and achieved his greatest success with the 1986 TV series *Ramayana*.

K.F.B. Packer, 68, Australian publishing, media and gaming tycoon, passed away on 26 December 2005. Packer was best known for founding the World Series Cricket, the forerunner of day and night cricket as well as cricket with coloured clothing. At the time of his death, he was the richest Australian with an estimated wealth of US$4.7 billion.

Eddie Barlow, 65, South African cricketer, passed away on 30 December 2005. He made his Test debut in 1961 and played in 30 Tests scoring 2,516 runs and taking 40 wickets; his career was shortened after South Africa was banned from international cricket in 1970.

Sheikh Maktoum bin Rashid Al Maktoum, 62, ruler of Dubai and vice-president and prime minister of the United Arab Emirates, died in Australia on 4 January 2006. He was reportedly suffering from heart problems. He became the ruler of Dubai and UAE prime minister on 7

October 1990, and was the co-owner of Dubai's Godolphin stables, renowned for its racehorses.

Nadira, 74, veteran actress, died at a Mumbai hospital after a prolonged illness that led to cardiac seizure on 8 February 2006. She portrayed various negative roles with panache in films of the 1950s and 1960s. Born in Israel as Florence Ezekiel, Nadira acted in over sixty films including *Aan*, *Waris*, *Shree 420*, *Pakeezah*, *Dil Apna Aur Preet Parayi* and *Saagar*.

Peter Benchley, 65, author of the bestseller *Jaws* that was the basis for the blockbuster film, died of complications from pulmonary fibrosis on 11 February 2006 at his home in Princeton, New Jersey. An advocate of shark conservation, he also served as a reporter for the *Washington* Post and *Newsweek*, and was a speechwriter for President Lyndon Johnson from 1967 until January 1969.

John Dennis Profumo, 91, the central figure in the 1963 Profumo Affair, one of the UK's most famous political scandals which contributed to the defeat of the Macmillan Conservative government the following year, died from a stroke on 9 March 2006. He succeeded in 1940 as fifth Baron Profumo of Italy, was a member of Parliament (Conservative) during 1940-45 and 1950-63, was awarded an OBE in 1944, and the CBE in 1975.

Oleg Cassini, 92, American fashion designer, who designed the dresses that helped make Jacqueline Kennedy the most glamorous first lady in history, died on 17 March 2006 in Long Island, New York. Cassini also designed clothes for Joan Fontaine, Joan Crawford and other Hollywood stars and women of great wealth, and was responsible for the popularity of the Nehru jacket for men.

Bhrigu Kumar Phukan, 49, former Assam home minister and one of the stalwarts of the anti-foreigners uprising in the state, died of multiple organ failure at the All India Institute of Medical Sciences (AIIMS) in New Delhi on 20 March 2006. Phukan was elected to the state Assembly for three consecutive times from 1985 to 2001, and was one of the signatories to the 1985 Assam Accord between the AASU and the Centre that brought to an end the bloodshed during the six-year anti-foreigners agitation.

Anil Biswas, 62, a member of the politburo of the Communist Party of India (Marxist) and secretary of the party's West Bengal unit, died on 26 March 2006, eight days after suffering a stroke. A former editor of the party Bengali mouthpiece, *Ganashakti*, Biswas was the brain behind the party's important decisions in West Bengal politics, and widely credited for the gradual liberalization of the CPI(M) from its earlier hard line approach in West Bengal. He wrote over twenty books, most of them dealing with politics, ideology and political philosophy.

Bansi Lal, 78, four-time Haryana chief minister, died on 28 March 2006 after a prolonged illness. He was considered the architect of modern Haryana. First elected to the Haryana Legislative Assembly in 1967, he also served as minister in the Union Cabinet and held key portfolios like minister of defence (1975–77), minister of railways (1984–85) and minister of transport (1985–86).

Manohar Shyam Joshi, 73, a Sahitya Akademi Award winning Hindi novelist, journalist and television soap opera writer, died of a heart attack in Delhi on 30 March 2006. Joshi redefined the world of television in 1982 with *Hum Log* and *Buniyad*, and also penned scripts of several other hugely popular serials like *Kakaji Kahin*, *Mungeri Lal Ke Haseen Sapne* and *Zameen Aasmaan*. He also wrote the scripts of Hindi films like *Hey Ram*, *Appu Raja* and *Papa Kahte Hain*. He was also editor of

Saptahik Hindustan and *Weekend Review*.

Rajkumar, 76, a one-time child actor who became one of south India's most beloved film stars, died of cardiac arrest on 12 April 2006. Rajkumar appeared in more than 200 Kannada-language films in five decades, and had millions of fiercely devoted fans. He began his acting career in 1954 in *Bedara Kannappa*. His other hits include *Navakoti Narayana*, *Santha Tukaram*, *Veera Kesari* and *Katari Veera*. After he retired he continued to work behind the scenes as a producer. In 2000, Kumar was kidnapped by Veerappan and was finally rescued after 108 days. He won several national and state films awards, including the Dadasaheb Phalke award, and received the Padma Bhushan in 1987.

John Kenneth Galbraith, 97, economist, passed away in 29 April 2006. He was US ambassador to India from 1961 to 1963, professor of economics at Harvard University from 1949 until his retirement in 1975, and the first economist to be president of the American Academy of Arts and Letters. He published more than twenty books, notable among which are *The Great Crash: 1929*; *The New Industrial State*; and his autobiography, *A Life in Our Times*.

Pramod Mahajan, 56, the top strategist of Bharatiya Janata Party, died on 3 May 2006, nearly two weeks after being shot by his younger brother in an apparent family dispute. Mahajan was the general secretary of the party's parliamentary board, as well as of its central election committee, served as the chairman, Committee on Transport and Tourism (1994–96), was a member, Lok Sabha (1996–97), was defence minister in 1996 and political advisor to the prime minister in 1998. He helped create the 'India Shining' campaign, was the Union minister for telecommunication and information technology, and was elected to the Rajya Sabha three times (July 1986, July 1992 and July 1998).

Naushad Ali, 86, a Dadasaheb Phalke award winner and one of best-known music composers of the Hindi film industry, died at the Nanavati Hospital in Mumbai on 5 May 2006. Beginning his career in the 1930s, he introduced a unique fusion of devotional, classical and north Indian folk music, and composed the scores for some of the biggest hits of the 1950s and 1960s. Apart from *Mughal-e-Azam* (1960), he composed the music for *Andaz* (1949), *Baiju Bawra* (1952), *Mother India* (1957) and *Pakeezah* (1971).

Floyd Patterson, 71, who became the youngest world heavyweight champion at twenty-one, and the first fighter to regain the title by knocking out Sweden's Ingmar Johansson in the second of their three fights in 1960, died on 11 May 2006, following Alzheimer's disease and prostate cancer. He was the first Olympic champion to go on and win boxing's richest prize.

Robert Bruce Merrifield, 84, an American biochemist who won the 1984 Nobel Prize in Chemistry for a method he named solid-phase peptide synthesis, passed away on 14 May 2006 after a long illness.

Raymond Davis Jr, 91, who won the 2002 Nobel Prize in Physics for his contributions to the discovery of solar neutrinos, died on 31 May 2006 from complications of Alzheimer's disease. He was the first to detect the elusive neutrinos produced by the sun, was Research Professor at the University of Pennsylvania and a research collaborator in chemistry at Brookhaven National Laboratory, New York.

Budhi Kunderan, 66, Indian wicket-keeper batsman, passed away on 23 June 2006; he was suffering from lung cancer. He was picked to play for India even before he had played a single first-class game, was among the five

Indian batsmen who scored a double century in his first Ranji match, played 18 Tests for India, and was among the select band of wicketkeepers who have scored in excess of 500 runs in a Test series. He aggregated 525 runs against England in 1963-64.

Theodore Levitt, 81, American economist and professor at Harvard Business School, died on 28 June 2006. Levitt was editor of the *Harvard Business Review*, four-time winner of the McKinsey Awards competitions for best annual article in the *Harvard Business Review*, winner of the Academy of Management Award for the outstanding business books of 1962 for Innovation in Marketing, winner of the John Hancock Award for Excellence in Business Journalism in 1969, recipient of the Charles Coolidge Parlin Award as 'Marketing Man of the Year' 1970, and recipient of the George Gallup Award for Marketing Excellence 1976.

Fred Trueman, 75, English fast bowler, passed away on 1 July 2006, of lung cancer. He played 67 Test matches and took 307 wickets, was the first cricketer to take 300 Test wickets, finished with an average of 21.57 and a strike rate of a wicket every 49 balls in Tests, formed an incisive new-ball pairing with Brian Statham, and spent many years summarizing the play for the BBC's Test Match Special after his retirement.

Kenneth Lay, 64, former chairman and chief executive of Enron who was convicted of fraud and conspiracy in the giant energy company's collapse, died of a heart attack on 5 July 2006 at his home in Aspen, Colorado.

Roger Keith Barrett (Syd Barrett), 60, the singer-songwriter-guitarist who co-founded the British rock band Pink Floyd died of complications from diabetes on 7 July 2006 at his home in Cambridgeshire, England. Barrett joined Pink Floyd in 1965 but left three years later, after one album.

Raja Rao, 97, one of India's most distinguished English writers, died of heart failure at his home in Austin, Texas, on 8 July 2006. His works include *Kanthapura*, which explores turbulence in a South Indian village, the semiautobiographical *The Serpent and the Rope* and *The Cat and Shakespeare*. Raja Rao was emeritus professor of philosophy at the University of Texas, Austin, where he began teaching forty years ago.

Vasant Chavan, 63, Rajya Sabha MP and senior Nationalist Congress Party leader, died of cardiac arrest on 11 July 2006. He was a member of the Maharashtra Legislative Assembly (1980–85) and a member of the Council from 1986 to 2004.

V.P. Sathyan, 40, former captain of the Indian national football team, committed suicide on 18 July 2006. Sathyan had a successful club career with Kerala Police and also played for Mohun Bagan and Mohammedan Sporting.

Nandini Satpathy, 75, senior Congress leader and former Orissa chief minister, died of a cardiac arrest on 4 August 2006. She was elected twice to the Rajya Sabha, in 1962 and in 1968, and served in the first Indira Gandhi government as deputy minister for information and broadcasting. She was chief minister for two terms (1972-73 and 1974-76). She was elected to the state assembly for seven consecutive terms, and received the prestigious Sahitya Bharati Samman award in 1998 for outstanding contribution to Oriya literature. Her works include *Ketoti Katha* and *Saptadasi*.

James Van Allen, 91, space scientist at the University of Iowa, died in Iowa on 9 August 2006. One of the pioneers of the American space programme, he discovered the belts of radiation that encircle the Earth, gave his name to them and designed spacecraft instruments to observe the outer reaches of the solar system.

Shamsur Rahman, 76, prominent Bangladeshi poet, journalist and human rights advocate who in 1999 survived an attempt on his life by an Islamic fundamentalist group, died in Dhaka, Bangladesh, on 17 August 2006. His most famous poem *Shadhinota Tumi*, that inspired war heroes, was written in 1971 during Bangladesh's independence war against Pakistan.

Ustad Bismillah Khan, 90, legendary shehnai player and Bharat Ratna awardee, passed away on 21 August 2006, in Varanasi, after a heart attack. He was one of only three classical musicians to be awarded the Bharat Ratna. His recital had become virtually a mandatory part of the Independence Day celebrations telecast on Doordarshan every year, and he played in Afghanistan, Europe, Iran, Iraq, Canada, West Africa, USA, USSR, Japan, Hong Kong and almost every capital city across the world.

Wasim Raja, 54, Pakistani batsman, passed away on 23 August 2006. He made his debut in 1973 against New Zealand, and played 57 Tests scoring 2821 runs, taking 51 wickets.

Clyde Walcott, 80, West Indian batsman, passed away on 26 August 2006. He played 44 Tests scoring 3,798 runs with an average of 56.68. He scored a then-record West Indian aggregate of 827 runs in a series against Australia in 1954-55, including a record five centuries.

Hrishikesh Mukherjee, 83, one of Bollywood's best-known film directors for nearly five decades, passed away on 27 August 2006. Known for his simple folksy stories about the Indian middle class, their lives, tribulations and their relationships, his best known films are *Anari*, *Guddi*, *Anand*, *Abhimaan*, *Mili*, *Chupke Chupke*, *Khoobsurat*, and *Golmal*. His last film was the 1998 Anil Kapoor-Juhi Chawla starrer *Jhooth Bole Kauwa Kaate*. He received the Dada Saheb Phalke award in 2001.

Steve Irwin, 44, an Australian naturalist who won worldwide acclaim with his TV shows, was killed on 4 September 2006 by a sting ray barb through the chest while diving off Australia's north-east coast. He made almost fifty *Crocodile Hunter* documentaries, which appeared on Animal Planet, and won a worldwide audience. He was a high profile ambassador for Australian tourism in the United States, and was also the owner and operator of Australia Zoo in Beerwah, Queensland.

Kanshi Ram, 72, famous politician and founder of Bahujan Samaj Party (BSP), died on 9 October 2006. He shared the BSP's leadership with Mayawati. In 1970 he formed the All India Backward and Minority Employees Federation. He represented the eleventh Lok Sabha from Hoshiarpur Constituency and in 2001 publicly announced Mayawati as his successor.

Lalit Suri, 59, famous hotelier and a member of the Rajya Sabha, died on 10 October 2006. An alumunus of Sri Ram College of Commerce, New Delhi, he won a number of prestigious awards and has been responsible for a number of policy recommendations on the tourism sector. He was the chairman and managing director of Bharat Hotels, of which the Grand group of hotels, which is a major player in India's tourism and hotel sector, is a subsidiary. He commissioned his first hotel in the capital in 1988.

Pieter Willem Botha, 90, former South Africa president who led the country defying international condemnation of apartheid, died on 31 October 2006. Botha became a member of South Africa's all-white parliament in 1948. He was elected prime minister in 1978 after becoming chief of the then ruling National Party. He held the position of prime minister for six years and served as President from 1984 to 1989.

100 Indians Who Are Changing India

A.P.J. Abdul Kalam

born 1931

Scientist and President of India

Born in Rameswaram, Kalam specialized in Aeronautical Engineering from the Madras Institute of Technology. He made a significant contribution as Project Director to develop India's first indigenous Satellite Launch Vehicle (SLV-III), which successfully established the Rohini satellite into near earth orbit in July 1980 and made India a member of the exclusive Space Club. Kalam was responsible for the evolution of ISRO's launch vehicle programme, particularly the PSLV configuration.

After working for two decades in ISRO and mastering launch vehicle technologies, Kalam took the responsibility of developing Indigenous Guided Missiles at the Defence Research and Development Organization (DRDO) as the Chief Executive of the Integrated Guided Missile Development Programme (IGMDP). He was responsible for the development of the Agni and Prithvi missiles and for building indigenous capability in critical technologies through the networking of multiple institutions. He was the Scientific Adviser to the Defence Minister and Secretary, Department of Defence, Research & Development from July 1992 to December 1999. During this period he orchestrated the development of strategic missile systems and the Pokhran-II nuclear tests—which gave India nuclear capability—in collaboration with the Department of Atomic Energy. As Chairman of the Technology Information, Forecasting and Assessment Council (TIFAC), Kalam paved the way for the Technology Vision 2020, giving a road map for transforming India from the present developing status to a developed nation. He was awarded the Padma Bhushan in 1981, the Padma Vibhushan in 1990 and the country's highest civilian award the Bharat Ratna in 1997. In 2002, he was elected President of India.

Kalam is renowned for his unflagging energy and his educational initiatives for children and in the area of science and technology. He is the best-selling author of several books, including *Wings of Fire*, *India 2020* and *Ignited Minds*.

Kalam's tenure as President comes to an end in July 2007; he might not seek a second term, and might choose to return to his first love, teaching and working with children. There is no doubt that whether from the grassroots or as the country's first citizen, he will continue to inspire millions of Indians for many years to come.

A.R. Rahman

born 1966

Film music composer

Allah Rakha Rahman was born A.S. Dileep Kumar in Madras. Something of a child prodigy, he started learning to play the piano at the age of four and at the age of eleven, joined the troupe of composer Ilaiyaraja as a keyboardist. He later played on the orchestras of M.S. Vishwanathan and Ramesh Naidu, and accompanied Zakir Hussain and Kunnakudi Vaidyanathan on world tours. These experiences allowed him to obtain a scholarship to Trinity College at Oxford University, where he received a degree in Western classical music. He moved to advertising in 1987 and composed more than 300 ad jingles over the next five years.

Rahman made his debut as music composer in 1992 with Mani Ratnam's Tamil film *Roja*, which was subsequently dubbed in many languages. Ram Gopal Varma's *Rangeela* (1995) was the first Hindi movie to have Rahman as music director. The nineties saw one chartbusting soundtrack after another from Rahman, including *Bombay*, *Humse Hai Muqabla*, *Sapnay*, *Dil Se* and *Taal*. His triumphant journey continued in the new millennium with *Zubeidaa*, *Lagaan*, *Saathiya*, *Swades* and *Rang De Basanti*. Apart from the film music, Rahman has also composed the album *Vande Mataram*. Andrew Lloyd Webber, impressed with Rahman's unique style, hired him to compose the Broadway stage production *Bombay Dreams* (2002). Rahman, along with the Finnish folk music band Värttinä, has also composed the music for *The Lord of the Rings* musical, which opened in Toronto on 23 March 2006.

Rahman is known for his unique sense of melody and for his rhythmic arrangements. He has rewritten the book on Indian popular music—and will continue to do so in the years to come.

Aamir Khan

born 1965

Film actor and producer

Son of filmmaker Tahir Hussain, Aamir Khan began his career as a child actor in his uncle Nasir Hussain's 1973 blockbuster *Yaadon Ki Baraat*. He rose to stardom with the romantic film *Qayamat Se Qayamat Tak* (1988). This was followed by a series of hit films including *Dil* (1990), *Jo Jeeta Wohi Sikander* (1992), *Hum Hai Rahi Pyar Ke* (1993), *Rangeela* (1995), *Raja Hindustani* (1996), *Ghulam* (1998), *Sarfarosh* (1999), *Lagaan* (2001) and *Dil Chahta Hai* (2001). *Lagaan*, which Aamir also produced, was nominated for an Oscar in the Best Foreign Film category.

Since 1993, Aamir has made it his practice to work on only one film at a time in order to give his best to each film. He has rarely had more than one release a year, yet has ranked consistently among Bollywood's top three stars. After a four-year hiatus, Aamir Khan returned to the screen in 2005 with *Mangal Pandey*. He has had two big hits in 2006 with *Rang De Basanti* and *Fanaa*. In 2006 he came out in support of the Narmada Bachao Andolan—becoming the first in the film fraternity to seriously espouse a political cause.

A consummate method actor, Aamir Khan has created a series of iconic characters on celluloid over the past decade. He also has some of the most memorable ad campaigns in India—including Coca-Cola, Toyota Innova and Titan—to his credit. As his tagline in the Toyota Innova ad goes, he plays many roles—to perfection.

Abhay Vasant Ashtekar

born 1949

Theoretical physicist

An expert on quantum gravity, Abhay Ashtekar completed his undergraduate education in India. He studied under Robert Geroch at the University of Chicago, receiving his PhD in 1974 (his thesis was on 'Asymptotic Structure of the Gravitational Field at Spatial Infinity'). He is now the Eberly Professor of Physics and the Director of the Institute for Gravitational Physics and Geometry at the Pennsylvania State University.

As the creator of Ashtekar variables, Dr Ashtekar is one of the founders of loop quantum gravity. He has worked in this field for twenty-five years and is almost single-handedly credited with one of the most popular unifying theories. In the 1980s, Dr Ashtekar reformulated Einstein's theory of relativity to resemble a modified quantum theory that predicts that at very small scales (10^{-33} cm or a trillionth of a trillionth of a billionth of a centimeter), space is 'quantized'.

Now Ashtekar and two of his post-doctoral researchers, Tomasz Pawlowski and Parmpreet Singh, have developed a mathematical model that skates right up to the Big Bang—and steps through it. According to him there exists another universe with a space-time geometry similar to our own, except that instead of expanding, it is shrinking. He claims that 'in place of a classical Big Bang, there is in fact a quantum Bounce'.

One of the leading Indian scientists in the international arena, Abhay Ashtekar keeps India's flag flying high.

Abhishek Bachchan

born 1976

Film actor

Son of Amitabh and Jaya Bachchan, Abhishek Bachchan dropped out of Boston University to pursue an acting career. Although he made a strong debut in J.P. Dutta's *Refugee* in 2000, the movie was not considered a success. Over the next four years he went on to do many more movies, none of which had any significant impact at the box office. However, with his performance in Mani Ratnam's *Yuva* (2004) he proved his mettle and won a Filmfare Award for Best Supporting Actor. Since then his career has undergone a complete turnaround. In 2004 he starred in *Dhoom*, one of the biggest hits of the year. In 2005 he had four more hits, *Bunty Aur Babli*, *Sarkar*, *Dus* and *Bluffmaster*, and won his second Filmfare Award in the Best Supporting Actor category for *Sarkar*.

The tall, dark and unshaven figure of Abhishek Bachchan has become representative of the retrosexual male in India. His immense popularity among teenagers and twenty-somethings has also resulted in several big-brand endorsements, including Motorola and Ford Fiesta.

Abhishek owes his iconic status not just to his retrosexual image but also to his 'never say die' attitude, which finds ample resonance in the new India.

Adi B. Godrej

born 1942

Chairman of the Godrej Group

Adi Godrej received his undergraduate and master's degrees in management from the Massachusetts Institute of Technology, USA. Returning to India, he was the first business graduate in a company that had long symbolized Indian independence and initiative.

As a young family member, he faced the management challenge of bringing about change. Much of his work was devoted to modernizing and systematizing management structures and implementing process improvements. Today the Godrej Group is a diversified consumer and industrial products company whose origins are represented in its major security and personal products businesses.

Adi Godrej has also been involved in the company's philanthropic efforts, which centre on the environment, family planning, and education. Not only is the Godrej Group a major supporter of the World Wildlife Fund in India, it has developed a green business campus in the Vikhroli township of Mumbai, which includes a 150-acre mangrove forest and a school for the children of company employees.

Over the years, the Godrej Group has continued to stay in the forefront of Indian business and has now begun to globalize its operations. By partnering with world–class corporations—including Sara Lee, Procter & Gamble and General Electric—the Godrej businesses have remained in the vanguard of management practices. Additionally, the Godrej companies have emphasized brand building to an extent uncommon in India, where intangible assets have historically been undervalued.

Adi Godrej is a recipient of the Rajiv Gandhi Award (2002), the Globoil India Legend Award (2002) and the Scodet Lifetime Achievement Award (2003). He has also consistently featured on the *Forbes* list of the richest men in India.

Aditya Chopra
born 1971
Film producer and director

Son of producer-director Yash Chopra, Aditya Chopra started his career by assisting his father in Yash Raj Films' *Chandni*, *Lamhe* and *Darr*. His first film as director, *Dilwale Dulhania Le Jayenge* (1995), was made when he was twenty-three. *DDLJ* became one of the largest grossing films in Indian history. Aditya Chopra worked on the screenplay of Yash Chopra's *Dil To Pagal Hai* (1997) and wrote and directed a second film, *Mohabbatein*, which was released in 2000. He co-produced and wrote the story, screenplay and dialogue for *Veer-Zaara* (2004) which shattered box-office records for the year worldwide and earned him Filmfare Awards for Best Story and Best Dialogue.

Since 2004, Aditya Chopra has taken on the mantle of producer and under his baton, Yash Raj Films has released a series of well-made fun films with a youthful feel, which have all become hits. The success story began in 2004 with *Hum Tum* and *Dhoom*, and continued with *Bunty Aur Babli*, *Salaam Namaste* and *Neal 'N' Nikki* (2005) and *Fanaa* (2006). Now Vice-Chairman of Yash Raj Films, Aditya Chopra is the driving force behind all the expansion plans and visions of the company. Among his flagship ventures are a film development division which works on scripts by new writers, and a new 100-crore state-of-the-art studio.

Aishwarya Rai
born 1973
Film actress

Aishwarya Rai was crowned Miss World in 1994, and in 2000 was voted the Most Beautiful Miss World of All Time. Her first film was Mani Ratnam's Tamil film *Iruvar* in 1997, while her first Hindi film was *Aur Pyar Ho Gaya*, released the same year. Aishwarya has starred in some of the biggest hits of recent times, including *Taal* (1999), *Hum Dil De Chuke Sanam* (1999), *Devdas* (2002) and *Khakee* (2004). She won the Filmfare Best Actress Award for *Hum Dil De Chuke Sanam* and *Devdas*. She has also acted in a number of offbeat films, including *Kandukondain Kandukondain*, Rituparno Ghosh's *Chokher Bali* and *Raincoat*, and Gurinder Chadha's *Bride and Prejudice*. She made a sensational appearance in an item number in *Bunty Aur Babli* (2005) which catapulted the film to superhit status.

In 2003, Aishwarya was a member of the jury at Cannes and in 2004, she was chosen by *Time* magazine's asian edition as one of Asia's '100 Most Influential People'. Aishwarya has also been honoured with a lifesize wax replica at Madame Tussaud's, and endorses leading brands like Coke, Longines and Nakshatra.

Aishwarya Rai is considered one of the most beautiful women in the world and, after nine years in the film industry, retains a mystique and aura that no other Indian actress has. She might also become the first Indian actor or actress to make it in Hollywood.

Ajay G. Piramal
born 1955
Chairman, Nicholas Piramal India Ltd

Ajay Piramal completed the Advanced Management Programme from the Harvard Business School in 1992. He is now the Chairman and Pharmaceutical business head of Nicholas Piramal India Ltd. NPIL has registered dramatic growth over the last fifteen years through a string of acquisitions that include the Indian subsidiaries of multinationals such as Roche, Boehringer

Mannheim, Rhone Poulenc, and Hoechst Marion Roussel (research division), and the pharmaceutical division of ICI India Limited.

NPIL is part of the Rs 2500 crore Piramal Enterprises (PEL), one of India's largest diversified business houses with interests in Retailing, Textiles, Autocomponents and Engineering. NPIL is India's second largest Pharmaceutical and Healthcare company; as many as sixteen of its brands are among the top 300 in the Indian pharma industry, and it has an annual turnover of $ 250 million.

Ajay Piramal is one of the most recognizable names in the booming pharma industry in India today. He is a member of the Prime Minister's Council for Trade and Industry and the Prime Minister's taskforce on Pharmaceuticals and Knowledge-based Industries.

Amartya Sen

born 1933

Nobel laureate in Economics, distinguished professor and author

Amartya Sen was born in Santiniketan, West Bengal, and studied at Presidency College, Kolkata and Trinity College, Cambridge. He is currently the Lamont University Professor and Professor of Economics and Philosophy at Harvard University, and until recently was the Master of Trinity College, Cambridge. He has served as President of the Econometric Society, the Indian Economic Association, the American Economic Association and the International Economic Association. He was awarded the Nobel Prize in Economic Sciences in 1998 for his contributions to welfare economics. He was awarded the Bharat Ratna in 1999.

Professor Sen is one of the most respected economists in the world. He is renowned for his work on famine, human development theory, the underlying mechanisms of poverty, and political liberalism. He has produced pioneering studies of gender inequality, and his work in the field of development economics has had considerable influence in the formulation of the Human Development Report, published by the United Nations Development Programme (UNDP). Professor Sen has also devised methods of measuring poverty that yield useful information for improving economic conditions for the poor.

Amartya Sen established the Pratichi Trust, aimed at basic education and gender equity in India and Bangladesh, using his Nobel Prize money from 1998. He has now become an influential voice in addressing concerns over crises of political and social identity with his best-selling books *The Argumentative Indian* (2005) and *Identity and Violence* (2006).

Constantly redefining areas of inquiry and parameters of analysis, Amartya Sen represents the very best of India's intellectual tradition.

Amitabh Bachchan

born 1942

Film actor

Son of the well-known poet Harivansh Rai Bachchan, Amitabh Bachchan gave up a job as freight broker to pursue a career in acting. He got his first break in Bollywood with *Saat Hindustani* (1969) and won a Filmfare Award for Best Supporting Actor for his role in Hrishikesh Mukherjee's *Anand* (1970). But his first major hit was *Zanjeer* (1973), which established the anti-establishment 'angry young man' persona created by writers Salim-Javed.

Throughout the seventies and early eighties, Amitabh Bachchan's name on the marquee could be counted on to pull crowds into the theatres. He had at least one major hit every year for the next decade, including *Sholay* and *Deewaar* (1975), *Kabhi Kabhie* (1976), *Amar Akbar Anthony* (1977), *Don*, *Trishul* and *Muqaddar Ka Sikander* (1978).

In 1984, Amitabh Bachchan briefly entered politics in support of his longtime family friend Rajiv Gandhi but resigned after three years. He returned to films with *Shahenshah* (1988) and *Agneepath* (1990).

Amitabh's popularity waned in the nineties. However he bounced back as the anchor of the record-breaking quiz show on television *Kaun Banega Crorepati?* (2000) which made him a household rage once again across the nation. Today, once again, scripts are being written around him. In 2005 he stormed the charts with no less than eight releases and four major hits—*Black*, *Waqt*, *Bunty Aur Babli* and *Sarkar*. He also has a record number of brand endorsements.

Voted the Superstar of the Millennium years ago and awarded France's highest honour the Legion d'Honneur in 2006, Amitabh Bachchan continues to scale new barriers in popularity, encapsulating all that is great about Bollywood.

Amitav Ghosh
born 1956
Writer

Amitav Ghosh was born in Kolkata and grew up in Bangladesh (then East Pakistan), Sri Lanka, Iran and India. He did his schooling from the Doon School and completed his graduation from St. Stephens College, Delhi. He went to Oxford to study Social Anthropology and received a Master of Philosophy and a PhD in 1982. In 1980, he went to Egypt to do field work in the fellaheen village of Lataifa. The work he did there resulted in the non-fiction work *In an Antique Land* (1993).

Amitav Ghosh's first novel was *The Circle of Reason* (1986), followed by *The Shadow Lines* (1988). *The Circle of Reason* won the Prix Medici Etranger, one of France's top literary awards, and *The Shadow Lines*, which has been published in many languages, won the Sahitya Akademi Award. His next novel *The Calcutta Chromosome* (1996) won the Arthur C. Clarke Award and *The Glass Palace* (2000) won the Grand Prize for Fiction at the Frankfurt International e-Book Awards in 2001. Ghosh turned down his nomination for the Commonwealth Writers Prize for *The Glass Palace*, accusing the awards of racism. His latest novel, *The Hungry Tide* (2004) won the Hutch Crossword Award for Best Work of Fiction.

Amitav Ghosh lives in New York and teaches at Columbia University. He is counted among the best Indian writers writing in English today, and is one of the few Asian writers who are bestsellers abroad. With every new book, he scales new horizons in presenting strong content in nuanced, lyrical prose.

Anand G. Mahindra
born 1955
Vice-Chairman and Managing Director, Mahindra & Mahindra Ltd

In 1981 Anand Mahindra secured an MBA from the Harvard Business School. Now the business head of Mahindra & Mahindra Ltd, he is engaged in a comprehensive change programme to make the company an efficient and aggressive competitor in the new liberalized economic environment in India.

All of Mahindra & Mahindra's businesses—auto, software, real estate and finance—are setting new market standards and the group turnover has shot up. The tractor division of Mahindra is the only tractor manufacturing company in the world to secure the coveted Deming Application Prize (2003). Mahindra's success story in the utility vehicle sector can be measured by startling performance of two of their brands Scorpio and Bolero. The company continues to be a market leader in the utility vehicle segment with a market share of 43.7 per cent.

Now, with the acquisition of the aerospace engineering company Plexion and forging giant Am Forge, Mahindra is poised to storm the market as an auto conglomerate that designs, engineers and produces vehicles. Mahindra is entering the truck market with International Trucks and the car market with Renault. Tech Mahindra would also be listed on the stock market this year.

Anand Mahindra is the co-founder of the Harvard Business School Association of India, and a Director of the National Stock Exchange of India, appointed under the 'Public Representatives' category. He is one of the most dynamic and enterprising industrialists in India today.

Anil Ambani

born 1959

Chairman, Reliance Capital, Reliance Infocomm and Chairman & Managing Director, Reliance Energy Limited

Anil Ambani holds a Bachelor of Science degree from the University of Bombay and an MBA degree from the Wharton School at the University of Pennsylvania. Currently, he serves as a member of the Wharton Board of Overseers.

Anil Ambani joined Reliance in 1983 as Co-Chief Executive Officer and was the Vice-Chairman and Managing Director of Reliance Industries Limited before his split with his brother Mukesh Ambani. He is credited with having pioneered many financial innovations in the Indian capital markets. He led India's first forays into overseas capital markets with international public offerings of global depositary receipts, convertibles and bonds. He directed Reliance in its efforts to raise around $2 billion from overseas financial markets since 1991 with a 100-year Yankee bond issue in January 1997 being his chief achievement in this endeavour.

After the split with his brother, Anil Ambani now runs the newly christened Anil Dhirubhai Ambani Group, an offshoot of the Reliance empire, with interests in telecom, energy and financial services. The Anil Dhirubhai Ambani Group is among the top three industrial groups in India, with over Rs 5,000 crore in operating profits. With over 19 million subscribers, Reliance is the largest telecom player in the country. With his investments in media such as a 51 per cent stake in Adlabs, the acquisition of the life insurance company AMP Sanmar, and investments in power projects in Dadri, Orissa and Haryana, Anil Ambani has a presence in virtually every significant sector of the economy. He revolutionized telecom services in India and is looking to do the same with the power and insurance sectors.

Anna Hazare

born 1940

Social activist

A Ramon Magsaysay Award winner and Padma Vibhushan awardee, Anna Hazare is well known and respected as the man who turned the ecology and economy of the village of Ralegan Siddhi around. Since 1975 under his leadership, Ralegan Siddhi has been evolving as an epitomization of the Gandhian idiom of a self-sufficient village and as an elementary unit of social organization.

Anna Hazare has had a long history as a protester against corruption and other social evils. He was in the news in May 1994 when he undertook a protest fast at the Sant Dyaneshwar temple at Alandi, Maharashtra. Earlier, the same month, he launched the Bhrastachar Virodhi Janandolan (people's movement against corruption). He has gone on numerous fasts for various social and environmental causes. One of the proponents of the Right to Information Act, he went on a fast until death and threatened to return his Padma Vibhushan in 2006 when there was talk of the RTI Act being modified. He prevailed, and the Act was left untouched for the time being.

A true Gandhian who has contributed to society building at the grassroots level, and an activist and protester who is not afraid to make his voice heard, Anna Hazare is an Indian who the new generation can look up to.

Aroon Purie

born 1944

Chief Executive, The India Today Group

As Founding Editor and Editor-in-Chief of *India Today*, Chief Executive, The India Today Group and Chairman, TV Today Network Ltd, Aroon Purie sets the journalistic style for the largest and most respected magazine publishing group in India and for the premier twenty-four-hour news and current affairs channels, Aaj Tak and Headlines Today.

Aroon Purie is an alumnus of the London School of Economics and a Fellow of the Institute of Chartered Accountants (England & Wales). After reviving Thomson Press, he set up the company Living Media to publish *India Today*, and has edited the newsmagazine since its first issue in 1975. The India Today Group, which has grown out of the magazine, is one of the largest media conglomerates in India.

Aroon Purie is a recipient of the National Award and the Padma Bhushan. A noted journalist and media baron, he is one of the key individuals instrumental in shaping public opinion in the country.

Arun Jaitley

born 1952

Lawyer and politician

A former minister for commerce, industry, law and justice of the Union Government of India, Arun Jaitley graduated in Law from the Faculty of Law, University of Delhi in 1977. He is a designated Senior Advocate and was the Additional Solicitor General of India in the year 1990. He has authored several publications on legal and current affairs.

Arun Jaitley became the spokesperson of the Bharatiya Janata Party during the period preceding the 1999 general election. He joined the council of ministers in the NDA government as a Minister of State with independent charge of the newly created Department of Disinvestment in 1999. In 2000 he was elevated to Cabinet Minister with the charge of Law, Justice and Company Affairs with the additional charge of the Ministry of Shipping. In 2002 he became the General Secretary of the Bharatiya Janata Party and functioned as its national spokesman till January 2003. He rejoined the Union Cabinet as the Minister of Commerce & Industry and Law & Justice in January 2003. With the defeat of the National Democratic Alliance in the elections in May 2004, Jaitley returned to serving the Bharatiya Janata Party as a General Secretary, and to his legal career.

Arun Jaitley is a key spokesperson for right-wing politics in India, and a future leader.

Arun Shourie

born 1941

Journalist, politician and author

Arun Shourie studied at St Stephen's in Delhi and obtained his doctorate in Economics from Syracuse University in the United States. He has been an economist with the World Bank, a consultant to the Planning Commission and editor of the *Indian Express*. In a series of exposés, many of which he wrote himself, Shourie and the *Indian Express* uncovered corruption in the highest echelons of the government and exposed several major scandals.

Shourie is a member of the Bharatiya Janata Party and has held the office of the Minister of Disinvestment, Communication and Information Technology in the NDA government under Atal Bihari Vajpayee. As disinvestment minister, he led the sale of Maruti, VSNL and Hindustan Zinc, among others.

Shourie now devotes his energy to writing books and regular columns, which appear in different languages in some thirty newspapers across India. His writings have gained him a considerable following around the country, as well as several national and international honours. Among these are the Padma Bhushan, the Magsaysay Award, the Dadabhai Naoroji Award, the Astor Award, the K.S. Hegde Award and the International Editor of the Year Award.

A key opinion-maker and an outspoken critic, Arun Shourie's is one of the most important voices that are heard today on contemporary India.

Arundhati Roy

born 1961

Writer and activist

Arundhati Roy studied architecture at the Delhi School of Architecture, played a village girl in the award-winning movie *Massey Sahib*, and wrote the screenplays for the acclaimed *In Which Annie Gives it Those Ones* and *Electric Moon*. In 1992 Roy began writing her first novel *The God of Small Things*, which she finished in 1996. She received half a million pounds as an advance, and rights to the book were sold in twenty-one countries. In 1997 she took the literary world by storm when the book won the Booker Prize.

It has been nine years since the Booker win, but Arundhati Roy has not produced a second novel. Instead, she has concentrated on writing non-fiction which deals with social and political issues. These include the Narmada Dam project, India's nuclear arsenal and power company Enron's activities in India. She is a figurehead of the anti-globalization/alter-globalization movement and a vehement critic of neo-imperialism.

Roy was awarded the Sydney Peace Prize in May 2004 for her work in social campaigns and advocacy of non-violence. In January 2006 she was awarded the Sahitya Akademi Award for her collection of essays on contemporary issues, *The Algebra of Infinite Justice*, but declined to accept it. She has also published a second collection of essays, *An Ordinary Person's Guide to Empire*.

Looking at development agendas from a different perspective and expressing herself in impassioned prose, Arundhati Roy is one of the most important writers commenting on India today.

Ashoke Sen

born 1956

Theoretical physicist

A theoretical physicist who works on string theory, Ashoke Sen received his PhD from State University of New York at Stony Brook. He worked as a research scientist in Fermilab and later joined Tata Institute of Fundamental Research before finally moving to Harish Chandra Research Institute.

In theoretical physics, Ashoke Sen is renowned for co-discovering S-duality and proposing a successful explanation of open string tachyon condensation. He has co-written many papers on string field theory. His first major project in this field involved studying the relationship between the two-dimensional models describing string propagation in a given background field, and the space-time properties of these background fields. This provided a way of looking for space-time supersymmetric vacuums of string theory. His second major project in string theory involved developing a method for generating new classical solutions of string theory from a known classical solution, when the original solution is independent of some of the space-time coordinates. Later, he used this method to generate the most general electrically charged rotating black hole solution in four dimensional heterotic string theory. He also worked on a major project that involves an attempt to understand the Bekenstein-Hawking entropy of black holes from counting the microscopic states in string theory.

Ashoke Sen is one of the most important Indian scientists working in the international arena today. He was awarded the Padma Shri in 2001.

Azim Hashim Premji

born 1945

Chairman and CEO, Wipro Technologies

Azim Premji graduated in engineering studies from Stanford University in 1966, and was a member of the Prime Minister's Advisory Committee for Information Technology in India. Wipro, a company that initially dealt in hydrogenated cooking oils and consumer products, expanded into computer software under him, and is now ranked among the top 100 technology companies globally, with a turnover exceeding $ 2.3 billion.

Wipro is the world's largest independent R&D service provider and its BPO arm is the largest outsourcing company in India. Wipro was the first Indian company to embrace Six Sigma; the first software services company in the world to achieve SEI CMM Level 5; and the world's first organization to achieve PCMM (People Capability Maturity Model) Level 5.

In 2004, Azim Premji was rated among the 100 most influential people in the world by *Time* magazine. From 1999 to 2005, he has been rated the richest person in the country by *Forbes*. In 2005, Premji was awarded the Padma Bhushan. He also became the first Indian to be awarded the Faraday Medal by the Institution of Electrical Engineers. Recently, the *Financial Times* ranked him tenth among the top 25 influential people in the world.

In 2001, Premji personally established the Azim Premji Foundation, a non-profit organization with a vision of contributing quality universal education towards building a just, equitable and humane society. Currently, the Foundation is involved with 2.5 million children in thirteen states under various programmes. Premji spends about Rs 20 crore a year from his personal wealth on the Foundation.

As an information technology entrepreneur, a top-rung industrialist and a philanthropist, Azim Premji is an inspiration and a role model for millions of middle-class Indians.

Bimal Jalan

born 1941

Economist and writer

A former Governor of the Reserve Bank of India for two terms (1997-2003), Bimal Jalan was educated at Presidency College, Calcutta and then at Cambridge and Oxford universities. He has been associated with a number of academic institutions including the Indian Statistical Institute, Kolkata and the Institute of Economic Growth, Delhi as chairman. He is currently president of the National Council for Applied Economic Research in New Delhi. In 2003 he was nominated to the Rajya Sabha by the President of India for distinguished public service.

Jalan was the Chief Economic Adviser to the government in the 1980s, Banking Secretary between 1985 and 1989 and also Secretary to the Ministry of Finance. During his tenure as the Governor of the Reserve Bank of India, the organization successfully handled the impact of the East Asian crisis and its aftermath, substantially strengthening India's balance of payments position, maintaining a low inflation environment and promoting wide-ranging reforms in the financial sector.

Bimal Jalan is the author of several seminal books on the Indian economy including *India's Economic Crisis: The Way Ahead*, *The Indian Economy: Problems and Prospects*, and *India's Economy in the New Millennium: Selected Essays*. His most recent book on India was published in 2005. Titled *The Future of India: Politics, Economics and Governance*, it is an attempt to examine current political developments and their effect in determining India's economic future and public welfare.

Bimal Jalan is one of the country's most respected economists and public figures.

Buddhadeb Bhattacharya
born 1944
Chief Minister of West Bengal

Buddhadeb Bhattacharya graduated from Presidency College, Calcutta in 1964. In 1977, he was elected to the Legislative Assembly for the first time, from the constituency of Kashipur. This was also the first year that the CPI (M)-led Left Front came to power in West Bengal. In 1996, Bhattacharya was appointed information and culture minister of the state with additional authority over the home (police) ministry. He is considered to be one of the few leaders who can balance both the hardliners and liberals in the party and this eventually led to his being promoted to chief minister, when Jyoti Basu finally decided to step down in 2000.

Since becoming chief minister Buddhadeb Bhattacharya has liberalized Bengal's economy significantly, attracting a lot of foreign investment to the state. Many new industries and IT-related services have emerged under his leadership and he is seen as a Communist leader who is open to reforms. Recently Bhattacharya said that he does not want to unionize the IT industry, which drew criticism from the labour unions of Bengal who say that this will lead to the exploitation of IT workers. In the 2006 Assembly Elections, he led the Left Front to a record seventh consecutive win in the state.

A politburo member of the CPI(M), Bhattacharya represents the new liberal face of Communism in India.

Charles Correa
born 1930
Architect

Charles Correa is an architect, planner, activist, a theoretician and a major figure in contemporary architecture worldwide. He studied at the University of Michigan and Massachusetts Institute of Technology. In private practice in Bombay since 1958, his work covers a wide range, from the Mahatma Gandhi Memorial at the Sabarmati Ashram, to the Jawahar Kala Kendra in Jaipur, and the Madhya Pradesh State Assembly—as well as townships and public housing project in Delhi, Mumbai, Ahmedabad, Bangalore and other Indian cities. He has taught and lectured at many universities including MIT, Harvard, University of London, and Cambridge.

Charles Correa is known for the wide range of his architectural work in India and on urbanization and low-cost shelter in the Third World, which he articulated in his 1985 publication, *The New Landscape*. His design of the new Brain and Cognitive Science building at MIT was unveiled in December 2005; the 30,000 sq ft structure is the largest neuroscience centre in the world. He has received many awards including the Royal Institute of British Architects Gold Medal in 1984, the Indian Institute of Architects Gold Medal in 1987, the International Union of Architects Gold Medal in 1990, and the Praemium Imperiale for Architecture from the Japan Art Association in 1994. In 2006, he was awarded the Padma Vibhushan.

Correa is the Chairman of the Delhi Urban Arts Commission and is working on preserving and maintaining the aesthetics of the ancient city's skyline. He is without doubt the most respected architect in the country today.

Deepak Parekh
born 1944
Executive Chairman, HDFC Limited

Deepak Parekh graduated from Mumbai's Sydenham College in 1965, and qualified as a chartered accountant in England, working with Ernst & Young, Precision Fasteners, ANZ Grindlays and

Chase Manhattan in New York and Mumbai. He joined HDFC in 1987 and was appointed Chairman in 1993.

Today the Rs 150,000 crore HDFC Group, serving 1.2 crore customers, is one of the largest financial sector groups in the country, straddling home loans, insurance, banking and mutual funds. HDFC has also established itself as the first stop for foreign investors looking to invest in India. Both HDFC Ltd and HDFC Bank are listed on the BSE Sensex.

Deepak Parekh has been a member of the infrastructure task force of the Prime Minister's Office and chalked out the rescue plan for the former Unit Trust of India during its first crisis in the late nineties. He is today one of the country's most influential figures in the Banking sector.

E. Sreedharan

born 1932

Managing Director, Delhi Metro Rail Corporation

Technocrat E. Sreedharan is one of India's greatest civil engineers, the architect of the supposedly unbuildable Konkan Railway linking Mumbai and Mangalore, and designer of the Delhi Metro system.

He studied at the Victoria College in Kerala and then graduated as an engineer from the Government Engineering College, Kakinada (now JNTU). After a short tenure as a lecturer in civil engineering at the Kerala Polytechnic in Kozhikode and a year at the Bombay Port Trust as an apprentice, he joined the Indian Railways as an engineer. His first major engineering project, in 1963, was the rebuilding of the nineteenth-century Pambam railway bridge in Tamil Nadu following its destruction by floods. For the next three decades he worked across India—including planning and designing the Kolkata Metro, before being entrusted in 1990 with the building of the Konkan Railway. Although he officially retired from Indian Railways in 1990, Sreedharan was brought back to oversee the building of the $2 billion, ninety-station Delhi Metro, the first stage of which was completed—on budget and on time—in December 2002. Work on extensions to the Delhi Metro, which seems to be the answer to the traffic problems in the national capital and a boon for commuters, is now in progress.

Sreedharan has won numerous awards and accolades including Chevalier de la Legion d'Honneur (Knight of the Legion of Honour) by the government of France. He was named as one of the top twenty-five newsmakers of the world in 2005 by the US-based *Engineering News Record*, and also named an 'Asian Hero' by *Time* magazine.

Ela Bhatt

born 1933

Founder and general secretary of SEWA

After completing her graduation Ela Bhatt entered Sir L.A. Shah Law College and in 1954 received her degree in law and a Gold Medal for her work on Hindu Law. She became a lawyer and then a social worker and in 1968 was the chief of the women's section of the Textile Labour Association in Ahmedabad. In this position she became aware of the conditions suffered by poor self-employed women in the city and elsewhere in South and Southeast Asia. This led her to set up SEWA (Self-Employed Women's Association), South Asia's first labour and trade union for women, in Ahmedabad.

SEWA has created healthcare, microfinance, vocational training centres, a bank and an academy for its 530,000 members. Bhatt is presently campaigning for an insurance programme for SEWA members. As the guiding spirit behind SEWA, Bhatt has shown that the weak and the poor can, through their collective strength, overcome numerous handicaps.

Ela Bhatt was nominated by the President of India to the Rajya Sabha in 1986. She was a member of the Planning Commission of India (1989-91) and has been chairperson and a founder member of Women's World Banking since 1980. She was granted an honorary Doctorate degree in Humane Letters by Harvard University in June 2001. She received the Padma Shri in 1985, the Padma Bhushan in 1996 and the Ramon Magsaysay Award for Community Leadership in 1977.

Ela Bhatt is a guiding light in the women's empowerment movement in India.

G.R. Gopinath

born 1952

Managing Director, Air Deccan

One of the pioneers of the low-cost carrier model in India, Captain G.R. Gopinath is a graduate of the National Defence Academy and has served in the Indian Army. He is a recipient of the prestigious Rolex Award for ecological site farming and the Wipro PRSI Award.

Set up in 1995, Air Deccan set the benchmark in India for low-cost, no-frills flights that had fares lower than railway tickets and enabled people who had never been able to afford flights before to fly. The airline has carved a niche for itself in the Indian aviation scene with its reputation for providing speedy and reliable aero-services for company charters, tourism, medical evacuation, offshore logistics and a host of others. Air Deccan has flown over 5.8 million passengers since its inception. Recently, it placed an order for ninety-six new aircraft that will be delivered over a period of eight years. It currently operates to fifty-five destinations across the country with 265 daily flights.

Captain G.R. Gopinath has changed the face of Indian civil aviation by extending the dream of flying to a whole new consumer base.

Hafeez Contractor

born 1950

Architect

Hafeez Contractor did his graduate diploma in architecture from Mumbai in 1975 and completed his graduation from Columbia University. A popular architect, Hafeez commenced his career in 1968 with T. Khareghat as an apprentice architect. In 1977, he became the associate partner in the same firm. Between 1977 and 1980 Hafeez was a visiting faculty at the Academy of Architecture, Mumbai. It was in 1982 that he began with his own private practice and from that moment onwards there has been no looking back.

Among his numerous architectural projects the most notable are D.Y. Patil Stadium, Navi Mumbai; Domestic Airport, Santacruz; Birla Corporate Office, Worli; DLF Golf and Country Club, Gurgaon; Hiranandani Club House, Thane; Knowledge Park, Bangalore; Indraprastha Apollo Hospital, Delhi; Public School, Navi Mumbai etc. Hafeez Contractor is a member of the Bombay Heritage Committee and the New Delhi Lutyens Bungalow Zone Review Committee and a Technical Advisor of Apollo Hospital. He has won numerous awards including the Architect of the Year–Priyadarshani Award.

Hafeez Contractor is to be credited for giving a new, attractive look to several modern Indian cityscapes.

Himesh Reshammiya

born 1973

Film music composer and singer

Himesh Reshammiya started out in show business at the age of sixteen with television serials made for Zee TV. He made his debut as music composer in the 1998 film *Pyaar Kiya To Darna Kya*, but initially his career in the film industry was not a success story. However, things turned around with the melodious soundtracks for *Humraaz* (2002) and *Tere Naam* (2003), and he has not looked back since. Reshammiya's exaggerated rhythms and catchy tunes have made him today's most-listened-to Hindi film composer.

With *Aashiq Banaya Aapne*, Reshammiya also began to sing playback, and to appear in films with his trademark baseball cap and unshaven look. His detractors say he has a nasal voice, but Himesh's inimitable style of crooning caught on with the masses in a big way, and his special appearances became de rigeur in every other Bollywood release in 2006. In 2006, he also released a solo music album, *Aap Ki Suroor*, which became a mega-seller.

Reshammiya has won the Zee Cine Awards (2004) Best Music Director award for *Tere Naam*, and the 2005 Filmfare Award for Best Playback Singer (Male) for *Aashiq Banaya Aapne*. In his own way, he has redefined popular Hindi film music in a matter of two years, and has scaled heights of popularity unequalled by any musician in the recent past.

Hrithik Roshan

born 1974

Film actor

The son of actor-director Rakesh Roshan, Hrithik Roshan made his debut as a child artist in 1980 in *Aap Ke Deewane*. He achieved instant fame in his first film as a lead actor with *Kaho Naa Pyaar Hai* in 2000. His convincing performance in a double role, supplemented by his excellent dancing skills, earned him both the Filmfare Best Debut Award and the Filmfare Best Actor Award.

Hrithik came up with strong performances in *Fiza*, *Mission Kashmir* and *Kabhi Khushi Kabhie Gham*, but his next big hit came in 2003, again under his father's baton, with *Koi Mil Gaya*, where he played a mentally challenged person befriended by an alien. *Koi Mil Gaya* was a huge hit especially with children, and won Hrithik his second Filmfare Award for Best Actor. *Krrish*, the sequel to *Koi Mil Gaya*, which was released in 2006, had Hrithik playing a superhero, and again the film was a big hit, making Hrithik something of an iconic figure among kids.

One of the biggest stars in Bollywood today with a distinctive image and a tremendous following among children, Hrithik Roshan is redefining the concept of the Bollywood hero.

Indira Jaisingh

Lawyer and activist

Indira Jaisingh is a senior advocate at the Supreme Court who specializes in public interest litigation. She is one of the most famous women lawyers of the country, and has been the anchor of many legal crusades for the underdog.

A civil rights activist and Padma Shri awardee, Jaisingh has been involved in the case of the Tehri dam. She is also a passionate advocate of women's issues. A founding member and Director of the Women's Rights Initiative of Lawyers Collective, she was actively involved in lobbying the government on the Domestic Violence Bill.

Indira Jaisingh is at the forefront of the legal fight for women's rights and rights for the underprivileged in India today.

Jagdish N. Bhagwati

born 1934

Economist

Jagdish Bhagwati is currently University Professor, Economics and Law, at Columbia University and Senior Fellow in International Economics at the Council on Foreign Relations. He graduated from Cambridge University in 1956 with a first in Economics Tripos. He then continued to study at MIT and Oxford, returning to India in 1961 as Professor of Economics at the Indian Statistical Institute, and then as Professor of International Trade at the Delhi School of Economics. He returned to

MIT in 1968, leaving it twelve years later as the Ford International Professor of Economics to join Columbia. He was Economic Policy Adviser to the Director General, GATT (1991-93) and also served as Special Adviser to the UN on Globalization and External Adviser to the Director General, WTO. Currently, he is a member of the UN Secretary General's Advisory Group on the NEPAD process in Africa.

Professor Bhagwati is described as the most creative international trade theorist of his generation and is a leader in the fight for freer trade. Five volumes of his scientific writings and two of his public policy essays have been published by MIT press. His most recent book, *In Defence of Globalization* (2004), has received worldwide acclaim. He was conferred the Lifetime Achievement Award by the Indian Chamber of Commerce in 2004. His name is being bandied about as a potential winner of the Economics Nobel.

Jagdish Bhagwati is an internationally renowned economist who keeps India's flag flying high.

K. Subrahmanyam

born 1929

Strategic analyst

K. Subrahmanyam completed his Masters in Chemistry from Madras University in 1950 and joined the Indian Administrative Service in 1951. From 1966 to 1967 he served as a Rockefeller Fellow in Strategic Studies at the London School of Economics. After returning to India, he served as the Director of the Institute for Defence Studies and Analyses (IDSA) until 1975. He held a number of top government positions—including Chairman of the Joint Intelligence Committee, Home Secretary for Tamil Nadu and Secretary for Defence Production in the Ministry of Defence—before returning as Director of IDSA from 1980 to 1987. Between 1974 and 1986, he also served on a number of United Nations study groups on issues such as Indian Ocean affairs, disarmament and nuclear deterrence.

A former consulting editor of the *Economic Times*, K. Subrahmanyam is the author of several studies on nuclear proliferation and international security. He was appointed the head of the National Security Council Advisory Board (NSCAB) established by the Vajpayee government to draft the Indian nuclear doctrine. He was also the head of the Kargil panel, a commission set up by the government to analyse the Kargil war. In November 2005, Prime Minister Manmohan Singh appointed Subrahmanyam to head a task force on 'Global Strategic Developments'.

K. Subrahmanyam is the person directly responsible for shaping India's future strategic thinking.

K.V. Kamath

born 1947

Managing Director and CEO, ICICI Bank

A mechanical engineer from REC, Karnataka and an MBA from the Indian Institute of Management, Ahmedabad, K.V. Kamath's first job was with ICICI's project finance division, where he initiated and implemented the firm's computerization programme. His fondness for technology and its potential continued to be the focal point of his vision for the future, and helped him take ICICI Bank to a position of primacy, with a reputation for being the most technologically savvy banking company in India. At a time when banking was synonymous with the physical banking approach of public sector banks, Kamath introduced the ATM mode of banking that was soon duplicated by every other bank.

From 1988 to 1996 Kamath also worked with the Asian Development Bank in Manila. He is the recipient of the Asian Business Leader of the Year prize. He says that now his top challenge is to retain the talent ICICI trains, which is keenly sought by other financial services players.

Head of the fastest growing and largest private sector bank in India, K.V. Kamath is a man with a vision, and this has led him to concentrate now on retail lending and the rural market.

Kailash Satyarthi

born 1954

Social activist

Kailash Saytarthi is founder and chairperson of Global March Against Child Labour, a civil society movement of more than 2,000 international and national NGOs and trade unions in about 140 countries, that initiated the first internationally recognized child labour free social labelling system 'Rugmark'. His 'Bachpan Bachao Andolan', initiated in 1980, is a mass movement and coalition for total elimination of child labour. Satyarthi is a recipient of the Raoul Wallenberg Human Rights Award, the Friedrich Ebert Stiftung International Human Rights Award, the Robert F. Kennedy Human Rights Award and the Aachener International Peace Prize.

Kailash Satyarthi was nominated for the Nobel Peace Prize in 2006. With his crusade against child labour, he has set an example for meaningful social activism.

Kallam Anji Reddy

born 1940

Chairman, Dr Reddy's Laboratories Limited

Before founding Dr Reddy's Laboratories in 1984, Dr K. Anji Reddy served in the state-owned Indian Drugs and Pharmaceuticals Limited and was founder and Managing Director of both Uniloids and Standard Organics Limited. Dr Reddy's Laboratories has become one of the first companies to take up drug discovery research in India and the first non-Japanese Asian pharmaceutical company to be listed on NYSE. The company with revenues of Rs 1,947 crore (US $446 million) was India's second largest pharmaceutical company in 2005, with revenue growth rates of 25 per cent in international markets and 24 per cent in India in 2006. The company recently acquired Betapharm—the fourth-largest generics company in Germany—for a total enterprise value of 480 million euros.

Dr Reddy is a serving member of the Prime Minister's Council on Trade and Industry and has been nominated to the board of the National Institute of Pharmaceutical Education and Research (NIPER). He is also a Padma Shri awardee.

Dr K. Anji Reddy is at the forefront of India's healthcare revolution.

Kapila Vatsyayan

born 1928

Art scholar

Dr Kapila Vatsyayan is an eminent scholar of classical Indian dance, art and architecture. She received her PhD from Michigan University, and is the author of many books on performing arts, aesthetics and philosophy including *The Square and the Circle of Indian Arts*, *Bharata: The Natya Sastra*, and *Matralaksanam*. She has been on the faculty of the universities of Delhi, Pennsylvania, Columbia and Berkeley. She has also served as secretary to the government of India in the Ministry of Education and Department of Arts and Culture, in which she was responsible for the establishment of many institutions of higher education in India.

Kapila Vatsyayan was removed from her position as Academic Director of the Indira Gandhi National Centre for the Arts by the NDA government in 2000, but returned to the Centre in 2006. As vice-chairperson of the advisory committee in the Culture ministry, India's representative on UNESCO's executive board, and chief patron of the Asia project under the India International Centre, she is at the heart of Delhi's social circle.

Kapila Vatsyayan has won many honours and awards including the

Padma Bhushan. She is the country's foremost cultural administrator.

Kiran Desai
born 1971
Writer

Kiran Desai won the £50,000 Man Booker Prize for Fiction 2006 with *The Inheritance of Loss*, her second novel. She is the first Indian-born writer to win the prestigious literary award since Arundhati Roy, whose *The God of Small Things* won in 1997. At thirty-five, Kiran Desai is also the youngest woman ever to win the Booker in its thirty-eight-year history. Kiran Desai is the daughter of renowned writer Anita Desai, who has been shortlisted thrice for the Booker Prize, but has never won.

Kiran Desai was born in India in 1971, and was educated in India, in England, and the United States. She studied creative writing at Columbia University. Her first novel *Hullabaloo in the Guava Orchard*, published in 1998, won the Betty Trask Award for Best First Novel.

With one of the most prestigious literary awards under her belt, Kiran Desai is a young Indian writer with a global appeal.

Kiran Mazumdar-Shaw
born 1953
Chairman and Managing Director, Biocon Ltd

Kiran Mazumdar-Shaw is an alumnus of Bishop Cotton Girls' School, Mount Carmel College at Bangalore and Ballarat University in Melbourne. She became India's first woman Brewmaster in 1975. Her professional career started with the position of trainee brewer in Carlton & United Beverages in 1974 and she joined Biocon Biochemicals Limited in Ireland in 1978 as a Trainee Manager. Biocon is an integrated biotechnology enterprise focused on the development of biopharmaceuticals.

Kiran Mazumdar-Shaw became the country's richest woman in 2004, and has retained that position since. She was termed 'India's Biotech Queen' by the *Economist* and *Fortune*, and 'India's mother of invention' by *New York Times*. She received the Padma Bhushan in 2005 and a Lifetime Achievement Award from the Indian Chamber of Commerce the same year. She is the Chairperson and Mission Leader of CII's National Task Force on Biotechnology and member of the Prime Minister's Council on Trade and Industry in India.

As India's leading businesswoman, Kiran Mazumdar-Shaw is an inspiration to the new generation of corporate aspirers.

Kishore Biyani
born 1961
CEO, the Future Group

Kishore Biyani's academic qualifications include a commerce degree and a post-graduate diploma in marketing. He started off his entrepreneurial career with selling branded men's wear products. He went on to launch Pantaloon Shoppe, a franchisee chain, in the early 1990s. He led the company's entry into the retail space with the launch of its first fashion store, Pantaloons, in August 1997 in Kolkata.

Over the years, Pantaloon Retail has emerged as the largest retailer in India. Kishore Biyani now heads the Future Group, which is designed to cater to the entire Indian consumption space. He prides in being an Indian and advocates 'Indianness' as the core value driving his company. He also stresses on the importance of continuous introspection and is a firm believer in learning, unlearning and re-learning all the time.

Kumar Mangalam Birla
born 1967
Chairman, the Aditya Birla Group

Kumar Mangalam Birla completed his Chartered Accountancy in 1988 and in

1992 earned his Masters in Business Administration degree from London Business School. His $6 billion (revenues) global commodities group is into everything from metals to movies (it includes Hindalco, Grasim, Indian Rayon, Indo Gulf, UltraTech and Applause Entertainment).

Kumar Mangalam Birla is also on the boards of major Indian companies like Tata Iron and Steel Company and Maruti Udyog Limited. He holds several key positions on various regulatory and professional boards, including chairmanship of the advisory committee constituted by the Ministry of Company Affairs for 2006 and 2007, membership of the Prime Minister's advisory council on Trade and Industry, and chairmanship of the board of trade reconstituted by the Union Minister of Commerce and Industry. Most recently, the Ministry of Finance nominated him to the Central Board of Directors of the Reserve Bank of India. Among the numerous awards and honours conferred on him are the Ernst & Young Entrepreneur of the Year–India award (2005) and the *Economic Times* Business Leader of the Year award (2002-03).

As chairman of one of the fastest growing business houses in India with a market cap of Rs 50,000 crore, Kumar Mangalam Birla is one of the leaders who are redefining business and industry in India.

Kushal Pal Singh

born 1931

Chairman, DLF Ltd

After graduating in Science from Meerut College, Kushal Pal Singh went to the UK to study aeronautical engineering. In 1960, he joined American Universal Electric Company. Subsequently, he worked with Willard India Limited in collaboration with ESB Inc of Philadelphia manufacturing automatic and industrial batteries in India and became its Managing Director.

Joining his father-in-law's Delhi Land and Finance in 1971, Singh built DLF City in Gurgaon, his showpiece township on the outskirts of Delhi, by acquiring land from farmers and transformed DLF into India's biggest real estate developer. He was also appointed National Advisor of GE in 1989 and continued in this position till 1993 when he was made a member of GE's National Advisory Board in New York. He has held various professional positions in India including President, ASSOCHAM and President, PHD Chambers of Commerce and Industry). Presently, he is Director, Central Board of Reserve Bank of India, Member of the Executive Committee of Federation of Indian Chambers of Commerce and Industry (FICCI), Council Member, Eastern Regional Organization for Planning and Housing (EAROPH) and Founder Member, National Estate Development Council (NAREDCO). According to the 2006 *Forbes* list Kushal Pal Singh ranked 114th among the world's richest people.

DLF is building residential townships, business centres and entertainment and retail hubs across India at a frenetic pace, and K.P. Singh is actively defining the look and shape of tomorrow's India.

L.M. Thapar

born 1930

Chairman Emeritus, Ballarpur Industries Ltd

L.M. Thapar heads the L.M. Thapar group of companies that includes among others JCT Mills, Ballarpur Industries Limited, Crompton Greaves Limited, Tiger Bay restaurant and the *Pioneer*. L.M. Thapar completed his schooling from the Doon School and graduated in engineering from the University of Southern California, USA. He is also a fellow at the Indian National Academy of Engineering.

Thapar took over the stewardship of the Thapar Group in 1962. He is a past president of PHD Chamber of Commerce and Industry and became the first president of the restructured 'new ASSOCHAM', one of the apex chambers of the country in 1988. He has also been chairman of the Indo-Canada, Indo-USSR and Indo-US joint business councils. He has been on the executive board of the International Chamber of Commerce and is also a member of the UN Commission on Transnational Corporations. He has also been the Chairman of the Board of Governors of the Indian Institutes of Technology at Kharagpur and Kanpur, and has served as chairman of the Thailand-based Phoenix Pulp and Paper.

L.M. Thapar is one of India's leading industrialists.

Lakshmi N. Mittal

born 1950

Chairman and CEO, Mittal Steel

Based in London, L.N. Mittal is, according to the *Sunday Times*, the richest man in the UK and the third richest man in the world today, with a net worth of US$ 14.8 billion.

L.N. Mittal graduated from St Xavier's in Kolkata with a commerce degree in 1969 and founded his company in 1976. Today Mittal Steel is the only truly global steel producer in the world with operations in fourteen countries, spanning four continents. In June 2006, Mittal Steel reached an agreement with Arcelor SA over a 26.9 billion euro merger. The new company, in which Mittal Steel holds a 45 per cent stake, is called Arcelor-Mittal and is the largest steel company in the world. Other related activities of Mittal Steel include shipping, power generation and distribution, and mining.

Mittal was awarded *Fortune* magazine's European Businessman of the Year award in 2004 and prior to that, the Steelmaker of the Year award by New Steel in the USA in 1996 and the Willy Korf Steel Vision Award in June 1998. He is a member of the Foreign Investment Council in Kazakhstan, the International Investment Council in South Africa, the World Economic Forum's International Business Council and the International Iron and Steel Institute's Executive Committee. He is a Director of ICICI Bank Limited and is on the Advisory Board of the Kellogg School of Management in the US.

L.N. Mittal is an Indian industrialist with a truly global reach.

Lal Krishna Advani

born 1929

Politician

The former president of the Bharatiya Janata Party (BJP) and leader of the Opposition in the current Lok Sabha, L.K. Advani completed his graduation in Law from Bombay University. At the time of partition, he was the RSS organizer in Karachi. When Jana Sangh was founded in 1951, Advani became its Rajasthan State Secretary and continued there till 1957 before he moved to Delhi to become the Delhi Jana Sangh Secretary; during this period he was also the Secretary to the Jana Sangh Parliamentary Group. He was elected president of Jana Sangh in 1973 and continued till 1977, before being appointed Information and Broadcasting minister in the Janata government. During his tenure he abolished press censorship and repealed anti-press legislation.

Advani was a member of the Rajya Sabha from 1970 to 1989, and has been elected to the Lok Sabha five times. In 1991, he was appointed leader of the Opposition in the Lok Sabha. From 1998 to 2004 he was the deputy prime minister and home minister in the Vajpayee government. After the BJP went out of power, he returned to his role of leader of the Opposition.

An outspoken and influential leader, Advani has consistently made the headlines with his comments on subjects ranging from Ayodhya to Jinnah's secularism. Though he is no longer a prime ministerial candidate, he remains the most recognizable face of right wing politics in India.

Lalu Prasad Yadav

born 1947

Union Railway Minister

Lalu Prasad Yadav has a Master's degree in Political Science from Patna University as well as a law degree. Socialist leader Jayaprakash Narayan, who led a student movement in Bihar in the early seventies, groomed Yadav as a politician. In 1977, at the age of twenty-nine, he became a Lok Sabha MP for the first time. After being in the Bihar Legislative Assembly for two terms, in 1989 he became the leader of the Opposition.

Lalu Prasad Yadav became the chief minister of Bihar in 1990, a post he held till 1997. When in 1997 he was forced to resign on widespread corruption charges (after his name cropped up in the fodder scam), he handed over the reins of the state to his wife. He served prison sentences before being re-elected to the twelfth Lok Sabha for a third term. In 1997, after breaking away from the Janata Dal, Lalu Prasad Yadav formed Rashtriya Janata Dal, of which he is the president. The RJD is part of the governing United Progressive Alliance at the Centre, and much to the surprise of many, Lalu Prasad Yadav has turned the stumbling behemoth of the Railways into a Rs 11,000-crore cash-rich organization.

It is difficult to think of Bihar without thinking of Lalu, and this is perhaps because his real passion seems to be surviving in politics, a skill he has mastered like few others. Critics hold him responsible for the worsening socio-political scenario of Bihar while he and his wife governed the state, but he has his legions of admirers, who are ready to die for him even after the RJD's ouster from power in the Bihar Assembly elections in 2005.

M. Karunanidhi

born 1924

Chief Minister of Tamil Nadu

M. Karunanidhi began his career as a script-writer working in the Tamil film industry, but shot to popularity in politics due to his wit and great oratorical skills. He became famous for writing historicals and mythological stories that helped propagate the socialist and rationalist ideals of the Dravidian movement to which he belonged. Since 1969 Karunanidhi has been the president of the Dravida Munnetra Kazhagam. He has championed the cause of the Tamil language in the past and has rallied against the 'imposition' of Hindi in Tamil Nadu.

In his political career spanning over sixty years Karunanidhi has never lost in any election; he has been elected to the state Legislative Assembly eleven times and once to the now-abolished Tamil Nadu Legislative Council. Before his current tenure (from 13 May 2006) he has served as the chief minister of Tamil Nadu four times. However, allegations of corruption have dogged his years in power. On 30 June 2001 he was arrested for alleged involvement in the 'flyover scam', an act that raised a lot of humanitarian questions. Although later released on health grounds, his arrest provoked massive riots, and brought the state government of Tamil Nadu, led by J. Jayalalithaa, into direct conflict with the Central government.

Having got the better of his political rival J. Jayalalithaa, and riding on a crest of popularity in Tamil Nadu, M. Karunanidhi is one of the most charismatic and influential politicians defining both regional and national politics today.

M.K. Narayanan

born 1934

National Security Advisor

M.K. Narayanan is an expert in security matters and a specialist on Sri Lankan affairs. Narayanan headed the Intelligence Bureau (IB) from 1989 to 1990, before heading the Joint Intelligence Committee. He became chief of the IB again in 1991, before retiring in 1992. He was called out of retirement by Prime Minister Manmohan Singh and appointed Special Advisor for Internal Security to the Prime Minister in May 2004.

As National Security Advisor, Narayanan is behind all security measures undertaken by the Government of India.

M.S. Swaminathan

born 1925

Agricultural scientist

Known as the 'Father of the Indian Green Revolution', M.S. Swaminathan was a graduate of Cambridge in 1952 with a PhD in genetics. He was behind the Green Revolution that made India self-sufficient in crop production in 1968. Swaminathan was the Chairman of the UN Science Advisory Committee set up in 1980 to take follow-up action on the Vienna Plan of Action. He has also served as Independent Chairman of the FAO Council and president of the International Union for the Conservation of Nature and Natural Resources, and is the current president of the Pugwash Conferences on Science and World Affairs. He has received the Magsaysay Award for Community Leadership in 1971 and the Padma Vibhushan in 1989.

Head of the M.S. Swaminathan Research Foundation, M.S. Swaminathan is still at the forefront of agricultural reforms in the country. Following the 2004 Indian Ocean earthquake, he advised the Government of India to plant mangrove trees along the shoreline to minimize damage from future tsunamis.

Mahendra Singh Dhoni

born 1981

Cricketer

Wicket-keeper Mahendra Singh Dhoni is a breathtaking talent and the latest sensation in Indian cricket. His explosive batting has been instrumental in many an Indian win in recent times and he has consistently treated the leading bowlers in contemporary cricket with amazing disdain. This led to his reaching the number 1 position among batsmen in the ICC rankings in 2006.

Though Dhoni made his first-class debut in the 1999-2000 season, it was with his two centuries against Pakistan A, in the triangular tournament in Kenya in 2004, that he established himself as a clinical destroyer of bowling attacks. In just his fifth one-dayer, against Pakistan, he scored a dazzling 148 and followed that up with a colossal 183 not out against Sri Lanka, when he broke Adam Gilchrist's record for the highest score by a wicket-keeper in ODIs. He made an instant impact at the Test level too, pounding 148 at Faisalabad, in only his fifth Test, when India were struggling to avoid the follow on, and established himself as one of the critical members of a revitalized side. His critics might say that he has performed well only on the docile pitches of the Indian subcontinent and that his biggest test is yet to come, but it has to be accepted that he has created terror in the hearts of bowlers throughout the world in a very short time.

Hailing from Ranchi, Dhoni is the idol of every small-town kid who dreams of making it big and becoming a national hero.

Mallika Sarabhai

Classical dancer

Mallika Sarabhai is one of the most renowned Kuchipudi and Bharatnatyam dancers in India. Mallika is the daughter of reputed dancer Mrinalini Sarabhai and renowned scientist Vikram Sarabhai.

Multi-faceted Malika Sarabhai holds an MBA and a doctorate from IIM, Ahmedabad. She started to learn dancing at a very young age and started her film career in parallel cinema when she was just fifteen. Mallika played the role of Draupadi in Peter Brook's film *Mahabharata*. She is a noted film-maker, a familiar TV anchor, an editor, a publisher, and a social activist espousing various causes. She is also a CEO of a TV channel. Along with Mrinalini Sarabhai, she co-directs the Darpana Academy of Performing Arts, Ahmedabad. Mallika has won many awards and accolades including the French Palme D'Or.

Mallika Sarabhai is internationally renowned as a classical dancer and respected as a social activist. She recently made headlines when she complained that the Narendra Modi government in Gujarat was harassing her due to her public criticism of its role during the riots.

Manish Malhotra
Fashion designer

Manish Malhotra is a fashion designer famous for revolutionizing the fashion scene in the Hindi film industry. He started his career with costume designing for Juhi Chawla in the film *Swarg*. He now designs clothes for almost every major Bollywood star. His work has been greatly appreciated and he has received several awards including the first and only Filmfare Award for Costume Design for Urmila Matondkar's look in *Rangeela*. He was exclusively asked to design clothes for Michael Jackson for his appearance during the Bollywood Awards held in New York. Apart from several Indian actresses, international model Naomi Campbell is also his client.

Manish Malhotra decided to branch into mainstream designing in 1998 with his high-profile couture store Reverie. His plans include a prêt-a-porter line for women along with his couture label and also a couture and prêt line for men.

Bollywood owes much of its great new stylish look to Manish Malhotra.

Manmohan Singh
born 1932
Prime Minister of India

Manmohan Singh earned an Honours degree in Economics from the University of Cambridge in 1957, and a DPhil in Economics from Nuffield College at Oxford University in 1962. He was a professor of Punjab University and the Delhi School of Economics and also served at the UN, the IMF and other international bodies.

In 1971, Dr Singh joined the Government of India as Economic Advisor in the Commerce Ministry. Among the many government positions he has occupied are Secretary in the Ministry of Finance, Deputy Chairman of the Planning Commission, Governor of the Reserve Bank of India, Advisor to the Prime Minister and Chairman of the University Grants Commission. He spent five years between 1991 and 1996 as India's finance minister and was first elected to the Rajya Sabha in 1991, representing the Congress there since. He was the leader of the Opposition between 1998 and 2004. In 2004, after the United Progressive Alliance came to power, he became the prime minister.

Manmohan Singh has won several awards for his work and contribution to society, including the Padma Vibhushan, the Euro Money Finance Minister of the year award and the Asia Money Finance Minister of the Year award. As finance minister of India he introduced the concept of service tax and is widely regarded as the architect of India's original economic liberalization programme that was enacted in 1991 by P.V. Narasimha Rao's administration.

Manmohan Singh is India's first prime minister who is not a politician but a technocrat. In his time at the head of government, he has demonstrated astute administrative skills and admirable statesmanship.

Maqbool Fida Husain

born 1915

Painter

M.F. Husain is India's most charismatic and popular painter. In the initial years he sustained himself in Bombay by painting cinema hoardings and his struggle continued until his paintings were first exhibited in Bombay. In 1952, his first solo exhibition was held at Zürich and over the next few years, his work was widely exhibited in Europe and USA. His first film, *Through the Eyes of a Painter* (1967) won a Golden Bear at the Berlin Festival. He has directed two other films: *Gaja Gamini* (with his 'muse' Madhuri Dixit as the main lead) and *Meenaxi: A Tale of Three Cities*.

M.F. Husain was nominated to the Rajya Sabha in 1987. Over the past two decades he has slowly grown into a public figure, known for its artistic skill, his controversial depictions, and his barefoot image. He is presently India's highest paid painter. At a recent auction one of his paintings fetched US$ 2 million. In February 2006, he was arrested and charged with hurting sentiments of people following his controversial nude paintings of Hindu gods and goddesses.

Forbes magazine has described Husain as 'the Picasso of India'. At ninety-one, he is a central figure in the contemporary Indian art scene, and that tells its own story.

Medha Patkar

born 1954

Environmental activist

Co-founder of the Narmada Bachao Andolan and convener of the National Alliance of People's Movements, Medha Patkar completed her Masters degree in Social Work from Tata Institute of Social Sciences and spent three years there as a member of the faculty. She left her position on the faculty of TISS as well as her unfinished PhD when she became involved with the tribal and peasant communities in Maharashtra, Madhya Pradesh and Gujarat. This involvement eventually gave rise to the Narmada Bachao Andolan.

The NBA movement started as a fight for information about the Narmada Valley development projects and the fight continued for rehabilitation for the displaced people ousted by the Sardar Sarovar Dam and other major dams along the Narmada river. In a great confrontation between NBA supporters and pro-dam forces in 1991, Patkar's twenty-one-day fast brought her close to death. Patkar went on a fast-to-death again in 2006 to protest against the increase in the height of the Narmada dam, and was eventually arrested.

Medha Patkar received the Right Livelihood Award in 1991. She has received numerous other awards, including the Goldman Environment Prize and the Human Rights Defender's Award from Amnesty International. She has also been a member of the World Commission of Dams.

Medha Patkar is one of India's most vocal advocates of the need to prioritize environment-related issues in development projects.

Montek Singh Ahluwalia

born 1943

Deputy Chairman of the Planning Commission

Montek Singh Ahluwalia earned his BA (Hons.) degree from St Stephen's College and his MA and MPhil degrees as a Rhodes scholar from the University of Oxford. He was the first director of the Independent Evaluation Office, International Monetary Fund, having assumed office in 2001. Before that he was a Member of the Planning Commission in New Delhi as well as a Member of the Economic Advisory Council to the Prime Minister. He had previously served as Finance Secretary, Secretary at the Department of Economic Affairs, Commerce Secretary,

Special Secretary to the Prime Minister and Economic Advisor to the Ministry of Finance.

M.S. Ahluwalia has been a key figure in India's economic reforms. According to him the greatest challenge confronting the nation is to sell economic reform policies in a manner that individuals begin to perceive them as inclusive—that it has something in it for them.

As Deputy Chairman of the Planning Commission, M.S. Ahluwalia is in charge of some Rs 150,000 crore of spending power, which makes him one of the most powerful individuals in the country.

Mukesh Ambani

born 1957

Chairman and Managing Director, Reliance Industries Ltd

Mukesh Ambani graduated in Chemical Engineering from the University of Mumbai and completed an MBA degree from Stanford Business School. He joined Reliance in 1981 and initiated its integration into polyester fibres and petrochemicals, leading to the creation of the world's largest grassroots petroleum refinery at Jamnagar.

Today Reliance Industries is India's largest private sector company with revenues touching Rs 100,000 crore. Despite losing half his empire to brother Anil in the Reliance split, Mukesh Ambani has been able to raise the Reliance Group's market capitalization from Rs 60,000 crore to Rs 109,000 crore.

Mukesh Ambani was given the Asia Society Leadership Award by the Asia Society, Washington in 2004 and was co-chairman of the World Economic Forum in 2006. His wealth is estimated at US$ 8.5 billion.

Mukesh Ambani is steering Reliance's initiatives on a world scale offshore deep water oil, gas exploration and production programme, a pan-Indian petroleum retail network involving 5,800 outlets, and a research-led life sciences initiative covering medical, plant and industrial biotechnology.

Mulayam Singh Yadav

born 1939

Chief Minister of Uttar Pradesh

Having passed his MA and BT examinations from the University of Agra, Mulayam Singh Yadav was greatly inspired and influenced by the socialist thoughts and ideology of Ram Manohar Lohia and in 1954, aged fifteen years, he was sent to jail for the first time for taking part in Lohia's 'Nahar Rate Movement'. Since then he has spent over three years in jail, most notably for nineteen months during the Emergency and in 1992 for launching a state-wide movement in the interest of the farmers.

He has been repeatedly elected to the UP legislative assembly since 1965 and first became a state minister in 1977. In 1980, he became the president of the Lok Dal in Uttar Pradesh, which later became part of the Janata Dal. In 1982, he was elected leader of the Opposition in the Uttar Pradesh Legislative Council; he first became chief minister of Uttar Pradesh in 1989. In 1992 he formed the Samajwadi Party and between 1996 and 1998 he was the defence minister in the Union Cabinet.

Mulayam Singh Yadav is a fierce supporter of Indian languages and stresses the need to remove the use of English from public life. He is a leader of considerable stature who has proved to be a driving force in UP and has brought Dalit politics to the forefront.

N.R. Narayana Murthy

born 1946

Industrialist

N.R. Narayana Murthy retired from his position as Executive Chairman of the Board and Chief Mentor of Infosys Technologies on 20 August 2006.

Narayana Murthy holds a BE from the University of Mysore and an MTech from IIT, Kanpur. He served as the Chief Executive Officer of Infosys between 1981 and 2002. Under his leadership, Infosys was listed on NASDAQ in 1999. He is chairman of the governing body of the Indian Institute of Information Technology, Bangalore and the Indian Institute of Management, Ahmedabad. He is a member of the Board of Overseers of the University of Pennsylvania's Wharton School, Cornell University Board of Trustees, Singapore Management University Board of Trustees, INSEAD's Board of Directors and the Asian Institute of Management's Board of Governors. He was Chairman of the Committee on Corporate Governance appointed by the Securities and Exchange Board of India (SEBI) in 2003. He also served as a member of the Central Board of the Reserve Bank of India between 2000 and 2006. He serves as a member of the Prime Minister's Council on Trade and Industry, and as a member of the Board of Directors of the United Nations Foundation.

Time magazine named Narayana Murthy as one of the ten leaders who are helping shape the future of technology in 2004. Now that he has relinquished office, India's IT visionary will surely find new ways to change and inspire the nation.

Nandan Nilekani

CEO and Managing Director, Infosys Technologies Ltd

Nandan Nilekani, who received his bachelor's degree in electrical engineering from IIT, Mumbai, is one of the founders of Infosys and has served as a director on the company's board since its inception in 1981. He was appointed Chief Executive Officer of Infosys in March 2002. He has strengthened Infosys as a global brand that has doubled its revenues in two years to cross the US$ 2 billion mark in 2006.

Nilekani co-founded the National Association of Software and Service Companies (NASSCOM) as well as the Bangalore Chapter of The IndUS Entrepreneurs (TiE). In January 2006, Nilekani became one of the youngest entrepreneurs to join twenty global leaders on the prestigious World Economic Forum (WEF) Foundation Board; he was also awarded the Padma Bhushan the same year.

Time magazine lists him as one of the 100 most influential people in the world. If India's IT future is in the hands of any one person, it is Nilekani's.

Narendra Modi

born 1950

Chief Minister of Gujarat

Narendra Modi completed his schooling in Vadnagar and got his masters degree in Political Science from Gujarat University. In 1984 he became one of the select few individuals to be deputed to the Bharatiya Janata Party (BJP) by the RSS. He joined the Bharatiya Janata Party in 1987 and was an important link between the RSS and the BJP. In 1988 he became the General Sectretary of the state BJP unit. As he had a formidable reputation as a party organizer he was made the National Secretary of the party, in charge of five states, in 1995. He is known to be one of L.K. Advani's favourite protégés.

When Keshubhai Patel was forced to step down in the fall-out from the earthquake in Gujarat in January 2001, Narendra Modi became the chief minister of Gujarat. In February 2002, when he was the CM, communal riots broke out in the state claiming hundreds of lives. Various human rights organizations and major Indian newspapers accused Modi of supporting, and in some cases instigating, the riots. But following the riots, Modi was sworn in as chief minister again after a landslide victory in the Assembly polls.

A right-wing hardliner known for his fundamentalist sentiments, Modi is nevertheless one of the strongest and most popular chief ministers in the country today.

Naresh Goyal

born 1949

Chairman, Jet Airways

In 1967, after completing his graduation in Commerce, Naresh Goyal joined the travel business with the GSA for Lebanese International Airlines. From 1967 to 1974 he underwent extensive training in all facets of the travel business through his association with several foreign airlines. In May 1974, he founded Jetair (Private) Limited with the objective of providing sales and marketing representation to foreign airlines in India.

Taking advantage of the opening of the Indian economy and the enunciation of the Open Skies Policy by the Indian government in 1991, Goyal set up Jet Airways for the operation of scheduled air services on domestic sectors in India, which commenced commercial operations on 5 May 1993. In thirteen years, Jet Airways has emerged as India's largest private domestic airline, valued at Rs 11,000 crore. Jet Airways has partnerships with as many as 123 airlines worldwide.

Naresh Goyal has won the Entrepreneur of the Year Award for Services from Ernst & Young. Following the 2005 IPO of Jet Airways, *Forbes* magazine declared him the sixteenth richest person in India with a net worth of US$ 1.9 billion.

Though Jet's deal to acquire Sahara fell through and numerous private airlines have mushroomed in the last couple of years, Naresh Goyal's organization holds its position of primacy in the Indian skies.

Nitish Kumar

born 1951

Chief Minister of Bihar

Nitish Kumar has a Bachelor's degree in Engineering from Bihar College of Engineering, Patna. In the mid-1970s he became involved in the JP Movement led by Jayaprakash Narayan. He was elected to the Bihar legislative assembly in 1985. In 1989, he became the Secretary-General of the Janata Dal in Bihar and in the same year was also elected to the Lok Sabha for the first time. So far, he has served as Lok Sabha MP for six terms. At various points of time he has served as Union Cabinet Minister of Railways, Surface Transport, and Agriculture.

In 2000, Nitish Kumar became chief minister of Bihar but had to resign after only seven days. In November 2005, the success of the Janata Dal (U)–BJP combine in the Bihar Assembly elections brought to an end the fifteen-year rule of the Lalu Prasad Yadav-led Rashtriya Janata Dal in the state.

After doing the undoable—ousting the RJD from power in Bihar—Nitish Kumar's next challenge is to introduce a semblance of administrative order in the state.

Piyush Pandey

born 1955

Advertising creative director

One of India's most celebrated creative ad men, Piyush Pandey is presently the Executive Chairman and National Creative Director for Ogilvy & Mather, India and South Asia. He obtained his Master's degree from St Stephen's College, Delhi and represented Rajasthan in the Ranji Trophy and worked as a tea taster before joining O&M in 1982. Under his leadership, O&M India has won a dozen Lions and has been named India's most creative agency nine times in the last ten years.

Piyush Pandey has won over 600 national and international awards and has been named the most influential man in Indian advertising three years in a row by the *Economic Times*. Ad Club Mumbai voted his commercial for the adhesive brand Fevikwik as the commercial of the century and his work for

Cadbury's as the campaign of the century. He is the only Indian to have won a double Gold at Cannes and a triple Grand Prize at the London International Awards. In June 2004, he was invited to be the President of the Jury for Outdoor & Press and Film at the Cannes International Advertising Festival, a first for an Asian.

Piyush Pandey has consistently been taking advertising creativity to new heights. He was nominated to the O&M worldwide board in September 2006.

Prakash Karat

born 1948

General Secretary, CPI(M)

Prakash Karat joined the CPI(M) in 1970 and worked underground for one and a half years during the Emergency. He was arrested twice and spent eight days in prison. He was the president of the Students' Fedration of India (SFI) between 1974 and 1979, was elected to the Central Committee of CPI(M) in 1985, and became a member of the politbureau in 1992. He is married to Brinda Karat who is also a member of the Central Committee of the CPI(M).

Prakash Karat became General Secretary of the CPI(M) after Harkishen Singh Surjeet stepped down from the post in 2005. He ushers in a new generational change within the CPI(M) and as a behind-the-scenes politician, analysts say, he will have a major role to play in shaping up the coalition relationship with the Congress-led United Progressive Alliance government.

Pranab Mukherjee

born 1935

External Affairs Minister

Having majored in History and Political Science and later graduating in Law, Pranab Mukherjee began his career as a lecturer and made his major break in politics by getting elected to the Rajya Sabha in 1969. Since then he has got re-elected to the Upper House four times and has been West Bengal Congress president more than once. In the national context, he has held key portfolios in the Central government like Finance, Commerce, Steel and Mines, and External Affairs from the 1970s to 1990s.

In 2004, Pranab Mukherjee was elected from Jangipur Lok Sabha constituency in West Bengal and returned to electoral politics after twenty-four years. He became defence minister in the UPA government, a post he held till he was made external affairs miister in October 2006. He has headed various Group of Ministers (GoMs) in the UPA government. He is also considered one of the key figures in formulating long-term economic policies of the nation.

One of the seniormost ministers in the Union Cabinet and one of the most experienced parliamentarians in the country, Pranab Mukherjee is part of the strategic core of policy-making that is redefining India.

Prannoy Roy

born 1949

Chairman and Director, NDTV

One of the leading psephologists and political analysts in India today, Prannoy Roy attended Doon School and received a scholarship to study at Haileybury, a leading public school in England, where he completed his A-levels, and the prestigious Leverhulme fellowship for his doctorate. He graduated in Economics from the University of London's Queen Mary College and received his PhD from the Delhi School of Economics where he also taught for a year. He is a qualified Chartered Accountant and has worked with PriceWaterhouseCoopers, India before moving to television. From 1985 to 1987 he was also associated with the Ministry of Finance as an economic advisor.

Prannoy Roy has been involved with the television media since 1980 as a commentator on elections and rose to fame with the news programme 'The World This Week' and his election coverage on Doordarshan. His company NDTV started with producing news programmes for Star TV and then started out on its own. NDTV is India's leading English language television news channel and commands over 30 per cent of the market share.

Prannoy Roy has been adjudged the television personality of the millennium by an *Indian Express* poll and has contributed to various national and international publications. He revolutionized news programming in India and is at the forefront of India's media revolution.

Raghav Bahl

Managing Director, Television Eighteen India Ltd

Raghav Bahl graduated in Economics from St Stephen's College, Delhi and completed his MBA from Delhi University. He began his professional career as a management consultant with A.F. Ferguson and Co. His second job was with American Express Bank. He started his career in media in 1985 as a correspondent and anchorperson for Doordarshan. He was the anchorperson and production consultant for India's first monthly video newsmagazine, *Newstrack*, produced by the India Today group. From 1991 to 1993 he was the Executive Director of Business India Television and produced the *Business India Show* and *Business A.M.* on Doordarshan. He has written articles for a number of publications and won the Sanskriti Award for Journalism in 1994.

Raghav Bahl's TV18 network, which began as a single-channel company, is now a Rs 1,100 crore media house that includes the TV channels CNBC-TV18, Awaaz, CNN-IBN and IBN 7, as well as several websites. Raghav Bahl is a senior anchorperson on CNBC-TV18. He is also a member of World Economic Forum.

The man behind Television Eighteen, India's leading television news and analysis network, Raghav Bahl is changing awareness levels and perception across the nation.

Rahul Bajaj

Chairman and Managing Director, Bajaj Auto Ltd

Rahul Bajaj holds a Bachelor's degree in Economics and is an alumnus of St Stephen's College and Harvard Business School. He became only the second Indian recipient of the Harvard Business School Alumni Achievement award in 2005. He has been the Chairman of the Technology Development Advisory Group and the India Development Council for Automobiles and Allied Industries between 1975 and 1977. The Government of India conferred the Padma Bhushan on him in 2001. In June 2006, he was nominated to the Rajya Sabha from the state of Maharashtra.

Rahul Bajaj heads the Bajaj Group, which comprises twenty-seven companies. Bajaj Auto Limited has been India's premier two- and three-wheeler manufacturer since 1968.

Bajaj has sold over 2.3 million bikes and has redefined transportation for the urban and semi-urban middle class in India.

Rahul Dravid

born 1973

Captain, Indian cricket team

The present Indian captain is one of the greatest batsmen the game has ever produced. His copybook technique and sound temperament have made him one of the most difficult batsmen to dismiss in world cricket. Dravid is the second highest run scorer for India in Tests and third highest in ODIs. He has been very successful while playing away from home and some of his best knocks have been played while on tour.

In October 2005, appointed captain of the one-day side, he began with a thumping 6-1 hammering of Sri Lanka in a home series, and was soon given responsibility of the Test side as well, taking over from the controversy-shrouded Sourav Ganguly. After two disappointing defeats to Pakistan and England, Dravid masterminded a historic series win in the West Indies, the first since 1970-71. His captaincy has received critical acclaim and he hopes to lead India to World Cup glory in 2007.

Rajkumar Hirani

Film director

Born in Nagpur, Rajkumar Hirani completed his diploma in cinema in 1987 from the Film and Television Institute of India at Pune with a specialization in editing. His production house named Canvas Films worked on several popular advertising campaigns, and Hirani also edited *Mission Kashmir* for Vidhu Vinod Chopra, winning the Best Editor Award at the Zee Cine Awards.

Munnabhai MBBS, Rajkumar Hirani's first film as director, made under the Vinod Chopra Films banner, was released in 2003, and made history of sorts. The comedy with a message gained immense popularity and Munna and Circuit became household names across the country. A leading Indian news channel voted it the best comedy ever made in India. The film was remade in three Indian languages and the English language rights have been sold to a major Hollywood studio—the first time that the remake rights of an Indian film have been acquired by Hollywood.

Lage Raho Munnabhai, Hirani's sequel to *Munnabhai MBBS*, released in 2006, made history yet again by making 'Gandhigiri' a catchword, and by making Mahatma Gandhi's philosophies of truth and non-violence relevant to and fashionable for the new generation.

Rajnath Singh

born 1951

President, Bharatiya Janata Party

Rajnath Singh has been associated with the RSS from 1964, and served it in various capacities. During the Emergency, he spent ten months in prison, and subsequently got elected as MLA from the Mirzapur constituency in the 1977 UP Assembly elections. In the next few years, he was appointed as the state BJP Secretary in Uttar Pradesh, became a Member of the BJP's National Executive, and in 1990, served as BJP's state Vice President in UP.

In 1991, he was the education minister in the first BJP government in UP and established the Anti-copying Act, included vedic mathematics in syllabi and revised the history textbooks. He served as the UP BJP president in 1997 and in 2003 became Union Minister of Agriculture and subsequently for Food Processing. During this period he initiated some significant projects like the Kisan Call Centre and the Farm Income Insurance Scheme.

After the NDA went out of power in 2004, Rajnath Singh returned to party politics and replaced L.K. Advani as BJP party president on 2 January 2006. As head of India's leading Opposition party, he has an acute influence on Indian politics.

Ram Gopal Varma

born 1962

Film director and producer

One of India's leading film directors today, Ram Gopal Varma dropped out from Siddhartha Engineering College in Vijayawada before beginning his career as a video storeowner. Varma started his film career in Telugu cinema and made a huge mark with his debut film *Shiva* (1990). Soon he started his own production banner Varma Corporation Limited, which produced Telugu films. His first huge success in Hindi cinema came with the 1995 commercial blockbuster *Rangeela*, and in 1998 he released the groundbreaking *Satya*, a crime epic set in the Mumbai underworld, followed in 2002 by the acclaimed *Company*. He has directed several other cutting-edge films like *Bhoot*, *Naach* and *Sarkar*, and his production house has enabled a number of bright young directors to make 'different' films.

A maverick producer-director who is not afraid to court controversy and has always been outspoken about his views, Ram Gopal Varma is now remaking *Sholay*, set in Mumbai. His films continue to explore techniques and territories new to Indian cinema.

Ratan Naval Tata

born 1937

Chairman, Tata Group

Ratan Tata received a degree in Architecture and Structural Engineering from Cornell University and completed an advanced management programme from Harvard University, after which he joined the family business in 1962, taking over as Group Chairman in 1991.

Today, the Tata Group has the largest market capitalization in the Indian share market (over Rs 200,000 crore). Tata Tea is the world's largest integrated tea company, TCS is Asia's largest software company, and Tata Steel is India's second largest steel producer. The indigenously produced Tata Indica, Ratan Tata's brainchild, has been immensely successful. Tata Sons is also the country's largest private sector employer with over 220,000 employees.

Ratan Tata has pumped more than Rs 4,500 crore into acquisitions since 2002. Tata Steel recently made news by buying the British steel firm Corus.

The Government of India honoured Ratan Tata with the Padma Bhushan in 2000. He is a member of the central board of the Reserve Bank of India and of the Prime Minister's Council on Trade and Industry. His future plans include the development and introduction of a car that would be marketed for just Rs 1 lakh.

Ratan Tata has been defining Indian industry and building the Indian economy for decades, and will continue to do so in the future.

Romila Thapar

born 1931

Historian

One of the world's most eminent Marxist historians, Romila Thapar studied Literature at Punjab University and then went to the School of Oriental and African Studies in London to read History. She received her doctorate degree in 1958. Before her appointment as Professor of Ancient Indian History in the Centre for Historical Studies at Jawaharlal Nehru University (1970-91), where she is now Emeritus Professor of History, Romila Thapar was lecturer at the University of London, and a reader in Ancient Indian History at the University of Delhi.

Thapar's *History of India*, first published in 1966, has been in print ever since. She is the author of several other major works on Indian history. She has twice refused the Padma Bhushan (on the principle that she does not accept state awards). In 2004 the US Library of Congress appointed her as the first holder of the Kluge Chair in Countries and Cultures of the South. In 2006, she actively supported Michael Witzel of Harvard in the Californian Hindu textbook controversy.

Romila Thapar has pioneered the exploration of early Indian cultural history in its interconnections with social and economic history, and of Indian historiography. She has written extensively on the need for defending scholarly interpretations of the Indian past, given the national and ethnic demands of the present.

Sachin Tendulkar

born 1973

Cricketer

A natural and breathtaking talent, Sachin Tendulkar is one of the greatest players ever to grace the cricket field. His brilliant technique has earned accolades from cricketers and journalists across the world including Sir Don Bradman. He is the highest run-getter in ODIs and the leading centurion in both forms of the game, and has scored hundreds against every Test playing nation. His intelligent bowling has also been an advantage to Indian cricket and pulled the team out of trouble in times of need.

Sachin Tendulkar has been an icon for the nation for more than a decade now. His endorsement deals have been record-breaking as well. He recently signed a new three-year marketing deal with Iconix reportedly worth around US$ 40 million.

Recovering from injury—after many had written him off—and returning to play his majestic cover drives and straight drives once again, Sachin Tendulkar continues to be the country's most adored citizen.

Sam Pitroda

born 1942

Chairman and CEO, WorldTel Ltd

Sam Pitroda did his Masters in physics and electronics in Baroda and then went to the US and did his Masters in electrical engineering from the Illinois Institute of Technology in Chicago. He worked in GTE, Chicago and founded Wescom Switching. He returned to India and founded the Centre for Development of Telematics in 1984. In 1987 he became Chief Technology Advisor to the Prime Minister of India and in 1989 was elected the first chairman of India's Telecom Commission.

Sam Pitroda is considered to have been largely responsible for India's communications revolution. In 1995, he founded WorldTel—a global organization backed by the ITU—to help develop telecom infrastructure in less developed countries. He is a recipient of India's National Citizen's Award for work on telecom from the Prime Minister of India, the IIT Alumni Medal and the International Distinguished Leadership Award. He is also the chairman of India's National Knowledge Commission.

Along with being a pioneer in telecom, Sam Pitroda has made a strong case for food, clean water, and adequate shelter for the underprivileged sections of society.

Samir Jain

Vice-Chairman, the Times of India

Samir Jain joined Bennett & Coleman in 1984. In the 1990s, he took the *Times of India* to new heights: in his attempt to break the near monopoly enjoyed by *Hindustan Times* in the Delhi and northern region, he launched a price war and offered special rates for taking out ads in combined editions and publications across the Bennett & Coleman stable. He succeeded in rapidly expanding the newspaper's circulation in Delhi, and extended this strategy with success to Bangalore, Hyderabad and elsewhere.

The Times Group listed Entertainment Network India, a radio broadcasting arm that operates the very popular Radio Mirchi, as an IPO, and in 2006 launched Times Now, a television news channel, in a joint venture with Reuters.

One of India's media barons, Samir Jain is one of the individuals who determines how news is packaged and presented to millions of Indians.

Sania Mirza

born 1986

Tennis player

C.G. Krishna Bhupathi, Mahesh Bhupathi's father, was Sania Mirza's coach when she started playing lawn tennis at the age of six. Sania turned professional in 2003 and won the Wimbledon Championships Girls' Doubles title, teaming up with Alisa

Kleybanova of Russia. She became the first and till date the only Indian woman to reach the fourth round of a Grand Slam tournament at the 2005 US Open. She is the first Indian to get into the Top 50 WTA rankings and is presently the highest ranked female tennis player ever from India (she had a rank of 31, her highest ever, in mid-October 2005). She is also the first Indian sportswoman to feature on the cover of *Time* magazine (South Asian edition) and was included in its 2005 list of Asia's 50 heroes. She won the Arjuna award in 2004 and in 2006 was honoured with a Padma Shri.

Making an impression in the international sporting arena where Indians and especially Indian women are hardly represented, Sania Mirza is an inspiration to millions of fans, and a youth icon.

Sanjeev Kapoor

born 1964

Chef

Sanjeev Kapoor is the host of *Khana Khazana,* a popular cookery programme shown on Zee TV since 1993, and author of several cookbooks. A line of branded products and franchise restaurants in India and abroad are named after him. He started his professional career in the ITDC under their kitchen management scheme. After working in many hotels, he became the Executive Chef of the Centaur Hotel in Mumbai. He won the Best Cookery Show award given by the Indian Television Academy (ITA) in 2001, and also received the Best Executive Chef of India Award from H&FS and the Mercury Gold Award from IFCA.

The man who made cooking fashionable on Indian television and in high-end kitchens, Sanjeev Kapoor has recently launched a multimedia CD-ROM on Indian foods. He has contributed substantially to making Indian cuisine one of the favoured cuisines across the world.

Sharad Pawar

born 1940

Union Minister

A former member of Indian National Congress who was expelled from the party for raising the question of the foreign origin of Sonia Gandhi, Sharad Pawar is the president of the Nationalist Congress Party formed by him in 1999. He entered the Maharashtra Legislative Assembly for the first time in 1967 and served as chief minister of Maharashtra four times. He was appointed the Union Defence Minister in 1991. After the 2004 Lok Sabha elections, he joined the UPA government as minister for Agriculture and Food. So far, he has been elected to six Lok Sabhas and has served on several parliamentary committees as member. In 2005, he was elected president of the Board of Control for Cricket in India (BCCI).

One of India's seniormost politicians, Sharad Pawar plays an important role in shaping the country's policy-making.

Sheila Dikshit

born 1938

Chief Minister, Delhi

Sheila Dikshit received her MA degree from Delhi University. During the period between 1984 and 1989, she served as a Lok Sabha MP. She was a Union Minister during 1986-1989, first as the Minister of State for Parliamentary Affairs and later as a Minister of State in the Prime Minister's Office. She is also the Secretary of the Indira Gandhi Memorial Trust.

Sheila Dikshit has championed the cause of women at various forums and also led movements for granting of equal rights to women. She represented India on the UN Commission on Status of Women for five years (1984-89).

Since 1998, when the Congress came to power in the national capital, Sheila Dikshit has been chief minister of Delhi and has overseen Delhi's transformation to a cleaner, greener city.

Shekhar Gupta
Editor-in-Chief, Indian Express

Shekhar Gupta began his career as a reporter with the *Indian Express* in 1977. He joined *India Today*, India's premier newsmagazine, in 1983. In 1995 he left to join the *Indian Express* as its Executive Editor.

Shekhar Gupta has reported from regions of conflicts in India and has written extensively on contemporary South Asian politics and security. He uncovered LTTE training camps in India, and nailed the lie of official intelligence agencies in a spy scandal. Seven years before 9/11, he travelled across Afghanistan, Pakistan, Germany, the US and the UK to report extensively on the threat from Islamic fundamentalism, and its links with Osama bin Laden. He has also worked as a Research Associate at the International Institute of Strategic Studies (IISS).

Shekhar Gupta writes a weekly column in the *Indian Express*, and has an interview programme, 'Walk the Talk', on NDTV.

One of India's leading journalists and editors, Shekhar Gupta continues to shape public opinion through reportage and analysis.

Shreeram Shankar Abhyankar
born 1930
Mathematician

A mathematician known for his contributions to singularity theory, S.S. Abhyankar's name is associated with Abhyankar's conjecture of finite group theory. He earned his BSc in Bombay in 1951, his Masters at Harvard in 1952, and his PhD at Harvard in 1955. He is Marshall Distinguished Professor of Mathematics and Professor of Computer Science and Industrial Engineering at Purdue University, Indiana, USA.

Professor Abhyankar is a fellow of the Indian Academy of Science and an editorial board member of the *Indian Journal of Pure and Applied Mathematics*. He has won numerous awards and honours. His current research is in the area of computational geometry (the study of algorithms to solve problems stated in terms of geometry) and algorithmic algebraic geometry.

S.S. Abhyankar is one of the leading Indian academicians of international repute.

Shobhana Bhartia
Vice Chairperson, Hindustan Times Media Ltd

The daughter of K.K. Birla, one of India's most well-known industrialists, Shobhana Bhartia is an alumnus of Loreto House and Loreto College, and joined the *Hindustan Times* in 1986. In the fight with the *Times of India* over circluation primacy, she launched the Mumbai edition of the HT, and diversified into FM radio. A television channel is also on the cards.

Shobhana Bhartia is the chairperson of the Press Trust of India and deputy chairperson of the Executive Committee, Audit Bureau of Circulations. She is a member of the Executive Committee, the Indian Newspaper Society and Commonwealth Press Union, London, and a member of the Board of Governors of NIFT. The World Economic Forum in Davos, Switzerland named her the Global Leader of Tomorrow in 1996. She is a recipient of the Padma Shri and in 2006 was nominated to the Rajya Sabha.

Shobhana Bhartia is the first woman chief of a national newspaper in India and contributes substantially to shaping public opinion in the country.

Somnath Chatterjee
born 1929
Speaker of the Lok Sabha

An eminent parliamentarian, Somanth Chatterjee has an MA (Cantab) and Barrister-at-Law degree from Middle Temple in the UK. He started his professional career as a barrister at the Calcutta High Court. He became a member of Communist Party of India

(Marxist) in 1968 and a Lok Sabha MP for the first time in 1971. Since then, he has been elected to ten Lok Sabhas.

From 1989 to 2004, when he became the Speaker, Somnath Chatterjee was leader of the parliamentary party of the CPI(M). He has served several parliamentary committees, both as chairman and as member. From 1999 to 2004, he was chairman of the West Bengal Industrial Development Corporation and was also actively involved in other state government projects.

One of India's most experienced parliamentarians, Somnath Chatterjee now presides over the country's apex policy-making chamber.

Sonia Gandhi

born 1946

President, Indian National Congress

The Italian-born wife of former prime minister Rajiv Gandhi, whose Italian origin embroiled her in controversy, became a full-fledged Indian citizen in 1984 after the death of Indira Gandhi. In 1991, following Rajiv Gandhi's death, Congress leaders entreated her to take over the party's leadership and become its candidate for prime minister, but she refused. Sonia Gandhi became a primary member of Congress a few months before the Calcutta Congress Plenary Session in August 1997. She became Congress president in 1998 and was elected to parliament in 1999, where she became leader of the Opposition. In 2004, after the Congress's success in the general elections, she was offered the prime ministership, which she declined in favour of Dr Manmohan Singh, retaining the post of the Leader of the Majority and the Chairperson of Congress Parliamentary Party. She is also the chairperson of the coordinating committee of the ruling United Progressive Alliance.

In 2006, she had to resign from the Lok Sabha for holding an office of profit, being the chairperson of the National Advisory Council. She was re-elected from her constituency Rae Bareli in May 2006.

Sonia Gandhi was named the third most powerful woman in the world by *Forbes* magazine in 2004. She has demonstrated an astute political acumen, staying out of executive power and choosing to concentrate on strengthening the Congress party and the ruling coalition.

Sri Sri Ravi Shankar

born 1956

Spiritual leader

Founder of the International Art of Living Foundation, Sri Sri Ravi Shankar has been the driving force behind numerous charitable organizations such as the International Association for Human Values and 5H. He travels to more than thirty-five countries every year to reinforce the message that all religions and the great spiritual traditions share common goals and values. He is the recipient of numerous honours including the Dara Shikoh National Award for Harmony 2005 given by the Inter Faith Harmony Foundation of India, the 2005 Global Humanitarian Award given by the state of Illinois, the Guru Mahatmya award of the government of Maharashtra, and the title of Yoga Shiromani (Supreme Jewel of Yoga) awarded by the President of India. He was also a contender for the Nobel Peace Prize in 2006.

Redefining spiritual traditions and techniques through his Art of Living programme, Sri Sri Ravi Shankar is one of the world's leading spiritual leaders and well-being proponents.

Subhash Chandra

born 1950

Chairman, Zee Telefilms Ltd

Subhash Chandra stopped studying after high school and at the age of nineteen started his own vegetable oil unit which, within the span of a few years, showed a turnover of US$ 2.5 million. A visit to a packaging exhibition in

1981 resulted in the formation of the innovative Essel Packaging Limited. Other visits to amusement parks abroad encouraged him to establish Asia's largest amusement park in India—EsselWorld in Mumbai.

In October 1992 he started Zee TV which was one of the first private satellite television channels in India. Zee was recognized as the 'Emerging Company of the Year' by the *Economic Times* in 1998 and Subhash Chandra himself was awarded the 'Entrepreneur of the Year' award by Ernst & Young and 'Businessman of the Year' by *Business Standard* in 1999. Zee TV still commands a big slice of the television ratings, and the Essel Group of Companies has also entered the newspaper market with *DNA*.

Subhash Chandra has made his mark as an influential philanthropist in India setting up TALEEM (Transnational Alternate Learning for Emancipation and Empowerment through Multimedia). He is also a trustee for the Global Vippassana Foundation, set up for guiding people towards spiritual fulfilment.

One of India's media barons, Subhash Chandra continues to define the parameters of information and entertainment in the country.

Subramaniam Ramadorai

born 1944

CEO and Managing Director, Tata Consultancy Services Ltd

An alumnus of the University of Delhi, IIS Bangalore and the University of California at Los Angeles, S. Ramadorai joined TCS in 1972 as a programmer and took over as the CEO and Managing Director in 1996. He is a member of the board of directors of Hindustan Lever, Nicholas Piramal, Tata Industries and several other companies. He has received the Distinguished Achievement Award from IIS Bangalore, and a fellowship from the Institute of Management Consultants of India. He is the winner of the CNBC Asia-Pacific's prestigious Asia Business Leader of the Year award as well as the Management Man of the Year award.

S. Ramadorai is at the forefront of India's burgeoning IT industry.

Sunil Mittal

born 1957

Chairman and Managing Director, Bharti Group

Son of a parliamentarian, Sunil Mittal joined Harvard Business School after graduating from Punjab University. He has risen from humble beginnings in the 1970s as a bicycle parts dealer, forming the Bharti Cellular Limited (BCL) in 1995 to offer cellular services under the brand name Airtel. In 2001, the company entered into a joint venture with Singapore Telecom International for a $650-million submarine cable project, the country's first ever undersea cable link connecting Chennai and Singapore. Bharti Tele-Ventures is now India's leading provider of telecommunications services, with over 17 million mobile subscribers and a presence in all twenty-three mobile phone circles in the country.

Sunil Mittal is estimated to be the third richest man in the country. He is a member of the National Council of Confederation of Indian Industry (CII) and the Federation of Indian Chambers of Commerce & Industry (FICCI), Chairman, Indo-US Joint Business Council, and a member of the Advisory Committee constituted by the Ministry of IT. Not content with being a telecom tycoon, he is giving shape to a new thrust to non-telecom businesses such as agriculture, insurance and airport infrastructure.

If one man could be credited with revolutionizing personal communication in India, it would be Sunil Mittal.

Swami Ramdev

Yoga specialist

Born at Alipur in Haryana, Swami Ramdev is known for his relentless efforts to popularize Yoga. He established the Divya Yoga Mandir Trust in 1995, along with Acharya Karamveer and Acharya Balkrishna. He has devised a set of six simple Pranayama or breathing exercises. Viewers of his TV show and attendees at his camp have reported significant improvements in their health. He also founded the Patanjali Yogpeeth Trust.

Initiated into the ascetic order of Swami Shankerdevji Maharaj, Swami Ramdev teaches that God resides in every human being and that the body is God's temple. He is a firm believer in the concept of *Vasudaiv kutambakam* (the world is one family).

Swami Ramdev's practical approach to Yoga has won him thousands of admirers throughout India and made him a living symbol of Indian culture.

Valmik Thapar

born 1952

Wildlife conservationist

Valmik Thapar is one of India's foremost chroniclers of natural history and the Executive Director of the Ranthambhore Foundation, which he started in 1987. He graduated from Delhi University in Anthropology. He has produced and directed several films including *Tiger Crisis*, *Land of the Tiger*, *Tigers' Fortress*, *Danger in Tiger Paradise* and *Search for Tigers* for the international media such as the BBC, Animal Planet, Discovery and National Geographic, and has authored a number of books, chiefly on India's national animal. His organization is devoted to maintaining the ecological balance necessary for man to live in harmony with nature.

Having made some extraordinary discoveries about the tiger, Valmik Thapar has been the country's most passionate crusader against poaching, and is committed, as a member of the Tiger Task Force, to bringing the tiger back in numbers.

Venugopal Dhoot

born 1951

CEO and Managing Director, Videocon Electronics

Venugopal Dhoot graduated in Electrical Engineering from Pune Engineering College. Videocon has established itself as 'the Indian multinational'—it is India's largest television and washing machine maker. To strengthen and maintain its leadership status, the Videocon group has clearly charted out its course for the future which involves aggressive R&D. The group also plans a significant involvement in the oil and gas business.

Dhoot is the chairman of the FICCI Consumer Goods Committee and president of the Electronic Industries Association of Marathwada. He is an adviser to the government of Orissa for industrial development in the state.

A true blue Indian industrialist, Venugopal Dhoot has impacted the consumer durables market in a significant way.

Vijay Mallya

born 1955

Chairman, United Beverages Group

Son of the famous industrialist Vittal Mallya, Vijay Mallya took over as chairman of the UB Group in 1983 and grew it into a multinational conglomerate of over sixty companies. The $2 billion United Beverages is now the world's second largest liquor company.

Mallya has also started a domestic airline in India called Kingfisher Airlines. He is on the board of several public companies in India and abroad and has received several awards both in India and overseas, the most notable being the Sir M. Visvesvaraya Memorial Award in 2001 from the Federation of Karnataka Chambers of Commerce and Industry. He was conferred a Doctorate in Philosophy in Business Administration by the University of Southern California and nominated as a Global

Leader for Tomorrow by the Geneva-based World Economic Forum. He owns a personal Boeing, as well as a yacht that once belonged to Elizabeth Taylor, and bought several priceless items related to former Mysore ruler Tipu Sultan. He is also a member of the Rajya Sabha.

One of the country's foremost businessmen, Vijay Mallya is also a proponent of the new-gen ethic of working hard and living well.

Vikram Chandra

born 1961

Writer

Vikram Chandra's first novel *Red Earth and Pouring Rain* (1995) won the David Higham Prize for Fiction and the 1996 Commonwealth Writers Prize for Best First Book. His *Love and Longing in Bombay* (1997), a collection of short stories, won the Commonwealth Writers Prize for Best Book (Eurasia region). His latest novel *Sacred Games* (2006) is set in the Mumbai underworld. Vikram Chandra is also a teacher of creative writing at University of California, Berkeley.

With *Sacred Games* Vikram Chandra achieved what many thought impossible—his is perhaps the best book on Mumbai yet, and it's a best-selling thousand-page literary thriller. He seems to have upturned every convention on its head, and emerged a clear winner.

Vikram Seth

born 1952

Writer

Vikram Seth received his early education from Doon School and then left India to study at Oxford University where he earned a degree in philosophy, politics, and economics. He enrolled, but left incomplete his PhD in Economics at Stanford University. After that he studied classical Chinese poetry at Nanjing University. In 1986, Vikram Seth published his first novel *The Golden Gate*, set in San Francisco and written in verse. *A Suitable Boy* (1993), his 1349-page epic, won the W.H. Smith Literary Award and the Commonwealth Writers Prize. His third novel *An Equal Music* was published in 1999. He has also published a travelogue, *From Heaven Lake: Travels Through Sinkiang and Tibet*, which won the Thomas Cook Travel Book Award, and several volumes of poetry. His latest work is *Two Lives*, a family memoir, published in 2005. For his contribution to literature, Vikram Seth received the award of the Commander of the Order of the British Empire in February 2001.

Writing in different genres, Vikram Seth has made his distinctive authorial voice heard over the last twenty years. In 2006 he came out in support of gay rights, marking the first major intervention by an Indian in this area.

Vir Sanghvi

born 1955

Editorial Director, Hindustan Times

Vir Sanghvi started writing for *India Today* in 1976, when he was a student at Oxford University. In 1978, at twenty-two, he became the founder editor of *Bombay* magazine. Subsequently he was editor of *Imprint* and *Sunday* magazines. Sanghvi became the consulting editor for Ananda Bazaar Patrika group in 1997. From 1999 to 2004 he was editor of *Hindustan Times*. Apart from his editorials and articles, Sanghvi writes a popular column on food, and hosts the television show 'Face the Music'. The World Economic Forum in Davos named Sanghvi 'Global Leader of Tomorrow'.

One of India's best-known journalists and television anchors, Vir Sanghvi is instrumental in shaping public opinion across the country.

Yogi Deveshwar

born 1947

Chairman, ITC Ltd

An engineering graduate from IIT, Delhi, Yogi Deveshwar joined ITC in 1968.

He joined the board in 1984, taking charge of Welcomgroup as its chairman. In 1991 he took over as chairman of the tobacco division. Deveshwar transformed the largest tobacco company in India into an FMCG major, with only 60 per cent of his company's earnings coming from the sale of cigarettes. He is also the chairman of Surya Nepal Pvt Ltd and is a director on the Board of International Travel House Limited.

He has also served as the chairman and managing director of Air-India, and was a member on the board of Indian Airlines, International Airports Authority of India, Airports Authority of India and Air Mauritius Ltd. He is the chairman of the Board of Governors of IIM Calcutta and has also been the president of CII. He received the Meridien Hotelier of the Year Award and the Marketing Man of the Year from A&M. Ernst & Young has also honoured Deveshwar with the Manager Entrepreneur of the Year Award in 2001.

The head of one of India's corporate giants, Deveshwar is a businessman with remarkable vision.

Cover Story: Sixty Years of Indian Independence

The Fall of a Dynasty, Delhi, 1857

William Dalrymple

At 4 p.m. on a hazy, humid winter's afternoon in Rangoon in November 1862, soon after the end of the monsoon, a shrouded corpse was escorted by a small group of British soldiers to an anonymous grave at the back of a walled prison enclosure.

This enclosure lay overlooking the muddy brown waters of the Rangoon river, a little downhill from the great gilt spire of the Shwe Dagon pagoda. Around the enclosure lay the newly constructed cantonment area of the port—an anchorage and pilgrimage town that had been seized, burned and occupied by the British only ten years earlier. The bier of the State Prisoner—as the deceased was referred to—was accompanied by two of his sons and an elderly, bearded mullah. No women were allowed to attend, and a small crowd from the bazaar who had somehow heard about the prisoner's death were kept away by armed guards. Nevertheless, one or two managed to break through the cordon to touch the shroud before it was lowered into the grave.

The ceremony was brief. The British authorities had made sure not only that the grave was already dug, but that quantities of lime were on hand to guarantee the rapid decay of both bier and body. When the shortened funeral prayers had been recited—no lamentations or panegyrics were allowed—the earth was thrown in over the lime, and the turf carefully replaced so that within a month or so no mark would remain to indicate the place of burial. A week later the British Commissioner, Captain H.N. Davies, wrote to London to report what had passed, adding:

> Have since visited the remaining State Prisoners—the very scum of the reduced Asiatic harem; found all correct. None of the family appear much affected by the death of the bed-ridden old man. His death was evidently due to pure decrepitude and paralysis in the region of the throat. He expired at 5 o'clock on the morning of the funeral. The death of the ex-King may be said to have had no effect on the Mahomedan part of the populace of Rangoon, except perhaps for a few fanatics who watch and pray for the final triumph of Islam. A bamboo fence surrounds the grave for some considerable distance, and by the time the fence is worn out, the grass will again have properly covered the spot, and no vestige will remain to distinguish where the last of the Great Moghuls rests.

The State Prisoner Davies referred to was more properly known as Bahadur Shah II, known from his pen-name as Zafar, meaning 'Victory'. Zafar was the last Mughal Emperor, and the direct descendant of Genghis Khan and Timur, of

Akbar, Jahangir and Shah Jahan. He was born in 1775, when the British were still a relatively modest and mainly coastal power in India, looking inwards from three enclaves on the Indian shore. In his lifetime he had seen his own dynasty reduced to humiliating insignificance, while the British transformed themselves from vulnerable traders into an aggressively expansionist military force.

Zafar came late to the throne, succeeding his father only in his mid-sixties, when it was already impossible to reverse the political decline of the Mughals. But despite this he succeeded in creating around him in Delhi a court of great brilliance. Personally, he was one of the most talented, tolerant and likeable of his dynasty: a skilled calligrapher, a profound writer on Sufism, a discriminating patron of painters of miniatures, an inspired creator of gardens and an amateur architect. Most importantly he was a very serious mystical poet, who wrote not only in Urdu and Persian but Braj Basha and Punjabi, and partly through his patronage there took place arguably the greatest literary renaissance in modern Indian history. Himself a ghazal writer of great charm and accomplishment, Zafar provided a showcase for the talents of India's greatest lyric poet, Ghalib, and his rival Zauq—the Mughal Poet Laureate, and the Salieri to Ghalib's Mozart.

While the British progressively took over more and more of the Mughal Emperor's power, removing his name from the coins, seizing complete control even of the city of Delhi itself, and finally laying plans to remove the Mughals altogether from the Red Fort, the court busied itself in the obsessive pursuit of the most cleverly turned ghazal, the most perfect Urdu couplet. As the political sky darkened, the court was lost in a last idyll of pleasure gardens, courtesans and *mushairas*, or poetic symposia, Sufi devotions and visits to pirs, as literary and religious ambition replaced the political variety.

The most closely focused record of the Red Fort at this period is the court diary kept by a news writer for the British Resident, now in the National Archives of India, which contains a detailed day-by-day picture of Zafar's life. The Last Emperor appears as a benign old man with impeccable manners—even when treated with extreme rudeness by the British. Daily he has olive oil rubbed into his feet to soothe his aches; occasionally he rouses himself to visit a garden, go on a hunting expedition or host a *mushaira*. Evenings were spent 'enjoying the moonlight', listening to singers or eating fresh mangoes. All the while the aged emperor tries to contain the infidelities of his young concubines, one of whom becomes pregnant by the most distinguished of the court musicians.

Then, on a May morning in 1857, three hundred mutinous sepoys and cavalrymen from Meerut rode into Delhi, massacred every Christian man, woman and child they could find in the city, and declared Zafar to be their leader and emperor. Zafar was no friend of the British, who had shorn him of his patrimony, and subjected him to almost daily humiliation. Yet Zafar was not a natural insurgent either. It was with severe misgivings and little choice that he found himself made the nominal leader of an Uprising that he strongly suspected from the start was doomed: a chaotic and officerless army of unpaid peasant soldiers set against the forces of the world's greatest military power, albeit one that had just lost the great majority of the Indian recruits to its Bengal Army.

The great Mughal capital, caught in the middle of a remarkable cultural flowering, was turned overnight into a battleground. No foreign army was in a position to intervene to support the rebels, and they had limited ammunition, no money and few supplies. The chaos and anarchy that erupted in the countryside proved far more effective at blockading Delhi than the efforts at besieging the city attempted by the British from their perch on the Ridge. The price of food escalated and supplies rapidly dwindled. Soon both the people of Delhi and the sepoys were on the edge of starvation.

The siege of Delhi was the Raj's Stalingrad: a fight to the death between two powers, neither of whom could retreat. There were unimaginable casualties, and on both sides the combatants were driven to the limits of physical and mental endurance. Finally, on 14 September 1857, the British and their hastily assembled army of Sikh and Pathan levees assaulted and took the city, sacking and looting the Mughal capital, and massacring great swathes of the population. In one *muhalla* alone, Kucha Chelan, some 1,400 citizens of Delhi were cut down. 'The orders went out to shoot every soul,' recorded Edward Vibart, a nineteen-year-old British officer.

> It was literally murder ... I have seen many bloody and awful sights lately but such a one as I witnessed yesterday I pray I never see again. The women were all spared but their screams, on seeing their husbands and sons butchered, were most painful ... Heaven knows I feel no pity, but when some old grey bearded man is brought and shot before your very eyes, hard must be that man's heart I think who can look on with indifference...

Those city dwellers who survived the killing were driven out into the countryside to fend for themselves. Delhi was left an empty ruin. Though the royal family had surrendered peacefully, most of the emperor's sixteen sons were captured, tried and hung, while three were shot in cold blood, having first freely given up their arms, then been told to strip naked: 'In 24 hours I disposed of the principal members of the house of Timur the Tartar,' Captain William Hodson wrote to his sister the following day. 'I am not cruel, but I confess I did enjoy the opportunity of ridding the earth of these wretches.'

Zafar himself was put on show to visitors, displayed 'like a beast in a cage', according to one British officer.' Among his visitors was the *Times* correspondent, William Howard Russell, who was told that the prisoner was the mastermind of the most serious armed act of resistance to Western colonialism. He was a 'dim, wandering eyed, dreamy old man with a feeble hanging nether lip and toothless gums,' wrote Russell.

> Was he, indeed, one who had conceived that vast plan of restoring a great empire, who had fomented the most gigantic mutiny in the history of the world? Not a word came from his lips; in silence he sat day and night with his eyes cast on the ground, and as though utterly oblivious of the conditions in which he was placed ... His eyes had the dull, filmy look of very old age ... Some heard him quoting verses of his own composition, writing poetry on a wall with a burned stick.

Russell was suitably sceptical of the charges being levelled against Zafar: 'He was called ungrateful for rising against his benefactors,' he wrote.

> He was no doubt a weak and cruel old man; but to talk of ingratitude on the part of one who saw that all the dominions of his ancestors had been gradually taken from him until he was left with an empty title, and more empty exchequer, and a palace full of penniless princesses, is perfectly preposterous...

Nevertheless, the following month Zafar was put on trial in the ruins of his old palace, and sentenced to transportation. He left his beloved Delhi on a bullock cart. Separated from everything he loved, broken-hearted, the last of the Great Mughals died in exile in Rangoon on Friday, 7 November 1862, aged eighty-seven.

With Zafar's departure, there was complete collapse of the fragile court culture he had faithfully nourished and exemplified. As Ghalib noted: 'All these things lasted only so long as the king reigned.' By the time of Zafar's death, much of his palace, the Red Fort, had already been torn down, along with great areas of the Mughal Delhi he loved and beautified. Meanwhile the great majority of its leading inhabitants and courtiers—poets and princes, mullahs and merchants, Sufis and scholars—had been hunted down and hanged, or else dispersed and exiled, many to the Raj's new, specially constructed gulag in the Andaman Islands. Those who were spared were left in humiliating and conspicuous poverty. As Ghalib, one of the few survivors from the old court, lamented, 'The male descendants of the deposed King—such as survived the sword—draw allowances of five rupees a month. The female descendants if old are bawds, and if young, prostitutes.'

> The city has become a desert ... By God, Delhi is no more a city, but a camp, a cantonment. No Fort, no city, no bazaars, no watercourses ... Four things kept Delhi alive—the Fort, the daily crowds at the Jama Masjid, the weekly walk to the Yamuna Bridge, and the yearly fair of the flower-men. None of these survives, so how could Delhi survive? Yes [it is said that] there was once a city of that name in the realm of India...
>
> We smashed the wine cup and the flask;
> What is it now to us
> If all the rain that falls from heaven
> Should turn to rose-red wine?

Assault—with Salt: The Dandi March

Rajmohan Gandhi

How did one coax an aggrieved yet disarmed, heterogeneous and divided populace to wage an assault on a powerful Empire? On 18 January 1930 Tagore called at the ashram and asked Gandhi about his strategy. 'I am furiously thinking night and day,' replied Gandhi, 'and I do not see any light.' However, the Working Committee authorized Gandhi to plan and direct the promised battle. His colleagues had no agreed plan of their own, and in any case they had learnt over the years to respect Gandhi's judgement.

In the middle of February his 'furious' search ended: the intuition came to him 'like a flash' that the assault should be over salt.

Salt? By taxing the manufacture and sale of salt, the government was injuring 'even the starving millions, the sick, the maimed and the utterly helpless'. Nature had gifted salt to India, but Indians could not collect or use it without paying a tax much higher than the cost of removal. All were hurt by the salt law, and all could defy it. Satyagrahis near the coast could defy the law simply by walking to where the salt lay and scooping it up. Indians in the interior could perform satyagraha by buying or selling 'illegal' salt.

Gandhi pictured a march to the sea by his ashramite army, with himself at the head, if the British did not arrest him earlier. The defiance would provide striking scenes, exert maximum pressure with the minimum risk of violence, and would be hard for the British to crush: could they police the entire coastline? Gandhi thought that satyagraha could spread quickly from the ashramites to the general public, as had happened sixteen years earlier in South Africa.

In the climate of 1930, the salt tax held another virtue for Gandhi: all could jointly oppose it, Hindus and Muslims, peasants and the landless. The poor needed salt more than the rich, who got it from all their foods. As Gandhi put it:

> Next to air and water, salt is perhaps the greatest necessity of life. It is the only condiment of the poor. Cattle cannot live without salt. Salt is a necessary article in many manufactures. It is also a rich manure.

Moreover, unlike defiance over land revenue, a salt defiance would not cost peasants their land or cattle. The British had indeed yielded over land revenue in Bardoli, but that was because the Bardoli satyagraha had been carefully disconnected from any campaigns for Swaraj. Now Swaraj was the central goal, and the British would not be merciful. Looking for a fight that would not ruin participants, Gandhi picked on salt.

It had long been germinating in his mind. Almost forty years earlier, as a student in London in 1891, he had spoken of 'salt, a heavily taxed article'. In 1909 his *Hind Swaraj* had referred to it; and he had mentioned it on numerous other occasions. It was a question, moreover, that Naoroji and, later, Gokhale had raised. Thanks to the salt tax—the simplest and most regressive form of taxing every Indian, including the poorest—British salt was easy to sell in India, and the government of India obtained two per cent of its revenue.

Also, salt was a powerful emblem, featuring in proverb, scripture and everyday speech, and the only inorganic thing that all humans ate. It preserved, disinfected, embalmed.

Clarity about salt changed Gandhi. Thereafter, an observer thought, Gandhi spoke at ashram prayer-meetings with 'a peculiar glow in his look and voice, as of one pregnant with inspired inner thought and prayer'.

For several days he kept the idea to himself and some close colleagues. Confidentiality was essential for preparation and also for preventing premature arrests. But several associates were informed in February, and asked to select a route for the march and its destination on the shore, where salt would be illegally collected.

In the last week of February Gandhi spelt out guidelines for a satyagraha without mentioning that it would be over salt. And in a letter to the Viceroy written on 2 March (but not made public for a week or so) he listed the removal of the salt tax as one of eleven demands the British would have to concede if they did not want to face satyagraha. After repeating the indictment of a 'four-fold' ruination, he demanded

> 1) Total prohibition, 2) A better rupee/shilling ratio, 3) Halving of land revenue, 4) Abolition of salt tax, 5) Halving of military expenditure, 6) Reduction in official salaries, 7) Tariffs on foreign cloth, 8) Reservation of coastal shipping for Indian ships, 9) Release of political prisoners save those convicted for murder or attempted murder, 10) Abolition of the Criminal Intelligence Department or control over it by elected representatives, and 11) The right of Indians to licensed firearms.

The writer is revealed as a formidable nationalist far removed from the image of an ascetic plying his spinning wheel. This ahimsa advocate is not willing to give up any Indian right, not even the right to a gun. Equally, the list reminded Indians that their fight was for more than a pair of words ('complete independence')—it was for a better life for the common Indian.

Addressed to 'Dear Friend', Gandhi's demands were couched in nonviolent language, yet the letter was even stronger than the one sent ten years earlier to Chelmsford. Irwin was reminded, among other things, of the huge salary he was drawing from Indian revenues.

There was no reply from Lord Irwin, but on 12 March Gandhi received a four-line letter from Cunningham, the Viceroy's secretary, stating that Lord Irwin 'regrets to learn that you contemplate a course of action which is clearly bound to involve violation of the law and danger to the public peace'.

On 5 March, from the ashram prayer ground, Gandhi made the first public announcement about the choice of salt. His political colleagues were shocked. Neither Jawaharlal nor his father was impressed, and a displeased Vallabhbhai stayed away from early planning meetings called by Gandhi.

The truth was that in February 1930 no part of India was agitating over the salt tax, which seemed a minor irritant to educated Indians, including many of Gandhi's associates. Indulal Yagnik, for example, spoke dismissively of striking 'the fly of the salt act' with the 'sledge hammer of satyagraha'.

There was chuckling in British and pro-British circles. 'Let Gandhi soon eat his own salt,' was one remark. After Gandhi announced his plan, *The Statesman*, Calcutta's British-owned journal, wrote:

> It is difficult not to laugh, and we imagine that will be the mood of most thinking Indians. There is something almost childishly theatrical in challenging in this way the salt monopoly of the Government.

After reconnoitring southern Gujarat, Mohanlal Pandya and Ravishankar Vyas selected a coastal village in Surat district, Dandi, where waves from the Arabian Sea usually left layers of salt, as the destination for the marchers. Dandi was more than 200 miles south from the ashram and close to Bardoli. Pandya and Vyas also proposed villages and towns in Kheda, Bharuch and Surat districts that the satyagrahis should walk through on their way to Dandi.

Gandhi vetted the list, picking villages where he thought he could (a) draw officials away from the Raj, (b) promote khadi and sanitation, (c) attack untouchability, and (d) advance Hindu-Muslim friendship. But the route and destination were not announced until 9 March.

He was equally particular that only the disciplined and the committed would march. Since they would be defying laws in pursuance of Gandhi's tough letter to the Viceroy, they were bound to invite arrest, perhaps for long terms. Beatings were likely and death could not be ruled out. Fifteen years after its founding, the Satyagraha ashram would show whether it lived up to its name.

Gandhi laid down detailed rules for the marchers. They should be willing to suffer unto death, cause no violence, injury or insult to British rulers or their Indian servants, and refrain from swearing or cursing. They should neither salute nor insult the Union Jack. If a communal fight appeared likely to start, the satyagrahis should intervene and prevent it.

When arrested, they should obey prison rules and not demand special facilities from the authorities or maintenance for dependents from the Congress. But they should refuse to shout slogans like 'victory to the government' or eat food that was unclean or rudely served.

Sensing a strong response from beyond the ashram as well, Gandhi expected an early arrest and left clear instructions for 'When I am Arrested'. Vallabhbhai, whose doubts were short-lived, would lead the marchers in Gandhi's absence.

Once the idea of a salt attack was announced (5 March), the British debated whether to put Gandhi away immediately or when he actually violated the Salt Act. Arresting now would add to his prestige and provoke an instant reaction. It would be cleverer to let his weird plan flop before arresting him. The British assumed, too, that a coastal corner of Kheda district, where Vallabhbhai's fellow Patidars were firm foes of their rule, would be the chosen site.

On 7 March, Vallabhbhai, who was passing through the Kheda village of Ras, was arrested there, to his and Gandhi's surprise. After he had agreed, following pressure from Ras's residents, to address them, officials tailing Patel handed him an order not to speak. By this time thousands had gathered to hear him. When Patel said he would speak to them, he was arrested. Alfred Master, collector of Kheda and the district magistrate, sentenced Patel for three months.

On 8 March Gandhi addressed 50,000 incensed Indians on the banks of the Sabarmati, said that his 'right hand' had been removed, and asked the audience to pledge themselves to 'follow Sardar Vallabhbhai to jail, or win complete independence', but 'only if you have the strength to act upon' the pledge. Thousands raised their hands in affirmation.

On 9 March Gandhi announced that in three days he and more than seventy others would begin a march to the Surat coast and hope to reach there early in April, in time for observing the National Week, as the April 6-13 period had been called from the time of the stir that culminated in Jallianwalla on 13 April 1919.

Gandhi knew he would soon be jailed, and death too was possible. He and the other marchers were stepping out of the ashram for good, to return, if alive, only after India was free. On the evening of 11 March he said:

> Even if the Government allows me to march tomorrow morning, this will be my last speech on the sacred banks of the Sabarmati. Possibly these may be the last words of my life here...
>
> But let there be not a semblance of breach of peace even after all of us have been arrested... Let no one commit a wrong in anger. This is my hope and prayer. I wish these words of mine reached every nook and comer of the land... I shall eagerly await the news that ten batches are ready as soon as my batch is arrested.

After his arrest, he said, Jawaharlal, the Congress president, would advise, but regional commanders were already in place, including Rajagopalachari in the south, Rajendra Prasad in Bihar, J.M. Sen Gupta in Bengal, Ghaffar Khan in the Frontier, Mahadev Desai for Gujarat outside the march route. If the commanders were arrested, the battle would throw up new leaders, Gandhi said.

In the early morning of 12 March, joy and sadness, pride and fear, and prayer songs marked the departure of Gandhi and seventy-eight (or, by another count, eighty) others. All the marchers received garlands and tilak from young girls. Those bidding farewell recalled settings-forth from history and the epics, and many among the tens of thousands who crammed Ahmedabad's streets cried, thinking they were seeing the marchers for the last time.

Kasturba pressed a tilak on Gandhi's forehead and garlanded him with handspun yarn. Kalelkar gave him a bamboo staff. Precisely at 6.30 a.m. the march commenced. All the marchers wore khadi and most donned a simple white khadi cap. Everyone including Gandhi (who did not wear the cap) carried a shoulder-bag containing a bedroll, a change of clothes, a takli for spinning, a diary and a drinking mug. His pocket-watch hanging conspicuously from the waist,

Gandhi, now sixty-one, was the oldest walker of the lot but also the most experienced and indeed among the quickest, though suffering from blisters and fatigue. Throughout the long march of around 220 miles, most of the others struggled to keep up with him.

This marching army was also a moving ashram: its general (or father) required of each marcher that he would daily pray, spin and write into a diary, which Bapu could ask to read. With Gandhi continuing to write numerous letters a day and several articles a week, it was a mobile office as well.

Gandhi also spelt out, ahead of the march, what he expected from a village en route: the simplest food (which the marchers were ready to cook); clean space for sleeping; and 'an enclosed space for the satyagrahis to answer calls of nature'. Arrangements were not left wholly to chance. Eighteen students of Ahmedabad's Gujarat Vidyapith went ahead of the marchers to help hosts organize spaces for cooking, sleeping and praying, and to help dig latrine trenches.

Many places en route gave a hugely enthusiastic response. Some towns (including Nadiad, Borsad, Bharuch and Surat) emptied into 'festooned streets sprinkled against dust' when the marchers passed through, and often there were immense meetings. But a few villages on Gandhi's route were cautious, in part because of his stand over the 'untouchables'. At the village of Dabhan (15 March), Gandhi 'walked straight through the village past the temple and the village square' to the quarters of the 'untouchables', where 'he drew water from the well and bathed', embarrassing but also challenging his high-caste reception committee, who had not expected Gandhi to draw water even from their 'pure' well: a servant should perform that sort of task.

By now Sykes, the Bombay governor, wanted to arrest Gandhi, as did Alfred Master and Master's superior in Ahmedabad, Joseph Garrett, but Irwin and his advisers hesitated. They had been informed that Gandhi's blood pressure was 'dangerous' and his heart 'none too good' and that with the physical and mental load he was carrying he could die before reaching Dandi.

Also, some of his Indian friends, including, it seems, Vithalbhai Patel, the central assembly president, had told Irwin that the salt march, more humorous than dangerous, was bound to invite ridicule. Arresting Gandhi, on the other hand, would not only glorify him; it could trigger widespread unrest.

So on 5 April, twenty-four days after leaving the ashram, Gandhi and his army reached Dandi without being arrested. Admitting that he had been 'wholly unprepared for this exemplary non-interference' from the government, Gandhi credited the policy to 'world opinion which will not tolerate repression' even of 'extreme political agitation' when that agitation remained nonviolent. But he did not think that 'actual breach of the salt laws' would be tolerated by the British.

Journalists from India and beyond had gathered in Dandi. For them Gandhi wrote out a crisp sentence: 'I want world sympathy in this battle of Right against Might.'

Early next morning, on the first day of National Week, Gandhi bathed in the ocean, stepped up to where the salt lay, scooped some of it up with his fingers, straightened himself, and showed what he had collected to the multitude around him. It was neither a large quantity nor very pure—the Raj's police had done its best to clear the spot of clean salt.

Yet the 'unlawful deed' had been done. A satyagraha had been executed, and in the days and weeks that followed, in one form or another, hundreds of thousands emulated it across India. The response was even larger than what

Gandhi had hoped for. As Jawaharlal would later put it, 'It seemed as though a spring had been suddenly released.'

The restraint that Gandhi had imposed on himself and his associates for six years—the retreat into ashrams, the focus on constructive work and on the evil of untouchability—had contributed to the power of the release. After the long self-suppression, satyagraha spread like 'prairie fire' (to use the second metaphor that Jawaharlal employed) from Gandhi and his marchers to India as a whole.

In hundreds of places across India, salt was illegally made, or carried, or sold, or bought. Often the action was en masse. In south Kheda's coastal village of Badalpur, around 20,000 people illegally picked up salt on 13 April, under a full moon. By mid-June there were resignations in over half of Kheda's villages: the district had de-recognized the Raj.

Bengal witnessed a 'spectacular' march, and in the south Rajagopalachari led an army of 100 carefully selected satyagrahis on a 145-mile trek to Vedaranyam on the Bay of Bengal. Those providing food or accommodation to the marchers were harassed and in several cases imprisoned, but the populace supported C.R. On 30 April his marchers were able to defy the law, make salt and invite arrest.

A bigger eruption occurred at India's opposite end, in the far North-West. Offended by the arrest on 23 April of their beloved leader, Ghaffar Khan, hundreds of Khudai Khidmatgars protested in Peshawar, standing up to machine guns, horses and lathis. Ordered to open fire at a crowd of unarmed Pakhtuns in Peshawar's Kissa Khwani Bazar, Indian soldiers of the Raj's Garhwal Rifles disobeyed the order, staging *their* nonviolent revolt. For five days Peshawar belonged to the Khidmatagars, not to the British.

Admitting 'surprise' at 'the dimensions' of the movement, Irwin and his officers curbed the press, banned *Young India* and *Navajivan,* banned the Working Committee and other Congress-affiliated bodies, and decided to rule through ordinances, bypassing the Central Assembly where Indian members, whether Swarajist or liberal, were increasingly sympathetic to the disobedience.

Still leaving Gandhi and his band alone, the British imprisoned many elsewhere while also using physical force to recover illegal salt. Beatings were judged cheaper and more effective than jail terms. Another British tactic was to remove salt from expected sites of attack. Left free in Dandi but denied salt to collect, the original marchers felt frustrated. Some were permitted to go elsewhere to join or ignite defiance, but the majority remained around Gandhi, whose answer to the lull in Dandi was two-fold.

First, he permitted women to join the struggle. Then, he scouted the area around Dandi and came up with his second riposte: a raid on three great salt heaps in a government depot in Dharasana, about twenty-five miles south of Dandi. Towards the end of April he announced at meetings with journalists that he would lead the raid on the depot.

By this time thousands had been arrested across the land, including Jawaharlal, Jamnalal Bajaj, Ravishankar Vyas, Darbar Gopaldas and Mahadev Desai, and two of Gandhi's sons, Ramdas, arrested not far from Dandi, and Devadas, who was taken in Delhi for selling contraband salt. In addition, hundreds had been beaten because they did not let go of the salt in their hands. Peshawar had erupted, and C.R. and his 100 were closing in on Vedaranyam.

The declaration of a raid by Gandhi was reported in Indian, British and American newspapers, and Irwin was bound to arrest the rebel-in-chief. Still, Gandhi wanted to inform the Viceroy directly of his intention. In an improvised hut in Karadi, where he was camping, five miles east of Dandi, Gandhi worked on a letter to Irwin until late on the night of 4 May. Unless the salt tax was removed and private salt-making allowed, he and his companions, Gandhi wrote, would 'set out for Dharasana' and 'demand possession of the Salt Works'.

But Irwin was not waiting for a letter. About forty minutes after midnight, three officers (two British and an Indian), accompanied by between twenty and thirty rifle-carrying Indian policemen, entered the camp, walked quietly past marchers sleeping under stars and mango trees, and stepped inside Gandhi's hut. By now sound asleep, with a marcher and a woman visitor sleeping on the floor on either side of his bedstead, Gandhi was woken up by lights flashed into his face.

'Do you want me?' Gandhi asked, even though he knew the answer. In response to another question, he was informed that his arrest was occurring under Regulation 25 of 1827, which authorized arrest without a trial. A new speech by him from the dock was not what the Raj wanted.

By this time everybody was up in Karadi but prevented by the police from reaching close to Gandhi, who instructed grandson Kanti to prepare a bedroll he could take, and Valji Desai to send to *Young India* the nearly-completed letter for Irwin.

'May I wash and brush my teeth?' Gandhi asked the Raj's officers. He could but should be quick, was the answer. In a few minutes Gandhi was ready, having also picked up a couple of taklis and a bundle of cotton slivers. As Tom Weber, the Salt March's Australian researcher, puts it, it was 'a cool and organized performance for an old man who had had less than two hours' sleep'.

Obtaining the officers' permission, Gandhi asked Pandit Khare to sing *Vaishnava Jana*, the bhajan with which the march had commenced. With head bowed and eyes closed the prisoner heard the song. Then he was removed. Fifty-eight years later, one of the Karadi men present at the arrest would break down while describing the scene .

The marchers had treasured their time with Gandhi, feeling that 'they were something special' to him. 'I felt like a son to him' or 'He was like a father to me' would be general memories, but there was also a feeling of being individually needed by Gandhi, e.g. to take care of his correspondence if Pyarelal was not around, or to assist if Gandhi had a problem with spinning.

Driven in a lorry to a level-crossing a few miles away, Gandhi was transferred there, in darkness, to the Frontier Mail, which made an unscheduled stop on its long journey from the North-West Frontier to Bombay. Some hours later, at 6.40 in the morning of 5 May, the Frontier Mail made another unscheduled halt north of Bombay, just short of Borivli.

Swiftly and quietly, Gandhi was removed to a Buick and driven all the way to Yeravda jail in Poona, a journey of 125 miles, but not before being greeted by two American journalists who had correctly guessed that the Buick and the British soldiers they had noticed around the rail track north of Borivli were meant for Gandhi. He recognized the journalists and gave them, on being asked, a short message for Americans: they should 'study the issues closely and judge them on their merits'.

A doctor accompanied the police party that took Gandhi to Yeravda, where goat's milk was made available for him, and he was allowed to spin and use a sewing machine as well. He expressed appreciation, but others could not help thinking that Gandhi had been arrested under cover of darkness by rulers who feared the multitude, because they took him for a prophet.

As had been arranged, the Muslim jurist, Abbas Tyabji, who was seventy-five and owned a flowing snow-white beard, took over the leadership of the marchers, who were joined also by Jugatram Dave. On the morning of 12 May, after being blessed by Kasturba and Mrs Tyabji, the marchers set off for the Dharasana salt depot. After they had walked a few minutes, several hundred policemen surrounded the marchers and ordered them to turn back. Though some thought that refusal could invite fire, all shouted that they were not turning back.

They were arrested and sentenced: Tyabji for six months' simple, Dave for six months' rigorous, and the rest for three months, except for four adjudged to be minor, who were cautioned and let off, and who promptly joined another party planning to raid Dharasana.

Here the salt heaps were successfully defended by a cordon of ditches and barbed wires and by twenty-six rifle-holding soldiers and about 400 policemen, commanded by six British officers. On 21 May Sarojini Naidu, Manilal Gandhi, Imam Bawazeer and Pyarelal led around 2,500 satyagrahis in an attack that fetched headlines across the world even if no salt was collected.

Successive columns wading through ditches and trying to reach the barbed wires were attacked with iron-tipped lathis. Scores were brutally hit in the head and shoulders but not one raised a hand against the police. The ground where they fell was soon blood-soaked. So were the blankets in which first-aid satyagrahi teams removed the injured to a 'hospital' tent nearby.

Little salt was captured in Dharasana, but, as J.C. Kumarappa claimed in *Young India* (29 May), 'Our primary object was to show the world at large the fangs and claws of the Government in all its ugliness and ferocity. In this we have succeeded beyond measure.' Smaller raids and beatings continued for a few more days, and a Gujarat Congress report would claim that in all 2,699 volunteers were sent into the field, 1,333 wounded, and four died of injuries.

A bigger raid took place in Bombay city on 1 June, targeting salt pans in Wadala. Around 15,000 assembled in support, and a number, including women and children, 'splashed through slime and mud to reach the salt pans'. This time a large quantity of salt was collected. There were lathi charges on the crowd, the infantry too was called, and numerous arrests made, but Bombay was experiencing a sense of independence.

In Delhi, Harry Haig, home secretary to the Government of India, privately conceded that the Congress seemed to run the streets of Bombay, noting that the numbers and discipline involved in Congress marches and 'the brushing aside' of police control of traffic 'have combined to produce a vivid impression of the power and success of the Congress movement'.

Elsewhere, too, the Raj's prestige slipped, if not as dramatically. It slipped despite bans on several units of the Congress, despite large-scale arrests, and despite ten ordinances that Irwin promulgated between mid-April and mid-December, exercising an 'arbitrary rule... wielded by no previous Viceroy'.

When Jawaharlal was arrested, his father became acting president of the Congress. When, in June, he too was arrested, Motilal Nehru named Vallabhbhai Patel, whose release came at the end of June, to the chair. By this time even Malaviya, always wary of confrontation, had resigned from the Central Assembly. On his request, Vallabhbhai nominated Malaviya to the Congress's illegal Working Committee. At the end of July, Vallabhbhai, Malaviya, and several others were arrested in Bombay for refusing an order to disperse. Released but rearrested in

December 1930, Patel named Rajendra Prasad to succeed him as acting Congress president.

About 90,000 Indians were arrested for defying laws during the 1930 movement. Except in the Frontier province, the proportion of Muslims courting arrest was, however, small, and Sikhs too seemed to stay away from the fight. Nonetheless 'unlawful' salt was collected, moved, sold or bought all across India, foreign cloth was boycotted, and previously bought foreign cloth set aflame. Import of cotton piece-goods came down by 75 per cent, khadi sales rose by 60 per cent and liquor sales were curbed by an expanding corps of picketing women.

Despite Gandhi's injunctions, violence from the Indian side occurred in Karachi (where two Congress volunteers died of injuries sustained while restraining a mob), in Calcutta, in Peshawar and in Chittagong in eastern Bengal, where an armed band raided the police armoury, killed guards and ran off with weapons and ammunition.

But these incidents were eclipsed by the scale of India's nonviolent assault in 1930. Referring to it the following year, Churchill charged that the Indians had 'inflicted such humiliation and defiance as has not been known since the British first trod the soil of India'. Another old Harrovian, Jawaharlal, would write in his autobiography that he 'felt a little abashed and ashamed for having questioned the efficacy of this method when it was first proposed by Gandhiji'. Writing, one prisoner to another, to Gandhi, Nehru said (28 July 1930):

> May I congratulate you on the new India you have created by your magic touch! What the future will bring I know not but the past has made life worth living and our prosaic existence has developed something of epic greatness in it.

From Independence to Freedom

Prem Shankar Jha

At midnight on 14–15 August 1947, India shed 190 years of colonial subjugation and became an independent country. In the Durbar Hall of what was to be rechristened Rashtrapati Bhavan, Nehru announced India's tryst with destiny. But only hours later, Indians realized that they had been administered a poisoned pill. Independence came with Partition, and the partition turned out to be a surgical operation without anaesthesia. In Punjab and Bengal the line of separation followed the borders not even of districts but of tehsils. The new lines divided families, separated buyers from sellers and sundered friendships that had endured for generations. People felt betrayed for no one had been consulted, no one had been warned and no one was given a chance to express second thoughts or to reconsider their choice. Partition came with the finality of a hammer blow. Without hope of reprieve, all that people had left was their anger. And they vented it on the 'other community' whom they blamed for their suffering.

What followed has become one of the darker chapters of human history. Millions died. Many millions more were forced to leave their homes and start a new life as destitutes in another nation. No two countries were so benighted at birth. It was almost as if in parting the British had done their best to ensure that these independent nations would fail. But India did not fail. Today it is possible to look back and say that India not only survived but has, in a modest way, flourished.

Borrowing from Amartya Sen, we can justifiably claim that we have successfully made the voyage from independence to freedom. In his thought-provoking work *Development as Freedom* Sen argues that Freedom is at once the ultimate goal of all social and economic arrangements and the most efficient means of realizing general welfare. The key to this is an ever-widening range of choice. It is the widening capacity to choose—an abode, a place of education, a profession and a way of life—that gives meaning to freedom. It also gives meaning to the very notion of development.

Today there are a host of statistics that demonstrate our modest yet substantial success. Indians live two and a half times longer than they did at Independence; they eat on an average a third more than they did and their diet has become infinitely more varied; they are on an average seven times better off than they were in 1947; and the proportion of Indians below the poverty line has fallen from more than half to less than a quarter. But these capture only the lesser part of our achievement. The more important part is the quiet, virtually unnoticed revolution that has occurred in our thinking.

The resignation to one's lot in life, and the fatalism with which Indians accepted adversity, is now a fading memory. Today most, if not yet all, Indians firmly believe that their fate lies in their own hands. From the farmer who gambles all on finding water under his land to the farm labourer who scrapes together Rs 50 to 150 a month to pay for private schooling for his child, to the proud parents who sell some of their land to meet the expenses of their college-going son, to the Dalits who cry 'enough is enough' and demand their place in the sun, people are exploring possibilities that their parents had not believed even existed.

All over India this restless search for a better future is uniting instead of dividing the country. Today anywhere between 60 and 80 million persons work outside their home states. Many, like the Bihari labourers in Punjab and western Uttar Pradesh, have settled down in their host states permanently. But in sharp contrast to many other countries, this has provoked no hostility in the latter. In the same way hundreds of thousands of students have secured places in colleges and medical schools and institutes of technology far from home. This too has not raised sub-national hackles in any part of the country. The changes have been so gradual that we have often failed to notice them. But over the past five decades they have knit the country together into a single economic and emotional unit. They have given substance to what it means to be an Indian, and created an identity that encompasses but far transcends our ethnic origins. The vast majority of the people in the country now share this 'Indianness', once a preserve of the elite.

The organic development of an Indian identity would not have been possible without political stability. Indians take for granted the sanctity of their Constitution and the civic rights it confers on them. They find it unsurprising that a government that is defeated in Parliament by a single vote, cast by a member whose right to exercise his vote was open to dispute, should abide by its rules and resign (that is what Atal Behari Vajpayee did in 1999). They cannot imagine that the verdict of a general election will not be respected.

They have only to look around the post-decolonization world to see how unique our achievement has been. Very few of the 140 newly emergent states have succeeded in developing a stable political system, let alone a democratic one. According to Freedom House, an American think tank that has been charting the growth of democracy across the globe, in 1993 there were only seventy-two nations that it considered free and more or less democratic. It classified another fifty-three as partly free (whatever that may mean) and fifty-five as not free. The first figure does not look too bad, until one examines its composition. It includes only sixteen decolonized countries. Of these India is by far the largest, most complex and stable.

The deep sense of security that democracy and stability have given to ordinary Indians has enabled a growing proportion of them to give a positive political and economic content to the independence they won. They have been able to plan with confidence, educate their children and imbue them with optimism and hope. As the notion of 'India' has taken concrete shape in their minds, two new generations have grown to consider the whole of India, and not just the region of their mother tongues, as their rightful domain. We owe all this partly to the extraordinary foresight of the leaders of the freedom movement, above all Mahatma Gandhi, and to the framers of our Constitution. We also owe it to the flexibility, respect for plurality and a willingness to accommodate differences that was shown by Nehru and his successors. Partly by design and partly through experiment, India developed a unique form of nationhood that depended upon accommodation and compromise and not force to define itself.

Indian federalism is similar in form but very different in content to the federalism of the United States or Australia. In the latter, federation is not much more than an administrative arrangement that often reflects the fact that the federating states joined the union at different points in time. Indian federalism, by contrast, is built on the historical foundations of the Empire State in which, for hundreds of years at a time, starting from the Mauryas and ending with the British, a single paramount power ruled a host of ethnic sub-states, each of which had its own history, culture and traditions of independence. The Empire State succeeded so long as it respected the autonomy of its constituent units. The modern Indian state has also succeeded because it has respected, by and large, the autonomy of the states that is enshrined in the Constitution. India's is therefore an 'ethnic' federalism, in which each constituent 'state' is, more or less, a lineal descendant of one or more of the ethnic sub-states of the old Empire State.

The principal characteristics of India's ethnic federalism are that the entire state is one economic zone in which not just capital but also labour is free to move anywhere in search of work. In practice this freedom, which is enshrined in the Constitution, is constrained to varying degrees in the weaker economic states by rules that require employers to give a minimum proportion of the jobs to people from that state. Such rules are observed sketchily at the best of times but provide an important psychological reassurance to the host populations in each state.

Similar restrictions also hedge the freedom to buy land and start a business in a few of the weaker states. But here too a wide variety of exceptions and loopholes ensure that their impact is mainly psychological.

On the other hand, there are very real safeguards for peoples' ethnic identities. The Constitution leaves education, agriculture and law and order entirely in the hands of the state governments. People thus learn their own mother tongues and their own histories in school. The laws they are governed by fully reflect their own traditional laws and customs. Keeping agriculture, where most of the oldest customary law is to be found, firmly under the aegis of the states doubly safeguards this position.

There is an elaborate system of financial devolution. Certain taxes, such as custom duties, are collected by the Centre and kept by it. Others, such as sales tax, are collected and retained by the states. But the main taxes, the income tax and excise duties, are collected by the Centre and shared with and between the states according to a formula revised every five years by a statutorily appointed finance commission. Overall, the share of the states in the total tax revenues of the nation has risen steadily and has more or less stabilized at slightly more than half. The allocation of Centrally collected tax revenues and Central assistance to the states has contained a strong element of redistribution in favour of the weaker units. This has not in practice levelled the playing field completely. Private investment has through the past forty years tended to concentrate in a handful of industrially advanced or mineral-rich states. But the psychological reassurance these measures have provided have played a very large part in keeping India free from ethnic conflict and steadily strengthening the bonds of nationhood.

Two other methods used to harmonize the demands of ethnicity and nationhood need mention. Not long after the linguistic reorganization of states in 1957, it became clear that this had not completely resolved the problem of ethnicity. Several of the new states contained ethnic sub-groups who found themselves even more disadvantaged in the face of a now more homogenous majority. This problem first came up in the North-East, where Assam contained a large number of distinct tribal groups. The initial solution, after local agitations outlined the need for one, was the subdivision of this composite state into smaller ones. Thus a hill state, Meghalaya, was carved out of Assam. But it soon became clear that every division created a new minority and a fresh demand for a new state. Thus in the early 1980s the government decided to create a third tier of devolution or autonomous development councils within states on a case by case basis. These autonomous councils are self-governing in education, culture, local law and order, maintenance and development planning and other matters at the district level.

Between 1989 and 1992, the Centre created the fourth and final (but misnamed third) tier of democratic institutions. It made elections to panchayats mandatory every five years, devolved a sizeable part of the states' developmental allocations to them and gave them autonomy in framing local development programmes, implementing various state and Centrally planned schemes for employment generation, shelter and primary education, and vested them with limited powers of taxation and fund-raising. It is too soon to tell how the new panchayat system will function but, apart from making local administration far more responsive to local needs and improving the delivery of developmental programmes, it holds out the promise of localizing the last and potentially most disruptive form of ethnic conflict in the country: a conflict between castes.

However finely you slice the cake, devolution of the above kind only empowers ethnic groups that enjoy a measure of geographical concentration. It cannot help those who enjoy some distinct common feature of identity but are thinly spread out over a large part of the country. This is the case with India's religious groups. Even among the Sikhs, who are the most geographically concentrated of India's religious minorities, between a quarter and a third live outside Punjab. To accommodate the yearning for security of identity India has also followed another method of accommodation through acceptance of separate personal laws. It has, however, not allowed the establishment of a separate system for the adjudication of those laws. There are no Shariat or other religious courts in India.

The success of India's ethnic federalism carries within it many lessons for the rest of the world. At the dawn of the new century a huge question mark hangs over the world. What will be the future of the nation state? This question has already been posed forcefully by events in Yugoslavia, Russia, Indonesia and various parts of Africa. It is bound to come up elsewhere as two developments alter radically the world we live in. The first is globalization: the emergence of a single, increasingly integrated global society. The second is the resurgence of ethnicity. The first is pushing the industrialized parts of existing nations inexorably closer together into what have been called Region or Network States. The second is threatening to pull established nations apart. The target of both is the nation state. Since the nation state will not go out quietly, both developments are loaded with potential for violence. The violence caused by the resurgence of ethnicity is already very much in evidence. The potential for violence contained in the process of globalization, and its assault on the nation state, has still to be fully appreciated.

Ironically both are children of the same 'revolution', the freeing of technology from the shackles of capital. The emergence of technology (as distinct from capital) as the key determinant of social, economic and political relations can be traced back to the rise of the monopoly firm in the last quarter of the nineteenth century and to what Schumpeter called the 'institutionalisation of innovation'. The resources the monopolies could devote to applied research moved technological innovation from the factory floor to the research laboratory and the pilot plant. Technology thus acquired a life of its own. And as the fruits of technology multiplied, the pace of change accelerated.

The harnessing of technology to production requires competition. Only the spur of competition makes investors replace older generations of equipment with newer, more efficient ones at the earliest opportunity. It is therefore not surprising that countries with competitive economies have forged ahead while those that shunned competition and relied on one or other form of centrally planned command economic systems fell by the wayside.

Technology is the force behind the emergence of the global market. Over the past century and a half it has not only reduced transport and communications costs to a minute fraction of what they used to be, but has literally collapsed distance and time. This was the essential prerequisite for the emergence of globally integrated production. It made possible hands-on management of production at a large number of remote production centres from a single global or a few regional headquarters. The rapid growth of global integration has been reflected in a 3–4 per cent faster rate of growth of world trade than of world gross national product (GNP) in the last half century. The ratio of trade to GNP has gone up from somewhere around 15 per cent in 1950 to around 45 per cent today. Fully one-third of world trade is made up of inter-branch sales within transnationals.

As recently as twelve years ago, the global marketplace was geographically still quite small. In all perhaps two dozen countries had open, market-driven economic systems. But the collapse of the socialist economies, and the abandonment of the command economy in all but one or two developing countries, has added another 100-odd countries to the list. Today the world is moving at breakneck speed towards becoming a single integrated global market.

Global integration has brought immense pressure to bear on the sovereignty of the nation state by making it necessary to harmonize national economic laws, such as on patents and copyright, minimize barriers to trade, investment and financial flows, and leave the determination of key economic variables like the exchange rate and the domestic rate of inflation to the market. Since conflict threatens trade, and this affects the fortunes of shareholders and workers in dozens of countries, the avoidance of conflict had become a second justification for the abrogation of national sovereignty.

The other major force that has been unleashed by the information revolution that lies at the core of globalization is ethnicity. Ethnic loyalties have resurfaced not only in the newly emergent nations, where the process of nation building on the European model is far from complete, but also in many older and supposedly homogeneous nations of Europe. So widespread is this resurgence that one can legitimately ask whether ethnic groups had ever been really homogenized or whether the political and even social expression of ethnic identities had been simply suppressed in nation states that had been built through conquest and coercion.

To inherited ethnic divisions within nation states must be added new ones that have been created by large-scale immigration, such as of Turks to Germany, North African Muslims to France and Hispanic peoples to the United States. All these have clearly defined identities and deep loyalty to their own groups. Thus both old and new ethnic groups demand accommodation through a redefinition of the European model of the nation state.

The European nation state is ill-equipped to cope with either the integrative pull of the global market or the disintegrative push of ethnicity. The former exerts a steady pressure towards the softening of frontiers to cope with ever-greater cross-border flows of not only goods and services but also people. But the European nation state was predicated to have hard frontiers. And it lent itself far more easily to economic autarchy, enshrined first in mercantilism and then doctrines of protection of infant industries to foster industrialization, and finally in socialism, than to a world without economic frontiers.

When such a state seeks to increase its linkages with the rest of the world it is much more comfortable in a hierarchy than a democracy. When it promotes the pursuit of peace, it tends to do so in the role of a policeman, rather than seeking peace through accommodation. Ensuring global peace comes, by degrees, to mean ensuring a monopoly of coercive power. Free trade comes to mean the lowering of barriers in the developing countries but putting up non-tariff barriers in the industrialized countries. Each and every one of these endeavours is pregnant with the threat of conflict.

This mindset is most visible in the interdiction of the free movement of labour. In the nineteenth century, when the transformation of European states into nation states had not been completed under the impetus of nationalism, labour moved relatively freely across European borders, and with complete freedom to North and South America. It was commodities and capital whose movement was impeded or discouraged. Today, literally everything can move across barriers—goods, services and capital—but not labour. This interdiction remains despite the fact that the high-wage countries are the prime sufferers from it. For as wage differentials have widened between the rich and poor nations so has the exodus of capital from the former to the latter. As a result, the mature industrialized countries face de-industrialization while many low-wage countries that have been most successful in attracting capital have experienced 7 and 8 per cent rates of growth.

The problems of the unitary state in dealing with resurgent ethnicity are even more severe. The European nation state was created by eliminating cultural differences between its constituent ethnic groups and creating a new, more homogeneous, identity based upon the culture of the dominant ethno-national group. Even where this worked, it widened the cultural gap between the newly created 'nation' and similarly created nations across the border. Since the entire process was artificial, especially where older ethnic groups lived on both sides of the border, it could only be maintained by force. Demands for greater autonomy based on ethnic resurgence thus threaten the very base of the European nation state. They can only be dealt with by suppression or by surgical excision, that is, the grant of independence.

Not surprisingly, European theories of the state postulate only a relationship between the individual and the state, and cannot easily accommodate the existence of an intermediate tier of loyalty between the two. To the European, the possibility of there being different laws for an identifiable sub-group than for the rest of the nation is close to anathema. But this is the very least that recognition of ethnicity demands. As a result, there is a predisposition to treat every demand for ethnic self-assertion as a demand for secession—independence if it is viewed sympathetically, and insurrection if it is not.

In Yugoslavia the world has already seen a harrowing example of the violence that can be unleashed by the clash of globalization with the European model of the nation state. Tito's Yugoslavia was a young state. It was born out of a shared opposition to Germany during the Second World War. It found a unifying ideology in communism, which helped to neutralize the deep-seated historical animosities between Serbs and Croats, Slovenes, Albanians and other ethnic minorities that had plagued the Balkans during the past six centuries. In contrast to the unitary European nation state, it made accommodation between ethnic groups in a federal state the basis of its nationhood. Had the socialist experiment been an economic success, Yugoslavia would have consolidated its nationhood on this basis and inherited ethnic animosities would have abated over time. This did in fact happen in the 1950s and 1960s, when Tito was alive, and the Yugoslav economy recorded impressive rates of growth. But two oil shocks and the death of Tito loosened the bonds of nationhood to the point where Yugoslavia was unable to withstand the assault of globalization on its frail nationhood when it came in the 1980s.

The way in which globalization overwhelmed socialist economies has been described by Manuel Castells in his three-volume study of capitalism in the Information Age. In brief, the vertical decision-making structures created by such 'statist' economies simply did not have the speed and flexibility in making economic decisions that were required to survive in the age of hyper-competition. Various efforts in the 1960s and 1970s to devolve decision-making responsibility on the enterprises were only partially successful in remedying this problem and created new ones in their train. Above all, the compulsion to integrate existing national economies with the emerging global economy began to pull the different parts of Yugoslavia apart. The more industrialized Slovenia and Croatia were drawn inexorably towards highly industrialized Western Europe. For them the autarchic political and economic structure of the socialist state became an impediment to progress. Their growing disillusionment with the socialist

Yugoslav state took the form of increased unwillingness to pay their share of taxes to Belgrade and demands for increased autonomy. The ethnic distinctness of the Slovenes and Croatians gave these demands a distinctly 'nationalistic' tinge and provoked a revival of the hitherto dormant Serb nationalism in Serbia. The latter found its leader in Slobodan Milosevic. The tragedy that followed is too well known to need repetition.

Yugoslavia also demonstrates the inability of those schooled in the principles of the European nation state to find a workable resolution of the conflict. Of the three states, Slovenia, Croatia and Bosnia, that were created in 1991, only Slovenia is arguably better off than it was before. There is a near-unanimity of views that the best solution to the Yugoslav crisis would have been to find a solution based upon still greater autonomy for its constituent republics. Since economic autonomy would have required the replacement of socialism and statism with a market economy and democracy, most of the anger unleashed in the West by the Yugoslav tragedy has focussed on Milosevic as the solitary barrier to all three developments. This predisposition lay behind NATO's intervention in Kosovo. But far from creating a viable autonomous Yugoslav republic in Kosovo, the intervention has created a de facto independent country that is an economic basket case.

The reconciliation of globalization and the nation state clearly lies in the development of some form of 'ethnic' federalism—a devolution of power within the state to identifiable ethnic groups, and consequently a loosening of its political and economic bonds, but one that does not, except in rare circumstances, go so far as to dissolve the bonds of the state itself. Only such a structure holds out the hope of simultaneously bringing existing nations states together while loosening their own internal bonds, without passing through an intermediate and costly phase of violence. Will this process be smooth or will there be many more Bosnias and Chechnyas until a solution is found?

This is where nations built on the European unitary model could profit from studying India's experience in nation building. Taken in its entirety, the Indian democratic system represents the most complex and at the same time most flexible system of devolution and power sharing that the world has ever known. The measure of its success is not that there has been no ethnic conflict in India but that, given its bewildering diversity, it has had so little. Accommodation has been reached with little violence. Taking the Punjab, Kashmir and Assam insurgencies together, in all no more than 20 to 35 million people were affected out of a population of more than a billion. The Punjab insurgency, which never affected more than a tiny minority of the Sikhs, was brought under control within ten years, with a loss of about 40,000 lives, of whom 25,000 were Sikh civilians killed by the insurgents for their refusal to cooperate. The far more serious sixteen-year-long Kashmir insurgency is likely to end in a three-way accommodation between Pakistan, India and representative Kashmiris that does not involve a redrawing of frontiers. The United Liberation Front of Assam (ULFA) mini-insurgency in Assam has been more or less snuffed out through a combination of force and accommodation.

There are four broad lessons that others can learn from India's experience. The first is that ethnic diversity is not a threat to nationhood. Accommodating it by explicitly recognizing intermediate tiers of loyalty between the individual and the state can strengthen it rather than the other way about. The second is that devolution of power to one or more federal tiers is perhaps the best way to obtain accommodation. But this only works when the ethnic minority is geographically concentrated. When it is not, the only way that may remain open is to accept the existence of separate personal laws. This should however be confined to the personal, that is, civil, domain and not cover crimes that come under the penal code. The separation of judiciaries, to create two completely parallel systems of law, is probably not desirable either.

Third, like any sovereign nation, the world will not be able to remain at peace indefinitely if it continues to maintain and strengthen barriers to the free movement of labour. That is the single glaring difference between the Indian microcosm and the global macrocosm today. In India, labourers from underdeveloped Bihar move freely to places as far away as Nagaland in the extreme east, Goa in the south and Punjab in the north to find work, without fear or resistance. Fourth, just as the Indian federation needs a paramount state, the global federation too needs a paramount authority. But that paramount authority has to be first democratic and not hierarchical in that the smallest state within it must have the same rights under the global constitution as the largest. Power and influence are another matter.

Lastly, just as the Central Government in India constantly seeks to do so, a paramount state must consciously perform a redistributive function between the economically strong and the economically weak.

Speaking at a seminar in Harvard in April 1995, Professor Stanley Hoffman expressed anxiety about where the world was headed. He said, '. . . We are putting all our eggs in the basket of competition. But international competition creates both international winners and international losers. And today the losers are in danger of being forgotten.'

One has only to compare the emerging international order with the one described above to see how far it is from ensuring a genuinely stable peace.

Does Ideology Matter?

Sitaram Yechury

A philosopher who was declared by the BBC as the thinker of the just-concluded second millennium once remarked that the difference between a bee and even the worst of architects is that the architect, unlike the bee, erects a structure in the mind before translating it into reality.

Human civilization has taken considerable time to attain the stage of the architect. However, having got there, the contours of human evolution are determined by a continuous clash of ideas in all spheres of endeavour. The philosophical divide between materialism and idealism is often erroneously portrayed as matter versus mind. It is, in fact, a battle between the mind or consciousness as the highest form of matter and consciousness independent of the human body and, in that sense, cosmic in nature. While advances in modern science from astrophysics to micro-genetic engineering reconfirm the former, the battle between sets of ideas, or ideology, continues to shape advances in every field. The answer to Descartes's famous postulate 'I think, therefore, I am' is 'I am, therefore, I think'.

Ideology represents the structure of ideas that seeks to influence the course of human development. It not merely remains relevant, but has become pivotal in shaping the future. Presuming that the goal of humanity is to seek emancipation from all forms of bondage, the realization of that quest lies in Marxism.

Marxism is unique in that it can be transcended only when its agenda is realized. This is because its understanding of capitalism is by itself thorough enough for it to comprehend the historical possibilities that lie beyond it. Hence Marxism will be rendered superfluous only when capitalism, the object of its analysis, is itself superseded.

Put another way, the uniqueness of Marxism lies in the fact that all so-called theoretical advances, which supposedly render it obsolete, actually represent throwbacks to still earlier theories superseded by it. Alternatively, these are exaggerations of some particular aspects inherent in Marxism, but dressed in a new garb. These should properly be assimilated within Marxism. 'Post-modernist' or 'post-Marxist' theories which, at their best, emphasize a moral-ethical stance on social issues, represent pre-Marxist notions of social reformism, egalitarianism or progressive interventionism. On the other hand, certain reformist theories like Keynesianism, based on insights into the functioning of the capitalist economy, unknowingly recall insights actually contained in though not adequately developed within Marxism. It is not surprising that the Polish economist Michael Kalecki, by training an engineer whose only introduction to economics was Marx's *Capital*, independently arrived at the so-called Keynesian Revolution.

Marx was not unique on account of subjective qualities that made him superior to other thinkers. What was remarkable was his approach to the analysis of capitalism and the unearthing of certain tendencies that he said were 'immanent' in capitalist social relations. The capitalist system functions in a manner that is not merely independent of the will and consciousness of its participants. Indeed, it makes the participants, whether capitalists or workers, victims of 'alienation' and mere personifications of the elements through which its inherent logic works itself out. Marx referred to the capitalist as 'capital personified'. You cannot therefore have a 'kind capitalist', a 'humane capitalist' or a 'decent capitalist'. The logic of capital works to destroy such individual traits and make every capitalist a mere medium for its realization. The superiority of Marxism and its uniqueness arise from the fact that it alone sees capitalism and analyses it in this manner. Marxism discovered that, unlike all previous modes of production, the basic feature of capitalism is that it is propelled by its immanent tendencies, which cannot be altered by the volition of its individual participants. Once Marxism discovered this basic feature of capitalism, it left no scope for another discovery of the same feature.

True, when socialism appears to be a powerful threat, some of these immanent tendencies may be temporarily held in check through the political process. But in the absence of any supersession of capitalism these tendencies cannot be overcome. They resume their inexorable logic by breaking through such temporary barriers.

Pre-Marxian writers like Adam Smith and Ricardo had also seen capitalism as a system driven by objective laws independent of human will and consciousness. But they envisaged this as the end of history (another example of how the modern perception of Fukuyama and others is a throwback to a pre-Marxian idea). They characterized capitalism as a self-actuating order that was on the whole benign and historically durable notwithstanding a tendency for falling rates of profit (which could be kept in check). But Marx saw this universally alienating system as producing increasing wealth at one pole and increasing misery at the other in a manner that made its supersession historically necessary and possible. Only with such supersession in fulfilment of the Marxist agenda would the stage be set for a supersession of Marxist theory itself.

But what is the evidence that capitalism will be superseded? It is possible that it might linger on and on, and Marxism itself might remain unsuperseded and unrealized, like some eternal cosmic play. This, however, is a matter beyond proof. Besides, the relations underlying capitalism ensure that even as the system grows quantitatively, antagonisms are accentuated. Matters must inevitably move towards a denouement, which is typical not of some eternal cosmic play but of a play with a climax. Even the belief that such a climax must entail a supersession of capitalism and not result in an orgy of destruction within it presupposes a faith in the possibility of human freedom. I have this faith. I see in Marxism the highest development of any theory for comprehending the contemporary human condition and the manner in which freedom is shackled under capitalism. It is precisely for this reason that I remain committed to Marxism.

Two preliminary clarifications are in order here. First, quite obviously, I do not see Marxism as a dogma. On the contrary I see it as an approach to the analysis of history in general, and of capitalism in particular. It is on this basis, building on the foundation provided by Marx, that we continuously reconstitute our theory for understanding the present conjuncture and the possibilities it holds for the future. Far from being a closed theoretical system, Marxism represents a process of continuous theorization, on the basis of certain premises (which are themselves not rigid or fixed), to apprehend what is, what may come into being and what may be made to come into being through praxis. The earlier reference to Keynesianism illustrates the point. The broad contours of Keynesian theory were already latent within the corpus of Marxism, but it remained in the background because the nature of the conjuncture and the demands of praxis within it kept it there. Different circumstances however brought it centre stage. Thus, while the basic approach of Marxism remains unchanged, the propositions that occupy centre stage within it at any particular time keep changing.

Secondly, the realization of the Marxist agenda is a prolonged historical process which must necessarily involve significant advance and retreat. The Bolshevik Revolution marked the start of a period of dramatic advances. The present is a period of massive retreat. To go on to argue on the basis of its current retreat that Marxism is dead would be absurdly short-sighted. The clearest proof of this comes from the fact that the period of Marxism in retreat, involving not only the collapse of the old socialist societies but also the 'rolling back' of a host of experiments in radical state intervention which had been stimulated by the prevalence of socialism, has not brought an end to exploitation and misery. On the contrary, these have intensified as capitalism has been relieved of the socialist threat.

In fact Marx himself had seen proletarian revolution as a protracted, cautious and circumspect process, totally devoid of the swiftness and apparent brilliance of bourgeois revolutions. Setbacks, even severe setbacks, are a part of this prolonged process.

However, we cannot be oblivious of the great achievements of old socialism, namely, saving the world from the spectre of fascism. The decolonization of the third world—not just political decolonization but the acquisition of control over its own resources, markets and production structures (a process being currently reversed through 'liberalization' and 'globalization')—would also not have been possible without the socialist counterweight to capitalist imperialism. Likewise, the building of the most extensive welfare state systems known to mankind and the enlarging of our notions of what is possible by establishing a new mode of production came into being for the first time in human history not spontaneously but through conscious action.

The socialist collapse, however, has ushered in a period of transition characterized by a sharp increase of exploitation and misery. Those who had argued that 'capitalism had changed', that henceforth only the humane face of welfare capitalism would be seen, and had concluded that Marxism was wrong, are themselves being proved wrong, with soaring unemployment in advanced countries and a progressive curtailment of the welfare state. Many argued that capitalism needed no colonies, that colonies were, if anything, a millstone round its neck and concluded that Marxism was wrong. They too are being proved wrong, as the sovereignty of third world states is being progressively throttled. But these are mere descriptions. How do we analytically locate these in relation to the trajectory of capitalist development?

An immanent tendency under capitalism is the centralization of capital. Increasingly, in the later phases of capitalism, small numbers of persons come to control enormous amounts of finance, reflecting the emergence of finance capital. Hilferding, Hobson, Lenin and others had written on the subject before or around the First World War. They traced the origin of that war to the conflict between rival nation-based and nation-state-aided finance capital oligarchies of the advanced countries. These financial oligarchies pressurized the state into exclusively promoting their interests rather than supposedly looking after the interests of society as a whole. Significantly, during the Great Depression, proposals for state intervention to reduce unemployment were thwarted by opposition from the financial oligarchies.

The weakening of financial oligarchies in the wake of the Second World War, the socialist challenge, and the strength and determination of the working class in advanced countries seeking a 'new deal' (which explains the defeat of Churchill in Britain's post-war election) saw a temporary phase in the history of capitalism during which decolonization, demand management through state intervention, and welfare measures could be carried out. Subsequently, however, not only did finance capital gradually get consolidated, but the inherent tendency towards centralization meant the emergence of a new form of finance capital. This was international in nature and went beyond what Hilferding, Hobson and Lenin had written about. This meant the concentration of enormous amounts of globally mobile finance in search of quick (speculative) gains, intent on breaking down barriers to its own free movement across the world and hence, by implication, to the free movement of commodities and all other forms of capital. This new form of international finance capital incorporated multinational corporations, which today engage in both production and speculation. International finance capital is the primary driver of 'liberalization' and 'globalization'.

International finance capital is mobile and confronts nation states, rendering effective its opposition to state intervention (other than what promotes its own interest). It simply moves out of any country that does not bend before its diktat, thereby engendering a liquidity crisis. This consequently impels host countries to retreat from state intervention in demand management. In the post-war period stretching over two decades and more, this strategy brought down unemployment in advanced capitalist countries to very low orders of magnitudes and stimulated the biggest boom in the history of capitalism. It also entailed cuts in welfare measures. In short, it has precipitated deflation and hence stagnation and unemployment in the capitalist world, which in turn has resulted in lower commodity prices and a peasant agriculture crisis the world over. This crisis has been accentuated by increases in input costs stemming from the withdrawal of subsidies and state-directed institutional credit for peasant agriculture within the third world itself—all under the diktat of international finance capital.

Thus the emergence of international finance capital to a position of hegemony brings in its wake unemployment, wage cuts and a sharp accentuation of wealth and income disparities in the advanced capitalist world. It also brings recession and the closure of small businesses everywhere, especially in the third world. Apart from vastly increased inequalities and industrial unemployment in the third world, it also spells acute misery for peasants and agricultural labourers.

International finance capital works everywhere to subvert democracy. The very idea of the nation state being a prisoner of the whims and caprices of a bunch of international speculators in the name of maintaining 'investors' confidence in the economy', rather than promoting the interests of the broad masses of the people, is of course basically undemocratic. And in so far as unemployment typically breeds fascism, fundamentalism and other divisive tendencies in society, it indirectly promotes and wilfully exploits anti-democratic tendencies everywhere.

The very process of capital accumulation in the era of globalization takes a new turn. In general, big capital can grow in one of two ways: either by setting up new productive enterprises, or by buying up small firms and small and petty producers or simply expropriating them. The latter route results in centralization of capital (when big capital takes the place of several small entrepreneurs) or of primitive accumulation of capital (when small and petty producers are simply expropriated by large capital and their assets taken over for virtually nothing). In the era of globalization, with pervasive deflation imposed by international finance capital that restricts the expansion of markets, growth through setting up new productive enterprises plays a secondary role compared to growth through expropriation of small capitalists or petty producers. Grabbing public sector property at throwaway prices is a prime example of such expropriation and is a direct fallout of the finance-dictated process of state-disengagement from the sphere of production. In addition, frantic efforts are made to coerce states to 'privatize' common property, natural resources, mineral wealth and scarce endowments like land and water. The phenomena of agribusiness grabbing land, of water resources being privatized and of oil and natural gas reserves being handed back to multinational corporations are all examples of such primitive accumulation of capital carried out in the name of 'development' but which is really a gigantic process of plunder.

Decolonization had, above all, meant recapturing control by newly independent third world states of their own resources from big metropolitan companies. Not only has this process been reversed but a whole new set of items has been added to the list of resources over which metropolitan companies have acquired control virtually gratis with the direct or indirect support of international finance capital. This is nothing else but a process of recolonization of third world economies.

The impact of these phenomena is far-reaching. A few figures will show what has been happening in India since 'liberalization' in 1991. This is important for the following reason. Most observers agree that Latin America and Africa have been severe victims of 'globalization'. The widespread lament about 'lost decades' in the context of these two continents relates to the absolute fall in per capita incomes witnessed during the years following 'globalization'. And it should surprise nobody that at least seven Latin American countries have recently elected left-wing governments in a bid to reverse the process of 'liberalization' and 'globalization'. But India and China are supposed to be 'success stories'. The example of China, with its very different economic system, may not be apposite in arguing the case for 'globalization'. But the claim that 'India is shining' warrants a close look at the Indian experience over the 1990s and later.

Unemployment, always a problem in India, has become sharply accentuated in recent years. This is especially true of rural unemployment. Between 1993-94 and 1999-2000, years for which we have detailed data from the National Sample Survey's quinquennial reports, rural employment grew at the annual rate of 0.58 per cent or far below the rate of growth of the rural population. Of the many contributory factors, the most obvious was the decline in the rate of growth of agriculture through the 1990s, and especially of food grain which are highly labour-intensive crops. The 1990s constitute the first decade since Independence that saw per capita food grain output decline in absolute terms. Obviously, unemployment must have worsened on this score. Likewise, even within the food grain sector there has been a certain decline in the labour coefficient per unit of output on account of mechanization. But over and above all these, there has been an additional factor of paramount importance, namely the cutback in government expenditure, especially in the countryside, owing to neo-liberal policies.

Notwithstanding the decline in per capita food grain output, the government was saddled with massive food grain stocks which had grown to 63 million tonnes by July 2002 (against an assumed 'norm' or reserve requirement of 24.3 million tonnes). Stocks came down subsequently on account of disbursements for drought relief and because the National Democratic Alliance (NDA) government chose to dump food grain on the international market at throwaway prices lower than what is charged to people living below the poverty line. Nor did these exports go towards augmenting food consumption abroad. They were instead diverted to feed livestock that went into human consumption. Thus what the Indian people could not access was fed to animals in the advanced countries!

What this suggests is a drastic squeeze in the purchasing power of the rural poor, over and above that occasioned by the drop in the growth rate of food grain production. And this squeeze resulted from a cutback in government expenditure. The curtailment in rural development expenditure was phenomenal, declining as a proportion of GDP from an average of over 11 per cent during the Eighth Plan period, that is, during the latter half of the 1980s, to around 5 per cent. With a deflation of this order it is not surprising that rural employment was badly hit.

The accentuation of rural unemployment has been accompanied by an increase in poverty that has been systematically ignored. The piling up of food grain stocks until July 2002, alongside a declining per capita food grain output, implies a drastic reduction in food grain availability. This has depressed the current level of per capita food grain availability for the country as a whole to about what obtained on the eve of the Second World War.

At the beginning of the twentieth century, per capita food grain availability in the country was around 200 kg per annum. The last half-century of colonial rule was so disastrous for the people that by the time of Independence it had declined to around 150 kg per annum. With all the efforts made after Independence this figure went up to about 180 kg per annum by the end of the 1980s. In the 1990s, especially during the latter half of the decade, it declined sharply. In 2000-01 it touched 151 kg, went up to 158 kg in 2001-02 and remained at 157 kg in 2002-03 (the latest year for which data are available), the average for the triennium coming to about 155 kg. If this is the national average, the situation in the countryside, especially among the rural poor, can be well imagined.

This fall, as mentioned earlier, is far greater than the decline in per capita output. It is a result of the fall in purchasing power in the hands of the rural poor associated with declining employment opportunities. The prevalence of hunger in rural India today is the highest since Independence. Rural poverty has consequently reached extremely high levels.

Poverty in India is defined in terms of a calorie 'norm' of 2400 calories per person per day for rural India. By this yardstick, as much as 75 per cent of the rural population fell below the poverty line in 1999-2000, a considerable increase over the 1973-74 level of 56 per cent. The unemployment picture, in other words, is in complete conformity with the poverty story. It would be no exaggeration to say that the rolling back of 'planning and state intervention' (no matter how flawed these were) in India and the unleashing of predatory capitalism under the diktat of international finance capital, in conformity with the developments elsewhere, have given rise to a deep-seated agrarian crisis and extraordinary rural distress.

A struggle against this accentuation of misery is absolutely essential. Linked as it is to the immanent tendencies of contemporary capitalism, this struggle cannot but set for itself the conscious objective of transcending capitalism. Though the precise manner of such transcendence, the stages through which it may come about and linkages between struggles in different countries are matters that cannot be answered speculatively but require theoretical resolution on the basis of concrete praxis, the necessity of such transcendence is indubitable for anyone who is concerned with human freedom. And to effect such a transcendence, the theory that provides illumination will have to be located within the Marxist approach, since, as mentioned earlier, there is no 'going beyond Marxism' as long as capitalism exists.

If the struggle for emancipation of mankind from its current predicament is not undertaken by means of a conscious effort to transcend capitalism through praxis based on a Marxist approach, it is quite likely that accentuating misery may find expression in all manner of destructive and futile tendencies like terrorism, religious extremism, and ethnic and other forms of fundamentalism. The denouement can be revolutionary and recreate our social structure in a manner that frees people to realize their potential, or it can lead to an endless cycle of senseless violence that only succeeds in compounding popular grief. Marxism is our only hope against this latter alternative. It is naive for some to think that history has come to an end. Immense battles are shaping up and it is important to choose the side of reason and humanity. It is this belief that sustains my commitment to Marxism.

Managing National Security

Manoj Joshi

Running like a trail of DNA through all of India's institutions is its colonial past. We are familiar with the baleful workings of the Police Act of 1861 and the 1885 Telegraph Act. But not many know how the shadow of the inauspicious quarrel between the Viceroy of India, Lord Curzon, and the Commander-in-Chief, Lord Kitchener, still falls across the corridors of South Block, much to the detriment of the country's security management.

Until 1904-05 the Viceroy was clearly recognized as the head of the Indian government, and the C-in-C as number two. Both were subordinate to London through the Secretary of State for India and the Secretary of War, who were members of the British Cabinet and responsible to the Parliament.

The armed forces operated under dual control, with the C-in-C responsible for operations and the Military Member of the Viceroy's Council, an appointee of the Viceroy, charged with the administration of the armed forces. Whereas Curzon saw the MM as his military adviser, Kitchener viewed his presence as a slight to his own authority. The Viceroy also saw in the C-in-C's position a threat to the Government of India's constitutional control over the Indian Army. Unfortunately for Curzon, the Cabinet in London backed Kitchener and downgraded the office of the MM, leading to the Viceroy's resignation.

Kitchener then became C-in-C and MM, which meant he was both army chief and defence minister, a situation that obtained till 1946. On paper, the Commander-in-Chief was subordinate to the Viceroy, but more or less ran the military administration, laid down policy and oversaw its execution. Until Independence, the security of India was a major concern of Whitehall, but India was also a prime instrument of British imperial policy. Forces based in India were responsible for the security of all British possessions along the Indian Ocean littoral and beyond. But Indians were kept out of all higher military direction and intelligence services. Moves to devolve greater constitutional authority to India usually excluded these areas. The Government of India Act of 1935 kept defence from the purview of the legislature with its limited electoral franchise. Indeed, the key issue on which the Congress resigned from the provincial ministries in 1939 was the Viceroy's decision to plunge India into the Second World War without even a pretence of consultation with nationalist opinion and the elected representatives.

During the war a department of defence was created, but its remit was limited to civil defence, internal security and the management of cantonments. In any event, the personnel remained largely British. The war years, particularly the Quit India movement of 1942, encouraged the British to keep the department under even tighter control. The result was that while there were hundreds of Indians who gained varied experience in running civilian departments prior to Independence, there was an acute paucity of civil servants who had any kind of comparable experience in managing the defence department or the intelligence services. An even bigger gap emerged in the critical area of external intelligence. According to D.K. Palit, there was not a single file left on external intelligence in the offices of the Intelligence Bureau (IB) and the Director, Military Intelligence. The IB was primarily concerned with internal security and was headed by police officers. This tradition was continued after Independence.

Britain had initially hoped to evolve common defence arrangements with India and Pakistan. At Independence, both dominions actually had a single C-in-C in Sir

Claude Auchinleck, but they viewed his task as facilitating the transfer of power and the division of the armed forces rather than managing and leading these forces. British officers were at the senior-most levels of command of all forces on both sides when the Kashmir war broke out in October 1947. The record shows that these British officers moderated the conflict but also promoted British interests.

As Independence approached, Nehru persuaded Mountbatten to spare his aide, Lord Ismay, to advise on India's higher defence management. Ismay suggested a three-tier system with the Political Affairs Committee of the Cabinet at the apex and the Defence Minister's Committee and the Chiefs of Staff Committee (COSC) at the next two levels. Ancillary groups such as the Joint Intelligence Committee, the Defence Science Advisory Committee and the Joint Planning Committee were created to assist. It was also decided to appoint C-in-Cs for each of the three services and link them through a Chief of Staffs Committee. The essence of Ismay's proposals was the need to maintain civilian supremacy over the armed forces.

Even before a new constitution was written, the Constituent Assembly assumed full powers to vote expenditure, legislate and exercise parliamentary oversight in regard to all subjects, including defence. The Interim Government had, meanwhile, assumed full executive control, with Baldev Singh as defence minister. The C-in-C became adviser to the defence minister and was part of the Defence Minister's Committee along with the Defence Secretary and the financial adviser. The status of the service chiefs suffered derogation in relation to that of the civilian Defence Secretary and other civilian officers.

These were the somewhat unpromising beginnings that led to a weak relationship between civil and military officials and poor management of the armed forces by the bureaucracy. Moving from exclusion to full control was exhilarating for the Indian political class, but it was heady wine.

The Defence Committee of the Cabinet (DCC) was active through the entire Kashmir war that began in October 1947. Among its members were Governor-General Lord Mountbatten, Prime Minister Nehru, Deputy Prime Minister Vallabhbhai Patel, the defence and finance ministers, and the minister-without-portfolio Gopalaswami Ayyangar, heading the Armed Forces Nationalisation Committee with special responsibility for security in East Punjab. Those in attendance included the three service chiefs, the Secretary-General of the Ministry of External Affairs, Girja Shankar Bajpai, the Secretary Ministry of States, V.P. Menon, and the Defence Secretary, H.M. Patel.

The military campaign in Jammu and Kashmir launched on 27 October 1947, following the tribal invasion from Pakistan, was executed with competence and confidence. One reason for this was the presence of Mountbatten, a seasoned war leader, and that of Sardar Patel, a strong foil to Nehru and some of the officials.

By the time the war ended on 1 January 1949, much had been achieved. The Constituent Assembly had got under way and the 560-odd princely states had been integrated into the Union, despite some fuss in Junagadh and Hyderabad. The country's armed forces had been consolidated and their 'Indianization' led to Cariappa taking over as the first Indian Commander-in-Chief.

In the case of Kashmir and Hyderabad, Patel played a key role, personally travelling to the war zone, briefing the DCC and pushing for key goals. On 7 November 1950, a month after the Chinese occupation of Tibet, he wrote at

Bajpai's urging his celebrated letter to Nehru outlining measures to counter a perceived Chinese threat. As a result, a committee was set up under the deputy minister of defence, Major-General (retd.) Himmatsinghji. It recommended a number of steps to defend the Himalayan border. Unfortunately the Sardar passed away and the report remained virtually unimplemented. Only one questionable recommendation was acted upon. The field military intelligence organization was abolished and its functions taken over by the Intelligence Bureau.

Patel's premature passing clearly unbalanced the apex of the Indian national security management system. Since Gandhi too had passed away, Nehru remained by far the tallest leader in the country. The Cabinet system operated only in name, especially in matters relating to defence and foreign affairs. The prime minister relied a great deal in respect of these issues on advisers like the Intelligence Bureau chief, B.N. Mullik, K.M. Panikkar and Krishna Menon. He saw himself as the foremost authority on foreign affairs and had a marked aversion for the military brass. Nehru did not take Parliament into confidence over important issues like the Chinese road built through Aksai Chin. Nor did Parliament play the role it could have. Indeed, parliamentary leaders like Acharya Kripalani maintained pressure on the government not to spend too much on defence.

Even the parsimonious inheritance that India's defence and intelligence apparatus got from their erstwhile colonial masters was squandered through the 1950s. The divide between the civilian and military managers widened, while a chasm opened up between civil and military intelligence. Many of these issues coalesced in the country's flawed China policy. A.G. Noorani has written on Nehru's whimsical management of Sino-Indian negotiations. The minister of defence, Krishna Menon's handling of the army high command reached a nadir in the episode that led to Thimayya putting in his papers as army chief in 1959 and then retracting his resignation.

Nehru, Menon and Mullik have been blamed for the 1962 debacle, but the attitude of the army brass was no better. During the Raj, the army had little problem, being no more than the tactical arm of the British Empire. The responsibility of strategizing and planning on a larger canvas had now fallen on the Indian military, and it failed.

Palit has cited the Chiefs of Staff Paper of January 1961 which said that the charter given by the government was that the forces were 'to be prepared for and to resist external aggression, mainly by Pakistan' and almost as a post script noted that, 'We are required by the government to resist and evict any further incursions or aggressions by China on our territory.' The paper, according to Palit, had another important qualifying statement: 'Should the nature of the war go beyond that of a limited war . . . and develop into a full scale conflagration amounting to an invasion of our territory, then it would be beyond the capacity of our forces to prosecute war . . . beyond a short period, because of limitations on size, the paucity of available equipment, and the lack of adequate logistical support.' In other words, the chiefs of staff had virtually decided in advance that they could not fight a major war with China.

The China war brought another personality into the security management, namely, the Supreme Commander. President Radhakrishnan was instrumental in Menon's removal as defence minister and in preventing Nehru from appointing Lt. General B.M. Kaul as army chief after General P.N. Thapar's resignation. Nehru ran the war much as he saw fit, taking ad hoc decisions such as allowing an ill

General Kaul to return to Tezpur as 4th Corps Commander or refusing to consider the use of the air force to block the Chinese advance. He took his most dramatic decision, after the debacle at Se La, in the Kameng sector of Arunachal, to appeal for a virtually unlimited military partnership between India and the United States without reference to the Cabinet. According to S. Gopal, Nehru's biographer, the only person he consulted was Foreign Secretary M.J. Desai.

Nehru's successor, Lal Bahadur Shastri, relied on the Cabinet system and his political colleagues, particularly Defence Minister Y.B. Chavan and External Affairs Minister Swaran Singh, in providing higher direction for the 1965 war. The Emergency Committee of the Cabinet proved capable of taking tough decisions, such as the one to use the air force to blunt the Pakistani offensive in Chhamb and subsequently to launch an offensive across the international boundary towards Lahore. Another important political directive was the order to the armed forces not to act against East Pakistan.

Unfortunately, the abilities of the army chief, General J.N. Chaudhuri, were exaggerated. Air Chief Marshal P.C. Lal has pointed out in his memoirs that even after the clashes in the Rann of Kutch, 'No contingency plans were drafted, nor were the three Services asked to define the parts that they would have to play in the event of a war.' He was 'informed' by Chaudhuri that plans had been discussed with the political leadership, 'and necessary sanction obtained', but what these were the army chief did not bother to inform his air force colleague.

The Indian Army battled thousands of Pakistani infiltrators through August and launched substantive operations, capturing the Haji Pir Pass, but there was no coordination with the air force. Only when Pakistan launched Operation Grand Slam on 1 September, and its armour rolled over the Indian positions in Chhamb and moved towards Akhnur, did Chaudhuri turn to the Indian Air Force and demand assistance. Yet, on 6 September when the army began a major counteroffensive towards Lahore, the air force was not informed, resulting in a fiasco. Lt. General Harbakhsh Singh has written how Chaudhuri panicked after the Pakistani army launched an offensive in Khem Karan and ordered a retreat to the Beas bridge, which would have meant abandoning the Amritsar doab. Fortunately, Harbakhsh Singh refused and his forces on the ground converted a looming disaster into the only victory of the war.

Just how poorly the higher command functioned is illustrated by Chaudhuri's final blunder. On 20 September, as Palit recounts, the army chief was summoned by Prime Minister Shastri and told that the government was willing to hold off declaring a ceasefire as demanded by the United Nations, if there was chance of significant military gain. Without bothering to consult his staff, Chaudhuri declared that the army was short of ammunition and therefore advised the acceptance of a ceasefire. In fact, as K. Subrahmanyam has revealed, it was Pakistan that had run out of ammunition. With sufficient second- and third-line ammunition, India could have converted the war into an outright victory, instead of the stalemate it turned out to be when a ceasefire was declared on 22 September.

By the time the 1971 war took place, Indira Gandhi, who succeeded Shastri in 1966, was the undisputed leader of the country and her party. According to Air Marshal Lal, who commanded the Indian Air Force, everything worked smoothly. The political authorities kept the service chiefs in the picture and the Chiefs of Staff Committee and the other inter-services committees functioned well. Yet Indian assessments were not very accurate. The initial plan was for a conventional attrition-type invasion of East Pakistan. The redeeming feature was that once the door to Dhaka appeared to open, with Lt. General Sagat Singh's heliborne move across the Meghna, the Indian Army revised its plans and went for the kill.

Poor leadership and execution marked the Indian Army's performance in the western theatre. Higher command confusion led to the loss of Chhamb. The initial plans called for an offensive towards Kharian from Chhamb. But the orders were that they should not strike before the Pakistanis so that India was not seen as an aggressor. However, at the last minute, on 30 November, Manekshaw and D.P. Dhar came to the area and, at a meeting, it was decided that Indian forces should remain on the defensive. Orders were issued on 1 December, but the division concerned was caught between implementing two opposing sets of orders when the Pakistanis attacked on 3 December, resulting in the loss of territory across the Munnawar-Tawi.

The handling of the Bangladesh crisis brought out structural changes in higher defence management following the changed political circumstances in the country. The prime minister had regained the supremacy he enjoyed in the Nehruvian era. But whereas Nehru's primacy sat comfortably with his colleagues, at least till the 1962 debacle, Indira Gandhi had won hers through a fierce political battle. The result was that, though she went through the motions of running a Cabinet-based higher command system, real power came to rest in a coterie that resented any criticism. Besides the favourite courtier of the hour, it comprised key officials such as P.N. Haksar, the Prime Minister's Principal Secretary; D.P. Dhar, ambassador to Moscow and later chairman of the Policy Planning Division of the External Affairs Ministry; R.N. Kao, head of the new external intelligence agency, RAW; P.N. Dhar, who later replaced Haksar; and T.N. Kaul, the Foreign Secretary. As the Bangladesh crisis deepened, the planning forum included the Cabinet Secretary, T. Swaminathan; the army chief, General Manekshaw; Home Secretary Govind Narain; Finance Secretary I.G. Patel; and Defence Secretary K.B. Lall.

Yet, even to this day we do not know how certain decisions were taken though formal approval was given by the Cabinet Committee on Political Affairs. K. Subrahmanyam has observed that in his years in the highest echelons of government he never found even a scrap of paper giving the background and aims of India's first nuclear test at Pokhran in 1974.

When she returned to power in 1980, Indira Gandhi's decision-making became more personalized and opaque. She depended a lot on her sons, first Sanjay and then Rajiv Gandhi, who in turn had their own advisers. Short-term electoral gains were pursued: outflanking the Akalis in Punjab by supporting Sikh extremism and undermining Farooq Abdullah in Jammu and Kashmir by replacing him with a Jamaat-e-Islami-supported government of Ghulam Mohammed Shah. Both actions had profoundly negative consequences for national security management. The old policy planning mechanism was once again brought into play, with G. Parthasarthi as its head, to contend with the developments in the region, primarily Afghanistan, Pakistan and Sri Lanka.

Though important decisions were taken with regard to the defence and security of the country, there was no change in institutional arrangements to address new and more complex challenges. The armed forces continued to remain outside the governmental system and the key decisions were taken by the leadership either through informal consultations or through individuals like Parthasarthi, or close advisers like R. Venkataraman, who later became President.

The infirmities of this model became apparent in the mid 1980s as India lurched from backing the Tamil militants in Sri Lanka to becoming honest broker between the Sinhalese and Tamils and then fighting the Liberation Tigers of Tamil Eelam (LTTE). Higher management was done in New Delhi through a core group chaired by Natwar Singh, then minister of state for external affairs, and comprising the vice-chiefs of the three services, the heads of RAW and IB, and Joint Secretary–level officers of the ministry of external affairs and the Prime Minister's Office. Just how dysfunctional the system was soon became apparent. The Indian Peace Keeping Force, which was sent to show the flag and receive the weapons decommissioned by the LTTE under the Indo-Sri Lanka Accord, ended up fighting a jungle war against the LTTE for the next two years. Perhaps the sorriest episode in this was the manner in which the RAW undermined the army's efforts, sometimes with the acquiescence of New Delhi.

Rajiv Gandhi, suddenly pitchforked into power, adopted a higher defence management system not too different from that of his mother, relying on two close aides, Arun Nehru and Arun Singh. However, two crises—both linked to military exercises, Operations Brasstacks and Chequerboard—brought out the weaknesses in the system. Both had been approved by the Cabinet Committee for Political Affairs, but the Pakistani and Chinese response to these unusually large and innovative exercises was not anticipated. Arun Singh, though only minister of state in the ministry of defence, virtually ran the ministry. His unusual energy, combined with the vigour of the army chief, General Sundarji, nearly took India to war with Pakistan and China in early 1987. Whether the exercises were the casus belli, or the exaggerated Pakistani and Chinese reaction, can be debated, but the higher national security management system failed to anticipate events. Instead of correcting this, Rajiv Gandhi chose to revert to the earlier system of keeping the armed forces under tight bureaucratic control, with K.C. Pant as the new defence minister.

The institutional weaknesses of the system became apparent in the ensuing period when internal security matters gained salience. The symbolic appointment of Mufti Mohammed Sayeed as home minister in the face of the growing unrest in Kashmir was followed by the shelving of the salient recommendations of the Arun Singh Committee on reform in higher defence management. P.V. Narasimha Rao's bid to create a new National Security Council proved abortive.

The National Democratic Alliance (NDA) led by the Bharatiya Janata Party (BJP) came to power and ordered a nuclear weapons test. The decision-making was again very secretive, perhaps occasioned by the awareness that any attempt to get Cabinet approval could result in an information leak. In the event, the key decision-makers were the prime minister, Atal Behari Vajpayee, his Principal Secretary, Brajesh Mishra, and the heads of the Defence Research and Development Organisation and the Department of Atomic Energy.

Subsequent to the test, the government moved fast to create institutions necessary for a more holistic view of security by creating a National Security Council, assisted by a National Security Advisory Board and a Strategic Policy Group. A new position of National Security Adviser was created, though it was throughout the NDA period headed by Brajesh Mishra. The composition of the National Security Council was the same as that of the Cabinet Committee on Security, namely, the prime minister, and the ministers of finance, external affairs and defence, with the addition of K.C. Pant, the deputy chairman of the Planning Commission.

The National Security Adviser was assisted by a secretariat no different from the old Joint Intelligence Committee. He was also called upon to supervise the Intelligence Bureau and the RAW. He was later given the responsibility of chairing the executive council of the National Nuclear Command Authority and was appointed Secretary of the Cabinet Committee on Security.

The second tier of the National Security Council, the Strategic Policy Group, consisted of the Cabinet Secretary, the three service chiefs, the Foreign Secretary, Home Secretary, Defence Secretary, Secretary (Defence Production), Finance Secretary, Secretary (Revenue), the Reserve Bank Governor, the IB and RAW chiefs, the head of the Atomic and Space agencies and the scientific adviser to the defence minister. This sought to institutionalize the presence of the armed forces within the deliberative organs of government.

The third element was the National Security Advisory Board consisting of people outside government with expertise in a range of areas. Its role is to provide long-term assessments and analyses for the National Security Council and recommend solutions and policy options for issues raised by it.

However, the system received two shocks: the Kargil incursion in 1999 followed by the hijacking of IC 814 to Kandahar, compelling the government to release Masood Azhar, Umar Sheikh and Mushtaq Zargar. The failures in the face of the hijack were palpable. The Kargil Review Committee that was set up came up with a detailed report that pretty much covered the entire gamut of decision-making and its failures and made a series of wide-ranging recommendations. As a result, the government constituted a Group of Ministers (GOM) in April 2000 to make a thorough review of the national security system in its entirety, including higher defence management, border security, internal security and intelligence.

The GOM report was approved by the government in May 2001, with one modification. A final view on the recommendation to institute a Chief of Defence Staff was left to be taken after consultations with various political parties. Signalling its determination to ensure 'jointness' within the three armed services, the government set up an Integrated Defence Staff, headed by a Chief of Integrated Staff, to support the Chiefs of Staff Committee and its chairman in the optimal performance of their roles and functions. The first Joint Andaman and Nicobar Command was established in October 2001 under a Commander-in-Chief who exercises control over all force components of the three services and the Coast Guard located in the island territories.

A Strategic Forces Command, to manage the country's nuclear assets, and a new Defence Intelligence Agency were also created. Structural changes were also announced to streamline procurement and research and development.

In January 2003 the government announced a new set of decisions relating to security management after the military standoff with Pakistan following the terrorist attack on Parliament House. A Nuclear Command Authority was created with a Political Council and an Executive Council, to lend weight to India's minimum credible nuclear deterrence posture. The Political Council is chaired by the prime minister. It is the sole body that can authorize the use of nuclear weapons. The Executive Council is chaired by the National Security Adviser. It provides inputs for decision-making by the Nuclear Command Authority and executes the directives given to it by the Political Council. A C-in-C Strategic Forces Command was also appointed to manage and administer the strategic forces.

The key to India's indifferent record in national security management perhaps lies in the poor quality of its strategic culture and a status quoist mentality that has encouraged defensive rather than proactive responses. This shortcoming is manifest not only in the armed forces but, equally important, within the political class and civilian bureaucracy. This is all too evident in the intellectual output of the country's universities or the writings of civilian and military commentators.

Despite recent reforms, the national security decision-making process leaves much to be desired. The same is true of the military organization. If the military high command is inadequately involved in national security decision-making, it also remains parochially divided along service lines. This suits politicians and bureaucrats alike, since it divides the armed forces and enhances their own position.

The 2001 National Democratic Alliance's GOM Report constitutes a most extensive body of national security reforms. Yet, key recommendations like the appointment of a Chief of Defence Staff remain unimplemented. The United Progressive Alliance government's explanations as to why it is not going ahead are not credible. They appear to be part of the same chimera that persuaded Nehru to keep the armed forces outside the government decision-making system, namely, fear of a coup!

Dread of the man on a horseback runs like a thread through Indian civilian attitudes towards the armed forces. This was possibly understandable in the early decades of independence when many newly independent countries, especially Pakistan, came under the heel of military dictators. But it is ridiculous in the twenty-first century, when the probity of the Indian armed forces on this score has been tested by time and circumstances, and when Indian democracy has struck deep roots.

It would be comfortable to interpret this narrative as a slow and steady evolution of the country's national security management. But, as the record shows, as each crisis passes, the system reverts to its previous state of lassitude. The new lines in an authority chart that come up tell us little about how effectively a higher command organization will meet the next challenge. But one thing is certain. In today's networked world, India cannot continue to handle its security through methods that brought grief in Namka Chu and Kandahar, or failed to avert the 13 December attack on Parliament.

India cannot deal with terrorist or weapons of mass destruction threats in a linear or sequential fashion. Crises in such an environment often require time-urgent interventions and responses and have horrific strategic implications. The technology of network-enabling capabilities—television, telephone, satellites, computers—may lead political leaders to believe that they have a better understanding of the battle space than is actually the case. In reality, the volume of information and the response time could make civilian and even top-level military control less, not more, effective. Arbitrating quickly and surely between the priorities of politicians, military commanders and diplomats, amid almost simultaneous action by adversaries and the pressure of 'public opinion', is the challenge facing future national security management in the country. To meet this, we need finally and firmly to bid goodbye to the Curzon–Kitchener–Ismay era.

Global and Medieval: India's Schizophrenic Economy

Edward Luce

India, as many Indians like to remind you, is a unique country. But what makes it particularly unusual, especially in comparison to China, is the character of its economy. In spite of much breast-beating in the west, China is developing in the same sequence as most western economies have done: it began with agricultural reform, moved to low-cost manufacturing, is now climbing up the value-added chain, and probably, at some stage in the next ten to twenty years, will break into internationally tradeable services on a larger scale. India is growing from the other end.

Its service sector accounted for significantly more than half of its economy in 2006, with agriculture and industry accounting for roughly equal shares of what remained. This resembles how an economy at the middle-income stage of its development, such as Greece or Portugal, should look. But Greece and Portugal do not have to worry about a vast army of 470 million labourers in their hinterlands. India's problem, and its peculiar way of addressing it, presents the country with a daunting challenge. The cure may be economic, but the headache is social.

When India started to liberalize its economy in 1991, there was effectively only one television channel on offer: Doordarshan, the state broadcaster. By 2006 there were more than 150 channels and three or four new ones were being added every month. In 1991 Doordarshan reached just a small minority of homes. Such is the electricity supply in much of rural India that even villages that had a TV set would only intermittently get good reception. India's general election of 2004 marked the first national poll in which the majority of the electorate could watch the spectacle on television. Roughly a third of these, more than 150 million people, had multi-channel cable television piped into their homes.

What today's villagers and small-town dwellers in India see seductively paraded before them as they crowd around their nearest screens are things most of them have little chance of getting in the near future: the cars, foreign holidays, smart medical services and electronic gadgets that dominate TV commercials. Most of these products are not meant for them at all. Such items are well beyond the reach of the majority in a country where the average per capita income in 2006 was still below $750. Sooner or later, if you are unable to get what you are repeatedly told you should want, something has to give. India's more far-sighted policy-makers frequently remind themselves that if the country is to forestall a social backlash, rising crime and further lawlessness, which blights life in many of its poorer states, they must ensure that economic growth keeps accelerating. On every occasion I have interviewed Manmohan Singh, the quiet, bespectacled Sikh who was India's Finance Minister in 1991, when the country began to loosen its regulatory stranglehold on the economy, and who became Prime Minister in 2004, he emphasized the same argument: 'The best cure for poverty is growth.' Judging by India's own record, it is hard to disagree.

India's economy has on average expanded at 6 per cent a year since 1991, almost double the 'Hindu rate of growth' it experienced in its first four decades after independence. This sharp economic acceleration has coincided with a steady fall in the rate of India's population growth, so the relative growth of individual incomes is even better than the economic growth figures would suggest. Put vividly: the difference between India's abysmal decade that began in 1972 and the more impressive decade that began in 1995 is the difference between countrywide unrest—which led Indira Gandhi to declare the Emergency, in which she suspended democracy amid an epidemic of national strikes, protests and rising violence—and the relatively normal functioning of democracy after Dr Singh ushered in economic reform. In the first decade India's economy grew by 3.5 per cent a year while its population grew by 2.3 per cent. In the second the economy grew by 6 per cent a year while population growth fell to just 2 per cent. It would have taken fifty-seven years for an Indian family to double its income in Gandhi's decade. In Dr Singh's decade it would take just fifteen years. In an age when you can watch exactly how the other half lives on a flickering screen, it is the difference between anarchy and stability.

Yet, on its own, faster growth is not enough: growth, as economists say, is a necessary but not sufficient condition for removing poverty. Equally important is the quality of growth—whether it is capital intensive, as it has been in India, in which case it will not employ many people, or labour intensive, as in China, which will give much larger sections of the television-viewing population a stake in the growth they see dangled in front of them.

Dr Singh has outlined India's twin economic challenges of today: the need to modernize agriculture and the related objective of providing more manufacturing jobs for India's under-employed peasantry. Perhaps the biggest mental hurdle to both is the Indian elite's continuing love affair with the village. It has become popular for journalists and academics in India to write off Gandhi's philosophy as officially dead. Certainly, as a political ideology, Gandhianism in today's India is an orphan: none of India's many political parties officially endorses the Mahatma's philosophy of the village. But as a social attitude his view of the village lives on notably in much of India's civil service; it can be heard coming from the mouths of many of India's senior diplomats and judges, and it is still mainstream among India's non-governmental organizations, the tens of thousands of charities which in many parts of rural India provide the village schools, basic medicines and the arts and crafts livelihoods which the Indian state often fails to deliver.

Gandhianism can also be taken as shorthand for an even more deeply rooted attitude that is quite common among privileged and upper-caste Indians, who, at many levels—some not openly stated—view the brash new world of metropolitan India as a challenge to their traditional domination of culture and society. This attitude is also a continuing echo of the anti-colonial struggle against the British, in which the village and the home were seen as those parts of Indian culture which were least touched by colonial influence.

However, it is hard to imagine any villager voluntarily turning. down the opportunity to have electricity or the other comforts of a consumer lifestyle. Nor is it easy to imagine a rural economic model that could sustain 700 million Indian villagers in security and in a condition of social enlightenment. Indians will continue to move to the city. Many more would move if there were secure jobs to be found.

Less than 7 per cent of India's dauntingly large labour force is employed in the formal economy, which Indians call the 'organized sector'. That means that only about 35 million people out of a total of 470 million have job security in any meaningful sense; and only about 35 million Indians pay income tax, a low proportion by the standards of other developing countries. The remainder, in more senses than one, are in the 'unorganized economy'. They are milking the family cow, making up the seasonal armies of mobile casual farmworkers, running small shops or street-side stalls, making incense sticks and *bidis*, driving rickshaws, working as maids, gardeners and nightwatchmen, and bashing metal as mechanics in small-town garages.

Of the 35 million or so Indians with formal sector jobs—which are, to some extent, registered, monitored, measured and audited—21 million are direct employees of the government. These are the civil servants, the teachers, the postal workers, the tea-makers and sweepers, the oil sector workers, the soldiers, the coal miners and the ticket collectors of the Indian government's lumbering network of offices, railway stations, factories and schools.

This leaves around 14 million working in the private 'organized' sector. Of these, just over a million—or about 0.25 per cent of India's total pool of labour—are employed in information technology, software, back-office processing and call centres. Software is clearly helping to transform India's self-confidence and the health of its balance of payments situation with the rest of the world, but the country's IT sector is not, and is never likely to be, an answer to the hopes of the majority of its job-hungry masses. Nor do foreign companies employ large numbers of Indians—estimates vary between one and two million people, depending on the definition of a 'foreign' company. The remainder are employees of Indian private sector companies.

Understanding the difference between organized and unorganized India is the key to realizing why the country's economy is so peculiar: at once confident and booming yet unable to provide secure employment to the majority of its people. Contrary to much conventional wisdom in the west, which often quite wrongly sees Indian employees of foreign multinationals as exploited sweatshop labour, the fourteen million who work for Indian or foreign private companies are the privileged few—India's aristocracy of labour. In 1983, as India was entering the twilight of its *swadeshi* phase, the average labour productivity of the worker in the private organized sector was six times that of his counterpart in the unorganized sector. By 2000, that had risen to nine times. The disparity in earnings was similar. This is a world of difference. Crossing from one world to the other requires good education and skills, or a huge dose of luck. It does not happen often enough.

If India is to build a better bridge between the old world and the new it must provide jobs for unskilled and semi-skilled employees in its manufacturing sector. In terms of scale, India can be measured only against China. In 2005 India employed just seven million people in the formal manufacturing sector, compared to more than a hundred million in China. Given the large investment and the priority that Nehru accorded to industrialization, many people find it puzzling that sixty years later India's manufacturing sector employs so few people. That is because Nehru's strategy was essentially capital intensive: he aimed to develop India's technological capacity, rather than employ the maximum number of people. But it does not follow that Indian manufacturing is correspondingly weak or uncompetitive. Measured by quality, if not quantity, many of India's home-grown private sector manufacturers are considerably more impressive than their counterparts in China. Again, in this respect, India finds itself higher on the ladder than one would perhaps expect it to be. It is just that most of its population are still standing at the bottom.

Another questionable legacy of the well-meaning society Nehru wanted to build is that India has some of the strictest labour laws in the world, making it virtually impossible to sack an employee, even if the person you want to fire is a chronic absentee. Some parts of Nehru's model, such as the Orwellian Licence Raj, have now been dismantled, but others, such as the absurdly strict labour laws (which became even stricter under Indira Gandhi in 1976), remain. This means that companies are reluctant to hire large numbers of people even when they are expanding because they fear being stuck with boom-era payrolls during the next recession, which would push them into bankruptcy and endanger everyone's job. But it also means companies prefer to outsource as much of their work as possible to small, unaudited outfits in the 'unorganized sector' so they can escape the labour laws, which are effectively unenforceable in India's labyrinthine informal economy. Other legacies also have yet to be abolished, such as the 'Inspector Raj' of constant inspections that plagues much of Indian business. As Gurcharan Das, former head of Procter & Gamble India wrote: 'In my thirty years in active business in India, I did not meet a single bureaucrat who really understood my business, yet he had the power to ruin it.'

There are also unintended consequences to another of Nehru's critical legacies—the decision to pour as much money into English-medium universities for the middle classes as he did into primary schools for the villages. The elite Indian IIT engineering graduates who are not in Silicon Valley or Massachusetts, are working for companies like Tata Steel and Reliance Industries. Because of its impressive university system, India's scientific and technical capacity is ranked third in the world, behind the United States and Japan but ahead of China. In contrast to India, though, China has invested much more heavily in elementary schools for those at the bottom of the social ladder. India produces about a million engineering graduates every year, compared to fewer than 100,000 in either the United States or Europe. However, India's literacy rate is only 65 per cent whereas China's is almost 90 per cent.

India has a highly unusual economy. Its complex steel plants are helping put their Japanese and American counterparts out of business. Its elite private hospitals conduct brain surgery on rich Arab clients and perform hip replacements on elderly British 'medical tourists' who are frustrated by the long waiting-lists in Britain's National Health Service. Employees at India's call centres are empowered by telephone or computer to accept or reject insurance claims of up to $100,000 from American policy-holders half a world away. And its drugs sector is on the cusp of producing new products as a result of indigenous research and development skills. Yet large numbers of India's farmers still subsist at African standards of living. Fewer than one million Indians annually produce more in IT and software export revenues than several hundred million farmers earn from agricultural exports.

It is true that India's higher economic growth rates in the last fifteen to twenty years have helped lift more people out of poverty than was the case in previous decades. According to the government of India, the proportion of Indians living in absolute poverty dropped from 35 per cent to just over 25 per cent between 1991 and 2001. The percentage is likely to have dropped further since then. Some parts of India, particularly its southern states and the west of the country, where the system of administration is widely regarded to be of a higher quality, have generated many more jobs than before, in both the organized and the unorganized service and manufacturing sectors.

However, contrary to what demographers would expect and what has happened in other developing economies, India's rate of urbanization has actually *slowed* while its economic growth has accelerated. In 1981, 23.7 per cent of India was urban; by 2001, this had risen only to 27.8 per cent. Of course, the numbers of people moving to the cities are still large by the standards of other countries: seventy million Indian villagers migrated between 1991 and 2001. Nevertheless, 'The surprise is that just when the urbanization process was expected to accelerate, it slowed down,' writes Rakesh Mohan, the deputy governor of India's central bank and one of the country's leading economists. 'This has been caused by both faulty national economic policies that have discouraged urban employment growth, particularly industrial employment, and by rigidities that have inhibited urban infrastructure investment.'

Some of India's business leaders believe the economic gap between rural and urban India cannot persist without eventually provoking a backlash. In 2004 Manmohan Singh asked Nandan Nilekani, the chief executive of Infosys, one of India's most successful IT companies, to join a task force on urbanization. Unusually among Indian leaders, Singh believed more rapid urbanization and a stronger manufacturing sector were essential to India's future success. Nilekani, who had put one million dollars of his own money into a project to improve urban governance in Bangalore, where Infosys is based, accepted without hesitation.

Many people who visit India are struck by the squalor of the urban slums that assault their senses almost immediately after they leave the airport. They find it hard to understand why so many Indians would voluntarily want to live in such conditions when they could be milking the family cow back in the village. But most of the migrants have voted with their feet (some have been involuntarily displaced by natural disasters or dams). In their view even the most squalid slum is better than living in a village. In spite of the inadequacies of India's urban planning and the. absence of secure employment, the city offers economic and social opportunities to the poor and to the lower castes that would be inconceivable in most of rural India. More than 100 million rural Indians do not own any land, and many of them are likely to move to the cities in the years ahead, whether slum conditions have improved or not.

'The answer is not to send people back to village, which anyway you can't do in a democracy,' Nandan Nilekani explained. 'It is to improve the quality of urban governance and to provide the poor with real jobs.'

India's economy offers a schizophrenic glimpse of a high-tech, twenty-first-century future amid a distressingly medieval past. But even more perplexing is that it is among India's elites—those who have been the largest beneficiaries of the liberalization of the economy since 1991—that you find the most robust defenders of an old mindset that could be described as modernity for the privileged, feudalism for the peasantry. However, most of the evidence suggests that the peasantry—including those in north India—does not necessarily acquiesce in this view. Many poor farmers get informal jobs in the city that enable them to send money to their families back in the village. The families remain behind because the jobs are not secure. This is one reason why India's official rate of urbanization has slowed.

Science Inspires Action

A.P.J. Abdul Kalam

National Science Day is celebrated on the 28th of February every year, the day in the year 1930 that Nobel Laureate Sir C.V. Raman announced a landmark discovery which is finding applications today in the area of continuous wave all-silicon laser. On this day, the nation pays tribute and expresses its gratitude to all the scientists who have made our dream of using the science and scientific discoveries as vehicles for economic development, a reality. Celebration of science will attract many young children to take up science as a career. This is the day, our scientists may like to rededicate themselves to create high quality scientific research output from India and make the nation proud. Science Day is the day to remind us that the important ingredient for societal transformation would mainly come from science.

Science as we see it

Today science has touched every person in all walks of life—be it rural or urban. When you visit a doctor with absolute faith that he will find a cure for every illness and when he or she does, you see science in action. When your harvest is bountiful and when you are able to make increased productivity than our forefathers in the same land, you see science in action. When natural disasters occur and when your life is saved due to a preemptive action due to forecast, you see science in action. When you talk to your sons and daughters anywhere in the planet from your cell phone or the STD booth, or through VOIP, you see science in action. When you enjoy the television shows from the comforts of your home, you see science in action. When you realize that the world is a global village and you have all the world of information available to you, you see science in action. I am sure if you seriously pursue science as a career, you will ensure that our future generation will see more actions of science that will make their life happy, prosperous and safe.

In the Indian Science Congress 2006, I have highlighted the various scientific achievements made by our scientists in the recent past. Today, I will focus on research by academic institutions, R&D organizations, scientists and students on the missions which will enable India to realize the goal of energy independence well before 2030. I have selected four research areas of importance that will make a change in our society. Government, academia and research foundations have to provide all the necessary assistance for the research areas.

The areas of research are:

- CNT based solar cells for higher efficiency
- Increasing the Bio-fuel oil content
- Efficient thorium based nuclear fuel
- Efficient hydrogen fuel, power package

CNT based solar cells for higher efficiency

One of the important needs for achieving energy independence by 2030 is to increase the power generated through renewable energy sources from the existing 5 per cent to 25 per cent. Particularly, the energy produced through solar energy has to increase substantially. The low efficiency of conventional photo voltaic cells has restricted the use of solar cells for large applications for power generation. Research has shown that the Gallium Arsenide (GaAs) based PV cell with multi junction device could give maximum efficiency of only 30 per cent. Hence it is essential to launch a research mission on Carbon Nano Tube (CNT) based PV cell which has got higher level of promise in efficiency.

The CNTs provide better electron ballistic transport property along its axis with high current density capacity on the surface of the solar cell without much loss. Higher electrical conductivity and mechanical strength of CNT could improve the quantum efficiency to the order of 35 per cent. But, this is not sufficient. Recent research has shown that the alignment of the CNT with the polymer composites substrate is the key issue and this aligned CNT based PV cells would give very high efficiency in photovoltaic conversion. The polymer composites increase contact area for better charge transfer and energy conversion. In this process, the researchers could achieve the efficiency of about 50 per cent at the laboratory scale. Our scientists have to take up this challenge and come up with the development of a CNT based PV cell with an efficiency of at least 50 per cent within the next three years so that it can go into commercial production within five years. In addition, they can also take up the development of organic solar cells, dye-sensitized solar cells and third generation solar cells. There are lots of opportunities for research in fundamental science in this area and I would like to see these opportunities used by a wider spectrum of our universities and research laboratories in a cóherent, consorted way with a mission mode programme.

Increasing the Bio-fuel oil content

We have nearly 60 million hectares of wasteland, of which 30 million hectares are available for energy plantations like Jatropha. Once grown, the crop has a life of fifty years. The cost of bio-diesel produced from Jatropha works out to Rs 20 per litre at present. Government has permitted the use of mixing of maximum 10 per cent bio-fuel with diesel for cars. In respect of heavy vehicles and tractors 100 per cent usage of bio-fuel has shown satisfactory results. Bio-diesel is carbon neutral and many valuable by-products flow from this agro-industry. Intensive research is needed to burn bio-fuel in internal combustion engines with high efficiency, and this calls for a focused R&D programme to be initiated on a war footing. Indian Railways has already taken a significant step of running two passenger locomotives (in the Thanjavur to Nagore section in Tamil Nadu) and six trains of diesel multiple units (in the Tiruchirapalli to Lalgudi, Dindigul and Karur sections in Tamil Nadu) with a 5 per cent blend of bio-fuel sourced from its in-house esterification plants. In addition, they have planted 1.5 crore Jatropha saplings in railway land which is expected to give yields from the current year. States like Chhattisgarh, Mizoram, Tamil Nadu and Andhra Pradesh have taken up large scale plantation of Jatropha. Similarly many states in our country have energy plantations. What is needed is to increase the output of bio-fuel from Jatropha from the existing average 2 tonnes per hectare to 4 to 6 tonnes per hectare. Oil is a very important and potential product of Jatropha curcas and the oil content of most Jatropha varieties range between 25 and 35 per cent. Research need to be undertaken to develop varieties with more than 45 per cent oil content so that recovery is possible with maximum of 35 per cent under mechanical expelling. This can be attempted through selection, intra-specific, inter-specific hybridization and mutation breeding. Research focus has to be on developing high-yielding varieties with a capacity to produce 4 to 6 kg seed yield per plant or 4 to 6 tonnes per hectare per annum. Though Jatropha grows in a wide range of climatic conditions, it exhibits a wide range of variations in different climates. The variation is believed to be mostly climate related coupled with available soil water moisture. Hence research initiatives should be aimed at production of flowering and fruiting with minimal moisture content in the soil.

Breeding for production of flowers and fruits twice a year helps to increase the overall productivity. Our agricultural scientists have to mount research missions in these areas which will enable the nation to realize energy independence progressively. They must also collaborate with our combustion experts and produce the most fuel efficient engines that are compatible with the bio-fuel produced from Jatropha.

Efficient thorium based nuclear fuel

Large scale generation of power through nuclear fuel is vital for our energy independence programme. We have to study the thorium based programme in relation to the ongoing programmes of the Department of Atomic Energy (DAE). Going critical of fast breeder reactor which is in an advanced stage of construction, development of Advanced Heavy Water Reactor (AHWR) and Accelerator Driven System (ADS) technologies have to be pursued in an integrated way. There are many scientific and technological challenges.

Fast reactors: Fast reactors can make a significant contribution to India's energy requirements, but the rate of increase in fast reactor installed capacity has to follow a certain growth path as plutonium-239, the fuel for the fast reactors, gets generated in nuclear reactors. Thus the rate of new fast reactor capacity addition has to be determined by the rate at which plutonium can be bred. The breeding depends on the fast reactor design and the chemical form of plutonium fuel. Metallic fuel gives much higher breeding ratio whereas plutonium in oxide form gives a lower breeding ratio. So our basic research has to be on the development of metallic fuel on priority. It is only after we have established enough fast reactor capacity, that we can shift to thorium based systems and continue to get power from thorium reactors for a long time.

Thorium technologies: The country has already set up a facility for reprocessing thorium and has designed an Advanced Heavy Water Reactor (AHWR), which aims to derive two-third of its power from thorium and one third from plutonium generated from Fast Breeder Reactor (FBR). Implementation of the AHWR project and development of associated fuel cycle facilities will provide industrial scale experience in the handling of thorium. An important basic research area would be to develop reactor systems based on thorium wherein power derived from thorium can be increased and external input of fissile material can be minimized. It will definitely lead to early utilization of thorium in power production.

Accelerator Driven Systems: The other possibility for thorium utilization is through Accelerator Driven Systems (ADS). ADS have two main components: an accelerator and a reactor. A reactor system using only thorium as fuel cannot become critical as thorium is not a fissile material. To make it critical, an external supply of neutrons is needed. A 'spallation' source can provide an external source of neutrons to achieve criticality in an otherwise sub-critical system. Protons, when accelerated to high energy in an accelerator and made to collide with a target of high atomic number element (such as lead, tungsten, uranium etc.), cause detachment of a large number of neutrons from these nuclides in a process called spallation. The development of an appropriate proton accelerator is the first step towards the development of ADS. The research results will lead to building an accelerator and subsequently the use of the accelerator for detachment of neutrons from heavy elements. Accelerator technology has many other applications. For example, accelerators are useful in health care for treatment of cancer and in basic research as tools to study the structure of atoms. Accelerators are also useful in the industry for chemical processing, where irradiation by accelerators can be used to improve the mechanical and electrical properties of cable insulation.

Efficient hydrogen fuel

During my visit to Iceland, I had a unique experience, which I would like to share with you. The President of Iceland and I, along with our teams, were traveling in a hydrogen fuelled bus. The bus also took us to a hydrogen fuel station and we filled up hydrogen gas in the fuel tank and continued our journey and discussions. I am aware that, hydrogen operated motorcycles, three wheelers and small generators have been developed in the country. In addition, Polymer Electrolyte Membrane Fuel Cell (PEMFC) and Phosphoric Acid Fuel Cell (PAFC) technologies and fuel cell-battery hybrid van have been developed. Hydrogen production from distillery waste and other renewable methods have also been developed. Hydrogen storage in metal hydrides has also been demonstrated. At present, research is in progress to further improve the performance and technology of these vehicles and generators. Particularly the fuel cell powered automobiles will become a reality in the world. In India, an electric car company in collaboration with DRDO has developed a hybrid vehicle which can be run with a fuel cell and the cost per kilometre will be just 40 paise in addition to the pollution free operation of the car. Also, we should know that ISRO launch vehicles use liquid oxygen and hydrogen fuel. Production of liquid hydrogen is being done in Mahendragiri Space Centre. I would urge the research community to concentrate on the areas such as high pressure storage of hydrogen, liquid storage, storage in nano-structure, development of safety codes and standards and development of dedicated engine for hydrogen fuel.

How we can meet these research and development challenges?

I would like to recall two experiences. India's nuclear programme has always been under technological denial for decades from many countries. Every one of the nuclear scientists and science leaders realized that self-reliance is the most promising route to development. Nuclear scientists have always shown the country how nuclear technology can be used for increasing the agricultural produce, medical application and nuclear power generation. Let me share one of my experiences when I was chief of the Aeronautical Development Agency (ADA). It was 1998; India achieved a very important national milestone. This resulted in many nations imposing technology denials and economic sanctions. Particularly, the Light Combat Aircraft programme came to a halt because of collaborating countries breaking the agreements on the development contracts undertaken. I took an emergency meeting of the ADA Board and we formed a National Team for LCA control system with twenty members drawn from seven organizations in the country with a two years' project schedule. In eighteen months, we realized a world class digital fly by wire control system for the LCA. Now, four LCA aircraft are flying and the fifth one is getting ready for flight test. Cumulative flying hours logged by the four aircraft is over 500 hours. The batch production of LCA TEJAS is to commence. The message I would like to give to our nuclear scientists on the day of commemoration of the discovery of Raman Effect is:

Nationally we have the best minds,
Enlist the national team,
The government and the people are with you,
Progress with your vast knowledge and experience,
You will succeed.

Conclusion

Discovery in science provides the greatest inspiration and happiness to the scientists and scientific community. When Einstein discovered the theory of relativity and the equation $e=mc^2$, when Sir C.V. Raman discovered the Raman Effect that explains that molecular scattering is the reason for ocean to be blue, and when Subramaniam Chandrasekar discovered the Black Hole and Chandrasekar Limit, it virtually led to bliss for all these scientists and their teams. No one probably thought of the magnitude of the application of these discoveries at the time they were discovered. The nuclear energy, light spectroscopy, calculation of the life of the sun, all were understood subsequently due to further scientific discoveries. The science leads to development of technologies. Availability of technologies leads to products. It should be the mission of our young and experienced scientists to see that they make scientific discoveries, which will lay the foundation for future technologies of the country leading to new cost effective products for our billion plus people, and also improving the quality of life of our people.

Panchayati Raj in India: The Greatest Experiment in Democracy Ever

Mani Shankar Aiyar

For the first time in independent India, a Union ministry of panchayati raj was set up in May 2004 and I was given the proud privilege of being named the first minister of panchayati raj. My life-long interest in panchayati raj as the salvation for rural poverty and injustice was stoked by the late Professor Balbir Singh in his Indian economics class at St Stephen's. I joined St Stephen's in 1958, the year after the publication of the Report of the Balwantrai Mehta Study Group, the progenitor of contemporary panchayati raj. It is tragic that five decades after Balbir Singh lit the spark of development through democracy in our hearts, we are still struggling to find answers to questions raised—and answered—fifty years ago. Fortunately, thanks to Rajiv Gandhi, we now have constitutional sanctity for panchayati raj but are still a long way from realizing on the ground, and at the grassroots, the rural revolution which animates the vision of Part IX of the Constitution entitled, simply, 'The Panchayats'. This is the most exciting development in India in terms of deepening democratic traditions and promoting participatory development.

We have now experienced more than a decade of economic reforms after the passing of these amendments. But these reforms have hardly touched the lives of the common people. Even if there is no great anger against reforms on the part of the people at large, there is no enthusiasm either. This is because the reformers regard panchayats as being as irrelevant to their purposes as the people regard reforms as being irrelevant to their lives. Reformers have no great objection to panchayats; the tragedy is they regard panchayats as a sideshow or merely as agents who will implement plans and priorities set out from the top. Not until economic reforms are integrated with planning and implementation through these institutions of self-government will grassroots empowerment lead to grassroots development. This then is the right moment to ensure that both move together in tandem. Indeed, panchayati raj needs to be made the fulcrum of the reform process for rural resurgence in India. It was after all launched the same year that saw the reforms process take off.

Rajiv Gandhi used to say that while we were without doubt the world's largest democracy, we were also the world's least representative democracy, with a mere 5000 elected representatives in Parliament and the state assemblies to represent a billion people. That has changed irresistibly, ineluctably, irreversibly. Today with elections having been held to approximately 250,000 panchayats, we are not only the largest but also the most representative democracy in the world. We are also the only country to ensure that out of the 3 million elected office bearers that we have more than one million are women. That is an achievement without precedent in history and without parallel in the world.

When we look at the achievements of the previous decade it is clear that this innovation has empowered the village community. Along with widening the democratic base of India's polity and bringing about significant changes in India's federalism, panchayati raj has led to an amazing development—the emergence of women as leaders. Their participation at the three levels, district, sub-district and village, has not only led to their personal growth but also enabled them to respond to the needs of the more vulnerable sections of the village community.

The constitutional mandate for the marginalized sections—Scheduled Castes and Scheduled Tribes—has provided them also with political space. The panchayats in tribal areas of nine states, in what is called the Fifth Schedule Areas, have been given a special legal dispensation over what is available elsewhere. This special law is called the Panchayats (Extension to Scheduled Areas) Act, 1996 (PESA) and it has been enacted in consonance with an enabling provision in the Constitution. PESA accords full recognition to the rights of tribal communities over natural resources, respects their traditional institutions and gives them vast powers of self-governance. This remarkable law is the first to empower people to redefine their own administrative boundaries.

The powers that are vested in the village assembly, the gram sabha, authorize it to approve all development plans, control all functionaries and institutions in social sectors, as well as manage waterbodies and other natural resources, have ownership of minor forest produce, prevent alienation of land, manage village markets and resolve disputes. The village assembly and panchayat are required to be consulted prior to any move to acquire land or grant any mineral concessions. This revolutionary law has, at one stroke, provided for the empowerment of tribal communities and their political participation and strengthened healthy traditional practices. By providing that at least 50 per cent of the members in the panchayat must be tribals, and that the chairperson must always be a tribal, this law gives tribals the necessary critical mass to ensure that decisions taken in panchayats are not indifferent to or opposed to their interests. The implementation of this law requires much hard work as it entails the loosening of political and bureaucratic control over natural resources in tribal areas.

Panchayati raj has not only sought to empower those who are marginalized. It is basically actuated by the spirit of empowerment of the village community. By providing for the gram sabhas, it has created equal opportunity for all citizens of the village to critically appraise the proposals of the elected body, the village panchayat. The gram sabha has been endowed with powers to identify beneficiaries under various poverty alleviation programmes, to draw up the annual plan and to pass (or withhold approval of) the annual accounts. Therefore, as a body, the gram sabha, which is the collective body of adults resident in the village, voices the hopes and aspirations of the whole village and the underprivileged, prioritizes their needs and allocates resources. It is the body to which the panchayat is accountable and an instrument of direct, as against representative, democracy. The contours of its powers are being drawn and redrawn, but these powers are vast.

Therefore, it can be said that all the components exist for a truly representative governance mechanism for planning and implementing economic development and social justice through panchayats in rural India. However, it is in actualizing this mechanism that progress has been slow and fitful. A great deal remains to be done, and the responses of state authorities and Central ministries have varied. While quite a few have responded with commitment and innovativeness to make the system strong and sustainable, others need to give panchayats their well-deserved place in the sun. The constitutional underpinnings are already there. The Constitution is remarkably explicit regarding the composition of panchayats, their continuity and accountability. It also provides for their power and authority, calling upon state governments to enable them 'by law' to function as 'institutions of self-government' and for the constitution of District Planning Committees (DPCs), which are to make possible planning from below. Article 243G, relating to the powers, authority and responsibilities of panchayat, is the heart of Part IX and the kernel of panchayati raj. Tragically, very few states have even attempted to approximate the goals of Article 243G. Not till this Article is fully implemented in letter and spirit can it be said that we have progressed towards fulfilling the dreams of Mahatma Gandhi and the framers of Part IX.

However, in most states, devolution and decentralization is by executive order under the law rather than 'by law' per se. It must be ensured that all states undertake devolution 'by law', as called for in the Constitution, so that no retrogression in devolution is possible without the explicit concurrence of the state legislature.

It is essential that state governments establish expert bodies to designate clearly the functions to be exercised at each tier of the three-tier system so that there is no confusion and no overlapping between different tiers and development work is synergized at all three levels. Such demarcation of responsibilities at different levels of the system will also facilitate the devolution of functionaries and finances to the appropriate level of the panchayati raj system. Effective devolution requires the devolution of functions with functionaries and finances (the three Fs mentioned above). The sine qua non of effective panchayati raj is the demarcation of responsibilities between the three tiers for each devolved function to go hand in hand with the devolution of functionaries and finances to that level.

The two key functions of the panchayats at each level are defined in Article 243G as the preparation of plans for economic development and social justice, and the implementation of schemes for economic development and social justice.

Unless planning and implementation are undertaken by the panchayats, such panchayats cannot qualify as 'institutions of self-government'. Of course, the Article provides that such planning and implementation will be 'subject to such conditions' as may by law be stipulated. But the central function of panchayats is planning and implementation. Planning is required to be undertaken at every tier of the panchayati raj system, not at the level of the DPC alone. Indeed, the very wording of Article 243ZD, dealing with the District Planning Committees, says the DPC is to 'consolidate the plans prepared by the Panchayats'. The Eleventh Five Year Plan, presently under preparation, must be based on plans prepared by the three tiers of the panchayati raj system (and the municipalities) and consolidated at the district level by the DPCs. It is not till the Planning Commission fulfils its constitutional obligation of making district planning through elected DPCs the basis of all planning that the objectives of clause (a) of Article 243G can be fulfilled.

To assist panchayats in the preparations of plans, state planning bodies should extend technical assistance and the Union and state governments must encourage the involvement of non-governmental organizations (NGOs) in the exercise. Local educational institutions, especially college faculties, local professionals (architects, engineers, doctors, etc.) and retired bureaucrats/technocrats would have a crucial role to play in facilitating scientific planning at all three levels of the panchayati raj system.

In addition to such 'conditions' as may by law be stipulated, state governments must give panchayats at different levels a clear idea of the financial resources available, both tied and untied, to make panchayat-level planning realistic and resource based. This should also encourage panchayats to search for their own resources for need-based projects or programmes which might otherwise have to be postponed or abandoned.

To involve women in the planning process, consultation with the village-level mahila sabha should be built into the planning process.

Equally, implementation is a key responsibility of the panchayats. But this has to be by panchayats functioning as 'institutions of self-government', not as handmaidens of the line departments. In respect of all devolved subjects, implementation must be the responsibility of the panchayats at the appropriate level, with the bureaucracy and technocracy assisting the elected authority in implementation and answerable to the panchayat concerned, not the line department of the state government. That is the way forward. Indeed, for all subjects that have been fully devolved to the panchayats, the line department concerned should be abolished, with the minister retaining only such secretarial staff as is necessary to monitor developments and report to the legislature.

Yet, in most states, there is no planning by panchayats and implementation has been reduced to a nexus between the contractor, the chairperson of the panchayat and the bureaucrats and technocrats of the line departments. In consequence, instead of evolving as 'institutions of self-government', the panchayats have been reduced to functional impotence. Corruption is engendered when chairpersons exercise their authority without the involvement and sanction of the members of the panchayat at all levels and that of the gram sabha at the village level.

Corruption in panchayats at all levels has become rampant in most states because chairpersons are not responsible to the committees of the panchayats or to the general body of the panchayats. In association with the bureaucracy, chairpersons have tended to usurp functions that properly belong to the panchayat as a whole. It is therefore of crucial importance to establish standing and ad hoc committees of the panchayats at each level so that proposals are processed by such committees and then brought before the general body of the panchayat for approval before, during and after the execution of works. Utilization certificates should be issued by the panchayat as a whole and, at the village level, after securing the endorsement of the gram sabha. It is only if this is done that the gram sabhas will have functional relevance, the elected members of the panchayats real and meaningful work to do, and the chairperson operate as chairperson-in-council, thus reducing, if not always completely eliminating, the scope for nepotism and corruption.

The gram sabha must be deeply involved in implementation at all levels because it is the best form of social audit, both pre-implementation and post-implementation. This is also the most effective way of cutting down corruption and nepotism and ensuring transparency and accountability, as well as functioning democracy. In laying down the procedure for panchayat-level implementation at all levels of the panchayati raj system, state governments should specify the role and functions of the panchayats, preferably in line with the role assigned to the gram sabhas in Parliament's Panchayats (Extension to Scheduled Areas) Act, 1996 even for non-Fifth-Schedule areas, especially as regards beneficiary identification, approval of implementation proposals and the issue of utilization certificates.

Present procedures for auditing the accounts of panchayats are serving little purpose because the sheer volume of work is resulting in inordinate delays in audit and action taken thereon. These delays are fuelling corruption and malfeasance in the panchayats. In the light of the experience gained over the last decade, the Comptroller and Auditor-General should be invited to review the arrangements which have been put in place for the audit of the accounts of the panchayats and to make recommendations for quicker, more transparent and effective audit that would deter malpractice.

It is only social audit through the gram sabhas that can effectively ensure adherence to prescribed procedures and transparency in the spending of panchayat moneys. The authorized functions of the gram sabha should specify their responsibilities in regard to social audit.

In elections to the panchayats, there are widespread complaints of electoral malpractice, including the harassment of women candidates, and excessive expenditure, as well as disturbing reports of the criminalization of the panchayati raj system in parts of the country. The Election Commission may be invited to review the experience of the conduct of panchayat elections in different parts of the country with a view to making recommendations that would promote free and fair elections, restraint on election expenditure, ending harassment of women candidates and others belonging to the weaker sections, and the sharp curtailing of criminalization in the panchayati raj system. Moreover, state election commissions should undertake similar reviews.

Whereas the independence and autonomy of the Election Commission at the Centre is beyond question, not all state legislatures have made adequate provision for the independence and autonomy of state election commissions. As independence and autonomy of election commissions constitute the quintessence of democratic practice, in the light of the experience gained hitherto, state legislatures should re-examine the existing legislative provisions in relation to state election commissions.

Legislating on issues relating to panchayats is a responsibility of individual state governments since local government figures in the State List. The Union ministry of panchayati raj provides the constitutional framework and also assumes the responsibility of ensuring adherence to the Constitution. Hence the need for creative, constructive interaction between the Government of India in the Union ministry of panchayati raj and state governments. Towards this end, the ministry convened a Conference of Chief Ministers of States. Acknowledging the fact that Panchayati Raj institutions are the key level of government at the critical interface between the mass of people and the institutions that govern them, this conference identified eighteen dimensions which require critical inputs and discussion with state governments. The conference resolved to hold Seven Round Table Conferences of State Ministers of Panchayati Raj between July and

December 2004. These round tables covered a multitude of topics relating to panchayats and passed 150 recommendations which constitute a joint action plan for the Centre and the states. Following up these recommendations and implementing them in right earnest by state governments with support from the Centre, they have the potential to change the face of governance in rural India.

Education: At the Crossroads

Pratap Bhanu Mehta

The Indian education system is at a crossroads. India has a relatively young population, with over five hundred million citizens under thirty. The demand for education, and the recognition that it is vital for personal advancement and empowerment, has now penetrated all levels of society. With the economy projected to grow at an average of eight per cent, the demand for skilled labour is exploding. The transition from an agrarian/rural economy to an urban/industrial economy can be facilitated only by education. The debate over the choice between primary education on the one hand, and tertiary on the other is a spurious one: India needs both robust primary education and innovative higher education.

Yet the manifest need for attention to education is scarcely matched by action. While enrollment rates are up to ninety per cent, more than thirty per cent of India's citizens remain illiterate. While there are islands of excellence, the average quality of schooling remains poor. One recent study of a high achievement state like Karnataka showed that average learning achievements for fifth graders were lower than what they should be for first graders. While the government runs decent schools at the secondary level like Kendriya and Navodaya Vidyalayas, teacher absenteeism is as high as thirty percent. The system of vocational education is in a state of extraordinary disrepair. While some efforts have been made to rejuvenate ITIs through public private partnerships, these cater to barely more than a few hundred thousand students. Our gross enrollment ratios in higher education are close to eight per cent, compared to an average of twenty per cent in East Asia. While in terms of gross numbers India produces the world's largest number of engineers, their average quality does not serve the needs of the economy. Every sector of the economy, from IT (as the NASSCOM report published this year showed) to textiles, from aviation engineering to nursing, is projecting a shortfall of skilled talent. India's position in the basic sciences, as judged by the number of articles published in top referred journals, is slipping. Arguably, the shortage of human resources might turn out to be one of the biggest obstacles to sustaining growth. Education is also the medium through which inequities in society are produced. Because islands of excellence are few, and the best and the brightest have the ability to secede from the system by going abroad, inequalities are widening.

The reasons for India's poor performance in education are complex. Arguably, keeping the population deprived of education has often served the interest of ruling elites since education, by disrupting the existing social equilibrium, would also undermine their power. This is true of old 'brahminical' elites as it is of their successor leaders from backward castes, who have equally neglected the education of the disempowered. There simply has never been any political commitment to education, pure and simple. When the government occasionally shows glimmers of commitment it is hobbled by three factors. First, while most people agree that spending on education should rise up to at least six per cent of GDP from the current three point six per cent, the pattern of wasteful government expenditure on subsides, makes reallocating priorities difficult. Second, the government's own accountability structures make its spending less effective than it should be. By one estimate the government spends almost four thousand rupees per child enrolled in school education. This should be sufficient to produce decent if not spectacular results. Yet teacher absenteeism and other leakages make this expenditure less effective. Third, the government's approach to education is hobbled by an overbearing statism. Education is the last bastion of the licence–permit raj that created artificial shortages in so many sectors of the economy. In higher education for instance we are perhaps the only country in the world where the state regulates everything: whom you should admit, what you should charge them and what you should teach them. There are huge entry barriers: universities can be set up only through acts of legislation, approval for starting professional courses is cumbersome and based on an archaic conception of disciplines, accreditation systems are extremely weak and arbitrary, and government permits very little differentiation between institutions in terms of the salaries they are allowed to offer or the fees they can charge. High fees and substandard education are symptoms of a supply shortage. On the other hand, except for a couple of dozen universities, the public university system remains abysmal on all measures of performance, whether in teaching or research. Again the core problem is that these institutions have a series of perverse incentives, have an administrative structure that empowers government more than educational professionals, and have absolutely no drive to distinguish themselves.

In some ways the debate over public versus private education in India is misleading. At one level the paradox is that there is a huge amount of de facto privatization in the system: more than seventy per cent of the available seats in engineering and more than fifty per cent in medical schools are in the private sector. At the school level, even in a state like Kerala more than fifty per cent students are enrolled in private institutions, and this number is rising in all states. But a lot of this privatization takes pathological forms as well since the rules for granting approvals are not transparent. In short, India will need greater public investment, a regulatory structure more conducive to better quality private participation, and reform of accountability in public institutions if it is to meet the enormous challenges its demography poses. The five hundred million young people can be an asset, or a ticking time bomb. And a lot will depend on educational opportunities provided to them.

Any democratic society has to be concerned about the inequality of access to education. The demand for affirmative action measures like reservations stems from a genuine concern. Given the vast inequalities in background conditions of Indian citizens, some form of affirmative action, even radical affirmative action, is inevitable. But a society also has to honestly confront four questions in designing affirmative action programmes: Are numerically mandated quotas the most effective form of affirmative action? Who should be the beneficiaries of affirmative action? Are quotas as they currently exist, largely a ruse to divert attention away from the fact that all the things that need to be done to ensure effective access are not being done? And what happens to a society when identity is used by the state as an axis of distributing goods? It would a fair summary to say that while most of Indian society supports some form of affirmative action, it is deeply divided on all four of these questions. The tragedy is that institutional forms in India do not allow for experimentation with a variety of affirmative action programmes. For instance, numerically mandated quotas are just one form. Others have proposed schemes that involve the construction of a deprivation index that awards handicap points based on a variety of deprivations students face: income, region, gender, rural, minority and so forth. These indexes do not privilege only one axis of distribution and are in principle more supple and responsive to the different dimensions of deprivation. Would these be better in picking out potential in Indian society?

There is a great deal of debate over intended beneficiaries as well. There is more consensus that Scheduled Castes and Tribes are more straightforwardly a candidate for a target group than other Backward Castes. The history of oppression they have faced is of a different order than OBCs and it is a travesty of justice that we think of all targeted groups as belonging to the same narrative. There is also more division over the inclusion of the so-called creamy layer in reservations. As an empirical fact most reservations, both within SCs and OBCs, are cornered by a relatively small elite group within them. Should members of these castes, who have attained relatively empowered status, be excluded from reservations, as the Supreme Court has often suggested? The trouble is that the answer to this question depends upon what you think the point of affirmative action is. If it is representation of different groups, then the exclusion does not make sense. If it is to compensate for lack of economic opportunities, then there is a case for exclusion. But if this is the rationale, then it is not clear why caste should be privileged in the first place as an axis of distribution. There is good evidence that income is the best predictor of opportunities of accessing education. If this is the case, empowering students with financial resources, or a robust public education system is a far surer means of ensuring access than palliative measures like reservation. But alas, the Indian education system is hobbled by the absence of the virtue it needs most: honest self-appraisal.

The Woman Citizen

Urvashi Butalia

In many ways women in India have a better deal—at least on paper—than they do in many other countries. The Constitution guarantees them equality, they have the vote, abortion is legal, they have some form of protective legislation. As a result of the 73rd and 74th amendments to the Constitution (by which 33 per cent of elected posts in municipal and village elections are reserved for women) there are now over a million women in positions of power at this level. Some of the most powerful people in the corporate world are women, a number of India's women politicians have shown themselves to be astute and clever, and some of the most important protest movements in recent years—such as the Narmada anti-dam movement and the Right to Information movement—have not only been led by women, but are made up substantially of women cadres.

But there is an important flip side to this rather positive picture: despite having proved themselves to be not only equal to, but often better than, men, women in India continue to suffer the worst kind of discrimination and violence, and attitudinal biases against them remain. This is the case not only among ordinary people but also in the view of the State where the woman citizen is by and large defined as a secondary citizen for whom citizenship and the rights that come with it are mediated through the family, or through her husband. Whether it is in marriage laws, or cases of custody, or inheritance, or indeed in the workplace, most legislation views the woman not as an independent entity but someone who comes second to the man, or to her family. Until recently, virtually all marriage laws gave more rights to men than to women: under the Christian Marriage Act, for example, while the man could sue for divorce on a number of grounds, for the woman it was almost impossible. This has now changed after years of hard work by women's groups, particularly Chrisitan groups, and with some support from the religious establishment. The Hindu Marriage Act has only recently recognized women's right to property, and the rape law still does not recognize marital rape as a crime or an offence—the assumption being that in a marriage the man has the right to do what he likes with his wife.

India's record on violence against women is not something to be proud of. According to national figures, there is one crime committed against women in India every three minutes, one case of cruelty by husbands or relatives takes place every nine minutes, one dowry death takes place every seventy-seven minutes, and the number of rape cases has gone up exponentially over the last few years. The last decade has seen a ten per cent increase in overall literacy in the country, taking the figure up to 64.8 per cent. Female literacy, however, remains at 54.16 per cent. Sex ratio figures tell their own dismal story, with some states, such as Haryana and Punjab, showing a figure of 704 women for every 1000 men—despite legislation that bans pre-natal sex selection tests, unscrupulous doctors are more than willing to conduct such tests and help parents abort female foetuses. If women as a whole are marginalized, tribal and Dalit women are much more so, belonging, as they do, to groups or clans that are already on the margins of society and strongly discriminated against.

From time to time the State has demonstrated its willingness to take account of this situation and has also occasionally played a role in setting right this skewed balance. In the early seventies, the Sixth Five-Year Plan introduced, for the first time, a separate chapter on women. Around the same time, the government commissioned a report on the status of women. Titled 'Towards Equality', and published in 1974, this report of the Committee on the Status of Women brought some startling information about women to the public eye. 1992 saw the bringing in of the 73rd and 74th Amendments and in 1997, in response to a writ petition filed by twelve women's groups in Delhi, the Supreme Court issued a set of guidelines on sexual harassment at the workplace. The most recent pro woman legislation to be introduced is the Protection of Women against Domestic Violence Act, that came into being in October 2006, and that recognizes a crime that is widespread but that has so far remained invisible.

Since the Sixth Five-Year Plan women's concerns have formed part of virtually all policy documents in India. As well, every political party has something to say about women in its manifesto. But these declarations do not always translate into action—so for example, despite their stated commitment to women, almost all political parties have strongly resisted the attempt to extend reservation of elected seats for women in the national parliament.

Thus, while in the eyes of the State and the bureaucracy, as well as within political parties, the overall attitude to the woman citizen remains ambivalent, and somewhat contradictory, it is from within the women's movement that the strongest battle for recognition for women as equal citizens has been fought. India has a strong and dynamic women's movement that is spread out in many states and that continues to deal with many different issues, be they health, sanitation, political power, food, water, violence, sexuality, fundamentalism and so on. It is because of the efforts of women activists that the laws on rape and dowry were changed after years of neglect; equally it is women activists who have been fighting for a gender just system of legislation in India, it is they who fought to bring in legislation banning sex pre-selection, and it is they who continue to fight on a host of other fronts.

However, no matter how hard women's groups work, and how much difference they succeed in making in policy documents and in commitments on paper, little will change for Indian women unless there is a will, and an implementation machinery, as well as trained officers, who can put some of the progressive legislation in place. And even if that is done, little will change unless people begin to recognize that women are not secondary citizens, but equal citizens whose work, whether in the home or outside, contributes substantially to the overall economy of the country, and without whom, this economy, and its invisible backing, would collapse. For India to be in the twenty-first century as a modern country, it needs to show and prove its commitment to its women citizens.

The New Non-Resident Indian

Sanjay Suri

'And Mrs Sidhu?' Mr Sidhu stepped aside a little grandly to let Kamlesh step up to the BA check-in counter at Delhi airport. He needed occasional reminders that she was with him after all. Like good Indian couples they usually stepped out into the world in a row of two.

Kamlesh was his Mrs, he her Mister, and about no one else's. At twenty-two when he left Ludhiana for London, never to return except with a return ticket in his bag, he was just Gursharan. Later he found that loaders at Heathrow aren't misters. Most of his life he was pleased enough getting just Seedo'd by whites. But in Ludhiana that changed. On his annual holiday to India he became Mr Sidhu.

Now his time was up. A look at his watch told him as he stepped towards immigration control, wife presumably following, that in about three hours he'd lose his NRI status. His flight would depart for London, his daughter would drive him from Heathrow to resume retirement at his three-bedroom house in Hounslow with a carpet and an upstairs and downstairs. There he would watch Zee TV, ask what's for lunch, and dress for doing the grocery. Suddenly, he didn't want to go.

London was never such a great place to stay in, really, just a great place to visit India from. He was coming from where everyone in Punjab wanted to get to, he was special. In migrating he had pole-vaulted over the entire caste system. As NRI he was the new Brahmin—when he visited India. As the eventual middle class man of London suburbia he was one among so many. In London he was tolerated, in Ludhiana he was feted. He was, all these years, anyhow. But after this time he was not sure any more. Ludhiana felt different, India was different. In a way that made him not so special any more.

He'd been seeing this change over his last few visits, but for the Diwali visit this year more than any other. Annually through his life in England he'd complained to Kamlesh about all the shopping they'd do for everyone every time they went back to India. They would travel free, but how he loved to say, 'All the money I save on ticket I spend on shopping.' And since he could get more baggage past his friends at the airport than paying passengers, there was that much more to take for his and Kamlesh's tabbars.

For that one time a year, it was a pleasure to shop for others, not himself or his own family. Because every gift was announcement of the superior world he occupied abroad. The things you don't get in India, the things that lead to countdowns before the opening of a suitcase. That unpacking made him more than any local mister in Ludhiana.

This time the opening of the suitcase had been a lot less suspenseful. There had been fewer calls too before he left London, fewer lines starting 'Saddey vaastey...' Now his sala drove a Ford, a good deal later and newer than his own in Hounslow. The roads were wider and straighter, everyone had money to spend, the malls made his packed suitcases look empty. No more was he a privileged citizen of Consumerland. He could now save himself some money on the shopping, but he'd lost his status as Santa.

This time he was in fact returning with shopping of the sort he'd never dreamt he could in India. There was winter wear, designer stuff, the brands he could never buy in England. And he was returning with memories of parties, places far, far warmer, and smarter, than any he knew in that in his brown west London; he'd been to non-brown London only a few times all his life. Yes, Ludhiana was still substantially tacky, but where it was smart, it was smarter than anything he knew in London.

Kamlesh had followed him to a couple of chairs in the waiting hall. He put his bags down, and walked up to pick up samosas and tea. No more did anyone ask for dollars, now that they were inside the terminal. With some misgivings, Sidhu had seen the difference disappear between rupee and sterling. His sala had traveled to Europe with his wife, they had used their Indian visa card to do their shopping. The rupee was making it to the western world. Just about every difference he'd seen, even celebrated, all his life was dissolving before his eyes. Now every Indian he knew in India was becoming NRI-like. And if Ludhiana had power and electricity all the time, and fast new roads, then what was left special about living in England?

But his new India was doing something for him in England. He wanted to meet some white guy, just any from his old work place, to say that Tata was buying Corus, the company that was once British steel. This new image had given him a talking point, but with no one around to put it to. What a change. All his life he had visited India and boasted he was from Britain, now he wanted to go to England and boast of India. How he wanted to enjoy this cleverness by association. The more those clever guys would do in Bangalore, the taller he could now feel doing nothing.

What strange things he was now hearing. That India invests more in UK than UK in India. That India is now the second largest investor in UK, that about 500

Indian companies are now doing business in Britain, offering thousands of jobs to Brits. That British universities now look to Indian centres for biotechnology. And all done by a sardarji who did not try to run to UK like the rest. He was making India as smart as UK, at places smarter.

It was time for the flight back, maybe he was headed the wrong way because India had finally taken off. Through years of habit, he checked his belongings. Yes, passport, wallet, ticket. Well, ticket. For the first time he asked himself if he could now go to India on a one-way ticket. Nice retirement home, India. Nice place also to live and do business in. Annoying that India should have done this a generation or two too late for him. Could he come next time on a one-way ticket? He saw no reason why not, and began to see many reasons why. In India he had variously been mister, uncle and sahib. In England he was nobody to anybody, as Hounslow was nothing amidst anywhere. But you can't give up England for India. Or can you? He fastened his belt and tried not to think.

We Don't Like Cricket, We Love It

John Wright

In India's teeming cities, kids always find somewhere to play cricket: in narrow side streets, between buildings, beside railway tracks, in parking lots and, on Sundays, in the empty business districts. Legend has it that Sunil Gavaskar's technique was the result of playing in an alley where you had to play straight because hitting a wall or a window was out. In the countryside, they even play in paddy fields and in the sand on dunes. We once drove past a game going on around a dead horse. Andrew Leipus reckoned it must have dropped a catch.

The Azad Maidan is a Mumbai rarity: an open patch of clay and grass in the middle of the city. The Maidan is home to twenty cricket clubs, each with its own pitch and pavilion, which may be nothing more than a tent. You don't take your deck chair to the Maidan, because space is at a premium. There might be twenty games going on in an area ten times the size of a rugby field, so there's a lot of overlap: being at long-on in one game could place you at bat-pad in another. It's non-stop action–bowlers charging in, batsmen throwing the bat, fielders throwing themselves, puffs of red dust raised by forty batsmen pounding up and down twenty pitches, and a barrage of advice from the sidelines. In a corner of the ground, a mob of people mill around waiting their turn to have a hit or a bowl against a wall. At 6 a.m. that morning there would have been a queue of people, young and not-so-young, wanting a go in the practice nets run by the clubs.

In the–relatively speaking–smaller towns there might be one turf wicket or there might be none. During my first one-day series, we played in Bhubaneswar, a city of more than a million people. I got some odd looks when I told the team there'd be fielding practice the next morning; they said there was nowhere to do it. Our fielding had been awful, so I vowed to find a ground. I was up at the crack of dawn next day and set off with the liaison man to find a suitable venue. We went to the soccer ground, where the grass was too long; then to the athletics stadium, where there was no grass at all and the surface was like a gravel road. Our Test opener, S.S. Das, was a local boy so I asked to be taken to his club ground. I'd been told it was unsuitable but figured it couldn't be any worse than what I'd seen. There was a concrete strip with a mud outfield that was so uneven you could get seasick walking out to bat. I couldn't comprehend how a product of that environment could develop into an international cricketer. I noticed some players, when venturing onto a Test arena, would touch the ground, then place their hand on their heart and forehead. This very Indian gesture is a mark of respect for the place in which you practice your craft and earn your living. Many of India's classical musicians and dancers do the same when they go on stage.

Even though–or perhaps because–they start out playing the game in such insalubrious settings and straitened circumstances, India's best players possess great flair and, in some special cases, pure artistry. Rahul Dravid can appear unassertive, even passive, but looks are deceptive: the air of tranquillity is accompanied by a precision-tooled technique and an iron will that combine to blunt, then dismantle, bowling attacks. Sachin Tendulkar has the entire repertoire and can choose between subtlety and aggression, wrist and muscle, or touch and power, like a golfer selecting a club. V.V.S. Laxman is the cricketing equivalent of a faith-healer; his hands seem to possess magical properties enabling him to dispatch the ball in whichever direction takes his fancy. Sourav Ganguly strokes the ball as if not wanting to damage it and hits spinners for six down the ground with the nonchalance of a man tilting a top hat, as the great cricket writer Alan Ross wrote of Colin Cowdrey. And then there's Virender Sehwag, cricket's Jumping Jack Flash. When he goes off, you do not leave your seat, regardless of hunger, thirst or calls of nature.

India stops for cricket. When a team is announced, they break away from the news or current affairs programmes and cross live to their cricket reporter. Every news channel scrolls live cricket scores across the bottom of the screen along with the weather, the stock market and breaking news. When there was a terrorist attack on the Parliament in New Delhi during a Test match in 2001, it took some channels a while to realize that it probably wasn't appropriate to keep running the cricket score.

When Harvinder Singh, a fast bowler from Punjab, made his debut in a one-day tournament in Toronto, the appliance shops in his hometown stayed open well past midnight so that people who didn't own a TV could watch the local hero. During the 2003 World Cup, the residents of a village in northern India that didn't have cable TV chipped in Rs 30,000 to get a 6.5 km cable run in from the nearest town. They put TV sets on tractors in community areas and had generators and car batteries on standby in case they lost electricity. When that happened during one match, they restored the picture by connecting the TV to a high-voltage overhead wire.

During a Test in Delhi, Sehwag dived for a catch at mid-wicket and stayed down. He thought he'd broken his shoulder, but it turned out to be a sprained joint. However, Andrew decided on a precautionary x-ray to make sure nothing else had been damaged, so Sehwag was bunged into a standby ambulance that contained so many doctors that Andrew had to hitch a ride with the police escort, several jeeps full of heavily-armed cops. They barrelled over to the hospital, sirens blaring, and lights flashing, as if they were rushing the President to the operating theatre after an assassination attempt. At the hospital, Leipus had to fight his way through a scrum of specialists to get to Sehwag. When the patient mentioned that he was feeling a bit faint, i.e. claustrophobic, the specialists insisted that he remain overnight for observation. As Leipus said, it was just India looking after one of its princes.

Not that long ago hockey was the sport in which India strutted on the global stage. But since India won the last of its eight Olympic gold medals in 1980, international success has been hard to come by and the sport has been in decline. India's cricketers won the World Cup in 1983 and the World Championship tournament in Australia two years later, and since then cricket has steadily cemented its position as India's no. 1 sport.

The potent combination of television and the one-day game has been a major factor in cricket's rise. TV has taken the game to far-flung comers of the country, where previously it was hardly played at all. The players now emerging from these regions have learned the game by watching and copying, which in some ways is preferable to being taught how to play by coaches. As a result, the likes of Sehwag or the wicketkeeper-batsman Mahendra Singh Dhoni can come out of nowhere with methods based on instinct and improvisation, and without the fear of failure that can be instilled by over-coaching and a conventional career path.

Indian cricket was far removed from the environment that I had played and coached in. It was involved and exciting. People would come to watch us practice in their thousands. On the drive to some grounds, I could see families gathered either at the side of the road or leaning over balconies or on other vantage points, just to see our bus go past. Mothers holding their babies, dads dressed in singlets, young kids smiling and waving. Brash young men on motorcycles would race right up alongside the bus, risking life and limb to wave frantically at their favourites. All the buses had curtains on them so the players could get some privacy.

There is no typical India or typical Indian. I've been a guest at the Maharajah of Gwalior's palace and at the ultra-modern headquarters of Infosys, the Bangalore-based software giant whose revenue in 2005–06 was US$2.15 billion. All of this is India, and the boys I worked with belonged to a country of a billion people where languages, customs and the landscape changed every few hundred kilometres.

I tried to understand the country through the Indian dressing room. It had Hindus, Muslims, Christians and Sikhs. Some were very religious, others less so. On checking into a hotel room, some players would put up pictures of their gods on the television or bedside table and pray at these mini-shrines every day. India has twenty-two official languages and, on a given day, there could be eight languages, other than English, spoken in our dressing room. Our run-outs sometimes suggested that the boys were perhaps not calling in the same tongue. Ganguly and Laxman, who weren't exactly greyhounds to start with, once managed to have a head-on collision. Unless they were talking to the opposition, the players generally swore in Hindi. Some boys were vegetarian, some weren't. Some ate rice, others ate wheat. From an outsider's point of view, you wondered what one corner of India had in common with the other. In our dressing room, it was cricket.

Historically, Indian cricket has had a heavy focus on the individual star but as public expectation grows there's an increasing emphasis on the result rather than individual performances. Getting the boys to play as a team was a priority. I used to tell them their fans deserved a fighting team rather than fighting individuals. The worst times for me were when team pride and a sense of obligation to the fans weren't in evidence; but when they went into battle together and fired up, the crowd's response was something to see.

Indian fans don't spend much time in a state of emotional equilibrium. If they're not in ecstasy, they're in despair. If we'd won, the people at the airports we passed through en route to the next game were all smiles; if we'd lost, the atmosphere would be subdued but never, it must be said, hostile. Paradoxically perhaps, Indian fans are demanding but forgiving. They have short memories and come the next game, they're once again full of hope and willing to invest the same amount of emotional energy.

It's actually not that easy to see big games live. Tickets are expensive, prohibitively so for the person in the street. In Chennai you paid Rs 200 for a 'squatting' seat, i.e. to plonk your backside on a small area of concrete. For a seat, you'd pay three times as much. The cheapest seats for a one-dayer at Eden Gardens were about Rs 700, although students and cricketers got them for as little as Rs 150. That was all very well but getting your hands on those tickets meant queuing up for hours, if not overnight, because there were never enough to go around. In the major centres, like Mumbai, only 10 per cent of the seats were available to the public, with the rest set aside for the host association's league or member clubs, donors, sponsors and other state associations. On top of that, thousands of complimentary tickets would be distributed to local government bigwigs and politicians, the police, the stadium's suppliers of commodities, such as electricity and water, and anyone else who had to be kept happy.

When India played South Africa in a one-dayer in late 2005, the queue began to form early on Friday, at a ticket outlet that opened on Saturday morning, for a game on Monday. By the time the outlet opened, the queue was a kilometre long. An eleven-year-old boy and his father travelled 90 km and spent the night on the street to give themselves a chance of getting 300-rupee 'squat' seats. The police on duty were worried that the boy might get hurt if there was a rush when the booth opened, so they moved him to the head of the queue and gave him a chair to sit on. He got the first ticket and had his photo in the local paper. The father told the paper his son wanted to be a cricketer and the family was planning to move closer to Mumbai to give him a better chance.

Getting a ticket was only half the battle. If you wanted to see the first ball bowled, you had to be queuing to get into the ground at least two hours before the start of play. Often, when we played in the smaller centres, there were ticketing fiascos that led to angry ticket-holders clashing with police because the ground was full and they weren't allowed in. The president of one association was arrested for circulating 25,000 fake tickets, which led to 10,000 disgruntled ticket-holders protesting outside the stadium and getting a tickle-up from the police for their pains. One of those on the receiving end happened to be a lawyer who promptly sued.

To a Westerner, getting in to watch the game seems a mixed blessing. Ordinary spectators aren't allowed to take in bags or cameras, and often not even food or water. Alcohol is only available in the corporate boxes and special clubhouse areas. Buying something to eat and drink means queuing up–yet again. If the food is rubbish or costs too much or runs out, well, that's just too bad. These people put up with a lot to watch India play and I could understand their resentment when their support and stoicism were rewarded with an insipid performance.

India has an unspoilt enthusiasm for cricket and the numbers are mind-boggling. They reckon the minimum TV audience for a big one-day international is 200 million, which works out at four people in front of every accounted-for TV set in the country. Occasionally, it hits 400 million which roughly equates to the combined populations of the United States, Britain and France. ESPN Star, the network that covered most of our overseas tours, created a fantasy league competition called Super Selector that you played via the internet. An hour after the first episode, they had 8,000 registered players. By the next morning they had 30,000. The producers in India asked the UK company running Super Selector's computer servers to upgrade their systems because they anticipated a lot of traffic. They were told that the company had fifteen years' experience of handling fantasy league traffic and knew what it was doing. Within two months the system crashed. By then Super Selector had 450,000 players, which was about thirty times as much traffic as the UK company had ever handled.

Cricinfo, the game's biggest website, is also the largest single-sport website in the world, which is amazing given how few countries play cricket to a serious level. I'm sure a high proportion of their hits come from India and Indian expatriates. During the India-Pakistan tests in March 2005, the website was accessed by 4.6 million separate computers. When India played Sri Lanka six months later, the figure was up to 5.8 million.

I soon realized that India doesn't stop at its borders. There are one billion Indians in India and then there's the Indian diaspora, the many millions of Indians scattered around the world. Cricinfo's second biggest source of traffic is that well-known cricketing hotbed, the USA. Obviously, there are all sorts of expatriates in America, but I'd wager that a lot of those American residents logging on to Cricinfo are Indian. Indians living in the UK formed the Bharat Army which descended on South Africa for the World Cup, and when we toured Australia in 2004 we had the Swami Army, made up of Indians studying at Australian institutions.

I don't think any other touring team in the world gets the kind of reception Indian cricketers do everywhere. Indians in the far corners of the world think nothing of inviting a group of 17–20 people home for dinner. In the West Indies, a doctor and his wife took the week off just to cook for the team. In Zimbabwe, Praful and Clement travelled from Botswana to Zimbabwe to see a one-day game and then shouted the entire team a night's stay on a game farm.

The Indians I met on tour welcomed me as one of their own. Arvind, an accountant, and his wife Kapila, a doctor, were from Johannesburg. They reckoned that since the end of 2003 they'd travelled 80,000 km to watch the Indian team, giving up holidays and putting in long hours at work to be able to go to India's games in South Africa. There's a group of UK businessmen, led by Jayesh Patel, who started by following Indian touring teams around England and have now graduated to jetting in to wherever the action is. 'It's like India's calling us,' they say. On the spur of the moment they flew out to watch the Mumbai test against Australia in 2004. It was all over in three days, but India won, so they didn't feel short-changed. One of the group prides himself on watching every minute of every match India plays, either live or on TV, regardless of sleep deprivation or disruption to his body clock. I heard of Indian fans who by mid-2005 had already booked yachts so they can sail from island to island during the 2007 World Cup in the West Indies.

But the people who never cease to amaze you are the ordinary Indians whose love for the game and their team withstands pressures and circumstances that Westerners struggle to comprehend. People would stop me in the street to thank me for being 'our' coach. It was humbling, but also guilt-inducing, because many of those who thanked me for doing a well-paid job that I loved led lives of day-to-day struggle. The gratitude and support I received from ordinary Indians was the most positive force I've ever encountered, in that it simultaneously lifted me and kept my feet on the ground. More than anything else, that was what kept me going through the hard, lonely times.

I still find it hard to put India's passion for cricket into perspective. I've heard it compared to rugby in New Zealand. Others say that cricket and cinema are India's two great forms of popular entertainment, and many Indians respond to cricket as they would to a colourful Bollywood melodrama. Then there's the big-picture view. In his address to the team in 2001, Harsha Bhogle told them that only two things united India: cricket and the army. Like Brazil and football, and New Zealand and rugby, cricket is intrinsic to how Indians see themselves and is, therefore, part of the image they present to the world.

Cricket is increasingly becoming an expression of national identity, an essential part of the new India. (There are certainly far more Indian flags being waved at cricket grounds these days than when I toured in 1989.) Just as India is flexing its muscles in regional and global affairs, those who run Indian cricket are determined to use their financial clout to make India a major–perhaps *the* major–player in the game. It mightn't be a case of No More Mr Nice Guy but the days when India could be condescended to and treated like a lightweight by the international cricket community are gone for good.

Nationalism in Popular Hindi Cinema

Namrata Joshi

'Ik pair future mein te ik pair past mein rakh ke hum aaj par moot rahe hain'
(With one leg in the future and the other
in the past we are peeing on the present)
—From Rakyesh Omprakash Mehra's *Rang De Basanti*

It's a dialogue that reverberated across the country's cinema halls early this year and was reciprocated with many approving wolf-whistles and cat-calls. What have we made of our country? Can nothing become of this nation? Has our Great Indian Dream come undone? The stridency of the sentiment instantly struck a chord with the cynical Indian middle class that is known to be largely pessimistic about the country and its problems, especially those that affect it the most—unemployment, inflation, corruption.

Cut to 1948. Ramesh Saigal's *Shaheed*, perhaps the first nationalist film of post-Independence India, reflected an entirely different spirit: not an overwhelming scepticism but an attitude of do or die. Country was paramount, you were not meant to ask what it had given you but had to sacrifice yourself for building it up from the scratch. It meant letting go of close family relationships if they came in the way, it meant a revolutionary son taking on a colonial father within the confines of their own home. The code of martyrdom ruled supreme and the popular song was '*Watan ki raah mein watan ke naujawan shaheed ho*' (the youth of the nation must become a martyr for its cause).

Popular cinema may not change the state of the nation; it may be ineffective in dealing with the complexity of our polity and society. However, its presumed naiveté, sentimentality and facile narratives notwithstanding, it has a quaint way of managing to reflect the mood of the nation. So, from the unwavering faith in one's homeland to an utter disillusionment it's been a long journey into the heart of cinematic nationalism.

Shaheed's metaphor of 'nation before self' was reflected in many a film of the '50s. In Mehboob Khan's *Mother India* (1957) the village became a microcosmic representation of the country and a mother's ultimate sacrifice of her son for the sake of the community was underlined with a patriotic significance. Cinema was about coming together; it was about solidarity, nation-building, progressing and moving ahead. Nationalism was a heady idealism, energetic and vibrant. Take Satyen Bose's *Jagriti* (1954) which exhorted children to worship the nation and its martyrs; it asked them to handle the nation with care: '*Hum laaye hain toofan se kishti nikal ke, is desh to rakhna mere bachchon sambhal ke*'. Years later this old-worldly spirit got reflected again in Ashutosh Gowariker's *Lagaan* (2001), a feel-good fable about the unbeatable might of underdog India.

Back in the '50s a series of films had also started talking of a young nation's problems. *Shree 420* (1955) captured post-Independence conflict of cultures in India, it talked of migration to the cities and the consequent unemployment, materialism and corruption. It was a romantic paean to the innocent, real India of the villages as against the Westernized modernity of the emerging cities. How would India combine the necessary modernity and economic productivity with its traditional ethos? A whole new genre of cinema addressed this issue: Bimal Roy's *Do Bigha Zameen* (1953), Sombhu Mitra/Amit Moitra's *Jagte Raho* (1956) and B.R. Chopra's *Naya Daur* (1957); Roy's *Naukri* (1954) focused on the plight of the educated unemployed and Saigal's *Phir Subah Hogi* (1958) dealt with the homeless, the slum and pavement dwellers and the dispossessed: '*Chino Arab humara, Hindustan humara. Rehne ko ghar nahin hai, sara jahan humara*' (China, Arab, India is ours; we don't have a home to stay but the entire world is ours).

However, even when these filmmakers reflected the growing cynicism with Nehruvian socialism the critiques remained humanist than braying. There was the possibility of revival. 'Woh subah kabhi to aayegi (the dawn will come) was the refrain of hope in Phir Subah Hogi. The bedrock of idealism, innocence, compassion and solidarity was always there to fall back on; there was a tremendous faith in collective change. Remember Saathi haath badhana (Friend lend a hand), the call for reform in Naya Daur?

In the 1960s, in the aftermath of the Indo-Pak war of 1965, Manoj Kumar donned the character of Bharat and probed, rather self-righteously, into the urban-rural schism yet again. *Upkar* (1967) (which he himself referred to as a '16,000-foot-long celluloid flag of India') was a cinematic interpretation of Lal Bahadur Shastri's slogan '*Jai Jawan Jai Kisan*'. It said that the peasant's hard work was as important for the nation's progress as the dams and the factories. *Purab Aur Paschim* (1970) played on the East-West polarity by pitching a traditional, religious India against a debauched, hedonistic West. The message was for the expatriates to return to the roots.

A similar sentiment echoed once again in Aditya Chopra's *Dilwale Dulhania Le Jayenge* (1995) and nationalism in the age of globalization came in vogue. You could dress up in Tommy Hilfigers but were 'Indian' enough not to sleep with your girlfriend before marriage; you could tour through Europe but found love and peace in Punjab's yellow mustard fields. In Karan Johar's *Kabhi Khushi Kabhie Gham* (2001) nationalism was all about pugnaciously making the Brits sing '*Jana Gana Mana*' in the very heart of London. Nationalism was about maintaining cloying Indian values and traditional souls within a global exterior.

Things changed with Ashutosh Gowariker's *Swades* (2004), a film that bridged the global-rural Indian divide. The global Indian here believed in affirmative action, community development, empowerment, self-reliance and self-governance. He left his treasured job in NASA to return to his village and initiated change—bridged the caste divide, solved water and power problems and saved the local school. *Swades* marked a coming back full circle to the *Naya Daur* of yore.

The 1962 Indo-China war gave Hindi films another genre to reinforce nationalism: that of the war movies. Chetan Anand's *Haqeeqat* (1964) denounced China even as it tried to raise the morale of a fatigued, defeated army. Since then war in Bollywood, right till J.P. Dutta's *Border* (1997) and Farhan Akhtar's *Lakshya* (2004) has given us several patriotic tokens: the desh-bhakti geet, the secular Hindu-Muslim-Sikh-Christian soldiers, the sacrifice for the nation.

The genre mutated into a new clarion call to patriotism in Anil Sharma's *Gadar* (2001). The film played on the animus against Pakistan, became a pitched battle between 'them' and 'us' in which the hero Sunny Deol even wrenched out a handpump and single-handedly demolished many Pakistanis. It marked the arrival of a new nationalistic aesthetic based on hatred, where patriotism became all about unbridled violence, physical as well as verbal. This genre soon changed direction with Yash Chopra's *Veer Zaara* (2005), which gave way to pacifism, and was about reconciliation with the neighbour. Nationalism implied a large-heartedness to accept the other and saw the two nations as an estranged family trying to rediscover the lost bonds.

On 15 August 2006 independent India entered its sixtieth year. By sheer coincidence two of the most well loved Hindi films this year—*Rang De Basanti* and Rajkumar Hirani's *Lage Raho Munnabhai*—have taken us back to the exhilarating days of the independence struggle and tried to reinvent the golden period of the nation's history for the new millennium. In doing so they have also added a new dimension to the concept of nationalism in Hindi cinema.

Both films reflect India's problematic present. The former brings out the anger with our political system, the latter looks at the society, the problems within us as people articulated in one simple line: '*Desh to apna ho gaya par log paraye hain*' (the country became ours but its people have become strangers). Both are about soul-searching, reflecting the deep sense of loss fostered by the following decades of a free nation's life.

Their brand of nationalism doesn't blindly accept everything 'Indian'. It is also about questioning the nation and the state of affairs. It's not about the enemy out there in the heights of Kargil but deep within us. Or, as Mehra puts it: 'It's about the enslavement by one's own, from within.'

Rang De Basanti sees Bhagat Singh and Chandrasekhar Azad in the materialistic, hedonistic youth of today. It makes for interesting parallels and departures. There is a sense of loss about moving away from the days of idealism and a simultaneous hope of a spark of resistance; that our yesterday, perhaps, can alter the today. But it's a hope that's guarded and embedded in cynicism.

It shows a significant shift in our attitude. Our history, leaders and our country is something we have not toyed with. They have been absolutely sacrosanct. *Lage Raho Munnabhai* and *Rang De Basanti* have had the audacity to play around with them; they have had fun with history. *Rang De Basanti* doesn't just articulate the angst and rootlessness of the young but plays out their banter, their music, bikes, jackets and beer. It's a nationalism that allows for fun, is edgy, entertaining and cool.

Lage Raho Munnabhai takes the most revered figure in our history, puts him on the same footing as the good-hearted lumpens, Munna and Circuit, and makes him 'one of us', a man of the masses rather than the preserve of intellectuals. It makes us laugh at our foibles along with the Mahatma. It may not be a rigorous depiction of the Civil Disobedience movement but brings Gandhi in tune with the times—reinventing his ideology as that of 'corporate social responsibility', says sociologist Shiv Vishwanathan.

Both the films also talk of an urgent need for renewal and urge the people to take the responsibility: '*Koi desh perfect nahin hota, usse perfect banana padta hai*' (no country is perfect, it has to be made perfect). In that sense, despite the disillusionment and questioning both films end up reiterating that it's not a nation that is ever at fault but what we as citizens make of it. It's a nationalism of affirmative action; just waving the tricolour and mouthing slogans won't do.

Hot Jobs of the Future

Usha Albuquerque

Step into any shopping mall and the buzz of activity, people, money and dazzling new products is new and palpable. There is buoyancy in the air and it shows. Over the last couple of years, India's economy has emerged out of the gloom of the seventies and eighties to rank today as one of the emerging markets of the future. Analysts have predicted that in the next thirty-forty years the four emerging economies of the BRIC countries—Brazil, Russia, India and China—could be larger than the G6 in dollar terms. And India is expected to grow the fastest, the Indian economy projected to be larger than Japan's by 2032!

A growing economy, the stock market booming, means more jobs. The growth has started in the cities with jobs chasing people, offering hope and guidance for those on the threshold of their careers. Ten years ago 80 per cent of jobs were in the area of manufacturing, while today the majority are in the services sector. Government jobs that were at a premium ten years ago are today the lowest priority for those looking at a wide choice of other exciting options. For the educated and ambitious, even the high profile IAS/IPS option is not a preferred choice any more. With government downsizing, there are less jobs, and little of the power and status that many hopefuls once coveted.

According to job portals and head hunters there are thousands of new job vacancies in several private and global sectors—at least 2.2 million more jobs will be created over the next two years. Never before have there been as many career options as there are today. Never before has there been as much information as there is available today. Moreover in this dynamic work scene, no job lasts for a lifetime. Jobs continually grow and evolve from opportunities as they present themselves.

So where are these millions of jobs, and how can you prepare for them?

The buzz in the shopping malls and markets indicates that the retail industry is slated to be the biggest generator of mass jobs. Followed by IT and IT enabled services such as the BPOs and KPOs, telecom services, financial services, hospitality and entertainment, healthcare and education; these are just some of the booming work areas.

Seeing the spanking new shopping malls, it's not difficult to guess why. Shoppers today have the option of dealing with enthusiastic young people waiting to attend to you at a mall, with a wide range of products, so different from the dour cranky shopkeeper of yesteryear.. They are trained, efficient and extremely courteous. As India gets ready to open its doors to the Wal-marts of the west, the retail business will have recruited almost 5 lakh trained hands as well as another 8-10 times that number indirectly in the related supply chains. With the growing middle class and the increasing purchasing power, the retail sector is all ready to boom. Retail companies like Pantaloons have plans to take on around 7,000 personnel in the next two years, while Shopper's Stop is looking for 3,000 more, and companies like Reliance and Tatas have huge plans to get into this sector too. With 5,000 people required to man a single mall, and 250 malls expected to be set up in the next five years, organized retail in India can provide new jobs to 50,000 young graduates and diploma holders. The retail business is looking for people at all levels, from the school pass-out with basic skills to the supply chain and retail management professionals.

And it's not only shopping malls which are attracting the youth with good job possibilities. In fact with the huge growth of the cell phone market, telecom jobs are possibly the fastest off the block. Barely five years ago there were around 15 million mobile users in India; currently this figure is estimated to be 70 million and increasing so rapidly that it is predicted to double in the next two years. Moreover, an additional 50 million new land lines are also to be added in the coming years and the whole country is expected to be connected by broadband / digital cable very soon. Riding on the back of falling call charges, a large number of private players and government deregulation, telecom is witnessing a huge demand for people. As new telecom circles get added on, there is a demand for people to man these services. The top jobs are open in the area of marketing of different telecom services as well as for qualified telecom engineers. Apart from all these areas there are also opportunities in networking, telecom protocols such as ISDN, wireless protocols such as GSM, as well as those providing the cables, the hardware and equipment. Big players like Bharti, Tata Infocomm and Hutch have a lead in this sector, but Reliance is fast catching up with the size and scale of its investment in telecom. Reliance's broadband services are already making their way through hundreds of Indian cities, recruiting thousands of electronics and telecom engineers and technicians to lay the network and more than 5,000 more to operate and maintain the services. The Ambanis are also opening 2,000 Web World Express shops across the country, each requiring at least five people to handle marketing and customer services. So over the next two-three years Reliance will hire around 42,000 people and provide indirect employment to another 4-5 lakh.

While IT and IT enabled services have moved down marginally from the number 1 position of top recruiter last year, it is estimated to take on 2.75 lakh new recruits by the end of this year. The software industry is growing at a rate of 50 per cent while IT exports account for 30 per cent of our total exports. As more and more areas of work get computerized there will be a continuous demand for both software and hardware professionals. Only 120,000 software engineers and 1 million software technicians are trained every year when the demand is for 2 million engineers and 4 million technicians. So IT is bound to grow and with it the technologies of the future. Already Indian companies handle the software needs of 400 of the Fortune 500 companies, and this is likely to grow still further with large companies bagging bigger contracts and driving new projects and development work in India. Top IT companies are also shifting operations to cities other than the metros such as Cochin, Pune, Chandigarh, Vishakapatnam and even Goa. But there continues to be a large gap between the demand for qualified technical personnel and available supply.

While the top jobs continue to be software engineering, software systems / programming jobs and the hardware jobs, Internet and e-mail commerce applications, network management, database administration and integration, as well as IT-enabled jobs in call centres and BPOs are also recruiting young people in huge numbers. Large companies like Infosys, Wipro and TCS continue to take on professionals—software engineers, BCAs, MCAs, and even data programmers—in large numbers, while the ITES companies like Convergys India and Daksh are facing an increasing shortfall, due to the lack of available manpower both in terms of skills and numbers. Currently covering business areas such as banking, financial services and insurance, call centres and BPOs are also diversifying their business and providing a larger share of non-voice services. However, despite the high attrition rates, by the year 2008, it is expected that they will create employment for 270,000 people generating revenues worth Rs 20,000 crore. Along with the quantitative jobs generated by sectors like call centres and retail there is also a simultaneous demand for qualitative jobs. KPOs or Knowledge Process Outsourcing jobs are being set up in smaller numbers in areas like knowledge management, IT consulting, IT development, pharma research and oil and gas exploration. MNC offshoring development centres of firms like Goldman Sachs and Accenture and high end BPOs which offer back-end research for top investment banks are looking for highly skilled personnel with qualitative skills.

While the red hot banking and finance sector continues to attract commerce graduates and management wannabes, it is retail banking that offers the maximum opportunities. As domestic and international banks get more aggressive on the retail front, they will require at least 30,000–40,000 executives with good presentation skills in areas where customer interface is important. Customer services in fact is the new mantra for all companies looking to attract new buyers and new markets. Fast food eateries, department stores, banks, call centres, telecom outlets and even petrol pumps are sporting a new breed of customer care professionals—with confidence and presentation skills. Reliance and the Essar group are looking at putting up diesel and petrol vending pumps across the country in the next two years for which they will require an army of trained customer services personnel, around 8-10 people per pump, both technical and managerial.

Insurance is yet another area waiting to explode. There are around seventeen insurance companies in the market today. Many more private companies like Reliance and Sahara will soon enter the fray. Growing at 15 per cent per year, only 24 per cent of our population have been covered for life insurance and there are still over 300 million potential clients. Health insurance is another area that has hardly been tapped in our country. And there is still a lot of scope for risk coverage of other items, such as homes, vehicles, intellectual property, films, books etc. and an estimated requirement of over 20,000 new jobs in next two years. The prestigious jobs here are for professionals in marketing & sales and MBAs and for insurance agents, surveyors and loss assessors.

Other sectors feeling the pinch of available manpower are the pharmaceuticals, healthcare and hospitality industries. Star hotels immediately need almost 15,000 trained professionals. With the huge growth in domestic tourism—some 50 million Indians go on holiday every year, and with the steady inflow of international tourists there is a demand for qualified chefs, F&B and housekeeping managers, as well as airline flying and cabin crew. And with each hotel room generating a ripple of indirect jobs in construction, transport, restaurant and catering services, souvenir, guide and travel websites services, and with rejuvenated government tourism departments catching up on lost years, this is another milk cow that hasn't yet been exploited to the full.

And it's not just hotels and travel service players who stand to gain; even private hospitals are sprucing up to take in foreign patients. With the government in no position to spend more on medical care, the Rs 60,000 crore healthcare services market is being taken over by the private sector. A CII–McKinsey study sees the healthcare sector growing at 13 per cent per annum. No wonder large companies like Apollo, Wockhardt, Max, Fortis, Tata and Duncans are setting up state-of-the-art hospitals and clinics across the country. All this action translates into growing opportunities for healthcare professionals, not just doctors, nurses and technicians, but managers and administrators as well.

As people become more health-conscious, the money they are willing to spend on health care has shot up. And this is not only in India. The US faces a shortfall of over 4 lakh professionals and countries like the UK, Australia and New Zealand are also looking for healthcare professionals from India. Those unable to get timely treatment in their own countries are coming to India for cost-effective medical treatment. Indian doctors, nurses and radiologists are in demand both in India and overseas. Indian nurses are greatly sought after today in countries like the USA, UK, Germany, Japan, the Philippines, Norway and Sweden. In fact 20 per cent of nurses passing out of nursing schools in India go abroad. Male nurses too are in demand in physiotherapy units, trauma care centres, intensive care and coronary care units.

There is also a growing need for manpower particularly in the research departments of pharmaceutical companies such as Ranbaxy and Dr Reddy's. Several pharma companies are putting a thrust on research and intellectual property, going global to attack the generics market. Highly qualified research scientists, quality assurance specialists, biotechnologists as well as legal professionals are being sourced for top-notch jobs both in India and abroad. In addition to specialized areas of scientific research, many pharmaceutical companies in the highly competitive generics markets require legal professionals with dual degrees in patent law and science to tackle the nuances of litigation.

This increased focus on health and well-being has greatly benefited the personal care and fitness industry too. More and more beauty salons are opening up for both men and women, even in smaller cities and towns. Looking good is no longer a luxury. Hair styling, beauty treatment, skin care and fitness have provided vast opportunities for young people, who can choose not only to work in a salon, but also join beauty consultants catering to the film and advertising industry or fashion houses.

Fitness too is a whopping Rs 2,000 crore industry. Personal fitness trainers are the rage. Aishwarya Rai has one, so does Sachin Tendulkar. Companies too undertake corporate fitness programmes. Companies like Infosys have in-house gyms manned by experts. Courses in fitness training and physical education are available. Among the better ones are those run by Reebok in the four metros, while fitness centres like VLCC and Talwalkar also offer training programmes.

Another area catering to the increasing discretionary income is that of entertainment. Over the last couple of years huge investments have been made in providing a range of leisure activities, performing arts programmes, music and film shows and theme events. Reality and countdown shows have provided a platform for a range of talents. So whether it is film or television, music or cultural performances, different areas of entertainment are expected to provide a range of jobs for those willing to bet on a not-so-formal job profile. Leisure and family entertainment centers, water parks, theme parks, clubs, bowling alleys, pool parlours etc. are also likely to throw up many career opportunities, as they are estimated to grow to Rs 1000 crores in the next five years. Event management is another huge segment which has seen a 100 per cent growth in the last three years. Resorts and clubs are in demand for corporate seminars and getaways, and will look for professionals in the area of marketing, public relations and leisure management. So if you are a born entertainer, have wild whacky ideas, and are good at communicating, the media and entertainment industry is ready to welcome you.

Little recognized, and certainly not on the list of options for the high achievers, education is one of the areas where lots of new jobs are being created. Never before has education become as relevant as it is today. As the demand for better educational facilities and professional and skills training institutes increases, many corporates are looking at the financial viability of setting up schools, colleges and institutes of higher learning. The reservation debate has also shown up the crying need for more educational facilities. With this demand for more educational institutions comes that of trained manpower to provide training to aspirants at all levels. And as the demand for good trainers grows along with increased remuneration, there are many, even from the corporate environment, looking at avenues in teaching and academics. In addition to academics there is a whole new area of educational marketing which looks promising for those with the right aptitudes. Foreign institute representations, promotion of institutions and counseling for further studies are other major areas of future growth.

But for all the new jobs being created there still remains 4 million graduates unemployed—not for lack of jobs, but unemployability. Several studies indicate that the mismatch between the supply and demand of professionals is in terms of the skill-sets learning by fresh entrants in the job market. So for those looking to cash in on the huge opportunities in the Indian job market, it may be wise to keep in mind while working on academic qualifications, to also develop competencies in problem solving, analytical skills, group learning and working in a team-based environment. Such skills along with strong communication abilities, presentation skills and solid work ethics can enable any young graduate to confidently apply for the jobs of the future.

Therefore those stepping out into the vast cavernous world of work need to look ahead with purpose. Concentrate on the areas best suited to you. A clear focus on your career direction will enable you to open your mind to the incredible choice of career options that exist and are being continuously created all the time, in every subject area. At the same time, these should help you figure out the skills you need to develop so as to be ready for the jobs in areas that are in demand today, and will hold good for the future.

Timeline of Indian History

Beginning of Time to 1994

100,000–75,000 BC: Paleolithic period.

9000 to 4000 BC: Mesolithic period: Paintings on walls of the rock shelters of Bhimbetka in the foothills of the Vindhya mountains begin to appear.

6000 BC: Neolithic settlements in Baluchistan.

2800–2700 BC: Beginning of Indus Valley Civilization; Kot Dijian phase.

c.2700 BC: Approximate date of Indus Valley seals found at Kish.

2650 BC: Mature Harappan phase begins.

2600–1700 BC: Civilization of the great cities in the Indus Valley (Mohenjodaro, Harappa), Punjab (Kalibangan) and Gujarat (Lothal).

2000–1600 BC: Aryans invade the Indus Valley region. Research in 1999 reported that gene patterns confirmed that Caucasoid invaders entered this region during this period.

c.1375 BC: Worship of Aryan deities in the land of the Mitanni, in the region from the Iranian mountains to the Mediterranean.

1400–900 BC: Early Vedic period (*Rig Veda*).

1000 BC: Iron in India.

900–500 BC: Later Vedic period (*Brahmanas*).

817 BC: Traditional date of the birth of Parsvanatha, the twenty-third tirthankara in the Jain tradition.

c.800 BC: *Baudhayana Sulbasutra* is composed. *Sulbasutras* are appendices to the Vedas which give rules for constructing altars. They contained a wealth of geometrical knowledge.

800–500 BC: The Upanishads are thought to have been composed around this time.

c.750 BC: *Manava Sulbasutra* is composed.

c.600 BC: *Apastamba Sulbasutra* is composed.

6th century BC onwards: Early urbanization in the eastern Gangetic valley.

6th century BC: The life and times of Mahavira, the founder of Jainism.

c.563 BC: Gautama Siddhartha Buddha, the founder of Buddhism, is born in what is today Nepal, possibly in Lumbini.

c.543–491 BC: Magadha under King Bimbisara.

537 BC: Cyrus the Persian campaigns west of the Indus.

517–509 BC: Darius the Persian conquers the Indus Valley region making the area a province of the Persian empire.

c.500 BC: The *Ramayana* composed.

500–200 BC: The *Mahabharata* put into its final form.

c.491–459 BC: Ajatshatru's rule of Magadha. Ajatshatru is believed to have killed his father Bimbisara in c.491 BC.

Between 520 BC and 400 BC, famous grammarian Panini (major work *Astadhyayi*) born in Shalatula (now in Pakistan). He is now considered by many as the forerunner of the modern formal language theory used to specify computer languages.

486 BC: Traditional date of Buddha's nirvana. First Buddhist Council at Rajagriha, under the patronage of King Ajatshatru.

386 BC: Second Buddhist Council at Vaishali.

364 BC: Nanda dynasty under Mahapadma.

327–326 BC: Invasion of India by Alexander.

325 BC: Alexander leaves India.

321 BC: Maurya dynasty founded by Chandragupta (Maurya).

c.305 BC: Indian expedition of Seleucus Nikator, a general of Alexander's army.

302 BC: Kautilya, minister to Chandragupta Maurya, writes *Arthasastra*, a compendium of laws, administrative procedures and political advice for running a kingdom.

c.273–232 BC: The reign of the Mauryan emperor Ashoka.

250 BC: Third Buddhist Council at Pataliputra.

c.206 BC: Indian expedition of Antiochos III, king of Syria.

c.200 BC: *Katyayana Sulbasutra* is composed.

185 BC: Pushyamitra kills the last Maurya and establishes the Sunga dynasty.

175 BC: Foundation of the Indo-Greek empire.

c.180 BC: *Varttikas*, or the supplementary rules to Panini's work written by Katyayana.

c.155 BC: Bactrian king Menander invades north-western India.

c.150 BC: *Mahabhashya* of Patanjali written.

c.145–101 BC: Rule of Elara Chola, a general and possibly a prince of Cholas who conquered Sri Lanka.

138–88 BC: Conflict of the kings of Parthia with Sakas in eastern Iran.

c.100 BC: Gandhara school of sculpture flourishes; appearance of a Buddha image based on the Greek god Apollo.

c.100 BC: Deccan domination by the Andhras (also known, according to Prakrit inscription, as Satavahanas or Satakarni) begins.

58 BC: Epoch of the Krita–Malava–Vikrama era.

57–38 BC: Squared letters appear on Parthian coins.

c.30 BC: End of Sunga–Kanva rule in eastern Malwa. Satavahana supremacy in the Deccan.

c.26–20 BC: Pandya ambassador in Roman emperor Augustus's court.

AD 20–46: Gondopharnes, Indo-Parthian king in Taxila.

Early 1st century AD: Kujala Kadphises unites the Yue-chi tribes and establishes Kushana empire.

1st century AD: Intensive trade connections with the Roman empire.

c.AD 64: Chinese emperor Ming-ti sends for Buddhist texts.

c.AD 70: Saka satrap Bhumaka establishes Scythian power on the north-west coast of India.

AD 78: Saka era begins, generally associated with Kushan ruler Kanishka I. Decline of the Parthian rulers and consolidation of the Kushan power in the Indus valley.

c.AD 100: Kanishka convenes Fourth Buddhist Council at Jalandhar or in Kashmir.

AD 89–105: Kushan king repulsed by the Chinese General Pan Chao.

c.AD 120: A Western Satrap dynasty (c.AD 120–c.AD 395) in Ujjain in Malwa founded by Bhumaka's son Chashtana.

AD 125 onwards: Resurgence of Satvahanas under Gautamiputra and Vasishtiputra.

c.AD 126: Saurashtra conquest of Gautamiputra Sri Satakarni.

AD 130–150: Accession of Saka ruler Rudradaman I, Chashtana's grandson.

AD 148–170: An-Shih-Kao translates a work by Kanishka's chaplain.

AD 1st or 2nd century: *Buddhacarita* ('Acts of the Buddha') written by poet Ashvaghosha.

1st to 4th century AD: Sangama literature compiled in Tamil Nadu.

AD 248: Epoch of the Traikutaka–Kalachuri era.

AD 250: Disintegration of the Satvahana empire.

276–293: Sassanian conquest of parts of north-west India.

4th century AD: Development of Vajrayana Buddhism. Final form of Bhagavad Gita.

320–550: Gupta dynasty.

c.320–330: Rule of Chandragupta I from Pataliputra.

335–375: Samudragupta's reign, expansion of Gupta kingdom throughout north India and extending to south India.

c.360: Ceylonese embassy to Samudragupta.

c.379: Accession of Chandragupta II.

c.388–401: Chandragupta II Vikramaditya ends the satrapy of Ujjain by conquest of Malwa, Gujarat and Saurashtra.

AD 3rd century: Pingala, author of *Chandasutra* explores the relationship between combinatorics and musical theory.

405–411: Travels of Fa-Hien in the Gupta empire.

c.410: Iron Pillar constructed in Delhi, possibly by Chandragupta II Vikramaditya.

c.415–455: Accession and rule of Kumara Gupta I.

436: Simhavarman, the Pallava king of Kanchi, mentioned in the *Lokavibhaga*.

455: Accession of Skanda Gupta. Defeat of White Huns by Skanda Gupta.

c.458: Decimal number system first published in *Lokavibhaga*.

c.465: Harisena of the Vakataka dynasty begins work at the Ajanta caves.

467: Latest known date of the rule of Skanda Gupta.

473: Accession of Kumara Gupta II.

476: Birth of the astronomer Aryabhatta, author of *Âryabhatîya*.

c.477–495: Reign of Budhagupta.

500–527: Huns rule over north India; decline of the classical urban culture of the north.

c.505: Famous astronomer and mathematician Varahamihira, author of *Pancasiddhantika*, is born.

510: Huns led by Mihiragula conquer Punjab, Gujarat and Malwa from the Guptas.

533: Yashodarman, king of Malwa, organizes a national uprising against the Hun ruler Mihiragula.

543–544: Gupta rule continues in north Bengal. Rise of the Chalukyas of Vatapi.

566–567: Accession of the Chalukya ruler Kirtivarman I.

574: Rise of the Pallavas of Kanchipuram.

598: Famous mathematician Brahmagupta, author of *Brahmasphutasiddhanta* and *Khandakhadyaka*, is born. Sometime in the seventh century he calculated the earth's circumference to be 36,800 kms.

Late 4th–early 5th century: Kalidasa, Sanskrit poet and dramatist, who wrote *Abhijnanasakuntalam*, was possibly active during this period.

About 600: Famous mathematician Bhaskara I, the author of *Mahabhaskariya*, the *Laghubhaskariya* and the *Aryabhatiyabhasya*, is born.

606: Accession of Harsha.

609: Coronation of the Chalukya ruler Pulakesin II.

619–620: Supremacy of Sasanka of Gauda in eastern India.

630: Pulakesin II defeats Harsha; end of north India's hegemony.

630–643: Chinese traveler Hiuen-Tsang in India.

634: Reference to the fame of Kalidasa and Bharavi in the Aihole inscription.

637: Arab raid against Thana.

639: Foundation of Lhasa by Srong-tsan-Gampo.

641: Harsha's embassy to China.

c.642: Death of Pulakesin II.

c.642–668: Rule of Narasimhavarman I, the great Pallava. In AD 642 he defeated Pulakesin II and took over Badami (Vatapi).

643: Harsha's meeting with Hiuen-Tsang.

c.646–647: Death of Harsha.

650: The Pallavas, who ruled from their capital at Kanchipuram, are defeated by the Chalukyas.

670: The Pallavas build a new city at Mamallapuram.

675–685: Itsing, a Chinese traveller, stays at Nalanda.

c.700: Conversion of King Srimaravarman to Saivism by Tirujnana Sambandhar, the first of sixty-three *Nayanars* or Tamil saints.

711: Invasion of Sind by Muhammad bin Qasim.

712: Arab conquest of Nirun and Aror. Defeat and death of Dahir, the ruler of Sind.

713: Capture of Multan by Arabs.

c.722: The defeat of Narasimhavarman II at the hands of the Chalukya king, Vikramaditya II, marking the downfall of Pallava power.

730–756: Rule of Nagabhatta I of the Pratihara dynasty. He ruled over Broach and Jodhpur, and extended his dominion till Gwalior; was also known for repulsing the invasion of the Mlecchas.

731: Yasovarman (c.730-c.740), king of Kanauj and an author who patronized the Prakrit poet Vakpatiraja and Sanskrit poet Bhavabhuti, sends an ambassador to China.

733: Lalitaditya Muktapida, ruler of Kashmir, receives investiture as king from the emperor of China.

c.733–46: Rule of the Chalukya king Vikramaditya II. He took Kanchi thrice. His queen commissioned 'the best southern architect' to build the temple of Virupaksha.

c.753: Rise of the Rashtrakuta empire.

c.760: Pala rule begins in Bengal.

783: Vatsaraja establishes Gurjara–Pratihara dynasty of Rajasthan.

793–815: The rule of Govinda III, a Rashtrakuta king. He defeated the Pratihara king Nagabhatta II. Both the Palas and the ruler of Kanauj submitted to his protection.

c.836: Accession of Bhoja I, king of Kanauj.

c.846: Rise of Cholas and defeat of Pallavas.

855: Accession of Avantivarman of Kashmir.

c.870: Famous mathematician Sridhara, author of two mathematical treatises, *Trisatika* (sometimes called *Patiganitasara*) and *Patiganita*, is born.

c.871–907: The rule of Aditya I, a Chola king.

892: Coronation of Bhima I, an eastern Chalukya ruler.

893: Mahendrapala I, a Pratihara king, consolidates the territories he inherited, besides adding to them parts of north Bengal, Magadha, and western Assam.

907: Accession of the Chola ruler Parantaka I.

914: Continuance of Pratihara rule in Saurashtra.

933: Devasena writes *Shravakachar*, considered the first Hindi book, in Apabhramsha.

945: Coronation of Amma II (Vijayaditya VI), an eastern Chalukya ruler.

c.950–1003: Rule of Queen Didda of Kashmir.

c.954–1002: Chandella dynasty builds numerous Vaishnava temples, notably at Khajuraho, under Yasovarman (c.930–54) and Dhanga (954–1002).

c.962: Alptigin, a Turkish warrior slave, seizes the Afghan fortress of Ghazni and founds the Ghaznavid dynasty.

973: Foundation of the later Chalukya empire of Kalyana.

977: Accession of Sabuktigin, son of Alptigin, as the ruler of Ghazni.

985: Accession of the Chola king Rajaraja the Great.

986–987: First invasion of Sabuktigin in the provinces of Kabul and Punjab.

c.995: Accession of Sindhuraja Navasahasanka to the throne of the Paramaras in Malwa.

997: Death of Sabuktigin.

998: Accession of Sultan Mahmud in Ghazni.

c.1000: Mahmud of Ghazni leads an expedition to India. Lingaraja temple is built at Bhubaneswar. Saktivarman become the ruler of the eastern Chalukyas. Rajaraja I builds the Rajarajeswara temple at Tanjore. Immadi Narasimha Yadava Rayalu, a king who reigns at Narayanavanam in the Karvetnagar zamindari, builds the Chandragiri fort.

1001: Defeat of Jaipal, ruler of Punjab at the hands of Sultan Mahmud. Al Baruni comes to India with Mahmud of Ghazni.

1003: Regent queen of Kashmir, Queen Didda, passes away.

1004: Mahmud of Ghazni attacks Bhera.

1005: Mahmud of Ghazni entrusts his Indian holdings to Sukhpala. Mahmud captures Bhatinda.

1006: Mahmud of Ghazni captures Multan.

1008: Mahmud of Ghazni defeats Anandapala's troops in the Second Battle of Peshawar.

1012–1044: Rajendra Chola I rules the area now known as Tamil Nadu.

1013: Mahmud of Ghazni captures Nandana, in the vicinity of Multan.

1014: Rajaraja Chola dies.

1018: Kanauj seized by Mahmud of Ghazni. This marks the end of the Pratihara dynasty.

c.1018–1055: Four-decade rule of Bhoja of Dhara in Malwa begins. He is known to have engraved *Kurmashataka*, a poetical work in Prakrita on stone slabs.

1025: Rajendra I of Chola sends a naval expedition against the maritime empire known as Sri Vijaya.

1026: Sarnath inscription of the time of Mahipala I of Bengal. Fall of Nidar Bhim of the Shahiya dynasty. Sack of Somnath (during the reign of Bhimdeva I) by Mahmud of Ghazni.

1027: Bhimadeva I, the Chalukya king, builds the Sun Temple at Modhera (Gujarat).

1029: The Khajuraho temples are completed by the Chandelas.

1030: Death of Sultan Mahmud of Ghazni. Rajendra Chola erects the temple of Gangaikondacholapuram in the area now known as Tamil Nadu. Al Baruni writes *Tahqiq-i-Hind*.

1032: Vimala Shah, the minister of the Chalukya (Solanki) king of Gujarat, completes the first of the Dilwara Jain temples in Mount Abu.

1038: Nayapala succeeds to the throne of Bengal. Atisha Dipankara, a Buddhist scholar, visits Tibet.

1039: Death of Gangeyadeva Kalachuri in Tripura who introduced the seated Lakshmi coins.

c.1040: Coronation of Lakshmikarna of the Kalachuri dynasty. Famous mathematician Bhaskara II, author of *Lilavati*, on arithmetic and geometry, and *Bijaganita* is born.

1052: Tomar ruler Anangpal builds a Rajput citadel and town containing the Lal Kot (red fort) in the area now known as Delhi.

1070–1122: Somadeva Bhatta writes *Kathasaritasagara*. Rajendra Chola, Kulottunga I rules in the area now known as Tamil Nadu.

1076–1127: Rule of Vikramaditya VI of Kalyana, now Basava Kaluyana in Bidar district in Karanataka.

c.1076–1148: Anantavarman Choda Ganga's reign begins in Orissa.

1089–1101: Rule of Harsha, one of Kashmir's last Hindu kings.

1090: Rise of the Gahadavalas in Kanauj.

1095: The Sena family, who came from the south, takes control of power in Bengal with Vijayasena.

c.1098: Kirtivarman Chandella comes to power in Bundelkhand.

1100: Construction of the Jagannath temple at Puri begins by Anantavarman Choda Ganga.

1150: Sena dynasty begins.

1153–64: Rule of Vigraharaja IV in parts of Rajasthan near Ajmer.

1156: Rawal Jaisal founds Jaisalmer.

1175: Muhammad of Ghur invades India and captures Multan.

1178: Muhammad of Ghur defeated in Gujarat.

c.1185–1205: The rule of Lakshmana Sena of Bengal. Jayadeva writes *Gitagovinda*.

1191: First battle of Tarain between Rajputs under Prithviraj Chauhan and Muhammad of Ghur.

1192: Second battle of Tarain. Fall of Prithviraj Chauhan.

1192–93: Qutb-ud-din Aibak takes Delhi. Begins constructing the Qutb Minar.

1202: Turkish conquerors defeat Sena ruler and overrun Bengal.

1206: Death of Muhammad of Ghur and accession of Qutb-ud-din Aibak in India.

1210: Death of Qutb-ud-din Aibak. Accession of Aram Shah.

1210–11: Accession of Iltutmish.

1221: Invasion of the Mongols under Chengiz Khan.

c.1228: Ahom rule begins in Assam.

1231–32: Completion of the Qutb Minar under Iltutmish.

1236: Death of Iltutmish. Accession and deposition of Iltutmish's son Rukn-ud-din Firuz Shah. Accession of Iltutmish's daughter Raziyya.

1240: Deposition and murder of Raziyya. Accession of Mu'iz-ud-din Bahram.

1241: Capture of Lahore by the Mongols.

1246: Deposition and death of Ma'sud, Sultan of Delhi. Accession of Nasir-ud-din Mahmud to the throne of Delhi.

1266: Death of Nasir-ud-din Mahmud. Accession of Ghiyas-ud-din Balban, a slave of Iltutumish, who became a Chaglan, a group of forty most influential people in Iltutmish's court.

1279: Latest known date of Rajendra IV Chola's rule in Tamil Nadu. Rebellion of Tughril in Bengal.

1286: Death of Ghiyas-ud-din Balban. Accession of Mu'iz-ud-din Kaiqubad, grandson of Balban, whom he succeeded in 1286 on the throne of Delhi in the absence of his father Nasiruddin Bughra Khan, who was then in Bengal.

1288: Marco Polo, the Venetian traveller, visits Kollam in Kerala.

1290: Death of Kaiqubad. Accession of Jalal-ud-din Firuz Khalji.

1292: Ala-ud-din Khalji captures Bhilsa. Mongol invasion somewhere between Delhi and the Khyber pass.

1294: Devagiri in the Deccan pillaged by Ala-ud-din Khalji.

1296: Accession of Ala-ud-din Khalji.

1297: Conquest of Gujarat (from Karnadeva II) by Ala-ud-din Khalji.

1297–1306: Delhi Sultanate repulses several attacks by the Mongols.

1301: Capture of Ranthambore by Ala-ud-din Khalji.

1302–03: Capture of Chittor by Ala-ud-din Khalji. Mongol invasion under Targhi.

1305: Conquest of Malwa, Ujjain, Mandu, Dhar and Chanderi by the Khaljis.

1306–07: Malik Kafur's (a general of Ala-ud-din Khalji) expedition to Devagiri.

1308: Khalji expedition to Warangal.

1310: Malik Naib's (Malik Kafur) expedition into the south Indian peninsula.

1316: Death of Ala-ud-din Khalji. Accession of Shihab-ud-din Umar. Death of Malik Naib.

1318: Assassination of Malik Kafur, deposition of Shahabuddin Umar, accession of Qutbuddin Mubarak.

1320: Assassination of Qutbuddin Mubarak, usurpation of power by Khusro Khan, a Hindu convert. Khusro Khan overthrown by Ghazi Malik (later known as Ghiyas-ud-din Tughluq). Foundation of Tughlaq dynasty by Ghiyas-ud-din Tughluq.

1321: Expedition to Warangal under Muhammad Jauna, the son of Ghiyas-ud-din Tughluq. Rebellion of Muhammad Jauna.

1323: Second expedition to Warangal under Muhammad Jauna. Mongol invasion in northwest India.

1325: Accession of Muhammad bin Tughluq (Muhammad Jauna).

1327: Destruction of Kampili, in Vijayanagar, by Muhammad bin Tughluq. Transfer of the capital from Delhi to Daulatabad.

1328: The Mongols invade India but are repelled by Delhi sultanate.

1329: Qarachil expedition of Muhammad bin Tughluq to gain access to Tibet. Issue of brass and copper coins by Muhammad bin Tughluq.

1333–34: Arrival of Ibn Batuta in India.

1334: Sayyid Jalal al-Din Ahsan of Kaythal, who had been appointed governor of Ma'bar, leads a rebellion at Madura. Capture of Anegundi by Muhammad bin Tughluq.

1336: Traditional date of the foundation of Vijayanagar.

1338: Separate sultanate of Bengal.

1342: Ibn Batuta leaves Delhi on his mission to China.

1345: Accession of Shams-ud-din Iliyas in Bengal.

1347: Ala-ud-din Bahman Shah proclaimed king of the Deccan.

1350: Famous mathematician Madhava of Sangamagramma is born.

1351: Death of Muhammad bin Tughluq. Accession of Firuz Tughluq.

1353: Firuz Tughluq's first expedition to Bengal.

1359: Firuz Tughluq's second expedition to Bengal.

1360: Firuz Tughluq's expedition to Orissa.

1361: Capture of Nagarkot or Kangra by Firuz Tughluq.

1363: Firuz Tughluq's first expedition to Sind.

1370: Vijayanagara conquers sultanate of Madurai.

1374: Bukka, ruler of Vijayanagar, sends an embassy to the emperor of China.

1377: Vijayanagar kingdom destroys sultanate of Madura.

1382: Rebellion of Raja Ahmad or Malik Raja in Khandesh.

1388: Death of Firuz Tughluq. Accession of Ghiyas-ud-din Tughluq II.

1389: Death of Ghiyas-ud-din Tughluq II.

1398: Timur invades India. He sacks Delhi on 17 December.

1399: Timur leaves India.

1403: Separate sultanate of Gujarat.

1414: Khizr Khan, governor of Multan appointed by Timur, takes possession of Delhi and founds the Sayyid dynasty. Raja Ganesha, a Hindu landlord of Bhaturia and Dinajpur becomes the king of Bengal by usurping power from the weak Iliyas Shahi sultans.

1424: Capture of Warangal by Ahmad Shah Bahmani, a ruler of the Bahmani dynasty.

1429: Transfer of the Bahmani capital from Gulbarga to Bidar.

c.1430–69: Rule of Rana Kumbha in Chittor.

1435–67: Kapilendra establishes Suryavamsha dynasty of Orissa.

c.1444: Famous astronomer Nilakantha Somayaji, author of *Tantrasamgraha*, is born.

1451: Bahlul Lodi ascends the throne of Delhi.

1459: Foundation of Jodhpur by Rao Jodha.

1469: Birth of Guru Nanak.

1486–1543: Life of Chaitanya, Bengali founder of popular Vaishnava sect.

1486–87: Fall of the Sangama dynasty of Vijayanagar. Beginning of the rule of the Saluva dynasty in Vijayanagar.

1489: Accession of Sikandar Lodi.

1489–90: Foundation of the Adil Shahi dynasty of Bijapur.

1490: Establishment of the independent Nizam Shahi dynasty of Ahmadnagar.

1493: Husain Shah elected king of Bengal.

1494: Accession of Babur in Farghana.

1497–98: First voyage of Vasco da Gama; he lands at Calicut.

1504: Babur occupies Kabul.

1505: Beginning of the rule of the Tuluva dynasty in Vijayanagar.

1509: Accession of Krishnadeva Raya to the Vijayanagar throne.

c.1509–27: Rule of Rana Sanga in Mewar, Rajasthan.

1510: The Portugese capture Goa. Albuquerque is the governor.

1511: Babur captures Samarqand again.

1513: Death of Albuquerque.

1517: Death of Sikandar Lodi. Accession of Ibrahim Lodi.

1518: Quli Qutb Shah, a Turkish governor of the Bahmani kingdom, declares his independence and moves his capital to Golconda where he establishes the Qutb Shahi dynasty.

1526: First battle of Panipat between Babur and Ibrahim Lodi.

1527: Battle of Khanua between Babur and Rana Sanga.

1528: Babri Masjid built in Ayodhya by Mir Baqi, a nobleman from Babur's court.

1529: Battle of Gogra between Babur and the allied Afghans of Bengal and Bihar.

1529–30: Death of Krishnadeva Raya.

1530: Death of Babur and accession of Humayun.

1533: Bahadur Shah, ruler of Gujarat, captures Chittor.

1534: Humayun marches to Malwa.

1535: Defeat of Bahadur Shah of Gujarat and his flight to Mandu.

1537: Death of Bahadur Shah of Gujarat. Pope Paul II makes Goa an Episcopal See.

1538: Sher Khan, the regent of Jalal Khan Lohani, defeats Ghiyasuddin Mahmud Shah, last sultan of the Husain Shahi dynasty of Bengal. Humayun enters Gaur. Death of Guru Nanak.

1539: Sher Khan defeats Humayun at Chaunsa and assumes sovereignty.

1540: Humayun's defeat near Kanauj.

1542: Birth of Akbar. Sher Shah (formerly Sher Khan) builds a fort in Patna and makes it the capital of Bihar. Sher Shah first mints the rupee, a silver coin.

1544: Humayun arrives in Persia.

1545: Death of Sher Shah. Accession of Islam Shah, son of Sher Shah, to the throne of Delhi.

1552: Death of Guru Angad, the second Sikh Guru.

1554: Death of Islam Shah. Accession of Muhammad Adil Shah, son of Islam Shah, to the throne of Delhi.

1555: Humayun recovers the throne of Delhi. Tashi Namgyal ascends Ladakhi throne of 'Lion' and reunifies the kingdom.

1556: Death of Humayun and accession of Akbar. Second battle of Panipat between Akbar and Hemu; Akbar is the winner. Italian traveller and art collector Niccolao Manucci arrives in India.

1560: Fall of Bairam Khan.

1561: Mughal invasion of Malwa.

1562: Akbar marries a princess of Amber.

1564: Abolition of the jizya. Death of Rani Durgavati and annexation of the Gond kingdom by the Mughals.

1565: Battle of Talikota; Vijayanagar is ransacked by sultans of the Deccan.

1568: Akbar's army captures the fort of Chittor.

1569: Akbar's army captures of Ranthambore and Kalinjar. Birth of Salim, son of Akbar.

1571: Foundation of Fatehpur Sikri by Akbar.

1572: Akbar annexes Gujarat.

1573: Surat surrenders to Akbar.

1574: Death of Guru Amardas, the third Sikh guru.

1575: Battle of Tukaroi between Daud Khan Karrani, ruler of Bengal, and Munim Khan, Akbar's army general; Karrani is defeated.

1576: Subjugation of Bengal. The battle of Gogunda or Haldighat; Rana Pratap defeated by Akbar.

1577: Akbar's troops invade Khandesh.

1580: Accession of Ibrahim Adil Shah II in Bijapur. First Jesuit mission at Agra. Rebellion in Bihar and Bengal by Daud Khan Karrani.

1581: Akbar's march against Mirza Muhammad Hakim in Kabul and reconciliation with him. Death of Guru Ramdas, fourth Sikh guru.

1582: Din-i-Ilahi or Divine Faith promulgated by Akbar.

1589: Death of Todar Mal, finance minister of Akbar, and Bhagwan Das, Todar Mal's colleague in charge of Lahore.

1591: Mughal conquest of Sind.

1592: Annexation of Orissa by Akbar.

1595: Siege of Ahmadnagar by Mughal army. Acquisition of Qandahar by Akbar. Annexation of Baluchistan by Akbar. Death of Faizi, a poet in the court of Akbar, in Lahore.

1597: Death of Rana Pratap of Mewar.

1600: Governor and Company of Merchants of London Trading into the East Indies or British East India Company formed by royal charter. Ahmadnagar stormed by Mughal army.

1601: Golden Temple at Amritsar is completed.

1602: Death of Abul Fazl. Formation of the United East India Company of the Netherlands.

1604: Adi Granth, the holy book of Sikhs, compiled.

1605: Death of Akbar and accession of Jahangir.

1606: Rebellion of Khusrau , son of Jehangir. Qandahar invaded by the Persians. Execution of the fifth Sikh guru, Arjan Dev, by Jahangir.

1607: Qandahar relieved by the Mughals. Sher Afghan, first husband of Nur Jahan, killed. Second revolt of Khusrau. First trading post set up in Surat by Dutch East India Company.

1608: Malik Ambar, the prime minister of Murtaza Nizam Shah II, and the founder of the city of Aurangabad takes Ahmadnagar.

1609: Dutch factory at Pulicat.

1611: Jahangir marries Nur Jahan. The English establish a factory at Masulipatam.

1612: Prince Khurram marries Mumtaz Mahal. First English factory at Surat.

1613: Jahangir's firman to East India Company to establish a factory at Surat.

1615: Submission of Mewar to the Mughals. Arrival of Sir Thomas Roe, an ambassador of King James I, in India.

1616: Sir Thomas Roe received by Jahangir. The Dutch establish a factory at Surat.

1617: Revolt in southern states of empire subdued by Prince Khurram, who receives title of Shah Jahan.

1618: Sir Thomas Roe, after obtaining firmans for English trade, leaves the Imperial Court.

1620: Jahangir captures Kangra Fort.

1625: Dutch factory at Chinsura.

1626: Death of Malik Ambar. Rebellion of Mahabat Khan.

1627: Jahangir dies and Shah Jahan assumes the throne.

1628: Shah Jahan proclaimed emperor.

1629: Rebellion of Khan Jahan Lodi, governor of Deccan.

1631: Death of Mumtaz Mahal. Shah Jahan commissions building of her tomb, the Taj Mahal.

1632: Mughal invasion of Bijapur. Grant of the 'golden firman' to the English Company by the sultan of Golconda. Construction of Taj Mahal begins at Agra.

1633: End of Ahmadnagar dynasty.

1636: Shahji, father of Shivaji, enters the service of Bijapur. Aurangzeb appointed subedar of the Deccan by Shah Jahan.

1639: Foundation of Fort St. George at Madras by the English. Shuja appointed subedar of Bengal.

1645: Shah Jahan grants the English exemption from customs duty on trade as a reward for curing Princess Jahanara.

1646: Shivaji captures Torna.

1648: Taj Mahal completed.

1651: English factory started at Hugli. Firman granted to the English Company by Shuja to trade in Bengal.

1653: Aurangzeb reappointed viceroy of the Deccan. The Dutch start a factory at Chinsura.

1656: Death of Muhammad Adil Shah of Bijapur. Another firman granted to the English by Shuja. Job Charnock first comes to Bengal, serves for a while in Cossimbazar, is then sent to Patna. He later returns to Cossimbazar.

1657: Invasion of Bijapur by Aurangzeb. Aurangzeb captures Bidar and Kalyani. Illness of Shah Jahan. The war of succession between Aurangzeb and his brothers begins.

1658: Aurangzeb executes his brothers, imprisons his father and ascends throne.

1659: Murder of Afzal Khan, a general of Bijapur court, by Shivaji.

1659–66: Bernier at the court of Aurangzeb.

1660: Mir Jumla appointed governor of Bengal.

1661: Cession of Bombay to the English by the Portuguese. Execution of Murad. Mughal capture of Cooch Behar.

1663: Death of Mir Jumla. Shaista Khan appointed governor of Bengal by Aurangzeb.

1664: Shivaji sacks Surat. Colbert, the French minister, founds an India Company. Shivaji assumes royal title.

1666: Death of Shah Jahan. Capture of Chittagong by Bujurg Umid Khan, eldest son of Mughal Subahdar Shaista Khan. Shivaji's visit to Agra and escape. Birth of Sikh guru Gobind Singh.

1668: First French factory started at Surat.

1670: Shivaji raids Surat.

1672: Satnami Sikh rebellion against Mughals. Shaista Khan's firman to the English Company.

1674: Francois Martin founds Pondicherry. Shivaji assumes the title of Chhatrapati.

1675: Execution of Teg Bahadur, guru of the Sikhs, by Aurangzeb.

1677: Shivaji's conquests in the Carnatic. East India Company's charter of 1677 allows them to mint money.

1678: Marwar occupied by the Mughals.

1679: Reimposition of the jizya by Aurangzeb. Mughal attack on Marwar.

1680: Death of Shivaji. Aurangzeb's firman to the English Company.

1681: Aurangzeb goes to the Deccan. Establishes Aurangabad as new Mughal capital.

1687: Fall of Golconda.

1688: Madras gets a municipal corporation.

1689: Execution of Shambhaji, son of Shivaji. Rajaram, brother of Shambhaji, succeeds but retires to Jinji.

1698: The English obtain zamindari of Sutanati, Calcutta and Govindapur from Sabarna Raychaudhuris of Bengal.

1699: First Maratha raid on Malwa. Guru Gobind Singh creates Khalsa.

1700: Death of Rajaram and regency of his widow Tara Bai. Aurangzeb appoints Murshid Quli Khan diwan of Bengal.

1701: French East India Company establishes post at Calicut.

1703: The Marathas enter Berar.

1706: The Marathas raid Gujarat and sack Baroda. Murshid Quli Khan shifts capital of Bengal from Dhaka to Murshidabad.

1707: Death of Aurangzeb. Battle of Jajau between sons of Aurangzeb.

Accession of Shah Alam I as the Mughal emperor in Lahore.

1708: Shambhaji's son Shahu becomes the king of the Marathas. Death of Guru Gobind Singh.

1712: Death of Shah Alam I. Accession of Jahandar Shah, third son of Shah Alam I, as Mughal emperor.

1713: Jahandar Shah murdered. Farrukhsiyar becomes Mughal emperor.

1714: Shahu dies of smallpox and his minister or Peshwa, Balaji Vishwanath, takes over the Maratha throne.

1716: Execution of Banda, the Sikh leader.

1717: Farrukhsiyar's firman to the English Company.

1719: Farrukhsiyar put to death. Accession of Muhammad Shah, grandson of Shah Alam I, as Mughal emperor.

1720: Accession of Peshwa Baji Rao at Poona. Fall of the Sayyid brothers Rafi-ud-Darajat and Rafi-ud-Dallah, kingmakers during the late Mughal period. They were killed by Muhammad Shah.

1720–40: Peshwa Baji Rao I extends Maratha rule to north India, raids Delhi.

1724: Saadat Khan appointed governor of Avadh by Mughal emperor Muhammad Shah. Hyderabad becomes essentially independent of Delhi under Governor Nizam-ul-Mulk. Qamar-ud-din becomes wazir of Mughal emperor Muhammad Shah.

1727: East India Company establishes first post office in Calcutta.

1727–39: Rule of Shujauddin Muhammad Khan as governor of Bengal after the death of his father-in-law Murshid Quli Khan.

1739: Nadir Shah sacks Delhi. Death of Shujauddin Muhammad Khan and accession of Sarfaraz in Bengal. The Marathas capture Salsette and Bassein, in what is now Mumbai, from the Portuguese.

1740: Alivardi Khan becomes governor of Bengal. Accession of Balaji Rao Peshwa in Poona.

1742: Maratha invasion of Bengal. Dupleix becomes governor of Pondicherry. Murder of Safdar Ali, nawab of the Carnatic.

1744–48: War between the English and the French in Europe. This led to the conflict between the two parties in the Carnatic resulting in the First Carnatic War.

1746: Labourdonnais, governor of Mauritius, reaches India and occupies Madras, in spite of the opposition of the British fleet; the French colours are displayed on Fort St. George.

1747: Invasion of Ahmad Shah Abdali in Lahore.

1748: Death of Nizam-ul-Mulk. Death of Muhammad Shah of Delhi and accession of his son Ahmad Shah.

1749: Death of Shahu. Through the Treaty of Aix-la-Chapelle between the French and the British, Fort St. George is restored to the British.

1750: Defeat and death of Nasir Jung, ruler of Hyderabad.

1750–54: War of the Deccan and Carnatic succession between Chanda Sahib, supported by the French, and Anwar-ud-din, claimant to the throne of Carnatic.

1751: Treaty of Alivardi with the Marathas. Robert Clive captures Arcot.

1754: Recall of Dupleix. End of the Second Carnatic War (1750–54). Accession of Alamgir II as Mughal emperor.

1755: Delhi plundered by Afghan invader Ahmed Shah Durrani.

1756: Death of Alivardi Khan. Accession of Siraj-ud-daulah in Murshidabad.

1756–63: Seven Years War of Austrian succession in Europe and Third Carnatic War between the English and the French in India.

1757: Sack of Delhi and Mathura by Ahmad Shah Abdali. The English capture Chandernagore. Battle of Plassey between Siraj-ud-daulah and the

British led by Robert Clive. Mir Jafar made Nawab of Bengal by the victorious British.

1758: Thomas-Arthur, Comte de Lally, French general, reaches India. The Marathas march beyond Punjab to reach Attock in Paktoonistan.

1759: Siege of Masulipatam; the town, garrisoned by the French under Marshal de Conflans, is attacked by an English force of 2,500 men under the command of Colonel Forde. After a two-hour bombardment, the post capitulates after putting up a largely symbolic fight.

1760: Battle of Wandiwash; French lose control of the Deccan to the English. Lally defeated by General Sir Eyre Coote and forced to retire to Pondicherry, where he is besieged. Marathas led by Sadashiv Rao Bhau invade Udgir and defeat the Nizam forces by taking Burhanpur, Daulatabad, Ahmadnagar and Bijapur. Mir Qasim, Nawab of Bengal.

1761: Third battle of Panipat between Ahmad Shah Abdali and the Marathas. Fall of Pondicherry; with no hope of reinforcements from France, Lally capitulated to Clive's troops. Shah Alam II becomes Mughal emperor. Accession of Madhava Rao Peshwa in central Maharashtra. Rise of Hyder Ali in Mysore. Clive is ill and leaves for England.

1763: Treaty of Paris. Pondicherry returns to France, but its fortifications are razed and limits set on French military strength on the Coromandel coast; French stations in Bengal are to be strictly commercial.

1764: Battle of Buxar. The British defeat Mir Qasim.

1765: Robert Clive is the governor of Bengal. Death of Mir Jafar. Grant of the Diwani of Bengal, Bihar and Orissa to the British governor of Bengal, Robert Clive, by the Mughal emperor, Shah Alam II. Treaty of Allahabad between Robert Clive and the nawab of Avadh.

1766: Grant of the Northern Sarkars, a district between the mouth of the Krishna and Puri, in Orissa, to the English by the nizam.

1767: Departure of Clive to London.

1767–69: The First Anglo–Mysore War. The British conclude a humiliating peace pact with Hyder Ali.

1769: The French East India Company is dissolved.

1770: The Great Bengal Famine.

1772: Warren Hastings appointed governor of Bengal. Death of Madhava Rao Peshwa.

1773: The Regulating Act passed by the British Parliament.

1774: The Rohilla War in Rohilkhand near Avadh. Warren Hastings becomes first governor general. Establishment of Supreme Court of Judicature in Calcutta by the British.

1775: Trial and execution of Nanda Kumar, a titled member of the Mughal aristocracy who became a naib immediately after the acquisition of the Diwani by the company, for forgery, allegedly at the instigation of Warren Hastings.

1775–82: The First Anglo–Maratha War.

1776: The Treaty of Purandhar, between the British and the Marathas.

1780–84: Second Anglo–Mysore War. The British defeat Hyder Ali. Birth of Ranjit Singh (1780) at Gujranwala.

1780: First Indian newspaper, an English weekly named *Bengali Gazette*, published from Calcutta.

1781: Deposition of Chait Singh, Raja of Benaras. Act passed to amend the Regulating Act.

1782: Affair of the Begums of Avadh, where Hastings forced them to surrender the treasure they inherited. The treaty of Salbai, between the Marathas and the British. Death of Hyder Ali.

1783: Death of Sir Eyre Coote. Fox's India Bills, introduced in the House of Commons by Charles James

Fox, one of which effectively puts the political government of India under the control of a commission appointed by Parliament. The other bill puts the management of the Company's commerce under another commission.

1784: Treaty of Mangalore between Tipu Sultan and the East India Company. Pitt's India Act; it divides the control of governance and trade, with clearly demarcated borders between the Crown and the Company. After this point, the Company function as a regularized subsidiary of the Crown, with greater answerability for its actions. Judge and linguist Sir William Jones founds Calcutta's Royal Asiatic Society.

1785: Resignation of Warren Hastings.

1786: Lord Cornwallis becomes governor general.

1790–92: Third Mysore War between Tipu Sultan and the British–Maratha–Nizam combine.

1792: Treaty of Seringapatam; Tipu's sons taken as hostage, he suffers huge monetary and territory losses.

1792: Ranjit Singh succeeds his father Mahan Singh as leader of Sukrchakhia misl.

1793: Cornwallis administration concludes Permanent Settlement—a contract between the East India Company and the Bengal landholders allowing the latter to be admitted into the state system as the absolute owners of landed property. The landowners are endowed with the privilege of holding their proprietary right at a rate which is to continue unchanged for ever. Renewal of the Company's Charter.

1794: Death of Mahadji Scindia of Gwalior.

1795: Death of Ahalya Bai Holkar; she ruled from Indore.

1797: Zaman Shah, ruler of Kabul, attacks Lahore. Death of Asaf-ud-daulah, nawab of Avadh.

1798: Wazir Ali becomes the nawab of Avadh after the death of Asaf-ud-daulah. British Lord Mornington (Wellesley) becomes governor general. Wellesley signs Subsidiary Alliance Treaty with the nizam.

1799: Fourth Anglo–Mysore War. Death of Tipu. Partition of Mysore. Ranjit Singh's appointment to the governorship of Lahore. William Carey opens Baptist Mission at Serampore.

1800: Death of Nana Phadnavis, a minister of the peshwa. Establishment of Fort William College by Wellesley. First multilingual press set up in Serampore.

1801: Annexation of the Carnatic by the British.

1802: Treaty of Bassein between Peshwa Baji Rao II and the East India Company.

1803–05: The Second Anglo–Maratha War: British defeat the Marathas at Assaye.

1805: British siege of Bharatpur fails. Recall of Wellesley.

1806: Vellore Mutiny: Revolt in Madras army over order to change head-dress, instigated by Tipu's sons and retainers.

1808: Mission of Malcolm to Persia and of Elphinstone to Kabul.

1809: Treaty of Amritsar between the Sikhs and the British defines the river Sutlej as the boundary between the two.

1813: Renewal of the Company's Charter by the British government.

1814–16: The Anglo–Gurkha War.

1817–18: British campaign against the Pindaris, irregular armies of looters in central India; Pindari forces dispersed.

1817–19: The last Anglo–Maratha War between the British and the armies of Peshwa Baji Rao II, Bhonsles of Nagpur, Holkars of Indore. Baji Rao II defeated and sent to Kanpur as a prisoner.

1819: Monststuart Elphinstone appointed governor of Bombay.

1820: Thomas Munro appointed governor of Madras. Missionaries at

Serampore bring out the first ever Bengali weekly *Samachar Darpan*.

1822: *Bombay Samachar*, a Gujarati daily, is published; it is the longest surviving daily in India.

1823: General Committee of Public Instruction formed in Calcutta. Sanskrit College founded in Calcutta.

1824: Sepoys at Barrackpore revolt citing small pay and religious reasons when asked to move to Arakan. Many of them hanged and some shot dead.

1824–26: The First Anglo–Burmese War.

1827: Death of Sir Thomas Munro, governor of Madras. Sir John Malcolm appointed governor of Bombay.

1828: Lord William Bentinck becomes governor general. Bengali reformer Raja Ram Mohun Roy founds the Brahmo Samaj, initially known as the Brahmo Sabha, in Calcutta.

1829: Prohibition of sati by Governor General William Bentinck.

1829–37: Suppression of Thuggees, gangs of roving criminals who looted and strangled their victims, primarily in Bengal, by British officer William Sleeman.

1831: Raja Ram Mohun Roy in England as the ambassador of the Mughal emperor, Akbar Shah II. Raja of Mysore deposed and its administration taken over by the East India Company. Meeting of Ranjit Singh and Governor General Bentinck at Rupar: Ranjit Singh agrees to let British traders use the Sutlej river.

1832: Annexation of Jaintia by the British.

1833: Renewal of the Company's charter by the British Parliament. The Charter Act of 1833 also requires the Company to divest itself of administering religious endowments. The English are now allowed to acquire land in India.

1834: Annexation of Coorg by the British. Law Commission appointed with Thomas B. Macaulay at its head. Formation of the Agra Province by the Charter Act of 1833; Metcalfe is the first governor.

1835: Bentinck announces that the British government should promote European literature and science by making English the language of higher education. Macaulay's *Minute on Education* argues that English should be taught instead of Sanskrit and Arabic. English is declared the official language of the East India Company's administration. Civil service jobs in India are opened to Indians. After Bentinck is removed Charles Metcalfe serves as acting governor general for one year; he removes the existing restrictions on the press. First tea garden opened at Lakhimpur, Assam.

1838: British ask Ranjit Singh to help Shah Shuja regain his throne at Kabul. A tripartite treaty is signed in July 1838.

1839: Death of Ranjit Singh. India gets twenty-one-mile-long telegraph line between Calcutta and Diamond Harbour.

1839–42: Persian army lays siege to Herat, leading to the First Anglo–Afghan War.

1843: Conquest of Sind. Gwalior War and adoption of the child-heir Jayavi Rao Scindia to the vacant throne. Panjim becomes capital of Goa.

1844: India's oldest teak plantation set up in Nilambur in Malabar.

1845: Commercial Bank of India founded.

1845–46: First Anglo–Sikh War.

1848: Lord Dalhousie becomes governor general.

1848–49: Second Anglo–Sikh War results in the defeat of the Sikhs and annexation of Punjab.

1849: Opening of a Hindu girls' school in Calcutta by John Drinkwater Bethune.

1850: First English translation of *Rig Veda* by H.H. Wilson.

1851: British India Association formed. Madras Medical College established. Geological Survey of India established.

1852: Second Anglo–Burmese War. First Indian stamp, Scinde Dawk, issued at Karachi.

1853: Railway line opened from Bombay to Thane. Telegraph line from Calcutta to Agra. Annexation of Nagpur by Lord Dalhousie using the 'Doctrine of Lapse'. Cession of Berar to the British. Renewal of the Company's charter. Indian Civil Services examination introduced. Bengal Chamber of Commerce comes into being.

1854: Sir Charles Wood's Education Despatch, aimed at creating a properly articulated system of education, from the primary school to the university. India's first railway bridge built over Thane creek. First textile mill opened at Tardeo, Bombay.

1855: Santhal insurrection breaks out under the leadership of two brothers Sidhu and Kanhu in Chhota Nagpur area. Revolt crushed by the British.

1856: Annexation of Avadh by Dalhousie; Wajid Ali Shah leaves for Calcutta. Remarriage of widows legalized.

1857: The revolt of 1857. Uprising of Indian sepoys at Barrackpore, Meerut, Lucknow and Kanpur joined by Rani of Jhansi, Nana Saheb, Tantia Tope. Bahadur Shah Zafar declared emperor; revolt crushed and emperor exiled. The University Act passed by the Indian Legislative Council for the establishment of a university at Calcutta.

1858: The Government of India Act: British India placed under the direct government of the Crown. Queen Victoria's Proclamation. Port Blair becomes a penal settlement.

1859: Indigo Revolt: Violent movement all over Bengal against European indigo planters.

1861: The Indian Councils Act passed, enables participation of Indians in the governor general's council. The Indian High Courts Act establishes high court of judicature. Introduction of a professional police organization under the Police Act of 1861. Paper Currency Act gives India a legal tender paper currency. Jhansi is ceded to the Scindias.

1862: Introduction of the Indian Penal Code (IPC) on 1 January 1862. Earl of Elgin is the new viceroy.

1863: Bombay–Burma Trading Corporation and National Bank of India established.

1865: The Orissa famine. Opening of telegraphic communication between India and Europe.

1867: Debendranath Tagore buys a vast tract of land in Birbhum district of Bengal and sets up an ashram now famous as Santiniketan.

1868: The Punjab Tenancy Act. Railway line opened from Ambala to Delhi. Vernacular Press Act passed.

1869: Lord Mayo becomes viceroy.

1870: Lord Mayo's Provincial Settlement. First submarine telegraph cable laid from UK to Bombay.

1872: First census in colonial India. Lord Mayo assassinated. Bombay Municipal Corporation established.

1874: The Bihar famine.

1875: Gaikwad of Baroda's succession case: Sayaji Rao III becomes ruler. Prince of Wales visits India.

1876: British Parliament passes the Royal Titles Act creating Queen Victoria Empress of India. Lord Lytton is the new viceroy.

1877: Delhi Durbar: Queen of England is proclaimed the Empress of India.

1878: Outbreak of the Second Anglo–Afghan War. The Vernacular Press Act intended to muzzle the periodicals in Indian languages.

1881: The Factories Act passed; minimum age of workers raised. Mysore restored to Wodeyars by the British.

1882: The Hunter Commission, officially known as Indian Education Commission, is the first education commission in India. Telephone exchanges opened at Bombay, Calcutta and Madras.

1883: The Ilbert Bill bans the protected status of the whites and seeks equality of all subjects, native or otherwise, in the eye of law. India's first public theatre, Star, inaugurated in Calcutta.

1885: Foundation of Indian National Congress by Alan Octavian Hume. Bengal Tenancy Act. Bengal Local Self-Government Act. Third Anglo–Burmese War.

1888: Durand Cup, the world's third oldest football tournament, started in Shimla.

1889: Abdication of Maharaja Pratap Singh of Kashmir.

1891: The Factories Act is passed covering all factories employing more than fifty workers. The Age of Consent Act is passed.

1892: The Indian Councils Act is passed to regulate Indian administration.

1893: The Indian Football Association is established. Swami Vivekananda delivers his landmark speech at the Parliament of Religions in Chicago.

1894: Cornelia Sorabjee becomes the first Indian woman law graduate.

1896: Lumiere Brothers' Cinematographic shows a motion picture for the first time in India at Watson's Hotel, Bombay.

1896–97: Plague in Bombay. A great famine sweeps through India.

1899: Lord Curzon becomes the viceroy. Mahatma Gandhi organizes Indian Ambulance Corps for the British during the Boer War in South Africa. Sir M. Monier Williams's Sanskrit–English Dictionary published.

1901: North-West Frontier Province is created by the British. The Imperial Cadet Corps is established. Indian Mines Act enacted. J. Watson Harod opens the first branch of the Gramaphone Company Limited in Calcutta. These are the first gramaphones in India. Rabindranath Tagore inaugurates the ashram school at Shantiniketan. Queen Victoria dies and a plan to built the Victorial Memorial is drawn up.

1902: The first wireless communication is established between Sagar Islands and the Sandheads in Diamond Harbour near Calcutta.

1903: India's first five-star hotel, the Taj Mahal at Bombay, starts doing business.

1904: British Expedition to Tibet. Universities Act: Allowing the universities to be centres of research and learning from merely a rewarding agency. Co-operative Societies Act passed. The British establish an Archaeological Department in India. Gandhi establishes the weekly journal, *Indian Opinion*. Organizes Phoenix Settlement near Durban.

1905: The First Partition of Bengal. Swadeshi campaign, boycott of British goods in protest. Lord Minto becomes governor general. Aga Khan III meets Minto in Simla and demands political rights to Muslims in India. Morley becomes Secretary of State for India. The first rifle factory is established at Icchapore. Hafiz Abdul Majeed founds Hamdard. Prince of Wales (later George V) lays the foundation stone for the Prince of Wales Museum in Bombay.

1906: Foundation of the Muslim League by Aga Khan III in Dhaka. Congress declaration regarding Swaraj. First satyagraha campaign began with meeting in Johannesburg by Mahatma Gandhi in protest against proposed Asiatic ordinance directed against Indian immigrants in Transvaal.

1907: Madame Bhikaji Cama unfurls the flag of India at the Stuttgart Congress of the Second International in August. Spirit of the National Congress into Moderates and Extremists. Tata

Iron and Steel Company (TISCO) is founded with Indian capital at Sakchi.

1908: Newspapers Incitement to Offences Act gives a magistrate the power to seize a newspaper if it published anything malicious. Khudiram Bose is sentenced to death for assassination attempt on Magistrate Kingsford which resulted in the killing of two British ladies. The Explosive Substances Act is enacted. The Calcutta Stock Exchange is inaugurated.

1909: The Morley–Minto Reforms: Officially known as India Act of 1909, it introduced separate electorate for the Muslims, inclusion of an Indian on the central and provincial councils and also on the council of the Secretary of State for India. The Indian Institute of Science in Bangalore is set up.

1910: Lord Crewe becomes the Secretary of State for India. Mahatma Gandhi establishes Tolstoy Farm near Johannesburg.

1911: The Delhi Durbar and announcement that Imperial capital moves to Delhi from Calcutta. Partition of Bengal modified. Mohun Bagan Club of Calcutta defeats East Yorkshire Regiment 2–1 in the IFA Shield final. Jinnah first introduces the Wakf Bill in the Imperial Legislative Council.

1912: Tata Iron and Steel Company begins production.

1913: Government of India Resolution on Educational Policy passed. The self-educated Indian genius Srinivasa Ramanujan sends a long list of brilliant theorems to British mathematician G.H. Hardy, and begins to come to the attention of academia. *Raja Harishchandra*, the first totally indigenous Indian feature film, is released. Rabindranath Tagore is awarded the Nobel Prize for literature.

1914: Indian Science Congress holds its first session at Calcutta.

1915: Defence of India Act passed to deal with revolutionary and German-inspired threats. Gopal Krishna Gokhale, leader of the 1907 split in Congress and former member of Imperial Legislative Congress, dies. Mahatma Gandhi establishes Sabarmati ashram near Ahmedabad.

1916: The Lucknow Pact of the Indian National Congress and the All-India Muslim League to strengthen the demand for self-government. The Home Rule League founded by Lokmanya Bal Gangadhar Tilak in Poona. Annie Besant founds Home Rule League in Madras. Foundation of the Women's University at Poona.

1917–18: Indians made eligible for the King's Commission. Report of the Industrial Commission is submitted. The Champaran Satyagraha, led by Gandhi, begins in Bihar in support of indigo peasants. Anne Besant is the president of Congress. Montagu–Chelmsford Report appears in the summer of 1918, aiming at introducing partial responsible government in the provinces of British India. The Indian National Liberal Federation is set up by moderate members of Congress.

1919: The Jallianwala Bagh massacre happens on 13 April at Amritsar. Rowlatt Act is passed to give the Government of India summary powers to curb seditious activities. Rabindranath Tagore renounces knighthood protesting against the Jallianwala Bagh massacre. *Orphans of the Storm* is the first film to be certified by the Censor Board in India. Montagu–Chelmsford Reforms (implemented in 1921) provides step to self-government within empire with greater provincialization. Moplah Revolt on Malabar coast.

1920: The Khilafat Movement initiated by the Ali brothers, Muhammad Ali and Shawkat Ali. The Non-Co-operation Movement begins as a spin off of the Khilafat Movement. Gandhi elected president of All-India Home Rule League. Gandhi appeals for satyagraha resolution at the Congress session in Delhi. First Indian Khilafat delegation reaches London.

1921: The Moplah's rebellion starts on the Malabar coast. The Prince of Wales visits India. The Duke of Connaught lays foundation stone of All-India War Memorial or India Gate. The discovery of the Indus Valley Civilization in Sind. Subramania Bharti, the Tamil poet, dies a tragic death.

1922: The Royal Military College opens in Dehra Dun. Delhi University is incorporated. Tagore's school at Shantiniketan becomes Vishva Bharati University. Thirty-eighth Session of Indian National Congress at Gaya. India granted the right to be represented at the International Labour Organization. Civil Disobedience Movement launched, followed by violence at Chauri-Chaura which leads Gandhi to suspend the movement.

1923: Swarajists led by Motilal Nehru and C.R. Das decide to participate in Indian Council elections. Franchise for women in the United Provinces and Rajkot. First May Day celebrations in Madras. Radio clubs of Bombay and Calcutta broadcast their programmes.

1924: Fortieth Session of the Congress at Belgaum, Gandhi presides. First All-India Communist Conference in Kanpur. The Gateway of India opened by Viceroy Earl of Reading. Subhas Chandra Bose is elected Mayor of Calcutta Corporation. Sir John Marshall discovers relics of Indus Valley Civilization.

1925: Vaikom satyagraha led by Kerala Provincial Congress Committee starts near Travancore to allow 'untouchables' to use roads round a temple. Elected legislative council at Cochin. RSS is founded at Nagpur by K.B. Hegdewar. Reforms Enquiry Committee Report. C.R. Das dies at Darjeeling. Franchise for women in Bengal. Electric Railway declared open in Bombay. Moderate Congress leader Surendranath Bannerjee dies at Barrackpore. Maharaja Hari Singh is the new ruler of Kashmir. Indian Hockey Federation is born. Lord Irwin succeeds Earl Reading as viceroy and governor general of India.

1926: Royal Indian Navy is created. Lord Reading's letter to the seventh nizam asserts sovereignty of the British government. Factories Act. Kakori Case: Ashfaqullah, Rajendra Lahiri and Ram Prasad Bismil are accused of conspiring to blow up the viceroy's train at Kakori. Shri Aurobindo Ashram is set up in Pondicherry.

1927: Indian Navy Act. British Parliament appoints Simon Commission to study the political reforms in India. Accused in the Kakori Conspiracy case Ashfaqullah, Rajendra Lahiri and Ram Prasad Bismil are hanged. FICCI is established by Purshottamdas Thakurdas, G.D. Birla and others. Jawaharlal Nehru succeeds in passing a resolution declaring complete independence as the goal of Congress at the Madras session.

1928: Simon Commission arrives in India; Congress boycotts the Commission; hartal observed in all major Indian cities. Lala Lajpat Rai dies after receiving blows during his protest against Simon Commission. No-tax satyagraha campaign is launched at Bardoli, led by Sadar Patel. Bhagat Singh, Ajoy Ghosh and Jatindranath Sanyal set up Hindustan Socialist Republican Army(HSRA). India wins hockey gold at Amsterdam Olympics. The Nehru Report: Motilal Nehru chairs an all-party meeting and publishes a report defining Dominion Status as the form of government desired by India. Gandhi moves resolution at Congress session at Calcutta, calling for complete independence within one year, or else the beginning of another all-Indian satyagraha campaign.

1929: Lord Irwin promises Dominion status for India. Congress calls for full independence. All-India Trade Union Congress splits National Trade Union Federation is established; Jawaharlal

Nehru and the Communists stay with AITUC; moderates leave. HSRA members try to kill Lord Irwin by blowing up his train. Bhagat Singh and Batukeswar Dutta arrested for throwing a bomb in the central legislative assembly in Delhi. Child Marriage Restraint Bill better known as Sarda Act passed raising the age for marriage from fifteen to eighteen for girls and from eighteen to twenty-one for boys. Lahore session of the Congress; Jawaharlal Nehru hoists the national flag at Lahore. Weekly air mail service between India and UK inaugurated. Appointment of the Royal Commission on Indian Labour. Viceroy House, now Rashtrapati Bhawan, has its first occupant, Lord Irwin. Abdul Gaffar Khan, or Frontier Gandhi, a Pakhtoon leader and aide of Gandhi, organizes Khudai Khitmatgar. Teen Murti Bhawan is built to house the British Commander-in chief in India.

1930: Congress Working Committee meeting at Sabarmati Ashram asks Gandhi to launch Civil Disobedience Movement. Salt satyagraha, Gandhi's Dandi March. C. Rajagopalachari leads a salt march from Trichinopoly to Vedaranniyam. Jawaharlal Nehru is arrested; soon Gandhi's arrest is ordered. Gandhi's arrest leads to massive protests, especially Bombay and Calcutta. Simon Commission submits report, does not mention Dominion Status; British prime minister Ramsay McDonald 'rejects' the commission's findings. First Round Table Conference opens in London: Congress leaders are absent from the conference which is supposed to decide the future of India. Bhagat Singh, Rajguru and Sukdev are sentenced to death in the Lahore conspiracy case. Chittagong armoury raid led by Surya Sen. Child Marriage Act comes into effect. C.V. Raman wins the Nobel prize in physics. Great Depression (fall of agrarian prices) hits India.

1931: Gandhi–Irwin Pact signed, ends the civil disobedience movement. Gandhi sails from Bombay, accompanied by Mahadev Desai, Naidu, Mirabehn and Pandit Madan Mohan Malaviya for the second Round Table Conference. The Indian Statistical Institute (ISI) founded by Professor P.C. Mahalanobis in Kolkata. Motilal Nehru dies in Lucknow. Mother Teresa takes her vows in Darjeeling. India's first talkie *Alam Ara* directed by Ardeshir M. Irani is released. Karachi session of Congress appoints Gandhi as its representative at the Round Table conference. Lord Willingdon is the new Viceroy of India.

1932: Gandhi arrested in Bombay with Sardar Patel and detained without trial at Yeravada prison. Madan Mohan Malviya arrested on the eve of Congress session in Delhi. Third Round Table Conference in London. The Communal Award creates separate electorates for 'depressed' classes; Gandhi protests and starts fast at Yeravada jail. The Poona Pact modifies the communal award. Sheikh Abdullah establishes All J&K Muslim Conference. The Indian Military Academy set up in Dehra Dun. J.R.D. Tata pilots pioneering flight from Karachi to Bombay. India are the hockey champions at the Los Angeles Olympics. India plays its first Test Match in England; India loses the Test.

1933: Publication of the White Paper on various issues discussed at the Round Table Conference. Gandhi begins weekly publication of *Harijan* in place of *Young India*. Civil Disobedience Movement restarts. Indian National Airways launches daily air service between Calcutta and Dacca. Gandhi on a ten-month tour of every province in India to help end untouchability. Kasturba Gandhi arrested and imprisoned for sixth time in two years. First Test match on Indian soil at Bombay, Lala Amarnath is the first Indian to score a century.

1934: Civil Disobedience Movement called off. Gandhi escapes attempt on life at Poona. The Indian Factories Act, 1934. The Bihar earthquake. Joint Committee on Indian Constitutional Reform. Ranji Trophy is instituted.

1935: New Government of India Act passed. Golden Jubilee year of the Indian National Congress. Reserve Bank of India is formally inaugurated on 1 April. India's first national park, the Corbett National Park, is created in Uttar Pradesh. R.K. Narayan publishes his first novel *Swami and Friends*. Subrahmanyan Chandrasekhar calculates mass limit for stellar collapse of a white dwarf star.

1936: Death of King-Emperor George V. Accession and abdication of Edward VIII. Accession of George VI. Jawaharlal Nehru is the president at the fifty-second session of Congress at Lucknow. All-India Kisan Sabha is formed. Madame Cama who unfurled the first Indian flag at the International Socialist Congress in Stuttgart, dies. India wins hockey gold at Berlin Olympics. Author Munshi Premchand dies. All India Radio inaugurated. Lord Linlithgow succeeds Lord Willingdon as Viceroy. First-ever elections in India.

1937: Inauguration of Provincial Autonomy. First elections held, won by Congress. Congress ministries in the majority of Provinces. C. Rajagopalachari forms a ministry in Madras. Hindu Women's Right to Property Act passed. Scientist J.C. Bose dies.

1938: Subhas Chandra Bose elected president of the Congress at Haripura session. Vinoba Bhabe establishes ashram at Poona. Bharatiya Vidya Bhavan founded in Bombay by K. M. Munshi.

1939: Second World War begins (3 September). Resignation of Congress Ministries and the beginning of political deadlock in India. U.N. Brahmachari establishes India's first blood bank at Calcutta. Subhas Chandra Bose resigns from Congress, forms Forward Bloc.

1940: Lahore Resolution ('Pakistan Resolution') of the Muslim League, 'two nations' theory articulated by Jinnah. Udham Singh murders Michael O'Dwyer in London. Singh hanged at a later date. Wardha session of CWC approves Gandhi's proposal for individual civil-disobedience. Maulana Azad is Congress president.

1941: Subhash Chandra Bose reaches Germany. First shipbuilding yard is completed at Vishakhapatnam. Rabindranath Tagore dies.

1942: Fall of Singapore to Japan. Evacuation of Rangoon followed by influx of refugees into India. Gandhi meets Sir Stafford Cripps in New Delhi but calls his proposals a post-dated cheque; they are ultimately rejected by Congress. Congress adopts the Quit India resolution. August Revolution and arrest of Indian Leaders. Forward Bloc is banned; Subhas Chandra Bose meets Hitler in Berlin.

1943: Lord Wavell is the new viceroy. Subhas Chandra Bose is in Tokyo. Bose organizes the Indian National Army; creates the provincial government of free India in Singapore. Gandhi on a twenty-one-day fast at Aga Khan Palace to end deadlock of negotiations between Viceroy and Indian leaders. Lord Mountbatten is Supreme Commander of South-east Asia. Hyderabad bans the Communist party in the state. Howrah Bridge over river Hooghly in Bengal is completed. C.D. Deshmukh is the first Indian governor of the Reserve Bank of India. Bombay Talkies' *Kismet* begins its three year eight month record run at Calcutta. Famine in Bengal; many die.

1944: Kasturba Gandhi dies in detention at Aga Khan Palace. Gandhi freed from jail. Gandhi–Jinnah talks opened in Bombay on Rajagopalachari's proposals for solution of constitutional deadlock. Talks break down on Pakistan issue. Battle of Kohima between the Japanese and Allied forces. Justice Party adopts a resolution to form a separate Dravida Nadu.

1945: Lord Wavell's broadcast announcing the British government's determination to go ahead with the task of fitting India for self-government. Lord Wavell invites Congress and Muslim League to Shimla for talks; talks fail. Subhas Chandra Bose mysteriously disappears after an 'air-crash' over Formosa. Telco launched. First trial of Indian National Army men opened.

1946: Mutiny in Royal Indian Navy. Announcement of special mission of Cabinet Ministers to India. Cabinet Mission's plan announced. British Cabinet's plan for interim government announced. Muslim League decides to participate in the interim government; Congress announces acceptance of the long-term part of 16 May plan, but refuses invitation to participate in interim government. Muslim League withdraws its acceptance and decides on a policy of direct action. This leads to outbreak of mob violence in Calcutta and Noakhali. Gandhi on a four-month tour of forty-nine villages in East Bengal to quell communal rioting over Muslim representation in provisional government. Interim government formed. Muslim League members sworn in. Constituent Assembly's first meeting. Dr Rajendra Prasad elected president of the Constituent Assembly. Madan Mohan Malviya dies. Sheikh Abdullah organizes the Quit-Kashmir movement against Maharaja Hari Singh. Communist-led Telengana movement in Andhra. Indian Telephone Industries is established. Tata Airlines renamed Air-India. Nehru publishes *The Discovery of India* from the Ahmadnagar fort prison.

1947: British PM Clement Attlee's historic announcement of transfer of power to 'responsible Indian hands' not later than June 1948. Lord Mountbatten's appointment as Viceroy of India in succession to Lord Wavell. Announcement of Lord Mountbatten's plan for Partition of India. Indian Independence Act is passed. Creation of dominions of India and Pakistan act passed by British Parliament. Sir Cyril Radcliffe's Boundary Commission set up to create the borders in Bengal and Punjab in June; Radcliffe awards are announced a month later. Jinnah insists on the creation of Pakistan; Muslim League begins 'Direct Action'. Pakistan is created by partitioning India on 14 August 1947. Patel's efforts to include princely states in the Indian Union begin. India wins freedom on 15 August; Jawaharlal Nehru is the country's first PM. Hundreds of thousands die in widespread communal violence after partition. India appeals to UN to intercede in the Kashmir dispute. Junagarh accedes to Pakistan. Kashmir becomes part of India. The accession, not recognized by Pakistan, leads to Indo–Pak conflict. C.N. Annadurai forms DMK. Sarojini Naidu is the governor of UP. Vijaylakshmi Pandit is the ambassador to UN. Shanmukham Chetty presents independent India's first budget. Kundanlal Saigal dies in Jalandhar.

1948: Mahatma Gandhi killed by Nathuram Vinayak Godse on 30 January at Birla House in Delhi. Sri Chakravarti Rajagopalachari appointed governor general of India. Reserve Bank of India nationalized. Death of Qaid-i-Azam Mohammad Ali Jinnah. Troops of Government of India enter Hyderabad state. War with Pakistan over disputed territory of Kashmir. Integration of princely states into Indian Union. B.R. Ambedkar presents first Draft Constitution to Constituent Assembly.

1949: Ceasefire in Kashmir. India's ceasefire line with Pakistan demarcated. New Constitution of India adopted and signed.

1950: New Constitution comes into force on 26 January; India becomes a republic. Rajendra Prasad becomes the first president of Republic of India. Inauguration of the Supreme Court.

India's first home minister Sardar Patel dies. Nehru–Liaqat pact on minorities. Sri Aurobindo is dead.

1951: Inauguration of First Five-Year Plan. First census is carried out in independent India. Debate on Kashmir begins in UN security Council. Shyama Prasad Mookherjee establishes Bhartiya Jan Sangh.

1952: First general election of independent India. Accession of Queen Elizabeth II. Chandernagore incorporated into India. Dr Rajendra Prasad is elected President of India. G.V. Mavalankar becomes the first Speaker of the Lok Sabha. First Five-Year Plan. Construction of Chandigarh begins. Sheikh Abdullah's ministry in Kashmir confirms accession to India. India launches its family planning programmes.

1953: New state of Andhra inaugurated. Chandigarh inaugurated as capital of Punjab. Mount Everest scaled by Edmund Hillary and Tenzing Norgay. Prime Minister of Kashmir, Sheikh Abdullah, imprisoned. Prime Ministers of India and Pakistan agree to appoint a plebiscite administrator for Kashmir. First backward classes commission headed by Kaka Kalelkar instituted.

1954: Pondicherry, Karaikal, Mahe, Yanon incorporated into India. The Filmfare Awards are instituted. China and India sign the Panchsheel agreement. Special Marriages Act introduces divorces by mutual consent.

1955: Hindu Marriage Act. Congress session at Avadi adopts resolution signalling a socialistic pattern of growth for the country. Satyajit Ray's first feature film *Pather Panchali* released. Kalelkar Commission report fails to recommend reservations for the backward classes.

1956: Nationalization of insurance companies. Pakistan proclaimed an Islamic republic. Hindu Succession Act. Reorganization of states along linguistic lines. India becomes the first Asian country to reach the semi-finals of the Olympic football tournament. Inauguration of Second Five-Year Plan. Chairman Drafting Committee of Indian Constitution B.R. Ambedkar dies.

1957: Second general election held. Introduction of the decimal system of coinage. First Communist government in a state of India—E.M.S. Namboodiripad becomes the chief minister of Kerala.

1958: Introduction of the metric system of weights. Union Finance Minister T.T. Krishnamachari resigns over share scandal. Maulana Abul Kalam Azad is dead.

1959: The Dalai Lama enters Indian territory for political asylum. Namboodiripad's Kerala government is dismissed; President's Rule is imposed. Sino-Indian border disputes. Swatantra Party formed by C. Rajagopalachari. Indo-Portuguese dispute. Arrival of Dwight D. Eisenhower, President of the USA, in New Delhi.

1960: Meeting of the Afro–Asian Conference at New Delhi. Indus Water Treaty with Pakistan. Nehru–Ayub Khan talks. Bifurcation of Bombay into Maharashtra and Gujarat states. Visits of President Voroshilov and Premier Khrushchev of the USSR and President Nasser of the UAR.

1961: Arrival of Queen Elizabeth and the Duke of Edinburgh at New Delhi. Nehru–Chow En Lai talks in Delhi. Operation Vijay and liberation of Goa, Daman and Diu from Portugal.

1962: Dr S. Radhakrishnan and Dr Zakir Hussain sworn in as President and vice-president of India. Chinese invasion of India. Border war with China. Third general election; Indian National Congress forms government, Nehru is prime minister again.

1963: Rajendra Prasad dies.

1964: Jawaharlal Nehru dies (24 May); Lal Bahadur Shastri becomes the new PM. CPI splits into CPI and CPI(M).

1965: Indo–Pak war in the Rann of Kutch. General Thimayya dies in Cyprus, leading UN Peacekeepers.

Hindi is declared the official language of the Union. DMK leads agitation in Madras. Durgapur Steel Plant becomes operational. First Indian expedition on Everest, led by Commander M.S. Kohli.

1966: Indo–Pak Tashkent accord. Death of Lal Bahadur Shastri at Tashkent. Indira Gandhi is the new PM. Bal Thackeray forms Shiv Sena. Mihir Sen swims across the English Channel. Artist and designer of the Bharat Ratna medallion Nandalal Bose dies. Reita Faria is crowned Miss World. Homi Bhabha, chairman Atomic Energy Commission, dies in an air-crash.

1967: Fourth general election, Congress wins majority. Dr Zakir Hussain becomes President. First DMK ministry in Madras. Socialist leader Ram Manohar Lohia dies. Earthquake in Maharashtra, 100 dead. India's first cricket captain C.K. Nayudu is dead.

1968: Nobel in physiology and medicine for Hargobind Khurana. Green Revolution begins. Fourth Five-Year Plan postponed. Ustad Bade Ghulam Ali Khan passes away. India's first overseas Test series win, against New Zealand; Mansoor Ali Khan Pataudi is the captain.

1969: President Dr Zakir Hussain passes away. V.V. Giri elected president of India. Congress splits over V.V. Giri's election as President. Indira Gandhi at the helm of Congress. Morarji Desai resigns from cabinet. Fourteen banks nationalized. Death of C.N. Annadurai.

1970: Prime Minister Indira Gandhi inaugurates Meghalaya. A Bill for setting up of 'North-Eastern Council', to co-ordinate the development and security of Assam, Meghalaya, Manipur, and Tripura passed. Prime Minister Indira Gandhi addresses the Silver Jubilee Session of the United Nations. Supreme court holds nationalization of banks illegal. Privy Purses and special privileges of former Indian rulers abolished. Foundation of Auroville near Pondicherry.

1971: Fifth general election, Indira Gandhi is re-elected PM. Indo–Soviet twenty-year Treaty of Peace, Friendship and Co-operation. Pakistan declares war on India after gunning down of its aircraft near Calcutta. Indian Army in East Pakistan in support of Mukti Bahini fighting for independence. Pakistan surrenders; Bangladesh is born and recognized by India. India under Ajit Wadekar wins the first-ever Test series in England.

1972: Indira Gandhi and Zulfikar Ali Bhutto sign an Agreement at Simla committing both 'to abjure the use of force in resolving differences'. Mizoram inaugurated as a Union Territory. Arrival of Bangladesh leader Sheikh Mujibur Rehman in Calcutta, and his talks with Prime Minister Indira Gandhi. Indira Gandhi visits Dhaka and a joint statement is issued by India and Bangladesh; India and Bangladesh sign a twenty-five year treaty of friendship, Co-operation and Peace.

1973: India's first Field Marshal is Sam Manekshaw. Coal mines nationalized. Foreign Exchange Regulation Act (FERA) passed.

1974: India carries out an underground nuclear experiment in Pokhran. Fakhruddin Ali Ahmad sworn in as the President of India. Joint Communique by India and Bangladesh; Indo-Pakistan Trade Agreement.

1975: Dr S. Radhakrishnan, former President of India, passes away in Madras. Railway Minister L.N. Mishra killed in a bomb blast at Samastipur railway station. Allahabad High Court upholds Raj Narain's petition against Indira Gandhi on electoral malpractices. National Emergency declared. Sikkim joins India. *Aryabhatta*, the first Indian satellite, launched from the Soviet Union. An Ordinance amending the Maintenance of Internal Security Act issued. Announcement of a package of economic measures—the Twenty-Point Economic Programme.

1976: Parliament approves a Bill extending the life of the Lok Sabha up to 1978. Private Oil companies nationalized. Urban Land Ceiling Regulation Act passed. Doordarshan is separated from Akashvani. Singer Mukesh is dead.

1977: President Fakhruddin Ali Ahmed passes away in New Delhi. Vice-President B.D. Jatti sworn in as acting President. General Elections: Morarji Desai, Atal Bihari Vajpayee, Madhu Dandavate elected to the Lok Sabha; Indira Gandhi defeated in Rae Bareli. Indira Gandhi resigns as PM after triumph of the Janata Party and its allies in the sixth general elections. Morarji Desai elected leader of the Janata Party and sworn in as Prime Minister. Internal emergency promulgated on 25 June 1975 withdrawn. Press censorship removed. Government revokes the external emergency promulgated on 3 December 1971. N. Sanjeeva Reddy elected unopposed as president of India. Indira Gandhi arrested in New Delhi by CBI on charges of corruption, released unconditionally. Government files petition in Delhi High Court challenging the release order of Indira Gandhi. Prime Minister Morarji Desai and the Soviet President Leonid Brezhnev sign a joint declaration in Moscow. India and Bangladesh sign Farakka agreement on water sharing in Dacca. The 44th Constitution Amendment Bill passed by the Lok Sabha.

1978: Congress splits; Indira Gandhi forms Congress(I); gets 'hand' as electoral symbol. Indian Coast Guard is set up. The Lok Sabha expels Indira Gandhi from the house and sentences her to imprisonment; she is released a week later.

1979: Mother Teresa receives the Nobel Peace prize. Famous hockey player Dhyan Chand passes away. No-confidence motion against Morarji Desai; Desai resigns. Charan Singh sworn in as Prime Minister of India; resigns. Lok Sabha is dissolved, elections announced. Second backward classes commission constituted; B.P. Mandal is the chairman. Socialist leader Loknayak Jaiprakash Narayan is dead.

1980: Indira Gandhi storms back to power. Mother Teresa receives the Bharat Ratna award. Prakash Padukone wins the All-England Badminton Championship. Famous singer Mohammed Rafi passes away. Congress leader Sanjay Gandhi dies in an aircrash. Mandal Commission report tabled. Atal Bihari Vajpayee and Lal Krishna Advani inaugurate Bharatiya Janata Party(BJP).

1981: Census begins all over the country. President's Rule is imposed in Assam. Famous actor Nargis Dutt passes away. Salman Rushdie's *Midnight's Children* wins Booker Prize.

1982: Giani Zail Singh is elected President of India. Acharya Vinoba Bhave dies. 'Palace on Wheels' begins its journey. India hosts the Ninth Asian Games in New Delhi. Jammu and Kashmir chief minister Sheikh Abdullah is dead; Farooq Abdullah is the new chief minister.

1983: Non-Aligned summit begins in New Delhi. Industrialist G.D. Birla passes away. Bhanu Athaiya wins Oscar for costumes in *Gandhi*. Indian cricket team led by Kapil Dev lifts the Prudential World Cup. Sunil Gavaskar breaks Sir Don Bradman's record of maximum Test centuries. The Vishwa Hindu Parishad (VHP) launches a campaign to build a temple on the disputed site in Ayodhya.

1984: President's Rule imposed in Punjab. Operation Blue Star is launched, Jarnail Singh Bhindranwale and his supporters who were hiding in the holy Golden Temple are flushed out by army operation in which Bhindranwale is killed. Indira Gandhi is assassinated by two security guards. Outbreak of riots in Delhi; Sikhs are targeted. Bachendri Pal is the first Indian woman on top of Mt Everest. Lok Sabha elections held; Congress led by Rajiv Gandhi gets an overwhelming majority. Rajiv Gandhi is sworn in as the prime minister of India.

Squadron Leader Rakesh Sharma become India's first cosmonaut. Bhopal gas tragedy kills 2,500.

1985: Supreme Courts invokes Article 125 in the Shah Bano case. Rajiv Gandhi and Akali leader Harchand Singh Longowal sign Punjab agreement. PM announces Assam accord. M. Azharuddin become the first batsman in the world to hit three centuries in successive Tests on his debut. Indian cricket team wins the Benson and Hedges World Championship cricket tournament. Indira Gandhi National Open University is established. Narmada Bachao Andolan begins. The 52nd Amendment of Constitution; Anti-Defection bill.

1986: Parliament enacts the Muslim Women (Protection of Rights on Divorce) Act, 1986 that gives a Muslim woman the right to maintenance for the period of *iddat* after the divorce. 'First' Indian test-tube baby born in Bombay. Noted actor Smita Patil passes away. General K.M. Cariappa is conferred the rank of Field Marshal. Fourth Pay Commission submits its report. President's Rule imposed in J&K. Government signs Mizo Accord with Laldenga. Rukmini Devi Arundale, founder of Kalakshetra, passes away. Mikhail Gorbachev visits Delhi. SAARC summit in Bangalore.

1987: Goa becomes the twenty-fifth state of India. India deploys troops for peacekeeping operation in Sri Lanka. Noted ornithologist Salim Ali passes away. Sunil Gavaskar scores 10,000th Test run. R. Venkataraman is elected President of India. Playback singer Kishore Kumar passes away.

1988: Janata Dal is formed in Bangalore. Securities and Exchange Board of India (SEBI) comes into existence. Raj Kapoor passes away. Morarji Dasai is bestowed the title of Nishan-e-Pakistan.

1989: More than seventy members of parliament resign over the Bofor's gun deal issue. Prime Minster Rajiv Gandhi tenders his resignation. Lok Sabha elections announced; Congress is the largest party in the parliament. Ram Janambhoomi foundation stone laid at Ayodhya. V.P. Singh of the newly formed Janata Dal is sworn in as the Prime Minister of India. The Constitution (61st Amendment) Act lowers the voting age from twenty-one to eighteen. Supreme Court orders Union Carbide Corporation to pay a compensation of $470 million for the Bhopal Gas tragedy. Mufti Mohammad Sayeed's daughter, Rubaiyya Sayeed, kidnapped in Kashmir; Rubaiyya released in exchange of five secessionists. Osho Rajneesh is dead.

1990: Bofors kickback case FIR registered. Mandal Commission Report on reservation implemented; violence erupts. PM V.P. Singh resigns after losing no-confidence motion in Parliament. Chandra Shekhar becomes Prime Minister of India. Film director V. Shantaram passes away. BJP president L.K. Advani begins his Rath Yatra to win support for building temple at Ayodhya. Indian troops withdrawn from Sri Lanka.

1991: Congress withdraws support from the Chandra Shekhar government. Lok Sabha elections announced. Rajiv Gandhi dies in a powerful bomb explosion in Sriperambudur during election campaign. Congress gets a majority in the Lok Sabha elections. P.V. Narasimha Rao is the new prime minister. Liberalization initiated by finance minister Dr Manmohan Singh. Satellite TV makes its debut in the wake of Gulf War. Census in India. Earthquake in Uttarkashi with many casualties.

1992: Satyajit Ray receives an Oscar for lifetime achievement. Prithvi missile launched. Shankar Dayal Sharma becomes President of India. Destruction of Babri Masjid on 6 December leads to communal violence all over the country. Famous vocalist Kumar Gandharva passes away. Satyajit Ray passes away.

1993: Riots in Mumbai. Rupee made convertible on trade account. More than 300 people killed in bomb blasts in Mumbai. Latur and Osmanabad earthquake kill thousands. J.R.D. Tata passes away. Women army officers are commissioned into non-combatant departments of the Indian Army.

1994: R.D. Burman passes away. ONGC becomes a public limited company. Chimanbhai Patel passes away. Manmohan Desai passes away. Devika Rani Roerich passes away. Lt. Gen. Satish Nambiar is new Army Chief. S. Bangarappa sets up Karnataka Congress Party. Wilfred D'Souza is new Goa chief minister. Sushmita Sen is crowned Miss Universe. Kiran Bedi wins Magsaysay Award. Rupee becomes fully convertible on current account. Cable Television Regulation Ordinance issued. The Gandhi Peace Prize is set up. Government notifies increase in the ceiling on election expenses on Lok Sabha and assembly polls. A.M. Ahmadi sworn in as Chief Justice. Aishwarya Rai is crowned Miss World. Shankar Roy Choudhury becomes new Chief of Army Staff. Giani Zail Singh passes away. H.D. Deve Gowda becomes Karnataka chief minister. NTR becomes Andhra Pradesh chief minister. P.K. Chamling becomes Sikkim chief minister.

1995: India becomes a member of the World Trade Organization (WTO). AIR launches its FM service in Delhi. Gegong Apang is sworn in as chief minister of Arunachal Pradesh. Former prime minister Morarji Desai passes away. VSNL launches Internet Access Service. President's Rule is imposed in Bihar. Music composer Salil Chowdhury passes away. A.K. Anthony is sworn in as Kerala chief minister, succeeding K. Karunakaran. President's Rule is imposed in Uttar Pradesh. Punjab chief minister Beant Singh is assassinated. South African president Nelson Mandela and Prime Minister Narasimha Rao sign an agreement on Intergovernmental Joint Commission for Political, Trade, Economic, Cultural, Scientific and Technical Co-operation. Industrialist Aditya Birla passes away. Harcharan Singh Brar is sworn in as chief minister of Punjab. The first exclusive Indian communications satellite, INSAT-2C, is launched. Mayawati becomes chief minister of Uttar Pradesh.

Last Ten Years in Review

1996

January: Victoria Terminus station, Mumbai, is renamed Chhatrapati Shivaji Railway Terminus. N. T. Rama Rao passes away.

February: Gold price zooms to all-time record high of Rs 5,600 per 10 grams. Sahib Singh Verma sworn in as Delhi's chief minister, succeeding Madanlal Khurana.

March: Chaudhary Randhir Singh is appointed governor of Sikkim.

April: Union Minister P. Chidambaram resigns. Supreme Court rules that political parties without audited accounts cannot take advantage of an election law that exempts tax expenditure on candidates. Assam chief minister Hiteshwar Saikia passes away. Dr Bhumindhar Barman becomes new chief minister of Assam.

May: Controversial godman Chandraswami is arrested. Reliance Industries become India's first private sector company to post a total income of over Rs 8,000 crore. Tamil Nadu chief minister J. Jayalalithaa resigns. Prime Minister P. V. Narasimha Rao and his council of ministers resign. M. Karunanidhi (DMK) sworn in as Tamil Nadu chief minister. Lok Sabha election results are announced (534 out of 537)—BJP (161) is the largest single party. President invites BJP leader A.B. Vajpayee to form government at the Centre. Eleventh Lok Sabha constituted. Joint Opposition candidate Purno A. Sangma (Congress MP from Meghalaya) is elected Speaker of Eleventh Lok Sabha. Prime Minister A.B. Vajpayee seeks vote of confidence. Thirteen-day-old BJP led minority coalition government headed by A.B.Vajpayee quits. Janata Dal leader H.D. Deve Gowda, the thirteen-party United Front's consensus candidate for prime minister, presents to the President letters from 190 member of Parliament, pledging support to him.

June: Former President N. Sanjiva Reddy passes away. H.D. Deve Gowda's twenty-one-member Central Cabinet is sworn in. India's third currency-note press inaugurated in Mysore. Ram Vilas Paswan appointed leader of the House in Lok Sabha and I. K. Gujral in Rajya Sabha.

July: Janata Dal expels Maneka Gandhi from primary membership of the party. Chief Election Commissioner T. N. Seshan wins Magsaysay award. Veteran freedom fighter Aruna Asaf Ali pases away.

August: Leander Paes wins a bronze at Atlanta Olympics. Supreme Court asks Harshad Mehta to pay Rs 217 crore to income tax department.

September: President's Rule imposed in Gujarat. Narasimha Rao resigns from Congress Party president's post.

October: Mother Teresa is made honorary US citizen. President's Rule reimposed in Uttar Pradesh.

November: Indian cricket team wins Titan Cup, beating S. Africa.

December: M.S. Gill is appointed as the new Election Commissioner. Mahashweta Devi is selected for the Jnanpith Award.

1997

January: Thirty-year Ganga water sharing treaty between India and Bangladesh takes effect. Former Tamil Nadu in chief minister Jayalalithaa released on bail after twenty-seven days in prison. CBI charge-sheets former Haryana chief minister Bhajan Lal, former Union ministers, Ajit Singh, Ram Lakhan Singh Yadav and five others in the Rs 3.5-crore Jharkhand Mukti Morcha MPs bribery case.

February: Shiromani Akali Dal (Badal) president, Parkash Singh Badal, sworn in chief minister of Punjab for the third time. J. M. Lyngdoh is appointed Election Commissioner. Justice J. S. Verma is appointed Chief Justice of India. CBI arrests Chandraswami for alleged offences in violation of Foreign Contributions (Regulation) Act, 1976.

March: Congress (I) withdraws support to ten-month-old Deve Gowda government.

April: The Deve Gowda government loses its vote of confidence. Interest rates on domestic term deposits brought down from 10 per cent to 9 per cent by the RBI. I.K. Gujral is sworn in as prime minister and wins vote of confidence in parliament.

May: Sonia Gandhi enrols as a primary member of Congress(I). Special judge, V.B. Gupta, discharges Arjun Singh, N. D. Tiwari, Madhavrao Scindia and R. K. Dhawan, former Union ministers, in the Jain Hawala case.

June: INSAT-2D, India's fourth indigenous communications satellite, put into orbit by Ariane launch vehicle from Kourou in French Guyana. Sitaram Kesri elected president of the Congress(I). Film-maker Basu Bhattacharya passes away.

July: Tamil actor Sivaji Ganesan gets 1996 Dada Saheb Phalke award. Janata Dal splits. Laloo Prasad Yadav announces formation of Rashtriya Janata Dal. Environmental activist Mahesh

Chander Mehta wins Ramon Magsaysay Award. Vice-President K.R. Narayanan wins presidential election by a record margin. Laloo Prasad Yadav resigns as Bihar chief minister after CBI-designated court issues an arrest warrant against him in the fodder scam case. Laloo Prasad Yadav's wife Rabri Devi is sworn in as the chief minister of Bihar and proves her majority in assembly.

August: The governor of Andhra Pradesh, Krishan Kant, is elected India's new vice-president. The Jain Commission, which looked into the events that led to the assassination of Rajiv Gandhi, submits interim report to government.

September: Mother Teresa passes away. Prasar Bharati Act comes into force. Kalyan Singh sworn in as chief minister of Uttar Pradesh. Gen. V. P. Malik takes over from Gen. Shankar Roychowdhury as Chief of Army Staff. Pravin Thipsay becomes India's third chess grand master.

October: India's first woman police officer, Kiran Bedi, is awarded Joseph Beuys prize for her work in reforming the country's largest prison, Tihar Jail. Arundhati Roy wins the Booker Prize for her novel *The God of Small Things*.

November: Diana Hayden becomes Miss World. Dr A.P.J. Abdul Kalam, scientific advisor to defence minister, awarded the Bharat Ratna.

December: 'Biju Janata Dal' formed. Congress leader in West Bengal,

1998

January: Defence Research and Development Organisation (DRDO) and the Indian Air Force (IAF) jointly conduct stealth aircraft experiments resulting in the achievement of 94 per cent radar invisibility.

February: Reserve Bank of India (RBI) allows exporters to receive interest-bearing advance payments not exceeding 100 basis points over Libor (London Inter-Bank Offered Rate) from their overseas buyers.

March: BJP forms government in Gujarat. The final report of the Jain Commission on the conspiracy aspect of Rajiv Gandhi's assassination is submitted to the Union home ministry by the one-man panel. Atal Bihari Vajpayee is sworn in as prime minister along with a forty-two-member, two-tier ministry. Communist leader and Kerala's former chief minister, E.M.S. Namboodiripad, passes away.

April: Supreme Court rules that the services of a confirmed employee in both private and government sectors cannot be legally terminated by a simple notice. Kushabhau Thakre is the new BJP president.

May: In Assam, the government decides to make Dispur the permanent state capital. Apart from the creation of a special non-lapsable fund of around Rs 1,500 crore each year, Prime Minister Atal Behari Vajpayee announces a series of other measures as part of his special north-east package. The Union government decides to scrap the Urban Land Ceiling Act (ULCA) and raise the retirement age of Central government employees from fifty-eight to sixty. India conducts nuclear test at Pokhran.

June: India and Russia reach an agreement on the Russian sale of six 9K81 S-300V mobile air defence systems to India for deployment at front and army level.

July: Centre announces a Rs 250 crore assistance to Jammu and Kashmir to help overcome the state's financial crisis and resolves to meet the state's expenditure to combat militancy. Pratapsingh Rane government in Goa is dismissed and Wilfred De Souza sworn in as the new chief minister to head the new coalition. Lok Sabha passes Prasar Bharati Bill by voice vote.

August: Goa chief minister Dr Wilfred D'Souza disqualified from the membership of the House. Government launches the 'Kar Vivadh Samadhan Scheme' for quick and voluntary settlement of over five lakh direct and indirect tax disputes amounting to arrears of Rs 52,000 crore.

September: The Bihar Assembly rejects the Vananchal Bill.

October: Amartya Sen is awarded the 1998 Nobel Prize in Economics.

November: The Union Cabinet clears the way for a bill to allow foreign insurance companies to take a 26 per cent stake in new insurance ventures in India. It also allows FIIs to pick up an additional 14 per cent in these organizations. Congress leader in Goa assembly, Luizinho Faleiro is sworn in as chief minister.

December: Women's Reservation Bill is introduced in the Lok Sabha. Union Cabinet okays automatic approval of foreign equity up to 100 per cent for undertaking construction and maintenance of roads, highways, bridges, toll roads and vehicular tunnels as also ports and harbours.

1999

January: The government reduces interest rates on small savings schemes, deposit schemes for retired government/PSU employees and relief bonds. Arunachal Pradesh chief minister Gegong Apang resigns as a confidence vote is defeated by a margin of 0–36 votes.

February: Shiv Sena leader Narayan Rane is sworn in as the fifteenth chief minister of Maharashtra. Anil Kumble creates history by becoming only the second bowler in 123 years of Test cricket to take all 10 wickets in an innings. Supreme Court allows resumption of the construction of Narmada Dam after almost five years. Lok Sabha ratifies President's Rule in Bihar.

March: In Bihar, Congress helps RJD leader Rabri Devi to win a vote of confidence.

April: The Twelfth Lok Sabha is dissolved.

May: Sensex crosses the 4,000 mark. The BJP and its allies decide to name themselves the National Democratic Alliance (Rashtriya Jantantrik Gathbandhan). Congress expels rebel leaders Sharad Pawar, P. A. Sangma and Tariq Anwar for six years. Government hikes salaries of PSU employees. India launches air- strikes in Kargil.

June: Union government imposes an indefinite ban on receiving signals of the Pakistan Television (PTV) in India. Leander Paes and Mahesh Bhupathi win French Open men's doubles at the Roland Garros. USA lifts sanctions against India.

July: Indian forces regain control of Tiger Hill after a prolonged fight. Leander Paes and Mahesh Bhupathi win the Wimbledon Men's doubles title. Election Commission announces the general elections for the thirteenth Lok Sabha will be held starting from 4 September. On the advice of the Election Commission, the President of India issues a notification debarring Shiv Sena leader Bal Thackeray from contesting elections and disenfranchising him till 10 December 2001.

August: Election Commission rejects the Sharad Pawar-led Nationalist Congress Party's plea for allotment of the 'charkha' symbol and orders its freezing. Prime Minister Atal Bihari Vajpayee accepts the resignation of Railway Minister Nitish Kumar.

September: Kapil Dev replaces Anshuman Gaekwad as India coach.

October: President K. R. Narayanan formally invites Atal Bihari Vajpayee to be the next prime minister. India, UAE sign extradition treaty. Several hundred people are feared killed and over 15 million affected as a super-cyclone, with a velocity of more than 260km per hour, hits ten coastal districts of Orissa for more than eight hours.

November: The Darjeeling Himalayan Railway is included on the UNESCO list of World Heritage sites.

December: Yukta Mookhey becomes Miss World. Indian Airlines flight IC-814 with 178 passengers and eleven crew aboard is hijacked.

2000

January: The special court for CBI cases allows the investigating agency to retain the final set of Swiss Bank documents relating to the Bofors pay-off case for conducting further investigation. Sensex rises sharply by over 369 points to reach an all-time high of 5,375. The Uttar Pradesh Assembly passes the UP Regulation of Public Religious Buildings and Places Bill, 2000, to regulate the use and construction of public buildings and places for religious purposes. T.S. Krishnamurthy is the new Election Commissioner. The government announces an across-the-board 1per cent cut in the deposit rates on all small savings schemes like Public Provident Fund (PPF), National Savings Certificates, Kisan Vikas Patras, Post Office fixed deposit and Post Office recurring deposit schemes. Prime Minister Atal Bihari Vajpayee announces a Rs 10,271-crore 'Agenda for Economic Development' for the north-east and Sikkim. The Indian team wins the Under-19 World Cup for cricket.

February: Dara Singh alias Ravinder Kumar Pal, wanted in fourteen cases including the murder of the Australian missionary Graham Stuart Staines and his two sons, is arrested. National cricket selectors appoint Sourav Ganguly as the captain.

March: Nitish Kumar is sworn in as chief minister of Bihar by the governor V.C. Pande. A twenty-five-member BJD–BJP coalition ministry headed by the BJD president, Naveen Patnaik, is administered the oath of office by the Orissa governor, M.M. Rajendran. Meghalaya chief minister, B. B. Lyngdoh, resigns, making way for the Speaker, E. K. Mawlong. Bihar chief minister Nitish Kumar resigns and is replaced by RJD's Rabri Devi. Government announces the creation of two special economic zones (SEZs) on the Chinese model in Gujarat and Tamil Nadu.

April: The Reserve Bank of India announces a cut in the bank rate from 8 per cent to 7 per cent. The government approves fifty-seven cases of foreign direct investment. Jhumpa Lahiri wins the Pulitzer Prize for fiction for her debut collection of short stories *Interpreter of Maladies*. Nishant, the indigenously built unmanned air vehicle (UAV), is test-flown from the interim test range.

May: Lara Dutta becomes Miss Universe 2000. Former Indian cricketer Manoj Prabhakar releases secret video that reveals the results of his 'undercover investigations' carried out with the help of tehelka.com.

June: Senior Congress leader and former Union minister Rajesh Pilot killed in a car accident. CBI issues summons to several cricketers, including Indian coach Kapil Dev, former skipper Mohammed Azharuddin, former manager Ajit Wadekar and commentators Ravi Shastri and Sunil Gavaskar in the match-fixing case. The government announces disinvestment of its equity in thirty-three state-owned companies, including privatization or outright sale of twenty-six public sector undertakings (PSUs) during the current financial year.

July: India's first missile-firing submarine, INS *Sindushastra*, is commissioned in St. Petersburg, Russia. RBI launches a series of measures to halt the slide of the rupee against the US dollar. Sandalwood smuggler Veerappan kidnaps famous actor Rajkumar along with three others.

August: Lt Gen. Sundararajan Padmanabhan is announced as the next Chief of the Army Staff replacing Gen. V.P. Malik. Bangaru Laxman is elected unopposed as the new BJP president. The Union Power Minister P.R. Kumaramangalam passes away. Prime Minister Atal Bihari Vajpayee announces a package of measures to strengthen the small-scale sector including raising the ceiling on loans from Rs 10 lakh to Rs 25 lakh and bringing service-oriented units into the ambit of the priority lending programme.

September: Weightlifter Karnam Malleswari wins a bronze at the Sydney Olympics. A special court convicts former prime minister P. V. Narasimha Rao and Buta Singh in the 'Jharkhand Mukti Morcha case' on charges of bribing members of Parliament to buy votes to save the minority Congress government in the no-confidence motion in 1993. Election Commission derecognizes CPI(M) as a national party but keeps alive its registration as a state party in Kerala, Tripura and West Bengal.

October: CBI alleges that Azharuddin had fixed matches while Ajay Jadeja and Nayan Mongia helped him.

November: The Union Cabinet allows the private sector to operate direct-to-home (DTH) television services that will enable subscribers to view over 100 channels through a small satellite dish and a TV set-top box containing a SIM card. The Board of Control for Cricket in India suspends five cricketers: Mohammad Azharuddin, Ajay Jadeja, Nayan Mongia, Ajay Sharma and Manoj Prabhakar. Uttaranchal is born as the twenty-seventh state of the country. Jharkhand becomes the twenty-eighth state of the Indian Union. Veerappan releases Kannada actor Rajkumar and his relative Nagesh.

December: Priyanka Chopra become Miss World. Azharuddin, Sharma banned for life by the BCCI. Government introduces a bill in the Lok Sabha that seeks to reduce its equity in nationalized banks from 51 to 33 per cent and empowers it to supersede the board of directors of public sector banks and constitute a financial restructuring authority. India and Russia sign their biggest-yet defence deal for licensed production of the SU-30MKI fighter jets.

2001

January: India's indigenously built Light Combat Aircraft (LCA) Technology Demonstrator I (TD I) undertakes its landmark first flight. The pilotless target aircraft, Lakshya, is successfully inducted into the IAF. India successfully carries out the second test of the Agni-II missile. Over 2 crore take a dip at Sangam in the Kumbh Mela. Union Cabinet permits the Enron Power Development Corporation to increase its stake in the Dabhol Power Project in Maharashtra since the other major partner, the Maharashtra State Electricity Board (MSEB), expressed its inability to pick up equity in the second phase of the project. Senior BJP leader Vijayaraje Scindia passes away. Major earthquake measuring 6.9 on the Richter scale strikes Gujarat. Prime Minister A.B. Vajpayee sanctions Rs 10 crore for immediate assistance. World Bank offers an immediate assistance of $300 million for emergency rehabilitation work in Gujarat.

February: Cabinet Committee on Disinvestment decides to reduce the government's share in Videsh Sanchar Nigam Limited (VSNL) to 26 per cent from the present 52.97 per cent. World's biggest census begins in India. Sitar maestro Pandit Ravi Shankar is bestowed the award of honorary Knight Commander of the Order of the British Empire by the Queen in recognition of his service to music. India and Russia sign a historic accord on massive Indian investment in the Sakhalin oil and gas fields. Cabinet Committee on Disinvestment formally decides to dilute the government's equity holding in the Maruti Udyog Limited (MUL). Reserve Bank of India cuts the bank rate and the credit reserve ratio (CRR) by 0.5 per cent. Veteran CPI leader and longest- serving parliamentarian Indrajit Gupta passes away. West Bengal Chief Minister Jyoti Basu retires from electoral politics.

March: Bombay Stock Exchange president, Anand Rathi, resigns in the wake of allegations of his involvement in a bear cartel. P. Gopi Chand wins the All-England badminton championship. Harbhajan Singh becomes the first Indian to claim a hat-trick in Test cricket, against Australia. Chokila Iyer assumes charge as India's first-ever woman foreign secretary, replacing Lalit Mansingh. V.V.S. Laxman becomes India's highest individual scorer (281) in a Test innings in the Kolkata Test against Australia. Defence Minister George Fernandes resigns from the Vajpayee government. Indian cricket team ends Australia's winning streak in Tests by winning the Kolkata Test. Former South African president Nelson Mandela honoured with the Gandhi Peace Prize by President K.R. Narayanan. External Affairs Minister Jaswant Singh as India's new defence minister replaces George Fernandes. Lata Mangeshkar receives the Bharat Ratna award. Indian cricket team retains the Border–Gavaskar trophy winning the Chennai Test. Amitabh Bachchan receives the Padma Bhushan. India's population is over 1.02 billion. Central Bureau of Investigation (CBI) arrests Ketan Parekh, leading stock broker, in connection with the Rs 130 crore pay-order scam.

April: Government decides to give an additional 2 per cent dearness allowance to the Central Government staff and 2 per cent dearness Relief to pensioners. NASSCOM president Dewang Mehta passes away. Securities and Exchange Board of India permanently debars Harshad Mehta from dealing in securities and orders his prosecution in connection with the 1998 price manipulations in the scrips of BPL, Videocon and Sterlite.

May: Centre permits the Food Corporation of India (FCI) to offer for export 30 lakh tonnes of rice during the current financial year. Bismillah Khan receives the Bharat Ratna. AIADMK, headed by Jayalalitha, secures a landslide victory in the Tamil Nadu Assembly election with 196 of the 234 seats. Congress-led United Democratic Front wins the Assembly elections in Kerala, securing a record two-thirds majority. Left Front wins again in the assembly elections of West Bengal. Congress–TMC combine emerges as the largest group in the Pondicherry Assembly elections, but falls short of an absolute majority. Renowned novelist R.K. Narayan passes away. Gold prices zoom to a fourteen-month high on the bullion market when standard gold touches Rs 4,600 per 10 grams.

June: Government declares use of its emblem and name of a Central ministry by private websites as illegal. Air Marshal S. Krishnaswamy is appointed the new Vice-Chief of Air Staff. Mahesh Bhupathi and Leander Paes win their second French Open men's doubles title. James Michael Lyngdoh takes over as the Chief Election Commissioner of India.

July: Excise department slaps a Rs 200-crore duty evasion show-cause notice on the country's premier car maker, Maruti Udyog Limited. Centre slashes by about 30 per cent the central issue price of wheat and rice sold to the 'above the poverty line' population (APL) through the public distribution system (PDS). Bangladesh passenger train, the first in thirty-six years, arrives at the Indian border. Fifty lakh people affected in Orissa floods. Samajwadi Party member of parliament, Phoolan Devi, is killed.

August: Milkha Singh declines the Arjuna Award for lifetime contribution. Supreme Court quashes the reservation for the graduates of All-India Institute of Medical Sciences (AIIMS) for post-graduate courses, throwing open almost 100 seats for meritorious students from across the country. Central Bureau of Investigation (CBI) receives the translated version of documents from Sweden relating to the Bofors pay-off case.

September: The indigenous anti-tank guided missile, Nag, is successfully test-fired from the interim test range at Chandipur-on-Sea. Special court sentences the stock broker, Hiten Dalal, and the former general manager of Canbank Mutual Fund (CBMF), B.R. Acharya, to three years' rigorous imprisonment for various offences including defrauding the CBMF of Rs 32.5 lakh during 1991–92. Mira Nair's *Monsoon Wedding* is awarded the Golden Lion for best picture at the Venice film festival. Government announces a 2 per cent increase in the dearness allowance for serving Central government employees and a similar hike in the dearness relief for pensioners. India's indigenous ship-to-ship missile, Dhanush, successfully launched from a navy vessel at sea.

October: Congress leader Madhavrao Scindia dies in an accident. Lt Gen. Pankaj Joshi takes over as the country's first Chief of Integrated Defence Staff (CIDS) and Lt Gen. N.C. Vij as the new Vice-Chief of Army Staff. Gujarat chief minister Keshubhai Patel submits his resignation to the governor, paving the way for Narendra Modi to take over. George Fernandes returns to the Union government as minister of defence. Asha Bhosle receives the Dada Saheb Phalke Award. Reserve Bank of India (RBI) cuts the bank rate by 50 basis points to 6.5 per cent—the lowest since May 1973. The cricket board's internal inquiry into the match-fixing scandal exonerates Kapil Dev from any wrongdoing and closes all cases pending against him. Government decides to sell six hotels owned by the India Tourism Development Corporation (ITDC).

November: Supreme Court orders a ban on smoking in public places throughout the country. Central Bureau of Investigation (CBI) arrests Harshad Mehta and his two brothers, Ashwin and Sudhir. Dr A.P.J. Abdul Kalam steps down as the principal scientific adviser to the government after over four decades of distinguished service in the government. President K.R. Narayanan confers the Indira Gandhi Award for Peace, Disarmament and Development on Mary Robinson, United Nations High Commissioner for Human Rights.

December: Acting CBI director P.C. Sharma is appointed full-time chief of the organization. Supreme Court makes fastening of seat belts mandatory for front-seat occupants in cars. Ashok Kumar, who dominated the Hindi celluloid scene with his inimitable acting for over seven decades, passes away. 250-km extended range version of the Prithvi missile, developed for the Indian Air Force, is successfully test-fired from the interim test range at Chandipur-on-Sea. Suicide squad storms Parliament; five militants killed; army deployed. Admiral Madhvendra Singh succeeds Admiral Sushil Kumar.

2002

January: STD and ISD services are withdrawn from all private public call offices (PCOs) and cybercafes in the Kashmir Valley following reports of misuse by militants. Pakistan government relaxes ban on Indian TV channels. Pakistan President Pervez Musharraf bans the Lashkar-e-Taiba and Jaish-e-Mohammad. The Indian Railways bans smoking in trains, railway stations and all railway offices. In West Bengal, gunmen kill four policemen and critically wound twenty persons in front of the American Center in Kolkata. A third-generation communication satellite, INSAT-3C, is successfully launched into space on board the European launch vehicle, Ariane-4. The former Indian Air Force chief, Arjan Singh, becomes the first-ever Marshal of the Indian Air Force. Mark Mascarenhas, WorldTel chief and marketing agent of cricketer Sachin Tendulkar, passes away. Supreme Court directs all states to confiscate ultrasound machines used to determine the sex of the foetus in clinics running without a licence.

February: Cabinet Committee on Disinvestment (CCD) decides on selling 25 per cent equity in the Videsh Sanchar Nigam Limited (VSNL) to Tata Group. Union Cabinet approves a voluntary retirement scheme for permanent government employees rendered surplus in keeping with the announcement made by Finance Minister Yashwant Sinha in his Budget speech the previous year. United Arab Emirates deports Aftab Ansari alias Farhan Malik, prime suspect in the American Center attack in Kolkata. *Lagaan* is nominated in the best non-English-language film category for the Oscars. Russian and Indian energy officials sign a $1.5 billion contract for the delivery of two Russian reactors for a new Indian nuclear power plant. Foreign exchange reserves cross $50 billion. Jyotiraditya Scindia wins from Guna in the Lok Sabha by-elections. Gujarat chief minister, Narendra Modi, wins the by-election from Rajkot-II assembly constituency. Goa governor Mohamad Fazal dissolves the state assembly.

March: Veteran Congress leader, Narain Dutt Tiwari, is sworn in as the first elected chief minister of Uttaranchal. Lok Sabha Speaker G.M.C. Balayogi killed in a helicopter crash. The boards of the Reliance Industries Ltd and Reliance Petroleum Ltd unanimously approve the merger of RPL with RIL. Union Cabinet approves 100 per cent foreign direct investment (FDI) in films and advertising but holds back a decision on permitting FDI in print media. India's medium range surface-to-air missile, Akash, is successfully test-fired from the interim test range (ITR) in Orissa's Chandipur. BSP politician Mayawati resigns from Lok Sabha to focus on Uttar Pradesh. Congress leader Ibobi Singh is sworn in as the Manipur chief minister. Lok Sabha passes the Prevention of Terrorism Ordinance (POTO) bill. The Union Cabinet decides to grant 4 per cent additional dearness allowance to Central government employees and a similar increase in dearness relief for pensioners. The indigenous pilotless target aircraft (PTA) Lakshya is successfully test-flown from the interim test range at Chandipur-on-Sea.

April: President K.R. Narayanan approves the appointment of Justice B.N. Kirpal as the Chief Justice of India with effect from 6 May. The Supreme Court directs the Uttar Pradesh government to hand over the security of the Taj Mahal in Agra to the Central Industrial Security Force (CISF) from 1 May. Union Coal Minister Ram Vilas Paswan resigns from the Cabinet.

May: Government appoints the former director-general of Punjab police, K. P. S. Gill, as Narendra Modi's security adviser. Chairman of the Oberoi Group, M. S. Oberoi, passes away. Urdu poet and recipient of the Sahitya Akademi fellowship, Kaifi Azmi, passes away. Ketan Parekh and his cousin, Kartik Parekh, and Jatin Sarvaiya are arrested by the economic offences wing of the Mumbai police for cheating a Mauritius-based company. Mayawati wins trust vote in Uttar Pradesh.

June: BJP legislature party leader, Manohar Parrikar, is sworn in as the new chief minister of a BJP-led coalition government in Goa. Former vice-president and acting President, B.D. Jatti, passes away. Democratic Front government in Maharashtra, headed by Vilasrao Deshmukh, wins the vote of confidence in the Assembly. The anti-tank guided missile, Nag, is successfully test-fired from the interim test range (ITR) at Chandipur-on-Sea. Cabinet clears 26 per cent foreign direct investment (FDI) in print media. Union Home Minister L. K. Advani becomes the deputy prime minister.

July: Yashwant Sinha becomes new foreign minister and Jaswant Singh becomes new finance minister. Chairman of Reliance Industries Ltd, Dhirubhai Ambani, passes away. Seventy-one-year-old scientist, A.P.J. Abdul Kalam, becomes the new President of India. Gujarat Governor Sunder Singh Bhandari dissolves the state assembly and accepts the resignation of Gujarat chief minister Narendra Modi. VSNL cuts its international call rates by up to 40 per cent. Vice-President Krishan Kant passes away. Mukesh Ambani becomes the new Reliance Industries Ltd chairman.

August: Indian Railways starts the facility of booking train tickets through the Internet. NDA candidate, Bhairon Singh Shekhawat, is elected the country's twelfth vice-president. Vice-captain of the Indian women's cricket team visiting England, Mithali Raj, scores an unbeaten 210, the highest individual Test score.

September: Cinema and theatre director, actor and musician, B.V. Karanth, passes away. Supreme Court directs Karnataka to release 1.25 tmcft (thousand million cubic feet) of water everyday to Tamil Nadu from its four reservoirs. Sachin Tendulkar becomes the youngest cricketer in the world to play 100 Test matches. India's Mahesh Bhupathi wins the US Open men's doubles title along with Max Mirnyi of Belarus. India's first exclusive meteorological satellite (METSAT) is launched using the Polar Satellite Launch Vehicle PSLV–C4, from Sriharikota. Jagmohan Dalmiya is unanimously re-elected BCCI president. Goa governor Mohammad Fazal is transferred and appointed governor of Maharashtra for the rest of his term. Short-range supersonic surface-to-air missile, Trishul, is successfully test-fired from the interim test range (ITR) at Chandipur-on-Sea. Trials of the country's first-ever sea-to-surface missile, Dhanush, successfully completed. Noted industrialist and founder chairman of the Apollo group, Raunaq Singh, passes away.

October: The Vatican approves of a miracle attributed to Mother Teresa, moving her one step closer to sainthood. The President appoints Justice Gopal Ballav Pattanaik as the new Chief Justice of India. Delhi Police chargesheet the suspended Haryana inspector-general of Police (Prisons), R.K. Sharma, for conspiring to murder the *Indian Express* journalist, Shivani Bhatnagar. Reserve Bank of India cuts bank rate by 25 basic points from 6.50 per cent to 6.25 per cent.

November: Election Commission directs the Gujarat government to remove all hoardings and posters 'on communal lines' that are displayed in the state. People's Democratic Party (PDP) president, Mufti Mohammad Sayeed, is sworn in as the chief minister of Jammu and Kashmir.

December: The Union Cabinet decides to increase the fine for ticketless travel in trains fivefold—from Rs 50 to Rs 250. Jurist, statesman and former ambassador to the US, Nani Ardeshir Palkhivala passes away. Yash Chopra is selected for the 2001 Dada Saheb Phalke Award. BJP wins the Gujarat Assembly elections, winning 126 seats in the, 182-member House. Parliament, in an effort to promote greater transparency, openness and accountability in administration, approves the Freedom of Information Bill which envisages access to government information and files to every citizen. Justice Visheshwar Nath Khare is sworn in as the thirty-third Chief Justice of India. Narendra Modi begins his second stint as the Gujarat chief minister. Metro Railway in Delhi starts operations. Ratan Tata gives up all his executive posts in the Tata group. He becomes the non-executive chairman.

2003

January: World athletics body absolves Sunita Rani, distance runner, of doping charges. Government appoints Justice S.N. Phukan as the new chief of the Tehelka enquiry commission. India successfully test-fires the 800-km-range Agni missile. IPS officer, Kiran Bedi, becomes the first woman and the first Indian to be appointed as a United Nations civilian police adviser. Sushil Kumar Shinde sworn in as the Maharashtra chief minister. Medium-range surface-to-air missile Akash is successfully test-fired from the interim test range (ITR) at Chandipur-on-Sea. Poet Harivanshrai Bachchan passes away. Government decides to carry out a strategic sale of the Hindustan Petroleum Corporation Limited. Bharatiya Vidya Bhavan receives the Gandhi Peace Prize for 2002. A special court convicts stockbroker Hiten Dalal and three others, sentencing them to seven years' rigorous imprisonment for allegedly defrauding the Canbank Mutual Fund.

February: Reserve Bank of India announces that the non-banking finance companies (NBFCs) not having the minimum net-owned fund (NOF) of Rs 25 lakhs as on 9 January would not be allowed to continue with their businesses. Reserve Bank of India reduces interest rate on saving accounts offered by banks and repurchase rate for government securities by 0.5 per cent.

March: India beats Pakistan in the World Cup and Sachin Tendulkar becomes the first player in one-day internationals to cross 12,000 runs. India successfully launches an indigenously built torpedo. Union Finance Minister Jaswant Singh rolls back the increases in fertilizer prices he had announced in the Union Budget on 28 February. Indian cricket team enters World Cup final but Australia retains the World Cup with a 125-run win in the final. The Election Commission issues revised directions, making it mandatory for candidates to declare their educational background, assets and criminal antecedants.

April: India's first confirmed case of Severe Acute Respiratory Syndrome (SARS) found in Goa. Reserve Bank of India cuts bank rate by 25 basic points, reducing it to 6 per cent. India's first stealth warship *Shivalik* is launched. Delhi High Court awards compensation of about Rs 18 crore to the families of the fifty-nine dead and 103 injured in the Uphaar fire case of 13 June 1997.

May: Air-to-air missile, Astra, is test-fired. Shivshankar Menon is appointed India's high commissioner to Pakistan. India announces the resumption of the suspended Delhi–Lahore bus service. Delhi High Court announces that former Indian cricketer Ajay Jadeja is free to play all matches in the country's domestic circuit, if selected. Duty on import of set-top boxes reduced.

June: Maruti Udyog Limited opens its maiden public issue of shares. Surface-to-air high-altitude interception missile, Akash test-fired from a mobile launcher. The Union Cabinet clears a proposal to include new castes and communities in the Central list of other backward classes in respect of Andhra Pradesh, Karnataka, Rajasthan, Delhi, Chandigarh, Haryana, Orissa and West Bengal. Nalin Surie is appointed India's new ambassador to China. The International Cricket Council (ICC) decides to withhold the $9 million due to India for playing in the World Cup after the players sign an amended sponsorship contract.

July: The Madhya Pradesh government issues a notification to increase the reservation for other backward classes (OBCs) to 27 per cent in the state. Leander Paes and Martina Navratilova win the Wimbledon mixed doubles title. Sania Mirza becomes the first Indian woman to win a Grand Slam title. East Bengal becomes the first Indian club to win an international tournament on foreign soil when it beats BEC Tero Sasana of Thailand. Chief Election Commissioner J.M. Lyngdoh and social worker Shantha Sinha honoured with the Ramon Magsaysay Award.

August: The Supreme Court bans the collection of capitation fees by professional colleges. The Archaeological Survey of India submits its final report relating to Ayodhya excavations before the Allahabad High Court.

September: INSAT-3E, the communication satellite of the Indian Space Research Organization, is launched successfully from a spaceport in Kourou, French Guyana, by a European Ariane-5 launch vehicle. India wins the sixth Asia Cup hockey title for the first time. BSP splits after thirty-seven rebels join Samajwadi party. The Mulayam Singh Yadav government wins vote of confidence in the Uttar Pradesh Legislative Assembly. The special CBI court hearing the Babri Masjid demolition conspiracy case discharges deputy prime minister L.K. Advani.

October: Uttar Pradesh chief minister, Mulayam Singh Yadav, inducts ninty-one new ministers into his Cabinet. CBI files a charge sheet against the Chhattisgarh chief minister Ajit Jogi for using a forged note. Anjali Bhagwat wins the air rifle gold in the World Cup Finals. Government of India resumes cricketing and other sporting links with Pakistan. Pankaj Advani wins the World snooker title at the IBSF World Snooker Championship. The Election Commission makes it mandatory for candidates contesting the assembly polls in five states to show accounts of poll expenditure to the observers or returning officers.

November: Sushil Sharma held guilty in the 'tandoor case' and is awarded the death sentence. Sensex crosses the 5,000 mark for the first time in forty-two months. India win Asian Under-19 cricket trophy. Tamil Nadu government sacks 587 employees for going on strike. BCCI suspends Maharashtra cricketer Abhijit Kale on alleged bribery charges. IIM Common Aptitude Test (CAT) is cancelled following the leaking of question papers. CBI exonerates Indian Institute of Management faculty. Light Combat Aircraft (LCA) prototype makes its first flight at subsonic speed. Abu Salem and Monica Bedi are given jail sentences in Portugal.

December: Former Mumbai Police Commissioner R.S. Sharma is arrested in the fake stamp paper scam case. More castes are added to the Central 'Other Backward Classes' lists. Vasundhara Raje becomes the first woman chief minister of Rajasthan. CBI registers a corruption case against the former Chhattisgarh chief minister Ajit Jogi. Dev Anand selected for the Dada Saheb Phalke Award. MP Cabinet decides to ban cow slaughter. India wins the second Test against Australia, its first Test win in Australia after twenty-two years. POTA Amendment Bill passed in Lok Sabha. Chhattisgarh bans cow slaughter in the state. Foreign exchange reserves cross $100 billion. Parliament passes Dual Citizenship Bill.

2004

January: SAARC nations agree on free trade regime. Sensex reaches all-time high of 6,026 points. Union Cabinet raises the FDI limit in oil refining to 100 per cent while the cap for oil marketing companies is increased from 74 per cent to 100 per cent. Cabinet Committee on Security approves the Rs 2,800 crore deal for the Russian aircraft-carrier Admiral Gorshkov. Padma Shree awarded to Sourav Ganguly and Rahul Dravid. Padma Vibhushan awarded to Amrita Pritam, M.N. Venkatachaliah and Jayant Vishnu Narlikar. Central Government bans import of domestic and wild birds. Restrictions on imports of gold and silver removed. India becomes the first developing country to import LNG.

February: HRD Ministry passes an order asking IIMs to reduce its fees to Rs 30,000. Rajiv Gandhi acquitted in Bofors case. Retest of the CAT held successfully. Sania Mirza wins first WTA title, the Hyderabad Open. RBI hikes limit on gifts to Rs 5 lakh. Government decides to roll back CAS. Election Commission bans political advertisements in electronic media.

March: Confederation of Indian Industry (CII) and the Lahore Chamber of Commerce and Industry (LCCI) sign memorandum of understanding (MoU) to exchange information on all economic and commercial matters. Major Rajyavardhan Singh Rathore wins a gold medal at the Shooting World Cup in Sydney. Jammu and Kashmir Assembly unanimously passes a Bill that disqualifies women from being permanent residents of the state after marriage with non-permanent residents. India and Israel sign their biggest-ever bilateral defence deal worth $1.1 billion. Election Commission orders the immediate removal of 'India Shining' and other state-sponsored advertisements. Prasar Bharati signs a Memorandum of Understanding (MoU) with the Indian Space Research Organisation (ISRO) for supply of Ku Band transponders for Doordarshan's Direct-to-Home (DTH) service. India registers its first-ever ODI series win in Pakistan. IIM-Kozhikode chairman, A.C. Muthiah, announces a cut in the annual fees.

April: Supreme Court bans surrogate advertisements on electronic media. Election Commission suggests ordinance to ban opinion polls. Election Commission asks the media organizations to furnish it with details of the revenue collected from each political party and candidate for their political advertisements so that it could be added to their election expenditure. IIM-Ahmedabad challenges fee cut. Infosys Technologies become India's first listed IT firm to have crossed $1 billion in turnover. India records its first-ever Test series win in Pakistan. Virender Sehwag scores 309 against Pakistan, the highest Test score by an Indian. Reliance Industries become the first private sector Indian company to cross the one billion milestone in net profit.

May: Congress emerges as largest party, United Progressive Alliance gets majority in Lok Sabha elections. President appoints Manmohan Singh as the prime minister. The CPI(M) Politburo unanimously decides on Somnath Chatterjee for the post of Speaker of the fourteenth Lok Sabha. Foreign exchange reserves touch $118.62 billion. India's first indigenously built civilian aircraft, Saras, achieves its maiden test flight. Union Human Resource Development Ministry asks the Indian Institutes of Management (IIMs) to evolve a uniform fee structure. Viswanathan Anand wins his third Chess Oscar.

June: L.K. Advani is unanimously elected leader of the BJP's parliamentary party. Union Finance Ministry appoints National Securities Depository Ltd. for providing Permanent Account Numbers (PAN) to new taxpayers in 139 cities. Tata Consultancy Services files IPO prospectus. The Board of Governors of the Indian Institute of Management Indore (IIM-I) decides to charge the same fee for the academic session 2004–05. TRAI directs all the cellular operators to inform their prepaid subscribers through SMS whenever they roam into another area and charge roaming fees.

July: PM announces assistance to each family in Andhra Pradesh whose breadwinner has committed suicide.

Foreign exchange reserves cross $120 billion. Eighty-seven schoolchildren burnt to death and twenty-three seriously injured in a fire at a primary school in Kumbakonam town of Thanjavur district in Tamil Nadu.

August: The Supreme Court rules that a doctor cannot be held criminally liable if a patient dies due to an error of judgment or carelessness or for want of due caution although she/he can be liable to pay compensation. The Union Cabinet announces the repeal of the controversial Prevention of Terrorism Act (POTA) before it lapses on 23 October. Major Rajyavardhan Singh Rathore gets the silver medal for India in shooting (double trap category) at the Olympic Games.

September: Supreme Court orders the Directorate-General of Health Services to complete counselling for the 161 seats fallen vacant under the 15 per cent all-India quota in government medical and dental colleges. Puneeta Arora, the new Commandant of the Armed Forces Medical College, becomes the first woman in the three services to reach the second highest rank in the armed forces. The first-ever census data on religion is released. The government allows the transfer of essential items such as butter, cheese, processed foods, aerated water and petrochemical products from the factory of production to warehouse, without the payment of excise duty. Rahul Dravid wins 'Player of the Year' and 'Test Player of the Year' award at the inaugural ICC Awards. Government permits duty-free imports of raw sugar for domestic consumption. Jagmohan Dalmiya is nominated the BCCI's Patron-in-Chief for three years after his term as the BCCI president ends on 30 September. Anju Bobby George is chosen for the Rajiv Gandhi Khel Ratna award for 2003. EDUSAT, India's first exclusive satellite for educational services, placed in orbit. Noted physicist and key leader of India's nuclear programme, Raja Ramanna, passes away. Tata Motors become the first company in the Indian engineering sector to list its securities on the New York Stock Exchange (NYSE). Author Mulk Raj Anand passes away. Ranbir Singh Mahendra of Haryana is elected president of the Board of Control for Cricket in India. International Olympic Committee imposes life bans on weightlifters Pratima Kumari and Sanamacha Chanu.

October: The Industrial Development Bank of India becomes a deemed banking company. The Union Cabinet decides to raise the Foreign Direct Investment limit in domestic airlines to 49 per cent. The UPA government unveils the State Wide Area Network Policy (SWAN) to give the nation an effective system of e-governance. The Cabinet Committee on Economic Affairs approves the proposal for the creation of an Investment Commission. Inflation rate dips to 7.80 per cent. Finance Ministry exempts 'shipping lines' from furnishing a bank guarantee for transhipment of export and import cargo. NTPC issue attracts US $15 billion Broadband policy is announced. The Tata group signs a $2 billion investment deal with Bangladesh.

November: The VSNL signs a Rs 500-crore-pact with Cisco Systems for deployment of India's largest broadband Metro Ethernet solution for Tata Indicom Broadband Services, in Mumbai. The Supreme Court rules that computer software is liable to be taxed under the provisions of the Sales Tax Act. Sensex hits 6,000-mark. Forex reserves cross $122 b mark. Six out of twelve directors of Reliance Energy Limited resigns from the Board of the company, which is headed by Anil Ambani.

December: Indian cricketers sign contract for graded payment. The Department of Telecom (DoT) makes mobile service fully operational in Jammu and Kashmir and the north-eastern states. Anil Ambani questions elder brother Mukesh's claims on ownership issue. The Union Cabinet approves the draft National Rural Employment Guarantee Bill, the draft Right to Information Bill, 2004. For the first time in the history of the BSE, the Sensex breaches the 6,400 mark. The government appoints Ratan Tata as chairman of the Investment Commission. Prime Minister Manmohan Singh launches DD Direct Plus, the country's only free-to-air direct-to-home (DTH) service, with thirty-three television and twelve radio channels.

2005

January: India, Pakistan exchange lists of nuclear installations. Anil Ambani quits as IPCL vice-chairman. The National Security Adviser J.N. Dixit passes away. Union Communications Minister Dayanidhi Maran launches '.in' Internet domain for India. Prime Minister Manmohan Singh, announces dual citizenship to all those who migrated from the country after it became a republic on 26 January 1950, provided their home countries allowed them to do so. Mrinal Sen is chosen for the Dada Saheb Phalke Award for 2003. India, U.S. announces open-skies aviation agreement. The Election Commission bans photography and videography inside polling stations. Godhra fire accidental, says Justice U.C. Banerjee Committee. The Union Cabinet approves Rs 2,731-crore relief and rehabilitation package for victims of the tsunami in Tamil Nadu, Andhra Pradesh, Kerala and Pondicherry. Parveen Babi passes away. J.N. Dixit and R.K. Laxman awarded the Padma Vibhushan. The Cabinet decides to set up a National Investment Fund—a corpus made of proceeds from disinvestment of PSUs. General Joginder Jaswant Singh takes over as the Chief of the Army Staff.

February: Senior Congressman Pratap Singh Rane is sworn in as the sixteenth chief minister of Goa, replacing Manohar Parrikar. Foreign direct investment in telecom allowed up to 74 per cent. Madras High Court orders the release of the junior Sankaracharya of the Kanchi Mutt, Sri Vijayendra Saraswathi, on conditional bail in the Sankararaman murder case. Sania Mirza breaks into the top 100 of the world and has been ranked number ninty-nine with 371 points by the WTA Tour in India. Pakistan agrees to allow travel across the Line of Control (LoC) by bus between Srinagar and Muzaffarabad. The Union Cabinet approves a Rs 821.88-crore relief and rehabilitation package for the tsunami-hit Andaman and Nicobar Islands. The Supreme Court holds that a member of the Scheduled Caste/Scheduled Tribe will not lose his status as SC/ST on migration to another state. The government allows 100 per cent foreign direct investment in the construction industry through the automatic route. Bihar chief minister, Rabri Devi, quits. With an increased allocation from Rs 8,420 crore in the current year to Rs 10,280 crore, Finance Minister P. Chibambaram presents the budget. Finance Minister imposed a banking transaction tax of Rs 10 on cash withdrawals of over Rs 10,000 in a single day.

March: Jharkhand Mukti Morcha (JMM) leader, Shibu Soren, is sworn in as the third chief minister of Jharkhand. Goa chief minister Pratapsinh Rane wins the vote of confidence in the Assembly. The Board of Control for Cricket in India awards Sony Entertainment Television the satellite rights for the India–Pakistan cricket series. Bhupinder Singh Hooda sworn in Haryana chief minister. Sania Mirza moves to an all-time career-high seventy-seventh spot in the latest WTA tour rankings. President A.P.J. Abdul Kalam approves the Union Cabinet's decision recommending President's Rule in Bihar following the stalemate in government formation. Jharkhand chief minister Shibu Soren resigns and replaced by Arjun Munda. The World Bank agrees in principle to provide $ 500 million for India's National e-Governance Plan (NEGP) over the next four years. Sachin Tendulkar becomes only the fifth cricketer and the second from India to reach 10,000 Test runs. India and China finalize a Memorandum of Understanding on the sharing of hydrological data about the Sutlej river during the flood season. The finance minister announces a deduction of Rs 1 lakh from taxable income for senior citizens (SC). Buta Singh is sworn in as acting governor of West Bengal. The Chattrapati Shivaji Terminus (formerly Victoria Terminus) in Mumbai finds a place in the World Heritage List.

April: Twenty-one states shift to the Value-Added Tax regime. Srinagar–Muzaffarabad bus service flagged off. India and China agree to an eleven-point 'political parameters and guiding principles' to resolve their long-standing boundary dispute. India, U.S. sign 'open skies' agreement. FIFA, the world body governing football, forwards a donation of $1 million for reconstruction of sporting facilities in the tsunami-affected countries. Indians win eleven golds in the seventeenth Asian powerlifting championship.

May: All-India Muslim Board adopts Nikahnama. Finances Minister raises IT exemption limit for women, senior citizens and Savings accounts exempted from cash withdrawal tax. India receives $ 465 million as IDA credit from the World Bank for reconstruction and recovery efforts in Tamil Nadu and Pondicherry. Nobel Laureate Amartya Sen receives the Tagore Peace Award of the Asiatic Society for 2004 in recognition of his creative contribution to the development of human understanding towards global peace. Two replicas of the stolen Nobel medallion of Rabindranath Tagore is handed over to the Visva-Bharati University by Sweden's Nobel Foundation. The Lok Sabha passes the Right to Information Bill. Navin B. Chawla is appointed Election Commissioner to fill the vacancy in the Commission caused by the elevation of B.B. Tandon as Chief Election Commissioner. Greg Chappell appointed coach of the Indian cricket team. President Kalam signs Proclamation in Moscow to dissolve Bihar Assembly. Sunil Dutt passes away. Sonia Gandhi is re-elected Congress chief. From August 1, smoking to be banned in movies, television serials. Amendments to the Tobacco Control Act notified.

June: The Banking Cash Transaction Tax on cash withdrawals and receipts of term deposits in banks comes into effect. The government decides to enhance the foreign investment cap under non-news category from 74 per cent to 100 per cent in Indian entities publishing scientific, technical and speciality magazines, periodicals and journals. Tamil Nadu government abolishes the Common Entrance Test (CET) for admission to medical and engineering courses from this year. Bharatiya Janata Party president L.K. Advani resigns from his party post, following the controversy over his description of Pakistan's founder Mohammad Ali Jinnah as 'secular' and his remark that the demolition of the Babri Masjid was the 'saddest day' of his life. BJP rejects L.K. Advani's resignation. Manmohan Singh becomes the first Prime Minister to visit Siachen. India signs $18-billion gas deal with Iran. The Ministries of Health and Family Welfare and Information and Broadcasting (I&B) decide to delay the imposition of the ban on smoking scenes in television serials and movies by two months from 1 August this year to Gandhi Jayanti (2 October). The Union cabinet allows printing of facsimile editions of foreign newspapers and periodicals and increasing the syndication limits in Indian newspapers. The Union Cabinet approves amendments to the Citizenship Act, 1955, allowing all Persons of Indian Origin (PIOs) access to dual citizenship as long as their home countries permitted it in some form or the other. Kerala bans camera cellphones in educational institutions. Anil D. Ambani is appointed chairman of Reliance Infocomm Ltd (RIC). Sensex crosses 7,200 mark. Rajendra Singh Lodha is elected chairman of the board of directors of Birla Corporation Ltd (BCL), the flagship company of the M. P. Birla group. The Cabinet decides to allow foreign radio stations to pick up stakes in private FM stations within the existing ceiling of 20 per cent of foreign capital but the ban on private stations to broadcast news continues.

July: Prasar Bharati evolves a new policy to promote sports by slashing charges for live telecast. Shiv Sena supremo Bal Thackeray expells leader of the opposition in the Maharashtra Assembly, Narayan Rane, from the party. Mahesh Bhupathi and Mary Pierce win the 2005 Wimbledon mixed doubles title. Six heavily-armed terrorists makes an attempt to storm the high-security makeshift Ram temple and a killed by the security forces before they could strike at the shrine. The Union Cabinet withdraws the restriction on use of the national flag by the public as a portion of costumes. Centre agrees to pay a monthly 'ad hoc' compensation in case their revenue from the Value Added Tax (VAT) fell short of their projections on the basis of collections in earlier years through the erstwhile sales tax regime. The Nilgiri Mountain Railway (NMR) line between Udhagamandalam and Mettupalayam is granted World Heritage Site status by UNESCO. The Supreme Court issues certain directions to control noise pollution caused by crackers, vehicles and loudspeakers, among other sources. The Maharashtra Legislative Assembly passes the controversial Bombay Police (Amendment) Bill prohibiting dance bars in the state. The Valley of Flowers, part of the Nanda Devi National Park in the western Himalayas, is included on the world heritage list by the World Heritage Committee of UNESCO. In one of the worst disasters in the history of India's petroleum industry, the offshore oil platform in the Bombay High area catches fire; four killed. All-time record rain in Mumbai; death toll crosses 100; thousands of Mumbai commuters stranded; Army, Navy called out. Sensex surpasses 7,600-mark. Prime Minister Manmohan Singh announces an immediate grant of Rs 500 crores to Maharashtra. Maharashtra rain toll put at 749. Pakistan bans import of films made in India.

August: Dr. V. Shanta, Chairperson of the Cancer Institute, Adyar, wins the Ramon Magsaysay Award for Public Service for 2005. Sania Mirza moves upto career-best ranking of 59 in the latest list released by the WTA. Parliament approves the extension of President's Rule in Bihar by another six months. Heavy rain continues in Maharashtra. Death toll in state goes up to 962. Pakistan lifts ban on sugar imports from India. The Centre announces a second instalment of Rs 500 crores for flood relief in Mumbai and eighteen districts of Maharashtra. The Supreme Court holds that a doctor would be liable for criminal prosecution only for 'gross negligence' or if he did not possess the requisite skill. Pollution Board approves using waste plastic to lay roads. The Supreme Court holds that admissions to unaided minority and non-minority professional educational institutions should be made only on the basis of a common entrance test. Parliament approves the Citizenship (Amendment) Bill. Parliament approves the Payment of Wages (Amendment) Bill, 2004. Reliance files demerger scheme. Sensex touches 7,900-mark. The National Rural Employment Guarantee Bill, 2005, seeking to provide 100 days' assured employment every year to every rural household in 200 districts, is unanimously passed by the Lok Sabha with fifty-two amendments Maharashtra bans plastic bags. Rajyavardhan Singh Rathore gets the Rajiv Gandhi Khel Ratna Award for the year 2004. The Protection of Women from Domestic Violence Bill, 2005, is unanimously passed by the Lok Sabha. P. Chidambaram unveils first-ever 'Outcome Budget'. The Drugs Controller of India approves the sale of 'emergency contraceptives' across the counter, not available without a prescription until now.

September: The government decides to divest 8 per cent shareholding in Maruti Udyog Limited (MUL). Malayalam filmmaker Adoor Gopalakrishnan is selected for the Dada Saheb Phalke Award for 2004 Mahesh Bhupathi wins his seventh Grand Slam title with Daniela Hantuchova in the U.S. Open. Sania Mirza jumps to a career-best ranking of thirty-four in the list released by the WTA. Nafisa Ali is nominated chairperson of the Children's Film Society of India (CFSI). Sourav Ganguly confirms that he was asked to step down as captain of the Indian cricket team before the first Royal Stag Test match against Zimbabwe. The Supreme Court declares that life imprisonment is not equivalent to imprisonment for fourteen or twenty years. The President gives assent to the National Rural Employment Guarantee Bill, 2005, applicable to the whole of India, except Jammu and Kashmir. India wins its first overseas series victory in nineteen years as Zimbabwe is defeated by 10 wickets in the second Royal Stag Test at the Harare Sports Club. The leaking of Greg Chappell's confidential e-mail addressed to BCCI president triggers cricket controversy. Amol Palekar's *Paheli* is chosen as India's official entry for the 2006 Academy Awards. Sensex crosses 8,600 level. The Supreme Court reiterates that lawyers have no right to go on strike nor give a call for boycott nor even a token strike to espouse their causes.

Timeline of World History

Beginning of Time to 1994

4.4–4.3 million BC: Earliest known hominid fossils of *Ardipithecus ramidus* found in 1994 in Aramis, Ethiopia, by Tim White. Gen Suwa and Berhane Asfaw date back to this time.

4.2 million BC: First *Australopithecus anamensis* discovery in the Kanapoi region of East Lake Turkana, Kenya, in 1965 by a Harvard University expedition date back to this time.

Approximately 4 million BC: Discovery of tiny foot bones and tiny pelvic fossils indicates that the ancestors of humans walked upright by this time.

3.2 million BC: Appearance of *Australopithecus afarenis*. A near-complete female hominid skeleton nicknamed Lucy was found in Ethiopia in 1974 by Donald Johanson and others.

2.5 million BC: Appearance of *Homo habilis*. This species had a larger brain than its ancestors and is widely believed to have used tools. Sileshi Semaw and Jack Harris published research on the tools in 1997.

1.8 million BC: Appearance of *Homo erectus*, who had a brain capacity of nearly 1,000ml.

1.7 million BC: *Homo erectus* leaves Africa. Researchers of ancient DNA, however, avidly debate this theory.

200,000 BC: In 1987, Rebecca Cann, Mark Stoneking and Allan Wilson report in the journal *Nature* that a common ancestor to all *Homo sapiens* was a woman who lived in Africa 200,000 years ago. They called her African Eve.

100,000 BC: Appearance of *Homo sapiens* in South Africa. Many believe the 'human' migrations from Africa to Asia began during this period.

c.50,000 BC: *Homo sapiens* reaches Australia.

70,000 BC: Possible appearance of Neanderthal man. This species could make fire and use advanced tools.

35,000 BC: Neanderthal man replaced by later groups of *Homo sapiens* such as Cro-Magnons in Europe.

20,000 BC: The accepted date for Neanderthal extinction.

18,000 BC: Cro-Magnons replaced by later cultures.

15,000 BC: Possible human migrations across the Bering Strait into the Americas.

10,000 BC: Signs of semi-permanent agricultural settlements in Africa, Asia and Europe.

10,000–4,000 BC: Settlements turn into proto-cities and development of skills such as the wheel, pottery and improved methods of cultivation in Mesopotamia and elsewhere.

5500–3000 BC: Predynastic Egyptian cultures develop (5500–3100 BC). Agriculture in Egypt (c. 5000 BC). Earliest-known civilization arises in Sumeria (4500–4000 BC). First phonetic writing appears (c. 3500 BC). Sumerians develop a city state civilization (c. 3000 BC). Egyptians and Sumerians start using copper. Neolithic age in Western Europe.

3000–2000 BC: Pharaonic rule begins in Egypt. King Khufu (Cheops), fourth dynasty (2700–2675 BC), completes construction of the Great Pyramid at Giza (c. 2680 BC). The Great Sphinx of Giza (c. 2540 BC) is built by King Khafre. The earliest Egyptian mummies. Invention of Papyrus. Phoenician settlements on the coast of what is now Syria and Lebanon. Semitic tribes settle in Assyria. Sargon, the first Akkadian king, builds the Mesopotamian empire. The Epic of Gilgamesh is composed (c. 3000 BC). Abraham leaves Ur (c. 2000 BC). Astronomical studies begin in Egypt, Babylon, India, China.

3000–1500 BC: Stonehenge erected in Britain. Its purpose, possibly astronomical, is still a matter of conjecture.

2000–1500 BC: Hyksos invaders drive Egyptians from Lower Egypt (seventeenth century BC). Amosis I frees Egypt from Hyksos (c. 1600 BC). Assyrians rise to power—rise of the cities of Ashur and Nineveh. Twenty-four-character alphabet developed in Egypt. Israelites enslaved in Egypt. Cuneiform inscriptions used by Hittites. Peak of Minoan culture on the Isle of Crete and the appearance of the earliest form of written Greek. Hammurabi, the king of Babylon, develops oldest existing code of laws (eighteenth century BC).

1500–1000 BC: Ikhnaton develops a monotheistic religion in Egypt (c. 1375 BC). His successor, Tutankhamen, returns to the earlier gods. Moses leads the Israelites out of Egypt into Canaan. The Ten Commandments. The Greeks destroy Troy (c. 1193 BC). End of Greek civilization in Mycenae with the invasion of the Dorians. Chinese civilization develops under the Shang dynasty. The Olmec civilization exists in Mexico.

1000–900 BC: Solomon succeeds King David, builds Jerusalem temple. After Solomon's death, the kingdom is divided into Israel and Judah. Old Testament books of Bible begin to be written. Phoenicians colonize Spain with a settlement at Cadiz.

900–800 BC: Phoenicians establish Carthage (c. 810 BC). The *Iliad* and the *Odyssey* composed, perhaps by the Greek poet Homer.

800–700 BC: First recorded Olympic games (776 BC). The legendary founding of Rome by Romulus (753 BC). Assyrian King Sargon II conquers the Hittites, Chaldeans and Samaria (end of the kingdom of Israel). Chariots introduced into Italy by Etruscans.

700–600 BC: End of Assyrian empire (616 BC)—Nineveh destroyed by Chaldeans (Neo-Babylonians) and Medes (612 BC). Founding of Byzantium by Greeks (c. 660 BC). Building of the Acropolis in Athens. Lifetime of Solon, the Greek lawmaker (640–560 BC). Time of Sappho of Lesbos, Greek poet (c. 610–580 BC). Times of Lao-tse, Chinese philosopher and founder of Taoism (born c. 604 BC).

600–500 BC: Babylonian King Nebuchadnezzar builds his empire and destroys Jerusalem (586 BC). Babylonian captivity of the Jews (starting 587 BC). Hanging Gardens of Babylon are designed. Cyrus the Great of Persia creates a great empire, conquers Babylon (539 BC) and frees the Jews. Athenian democracy develops. It is said Thales correctly predicted a solar eclipse (c.585 BC). Anaximander is said to have made the first map of the world in this time. Greeks discovered electric attraction produced by rubbing amber. Lifetime of Aeschylus, Greek dramatist (525–465 BC). Pythagoras, Greek philosopher and mathematician, probably lived between 582 and 507 BC. Confucius (551–479 BC) develops his ethical and social philosophy in China. The *Analects* or Lunyü ('collected sayings') are compiled by the second generation of Confucian disciples.

500–400 BC: The Greeks defeat the Persians: battles of Marathon (490 BC),

Thermopylae (480 BC), Salamis (480 BC). Peloponnesian Wars between Athens and Sparta (431–404 BC). Sparta emerges victorious. Pericles comes to power in Athens (462 BC). Flowering of Greek culture during the Age of Pericles (450–400 BC). The Parthenon is built in Athens as a temple of the goddess Athena (447–432 BC). Ictinus and Callicrates are the architects and Phidias is responsible for the sculpture. Sophocles, Greek dramatist lived between c.496 and 406 BC. Hippocrates, the Greek 'Father of Medicine', born around 460 BC). Xerxes I, king of Persia, rules in the period between 485 and 465 BC.

400–300 BC: Pentateuch or the first five books of the Old Testament evolve in their final form. Philip of Macedon is assassinated after subduing the Greek city states (336 BC); his son Alexander the Great (356–323 BC) succeeds him. Alexander destroys Thebes (335 BC) and conquers Tyre and Jerusalem (332 BC). Alexander occupies Babylon (330 BC), invades India, and dies in Babylon. Alexander's empire is divided among his generals; General Seleucus I establishes his Middle East empire with capitals at Antioch (Syria) and Seleucia (in Iraq). The trial and execution of Greek philosopher Socrates (399 BC). Socrates's student Plato records the *Dialogues* (c. 427–348 BC). Euclid's work on geometry, *Elements of Geometry* is composed (323 BC). Aristotle, Greek philosopher, lived sometime between 384 and 322 BC. Leucippus and Democritus proposed that matter is made of small, indestructible particles. They called these particles atoms.

300–251 BC: Aristarchus of Samos proposes that the earth revolves around the Sun and calculates diameter of the Earth. First Punic War (264–241 BC): Rome defeats the Carthaginians and begins its domination of the Mediterranean. Temple of the Sun at Teotihuacán, Mexico, is built (c. 300 BC). Invention of the Mayan calendar in Yucatán. First Roman gladiatorial games are played (264 BC). Archimedes, Greek mathematician, lived and worked between 287 and 212 BC.

250–201 BC: Second Punic War (219–201 BC): Hannibal, Carthaginian general, crosses the Alps (218 BC), reaches the gates of Rome (211 BC), retreats, and is defeated by Scipio Africanus at Zama (202 BC). Great Wall of China built (c. 215 BC).

200–151 BC: Romans defeat Seleucid King Antiochus III at Thermopylae (191 BC). The beginning of Roman world domination.

150–101 BC: Third Punic War (149–146 BC): Rome destroys Carthage, killing 450,000 and enslaving the remaining 50,000 inhabitants. Roman armies conquer Macedonia, Greece, Anatolia, Balearic Islands, and southern France. The Venus de Milo is sculpted (c. 140 BC). Cicero, Roman orator, lived between 106 and 43 BC.

100–51 BC: Julius Caesar (100–44 BC) invades Britain (55 BC) and conquers Gaul (France) (c. 50 BC). Spartacus leads a slave revolt against Rome (71 BC). Romans conquer the Seleucid empire. Roman General Pompey conquers Jerusalem (63 BC). Cleopatra sits on the Egyptian throne (51–31 BC). Chinese develop the use of paper (c. 100 BC). Virgil, Roman poet, lived between 70 and 19 BC. Lifetime of Horace, the Roman poet (65–8 BC).

50–1 BC: Caesar crosses Rubicon to fight Pompey (50 BC). Herod made Roman governor of Judea (37 BC). Caesar murdered (44 BC). Caesar's nephew, Octavian, defeats Mark Antony and Cleopatra at Battle of Actium (31 BC), and establishes Roman empire as Emperor Augustus; rules 27 BC–AD 14. Pantheon built for the first time under Agrippa, 27 BC. Lifetime of Ovid, Roman poet (43 BC–AD 18).

1–49 AD: Birth of Jesus Christ (variously given from 4 BC to AD 7). After Augustus, Tiberius becomes emperor (dies AD 37), succeeded by Caligula (assassinated AD 41), who is followed by Claudius. Crucifixion of Jesus (probably AD 30). Han dynasty in China founded by Emperor Kuang Wu Ti. Buddhism introduced in China.

50–99 AD: Claudius poisoned (AD 54), succeeded by Nero (who commits suicide in AD 68). Missionary journeys of Paul the Apostle (AD 34–60). Jews revolt against Rome; Jerusalem destroyed (AD 70). Roman persecutions of the Christians begin (AD 64). Colosseum built in Rome (AD 71–80). Trajan rules AD 98–116. Roman empire extends to Mesopotamia, Arabia, Balkans. First Gospels of St. Mark, St. John, St. Matthew.

100–149 AD: Hadrian rules Rome (AD 117–38); codifies Roman law, rebuilds the Pantheon, establishes a postal system, as well as builds a wall between England and Scotland. Jews revolt under Bar Kokhba (AD 122–35); final Diaspora (dispersion) of Jews begins.

150–199 AD: Marcus Aurelius rules in Rome (AD 161–80). Oldest Mayan temples in Central America constructed at this time (c. AD 200). Ptolemy studies mathematics, science, geography; proposes that the earth is the centre of the solar system.

200–249 AD: Goths invade Asia Minor (c. AD 220). Roman persecutions of Christians increase. Persian (Sassanid) empire re-established. End of Chinese Han dynasty. Chinese mathematicians calculate the value of pi to five decimal places.

250–299 AD: Invasions of the Roman empire by Franks and Goths. Buddhism spreads in China. Chinese mathematicians invent the magnetic compass. Classic period of Mayan civilization (AD 250–900); development of hieroglyphic writing, advances in art, architecture and science.

300–349 AD: Constantine the Great (rules AD 312–37) reunites eastern and western Roman empires, with a new capital (Constantinople) on the site of Byzantium (AD 330); issues Edict of Milan legalizing Christianity (AD 313) and becomes a Christian on his deathbed (AD 337). Council of Nicaea (AD 325) defines orthodox Christian doctrine.

350–399 AD: Huns invade Europe (c. AD 360). Theodosius the Great (rules AD 392–95) is the last emperor of a united Roman empire. Roman empire permanently divided in AD 395: western empire ruled from Rome; eastern empire ruled from Constantinople.

400–449 AD: Western Roman empire disintegrates under weak emperors. Alaric, king of the Visigoths, sacks Rome (AD 410). A mob of rioters burns down the Library of Alexandria, and much of the recorded knowledge of the western world is lost (415 AD). Attila the Hun attacks Roman provinces (AD 433). St. Augustine's *City of God* is written (AD 411).

450–499 AD: Vandals destroy Rome (AD 455). Western Roman empire ends as Odoacer, German chieftain, overthrows the last Roman emperor, Romulus Augustulus, and becomes the king of Italy (AD 476). Ostrogothic kingdom of Italy established by Theodoric the Great (AD 493). Clovis, ruler of the Franks, is converted to Christianity (AD 496). First schism between western and eastern churches (AD 484). Beginning of the 'Dark Ages' in Europe.

500–549 AD: Eastern and western churches reconciled. Justinian I the Great (483–565), becomes Byzantine emperor (527), issues his first code of civil laws (529), conquers North Africa, Italy, and part of Spain. Plague in Europe. Arthur, legendary king of the Britons, is killed (c. 537).

550–599: Beginnings of European silk industry after Justinian's missionaries smuggle silkworms out of China (553). The times of Prophet Muhammad, founder of Islam (570–632). Buddhism introduced in Japan (c. 560). St. Augustine of Canterbury brings Christianity to Britain (597). After killing about half the population, plague in Europe subsides (594).

600–649: Prophet Mohammed flees from Mecca to Medina (the *Hejira*); first year of the Muslim calendar (622). Arabs conquer Jerusalem (637). Arabs conquer the Persians (641). Lifetime of Fatima, Prophet Mohammed's daughter (606–632).

650–699: Arabs attack North Africa (670) and destroy Carthage (697). Venerable Bede, an English monk, lived between 672 and 735.

700–749: Arab empire extends from Lisbon to China (by 716). Charles Martel, Frankish leader, defeats Arabs at Tours/Poitiers, halting the Arab advance in Europe (732). Charlemagne (742–814) is born. Introduction of pagodas in Japan from China.

750–799: Charlemagne becomes king of the Franks (771). Caliph Harun al-Rashid, immortalized in the *Arabian Nights*, rules the Arab empire from Baghdad (786–809): often noted as the 'golden age' of Arab culture. Vikings begin attacks on Britain (790) and land in Ireland (795). City of Machu Picchu flourishes in Peru.

800–849: Charlemagne crowned the first Holy Roman Emperor in Rome (800). Charlemagne dies (814), succeeded by his son, Louis the Pious, who divides France among his sons (817). The Arabs conquer Crete, Sicily, and Sardinia (826–827).

850–899: Norse attack as far south as the Mediterranean. However, they are repulsed (859). They discover Iceland (861). Alfred the Great is the king of Britain (871), defeats Danish invaders (878). Russian nation founded. Prince Rurik establishes his capital at Novgorod (c. 862–879).

900–949: Beginning of Mayan post-classical period, which lasted till the Spanish conquest (900–1519). Vikings discover Greenland (c. 900). Arab Spain under Abd ar-Rahman III becomes a centre of learning (912–961). Otto I crowned in Aachen as king of Germany (936). West Saxon victory by the army of King Athelstan and his brother Edmund over the combined armies of Olaf III Guthfrithson, Viking king of Dublin and Constantine, and king of Scotland at the battle of Brunanburh(c. 936). Song dynasty (960–1126) reunifies China. Toltecs in Central America learn metal-smelting.

950–999: Mieszko I (c. 960–92), the first prince of the Piast dynasty, is the founder of the Polish state. Eric the Red, Viking explorer, sets up a colony in Greenland (c. 986). Reign of Hugh Capet, first Capetian king of France (987–96). Musical notation systematized by Guido D'Arezzo, a Benedictine prior of the Camaldolite monastery of Avellana around 990–1050. Vikings and Danes attack Britain repeatedly (988–99). Otto I crowned Holy Roman Emperor by Pope John XII (962).

c.1000–1300: Classic Pueblo period of Anasazi culture.

c. 1000: Viking explorer Leif Eriksson reaches North America. Hungary and Scandinavia convert to Christianity. The old English epic *Beowulf* is written.

c. 1008: Murasaki Shikibu writes one of the world's first novels, *The Tale of Genji*.

1013: Danes take control of England.

1040: Macbeth murders Duncan, king of Scotland.

1053: Norman conquest of Italy. Norman invader Robert Guiscard establishes kingdom in Italy.

1054: Final separation between Eastern (Orthodox) and Western (Roman) churches.

1066: William of Normandy invades England, defeats last Saxon king, Harold II, at Battle of Hastings. He is later crowned William I of England, or William the Conqueror.

1068: Construction on the cathedral in Pisa, Italy, begins.

1095: At the Council of Clermont, Pope Urban II calls for a holy war to seize control of Jerusalem from the Muslims. This launches the First Crusade (1096).

1144: Second Crusade begins.

c. 1150: Angkor Wat is completed.

1150–67: The Universities of Paris and Oxford are established.

1162: Thomas á Becket becomes Archbishop of Canterbury.

1169: Ibn-Rushd begins translating the works of Aristotle.

1170: Followers of Henry II, king of England, assassinate Thomas á Becket.

1189: Richard I (Richard the Lionhearted) succeeds Henry II in England. Third Crusade.

1199: Richard the Lionhearted is killed in France. King John succeeds him to the English throne.

1312–37: In Africa, the Mali empire reaches its zenith under King Mansa Musa.

c. 1325: The beginning of the Renaissance in Italy. Development of *Noh* drama in Japan. Aztecs establish Tenochtitlán on the site of modern Mexico City. Peak of Muslim culture in Spain.

1337–1453: The Hundred Years War. English and French kings fight for control of France.

1347–51: Nearly 25 million people die in Europe's 'Black Death', a bubonic plague epidemic.

1368: Ming dynasty begins in China.

1376–82: John Wycliffe, pre-Reformation religious reformer, and his followers translate the Latin Bible into English.

1378–1417: The Great Schism resulting in rival popes in Rome and Avignon, France, fighting for control of Roman Catholic Church.

c. 1387: Chaucer writes his *Canterbury Tales*.

1407: One of the world's first public banks, Casa di San Giorgio, is founded in Genoa.

1415: King of England Henry V defeats the French at Agincourt. Jan Hus, Bohemian preacher and follower of Wycliffe, burned at the stake in Constance as heretic.

1418–60: Portugal's Prince Henry the Navigator sponsors exploration of Africa's coast.

1428: Joan of Arc leads the French against the English.

1430: The Burgundians capture Joan of Arc and turn her over to the English.

1431: Joan of Arc burned at the stake as a witch after an ecclesiastical trial.

1438: Rule of the Incas in Peru.

1450: Florence becomes centre of the Renaissance arts and learning under the Medicis.

1453: The Byzantine empire comes to an end when the Turks conquer Constantinople and found the Ottoman empire.

1455: The War of the Roses, a civil war between rival noble factions, start in England. It lasts till 1485. Johann Gutenberg invents the movable type at Mainz, Germany, and completes the first printed Bible.

1462: Ivan the Great begins his rule over Russia as its first czar. He rules till 1505.

1492: Troops of Queen Isabella I of Castile and King Ferdinand II of Aragon defeat the Moors. Christopher Columbus becomes the first European to visit the Caribbean Islands.

1493–96: Columbus's second voyage, to Dominica, Jamaica, Puerto Rico.

1498: Columbus's third voyage, to the Orinoco region.

1502–04: Columbus's fourth voyage, to Honduras and Panama.

1497–98: Portuguese explorer Vasco da Gama sails around the southern tip of Africa and discovers the sea route to India. John Cabot, Italian navigator and explorer in English employment, reaches and explores the Canadian coast. First black slaves in America are brought to the Spanish colony of Santo Domingo.

c. 1503: Leonardo da Vinci paints the *Mona Lisa*.

1504: Michelangelo sculpts his *David*.

1506: Construction of St. Peter's Church begins in Rome. Artists and architects like Michelangelo, Leonardo da Vinci, Bramante, Raphael and Bernini are involved in its design and decoration.

1509: Henry VIII ascends the English throne. Michelangelo paints the ceiling of the Sistine Chapel.

1513: Vasco Nunez de Balboa becomes the first European to see the Pacific Ocean. Machiavelli writes *The Prince*.

1517: Turks gain control of Arabia and conquer Egypt. German theologian Martin Luther posts his ninety-five theses denouncing church abuses on a church door in Wittenberg. This starts the Reformation in Germany.

1519: Hernando Cortes conquers Mexico for Spain. Portuguese explorer Ferdinand Magellan sets out to circumnavigate the world. Charles I of Spain becomes Holy Roman Emperor Charles V. Ulrich Zwingli begins Reformation in Switzerland.

1520: Suleiman I ('the Magnificent') becomes sultan of Turkey. He invades Hungary in 1521, Rhodes in 1522, attacks Austria in 1529, annexes Hungary in 1541, and Tripoli in 1551. He makes peace with Persia in 1553. In 1560, he destroys the Spanish fleet. He passes away in 1566. Pope Leo X excommunicates Martin Luther.

1521: Magellan reaches the Pacific but is killed in a skirmish with Philippine natives.

1522: One of Magellan's ships continues the circumnavigation under the leadership of Juan Sebastián del Cano and reaches Spain.

1524: Sailing under the French flag, Verrazano explores the coast of New England and New York Bay.

1527: Troops of the Holy Roman Empire attack Rome and imprison Pope Clement VII. This is regarded as the end of the Italian Renaissance. The Medici family is expelled from Florence.

1533: Spanish conquistador Francisco Pizarro marches to Peru and kills the last Inca ruler, Atahualpa.

1535: Reformation begins in England as Henry VIII makes himself head of the Church of England after a dispute with the Pope. Sir Thomas More, Lord Chancellor of England, executed as a traitor for his refusal to acknowledge the king's religious authority. Jacques Cartier sails up the St. Lawrence river, which forms the basis of French claims to Canada.

1536: Henry VIII executes his second wife, Anne Boleyn. John Calvin establishes the Reformed and Presbyterian form of Protestantism in Switzerland, writes *Institutes of the Christian Religion*.

1541: John Knox leads Reformation in Scotland and establishes the Presbyterian Church there in 1560.

1543: Nicolaus Copernicus publishes *On the Revolution of Heavenly Bodies*. It details his heliocentric or Sun-centred theory of the solar system.

1547: Ivan IV ('the Terrible') crowned czar of Russia.

1553: Queen Mary I restores Roman Catholicism in England.

1558: Queen Elizabeth I ascends the throne in England and rules till 1603. She restores Protestantism in England, establishes state Church of England, or Anglicanism.

1561: The Edict of Orleans stops the persecution of Huguenots, or members of the Protestant Reformed Church in France.

1570: Japan allows the visits of foreign ships. The Pope excommunicates Queen Elizabeth I. Turks attack Cyprus and declare war on Venice.

1571: Spanish and Italian fleets defeat the Turkish fleet at the Battle of Lepanto.

1572: Peace of Constantinople ends Turkish attacks on Europe. French religious wars between Catholics and Protestants restart with St. Bartholomew's Day Massacre, the killing of thousands of Huguenots at Vassy.

1580: Francis Drake returns to England after circumnavigating the world.

1582: Pope Gregory XIII implements the Gregorian calendar.

1583: William of Orange rules the Netherlands.

1584: William of Orange assassinated on the orders of Philip II of Spain.

1587: Mary, Queen of Scots, executed for treason on the orders of Queen Elizabeth I.

1588: The English defeat the Spanish Armada and hence thwart a Spanish invasion of England. Henry, king of Navarre and Protestant leader, recognized as Henry IV, first Bourbon king of France.

1590: Henry IV assassinated. Edmund Spenser writes *The Faerie Queen*. Galileo conducts experiments with falling objects.

1592–1613: William Shakespeare's plays enacted in London.

1598: The Edict of Nantes grants religious freedom to the Huguenots.

1598: Tycho Brahe of Denmark describes his astronomical experiments.

1603: Elizabeth I passes away. James I of Scotland become King James I of England and Scotland. Japanese ruler shifts the capital to Edo (present-day Tokyo). Shakespeare writes *Hamlet*.

1605: Cervantes writes *Don Quixote de la Mancha*.

1607: Jamestown, Virginia, established as the first permanent English colony on American mainland.

1609: Samuel de Champlain establishes the French colony of Quebec.

1610: Galileo observes the moons of Jupiter through his telescope.

1611: Gustav II Adolph, or Gustavus Adolphus, elected king of Sweden. King James Version of the Bible is published in England. Rubens paints his *Descent from the Cross*.

1614: John Napier discovers logarithms.

1618–48: The Thirty Years War is fought in Europe as Protestants fight against Catholic oppression. The key players were Denmark, Sweden, Spain, Germany and France.

1618: Johannes Kepler postulates the last of three laws of planetary motion.

1619: A Dutch ship brings the first African slaves to British North America.

1620: The Pilgrim Fathers land in present-day USA after a three-month voyage in *Mayflower*. They had set sail from Plymouth, England.

1623: Dutch West India Company establishes New Netherland on the east coat of North America.

1626: Completion of St. Peter's Church in Rome.

1632: Lord Baltimore founds Maryland.

1633: The Inquisition forces Galileo to recant his belief in Copernican theory of the solar system.

1642–46: Civil war breaks out in England between the supporters of Charles and the parliamentary forces, the New Model Army, also called Roundheads. Parliamentary leader Oliver Cromwell defeats the Royalists in 1646. The monarchy is overthrown.

1648: Charles I is put to trial. He is beheaded in 1649.

1653: Oliver Cromwell becomes Lord Protector of England, Scotland and Ireland.

1644: End of Ming dynasty in China and the Manchus come to power. Descartes writes *Principles of Philosophy*.

1658: Oliver Cromwell passes away and his son Richard takes over as Lord Protector.

1659: Richard Cromwell resigns and the Puritan government collapses.

1660: Restoration of monarchy in England under King Charles II.

1661: In France, Louis XIV begins personal rule as an absolute monarch and starts construction of his palace at Versailles.

1664: In North America, the British take New Amsterdam from the Dutch. New Amsterdam eventually grows into present-day New York City. Isaac Newton conducts experiments with gravity.

1665: The Great Plague kills 75,000 in London.

1666: Great Fire of London. Molière writes *Misanthrope.*

1667: Milton writes *Paradise Lost.*

1683–99: War of European powers against the Turks. Vienna survives a three-month Turkish siege.

1684: Gottfried Wilhelm Leibniz's calculus is published.

1685: James II succeeds Charles II in England.

1687: Newton's *Philosophiae Naturalis Principia Mathematica* (Mathematical Principles of Natural Philosophy), *Principia* or *Principia Mathematica* for short) is published, containing the statement of Newton's laws of motion and his law of universal gravitation.

1688: William of Orange invited to England amid apprehensions that James II will restore Catholicism. James II escapes to France. William III and his wife, Mary, are crowned rulers of England. In France, Louis XIV revokes the Edict of Nantes of 1598, leading to an exodus of thousands of Protestants.

1689: Peter the Great becomes czar of Russia and tries to westernize the country and develop Russia as a military power.

1690: William III of England defeats former King James II and Irish rebels at Battle of the Boyne in Ireland.

1701: War of Spanish Succession begins.

1707: United Kingdom of Great Britain formed as England, Wales, and Scotland are joined together by a parliamentary Act of Union.

1714: The Peace of Utrecht ends the War of Spanish Succession and marks the rise of the British empire as Britain gains Newfoundland, Hudson's Bay Territory, and Acadia from France, and Gibraltar and Minorca from Spain.

1729: Bach composes *St. Matthew's Passion.* Isaac Newton's *Principia* translated from Latin into English.

1740: Capt. Vitus Bering, a Dane in Russian employment, discovers Alaska. Frederick II 'the Great' becomes king of Prussia.

1746: British defeat Scots under Stuart Pretender Prince Charles at Culloden Moor.

1755: Samuel Johnson's *Dictionary* is published for the first time. More than 60,000 die in an earthquake in Lisbon, Portugal.

1756–63: Seven Years War (called French and Indian Wars in America). Britain and Prussia defeat France, Spain, Austria, and Russia. It results in France losing its North American colonies, Spain handing over Florida to Britain in exchange for Cuba.

1759: British capture Quebec from the French. Voltaire writes *Candide.* Haydn composes *Symphony No. 1.*

1762: Catherine II 'the Great' becomes czarina of Russia. Jean Jacques Rousseau writes *Social Contract.* Mozart tours Europe as six-year-old prodigy.

1765: James Watt invents the steam engine. Britain imposes the Stamp Act on the American colonists.

1769: Sir William Arkwright patents a spinning machine. This is considered to be one of the first steps of the Industrial Revolution.

1770: The Boston Massacre, in which British troops open fire on an American mob. The event helped spark the American Revolution.

1772: Joseph Priestley and Daniel Rutherford independently discover nitrogen. Partition of Poland occurs. It takes place again in 1793 and in 1795. Austria, Prussia, and Russia divide the country and end its independence.

1773: The Boston Tea Party, in which a group of about sixty local Boston residents, named Sons of Liberty destroy the cargo of tea imported by the British authorities and throw it into the Boston Harbour. This event is considered as one of the starting points of the American Revolution.

1775: The American Revolution begins with battle of Lexington and Concord. Joseph Priestley discovers hydrochloric and sulphuric acids.

1776: US Declaration of Independence. Adam Smith writes *Wealth of Nations*. Edward Gibbon writes *Decline and Fall of the Roman Empire*.

1778: Capt. James Cook 'discovers' Hawaii.

1781: Immanuel Kant writes *Critique of Pure Reason*. German-born astronomer and musician William Herschel discovers Uranus, the seventh planet of the solar system.

1784: Russia annexes Crimea.

1787: Antoine Lavoisier conducts his work on chemical nomenclature. Mozart composes *Don Giovanni*.

1788: The French Parliament presents its grievances to King Louis XVI who agrees to hold the *Estates-General* in 1789 for the first time since 1613.

1789: French Revolution begins with the storming of the Bastille prison. George Washington is elected US President with all sixty-nine votes of the electoral college; takes oath of office in New York City.

1790: Lavoisier formulates *Table of 31 chemical elements*.

1793: Louis XVI and Marie Antoinette are executed. The Reign of Terror begins in France. Eli Whitney invents the cotton gin resulting in the growth of the cotton industry.

1794: Reign of Terror ends in France with the execution of Maximilien Robespierre.

1796: French general Napoléon Bonaparte leads the French Army to victory against the Austrians. Edward Jenner introduces smallpox vaccine.

1798: Napoleon's fleet is defeated by the British at the Battle of the Nile, also known as the Battle of Aboukir Bay.

1799: Napoleon leads a coup that establishes himself as the effective ruler of France, as the First Consul.

1800: Napoleon conquers Italy. Strengthens his position as First Consul. In USA, the federal government moves to Washington DC. William Herschel discovers infrared radiation. Alessandro Volta develops the voltaic pile, a forerunner of the electric battery, which produces a steady electric current.

1801: United Kingdom of Great Britain and Ireland established with one monarch and one Parliament, but Catholics are excluded from voting.

1803: US negotiates the Louisiana Purchase from France. It pays $15 million to increase its territory by 827,000 sq. mi. (2,144,500 sq. km).

1804: Napoleon proclaims himself emperor of France and codifies French law under *Code Napoleon*.

1805: Lord Nelson defeats the combined French–Spanish fleets in the Battle of Trafalgar. Napoleon wins over Austrian and Russian forces at the Battle of Austerlitz.

1807: Robert Fulton carries out the first successful steamboat trip on *Clermont* between New York City and Albany.

1808: French armies occupy Rome and Spain. UK helps Spanish guerrillas against Napoleon in the Peninsular War. The US Congress bans the importation of slaves.

1812: Napoleon invades Russia in June but is forced to retreat in the severe winter. This results in the death of most of Napoleon's soldiers.

1814: The allied forces of Britain, Austria, Russia, Prussia, Sweden, and Portugal defeat the French. Napoleon is exiled to Elba, an island off the Italian coast. Bourbon King Louis XVIII takes over the French throne. George Stephenson builds the first practical steam locomotive.

1815: Napoleon returns to Paris on 20 March. Napoleon is defeated at the Battle of Waterloo, his last battle, on 18 June. King Louis XVIII is restored to the French throne on 28 June. Napoléon formally surrenders on board the British vessel HMS *Bellerophon* on 15 July. Napoléon is imprisoned and then exiled by the British to the island of Saint Helena from 15 October. Congress of Vienna is held. The political map of Europe is redrawn following the defeat of Napoleonic France.

1819: Simón Bolivar liberates New Granada (former Spanish colony in South America consisting of present-day Colombia, Venezuela, and Ecuador) from Spanish rule.

1821: Panama, Guatemala, and Santo Domingo proclaim independence from Spain.

1822: Greece proclaims independence from Turkey and becomes a republic. Turkey invades Greece. Brazil declares its independence from Portugal.

1825: Portugal recognizes Brazil as an independent nation.

1828: Russia declares war on Turkey. France and UK support Greece.

1829: War ends and Turkey recognizes Greek independence. Brazil becomes independent of Portugal.

1823: US Monroe Doctrine warns European nations not to interfere in the western hemisphere.

1824: Mexico becomes a republic. Simón Bolívar liberates Peru. Beethoven composes the *Ninth Symphony.*

c. 1826: Date of earliest known surviving photograph taken by Joseph-Nicéphore Niepce, considered to be the first successful permanent photograph.

1830: France invades Algeria. Louis Philippe becomes 'Citizen King' after a revolution forces Charles X to abdicate.

1831: Polish revolt against Russia fails. Belgium breaks away from the Netherlands.

1833: Slavery abolished in the British empire.

1834: Charles Babbage invents 'analytical engine', a precursor of the computer.

1836: Charles Dickens writes *Pickwick Papers*.

1837: Victoria becomes queen of Great Britain.

1839–42: First Opium War between Britain and China.

1840: Lower and Upper Canada united.

1843: Wagner composes his opera *The Flying Dutchman.*

1844: Samuel F. B. Morse patents the telegraph.

1846: The eighth planet in the solar system, Neptune, is discovered. USA declares war on Mexico and annexes California and New Mexico. Elias Howe patents the sewing machine. Failure of potato crop causes famine in Ireland.

1848: Revolt in Paris leads to the abdication of Louis Philippe and election of Louis Napoleon as President of French Republic.

1848–49: Royalist troops suppress revolutions in Venice, Vienna, Berlin, Milan, Rome, and Warsaw. US–Mexico War ends with Mexico giving up claims to Texas, California, Arizona, New Mexico, Utah, and Nevada. Karl Marx and Friedrich Engels compile the *Communist Manifesto*.

1849: Gold rush begins in California.

1850: In USA, Henry Clay opens debate on slavery and warns the South against secession from the Union.

1851: Herman Melville writes *Moby Dick.*

1852: South African Republic is established. Louis Napoleon proclaims himself Napoleon III. Harriet Beecher Stowe writes *Uncle Tom's Cabin.*

1853: Crimean War begins as Turkey declares war on Russia.

1854: UK and France join Turkey in war on Russia. Japanese allow American trade. Lord Alfred Tennyson writes *Charge of the Light Brigade*.

1855: Armed clashes between pro- and anti-slavery groups take place in Kansas, USA.

1856: Gustave Flaubert writes *Madame Bovary*.

1857: US Supreme Court rules that a slave is not a citizen.

1858: Pro-slavery Constitution rejected in Kansas. Republican politician Abraham Lincoln makes strong anti-slavery speech in Springfield, Illinois.

1859: The process of unification of Italy starts under the leadership of Sardinian premier Count Cavour. Construction of the Suez Canal starts. Jean-Joseph-Étienne Lenoir builds first practical internal-combustion engine. Edward Fitzgerald translates *The Rubaiyat of Omar Khayyam*. Charles Darwin writes *Origin of Species*.

1860: South Carolina breaks away from the Union.

1861: US Civil War begins. Alabama, Florida, Georgia, Louisiana, Mississippi and Texas break away from the Union and join with South Carolina to form the Confederate States of America, with Jefferson Davis as President. Arkansas, North Carolina, Tennessee and Virginia secede and join the Confederacy. First Battle of Bull Run (Manassas). Abraham Lincoln inaugurated as US President. Independent Kingdom of Italy proclaimed under Sardinian king Victor Emmanuel II. Serfs emancipated in Russia. Louis Pasteur postulates his theory of germs.

1862: US Civil War continues.

1863: Battle of Gettysburg.

1864: Gen. Sherman's Atlanta campaign.

1865: Confederate general Robert E. Lee surrenders to Union Army General Ulysses S. Grant at Appomattox to end the US Civil War. President Lincoln is assassinated. Joseph Lister begins antiseptic surgery. Gregor Mendel postulates *Law of Heredity*. Lewis Carroll writes *Alice's Adventures in Wonderland*.

1866: Alfred Nobel invents dynamite. Prussia and Italy defeat Austria in Seven Weeks War.

1867: Austria–Hungary Dual Monarchy established. Dominion of Canada is established. USA buys Alaska from Russia for $7,200,000. South African diamond field discovered. 675-year shogun rule comes to an end in Japan. Volume I of Marx's *Das Kapital* is published. Johann Strauss II composes *Blue Danube*.

1868: Revolution in Spain deposes Queen Isabella who then flees to France. In US, the Fourteenth Amendment giving civil rights to blacks is ratified.

1869: Suez Canal opens. German Lothar Meyer and Russian Dmitry Ivanovich Mendeleev almost simultaneously develop the first periodic table.

1870: Franco–Prussian War starts. Revolt in Paris. Third Republic is proclaimed in France.

1871: Franco–Prussian War ends. France surrenders Alsace–Lorraine to Germany. German empire proclaimed with Prussian king as Kaiser Wilhelm I. Henry Morton Stanley meets David Livingstone in Africa.

1872: Jules Verne writes *Around the World in 80 Days*.

1873: Economic crisis in Europe.

1875: The first performance of Georges Bizet's *Carmen*.

1876: Alexander Graham Bell patents the telephone.

1877: Russo-Turkish War starts. Thomas Alva Edison patents the phonograph. Pyotr Ilyich Tchaikovsky composes *Swan Lake*.

1878: Russo–Turkish War ends. Congress of Berlin revises Treaty of San Stefano that ended the Russo–Turkish War and redivides south-east Europe.

1879: UK and the Zulus fight the Anglo–Zulu War.

1880: Construction of the Panama Canal begins. US–China treaty allows USA to restrict immigration of Chinese labour.

1881: US President James Garfield assassinated.

1882: UK conquers Egypt. Germany, Austria, and Italy form Triple Alliance. In Berlin, Robert Koch announces the discovery of the tuberculosis germ.

1883: In Barcelona, Spain, architect Antoni Gaudi begins to build his masterpiece, the La Sagrada Familia cathedral.

1884–85: The Berlin West Africa Conference is held in Berlin at which major European nations discuss expansion in Africa.

1886: UK annexes Burma, now Myanmar. The Statue of Liberty is dedicated. Karl Benz patents his first successful petrol-driven automobile.

1887: Queen Victoria's Golden Jubilee. Sir Arthur Conan Doyle writes his first Sherlock Holmes story, *A Study in Scarlet*.

1888: John Boyd Dunlop develops commercially practical pneumatic tyres. 'Jack the Ripper' murders take place in London. The true identity of the murderer is yet to be ascertained.

1889: The Eiffel Tower is built for the Paris exposition.

1890: Elizabeth Jane Cochran, better known as Nellie Bly, pioneer of undercover journalism, travels round the world in 'seventy-two days, six hours, eleven minutes and fourteen seconds', mimicking Jules Verne's book *Around the World in Eighty Days*.

1892: Rudolf Diesel invents and patents the Diesel engine.

1893: New Zealand becomes first country in the world to grant women the right to vote.

1894: Sino–Japanese War begins. In France, Capt. Alfred Dreyfus convicted on false treason charge.

1895: Sino–Japanese War ends with China accepting defeat in the Treaty of Shimonoseki. German physicist Wilhelm Roentgen discovers X-rays. Auguste and Louis Lumière show their first motion pictures in Paris.

1896: Alfred Nobel's will establishes the Nobel Prizes for peace, science, and literature. Guglielmo Marconi receives his first wireless patent in UK. First modern Olympic Games are held in Athens, Greece.

1897: Theodor Herzl launches the Zionist movement.

1898: Pierre and Marie Curie discover radium and polonium. US Battleship *Maine* is sunk in Havana Harbour. Spanish–American War begins and USA destroys a Spanish fleet near Santiago, Cuba.

1899: Boer War, or South African War, starts as a conflict between British and the Boers.

1900: Sigmund Freud writes *The Interpretation of Dreams*.

1901: The first Nobel Prizes are awarded. Queen Victoria passes away. Her son, Edward VII, succeeds her to the British throne. US President William McKinley assassinated.

1902: Boer War ends in British victory.

1903: The Wright brothers, Orville and Wilbur, fly their first powered, controlled, heavier-than-air plane at Kitty Hawk.

1904: Russo–Japanese War begins. UK and France settle their differences by signing a series of agreements, the Entente Cordiale. Ernest Rutherford and Frederick Soddy postulate the General Theory of Radioactivity.

1905: Russo–Japanese War ends in defeat for Russia and Japan gains control of Korea but restores southern Manchuria to China. The Russian Revolution of 1905 begins when troops open fire on unarmed demonstrators in St. Petersburg. Strikes and riots follow and sailors on battleship *Potemkin* mutiny. In response, Czar Nicholas II announces reforms including first Duma or Parliament. Albert Einstein publishes Special Theory of Relativity and other significant theories in physics.

1906: San Francisco earthquake on the San Andreas Fault destroys much of San Francisco. Norwegian explorer Roald Amundsen fixes magnetic North Pole.

1907: Second Hague Peace Conference of forty-six nations adopts ten conventions on rules of war. Pablo Picasso's *Les Demoiselles d'Avignon* introduces cubism.

1908: Earthquake kills 150,000 in southern Italy and Sicily. Union of South Africa established as a confederation of colonies.

1909: American explorers Robert E. Peary and Matthew Henson are reported to have reached the North Pole.

1910: South Africa becomes a British dominion.

1911: Ernest Rutherford discovers the structure of the atom. Roald Amundsen reaches the South Pole. Italy defeats Turks in the Turkish–Italian War and annexes Tripoli and Libya. Chinese Republic is proclaimed after a revolution overthrows the Manchu dynasty. Sun Yat-sen is named President. A revolution in Mexico results in the replacement of President Porfirio Diaz with Francisco Madero.

1912–13: Balkan Wars take place. Turkey defeated by an alliance of Bulgaria, Greece, Montenegro, and Serbia. In the second war of 1913, Bulgaria is defeated after it attacks Serbia and Greece and Romania intervenes and Turks recapture Adrianople.

1912: The *Titanic* sinks on its maiden voyage.

1913: Greece annexes Crete. Francisco Madero, President of Mexico, assassinated. George I, king of Greece, assassinated.

1914: Austrian Archduke Francis Ferdinand and wife Sophie are assassinated in Sarajevo. Austria declares war on Serbia, Germany on Russia and France, and Britain on Germany. World War I begins. Panama Canal is officially opened.

1915: World War I continues. German submarine sinks British passenger liner and cargo ship *Lusitania*. This event plays a key role in the entry of the USA into World War I. Second Battle of Ypres takes place. Genocide of estimated 600,000 to one million Armenians by Turkish soldiers. Albert Einstein publishes *General Theory of Relativity*.

1916: World War I continues. Battle of Verdun and Battle of the Somme take place. USA buys the Virgin Islands from Denmark for $25 million. British troops suppress Easter Rebellion in Ireland.

1917: World War I continues. USA declares war on Germany. First US combat troops arrive in France. Third Battle of Ypres takes place. Russian Revolution of 1917 ends the rule of the Romanov family in Russia. February Revolution forces Czar Nicholas II to abdicate. A provisional government takes office in Russia with Alexander Fedorovich Kerensky as prime minister. Bolsheviks seize power in armed coup d'état led by Lenin and Trotsky in Russia. Kerensky flees the country. Balfour Declaration promises Jewish homeland in Palestine. US declares war on Austria and Hungary. Armistice signed between new Russian Bolshevik government and Germans. Sigmund Freud writes *Introduction to Psychoanalysis*.

1918: Bolsheviks execute Czar Nicholas II and his family. Russian Civil War breaks out between Reds (Bolsheviks) and Whites (anti-Bolsheviks). Second Battle of the Marne. German Kaiser abdicates. Hostilities cease on the Western Front. Worldwide influenza epidemic kills nearly 20 million.

1919: Third International (Comintern) establishes Soviet control over international communist movements. Allies and Germany sign Versailles Treaty incorporating Woodrow Wilson's draft Covenant of League of Nations. Aviators John Alcock and Arthur Brown make the first transatlantic non-stop flight.

1920: Bolsheviks emerge victorious in the Russian Civil War. League of Nations holds its first meeting at Geneva, Switzerland. Treaty of Sèvres dissolves the Ottoman empire.

1921: US Congress formally ends war. Reparations Commission fixes German liability for World War I at 132 billion gold marks. German inflation begins. Major treaties signed at Washington Disarmament Conference limit naval tonnage and pledge to respect territorial integrity of China.

1922: Benito Mussolini marches on Rome and forms a fascist government. Irish Free State, a self-governing dominion of British empire, is officially proclaimed. Kemal Atatürk, founder of modern Turkey, overthrows the country's last sultan. James Joyce writes *Ulysses.*

1923: Adolf Hitler's 'Beer Hall Putsch' coup attempt in Munich fails. French and Belgian troops occupy Ruhr region of Germany to enforce reparations payments. Earthquake destroys large parts of Tokyo.

1924: Death of Lenin. Stalin wins Russian power struggle and rules as Soviet dictator until death in 1953. Adolf Hitler is sentenced to five years in prison where he writes *Mein Kampf,* his autobiography.

1925: Locarno conferences seek to secure European peace through mutual guarantees. John Logie Baird, Scottish inventor, transmits human features by television.

1926: Gertrude Ederle of USA becomes the first woman to swim English Channel. Ernest Hemingway writes *The Sun Also Rises.*

1927: German economy collapses. Socialists riot in Vienna. General strike follows acquittal of Nazis for political murder. Leon Trotsky expelled from Russian Communist Party. Charles A. Lindbergh flies the first successful solo non-stop flight from New York to Paris. Philo T. Farnsworth demonstrates working television model. Georges Lemaître proposes Big Bang Theory. *The Jazz Singer,* with Al Jolson, is the first part-talking motion picture.

1928: Sixty-five nations sign the Kellogg-Briand Pact, outlawing war. Alexander Fleming discovers penicillin. Richard E. Byrd starts expedition to the Antarctic. *Oxford English Dictionary* published after forty-four years of research.

1929: Leon Trotsky expelled from USSR. Lateran Treaty establishes an independent Vatican City. In USA, stock market prices collapse resulting in the first phase of Depression and global economic crisis. Edwin Powell Hubble proposes theory of expanding universe. St. Valentine's Day gangland massacre in Chicago.

1930: UK, USA, Japan, France, and Italy sign naval disarmament treaty. Nazis achieve gains in German elections. US physicist Ernest O. Lawrence develops the cyclotron. Clyde W. Tombaugh discovers Pluto, the ninth planet in the solar system.

1931: Spain becomes a republic with the ouster of King Alfonso XIII. In Germany, the Nazi Party gets the support of German industrialists. Mukden Incident, also called Manchurian Incident, in which the Japanese blow up a section of a Japanese railroad near Mukden (present-day Shenyang) in northern Manchuria, begins Japanese occupation of Manchuria. The *Star Spangled Banner* officially becomes US national anthem.

1932: Nazis lead in German elections with 230 Reichstag seats. Famine in USSR. Amelia Earhart becomes the first woman to fly solo across the Atlantic Ocean.

1933: Adolf Hitler is appointed German chancellor and assumes dictatorial powers. Germany and Japan withdraw from League of Nations. President Franklin D. Roosevelt launches New Deal to revive US economy. Prohibition repealed in USA. USA recognizes USSR.

1934: Nazis assassinate Chancellor Englebert Dollfuss of Austria. Hitler becomes Führer. USSR admitted to League of Nations. In China, Mao Zedong begins the Long March north with 100,000 soldiers.

1935: Saar becomes a part of Germany following a plebiscite. Nazis repudiate Versailles Treaty and introduce compulsory military service. Mussolini invades Ethiopia. President Roosevelt opens second phase of New Deal in USA.

1936: Germany occupies Rhineland. Italy annexes Ethiopia. Rome–Berlin Axis is proclaimed. Leon Trotsky is exiled to Mexico. King George V dies and is succeeded by his son, Edward VIII who abdicates the throne in the same year to marry an American-born divorcée. His brother, George VI succeeds him. Spanish civil war begins. War breaks out between China and Japan. Japan and Germany sign anti-Comintern pact.

1937: Hitler repudiates war guilt clause of Versailles Treaty. Italy withdraws from League of Nations. Japan invades China and conquers most of its coastal area. Amelia Earhart lost somewhere in the Pacific on her round-the-world flight. Picasso paints the *Guernica* mural.

1938: Hitler marches into Austria. Political and geographical union of Germany and Austria is proclaimed. The Munich Pact is signed whereby UK, France and Italy agree to allow Germany partition Czechoslovakia.

1939: Germany invades Poland, occupies Bohemia and Moravia. Germany renounces pact with England and concludes ten-year non-aggression pact with USSR. Russo–Finnish War begins. World War II begins. President Roosevelt proclaims US neutrality. Albert Einstein writes to President Roosevelt about the feasibility of an atomic bomb. *Gone with the Wind* premieres. General Franco's fascist forces defeat loyalist forces in the Spanish civil war.

1940: World War II continues. Japan joins the Axis powers. Hitler invades Norway, Denmark, the Netherlands, Belgium, Luxembourg and France. Winston Churchill becomes Britain's prime minister. Leon Trotsky is assassinated in Mexico. USSR annexes Estonia, Latvia and Lithuania. Russia and Finland sign a peace treaty whereby Finland loses one-tenth of its territory.

1941: World War II continues. Germany attacks the Balkans and Russia. Japanese surprise attack on US fleet at Pearl Harbour brings US into World War II. USA and UK declare war on Japan. Manhattan Project on atomic bomb research begins.

1942: World War II continues. Declaration of United Nations signed in Washington DC. Nazi leaders attend Wannsee Conference to discuss the 'final solution to the Jewish question', the systematic extermination of Jews now called the Holocaust. Enrico Fermi achieves nuclear chain reaction. More than 120,000 Japanese and persons of Japanese ancestry living in western US moved to 'relocation centres', some for the entire duration of the war.

1943: World War II continues. British prime minister Churchill and US President Roosevelt meet at the Casablanca Conference. Italian dictator Mussolini is deposed and killed.

1944: Allied forces invade Normandy on D-Day. Bretton Woods Conference creates International Monetary Fund and World Bank. USA, British Commonwealth and USSR propose establishment of United Nations at the

Dumbarton Oaks Conference. Battle of the Bulge, or the Ardennes Offensive, the last major German offensive on the Western Front.

1945: Roosevelt, Churchill, Stalin meet at the Yalta Conference and plan the final defeat of Germany. President Roosevelt dies. Adolf Hitler is believed to have committed suicide. Germany surrenders. 8 May is declared V-E Day. Harry Truman, Churchill and Stalin meet at the Potsdam Conference to establish the basis of German reconstruction. US drops atomic bombs on the Japanese cities of Hiroshima and Nagasaki forcing Japan to surrender on V-J Day, 2 September. World War II ends. The United Nations is established. First electronic computer, ENIAC, is built.

1946: The First meeting of UN General Assembly opens in London. League of Nations is dissolved. Winston Churchill's 'Iron Curtain' speech warns of Soviet expansion. Italy abolishes monarchy. The verdict is passed in the Nuremberg war trial. Twelve Nazi leaders (including one tried in absentia) are sentenced to death, seven are imprisoned, three are acquitted. Hermann Goering commits suicide a few hours before ten other Nazi leaders are executed. Juan Perón becomes President of Argentina.

1947: Peace treaties for Bulgaria, Finland, Hungary, Italy, and Romania are signed in Paris. Soviet Union rejects US plan for UN atomic energy control. President Truman proposes Truman Doctrine to help Greece and Turkey in resisting communist expansion. Marshall Plan for European recovery is proposed. It envisages a coordinated programme to help European nations recover from the war. US Air Force pilot Chuck Yeager becomes the first person to break the sound barrier. Anne Frank's *The Diary of a Young Girl* is published.

1948: UK grants independence to Burma, now Myanmar and Ceylon, now Sri Lanka. Communists seize power in Czechoslovakia. Organization of American States (OAS) Charter is signed at Bogotá, Colombia. Nation of Israel proclaimed. Arab armies attack the newborn state the following day. The Berlin Blockade begins when the Soviet Union block Western rail and road access to Berlin from 24 June 1948–11 May 1949. This leads to an Allied airlift of essential supplies to the Western-held sectors of Berlin. Independent Republic of Korea is proclaimed. Verdict in Japanese war trial: eighteen are imprisoned, Tôjô Hideki (Japanese PM and general during the war) and six others are hanged. United States of Indonesia is established. Alger Hiss, former US State Department official, indicted on perjury charges after denying passing secret documents to a communist spy ring and sentenced to five-year prison term. Alfred Kinsey publishes *Sexual Behavior in the American Male*. Tennessee Williams's *A Streetcar Named Desire* wins Pulitzer.

1949: Berlin Blockade ends ceasefire in Palestine. Truman proposes Point Four Program to help world's less developed areas. Israel signs armistice with Egypt. Start of North Atlantic Treaty Organization (NATO). Federal Republic of Germany (West Germany) is established. First successful Soviet atomic test. Chairman Mao Zedong formally proclaims Communist People's Republic of China. German Democratic Republic (East Germany) is established under Soviet rule. South Africa institutionalizes apartheid.

1950: Start of the Korean War following North Korean invasion of South Korea. Assassination attempt on President Truman by Puerto Rican nationalists. McCarthyism begins. Alger Hiss is convicted in second trial.

1951: Forty-nine nations sign Japanese peace treaty in San Francisco. Libya becomes independent.

1952: British monarch George VI dies and his daughter becomes Queen

Elizabeth II. Japan officially regains independence, marking the end of the period of Occupied Japan. Military coup in Egypt ousts King Farouk.

1953: Gen. Dwight D. Eisenhower becomes President of USA. Stalin dies. Dag Hammarskjöld becomes UN Secretary General. Edmund Hillary of New Zealand and Tenzing Norgay of Nepal become the first to reach the summit of Mt. Everest. Egypt becomes a republic. Korean armistice is signed. USSR explodes a hydrogen bomb. Tito becomes President of Yugoslavia. James Watson, Francis Crick, and Rosalind Franklin discover structure of DNA. Ernest Hemingway wins Pulitzer for *The Old Man and the Sea.*

1954: Soviet Union grants sovereignty to East Germany. Dien Bien Phu, French military outpost in Vietnam, falls to Vietminh army. Eight-nation Southeast Asia defence treaty (SEATO) is signed at Manila. Dr Jonas Salk starts innoculating children against polio. Algerian War of Independence against France begins.

1955: Churchill resigns as British prime minister and Anthony Eden succeeds him. West Germany becomes a sovereign state. Western European Union (WEU) comes into being. Warsaw Pact, East European mutual defence agreement, is signed. Juan Peron ousted in Argentina.

1956: First aerial hydrogen bomb tested over Namu islet, Bikini Atoll. Egypt takes control of Suez Canal. Hungarian rebellion forces Soviet troops to withdraw from Budapest. Israel attacks Egypt's Sinai peninsula. Hungarian prime minister Imre Nagy announces Hungary's withdrawal from Warsaw Pact. Soviet troops occupy Budapest. British and French forces invade Port Said on the Suez Canal. Ceasefire forced by US pressure stops British, French and Israeli advance. Morocco gains independence.

1957: Eisenhower Doctrine calls for aid to mid-east countries which resist armed aggression from Communist-controlled nations. Russians launch *Sputnik I,* the first Earth-orbiting satellite.

1958: European Economic Community (Common Market) comes into effect. First US Earth satellite, *Explorer I,* is launched into orbit. Egypt and Syria merge to form United Arab Republic. US President Eisenhower orders US Marines into Lebanon at the request of President Chamoun. New French constitution adopted.

1959: Cuban President Batista resigns and flees the country as Fidel Castro takes over the country. The Dalai Lama escapes Tibet and arrives in India.

1960: American U-2 spy plane, piloted by Francis Gary Powers, is shot down over Russia. USSR sentences Gary Powers to ten years in prison. Israelis capture Nazi leader Adolf Eichmann in Argentina. Senegal, Ghana, Nigeria, Madagascar, and Zaire (Belgian Congo) gain independence. Cuba starts to confiscate $770 million of US property. John F. Kennedy becomes US President.

1961: USA severs diplomatic relations with Cuba. Maj. Yuri A. Gagarin of USSR becomes the first man in orbit around Earth. An invasion by an estimated 1,200 anti-Castro exiles aided by USA is crushed. Alan B. Shepard Jr. is the first American in space. Berlin Wall is erected between East and West Berlin to stop East Germans from crossing over into West Germany. USSR tests fifty-megaton hydrogen bomb.

1962: Nazi leader Adolf Eichmann is executed in Israel. Lt Col. John H. Glenn Jr. becomes the first American to orbit Earth. Algeria gains independence. Cuban missile crisis. Burundi, Jamaica, Western Samoa, Uganda, and Trinidad and Tobago become independent. Gary Powers is freed in exchange for Soviet spy.

1963: France and West Germany sign treaty of cooperation. Pope John XXIII dies and is succeeded by Cardinal Montini who becomes Pope Paul VI.

Profumo scandal in UK. Martin Luther King Jr delivers his 'I have a dream' speech at a civil rights rally attended by 200,000 people in Washington, DC. US President John F. Kennedy assassinated. Kenya becomes independent.

1964: Nelson Mandela is sentenced to life imprisonment in South Africa. President's Commission on the Assassination of President Kennedy issues Warren Report and concludes that Lee Harvey Oswald acted alone.

1965: Malcolm X, US black-nationalist leader, shot dead in New York City.

1966: The People's Republic of China explodes its first hydrogen bomb.

1967: Biafra secedes from Nigeria. Six-Day War ends with Israel occupying Sinai peninsula, Golan Heights, Gaza Strip, and east bank of Suez Canal. Dr Christiaan N. Barnard and his team of South African surgeons perform the world's first successful human heart transplant but the patient dies eighteen days later.

1968: Tet offensive and My Lai massacre take place in Vietnam War. Martin Luther King Jr., civil rights leader, is killed in Memphis. Sen. Robert F. Kennedy, younger brother of President John F. Kennedy is assassinated. Russian and Warsaw Pact forces invade Czechoslovakia to remove a liberal regime.

1969: Stonewall riot in New York City marks beginning of gay rights movement. *Apollo 11* astronauts—Neil A. Armstrong, Edwin E. Aldrin Jr. and Michael Collins are the first men to walk on Moon. Woodstock Festival ARPAnet, forerunner of Internet, goes online.

1970: Biafra surrenders after a thirty-two-month fight for independence from Nigeria. Rhodesia declares itself a racially segregated republic. US troops invade Cambodia.

1971: UN gives its seat to Communist China and expels Nationalist China (Taiwan).

1972: UK takes over direct rule of Northern Ireland. In USA, police arrests five men who were trying to plant listening devices at the Democratic National Committee headquarters in Washington DC's Watergate complex. This starts the Watergate scandal. Eleven Israeli athletes are killed at the Munich Olympic Games after eight members of an Arab terrorist group invade the Olympic Village.

1973: Vietnam War ends with signing of peace pacts. In USA, President Nixon appears on national TV and accepts responsibility, but not blame, for the Watergate scandal. Greek military junta abolishes monarchy and proclaims a republic. Chile's Marxist President Salvadore Allende is ousted. Yom Kippur War is fought between Israel, Egypt and Syrian forces.

1974: In USA, the House Judiciary Committee adopts three articles of impeachment charging President Nixon with obstruction of justice, failure to uphold laws, and refusal to produce material subpoenaed by the committee. Richard M. Nixon announces he will resign the next day, the first US President to do so.

1975: Pol Pot and Khmer Rouge take over Cambodia. Two assassination attempts take place on US President Gerald Ford.

1976: Israeli airborne commandos attack Uganda's Entebbe Airport and free 103 hostages held by pro-Palestinian hijackers of Air France plane.

1977: Chinese leader Deng Xiaoping is restored to power as 'Gang of Four' is expelled from the Communist Party.

1978: Rhodesia's prime minister Ian Smith and black leaders agree on a transfer to black majority rule. Former Italian prime minister Aldo Moro kidnapped by Left wing terrorists and killed. Pope Paul VI dies and is succeeded by new Pope, John Paul I, who also dies after thirty-four days in office. He is succeeded by Karol Wojtyla of

Poland as Pope John Paul II. Egypt's President Anwar Sadat and Israeli PM Menachem Begin sign a peace deal.

1979: Vietnam and Vietnam-backed Cambodian insurgents announce the fall of Phnom Penh, capital of Cambodia and the collapse of the Pol Pot regime. The Shah of Iran leaves the country and revolutionary forces under Muslim leader Ayatollah Ruhollah Khomeini take over the country. Margaret Thatcher becomes new British prime minister. Nicaraguan President Gen. Anastasio Somoza Debayle resigns and flees to Miami, paving the way for Sandinistas to take over the country. Iranian militants seize US embassy in Teheran and take hostages. Soviet Union invades Afghanistan.

1980: Six US embassy aides escape from Iran. US breaks off diplomatic ties with Iran. Ousted Nicaragua ruler. Anastasio Somoza Debayle, assassinated in Asunción, capital of Paraguay. Eight-year Iran–Iraq war begins. John Lennon of the Beatles is shot dead in New York City. Smallpox eradicated.

1981: US–Iran agreement frees fifty-two hostages held in Teheran since 1979. Assassination attempt on Pope John Paul II. AIDS is first identified.

1982: UK defeats Argentina in Falklands war. Israel invades Lebanon in attack on PLO. Princess Grace of Monaco dies of injuries in a car crash.

1983: Benigno S. Aquino Jr., political rival of Philippines President Marcos, is killed in Manila. A South Korean Boeing 747 jetliner bound for Seoul apparently flies into Soviet airspace by mistake and is shot down by a Soviet fighter aircraft, killing all 269 on board. More than 200 US marines are killed in an explosion in Beirut. US and its Caribbean allies invade Grenada.

1984: US and the Vatican exchange diplomats after 116 years. Italy and Vatican agree to end Roman Catholicism as state religion. Soviet Union and its allies withdraw from the Summer Olympic Games in Los Angeles.

1985: Mikhail Gorbachev becomes Soviet leader. Two gunmen capture an American airliner with 133 on board, 104 of them Americans. Italian cruise ship *Achille Lauro* hijacked with eighty passengers and crew on board. Egyptian Boeing 737 airliner seized after take-off from Athens. Fifty-nine die after Egyptian forces storm the plane on Malta.

1986: Spain and Portugal join European Economic Community. USA freezes Libyan assets in the US. US Space shuttle *Challenger* explodes after launch at Cape Canaveral, killing all seven on board. Haiti President Jean-Claude Duvalier flees to France. President Marcos flees the Philippines after ruling for twenty years and is succeeded by Corazon Aquino. Swedish prime minister Olof Palme is shot dead. Austrian President Kurt Waldheim's secret past as a Nazi army officer is revealed. US military aircraft attack Libyan targets. Desmond Tutu is elected archbishop in South Africa. Major nuclear accident at Soviet Union's Chernobyl power plant.

1987: Iraq apologizes after its missiles killed thirty-seven in attack on US frigate *Stark* in the Persian Gulf. World War II Nazi leader Klaus Barbie sentenced to life imprisonment by French court for war crimes. In USA, Oliver North Jr. tells congressional inquiry that senior officials approved his secret Iran–Contra operations. Admiral John M. Poindex-ter, former national security adviser, testifies that he authorized use of Iran arms sale profits to aid Contras. Secretary of State George P. Shultz testifies he was deceived repeatedly on Iran–Contra affair. Defence Secretary Caspar W. Weinberger reveals official deception and intrigue. President Reagan accepts responsibility for Iran arms–Contra policy. Severe earthquake strikes Los Angeles.

1988: USA and Canada reach free trade agreement. Robert C. McFarlane, former national security adviser, pleads guilty in Iran–Contra case. US Navy ship shoots down Iranian airliner in Persian Gulf after mistaking it for a military aircraft, killing 290. Explosion on board his official aircraft kills Pakistani President Mohammad Zia ul-Haq. Pan-Am 747 crashes in Lockerbie, Scotland, killing all 259 on board and eleven on ground.

1989: US planes shoot down two Libyan fighters over international waters in Mediterranean. Emperor Hirohito of Japan dies. Iran's Ayatollah Khomeini declares author Salman Rushdie's book *The Satanic Verses* offensive and issues a fatwa on him. Tanker *Exxon Valdez* discharges 11 million gallons of crude oil into Alaska's Prince William Sound. Tens of thousands of Chinese students take over Beijing's Tiananmen Square in a pro-democracy demonstration. Thousands are killed when the Chinese authorities decide to adopt a hard-line approach towards the demonstrators. US jury convicts Oliver North in Iran–Contra affair. Mikhail S. Gorbachev becomes Soviet President. P.W. Botha quits as South Africa's President. Deng Xiaoping resigns as China's leader. Berlin Wall comes down. Czech Parliament ends Communist domination in the country. Uprising in Romania ousts communist government. President Ceausescu and his wife are executed. US troops invade Panama to capture its leader Gen. Manuel Noriega on drug-related charges. The Dalai Lama wins the Nobel Peace Prize.

1990: Start of the World Wide Web and the Internet. Gen. Manuel Noriega surrenders in Panama. Yugoslav communists end forty-five-year grip on power. Communists give up power in USSR. South Africa frees Nelson Mandela after more than twenty-seven years in prison. Hubble Space Telescope is launched. Iraqi troops invade Kuwait leading to Persian Gulf War. East and West Germany are reunited. Soviet President Gorbachev assumes emergency powers. Margaret Thatcher resigns as British prime minister after three terms in office; John Major is new prime minister. Solidarity Party leader Lech Walesa wins Poland's run-off presidential election. Haiti elects leftist priest Jean Bertrand Aristide as President in its first democratic election.

1991: US and Allies at war with Iraq. Warsaw Pact dissolves military alliance. Ceasefire ends Persian Gulf War. European countries end sanctions on South Africa. Communist government of Albania resigns. Jiang Qing, widow of Mao Zedong, commits suicide. South African Parliament repeals apartheid laws. Warsaw Pact is dissolved. Boris Yeltsin is inaugurated as the first freely elected President of Russian Republic. Lithuania, Estonia, and Latvia become independent. Haitian troops seize President Aristide in an uprising. USA suspends assistance to Haiti. Israel and Soviet Union resume relations after twenty-four years. USA indicts two Libyans in 1988 bombing of Pan Am Flight 103 over Lockerbie, Scotland. USSR breaks up after President Gorbachev resigns. Its constituent republics form Commonwealth of Independent States (CIS).

1992: Yugoslav Federation breaks up. President Bush of USA and President Yeltsin of Russia formally proclaim an end to 'Cold War'. US lifts trade sanctions against China. US recognizes three former Yugoslav republics. Former Panama leader Gen. Manuel Noriega is convicted in a US court and sentenced to forty years imprisonment on drug charges. Caspar W. Weinberger indicted in Iran–Contra affair. Last Western hostages freed in Lebanon. UN expels Serbian-dominated Yugoslavia. US forces leave the Philippines after nearly a century of American military presence. Czechoslovak Parliament approves its separation into two nations. In UK, Prince Charles and Princess Diana agree to separate. President Bush pardons former Reagan administration officials involved in Iran–Contra affair.

1993: Czechoslovakia breaks up into Czech Republic and Slovakia. Vaclav Havel is elected Czech President. USA begins airlifting of supplies to besieged Bosnia towns. President of Sri Lanka, Ranasinghe Premadasa, is assassinated. Iraq accepts UN weapons monitoring. Israel and Palestinian authorities reach an accord. President Yeltsin's forces crush a revolt in the Russian Parliament. Europe's Maastricht Treaty takes effect, creating the European Union. South Africa adopts majority rule constitution.

1994: NAFTA comes into effect. Vance–Owen peace plan for Bosnia and Herzegovina is announced. Eugene Ionesco passes away. Tutsi massacre in Rwandan capital Kigali. Nelson Mandela becomes South Africa's first black President after its first fully multiracial elections. Richard Nixon passes away. The Channel Tunnel opens. Ayrton Senna is killed. Jacqueline Kennedy passes away. Erich Honecker passes away. Israel and the Vatican establish full diplomatic ties. Fragments of Comet Shoemaker Levy 9 hit Jupiter. North Yemen occupies South Yemen capital Aden. Israel and Jordan sign the Washington Declaration. Kim Il-Sung passes away. Ferry MS *Estonia* sinks in Baltic Sea. NASA loses Magellan probe over Venus. Burt Lancaster passes away. Angolan government and UNITA rebels sign the Lusaka Protocol in Zambia. Sweden voters accept and Norwegian voters reject EU membership. Red Hat Linux 1.0 is released. Russia sends troops into Chechnya.

1995: Austria, Finland and Sweden enter the European Union World Trade Organization is established to replace GATT. Gerald Durrell, naturalist, zookeeper, author and television presenter, passes away. Steve Fossett becomes the first person to make a solo flight across the Pacific Ocean in a balloon. UK's oldest investment banking firm, Barings PLC, collapses after a securities broker, Nick Leeson, lost the bank $1.4 billion on unauthorized investments at the Tokyo Stock Exchange. Dr Bernard A. Harris, Jr. becomes the first African-American astronaut to walk in space. Nick Leeson is arrested for his role in the collapse of Barings Bank. The United Nations peacekeeping mission in Somalia ends. Astronaut Norman Thagard becomes the first American to travel to space on-board a Russian launch vehicle. The Schengen treaty comes into force. Ginger Rogers, actress, dancer, passes away. Jacques Chirac becomes the President of France. The Java programming language is launched to the public. The Bose–Einstein condensate is created for the first time. In New York City, the NASDAQ stock index closes above the 1,000 mark for the first time. Jerry Garcia, musician and lead guitarist of the Grateful Dead, passes away. A right-wing Israeli gunman, Yigal Amir, assassinates Israeli prime minister Yitzhak Rabin in Tel Aviv. The Nigerian government executes playwright and environmental activist Ken Saro-Wiwa along with eight others from the Movement for the Survival of the Ogoni People. The European Union and Israel enter into a comprehensive Treaty of Association negotiated and signed by Javier Solana and Shimon Peres. The Dow Jones Industrial Average closes above 5,000 (5,023.55) for the first time. The last new *Calvin and Hobbes* cartoon strip is published .

Last Ten Years in Review

1996

January: Yasser Arafat is elected president of the Palestinian Authority. Andreas Papandreou, prime minister of Greece, resigns due to health problems and a new government is formed under Costas Simitis. Polish Premier Jozef Oleksy resigns amid charges that he spied for Moscow. US First Lady Hillary Rodham Clinton testifies before a grand jury in the Whitewater scandal. President Jacques Chirac of France announces a 'definitive end' to French nuclear testing. An explosives-filled truck explodes at the Central Bank in Colombo, Sri Lanka, killing at least eighty-six and injuring 1,400. François Mitterrand, French politician and former President of France, passes away.

February: Recently defected Iraqi weapons programme leader and Saddam Hussein's son-in-law, Hussein Kamel, is murdered on his return to Iraq.

March: Iraqi authorities cause a delay of seventeen hours in providing UNSCOM inspection teams access to five sites designated for inspection. John Howard becomes prime minister of Australia. US President Bill Clinton commits $100 million to an anti-terrorism agreement with Israel. The British government announces that bovine spongiform encephalopathy (BSE) or Mad Cow Disease is likely to have been transmitted to humans. The Republic of China (Taiwan) holds its first direct elections for president, electing Lee Teng-hui as president. The International Monetary Fund (IMF) approves a $10.2 billion loan to Russia for economic reform.

April: In USA, suspected 'Unabomber' Theodore Kaczynski is arrested.

May: In USA, ValuJet's Douglas DC-9 Flight 592 on a Miami–Atlanta trip crashes in the Florida Everglades region killing all on board. Russian President Boris Yeltsin meets with Chechnya rebels for the first time and negotiates a ceasefire in the ongoing First Chechnya War.

June: UNSCOM supervises the destruction of Al-Hakam, Iraq's main biological warfare agents production facility. USA fails to build support for military action against Iraq in the UN Security Council even as Iraq continues to refuse access to a number of sites. A bomb explosion hits Manchester City Centre in UK. Nineteen US servicemen are killed in a bombing attack at Khobar Towers in Saudi Arabia. Ella Fitzgerald, jazz singer, passes away. Andreas Papandreou, Greek former prime minister, passes away.

July: Dolly the sheep, the first mammal to be successfully cloned from an adult cell, is born. Iraqi officials block UN Inspector Ritter's attempt to conduct surprise inspections on the Republican Guard facility. Martina Hingis becomes the youngest person in history (age fifteen years and 282 days) to win at Wimbledon when she takes the Ladies Doubles event. A Paris-bound Boeing 747 operating as TWA flight 800 explodes off the coast of Long Island killing all 230 on board. The 1996 Summer Olympics start in Atlanta, Georgia, USA.

August: NASA announces that the ALH 84001 meteorite, believed to have originated from Mars, contains evidence of primitive life forms. In UK, Prince Charles and Princess Diana are formally divorced at the High Court in London. Iraqi forces launch an offensive into the northern no-fly zone and capture Arbil.

September: In Afghanistan, the Taliban capture capital city Kabul.

October: Opening statements in the O.J. Simpson trial begin in the USA.

November: Bill Clinton defeats Bob Dole in the US presidential election. UNSCOM inspectors discover buried prohibited missile parts. Iraq refuses to allow UNSCOM teams to remove remnants of missile engines for analysis outside of the country. NASA launches the Mars Global Surveyor. Mother Teresa gets honorary US citizenship.

December: In Afghanistan, Taliban forces retake the strategic Bagram air base. The Guatemalan government and leaders of Guatemalan National Revolutionary Union sign a peace accord that ends a thirty-six-year civil war. Saddam Hussein's son Uday Hussein is seriously injured in an assassination attempt. Carl Sagan, US astronomer, passes away.

1997

January: Yasser Arafat returns to Hebron after more than thirty years and joins celebrations over the handover of the last Israeli-controlled West Bank city. Bill Clinton starts his second term as President of the United States. Madeleine Albright becomes the first female Secretary of State after confirmation by the US Senate. Clyde Tombaugh, astronomer and discoverer of Pluto, passes away.

February: O. J. Simpson is found to have civil liabilities for the deaths of Nicole Brown Simpson and Ron Goldman. The so-called 'Big Three' banks in Switzerland announce the creation of a $71 million fund to aid Holocaust survivors and their families. Morgan Stanley and Dean Witter investment banks announce a $10 billion merger. Astronauts from the space shuttle Discovery carry out repair work on the Hubble Space Telescope. The last of the People's Republic of China's major revolutionary leaders, Deng Xiaoping, passes away.

March: US President Bill Clinton bans federal funding for any research on human cloning. Picasso's work *Tete de Femme* is stolen from a London gallery but is recovered a week later. In one of Japan's worst nuclear accidents, an explosion at a nuclear waste reprocessing plant exposes thirty-five workers to low-level radioactive contamination. Thirty-nine found dead in the Heaven's Gate cult suicide.

April: A 126-day hostage crisis at the residence of the Japanese ambassador in Lima, Peru, ends after government commandos storm and capture the building and rescue seventy-one hostages. Allen Ginsberg, US poet, passes away.

May: In UK, Labour Party victory in the general election ends eighteen years of Conservative rule. Labour Party leader Tony Blair appointed prime minister of the United Kingdom. An earthquake near Ardekul in north-eastern Iran kills at least 2,400. IBM's chess computer Deep Blue defeats Garry Kasparov.

June: Timothy McVeigh is sentenced to death for his role in the 1995 terrorist bombing of the Alfred P. Murrah Federal Building in Oklahoma City, Oklahoma. In Cambodia, Khmer Rouge leader Pol Pot orders the killing of his defence chief Son Sen and eleven of Sen's family members.

July: UK hands over sovereignty of Hong Kong to the People's Republic of China. NASA's Pathfinder space probe lands on the surface of Mars. NATO invites the Czech Republic, Hungary and Poland to join the organization in 1999. In Miami, Florida, USA, serial killer Andrew Phillip Cunanan kills fashion designer Gianni Versace outside his home. The F.W. Woolworth Company closes after more than 100 years in business.

August: Aviation giants Boeing and McDonnell Douglas complete their merger. Microsoft buys a $150 million share of Apple Computer. The Independent International Commission on

Decommissioning is set up in Northern Ireland, as part of the peace process. Diana, Princess of Wales, is severely injured in a car crash in Paris on 31 August and dies the next day.

September: Scotland votes to create its own Parliament after nearly 300 years of union with England. Agnes Gonxha Bojaxhiu, better known as Mother Teresa, passes away.

October: Iraq threatens to shoot down U-2 surveillance planes being used by UNSCOM inspectors.

November: Telecom giants WorldCom and MCI announce a US $37 billion merger to form MCI–WorldCom. Mary McAleese is elected President of Ireland. After nearly eighteen years of imprisonment, pro-democracy dissident Wei Jingsheng is released in the People's Republic of China releases for medical reasons.

December: Hong Kong starts killing all the chickens within its territory to stop the spread of a potentially lethal influenza strain.

1998

January: Russia begins to circulate a new ruble to curb inflation and promote confidence. The Lunar Prospector spacecraft is launched into orbit around the Moon. It finds evidence of frozen water on the moon's surface. Ramzi Yousef is sentenced to life in prison for planning the World Trade Center bombing. European nations agree to forbid human cloning. Paula Jones accuses President Bill Clinton of sexual harassment. Bill Clinton denies, on American television, that he had 'sexual relations' with former White House intern Monica Lewinsky. US First Lady Hillary Rodham Clinton appears on television calling the attacks against her husband part of a right-wing conspiracy. In USA, suspected 'Unabomber' Theodore Kaczynski pleads guilty and accepts a sentence of life without the possibility of parole.

February: An earthquake measuring 6.1 on the Richter scale hits north-east Afghanistan killing more than 5,000. Crown Prince Abdullah becomes the ruler of Jordan by decree of his father, King Hussein. Iraqi President Saddam Hussein negotiates a deal with UN Secretary General Kofi Annan, allowing the return of weapons inspectors to Baghdad and thus preventing US and British military action. Osama bin Laden publishes fatwa declaring jihad against all 'Jews and Crusaders'.

March: Data from the Galileo probe indicate that Jupiter's moon Europa has a liquid ocean under a thick crust of ice. An earthquake measuring 6.9 on the Richter scale hits south-eastern Iran. *Titanic* wins eleven Oscars at the Academy Awards ceremony. In USA, the government approves Viagra for use as a treatment for male impotence. Benjamin Spock, pediatrician, writer, Olympian, passes away.

April: UNSCOM reports to the UN Security Council that Iraq's declaration on its biological weapons programme is incomplete and inadequate. On Good Friday, the Belfast Agreement is signed between the Irish and British governments and most Northern Ireland political parties. In Japan, the Akashi-Kaikyo Bridge linking Shikoku with Honshu opens to traffic, becoming the largest suspension bridge in the world. The Cambodian dictator, Pol Pot, passes away.

May: Apple Computer unveils the iMac. Mercedes-Benz buys Chrysler for US $40 billion and forms Daimler Chrysler. The US Department of Justice and twenty US states file an anti-trust case against Microsoft. Indonesian President Suharto resigns after thirty-two years as President and seventh consecutive re-elections. Vice-President B. J. Habibie becomes new President. An earthquake of magnitude 6.6 on the Richter scale hits northern Afghanistan killing up to 5,000. Frank Sinatra, singer, actor, passes away.

June: An ICE high-speed train derails at Eschede, Germany, causing 101 deaths.

July: In St. Petersburg, Nicholas II of Russia and his family are buried in St. Catherine Chapel, eighty years after being killed by the Bolsheviks. A tsunami triggered by an undersea earthquake destroys ten villages in Papua New Guinea, killing an estimated 1,500, leaving 2,000 more unaccounted for and thousands more homeless. Former White House intern, Monica Lewinsky, receives transactional immunity in exchange for her grand jury testimony concerning her relationship with US President Bill Clinton.

August: Iraq officially suspends all cooperation with UNSCOM teams. Bombing of the US embassies in Dar es Salaam, Tanzania, and Nairobi, Kenya, kills 224 people and injures over 4,500. In retaliation, the United States military launches cruise missile attacks against alleged al-Qaeda camps in Afghanistan and a suspected chemical plant in Sudan. US President Bill Clinton admits in taped testimony that he had an 'improper physical relationship' with White House intern Monica Lewinsky. On the same day he admits before the nation that he 'misled people' about his relationship.

September: A McDonnell Douglas MD-11 airliner operating as Swissair flight 111 crashes near Peggy's Cove, Nova Scotia, while flying from New York City to Geneva. All 229 people on board are killed. The US Congress passes the 'Iraq Liberation Act' that states the US government's intention to remove Saddam Hussein from power in Iraq and replace the government with a democratic institution. Akira Kurosawa, Japanese film director, passes away. Florence 'Flo-Jo' Griffith-Joyner, track and field sprinter, passes away.

October: In South Africa, the Truth and Reconciliation Commission presents its report, condemning both sides for committing atrocities. 77-year old John Glenn, the first American to orbit Earth, becomes the oldest person to go into space when he is launched on board space shuttle, Discovery.

November: US President Clinton orders air strikes on Iraq but calls it off at the last minute when Iraq promises unconditional support to UNSCOM. UNSCOM inspectors subsequently return to Iraq. The US House of Representatives' Judiciary Committee begins impeachment hearings against US President Bill Clinton. Deutsche Bank announces a US $10 billion deal to buy Bankers Trust, thus creating one of the largest financial institutions in the world.

December: US President Clinton orders American and British air strikes on Iraq. UNSCOM withdraws all weapons inspectors from Iraq. Iraq announces its intention to fire upon US and British warplanes that patrol the northern and southern no-fly zones.

1999

January: The EU common currency, the Euro, is introduced. An earthquake measuring 6.0 on the Richter scale hits western Colombia killing at least 1,000.

February: The United States Senate acquits US President Bill Clinton in his impeachment trial. Kurdish rebels take over embassies across Europe and hold hostages after Turkey arrests Kurdish leader Abdullah Ocalan. Olusegun Obasanjo becomes Nigeria's first elected President since 1983. Former boxing champion Mike Tyson is sentenced to one year in prison for an August 1998 assault on two people following a car accident. King Hussein of Jordan passes away.

March: In its first-ever attack on a sovereign country, NATO launches air strikes on Federal Republic of Yugoslavia. A fire in the Mont Blanc Tunnel in Europe kills thirty-nine people and closes the tunnel for nearly three years. Hungary, Poland and the Czech Republic join NATO. Bertrand Piccard and Brian Jones become the first to circumnavigate the Earth in a hot-air balloon. The Angolan embassy in Lusaka, Zambia, is destroyed in an explosion. In New York City, the Dow Jones Industrial Average closes above the 10,000 mark for the first time. Stanley Kubrick, American film director and writer, passes away. Joe DiMaggio, American baseball player, passes away. American violinist Yehudi Menuhin passes away,

April: Serbian forces close Kosovo's main border crossings to prevent ethnic Albanians from leaving. Columbine High School massacre takes place as two teenagers named Eric Harris and Dylan Klebold open fire on their teachers and fellow students in Littleton, Colorado, killing twelve students and one teacher, after which they take their own lives. Nunavut, an Inuit homeland, part of the Northwest Territories, becomes Canada's third territory. Two Libyans suspected of causing the crash of Pan Am flight 103 in 1988 are handed over for trial in the Netherlands.

May: Elections are held in Scotland and Wales for the new Scottish Parliament and National Assembly for Wales. Ehud Barak is elected prime minister of Israel. The International Criminal Tribunal for the former Yugoslavia in The Hague, Netherlands, indicts Slobodan Milosevic and four others for war crimes and crimes against humanity committed in Kosovo. Leonardo da Vinci's masterpiece *The Last Supper* is put back on display in Milan, Italy, after twenty-two years of restoration work.

June: Federal Republic of Yugoslavia and NATO sign a peace treaty. The Kosovo War nears an end when NATO suspends its air strikes after Slobodan Milosevic agrees to withdraw Serbian forces from Kosovo. Operation Joint Guardian begins as NATO-led UN peacekeeping force KFor enter Kosovo. The government of Colombia announces it will include the estimated value of the country's illegal drug crops, over half a billion US dollars, in its GNP.

July: A plane piloted by John F. Kennedy Jr crashes off the coast of Martha's Vineyard. His wife Carolyn Bessette Kennedy and her sister Lauren Bessette were on board and all three are killed.

August: Russian President Boris Yeltsin removes his Sergei Stepashin, and his entire cabinet. An earthquake of magnitude 7.4 on the Richter scale hits north-western Turkey, killing more than 17,000 and injuring 44,000.

September: Former US Senator John Danforth is appointed the head of an independent investigation of the 1993 fire at the Branch Davidian compound in Waco, Texas.

October: A military coup led by Pakistani Army Chief General Pervez Musharraf ousts the government of Prime Minister Nawaz Sharif and takes control of Pakistan. The US Senate rejects ratification of the Comprehensive Test Ban Treaty (CTBT). EgyptAir Flight 990 on a New York City to Cairo flight crashes off the coast of Massachusetts, killing all 217 on board. The world human population crosses six billion.

November: Australians vote to keep the British Queen as their head of state.

December: UK devolves political power in Northern Ireland to the Northern Ireland Executive. Tori Murden becomes the first woman to cross the Atlantic Ocean by rowboat alone when she reaches Guadeloupe from the Canary Islands. Algerian Ahmed Ressam is arrested while crossing the United States–Canada border when United States Customs finds explosives in the trunk of his vehicle. He is later convicted in a plot to bomb Los Angeles International Airport on New Year's Eve.

2000

January: America Online (AOL) announces an agreement to buy Time Warner for $162 billion making it the largest-ever corporate merger. A UN tribunal sentences five Bosnian Croats up to twenty-five years for the 1993 killing of over 100 Muslims in a Bosnian village.

February: Charles M. Schulz, creator of the *Peanuts* comic strip, passes away.

March: The Constitution of Finland is rewritten. Chen Shui-bian is elected President of the Republic of China (Taiwan). Vladimir Putin is elected President in Russia.

April: Yoshiro Mori replaces the ailing Keizo Obuchi as prime minister of Japan. Microsoft is ruled to have violated US anti-trust laws.

May: Portions of Lebanese land are liberated after twenty-two years of Israeli occupation. Barbara Cartland, romance novel author, passes away. British actor Sir John Gielgud passes away.

June: Hafez al-Assad, President of Syria, passes away.

July: A Concorde supersonic passenger jet crashes soon after take-off from Paris killing all 109 aboard and five on the ground. Russian submarine *Kursk* sinks in the Barents Sea with the loss of all lives on board.

August: British actor Sir Alec Guinness passes away.

September: The 2000 Summer Olympics start in Sydney, Australia. The United Nations Millennium Summit begins in New York City.

October: In Aden, Yemen, the US destroyer USS *Cole* is severely damaged in a suicide attack launched by a small boat laden with explosives.

November: Iraq rejects new UN Security Council weapons inspection proposals Republican George W. Bush defeats Democrat Vice-President Al Gore in the US presidential election, but the final result is delayed for over a month because of disputed votes in Florida. Hillary Rodham Clinton is elected to the United States Senate. She is the first First Lady of the United States to win a public office. Jean Chrétien is re-elected as the Canadian prime minister. Netscape Navigator version 6.0 is launched. Bill Clinton becomes the first serving US President to visit Vietnam.

December: A series of bombs explode in various places in Metro Manila, Philippines, within a span of a few hours, killing twenty-two and injuring nearly 100 more. In Mexico, Vicente Fox becomes the new President.

2001

January: A major earthquake measuring 7.6 on the Richter scale hits El Salvador. George W. Bush succeeds Bill Clinton as President of the United States. In the Netherlands, a Scottish court convicts a Libyan agent but acquits another for their part in the bombing of Pan Am Flight 103 that crashed at Lockerbie, Scotland, in 1988. Laurent-Desire Kabila, President of the Democratic Republic of the Congo is assassinated.

February: British and US forces carry out bombing raids attempting to disable Iraq's air defence network. Likud Party leader Ariel Sharon wins election as prime minister of Israel. American submarine USS *Greeneville* accidentally strikes and sinks Japanese fishing vessel *Ehime-Maru*. NEAR Shoemaker spacecraft touches down on asteroid 433 Eros, becoming the first spacecraft to land on an asteroid. US and UK warplanes bomb Baghdad suburb. Foot-and-mouth disease crisis begins in UK. Cricket legend Sir Donald Bradman passes away.

March: Apple Computer's Mac OS X version 10.0 is released. Author Robert Ludlum passes away.

April: Former President of the Federal Republic of Yugoslavia, Slobodan

Milosevic, surrenders to police special forces. In the Netherlands, the Act on the Opening up of Marriage allowing same-sex couples to marry legally comes into effect for the first time in the world.

May: The Japanese cities of Urawa, Omiya and Yono merge to form the city of Saitama. Government officials in the People's Republic of China put Zhonghua Sun to death because she refused to be sterilized, in violation of the country's one-child policy. Thirty-two-year old Erik Weihenmayer, from Boulder, Colorado, USA, becomes the first blind person to reach the summit of Mount Everest.

June: King Birendra, Queen Aishwarya and other members of the Nepalese royal family are killed when Crown Prince Dipendra goes on a drunken shooting spree. The prince then shoots himself. Although the wounded prince is proclaimed the new king, he succumbs to his injuries and King Birendra's brother, Prince Gyanendra, is crowned the new king. Tony Blair's Labour Party is elected for a second term in UK general election. In USA, Timothy McVeigh is executed for the 1995 Oklahoma City bombing. General Pervez Musharraf takes over as President of Pakistan.

July: The world's first self-contained artificial heart implanted in a patient, Robert Tools. British politician and novelist Jeffrey Archer is sentenced to four years in prison for perjury and perverting the course of justice.

August: US President George W. Bush announces his support for federal funding of limited research on embryonic stem cells.

September: The United States Justice Department announces that it is no longer seeking to break-up Microsoft and will instead seek a lesser anti-trust penalty. In Afghanistan, Ahmed Shah Massoud, leader of the Northern Alliance, is assassinated. Around 3,000 killed in the 11 September 2001(9/11) attack on the World Trade Center in New York City, The Pentagon in Arlington, Virginia, and rural Pennsylvania. Christiaan Barnard, South African heart surgeon who was the first to perform a human-to-human heart transplant, passes away.

October: First case of anthrax attack in the USA is reported. US attack on Afghanistan begins. US President George W. Bush presents a list of twenty-two most wanted terrorists.

November: At the Doha Round of World Trade Organization conference, the Doha Declaration relaxes the international intellectual property laws. The supersonic commercial aircraft Concorde resumes flying after a fifteen-month break. Microsoft releases the X-*Box* console gaming system to the public. In New York City, an Airbus A300 carrying American Airlines Flight 587 crashes minutes after takeoff from John F. Kennedy International Airport, killing all 260 on board. Taliban forces abandon Kabul, the capital of Afghanistan, ahead of advancing Northern Alliance troops who then capture the city. In the first such instance since World War II, US President George W. Bush signs an executive order allowing military tribunals against any foreigners suspected of having connections to terrorist acts or planned acts on the United States. The first Harry Potter film, *Harry Potter and the Sorcerer's Stone*, is released. Nintendo releases the *Gamecube* console gaming system to the public. Former Beatle George Harrison passes away.

December: Enron files for Chapter 11 bankruptcy protection. The People's Republic of China gains permanent normal trade status with the United States.

2002

January: Euro banknotes and coins become legal tender in twelve member states of the European Union. Enron hearings begin. Kenneth Lay, CEO of the bankrupt Enron Corporation, resigns. Terrorist suspect John Walker Lindh's hearing begins.

February: Prince Willem-Alexander of the Netherlands, heir to the Dutch throne, marries Máxima Zorreguieta Cerruti in Amsterdam.

March: Elizabeth Bowes-Lyon, the British Queen Mother, passes away. Israeli ground troops invade the West Bank and Gaza Strip while dozens of tanks occupy Ramallah.

April: Ten nations deposit their ratifications for the International Criminal Court at a UN ceremony, bringing the total to sixty-six. A minimum of sixty was needed to bring the statute into force. Hugo Chávez returns to power in Venezuela barely days after a coup.

May: Jacques Chirac wins the French presidential elections. East Timor becomes an independent state. The media reports that the NASA space probe Mars Odyssey has found signs of huge ice deposits on the planet Mars. A wordless ceremony takes place at the World Trade Center site to mark the end of the recovery effort.

June: Accountants Arthur Andersen convicted of obstructing justice by shredding documents related to the Enron inquiry. The World Health Organization declares Europe polio-free. A major earthquake hits Iran with its epicentre at Bou'in-Zahra and having a magnitude of at least 6.0 on the Richter scale.

July: Assassination attempt on French President Jacques Chirac during Bastille Day celebrations. John Walker Lindh, the American who was found fighting for the Taliban in Afghanistan, pleads guilty to two charges. In the Netherlands, a new Cabinet is sworn in with Jan Peter Balkenende replacing Wim Kok as prime minister. An Israeli F-16 jet drops a bomb into a densely populated residential area of Gaza City killing 15 people including Salah Shehade, the leader of Hamas's military wing, a few hours after the spiritual leader of Hamas, Ahmed Yassin, offered to stop all suicide attacks in exchange for full Israeli withdrawal from the West Bank and Gaza Strip. WorldCom files for bankruptcy protection. First near-earth object to be given a positive rating on the Palermo Technical Impact Hazard Scale for potential Earth collision is 2002 NT7 with a potential impact on 1 February 2019. A series of bomb blasts occurs in the Christian districts of the city of Ambon in Indonesia. The Homeland Security Bill is passed by the US House of Representatives.

August: Explosions take place near the Parliament building in Bogota as Colombia's President Álvaro Uribe is being sworn in. At least ten people are killed. WorldCom announces it has discovered $3.3 billion in false accounting in addition to the $3.8 billion found earlier. Colombian President Álvaro Uribe declares state of emergency. Russian President Vladimir Putin announces that Belarus will be fully integrated into Russia and each of Belarus's six provinces will become a separate republic within the Russian Federation. US Airways declares bankruptcy.

September: President Hamid Karzai of Afghanistan survives an assassination attempt in Kandahar. Ramzi Binalshibh, a key al-Qaeda member who is believed to have taken part in the planning of the 11 September 2001 attack is held in Pakistan. Switzerland becomes a full member of the UN. Hundreds of thousands join marches in London, UK and Rome, Italy, and thousands march in Denver, Colorado, to protest the US plan to invade Iraq. East Timor becomes the 191st member of the United Nations. Colin Powell meets with the UN Security Council for stronger resolutions against Iraq. Iraq tells the UN it will allow weapons inspectors immediately and unconditionally. Belgium becomes the second European country to legalize euthanasia.

The governor of the Philippine state of Palawan sends Philippine soldiers to take possession of the uninhabited oil-rich Spratly Islands. Gerhard Schröder defeats Edmund Stoiber to remain the chancellor in Germany. Israel destroys buildings in Yasser Arafat's Ramallah headquarters after a suicide bomber killed five and wounded more than sixty on a Tel Aviv bus. The Bush administration pressures Congress to pass a resolution giving President Bush authority to use all means, including force, to remove Saddam Hussein and disarm Iraq. Archaeologists use a remote-controlled robot to access a sealed chamber within the Great Pyramid of Giza.

October: Suspected Chechen guerrillas take hundreds of hostages when they seize a theatre in Moscow. They demand the withdrawal of Russian troops from Chechnya. Later, special forces of the Russian army attack the Chechen separatists. Fifty of the fifty-three separatists and over 100 of the 800 hostages are killed. A bomb explodes outside a nightclub on the Indonesian island of Bali, killing around 200 people, most of them foreign holiday-makers. Around 200 more are injured. Hundreds of Israeli soldiers backed by tanks and other military vehicles take control of the Palestinian city of Jenin in response to a suicide bombing that killed fourteen people. The discovery of a planetoid named Quaoar circling the Sun is announced. The European Commission of the European Union announces that ten countries have met its criteria for entry, paving the way for an expansion of the EU from fifteen member states to twenty-five. The US Senate votes to give war powers to President George W. Bush. Former US President Jimmy Carter is awarded the Nobel Peace Prize. Leftist Luis Inacio 'Lula' da Silva wins Brazil's presidential election. A bomb explodes in suburban Manila, destroying a bus and killing at least three people, while twenty-three others are wounded. Kenyan President Daniel Arap Moi dissolves the country's Parliament to officially start the campaign for general elections and ending his tenure as one of Africa's longest-ruling leaders. Canadian author Yann Martel wins the Booker Prize for *Life of Pi*. In the Netherlands, the new cabinet of PM Balkenende resigns because of constant internal fighting. UK takes back control of the local government in Northern Ireland.

November: An earthquake kills twenty-nine in the town of San Giuliano di Puglia, in Campobasso, Molise, Italy. An earthquake of magnitude 7.9 strikes Denali fault in Denali National Park in Alaska. In Yemen an American missile destroys a car carrying what the United States claims were six al-Qaeda members, including the mastermind of the USS *Cole* attack, Qaed Salim Sinan al-Harethi. Israel's PM, Ariel Sharon, dissolves Parliament and calls for elections early next year. USA signs the International Treaty on Plant Genetic Resources for Food and Agriculture. Iran bans advertising of US products. Democratic Party members of the United States House of Representatives choose California Representative Nancy Pelosi as their minority leader. She is the first woman to lead a major American party. Human clinical trials of a new HIV vaccine developed by researchers at the US National Institute of Allergy and Infectious Diseases start. Three suicide bombers detonate themselves at a hotel in Mombasa, Kenya, killing a number of people including Israeli tourists. At the same time two anti-aircraft missiles miss a passenger aircraft taking off at Mombassa airport. Henry Kissinger is appointed chairman of the independent panel investigating the September 11 attacks on America. British intelligence agency MI5A uncovers a plot to release poison gas in the London underground railway network. The first UN arms inspectors' team arrive in Iraq and prepare for inspections for evidence of the development or possession of weapons of mass destruction. An Italian court sentences former prime minister Giulio Andreotti to twenty-four years in prison for his involvement in the 1979 murder of journalist Mino Pecorelli. The Miss World contest is shifted to London following riots and killings in Nigeria. The tanker *Prestige* which has been leaking oil off the north-west coast of Spain for several days, splits into two. Despite efforts, the oil reaches the coast. The controversial physician Severino Antinori claims that a project to clone human beings has succeeded, with the first human clone due to be born in 2003. The Clonaid organization also announces that they have five clones waiting to be born, one of whom would be born in December 2002. US President George W. Bush signs into law the creation of a new Department of Homeland Security.

December: President Pierre Buyoya of Burundi and Pierre Nkurunziza, leader of the Hutu insurgents' Forces for the Defence of Democracy (FDD), sign a ceasefire accord at Arusha, Tanzania, in a bid to end the nine-year civil war. In Venezuela, opposition intensifies its attempt to remove President Hugo Chávez from power. Israeli troops, tanks and helicopter gunships move into the Bureij refugee camp in the Gaza Strip. Two paintings by Vincent van Gogh are stolen from the Van Gogh Museum in Amsterdam. North Korea expels UN weapons inspectors, and announces plans to reactivate a dormant nuclear fuel-processing laboratory. A US federal judge orders Microsoft to distribute Sun Microsystem's Java programming language in its Microsoft Windows operating system. Scientists at California-based VaxGen Inc. finishes the first human trial of an AIDS vaccine. Palestinian leader Yasser Arafat announces the cancellation of presidential and legislative elections scheduled for January 2003. US officials state that Iraq has failed to account for all its chemical and biological agents and that Iraq is in material breach of a United Nations Security Council resolution. In the Congo, government, rebels and Opposition parties sign a peace accord to end four years of civil war and set up a transitional government. Former Bosnian Serb President Biljana Plavsic pleads guilty to crimes against humanity at The Hague tribunal for her part in persecuting Bosnian Muslims and Croats during the 1992–95 conflict. Former US vice-president and 2000 presidential candidate Al Gore announces that he will not seek election to the presidency in 2004. Henry Kissinger steps down as the chairman of a panel investigating the 11 September attacks citing conflict of interest with his clients. The European Union invites the Czech Republic, Cyprus, Estonia, Hungary, Latvia, Lithuania, Malta, Poland, Slovakia, and Slovenia to join when the EU is scheduled for its next expansion in May 2004. First flight of the ESC-A variant of the Ariane 5 ends in failure and the rocket and the two communications satellites it was carrying are destroyed a few minutes after lift-off from Kourou, French Guiana. The government of Indonesia and rebel leaders from the province of Aceh in north Sumatra sign a peace accord.

2003

January: Facing worldwide criticism and against the wishes of the majorities of their own electorates, leaders of Britain, Spain, Italy, Portugal, Hungary, Poland, Denmark, and the Czech Republic release a statement, the letter of the eight, demonstrating support for the United States' plans for an invasion of Iraq. Leopoldo Galtieri, former Argentine dictator, passes away. Maurice Gibb, musician, passes away. Gianni Agnelli, president of Italian carmaker Fiat, passes away.

February: The Space Shuttle Columbia disintegrates over Texas upon re-entry, killing all seven astronauts on board. The dead astronauts include Indian-born Kalpana Chawla and the first Israeli to go to space, Ilan Ramon. US Secretary of State Colin Powell addresses the UN Security Council on Iraq. Global protests against war on Iraq take place as more than six million people protest in over 600 cities worldwide. Dolly the sheep, the world's first cloned mammal, dies.

March: The United Arab Emirates, Bahrain and Kuwait urge Iraqi president Saddam Hussein to step down to avoid another war. Authorities in Pakistan capture Khalid Shaikh Mohammed, suspected mastermind of the 11 September 2001 attacks. Iraqi fighter aircraft threaten two US U-2 surveillance planes on missions for UN weapons inspectors forcing them to abort their mission and return to base. Arab media reports that Saddam Hussein has opened terrorist training camps in Iraq for Arab volunteers who are willing to carry out suicide bombings against US forces if a US-led attack takes place. Serbian prime minister Zoran Djindjic assassinated in Belgrade. WHO issues a global alert on SARS. Media reports claim that 350,000-year-old upright-walking human footprints have been found in Italy. Hu Jintao becomes President of the People's Republic of China, replacing Jiang Zemin. On 17 March US President George W. Bush gives an ultimatum: Iraqi leader Saddam Hussein and his sons must either leave Iraq within forty-eight hours or face military action at a time of the US's choosing. President Saddam Hussein and his sons do not comply with this ultimatum. On 19 March, the first American bombs are dropped on Baghdad. On 20 March, land troops from USA, UK, Australia and Poland invade Iraq. On 22 March, USA and UK begin their 'shock and awe' campaign with a massive air strike on military targets in Baghdad. Cricket World Cup in South Africa ends as Australia win over India. Boxer Roy Jones Jr. beats John Ruiz to become WBA champion. WHO doctor Carlo Urbani, who first identified SARS, dies of the disease.

April: US forces seize control of Baghdad. This event is considered to be the end point of the regime of Saddam Hussein. Retired US Army General Jay Garner becomes interim civil administrator of Iraq. Dr Robert Atkins, who developed the Atkins Nutritional Approach, passes away.

May: George W. Bush lands on the aircraft carrier USS *Abraham Lincoln* and gives a speech announcing the end of major combat in the Iraq War. A female homicide bomber blows up explosives strapped to her waist in a crowd of thousands of Muslim pilgrims, killing at least eighteen people in Chechnya. The attack is seen as an attempt on the life of President Akhmad Kadyrov. A draft version of the proposed European Constitution is unveiled. Three hundredth anniversary celebration of Saint Petersburg, Russia, begins.

June: A female bomber detonates a bomb near a bus carrying soldiers and civilians to a military airfield in Mozdok, a key staging point for Russian troops in Chechnya, killing at least sixteen people. Actor Gregory Peck passes away. Actress Katharine Hepburn passes away.

July: WHO declares that SARS has been contained. British government scientist Dr David Kelly's body is found a few miles from his home in UK. Actor and comedian Bob Hope passes away.

August: A bomber drives a truck filled with explosives into a military hospital near Chechnya, killing fifty people including Russian troops. Scientists announce that the ozone layer may be showing signs of recovery. NATO takes over command of the peacekeeping force in Afghanistan. This is its first major operation outside Europe. Jemaah Islamiah leader. Widespread power outage hits north-east USA and Canada. Former Ugandan dictator Idi Amin passes away. Sérgio Vieira de Mello, Brazilian diplomat and statesman, is killed in an attack on the UN coumpund in Baghdad. Charles Bronson, actor, passes away.

September: Swedish Foreign Minister Anna Lindh is stabbed to death in a Stockholm department store. Sweden rejects adopting the Euro in a referendum. Estonia approves joining the EU in a referendum. American movie director Elia Kazan passes away.

October: Ahmed Qurei is new Palestine prime minister. China launches its first astronaut, Yang Liwei, into orbit. D.B.C. Pierre wins the Booker Prize. Pope beatifies Mother Teresa. Final Concorde flight from New York to London takes place. Mahathir bin Mohamad retires, Badawi is the new PM of Malaysia.

November: President Kumaratunga suspends Sri Lankan parliament and deploys troops. UN votes in favour of a resolution to end sanctions against Cuba. Junichiro Koizumi wins the general elections in Japan. Arnold Schwarzenegger is sworn in as California governor. Michael Jackson surrenders to the police in USA. Georgian opposition supporters seize the Parliament building in the capital city T'bilisi.

December: Zimbabwe withdraws from the Commonwealth of Nations. US forces capture Saddam Hussein. Pervez Musharraf survives two assassination attempts. British scientists fail to make contact with its Mars probe, Beagle 2. A powerful earthquake destroys 70 per cent of the southern Iranian city of Bam, including the ancient Bam Citadel; the initial death toll is estimated at 40,000.

2004

January: The Republic of Ireland takes over the presidency of the European Union. The first of the NASA Mars Exploration Rovers, Spirit, successfully lands on the planet and starts transmitting signals. In Afghanistan, the Grand Council, the Loya Jirga, adopts a new Constitution of Afghanistan. Mikhail Saakashvili wins the Presidential elections of the Republic of Georgia. The inquest into the death of Diana, Princess of Wales, and Dodi Al-Fayed is officially opened. US lifestyle guru Martha Stewart pleads not guilty to five criminal counts that include conspiracy, obstruction of justice and securities fraud arising from a 2001 stock sale. Indonesia announces that millions of birds have died from avian flu in the last few months. The People's Republic of China announces an outbreak of the H5N1 strain of avian influenza in its Guangxi autonomous region. Senator John Kerry wins the New Hampshire primary round of the 2004 US presidential election. In UK, the Hutton Inquiry report is released and absolves the British government and Prime Minister Tony Blair of any wrongdoing in David Kelly's death. The discovery of a new form of matter, Fermionic condensate, is announced.

February: A team of Russian scientists and another of US scientists report the discovery of two new chemical elements. These are elements 113, given the temporary name Ununtrium (Uut), and element 115, designated Ununpentium (Uup). Pakistan removes Abdul Qadeer Khan, the founder of Pakistan's nuclear weapons programme, as a special adviser to the prime minister. Abdul Qadeer Khan later confesses to smuggling nuclear hardware, sharing secret designs necessary to develop a nuclear weapon, and giving personal briefings to nuclear scientists from Libya, Iran, and North Korea. Astronomers detect the presence of oxygen and carbon in the atmosphere of an extra-solar planet, provisionally named Osiris. Sri Lankan

President Chandrika Kumaratunga dissolves the parliament. Nearly 400 members of Yasser Arafat's Fatah faction of the PLO resign in protest over corruption and mismanagement. Senator John Kerry wins the caucuses in in the race for the Democratic presidential nomination. South Korean scientists announce what they claim to be the world's first successfully cloned human embryo. Scientists at the California Institute of Technology announce the discovery of a galaxy that is the farthest known object in the universe. Iran offers to sell nuclear reactor fuel on the international market under the supervision of the International Atomic Energy Agency. Haitian President Jean-Bertrand Aristide resigns as president of Haiti and escapes to Central African Republic.

March: Russian President Vladimir Putin names Mikhail Fradkov as his new prime minister. USA, France and Canada sends in hundreds of troops to Haiti. The Serbian parliament approves a new government headed by Vojislav Kostunica. Libya admits to having stockpiled 23 metric tons of mustard gas in its declaration to the Organization for the Prohibition of Chemical Weapons in The Hague. New Democracy led by Costas Karamanlis defeats the Panhellenic Socialist Movement led by George Papandreou in the 2004 Greek legislative election. Iraq's governing council unanimously approves the country's new constitution. Ten bombs explode on Madrid commuter trains killing nearly 200 people and wounding around 1,400 more. The South Korean Parliament votes to impeach President Roh Moo-hyun for his alleged breach of election rules. Prime Minister Goh Kun takes over the presidential functions. Newly elected Spanish Prime Minister José Luis Rodríguez Zapatero of the Spanish Socialist Workers' Party (PSOE) announces his government's opposition to the invasion and occupation of Iraq. Astronomers announce the discovery of Sedna, a Pluto-like planetoid. It is the most distant individual object known to orbit the Sun. Taiwanese President Chen Shui-bian and Vice-President Annette Lu are shot while campaigning in Tainan. Both survive with minor injuries. A bomb is discovered on the high speed TGV railway between Paris and Geneva near Troyes, France. NASA succeeds in its second attempt to fly the X-43A experimental aircraft from the Hyper-X project. It attains speeds above of Mach 7 making it the fastest ever hypersonic flight.

April: Four persons suspected of involvement in the 11 March 2004 Madrid bombings blow themselves up in an apartment building in Madrid when police raid the apartment. Canadian authorities order the slaughter of 19 million chickens in British Columbia due to bird flu fears. West Indies captain Brian Lara sets the highest score in Test cricket—400 not out on the third day of the fourth Test against England in Antigua. An Arabic channel broadcasts an audiotape, believed to be that of Osama bin Laden. The voice in the tape offers to halt terrorist operations in European countries that withdrew their troops from Muslim nations. Socialist Party leader José Luis Rodríguez Zapatero is sworn in as Spain's prime minister. Mordechai Vanunu, who leaked Israeli nuclear-weapons secrets in 1986, is released from prison after eighteen years. Reunification referendum held in Cyprus. 65 per cent of Turkish Cypriot voters accept and 75 per cent of Greek Cypriot voters reject the Annan Plan. Photographs showing US troops abusing and humiliating Iraqi prisoners at the Abu Ghraib prison outside Baghdad appear in the press. Six soldiers face court martial. Their commanding officer is suspended.

May: Cyprus, the Czech Republic, Estonia, Hungary, Latvia, Lithuania, Malta, Poland, Slovakia and Slovenia join the European Union. Over fifty former high-ranking United States diplomats address an open letter to George W. Bush complaining about the Bush administration's policy towards the Middle East. The United States Senate approves John Negroponte as the head of the new US embassy in Iraq. Hamas co-founder Mohammad Taha is released from an Israeli prison. Vladimir Putin is sworn in for his second four-year term as Russian President. US Defense Secretary Donald Rumsfeld testifies before the US Congress taking full responsibility and apologizing for the abuse of Iraqi detainees at the Abu Ghraib prison. Chechen President Akhmad Kadyrov is killed in a landmine bomb blast during a parade in Grozny. British tabloid newspaper The *Daily Mirror* acknowledges its photos of alleged British Army abuse of Iraqi prisoners as a hoax, tenders an apology and sacks its editor, Piers Morgan. Michael Moore's controversial film *Fahrenheit 9/11* wins the Palme d'Or at the Cannes Film Festival. Horst Köhler is elected President of Germany. The signing of a peace accord marks an end to the twenty-one-year civil war in Sudan.

June: Ghazi Mashal Ajil al-Yawer is named president of Iraq's incoming government. Norway bans smoking in all bars and restaurants. In USA, Central Intelligence Agency (CIA) director George Tenet tenders his resignation. George W. Bush presents the US Presidential Medal of Freedom to Pope John Paul II. North Korea bans its citizens from using mobile phones. Former US President Ronald Reagan passes away. The first transit of Venus since 1882 takes place. The ICC suspends the Zimbabwean cricket team from playing Test Matches till the end of 2004 due to their policy of racial bias in team selection. Software experts announce the development of a computer virus named 'Cabir' that is capable of infecting cellphones running on the Symbian OS with Bluetooth capabilities. The latest meeting of the European Council in Brussels ends in the agreement of a constitution for the European Union. The Philippine Congress announces the re-election of Gloria Arroyo to a second term as President of the Philippines in the 2004 general election. SpaceShipOne successfully achieves its maiden flight to the edge of outer space, thus becoming the first privately funded spacecraft to travel into space. US administrator in Iraq, Paul Bremer, hands over power in Iraq two days before the US-imposed deadline. The currencies of Estonia (the kroon), Lithuania (the litas), and Slovenia (the tolar) enter ERM II, the European Union's Exchange Rate Mechanism.

July: The Iraqi Special Tribunal holds the first hearing in the trial of Saddam Hussein. The first direct presidential election is held in Indonesia. The Cambodian parliament votes to reappoint Hun Sen as prime minister. Former chess World Champion Bobby Fischer is detained in Japan. The prime minister of the Palestinian Authority, Ahmed Qurei, submits his resignation. Yasser Arafat refuses to accept the resignation and Qurei later withdraws his resignation. Israeli prime minister Ariel Sharon calls on French Jews to move to Israel following a dramatic rise in French anti-semitism. In USA, the 9/11 Commission releases its unanimous final report that harshly criticizes US intelligence agencies. US Senator John Kerry formally accepts the 2004 Democratic presidential candidate nomination.

August: US authorities raise the security alert level for the World Bank and the International Monetary Fund (IMF) offices in Washington, DC, the New York Stock Exchange and companies in the New York City area after intelligence reports a possible al-Qaeda attack. The FBI warns that Mumbai, Delhi, or Bangalore could be the target of terrorist attacks. A non-radioactive steam leak at a Japanese nuclear power plant kills four and injures eight others. The South Korean government announces the shifting of the country's capital from Seoul to a new site at Gongju. British scientists at University of Newcastle-upon-Tyne become the first in Europe to be granted permission to clone human embryos. Lee Hsien Loong is sworn in as the third prime minister of Singapore. The 2004 Summer Olympics are held in Athens, Greece. Venezuelan President Hugo Chávez defeats a recall vote with 58 per cent support. 1,300 Iraqi delegates begin a three-day conference in Baghdad to select an interim National Assembly. The Cassini-Huygens spacecraft discovers two new natural satellites of Saturn. Germany apologizes for the genocide in Namibia on the 100th anniversary of the Herero uprising. *Nature* magazine reveals that five new satellites and a further candidate moon have been discovered orbiting Neptune. The Trans-Atlantic Exoplanet Survey (TrES) announces its first discovery of an extrasolar planet. China passes a law making it illegal to buy and sell blood, in a bid to tackle the HIV epidemic. Former Yugoslav President Slobodan Milosevic opens his defence at the trial that accuses him of genocide, crimes against humanity and war crimes.

September: Alu Alkhanov wins the presidential election in Chechnya. Iran informs the International Atomic Energy Agency that it plans to convert 37 tons of yellowcake uranium into a form that can be made into weapons. Armed men and women seize a school in Beslan, North Ossetia, Russia, and hold over 1,300 adults and children hostage. The standoff ends in tragedy; the official reports list 335 confirmed dead, including 156 children, and more than 700 wounded; 176 remain missing. Chechen warlord Shamil Basayev claims responsibility. US President George W. Bush accepts the Republican nomination for a second term in office. The UN war crimes tribunal in The Hague declares former Yugoslav President Slobodan Miloševic unfit to represent himself in his trial, and appoints two lawyers to his defence. The management of US film company Metro-Goldwyn-Mayer accepts a take-over offer from Sony in a deal worth just under US$3 billion. Afghan President Hamid Karzai survives an assassination attempt after a rocket is fired at his helicopter. The US Department of Homeland Security intercepts a United Airlines flight from London, so that Yusuf Islam, the musician formerly known as Cat Stevens, can be arrested and deported. Syria begins a 'phased redeployment' of its forces in Lebanon. USA formally lifts its general trade and aviation sanctions against Libya. The United States Senate confirms the nomination of Porter Goss as Director of the Central Intelligence Agency.

October: Former General Susilo Bambang Yudhoyono wins a landslide in the Indonesian presidential polls held on September 20. Americans David J. Gross, H. David Politzer and Frank Wilczeck win the 2004 Nobel Prize for Physics for showing how tiny quark particles interact. Alu Alkhanov (forty-seven), is sworn in Chechnya President. Wangari Maathai, a Kenyan woman (sixty-four) whose Green Belt Movement has planted 30 million trees in Africa, wins this year's Nobel Peace Prize. Afghanistan holds first direct Presidential polls. Australian prime minister, John Howard wins a fourth straight term in office, in general elections. Russia and China sign a pact settling the last stretches of a 4,300 km border between the two states, in Beijing. The Turkish Cypriot government led by Mehmet Ali Talat falls. The interim leader of Afghanistan, Hamid Karzai, wins majority in presidential polls.

November: Ukrainians vote in presidential polls. US President, George W.

Bush, wins a second four-year term after defeating his Democrat rival John Kerry. George Bush nominates Condoleezza Rice the new Secretary of State and Stephen Hadley National Security Adviser. The Ukrainian prime minister, Viktor Yanukovich, wins the runoff for the presidency. India and the ten ASEAN nations sign the 'ASEAN–India Partnership for Peace, Progress and Shared Prosperity' Pact at the third annual summit in the Laotian capital Vientiane.

December: The Ukrainian Parliament votes to dismiss the government. Miss Peru, Maria Julia Mantilla Garcia (20), is crowned Miss World 2004 at the southern Chinese beach resort of Sanya. Over 80,000 people are killed following a massive undersea earthquake off Sumatra in Indonesia. Over 28,000 are killed in Sri Lanka and 4,560 in Thailand as the quake-triggered tidal waves lash the regions.

2005

January: The Turkish currency is revalued at a rate of 1,000,000 'old' lira for 1 New Turkish lira. The United Nations accepts Singapore's offer to set up a UN Regional Coordination Centre to coordinate relief efforts to tsunami-affected areas. The United States Department of Defense announces a new investigation into allegations of prisoner abuse at the Camp X-Ray detention center in Guantanamo Bay, Cuba. World leaders gather in Jakarta, Indonesia, for an emergency summit with the United Nations. Japan sends its largest military deployment since World War II to tsunami-hit countries, with around 1,000 troops on standby. The Group of Seven Industrialised Nations (G7) agrees to a moratorium on the debt repayments of countries worst affected by the tsunamis in Asia. In Nairobi, Kenya, a peace treaty is signed between warring factions in the Sudanese civil war, which has claimed over 1.5 million lives in more than twenty years. Mahmoud Abbas is officially declared winner of the Palestinian presidential election. A smoking ban comes into effect in Italy, prohibiting tobacco smoking in public places. US space probe Deep Impact is successfully launched from Cape Canaveral. Paris Club, a group of officials from nine teen of the world's richest countries, offers a debt freeze to nations affected by 2004 Indian Ocean earthquake. The Huygens probe successfully lands on Saturn's largest moon, Titan. Croatian president Stipe Mesic is elected for a second term. A UN World Conference on Disaster Reduction in Kobe, Japan begins. Israel lifts a ban on contacts with new Palestinian leader, Mahmoud Abbas. US President George W. Bush is sworn in for his second term. The Republic of Ireland, one of the last countries to use non-metric speed limits, officially changes all road signage and regulations to use kilometres per hour. In Ukraine, the Supreme Court dismisses Prime Minister Viktor Yanukovych's appeal and confirms Viktor Yushchenko as new president. Mars rover, Opportunity, uses its spectrometers to prove that Heat Shield Rock is a meteorite, the first to be found on another planet Yulia Tymoshenko is appointed Prime Minister of Ukraine. Bill Gates donates $750 million through the Bill and Melinda Gates Foundation to the Global Alliance for Vaccines and Immunization, to provide vaccines to children in poor countries. Condoleezza Rice is confirmed in the US Senate; she is the first African-American woman to serve as US Secretary of State. The World Economic Forum begins in Davos, Switzerland. Hamas comes to power in local elections in Gaza. Voting takes place in Iraq, marking the first multi-party election in fifty years.

February: King Gyanendra of Nepal sacks the government of Sher Bahadur Deuba and assumes direct power. Star

Trek: Enterprise television series is cancelled, marking the end of eighteen consecutive years of Star Trek on television. Zurab Zhvania, prime minister of Georgia, dies of gas poisoning. Thai prime minister Thaksin Shinawatra wins an unprecedented second term as prime minister. A ban on tobacco smoking in public places begins in Cuba. The Greek parliament elects Karolos Papoulias as their new President. The French parliament votes in favor of relaxing the thirty-five-hour work week rules. North Korea announces that it has developed nuclear weapons for its self-defense, and suspends participation in multi-nation talks to discuss its arms programme. Saudi Arabia starts its first nationwide municipal elections, however only men in Riyadh are allowed to vote and only half of the municipal councils are open to voting; the monarchy will appoint the other half. The Kyoto Protocol on global warming, comes into effect. Iran and Syria announce the formation of a 'united front' The European Union introduces new laws that increase the rights of air passengers; they are now entitled receive higher compensation for overbooking, delays and cancellation of flights. Bhutan bans smoking in public places. New EU laws declare lottery scams illegal.

March: In Afghanistan, President Hamid Karzai appoints Abdul Rashid Dostum as his chief-of-staff In Burundi, a referendum approves the new constitution designed to end twelve years of civil war. President Saparmurat Niyazov of Turkmenistan orders the closure of all the hospitals in the country except those in the capital, as well as all rural libraries. Microsoft founder Bill Gates conferred the title of Knight Commander of the Most Excellent Order of the British Empire. Muslim cleric Abu Bakar Bashir is found guilty of conspiracy for his involvement in the 2002 Bali bombing and is awarded a two-and-a-half-year jail sentence. US businesswoman Martha Stewart is released from prison after serving a five-month sentence. Sony Corporation names its current US operations chief, British-born Howard Stringer, its first-ever non-Japanese Chairman and Chief Executive Officer. Kosovan prime minister Ramush Haradinaj resigns after the International Criminal Tribunal for the former Yugoslavia charges him with war crimes. USA withdraws from a part of the Vienna Convention that gave the International Criminal Court the right to intervene in cases of foreigners held in death rows in US jails. China begins human trials of AIDS vaccine. Bangladesh bans smoking in public places Israel formally hands Jericho to Palestinian Authority control. In Namibia, president Sam Nujoma is succeeded by Hifikepunye Pohamba. United Nations declares World Water Day, starting a decade-long Water-for-Life campaign for clean water. German airline Lufthansa announces its takeover of Swiss Airlines. The World Health Organization states that tuberculosis cases in some African countries have tripled since 1990.

April: Hamas and Islamic Jihad declare their 'in principle' intention to join the Palestine Liberation Organization (PLO) In Zimbabwe, the ruling Zanu-PF gains a two-thirds majority in the parliamentary election. Pope John Paul II passes away at the age of eighty-four. In Nepal, former prime minister Girija Prasad Koirala is released from house arrest. Kurdish leader, Jalal Talabani, is named as Iraq's President. Monaco's Prince Rainier III dies at age eighty-one. The Integrated Ocean Drilling Programme (IODP) announces that it has drilled a hole to the lowest level of the Earth's crust. In UK, Prince Charles marries Camilla Parker Bowles. The parliament of Kyrgyzstan approves the resignation of deposed President Askar Akayev. The European Parliament votes to allow Bulgaria and Romania to join the European Union in 2007. Najib Mikati becomes the new prime minister of Lebanon. Mehmet Ali Talat is elected as the new Turkish Cypriot President. German Cardinal Joseph Ratzinger is elected as the new Pope; he assumes the name of Pope Benedict XVI. The parliament of Kuwait gives initial support to a law that would allow women to vote. The parliament of Greece ratifies the European Union Constitution. The prime minister of Italy, Silvio Berlusconi, resigns in order to form a new government. The Ecuadorian parliament removes President Lucio Gutiérrez from power; Vice-President Alfredo Palacio is sworn in as new interim president. A rodent species representing a new family of mammals, Laonastidae, is discovered in Laos; this is the first new family of mammals discovered since 1974. The currencies of Cyprus, Latvia, and the Malta join the European Exchange Rate mechanism, one of the steps needed for a currency to join the Eurozone. King Gyanendra of Nepal ends the state of emergency but continues press censorship and ban on political activities.

May: Lenovo Group, the largest Chinese computer company acquires the personal computer business of IBM for US$ 1.25 billion in cash. In Nepal, 10,000 protesters march in Kathmandu against the policies of king Gyanendra and demand return of democracy. Europe's largest sporting. goods maker Adidas–Salomon sold its Salomon division for 485 million euros to Finnish company Amer Sports. In UK, the Labour Party wins a parliamentary majority but with a reduced margin; Tony Blair becomes the first Labour prime minister to lead his party to three election victories. Malcolm Glazer wins control of British football team Manchester United F.C. after securing a 70 per cent share. South Korea announces it will restart bilateral talks with North Korea after a gap of one year. The National Assembly of Kuwait votes 35–23 in favor of women's suffrage, effective for the 2007 Parliamentary Election. The United Nations World Food Programme declares that North Korea is in desperate need of food aid. The World Health Organization announces an ebola outbreak in the Democratic Republic of Congo. The Baku–T'bilisi–Ceyhan pipeline, the longest oil pipeline in the world, begins operations. The South African Geographical Names Council unanimously approves a recommendation to change the name of the country's executive capital Pretoria to Tshwane. In Egypt, a referendum is held for constitutional changes for presidential elections. In Germany, the CDU/CSU opposition combine elects Angela Merkel as its candidate for chancellor in the upcoming German federal election. Russian billionaire and businessman Mikhail Khodorkovsky is sentenced to nine years in prison in his tax evasion trial. In Bangkok, Thailand, the Canadian contestant Natalie Glebova is crowned Miss Universe 2005. In France, Prime Minister Jean-Pierre Raffarin resigns following the country's rejection of the Constitution for Europe China opens Three Gorges Dam to tourists.

June: Apple Computer announces shift from IBM to Intel processors for their Macintosh computer range. Siemens announces the sale of its mobile phone assets to the Taiwanese electronics company BenQ. In Syria, the ruling Baath party votes to end the forty-year long state of emergency. Bolivian President Carlos Mesaresighs; Eduardo Rodríguez becomes the new interim President. The G8 announces the cancellation of the multilateral debt of eighteen of the poorest countries in the world. Mike Tyson announces his retirement from boxing. Kuwait appoints Massuma al-Mubarak as the country's first female cabinet minister.

Kurdish parliament in Northern Iraq elects Masoud Barzani as a President of the region. In USA, a California court clears Michael Jackson on all counts of child molestation and related charges. Swedish diplomat Jan Eliasson is unanimously elected president of the United Nations General Assembly. Asafa Powell breaks the world record in the 100 metres. JP Morgan Chase and Co. announces a settlement of a lawsuit brought against it by Enron investors who claim that it helped the management of that company defraud them. Presidential election begins in Iran. In Bulgaria, the Socialists win the most votes in the general elections, but fall short of the requirement to form a government on their own. The Ugandan parliament votes to remove the law that restricts presidential tenure to two five-year terms. New York City officials release the design for the centerpiece building of the World Trade Center; the name of the building is proposed to be 'The Freedom Tower'.

July: The UK assumes the rotating presidency of the European Union. The impactor of NASA probe Deep Impact successfully hits comet Tempel 1. The International Olympic Committee names London as the host of the 2012 Summer Olympics. In Burundi, the former Hutu rebel group, Forces for the Defence of Democracy wins 58 per cent of the vote in parliamentary elections. Explosions take place on the London Underground and bus system; the entire transport network is shut down. The first case of avian influenza in the Philippines is reported in the Bulacan province. World leaders at the thirty-first G8 summit in Gleneagles, Scotland, pledge US$50 billion to fight poverty in Africa and US$3 billion to Palestinians for infrastructure development. In Monaco, Prince Albert is inaugurated as the new ruling prince. The European Court of Justice fines France •20 million ($24 million) for violating European Union fishing quotas. The English version of *Harry Potter and the Half-Blood Prince* is released at midnight local time across the UK, Ireland and North America. The People's Bank of China announces a 2 per cent revaluation of its currency, the Renminbi (yuan), and removes its peg to the US dollar. Microsoft announces that the next version of its Windows operating system, codenamed 'Windows Longhorn' till now, will be officially known as 'Windows Vista'. American cyclist and cancer survivor Lance Armstrong wins his seventh consecutive Tour de France. Armstrong announced that this will be his last tour. Bilateral negotiations resume between the US and North Korea. The Space Shuttle, Discovery, is successfully launched on mission STS-114, dubbed 'Return to Flight'. The United States, India, China, Japan, South Korea and Australia form an alliance named the Asia–Pacific Partnership on Clean Development and Climate, with the goal of reducing the emissions of gasses that lead to global warming.

August: New European Union directive banning tobacco advertising comes into effect. NASA announces that astronauts will carry out repairs on hull of the space shuttle, Discovery, to ensure its safety in re-entry. Mahmoud Ahmadinejad officially becomes the new president of Iran. Scientists in Seoul National University, South Korea, announce they have cloned a dog, named Snuppy. Iran resumes its nuclear programme at its uranium facility near the city of Isfahan. Space Shuttle Discovery returns safely and lands at Edwards Air Force Base in California. Pakistan's carries out a test launch of its first domestically designed cruise missile, the Babur missile. Kurmanbek Bakiyev is sworn in as Kyrgyzstan's new President. The parliament of Iraq grants an extension to leaders who are formulating the country's new Constitution. Russian cosmonaut Sergei K. Krikalev sets a record for spending the most days in space (nearly 748 days over twenty years). Singapore president S.R. Nathan wins a second term in office. The original handwritten manuscript of a paper by Albert Einstein, entitled 'Quantum theory of the monatomic ideal gas' is found in the archives of Leiden University's Lorentz Institute for Theoretical Physics. All Palestinian Authority Assets held in the United States have been frozen.

September: The Common Chimpanzee genome sequence is released. Hosni Mubarak wins the first multi-candidate presidential election in Egypt. Ukraine President Viktor Yushchenko removes Prime Minister Yulia Tymoshenko and most of the cabinet. In Norway, the Red–Green Coalition led by Jens Stoltenberg wins the 2005 legislature election. Israel withdraws the last of its troops from the Gaza Strip. Iranian President Mahmoud Ahmadinejad rejects an offer from the European Union to halt its nuclear programme while addressing the UN General Assembly. Federal elections held in Germany produce a hung parliament. North Korea agrees to abandon its nuclear weapons programmes and return to the Nuclear Non-Proliferation Treaty. Renault driver Fernando Alonso becomes the youngest ever Formula One champion. Swiss voters approve citizens from the ten newest European Union member countries to travel and work in Switzerland.

POLITICAL INDIA

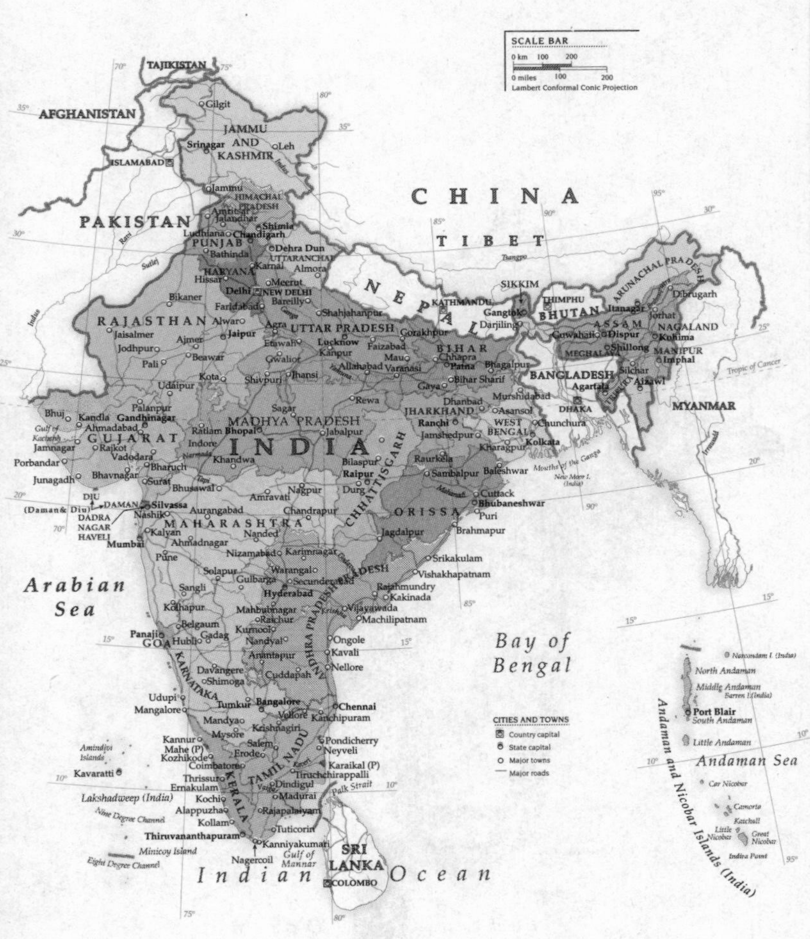

The following pertains to all maps showing the external boundaries and coastlines of India:

- © Government of India, 2002.
- Based upon Survey of India maps with the permission of the Surveyor General of India.
- The responsibility for the correctness of internal details rests with the publisher.
- The territorial waters of India extend into the sea to a distance of twelve nautical miles measured from the appropriate base line.
- The administrative headquarters of Chandigarh, Haryana and Punjab are at Chandigarh.
- The interstate boundaries between Arunachal Pradesh, Assam and Meghalaya shown on these maps are as interpreted from the North-Eastern Areas (Reorganisation) Act, 1971, but have yet to be verified.
- The external boundaries and coastlines of India agree with the Record/Master Copy certified by Survey of India.
- The topographical details within India are based upon Survey of India maps with the permission of the Surveyor General of India, the copyright 2002 of which vests with the Government of India.
- The interstate boundaries between Uttaranchal & Uttar Pradesh, Chhattisgarh & Madhya Pradesh and Jharkhand & Bihar have not been verified by the Government concerned.

PHYSICAL INDIA

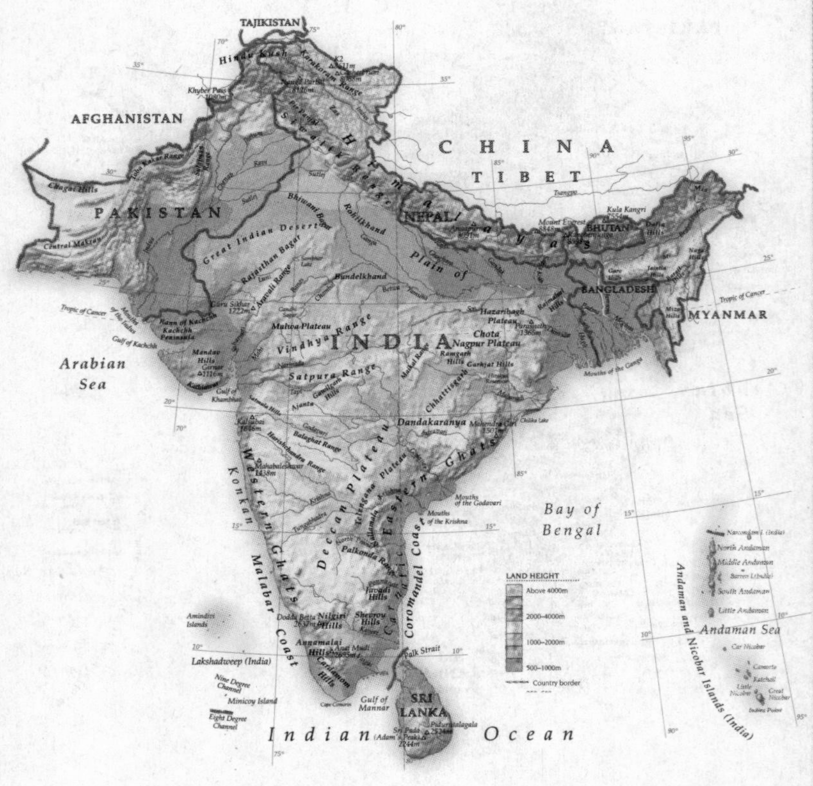

TAJIKISTAN
Hindu Kush
Karakoram Range
Khyber Pass
AFGHANISTAN
CHINA
TIBET
PAKISTAN
Great Indian Desert
Rajasthan Bagar
Aravalli Range
Bundelkhand
Rohilkhand
Plain of
NEPAL
BHUTAN
Mount Everest 8848m
Kula Kangri
BANGLADESH
MYANMAR
Tropic of Cancer
Rann of Kachchh
Kachchh Peninsula
Gulf of Kachchh
Arabian Sea
Mahwa Plateau
Vindhya Range
INDIA
Satpura Range
Hazaribagh Plateau
Chota Nagpur Plateau
Ramgarh Hills
Garhjat Hills
Mouths of the Ganga
Gulf of Khambhat
Ajanta
Chhattisgarh
Dandakaranya
Chilika Lake
Balaghat Range
Harishchandra Range
Mahabaleshwar 1438m
Konkan
Western Ghats
Deccan Plateau
Telangana Plateau
Eastern Ghats
Mouths of the Godavari
Mouths of the Krishna
Bay of Bengal
Palkonda Range
Coromandel Coast
Malabar Coast
Javadi Hills
Nilgiri Hills
Shevroy Hills
Annamalai Hills
Cardamom Hills
Amindivi Islands
Lakshadweep (India)
Nine Degree Channel
Minicoy Island
Eight Degree Channel
Palk Strait
Gulf of Mannar
SRI LANKA
Indian Ocean
Andaman Sea
Andaman and Nicobar Islands (India)
North Andaman
Middle Andaman
South Andaman
Little Andaman
Car Nicobar
LAND HEIGHT
Above 4000m
2000–4000m
1000–2000m
500–1000m
Country border

SCALE BAR
0 km 100 200
0 miles 100 200
Lambert Conformal Conic Projection

NORTHWESTERN INDIA

CHANDIGARH, HARYANA, HIMACHAL PRADESH, JAMMU & KASHMIR, PUNJAB

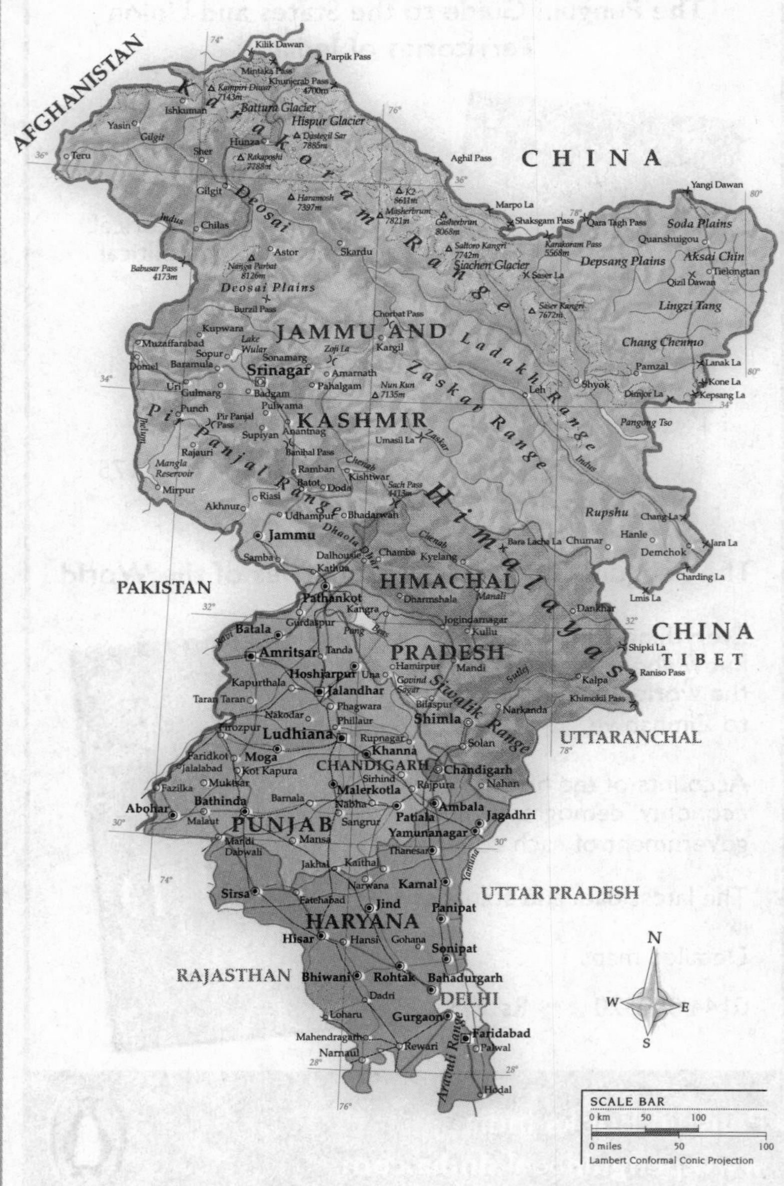

NORTHERN INDIA

DELHI, UTTAR PRADESH, UTTARANCHAL

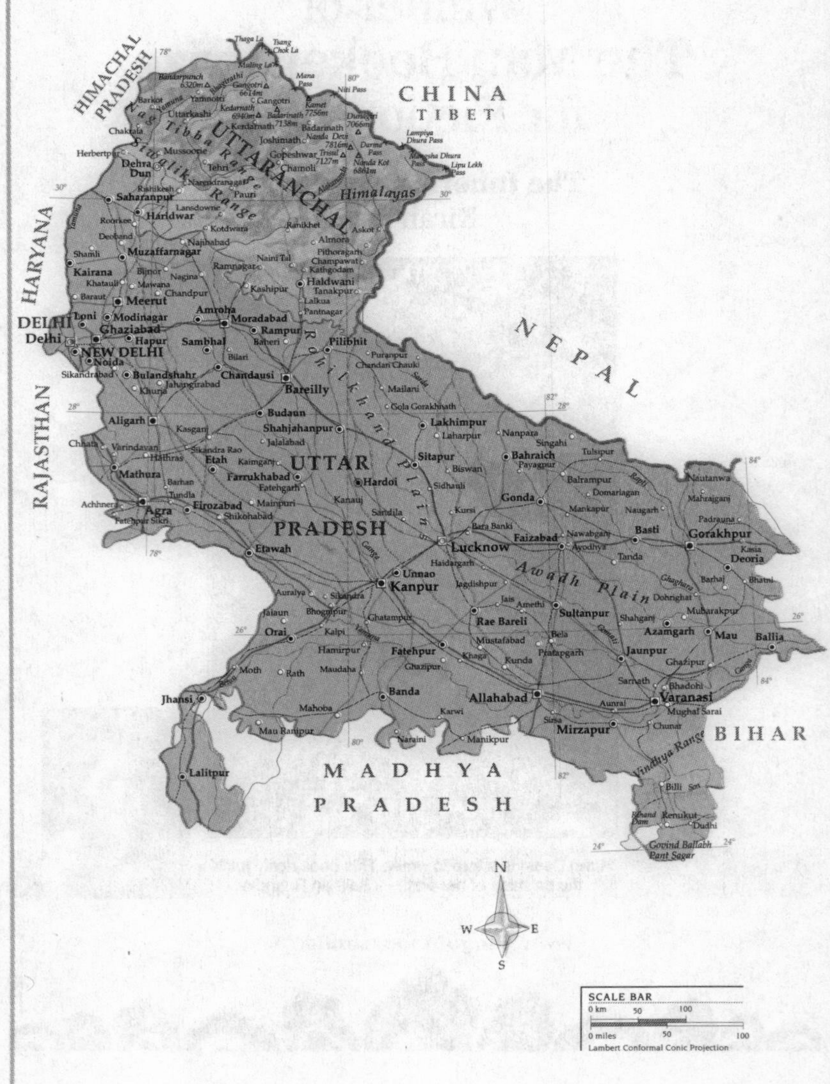

WESTERN INDIA

Dadra & Nagar Haveli, Daman & Diu, Gujarat, Maharashtra, Rajasthan

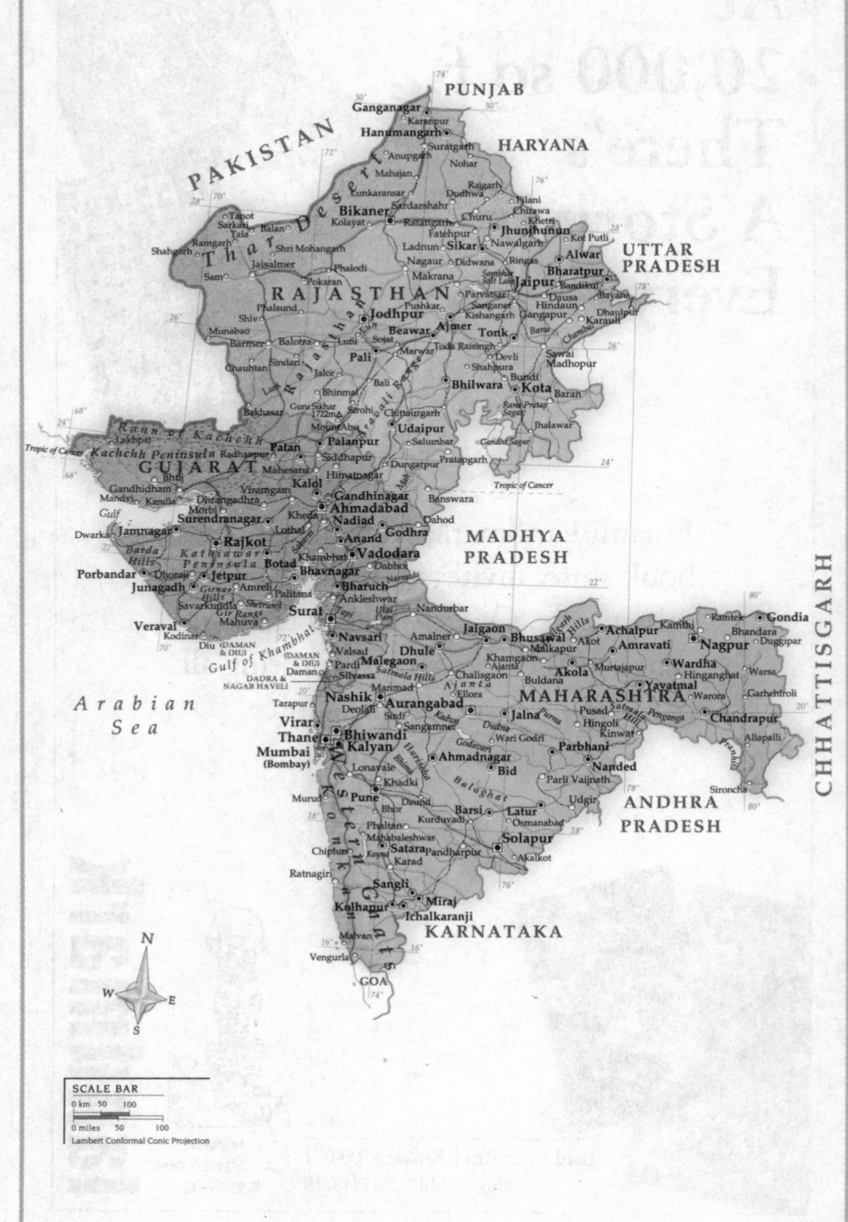

CENTRAL INDIA

MADHYA PRADESH, CHHATTISGARH

SCALE BAR
0 km 50 100
0 miles 50 100
Lambert Conformal Conic Projection

EASTERN INDIA

Bihar, Jharkhand, Orissa, Sikkim, West Bengal

NEPAL
BHUTAN
BANGLADESH
UTTAR PRADESH
CHHATTISGARH
ANDHRA PRADESH
SIKKIM
BIHAR
JHARKHAND
WEST BENGAL
ORISSA
Bay of Bengal

SCALE BAR
0 km 50 100
0 miles 50 100
Lambert Conformal Conic Projection

NORTHEASTERN INDIA

ARUNACHAL PRADESH, ASSAM, MANIPUR, MEGHALAYA, MIZORAM, NAGALAND, TRIPURA

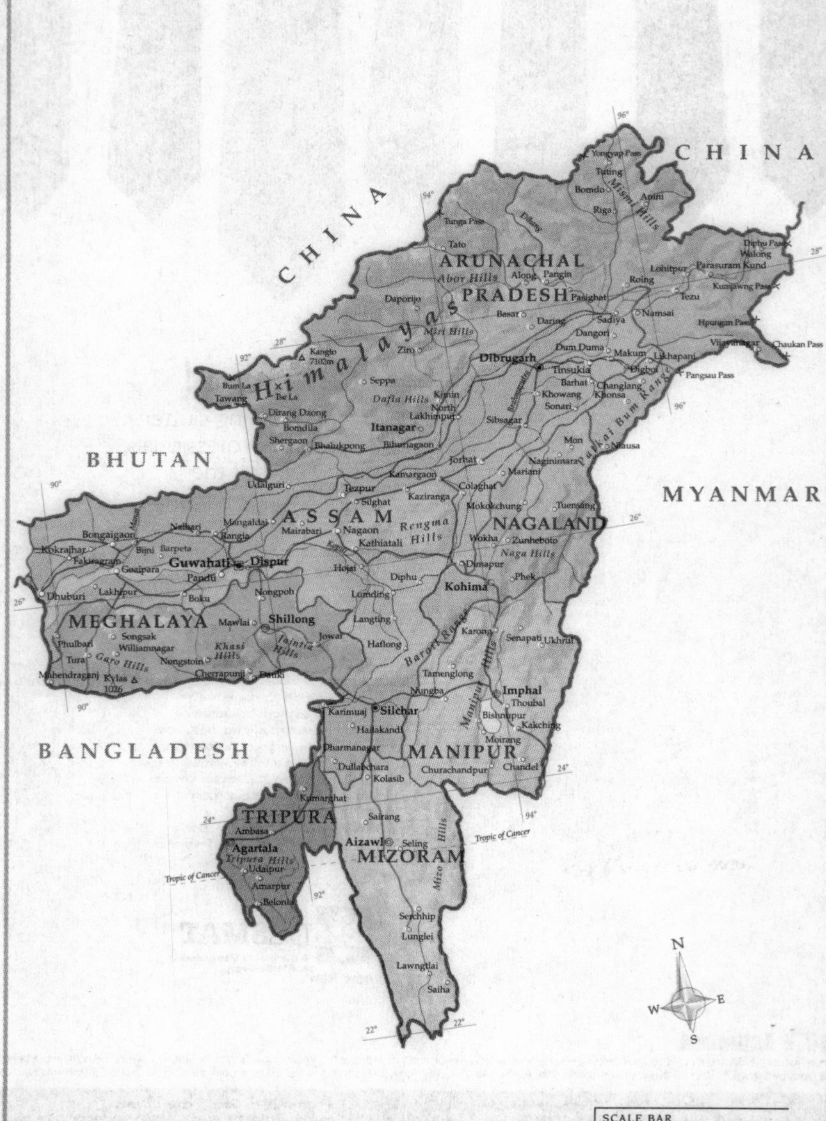

SCALE BAR

0 km 50 100

0 miles 50 100

Lambert Conformal Conic Projection

SOUTHERN INDIA

ANDHRA PRADESH, GOA, KARNATAKA, KERALA, PONDICHERRY, TAMIL NADU

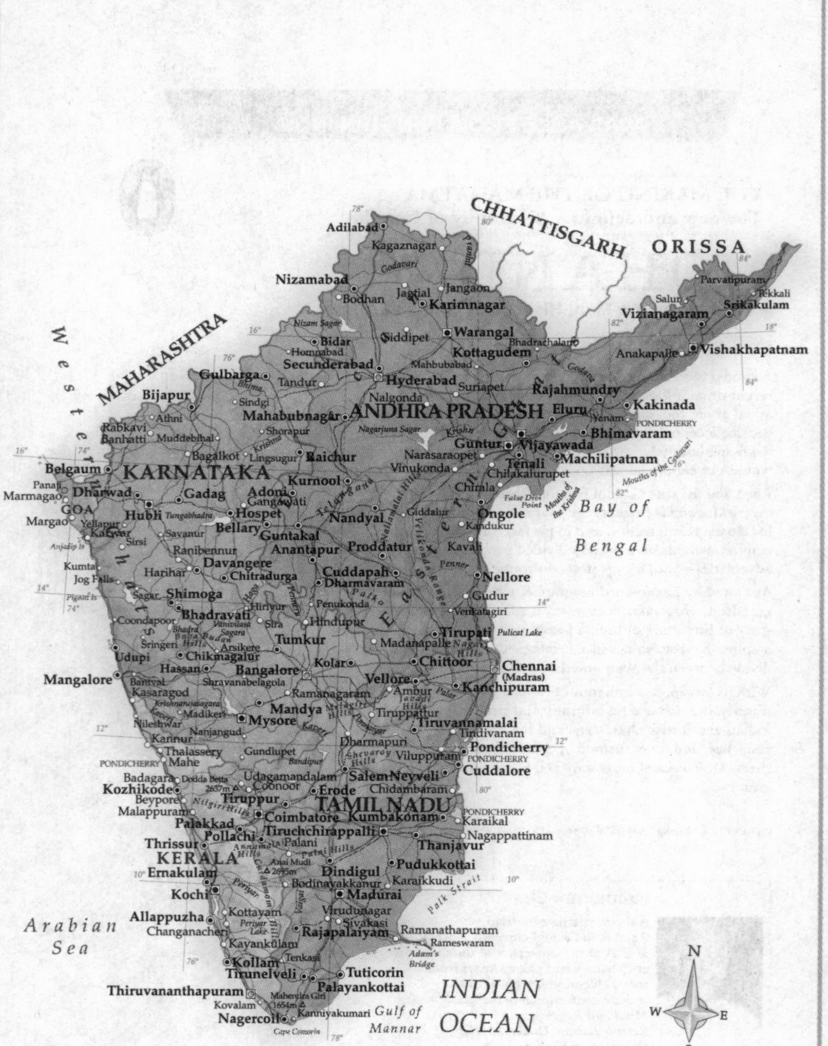

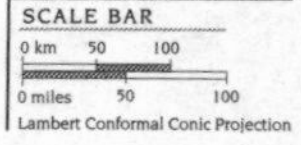

India

States

Between 26 January 1950 and 1 November 1956 there were four types of divisions in India: states (governor as head), states (under a rajpramukh), states (under a chief commissioner), and one territory; from 1956 there were only states and Union territories. Currently, there are twenty-eight states with Rajasthan being the largest and Goa the smallest in area.

Andhra Pradesh

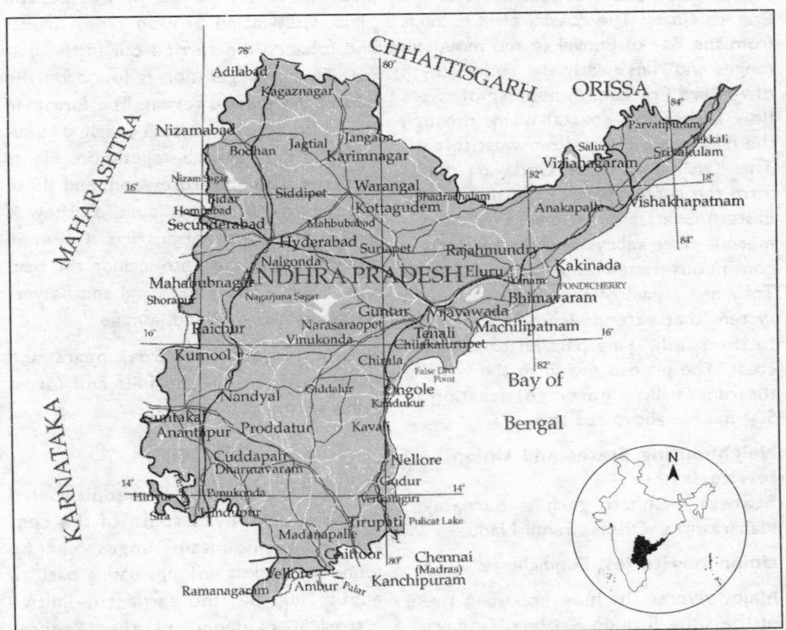

Key Statistics

Capital: Hyderabad.
Area: 276,754 sq. km.

Population: Total: 76,210,007, Male: 38,527,413, Female: 37,682,594.
Population density: 275 per sq. km.
Sex ratio: 978 females per 1000 males.

Principal languages: Telugu, Urdu, Hindi.

Literacy rates: Total: 60.5%, Male: 70.3%, Female: 50.4%.

Government

Governor: Rameshwar Thakur. He assumed office on 29 January 2006.

Chief Minister: Y.S. Rajasekhar Reddy (INC). He was sworn in on 14 May 2004.

Geography

Physical characteristics: Andhra Pradesh has three main physiographic regions: a coastal plain lying in the eastern part of the state, the Eastern Ghats, which form the western flank of the coastal plain, and a plateau west of the Eastern Ghats. The coastal plain extends from the Bay of Bengal to the mountain ranges and runs nearly the entire length of Andhra Pradesh. A number of rivers flow across the coastal plain, through the hills into the bay, from west to east. The Krishna and the Godavari deltas form the central part of the plains. The Eastern Ghats are broken up by the numerous river valleys and do not form a continuous range in Andhra Pradesh. They are a part of the larger mountain system that extends from central India to the south, lying parallel to the east coast. The plateau region to the west of the ranges has an average elevation of 500 metres above sea level.

Neighbouring States and Union territories:

States: Chhattisgarh, Karnataka, Maharashtra, Orissa, Tamil Nadu.

Union territories: Pondicherry.

Major rivers: The most important rivers of the state include Krishna, Godavari, Musi, Penneru and Tungabhadra.

Climate: In Andhra Pradesh, the summer is from March to June, the rainy season from July to September and the winter from October to February. Maximum and minimum temperatures in most parts of the state range from 23°C to 28°C and from 10°C to 12°C respectively. The coastal plain region experiences very warm summers with temperatures rising to 42°C in some places. Summers are cooler and winters colder still in the plateau region. Rainfall is largely due to the south-west monsoon winds and some places receive a maximum of 1,400mm of rain while other parts get less than half of that. Rainfall is heavier in the coastal areas but scanty in the northern and western parts of the plateau.

Flora and Fauna:

Flora: Forests occupy nearly 63,000 sq. km. in the state. Mangrove swamps and palm trees are found in the coastal plain. Cultivation of food crops, fruits, and tobacco are carried out in the deltas. Thorny vegetation is found on the hills of the plateau region. The forests in the state consist of both moist deciduous and dry savanna vegetation. Plants like teak, bamboo, rosewood, and those bearing wild fruits are found. Cashew is grown in the coastal districts. Common trees found in the state include the banyan, mango, neem and pipal and flowering plants like rose and jasmine.

Fauna: Tigers, leopards, bears and deer are found in the hills and forest areas of the state.

History

Although references to people called Andhras, who lived south of the central Indian mountain ranges, can be found in Sanskrit writings dating back to about 1000 BC, the earliest definitive historical evidence of the Andhras dates only from the times of the Mauryan dynasty, around the third century BC. Emperor Ashoka had sent Buddhist missions to the Andhras. Around the first century AD, the Satakarnis (or the Satavahanas) came to power. They were one of the most well known Andhra dynasties and ruled over almost the entire Deccan plateau. They even established trade relations with Rome. In the eleventh century, large expanses of Andhra were united under the reign of the eastern Chalukyas. The Kakatiya dynasty of Warangal spread Andhra power in the twelfth and thirteenth centuries. Their regime witnessed the rise of the Andhras as a commercial power to parts of South-East Asia. Muslim invasion of south India led to the downfall of Warangal in 1323. However, the rise of the kingdom of Vijayanagar to the south-west of Warangal prevented Muslim domination to some extent. The Vijayanagar kingdom is often regarded as the greatest kingdom in Andhra history. Its greatest ruler was Krishna Deva Raya who reigned from 1509 to 1529. However, the glory of the Vijayanagar kingdom came to an end when it succumbed to an alliance of the neighbouring Muslim states in 1565.

In 1687, the Mughal emperor Aurangzeb invaded Golconda and annexed it to the Mughal Empire. The Mughals appointed 'nazims' as agents of the Mughal emperor. For about thirty-five years the nazims ruled the area. Then came the Asaf Jahi nizams.

When the Europeans arrived in India and gained power, the nizams of Hyderabad sought their help against their rivals. In this process, they acquired French and later British support. In exchange, the British acquired vast stretches of land from the nizams. Over a period of time the British gained control over most parts of Andhra territory and only parts of the Telugu-speaking areas, the Telangana region, remained with the nizams. Even the French acquired a few towns.

At the time of Independence in 1947, the nizams held sway over Hyderabad and desired to gain independence. Hyderabad was then one of the most prosperous of the princely states and had substantial armed forces. For this purpose, Nizam Osman Ali enlisted the help of Kasim Razvi of the Ittehadul Muslimeen and its private army, the Razakars. Even as the Hindus of the state campaigned to join India, the Nizam banned the Congress party in the state. As 15 August 1947 approached, negotiations between India and the nizam reached a stalemate as Osman Ali refused to join India. Meanwhile, the nizam's police, the Razakars, and the supporters of the nizam, perpetrated a reign of terror in the state. On 29 November 1947, Hyderabad signed a Standstill Agreement with India. It established a period of status quo. Hyderabad was allowed to maintain the status that existed between the British and the nizam before 15 August 1947. The nizam sent representations to other nations to seek their support and even approached the United Nations Security Council.

The Indian armed forces launched Operation Polo on 13 September 1948. It ended just over 100 hours later, when the nizam asked his forces to cease fire, allowed Union troops into the Hyderabad territories and banned the Razakars. On 18 September, the Hyderabad Army surrendered and Major General J.N. Chaudhuri of the Indian Army was appointed military governor of the state. The merger of Hyderabad state with the Indian dominion followed. In January 1950, M.K. Vellodi, a senior civil servant, was appointed the chief minister of the state. The first general elections were held in 1952 and B. Rama Krishna Rao became the first popularly elected chief minister.

Meanwhile, the demand for a separate Andhra state gained momentum. To complicate matters, a local Gandhian leader, Potti Sreeramulu, fasted to death in 1953. On 1 October 1953, the Andhra state, which included the Telugu-speaking districts of the former Madras state, was formed with its capital at Kurnool. Andhra Pradesh was formed on 1 November 1956 when the erstwhile state of Hyderabad was split up and its Telugu-speaking districts were joined to the Andhra state. Neelam Sanjiva Reddy was the first chief minister of Andhra Pradesh.

In 1960, 221.4 square miles in the Chingleput and Salem districts of Madras state were transferred to Andhra Pradesh in exchange for 410 square miles from Chittoor district.

Politics

The Andhras had long cherished a demand for the formation of Visalandhra, which would incorporate the outlying Telugu-speaking areas of Orissa, Madhya Pradesh, Mysore and Madras into a greater Andhra state. However, the States Reorganization Committee, set up by the Government of India in 1953, favoured the formation of a separate state for Telangana. The Congress High Command favoured Visalandhra and prevailed upon the Andhra and Telangana lobbies to sort out their differences. The two parties entered into a Gentlemen's Agreement, one of the provisions of which was the creation of a Regional Council for the all-round development of Telangana. Consequent to this, the enlarged state of Andhra Pradesh was formed in 1956, merging nine Telugu-speaking districts with eleven districts of the Andhra state.

During the years 1969 and 1972, Andhra Pradesh was rocked by two political agitations popularly known as the Telangana movement and the Jai Andhra movement. The Telangana agitation was started by the people of the region when they felt that the Andhra leaders had flouted the Gentlemen's Agreement which facilitated the formation of Andhra Pradesh. The agitation took a new turn when Congress legislators from Telangana supported the movement. Dr Channa Reddy formed the Telangana Praja Samiti to lead the movement. But the movement petered out after it became clear that Prime Minister Indira Gandhi was not in favour of a separate Telangana state. In September 1971, Brahmanand Reddy, the then chief minister, resigned to make room for a leader from Telangana to become chief minister. P.V. Narasimha Rao became the new chief minister.

The Jai Andhra movement was a sequel to the Telangana agitation, and demanded that only 'mulkis' be appointed to posts in Telangana including Hyderabad city.

A mulki was defined as one who was born in the state of Hyderabad or resided there continuously for fifteen years and had given an affidavit that he abandoned the idea of returning to his native place. Even after the formation of Andhra Pradesh, the mulki rules continued to be in force in the Telangana region. As these rules stood in the way of the people of the Andhra region to compete for the posts, their validity was challenged in the High Court. A full bench of the High Court by a four–one majority held that the mulki rules were not valid and operative after the formation of Andhra Pradesh. But on an appeal by the state government, the Supreme Court declared on 3 October 1972 that the mulki rules were valid and were in force. The judgment created a great political crisis in the state. The people of the Andhra region felt that they were reduced to the status of second-class citizens in their own state capital. They felt that the only way to uphold their dignity was by severing their connection with Telangana and started a movement for the separation of the Andhra region from Andhra Pradesh. As the agitation continued, President's Rule was imposed in the state on 10 January 1973. Finally, a political settlement was arrived at under the aegis of the Central government. On 10 December 1973, President's Rule in the state was revoked and a popular ministry with Jalagam Vengala Rao as the chief minister was inducted.

N.T. Rama Rao, a leading figure of the film world, formed a regional party called Telugu Desam in January 1983 and contested the elections to the Andhra Pradesh Legislative Assembly held in 1983. His party became victorious and Rama Rao was sworn in as the tenth chief minister of the state. But on 16 August 1984, Nadendla Bhaskara Rao, a cabinet colleague of Rama Rao, succeeded in becoming the chief minister by engineering the dismissal of Rama Rao by the governor. However, Rama Rao was reinstated on 16 September 1984, consequent on the severe criticism on the action of The governor. In the elections of March 1985, Rama Rao proved that he continued to enjoy the confidence of the people by winning an absolute majority in the House.

The Congress returned to power in 1989 with a good majority. During the following five years, three chief ministers, Dr M. Channa Reddy, N. Janardhana Reddy and K. Vijaya Bhaskara Reddy held the reins of power. The discontentment of the Telugu public was reflected in pushing the Congress out and handing over the power again to the Telugu Desam party in 1994. In 1995 N.T. Rama Rao was succeeded by N. Chandrababu Naidu of the same party. In May 2004 the Congress won the Assembly elections and Y.S. Rajashekhara Reddy was sworn in as the chief minister.

Culture

One of the six classical dance forms of India, Kuchipudi, is indigenous to Andhra Pradesh. The state is also well known for its banjara embroidery, bidri metalwork, Budithi metalwork and Dokra metal craft. Nirmal in Adilabad district is famous for its Nakash craftsmen, who specialize in painting scenes from the *Mahabharata* and the *Ramayana*. The state is also known for its Ikat textiles. Besides these, Andhra Pradesh is also reputed for its wood and stone carvings, kalamkari fabrics, puppets, toys, dolls and filigree work.

Fairs and festivals: Hindu festivals such as Dasara, Deepavali, Sri Ramanavami, Krishna Janmastami, Vinayaka Chavithi (Ganesh Chaturthi) and Maha Sivarathri are celebrated in the state. But the celebrations of Ugadi (Telugu New Year's day), Sankranti, Dasara and Vinayaka Chavithi in the state are unique.

Economy, Industry and Agriculture

Economy: The net state domestic product at current prices for 2003–04 (provisional) was Rs 1,62,153 crores. The per capita net state domestic product at current prices for 2003–04 (provisional) was Rs 20,757.

Minerals and industry: The significant industries of the state include IT industry, auto-component manufacturing, chemical synthesis and process engineering, and horticulture. Smaller industries that have developed in the state from locally available agricultural raw materials include rice flour, rice-bran oil, soaps and detergents, cardboard and other packaging materials, paints and varnishes, and cattle feed.

Minerals found in the state include oil and natural gas, coal, limestone, iron ore, manganese, gold, diamonds, asbestos, ball clay, fire clay, graphite, dolomite, quartz, tungsten, feldspar and silica sand. Much of the state's mineral resources remain unexploited.

Agriculture: The production of food grains dominates agriculture in Andhra Pradesh and forms the mainstay of the state's economy. The state is one of the leading producers of rice and tobacco in the country. Sugar cane is also produced in the state. Other agricultural commodities now grown in different parts of Andhra Pradesh include pulses (peas, beans and lentils), chilli peppers, castor beans, sorghum, groundnut and cotton, as well as fruits like mangoes, grapes, bananas and oranges.

Power: Andhra Pradesh has one of the highest installed power capacities in the country.

Education

Prominent educational institutions of Andhra Pradesh include the Andhra University (Vishakhapatnam), Central Institute of English and Foreign Languages (Hyderabad), Dr B.R. Ambedkar Open University (Hyderabad), Dravidian University (Chitoor), University of Hyderabad (Hyderabad) , Jawaharlal Nehru Technological University (Hyderabad), Kakatiya University (Warangal), Maulana Azad National Urdu University (Hyderabad), Nagarjuna University (Guntur), Nizam's Institute of Medical Sciences (Hyderabad), N.T.R. University of Health Sciences (Vijayawada), Osmania University (Hyderabad), Potti Sreeramulu Telugu University (Hyderabad), Rashtriya Sanskrit Vidyapeetha (Tirupati), Sri Krishnadevaraya University (Anantapur), Sri Sathya Sai Institute of Higher Learning (Prasanthinilayam), Sri Padmavati Mahila Visvavidyalayam (Tirupati) and Sri Venkateswara Institute of Medical Sciences (Tirupati).

Tourism

Major tourist attractions:

1. Hyderabad: Charminar, Salarjung Museum, Hussein Sagar Lake, Durgam Ceruvu (Secret Lake), Shamirpet Lake, Qutb Shahi Tombs, Statue of Lord Buddha in Hussein Sagar Lake, Golconda Fort.
2. Tirupati: Lord Venkateswara Temple, Sri Agastheswara Swamy Temple, Govindarajaswami Temple, Goddess Alamelumanga Temple, Kodandarama Swamy Temple.
3. Vishakhapatnam: Simhachalam Temple, Rishikonda Beach, Dolphin's Nose.
4. Chittoor: Horsley Hills, Chandragiri Fort, Lord Venkateswara Temple, Sri Venkateswara Sanctuary, Govindarajaswami Temple.
5. Cuddapah: Bhagavan Mahavir Government Museum, Chand Phira Gumbadh, Gandikota Fort.
6. Vijayawada: Prakasam Barrage, Kanakadurga Temple, St. Mary's Church, Moghalrajapuram caves, Hazrat Bal Mosque, Kondapalli Fort, Victoria Jubilee Museum.

Airports:
International: Hyderabad.
Domestic: Rajahmundry, Tirupati, Vijaywada, Vishakhapatnam, Warangal, Cuddapah, Donakonda and Nadrigul.

National Parks: Kasu Brahma Reddy National Park in Hyderabad district (1.42 sq. kms), Mahavir Harina Vanasthal National Park in Rangareddi district (14.59 sq. kms), Mrugavani National Park in Rangareddi district (3.6 sq. kms), Sri Venkateshwara National Park in Chittoor and Cuddapah districts (353.62 sq. kms).

Administration

Legislature: Andhra Pradesh has a unicameral legislature with only the legislative assembly. The assembly has 295 seats including thirty-nine seats reserved for SCs, fifteen seats reserved for STs and one member who is nominated from the Anglo-Indian community.

The current party position is as follows:

Name of Party	Seats
Indian National Congress	185
Telugu Desam Party	47
Telangana Rashtra Samithi	26
Communist Party of India (Marxist)	9
Communist Party of India	6
All India Majlis-E-Ittehadul Muslimeen	4
Bharatiya Janata Party	2
Janata Party	2
Bahujan Samaj Party	1
Samajwadi Party	1
Independent	11
Nominated	1
Total	**295**

Judiciary: The seat of the Andhra Pradesh High Court is in Hyderabad. The present acting chief justice is Bilal Nazki.

Districts:

District	Area (sq. km)	Population	Headquarters	Urban Agglomerations
Adilabad	16128	2,479,347	Adilabad	Adilabad
Anantapur	19130	3,639,304	Anantapur	Anantapur
Chittoor	15151	3,735,202	Chittoor	Madanapalle, Tirupati
Cuddapah	15359	2,573,481	Cuddapah	Cuddapah
East Godavari	10807	4,872,622	Kakinada	Kakinada, Rajahmundry
Guntur	11391	4,405,521	Guntur	Narasaraopet
Hyderabad	217	3,686,460	Hyderabad	Hyderabad
Karimnagar	11823	3,477,079	Karimnagar	Ramagundam, Karimnagar
Khammam	16029	2,565,412	Khammam	Kothagudem, Khammam
Krishna	8727	4,218,416	Machilipatnam	Vijayawada
Kurnool	17658	3,512,266	Kurnool	Adoni, Kurnool, Nandyal
Mahbubnagar	18432	3,506,876	Mahbubnagar	Mahbubnagar, Gadwal
Medak	9700	2,662,296	Sangareddy	
Nalgonda	14240	3,238,449	Nalgonda	Miryalguda, Nalgonda, Suryapet
Nellore	13076	2,659,661	Nellore	Guduru, Kavali, Nellore
Nizamabad	7956	2,342,803	Nizamabad	
Prakasam	17626	3,054,941	Ongole	Chirala, Ongole
Rangareddi	7493	3,506,670	Hyderabad	Hyderabad
Srikakulam	5837	2,528,491	Srikakulam	Srikakulam
Visakhapatnam	11161	3,789,823	Visakhapatnam	Bheemunipatnam, Visakhapatnam
Vizianagaram	6539	2,245,103	Vizianagaram	Vizianagaram
Warangal	12847	3,231,174	Warangal	Warangal
West Godavari	7742	3,796,144	Eluru	Palacole, Tanuku, Eluru, Bheemavaram

Arunachal Pradesh

Key Statistics

Capital: Itanagar.
Area: 83,743 sq. km.
Population: Total: 1,097,968, Male: 579,941, Female: 518,027.
Population density: 13 per sq. km.
Sex ratio: 893 females per 1000 males.
Principal languages: Nissi/Daffla, Nepali, Bengali.
Literacy rates: Total: 54.3%, Male: 63.8%, Female: 43.5%.

Government

Governor: S.K. Singh. He was sworn in on 16 December 2004.

Chief Minister: Gegong Apang (INC). He was sworn in on 16 October 2004.

Geography

Physical characteristics: Arunachal Pradesh is a land of lush green forests, deep river valleys and plateaus. The land is mostly mountainous with the Himalayan ranges lying along the northern borders criss-crossed with north–south running ranges. These divide the state into five river valleys: the Kameng, the Subansiri, the Siang, the Lohit and the Tirap. A series of foothills lie in the southernmost part of the

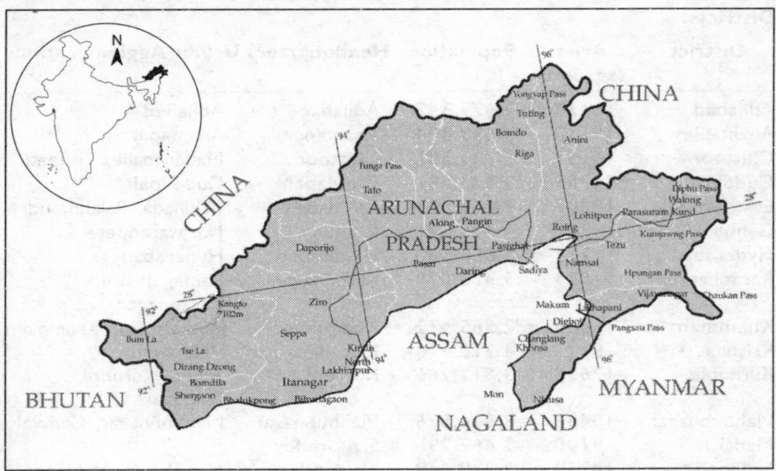

state, rising from the Assam plains to touch altitudes of 300 to 1,000 metres. These hills rise northward to the Lesser Himalayas to reach heights of more than 3,000 metres. The main ranges of the Great Himalayas lie further north, along the Chinese border.

Neighbouring States and Union territories:

International borders: Bhutan, China, Myanmar.

States: Assam, Nagaland.

Major rivers: The Brahmaputra, known as the Siang in Arunchal Pradesh, and its tributaries which include the Lohit, Subansiri, Dibang, Kameng, Tirap, Kamla, Siyum, Noa-Dihing and Kamlang.

Climate: The climate of Arunachal Pradesh varies from subtropical in the south to alpine in the north. Arunachal Pradesh receives heavy rainfall varying from 1,000mm in the higher altitudes to 5,750mm in the foothills. Average rainfall is more than 3,500mm. It is spread over eight to nine months with the exception of a dry period in winter. The average temperature ranges from 15 to 21°C during winter and 22 to 30°C during monsoon. Between June and August the temperature sometimes rises to 40–42°C (in some regions).

Flora and Fauna:

Flora: Almost 60 per cent of the state is covered with evergreen forests. Arunachal Pradesh has seven types of forests. These are: tropical, subtropical, pine, temperate, alpine, bamboo and degraded forests. Besides these forests, there are grasslands in the riverine plains and higher altitudes.

The state is home to a variety of timber species, orchids, oaks, rhododendrons, medicinal plants, ferns, bamboos and canes.

Fauna: Arunachal Pradesh has a rich wildlife population. It is home to the mithun, elephant, tiger, leopard, snow leopard, clouded leopard, white-browed gibbon, red panthers, musk deer, gaur and wild buffalo. The species of primates found in the state include the slow loris, hoolock gibbon, rhesus macaque, pigtailed macaque, Assamese macaque, stump-tailed macaque, and capped langur. Three species of goat-antelopes, serow, goral and takin, are found in the state. Significant species of birds found in the state are the hornbill, Sclater's monal, white-winged duck, Bengal florican, Temminck's tragopan and green pigeon.

History

The history of Arunachal Pradesh is rich in myths and traditions. The recorded history of this state is available only from the sixteenth century onwards. It was at this point of time that the Ahom kings began to rule Assam. The modern history of the state begins with the imposition of British rule in Assam following the Treaty of Yandaboo (1826). Between 1947 and 1962, it was a part of the North-East Frontier Agency that was constitutionally a part of Assam. Because of its strategic importance, the ministry of external affairs administered Arunachal Pradesh till 1965, with the governor of Assam acting as an agent to the President of India. The administrative head was the advisor to the governor. Later, in August 1965, the Ministry of Home Affairs gained administrative control. In 1972, it became a Union territory under the name of Arunachal Pradesh. In 1975, it got its own legislature. Arunachal Pradesh attained full-fledged statehood on 20 February 1987. At that time, Gegong Apang was its chief minister.

Politics

Though the history of the political process in Arunachal Pradesh dates back to 1875 when the British-Indian government started to define the administrative jurisdiction by drawing an Inner Line in relation to the frontier tribes inhabiting the North Frontier Tract, the area was kept outside the purview of regular laws of the country. Thereafter, the British followed the policy of gradual penetration to bring more areas under normal administration. By the year 1946, the North-East Frontier Tracts were reorganized into four Frontier Tracts namely Sadiya, Lakhimpur, Tirap and Sela Sub Agency and Subansiri, and administrated by the governor of Assam in his discretion. The government of Assam administered the North-East Frontier Tracts during the period 15 August 1947 to 26 January 1950. In 1950, Frontier Tract, Tirap Frontier Tract, Abor Hill District and Mishimi Hills Districts were transferred to the government of Assam. In 1951, the units of the tracts were reconstituted again and Tuensang Frontier Division was created, which later merged with Nagaland. The remaining portion of the Tracts after the introduction of the North-East Frontier (Administration) Regulation 1954 was designated as the North-East Frontier Agency, the NEFA. Thereafter, the administration was brought under the Ministry of External Affairs and in August 1965, it was brought under the supervision and control of the Ministry of Home Affairs. It remained so till the attainment of Union territory status by Arunachal Pradesh in 1972. It was only in 1975 that by virtue of the enactment of 37th Constitutional Amendment Act that the Pradesh Council was constituted as a separate Legislative Assembly. In November 1979, the Assembly was dissolved and President's Rule was imposed which continued till January 1980. On 18 January 1980 Gegong Apang became the chief minister. He was the chief minister for a record nineteen years. The union territory of Arunachal Pradesh became a full-fledged state with effect from 20 February 1987.

Culture

The various tribes of Arunachal Pradesh have their own dance forms. Some of the more popular folk dances include Roppi (Nishing Tribe), Aji Lamu (Monpa), Hiirii Khaniing (Apatani), Chalo (Nocte), Lion and Peacock dance (Monpa), Ponung (Adi), Popir (Adi), Pasi Kongki (Adi) and Rekham Pada (Nishing). Most of the dance forms of the state are group dances performed by both men and women. However there are some dance forms, such as the war dances of the Adis, Noctes and Wanchos, Igu dance of the Mishmi priests and ritualistic dance of the Buddhist tribes, that are exclusive male dances. The state has a notable tradition of bamboo and cane handicrafts, as well as pottery, carpet weaving and woodcarving. Handloom is a significant aspect of the state's culture and tradition.

Fairs and festivals: Important festivals of the state include Lossar, Si-Donyi, Mopin, Solung, Nyokum, Dree, Sipong Yong, Reh, Boori-boot, Kshyatsowai, Tamladu, Sarok, Chalo-loku, Nichido, Sangken, Mopin and Oriah. Parashuram Kund Mela (Parashuram Kund) and Malinithan Mela (Likabali) are two notable fairs of the state.

Economy, Industry and Agriculture

Economy: The net state domestic product at current prices for 2003–04 (provisional) was Rs 1,971 crores. The per capita net state domestic product at current prices for 2003–04 (provisional) was Rs 17,393.

Minerals and industry: Notable among the industries of the state are timber-based industries, tourism, tea-based industries, coal mines and fruit-processing plants.

Coal reserves at the Namchik-Namphuk coalfield are estimated at 90 million tonnes. Petroleum crude reserves are estimated at 1.5 million tonnes. Besides these, there are reported deposits of iron, copper, limestone, graphite, dolomite, quartzite, kyanite and mica.

Agriculture: The major crops grown in the state are rice, maize, millet, wheat, pulses and sugarcane. There are rubber, coffee and tea plantations. The state also grows banana, ginger, chillies, turmeric, pineapple, plum, orange, apple, walnut, guava, grapes and potato.

Power: Most of the state's power requirements are met by hydroelectric power plants. As a matter of fact, the hydel power potential of Arunachal Pradesh is estimated at 30,000 MW. There are a large number of mini and micro hydel power plants in the state. A certain amount of the state's power needs are met by diesel power plants.

Education

Educational institutes: Arunachal University (Itanagar), North-Eastern Regional Institute of Science and Technology (Itanagar).

Tourism

Major tourist attractions: Tawang monastery, Bhismaknagar, Malinithan, Parashuram Kund, Tipi Orchid Research Centre, Akashiganga, Gekar Sinyi (Ganaga lake), Talley Valley, Dr D. Ering Wildlife Sanctuary, Bomdila.

Airports: Along, Daporijo, Pasighat, Teju, Ziro.

National Parks: Mouling National Park in Upper Siang district (483 sq. km) and Namdapha National Park in Changlang district (1985.23 sq. km).

Administration

Legislature: The state has a sixty-seat legislative assembly, out of which fifty-nine are reserved for STs. Elections were held in October 2004. The current party position is:

Name of Party	Seats
Indian National Congress	34
Bharatiya Janata Party	9
Nationalist Congress Party	2
Arunanchal Congress	2

Independent 13
Total 60

Judiciary: Arunachal Pradesh is under the jurisdiction of the Itanagar Bench of the Gauhati High Court at Guwahati, Assam. Binod Kumar Roy is the current chief justice.

Districts:

District	Area (sq. km)	Population	Headquarters	Urban Agglomerations
Anjaw	-	-	Hawai	
Changlang	4,662	124,994	Changlang	–
Dibang Valley	1,302	57,543	Anini	–
East Kameng	4,134	57,065	Seppa	–
East Siang	3,895	87,430	Pasighat	–
Kurung Kumey	NA	NA	Laying-Yangte	–
Lohit	11,402	143,478	Teju	–
Lower Subansiri	9,548	97,614	Ziro	–
Papum Pare	3,462	121,750	Yupia	–
Tawang	2,172	34,705	Tawang	–
Tirap	2,362	100,227	Khonsa	–
Upper Siang	6,590	33,146	Yingkiong	–
Upper Subansiri	7,032	54,995	Daporijo	–
West Kameng	7,422	74,595	Bomdila	–
West Siang	8,033	103,575	Along	–

Assam

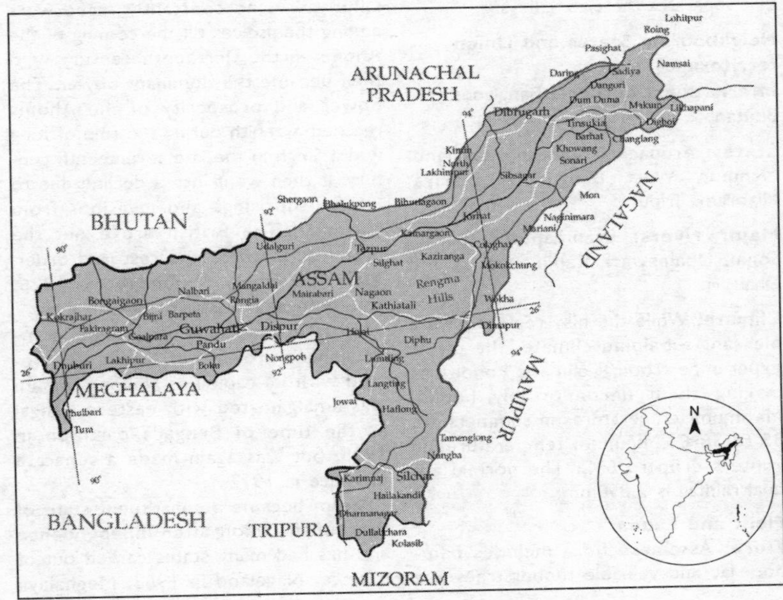

Key Statistics

Capital: Dispur.
Area: 78,438 sq. km.
Population: Total: 26,655,528, Male 13,777,037, Female: 12,878,491.
Population density: 340 per sq. km.
Sex ratio: 935 females per 1000 males.
Principal languages: Assamese, Bengali, Bodo/Boro.
Literacy rates: Total: 63.3%, Male: 71.3%, Female: 54.6%.

Government

Governor: Lt Gen. (Retd) Ajai Singh. He was sworn in on 5 June 2003.

Chief Minister: Tarun Gogoi. He was sworn in on 18 May 2001.

Geography

Physical characteristics: Assam can be broadly divided into three geographical units: the alluvial Brahmaputra Valley covering large parts of the state in the north, the Barak Valley in the southern part of the state, and the hilly region that separates the two valleys.

Neighbouring States and Union territories:
International borders: Bangladesh, Bhutan.

States: Arunachal Pradesh, Nagaland, Manipur, West Bengal, Meghalaya, Mizoram, Tripura.

Major rivers: Brahmaputra, Barak, Sonai, Dhaleswari, Kapili, Jamuna and Dhansiri.

Climate: While the hilly regions have a pleasant subalpine climate, the plains experience tropical climatic conditions making them uncomfortably humid. Maximum temperatures in summers are 35 to 38°C. Minimum temperatures in winters drop to 6°C. The normal annual rainfall is 2,850mm.

Flora and Fauna:
Flora: Assamese flora includes bamboo, lac and valuable timber trees like sal and teak. The state's forests have about seventy-four species of trees, of which two-thirds are commercially exploited.

Fauna: Wildlife found in Assam includes the one-horned rhinoceros, elephant, wild buffalo, wild boar, swamp deer, sambar, hog deer, sloth bear, tiger, leopard, leopard cat, jungle cat, hog badger, capped langur, hispid hare, pygmy hog and golden langur, hoolock gibbon, jackal, goose, hornbill, ibis, pelican, duck, cormorants, egret, river chats (white-capped redstars), forktail, heron and fishing eagle.

History

In ancient times, Assam was a part of the kingdom of Kamarupa that had its capital at Pragjyotishpura. Chinese traveller Hiuen-Tsang's account of AD 640 describes a powerful Kamarupa under King Bhaskaravarman. From the seventh to thirteenth century, the region was ruled by different dynasties—the Palas, Koches, Kacharis, and the Chutiyas—who constantly raged wars among themselves till the coming of the Ahoms in the thirteenth century who then became the dominant power. The power and prosperity of the Ahoms reached a zenith during the rule of King Rudra Singh in the late seventeenth century. It then went into a decline due to internal uprisings and invasions from Myanmar. The British drove out the Myanmar invaders and restored order. After the Treaty of Yandabo in 1826, Assam became a part of British India.

In 1874, a separate chief commissioner's province of Assam was created with its capital at Shillong. Assam was amalgamated with eastern Bengal at the time of Bengal's partition in 1905, but was again made a separate province in 1912.

Assam became a constituent state of the Indian Union after Independence and has had many states carved out of it since: Nagaland in 1963, Meghalaya and Mizoram in 1971, and Arunachal Pradesh in 1972. Assam's first chief minister was Gopinath Bardoloi.

Politics

The legislature of Assam remained bicameral from 1937 to 1946. Under the India (Provincial Legislatures) Order 1947, the Legislative Council was abolished on 14 August 1947. The Assam legislature has been unicameral since then. In the years that followed, Assam was truncated to create several smaller states. Gopinath Bardoloi from the Congress party was the first chief minister of Assam who remained in office from 15 August 1947 to 6 August 1950. The Congress has ruled the state for the longest period since 1952. It lost to the Asom Gana Parishad in the 1985 Assembly elections held immediately after the Assam Accord was signed in the wake of a violent anti-foreigner agitation, which lasted from 1979 to 1985. However, the Congress returned to power in 1991 and ruled the state until 1996.

Following Indian Independence in 1947, the Assamese won control of their state assembly and launched a campaign to reassert the preeminence of Assamese culture in the region and improve employment opportunities for native Assamese. This led to the alienation of some tribal districts. In addition, many in the tribal districts were demanding independence from India. Thinking it would satisfy the tribals, the Indian government parititioned former Assamese territories into the tribal states of Nagaland, Mizoram, Meghalaya, Manipur and Arunachal Pradesh over the next twenty years. This was seen by Assamese leaders as a deliberate division of their constituency. Following the Pakistan war in 1971, nearly two million Bengali Muslim refugees migrated to Assam. Their illegal settlement and then their electoral support for Indira Gandhi's Congress government further aggravated Assamese fears of Bengali cultural domination and central government's ambitions to undermine Assamese regional autonomy. In the late 1970s and early 1980s, there were persistent disputes between the government and Assamese students and some Assamese political factions over the rights of illegal immigrants to citizenship and suffrage. The state government and the Government of India responded by the use of force to suppress the movement. Many demonstrators were killed. This led to some of India's worst communal violence since Partition towards the end of the movement. The central government's effort to hold a constitutionally mandated election to the state assembly in 1983 led to its near total boycott, a complete breakdown of order, and the worst killings since 1947. The election proved to be a complete failure with less than 2 per cent of the voters casting their votes in the constituencies with Assamese majority. The Congress party formed the government and on 27 February 1983 Hiteshwar Saikia became the chief minister of the state.

In 1985, a treaty was signed between the Assamese and the Government of India. According to it all those foreigners who had entered Assam between 1951 and 1961 were to be given full citizenship, including the right to vote; those who had done so after 1971 were to be deported; the entrants between 1961 and 1971 were to be denied voting rights for ten years but would enjoy all other rights of citizenship. This was followed by an election. A new party, Asom Gana Parishad, formed by the leaders of anti-foreigners movement, was elected to power, winning sixty-four of the 126 Assembly seats. Prafulla Mahanta became at the age of thirty-two the youngest chief minister of independent India. There was a lot of expectation among the people. But the victory of the AGP did not end the controversy over Assamese nationalism. The AGP was unable to implement the accord's provisions for disenfranchising and expelling illegal aliens, in part because parliament passed legislation making it more difficult to prove illegal alien status. The AGP's failure to implement the accord along with the general ineffectiveness with which it operated the state government undercut its popular support, and in November 1990 it was dismissed and President's Rule declared.

As the AGP floundered, other nationalist groups of agitators flourished. The United Liberation Front of Assam (ULFA) became the primary torchbearer of militant Assamese nationalism while the All Bodo Students' Union (ABSU) and Bodo People's Action Committee (BPAC) led an agitation for a separate homeland for the central plain tribal people of Assam (often called Bodos). By 1990 ULFA militants ran virtually a parallel government in the state, extorting huge sums from businesses in Assam, especially the Assamese tea industry. The ULFA was ultimately subdued through a combination of military action and generous terms of surrender for many of its leaders. The Government of India has classified it a terrorist organization and had banned it under the Unlawful Activities (Prevention) Act in 1990. On the other hand the ABSU/BPAC-led mass agitation lasted from March 1987 until February 1993 when the ABSU signed an accord with the state government that had been under Congress (I) control since 1991. The accord provided for the creation of a Bodoland Autonomous Council with jurisdiction over an area of 5,186 square kilometers and 2.1 million people within Assam. Nevertheless, the Bodo agitation continued in the mid-1990s as a result of the demands of many Bodo leaders, who insisted that more territory be included under the Bodoland Autonomous Council.

On 30 June 1991 Hiteshwar Saikia of the Congress party returned to power, becoming the chief minister for the second time and remained in power till 22 April 1996. Prafulla Kumar Mahanta regained the chief ministership in May 1996. He remained in power till 18 May 2001. In the 2001 elections the Congress(I) came back to power in Assam. It defeated the four-party alliance led by Asom Gana Parishad (AGP), winning seventy-one of the 125 seats. The alliance, which included the AGP, the BJP, the All Bodo Students Union (ABSU) and the Autonomous State Demand Committee (United) secured thirty-nine seats. Tarun Gogoi was sworn in as the fifteenth chief minister of Assam. Despite large-scale violence by ULFA and the National Democratic Front of Bodoland (NDFB), more than 70 per cent of the electorate exercised its franchise in largely peaceful polling.

Culture

Assam has a large number of tribal groups who exhibit great cultural variety. Among them are the Boro-Kacharis, Deoris, Misings, Dimassas, Karbis, Lalungs and Rabhas. The three Bihus or agricultural festivals—Rongali Bihu, Bhogali Bihu and Kongali Bihu—are an important aspect of Assamese culture. Apart from Bihu, popular dance forms include Ojapali, Satriya, Ghosa Dhemali, Ras Nritya and Bagrumba.

Handloom weaving of fine silk and cotton cloths is a popular activity. Other ethnic products include cane and bamboo articles, brass and bell-metal products, pottery, woodcraft, masks, jewellery and terracotta articles.

Fairs and festivals: Important festivals and fairs are the three Bihus, Durga Puja, Bathow Puja, Kherai Puja, Ali-ai-ligang, Po-rag, Baishagu, Bohaggiyo Bishu, Jonbeel Mela and Ambubasi Mela.

Economy, Industry and Agriculture

Economy: Net state domestic product at current prices for for 2003–04 (provisional) was Rs 35,943 crores. The per capita net state domestic product at current prices for 2003–04 (provisional) was Rs 13,139.

Minerals and industry: The industrial scenario in Assam is dominated by two major industries: tea and oil and natural gas. Other industries include jute, silk, fertilizers, petrochemicals, paper, matchsticks, cement, iron pipes, asbestos sheets and pipes, pan masala, cosmetics, plastics processing and moulded articles, polyester yarn, acrylic yarn, sugar, plywood, handloom and handicrafts.

The mineral wealth of Assam includes coal, petroleum, limestone, granite, sillimanite, iron ore, quartzite, feldspar and clay.

Agriculture: Rice, maize, wheat, jute, cotton, sugar cane and pulses are the major crops. Important plantation crops are tea, rubber and coffee. Major horticultural crops are banana, pineapple, orange, potato, sweet potato, papaya, cabbage, onion, tapioca, areca nut, coconut, ginger, jackfruit, guava and mango.

Power: Assam has great potential for the development of its power sector based on hydel, oil, natural gas and coal resources. At present the Assam State Electricity Board has a total installed capacity of 574 MW.

Education

Prominent educational institutions are Gauhati University, Guwahati; Dibrugarh University, Diburgarh; Tezpur University, Tezpur; Assam University, Silchar; Assam Agriculture University, Jorhat; Indian Institute of Technology, Guwahati and National Institute of Technology, Silchar.

Tourism

Major tourist attractions:

1. Kamrup: Guwahati (Kamakhya and Bhubaneswari Temples, Basishthashram, Navagraha Temple, Gandhimandap); Hajo (Hayagriva-Madhab Temple, Poa Macca); Chandubi; Sualkuchi; Madan Kamdev.
2. Darrang: Bhairabkunda.
3. Morigaon: Pobitora Wildlife Sanctuary.
4. Nagaon: Nagaon; Batadrawa; Laokhowa Wildlife Sanctuary.
5. North Lakhimpur: Pobha Wildlife Sanctuary; Garampani.
6. Golaghat: Kaziranga National Park.
7. Tinsukia: Dibru Saikhowa National Park; Digboi (National Oil Park, War Cemetery).
8. Sonitpur: Orang Wildlife Sanctuary; Nameri National Park; Bhalukpun; Tezpur (Bamuni Hill, Hazara Tank, Chitralekha Udyan, Cole Park, Agnigarh, Da-Parbatiya, Maha Bhairav Temple).
9. Barpeta: Barpeta Satra and Kirtan Ghar; Manas National Park.
10. Sibsagar: Sibsagar (Shivadol, Vishnudol and Devidol Temples, Kareng Ghar and Talatal Ghar, Gorgaon Palace, Rang Ghar, Joysagar Tank and Temples, Charaideo).
11. NC Hills: Haflong; Jatinga; Maibong; Umrangshu.
12. Jorhat: Majuli, the world's largest riverine island.

Airports: Guwahati, Tezpur, Jorhat, Dibrugarh, Silchar, North Lakhimpur.

National Parks: Kaziranga National Park in Golaghat, Nagaon districts (471.71 sq. km); Manas National Park in Barpeta, Bongaigaon districts (500 sq. km); Nameri National Park in Sonitpur District (200 sq. km); Dibru Saikhowa Naional Park in Tinsukia, Dibrugarh districts (340 sq. km); Orang National Park in Darrang and Sonitpur districts (78.808 sq. km).

Administration

Legislature: The Assam state legislative assembly has 126 members elected from as many constituencies. Of the 126 seats, eight are reserved for scheduled castes and sixteen for scheduled tribes. The present party position is as follows:

Name of Party	Seats
Indian National Congress	53
Asom Gana Parishad	24
Bharatiya Janata Party	10
Nationalist Congress Party	1
Autonomous State Demand Committee	1
Loko Sanmilon	1
Communist Party of India	1
Communist Party of India (Marxist)	2
Assam United Democratic Front	10
Asom Gana Parishad Pragtisheel	1
Independents	22
Total	**126**

Judiciary: The Gauhati High Court, Guwahati, is the high court of Assam, Nagaland, Meghalaya, Manipur, Tripura, Mizoram, and Arunachal Pradesh. The present chief justice is Binod Kumar Roy.

Districts:

District	Area (sq. km)	Population	Headquarters	Urban Agglomerations
Barpeta	3245	1,642,420	Barpeta	
Bongaigaon	2510	906,315	Bongaigaon	Bongaigaon
Cachar	3786	1,442,141	Silchar	Silchar
Darrang	3481	1,503,943	Mangaldoi	
Dhemaji	3237	569,468	Dhemaji	
Dhubri	2798	1,634,589	Dhubri	
Dibrugarh	3381	1,172,056	Dibrugarh	Dibrugarh
Goalpara	1824	822,306	Goalpara	
Golaghat	3502	945,781	Golaghat	
Hailakandi	1327	542,978	Hailakandi	
Jorhat	2851	1,009,197	Jorhat	Jorhat
Kamrup	4345	2,515,030	Guwahati	Guwahati
Karbi Anglong	10434	812,320	Diphu	
Karimganj	1809	1,003,678	Karimganj	
Kokrajhar	3169	930,404	Kokrajhar	
Lakhimpur	2277	889,325	North Lakhimpur	
Marigaon	1704	775,874	Marigaon	
Nagaon	3831	2,315,387	Nagaon	Lumding, Nagaon
Nalbari	2257	1,138,184	Nalbari	
North Cachar Hills	4888	186,189	Haflong	
Sibsagar	2668	1,052,802	Sibsagar	
Sonitpur	5324	1,677,874	Tezpur	Tezpur
Tinsukia	3790	1,150,146	Tinsukia	Digboi, Tinsukia

Bihar

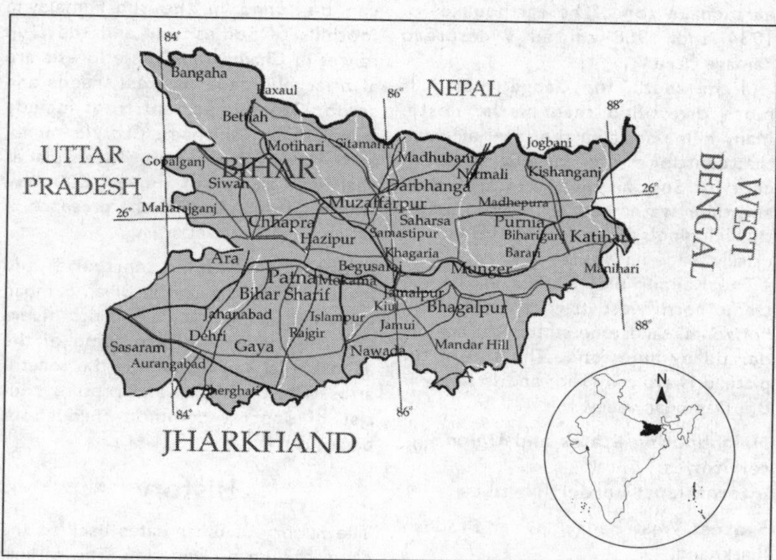

Key Statistics

Capital: Patna.
Area: 94,163 sq. km.
Population: Total: 82,998,509, Male: 43,243,795, Female: 39,754,714.
Population density: 880 per sq. km.
Sex ratio: 919 females per 1000 males.
Principal languages: Hindi, Urdu, Santhali.
Literacy rates: Total: 47%, Male: 59.7%, Female: 33.1%.

Government

Governor: Ramkrishnan Suryabhan Gavai. He assumed office on 22 June 2006.

Chief Minister: Nitish Kumar. He assumed office on 24 November 2005.

Geography

Physical characteristics: Located in the eastern part of the country, Bihar is a landlocked state. The outlet to the sea is through the port of Kolkata. The river Ganga flows through the middle of the Bihar plain from west to east and divides it into two halves.

Bihar lies midway between the humid West Bengal in the east and the sub-humid Uttar Pradesh in the west, which gives it a transitional position in terms of climate.

The north Gangetic plain consist of a flat alluvial region, and is prone to floods. The Kosi river, due to its tendency to cause dangerous floods, was previously referred to as the 'Sorrow of Bihar', before the construction of artificial embankments.

The soil in the Bihar plain is composed mainly of new alluvium, which is mostly non-chalky and heavy-textured (clay and clay loam) towards the east, and chalky and light-textured (mostly sandy loam) towards the west of the Old Burhi Gandak river.

Apart from floods, another hazard is that this region lies in the Himalayan earthquake zone. The earthquakes of 1934 and 1988 caused widespread damage here.

In the south, the Gangetic plain is more diversified than in the north. Many hills rise from the level alluvium that constitutes the Gangetic plain. Except for Son, all the rivers are small, and their water is diverted into irrigation channels. The soil of the land is usually made up of older alluvium.

The Kaimur plateau lies in the extreme north-west. It consists of nearly horizontal sandstone strata that are underlaid by limestone. The soil of the plateau is typically red, and is sandy in the Damodar valley.

Neighbouring States and Union territories:
International border: Nepal.

States: West Bengal, Uttar Pradesh, Jharkhand.

Major rivers: Ganga, Kamla-Balan, Mahananda, Saryu (Ghaghra), Gandak, Budhi Gandak and Bagmati.

Climate: Bihar's climate is in keeping with the Indian subcontinent's climatic pattern. Due to its great distance from the sea, Bihar enjoys a continental monsoon type of climate.

There are many factors that affect its climate. For one, the Himalayan mountains in the north affect the distribution of monsoon rainfall in Bihar. It records an average annual rainfall of about 1,200mm.

Also, Bihar extends from 22° to 27°N latitude, i.e. it lies in the tropical to subtropical region.

The cold weather season in Bihar lasts from December to February. Summer lasts from March to May. The southwest monsoon lasts from June to September, and the retreating southwest monsoon from October to November.

Flora and Fauna:
Flora: Deciduous forests in the state can be found in the sub-Himalayan foothills of Someshwar and the Dun ranges in Champaran. These forests are also largely made of grass, reeds and scrub. Other important trees include semal, khair, shisham, *Cedrela toona*, and *Shorea robusta* (sal). These places register a rainfall of above 1,600 mm, which is responsible for the presence of sal forests in certain areas.

Fauna: Many wildlife sanctuaries and reserves can be found in Bihar. Sambar, gaur, nilgai, munjtac, elephants, tigers and the Indian wolf are some of the animals that can be seen in the sanctuaries. The birds, fish and reptiles consist of species common throughout peninsular India.

History

The history of Bihar dates back to the dawn of human civilization. The earliest myths and legends of Hinduism are associated with Bihar, including the sanatana (eternal) dharma. Sita, the consort of Lord Rama, is believed to have been a princess from Bihar.

In the third century BC, the state was part of Ashoka's kingdom.

During the British rule in India, Bihar was a part of the Bengal Presidency and governed from Calcutta, and was separated from it in 1912. Together with Orissa, Bihar formed a single province, until the Government of India Act of 1935, which made Orissa into a separate province, and led to the formation of the province of Bihar as an individual administrative unit of British India.

At the time of Independence in 1947, Bihar was constituted with the same geographic boundary into the Republic of India. In 1956, during the linguistic reorganization of Indian states, the south-east area of Bihar known as

Purulia was separated from the state, and was added to the territory of West Bengal. Srikrishna Sinha became the first chief minister of Bihar.

In the year 2000, Bihar was bifurcated and the state of Jharkhand was carved out.

Politics

The Bihar Legislative Assembly came into existence in 1937. Bihar had a Congress government from 1937. After Independence, Srikrishna Sinha was the chief minister from 15 August 1947 to 31 January 1961. Unexpectedly, the Congress party could not win a majority of seats in 1967 elections. A coalition government came to power under the leadership of Mahamaya Prasad Sinha of the Bharatiya Kranti Dal. President's Rule was imposed for the first time in the state on 29 June 1968 when Bhola Paswan Shastri, succumbing to pulls and pressures from various constituents of his Sanyukta Vidhayak Dal (SVD), resigned. Bihar was brought under Central rule for the fourth time on 30 April 1977 when Jagannath Mishra's Congress government was dismissed after Morarji Desai became prime minister. With the failure of the Janata experiment and the return of Indira Gandhi, President's Rule was imposed for the fifth time on 17 February 1980, after which Jagannath Mishra became the chief minister for the second time and remained in the position till 14 August 1983. Laloo Prasad Yadav became the chief minister for the first time in 1990 and remained in power till the 1995 elections. Shortly after winning the 1995 election, Laloo Prasad Yadav came under pressure from senior leaders in the Janata Dal and its alliance partners to resign as chief minister following his alleged involvement in the fodder scam. He was charge-sheeted by the Central Bureau of Investigation (CBI), but remained in power until July 1997 when he floated the Rastriya Janata Dal, resigned as chief minister and appointed his wife Rabri Devi his successor. Rabri Devi had three tenures as chief minister. In between her second and third tenures Nitish Kumar was the chief minister for seven days in March 2000. After the 2005 election which resulted in a hung Assembly, Bihar was brought under President's rule for the eighth time on 8 March 2005. The JDU–BJP alliance won the Bihar Assembly election in November 2005. Nitish Kumar was sworn in as the chief minister of the state on 24 November 2005. Twenty-six ministers, sixteen of cabinet rank and ten ministers of state, took oath along with Chief Minister Nitish Kumar. The victory of the JDU–BJP alliance led by Nitish Kumar brought an end to the fifteen-year rule of the Lalu Prasad Yadav-led Rashtriya Janata Dal in the state.

On 26 January 2006, governor of Bihar, Sardar Buta Singh sent his resignation to President A.P.J. Abdul Kalam. The next day, he was replaced by the governor of West Bengal, Gopalkrishna Gandhi. On 22 June 2006, Ramkrishnan Suryabhan Gavai assumed office.

A students' agitation which began in Bihar in 1974 is popularly known as the Jayaprakash Narayan or JP movement. Today's Bihar is dominated by leaders who were once the chief actors in the JP movement—Lalu Prasad Yadav of the Rashtriya Janata Dal (RJD), Sushil Modi of the Bharatiya Janata Party (BJP), Ram Jatan Sinha of the Congress, and Nitish Kumar of the Janata Dal (United). The JP movement's ideological thrust was to fashion a new Bihar, free from corruption and casteism. The movement catalysed some revolutionary social changes, such as inter-caste marriages and the breaking of the sacred thread worn by upper-caste Hindus. Jayaprakash Narayan wanted a 'total revolution', not political change alone but also transformations in the social and cultural attitudes of the people. But even today the caste factor is the most potent social and political force in the state. Bihar has never been free of caste in politics. Even during the freedom movement, Bhumihars dominated politics; there were intense rivalries in Congress politics between Bhumihars and Rajputs, on the one hand, and Brahmins on the other. Even the state's greatest politicians couldn't rid themselves of narrow casteism. Veteran Congress leader Srikrishna Sinha, the first chief minister of Bihar, credited with the abolition of the zamindari system, was accused by Jayaprakash Narayan of promoting people from the Bhumihar caste and, thus, creating bottlenecks in the progressive evolution of politics and society. Even today, elections in Bihar are contested with formulations of caste-based alliances.

Culture

Writers from Bihar like Shiva Pujan Sahay, Ram Briksha Benipuri, Raja Radhika Raman Singh, Ramdhari SIngh Dinakar, and Divakar Prasad Vidyarthy contributed greatly to Hindi literature and culture, which flourished around the mid-nineteenth century, with Bhartendu Babu Harischandra's drama *Harischandra*. 'Indumati' by Pundit Kishorilal Goswami was published in 1900, and is considered to be one of the very first short stories in Hindi.

Bihar also has a variety of dance forms including religious dances and the dances of the tribals and the famous Chhau dance. Karma, Jatra and Paika dances are some other important dances.

Fairs and festivals: Bihar has a long tradition of festivals. The most popular festival Chatt Puja, is a unique form of worship of the sun god. The people of Bihar have immense faith in this festival, celebrated twice a year, once in Chaitra (according to the Hindu Calendar, in March) and in Kartik (November).

The other popular festivals include Sama-Chakeva festival, Ramnavami and the Makar Sankranti, also known as the Tila Sankranti, to mark the beginning of summer.

Economy, Industry and Agriculture

Economy: The net state domestic product at current prices in 2003–04 (provisional) was Rs 50,381 crores, whereas the per capita net state domestic product at current prices in 2003–04 (provisional) is Rs 5,780.

Minerals and industry: Some of the major industries in Bihar are agro-based industries, oil refineries, textiles, engineering, and oil mills.

Industries that are dependent on agriculture are the edible oil mills located at Araria, rice mills located in Buxar Karbisganch in Purnia district, spice industires, sugar mills located at Banmankhi in Purnia district, jute mills and other agro-based industries.

One of the biggest oil refineries in the country is situated at Barauni in Bihar. It is managed and controlled by the Indian Oil Corporation Ltd, and was built in collaboration with the erstwhile Soviet Union at a cost of Rs 49.40 crores, and went into operation in 1964.

After West Bengal, Bihar is the largest producer of jute and jute textiles. This is largely due to the availability of sufficient power, raw jute, water, transportation, and cheap labour. Jute mills are located in Katihar and Muktapur in Samastipur district, and at Karsbisganj in Purnia district.

Engineering industries are located at Madora in the district of Saran, Muktapur in Samastipur district, Dumaro in Bhojpur district, and Fatuha in Patna district. Railway carriages and goods factories are located in Rohtas district at Dehri-on-Son.

Due to the availability of kendu leaves and cheap labour, biri manufacturing industries are located at Bihar Sarif in

Nalanda district. Bihar is also the sixth largest producer of tobacco in the country.

The important minerals found in Bihar are limestone, pyrites, quartzite and steatite.

Agriculture: Bihar has plenty of farmlands and orchards. The important crops include paddy, sugarcane, wheat and lentils. Jute or hemp, a source of tough fibres used for gunny bags, is also grown. Some of the important fruits grown in the state are banana, jackfruit, mangoes, and litchis.

Paddy is the important crop in all the regions. Supplementary crops include oilseeds, pulses (legumes), barley, gram, wheat and corn (maize). Sugar cane is grown in a well-defined belt in the north-west.

Vegetables include potatoes grown near Bihar Sharif, in Patna district, which produces the best variety of seed potato in India. Other important cash crops include tobacco and chillies that are grown on the banks of the Ganga.

Power: Thermal power is the main source of electricity in the state. Hydroelectric power ranks a distant second.

Education

Prominent institutes of higher education include B.N. Mandal University (Madhepura), Babasaheb Bhimrao Ambedkar Bihar University (Muzaffarpur), Jai Prakash Vishwavidyalaya (Chapra), Kameshwar Singh Darbhanga Sanskrit University (Darbhanga), Lalit Narayan Mithila University (Darbhanga), Magadh University (Bodh Gaya), Nalanda Open University (Patna), Patna University, Rajendra Agricultural University (Samastipur), Tilka Manjhi Bhagalpur University (Bhagalpur) and Veer Kunwar Singh University (Arrah).

Tourism

Major tourist attractions: Bodh Gaya, Rajgir, Nalanda, Vaishali, Pawapuri, Lauria Nandangarh, Vikramshila.

Airports: Patna, Gaya.

National Parks: Valmiki National Park in Pashchim Champaran district (335.65 sq. km).

Administration

Legislature: Bihar has a bicameral legislature consisting of the Vidhan Parishad and the Vidhan Sabha. The governor is appointed by the President of India and acts as the head of the state. The chief minister heads the council of ministers. There are 243 seats in the Vidhan Sabha, of which thirty-nine seats are reserved for SC candidates. No seats are reserved for ST candidates.

The current party position is as follows:

Name of Party	Seats
Bharatiya Janata Party	37
Indian National Congress	10
Nationalist Congress Party	3
Communist Party of India	3
Bahujan Samaj Party	2
Communist Party of India (Marxist)	1
Rashtriya Janata Dal	75
Janata Dal (United)	55
Communist Party of India (Marxist-Leninist) (Liberation)	7
Samajwadi Party	4
Lok Jan Shakti Party	29
Independent	17
Total	**243**

Judiciary: The main seat for the judiciary is the high court of judicature at Patna. The chief justice is Ravi S. Dhawan.

Districts:

District	Area (sq. km)	Population	Headquarters	Urban Agglomerations
Araria	2,830	2,124,831	Araria	
Aurangabad	3,305	2,004,960	Aurangabad	
Banka	3,020	1,608,778	Banka	
Begusarai	1,918	2,342,989	Begusarai	Begusarai
Bhagalpur	2,569	2,430,331	Bhagalpur	Bhagalpur
Bhojpur	2,474	2,233,415	Arrah	
Buxar	1,624	1,403,462	Buxar	
Darbhanga	2,279	3,285,473	Darbhanga	
Gaya	4,976	3,464,983	Gaya	Gaya
Gopalganj	2,033	2,149,343	Gopalganj	
Jamui	3,098	1,397,474	Jamui	
Jehanabad	1,569	1,511,406	Jehanabad	
Kaimur (Bhabua)	3,362	1,284,575	Bhabua	
Katihar	3,057	2,389,533	Katihar	Katihar
Khagaria	1,486	1,276,677	Khagaria	
Kishanganj	1,884	1,294,063	Kishanganj	
Lakhisarai	1,228	801,173	Lakhisarai	
Madhepura	1,788	1,524,596	Madhepura	
Madhubani	3,501	3,570,651	Madhubani	
Munger	1,419	1,135,499	Munger	
Muzaffarpur	3,172	3,743,836	Muzaffarpur	
Nalanda	2,355	2,368,327	Biharsharif	
Nawada	2,494	1,809,425	Nawada	
Pashchim Champaran	5,228	3,043,044	Bettiah	
Patna	3,202	4,709,851	Patna	Patna
Purba Champaran	3,968	3,933,636	Motihari	Motihari
Purnia	3,229	2,540,788	Purnia	Purnia
Rohtas	3,851	2,448,762	Sasaram	
Saharsa	1,702	1,506,418	Saharsa	
Samastipur	2,904	3,413,413	Samastipur	Samastipur
Saran	2,641	3,251,474	Chapra	
Sheikhpura	689	525,137	Sheikhpura	
Sheohar	443	514,288	Sheohar	
Sitamarhi	2,200	2,669,887	Sitamarhi	Sitamarhi
Siwan	2,219	2,708,840	Siwan	
Supaul	2,410	1,745,069	Supaul	
Vaishali	2,036	2,712,389	Hazipur	

Chhattisgarh

Key Statistics

Capital: Raipur.

Area: 135,191 sq. km.

Population: Total: 20,833,803, Male: 10,474,218, Female: 10,359,585.

Population density: 154 per sq. km.

Sex ratio: 989 females per 1000 males.

Principal language: Hindi.

Literacy rates: Total: 64.7%, Male: 77.4%, Female: 51.9%.

Government

Governor: Lt Gen. K.M. Seth, (Retd). He was sworn in on 2 June 2003.

Chief Minister: Dr Raman Singh (BJP). He was sworn in on 8 December 2003.

Geography

Physical characteristics: The state can be divided into three agro-climatic zones. These are the Chhattisgarh plains, the northern hills of Chhattisgarh and the Bastar plateau.

The Satpura mountain range lies in the northern part of the state; the plains of river Mahanadi and its tributaries lie in the central part of the state, while in the south lies the plateau of Bastar. Uttar Pradesh borders the state towards the north; Jharkhand in the north-east; Orissa in the east; Andhra Pradesh in the south and south-east; Maharashtra in the south-west and Madhya Pradesh in the west.

Neighbouring States and Union territories:

States: Madhya Pradesh, Jharkhand, Orissa, Uttar Pradesh, Andhra Pradesh, Maharashtra.

Major rivers: The Mahanadi and the Indravati are the two most important rivers of the state. The Narmada, the Son, the Hasdeo, the Sabari, the Sheonath, the Ib and the Arpa also provide water to the state.

Climate: Chhattisgarh has a generally sub-humid climate. It has hot, dry summers and cold winters. Annual rainfall ranges from 1,200 to 1,500mm.

Flora and Fauna:

Flora: Chhattisgarh has deciduous forests of two types: tropical moist deciduous forests and tropical dry deciduous forests. The state has about twenty-two forest subtypes. The two major tree species in the state are sal and teak. The other notable species are saja, dhawra, mahua, bija, tendu, amla, karra and bamboo.

Fauna: The notable species of animals found in Chhattisgarh are tiger, gaur, sambar, wild buffalo, hill mynah, chital, nilgai, wild boar and leopard.

History

In ancient times, the region that is today Chhattisgarh was called Dakshin Kosala. Its history can be traced back to the *Ramayana* and the *Mahabharata*. It was called Ratanpur during the reign of the Mughals.

In the tenth century AD, a powerful Rajput family ruled at Tripuri, near Jabalpur. A member of the Kalchuri dynasty, Kalingraja, settled at Tuman around AD 1000. His grandson Ratanraja founded Ratanpur, which became the capital of a large part of the area now known as Chhattisgarh. This Rajput family called itself the Haihaya dynasty and it continued to rule Chhattisgarh for six centuries until about the fourteenth century, when it disintegrated.

In the middle ages, the Chalukya dynasty established its rule in Bastar. The Chalukya ruler Annmdev established his dynasty in Bastar in 1320.

One branch of the dynasty continued at Ratanpur, while the other settled in Raipur. At the end of the sixteenth century the latter branch acknowledged the domination of the Mughals.

In 1741, the Marathas attacked Chhattisgarh and destroyed the Haihaya power. In 1745, they conquered the region and deposed Raghunathsinghji, the last survivor of the Ratanpur house. In 1758, the Marathas ultimately annexed Chhattisgarh and it came directly under Maratha rule. The Maratha rule was a period of chaos and misrule, marked by widespread loot and plunder by the Maratha army. The Gonds resisted the Marathas, leading to conflicts and hostility between them. In the early nineteenth century, the Pindaris from Gwalior attacked and plundered the region.

In 1818, Chhattisgarh came under British control for the first time. When the province of Nagpur lapsed to the British government in 1854, Chhattisgarh was put under a deputy commissioner and Raipur made the headquarters. The tribals of Bastar resisted British overlordship and this resulted in the Halba Rebellion, which lasted nearly five years (1774–79).

A demand for a separate Chhattisgarh state was first raised in 1924 by the Raipur Congress unit. It was later raised at the Tripuri session of the Indian National Congress. In 1955, a demand for a separate state was made in the Nagpur assembly of the then state of Madhya Bharat.

On 18 March 1994, a resolution for a separate Chhattisgarh was tabled in the Madhya Pradesh Vidhan Sabha. Both the INC and the BJP supported the resolution and it was unanimously approved.

In 1998, the Union government drafted a bill for the creation of a separate state of Chhattisgarh carved out from sixteen districts of Madhya Pradesh. The Madhya Pradesh assembly unanimously approved the draft bill in 1998, with some modifications.

Chhattisgarh became a separate state on 1 November 2000. Ajit Jogi was the first chief minister of Chhattisgarh.

Politics

The Congress government of Madhya Pradesh took the first institutional and legislative initiative for the creation of Chhattisgarh. On 18 March 1994, a resolution demanding a separate Chhattisgarh was tabled and unanimously approved by the Madhya Pradesh Vidhan Sabha. Both the Congress and the Bhartiya Janta Party supported the resolution. The election manifestos of the Congress and the BJP for both the 1998 and the 1999 parliamentary elections as well as the Madhya Pradesh assembly election of 1998 included the demand for the creation of a separate Chhattisgarh. The state of Chhattisgarh came into existence on 1 November 2000, with the enactment of the Madhya Pradesh (Reorganization) Act, 2000, by the parliament. The state fulfils the long-cherished demand of the tribal people. This is the twenty-sixth state of India. Ajit Jogi of the Congress was sworn in the first chief minister of the state. In the 2003 Assembly elections the BJP won fifty seats in the ninety-member Chhattisgarh state assembly, while the ruling Congress party had to content itself with a mere thirty-seven seats. Raman Singh, president of the BJP in Chhattisgarh, was sworn in as the chief minister on 7 December 2003.

Culture

The state is well known for its tribal art forms, dance forms and handicrafts. These include handicrafts made out of wood, bamboo, terracotta, bell-metal items, wrought-iron items and cotton fabrics. The state is also renowned for its Kosa silk fabric. Local dance forms include the Suga dance, Saila, Ravat Nacha and Karma.

Fairs and festivals: Besides Diwali, Dussehra and Holi, various districts have their own distinct festivals. These include Charta, Navakhana, Surhul, Mati Puja, Goncha, Madai Hareli, Pola, Cherchera, Dev Uthni, Gouri-gour and Surti Teeja.

Economy, Industry and Agriculture

Economy: The net state domestic product at current prices for 2003–04 (provisional) was Rs 32,400 crores. The per capita net state domestic product at current prices for 2003–04 (provisional) was Rs 14,863.

Minerals and industry: The famous Bhilai Steel Plant is located in this state. Apart from this, there are cement plants, food-processing plants, engineering works, chemical plants, plastics units, and fabrication units.

The minerals mined in the state include iron ore, coal, corundum, bauxite, diamond, gold, dolomite, limestone, tin and granite.

Agriculture: The most important crops are paddy, maize, pulses like tur and kulthi, kodo-kutki, small millets, oilseeds like sunflower, groundnut, soyabean and niger. The state also produces jowar, gram, urad, moong and moth in the rabi season.

Power: Most of the state's power comes from thermal power plants, while hydroelectric plants generate the rest.

Education

Educational institutes: The most well known among the institutes of higher education in the state are Pandit Ravishankar Shukla University (Raipur), Guru Ghasidas University (Bilaspur), Indira Gandhi Agriculture University (Raipur), Indira Kala Sangeet University (Khairagarh), Jawaharlal Nehru Krishi Vishwavidyalaya (Jabalpur) and Rani Durgavati Vishwavidyalaya (Jabalpur).

Tourism

Major tourist attractions: Chitrakot waterfalls, Bastar dist.; Tirathgarh Falls, Bastar dist.; Kutumsar caves and Kailash Gufa, Bastar dist.; Danteshwari Temple, Bastar dist.; Ratanpur, Bilaspur dist.; Mallhar, Bilaspur dist.; Deorani-Jethani Temple, Talagram, Bilaspur dist.; Maitry Bagh, Durg dist.; Amrit Dhara waterfalls, Koriya dist.; Ramdaha waterfalls, Koriya dist.; Gavar Ghat waterfalls, Koriya dist.; Akuri Nala, Koriya dist.; Radha Krishna Temple, Raipur dist.; Chandi Temple, Raipur dist.; Swastik Vihar Monastery, Raipur dist.; Anand Premkuti Vihar monastery, Raipur dist.; Maa Bambleshwari Temple, Dongargarh, Rajnandgaon dist.; Thinthini Patthar, Surguja dist.

Airports: Raipur, Bilaspur.

National Parks: Indravati National Park in Dantewada dist. (1,258.37 sq. km), Sanjay National Park in Surguja and Koriya dists (1,471.13 sq. km) and Kangerghati National Park in Kanker dist. (200 sq. km).

Administration

Legislature: Chhattisgarh has a unicameral legislature. There are ninety seats in the Legislative Assembly, of which ten are reserved for SCs and thirty-four for STs. The tenure of the present House ends on 21 December 2008. The current party position is:

Name of Party	Seats
Bharatiya Janata Party	50
Indian National Congress	37

Bahujan Samaj Party	2
Nationalist Congress Party	1
Total	**90**

Judiciary: Chhattisgarh High Court is at Bilaspur. Ananga Kumar Patnaik is the chief justice.

Districts:

District	Area (sq. km)	Population	Headquarters	Urban Agglomerations
Bastar	14,974	13,02,253	Jagdalpur	Jagdalpur
Bilaspur	8,270	19,93,042	Bilaspur	Bilaspur, Mungeli
Dantewada	17,634	7,19,065	Dantewada	
Dhamtari	3,385	7,03,569	Dhamtari	
Durg	8,549	28,01,757	Durg	Dalli-Rajhara, Durg, Bhilainagar
Janjgir-Champa	3,852	13,16,140	Janjgir	
Jashpur	5,838	7,39,780	Jashpur	
Kanker	6,506	6,51,333	Kanker	Kanker
Kawardha	4,223	5,84,667	Kawardha	Kawardha
Korba	6,599	10,12,121	Korba	
Korea	6,604	5,85,455	Baikunthpur	Chirmiri
Mahasamund	4,789	30,09,042	Mahasamund	
Raigarh	7,086	12,65,084	Raigarh	Raigarh
Raipur	13,083	30,09,042	Raipur	Raipur, Tilda Newra
Rajnandgaon	8,068	12,81,811	Rajnandgaon	
Surguja	15,731	19,70,661	Ambikapur	Ambikapur

Goa

Key Statistics

Capital: Panaji.
Area: 3,702 sq. km.
Population: Total: 1,347,668, Male: 687,248, Female: 660,420.
Population density: 363 per sq. km.
Sex ratio: 961 females per 1000 males.
Principal languages: Konkani, Marathi, Kannada.
Literacy rates: Total: 82.32%, Male: 88.88%, Female: 75.51%.

Government

Governor: S.C. Jamir. He became the governor on 2 July 2004.

Chief Minister: Pratapsingh R. Rane (INC) was sworn in on 2 February 2005. On 4 March 2005 the Assembly was dissolved and President's Rule was declared. Pratapsingh Rane was reinstated on 7 June for the fourth time.

Geography

Physical characteristics: Goa, situated on the Konkan coast of India, has a coastline of 131 km. It has a partly hilly terrain, with the Western Ghats rising to nearly 1,200 metres in some parts of the state. In the north, the Terekhol river separates Goa and Maharashtra. Karnataka lies to the south, with the Arabian Sea to the west and the Western Ghats to the east. The island of Goa lies between the mouths of the Mandovi and Zuari rivers, which are connected on the landward side by a creek. The island is triangular in shape, with a cape in the form of a rocky headland that divides

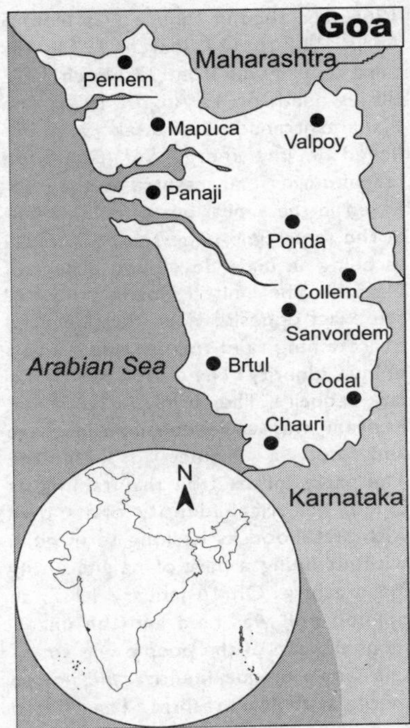

the harbour of Goa into two parts—Aguada at the mouth of the Mandovi, on the north, and Mormugao or Marmagao at the mouth of the Zuari, on the south.

Neighbouring States and Union territories:

States: Maharashtra, Karnataka.

Major rivers: Mandovi and Zuari.

Climate: Summer temperatures vary from 24°C to 32.7°C. Winter temperatures vary from 21.3°C to 32.2°C. Rainfall 3,200mm (June–September).

History

Goa first appears in the Puranas as Gove, Govapuri and Gomant. The medieval Arab geographers called it Sindabur. The Portuguese called it Velha Goa. From the second century AD to 1312, it was ruled by the Kadamba dynasty. The Muslim invaders of the Deccan held sway between 1312 and 1367, after which it was annexed by the Hindu kingdom of Vijayanagar. Later, it was conquered by the Bahmani dynasty, which founded Old Goa in 1440. After 1482, Goa passed into the hands of Yusuf Adil Khan, the king of Bijapur. It was during his reign that the Portuguese first reached India. In March 1510 the city surrendered to the Portuguese under Afonso de Albuquerque. A violent struggle between the Portuguese and Yusuf Adil Khan ensued, but the Portuguese had the last laugh. Goa was the first territorial possession of the Portuguese in Asia. It later became the capital of the entire Portuguese empire in the East.

In 1603 and 1639 the Dutch Navy blockaded the city, but never managed to capture it. In 1683 a Mughal army saved it from capture by the Maratha. The latter attacked the area again in 1739 but it was saved once again.

In 1809, the British temporarily occupied the city, as a result of Napoleon's invasion of Portugal.

At the time of Independence in 1947, Goa was still a Portuguese colony. In 1961, Indian military forces invaded and occupied Goa, Daman, and Diu. They were incorporated into the Indian Union in 1962. On 30 May 1987, Goa was granted statehood, Daman and Diu remaining as a separate Union territory. Goa's first chief minister was Pratapsingh Rane.

Politics

Portuguese rule was so oppressive and exploitative that during 450 years of Portuguese rule, there were forty armed revolts in Goa. Although these revolts were put down with a heavy hand, the urge for freedom could not be suppressed forever. A movement for the liberation of Goa gained momentum in the 1900s. The main leaders of the movement were Tristao Bragansa Cunha, Purushottam Kakodkar, Laxmi Kant Bhembre, Divakar Kakodkar and Dayanand Bandodkar. The liberation movement became stronger after Indian Independence in 1947.

India's new government claimed Goa in 1948. In 1955, nonviolent protesters attempted a peaceful annexation. The resulting casualties led to a breakdown of relations between India and Portugal. Indian troops invaded Goa in December 1961. Within three days Goa was integrated into India in a near bloodless operation—Operation Vijay—on 19 December 1961. The other Portuguese territories of Daman and Diu were also taken over at around the same time and thus was formed the Union territory of Goa, Daman and Diu which became a part of the Indian Union. Initially the liberated territory was under the army administration of Lt Gen. Candeth, the military governor who was assisted by the chief civil administrator. On 8 June 1962, the military government gave place to civil rule. The lieutenant governor formed an informal Consultative Council consisting of twenty-nine nominated members to assist him in the administration of the territory. Goa attained full statehood on 30 May 1987 when Daman and Diu retained a separate identity as a Union territory.

In 1963, the Maharashtrawadi Gomantak Party, which had won the first Assembly elections, was led by Dayanand Bandodkar. On 20 December 1963, the first chief minister of Goa, Daman and Diu (Union territory), Dayanand Bandodkar, was sworn in. He had three tenures as the chief minister of Goa, Daman and Diu. Bhausaheb Bandodkar was the chief minister from 20 December 1963 to 2 December 1966. His second tenure was from 5 April 1967 to 23 March 1972. His third tenure was from 23 March 1972 till his death on 12 August 1973. The Maharashtrabadi Gomantak Party believed in the merger of Goa with neighbouring Maharashtra as they believed in the similarities of culture but at the same time underscored Konkani as being an underdeveloped dialect of Marathi. The United Goans party had the exact opposite view; they believed in retaining and preserving Goa's unique identity. They were led by Dr Jack Sequeira. They firmly believed that Konkani was an independent language and not a dialect of Marathi. The party insisted on maintaining its unique historical identity of its own with statehood as its long term goal, without being a part of neighbouring Maharashtra. On 16 January 1967, an opinion poll was held and the unanimous opinion of the people was to retain Goa's unique identity and not to merge with Maharashtra. The United Goans party won the elections by 34,021 votes.

After the death of Dayanand Banodkar, his daughter, Shashikala Kakodkar, was voted into power and she became the chief minister (India's first woman to do so). She was in power until April 1979. After a brief eight months of President's Rule, elections were held in January 1980. For the first time, the MG party was voted out of power and the mainstream Congress party came to power with the election of Pratapsingh Rane of the Congress party as chief minister. This was the first time the Congress party had made an entry into Goa's political scene. A scion of the Rane family of Sattari, Pratapsingh Rane remained in power, winning the election again in 1985 and 1990. Goa attained another political milestone by becoming a state on 30 May 1987. Daman and Diu remained as a separate Union territory. Pratapsingh Rane was sworn in as the first chief minister of the new Goa state. In 1992 Konkoni was declared as the official language of the state of Goa.

On 27 March 1990 Churchill Alemao of United Goans Democratic Party took over as the chief minister of Goa. His rule lasted for eighteen and a half days, till 14 April 1990. From 14 April 1990 to 14 December 1990, Dr Luis Proto Barbosa was the chief minister of Goa, followed by President's Rule. On 25 January 1991 Ravi Naik took over as the chief minister until 18 May 1993. Ravi Naik was followed by Dr Wilfred or Willy D'Souza from 18 May 1993 to 2 April 1994. Shri Ravi Naik came back as chief minister from 2 April 1994 to 8 April 1994. Ravi Naik's second tenure as the chief minister lasted for six and a half days. Once again Dr Wilfred D'Souza was the chief minister from 8 April 1994 to 16 December 1994. Pratapsingh Rane's fifth tenure as the chief minister of Goa came on 16 December 1994 and lasted till 29 July 1998. Dr Wilfred D'Souza came for the third time as the chief minister from 29 July 1998 to 23 November 1998. On 26 November 1998, Luizinho Faleiro took over as the chief minister and ruled till 8 February 1999, followed by President's Rule. On 9 June 1999, once again Luizinho Faleiro took over as the chief minister till 24 November 1999. From 24 November 1999 to 24 October 2000, Francisco Sardinha was the chief minister. From 24 October 2000 to 3 June 2002, Manohar Parrikar of the Bharatiya Janata Party was the chief minister. Parrikar's second tenure as the chief minister was from 3 June 2002 till 2 February 2005. Again Pratapsingh Rane was sworn in as chief minister on 2 February 2005. President's rule was proclaimed on 4 March. A by-election in June 2005 saw the Congress come back to power after winning three of the five seats that went to polls. Pratapsingh Rane returned as chief minister on 7 June 2005 for the fourth time.

Culture

Goa is well known for its folk dances like Dhalo, Fugdi, Mando, Corridinho and performing folk arts like Khell-Tiatro and Jagar-perani. It is also well known for rosewood and teak furniture, terracotta figurines, brass items and jewellery designs. Folk paintings of Goa mostly depict scenes from the *Mahabharata*, the *Ramayana* and the Puranas and also scenes from the New Testament. Goa is also an important centre for Konkani literature.

Fairs and festivals: The Goan Hindu community celebrates Ganesh Chathurti, Krishna Janmashtami, Rakshabandhan, Gudi Padwa, Diwali, Dussehra, Holi, and Ramnavami.

In Goa, the most widely celebrated festival is Ganesh Chaturthi, or Chovoth. In the month of Phalgun, Goa celebrates Holi, or Shigmoutsav. In the month of Shravan, the town of Vasco celebrates Vasco Saptah. The Lairai Jatra takes place in early May. The Goa Carnival is usually celebrated in February or March.

Economy, Industry and Agriculture

Economy: The net state domestic product at current prices in 2002–03 was Rs 7,412 crores. The per capita net state domestic product at current prices in 2002–03 was Rs 53,092. Goa has the highest per capita income in India.

Minerals and industry: There are over 5,000 small-scale industrial units in the state. Mineral resources of the state include bauxite, iron ore and ferro-manganese.

Agriculture: Rice, millets and pulses are the most widely grown food grains. Coconuts, cashew nuts and oilseeds are also grown.

Education

Educational institutes: Prominent institutes of higher education include Goa University, National Institute of Oceanography, National Institute of Water Sports, Goa Institute of Management and the Indian Council of Agricultural Research.

Tourism

Major tourist attractions: Calangute Beach, Colva Beach, Dona Paula Beach, Miramar Beach, Anjuna Beach, Palolem Beach, Vagator Beach, Arambol Beach, Agonda Beach, Basilica of Bom Jesus, Se Cathedral, Church of St. Francis of Assisi, Dudhsagar waterfalls, Aguada Fort.

Airports: Goa, Mormugao.

National Parks: Bhagwan Mahavir (107 sq. km).

Administration

Legislature: Goa has a unicameral legislature, with a legislative assembly. There are forty seats in the assembly, including one seat reserved for SCs. The term of the current assembly expires on 11 June 2007. The present party position in the assembly is as follows:

Name of Party	Seats
Bharatiya Janata Party	17
Indian National Congress	16
United Gomantwadi Democratic Party	3
Maharashtrabadi Gomantak Party	2
Nationalist Congress Party	1
Independent	1
Total	**40**

Judiciary: Goa falls under the jurisdiction of the Goa bench of the Mumbai High Court. The chief justice is Dalveer C. Bhandari. There is one district court and other subordinate courts.

Districts:

District	Area (sq. km)	Population	Headquarters	Urban Agglomerations
North Goa	1,736	757,407	Panaji	Panaji
South Goa	1,966	586,591	Margao	Margao, Mormugao

Gujarat

Key Statistics

Capital: Gandhinagar.

Area: 196,024 sq. km.

Population: Total: 50,671,017, Male: 26,385,577, Female: 24,285,440.

Population density: 258 per sq. km.

Sex ratio: 920 females per 1000 males.

Principal languages: Gujarati, Hindi, Sindhi.

Literacy rates: Total: 69.1%, Male: 79.7%, Female: 57.8%.

Government

Governor: Nawal Krishna Sharma. He was sworn in on 24 July 2004.

Chief Minister: Narendra Damodardas Modi. He was sworn in on 22 December 2002.

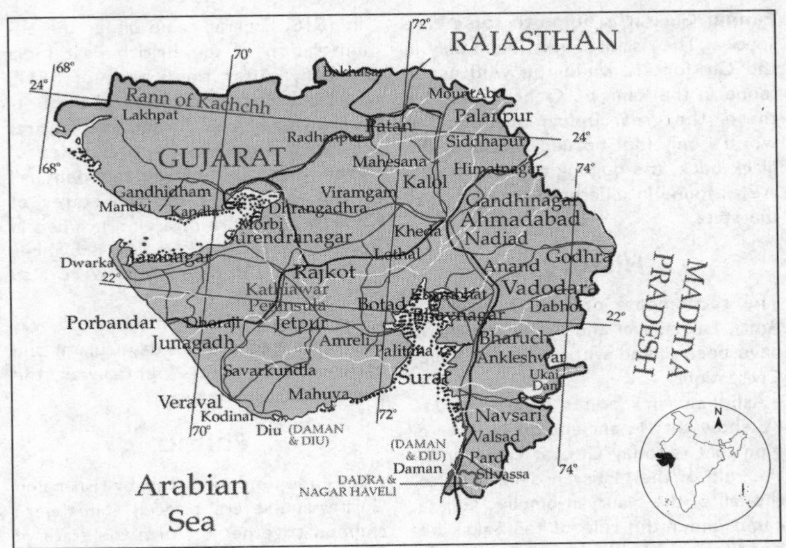

Geography

Physical characteristics: One of the most striking geographical features of the state is the Rann of Kachchh, a vast salt marsh that stretches for about 18,000 sq km. In the dry season, it is a sandy salt plain prone to dust storms, but during the rainy season even light rainfall floods the Rann and the region becomes an island.

The expansive Kathiawar Peninsula lies to the south of Kachchh, between the Gulf of Kachchh and the Gulf of Khambhat. This is another arid region and the coastal region gives way to a low area of wooded hilly region in the central part. The rivers of the state are mostly seasonal streams. The north-eastern part of the state is primarily a region of plains and low hills. The highest point in the state is in the Girnar hills (1,117 metres).

Neighbouring States and Union territories:
International border: Pakistan.

States: Rajasthan, Maharashtra, Madhya Pradesh.

Union territories: Daman and Diu, Dadra and Nagar Haveli.

Major rivers: Narmada, Tapti, Mahi, Sabarmati, Banas and Bhadar are the most important rivers. Other rivers include Heran, Orsang, Karad, Saidak, Mohar and Vatrak.

Climate: The climate in Gujarat varies from humid in the coastal areas, to very hot in areas like Kachchh. It can get extremely hot in the summers and extremely cold in the winters.

The climate of Gujarat is moist in the southern districts and dry in the northern region. The state's climate can be divided into a winter season from November to February, a summer season from March to May and a south-west monsoon season from June to September.

Flora and Fauna:
Flora: Roughly 10 per cent of the area of Gujarat is under forest cover. The state's flora includes dry deciduous forests, moist deciduous forests, grasslands, wetlands and marine ecosystems.

Fauna: Gujarat is home to some rare species. The Asiatic lion is found only in the Gir forest, while the wild ass is found in the Rann of Kachchh. Besides these, the great Indian bustard, the world's only four-horned antelope, the black buck, the dugong and the boralia are all found in different habitats across the state.

History

The settlements of Lothal, Rangpur, Amri, Lakhabaval and Rozdi in Gujarat have been linked with the Indus Valley Civilization.

Ashokan rock edicts of around 250 BC show that in ancient times, the region that is today Gujarat came under the rule of the Mauryan dynasty. After the fall of the Mauryan empire, Gujarat came under the rule of the Sakas between AD 130–390. At its height, the Sakas held sway over what is today Malwa, Saurashtra, Kachchh and Rajasthan.

In the fourth and fifth centuries, Gujarat constituted a part of the Gupta empire. The Guptas were succeeded by the Maitraka dynasty of the kingdom of Valabhi. The Maitrakas ruled over Gujarat and Malwa for three centuries. They were succeeded by the Gurjara-Pratiharas of Kannauj, who ruled during the eighth and ninth centuries. Following the Gurjara-Pratiharas came the Solanki dynasty, which was followed by the Vaghela dynasty. In about 1297, Ala-ud-Din Khalji, the sultan of Delhi, defeated Karnadeva Vaghela and the area came under Muslim influence. In 1401, Zafar Khan, whom the Tughluqs had appointed governor of the province, declared independence. His grandson Ahmad Shah, founded Ahmedabad in 1411. From the end of the sixteenth century to the mid-eighteenth century, Gujarat was under Mughal rule. Then came the Marathas who overran the region in the mid-eighteenth century.

In 1818, Gujarat came under the administration of the British East India Company. After the Revolt of 1857, the area became a province of the British crown and was divided into Gujarat province and numerous smaller states.

When India became independent, all of Gujarat except for the states of Kachcha and Saurashtra was included in Bombay state. In 1956, the provinces of Kachcha and Saurashtra were also included.

On 1 May 1960, Bombay state was bifurcated into present-day Gujarat and Maharashtra. Jivraj Mehta was the state's first chief minister.

Politics

After Independence, the British-ruled Gujarat and several princely states were clubbed together to form the state of Bombay. The States Reorganization Act was passed by Parliament in November 1956. Bombay state was enlarged by merging the states of Kachchh and Saurashtra and the Maratha-speaking areas of Hyderabad with it. The strongest reaction against the States Reorganization Act came from Maharashtra where widespread rioting broke out; eighty people were killed in Bombay city in police firings in January 1956. Under pressure, the government decided in June 1956 to divide Bombay state into two linguistic states of Maharashtra and Gujarat with Bombay city forming a separate, centrally administered state. This move too was, however, opposed by the people of both Maharashtra and Gujarat. The government finally agreed in May 1960 to bifurcate the state of Bombay into Maharashtra and Gujarat, with Bombay city being included in Maharashtra, and Ahmedabad being made the capital of Gujarat.

On bifurcation of the Greater Bombay state on 1 May 1960, under the Bombay Reorganization Act, 1960, the new state of Gujarat came into existence.

The Congress dominated Gujarat's corridors of power for most of the time from 1960 to 1995. Chimanbhai Patel and Chhabildas Mehta were the last Congress chief ministers of the state. Keshubhai Patel of the BJP became chief minister after elections in 1995. Narendra Damodardas Modi took over as the fourteenth chief minister of Gujarat on 7 October 2001 after Keshubhai Patel stepped down on the directive of BJP high command. He is the current chief minister. The imposition of President's Rule on five occasions so far and frequent outbreaks of communal violence has played a vital role in shaping the state's politics over the years. On 27 February 2002, a sleeper coach in the Sabarmati Express, coming from Faizabad and proceeding towards Ahmedabad, caught fire a few minutes after it left the Godhra railway station. The coach that was ravaged in the fire was occupied predominantly by members and sympathizers of the Sangh Parivar, called kar sevaks, who were returning after a pilgrimage to Ayodhya. This incident was a precursor to a spate of widepsread riots in the state, which lasted nearly three months.

Culture

Gujarat is famous for its Garba dance form, which is performed on Navratri. The state is also famous for its bandhni tie-and-dye technique, Patola saris, toys of Idar, perfumes of Palanpur, the handloom products of Konodar and woodwork from Ahmedabad and Surat.

Fairs and festivals: The festivals of the state include the International Kite Festival of Ahmedabad, Somnath Festival, Navratri, Tarnetra Festival and Janmastami.

Economy, Industry and Agriculture

Economy: The net state domestic product at current prices for 2003–04 (provisional) was Rs 142,559 crores. The per capita net state domestic product at current prices for 2003–04 (provisional) was Rs 26,979.

Minerals and industry: The important minerals found in the state are bauxite, manganese, limestone, lignite, bentonite, dolomite, crude oil, granite, silica, china clay and fireclay.

The major industries in the state are petrochemicals, engineering, electronics, chemicals and fertilizers. Surat is an important centre for the diamond trade while Anand is home to Amul, the milk giant.

Agriculture: Major food crops in the state are rice, wheat, jowar, bajra, maize, tur, gram and groundnut. The most important non-food crops are cotton and tobacco.

Power: Gujarat gets its power mainly from thermal power plants, as well as partially from nuclear and hydroelectric power plants.

Education

Educational institutes: Notable institutes for higher education in the state include the Indian Institute of Management (Ahmedabad), Gujarat University (Ahmedabad), Gujarat Agricultural University (Sardar Krushinagar), Maharaja Sayaji Rao University (Vadodara), North Gujarat University (Patan), Saurashtra University (Rajkot), Indian Institute of Rural Management (Anand), Mudra Institute of Communications (Ahmedabad).

Tourism

Major tourist attractions: Mandvi Beach, Palitana Temple, Hatheesing Temple, Akshardham Temple, Somnath Temple, Sasan Gir, Modhera Sun Temple, Lothal, Bala Sinor, Saputara Hill Station.

Airports:
International: Ahmedabad.

Domestic:: Bhuj, Kandla, Jamnagar, Keshoo, Bhavnagar, Rajkot , Vadodara, Palanpur, Porbandar.

National Parks: Marine National Park and Sanctuary in Jamnagar dist. (162.89 sq. km and 295.03 sq. km respectively); Gir National Park and Sanctuary in Junagadh dist. (258.71 sq. km and 1153.42 sq. km respectively); Velavadhar National Park in Bhavnagar dist. (34.08 sq. km) and Vansda National Park in Valsad dist. (23.99 sq. km).

Administration

Legislature: Gujarat has a unicameral legislature. There are 182 seats of which thirteen are reserved for SCs and twenty-six for STs. The tenure of the present house ends on 26 December 2007.

The party position in the current Vidhan Sabha is as follows:

Name of Party	Seats
Bharatiya Janata Party	128
Indian National Congress	49
Janata Dal	2
Independents	2
Vacant	1
Total	**182**

Judiciary: The High Court of Gujarat is at Ahmedabad. The chief justice is Bhawani Singh, sworn in on 25 August 2003.

Districts:

District	Area (sq. km)	Population	Headquarters	Urban Agglomerations
Ahmedabad	8,086	5,808,378	Ahmedabad	Ahmedabad, Dholka
Amreli	7,397	1,393,295	Amreli	Amreli
Anand	2,940	1,856,712	Anand	Anand, Khambhat
Banas Kantha	10,757	2,502,843	Palanpur	Palanpur
Bharuch	6,527	1,370,104	Bharuch	Anklesvar, Bharuch
Bhavnagar	9,980.9	2,469,264	Bhavnagar	Bhavnagar, Mahuva
Dahod	3,646.1	1,635,374	Dahod	Dahod
Gandhinagar	2,163.4	1,334,731	Gandhinagar	Ahmadabad, Kalol
Jamnagar	14,125	1,913,685	Jamnagar	Jamnagar
Junagadh	8,846	2,448,427	Junagadh	Junagadh, Mangrol, Veraval
Kutch	45,652	1,526,321	Bhuj	Bhuj
Kheda	4,218.8	2,023,354	Nadiad	Dakor, Nadiad
Mahesana	4,382.8	1,837,696	Mahesana	Kadi, Mahesana, Vijapur, Visnagar
Narmada	2,755.5	514,083	Rajpipla	
Navsari	2,209.2	1,229,250	Navsari	Bilimora, Navsari
Panch Mahals	5,219.9	2,024,883	Godhra	Godhra, Halol, Kalol
Patan	5,730.4	1,181,941	Patan	Patan, Sidhpur
Porbandar	2,297.8	536,854	Porbandar	Porbandar, Ranavav
Rajkot	11,203	3,157,676	Rajkot	Gondal, Morvi, Rajkot
Sabar Kantha	7,390	2,083,416	Himatnagar	Idar
Surat	7,657	4,996,391	Surat	Surat
Surendranagar	10,489	1,515,147	Surendranagar	Wadhwan
The Dangs	1,764	186,712	Ahwa	
Vadodara	7,549.5	3,639,775	Vadodara	Padra, Vadodara
Valsad	3,034.8	1,410,680	Valsad	Valsad

Haryana

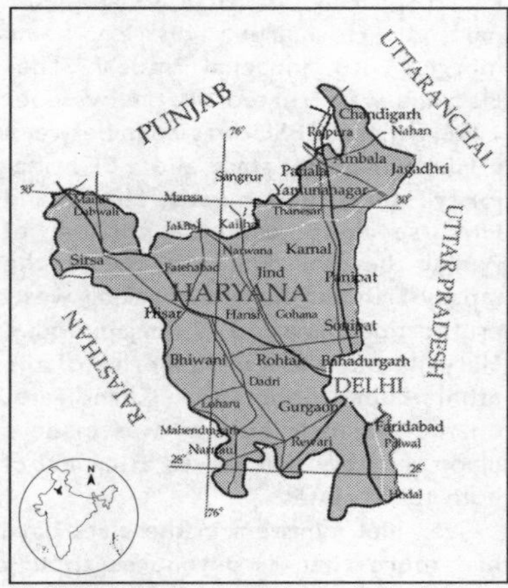

Key Statistics

Capital: Chandigarh.
Area: 44,212 sq. km.
Population: Total: 21,144,564, Male: 11,369,953, Female: 9,780,611.
Population density: 477 per sq. km.
Sex ratio: 861 females per 1000 males.
Principal languages: Hindi, Punjabi, Urdu.
Literacy rates: Total: 67.9%, Male: 78.5%, Female: 55.67%.

Government

Governor: A.R. Kidwai. He became governor on 5 July 2004.

Chief Minister: Bhupinder Singh Hooda (INC). He was sworn in on 5 March 2005.

Geography

Physical characteristics: Haryana is surrounded by Himachal Pradesh in the north, Punjab in the west, Uttar Pradesh in the east and Delhi and Rajasthan in the south. The state has four main geographical features: (i) The Shivalik hills in the north, source of main seasonal rivers; (ii) The Ghaggar–Yamuna plain, which is divided into two parts—the higher one called Bangar and the lower one Khadar; (iii) A semi-desert plain, bordering the state of Rajasthan and (iv) The Aravalli hills in the south, a dry area with uneven landscape.

Neighbouring States and Union territories:
States: Rajasthan, Punjab, Uttar Pradesh, Uttaranchal, Himachal Pradesh.

Union territories: Chandigarh, Delhi.

Major rivers: The Yamuna, Haryana's only perennial river, flows along the eastern boundary of the state. Ghaggar, the main seasonal river, flows along the northern boundary. Some other important seasonal rivers are Markanda, Tangri and Sahibi.

Climate: Haryana has very hot summers with maximum temperatures going up to 50°C in May and June in some areas. December and January are the coldest, minimum temperatures dropping as low as 1°C in parts of the state.

Rainfall is varied with the Shivalik region receiving the most rain and the Aravalli region being the driest. Nearly 80 per cent of the total rainfall occurs in the monsoon season, from July to September. The tributaries of the Yamuna and Ghaggar cause occasional floods.

Flora and Fauna:
Flora: Forests, mostly thorny dry deciduous forest, cover about 3.5 per cent of the total area. Common trees are babul, neem, shisham, pipal and banyan.

Fauna: Animals and birds found in the state include leopard, jackal, Indian fox, barking deer, sambar, chital, black buck, wild boar, seh or Indian porcupine, blue jay, northern green barbet, coppersmith, rose-ringed parakeet, kingfisher, Indian krait and Russell's viper.

History

The word Hariana occurs in a Sanskrit inscription dated AD 1328. The region now known as Haryana was the scene of many important battles in Indian history. These include the three battles of Panipat: the first in 1526, when Babur defeated Ibrahim Lodi to establish Mughal rule in India; the second in 1556, when Emperor Akbar's army defeated the Afghans; and the third in 1761, when Ahmad Shah Abdali defeated the Marathas.

In 1803, the area included in the present state was ceded to the British East India Company and was subsequently transferred to the North-Western Provinces in 1832. Haryana became a part of Punjab in 1858, and remained so well after independence. Demands for states on a linguistic basis started to gain momentum in the early 1960s. On 1 November 1966, with the passage of the Punjab Reorganization Act, Haryana became the seventeenth state of India. Bhagwat Dayal Sharma was the first chief minister of the state.

Politics

In 1956, the states of PEPSU had been merged with Punjab, which remained a trilingual state having three language speakers—Punjabi, Hindi and Pahari—within its borders. In the Punjabi-speaking part of the state, there was a strong demand for carving out a separate Punjabi Suba (Punjabi-speaking state). The State Reorganization Commission had refused to accept the demand for a separate Punjabi-speaking state on the ground that this would not solve the language problem of Punjab. Finally, in 1966, Indira Gandhi agreed to the division of Punjab into two Punjabi- and Hindi-speaking states of Punjab and Haryana, with the Pahari-speaking district of Kangra and a part of Hoshiarpur district being merged with Himachal Pradesh. Thus Haryana was created on 1 November 1966, when PEPSU was split between a Hindu majority state and a Sikh majority state. The mostly Hindu and Hindi-speaking eastern portion of Punjab became Haryana, while the mostly Sikh and Punjabi-speaking western portion remained as Punjab. Today, Haryana has the vast majority of the ethnic Hindu population. Chandigarh, on the linguistic border, was made a union territory that serves as capital of both these states.

Five chief ministers in the state have had more than two tenures though most of them did not last the complete tenure of five years. Jat strongman Devi Lal was chief minister twice. Congress Leader Bansi Lal assumed charge for the first time in 1968 and remained chief minister till 1975. He was again chief minister between 1987 and 1989. His last tenure was from 1996-99. Banarsi Dass Gupta who succeeded Bansi Lal in 1975 also was chief minister twice. Devi Lal succeeded him on 21 May 1977. Devi Lal had played an active and decisive role in the formation of Haryana as a separate state. In 1971 he left the Congress after being in it for thirty-nine years. In 1977 he was elected on a Janata Party ticket and became the chief minister of Haryana. He formed the Lok Dal and started the programme Nyaya Yudh under the Haryana Sangharsh Samiti which became hugely popular among the masses. In the 1987 state elections, the alliance led by Devi Lal won a record victory winning eighty-five seats in the ninety-member house. Bhajan Lal first became chief minister in 1979; he continued till 1985. He was again chief minister from 1991 to 1996. Om

Prakash Chautala served the state four times as chief minister. He was elected unanimously as the president of the Haryana unit of the Indian National Lok Dal in 1999. Chautala's Indian National Lok Dal was routed in the 2005 Assembly polls. Bhupinder Singh Hooda of the Congress took oath on 5 March 2005 as the nineteenth chief minister of Haryana.

Culture

Haryana has a tradition of folklore expressed through mimes, dramas, ballads and songs such as Phag dance, Loor, Saang, Chupaiya and so on.

Fairs and festivals: Prominent festivals of Haryana are Holi, Diwali, Teej, Gugga Pir and Sanjhi. Popular fairs include Gopal-Mochan fair, Masani fair and Surajkund crafts fair. The Mango Festival and the Kurukshetra Festival are other popular annual events.

Economy, Industry and Agriculture

Economy: The net state domestic product at current prices for 2003–04 (provisional) was Rs 66,325 crores. The per capita net state domestic product at current prices for 2003–04 (provisional) was Rs 29,963.

Minerals and industry: The manufacturing sector's contribution to the state economy was 21.3 per cent during 1998–99. Major industries include passenger cars, motorcycles, tractors, sanitary ware, GI pipes, scientific instruments and gas stoves. In thirty years, the number of large and medium units has gone up from 162 to 1023, while the number of small-scale units increased from 4,500 to 80,000. In recent years, many multinational companies have set up Business Process Outsourcing (BPO) operations in Gurgaon. Major minerals of the state are limestone, dolomite, china clay and marble.

Agriculture: Apart from meeting its own requirements, Haryana contributes about 45 lakh tonnes of food grain (mostly wheat and paddy) to the Central pool each year. Other important crops are sugar cane, cotton and maize.

Animal husbandry is a significant component of agriculture in the state. Apart from the Murrah breed of buffaloes, the state regularly supplies eggs, layer-chicks and broilers to other Indian states.

Power: Most of Haryana's power is generated by thermal power plants. The rest comes from hydroelectric plants.

Education

Educational institutes: Notable institutions include the Maharshi Dayanand University (Rohtak), Kurukshetra University (Kurukshetra), Guru Jambheshwar University (Hissar), Chaudhary Charan Singh Agriculture University (Hissar) and National Dairy Research Institute (NDRI) (Karnal).

Tourism

Major tourist attractions: Surajkund, Kurukshetra, Panipat.

Airports: Chandigarh.

National Parks: Sultanpur National Park in Gurgaon dist. (1.43 sq. km).

Administration

Legislature: The state has a unicameral legislature with ninety members. Out of this seventeen seats are reserved for SCs. The tenure of the current house ends on 8 March 2005. The current party position is as follows:

Name of Party	Seats
Indian National Congress	67
Indian National Lok Dal	9
Bharatiya Janata Party	2

Bahujan Samaj Party	1
Nationalist Congress Party	1
Independents	10
Total	**90**

Judiciary: The seat of the Punjab and Haryana High Court is at Chandigarh. The current chief justice is D.K. Jain.

Districts:

District	Area (sq. km)	Population	Headquarters	Urban Agglomerations
Ambala	1,574	1,013,660	Ambala	Ambala
Bhiwani	4,778	1,424,554	Bhiwani	
Faridabad	2,151	2,193,276	Faridabad	
Fatehabad	2,538	806,158	Fatehabad	
Gurgaon	2,766	1,657,669	Gurgaon	Gurgaon
Hisar	3,983	1,536,417	Hisar	Hisar
Jhajjar	1,834	887,392	Jhajjar	Bahadurgarh
Jind	2,702	1,189,725	Jind	
Kaithal	2,317	945,631	Kaithal	
Karnal	2,520	1,274,843	Karnal	Karnal
Kurukshetra	1,530	828,120	Kurukshetra	Thanesar
Mahendragarh	1,859	812,022	Narnaul	
Panchkula	898	469,210	Panchkula	Pinjore
Panipat	1,268	967,338	Panipat	Panipat
Rewari	1,582	764,727	Rewari	
Rohtak	1,745	940,036	Rohtak	Rohtak
Sirsa	4,277	1,111,012	Sirsa	
Sonipat	2,122	1,278,830	Sonipat	Sonipat
Yamunanagar	1,768	982,369	Yamunanagar	Yamunanagar

Himachal Pradesh

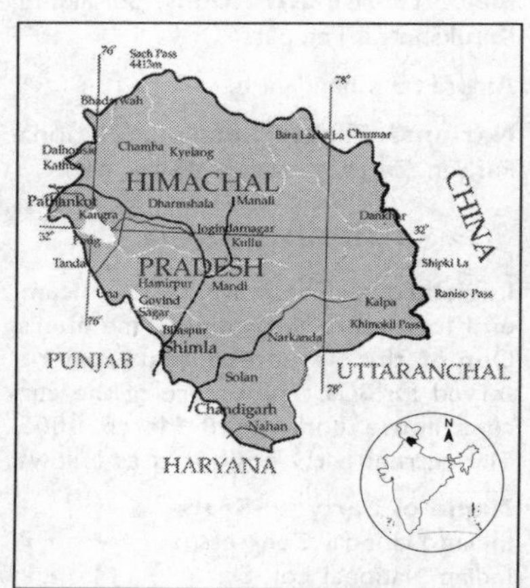

Key Statistics

Capital: Shimla.
Area: 55,673 sq. km.
Population: Total: 6,077,900, Male: 3,087,940, Female: 2,989,960.
Population density: 109 per sq. km.
Sex ratio: 968 females per 1000 males.
Principal languages: Hindi, Punjabi, Kinnauri.
Literacy rates: Total: 76.5%, Male: 85.3%, Female: 67.4%.

Government

Governor: Vishnu Sadashiv Kokje. He assumed the office of the governor on 8 May 2003.

Chief Minister: Virbhadra Singh (INC). He was sworn in on 6 March 2003.

Geography

Physical characteristics: Almost completely mountainous, with altitudes varying from 350 m to 6,975 m above sea level, Himachal Pradesh can be divided into five zones: (i) Wet sub-temperate zone (parts of Kangra, Mandi and Chamba districts); (ii) Humid sub-temperate zone (Kullu and Shimla districts; parts of Mandi, Solan, Chamba, Kangra and Sirmaur districts); (iii) Dry temperate alpine highlands (parts of Lahaul and Spiti district); (iv) Humid subtropical zone (Sirmaur district; parts of Chamba, Solan and Kangra districts); and (v) Sub-humid subtropical zone (parts of Kangra district).

Neighbouring States and Union territories:

International border: China.

States: Jammu and Kashmir, Uttaranchal, Punjab, Haryana, Uttar Pradesh.

Major rivers: Sutlej, Beas, Ravi, Chenab and Yamuna.

Climate: The climate varies from hot and humid in the valley areas to freezing cold in the alpine zone, which remains under snow for five to six months a year. Temperatures range from 40°C in plains during summer to –20°C in the alpine zone during winters. The average annual rainfall is about 1,600mm.

Flora and Fauna:

Flora: Vegetation varies from dry scrub forests at lower altitudes to alpine pastures at higher altitudes. Between these two extremes, there are zones of mixed deciduous forests with deodar, chil, oak, bamboo, kail, spruce and fir.

Fauna: Wildlife found in Himachal Pradesh includes musk deer (the state animal), Himalayan tahr, brown bear, snow leopard, ibex, western tragopan, sambhar, barking deer, wild boar, ghoral, leopard, monal (the state bird), cheer, snow cock and white crested kaleej.

History

The earliest known inhabitants of this mountainous region were a tribe called Dasas and later, Aryans. Successive Indian empires such as the Mauryans, the Kushans, the Guptas and the Mughals exercised varying degrees of control over the area. British domination of the region followed the Anglo-Sikh wars of the 1840s and continued for the next 100 years. After Independence, thirty princely states were united to form the chief commissioner's province of Himachal Pradesh, which went on to become a Union territory in 1956.

With the reorganization of Punjab in 1966, Kangra and some other hill areas of Punjab were included in Himachal Pradesh, though its status remained that of a Union territory. Himachal Pradesh became the eighteenth state of the Indian Union on 25 January 1971. Yashwant Singh Parmar was the first chief minister.

Politics

Himachal Pradesh was formed as a union territory in 1948 by the merger of thirty former Punjabi princely states. In 1951, it became a part 'C' state. In 1956, despite majority recommendation of the States Reorganization Commission for its merger with Punjab, Himachal Pradesh retained its separate identity, thanks to the famous dissenting note of the Chairman of the Commission, Justice Sh. Fazal Ali. But a great price had to be paid as Himachal was made a Union territory sans a Legislative Assembly and was placed under an administrator designated as lieutenant governor. Thereafter, the people and the political leadership of the state had to literally move heaven and earth for the restoration of a democratic edifice. Their efforts finally bore fruit in 1963, when a bill was passed by the Union parliament for providing Legislative Assemblies and Councils of Ministers to certain union territories including Himachal Pradesh. Himachal Pradesh attained statehood in the year 1971, emerging as the eighteenth state of the Indian Union. Virbhadra Singh of the Congress party, the current chief minister, has had three tenures as chief minister of Himachal Pradesh.

Culture

Dances of Himachal include the Rakshasa (demon) dance, Kayang, Jataru Kayang, Chohara, Shand, Shabu, Lang-dar-ma, Jhanjhar and Rasa. These are accompanied by instruments like the Ranasingha, Karna, Turhi, Kindari, Jhanjh and Ghariyal. Popular weaving and handicrafts traditions include the Kullu and Kinnauri shawls, tweeds and blankets, carpets, traditional dresses, metal craft and pottery. Himachal is also famous for the Kangra Valley School of Painting.

Fairs and festivals: Prominent fairs and festivals of the state include Kullu Dussehra, Shimla's Summer Festival, Lohri or Maghi, Basant Panchami, Mandi Shivratri, Holi, Nalwari fair, Baisakhi, Phulech (Festival of Flowers), Minjar fair and Lahaul Festival.

Economy, Industry and Agriculture

Economy: The net state domestic product at current prices in 2003–04 (provisional) was Rs 15,933 crores. The per capita net state domestic product at current prices in 2003–04 (advance estimate) was Rs 24,903.

Minerals and industry: Major industries of Himachal Pradesh are chemicals and chemical products, textile, electronics, steel and steel products, paper and paper products, cement, beverages and plastic products. Minerals found in the state include limestone (light grade), quartzite, gold, pyrites, copper, rock salt, natural oil, gas, mica, barytes and gypsum.

Agriculture: Himachal Pradesh is predominantly an agricultural state with nearly 70 per cent of the total population getting direct employment from agriculture. Important crops include maize, paddy, wheat, barley, vegetables, ginger and potato. Main fruits under cultivation are apple, pear, apricot, plum, peach, mango, litchi, guava and strawberry.

Power: Himachal has a huge identified hydroelectric potential in its five river basins. All of the state's power comes from hydroelectric plants.

Education

Educational institutes: Prominent educational institutions include Himachal Pradesh University, Shimla; Dr Y.S. Parmar University of Horticulture and Forestry, Solan; C.S.K. H.P. Krishi Vishva Vidyalaya, Palampur; Jaypee University of Information Technology (JUIT), Solan; Indian Institute of Advanced Studies, Shimla; National Institute of Technology, Hamirpur and Indira Gandhi Medical College, Shimla.

Tourism

Major tourist attractions:

1. Shimla: The Ridge, The Mall, Kali Bari Temple, State Museum, Chadwick Falls, Mashobra, Naldehra.
2. Chamba: Dalhousie, Laxmi Narayan Temple, Champavati Temple, Akhand Chandi Palace, Panchpula, Kalatop, Khajiar, Banikhet.
3. Kangra: Dharamshala, Kangra Fort, Palampur.
4. Solan: Kasauli, Chail.
5. Sirmaur: Nahan, Suketi Fossil Park, Paonta Sahib, Renuka.

6. Kullu: Manali, Bijli Mahadev shrine, Raghunathji Temple, Camping Sight Raison, Hadimba Temple, Tibetan monasteries, Rohtang pass.

7. Kinnaur: Sangla Valley, Chitkul, Recong Peo, Rakchham.

8. Lahaul and Spiti: Gondla, Tandi, Shashur Monastery, Kardang monastery, Thang Yug gompa.

Airports: Shimla, Kullu, Kangra (Gaggal).

National Parks: Great Himalayan National Park, Kullu (754 sq. km) and Pin Valley National Park, Lahaul-Spiti (675 sq. km).

Administration

Legislature: The Himachal Pradesh Legislative Assembly has sixty-eight seats, of which sixteen are reserved for SCs and three for STs. The term of the current house expires on 9 March 2008. The current party position is as follows:

Name of Party	Seats
Indian National Congress	43
Bharatiya Janata Party	16
Himachal Vikas Congress	1
Lok Jan Shakti Party	1
Loktantrik Morcha Himachal Pradesh	1
Independents	6
Total	**68**

Judiciary: The seat of the Himachal Pradesh High Court is in Shimla. The current chief justice is Justice V.K. Gupta.

Districts:

District	Area (sq. km)	Population	Headquarters	Urban Agglomerations
Bilaspur	1,167	340,735	Bilaspur	
Chamba	6,528	460,499	Chamba	
Hamirpur	1,118	412,009	Hamirpur	
Kangra	5,739	1,338,536	Dharamshala	
Kinnaur	6,401	83,950	Recong Peo	
Kullu	5,503	379,865	Kullu	
Lahaul and Spiti	13,835	33,224	Keylong	
Mandi	3,950	900,987	Mandi	
Shimla	5,131	721,745	Shimla	Shimla
Sirmaur	2,825	458,351	Nahan	
Solan	1,936	499,380	Solan	
Una	1,540	447,967	Una	

Jammu and Kashmir

Key Statistics

Capital: Summer (May–October)—Srinagar; Winter (November–April)—Jammu.
Area: 222,236 sq. km.
Population: Total: 10,069,917, Male: 5,300,574, Female: 4,769,343.
Population density: 99 per sq. km.
Sex ratio: 900 females per 1000 males.
Principal languages: Urdu, Kashmiri, Dogri.
Literacy rates: Total: 54.46%, Male: 65.75%, Female: 41.82%.

Government

Governor: Lt Gen. (Retd) Sriniwas Kumar Sinha. He took over as governor on 4 June 2003.

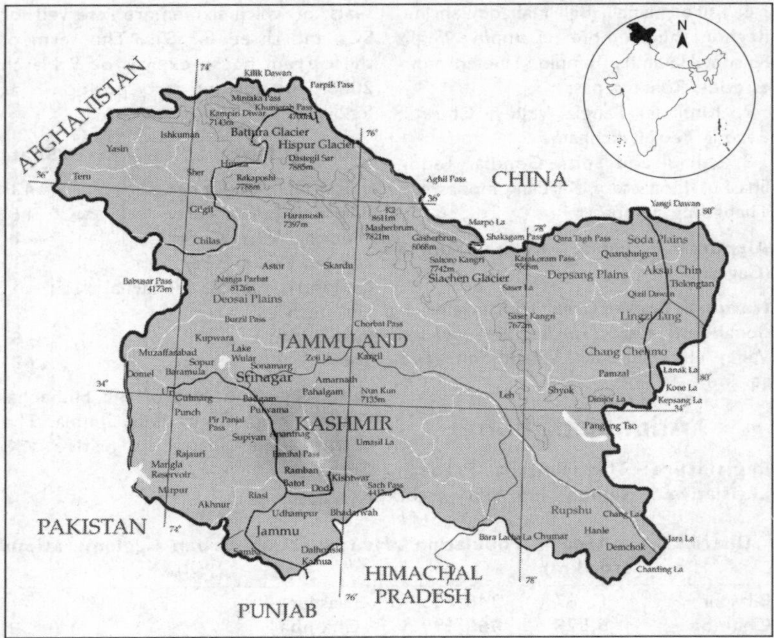

Chief Minister: Ghulam Nabi Azad (INC). He was sworn in on 2 November 2005.

Geography

Physical characteristics: The northern extremity of India, Jammu and Kashmir is bounded by Pakistan, Afghanistan and China from west to east. Himachal Pradesh and Punjab are on its south. The state has four geographical zones: (i) The submountainous and semi-mountainous plain known as Kandi; (ii) The Shivalik ranges; (iii) The high mountain zone constituting the Kashmir valley, the Pir Panjal range and its offshoots; (iv) The middle run of the Indus river comprising Leh and Kargil.

Neighbouring States and Union territories:

International border: Pakistan, Afghanistan, China.

States: Himachal Pradesh, Punjab.

Major rivers: Indus, Chenab, Jhelum and Ravi.

Climate: The climate varies from tropical in the plains of Jammu to semi-arctic cold in Ladakh. The mountainous tracts in Kashmir and Jammu have temperate climatic conditions. Annual rainfall varies from 92.6mm in Leh to 650.5mm in Srinagar and 1115.9mm in Jammu.

Flora and Fauna:

Flora: Flora in Jammu and Kashmir ranges from the thorn bush type in arid plains to the temperate and alpine flora in higher altitudes. Maple, horse chestnuts and silver fir are the common broad-leaf trees. Birch, rhododendron, berbers and a large number of herbs are found on higher altitudes. The state is also famous for its chinar tree that is found all over the valley. Other trees found in the state include almond, walnut, willow and cedar. The mountain ranges have deodar, pine and fir.

Fauna: Wildlife in the state include leopard, hangul or Kashmir stag, wild sheep, bear, brown musk shrew, musk rat, varieties of snakes, chakor, snow partridge, pheasants and peacock. The fauna in Ladakh includes yak, Himalayan ibex, Tibetan antelope, snow leopard, wild ass, red bear and gazelle. Besides these, the state is known for its trout population.

History

Legend has it that Kashyapa Rishi reclaimed the land that now comprises Kashmir from a vast lake. It came to be known as Kashyapamar and, later, Kashmir. Emperor Ashoka introduced Buddhism to the region in 3 BC. Subsequently, the valley became parts of the empires of Kanishka and Mihiragula. Around the seventh century AD, a local dynasty, the Karkotas, believed to have been founded by Durlabhavardhana, came to power in the region. According to Kalhana, the famous historian of Kashmir, this dynasty spread its power under the reign of Lalitaditya. He is believed to have defeated Kanauj, the Tibetans and even the Turks in the Indus area. His grandson, Jayapada Vinyaditya, achieved victories over Gauda and Kanauj. This dynasty came to an end around 855. The house of Utpalas followed. Its founder was Avantivarman. His son, Sankaravarmana, expanded the state's territorial limits and is believed to have even annexed a part of Punjab from the Gurjaras. A period of turmoil followed his death during which the widowed queen, Sugandha, attempted to rule. She faced fierce opposition from the Tantrins, a powerful military faction. They emerged as the virtual military dictators of the territory. But ultimately a group of Brahmanas elevated Yasaskara, a member of their order, to the throne of Kashmir. The line started by Yasaskara was succeeded by the dynasty started by Parva Gupta.

The Hindu rule over Kashmir came to an end in the fourteenth century. In around 1339 or 1346, a Muslim adventurer named Shah Mirza seized power and assumed the title of Shams-ud-din Shah. The Sultanate of Kashmir thus established ruled till about 1540 when a relative of Humayun, Mirza Haidar, annexed Kashmir. He ruled Kashmir virtually as a sovereign although in theory he ruled on behalf of Humayun. In 1551, the local nobles ousted Mirza Haidar. In around 1555, the Chakks seized the throne. Kashmir ultimately became a part of the Mughal empire in Akbar's reign.

In 1819, Kashmir was annexed to the Sikh kingdom of Punjab and later on to the Dogra kingdom of Jammu in 1846. In 1846, the treaties of Lahore and Amritsar that were signed at the conclusion of the First Sikh War made Raja Gulab Singh, the Dogra ruler of Jammu, the ruler of an extensive Himalayan kingdom. The state was under Dogra rule till 1947, when Maharaja Hari Singh signed the Instrument of Accession in favour of the Indian union.

Much drama surrounds Jammu and Kashmir's accession to the Indian Union. Jammu and Kashmir was one of the princely states of India on which British paramountcy lapsed at midnight on 15 August 1947. When power was transferred to the people in British India, the rulers of the princely states were given an option to join either India or Pakistan. The ruler of Jammu and Kashmir, Maharaja Hari Singh, did not exercise the option immediately. Instead, he offered a 'Standstill Agreement' to both India and Pakistan, pending a final decision. On 12 August 1947, the Prime Minister of Jammu and Kashmir sent identical communications to the governments of India and Pakistan, offering to enter into Standstill Agreements with both the countries. While Pakistan entered into a Standstill Agreement, India declined and instead asked the state to send its emissary for talks. Meanwhile, a 'Quit Kashmir' movement was active under the leadership of Sheikh Mohammad Abdullah. Sheikh Abdullah was against the Kashmir ruler's autocratic rule as well as an accession to Pakistan and enjoyed public support.

When Pakistani designs on acquiring the state failed, they sent in thousands of tribals along with regular Pakistani troops who entered the state on 22 October 1947. This finally caused the maharaja to sign the Instrument of Accession in favour of India on 26 October 1947, agreeing to the prescribed terms and conditions. On 30 October 1947, an emergency government was formed in the state with Sheikh Mohammad Abdullah as its head. The Indian Army was sent in and it successfully flushed out the invaders. On 1 January 1948, India took up the issue of Pakistani aggression in Jammu and Kashmir at the United Nations. Consequently, a ceasefire came into operation on the midnight of 1 January 1949. At the time of ceasefire, Pakistan was in illegal possession of 78,114 sq. km. It remains in possession of this territory even today.

On 5 March 1948, the maharaja announced the formation of an interim popular government with Sheikh Mohammad Abdullah as the prime minister. The maharaja then signed a proclamation making Yuvraj Karan Singh the regent. Pakistan waged two more wars, in 1965 and 1971, with the intention of annexing all of Jammu and Kashmir, but was beaten back.

In 1959, Chinese troops occupied the Aksai Chin part of Ladakh. In 1963, a Sino-Pakistani agreement defined the Chinese border with Pakistani Kashmir and ceded Indian-claimed territory to China.

Politics

Jammu and Kashmir was one of about 565 princely states of India on which the British paramountcy lapsed at the stroke of midnight on 15 August 1947. While the power was transferred to the people in British India, the rulers of the princely states were given an option to join either of the two dominions – India or Pakistan. Moreover, in the Indian Independence Act, 1947, there was no provision for any conditional accession. The ruler of Jammu and Kashmir, Maharaja Hari Singh, did not exercise the option immediately and instead offered a proposal of Standstill Agreement to both the dominions, pending a final decision on the state's accession. India did not agree to the offer and advised the maharaja to send his authorized representative to Delhi for discussions on the offer. The maharaja was already facing a formidable challenge from the people who had launched the Quit Kashmir movement under the leadership of Sher-i-Kashmir Sheikh Mohammad Abdullah against the maharaja's rule. The Quit Kashmir movement ran parallel to the national movement with Sheikh Mohammad Abdullah having close associations with the leaders of the national movement against British rule. National leaders like Mahatma Gandhi and Pandit Nehru too espoused the cause of the people of Kashmir seeking political freedom from autocratic rule. To deal with the people's upsurge, the maharaja had even detained Sheikh Abdullah on 20 May 1946. Faced with the new alarming situation arising out of repeated violations of the Standstill Agreement by Pakistan and blocking of the Pindi-Srinagar road, the Maharaja set him free on 29 September 1947. Mohammad Abdullah deputed his close aide Kh. G.M. Sadiq to Pakistan to tell Pakistani leaders about the sentiments of the people who could not be taken for granted and coerced to join them. This plain speaking did not deter Pakistan from pursuing its designs. At last, bowing before the wishes of the people as reflected by the Muslim dominated National Conference, and to resist the invaders, the maharaja signed the Instrument of Accession in favour of India on 26 October 1947. This was accepted by the governor-general of India, Lord Mountbatten, the next day. With Jammu and Kashmir becoming a legal and constitutional part of the Union of India, Indian troops were rushed to the state to push back the invaders and vacate aggressors from the territory of the state. On 30 October 1947 an emergency government was formed in the state with Sheikh Mohammad Abdullah as its head. The army fought a sustained battle with the intruders and after several sacrifices pushed them out of the Valley and other areas in the Jammu region. On 1 January 1948 India took up the issue of Pak aggression in Jammu and Kashmir in the UNO under Article 35 of its charter. The Government of India requested the Security Council to call upon Pakistan to put an end immediately to the giving of such assistance, which was an act of aggression against India. If Pakistan did not do so, the Government of India said it may be compelled, in self-defence, to enter Pakistani territory to take military action against the invaders. After long debates, a cease-fire came into operation on the midnight of 1 January 1949. At the time of the cease-fire, Pakistan was holding 78,114 sq. km of Kashmir territory illegally and this illegal possession of that territory (Pakistan Occupied Kashmir) continues even today. So far India and Pakistan have been to war three times in Kashmir (1947-1948, 1965, 1971) and clashed there again during the Kargil conflict of 1999.

On 5 March 1948, the Maharaja announced the formation of an interim popular government with Sheikh Mohammad Abdullah as the prime minister. Subsequently, the maharaja signed a proclamation making Yuvraj Karan Singh the regent. After attaining political freedom, Jammu and Kashmir marched ahead to strengthen the democratic structure. In 1951, the State Constituent Assembly was elected by the people. Close on the heels of this, the Delhi Agreement was signed between the two prime ministers of India and Jammu and Kashmir giving special position to the state under the Indian Constitutional framework. The Constituent Assembly elected the yuvraj as the sadar-i-riyasat on 15 November 1952, thus bringing to end the 106-year-old hereditary rule in Jammu and Kashmir. The State Constituent Assembly ratified the accession of the state to the Union of India on 6 February 1954 and the President of India subsequently issued the Constitution (Application to J&K) Order under Article 370 of the Indian Constitution extending the Union Constitution to the state with some exceptions and modifications. The state's own Constitution came into force on 26 January 1957 under which the elections to the state Legislative Assembly were held for the first time on the basis of adult franchise the same year. Since then eight assembly elections have been held in the state besides Lok Sabha elections where the people exercised their franchise freely.

Bakshi Ghulam Mohammad held the reins of government in the wake of Sheikh Abdullah's deposition in 1953. Bakshi had to face unprecedented challenges from the forces of disintegration and secessionism, which got a new lease of life after Sheikh Abdullah stepped down from office. He remained in power till 12 October 1963. The state's Constitution was amended on 30 March 1965 to rename the sadr-e-riyasat (president) as governor and the prime minister as the chief minister. Ghulam Mohammad Sadiq was the last prime minister and became the first chief minister of the state on 10 April 1965. Syed Mir Qasim held the post between December 1971 and February 1975. The founder president of National Conference Shiekh Mohammad Abdullah held the post twice from 1975 to 1982. He was succeeded by Farooq Abdullah who held the post thrice heading a National Conference government from 1982-84, 1987-90 and 1996-2002. In between, Abdullah's brother-in-law, Ghulam Mohammad Shah, held the top office in 1984-86. A nine-member ministry headed by People's Democratic Party president Mufti Mohammad Sayeed was sworn-in as chief minister in Jammu and Kashmir on 2 November 2002. After Mufti Mohammad Sayeed completed his three-year term as per the power-sharing agreement between the PDP–Congress alliance reached in late 2002, Congress leader Ghulam Nabi Azad replaced Mufti Sayeed on 2 November 2005. Azad had led the Congress in the Assembly elections in 2002, which saw the Congress winning twenty seats and in a post-poll tie-up with the PDP, which got sixteen seats, the first go at power enabling Mufti to become the chief minister. As per the power-sharing agreement, the PDP and Congress were to head the government for three years each.

Culture

Popular performing traditions of the Jammu region include Kud, a ritual dance performed in honour of local deities and the traditional theatre form Heren. Folk traditions in the Kashmir region include the theatre-style Bhand Pather and the Chakri form of music. There is also a rich tradition in Sufiana music. Jabro and Alley Yate are popular dance forms in the Ladakh region.

Fairs and festivals: Principal festivals of the state include Lohri, Baisakhi and Bahu Mela in the Jammu region; Id-ul-Fitr, Id-ul-Zuha and Miraj Alam in the Kashmir region; and Mela Losar and Hemis festival in the Ladakh region.

Economy, Industry and Agriculture

Economy: The net state domestic product at current prices for 2001–02 was Rs 13,697 crore. The per capita net state domestic product at current prices for 2001–02 was Rs 13,320.

Minerals and industry: Handicrafts production and export, mainly of papier mâchè, wood carving, carpets, shawls, copper and silverware, has been the traditional industry of the state. Other important industries include plastic products, cricket bats and other sports items, chemicals and basic drugs, electronics and precision engineering. The state has small mineral and fossil fuel resources largely concentrated in the Jammu region. There are bauxite and gypsum deposits in Udhampur district. Other minerals include limestone, coal, zinc, and copper.

Agriculture: Nearly 80 per cent of the state's population depends on agriculture. Major crops include paddy, wheat, maize, pulses, cotton and barley. Horticulture is also widespread. Large orchards in the Kashmir valley produce apples, pears, peaches, walnuts, almonds, cherries, apricots, strawberries and saffron.

Power: Nearly all of Jammu and Kashmir's power comes from hydroelectric plants.

Education

Educational institutes: Notable educational institutes include University of Jammu, Jammu, University of Kashmir, Srinagar and Sher-e-Kashmir University of Agricultural Sciences and Technology, Srinagar.

Tourism

Major tourist attractions:

1. Jammu: Bahu Fort, Mubarak Mandi complex, Ziarat Baba Buddan Shah,

Raghunath Temple, Vaishno Devi shrine, Mansar Lake, Patnitop.

2. Kashmir: Dal Lake, Hazratbal shrine, Shankarcharya Temple, Gulmarg, Pahalgam, Sonamarg, Charar-i-Sharief, Amarnath.

3. Ladakh: Buddhist gompas or monasteries at Hemis, Alchi, Thikse, and Spituk; Shey Palace, Jama Masjid, Leh Palace.

Airports: Srinagar, Jammu, Leh.

National Parks: Dachigam in Srinagar (141 sq. km); Hemis Leh (4100 sq. km) and Kishtwar Doda (310 sq. km).

Administration

Legislature: Jammu and Kashmir has a special status within the Union government: the state has its own Constitution (adopted in 1956) that affirms its integrity within the Republic of India.

The state assembly has a total of eighty-seven seats, with seven seats reserved for scheduled castes. As per Article 52 of the Constitution of Jammu and Kashmir, the term of the state assembly is for six years. The term of the current house expires on 20 November 2008. The current party position is as follows:

Name of Party	Seats
Jammu and Kashmir National Conference	28
Indian National Congress	20
Peoples Democratic Party	16
J and K National Panthers Party	4
Communist Party of India (Marxist)	2
Jammu and Kashmir Awami League	1
Democratic Movement	1
Bahujan Samaj Party	1
Bharatiya Janata Party	1
Independent	13
Total	**87**

Judiciary: The headquarters of the Jammu and Kashmir High Court is at Srinagar from May to October, and at Jammu from November to April. However, court sections of both Jammu and Srinagar wings of the High Court function throughout the year. The current chief justice is Sachchidanand Jha.

Districts:

District	Area (sq. km)	Population	Headquarters	Urban Agglomerations
Anantanag	3,984	1,170,013	Anantnag	Anantnag
Badgam	1,371	593,768	Budgam	
Baramula	4,588	1,166,722	Baramula	Baramula, Sopore
Doda	11,691	690,474	Doda	
Jammu	3,097	1,571,911	Jammu	Jammu
Kargil	14,036	115,227	Kargil	
Kathua	2,651	544,206	Kathua	Kathua
Kupwara	2,379	640,013	Kupwara	
Leh	45,110	117,637	Leh	
Pulwama	1,398	632,295	Pulwama	
Poonch	1,674	371,561	Poonch	
Rajauri	2,630	478,595	Rajauri	
Srinagar	2,228	1,238,530	Srinagar	Srinagar
Udhampur	4,550	738,965	Udhampur	Udhampur

Jharkhand

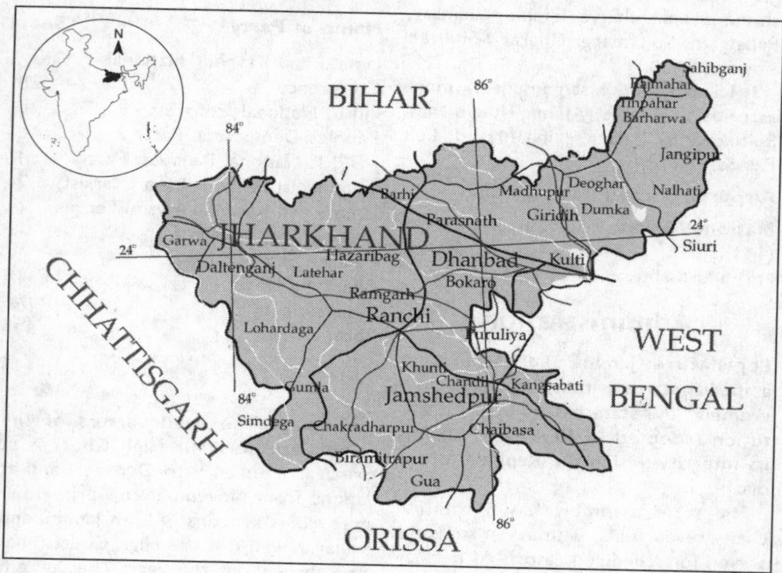

Key Statistics

Capital: Ranchi.
Area: 79,714 sq. km.
Population: Total: 26,945,829, Male: 13,885,037, Female: 13,060,792.
Population density: 338 per sq. km.
Sex ratio: 941 females per 1000 males.
Principal languages: Local languages like Santhali, Hindi, Urdu.
Literacy rates: Total: 53.6%, Male: 67.3%, Female: 38.9%.

Government

Governor: Syed Sibte Razi. He was sworn in on 10 June 2004.

Chief Minister: Arjun Munda (BJP). He was sworn in on 18 March 2003.

Geography

Physical characteristics: The Jharkhand region lies to the south of Bihar and encompasses Santhal Parganas and Chhota Nagpur. It is a plateau region about 1,000 metres above sea level, which features densely forested hill ranges. The highest part of the plateau is Netarhat (1,100 metres). The Parasnath hill is the highest point in the state (1,500 metres). Bihar lies to the north, Chhattisgarh and Uttar Pradesh to the west, Orissa to the south and West Bengal to the east of the state.

Neighbouring States and Union territories:
States: Bihar, West Bengal, Orissa, Chhattisgarh, Uttar Pradesh.

Major rivers: Damodar and Subarnarekha.

Climate: The state's climate is of the hot tropical type, with hot summers and cold winters. Most of the rainfall takes place in the period between July and September. Maximum temperatures range from 30°C to 44°C in summer; winter temperatures range from 1°C to 28°C.

Flora and Fauna:

Flora: Forests extend over 23,605 sq. km, which is 29.61 per cent of the state's total geographical area. Of this, 82 per cent is categorized as 'Protected Forest' and 17.5 per cent as 'Reserve Forest'. A small portion (33.49 sq. km) is not categorized.

The state's forests consist largely of the tropical moist deciduous type. The state is home to a large number of threatened orchids. Sal and bamboo are the two key constituents of the state's forests.

Fauna: Important members of the state's animal population include gaur, chital, tiger, panther, wild boar, sambar, sloth bear, nilgai and deer.

History

In 1929, the Simon Commission was presented with a memorandum that demanded the formation of a separate Jharkhand state. In December 1947, the All-India Jharkhand Party was formed and in 1951, it was elected to the Vidhan Sabha as the main opposition party. In 1971, A.K. Roy set up the MCC to demand a separate Jharkhand state. In 1973, N.E. Horo named his party the Jharkhand Party and presented the then prime minister with a memorandum for a separate Jharkhand state. The year 1980 saw the establishment of the Jharkhand Kranti Dal. In 1987, the home minister of India directed the Bihar government to prepare a detailed report on the profile of all districts of Chhota Nagpur and Santhal Parganas. In January 1994, Laloo Prasad Yadav declared that the Jharkhand Development Autnomous Council Bill would be passed in the budget session of the legislature. In 1995, the Jharkhand Area Autonomous Council was formed, comprising eighteen districts of Santhal Parganas and Chhota Nagpur, with Shibu Soren nominated as the chairman.

In July 1997, Shibu Soren offered his party's support to the minority government of Laloo Prasad Yadav, on the condition of a separate Jharkhand Bill in the Assembly. In August 2000, the bill to create a separate state of Jharkhand out of the state of Bihar was passed in the Lok Sabha by a voice vote. Later that month, the Rajya Sabha cleared the formation of Jharkhand as well. On 25 August, the then President, K.R. Narayanan, approved the Bihar Reorganization Bill, 2000. The state of Jharkhand came into existence on 15 November 2000. The state's first chief minister was Babulal Marandi.

Politics

The Jharkhand movement started with the organizational activities of the Chhotanagpur Unnati Samaj (CUS), founded in 1921, and subsequently of the Adivasi Mahasabha, founded in 1939. Among those who spearheaded the Jharkhand movement was Jaipal Singh, an Oxford-returned tribal Christian who helped the regional aspiration gain national recognition. On 28 December 1947, the All-India Jharkhand Party came into being under the leadership of Jaipal Singh. It was with the emergence of this party that the Jharkhand movement became purely political. In 1951, the Jharkhand party became the largest opposition party in the Bihar Assembly winning all the 32 seats from south Bihar and giving a fresh impetus to the demand for a separate Jharkhand state. The movement's original demand was for the formation of a separate state with sixteen districts of south Bihar's Chhota Nagpur and Santhal Pargana regions. The Jharkhand Party also wanted three contiguous, tribal-dominated districts of adjoining West Bengal, four districts of Orissa and two districts of Madhya Pradesh to be included in the proposed state. West Bengal, Orissa and Madhya Pradesh, however, refused to part with any territory. In 1955, the Jharkhand Party submitted a memorandum to the States Reorganization Commission, reiterating the statehood demand. But it was turned down by the Commission. Subsequently the Jharkhand Party suffered a series of splits. In 1970, Shibu Soren of Santhal Pargana quit the party to form the Jharkhand Mukti Morcha, with Benode Behari Mahato as its chairman. In 1971, A.K.Roy founded the Marxist M.C.C. to demand a separate Jharkhand state. In 1973, N.E. Horo named his party the Jharkhand Party and presented the prime minister a memorandum for a separate Jharkhand state. The year 1980 saw the establishment of the Jharkhand Kranti Dal. On 25 September 1986, the All-Jharkhand Students Union gave its first call for a Jharkhand bandh, which was a huge success. In 1987, the home minister of India directed the Bihar government to prepare a detailed profile of all districts of Chhota Nagpur and Santhal Pargana. In 1995, the Jharkhand Area Autonomous Council was formed comprising eighteen districts of Santhal Pargana and Chhota Nagpur and Shibu Soren was nominated as the chairman. In July 1997, Shibu Soren offered support to the minority government of Laloo Prasad Yadav with a condition of a separate Jharkhand bill in the assembly. In the year 2000 the bill to create a separate state of Jharkhand to be carved out of Bihar was passed in the Lok Sabha. The long cherished demand of people of the region was fulfilled and the new state Jharkhand was formed on 15 November 2000. Jharkhand is the twenty-eighth state of the Indian Union. Babulal Marandi of the Bharatiya Janata Party was sworn in as the first chief minister of Jharkhand. On 18 March 2003, Arjun Munda was sworn in as the chief minister. Sibu Soren replaced him after the assembly elections in 2005 but failed to prove his majority in the assembly and resigned. On 12 March 2005, Arjun Munda was again sworn in as the chief minister of the state.

Culture

Folk music forms of Jharkhand include Akhariya Domkach, Dohari Domkach, Janani Jhumar, Mardana Jhumar and Faguwa. Folk dance forms include Paika, Chhau, Jadur and Karma. Santhali Bhittichitra, Oraon Bhittichitra, Jado Patiya are some local forms of painting.

Fairs and festivals: Sarhul, Karma, Sohrai, Badna and Tusu (or Makar) are notable among the local festivals.

Economy, Industry and Agriculture

Economy: The net state domestic product at current prices in 2003–04 (provisional) was Rs 35,168 crores. The per capita net state domestic product at current prices in 2003–04 (provisional) was Rs 12,509.

Minerals and industry: Jharkhand has some of the richest deposits of minerals in the country. The steel plants at Bokaro and Jamshedpur are also in this state. Minerals mined in the state include iron ore, coal, copper ore, mica, bauxite as well as fireclay, graphite, kyanite, sillimanite, limestone and uranium.

Agriculture: The main crops grown in the state are paddy, wheat, pulses and maize.

Power: The state gets its power from both thermal and hydroelectric sources.

Education

Educational institutes: Prominent institutes in the state include Ranchi University, Siddhu Kanhu University (Dumka), Vinoba Bhave University (Hazaribag), Birsa Agricultural University (Ranchi), Birla Institute of Technology and Science (Ranchi), Xavier Labour Relations Institute (Jamshedpur), National Metallurgical Laboratory (Jamshedpur), Central Mining Research Institute (Dhanbad) and Research and Development Centre for Iron and Steel (Ranchi).

Tourism

Major tourist attractions: Dassam Falls, Netarhat, Hazaribag National Park, Baidyanath Temple, Deoghar, Basakinath Temple, Deoghar, Topchanchi Lake, Dhanbad.

Airports: Ranchi.

National Parks: Palamau National Park (Betla) in Palamau dist. (226.32 sq. km) and Hazaribag National Park in Hazaribag dist. (183.89 sq. km).

Administration

Legislature: Jharkhand has a unicameral legislature consisting of eighty-one seats, out of which nine are reserved for SCs and twenty-eight for STs. However, the tenure of the existing members of Legislative Council (MLCs) was carried over from Bihar at the time of the formation of the state, and were maintained.

The party position in the state assembly is as follows:

Name of Party	Seats
Bharatiya Janata Party	30
Indian National Congress	9
Nationalist Congress Party	1
Jharkhand Mukti Morcha	17
Rashtriya Janata Dal	7
Janata Dal (United)	6
United Goans Democratic Party	2
All India Forward Bloc	2
Communist Party of India (Marxist-Leninist) (Liberation)	1
All Jharkhand Students Union	2
Jharkhand Party	1
Independent	3
Total	**81**

Judiciary: The Jharkhand High Court is located at Ranchi. The chief justice is Altamas Kabir.

Districts:

District	Area (sq. km)	Population	Headquarters	Urban Agglomerations
Bokaro	2,861	1,775,961	Bokaro Steel City	Bokaro Steel City, Phusro
Chatra	3,706	790,680	Chatra	
Deoghar	2,479	1,161,370	Deoghar	Deoghar
Dhanbad	2,052	2,394,434	Dhanbad	Chirkunda, Dhanbad
Dumka	6,212	1,754,571	Dumka	
Garhwa	4,044	1,034,151	Garhwa	
Giridih	4,975	1,901,564	Giridih	Giridih
Godda	2,110	1,047,264	Godda	
Gumla	9,077	1,345,520	Gumla	
Hazaribag	6,147	2,277,108	Hazaribag	Hazaribag, Ramgarh
Jamtara	786.43	489,991	Jamtara	
Koderma	1,312	498,683	Koderma	
Latehar	3652	558,831	Latehar town	

Lohardaga	1,491	364,405	Lohardaga	
Pakur	1,806	701,616	Pakur	
Palamu	8,705	2,092,004	Daltonganj	
Pashchimi Singhbhum	9,907	2,080,265	Chaibasa	Chakradharpur, Jamshedpur
Purbi Singhbhum	3,533	1,978,671	Jamshedpur	Jamshedpur
Ranchi	7,698	2,783,577	Ranchi	Ranchi
Sahibganj	1,599	927,584	Sahibganj	
Seraikela-Kharsawan	NA	767,442 (1991 census)	Seraikela	
Simdega	3756	446,421	Simdega	

Karnataka

Key Statistics

Capital: Bangalore.

Area: 191,791 sq. km.

Population: Total: 52,850,562, Male: 26,898,918, Female: 25,951,644.

Population density: 275 per sq. km.

Sex ratio: 965 females per 1000 males.

Principal languages: Kannada, Urdu, Telugu.

Literacy rates: Total: 66.6%, Male: 76.1%, Female: 56.9%.

Government

Governor: Dharam Singh. He assumed office of the governor on 3 Feb 2006.

Chief Minister: H.D Kumaraswamy. He assumed office on 3 February 2006.

Geography

Physical characteristics: About 750 km from north to south and 400 km from east to west, Karnataka can be divided in four physiographic regions: (i) The northern plateau, with a general elevation of 300 to 600 metres from the mean sea level; (ii) The central plateau, with a general elevation of 450 to 700 metres; (iii) The southern plateau, with a general elevation of 600 to 900 metres; and (iv) The coastal region, comprising the plains and the Western Ghats.

Among the tallest peaks of the state are Mullayyana Giri, Bababudangiri and Kudremukh.

Neighbouring States and Union territories:

States: Goa, Maharashtra, Andhra Pradesh, Tamil Nadu, Kerala.

Major rivers: Krishna, Cauvery, North Pennar, South Pennar, Palar, Hemavati, Kalinadi, Gagavali and Tungabhadra.

Climate: The climate varies from hot with excessive rainfall in the coastal belt and adjoining areas to hot and seasonally dry tropical climate in the southern half, and to hot and semi-arid in the northern half. April and May are the hottest months with maximum temperatures going above 40°C. The period from October to March is generally pleasant over the entire state. The average annual rainfall for the state is 1,390mm, with Bijapur, Raichur and Bellary receiving the minimum rainfall and Shimoga and Kodagu receiving the maximum.

Flora and Fauna:

Flora: Around 20 per cent of the state area is under forests, with teak, rosewood, honne, mathi, bamboo and sandal trees in abundance.

Fauna: Wildlife found in Karnataka include gaur, sambar, barking deer, elephant, tiger, leopard, wild dog, sloth bear, black buck, open-bill stork, white ibis, egret, heron, partridge, peafowl, quail and hornbill.

History

Around the mid-third century BC, the Mauryas ruled over major parts of present-day Karnataka. After the Mauryas up until the eleventh century AD, the principal dynasties in the region were the Kadambas, the Gangas and the Pallavas. They were followed by the Chalukyas, the Hoysalas and the Rashtrakutas. After the thirteenth century, Mysore gradually came under the influence of the Vijayanagar empire.

Towards the end of the sixteenth century, the Vijayanagar empire declined, resulting in Mughal domination of the territory lying north of the Tungabhadra and the rajas of Mysore controlling the south. Hyder Ali rose to power in 1761 and his invasions extended Mysore's dominion. After his son Tipu Sultan was killed in 1799, the area came under British control which continued until Independence.

After Independence, Mysore state went through two territorial reorganizations: in 1953 and in 1956. The state was renamed Karnataka on 1 November 1973. Arcot Ramaswami Mudaliar was the first chief minister of Karnataka.

Politics

After Indian Independence, the Wodeyar Maharaja of Mysore acceded to India. In 1950, Mysore became an Indian state, and the former Maharaja became its rajpramukh or governor. After accession to India, the Woyedar family was given a pension by the Indian government until 1975, and members of the family still reside in part of their ancestral palace in Mysore. On 1 November 1956, Mysore state was enlarged to its present boundaries, incorporating the state of Coorg and the Kannada-speaking portions of neighboring Madras, Hyderabad, and Bombay states. On 1 November 1973 the name of the state was changed to Karnataka.

Karnataka's first Assembly started functioning from 18 June 1952 and lasted till 31 March 1957. During this period Karnataka had the highest dignitaries as its chief minister, including K.H. Hanumanthaiah, Kadidal Manjappa and S. Nijalingappa. Ramakrishna Hegde started his first term as chief minister from 1983. H.D. Deve Gowda was chief minister from 1994 to 1996, and subsequently became prime minister of India. J.H. Patel succeeded him as chief minister. S.M. Krishna became chief minister in 1999. After the 2004 Assembly elections, Dharam Singh came to power as chief minister. On 28 January 2006, the governor of Karnataka T.N. Chaturvedi invited the leader of the Janata Dal (Secular) H.D. Kumaraswamy, son of former Prime Minister of India H.D. Deve Gowda, to form the governor in the state after Dharam Singh resigned earlier in the day. He was sworn in as chief minister of the state on 3 February 2006. Although the single largest party with seventy-nine MLAS, almost twice the number of MLAS with JD (SJ), BJP conceded the chief minister's post.

Culture

Karnataka boasts a fascinating variety of folk theatre, called Bayalata. Dasarata, Sannata, Doddata, Parijata and Yakshagana are the most popular forms of Bayalata.

Fairs and festivals: Prominent festivals of the state include Ugadi, Dussehra, Kar Hunnive, Nagapanchami, Navaratri or Nadahabb, Yellu Amavasya, Ramzan and Deepavali. Major fairs are Sri Vithappa fair, Sri Shidlingappa's fair, the Godachi fair and Banashankari Devi fair.

Economy, Industry and Agriculture

Economy: The net state domestic product at current prices for 2003–04 (provisional) was Rs 118,329 crores. The per capita net state domestic product at current prices for 2003–04 (provisional) was Rs 21,696.

Minerals and industry: Prominent industries in Karnataka are aeronautics, automobiles, biotechnology, electronics, textiles, sugar, iron and steel, information technology, pharmaceuticals, leather, cement and processed foods. Minerals found in the state include gold, silver, iron ore, manganese, chromite, limestone, bauxite, copper and china clay.

Agriculture: Important crops include paddy, jowar, bajra, ragi, maize, pulses, groundnut, sunflower, soyabean, cotton, sugar cane and tobacco. Principal plantation crops are coffee, cashew, coconut, areca nut and cardamom.

Power: With an installed capacity of 3066 MW, a large part of Karnataka's power comes from hydroelectric plants. The rest comes from thermal and nuclear power plants.

Education

Educational institutes: Prominent educational institutions of Karnataka include the Indian Institute of Management, Bangalore; Indian Institute of Science, Bangalore; National Law School of India University, Bangalore; National Institute of Mental Health and Neuro-Sciences, Bangalore; University of Agricultural Sciences, Bangalore; Bangalore University, Bangalore; National Institute of Technology, Surathkal; Indian Statistical Institute, Bangalore; Central Institute of Indian Languages, Mysore; Gulbarga University, Gulbarga; Mangalore University, Mangalore; Manipal Academy of Higher Education, Manipal and University of Mysore, Mysore.

Tourism

Major tourist attractions:

1. Bangalore: Vidhana Soudha, Cubbon Park, Palace of Tipu Sultan, Ulsoor Lake.
2. Mysore: Mysore Palace, Srirangapatna, Gumbaz, St. Philomena's Church, Brindavan Gardens.
3. Badami: The cave temples.
4. Aihole and Pattadakal.
5. Madikeri: Tipu's Fort, Omkareshwara Temple, Abbey Falls.
6. Hampi: Virupaksha Temple, Vittala Temple.
7. Belur and Halebid: Chennakeshava Temple, Shiva Temple.
8. Beaches: Karwar, Marwanthe, Malpe.
9. Jog falls.
10. Bijapur.
11. Sravanabelagola.
12. Sringeri.
13. Nandi Hills.

Airports:

International: Bangalore

Domestic:: Belgaum, Hubli, Mangalore.

National Parks: Anshi (Uttarakanada) —250 sq. km.; Bandipur Tiger Reserve (Mysore)—874.20 sq. km.; Bannerghatta (Bangalore)—104.27 sq. km.; Kudremukh (South Kanada and Chikmagalur)—600.32 sq. km.; Nagarhole (Mysore Kodagu)—643.39 sq. km.

Administration

Legislature: The Karnataka legislature comprises two houses: the seventy-five-member legislative council and the 225 member legislative assembly. Of the 225 assembly seats, 224 are for elected members (thirty-three reserved for SCs, two for STs) and one for a nominated member. The current party position is:

Name of Party	Seats
Bharatiya Janata Party	79
Indian National Congress	65
Janata Dal (S)	58
Janata Dal (U)	5
Communist Party of India (Marxist)	1
Republican Party of India	1
Kannada Nadu Paksha	1
Kannada Chalarali Vatal Paksha	1
Independent	13
Nominated	1
Total	**225**

Judiciary: The seat of the Karnataka High Court is in Bangalore. The present chief justice is Nauvdip Kumar Sodhi.

Districts:

District	Area (sq. km)	Population	Headquarters	Urban Agglomerations
Bagalkot	6,575	1,652,232	Bagalkot	
Bangalore	2,190	6,523,110	Bangalore	Bangalore
Bangalore Rural	5,815	1,877,416	Bangalore	
Belgaum	13,415	4,207,264	Belgaum	Athni, Belgaum, Ramdurg
Bellary	8,450	2,025,242	Bellary	
Bidar	5,448	1,501,374	Bidar	Bidar
Bijapur	10,494	1,808,863	Bijapur	Bijapur
Chamarajnagar	5,101	964,275	Chamarajnagar	
Chickmagalur	7,201	1,139,104	Chickmagalur	
Chitradurga	8,440	1,510,227	Chitradurga	Chitradurga
Dakshina Kannada	4,560	1,896,403	Mangalore	Mangalore
Davanagere	5,924	1,789,693	Davanagere	Harihar
Dharwad	4,260	1,603,794	Dharwad	
Gadag	4,656	971,955	Gadag	
Gulbarga	16,224	3,124,858	Gulbarga	Gulbarga, Shahabad, Wadi
Hassan	6,814	1,721,319	Hassan	Arsikere, Channarayapattana, Hassan
Haveri	4,823	1,437,860	Haveri	
Kodagu	4,102	545,322	Madikere	
Kolar	8,223	2,523,406	Kolar	Robertson Pet
Koppal	7,189	1,193,496	Koppal	Gangawati
Mandya	4,961	1,761,718	Mandya	
Mysore	6,854	2,624,911	Mysore	Mysore
Raichur	6,827	1,648,212	Raichur	
Shimoga	8,477	1,639,595	Shimoga	
Tumkur	10,597	2,579,516	Tumkur	
Udupi	3,880	1,109,494	Udupi	Udupi
Uttara Kannada	10,291	1,353,299	Karwar	Ankola, Bhatkal, Karwar, Kumta, Sirsi

Kerala

Key Statistics

Capital: Thiruvananthapuram.

Area: 38,863 sq. km.

Population: Total: 31,841,374, Male: 15,468,614, Female: 16,372,760.

Population density: 819 per sq. km.

Sex ratio: 1,058 females per 1,000 males.

Principal languages: Malayalam, Tamil, Kannada.

Literacy rates: Total: 90.9%, Male: 94.2%, Female: 87.7%.

Government

Governor: R.L. Bhatia. He was sworn on 23 June 2004.

Chief Minister: V.S. Achuthanandan. He assumed office on 18 May 2006.

Geography

Physical characteristics: Kerala is a narrow strip of land on the south-west coast of India. The Lakshadweep Sea lies on the west, while the Western Ghats lie on the east. Karnataka is towards the north and north-east of the state while Tamil Nadu is to the east and the south. The Western Ghats are densely forested and have extensive ridges and ravines.

Anai peak (2,695 metres) is the highest peak of peninsular India. An interconnected chain of lagoons and backwaters is a feature of the coastline of Kerala.

Neighbouring states and Union territories:
States: Karnataka, Tamil Nadu.

Union territories: Pondicherry.

Major rivers: Periyar, Bharatapuzha, Chalakudi and Pamba.

Climate: Kerala has a tropical climate. The summer season is from February to May (24°C to 33°C). The monsoon season is from June to September (22°C to 28°C). The winter lasts between October and January (22°C to 32°C).

Kerala lies directly in the path of the south-west monsoon, but also receives rain from the north-east monsoon. Rainfall averages about 3,000 mm annually, although some parts receive much more.

Flora and Fauna:
Flora: The state has 1,081,509 hectares of forest area. These are mostly rain forest, tropical deciduous forest and upland temperate grassland.

Fauna: The animal population of the state includes sambar, gaur, Nilgiri tahr, elephant, leopard, tiger, hanuman, Nilgiri langur, spectacled and king cobras, peafowl, bonnet monkey, lion-tailed macaque and hornbill.

History

Kerala has been mentioned in a rock inscription, dating back to the third century BC, of the Mauryan emperor Ashoka as 'Keralaputra'. Jewish immigrants arrived in the area in the first century AD, while Syrian Orthodox Christians believe that St. Thomas the Apostle visited Kerala at around the same time. In the first five centuries AD, the region that is today Kerala was a part of Tamilakam and was at different times controlled by the eastern Pandya, Chola and the Chera dynasties.

Arab traders introduced Islam to the region in the latter part of the period between the sixth to eighth centuries AD. It was under the Kulasekhara dynasty that reigned between the years 800 and 1102 that Malayalam emerged as a distinct language.

In the early fourteenth century, Ravi Varma Kulasekhara of Venad established a short-lived domination over southern India. His death ushered in an era of confusion, characterized by chieftains who constantly fought each other.

In 1498, the Portuguese explorer Vasco da Gama landed near Calicut (now Kozhikode). In the sixteenth century, the Portuguese dominated trade and commerce in the Malabar region, successfully overtaking the Arab traders. Their attempts to establish political rule, however, were foiled by the hereditary rulers of Calicut, called zamorins.

In the seventeenth century, the Dutch ousted the Portuguese. But even their ambition of imposing Dutch supremacy in the region was foiled by Marthanda Varma in 1741, in the Battle of Kolachel. Marthanda Varma adopted a system of martial discipline and expanded the new state of Travancore.

However, by 1806, Cochin, Travancore and Malabar had all become subject states under the British Madras Presidency. At the time of Independence in 1947, the region that is today Kerala consisted of three separate territories: Cochin, Travancore and Malabar. On 1 July 1949, Cochin and Travancore were merged to form the Travancore–Cochin state. The present state of Kerala was formed on a linguistic basis, when Malabar along with the Kasargod taluka was added to the Cochin–Travancore state.

The new state was inaugurated on 1 November 1956. When Kerala was formed, the state was under President's Rule. Elections were held for the first time in 1957 and E.M.S. Namboodiripad became the first chief minister.

Politics

The move towards democracy and social change started in Kerala towards the end of the nineteenth century. By the early twentieth century, leaders like E.M. Sankaran Namboodiripad, A.K. Gopalan and T.M. Varghese used Communist ideologies to organize political mass movements both against British rule and the Travancore state. In 1949, the two separate states of Travancore and Cochin were united. On 1 November 1956, the boundaries of the newly united states were revised to include neighbouring Malayalam-speaking areas, and the whole territory was officially named Kerala. In the first elections that followed the Communists gained a majority and the first Kerala ministry was sworn in under the leadership of E.M. Sankaran Namboodiripad (known as EMS), head of the Communist Party of India—Marxist. On 16 March 1957 for the first time in the history of the world, the Communists had come to power through democratic means. The ministry, however, lasted only until July 1959. The ministry was dismissed because the opposition parties launched an agitation called 'Vimochana Samaram' (Liberation Struggle) which led to clashes between the police and mass protesters. The state came under Presidential Rule. In February 1960 the second Assembly was formed with the coalition of the Congress Party and the

Praja Socialist Party, with Pattom Thanu Pillai as chief minister. In 1967 E.M.S. Namboodiripad became the chief minister again with the Indian Communist Party (Marxist) getting an absolute majority in the assembly elections. In October 1969, EMS resigned and C. Achutha Menon became the chief minister. K. Karunakaran of the Congress became the chief minister in March 1977. In January 1980 seven political parties formed a coalition, the Left Democratic Front (LDF) under the leadership of the Communist Party of India-Marxist and won the election. E.K. Nayanar became the chief minister. In May 1982, an election was held and a political coalition, the United Democratic Front (UDF), under the leadership of the Congress, got the majority. K. Karunakaran became the chief minister again. Power exchanged hands between the LDF and UDF subsequently. In 2004, Oommen Chandy was sworn in as the nineteenth chief minister of Kerala.

Culture

The dance form of Kathakali, which is one of the six classical dance forms of India, is indigenous to the state of Kerala, as is Mohiniattam. There are also more than fifty well-known folk dances in Kerala. The most popular among these are the Kaliyattom, Kolam Thullal, Kolkli, Mudiettu. Poorakkali, Velakali, Kamapadavukali, Kanniyarkali, Parichmuttukali, Thappukali, Kuravarkali and Thiruvathirakali. Other folk dance forms include Arjuna Nritham, Thullal and Theyyam.

The state is also the birthplace of the Kalaripayuttu martial art form.

Aranmula is famous for its metal mirrors. The state is also famous for its brass lamps and Kathakali masks.

Fairs and festivals: Important festivals of the state are Onam, Vishu, Thiruvathira, Navarathri, Sivarathri, Oachira, Kettukazcha, Vallom Kali, Christmas, Easter, Bakrid, Idul Fitr, Miladi Sharif and Muharram.

Economy, Industry and Agriculture

Economy: The net state domestic product at current prices for 2003–04 (provisional) was Rs 80,116 crores. The per capita net state domestic product at current prices for 2003–04 (provisional) was Rs 24,492.

Minerals and industry: The state's industries are mostly based on its natural resources. It is noted for handloom, cashewnut processing, food processing, coir and handicrafts. Tourism is also a major industry. Other industries of the state include rubber, tea, ceramics, electronics, electronic appliances, engineering, bricks and tiles, tobacco products, precision engineering products, petroleum-based industries, drugs and chemicals, plywood and soaps and oils. The state's mineral resources include zircon, monazite, ilmenite, rutile, sillimanite, clay and quartz sand.

Agriculture: The agricultural pattern of Kerala is unique for the predominance of cash crops. The state is a major producer of coconut (the most important cash crop of the state), rubber, pepper, coffee, cardamom, ginger, cocoa, cashew, areca nut, nutmeg, cinnamon, cloves and tea. The state is also noted for the production of fruits like banana, plantain, mango, jackfruit and pineapple.

Power: Most of the state's power comes from hydroelectric sources, while the rest comes from thermal power plants.

Education

Educational institutes: The major institutes for higher education in the state include the Indian Institute of Management (Kozhikode), Kerala Institute of Tourism and Travel Studies (Thiruvananthapuram), Cochin University of Science and Technology (Kochi), Central Institute of Fisheries, Nautical and Engineering Training (Kochi), Central Marine Fisheries Research Institute (Kochi), Kerala Agricultural University (Trichur), University of Kerala (Thiruvananthapuram), University of Calicut (Kozhikode), Mahatma Gandhi University (Kottayam), Sree Chitra Tirunal Institute of Medical Sciences and Technology (Thiruvananthapuram), Sree Sankaracharya University of Sanskrit (Sree Sankarapuram), Kannur University (Kannur) and Central Plantation Crops and Research Institute (Kudlu, near Kasargod).

Tourism

Major tourist attractions: Vembanad Lake; Kappad Beach, Kozhikode; Kottayam; Kovalam Beach, Trivandrum; Munnar; Ponmudi; Cheeyappara and Valara waterfalls; Thattekkad Bird Sanctuary, Idukki; Thekkady; Kasaragod; Periyar; Silent Valley.

Airports:
International: Thiruvananthapuram, Nedumbassery (Kochi).

Domestic:: Kozhikode.

National Parks: Periyar National Park (part of the Tiger Reserve) in Idukki dist. (Tiger Reserve Area—777 sq. km, National Park—350 sq. km); Eravikulam National Park in Idukki dist. (97 sq. km); Silent Valley National Park in Palakkad dist. (89.52 sq. km).

Administration

Legislature: Kerala has a unicameral legislature. There are 140 seats in the Kerala Legislative Assembly. This includes thirteen seats reserved for SCs and one seat reserved for STs, and one member nominated by the governor from the Anglo-Indian community.

The current party position is as follows:

Name of Party	Seats
Indian National Congress	25
Communist Party of India (Marxist)	60
Muslim League Kerala State Committee	7
Kerala Congress (M)	7
Communist Party of India	17
Janadhipathiya Samrekshna Samiti	1
Janata Dal (Secular)	5
Democratic Indira Congress (Karunakaran)	1
Indian National League	1
Congress (Secular)	1
Kerala Congress	4
Revolutionary Socialist Party	3
Nationalist Congress Party	1
Kerala Congress (B)	1
Kerala Congress (Secular)	1
Independent	5
Total	**140**

Judiciary: The High Court of Kerala has its seat at Ernakulam. Its jurisdiction also includes the Union territory of Lakshadweep. The acting chief justice is K.S. Radhakrishnan.

Districts:

District	Area (sq. km)	Population	Headquarters	Urban Agglomerations
Alappuzha	1,414	2,105,349	Alappuzha	Alappuzha, Cherthala
Ernakulam	2,950	3,098,378	Ernakulam	Kochi
Idukki	4,476	1,128,605	Kuyilimala	
Kannur	2,966	2,412,365	Kannur	Kannur

Kasargod	1,992	1,203,342	Kasargod	Kanhangad, Kasargod
Kollam	2,491	2,584,118	Kollam	Kollam
Kottayam	2,208	19,52,901	Kottayam	Kottayam
Kozhikode	2,344	28,78,498	Kozhikode	Kozhikode, Vadakara
Malappuram	3,550	36,29,640	Malappuram	Malappuram
Palakkad	4,480	26,17,072	Palakkad	Chittur-Thathamangalam, Palakkad
Pathanamthitta	2,637	12,31,577	Pathanamthitta	
Thiruvananthapuram	2,192	32,34,707	Thiruvananthapuram	Thiruvananthapuram
Thrissur	3,032	29,75,440	Thrissur	Guruvayoor, Kodungallur, Thrissur
Wayanad	2,131	7,86,627	Kalpetta	

Madhya Pradesh

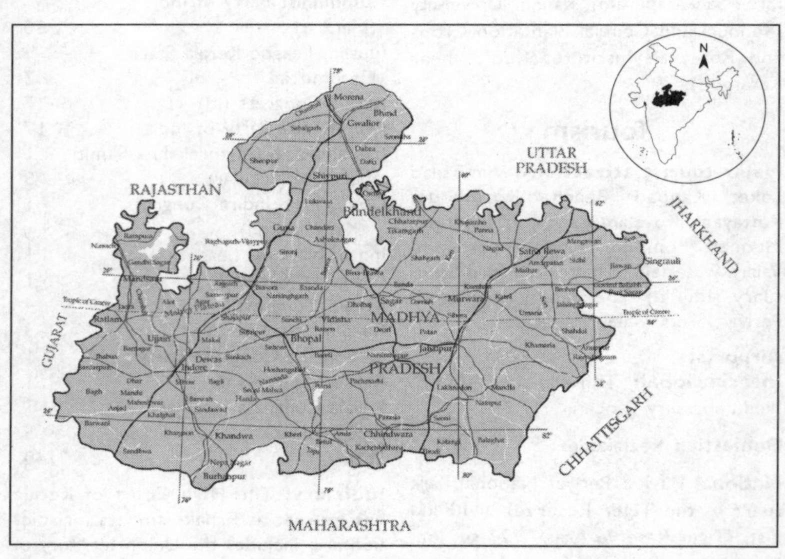

Key Statistics

Capital: Bhopal.
Area: 308,000 sq. km.
Population: Total: 60,348,023, Male: 31,443,652, Female: 28,904,371.
Population density: 196 per sq. km.
Sex ratio: 919 females per 1000 males.
Principal languages: Hindi, Bhili/Bhilodi, Gondi.
Literacy rates: Total: 63.7%, Male: 76.1%, Female: 50.3%.

Government

Governor: Balram Jakhar. He was sworn in as the governor of Madhya Pradesh on 30 June 2004.

Chief Minister: Shivraj Singh Chouhan. He was sworn in on 23 August 2004.

Geography

Physical characteristics: Madhya Pradesh is the second largest Indian state covering 9.5 per cent of the country's area. It lies between the Indo-Gangetic plain in the north and the Deccan plateau in the south. Its landscape, which is largely made up of wide-ranging plateaus, low hills and river valleys, ranges from 100 to 1,200 metres.

The land rises from south to north in the northern part of the state. In the southern part, its elevation increases towards the west. The Kaimur hills and the Vindhya range are situated in the north and the west respectively. To the north-west side of the Vindhya range is the Malwa plateau, which rises up to 100 metres. The Bundelkhand plateau lies to the north of the Vindhya range. There is also the Baghelkhand plateau in the north-east, and Madhya Bharat plateau in the extreme north-east. Various rivers originate from the state and flow into the adjoining states.

Neighbouring States and Union territories:
States: Gujarat, Maharashtra, Chhattisgarh, Rajasthan, Uttar Pradesh.

Major rivers: Narmada, Chambal, Betwa, Tapti and Wainganga are some of the major rivers.

Climate: The climate of Madhya Pradesh is mostly tropical, and largely governed by the monsoon. From March to May it experiences a hot, dry and windy summer, when the temperature can reach a maximum of about 48°C in some parts of the state. From June to September comes the south-west monsoon, when the rainfall fluctuates from region to region. The state has been divided into five crop zones and seven agro-climatic zones due to this reason. The total annual rainfall varies from 600mm (in the extreme northwestern areas) to about 1,200mm (southern areas). Winters (between October and February) are usually pleasant.

Flora and Fauna:
Flora: Madhya Pradesh is rich in forest resources. There are four important types of forest, namely the tropical dry forest, the tropical moist forest, the subtropical broadleaved hill forest, and the tropical thorn forest. Based on the composition of the forest and the terrain of the region, it is possible to classify forests into three types: teak forests, sal forests and miscellaneous forests. Bamboo, small timber, fodder and fuelwood also grow in many areas.

Fauna: Madhya Pradesh is famous for its tiger population and is known as the Tiger State. It has 19 per cent of the tiger population in India, and 17 per cent of the tiger population in the world. Satpura, Bandhavgarh, Pench, Panna, and Kanha are the five Project Tiger areas in the state. Apart from these projects, there is the Ghatigaon Sanctuary, which is set up for the conservation of the great Indian bustard, also known as the Son Chiriya. The Ken-gharial and Son-gharial sanctuaries are home to the mugger and gharial, while the Sardarpur Sanctuary houses the kharmor or lesser florican. Other creatures found in the state include the bison, panthers, chital (spotted deer), wild buffalo, sambar, black buck, bears and many species of birds.

History

Madhya Pradesh was founded on 1 November 1956, and forty-four years later, on 1 November 2000, the new state of Chhattisgarh was carved out of it. Madhya Pradesh occupies some of the oldest inhabited parts of India. At Bhimbhetka, close to Bhopal, some fascinating paintings are preserved in prehistoric caves dating back to the Paleolithic times.

The whole state came under the territory of the Guptas during the ascendancy of the Gupta dynasty. It also constituted part of Harshavardhan's empire. During the decline of the imperial power, small principalities created out of the province began fighting each other to establish their superiority. The Chandel dynasty emerged out of this, and later constructed the great temples of Khajuraho, creating a prosperous kingdom after the fall of the imperial power.

The Pratihara and Gaharwar Rajput dynasties followed the Chandels, but lost out to the expanding Muslim power. Emperor Akbar finally subdued all the other contenders in the region, and with Aurangzeb, Mughal rule was established in the region.

With the decline of the Mughals the Marathas reigned supreme, but they were finally replaced by the British who entered into treaty relationships with the rulers of the princely states in the area and went on to gain power over them.

After Independence, many such princely states were merged into the Union. With the reorganization of states, the boundaries were rationalized and the state of Madhya Pradesh came into existence. Pandit Ravishankar Shukla was the first chief minister of the state.

Politics

Madhya Pradesh was created in 1950 from the former British Central Provinces and Berar and the princely states of Makrai and Chhattisgarh, with Nagpur as the capital of the state. The state of Madhya Pradesh was formed on 1 November 1956, on the basis of the Report of the States Reorganization Commission by merging the territories of the states of Madhya Bharat, a union of princely states in the Malwa plateau region; Vindhya Pradesh, a union of states in the Vindhya region; Bhopal, a centrally administered princely state; the Hindi-speaking areas popularly known as Mahakoshal; and the Chhattisgarh region of the state of Central Provinces and Berar. Bhopal became the new capital. The state was bifurcated into two states, Madhya Pradesh and Chhattisgarh, on 1 November 2000.

Sunderlal Patwa of the Bharatiya Janata Party had two tenures as chief minister, in 1980 and from 1990 to 1992. From 1980 to 1985 Arjun Singh of the Congress party was the chief minister. He served as chief minister of the state again from 1988 to 1989. Motilal Vora of the Congress party became the chief minister twice, in 1985 and 1989. In 1993, Digvijay Singh of the Congress became chief minister. He was the longest serving chief minister in the history of Madhya Pradesh after winning the people's mandate for the second consecutive term in the year 1998. The victory of the ruling Congress party in the election in Madhya Pradesh was more significant because the political parties in power were losing elections in state after state in India in that year in the face of an anti-incumbency wave. Uma Bharti of the Bharatiya Janata Party was sworn-in on 8 December 2003 as the first woman chief minister of Madhya Pradesh. Babulal Gaur of the Bharatiya Janata Party was sworn in as the chief minister on 23 August 2004. On 28 November 2005 Babulal Gaur tendered his resignation to Governor Balram Jakhar and Shivraj Singh Chouhan was elected leader of the Bharatiya Janata Party legislature party. On 29 November 2005, Shivraj Singh Chouhan was sworn in as chief minister of Madhya Pradesh.

Culture

In Madhya Pradesh, the Gwalior gharana is one of the most important propagators of style in Indian music. Madhya Pradesh is famous for the rivalry of Tansen and Baiju Bawra, and is also well known for the patronage of the dhrupad singers by Raja Mansingh.

Other great musicians from Madhya Pradesh include the legendary Ustad Alauddin Khan, the guru of the famous sitarist Pandit Ravi Shankar; the sarod players Ali Akbar Khan and Ustad Hafiz Khan; and the *beenkar* Ustad Hussu Khan.

Madhya Pradesh is also famous for its craftsmen, including the sari weavers from Chanderi town, who are also regarded as true artists. Their silk and cotton saris, delicately woven with silver and gold threads, are extremely popular. Maheshwar in Madhya Pradesh is popular for sari making, while Bhopal is renowned for the bead work and embroidery, and Ujjain for its *chippa* work (block-printing by hand). Other popular forms of craft include woodwork, terracotta display and metalware in the tribal areas of Bastar.

In the year 1980, the state government constituted a separate department for culture in Madhya Pradesh.

Fairs and festivals: Shivratri in Khajuraho, Ujjain, Pachmarhi and Bhojpur, the annual festival of dances at Khajuraho, Bhagoriya in Jhabua, Dussehra in Bastar, the Malwa Festival in Mandu, Ujjain and Indore, Ramnavami in Orchha and Chitrakoot, and the Pachmarhi Festival are some of the important cultural events in Madhya Pradesh. Some of the important cultural festivals held in the state include the All-India Kalidasa Festival, Alauddin Khan Samaroh (Maihar), Tansen Samaroh (Gwalior), Lokranjan (Khajuraho), Miwar Utsav (Maheshwar), Khajuraho Dance Festival, Kumar Gandharva Samaroh (Dewas) and Shankara Samaroh.

Economy, Industry and Agriculture

Economy: The net state domestic product at current prices in 2003–04 (provisional) was Rs 89,236 crores. The per capita net state domestic product at current prices in 2003–04 (provisional) was Rs 14,011.

Minerals and industry: Madhya Pradesh is one of the largest producers of forest products, agricultural products, and minerals. Its important industries also include its modern biotech industries, horticulture, agro-industries, and its eco-tourist and tourist industry, which are especially aided by the presence of world heritage sites like Khajuraho and Sanchi, and various tiger reserves in the state.

The state consists of nineteen Industrial Growth Centres, and its infrastructure is an advantage, in terms of its railways and roads connecting all the important cities. The strongest optical fibre backbone is present in every district in Madhya Pradesh. Important minerals of Madhya Pradesh include limestone, bauxite, coal, manganese ore, diamond, base metals, dolomite, rock phosphate and granite.

Agriculture: In Madhya Pradesh, 49.5 per cent of its population depend on agriculture. The state produces about 2.19 million tonnes of sugar cane, 2.38 million tonnes of cotton, 3.969 million tonnes of oil seed, and nine million tonnes of food grain. Food grain production in Madhya Pradesh is about 260 kg per person, compared to the all-India production figure of about 200 kg per person per year. On the other hand, food grain yield in Madhya Pradesh, when compared to the all-India figure of 1.70 tonne per hectare (ha), is quite low at 1.14 tonnes per ha. Wheat, rice, a few varieties of coarse millets, and jowar (sorghum) are the main food crops in the state. Soyabean is produced on a large scale throughout the state.

Power: Thermal power is the main source of energy in the state. The rest of the energy is provided by hydroelectric sources.

Education

Educational institutes: Some of the important institutions of higher education are Awadhesh Pratap Singh University (Rewa), Barkatullah Vishwavidyalaya (Bhopal), Devi Ahilya Vishwavidyalaya (Indore), Dr Harisingh Gour Vishwavidyalaya (Sagar), Jawaharlal Nehru Krishi Vishwavidyalaya (Jabalpur), Jiwaji University (Gwalior), Lakshmibai National Institute of Physical Education (Gwalior), Madhya Pradesh Bhoj Open University (Bhopal), Maharishi Mahesh Yogi Vedic University (Jabalpur), Mahatma Gandhi Gramoday Vishwavidyalaya (Chitrakoot), Makhanlal Chaturvedi National University of Journalism (Bhopal), Rani Durgavati Vishwavidyalaya (Jabalpur) and Vikram University (Ujjain).

Tourism

Major tourist attractions: Khajuraho; Amarkantak; The marble rocks at Bhedaghat, near Jabalpur; Bhimbhetka; Bhojpur; Chanderi; Chitrakoot; Mandu; Omkareshwar; Sanchi; Pachmarhi.

Airports: Gwalior, Indore, Jabalpur, Bhopal, Khajuraho.

National Parks: Bandhavgarh National Park in Umaria and Jabalpur districts (448.85 sq. km) • Fossil National Park in Mandla district (0.27 sq. km), Kanha National Park in Mandla and Balaghat districts (940 sq. km), Madhav National Park in Shivpuri district (375.22 sq. km), Panna National Park in Panna and Chhatarpur districts (542.67 sq. km), Pench (Priyadarshini) National Park in Seoni and Chhindwara districts (292.85 sq. km), Sanjay National Park in Sidhi district (466.88 sq. km), Satpura National Park in Hoshangabad district (585.17 sq. km) and Van Vihar National Park in Bhopal district (4.45 sq. km).

Administration

Legislature: Madhya Pradesh has a unicameral legislature. There are 230 seats in the Madhya Pradesh assembly, of which thirty-three are reserved for SCs and forty-one for STs.

The current party position is as follows:

Name of Party	Seats
Bharatiya Janata Party	173
Indian National Congress	38
Samajwadi Party	7
Gondvana Gantantra Party	3
Bahujan Samaj Party	2
Rashtriya Samanta Dal	2
Communist Party of India (Marxist)	1
Nationalist Congress Party	1
Janata Dal—United	1
Independent	2
Total	**230**

Judiciary: The High Court of Madhya Pradesh has its seat at Jabalpur. Justice Rajiv Gupta is the acting chief justice of the Madhya Pradesh High Court.

Districts:

District	Area (sq. km)	Population	Headquarters	Urban Agglomerations
Anuppur	3,701	667,155	Anuppur	
Ashoknagar	4,674	688,992	Ashoknagar	
Balaghat	9,229	1,445,760	Balaghat	Balaghat, Wara Seoni
Barwani	5,422	1,081,039	Barwani	
Betul	10,043	1,394,421	Betul	Betul
Bhind	4,459	1,426,951	Bhind	
Bhopal	2,772	1,836,784	Bhopal	Bhopal
Burhanpur	NA	634,883	Burhanpur	
Chhatarpur	8,687	1,474,633	Chhatarpur	Chhatarpur

Chhindwara	11,815	1,848,882	Chhindwara	Chhindwara,
			Chiklikalan Parasia	Damoh 7,306
1,081,909	Damoh	Damoh		
Datia	2,691	627,818	Datia	
Dewas	7,020	1,306,617	Dewas	
Dhar	8,153	1,740,577	Dhar	
Dindori	7,470	579,312	Dindori	
East Nimar (Khandwa)	10,776	1,708,170	Khandwa	
Guna	11,064	1,665,503	Guna	
Gwalior	4,560	1,629,881	Gwalior	Gwalior
Harda	3,330	474,174	Harda	Harda
Hoshangabad	6,707	1,085,011	Hoshangabad	Itarsi, Pipariya
Indore	3,898	2,585,321	Indore	Indore, Mhow Cantt
Jabalpur	5,211	2,167,469	Jabalpur	Jabalpur
Jhabua	6,778	1,396,677	Jhabua	
Katni	4,950	1,063,689	Katni	
Mandla	5,800	893,908	Mandla	Mandla
Mandsaur	5,535	1,183,369	Mandsaur	Mandsaur
Morena	4,989	1,587,264	Morena	Joura, Sabalgarh
Narsinghpur	5,133	957,399	Narsinghpur	Gadarwara, Narsinghpur Neemuch
4,256	725,457	Neemuch	Neemuch	
Panna	7,135	854,235	Panna	Panna
Raisen	8,466	1,120,159	Raisen	Baraily
Rajgarh	6,153	1,253,246	Rajgarh	
Ratlam	4,861	1,214,536	Ratlam	Jaora, Ratlam Rewa
6,314	1,972,333	Rewa		
Sagar	10,252	2,021,783	Sagar	Bina-Etawa, Garhakota, Khurai, Sagar
Satna	7,502	1,868,648	Satna	Satna
Sehore	6,578	1,078,769	Sehore	Ashta, Sehore
Seoni	8,758	1,165,893	Seoni	
Shahdol	9,952	1,572,748	Shahdol	Burhar-Dhanpuri,
Shajapur	6,195	1,290,230	Shajapur	Shajapur
Sheopur	6,606	559,715	Sheopur	Sheopur
Shivpuri	10,277	1,440,666	Shivpuri	
Sidhi	10,526	1,830,553	Sidhi	
Tikamgarh	5,048	1,203,160	Tikamgarh	
Ujjain	6,091	1,709,885	Ujjain	Badnagar, Mahidpur, Ujjain
Umaria	4,076	515,851	Umaria	
Vidisha	7,371	1,214,759	Vidisha	Basoda
West Nimar (Khargone)	8,030	1,529,954	Khargone	Barwaha, Khargone

Maharashtra

Key Statistics

Capital: Mumbai.
Area: 307,713 sq. km.
Population: Total: 96,878,627, Male: 50,400,596, Female: 46,478,031.
Population density: 314 per sq. km.
Sex ratio: 922 females per 1000 males.
Principal languages: Marathi, Hindi, Urdu.
Literacy rates: Total: 76.9%, Male: 86.0%, Female: 67.0%.

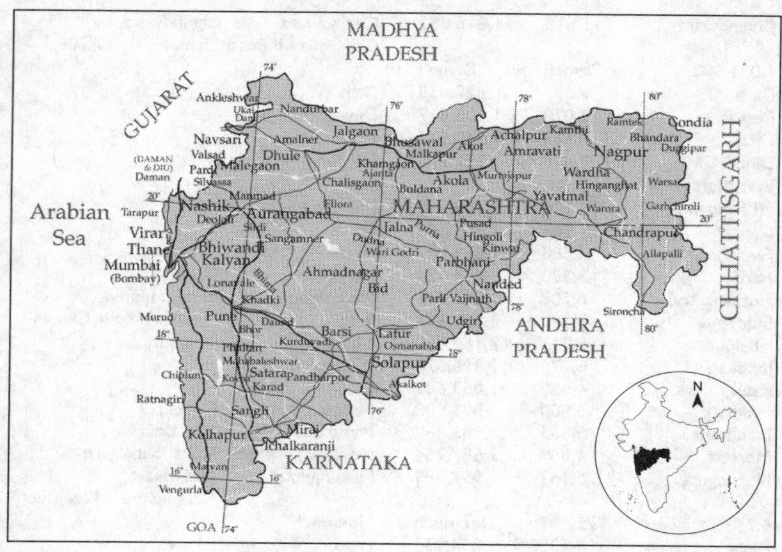

Government

Governor: S.M. Krishna. He was sworn in on 6 December 2004.

Chief Minister: Vilasrao Deshmukh (INC). He became the chief minister on 1 November 2004.

Geography

Physical characteristics: The dominant physical feature of the state is its plateau. The western upturned edges of this plateau rise to form the Sahyadri range. The major rivers and their main tributaries have eroded the plateau into alternating river valleys and intervening higher-level interfluves, such as the Ahmednagar, Buldhana and Yavatmal plateaus.

The Sahyadri range, with an average elevation of 1,000m, forms the topographical backbone of Maharashtra. Its steep cliffs descend to the Konkan coast in the west, while on the east it descends in steps through a transitional area called Mawal till it reaches the plateau level.

The Konkan area is a narrow coastal lowland that is hardly 50 km wide and 200m high. It lies between the Arabian Sea and the Sahyadri range.

The Satpuras that lie along the northern border and the Bhamragad-Chiroli-Gaikhuri range that lies along the eastern border serve as the natural limits of Maharashtra.

The flat topography of the state is a result of the outpouring of lava through fissures in the ground around 60 to 90 million years ago. This formed horizontal layers of basalt over extensive areas.

Neighbouring States and Union territories:

States: Gujarat, Madhya Pradesh, Karnataka, Andhra Pradesh, Goa, Chhattisgarh.

Union territories: Dadra, Nagar Haveli.

Major rivers: Godavari, Tapi, Wainganga, Penganga, Ulhas, Wardha and Bhima.

Climate: Maharashtra has a tropical monsoon climate. The summers are hot and commence from March onwards and continue till June, when the monsoon season arrives. This lasts till October when the transition to winter takes place. Seasonal rains from sea clouds are intensive and rainfall exceeds 4,000mm in the Sahyadri region.

The Konkan region also gets heavy rainfall, but the intensity follows a decreasing trend northwards. Rainfall is low east of the Sahyadris, around 700mm in the western plateau areas. The Sholapur–Ahmednagar region forms the heart of the dry zone. The rains increase marginally later in the season, mainly eastwards in the Marathwada and Vidarbha regions.

Flora and Fauna:

Flora: The forest cover of Maharashtra is 47,482 sq. km. It is interesting that the forest cover in the state has been showing increasing trends. Teak trees are found to occur over an area of approximately 10,180 sq. km, while bamboo plants cover an area of in excess of 10,100 sq. km.

The forests of the state are of the following types: (i) southern tropical semi-evergreen forests, (ii)) southern tropical moist deciduous forests, (iii) southern tropical dry deciduous forests, (iv) southern tropical thorn forests, and (v) littoral and swamp forests.

Fauna: Animals found in the state include tigers, bison, panthers, deer, antelopes, wild boar, blue bull, great Indian bustard, sloth bear, wild dog, jackal, hyena, chausingha, sambar, gaur, barking deer, ratel, pangolin, cheetal, mouse deer, flying squirrel and civet cat. Reptiles found in the state include monitor lizard, python, cobra, Russell's viper and pit viper.

A large variety of birds are found in the Sanjay Gandhi National Park. These include Tickell's flower pecker, sunbird, white-bellied sea eagle, paradise flycatcher, trogon, various species of kingfisher, woodpeckers, and drongos. Besides these, the green barbet, the parakeet, the Malabar whistling thrush and spotted babbler are also found.

History

The name Maharashtra appeared in a seventh-century inscription and in the account of the Chinese traveller, Hiuen-Tsang.

During the early period, the territory that forms the modern state of Maharashtra was ruled over by several Hindu kingdoms. The Satavahanas, the Rashtrakutas, the Yadavas, the Vakatakas, the Kalachuris and the Chalukyas. After 1307 came the Muslim dynasties.

By the middle of the sixteenth century, Maharashtra was broken up into several smaller states and ruled by several independent, warring Muslim rulers. Shivaji was born in 1627. He set up a large Maratha empire that rivalled the Mughals in might and power. During the eighteenth century, almost the entire region of western and central India, as well as large parts of north and even eastern India were brought under Maratha control. Ultimately, even the mighty Marathas had to give way to the British in the nineteenth century.

At the time of Independence in 1947, The Bombay Presidency became the state of Bombay with B.G. Kher as its first chief minister. On 1 May 1960, the state was divided into two parts creating Gujarat in the north and Maharashtra in the south, with Y.B. Chavan as its chief minister.

Politics

During British rule, portions of the western coast of India under direct British rule were part of the Bombay Presidency. In 1937, the Bombay Presidency became a province of British India. After Indian Independence in 1947, many former princely states, including the Gujarat states and the Deccan states, were merged with the former Bombay province. Bombay state was significantly enlarged on 1 November 1956, expanding eastward to incorporate the Marathi-speaking Marathwada region of Hyderabad state, the Marathi-speaking Vidarbha region of southern Madhya Pradesh, and Gujarati-speaking Saurashtra and Kutch. The southernmost, Kannada-speaking portion of Bombay state became part of the new linguistic state of Karnataka. Yashwantrao Chavan and later Morarji Desai were its only two chief ministers. Bombay state was partitioned into Gujarat and Maharashtra states on 1 May 1960, after an agitation for a separate Marathi state turned violent.

Yashwantrao Balwantrao Chavan of the Congress Party became the Bombay's chief minister (1956) and was the first chief minister of the new state of Maharashtra (1960-62). Shankarrao Bhaurao Chavan served two times as chief minister, from 1975 to 1977, and from 1986 to 1988. In 1978, Sharad Pawar toppled the Congress government in Maharashtra led by Vasantdada Patil and formed a government in coalition with the Janata Party under the banner of the Progressive Democratic Front. He was also chief minister from 1988 to 1991 and from 1993 to 1994. Sharad Pawar is the president of the Nationalist Congress Party, which he formed in 1999. Shiv Sena, a Hindu nationalist party strongly associated with Maratha identity, was founded in 1966 by Bal Thackeray who is the president of the party. The party came to power in 1995 in alliance with the BJP and Manohar Joshi was the chief minister till 1999. Vilasrao Deshmukh of the Congress became chief minister in 1999. He had to step down in January 2003 and make way for Sushilkumar Shinde, a prominent Dalit face of Congress, following factionalism in the state unit of the party. Vilasrao Deshmukh again came back to the office of chief minister on 1 November 2004.

Culture

The tamasha form of folk drama is indigenous to this state. Marathi literature is also well known. Mumbai is also the most important centre of the Indian film industry.

Fairs and festivals: Ganesh Chaturthi is one of the most important festivals of the state. Modern festivals of the state include Pune Festival, Banganga Festival, Elephanta Festival, Ellora Festival (near Aurangabad), Kalidas Festival (Nagpur).

Economy, Industry and Agriculture

Economy: The net state domestic product at current prices for 2003–04 (provisional) was Rs 294,001 crores. The per capita net state domestic product at current prices for 2003–04 (provisional) was Rs 29,204.

Minerals and industry: Mumbai is regarded as the financial capital of India. The state is home to a wide range of manufacturing industries such as chemicals, textiles, automobiles, food products, machinery, electrical products, printing and publishing, paper and paper products, tobacco and related products. The film and tourism industries have an important place in the economic and social life of Maharashtra.

The districts of Chandrapur, Gadchiroli, Bhandara and Nagpur constitute the main mineral-bearing areas of Maharashtra. Coal and manganese are the major minerals mined in the state. There are deposits of iron ore and limestone as well. Substantial deposits of ilmenite are found in the coastal area of Ratnagiri.

Agriculture: Major crops grown in the state are rice, jowar, bajra, wheat, pulses, oilseeds, cotton, sugar cane and turmeric. The main fruit crops are oranges, grapes, mangoes and bananas.

Power: The state gets most of its power from thermal power plants. Hydroelectric power plants are the second most important source while nuclear power plants are the third.

Education

Educational institutes: Prominent institutes of higher education in the state include the University of Mumbai, University of Pune, Nagpur University, Indian Institute of Technology (Powai), Jamnalal Bajaj Institute of Management Studies (Mumbai), Narsee Monjee Institute of Management Studies (Mumbai), SNDT Women's University (Mumbai), Amravati University (Amravati), Bharati Vidyapeeth (Pune), Central Institute of Fisheries Education (Mumbai), Deccan College Post Graduate and Research Institute (Pune), Dr Babasaheb Ambedkar Marathwada University (Aurangabad), Dr Babasaheb Ambedkar Technological University (Raigad), Dr Panjabrao Deshmukh Krishi Vidyapeeth (Akola), Gokhale Institute of Politics and Economics (Pune), Indira Gandhi Institute of Development Research (Mumbai), International Institute for Population Sciences (Mumbai), Kavikulguru Kalidas Sanskrit Vishwavidyalaya (Ramtek), Konkan Krishi Vidyapeeth (Ratnagiri) • Maharashtra University of Medical Sciences (Nashik), Mahatma Gandhi Antarrashtriya Hindi Vishwavidyalaya (Wardha), Mahatma Phule Krishi Vidyapeeth (Ahmadnagar), Marathwada Krishi Vidyapeeth (Parbhani), North Maharashtra University (Jalgaon), Shivaji University (Kolhapur), Swami Ramanand Teerth Marathwada University (Nanded), Tata Institute of Social Sciences (Mumbai), Tilak Maharshtra Vidyapeeth (Pune), Yahswantrao Chavan Maharasthra Open Univeristy (Nashik).

Tourism

Major tourist attractions: Mahabaleshwar, Lonavla, Elephanta Caves, Gateway of India, Ganapatiphule, Alibag, Raigad Fort, Sinhadurg Fort, Panchgani, Ajanta and Ellora.

Airports:
International: Mumbai.
Domestic: Pune, Nagpur, Akola, Sholapur, Kolhapur, Aurangabad.

National Parks: Sanjay Gandhi National Park in Thane dist. (86.96 sq. km). Gugamal National Park in Amaravati district. It is a part of Melghat Tiger Reserve. The Tiger Reserve covers an area of 1676.93 sq. km while the National Park has an area of 361.28 sq. km. Pench National Park in Nagpur dist. (257.26 sq. km). Navegaon National Park in Bhandara dist. (133.88 sq. km). Tadoba National Park in Chandrapur dist. (116.55 sq. km). The Andhari Wildlife Sanctuary (508.85 sq. km). Tadoba National Park together form the Tadoba-Andhari Tiger Reserve.

Administration

Legislature: Maharashtra has a bicameral legislature, which means that there is a legislative assembly as well as a legislative council. There are 288 seats in the assembly, of which eighteen are reserved for SCs and twenty-two for STs. Elections were held in October 2004.

The current party position is as follows:

Name of Party	Seats
Nationalist Congress Party	71
Indian National Congress	69
Shiv Sena	62
Bharatiya Janata Party	54
Jan Surajya Sharti	4
Communist Party of India (Marxist)	3

Peasants and Workers Party of India	2
Akhil Bharatiya Sena	1
Bharipa Bahujan Mahasangha	1
Republican Party of India (A)	1
Swatantra Bharat Paksha	1
Independent	19
Total	**288**

Judiciary: The Bombay High Court has jurisdiction over Maharashtra, Goa, and Daman and Diu. Besides Mumbai, it has benches at Aurangabad, Nagpur and Panaji (Goa). Dalveer Bhandari is the chief justice.

Districts:

District	Area (sq. km)	Population	Headquarters	Urban Agglomerations
Ahmednagar	17,048	4,088,077	Ahmednagar	Ahmednagar, Shrirampur
Akola	5,429	1,629,305	Akola	
Amravati	12,210	2,606,063	Amravati	
Aurangabad	10,107	2,920,548	Aurangabad	Aurangabad
Bhandara	3,895	1,135,835	Bhandara	
Beed	10,693	2,159,841	Beed	
Buldhana	9,661	2,226,328	Buldhana	
Chandrapur	11,443	2,077,909	Chandrapur	
Dhule	8,063	1,708,993	Dhule	
Gadchiroli	14,412	969,960	Gadchiroli	
Gondia	5,425	1,200,151	Gondia	
Hingoli	4,524	986,717	Hingoli	
Jalgaon	11,765	3,679,936	Jalgaon	Bhusawal
Jalna	7,718	1,612,357	Jalna	
Kolhapur	7,685	3,515,413	Kolhapur	Ichalkaranji, Kolhapur
Latur	7,157	2,078,237	Latur	
Mumbai	157	3,326,837	Mumbai	Greater Mumbai
Mumbai (Suburban)	446	8,587,561	Mumbai	Greater Mumbai
Nagpur	9,802	4,051,444	Nagpur	Kamptee, Nagpur
Nanded	10,528	2,868,158	Nanded	
Nandurbar	5,034	1,309,135	Nandurbar	
Nashik	15,530	4,987,923	Nashik	Nashik
Osmanabad	7,569	1,472,256	Osmanabad	
Parbhani	6,517	1,491,109	Parbhani	
Pune	15,643	7,224,224	Pune	Pune
Raigarh	7,152	2,205,972	Alibag	
Ratnagiri	8,208	1,696,482	Ratnagiri	
Sangli	8,572	2,581,835	Sangli	Sangli
Satara	10,480	2,796,906	Satara	
Sindhudurg	5,207	861,672	Oras	
Sholapur	14,895	3,855,383	Sholapur	
Thane	9,558	8,128,833	Thane	Bhiwandi, Greater Mumbai, Vasai
Wardha	6,309	1,230,640	Wardha	
Washim	5,153	1,019,725	Washim	
Yavatmal	13,582	2,460,482	Yavatmal	Yavatmal

Manipur

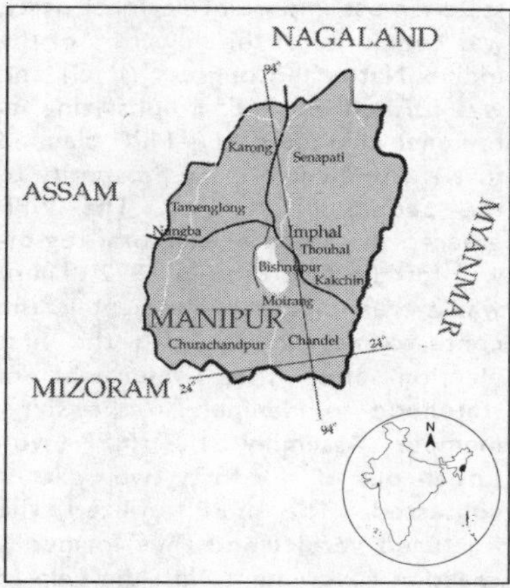

Key Statistics

Capital: Imphal.
Area: 22,327 sq. km.
Population: Total: 2,166,788, Male: 1,095,634, Female: 1,071,154.
Population density: 107 per sq. km.
Sex ratio: 978 females per 1000 males.
Principal languages: Manipuri, Thado, Tangkhul.
Literacy rates: Total: 70.5%, Male: 80.3%, Female: 60.5%.

Government

Governor: Shivender Singh Sidhu. He was sworn in on 6 August 2004.

Chief Minister: Okram Ibobi Singh (INC). He was sworn in on 7 March 2002.

Geography

Physical characteristics: Manipur can be divided into two distinct physical regions—the outlying area of rugged hills and narrow valleys, and the inner area of flat plains. The Loktak lake is an important geographic feature of the central plain area. The total area occupied by all the lakes is about 600 sq. km. The highest point of the state is the Iso peak near Mao (2,994m).

Neighbouring States and Union territories:
International border: Myanmar.

States: Assam, Mizoram, Nagaland.

Major rivers: Manipur (also called Imphal) and Barak.

Climate: The average annual rainfall varies from 933mm at Imphal to 2,593mm at Tamenglong. The temperature ranges from sub-zero to 36°C. Depending on the altitude, the climatic conditions vary from tropical to subalpine.

Flora and Fauna:
Flora: About 67 per cent of the geographical area of Manipur is hilly and covered with forests. The wet forests and the pine forests occur between 900–2700m above mean sea level. Manipur is home to 500 varieties of orchids. The siroi lily, which is the only terrestrial lily in India, grows on the hilltops of the Siroi Hill.

Fauna: The rich fauna of Manipur includes the sangai (or dancing deer), slow loris, hornbill, hoolock gibbon, the clouded leopard, Mrs Hume's barbacked pheasant, spotted linshang, blyths tragopan, Burmese peafowl and salamander.

History

In 1762, the ruler of Manipur, Raja Jai Singh, made a treaty with the British to thwart a Myanmarese invasion. Again in 1824, the services of the British were sought to expel invaders from Myanmar. Political turmoil continued for some time until 1891, when Chura Chand, a five-year-old member of the ruling family, was nominated as the raja.

The administration was henceforth conducted under British supervision for the next few years.

In 1907, the raja and the durbar regained control of the government. It is noteworthy that the vice-president of the durbar was a member of the Indian Civil Service. The administration was eventually transferred to the raja and the vice-president of the durbar became its president.

An uprising of the Kuki hill tribes in 1917 resulted in the adoption of a new system of government. The region was divided into three subdivisions. Each of these subdivisions was put under an officer from the government of the neighbouring state of Assam.

In 1947 Manipur joined the Indian Union and the political agency of Assam was abolished. In 1949 Manipur became a Union territory administered by a chief commissioner and an elected territorial council. In 1969, the office of the chief commissioner was replaced by a lieutenant governor. This in turn was converted to a governorship when Manipur became full-fledged state of the Indian Union on 21 January 1972. M. Koireng Singh was the first chief minister of Manipur.

Politics

The year 1934 marked a turning point in the political history of Manipur when a political organization called the Nikhil Manipuri Mahasabha under the Presidentship of Maharaja Chura Chand Singh came into existence. The Mahasabha was initially a social organization, but in 1938 it became the first political party of Manipur, thus becoming a harbinger of regional parties in Manipur. At the time of Independence, the king of Manipur was one of the few rulers who refused to sign the merger agreement but was later reportedly coaxed and compelled to sign on 21 September 1949, and subsequently endorsed the formal merger of Manipur with the dominion of India on 15 October 1949. The Manipur People's Party (MPP), the state's most important regional party, was composed of the defectors of the Indian National Congress (INC) and was formed in 1968. Emphasizing its regional character, the MPP claimed that it alone could bring prosperity to the people of Manipur. The MPP entered the arena of electoral tug-of-war for the first time in 1972. There was a tremendous excitement in the contest since it was also the first election after the conferment of statehood to Manipur. In the sixty-member Assembly, the MPP won fifteen out of the forty-two seats it contested. The MPP utilized the fractured verdict and thus formed a coalition government with the help of Socialist Party, Congress (O), and Independents. A ministry headed by Md Alimuddin under the name of United Legislature Party (ULP) was installed on 20 March 1972. However, dissensions soon cropped up in the government. As a result some members of the ULP ministry defected to the Opposition. Later on, the Opposition moved a non-confidence motion against the government. Subsequently, the Assembly was dissolved and President's Rule was imposed. In the next elections, no party was able to secure an absolute majority in the house and political instability continued to plague Manipur as before. On 29 June 1977 a new Janata ministry under Yangmaso Shaiza was installed. All the members of the Congress party and the MPP joined the Janata Legislature Party and the Janata Party's strength was raised to fifty-five in the House. Again, after the 1990 Assembly election, a new ministry was sworn in under the leadership of MPP stalwart R.K. Ranbir Singh making an event in the political history of Manipur of being the first non-Congress government in more than a decade. A Congress ministry came to power under Okram Ibobi Singh after the 2002 elections.

Culture

The Manipuri dance form is indigenous to the state. For example, the Anal community have the Kamdom and the Ludem dance forms, while the Chote community has the Hucham Pulak. Different communities and tribes have varied art forms, folk dances, folk songs and folklore of their own.

Fairs and festivals: Important festivals of the state include Ningol Chakouba, Yaoshang (the most important festivals of Hindus of the state), Ramzan Id, Kut (a festival of Kuki-Chin-Mizo), Gang-Ngai (a festival of Kabui Nagas), Chumpha (festival of Tangkhul Nagas), Christmas, Cheiraoba (the Manipuri New Year), Kang (the Rathayatra of Manipur) and Heikru Hitongba.

Economy, Industry and Agriculture

Economy: The net state domestic product at current prices in 2003–04 (provisional) was Rs 3,571 crores. The per capita net state domestic product at current prices (new series) in 2003–04 (advance estimate) was Rs 14,766.

Minerals and industry: Deposits of asbestos, copper ore, coal, bog iron, lignite, chromite, limestone, nickel ore and petroleum are present. Iron and steel products, consumer products and cement are also produced in the state.

Agriculture: About 80 per cent of the state's population depends on agriculture for their livelihood. Rice and maize are the most important food crops. Besides this, the state is well known for its fruit production—orange, pineapple, jackfruit, peach, plum, pears and banana. Potato, turmeric, ginger, black pepper, tapioca, cotton, oilseeds, jute and mesta, cashew nut, tea, mushrooms, orchids and areca nut are also grown.

Power: The state mainly utilizes hydroelectric power, but thermal power is also used.

Education

Educational institutes: Prominent institutes of higher education are the Manipur University and the Central Agricultural University, both located at Imphal.

Tourism

Major tourist attractions: Ima Market, Imphal; Khomghampat Orchidarium, Imphal; Manipur Zoological Gardens, Imphal; Bishnupur; Moirang; Loktak Lake and Sendra Island; Waithou Lake; Kangchup; Ukhrul; Tamenglong.

Airport: Imphal.

National Parks: Keibul Lamjao National Park in Bishnupur district (40 sq. km). It is the world's only floating national park and Shiroi Hill National Park in Ukhrul district (41 sq. km).

Administration

Legislature: Manipur has a unicameral legislature. There are sixty seats of which one is reserved for SCs and nineteen are reserved for STs. The tenure of the present house ends on 11 March 2007. The current party position is as follows:

Name of Party	Seats
Indian National Congress	20
Federal Party of Manipur	13
Manipur State Congress Party	7
Communist Party of India	5
Bharatiya Janata Party	4
Nationalist Congress Party	3
Samata Party	3
Manipur Peoples Party	2
Democratic Revolutionary Peoples Party	2
Manipur National Conference	1
Total	**60**

Judiciary: The state comes under the Mizoram bench of the Guwahati High Court. Binod Kumar Roy is the chief justice.

Districts:

District	Area (sq. km)	Population	Headquarters	Urban Agglomerations
Bishnupur	496	205,907	Bishnupur	
Chandel	3,313	122,714	Chandel	
Churachandpur	4,570	228,707	Churachandpur	
Imphal East	709	393,780	Porompat	Imphal
Imphal West	519	439,532	Lamphel	Imphal
Senapati	3,271	379,214	Senapati	
Tamenglong	4,391	111,493	Tamenglong	
Thoubal	514	366,341	Thoubal	
Ukhrul	4,544	140,946	Ukhrul	

Meghalaya

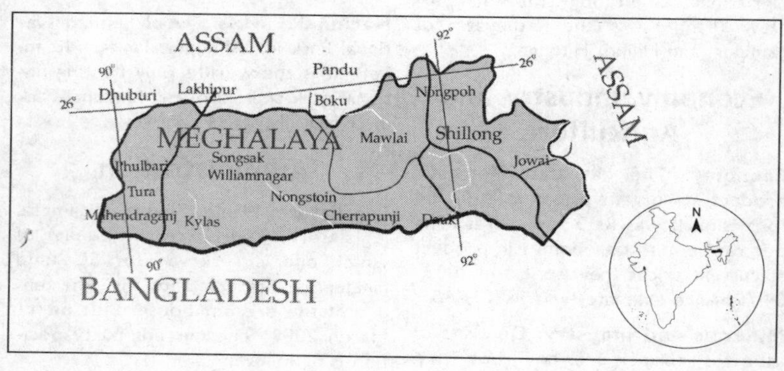

Key Statistics

Capital: Shillong.
Area: 22,429 sq. km.
Population: Total: 2,318,822, Male: 1,176,087, Female: 1,142,735.
Population density: 103 per sq. km.
Sex ratio: 972 females per 1000 males.
Principal languages: Khasi, Garo, Bengali, Assamese.
Literacy rates: Total: 62.6%, Male: 65.4%, Female: 59.6%.

Government

Governor: Mundakkal Matthew Jacob. He has been the governor of Meghalaya since 19 June 1995.

Chief Minister: J. Dringwell Rymbai. He was sworn in on 15 June 2006.

Geography

Physical characteristics: The state of Meghalaya is a region of uplands that was formed by a detached part of the Deccan plateau. In the western part of

Meghalaya, the Garo hills rise abruptly from the Brahmaputra valley to about 300 metres. They merge with the Khasi hills and Jaintia hills. These adjacent highlands together form a single tableland region that is separated by a series of eastward-running ridges. The steep southern face of the plateau overlooks the lowlands of Bangladesh. A number of rivers and streams flow out of the plateau, to create deep, narrow valleys with steep sides. These include the Umiam–Barapani, a major source of hydroelectric power for Assam and Meghalaya.

Neighbouring States and Union territories:
International border: Bangladesh.

States: Assam

Major rivers: Although there are a number of rivers in Meghalaya, none of them are fit for navigation. In the Garo hills, the Manda, the Janjiram and the Damring flow towards the north while the Ringge and the Ganol flow westwards. The south flowing rivers are the Simsang, the biggest river in Garo Hills, and the Bhogai.

Significant north-flowing rivers in the Khasi and Jaintia hills are the Khri, the Umkhem, the Umtrew and the Umiam. The Kulpi lies on the border between Jainita Hills and North Cachar hills. The Kynshi, the Umiam Mawphlang and the Umngot flow south into Bangladesh.

Climate: This region experiences tropical monsoonal climate, that varies from the western to the eastern parts of the plateau. The Garo hills district has a tropical climate characterized by high rainfall and humidity. Summers are generally warm while winters are moderately cold. The Khasi and Jaintia hills have high rainfall, moderately warm summers and severely cold winters when temperature sometimes dips to below freezing point in the higher altitudes. The mean summer temperature in Meghalaya is 26°C and the mean winter temperature is 9°C.

A maximum rainfall of 12,000mm has been recorded on the southern slope of Khasi hills along the Cherrapunjee–Mawsynram belt. The average annual rainfall is about 2,600mm in western Meghalaya, between 2,500 and 3,000mm in northern Meghalaya and about 4,000mm in south-eastern Meghalaya. There is substantial variation of rainfall in the central and southern parts of the state.

Flora and Fauna:
Flora: Meghalaya has a widely varied and unique flora. The vegetation of Meghalaya ranges from tropical and subtropical to temperate or near temperate. This is largely due to the diverse topography, abundant rainfall and climatic and soil conditions of the state.

The forest types found in the state are: (i) Tropical forests: tropical evergreen forests, tropical semi-evergreen forests, tropical moist and dry deciduous forests, and grasslands and savannas; and (ii) Temperate forests.

The different types of plants found in the state are: parasites and epiphytes, succulent plants, and trees and shrubs.

Meghalaya also produces timber, fuelwood, resin, fibre, latex, tannin, fodder, gums, shellac, essential oils, fats, edible fruits, honey and a large number of medicinal plants. Some of the important tree species that yield timber are Khasi pine, teak, sal, and bamboos. Meghalaya is also well known for a large variety of flowers, bay leaves, orchids and cinnamon.

Fauna: Meghalaya is home to a wide variety of animals. These include the elephant, serow, sambar, hoolock, leopard, golden cat, barking deer, pangolin, jungle cat, large Indian civet, binturong or bear cat and Himalayan black bear. Notable among the reptile population found in the state are Indian cobra, king cobra, coral snake, viper, green tree racer, red-necked kulback, copperhead, blind snake and python.

Some of the significant species of birds found in the state are hoopoe, black-breasted Kalij pheasant, jungle mynas, hill mynas, long-tailed broadbill, red jungle fowl, spotted forktail, Himalayan whistling thrush, Burmese roller, blue-throated barbet, and Himalayan black bulbul. Besides these, the great Indian hornbill, florican and black drongo are also found in the state. Meghalaya is also famous for its large butterfly population.

History

When the British came to Sylhet (now in Bangladesh) in 1765, the Khasis used to go to Pandua on the border of Sylhet to trade in various commodities in exchange for rice, salt and dried fish. At that time, limestone from the Khasi Hills was taken to Bengal. The British officials of the East India Company came in contact with the Khasis when they began trading in Khasi Hill limestone.

In 1824, the Burmese invaded Cachar and reached the border of the Jaintia Hills. The British sent a force to reinforce the Jaintia ruler's troops. This paved the way for a friendship treaty to be signed on 10 March 1824, whereby the Jaintia ruler accepted British protection. This led to other Khasi chiefs to allow the passage of the British troops through their territories. After the end of the Burmese invasion, the Khasi chiefs agreed to a British demand for a route through the Khasi and Jaintia hills that would connect Assam valley with Surma valley. The road was completed in March 1929, but only after suppressing an uprising led by U Tirot Sing. This led to the signing of several treaties with different Khasi chiefs. These treaties let the British slowly take control of the mineral deposits and at the same time subjugate the chiefs and also gain control of the judiciary. In 1862 the Jaintias rose in revolt under U Kiang Nongbah.

Shillong, the present-day capital of Meghalaya was made the capital of Assam in 1874. It remained so till January 1972, when Meghalaya was created. At the time of Independence in 1947, the rulers of the region acceded to India. The region was given special protection in the Indian Constitution. It was included within the state of Assam but was granted a substantial amount of autonomy. On 2 April 1970, Meghalaya became an autonomous state within Assam and attained full statehood on 21 January 1972. Captain Williamson A. Sangma was the state's first chief minister.

Politics

With the partition of Bengal in 1905, Meghalaya became a part of the new province of Assam and eastern Bengal. In 1912, when the partition of Bengal was reversed, Meghalaya became a part of the revived province of Assam. In 1921, following the Montagu-Chelmsford Report of 1917 and the Government of India Act of 1919 the governor-general-in-council declared the areas now in Meghalaya, excluding the Khasi states, as backward tracts. On 2 April 1970 an autonomous state of Meghalaya was created within the state of Assam by the Assam Reorganization (Meghalaya) Act, 1969. Williamson A. Sangma, the first chief minister of Meghalaya, had three tenures as chief minister, from 1970 to 1978, from 1981 to 1983 and from 1988 to 1990. In 1979, B.B. Lyngdoh split the All-Party Hill Leaders' Conference (APHLC) to form a coalition government with the Congress. Lyngdoh and Sangma agreed to share the chief minister's post for two years each. D.D. Lapang, the current chief minister, came to power in 2003.

Culture

A common and unique cultural tradition of all the tribes of Meghalaya is the matriarchal law of inheritance, whereby custody of property and succession of family position runs through the female line. It passes from the mother to the youngest daughter. The traditional costume of the state is the jainsem and the dhara, although Western clothes are gaining popularity amongst the younger generation.

The different tribes have their own set of traditions and art forms. Phawar is one of the basic forms of Khasi music. It is more of a chant than a song and is often composed on the spot to suit the occasion. Other forms of songs include the exploits of legendary heroes, ballads and verses based on historical events and laments for martyrs. Khasi musical instruments include the tangmuri, shaw shaw, nakra, ksing padiah, besli, sharati, shyngwiang and duitara.

Fairs and festivals: The different Khasi festivals are Ka Shad Suk Mynsiem, Ka Pom-Blang Nongkrem, Ka-Shad Shyngwiang-Thangiap, Ka-Shad-Kynjoh Khaskain, Ka Bam Khana Shnong, Umsan Nongkharai and Shad Beh Sier. The key Jaintia festivals include Behdienkhlam, Laho Dance and the sowing ritual ceremony. Other festivals commemorated by the Jaintias include the Tiger Festival, Bam Phalar/ Bam Doh, Rong Belyngkan, Durga Puja, Seng Kut Snem and Christmas. The main festivals of the Garos are Wangala, Den Bilsia, Rongchu gala, Mangona, Grengdik BaA, Mi Amua, Jamang Sia, Ja Megapa, Sa Sat Ra Chaka, Ajeaor Ahaoea, Chambil Mesara, Dore Rata Dance, Saram Cha'A, Do'KruSua and A Se Mania.

Economy, Industry and Agriculture

Economy: The net state domestic product at current prices in 2003–04 (provisional) was Rs 4,349 crores. The per capita net state domestic product at current prices in 2003–04 (provisional) was Rs 18,135.

Minerals and industry: The main industries of the state are tourism, iron and steel, consumer products, cement, handloom, silk production, lime and granite cutting and polishing. Small-scale industries in the state include wooden-furniture making, cane and bamboo works, tailoring, flour and rice mills, weaving and bakeries. There are six industrial estates, one designated industrial area and one export promotion industrial park in Meghalaya.

The significant mineral resources that are currently being exploited in the state are coal, limestone, clay and sillimanite. Other mineral resources found to occur in the state include phosphorite, glass sand, granite, quartz, feldspar, gypsum, gold, iron ore, uranium, base metal and gypsum.

Agriculture: Agriculture is the main occupation of the people of Meghalaya. Over 80 per cent of the total population is dependent on agriculture for their livelihood. Rice and maize are the major food crops. Millets and pulses are also grown, but in lesser quantities. Potato is a major cash crop of Meghalaya. Oilseeds such as rapeseed, mustard, soyabean and sesame are also grown. Important fruits grown here are orange, pineapple, lemon, guava, litchi, plum, peach, pear, jackfruit and bananas. Jute, mesta and cotton are the main fibre crops grown in the state. Areca nut and betelvine are also grown. The most prominent spices of the state are ginger, chillies, turmeric, black pepper and bay leaf. The jhum or 'shifting system' of cultivation is now being replaced with scientific methods, thereby bringing more land under permanent cultivation.

Power: Hydroelectric power plants meet all of Meghalaya's power requirements. However, the state has a high thermal power generation potential.

Education

Educational institutes: North-Eastern Hill University, Shillong; Sacred Heart Theological College, Hawlai; Jowai Polytechnic School and North-Eastern Indira Gandhi Regional Institute of Health and Medical Sciences.

Tourism

Major tourist attractions:

1. Khasi Hills: Cherrapunjee (Sohra), Shillong peak, Mawsynram, Ward's Lake, Sohpetbneng peak, Botanical garden, Lady Hydari park, Umiam Water Sports complex, Shillong Cathedral, Dwarksuid, Bishop and Beadon falls, Elephant falls, Sweet falls, Nongkhnum Island, Crinoline falls, Diengiei peak, Spread Eagle falls, Kyllang rock, Noh Kalikai falls, Ranikor.
2. Jaintia Hills: Megalithic remnants at Nartiang, Syndai, Syntu Ksiar, Jowai, Thadlaskein lake.
3. Garo Hills: Nokrek peak, Imilchang Dare waterfalls, Tura peak, Naphak Lake.

Airport: Umroi.

National Parks: Balphakram National Park in South Garo Hills district (220 sq. km) and Nokrek National Park in east, west and south Garo Hills districts (47.48 sq. km).

Administration

Legislature: Meghalaya has a sixty-seat unicameral legislature of which fifty-tive are reserved for STs. The term of the current house expires on 10 March 2008. The present party position is as under:

Name of Party	Seats
Indian National Congress	22
Nationalist Congress Party	14
United Democratic Party	9
Meghalaya Democratic Party	4
Bharatiya Janata Party	2
Hill State People's Democratic Party	2
Khun Hynnieutrip National Awakening Movement	2
Independent	5
Total	**60**

Judiciary: Meghalaya is under the jurisdiction of the Gauhati High Court at Guwahati, Assam. The principal seat of the High Court is at Guwahati and there is a circuit bench at Shillong. Binod Kumar Roy is the chief justice.

Districts:

District	Area (sq. km)	Population	Headquarters	Urban Agglomerations
East Garo Hills	260	247,555	Williamnagar	
East Khasi Hills	2,748	660,994	Shillong	Shillong
Jaintia Hills	3,819	295,692	Jowai	
Ri Bhoi	2,448	192,795	Nongpoh	
South Garo Hills	1,887	99,105	Baghmara	
West Garo Hills	3,677	515,813	Tura	
West Khasi Hills	5,247	294,115	Nongstoin	

Mizoram

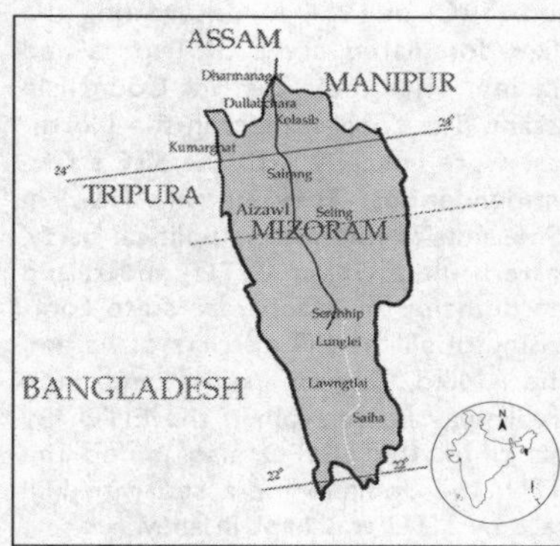

Key Statistics

Capital: Aizawl.
Area: 21,087 sq. km.
Population: Total: 888,573, Male: 459,109, Female: 429,464.
Population density: 42 per sq. km.
Sex ratio: 935 females per 1000 males.
Principal languages: Lushai/Mizo, Bengali, Lakher.
Literacy rates: Total: 88.49% (second highest in the country), Male: 90.69%, Female: 86.13%.

Government

Governor: Amolak Rattan Kohli. He took over as governor on 18 May 2001.

Chief Minister: Pu Zoramthanga (MNF). He was sworn in on 4 December 2003.

Geography

Physical characteristics: Mizoram is bounded by Myanmar on the east and south and Bangladesh on the west. It is a mountainous region with steep hills separated by rivers that create deep gorges between them. Phawngpui or the Blue Mountain is the highest peak (2,210m). The Tropic of Cancer runs through the state.

Neighbouring States and Union territories:
International borders: Myanmar, Bangladesh.

States: Assam, Tripura, Manipur.

Major rivers: Tlawṇg is the longest river of the state. Tlau, Chhimtuipui, Tuichang and Tuirial are other important rivers.

Climate: The hilly areas are cooler during summer, while the lower reaches are relatively warm and humid. The average maximum temperature in summer is 30°C. The average minimum temperature during winter is around 11°C. The months of May to September see heavy rains, with an average annual rainfall of 2500mm.

Flora and Fauna:
Flora: Three-fourths of the state's area is under forest cover. Prominent trees include the Himalayan maple, champak, ironwood, bamboo and gurjun. The region also abounds in various species of shrubs. About 150 species of orchids have also been identified.

Fauna: Wildlife found in the state include tiger, leopard, elephant, Malayan sun bear, Himalayan black bear, serow, wild boar, slow loris, Assamese macaque, capped langur, owl, pheasant, partridge, hawk, eagle, egret and heron.

History

Like many other north-east Indian tribes, the origin of the Mizos is shrouded in mystery. They are generally accepted as part of a great Mongoloid wave of migration from China. These include the Kuki, New Kuki and Lushai tribes. In 1895, the Mizo Hills were formally declared as a part of British

India and subsequently marked as Lushai Hills district, with Aizawl as the headquarters.

At the time of India's Independence, a subcommittee was formed under the chairmanship of Gopinath Bordoloi to advise the Constituent Assembly on the tribal affairs in the north-east. The region became a district of Assam.

In 1959, a great famine, known in Mizo history as the Mautam Famine, struck the Mizo Hills. The cause of the famine was the flowering of bamboos and the consequent manifold increase in the rat population which infested the villages and destroyed crops.

Movements for sovereignty for the region gained momentum in 1961, with the birth of the Mizo National Front (MNF). After a decade of insurgency, the region was declared a Union territory in 1972. Insurgency continued for another fourteen years, and ended with MNF leader Laldenga signing an accord with the Union government. Mizoram became India's twenty-third state on 20 February 1987. Laldenga was the state's first chief minister.

Politics

It was during the British regime that a political awakening among the Mizos in the Lushai Hills started taking shape. The first political party, the Mizo Common People's Union, was formed on 9 April 1946. At the time of Independence a sub-committee under the chairmanship of Gopinath Bordoloi was formed to advise the Constituent Assembly on the tribal affairs in the North-East. The Mizo Union submitted a resolution to this sub-committee demanding inclusion of all Mizo-inhabited areas adjacent to Lushai Hills. However, a new party called the United Mizo Freedom (UMFO) came up to demand that Lushai Hills join Burma after Independence. After the independence of India, Mizoram continued to be part of Assam. The Lushai Hills Autonomous District Council came into being in 1952. Representatives of the District Council and the Mizo Union pleaded with the States Reorganization Commission (SRC) in 1954 for integrating the Mizo-dominated areas of Tripura and Manipur with their District Council in Assam. The tribal leaders in the North-East were unhappy with the SRC's recommendations. They met in Aizawl in 1955 and formed a new political party, Eastern India Union (EITU) and raised the demand for a separate state comprising of all the hill districts of Assam. The Mizo Union split and the breakaway faction joined the EITU. By this time, the UMFO also joined the EITU; the demand for a separate Hill state by EITU was kept in abeyance.

A new political organization, the Mizo National Front (MNF) was born on 22 October 1961 under the leadership of Laldenga with the specified goal of achieving sovereign independence of Greater Mizoram. While the MNF took to violence to secure its goal of establishing a sovereign land, other political forces in the hills of Assam were striving for a separate state. The search for a political solution to the problems facing the hill regions in Assam continued. In 1966 the Mizos resorted to the use of armed struggle to put forth their demands to set up a homeland. The Mizo National Front was outlawed in 1967. A Mizo District Council delegation, which met Prime Minister Indira Gandhi in May 1971, demanded a full-fledged state for the Mizos. The Union government on its own offered to turn Mizo Hills into a union territory in July 1971. The union territory of Mizoram came into being on 21 January 1972. On 3 May 1972 L. Chal Chhunga was sworn in as the first chief minister of Mizoram. In 1986 a peace agreement was signed between the Government of India and the MNF. Mizoram was created as a separate state within India, and Pu Laldenga became chief minister. The formalization of Mizoram state took place on 20 February 1987. However, in 1989, the

MNF lost the first elections following the peace agreement. In 1998 and 2003 the MNF won the state assembly elections, and Pu Zoramthanga is currently the chief minister.

Culture

Popular dance forms of Mizoram are Khuallam, Cheraw or bamboo dance, Chailam and Tlangiam. These are accompanied by instruments like the gong and drum. Traditional crafts include exquisite cane and bamboo work and handloom weaving.

Fairs and festivals: Most Mizo festivals are connected with harvest or other agricultural operations. These include Mim Kut, Pawl Kut and Chapchar Kut.

Economy, Industry and Agriculture

Economy: The net state domestic product at current prices in 2002–03 was Rs 2027 crores. The per capita net state domestic product at current prices in 2002–03 was Rs 22,207.

Minerals and industry: Mizoram has no major industry. The small-scale sector comprises handloom, handicrafts, rice, oil and flour milling, mechanized bamboo workshops and sericulture. Major minerals include coal, limestone and natural gas.

Agriculture: Nearly 60 per cent of the population is engaged in agriculture. Shifting cultivation, or jhum, is the usual practice. Important crops include paddy, maize, soyabean, mustard, pulses, sugarcane, chilli, ginger, tobacco, turmeric, potato, banana and pineapple.

Power: The two main sources of power in the state are hydroelectric plants and diesel power plants.

Education

Educational institutes: The North-Eastern Hill University, which is headquartered at Shillong, has a campus at Aizawl.

Tourism

Major tourist attractions: The Blue Mountain (Phawngpui); The famous caves: Pukzing cave, Milu Puk, Lamsial Puk, and Kungawrhi Puk; Sibuta Lung; Thangliana Lung; Suangpuilawn Inscriptions; Mangkhai Lung; Buddha's image near Mualcheng village.

Airport: Aizawl.

National Parks: Murlen (200 sq. km) and Phawngpui (50 sq. km).

Administration

Legislature: The Mizoram Legislative Assembly comprises forty seats, of which thirty-nine are reserved for STs. The term of the current assembly expires on 14 November 2008. The party position of the current house is as follows:

Name of Party	Seats
Mizo National Front	21
Indian National Congress	12
Mizoram People's Conference	3
Zoram Nationalist Party	2
Hmar Peoples Convention	1
Maraland Democratic Front	1
Total	**40**

Judiciary: Mizoram falls under the jurisdiction of the Gauhati High Court. There is a permanent bench located at Aizawl. Binod Kumar Roy is the chief justice.

Districts:

District	Area (sq. km)	Population	Headquarters	Urban Agglomerations
Aizawl	3,576.3	339,812	Aizawl	–
Champhai	3,185.8	101,389	Champhai	–

Kolasib	1,382.5	60,977
Lawngtlai	2,557.1	73,050
Lunglei	4,538.0	137,155
Mamit	3,025.8	62,313
Saiha	1,399.9	60,823
Serchhip	1,421.6	55,539

Kolasib	–
Lawngtlai	–
Lunglei	–
Mamit	–
Saiha	–
Serchhip	–

Nagaland

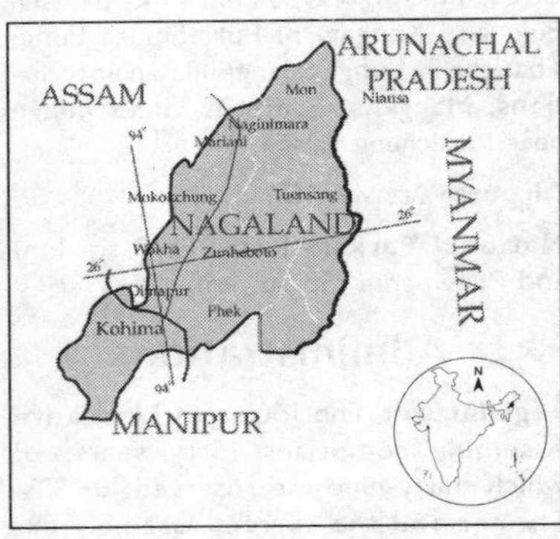

Key Statistics

Capital: Kohima.
Area: 16,579 sq. km.
Population: Total: 1,990,036, Male: 1,047,141, Female: 942,895.
Population density: 120 per sq. km.
Sex ratio: 900 females per 1000 males.
Principal languages: Ao, Sema, Konyak.
Literacy rates: Total: 66.6%, Male: 71.2%, Female: 61.5%.

Government

Governor: Shyamal Datta. He assumed the office of the governor of Nagaland on 28 January 2002.

Chief Minister: Neiphi-u Rio (NPF). He became chief minister on 6 March 2003.

Geography

Physical characteristics: Nagaland has state boundaries with Assam, Arunachal Pradesh and Manipur. On the east, it has an international boundary with Myanmar. The Naga Hills run through this state. Saramati (3840m) is the highest peak.

Neighbouring States and Union territories:
International border: Myanmar.

States: Arunachal Pradesh, Assam, Manipur.

Major rivers: Dhansiri, Doyang, Dikhu, Barak and tributaries of the Chindwin of Myanmar. Others include Milak, Zungki and Tizu.

Climate: Temperature varies between 16°C and 31°C in summer and between 4°C and 24°C in winter. The average rainfall is 2,000mm to 2,500mm. It rains heavily from May to August, as well as occasionally in September and October. November to April is the dry season.

Flora and Fauna:
Flora: Evergreen and coniferous forests, medicinal plants, bamboo, cane and orchids make up the state's flora.

Fauna: Animals like the Asian elephant, clouded leopard, binturong, musk deer, macaque, common langur, gaur (Indian bison), tiger, sambar, barking deer, hoolock, serow, sloth bear and wild boar can be found in the state. Reptiles include the monitor lizard, tortoise, reticulated python, king cobra, common krait, banded krait, viper and common cobra.

The greyheaded fishing eagle, crested serpent eagle, forest eagle owl, tragopan and hornbill are notable among the birds found in Nagaland. Amongst the animals, the Asian elephant, spotted linsang, tiger civet, sloth bear, tiger and the tailed pig are endangered species. The gaur or Indian bison is also facing extinction in Nagaland. The diverse hornbills and tortoise are also endangered.

History

Medieval chronicles of the Ahom kingdom of Assam talk of the Naga tribes. The Myanmar invasion of Assam in 1816 was followed by the establishment of British rule in 1826. By 1892, British administration covered the entire Naga territory, with the exception of the Tuensang area.

After Independence in 1947, Naga territory initially remained a part of Assam, after which there was a strong nationalist pressure for the political union of the Naga tribes. In 1957, an agreement was signed between the Naga leaders and the Indian government, following which the Naga Hill districts of Assam and the Tuensang division to the north-east were brought together under a single unit, directly administered by the Indian government. However, unrest continued and another accord was reached at the Naga People's Convention meeting of July 1960. According to this accord, it was decided that Nagaland should become a constituent state of the Indian Union. Nagaland became a state on 1 December 1963 and a democratically elected government took office in 1964. Shilu Ao was the first Chief Minister.

Politics

The Naga territory remained split between Assam and the North-East Frontier Agency after Indian independence in 1947, despite a vocal movement advocating the political union of all the Naga tribes. The government of the newly independent India refused to accept such a demand, and some Nagas took to armed rebellion in an effort to gain independence. The area remained in a rebellious political condition for much of the 1950s. A voluntary plebiscite was held in 1951 to determine whether the Nagas would join the Indian Union, or remain by themselves. The result was 99.9 in favour of independence. In persuance of their declared national decision, the Naga people launched a civil disobedience movement and successfully boycotted the general elections of free India. Nagaland was just a district in the state of Assam until 1957, known to others as 'The Naga Hills'. Not satisfied with such an obscure status, the leaders of various Naga tribes, in August 1957, formed the Naga People's Convention (NPC). In its first session held at Kohima on 21 August 1957, under the presidentship of Imkongliba Ao, the NPC proposed the formation of a separate administrative unit by merging the Tuensang division of NEFA with Naga Hills district. The government of India agreed to the proposal. In July 1960, a delegation of the NPC met Jawaharlal Nehru and discussed the formation of a separate state for the Nagas within the Indian Union to be known as Nagaland. On 18 February 1961 an interim body of forty-two members was constituted to function as the de-facto legislature. On 1 December 1963, President S. Radhakrishnan inaugurated the state of Nagaland. The first Assembly election in Nagaland was held in 1964 and the Naga National Organization (NNO) came to power. Following a grave political crisis in the state, President's Rule was imposed in Nagaland on 22 March 1975; Nagaland was under President's

Rule for thirty-two months, so far the longest in the country. The state has come under President's Rule several more times. Neiphi-u Rio, leader of the Democratic Alliance of Nagaland (DAN), was sworn in as the present chief minister on 6 March 2003.

Culture

Each of the several tribes and communities of Nagaland has its own unique folk dances, folk songs and folklore. They are skilful craftsmen specializing in woodcarving, weaving, spinning, metalwork and stonework. Pottery is considered a taboo among certain sections of the Ao community.

Fairs and festivals: The major festivals of the state are Sekrenyi of the Angamis, Moatsu of the Aos, Phom-Monyu of the Phom tribe and the Hornbill festival of Nagaland.

Economy, Industry and Agriculture

Economy: The net state domestic product at current prices in 2001–02 was Rs 3,864 crores. The per capita net state domestic product at current prices in 2001–02 was Rs 18,911.

Minerals and industry: The process of industrialization of the state is in its infancy. There is a need for more industries in the state. There are several plans in the pipeline to increase industrial investment and activity in the state. Coal, limestone, petroleum and marble are the main minerals found in the state.

Agriculture: Agriculture is the most important occupation of the people. Rice, wheat, maize and pulses are the chief agricultural products of the state. Fruits like banana, orange, passion fruit, pears, plum and jackfruit are grown. Vegetables like ginger, cabbage, chilli, tomato, potato and garlic are also grown.

Power: The main sources of power in the state are diesel power plants and hydroelectric plants.

Education

Educational institutes: Nagaland University is at Kohima.

Tourism

Major tourist attractions: Shangnyu village; Longwa village; Veda peak; Naginimora; Dzukou Valley; Kohima village; War Cemetry, Kohima; Dzulekie; Ruins of medieval Kachari kingdom, Dimapur; Chumukedima.

Airport: Dimapur.

National Parks: Intanki National Park in Kohima district (202.02 sq. km).

Administration

Legislature: Nagaland has a unicameral legislature. The Nagaland Legislative Assembly has sixty seats out of which fifty-nine are reserved for STs. The term of the present house runs out on 13 March 2008. The current party position is:

Name of Party	Seats
Indian National Congress	21
Nagaland Peoples Front	19
Bharatiya Janata Party	7
Nationalist Democratic Movement	5
Janata Dal (United)	3
Samata Party	1
Independent	4
Total	**60**

Judiciary: Nagaland falls under the jurisdiction of the Gauhati High Court with a bench at Kohima. Binod Kumar Roy is the chief justice.

Districts:

District	Area (sq. km)	Population	Headquarters	Urban Agglomerations
Dimapur	927	308,382	Dimapur	–
Kohima	3,114	314,366	Kohima	–
Mokokchung	1,615	227,230	Mokokchung	–
Mon	1,786	259,604	Mon	–
Phek	2,026	148,246	Phek	–
Tuensang	4,228	414,801	Tuensang	–
Wokha	1,628	161,098	Wokha	–
Zunheboto	1,255	154,909	Zunheboto	–

Orissa

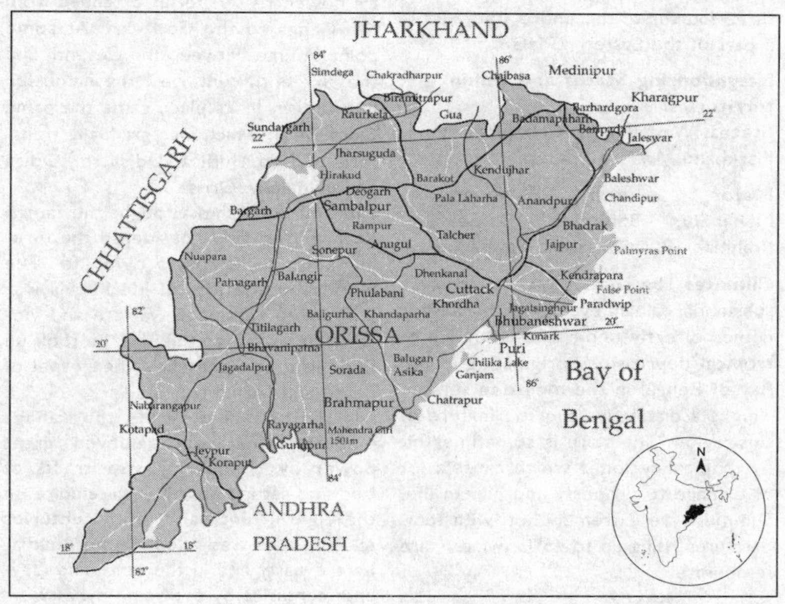

Key Statistics

Capital: Bhubaneswar.

Area: 155,707 sq. km.

Population: Total: 36,804,660, Male: 18,660,570, Female: 18,144,090.

Population density: 236 per sq. km.

Sex ratio: 972 females per 1000 males.

Principal languages: Oriya, Hindi, Telugu.

Literacy rates: Total: 63.1%, Male: 75.3%, Female: 50.5%.

Government

Governor: Rameshwar Thakur. He was sworn in on 16 November 2004.

Chief Minister: Naveen Patnaik (BJD). He was sworn in on 16 May 2004.

Geography

Physical characteristics: The state is surrounded by the Bay of Bengal on the east, Chhattisgarh in the west, Jharkhand and West Bengal in the north and Andhra Pradesh in the south. It has a coastline of about 450 km. Orissa is divided into five major physiographic regions: the central plateaus, the coastal plain in the east, the western rolling uplands, the middle mountainous and highland regions, and the flood plains. The middle mountainous and highland region covers about three-fourths of the entire state and is a part of the Eastern Ghats.

Neighbouring States and Union territories:
States: West Bengal, Chhattisgarh, Jharkhand, Andhra Pradesh.

Major rivers: Subarnarekha, Mahanadi, Baitarani, Burabalang, Brahmani, Rushikulya and Vamsadhara.

Climate: The coastal lowland receives substantial rainfall every year because it comes directly under the influence of tropical depressions originating in the Bay of Bengal in the monsoon season. This is a distinctive climatic feature of this region. The state is sometimes hit by tropical cyclones which cause a lot of damage to property and human life. Summers are extremely hot, with temperatures rising up to 45°C; winters are temperate.

Flora and Fauna:
Flora: The state has tropical semi-evergreen, tropical moist deciduous, tropical dry deciduous, littoral and swamp forests.

Fauna: Wildlife found in the state includes tiger, elephant, gaur, chital, leopard, mouse deer, flying squirrel, mugger, salt-water crocodile, monitor lizards, snakes, fishing cat, hyena, wild pig, water birds and Ridley sea turtle.

History

At various points in ancient and medieval times, the land corresponding roughly with modern Orissa was known as Utkala, Kalinga, and Odra Desa. These names were initially associated with peoples. The Okkala or Utkala, the Kalinga, and the Odra or Oddaka were mentioned in literature as tribes. Later on these names became identified with territories. For many centuries preceding and following the birth of Christ, Kalinga was a very strong political power. Its territories extended from the Ganga to the Godavari. At some point of time between the eleventh and the sixteenth centuries, the name fell into disuse. In its place came the name Odra Desa, which was gradually transformed into Uddisa, Udisa, or Odisa and ultimately, Orissa.

In 260 BC, Ashoka fought the famed Kalinga War, now considered the turning point in Ashoka's own life. The bloodshed and loss of life in this war led him to renounce warfare and violence. It was after this that he took up Buddhism and preached the gospel of peace and harmony.

In the first century BC, the Kalinga emperor Kharavela achieved great power by conquering vast tracts of land and setting up a Kalinga empire. In the eighth, ninth and tenth centuries AD, the area was ruled by the Bhuma-Kara dynasty and in the tenth and eleventh centuries by the Soma dynasty.

Between 1028 and 1434–35, Kalinga was ruled by the Ganga dynasty followed by the Surya dynasty. After the fall of the Surya kings, Orissa passed into the hands of the Afghan rulers of Bengal.

In the 1590s, the Mughal emperor Akbar conquered Orissa from the Afghans. With the decline and fall of the Mughal empire in the 1760s, a part of Orissa remained under the Bengal nawabs and the rest went to the Marathas. The Bengal region passed into British rule in 1757, after the Battle of Plassey. The British conquered the Maratha areas in 1803. After 1803, the British controlled the entire Oriya-speaking area and it was administered as two separate units, the Northern Division and the Southern Division. It was only in April 1936 that the British constituted Orissa as a separate province on a linguistic basis, with the exception of twenty-six princely states that stayed outside provincial administration. After Independence in 1947, all these princely states (except Saraikela and Kharsawan that merged with Bihar) became parts of Orissa. The first chief minister of Orissa was Harekrushna Mahatab.

Politics

Orissa became a separate province on 1 April 1936 by the Government of India (Constitution of Orissa) Order 1936. It comprised certain portions of the Bihar and Orissa Province, Madras Presidency and the Central Provinces. On 1 January 1948, twenty-four princely states merged with the province of Orissa. Harekrushna Mahtab became the first chief minister of Orissa in 1947 and was chief minister two more times. Biju Patnaik of the Congress first became chief minister in 1961. In 1967 a new party called Jana Congress was formed under the leadership of Harekrushna Mahtab and came to power. Utkal Congress was formed in 1969 when Biju Patnaik left the Indian National Congress. After the 1971 Orissa elections Utkal Congress took part in the Biswanath Das ministry in the state. In 1977 Utkal Congress merged into the Janata Party. The Jana Congress too merged into the Janata Party. In a mid-term poll, the Janata Party led by Biju Patnaik secured 110 seats out of 147. Nilamani Routray was made the chief minister. In 1981 the Congress party won a resounding victory and Janaki Ballav Patnaik became the chief minister. Under the leadership of Biju Patnaik, the Janata Dal won an astounding victory in the elections held in 1990. J.B. Patnaik was the chief minister again from 1995 to 1999. On 5 March 2000 Naveen Patnaik of the Biju Janata Dal was elected the chief minister. In 2004, the thirteenth Assembly election was held in Orissa. On 16 May 2004, Naveen Patnaik was sworn in as chief minister for the second time.

Culture

The state is home to the Odissi and Chhau dance forms as well as the Patachitra art form. It is the home of renowned weaves of saris like Sambalpuri, Katki, Behrampuri, Bomkai and Baraghat.

Fairs and festivals: The major festivals of the state include Dola Purnima (Holi), Ratha Yatra, Chandan Yatra, Snana Yatra, Konark Dance Festival, Puri Beach Festival, Bali Yatra and Dhanu Yatra.

Economy, Industry and Agriculture

Economy: The net state domestic product at current prices for 2003–04 (provisional) was Rs 47,002 crores. The per capita net state domestic product at current prices for 2003–04 (provisional) was Rs 12,388.

Minerals and industry: Orissa has substantial mineral resources such as dolomite, chromite, limestone, high quality iron ore, coal and manganese. The state is home to steel mills, non-ferrous smelting, paper mills, fertilizer industries, cement plants, foundries and glass works. The famous steel plant at Rourkela is in Orissa.

Agriculture: About 80 per cent of the area sown is under rice cultivation.

Other important crops are oilseeds, pulses, jute, sugar cane, and coconut. Adverse crop-growing conditions such as poor soil quality and low availability of sunlight combine to hamper agriculture in the state.

Power: Most of Orissa's power is generated by hydroelectric plants. The rest comes from thermal power plants.

Education

Educational institutes: Notable educational institutes in the state include Utkal University, Bhubaneswar; Fakir Mohan University, Balasore; Orissa University of Agriculture and Technology, Bhubaneswar; Regional Engineering College (National Institute of Technology), Rourkela and Xavier Institute of Management, Bhubaneswar.

Tourism

Major tourist attractions: Bhitarkanika National Park; Simlipal National Park; Lingaraj Temple, Bhubaneswar; Mukteswar Temple, Bhubaneswar; Rajarani Temple, Bhubaneswar; Shanti Stupa, Bhubaneswar; Jagannath Temple, Puri; Sun Temple, Konark; Barabati Fort, Cuttack; Chilka Lake; Puri beach.

Airports: Bhubaneswar, Jharsuguda.

National Parks: Simlipal (Mayurbhanj) —845.7 sq. km, Bhitarkanika (Cuttack) —367 sq. km.

Administration

Legislature: The state has a unicameral legislature of 147 members. Out of this, twenty-two seats are reserved for SCs and thirty-four for STs. The tenure of the current house ends on 29 June 2009. The current party position is:

Name of Party	Seats
Biju Janata Dal	61
Indian National Congress	38
Bharatiya Janata Party	32
Jharkhand Mukti Morcha	4
Orissa Gana Parishad	2
Communist Party of India	1
Communist Party of India (Marxist)	1
Independent	8
Total	**147**

Judiciary: The Orissa High Court is situated at Cuttack. The chief justice is Sujit Burman Ray.

Districts:

District	Area (sq. km)	Population	Headquarters	Urban Agglomerations
Anugul	6,375	1,139,341	Anugul	
Balangir	6,575	1,335,760	Balangir	Titlagarh
Baleswar	3,806	2,023,056	Baleswar	Baleswar
Bargarh	5,837	1,345,601	Bargarh	
Baudh	3,098	373,038	Baudh	
Bhadrak	2,505	1,332,249	Bhadrak	
Cuttack	3,932	2,340,686	Cuttack	Cuttack
Debagarh	2,940	274,095	Debagarh	
Dhenkanal	4,452	1,065,983	Dhenkanal	
Gajapati	4,325	518,448	Parlakhemundi	
Ganjam	8,206	3,136,937	Chatrapur	
Jagatsinghapur	1,668	1,056,556	Jagatsinghapur	
Jajapur	2,899	1,622,868	Panikoili	Byasanagar
Jharsuguda	2,081	509,056	Jharsuguda	
Kalahandi	7,920	1,334,372	Bhawanipatna	
Kandhamal	8,021	647,912	Phulbani	

Kendrapara	2,644	1,301,856	Kendrapara	
Kendujhar	8,303	1,561,521	Kendujhar	
Khordha	2,813	1,874,405	Khordha	Bhubaneswar, Jatani
Koraput	8,807	1,177,954	Koraput	
Malkangiri	5,791	480,232	Malkangiri	
Mayurbhanj	10,418	2,221,782	Baripada	Baripada
Nabarangapur	5,291	1,018,171	Nabarangapur	
Nayagarh	3,890	863,934	Nayagarh	
Nuapada	3,852	530,524	Nuapada	
Puri	3,479	1,498,604	Puri	
Rayagada	7,073	823,019	Rayagada	Gunupur
Sambalpur	6,657	928,889	Sambalpur	Sambalpur
Subarnapur	2,337	540,659	Subarnapur	
Sundergarh	9,712	1,829,412	Sundergarh	Raurkela

Punjab

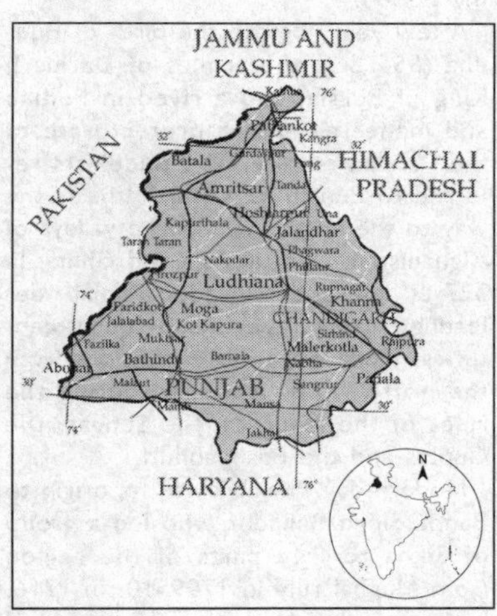

Key Statistics

Capital: Chandigarh.

Area: 50,362 sq. km.

Population: Total: 24,358,999, Male: 12,985,045, Female: 11,373,954.

Population density: 482 per sq. km.

Sex ratio: 876 females per 1000 males.

Principal languages: Punjabi, Hindi, Urdu.

Literacy rates: Total: 69.7%, Male: 75.2%, Female: 63.4%.

Government

Governor: Gen. S.F. Rodrigues. He was sworn in on 16 November 2004.

Chief Minister: Captain Amarinder Singh. He was sworn in on 27 February 2002.

Geography

Physical characteristics: Punjab is largely a flat plain that rises gently from about 150 metres in the south-west to about 300 metres in the north-east. Physiographically, it can be divided into three parts: (i) The Shivalik hills in the north-east rising from about 300 to 900 metres; (ii) The zone of narrow, undulating foothills dissected by seasonal rivers terminating in the plains and not flowing into bigger waterbodies and (iii) The flat tract with fertile alluvial soils. The low-lying floodplains lie along the rivers while the slightly elevated flat uplands lie between them. Sand dunes are found in the south-west and west of the Sutlej.

Neighbouring States and Union territories:

International border: Pakistan.

States: Haryana, Himachal Pradesh, Jammu and Kashmir, Rajasthan.

Union territories: Chandigarh.

Major rivers: Ravi, Beas, Sutlej and Ghaggar with their numerous small and seasonal tributaries.

Climate: Punjab has three major seasons. These are: (i) The hot weather from April to June with temperatures rising as high as 45°C; (ii) The rainy season from July to September with average annual rainfall in the state ranging between 960mm in the submontane region to 580mm in the plains and (iii) The cold weather from October to March with temperatures going down to 4°C.

Flora and Fauna:

Flora: The rapid growth of human settlement resulted in the clearing out of most of the forest cover of the state. Consequently, trees have been replaced by bush vegetation in the Shivalik hills. Attempts at afforestation have been made on the hills while eucalyptus trees have been planted along major roads.

Fauna: Wildlife faces intense competition from agriculture for its natural habitat. Many species of birds, some monkeys, rodents, and snakes have adapted to the farmland environment.

History

Punjab was the site of the Indus Valley Civilization. Archaeological excavations all over the state have revealed evidences of the cities belonging to the civilization that also included Harappa and Mohenjodaro, which are now in Pakistan. The *Mahabharata* contains rich descriptions of the land and people of Punjab. It is also believed that parts of the *Ramayana* were written around the Shri Ram Tirath Ashram near Amritsar and that it was in the forests of what is today Punjab that Lav and Kush, the sons of Rama, grew up.

Other important historical centres are at Ropar, Kiratpur, Dholbaha, Rohira and Ghuram. Sanghol, in Fatehgarh Sahib district near Ludhiana, is home to sites associated with the Mauryan dynasty. Relics found here record the presence of Buddhism in the region.

The Vedic and the later epic periods of the Punjab are of great significance. The *Rig Veda* was composed here. Numerous cultural and educational centres were established in the region during the period.

A few years before the birth of Buddha (556 BC), the armies of Darius I, King of Persia, had arrived in Punjab and made the area a protectorate of the Persian empire. The Buddhists referred to Punjab as 'Uttar Path' or the way to the north, namely the valleys of Afghanistan, Central Asia and China. In 327 BC Alexander invaded Punjab, defeating Raja Paurava. In subsequent centuries, there were more invasions from the north. This happened during the rules of the Mauryas, the Sungas, the Guptas and the Pushpabhuti.

Modern-day Punjab owes its origin to Banda Singh Bahadur who led a group of Sikhs to free parts of the region from Mughal rule in 1709–10. In 1716, however, the Mughals defeated and killed Banda Singh. This sparked off a prolonged struggle between the Sikhs and the Mughals and Afghans.

By 1764–65, the Sikhs established their dominance in the region. Ranjit Singh led Punjab into a powerful kingdom and also added the provinces of Multan, Kashmir, and Peshawar. In 1849, Punjab had passed into the hands of the British East India Company. It later became a province of the British empire in India.

Many Punjabis played significant roles during India's freedom struggle. These included Baba Ram Singh (of the Kuka or Namdhari movement fame), Lala Lajpat Rai, Madan Lal Dhingra, Bhagat Singh and Bhai Parmanand. The nationalist fervour was kept alive by several movements, such as the Singh Sabha, Arya Samaj and the Akali movements and by organizations like Bharat Mata Society, Naujawan Bharat Sabha and Kirti Kisan Sabha.

It was in Punjab that the infamous Jallianwala Bagh massacre took place at Amritsar on 13 April 1919. Hundreds of peaceful demonstrators were killed and over a thousand were injured when General Reginald Dwyer ordered his troops to open fire on civilians who had gathered in a peaceful protest meeting. This incident proved to be a turning point in the history of India.

At the time of Independence in 1947, the province was divided between India and Pakistan. The smaller eastern portion was allocated to India. Gopichand Bhargava was the first chief minister of the state. In November 1956 the Indian state of Punjab was enlarged by the addition of the Patiala and East Punjab States Union (PEPSU). Pepsu was a collection of the erstwhile princely states of Faridkot, Jind, Kalsia, Kapurthala, Malerkotla, Nabha, Nalagarh and Patiala.

The present-day state of Punjab came into existence on 1 November 1966 when Punjab was divided on a linguistic basis. The Hindi-speaking parts were formed into a new state, Haryana. The northernmost districts were transferred to Himachal Pradesh.

Politics

With the partition of India in 1947, the East Punjab Legislative Assembly came into existence. On 15 July 1948 eight princely states of East Punjab grouped together to form a single state called PEPSU (Patiala and the East Punjab States Union) which merged with Punjab on the Reorganization of States on 1 November 1956. Later, the state of Punjab was reorganized on 1 November 1966 when Haryana was carved out of it and some of its areas were transferred to Himachal Pradesh.

Following the partition of India in 1947, the Sikhs were concentrated in India in east Punjab. Sikh leaders demanded a Punjabi language majority state, which would have included most Sikhs. Fearing that a Punjabi state might lead to a separatist Sikh movement, the government opposed the demand. In 1966 a compromise was reached, when two new states of Punjab and Haryana were created. Punjabi became the official language of Punjab, and Chandigarh became the shared capital of the two states. However the agreement did not resolve the Sikh question.

The Congress ruled the state for the first two decades. From the late 1960s the Akali Dal won power in the state. Prakash Singh Badal formed an Akali government in Punjab in 1970. From 1972 to 1977 Zail Singh of the Congress party served as the chief minister; he later became the President of India. Prakash Singh Badal became the chief minister for the second time in 1977 and remained in the post till 1980.

From the early 1980s to the early part of the 1990s the state was ravaged by Khalistani terrorism. In 1977, Sant Jarnail Singh Bhindranwale, an obscure but charismatic religious leader, made his appearance. He preached strict fundamentalism and armed struggle for national liberation. His speeches inflamed both young students and small farmers dissatisfied with their economic lot. Tensions between Sikhs and New Delhi heightened during the early 1980s. Over the years that followed, Punjab was faced with escalating confrontations and increased terrorist incidents. The Akali Dal only achieved limited concessions from the government and Sikh separatists prepared for battle. In the Golden Temple enclosure 10,000 Sikhs took an oath to lay down their lives if necessary in the struggle. Renewed confrontations in October 1983 resulted in Punjab being placed under central government authority. The violence continued and hundreds of Sikhs were detained in the first part of 1984. Followers of Jarnail Singh Bhindranwale established a terrorist stronghold inside the Golden Temple. The prime minister Indira Gandhi then initiated Operation Blue Star, which took place on 5-6 June 1984. The Golden Temple was shelled and besieged by the army to dislodge the terrorists. The fighting continued for five days. Bhindranwale was killed and there was serious damage to sacred buildings. The intervention had disastrous consequences for the Sikh community and the whole country. Sikh-Hindu communalism was aggravated, Sikh extremism was reinforced, and political assassinations increased. On 31 October 1984 Indira Gandhi was assassinated in New Delhi by two Sikh bodyguards. A peace agreement was concluded between the Indian government and moderate Akali Dal Sikhs led by Harchand Singh Longowal in July 1985, which granted many of the Sikh community's longstanding demands. However the extremists regarded Longowal as a traitor to the Sikh cause and he was assassinated in August 1985. In 1987 the state government was dismissed and Punjab was placed under President's Rule. Extremists spread terror throughout Punjab and the Indian government mounted a campaign of anti-terrorist measures designed to restore the situation in Punjab to normal. In May 1988 the Punjab police and Indian paramilitary forces launched Operation Black Thunder against armed extremists who had again created a fortified stronghold within the Golden Temple. At least forty extremists and several police officers were killed during the battle. President's Rule was finally brought to an end following elections in February 1992, which were won by the Congress (I). However the elections were boycotted by the leading factions of Akali Dal and attracted an extremely low turnout. Beant Singh of the Congress (I) was sworn in as chief minister. On 31 August 1995 Beant Singh was killed by a car bomb in Chandigarh.

Rajinder Kaur Bhattal who became chief minister on 21 November 1996 was the first woman chief minister of Punjab. After the February 1997 state election, Prakash Singh Badal became chief minister a third time, chosen by the Akali Dal party. He remained in power till 27 February 2002. In the state elections in Punjab in 2002, the Congress Party won sixty-four out of 117 seats. Amarinder Singh was sworn in as chief minister.

Culture

Patiala and Muktsar are famous for *juttis*, the traditional shoes worn by Punjabis. Punjab's most famous example of handicraft, phulkari, is a shawl that is completely covered in silk embroidery, with folk motifs in jewel tones.

Punjabi ornaments include the sagi, which is a central head stud. There are many varieties of sagi. These include the sagi uchhi, sagi motianwali, sagi phul, sagi chandiari, sagi meenawali. The state is famous for its gold and silver ornaments and objects made out of these metals.

Punjab is also noted for its weaving of durries which are cotton bedspreads or floor spreads in a variety of motifs and designs. The state's needlework is also unique. These include baghs, phulkaris, handkerchiefs and scarfs. In Punjab, needlework is done on a wide variety of objects. Punjabi hand fans are also well known. Punjab is famous for its woodwork. These include elaborate decorated beds called pawas, low seats called peeras. Besides furniture, the state's woodwork is also noted for boxes, toys and decorative pieces.

The state's many dance forms include bhangra, gidda, jhumar, luddi, julli, dankara, dhamal, sammi, jaago, kikli and gatka.

In the eighteenth and nineteenth centuries a new school of classical music grew up around Patiala. This is known today as the Patiala gharana. The founders of this gharana were Ustaad Ali Bux and Ustaad Fateh Ali, singers at the Patiala darbar. Notable amongst their disciples were Ustaad Bade Ghulam Ali and his brother Barkat Ali. The gharana of tabla playing which is known as the Punjab style also developed in the state. Ustaad Alla Rakha was its best-known exponent.

Various songs are associated with Punjabi weddings. These include suhag, sehra, ghodi, sithaniya and patal kaavya, The instruments used in Punjabi folk art forms include the toombi, algoza, chheka, chimta, kaanto, daphali, dhad and manjira.

Fairs and festivals: Lohri, Baisakhi and Maaghi Da Mela are the most significant among the Punjabi festivals.

Economy, Industry and Agriculture

Economy: The net state domestic product at current prices for 2003–04 (provisional) was Rs 69,841 crores. The per capita net state domestic product at current prices for 2003–04 (provisional) was Rs 27,851.

Minerals and industry: The main industrial products of the state include engineering goods, pharmaceuticals, leather goods, food products, textiles, electronic goods, sugar, machine tools, hand tools, agricultural implements, sports goods, paper and paper packaging.

Agriculture: Agriculture is the most important component of Punjab's economy. As much as 97 per cent of the total cultivable area is under the plough. The main crops grown in the state are wheat, rice and cotton. Sugar cane and oilseeds are also grown. In recent times, impetus is being given to horticulture and forestry. The state has recorded the highest yield per hectare of wheat, rice, cotton and bajra. It also has the highest per capita milk and egg production in the country.

Power: Punjab gets its power requirements both from thermal and from hydroelectric sources.

Education

Educational institutes: Well-known institutions of higher education in Punjab include Baba Farid University of Health Sciences (Faridkot), Guru Nanak Dev University (Amritsar), Punjab Agricultural University (Ludhiana), Punjab Technical University (Jalandhar), Punjabi University (Patiala) and Thapar Institute of Engineering and Technology (Patiala).

Tourism

Major tourist attractions:

Religious centres: Golden Temple, Amritsar; Ram Tirth, Amritsar; Durgiana Mandir, Amritsar; Bhagwathi Mandir, Maisar Khanna, Bathinda city; Shiv Mandir, Gur-mandi, Jalandhar; Sodal Mandir, Jalandhar city; Panch Mandir, Kapurthala town; Kali Devi Temple, Patiala; Mazaar, Pir Baba Haji Rattan, Bathinda city; Rauza Sharif, Sirhind; Qadian; The Moorish mosque, Kapurthala city; Imam Nasir mausoleum and Jamma Masjid, Jalandhar city; Chilla Baba Seikh Farid, Faridkot city; Gurudwaras at Kiratpur Sahib; Gurudwaras at Anandpur Sahib; Bhaini Sahib; Radha Soami Dera Baba Jaimal Singh; Swetamber Jain Temple, Zira, Ferozepur district; Buddhist caves, Doong, Gurdaspur; Catholic Cathedral, Jalandhar cantt.

Archaeological centres: Ghuram, Patiala dist.; Sanghol, Fatehgarh Sahib dist.; Ropar; Dholbaha.

Forts: Govindgarh fort, Amritsar; Bathinda fort; Faridkot fort; Qila Mubark, Patiala; Bhadurgarh fort; Anandpur Sahib fort, Ropar; Phillaur fort, Ludhiana; Shahpur Kandi fort, near Pathankot.

Palaces: Summer Palace of Maharaja Ranjit Singh, Amritsar; Sheesh Mahal, Patiala.

Museums: Maharaja Ranjit Singh Museum, Amritsar; Sanghol Museum; Anglo-Sikh War Memorial, Ferozeshah; Government Museum, Hoshiarpur; Rural Museum, Punjab Agricultural University, Ludhiana; Qila Mubarak Patiala, Museum of Armoury and Chandeliers; Art Gallery at Sheesh Mahal, Patiala; Sports Museum, National Institute of Sports, Patiala; Guru Teg Bahadur Museum, Anandpur Sahib, Ropar.

Others: Jallianwala Bagh Martyr's Memorial, Amritsar; Bhagat Singh, Sukhdev and Rajguru Memorial, Ferozepur; The Sargarhi Memorial at Ferozepur; Desh Bhagat Hall, Jalandhar.

Airports:
International: Amritsar.
Domestic: Chandigarh, Ludhiana.

National Parks: None.

Administration

Legislature: The state has a 117-seat legislative assembly of which twenty-nine are reserved for SCs. The term of the current house expires on 20 March 2007. The party position is as under:

Name of Party	Seats
Indian National Congress	62
Shiromani Akali Dal (Badal)	41
Bharatiya Janata Party	3
Communist Party of India	2
Independent	9
Total	**117**

Judiciary: The High Court of Punjab and Haryana is at Chandigarh. The chief justice is D.K. Jain.

Districts:

District	Area (sq. km)	Population	Headquarters	Urban Agglomerations
Amritsar	5,094	3,074,207	Amritsar	Amritsar
Bathinda	3,382	1,181,236	Bathinda	Rampur Phul
Faridkot	1,469	552,466	Faridkot	Faridkot, Jaitu
Fatehgarh Sahib	1,180	539,751	Fatehgarh Sahib	Gobindgarh
Ferozepur	5,300	1,744,753	Ferozepur	Jalalabad, Zira
Gurdaspur	3,569	2,096,889	Gurdaspur	Batala, Gurdaspur, Pathankot, Qadian
Hoshiarpur	3,364	1,478,045	Hoshiarpur	
Jalandhar	2,634	1,953,508	Jalandhar	Jalandhar
Kapurthala	1,633	752,287	Kapurthala	Phagwara
Ludhiana	3,767	3,030,352	Ludhiana	
Mansa	2,169	688,630	Mansa	
Moga	2,216	886,313	Moga	Moga
Muktsar	2,615	776,702	Muktsar	
Nawanshahr	1,266	586,637	Nawanshahr	Nawanshahr
Patiala	3,627	1,839,056	Patiala	Patiala
Rupnagar	2,056	1,110,000	Rupnagar	Kharar, Nangal
Sangrur	5,021	1,998,464	Sangrur	Sunam

Rajasthan

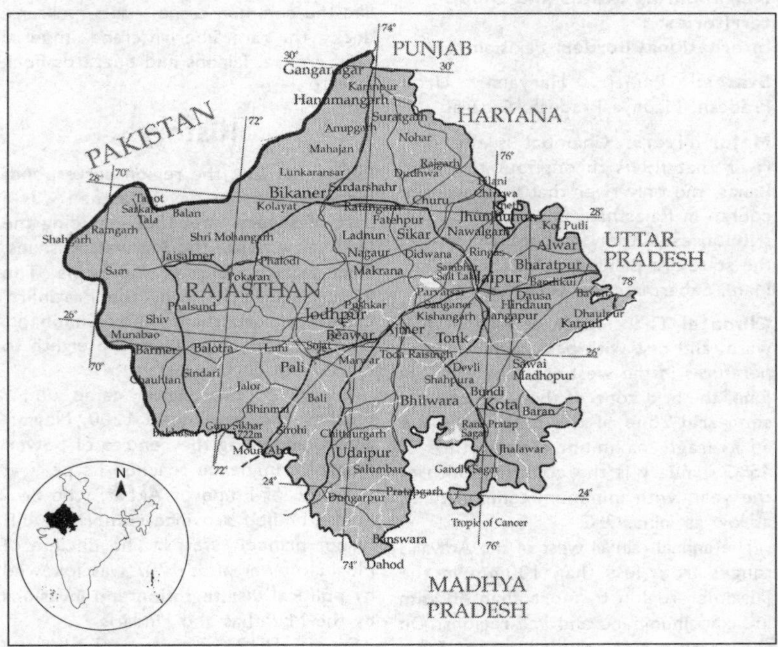

Key Statistics

Capital: Jaipur.
Area: 342,239 sq. km.
Population: Total: 56,507,188, Male: 29,420,011, Female: 27,087,177.
Population density: 165 per sq. km.
Sex ratio: 921 females per 1000 males.
Principal languages: Hindi, Bhili/Bhilodi, Urdu.
Literacy rates: Total: 60.4%, Male: 75.7%, Female: 43.9%.

Government

Governor: Pratibha Patil. She was sworn in on 8 November 2004.

Chief Minister: Vasundhara Raje Scindia (BJP). She is the first woman chief minister of the state, and was sworn in on 8 December 2003.

Geography

Physical characteristics: Rajasthan shares an international boundary with Pakistan in the west. On the Indian side there is a border with Punjab and Haryana in the north, Uttar Pradesh and Madhya Pradesh in the east and Gujarat in the south. The southern part of the state is about 225km from the Gulf of Kutch and about 400km from the Arabian Sea. The Aravalli mountain range divides the state into two regions. The north-west region mostly consists of a series of sand dunes and covers two-thirds of the state, while the eastern region has large fertile areas. The state includes The Great Indian (Thar) Desert.

Neighbouring States and Union territories:
International border: Pakistan.

States: Punjab, Haryana, Uttar Pradesh, Madhya Pradesh, Gujarat.

Major rivers: Chambal is the only river that flows throughout the year. Banas, the only river that has its entire course in Rajasthan, is one of its main tributaries. Other important rivers of the state are Banganga, Gambhiri, Luni, Mahi, Sabarmati and Ghaghar.

Climate: The climate of Rajasthan is warm and dry, with peak summer temperatures in the west reaching 49°C. In June, the arid zone of the west and the semi-arid zone of the mid-west have an average maximum temperature of 45°C. January is the coldest month of the year, with minimum temperatures as low as minus 2°C.

The annual rainfall west of the Aravallis ranges from less than 100mm in the Jaisalmer region to more than 400mm in Sikar, Jhunjhunu and Pali regions. On the eastern side, rainfall ranges from 550mm in Ajmer to 1,020mm in Jhalawar. Mount Abu in the south-west usually receives the highest rainfall. Notably, Rajasthan's climate and parched landscape are undergoing significant changes because of developmental efforts like the Indira Gandhi Nahar. As a result, Rajasthan is today a major producer of a number of agricultural crops.

Flora and Fauna:
Flora: The flora of Rajasthan includes the semi-green forests of Mount Abu, dry grasslands of the desert, the dry deciduous thorn forest of the Aravallis and the wetlands of Bharatpur. 16,367 sq. km of area is under forest cover.

Fauna: Notable among the fauna of Rajasthan are black buck, chinkara, tigers, the rare desert-fox, the endangered caracal, gharial, monitor lizard, wild boars, porcupine and the great Indian bustard.

In the winter months, migratory birds like the common crane, coots, pelicans, ducks, the rare Siberian crane, imperial sand grouse, falcons and buzzards flock to this state.

History

Before AD 700, the region corresponding with present-day Rajasthan was a part of several republics including the Mauryan empire, the Malavas, Kushans, Saka satraps, Guptas and Huns. The Rajput clans, primarily the Pratihars, Chalukyas, Parmars and Chauhans, rose to ascendancy from the eighth to the twelfth century AD.

A part of the region came under Muslim rule around AD 1200, Nagaur and Ajmer being the centres of power. Mughal dominance reached its peak at the time of Emperor Akbar, who created a unified province comprising different princely states. The decline of Mughal power after 1707 was followed by political disintegration and invasions by the Marathas and Pindaris.

From 1817–18, almost all the princely states of Rajputana, as the state was then called, entered treaties of alliance with the British, who controlled their affairs till the time of Independence. The erstwhile Rajputana, comprising nineteen princely states and the British-administered territory of Ajmer–Merwara, became the state of Rajasthan after a long process of integration that began on 17 March 1948 and ended on 1 November 1956. Rajasthan's first chief minister was Gokul Lal Asawa.

Politics

After Independence, Sardar Vallabhbhai Patel, deputy prime minister, persuaded the ruling princes of the Indian states to merge their principalities into the Indian Union. The merger of the states was considered a major triumph towards the establishment of a democratic nation. Though the twenty-two princely states of Rajputana region were declared to have been annexed to the Union of India on 15 August 1947, the process of merger and their unification became complete only in April 1949, in five phases. The Union of Rajasthan was inaugurated by Jawaharlal Nehru on 18 April 1948. The maharana of Udaipur was appointed as rajpramukh and the kota naresh was appointed as uprajpramukh of this Union. The formation of the Union of Rajasthan paved the way for the merger of big states like Bikaner, Jaisalmer, Jaipur and Jodhpur with the Union and the formation of Greater Rajasthan. It was formally inaugurated on 30 March 1949 by Sardar Vallabhbhai Patel. Rajasthan attained its current dimensions in November 1956. The princes of the former kingdoms were constitutionally granted handsome remuneration in the form of privy purses to assist them in the discharge of their financial obligations. In1970, Indira Gandhi, who had come to power in 1966, commenced undertakings to discontinue the privy purses, which were abolished in 1971. Mohanlal Sukhadia of the Congress held the post of chief minister for the longest duration, from 1954 to 1971. Bhairon Singh Shekhawat, the present vice-president of India, became the state's first non-Congress chief minister in 1977, and remained in office till 1980, when he was dismissed after the change of government at the Centre. He became chief minister again in 1990, only to be dismissed again on 15 December 1992, in the aftermath of the demolition of the Babri Masjid at Ayodhya. In 1998 the Congress (I) Legislature Party elected state party president Ashok Gehlot to be the chief minister. Gehlot, at forty-seven, was the youngest chief minister Rajasthan has had. BJP leader Vasundhara Raje came to power as the first woman chief minister of Rajasthan in 2003.

Culture

Communities of musicians like the Mirasis, Manganiyars and Langas have preserved the rich traditions that exist in folk music and dance, like the Maand style of singing. The state is also home to different schools of painting like the Mewar school, the Bundi–Kota *kalam*, and the Jaipur school. The Kishengarh school is best known for its Bani Thani paintings.

Fairs and festivals: The major festivals of the state include Holi, Diwali, the Desert Festival (Jaisalmer), Gangaur and Teej (Jaipur), Urs Ajmer Sharif (Ajmer) and the Pushkar Fair.

Economy, Industry and Agriculture

Economy: The net state domestic product at current prices for 2003–04 (provisional) was Rs 92,339 crores. The per capita net state domestic product at current prices for 2003–04 (provisional) was Rs 15,486.

Minerals and industry: Textiles are the major industry in the large and medium category of industries, followed by agro-food and allied products, as well as cement. Other important industries are chemical gases, lubricants and plastics, heavy machinery and metal and allied products. Tourism is also a major industry. More than half the heritage hotels in India are located in Rajasthan.

Major minerals include zinc, gypsum, silver ore, asbestos, mica, rock phosphate, limestone and marble. Recently, oil reserves have been discovered around Barmer. Rajasthan holds a share of about 24 per cent in the total national production of non-metallic minerals.

Agriculture: Rajasthan produces a wide variety of cereals, oilseeds, pulses, cash crop like cotton, vegetables and fruits. The state accounts for a large proportion of the seed spices grown in the country, mainly coriander, cumin, fennel, chillies and garlic. The state produces jowar, maize, wheat, rice and millet and it is amongst the largest producers of bajra in the country.

Power: The majority of the state's power requirements are met by thermal power plants. Besides these, nuclear and hydroelectric power plants also contribute to the state's power needs.

Education

Educational institutes: Notable educational institutes include Rajasthan University (Jaipur), Jai Narayan Vyas University (Jodhpur), Birla Institute of Technology and Science (Pilani), Vanasthali Vidyapeeth (Tonk), Kota Open University, Maharshi Dayanand Saraswati University (Ajmer), Mohanlal Sukhadia University (Udaipur), Rajasthan Agricultural University (Bikaner) and Rajasthan Vidyapeeth (Udaipur).

Tourism

Major tourist attractions:

1. Ajmer: The dargah of Khwaja Moinuddin Chisti, Adhai-din-ka-jhonpra, Taragarh fort, Pushkar.
2. Alwar: City Palace, Government Museum, Vijai Mandir Palace, Sariska Wildlife Reserve, Ranthambore National Park, Keoladeo Ghana National Park.
3. Bharatpur: Lohagarh Fort, Deeg Palace, Jawahar Burj and Fateh Burj.
4. Chittorgarh: Vijay Stambh, Rana Khumbha's Palace, Saas-Bahu Temple, Meerabai Temple.
5. Jaipur: The City Palace, Jantar Mantar, Hawa Mahal, Amer Palace, Jaigarh and Nahargarh.
6. Jaisalmer: The fort, Manak Chowk and havelis, Sam sand dunes.
7. Jodhpur: Mehrangarh fort, Umaid Bhawan Palace, Mandore.
8. Kota: Chambal Garden, Maharao Madho Singh Museum, Jag Mandir.
9. Mount Abu: Gaumukh Temple, Delwara Jain Temple, Guru Shikhar.
10. Udaipur: City Palace, Haldighati, Eklingji, Nathdwara, Kumbhalgarh fort, Ranakpur Jain Temples.

Airports: Jaipur, Udaipur, Jodhpur, Jaisalmer.

National Parks: Keoladeo Ghana National Park in Bharatpur dist. (29 sq. km), Ranthambhor National Park in Sawai Madhopur dist. (392 sq. km), Sariska Tiger Reserve in Alwar dist. (866 sq. km), Desert National Park in Jaisalmer dist. (3162 sq. km).

Administration

Legislature: The state has a unicameral legislature. The legislative assembly consists of 200 members, of which fifty-seven seats are reserved for SCs (thirty-three) and STs (twenty-four).

The party position of the current assembly is as follows:

Name of Party	Seats
Bharatiya Janata Party	120
Indian National Congress	56
Indian National Lok Dal	4
Bahujan Samaj Party	2
Janata Dal (United)	2
Communist Party of India (Marxist)	1
Lok Jan Shakti Party	1
Rajasthan Samajik Nyaya Manch	1
Independent	13
Total	200

Judiciary: The seat of the Rajasthan High Court is at Jodhpur, with a bench at Jaipur. The acting chief justice is Y.R. Meena.

Districts:

District	Area (sq. km)	Population	Headquarters	Urban Agglomerations
Ajmer	8,481.0	2,180,526	Ajmer	Ajmer, Beawar
Alwar	8,380.0	2,990,862	Alwar	Alwar
Banswara	5,037.0	1,500,420	Banswara	Banswara
Baran	6,992.0	1,022,568	Baran	
Barmer	28,387.0	1,963,758	Barmer	
Bharatpur	5,066.0	2,098,323	Bharatpur	Bharatpur
Bhilwara	10,455.0	2,009,516	Bhilwara	
Bikaner	27,284.0	1,673,562	Bikaner	
Bundi	5,550.0	961,269	Bundi	Lakheri
Chittorgarh	10,856.0	1,802,656	Chittorgarh	
Churu	16,830.0	1,922,908	Churu	Churu, Rajgarh
Dausa	3,432.0	1,316,790	Dausa	
Dholpur	3,033.0	982,815	Dholpur	Dholpur
Dungarpur	3,770.0	1,107,037	Dungarpur	
Sri Ganganagar	7,984.0	1,788,487	Sri Ganganagar	Sri Ganganagar
Hanumangarh	12,650.0	1,517,390	Hanumangarh	
Jaipur	11,143.0	5,252,388	Jaipur	
Jaisalmer	38,428.0	507,999	Jaisalmer	
Jalor	10,640.0	1,448,486	Jalor	
Jhalawar	6,219.0	1,180,342	Jhalawar	
Jhunjhunu	5,928.0	1,913,099	Jhunjhunu	Khetri, Pilani
Jodhpur	22,783.0	2,880,777	Jodhpur	Jodhpur, Phalodi
Karauli	5,524.0	1,205,631	Karauli	
Kota	5,443.0	1,568,580	Kota	Kota
Nagaur	17,718.0	2,773,894	Nagaur	Nagaur, Makrana
Pali	12,387.0	1,819,201	Pali	
Rajsamand	3,860.0	986,269	Rajsamand	
Sawai Madhopur	4,498.0	1,116,031	Sawai Madhopur	Sawai Madhopur, Gangapur city
Sikar	7,732.0	2,287,229	Sikar	Sikar, Khandela
Sirohi	5,136.0	850,756	Sirohi	Abu Road
Tonk	7,194.0	1,211,343	Tonk	Malpura
Udaipur	13,419.0	2,632,210	Udaipur	

Sikkim

Key Statistics

Capital: Gangtok.
Area: 7096 sq. km.
Population: Total: 540,851, Male: 288,484, Female: 252,367.
Population density: 76 per sq. km.
Sex ratio: 875 females per 1000 males.
Principal languages: Nepali, Bhutia, Lepcha.
Literacy rates: Total: 68.8%, Male: 76.0%, Female: 60.4%.

Government

Governor: V. Rama Rao. He was appointed on 23 September 2002.

Chief Minister: Pawan Kumar Chamling (SDF). He was sworn in on 21 May 2004.

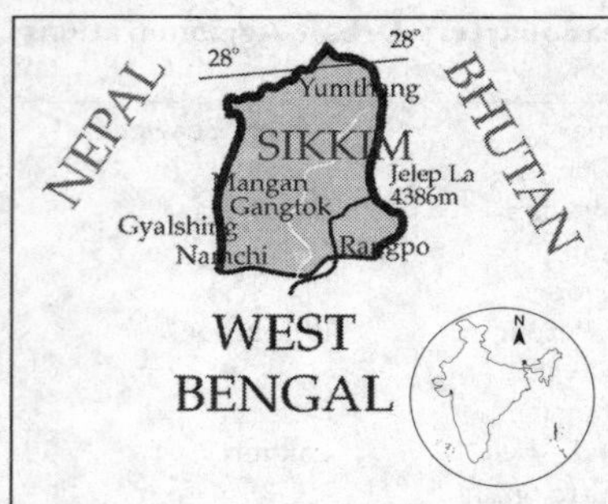

Geography

Physical characteristics: Sikkim is a small hilly state situated in the eastern Himalayas. It is a basin surrounded on three sides by steep mountain walls. It extends for approximately 114km from north to south and 64km from east to west. The state is surrounded by the Tibetan plateau towards the north, the Chumbi valley of China and Bhutan towards the east, Darjeeling district of West Bengal in the south and Nepal towards the west. The state is a part of the inner ranges of the Himalayas and as such it has no open valley or plains. Within a distance of 80 km, the elevation rises from 200 metres in the Teesta river valley to 8,598 metres at Kanchenjunga, India's highest peak and the world's third highest. The 31-km long Zemu glacier lies on the western side of the peak.

Besides the Kanchenjunga, other major peaks in the state include Jongsang (7,459m), Tent Peak (7,365m), Pauhunri (7,125m), Sinioulchu (6,887m), Pandim (6,691m), Rathong (6,679m), Talung (6,147m) and Koktang (6,147m). The Singalila range forms the barrier between Sikkim and Nepal in the west, while the Dongkya range is at the border with China on the east. There are many passes across this range that allow access to the Chumbi valley.

Neighbouring States and Union territories:

International borders: China, Nepal, Bhutan.

States: West Bengal.

Major rivers: The Teesta and Rangit are the two most important rivers of the state. Other significant rivers include Rongni Chu, Talung and Lachung. Sikkim is also home to many hot-water springs like Ralang Sachu, Phur-Cha, Yumthang and Momay.

Climate: The climate of Sikkim can be divided into tropical, temperate and alpine zones. For most of the year, the climate is cold and humid as rainfall occurs in each month.

In Sikkim, temperatures tend to vary with altitude and slope. The maximum temperature is usually recorded in July and August, while the minimum is usually registered during December and January. Fog is a common feature, mainly between May and September. Intense cold is experienced at high altitudes in the winter months and snowfall is also not uncommon during this period.

The state gets well-distributed heavy rainfall between May and early October. The wettest month is usually July in most parts of the state. Mean annual rainfall varies between a minimum of 82mm at Thangu and a maximum of 3,494mm at Gangtok. The intensity of rainfall during the south-west monsoon decreases from south to north. The distribution of winter rainfall is in the reverse pattern.

Flora and Fauna:

Flora: Forests cover 36 per cent of the land. The plants vary with altitude. The flora at altitudes between 1,500 m and 4,000 m is largely temperate forest of oak, birch, alder, chestnut, magnolia maple, and silver fir. The alpine zone lies above 4,000 m with plants like juniper, cypress and rhododendron. The perpetual snowline lies at 5,000 m. More than 4,000 species of plants have been recorded in Sikkim. Sikkim is also home to over 600 species of orchids.

Fauna: Notable among the animals found in Sikkim are the snow leopard, the red panda, the musk deer, the Himalayan black bear, the tahr, the yak, the wild ass and the blue sheep. The state is also home to many species of birds like vulture, eagle, whistling thrush, giant lammergeier, minivets, bulbuls and pheasants.

History

In prehistoric times, land that is today Sikkim was inhabited by three tribes—the Naongs, the Changs and the Mons. The Lepchas, who entered Sikkim later, absorbed them completely. The Lepchas were organized into a society by a person named Tur Ve Pa No who was eventually elected the leader or the king 'Punu', in 1400. After his death in battle three kings succeeded him—Tur Song Pa No, Tur Aeng Pa No and Tur Alu Pa No. After the death of Tur Alu Pa No, the monarchy came to an end. From then on, the Lepchas resorted to an elected leader. The area witnessed a major migration from Tibet later on.

In 1642, a young man named Phuntsok was crowned king. He was named Namgyal and also endowed with the title of Chogyal or religious king. The Namgyal dynasty ruled over Sikkim as hereditary rulers for about 332 years. Phuntsok Namgyal ruled over a vast territory, much larger than present-day Sikkim. In his times, the kingdom extended till Thang La in Tibet in the north, Tagong La near Paro in Bhutan in the east, Titalia on the West Bengal–Bihar border in the south and Timar Chorten on the Timar river in Nepal in the west. Even the Dalai Lama recognized Phuntsok Namgyal as the ruler of the southern slopes of the Himalayas and sent ceremonial gifts to him. At the time the capital city was at Yoksom.

In 1670, Phuntsok Namgyal's son, Tensung Namgyal, succeeded his father. He moved the capital to Rabdentse. Chador Namgyal, a minor son from Tensung's second of three wives, succeeded to the throne upon the death of his father. This led to much conflict as Pedi, the daughter from the first wife, challenged the succession and secretly invited Bhutan, her mother's homeland, to intervene. A loyal minister named Yungthing Yeshe ferreted away the minor king to Lhasa. In Tibet, Chador Namgyal made his mark as a scholar of Buddhist learning and Tibetan literature. He even became a state astrologer to the sixth Dalai Lama. When Bhutanese forces imprisoned Yugthing Yeshe's son, Tibet intervened and forced Bhutan to withdraw.

Chador Namgyal evicted the rest of the invading Bhutanese forces on his return. Although the Bhutanese made a second attempt to capture Sikkim territory, Chador Namgyal put up a worthy resistance but certain areas were lost forever. However, the old family feud returned to cost Chador Namgyal his life. He was killed in 1716 as a result of a conspiracy hatched by Pedi.

The next few years saw rebellions, internal conflicts and border disputes. Gurkhas encroached into Sikkimese territory under the leadership of Raja Prithvi Narayan Shah of Nepal. They also incited the rebellious factions within Sikkim. But they were repelled seventeen times. In 1775, a peace treaty was signed, whereby Gurkhas promised to refrain from attacks and also stay away from collaborating with the Bhutanese. Nevertheless, they violated the treaty when they took land in western Sikkim. The period also saw a Bhutanese invasion. They captured all areas east of the Teesta river, but later retreated following negotiations.

In the nineteenth century, the British struck up a friendship with Sikkim. This was largely due to the fact that they had a common enemy—the Gorkhas. The British defeated Nepalese forces in the Anglo-Nepalese War (1814–16). In 1817, British India signed the Treaty of Titalia with Sikkim. Consequently, territories that the Nepalis had taken away were restored to Sikkim. By the treaty, British India gained a position of great power and influence in the state and Sikkim almost became a British protectorate.

Sikkim even gifted Darjeeling to British India in return for an annual payment and Chogyal Tsudphud Namgyal signed the gift deed in 1835. The British however, did not pay the compensation. This led to a deterioration in relations between the two countries. There were also differences between the British government and Sikkim over the status of the people of Sikkim. The relations deteriorated to the extent that in 1849, when the superintendent of Darjeeling visited Sikkim along with a scientist on a research trip, they were taken prisoners. They were later freed after the British issued an ultimatum. In 1850, British India stopped the annual grant of Rs 6,000 to the maharaja of Sikkim and also annexed part of Darjeeling and a large portion of Sikkim.

When India became independent, the then Chogyal, Tashi Namgyal, obtained the status of a protectorate for Sikkim. However, local parties like the Sikkim State Congress wanted a democratic set-up and the accession of Sikkim to the Union of India. After Tashi Namgyal died in 1963, demands for the removal of the monarchy and the establishment of a democratic set-up intensified. By 1973, the agitation against the Sikkim Durbar had taken a serious turn and resulted in a collapse of the administration. This led the Indian government to intervene, and Sikkim was transformed from a protectorate to an associate state.

Politics

In 1947, after the British withdrew from India, Tashi Namgyal of the Chogyal dynasty was successful in getting a special status of protectorate for Sikkim. On 4 September 1947, the leader of Sikkim Congress, Kazi Lendup Dorji, was elected the chief minister of the state. The Chogyal however still remained as the constitutional figurehead monarch in the new setup. Troubles arose in 1973, when the Sikkim National Congress demanded fresh elections and establishment of a democratic set-up. The Kazi was elected by the council of ministers, which was unanimous in its opposition to the retention of the monarchy. After a period of unrest in 1972-73, matters came to a head in 1975, when Kazi appealed to the Indian parliament for representation and change of status to statehood. A referendum was held in which 97.5 per cent of the people voted to join the Indian Union. Sikkim became a full-fledged state of the Indian Union on 16 May 1975; it was India's twenty-second state. Kazi was elected chief minister. A popular ministry headed by Nar Bahadur Bhandari, leader of the Sikkim Parishad Party, came into power in 1979. Bhandari held on to power in the 1984 and 1989 elections. After the 1994 elections Pawan Kumar Chamling from the Sikkim Democratic Front became the chief minister of the state. The party has since held on to power by winning the 1999 and 2004 elections. In 2003, China officially recognized Indian sovereignty over Sikkim as the two nations moved toward resolving their border disputes. Sikkim no longer figures as an independent nation in the world map and index of the annual yearbook published by the Chinese Foreign Ministry.

Culture

Sikkim is famous for its mask dance that is performed by lamas in gompas. The state is also known for its handicrafts and handloom objects. The kagyat dance is performed every twenty-eighth and twenty-ninth day of the Tibetan calendar. The dance is one of solemnity interspersed with comic relief provided by jesters.

Fairs and festivals: Different communities in the state have different festivals. Saga Dawa is an auspicious day for the Mahayana Buddhists and they go to monasteries to offer butter lamps and worship. Monks take out a procession that goes around Gangtok with holy scriptures.

Phang Lhabsol is a unique festival that is celebrated to offer thanks to Mount Kanchenjunga. The biggest and most important festival of the Hindu–Nepali population is Dasain. It is celebrated in September/October and symbolizes the victory of good over evil. Tyohar or Dipavali is the festival of lights and is celebrated ten days after Dasain. Other festivals include Drupka Tseshi that is celebrated around August. Losoong is the Sikkimese New Year which is celebrated in the last week of December, while Losar is the Tibetan New Year and is celebrated around February.

Economy, Industry and Agriculture

Economy: The net state domestic product at current prices for 2003–04 (provisional) was Rs 1,233 crores. The per capita net state domestic product at current prices for 2003–04 (provisional) was Rs 21,586.

Minerals and industry: Sikkim is an industrially underdeveloped state. There are public–sector undertakings for the manufacture of precision instruments and watches. Besides these, there are handicrafts, handlooms, liquor, and pisciculture ventures in the state.

Agriculture: Maize, rice, wheat, barley, pulses, potato and cardamom are the most important crops grown in the state. The economy is based largely on agriculture and animal husbandry.

Power: The state mainly utilizes hydroelectric power.

Education

Educational institutions: The Sikkim Manipal University of Health, Medical and Technology Sciences is at Gangtok. Other institutes of learning in the state include the Directorate of Handicraft and Handloom and the Sikkim Research Institute of Tibetology (SRIT).

Tourism

Major tourist attractions:

1. North Sikkim: Singba Rhododendron Sanctuary, Yumthang, Chungthang, Singiek, Kabi Lungtsok.
2. South Sikkim: Namtse, Varsey Rhododendron Sanctuary, Borong Tsa-Chu hot spring, Maenam Hill, Ravangla.
3. East Sikkim: White Hall, Ridge Garden, Do-Drul Chorten, Rumtek Dharma Chakra Centre, Kyongnosla Alpine Sanctuary, Fambong La Wildlife Sanctuary.
4. West Sikkim: Pelling, Ruins of Rabdentse, Yuksom.

Airports: None.

National Parks: Kanchenjunga National Park in North Sikkim dist. (850 sq. km).

Administration

Legislature: There are thirty-two seats in the legislative assembly, out of which two are reserved for SCs and twelve for STs (for the Bhutia and Lepcha communities). One general seat is reserved for the Sangha community. The term of the current house expires on 14 October 2004. The current party position is:

Name of Party	Seats
Sikkim Democratic Front	31
Indian National Congress	1
Total	**32**

Judiciary: The High Court of Sikkim is at Gangtok. N. Surjawani Singh is the acting chief justice.

Districts:

District	Area (sq. km)	Population	Headquarters	Urban Agglomerations
East Sikkim	954.0	244,790	Gangtok	–
North Sikkim	4,226.0	41,023	Mangan	–
South Sikkim	750.0	131,506	Namchi	–
West Sikkim	1,166.0	123,174	Gyalshing	–

Tamil Nadu

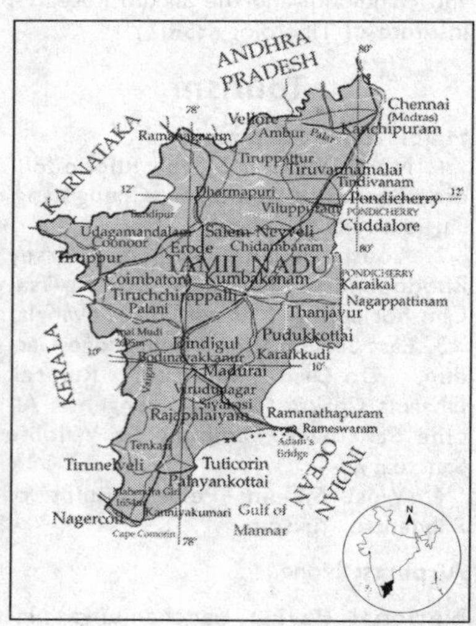

Key Statistics

Capital: Chennai.
Area: 1,30,058 sq. km.
Population: Total: 62,405,679, Male: 31,400,909, Female: 31,004,770.
Population density: 478 per sq. km.
Sex ratio: 987 females per 1000 males.
Principal languages: Tamil, Telugu, Kannada.
Literacy rates: Total: 73.5%, Male: 82.4%, Female: 64.4%.

Government

Governor: Surjeet Singh Barnala. He assumed the office on 1 November 2004.

Chief Minister: Kalaignar Muthuvel Karunanidhi. He was sworn in on 13 May 2006.

Geography

Physical characteristics: Tamil Nadu is divided between the flat areas along the eastern coast and the hilly regions in the north and west. The Kavery delta is the broadest part of the eastern plains, with the arid plains of Ramanathapuram and Madurai towards the south. The Western Ghats run along the state's western border, while the lower hills of the Eastern Ghats run through the centre.

Neighbouring States and Union territories:

States: Andhra Pradesh, Karnataka, Kerala..

Union territories: Pondicherry.

Major rivers: Kavery, Palar, Ponnaiyar, Pennar, Vaigai and Tamiraparani.

Climate: Excepting the hills, Tamil Nadu's climate can be classified as semi-arid tropic monsoonal. Maximum temperatures in the plains go up to 45°C in summer, with minimum temperatures in the winter hovering around 10°C. The average annual rainfall ranges between 650mm and 1900mm. The hill areas have maximum temperatures around 30°C in the summer and minimum temperatures as low as 3°C in the winter and also receive substantially higher rainfall.

Flora and Fauna:

Flora: Nearly 18 per cent of the area of Tamil Nadu is under forests. Dry deciduous forests, thorn forests, scrub, mangroves and wetlands cover most of the plains and lower hills. Moist deciduous and wet evergreen forests as also shoal and grassland occupy most of the hills in the moister parts, particularly in the Western Ghats. Sandalwood, pulpwood, rubber and bamboo are important forest products.

Fauna: Wildlife found in the state includes elephant, tiger, leopard, striped hyena, jackals, Indian pangolin, slender loris, lion-tailed macaque, sloth bear, bison or gaur, black buck, Nilgiris tatur, grizzled giant squirrel, dugong and mouse deer.

History

The early history of the region can be traced to a trinity of powers: the Cheras, the Cholas and the Pandyas. From the sixth to the ninth centuries, the Chalukyas and the Pallavas also established their dominance with a series of wars in the region. From the mid-ninth century, Chola rulers dominated the region, the most prominent among them being Rajendra I. Around the twelfth century, Muslim rulers also strengthened their position, leading to the establishment of the Bahamani sultanate. The Vijayanagar kingdom came into prominence in the mid-fourteenth century and ruled for nearly 300 years. The British control over the region began from the mid-seventeenth century and continued until Independence.

After Independence, the areas of present-day Tamil Nadu, Andhra Pradesh and some territorial areas of Kerala came under the governance of Madras state. In 1953, the Telugu-speaking areas of Madras state were carved out into the state of Andhra Pradesh. In 1956, the Madras state was further divided into the states of Kerala, Mysore and Madras. In August 1968, Madras state was renamed Tamil Nadu. O.P. Ramaswamy Reddyar was the first chief minister.

Politics

Modern Tamil Nadu has emerged from Madras Presidency of the British administration. At the time of Indian Independence, Madras state comprised of Tamil Nadu, Andhra Pradesh and some territorial areas of present Kerala. In 1953, however, the Madras state bifurcated into two states, Andhra state, comprising of Telugu-speaking areas, and Madras state, comprising of Tamil-speaking areas. The old capital city of Madras was retained in the Madras state. Under the States Reorganization Act, 1956, Madras state was further divided into the states of Kerala, Mysore and Madras. Later, on 1 April 1960, territories comprising Chittoor district in Andhra Pradesh were transferred to Madras state in exchange of territories from the Chingleput and Salem district. In 1968, Madras state was renamed Tamil Nadu.

Regional political parties have been strongest in Tamil Nadu, where they have dominated state politics since 1967. Regional parties in the state trace their roots to the establishment of the Justice Party by non-Brahmin social elites in 1916 and the development of the non-Brahmin Self-Respect Movement, founded in 1925 by E.V. Ramaswamy Naicker. As leader of the Justice Party, in 1944 Ramaswamy renamed the party the Dravida Khazagam (Dravidian Federation) and demanded the establishment of an independent state called Dravidasthan. In 1949, charismatic film script writer C.N. Annadurai, who was chafing under Ramaswamy's authoritarian leadership, split from the DK to found the DMK (Dravida Munnetra Khazagam) in an attempt to achieve the goals of Tamil nationalism through the electoral process. During the fifties and sixties, however, there were several developments which gradually led to a change in the basic political thrust of DMK. Naicker gave up his opposition to Congress when in 1954, K. Kamraj, a non-Brahmin, displaced C. Rajagopalachari, the dominant leader of the Congress party in Tamil Nadu and became the chief minister. He remained in power till 2 October 1963. DMK participated in the 1957 and 1962 elections. That a change was coming became visible when, in the 1962 elections, it entered into an alliance with Swatantra Party and CPI and did not make a separate Dravidasthan a campaign issue. Although the DMK dropped its demand for Dravidasthan in 1963, it played a prominent role in the agitations that successfully defeated attempts to impose the northern Indian language of Hindi as the official national language in the mid-1960s. With each election the DMK kept expanding its social base and increasing its electoral strength. With the deterioration of Annadurai's health, M. Karunanidhi became chief minister in 1969. Karunanidhi's control over the party was soon challenged by M.G. Ramachandran (best known by his initials, MGR), one of south India's most popular film stars. In the 1971 elections to the Lok Sabha and the state assembly, DMK teamed up with the Indira Gandhi-led Congress (R), which surrendered all claims to assembly seats in return for DMK's support to it in nine parliamentary seats, which it won. In 1972 MGR split from the DMK to form the All-India Anna Dravida Munnetra Kazhagam (AIADMK). Under his leadership, the AIADMK dominated Tamil politics at the state level from 1977 through 1989. The importance of personal charisma in Tamil politics was dramatized by the struggle for control over the AIADMK after MGR's death in 1988. MGR's wife Janaki Ramachandran, herself a film star, succeeded MGR and vied for control with Jayalalitha, an actress who had played MGR's leading lady in several films. The rivalry allowed the DMK to gain control over the state government in 1989. The AIADMK, under the leadership of Jayalalitha, recaptured the state government in 1991. From 1996 to 2001 Karunanidhi returned to power. Jayalalitha came back to power in 2001 and, on being jailed on charges of corruption, appointed O. Paneerselvam as the chief minister for a year. In 2002, Jayalalitha became the chief minister of Tamil Nadu again. On 13 May 2006, Kalaignar Muthuvel Karunanidhi was sworn in as chief minister of Tamil Nadu.

Culture

Tamil Nadu has more than 30,000 temples, for which reason the state is sometimes called 'a land of temples'. The festivals held in many of them attract large congregations of devotees throughout the year.

The Bharatnatyam form of classical dancing has its origin in the temples of Tamil Nadu and continues to be followed with a lot of fervour. Another reputed art form that has flourished over the ages is Carnatic music.

Fairs and festivals: Prominent festivals and fairs include Pongal, Chithirai Festival, Navarathri, Saral Vizha, Kanthuri Festival, Mahamagam Festival, Thyagaraja Festival and Mamallapuram Dance Festival.

Economy, Industry and Agriculture

Economy: The net state domestic product at current prices for 2003–04 (provisional) was Rs 148,907 crores.

The per capita net state domestic product at current prices for 2003–04 (provisional) was Rs 23,358.

Minerals and industry: Important industries of Tamil Nadu include cement, automobiles and auto components, railway coaches, leather, cotton textiles, sugar, software, biotechnology, agro-based industries and paper. Major minerals found in the state include garnet, lignite, magnesite, monazite, quartz/silica sand, gypsum, ilmenite, rutile, vermiculite, zircon, graphite.

Agriculture: Paddy, millets and other cereals, pulses, sugar cane, groundnut, gingelly, tea, rubber, cashew and cotton are the principal crops of the state.

Power: A large part of Tamil Nadu's power comes from thermal power plants and hydroelectric plants.

Education

Educational institutes: Prominent educational institutions of the state include Alagappa University, Karaikudi; Annamalai University, Annamalainagar; Bharathiar University, Coimbatore; Bharthidasan University, Tiruchirapalli; Chennai Medical College and Research Institute, Chennai; Indian Institute of Technology Madras, Chennai; University of Madras, Chennai; Madurai Kamraj University, Madurai; Periyar University, Salem; Sri Ramachandra Medical College and Research Institute, Chennai; Tamil Nadu Dr Ambedkar Law University, Chennai and Tamil Nadu Dr MGR Medical University, Chennai.

Tourism

Major tourist attractions:

1. Chennai: Planetarium, Vandalur zoo, Art gallery, Snake park, Marina beach.
2. Chidambaram: Poompuhar, Tarangambadi, The Church of Zion, Masilamaninathar Temple.
3. Coimbatore: Indira Gandhi National Park, Maruthamalai Temple.
4. Kancheepuram: Tiruttani, Vellore, Vedanthangal, Elagiri Hills.
5. Kanniyakumari: Suchindram, Nager-coil, Pechipara Dam, Padmanabhapuram, Valluvar statue, Udayagiri fort, Vivekananda rock.
6. Kodaikkanal: Palani, Hill range.
7. Madurai: Alagarkoil, Pazhamudircholai, Thiruparankunram, Thiruvadavur, Tiruvedagam.
8. Mamallapuram: Tirukkalukunram, Crocodile bank.
9. Pondicherry: Auroville, Cuddalore, Tiruvannamalai, Sathanur, Gingee fort.
10. Rameswaram: Kurusadai islands.
11. Thanjavur: Thiruvaiyaru, Swamimalai, Tirubuvanam, Kumbakonam, Kodikkarai.
12. Tiruchirappally: Srirangam, Thiruvanaikkaval, Gangaikondancholapuram.
13. Udagamandalam (Ooty): Mudumalai, Coonoor.

Airports:

International: Chennai.

Domestic: Tiruchirappally, Madurai, Coimbatore, Tuticorin.

National Parks: Guindy (Chennai)—2.82 sq. km, Indira Gandhi National Park (Coimbatore)—117.10 sq. km, Gulf of Mannar Biosphere Reserve and National Park—6.23 sq. km, Mudumalai (Nilgiris)—103.23 sq. km and Mukurthi (Nilgiris)—78.46 sq. km.

Administration

Legislature: The unicameral Tamil Nadu state assembly comprises 234 elected members and one nominated member (Anglo-Indian). Of the 234 seats forty-two are reserved for SCs and three for STs. The term of the current house expires on 21 May 2006.

The current party position is as follows:

Name of Party	Seats
All India Anna Dravida Munnetra Kazhagam	61
Dravida Munnetra Kazhagam	96

Pattali Makkal Katchi 18
Indian National Congress 34
Communist Party of India (Marxist) 9
Communist Party of India 6
Bharatiya Janata Party 4
Marumalarchi Dravida Mumetra Kazhagam 6
Viduthalai Chiruthaigal Katch 2
Desiya Morpokku Dravida Kazagham 1
Independent 1
Total **234**

Judiciary: Madras High Court, with its seat in Chennai, has jurisdiction over Tamil Nadu and Pondicherry. The present chief justice is Markandey Katju.

Districts:

District	Area (sq. km)	Population	Headquarters	Urban Agglomerations
Chennai	178.2	4,216,268	Chennai	Chennai
Coimbatore	7,470.8	4,224,107	Coimbatore	Coimbatore, Pollachi, Tiruppur
Cuddalore	3,645.0	2,280,530	Cuddalore	Chidambaram, Neyveli
Dharmapuri	4,497.8	1,286,552	Dharmapuri	
Dindigul	6,058.0	1,918,960	Dindigul	
Erode	8,209.0	2,574,067	Erode	Erode, Bhavani
Kanchipuram	4,433.0	2,869,920	Kanchipuram	Kanchipuram
Kannyakumari	1,684.0	1,669,763	Nagercoil	
Krishnagiri	5,143.0	1,546,700	Krishnagiri	
Karur	3,003.5	933,791	Karur	Karur
Madurai	3,497.8	2,562,279	Madurai	Madurai
Nagapattinam	2,715.8	1,487,055	Nagapattinam	
Namakkal	3,363	1,495,661	Namakkal	Erode, Bhavani, Mallasamudram
The Nilgiris	2452.5	764,826	Udhagamandalam	Coonoor, Devarshola
Perambalur	3,690	1,181,029	Perambalur	
Pudukkottai	4,651.0	1,452,269	Pudukkottai	
Ramanathapuram	4,129.0	1,183,321	Ramanathapuram	
Salem	5,219.6	2,992,754	Salem	Mallasamudram, Salem
Sivaganga	4,189.0	1,150,753	Sivaganga	Karaikkudi
Thanjavur	3,396.6	2,205,375	Thanjavur	Kumbakonam
Theni	3,243.6	1,094,724	Theni	
Thoothukudi	4,621.0	1,565,743	Thoothukudi	Thoothukudi, Tiruchendur
Tiruchirappalli	4,403.8	2,388,831	Tiruchirappalli	Tiruchirappalli
Tirunelveli	6,810.0	2,801,194	Tirunelveli	Ambasamudram, Tirunelveli
Tiruvallur	3,424.0	2,738,866	Tiruvallur	Tiruvallur
Tiruvarur	2,167.6	1,165,213	Tiruvarur	
Tiruvannamalai	6,191.0	21,81,853	Tiruvannamalai	
Vellore	6,077.0	3,482,970	Vellore	Arcot, Gudiyatham, Vaniyambadi, Vellore
Viluppuram	7,250.0	2,943,917	Viluppuram	
Virudhunagar	4,283.0	1,751,548	Virudhunagar	Sivakasi

Tripura

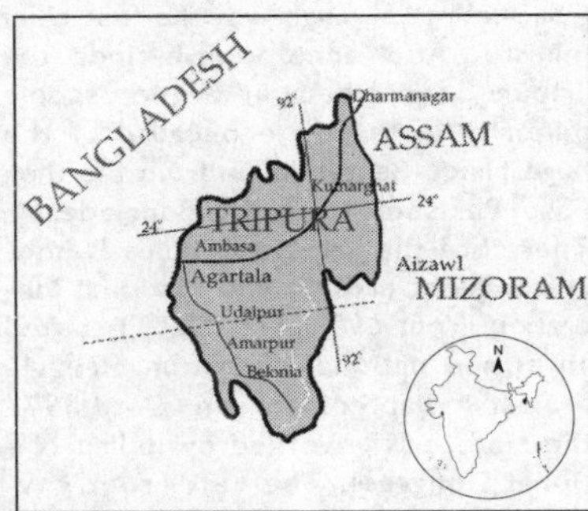

Key Statistics

Capital: Agartala.

Area: 10,491.69 sq. km.

Population: Total: 3,199,203, Male: 1,642,225, Female: 1,556,978.

Population density: 304 per sq. km.

Sex ratio: 948 females per 1000 males.

Principal languages: Bengali, Tripuri, Hindi.

Literacy rates: Total: 73.2%, Male: 81.0%, Female: 64.9%.

Government

Governor: Dinesh Nandan Sahaya. He assumed office on 2 June 2003.

Chief Minister: Manik Sarkar (CPIM). He was sworn in on 7 March 2003.

Geography

Physical characteristics: Tripura is a land of hills, plains and valleys. The central and northern part of the state is a hilly region that is intersected by four major valleys. These are the Dharma-nagar, Kailashahar, Kamalpur and Khowai valleys. These valleys are formations resulting from northward-flowing rivers. The valleys in the western and southern part of the state are marshy. The terrain is densely forested and highly dissected in southern Tripura. Ranges running north–south cross the valleys. These hills are a series of parallel north–south ranges that decrease in elevation southwards and finally merge into the eastern plains. These are the Deotamura range, followed by the Atharamura, Langtarai, and Sakhan Tlang ranges. Of these peaks, Deotamura is the lowest and the height of each successive range increases eastwards. The 74-km-long Jamrai Tlang mountains have the highest peak, Betalongchhip (1097m).

The Tripura plains are also called the Agartala plains. The plains lie in the south-western part of the state and extend over approximately 4,150 sq. km. The Tripura plains are situated on a part of the bigger Ganga–Brahmaputra lowlands to the west of the Tripura Hills. The plains have extensive forest cover and have numerous lakes and marshes.

Neighbouring States and Union territories:

International border: Bangladesh.

States: Assam, Mizoram.

Major rivers: Gomti, Muhuri, Howrah, Juri, Manu, Deo, Dhalai, Khowai, Feni and Longai.

Climate: Summer temperatures range between 20°C and 36°C. In winter, the range is between 7°C and 27°C. Average annual rainfall in 2,000 was 2,500mm.

Flora and Fauna:

Flora: In 2000–01, Tripura had a forest area of 6,292.68 sq. km or around 60 per cent of the total land area. Sal is found extensively in the state. There are rubber, tea and coffee plantations as well.

Fauna: Tiger, elephant, jackal, leopard, wild dog, boar, wild buffalo and gaur are the most notable members of the state's animal population.

History

The early history of Tripura is described in the *Rajamala*, an account of people who are supposed to be the early rulers of Tripura. The *Rajamala*, written in Bengali verse, was compiled by the courtiers of Dharma Manikya, one of the greatest rulers of Tripura.

During the reigns of Dharma Manikya and his successor, Dhanya Manikya, in the fifteenth and sixteenth centuries, rule of Tripura was extended over large portions of Bengal, Assam, and what is today Myanmar as a consequence of a string of military conquests.

It was only in the seventeenth century that the Mughal empire extended its rule over Tripura. The British East India Company gained control of parts of Tripura when it obtained the diwani of Bengal in 1765. But this was limited to the parts that were under Mughal control. From 1808 onwards, the rulers of Tripura had to be approved by the British government. In 1905, Tripura was attached to the new province of Eastern Bengal and Assam. It came to be known as Hill Tippera.

Politics

The princely state of Tripura was ruled by maharajas of Manikya dynasty. It was an independent administrative unit under the maharaja even during the British rule in India though this independence was qualified, being subject to the recognition of the British of each successive ruler. After India's independence, an agreement of merger of Tripura with the Indian Union was signed by the regent maharani on 9 September 1947. Tripura was merged with the Indian Union as a part 'C' state. Tripura became a union territory with effect from 1 November 1956. A popular ministry took power on 1 July 1963. On 21 January 1972, Tripura became a full-fledged state.

Sachindra Lal Singh was the first chief minister. After annexation by India the Tripuri people became a microscopic minority in the state because of the huge Hindu Bengali influx from the then East Pakistan (present Bangladesh). Therefore the Tripura Peoples Democratic Front (TPDF) and National Liberation Front of Tripura (NLFT) started an armed national liberation struggle against Indian colonialism. Until 1977 the state was governed by Indian National Congress. The Left Front governed from 1978 to 1988 and then returned to power in 1993. Comrade Nripen Chakraborty became the chief minister of the state's first Left Front government in 1978 and also of the second one in 1983. From 1988 to 1993 the state was governed by a coalition of Indian National Congress and Tripura Upajati Juba Samiti. A Left Front ministry was sworn-in on 7 March 2003 headed by Manik Sarkar, who assumed the office of chief minister for the second consecutive term.

Culture

Tripura has a rich heritage of folk dances of the different communities of the state. The main folk dances of Tripura are Garia, Maimita, Masak Sumani, Jhum and Lebang Boomani dances of the Tripuri community, Hozagiri dance of the Reang community, Cheraw and Welcome dances of the Lusai community, Bizu dance of the Chakma community, Sangraiaka, Chimithang, Padisha and Abhangma dances of the Mog community, Hai-Hak dance of the Malsum community, Wangala dance of the Garo community, Basanta Rash and Pung Chalam dances of Manipuri community, Garia dances of Kalai and Jamatia communities, Gajan, Sari, Dhamail, and Rabindra dances of the Bengali community. The state is also well known for its cane and bamboo handicrafts and household items such as furniture, baskets and ornaments.

Fairs and festivals: In Tripura, Garia and Gajan festivals, Manasa Mangal, Durga Puja, Rabindra Jayanti and Nazrul Jayanti are celebrated all over the state. Events of specific places include Ashokastami festival of Unakoti, Kharchi festival of Old Agartala, Dewali festival of Mata Tripureswari Temple in Udaipur, Rasha festival of Kamalpur, Kailashahar, Khowai and Agartala, Orange and Tourism festival of Jampui Hill range and the Pous Sankranti mela of Tirthamukh.

Economy, Industry and Agriculture

Economy: The net state domestic product at current pr ces in 2002–03 was Rs 6,085 crores. The per capita net state domestic product at current prices in 2002–03 was Rs 18,676.

Minerals and industry: Jute, tourism, handicrafts, handloom and food products are the most notable among the existing industrial ventures of the state. There are five industrial estates and two industrial growth centres in Tripura. Both the state and the Central governments offer various incentives for the setting up of new industrial ventures in Tripura. It is also being promoted as the international gateway to the northeast region of India, given its proximity to Bangladesh, mainly the latter's port at Chittagong.

The two most important mineral resources of Tripura are oil and natural gas. Other significant minerals are glass sand, shale, plastic clay and sand.

Agriculture: The main crops grown in the state are rice, sugar cane, cotton, jute and mesta. Key plantation crops are tea, rubber and coffee. Besides these, banana, pineapple, cashew nuts, orange, mango, guava, litchi, potato, papaya and tomato are also grown.

Power: Thermal power plants contribute the biggest share of the energy produced in the state. Hydroelectric power plants are the second most important source.

Education

Educational institutions: Tripura University is at Agartala.

Tourism

Major tourist attractions: Sephahijala Wildlife Sanctuary, Trishna Wildlife Sanctuary, Gumti Wildlife Sanctuary, Roa Wildlife Sanctuary, Rudra Sagar (Neer Mahal), Kamala Sagar, Brahmakund, Udaipur, Deotamura, Dumbur, Pilak, Jampui Hills, Unakoti, Tripura Sundari Temple, Ujjayanta palace.

Airports: Agartala, Kailashahar, Khowai, Kamalpur.

National Parks: None.

Administration

Legislature: The legislative assembly of Tripura has sixty seats, out of which twenty seats are reserved for STs and seven reserved for SCs. The term of the current house expires on 19 March 2008.

The current party position is as follows:

Name of Party	Seats
Communist Party of India (Marxist)	38
Indian National Congress	13
Indigenous Nationalist Party of Tripura	6
Revolutionary Socialist Party	2
Communist Party of India	1
Total	**60**

Judiciary: The jurisdiction is of the Agartala Bench of the Gauhati High Court. Binod Kumar Roy is the chief justice.

Districts:

District	Area (sq. km)	Population	Headquarters	Urban Agglomerations
Dhalai	2,212.3	307,417	Ambassa	–
North Tripura	2,100.7	590,655	Kailashahar	–
South Tripura	3,140.0	762,565	Udaipur	–
West Tripura	3,033.0	1,530,531	Agartala	–

Uttaranchal

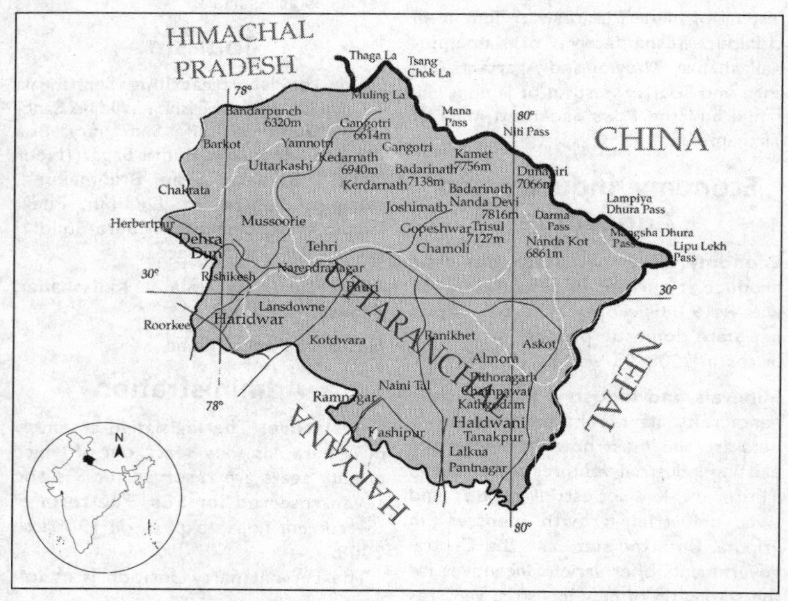

Key Statistics

Capital: Dehradun (provisional).

Area: 53,483 sq. km.

Population: Total: 8,489,349, Male: 4,325,924, Female: 4,163,425.

Population density: 159 per sq. km.

Sex ratio: 962 females per 1000 males.

Principal languages: Hindi, Garhwali, Kumaoni.

Literacy rates: Total: 71.6%, Male: 83.3%, Female: 59.6%.

Government

Governor: Sudarshan Agarwal. He was appointed on 8 January 2003.

Chief Minister: N.D. Tiwari. He was sworn in on 2 March 2002.

Geography

Physical characteristics: Uttaranchal is located in the foothills of the Himalayas. The state has international boundaries with China in the north and Nepal in the east. On its north-west lies Himachal Pradesh while Uttar Pradesh lies to the south. The region is mostly mountainous with a major portion covered with forests. Based on topographic characteristics, specific availability of land resources for urban development and economic mobility, the thirteen districts in Uttaranchal can be segregated into three broad categories. These are:

1. The high mountain region (these include significant portions of Uttarkashi, Champawat, Pithoragarh, Chamoli and Rudra-prayag districts).
2. The mid-mountain region (major parts of Pauri Garhwal, Tehri, Almora, Bageshwar districts).
3. The Doon, Terai region and Haridwar (lower foothills and plains of Dehradun, Nainital, Udhamsingh Nagar and Haridwar districts).

The significant peaks of the Great Himalayan range in the state are Nanda Devi, Panchachuli, Kedarnath, Chaukhamba, Badrinath, Trishul, Bandarpunch and Kamet. Pindari, Gangotri, Milam and Khatling are the important glaciers.

Neighbouring States and Union territories:
International borders: China, Nepal.

States: Himachal Pradesh, Uttar Pradesh.

Major rivers: Ganga, Yamuna, Ramganga and Kali (Sharda).

Climate: The climate of the state is generally temperate but varies greatly from tropical to severe cold, depending upon altitude. Different parts of the state experience temperature variations due to difference in elevation. Summers are pleasant in the hilly regions but in the Doon area, it can get very hot. It can get even hotter in the plains of the state. Temperature drops to below freezing point not only at high altitudes but also at places like Dehradun in the winters. Average rainfall experienced in the state is around 1,079mm. Average temperature ranges between a minimum of 1.9°C and a maximum of 40.5°C.

Flora and Fauna:
Flora: Different types of forests found in the state are: deodar forests, blue pine forests, chir forests, teak forests, bamboo forests, oak forests, fir and spruce forests, and sal forests.

The region is also rich in medicinal plants. These can be classified on the basis of the altitude at which they can be found growing.

1. Medicinal plants growing upto 1,000m: bel, chitrak, kachnar, pipali, babul, ashok, amaltas, sarpagandha, bhringraj, harar, behera, malu, siris, amla and mossli.
2. Medicinal plants growing from 1,000m to 3,000m: banspa, sugandhabala, tejpat, dalchini, jhoola, kuth, timru and painya.
3. Medicinal plants growing above 3,000m: atis, mitha, gugal, jamboo, mamira, gandrayan, bajradanti and salammishri.

Fauna: The animal population of Uttaranchal includes tiger, leopard, other members of the cat family, Indian elephant, dhole (wild dog), antelopes like nilgai and ghoral, Himalayan tahr, deer like hog deer, sambar, chital or spotted deer and barking deer and primates like rhesus monkey and langur. Other animals found in the state include jackals, foxes, civets, wild boar, sloth bear and black bear. Reptiles like the cobra and python are found in the state. Ramganga river is home to two species of crocodile, namely gharial and mugger, as well as fishes like the famous mahaseer and the malee.

Uttaranchal is also home to hundreds of species of birds including water fowl, many types of woodpecker and predatory birds like the Pallas's fishing eagle, harriers and kites. Peafowl, kalij pheasant, chir pheasant, red jungle fowl, minivets, shrikes, cuckoos, drongos and barbets are also found in the state. Corbett National Park is home to various species of birds like brown fish owl, Himalayan kingfisher, brown dipper and plumbeous/white-capped redstarts. The bird population of the National Park also includes the slaty-backed forktails and rufous-bellied hawk-eagles, blue whistling thrush and red jungle fowl, oriental white-eye, jungle owlet, Alexandrine parakeet, Himalayan swiftlet, lesser fish-eagle and great thick-knee, stork-billed kingfisher.

History

Uttaranchal has been mentioned in ancient texts as Kedarkhand and Kurmanchal. The region's history is older than that of the *Ramayana* and the *Mahabharata*. It is also a site of popular myths, like that of Lord Shiva appearing as Kirat, of Urvashi, Shakuntala as well as the Kauravas and Pandavas. In those days, the area that is today Garhwal was known as Kedarkhand, or the region of Kedarnath. On the other hand, Kumaon was Kurmanchal, the land of the Kurmavatar—Lord Vishnu in his incarnation as tortoise.

Rock paintings, rock shelters, palaeoliths and megaliths bear evidence of human habitation in this region from the prehistoric period. Various texts also mention a number of tribes that inhabited the region. These include the Sakas, Kol-Munds, the Nagas, Khasas, Hunas, Kirats, Gujars and Aryans. After the era of the Kols and the Kirats, the Khasas attained a position of dominance in the Garhwal and Kumaon Himalayas, till the arrival of the Rajputs and Brahmins from the plains.

With the arrival of the Aryans came the establishment of later Vedic culture and most of these people got absorbed into the caste system. The sages living in the region made it an important point of origin of Indo-Aryan culture.

What is Uttaranchal today was earlier a part of the United Provinces of Agra and Awadh. This province came into existence in 1902 and in 1935, it was renamed United Provinces. In 1950, it was renamed once again, this time as Uttar Pradesh. The socio-economic disparities of this region led to a demand for a separate state for many years. The students' protest at Pauri in August 1994 against 27 per cent OBC reservation in education subsequently led to widespread agitations. Later on, it turned into a full-fledged mass movement for a separate state.

Uttaranchal came into existence on 9 November 2000 as the twenty-seventh state of the Indian Union. Nityanand Swami was the first chief minister of the state.

Politics

The first demand for a separate Uttarakhand state was voiced by P.C. Joshi, a member of the Communist Party of India (CPI), in 1952. However, a movement did not develop in earnest until 1979 when the Uttarakhand Kranti Dal (Uttarakhand Revolutionary Front) was formed to fight for separation. In 1991 the Uttar Pradesh legislative assembly passed a resolution supporting the idea, but nothing came of it. In 1994, a student agitation against the state's implementation of the Mandal Commission report increasing the number of reserved government positions and university places for lower caste people (the largest caste of Kumaon and Garhwal is the high-ranking Rajput Kshatriya group) expanded into a struggle for statehood. Violence spread on both sides, with attacks on the police, police firing on demonstrators, and rapes of female Uttarakhand activists. In 1995 the agitation was renewed, mostly peacefully, under the leadership of the Uttarakhand Samyukta Sangharsh Samiti (Uttarakhand United Struggle Association), a coalition headed by the Uttarakhand Kranti Dal. The Bharatiya

Janata Party (BJP), seeing the appeal of statehood to its high-caste constituencies, also supported the movement, but wanted to act on its own. To distinguish its activities, the BJP wanted the new state to be called Uttaranchal, essentially a synonym for Uttarakhand. In 1995 various marches and demonstrations of the Uttarakhand movement were tense with the possibility of conflict not just with the authorities, but also between the two main political groups. Actual violence, however, was rare. Uttaranchal became the twenty-seventh state of the republic of India on 9 November 2000. The BJP came to power under the leadership of Nityanand Swamy. Narain Dutt Tiwari was sworn in as the chief minister on 2 March 2002.

Culture

The arts, crafts, dance forms and music of Uttaranchal revolve around gods and goddesses and seasonal cycles. In recent times, however, historical events of the freedom struggle and national life have come to be based as the topic for art forms.

Fairs and festivals:

1. Almora: Shrawan Mela (Jageshwar), Doonagiri Mela (Ranikhet), Gananath Mela, Dwarhat Mela, Kasar Devi Mela, Somnath fair.
2. Bageshwar: Uttarayani Mela, Shivratri fair, Kartik Purnima, Dussehra fair.
3. Champawat: Purnagiri fair, Devidhura fair, Mata Murti ka Mela.
4. Dehradun: Jhanda fair, Tapakeshwar fair, Lakshman Siddha fair, Bissu fair, Mahasu Devta's fair, Shaheed Veer Kesari Chand's fair, Lakhawar fair, Hanol Mela, Neelkanth Mahadev Mela.
5. Haridwar: Ardh Kumbh and Kumbh Mela, Kavand Mela.
6. Nainital: Vasantotsav, Nandadevi fair, Hariyali Devi fair, Ranibagh fair, Chhota Kailash fair, Garjiadevi fair, Sharadotsav, Holi Mahotsav.
7. Pithoragarh: Jauljibi and Thal fairs, Punyagiri Mela, Hatkalika fair.
8. Tehri Garhwal: Chandrabadni fair, Surkhanda Devi fair, Kunjapuri fair.
9. Udham Singh Nagar: Tharuwat Buxad Mahotsav, Ataria fair, Chaiti fair, Terai Utsav.
10. Uttarkashi: Magh Mela.

Economy, Industry and Agriculture

Economy: The net state domestic product at current prices in 2001–02 was Rs 11,361 crores. The per capita net state domestic product at current prices in 2001–02 was Rs 13,260.

Minerals and industry: Sheep development, weaving and fruit processing are the predominant industries of this industrially backward state. Most of the industrial enterprises of the state belong to the small-scale and household sector like khadi and handicrafts.

According to estimates, there are deposits of limestone, dolomite, magnesite, rock phosphate, gypsum and soapstone in different areas of the state.

Agriculture: Agriculture is the main source of livelihood of the rural population. The state grows foodgrains (like rice, wheat, barley, jowar, bajra, maize, manduwa, sanwan and kodo). It also grows pulses (like urad, moong-moth, masoor, gram, peas, arhar), oilseeds (like rape, mustard, sesame, groundnut, sunflower and soyabean). Besides these, sugar cane, potato, tobacco and cotton are also grown.

Power: The state's power requirements are mainly met by hydroelectric power plants. The state is home to the Tehri Dam Project.

Education

Educational institutions: Hemwati Nandan Bahuguna Garhwal University, Srinagar; G.B. Pant Kumaon University,

Nainital; Gurukul Kangri University, Haridwar; G.B. Pant University of Agriculture and Technology, Pantnagar; Roorkee Engineering University, Roorkee; Forest Research Institute, Dehradun; Indian Institute of Petroleum, Dehradun; Keshav Dev Malviya Institute of Petroleum Exploration, Dehradun; Oil and Natural Gas Corporation Ltd., Dehradun; Wadia Institute of Himalayan Geology, Dehradun; Wildlife Institute of India, Dehradun; Indira Gandhi National Forest Academy, Dehradun; Survey of India, Dehradun; Indian Institute of Remote Sensing, Dehradun; Instrument Research and Development Establishment, Dehradun; L.B.S. National Academy of Administration, Mussoorie; Defence Electronics Applications Laboratory, Dehradun; Indian Military Academy, Dehradun; Central Soil and Water Conservation Research and Training Institute, Dehradun; National Institute of Visually Handicapped, Dehradun; Rashtriya Indian Military College, Dehradun; Nehru Institute of Mountaineering, Uttarkashi, Central Building Research Institute, Roorkee.

Tourism

Major tourist attractions:

I. Nature tourism:

a. Wildlife: Askot Sanctuary, Corbett National Park, Govind Wildlife Sanctury, Nanda Devi National Park, Rajaji National Park, Valley of Flowers, Assan Barrage.

b. Glaciers: Bandarpunch glacier, Chorbari Bamak glacier, Dokriani glacier, Doonagiri glacier, Gangotri glacier, Pindari glacier, Maiktoli glacier, Sunderdhunga glacier, Milam glacier, Ralam glacier, Namik glaciers, Khatling Glaciers, Nandadevi glacier, Satopnath, Bhagirathi-Khark glacier, Tiprabamak glacier.

II. Pilgrimage tourism:

a. Yatras: Char Dham Yatra, Nanda Devi Yatra, Kailash Mansarovar Yatra.

b. Pilgrimage centres

i. Almora: Doonagiri Temple, Jageshwar Temple, Chitai Temple, Hairakhan.

ii. Bageshwar: Bagnath Temple, Chandika Temple, Shri Haru Temple, Gauri Udiyar.

iii. Chamoli: Badrinath, Hemkund Saheb, Gopeshwar, Prayags.

iv. Champawat: Baleshwar Temple, Gwal Devta, Devidhura, Kranteshwar Mahadev, Meetha Reetha Saheb, Purnagiri.

v. Dehradun: Bhadraj Temple, Surkhanda Devi, Jwalaji Temple, Nag Devta Temple, Parkasheshwar Temple, Bharat Mandir, Kailash Niketan Mandir, Satya Narayan Temple, Shatrughan Temple, Neelkanth Mahadev.

vi. Haridwar: Har ki Pauri, Sapt Rishi Ashram and Sapt Sarovar, Mansa Devi Temple, Chandi Devi Temple, Maya Devi Temple, Daksha Mahadev Temple.

vii. Nainital: Garjiya Devi Temple, Naina Devi Temple, Seeta Bani Temple.

viii. Pauri: Siddhibali Temple, Durga Devi Temple, Medanpuri Devi Temple, Shri Koteshwar Mahadev, Tarkeshwar Mahadev, Keshorai Math, Kamleshwar Temple, Shankar Math, Devalgarh, Dhar Devi.

ix. Pithoragarh: Dhwaj Temple, Narayan Ashram, Patal Bhaubaneshwar, Thal Kedar, Kapileshwar Mahadev.

x. Rudraprayag: Kedarnath Temple, Shankaracharya Samadhi, Gaurikund, Son Prayag, Panch Kedar, Madmaheshwar, Tungnath, Koteshwar, Guptkashi.

xi. Tehri Garhwal: Surkhanda Devi Temple.

xii. Udham Singh Nagar: Atariya Temple, Nanak Matta, Purnagiri, Chaiti.

xiii. Uttarkashi: Gangotri, Yamunotri.

III. Adventure tourism:

a. Skiing: Auli, Mundali, Dayara Bagyal, Munsya.

b. Water sports:

i. Still water sports: Asan Barrage Water Sports Resort, Nainital Lake Paradise, Nanaksagar Matta.

ii. Rafting:

a. Garhwal: River Yamuna: Barkot to Bernigad, Damta to Yamuna Bridge, Mori to Tuni (Khoonigad). River Alaknanda: Kaliasaur to Srinagar, Srinagar to Bagwan, Kaliasaur to Rishikesh. River Bhagirathi: Matli to Dunda, Harsil to Uttarkashi, Dharasu to Chham, Jangla to Jhala, Bhaldyana to Tehri. River Bhilangana: Ghansali to Gadolia. River Mandakini: Chandrapuri to Rudraprayag.

b. Kumaon: River Maha Kali, Kaudiyala Rafters Camp.

Airports: Dehradun, Pant Nagar.

National Parks: Corbett National Park in Nainital and Pauri Garhwal districts (520.82 sq. km), Gangotri National Park in Uttarkashi district (1,552 sq. km), Govind National Park in Uttarkashi district (472.08 sq. km), Nanda Devi National Park in Chamoli district (630.00 sq. km), Rajaji National Park in Dehradun Garhwal and Haridwar districts (820.00 sq. km), Valley of Flowers National Park in Chamoli district (87.50 sq. km).

Administration

Legislature: Uttaranchal has a unicameral legislature of seventy seats of which twelve are reserved for SCs and three for STs. The term of the current house ends on 17 March 2007. The present party position is as under:

Name of Party	**Seats**
Indian National Congress	36
Bharatiya Janata Party	19
Bahujan Samaj Party	7
Uttarakhand Kranti Dal	4
Nationalist Congress Party	1
Independent	3
Total	70

Judiciary: The High Court of Uttaranchal is at Nainital. The chief justice is Cyriac Joseph.

Districts:

District	Area (sq. km)	Population	Headquarters	Urban Agglomerations
Almora	3,082.8	630,446	Almora	Almora
Bageshwar	2,302.5	249,453	Bageshwar	
Chamoli	7,613.8	369,198	Gopeshwar	
Champawat	1,781.0	224,461	Champawat	
Dehradun	3,088.0	1,279,083	Dehradun	Dehradun, Mussouri, Rishikesh
Pauri Garhwal	5,399.6	696,851	Pauri	
Haridwar	2,360.0	1,444,213	Hardwar	Haridwar, Roorkee
Nainital	3,860.4	762,912	Nainital	Nainital, Haldwani-cum-Kathgodam
Pithoragarh	7,100.0	462,149	Pithoragarh	
Rudraprayag	1,890.6	227,461	Rudraprayag	
Tehri Garhwal	4,080.0	604,608	New Tehri	
Udhamsingh Nagar (Rudrapur)	2,908.4	1,234,548	Udhamsingh Nagar	
Uttarkashi	8,016.0	294,179	Uttarkashi	

Uttar Pradesh

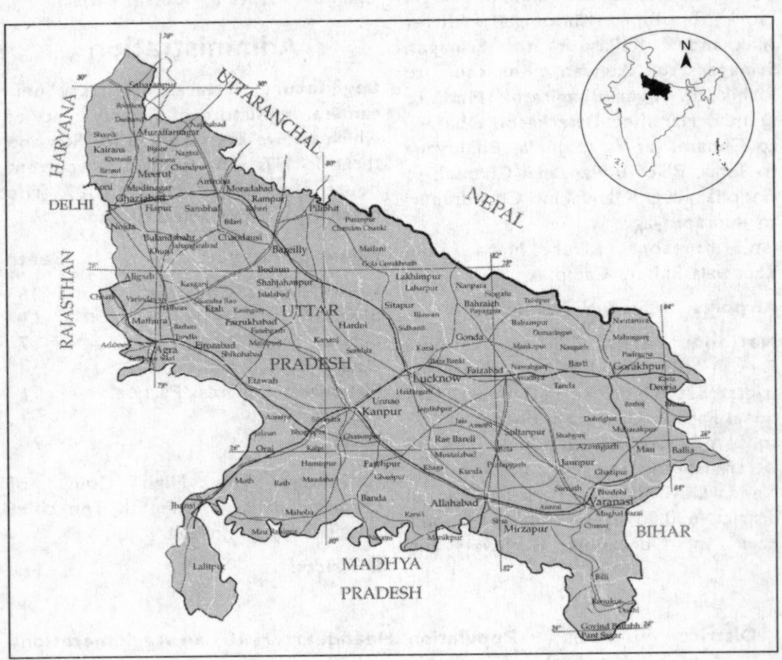

Key Statistics

Capital: Lucknow.
Area: 2,36,286 sq. km.
Population: Total: 166,197,921, Male: 87,565,369, Female: 78,632,552.
Population density: 689 per sq. km.
Sex ratio: 898 females per 1000 males.
Principal languages: Hindi, Urdu, Punjabi.
Literacy rates: Total: 56.3%, Male: 68.8%, Female: 42.2%.

Government

Governor: T.V. Rajeshwar. He was sworn in on 8 July 2004.

Chief Minister: Mulayam Singh Yadav (SP). He was sworn in on 29 August 2003.

Geography

Physical characteristics: On the basis of its physiography, the main regions of Uttar Pradesh are the central plains of the Ganga and its tributaries, the southern uplands, the Himalayan region, and the submontane region between the Himalayas and the plains.

The Gangetic plain occupies about three-fourths of the total area of Uttar Pradesh. It largely consists of a fertile plain which is featureless, and varies in elevation, rising up to 300 metres in the north-west, and 60 metres in the extreme east. It is composed of alluvial deposits which are brought down by the Ganga and its tributaries from the Himalayas.

The southern uplands constitute a part of the Vindhya range, which is rugged, largely dissected, and rises towards the south-east. The elevation in this region reaches up to 300 metres. The submontane region consists of the Bhabar, a narrow bed of alluvium and gravel, which along its southern fringes joins into the Terai area. The Terai area, which previously consisted of tall grass and thick forests, is a marshy and damp tract. A definite portion of the Terai region has been subject to deforestation.

The topography of the Himalayan region is vastly varied. There are deep canyons, turbulent streams, large lakes and snow-capped peaks.

Neighbouring States and Union territories:
International border: Nepal.

States: Uttaranchal, Madhya Pradesh, Haryana, Rajasthan, Himachal Pradesh, Bihar.

National Capital Territory: Delhi.

Major rivers: Ganga, Yamuna, Gomti, Ramganga, Ghaghara, Chambal, Betwa, Ken and Son.

Climate: Uttar Pradesh has a varying climate. The Himalayan region experiences a moderately temperate climate, while the southern uplands and the central plains experience tropical monsoon. The highest temperature recorded in the state was 49.9°C at Gonda in 1958. The average temperatures in the plains vary from 12.5°C to 17.5°C in January to 27.5°C to 32.5°C in May and June.

Uttar Pradesh registers a rainfall between 1,000–2,000mm in the east and 600–1,000mm in the west. Around 90 per cent of the rainfall occurs between June and September, during the time of the southwest monsoon. Floods are a recurring problem due to the concentrated rainfall during these four months, and cause heavy destruction to life, property and crops, especially in the eastern part of Uttar Pradesh. On the other hand, the periodic failure of monsoons leads to droughts and failure of crops.

Flora and Fauna:
Flora: The plains of Uttar Pradesh are rich in mineral deposits, which is diminishing due to the various requirements of the people. While natural forests can be found in the mountainous regions of Uttaranchal on a very large scale, Uttar Pradesh has very few patches of natural forest that lie scattered in the plains.

Tropical moist deciduous forests grow in regions that register 1,000 to 1,500 mm of annual rainfall and an average temperature between 26°–27°C. In Uttar Pradesh, these forests can be found in Terai. Deciduous trees of uneven sizes grow in regions of higher altitude. This is a special feature of these forests.

In the lower regions, there are climbers, bamboo and evergreen shrubs. The important trees that grow here are dhak, gular, jamun, jhingal, sal, palas, amla, and mahua semal. In all parts of the plains, especially in the central, eastern and western regions, tropical dry deciduous forests can be found, and they consist of trees that are mostly deciduous. Important trees include amaltas, anjeer, palas, bel, and sal. In other moist regions, and especially along river banks, sheesham, jamun, babool, imli (tamarind), peepal, mango, and neem can be found.

In the south-western parts of the state can be found tropical thorny forests, which are confined to areas that experience low humidity (below 47 per cent), low annual rainfall (between 500–700mm), and a mean annual temperature between 25° to 27°C. Euphorbias, thorny legumes, babool, and especially thorny trees can be found extensively in these areas. Short grasses grow during rains. In these regions, the trees are normally small, and form open dry forests. Some of the trees that can be found in this region are kokke, khair, dhaman, neem, phulai, and danjha. These trees also produce various types of gum and resin.

Fauna: Uttar Pradesh has a variety of fauna. Important species of fish include rohu, einghi, trout, cuchia, labi, parthan, mirror carp, kata, eel, hilsa, magur, mirgal, mahaser, vittal and tengan. Birds include pigeon, vulture, owl, nightingale, sparrow, parrot, nilkanth, cheel and peacock. Other common species found in the state are black deer, nilgai, kastura, sambar, chinkara, snow leopard, hill dog, elephant, mountain goat, cheetal, hyena, tiger, and black-brown bear.

The submontane region of the state is rich in animal life. Animals like wild boars, crocodiles, sloth bears, leopards and tigers, and birds like partridges, wild ducks, quails, peafowls, woodpeckers, doves, pigeons and blue jays can be found in these regions.

History

During the British rule in India, there were certain pockets in Uttar Pradesh that were governed by the English equity and Common Law. In 1773, the Mughal emperor transferred the districts of Banaras and Ghazipur to the East India Company.

The East India Company acquired the area of modern-day Uttar Pradesh over a period of time. The territories occupied from the nawabs, the Scindias of Gwalior and the Gurkhas were initially placed within the Bengal Presidency. In 1833, they were separated and the North-Western Provinces, originally called Agra Presidency, were created. In 1877, the kingdom of Awadh was united with the North-Western Provinces and the province was renamed North-Western Provinces of Agra and Oudh. In 1902, the province was renamed yet again, when it became 'United Provinces of Agra and Oudh'. In 1937, the name was shortened to United Provinces.

In 1947, the United Provinces became an administrative unit of independent India. In 1949, the autonomous states of Rampur and Tehri-Garhwal were incorporated into the United Provinces. When the new Constitution was adopted in 1950, United Provinces got its present name, Uttar Pradesh. Gobind Ballabh Pant was the first chief minister of Uttar Pradesh.

In 2000, the state of Uttaranchal was carved out from Uttar Pradesh.

Politics

The state was made a governor's province in 1921 and after some time its capital was shifted to Lucknow. Its name was changed to United Provinces in 1937. It got its present name of Uttar Pradesh in 1950. Uttar Pradesh has held the centre stage in the country's politics mainly because it provides the biggest chunk of eighty-five MPs in the 545-member Indian parliament. Its 425-member state assembly holds a perpetual live-wire political situation. Heavyweight chief ministers like Sampurnanand, C.B. Gupta, Sucheta Kriplani, Charan Singh, Tribhuvan Narain Singh, Kamlapati Tripathi, H.N. Bahuguna and N.D. Tiwari kept the Congress flag flying high in Uttar Pradesh for nearly thirty years. The state had by 1977 produced all the three prime ministers of the country. But by mid-March 1977, the political setting of Uttar Pradesh saw the Congress as a humiliated party. The Janata Party made a clean sweep of the eighty-five Lok Sabha seats, with 68 per cent of the voters backing it. Subsequent Assembly elections proved no different for the Congress. The Janata Party won 352 seats of the 425 seats in the assembly. But soon infighting and bickering crippled the Janata Party. The going proved tough for the first backward chief minister Ram Naresh Yadav.

Already bogged down with the Shia-Sunni riots of October 1977, Yadav seemed completely at a loss with the outbreak of communal violence in Varanasi on the Dussehra day. Banarsi Das was the chief minister from 1979 to 1980. This was a period of political instability. At this time Sanjay Gandhi capitalized on the Janata Party's failures and helped his mother Indira Gandhi to take over the reins of the country for the second time in January 1980. The Congress won fifty-one of the eighty-five UP Lok Sabha seats in 1980. Vishwanath Pratap Singh set his foot in big-time politics when he became the chief minister on 9 June 1980. Sanjay Gandhi himself handpicked his huge sixty-one-member ministry. The air crash on 23 June abruptly ended Sanjay Gandhi's soaring rise. This presented Singh with unexpected challenges from within the Congress in the state. Many severe tests were waiting. The violent Moradabad riots, which started on 13 August 1980, proved the worst ever. The riots continued for more than forty-five days and necessitated intermittent curfew situations in and around the district. A visibly upset V.P. Singh tendered his resignation but it was not accepted. 1981 was even worse for V.P. Singh. Sripati Misra was chosen as Singh's alternative in 1982. A virtual revolt by Congress MLAs sealed Misra's fate. The Congress chose its old hand N.D. Tiwari, a union minister, to replace Misra in August 1984.

The Vishwa Hindu Parishad had launched Ek-atmata Yatras in late 1983. These yatras criss-crossed Uttar Pradesh to receive an overwhelming response. There were repeated religious build ups in Ayodhya. The Vishwa Hindu Parishad's major onslaught was unveiled with the announcement of a Ram Janm Bhumi Mukti (freeing of the temple) agitation on 7 October 1984. A huge crowd of kar sevaks (RSS volunteers) collected at the banks of the Sarayu river in Ayodhya and vowed to sacrifice their lives for the cause. A truck carrying idols of Ram and Sita, called the Ram Rath yatra, started from Ayodhya to Lucknow the next day on its way to Delhi. The yatra had to be abandoned in Ghaziabad, on the Delhi borders, as Indira Gandhi was assassinated, riddled with bullets by her own bodyguards.

Rajiv Gandhi's entry worked as a soothing balm for hurt sentiments. The Congress won a whopping 415 of the total 542 Lok Sabha seats; the biggest ever haul by a single party. Uttar Pradesh responded in Rajiv's favour almost unilaterally. The party lost just three of the eighty-five Lok Sabha seats in the state with an incredible 50.71 per cent votes. The BJP, in turn, stood nowhere with merely 6.37 per cent votes. The Dalit Mazdoor Kisan Party (DMKP), formed by dissolving Lok Dal, was the only party which survived the hurricane with only three seats but a more respectable vote percentage of 24.47 per cent. But the Congress could not fair well in the Vidhan Sabha elections in 1985. One reason for the Congress's dip in performance compared to the 1980 elections could have been Rajiv's determination of lending a clean image to the party. Nearly half the 306 MLAs of 1980 were denied tickets and they worked against the party's interest in most cases during the campaign. The Congress won 268 seats. It was time for Narayan Datt Tiwari to move out. He made way for Bir Bahadur Singh as chief minister.

In 1989, the National Front comprising seven parties, on an electoral understanding with the BJP, came to power. The Congress's downfall in UP had begun. And so had the era of political instability in Uttar Pradesh. Mulayam Singh Yadav of the Samajvadi Party became the chief minister and remained in the post till 1991. His government fell when the government at the Centre changed. Mulayam Singh Yadav was succeeded by Kalyan Singh on 24 June

1991. The Kalyan Singh government was dismissed on 6 December 1992 after the demolition of the Babri Masjid at Ayodhya, and a governor's rule was imposed. Two governors—Satyanarain Reddy and Motilal Vora—ruled the state over the next nine months. On 5 December 1993 Mulayam Singh Yadav was back on the seat of chief minister. Mayawati of the Bahujan Samaj Party became the chief minister in 1995, but President's Rule was soon imposed in the state.

The 1997 Assembly elections produced a hung assembly. The BJP and the BSP carved out a peculiar unheard-of arrangement: the chief minister's position was to be shared by the two parties in rotation in the block period of six months each. The BSP was to get the chief minister's position first. Mayawati took over as chief minister once again on 20 March 1997. Kalyan Singh took over on 21 September 1997 and reversed some of the decisions made by the Mayawati government. Mayawati withdrew support from the Kalyan Singh government on 19 October. On 21 February 1998, twelve members of the rebel Congress group Loktantrik Congress Party (LCP), which was supporting the BJP government, called on the governor along with some other rebel MLAs of other splinter groups along with Mayawati and Congress Legislature Party leader Pramod Tewari. Representatives of the Samajvadi Party were also in the delegation. Congress MLAs submitted a memorandum claiming that the LCP had withdrawn support from the BJP. The governor of UP Romesh Bhandari immediately invited Jagdambika Pal to form the government. On 22 February the court reinstated the Kalyan Singh government by setting the governor's order null and void. The Vidhan Sabha met on 26 February as both the chief ministers occupied the podium along with the Speaker. Kalyan Singh proved his strength in the House and emerged the winner. Mayawati came to power for the third time on 3 May 2002. She was succeeded by Mulayam Singh Yadav on 29 August 2003.

Culture

Apart from possessing a variety of geographical regions and cultures, Uttar Pradesh is also one of the most ancient centres of Indian culture. The antiquities discovered at Mirzapur, Meerut and Banda or Bundelkhand connect its history to the early stone age and the Harappan culture. In the Vindhyan range, chalk drawings or dark red drawings by primitive men can be found.

The state also features popular holy shrines and pilgrim centres, and also plays an important role in education, culture, politics, tourism, industry, and agriculture. It is also well known for the contribution of its people to the national freedom movement.

Fairs and festivals: There are about 2,250 fairs that are held every year in Uttar Pradesh. Mathura has the largest number of fairs (eighty-six). Other major venues of fairs are Kanpur, Hamirpur, Jhansi, Agra and Fatehpur.

The Kumbh Mela at Prayag (Allahabad) attracts pilgrims and tourists from around the world. At Prayag, the Kumbh fair is held once in twelve years, and the Ardh Kumbh is held every six years.

Festivals of other religions are also celebrated in Uttar Pradesh, and it is renowned for its composite culture. As many as forty festivals are celebrated by various communities. Hindu festivals include Shivaratri, Makar Sankranti, Krishna Janmashtami, Karthik Purnima, Vijaya Dashmi, Holi, Deepawali, Ganesha Chaturthi, Ganga Dashahara, Ram Navami, Vaishakhi Purnima, Raksha Bandhan, Sheetla Ashtami, Naag Panchami, and Vasant Panchami.

Major Muslim festivals celebrated in the state are Shab-e-Barat, Barawafat, Bakr-Id, Id and Muharram. Christian festivals include Christmas, Good Friday, Easter and New Year's Day.

Some of the important fairs and festivals held in Uttar Pradesh include the Bateshwar Fair, festivals organized by the UP Tourism Department, the Ganga Mahotsava at Varanasi, the Buddha Mahotsava at Sarnath and Kushinagar, and the Water Sports Festival at Allahabad.

Economy, Industry and Agriculture

Economy: The net state domestic product at current prices for 2003–04 (provisional) was Rs 189,598 crores. The per capita net state domestic product at current prices for 2003–04 (provisional) was Rs 10,817.

Minerals and industry: Textiles and sugar refining, both long-standing industries in Uttar Pradesh, employ nearly one-third of the state's total factory labour. Most of the mills, however, are old and inefficient. Other resource-based industries in Uttar Pradesh include vegetable oil, jute and cement.

A number of large factories manufacturing heavy equipment, machinery, steel, aircraft, telephone and electronics equipment, and fertilizers have been set up in the state. An oil refinery at Mathura and the development of coalfields in the south-eastern district of Mirzapur are also major Union government projects.

The state government has promoted medium and small-scale industries. Industries that contribute most to the state's exports include handicrafts, carpets, brassware, footwear, and leather and sporting goods. Carpets from Bhadohi and Mirzapur are prized worldwide. Silks and brocades of Varanasi, ornamental brassware from Moradabad, chikan (a type of embroidery) work from Lucknow, ebony work from Nagina, glassware from Firozabad, and carved woodwork from Saharanpur are also important.

Tourism in the state has great potential, but much of it is untapped.

The minerals found in Uttar Pradesh include limestone, dolomite, glass-sand, marble, bauxite and uranium

Agriculture: The economy of Uttar Pradesh is largely dependent on agriculture. The main crops are rice, sugar cane, millet, wheat and barley. High-yielding varieties of seed for rice and wheat were introduced in the 1960s, along with a greater availability of fertilizers, and an increased use of irrigation in the state.

Two chief problems still affect the farmers, namely small, non-economic landholdings and lack of resources needed to invest in the state's technology, in order to increase production. The yield of milk is low, but livestock and dairy still manage to provide a supplementary means of income. Most of the agricultural landholdings are insufficient for the subsistence of the farmers in the state.

Forests in the state yield timber, which is used in construction, and also as firewood and raw materials for producing a number of industrial products like paper, matches and plywood. The government's reforestation programmes in Uttar Pradesh have contributed to some increase in the forest area, and the subsequent availability of forest products useful for industries.

Power: Uttar Pradesh is mainly dependent on thermal power, which provides the bulk of the energy to the state. However, hydroelectric and nuclear power (from the Narora Atomic Power Station) also contribute to the total power scenario.

Education

Educational institutes: Aligarh Muslim University (Aligarh), University of

Allahabad, Babasaheb Bhimrao Ambedkar University (Lucknow), Banaras Hindu University (Varanasi) , Bundelkhand University (Jhansi), Central Institute of Higher Tibetan Studies (Varanasi), Ch. Charan Singh University (Meerut), Chandra Shekhar Azad University of Agriculture and Technology (Kanpur), Chhatrapati Sahu Ji Maharaj Kanpur University (Kanpur), Dayalbagh Educational Institute (Agra), Deendayal Upadhyaya Gorakhpur University (Gorakhpur), Dr Bhim Rao Ambedkar University (Agra), Dr Ram Manohar Lohia Avadh University (Faizabad), Indian Institute of Technology (Kanpur), Indian Veterinary Research Institute (Izatnagar), University of Lucknow, Mahatma Gandhi Kashi Vidyapeeth (Varanasi), M.J.P. Rohilkhand University (Bareilly), Narendra Deva University of Agriculture and Technology (Faizabad), Purvanchal University (Jaunpur), University of Roorkee, Sampurnanand Sanskrit Vishwavidyalaya (Varanasi) and the Sanjay Gandhi Postgraduate Institute of Medical Sciences (Lucknow).

Tourism

Major tourist attractions: Chitrakoot, Ayodhya, Jhansi, Kushinagar, Kapilavastu, Varanasi, Sarnath, Fatehpur Sikri, Braj-Bhoomi, Vrindavan, Agra.

Airports: Lucknow, Kanpur, Varanasi, Agra.

National Parks: Dudhwa National Park in Lakhimpur Kheri district (490.00 sq. km).

Administration

Legislature: Uttar Pradesh has a bicameral legislature. The Lower House is called Vidhan Sabha and the Upper House Vidhan Parishad. The state legislative assembly has 403 seats, of which eighty-nine are reserved for the SCs. No seats are reserved for STs. The present party positions are:

Name of Party	Seats
Samajwadi Party	143
Bahujan Samaj Party	98
Bharatiya Janata Party	88
Indian National Congress	25
Rashtriya Lok Dal	14
Rashtriya Kranti Party	4
Apna Dal	3
Communist Party of India (Marxist)	2
Akhil Bhartiya Lok Tantrik Congress	2
Janata Dal (United)	2
Akhil Bharat Hindu Mahasabha	1
Janata Party	1
Lok Jan Shakti Party	1
National Loktantrik Party	1
Rashtriya Parivartan Dal	1
Samajwadi Janata Party (Rashtriya)	1
Independent	16
Total	**403**

Judiciary: The Allahabad High Court is the seat of judiciary. A.N. Roy is the chief justice.

Districts:

District	Area (sq. km)	Population	Headquarters	Urban Agglomerations
Agra	4,027.0	3,611,301	Agra	Agra
Aligarh	3,747.0	2,990,388	Aligarh	
Allahabad	5,425.1	4,941,510	Allahabad	Allahabad
Ambedkar Nagar	2,372.0	2,025,373	Akbarpur	
Auraiya	2,051.9	1,179,496	Auraiya	
Azamgarh	4,210.0	3,950,808	Azamgarh	Mubarakpur
Bagpat	1,389.4	1,164,388	Bagpat	
Bahraich	5,751.0	2,384,239	Bahraich	
Ballia	2,981.0	2,752,412	Ballia	
Balrampur	2,927.0	1,684,567	Balrampur	

Banda	4,418.1	1,500,253	Banda	Banda
Barabanki	3,825.0	2,673,394	Barabanki	Barabanki
Bareilly	4,120.0	3,598,701	Bareilly	Bareilly
Basti	3,033.8	2,068,922	Basti	
Bijnor	4,561.0	3,130,586	Bijnor	Bijnor, Kiratpur, Seohara
Budaun	5,168.0	3,069,245	Budaun	
Bulandshahr	3,717.7	2,923,290	Bulandshahr	
Chandauli	2,554.1	1,639,777	Chandauli	Mughalsarai
Chattrapati Shahuji Maharaj Nagar			Gauriganj	
Chitrakoot	3,205.9	800,592	Chitrakoot	
Deoria	2,535.0	2,730,376	Deoria	
Etah	4,446.0	2,788,270	Etah	
Etawah	2,288.2	1,340,031	Etawah	
Faizabad	2,764.0	2,087,914	Faizabad	Faizabad
Farrukhabad	2,279.5	1,577,237	Fatehgarh	Farrukhabad-cum-Fatehgarh
Fatehpur	4,152.0	2,305,847	Fatehpur	
Firozabad	2,361.0	2,045,737	Firozabad	Firozabad, Sirsaganj, Tundla
Gautam Buddha Nagar	1,268.6	1,191,263	Noida	
Ghaziabad	1,955.8	3,289,540	Ghaziabad	Modinagar
Ghazipur	3,377.0	3,049,337	Ghazipur	Ghazipur
Gonda	4,425.0	2,765,754	Gonda	
Gorakhpur	3,321.0	3,784,720	Gorakhpur	
Hamirpur	4,316.5	1,042,374	Hamirpur	
Hardoi	5,986.0	3,397,414	Hardoi	
Hathras	1,751.0	1,333,372	Hathras	Hathras, Sasni
Jalaun	4,565.0	1,455,859	Orai	
Jaunpur	4,038.0	3,911,305	Jaunpur	
Jhansi	5,024.0	1,746,715	Jhansi	Jhansi
Jyotiba Phule Nagar	2,320.5	1,499,193	Amroha	
Kannauj	1,994.5	1,385,227	Kannauj	
Kanpur Dehat	3,146.0	1,584,037	Akbarpur	
Kanpur Nagar	3,030.0	4,137,489	Kanpur	Kanpur
Kaushambi	1,835.9	1,294,937	Kaushambi	
Kheri	7,680.0	3,200,137	Kheri	
Kushinagar	2,910.0	2,891,933	Padarauna	
Lalitpur	5,039.0	977,447	Lalitpur	
Lucknow	2,528.0	3,681,416	Lucknow	Lucknow
Maharajganj	2,951.0	2,167,041	Maharajganj	
Mahoba	2,849.6	708,831	Mahoba	
Mainpuri	2,746.0	1,592,875	Mainpuri	Mainpuri
Mathura	3,332.0	2,069,578	Mathura	Mathura
Mau	1,713.0	1,849,294	Mau	Muhammadabad Gohna

Meerut	2,521.6	3,001,636	Meerut	Meerut
Mirzapur	4,522.0	2,114,852	Mirzapur	
Moradabad	3,646.5	3,749,630	Moradabad	Bilari
Muzaffarnagar	4,008.0	3,541,952	Muzaffarnagar	Muzaffarnagar, Purquazi
Pilibhit	3,499.0	1,643,788	Pilibhit	
Pratapgarh	3,717.0	2,727,156	Pratapgarh	
Rae Bareli	4,586.0	2,872,204	Rae Bareli	
Rampur	2,367.0	1,922,450	Rampur	
Saharanpur	3,689.0	2,848,152	Saharanpur	
Sant Kabir Nagar	1,442.3	1,424,500	Khalilabad	
Sant Ravidas Nagar	959.8	1,352,056	Bhadohi	
Shahjahanpur	4,575.0	2,549,458	Shahjahanpur	Shahjahanpur
Shravasti	1,126.0	1,175,428	Shravasti	
Siddharth Nagar	2,752.0	2,038,598	Navgarh	
Sitapur	5,743.0	3,616,510	Sitapur	
Sonbhadra	6,788.0	1,463,468	Robertsganj	Renukoot
Sultanpur	4,436.0	3,190,926	Sultanpur	
Unnao	4,558.0	2,700,426	Unnao	
Varanasi	1,578.0	3,147,927	Varanasi	Varanasi

West Bengal

Key Statistics

Capital: Kolkata.

Area: 88,752 sq. km.

Population: Total: 80,176,197, Male: 41,465,985, Female: 38,710,212.

Population density: 904 per sq. km.

Sex ratio: 934 females per 1000 males.

Principal languages: Bengali, Hindi, Urdu.

Literacy rates: Total: 68.6%, Male: 77.0%, Female: 59.6%.

Government

Governor: Gopalkrishna Gandhi. He was sworn in on 14 December 2004.

Chief Minister: Buddhadeb Bhattacharya (CPI[M]). He was sworn in on 18 May 2001.

Geography

Physical characteristics: Stretching from the Himalayas in the north to the Bay of Bengal in the south, West Bengal is primarily composed of plain land, except the north where the southern flank of the Himalayas extends into the state. Part of the Ganga–Brahmaputra delta constitutes the eastern part of West Bengal. From the northern highlands to the tropical forests of Sunderbans, variations in altitude result in great variety in nature and climate.

Neighbouring States and Union territories:

International borders: Bangladesh, Nepal, Bhutan.

States: Sikkim, Assam, Bihar, Jharkhand, Orissa

Major rivers: Hooghly and its tributaries (Mayurakshi, Damodar, Kangsabati and Rupnarayan) and Teesta, Torsa, Subarnarekha, Joldhara and Ranjit.

Climate: Climate in the state varies from the relatively cooler northern part

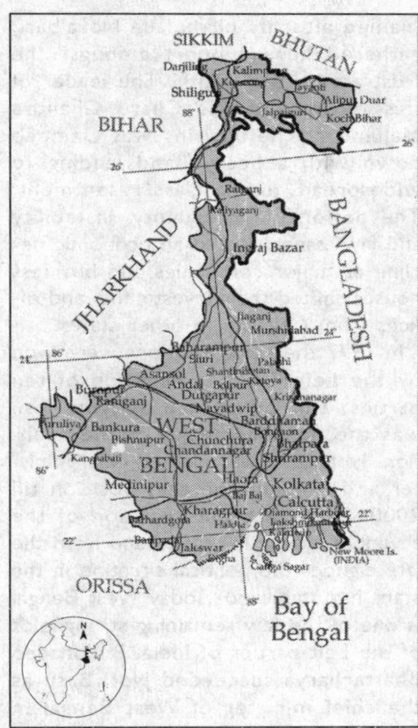

to the warm region in the south. Maximum and minimum temperatures vary between 30°C–44°C and 4°C–12°C respectively. Annual rainfall is about 4,000–5,000mm in the northern districts and about 1,100–1,600mm in the western districts. The average annual rainfall is 1,750mm.

Flora and Fauna:

Flora: The forests of West Bengal could be classified under seven categories: tropical semi-evergreen, tropical moist deciduous, tropical dry deciduous, littoral and swampy, subtropical hill forest, eastern Himalayan wet temperate, and alpine.

The Sunderbans, which derives its name from sundari trees, have large numbers of genwa, dhundal, passur, garjan and kankra trees.

Fauna: Wildlife found in the state include Royal Bengal Tiger, elephant, one-horned rhino, sambar, barking deer, spotted deer, hog deer, wild boar, rhesus monkey, mongoose, crocodile, bison, Olive Ridley sea turtle, python, salvator lizard, chequered killback, heron, egret, cormorant, fishing eagle, white-bellied sea eagle, seagull, tern, kingfisher, Eastern knot, curlew, sandpiper, golden plover, pintail, white-eyed pochard and whistling teal.

History

The state gets its name from the ancient kingdom of Vanga, or Banga. Around 3 BC, it formed part of the extensive Mauryan empire. The region was then taken over into the Gupta empire and later came under the rule of the Pala dynasty. From the thirteenth to the eighteenth centuries Bengal was under Muslim rule, and came under British control following Robert Clive's conquest over the region in 1757.

In 1773, Warren Hastings, the governor of Bengal, became the first governor-general of Bengal with powers over the Madras and Bombay Presidencies as well. In 1905, Bengal was partitioned into two provinces in spite of violent protests. Continued opposition to the partition led to the reunification of the state in 1911.

At the time of Independence, the eastern part of Bengal became East Pakistan (later Bangladesh) and the western part became the Indian state of West Bengal. The princely state of Cooch Behar was integrated with West Bengal in 1950. The state also gained some territory from Bihar after the reorganization of Indian states in 1956.

Politics

After India's independence, partition led to two nations, India and Pakistan with two halves—East Pakistan and West Pakistan. Bengal was partitioned and the western half became the state of West Bengal in the Indian Union. The eastern half of Bengal became East Pakistan and in 1971, became an independent nation—Bangladesh. The first chief minister of the Indian state of West Bengal, Dr Prafulla Chandra Ghosh, was sworn in as the chief minister on 15 August 1947. Dr Bidhan Chandra Roy became the new chief minister on 14 January 1948. Dr B.C. Roy is credited with the planning and implementation of many of West Bengal's major projects. In 1962, with the death of Dr B.C. Roy, Prafulla Chandra Sen, the food minister, became the chief minister and his government lasted till 1967. During the late sixties and early seventies widespread poverty and dissatisfaction led to a major political turbulence in the state. The breakdown of infrastructure and resentment against the Delhi-based Congress government led to the strengthening of the Left parties in West Bengal. The Communist Party of India (CPI), formed in 1920, split in 1964 and the Communist Party of India (Marxist) (CPIM) was formed. The United Front, a combination of Left and other parties came to power in West Bengal in 1967. Ajoy Mukherjee of the Bangla Congress became the new chief minister in the UF government. The government was short lived and Dr Prafulla Chandra Ghosh (the first chief minister and the food minister in Ajoy Mukherjee's cabinet) formed the Progressive Democratic Front and became the new chief minister. In 1969 the United Front returned to power with Ajoy Mukherjee as the chief minister for a second time. The second UF government survived till 1971, followed by a Congress coalition with Ajoy Mukherjee remaining the chief minister. The Congress Party returned to power in 1972 under the leadership of Siddhartha Shankar Ray. A leftist movement called the Naxalite movement (named after its birthplace Naxalbari) gathered huge support amongst the frustrated urban youth. The leader of this movement was Charu Chandra Majumdar. The uprising was clamped down with a heavy hand leading to widespread middle class resentment. The period of uncertainty, instability and lawlessness led to an economic decline as major companies and business houses shifted their investments and offices from Calcutta to other states.

In 1977 the state elections were won by the Left Front, a coalition of ten parties. The CPI(M) led by Jyoti Basu was the dominant party in the coalition. Jyoti Basu was elected chief minister and remained in that position till 2000. The turbulent situation of the seventies slowly improved and from the late eighties the political situation in the state has stabilized. Today West Bengal is one of the few remaining strongholds of the Left parties of India. Buddhadeb Bhattacharya succeeded Jyoti Basu as the chief minister of West Bengal in 2000. The main opposition in the state —the Indian National Congress (INC)—suffered a setback when a former Congress party member and popular leader Mamata Banerjee founded her own Trinamool (grassroots) Congress (TMC) Party in 1997. In the 1998 and the 1999 national elections she allied with the Bharatiya Janata Party. It is interesting to note that the BJP (founded in 1980) has its origins in the Bharatiya Jana Sangha which was founded by prominent Bengali leader Dr Shymaprasad Mukherjee (1901–1953). The 1999 national elections saw the Left maintaining its comfortable lead from the state, followed by the TMC, the INC and the BJP. The TMC won all the three seats from Calcutta. In 1999 Calcutta's name was changed to Kolkata by the state legislature. Just before the 2001 state assembly elections there was a realignment of political parties with the TMC dumping the BJP and joining hands with the INC.

The Kolkata media had predicted a tough fight by the TMC-INC alliance and a possibility of the government changing hands. However the Left Front won 199 of the 294 seats and was voted back to power for a record sixth time.

Culture

The rich traditions in art and culture in West Bengal are reflected in numerous ways in theatre, folk music, literature, films and paintings. The state has seen many great writers and artists, including the Nobel prize-winning poet Rabindranath Tagore.

Jatra, the hugely popular theatre form, has a range of themes: from mythological to historical to contemporary. Rabindrasangeet, consisting of songs written and composed by Tagore, has a strong influence on Bengali culture. Bengali filmmakers—most notably Satyajit Ray, Tapan Sinha and Mrinal Sen—have also earned worldwide acclaim.

Popular handicrafts include leather craft, brass and bell metal, articles from bamboo and cane, clay dolls, jute products and silver filigree. Handloom saris, notably the Baluchari and Dhakai, are well known.

Fairs and festivals: Important festivals of West Bengal include Durga Puja, Id, Diwali, Rasajatra, Navanna, Christmas, Saraswati Puja, Vasanta Utsav, Holi and Charak. Important fairs include Gangasagar Mela, Kenduli Mela, Jalpesh Mela, Rash Mela and Poush Mela.

Economy, Industry and Agriculture

Economy: The net state domestic product at current prices for 2003–04 (provisional) was Rs 173,674 crores. The per capita net state domestic product at current prices for 2003–04 (provisional) was Rs 20,896.

Minerals and industry: Major industries in the state include chemicals, cotton textiles, coal, iron and steel products, heavy and light engineering products, leather and footwear, papers, tea, jute products, breweries, drugs and pharmaceuticals, electrical and electronics, plastics, software and infotech, locomotives, vegetable oils, gems and jewellery, poultry products and frozen marine products.

The state is rich in coal deposits located in the districts of Bardhaman and Birbhum. Other mineral deposits include iron ore, manganese, silica, limestone, China clay and dolomite.

Agriculture: Principal crops include rice, food grains, oilseeds, jute, potato, tea, mango, pineapple, banana, papaya, orange, guava and litchi. With an annual production of 58,000 tonnes, floriculture is another important activity.

Power: With an installed capacity of 6877 MW, West Bengal is a power surplus state. It supplies power to its neighbouring states. Most of the state's power comes from thermal power plants, and a small amount from hydroelectric plants.

Education

Educational institutes: University of Calcutta, Kolkata; Jadavpur University, Kolkata; Visva Bharati, Santiniketan; Rabindra Bharati University, Kolkata; Indian Institute of Technology, Kharagpur; Indian Institute of Management, Kolkata; Indian Statistical Institute, Kolkata; Bengal Engineering College, Howrah; University of Burdwan, Burdwan; Netaji Subhash Open University, Kolkata; University of North Bengal, Darjeeling • Vidyasagar University, Medinipur; Marine Engineering and Research Institute, Kolkata; West Bengal University of Animal and Fisheries Sciences, Kolkata.

Tourism

Major tourist attractions:

1. Kolkata and Howrah: Victoria Memorial, Indian Museum, Kalighat Temple, Dakshineswar Kali Temple, Belur Math, Ramakrishna Mission Institute of Culture, St. John's Church, Birla planetarium, Shahid Minar, Howrah Bridge (Rabindra Setu), Vidyasagar Setu, Science City, Botanical gardens.
2. Santiniketan.
3. Darjeeling: Tiger Hill, Batasia Loop, Lloyds Botanical Garden.
4. Murshidabad: Nimak Haram Deohri, Khusbagh, Hazarduari, Plassey.
5. Dooars Valley: Jaldapara, Buxa Tiger Project, Gorumara and Chapramari wildlife sanctuaries.
6. Kalimpong: Dr Graham's Homes, Durpin Dara, Kalibari, Thongsha Gumpha, Tharpa Choling monastery.
7. Vishnupur: Rasmancha, Pancha Ratna Temple, Jorebangla Temple.
8. Siliguri.
9. Beaches: Digha, Shankarpur, Junput, Bakkhali, Sagardwip.

Airports:

International: Kolkata.

Domestic: Bagdogra.

National Parks: Neora Valley National Park (Darjeeling)—88.00 sq. km, Singalila National Park (Darjeeling)—78.60 sq. km, Sunderbans Tiger Reserve (South 24 Parganas)—1330.10 sq. km, Buxa Tiger Reserve (Jalpaiguri)—117.10 sq. km, Gorumara National Park (Jalpaiguri)—79.45 sq. km.

Administration

Legislature: The unicameral West Bengal legislature comprises 294 elected seats, of which fifty-nine are reserved for SCs and seventeen for STs. One member can be nominated by the governor to represent the Anglo-Indian community. The term of the current house expires on 13 June 2006. The present party-wise break-up is as follows:

Name of Party	Seats
Communist Party of India (Marxist)	176
All India Trinamool Congress	30
Indian National Congress	21
All-India Forward Bloc	23
Revolutionary Socialist Party	20
Communist Party of India	8
West Bengal Socialist Party	4
Gorakha National Liberation Front	3
Rashtriya Janata Dal	1
Jharkhand Party	1
Democratic Socialist Party	1
Independent	6
Total	294

Judiciary: The Calcutta High Court is the seat of judiciary. The present chief justice is V.S. Sirpurkar.

Districts:

District	Area (sq. km)	Population	Headquarters	Urban Agglomerations
Bankura	6,882.0	3,191,822	Bankura	
Bardhaman	7,024.0	6,919,698	Bardhaman	Asansol, Kalna, Katwa
Birbhum	4,545.0	3,012,546	Suri	
Cooch Behar	3,387.0	2,478,280	Cooch Behar	Dinhata, Cooch Behar
Darjeeling	3,149.0	1,605,900	Darjeeling	Darjeeling
East Midnapore	NA	NA	NA	NA
Hooghly	3,149.0	5,040,047	Chinsurah	Kolkata
Howrah	1,467.0	4,274,010	Howrah	Kolkata
Jalpaiguri	6,227.0	3,403,204	Jalpaiguri	Alipurduar
Kolkata	185.0	4,580,544	Kolkata	Kolkata

Malda	3,733.0	3,290,160	English Bazar	English Bazar
Murshidabad	5,324.0	5,863,717	Behrampore	Behrampore
Nadia	3,927.0	4,603,756	Krishnanagar	Birnagar, Chakdaha, Kolkata, Krishnanagar, Nabadwip, Ranaghat
North Twenty Four Parganas	4,094.0	8,930,295	Barasat	Gobardanga, Habra, Kolkata
North Dinajpur	3,140.0	2,478,280	Raiganj	Raiganj
Purulia	6,259.0	2,535,233	Purulia	
South Twenty Four Parganas	9,960.0	6,909,015	Alipur	Kolkata
South Dinajpur	2,219.0	1,502,647	Balurghat	Balurghat, Jaynagar-Mazilpur
West Midnapore	NA	NA	NA	NA

National Capital Territory

The approval of the Union Cabinet to grant statehood to Delhi has sparked off a fresh debate in political circles. Here are some essential facts about the National Capital Territory.

Delhi

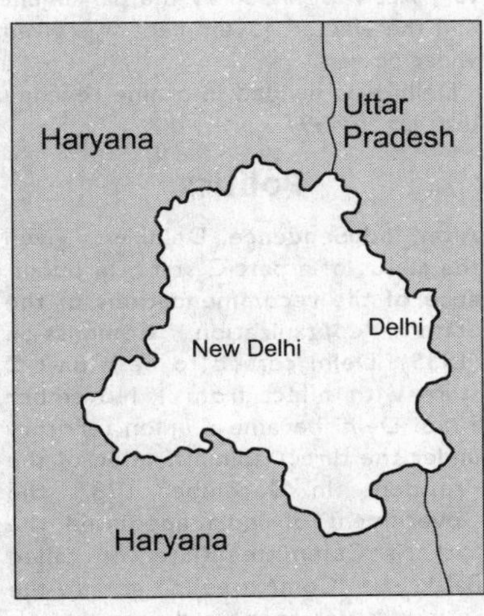

Key Statistics

Capital: Delhi.
Area: 1483 sq. km.
Population: Total: 13,850,507, Male: 7,607,234, Female: 6,243,273.
Population density: 9294 per sq. km.
Sex ratio: 821 females per 1000 males
Principal languages: Hindi, Punjabi, Urdu.
Literacy rates: Total: 81.7%, Male: 87.3%, Female: 74.7%.

Government

Lt Governor: Banwari Lal Joshi. He was sworn in as Lt Governor on 9 June 2004.

Chief Minister: Sheila Dikshit (INC). She was sworn in on 15 December 2003.

Geography

Physical characteristics: Delhi, the National Capital Territory of India, is divided into two zones: the extension of the Aravali Hills and the plains. Altitudes vary between 200 to 300 metres.

Neighbouring States and Union territories:

States: Haryana, Uttar Pradesh

Major rivers: Yamuna.

Climate: Delhi witnesses hot summers characterized by extreme dryness, with maximum temperatures going up to 46°C. Cold waves from the north make winters in Delhi very chilly, with minimum temperatures of around 4°C. Winters also witness thick fog on some mornings. Rainfall varies between 400–600mm.

Flora and Fauna:

Flora: Forest and tree cover constitutes about 151 sq. km of the area. The Ridge, with trees like dhak and amaltas, is classified as a tropical thorn forest. Delhi is also known for numerous flowering plants, mainly chrysanthemums, verbenas, violas, and phlox.

Fauna: The Indira Priyadarshini Wildlife Sanctuary at Asola is the main habitat for most animal species. These include nilgai, common mongoose, small Indian civet, porcupine, rufus tailed hare and monitor lizards. There's also a variety of birds including cormorants, egrets, grebes, falcons, partridges, quail, peafowl, waterhens, lapwings, sandpipers, woodpeckers, doves, parakeets, cuckoos, owls, nightjars, barbets, swallows, shrikes, orioles, drongos, mynahs, flycatchers, warblers, babblers, wagtails, pipits and buntings.

History

The earliest historical reference to Delhi date back to the first century BC, when Raja Dhilu built a city near the site of present-day Qutab Minar and named it after himself. Around AD 12, the city became the capital of Prithviraj Chauhan and passed into Muslim rule by the end of that century. It became the capital of Qutab-ud-din Aibak. The city was then ruled by the Khaljis followed by the Tughluqs. Babur established Mughal rule in India in 1526 with Delhi as the seat of his empire.

Mughal emperors Akbar and Jahangir moved their headquarters to Fatehpur Sikri and Agra respectively, but the city was restored to its former glory in 1638, when Shah Jahan laid the foundations of Shahjahanabad, which is now known as Old Delhi.

After the fall of the Mughal empire during the mid-eighteenth century, Delhi faced many raids by the Marathas and an invasion by Nadir Shah before the British rise to prominence in 1803. In 1912, the British moved the capital of British India from Calcutta to Delhi.

After Independence, Delhi remained a chief commissioner's province till 1956, when it was converted into a Union territory. The chief commissioner was replaced by a lieutenant governor.

In 1991, the National Capital Territory Act was passed by the parliament and the elected government was given wider powers.

Delhi was divided into nine revenue districts in 1997.

Politics

After Independence, Delhi was given the status of a part-C state. In pursuance of the recommendations of the State Reorganization Commission (1955), Delhi ceased to be a part-C state with effect from 1 November 1956. Delhi became a union territory under the direct administration of the President. In December 1987, the Government of India appointed the Sarkaria Committee (later on called Balakrishan Committee) to go into the various issues connected with the administration of the union territory of Delhi and to recommend measures for streamlining the administrative set-up. The committee submitted its report on

14 December 1989. After detailed enquiries and examinations, it recommended that Delhi should continue to be a union territory but should be provided with a Legislative Assembly and a Council of Ministers. The committee also recommended that with a view to ensuring stability and permanence, the arrangements should be incorporated in the Constitution to give the national capital a special status among the union territories. Delhi was granted a special statehood and an elected Legislative Assembly in 1991 under the 69th Constitutional amendment. Delhi is headed by a lieutenant governor nominated by the President of India and is administered by a chief minister appointed from the elected party.

In 1993, the BJP wrested the state from the Congress in a big way securing forty-nine of the seventy seats while Congress got just fourteen. The veteran BJP leader Madanlal Khurana became the chief minister. Sahib Singh Verma replaced him after a few years following intense infighting. Finally, just months before the 1998 polls, the high profile union minister Sushma Swaraj was brought in as the chief minister. The ruling BJP led by Sushma Swaraj was routed in the polls bagging just fifteen seats while the Congress walked away with fifty-two seats. The credit for the Congress victory went to its Delhi chief Sheila Dikshit, who became the chief minister. In the Assembly elections held in 2003 the Congress emerged victorious again and Sheila Dikshit remained chief minister of the National Capital Territory of Delhi.

Culture

Migrations from various parts of India has led to pockets of diverse culture coming together in Delhi. Many of the country's prominent cultural institutions are located in Delhi. Popular handicrafts include zari zardozi, stone carving, paper craft and papier mâchè, and metal engraving.

Fairs and festivals: Major festivals and fairs include Holi, Dussehra, Lohri, Deepawali, Qutub festival, Phoolwalon Ki Sair, Roshnara and Shalimar Bagh festivals, and Mango festival.

Economy, Industry and Agriculture

Economy: The net state domestic product at current prices in 2003–04 (provisional) was Rs 77,186 crores. The per capita state domestic product at current prices in 2003–04 (provisional) was Rs 51,664.

Minerals and industry: Delhi is the largest centre of small industries in India. These manufacture a wide variety of goods like plastic and PVC goods, sports goods, radio and TV parts, razor blades, textiles, chemicals, fertilizers, soft drinks, and hand and machine tools. The new industrial policy focuses on areas like electronics, telecommunications, software and IT-enabled services.

Agriculture: The main crops are wheat, jawar, bajra and paddy. Vegetable cultivation, floriculture and mushroom cultivation are also important activities. The main livestock products are milk, eggs and meat.

Power: Delhi's own resources amount to an installed capacity of about 1000 MW, all of which come from thermal power plants. The balance of the power demand, which exceeds 3000 MW, is met by purchases from NTPC and other sources.

Education

Educational institutes: All India Institute of Medical Sciences, University of Delhi, Indian Agricultural Research Institute, Indian Institute of Technology, Delhi, Indira Gandhi National Open University, Jamia Millia Islamia, Jawaharlal Nehru University, School of Planning and Architecture, Shri Lal Bahadur

Shastri Rashtriya Sanskrit Vidyapeetha, TERI School of Advanced Study and Indian Institute of Foreign Trade.

Tourism

Major tourist attractions: Red Fort, Purana Qila, Qutab Minar (World Heritage Site), India Gate, Bahai's House Of Worship, Rashtrapati Bhavan, Rajghat, Humayun's Tomb (World Heritage Site), Parliament House, Jama Masjid, Jantar Mantar, Firoz Shah Kotla, Safdurjung's Tomb, Dilli Haat, Mughal Gardens, Lodi Gardens, National Museum.

Airports:
International: Indira Gandhi International Airport.
Domestic: Palam Airport, Safdarjung Airport.

National Parks: None.

Administration

Legislature: Two acts passed by the Parliament have been instrumental in providing for a legislative assembly for Delhi and supplementing the provisions relating to it: the Constitution (69th Amendment) Act, 1991; and the Government of National Capital Territory of Delhi Act, 1991.

The Delhi Legislative Assembly has seventy members, all chosen by direct election from as many constituencies, of which thirteen are reserved for SCs. The term of the present house ends on 17 December 2008. Party position in the present assembly is as follows:

Name of Party	Seats
Indian National Congress	47
Bharatiya Janata Party	20
Nationalist Congress Party	1
Janata Dal (Secular)	1
Independent	1
Total	**70**

Judiciary: The Delhi High Court was established in 1966. The present chief justice is B.C. Patel.

Districts:

District	Area (sq. km)	Population
Central Delhi	25	644,005
East Delhi	64	1,448,770
New Delhi	35	171,806
North Delhi	60	779,788
North-east Delhi	60	1,763,712
North-west Delhi	440	2,847,395
South Delhi	250	2,258,367
South-west Delhi	420	1,749,492
West Delhi	129	2,119,641

Union Territories

There are six Union territories in India and only one—Pondicherry—has an Assembly.

Andaman and Nicobar Islands

Key Statistics

Capital: Port Blair.
Area: 8,249 sq. km.
Population: Total: 356,152, Male: 192,972, Female: 163,180.
Population density: 43 per sq. km.
Sex ratio: 846 females per 1000 males.
Principal languages: Bengali, Tamil, Hindi.
Literacy rates: Total: 81.3%, Male: 86.3%, Female: 75.2%.

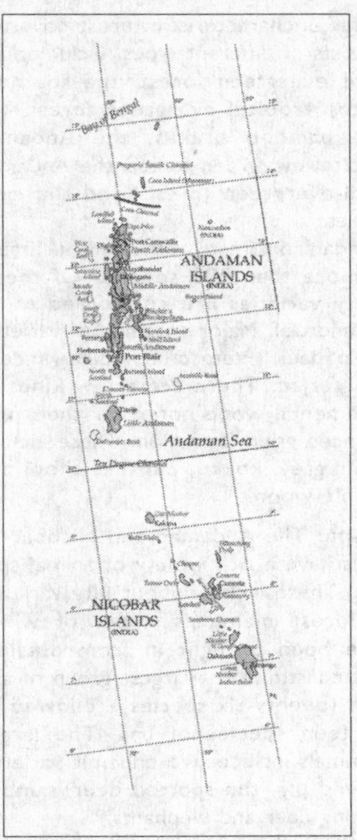

Government

Lieutenant Governor: The acting lieutenant governor is Madan Mohan Lakhera.

Geography

Physical characteristics: The Andaman and Nicobar Islands lie along an arc in a long broken chain, approximately north–south over a distance of about 800km.

The Andamans are a group of more than 300 islands and islets, of which only twenty-six are inhabited. The three main islands, namely North, Middle and South Andaman, are collectively known as Great Andaman, since they are closely positioned. The Andaman Islands have a rough landscape, with hills enclosing its longitudinal, narrow valleys. The islands are covered by dense tropical forests. The deeply indented coral-fringed coasts form tidal creeks and harbours, which are surrounded by mangrove swamps. Saddle Peak (737m) is the highest in the Andaman Islands. About 135 km from Port Blair is Barren Island, India's only active volcano.

The Nicobar Islands consist of a group of islands, of which twelve are inhabited and seven are uninhabited. The uninhabited islands in the central and southern group are Battimaly, Tileangchong and Merore, Trak, Treis, Menchal and Kabna respectively. Inhabited islands include Kamorta and Nancowry, which form the central group; Car Nicobar, which belongs to the northern group; and Great Nicobar, the largest and the southernmost of all. Undulating landscapes and intervening valleys characterize the physiography of these islands. However, Car Nicobar and Trinket are flat islands.

The Great Nicobar is hilly, and contains many fast-flowing streams. A few of the other islands have flat surfaces covered with coral. Great Nicobar rises to a height of 642m. It is isolated from the Nicobars and the Nancowries group by the Sombero channel.

The Ten Degree Channel (145 km wide) separates the Andamans from the Nicobars. The principal harbours in Andaman and Nicobar are Port Blair, Neil, Diglipur, Mayabandar and Rangat in the Andamans and Car Nicobar and Kamorta in the Nicobars. The Union Territory has a total of 572 islands and islets. To the extreme south of the Nicobars is Indira Point, the southernmost point of India.

Neighbouring States and Union territories: The Andaman and Nicobar Islands have no neighbouring states or union territories. They lie on the south-eastern margins of the Bay of Bengal. Port Blair is connected to Kolkata and Chennai by air as well as by sea routes.

Major rivers: Alexendra, Dagmar and Galathea rivers (Great Nicobar) and Kalpong (North Andaman) are the perennial freshwater rivers in these islands.

Climate: The Andaman and Nicobar Islands enjoy warm, moist and tropical climate. The abundant rainfall and the presence of the sea prevent the islands from experiencing extremes of heat, though the amount of rainfall may vary from island to island. Humidity is high, and varies from 66 per cent to 85 per cent. The temperature ranges from 18°C to 34°C. The islands receive an average annual rainfall of about 3,000mm from south-west and north-east monsoons, extending over a period of about eight months.

A reporting station was set up at Port Blair in 1868, in order to provide accurate meteorological data for shipping in the Bay of Bengal.

Flora and Fauna:

Flora: The Andaman and Nicobar Isalnds are covered with evergreen tropical rainforests containing some 2,200 varieties of plants. Out of these, 200 are endemic and 1,300 cannot be found in mainland India. North Andamans have wet evergreen forests that contain plenty of woody climbers. South Andaman forests have a luxuriant growth of orchids, ferns and other epiphytic vegetation, while the Middle Andamans mostly contain deciduous forests.

Evergreen forests are absent in north Nicobar, including Battimaly and Car Nicobar, but form the dominant vegetation in central and southern Nicobar. Grasslands, not found in the Andamans, are present in the Nicobar group, whereas deciduous forests common in Andamans, can hardly be found in the Nicobars.

This uncharacteristic forest coverage consists of different types, including the giant evergreen forest, the southern hilltop tropical evergreen forest, the wet bamboo brakes, the Andaman tropical evergreen forest, the Andaman semi-evergreen forests and the cane brakes.

Andaman forest is abundant in timber of more than 200 species. Of these, thirty varieties are considered to be commercial. Major commercial varieties are padauk (*Pterocarpus dalbergioides*), and gurjan. There are a few kinds of ornamental wood noted for their pronounced grain formation. These include silver grey, kokko, padauk, chooi and marble wood.

Fauna: The Andaman and Nicobar Islands have a rich variety of animal species. These include about fifty varieties of forest mammals, most of which have been brought in from outside. Rats constitute the largest group of animals (twenty-six species), followed by fourteen species of bat. The larger mammals include two endemic varieties of wild pig, the spotted deer, sambar, barking deer and elephants.

Other than mammals, there are more than 225 species of moths and butterflies in the Andaman and Nicobar islands. Shells, corals and fishes are also found in abundance.

History

The Andaman and Nicobar islands have been the home of aboriginals since prehistoric times. According to a British Survey conducted here in 1777, Negritos and Mongoloids occupied the Islands for many centuries, till people from outside arrived.

The history of these islands can be divided into four broad periods: British intrusion and settlement, the Japanese regime, and the post-independence period. In 1788, the governor-general of India, Lord Cornwallis, according to the recommendation of two of his navy officers, founded the British settlement in 1789 on Chatham Island near Port Cornwallis (which is now Port Blair, named after Lt Reginald Blair who conducted a survey of the area in 1789).

After the Revolt of 1857, the British government wanted to establish a penal settlement here, which they did in 1858. Two hundred prisoners, mostly rebels from the Indian Army, were kept in a jail at Viper island, which had a jail, gallows, and areas for residence. This jail was later abandoned in favour of the Cellular Jail built at Port Blair in 1906.

During the Second World War, the Japanese occupied Andamans on 21 March 1942 and kept the region under their control till 1945. Many innocent people were killed by the Japanese, including the massacre at Humfreygunj. The Japanese occupation however made the Andamans self-sufficient, in terms of food production. On 30 December 1943, Subhash Chandra Bose hoisted the National Flag at Port Blair, making it the first instance during British rule in India. The Japanese finally surrendered to the South East Asia Command at Port Blair on 8 October 1945.

The Andaman and Nicobar Islands together with the rest of India became independent on 15 August 1947.

Culture

Two distinct native cultures dominate the Andaman and Nicobar Islands. One is that of the Negrito population, and the other is of the Mongoloid Nicobarese and Shompen. Both before and after Independence, these cultures retained their separate identities.

The Onges of Negrito origin form the main aboriginal group in the Andamans. Their main occupations include honey collecting, fishing and food gathering and hunting. They are the only tribe who accept contact with people from outside the islands. Till 1998, the Jarwas remained hostile but now they voluntarily seek medical assistance.

In the Nicobars, the Shompens are the only aboriginals. They are averse to contact with people from outside the island. The largest group, the Nicobarese are probably a mixture of Malay, Mon, Shan and Burmese origins. They still engage in the barter system.

Fairs and Festivals: The noteworthy fairs and festivals in these islands include the Island Tourism Festival, Subhash Mela (organized to commemorate the birth anniversary of Subhash Chandra Bose) and Vivekananda Mela. Festivals like Panguni Uthiram and Pongal for the Tamils, Durga Puja for the Bengalis, and Onam for the Malayalis are also celebrated.

Economy, Agriculture and Industry

Economy: The net state domestic product at current prices for 2002–03 was Rs 1,040 crores. The per capita net state domestic product at current prices for 2002–03 was Rs 28,340.

Minerals and industry: The main industry is fisheries which, the Union territory occupying a coastline of 1912 km, has potential for further development. More than 1,100 species of fish are identified in these islands of which about thirty species are commercially exploited at present. The estimated annual exploited stock is around 1.6 lakh tonnes, while the level of exploitation is only 26,000 tonnes. Fish culture, fish processing and other industries like fish meal, fish pickling, and fish oil are encouraged.

Another important industry is tourism, with the islands coming up as major tourist attractions. This also generates large employment. The other industries include production of cane, bamboo, coir, coconut and rubber. Industries like boat building, automobile-body building, electronics and packaging are also coming up. The mineral wealth is negligible.

Agriculture: Paddy is the main food crop of the Andaman Islands. About 50,000 hectares of land is cultivated. Areca nut and coconut are the main cash crops of the Nicobar group of islands. Fruits such as sapota, pineapple, mango, papaya, orange and root crops are also grown in these islands. Coffee, rubber and tapioca are also important. About 7,171 sq. km of the total area is under forest cover.

Power: Presently, diesel power generation meets the requirements of commercial and household establishments in the territory.

Education

Educational institutes: The Andaman and Nicobar Islands has a few colleges affiliated to the Pondicherry University, and two polytechnics—the Dr B.R. Ambedkar Government Polytechnic at Port Blair, and the Second Government Polytechnic at Port Blair.

Tourism

Major tourist attractions:

1. Andaman: Long Island, Neil Island, Mayabander, Rangat, Diglipur, Little Andaman Island, Cellular Jail, Sippighat Farm, National Memorial Museum, Ross Island, Andaman Water Sports Complex.

2. Nicobar: Car Nicobar, Katchal, Great Nicobar. Scuba-diving and snorkelling are added attractions here.

Airports: Port Blair, Car Nicobar.

National Parks:

Andaman district: Mahatma Gandhi Marine National Park (281.50 sq. km), Rani Jhansi Marine National Park (256.14 sq. km), Middle Button Island National Park (0.64 sq. km), Mount Harriet National Park (0.46 sq. km), North Button Island National Park (0.44 sq. km), Saddle Peak National Park (32.54 sq. km), South Button Island National Park (0.03 sq. km).

Nicobar district: Campbell Bay National Park (426.23 sq. km), Galathea National Park (110.00 sq. km).

Administration

Legislature: The territory is administered by a lieutenant governor, appointed by the President of India.

Judiciary: The Union territory of Andaman and Nicobar Islands is under the jurisdiction of the Calcutta High Court. The chief justice of the Calcutta High Court is V.S. Sirpurkar.

Districts:

District	Area (sq. km)	Population	Headquarters	Urban Agglomerations
Andaman	6,408	314,239	Port Blair	–
Nicobar	1,841	42,026	Car Nicobar	–

Chandigarh

Key Statistics

Capital: Chandigarh.
Area: 114 sq. km.
Population: Total: 900,635, Male: 506,938, Female: 393,697.
Population density: 7,902 per sq. km.
Sex ratio: 777 females per 1000 males.
Principal languages: Hindi, Punjabi, Tamil.
Literacy rates: Total: 81.9%, Male: 86.1%, Female: 76.5%.

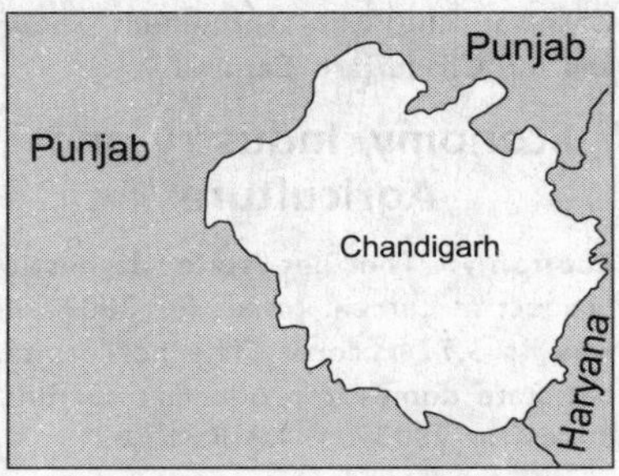

Government

Administrator: Gen. (Retd) S.F. Rodrigues. He was sworn in on 16 November 2004.

Geography

Physical characteristics: Situated at the foot of the Shivalik range, Chandigarh lies on the Indo-Gangetic plain. The Union territory is positioned between two seasonal hill torrents: the Patiali Rao and the Sukhna Choe.

The city of Chandigarh (area 56 sq. km) covers about half of the land area of the territory. It has the distinction of being the first planned city of independent India. The city, built in forty-seven rectangular sectors, has a modern infrastructure. No sector was given the unlucky number '13'. Every sector consists of shopping centres and marketplaces, and the sectors are interconnected by buses and auto-rickshaws. Most of the important government buildings are in Sector 1, in the northern part of the city, whereas the industrial areas are mainly located in the south-east.

Neighbouring States and Union territories:

States: Haryana, Punjab.

Major rivers: There are no major rivers.

Climate: Chandigarh has hot summers and cold winters. During summer, the maximum temperature goes up to 44°C, the temperature range being 37°C–44°C. In winter, the temperature is generally within 4°C–14°C. Chandigarh sees monsoon from July to September, with an average annual rainfall of 1110mm.

Flora and Fauna: The Union territory of Chandigarh has 3,245 hectares under forest area. These forest areas are mostly situated around Patiala ki Rao, Sukhna Choe and Sukhna Lake. On the outskirts of Chandigarh towards the hills, next to the village of Kansal, is a reserve forest. Another reserve forest, known as Nepli, is located at a short distance from Kansal forest, and has a variety of wild life including hyena, antelopes, jackals, nilgais, and hares.

History

After India attained independence in 1947, the province of Punjab was divided and its capital Lahore fell within the Pakistani borders. As a result, the Indian state of Punjab was left without a capital and the need to construct a new capital city was felt. In March 1948, a 114.59 sq. km tract of land at the foot of the Shivalik Hills was approved for the purpose. The chosen site was a tract of agricultural land marking the sites of twenty-four villages—one of which was called Chandigarh since it had a temple dedicated to the goddess Chandi. The chosen site got its name from that village.

American town planner Albert Mayer was initially approached by the government of Punjab to create the new capital. Though he showed a lot of initial interest and also conceived a master plan for the city, he could not continue with the project due to the death of Matthew Nowicki, an architect who was involved with Mayer in the execution of the plan. In 1950, renowned French architect Le Corbusier was selected to replace Mayer, which he successfully did, giving India its first 'planned' city. Other than Corbusier, the work was carried out by three other foreign architects—Maxwell Fry, his wife Jane Drew and Corbusier's cousin Pierre Jeanneret.

On 21 September 1953, the capital of Punjab was officially shifted to Chandigarh from Shimla, and President Dr Rajendra Prasad inaugurated the city on 7 October 1953. When Punjab was again divided in 1966, leading to the creation of Haryana, Chandigarh became the capital of both Punjab and Haryana. However, the city became a Union territory, administered by the Government of India, and Mani Majra town and some villages of Kharar tehsil of Ambala district were added to the city.

Culture

The city of Chandigarh has a cosmopolitan character. It is home to many painters and writers, and houses frequently held exhibitions and performances by musicians, dancers, singers and actors. The city also has many associations and halls devoted to the culture of other states. Numerous institutions in the city offer instruction in classical, folk and instrumental music. Chandigarh also has several noted potters, sculptors, photographers and graphic designers. Street theatre is quite popular in Chandigarh, and there are many active groups in the realm of theatre.

Fairs and festivals: Other than the traditional religious festivals, Chandigarh celebrates several unique festivals. The Festival of Gardens (initially called the Rose Festival) is one of the main cultural events in Chandigarh and attracts thousands of visitors. On April Fools' Day, poets from all over the country gather to take part in the 'Maha Moorkh Sammelan'. The other popular festivals are Baisakhi, the Mango Festival, Indo-Pak Mushaira, Teej, the Plaza Carnival, the Chrysanthemum Show and the Chandigarh Carnival.

Economy, Industry and Agriculture

Economy: The net state domestic product at current prices for 2003–04 was Rs 5,774 crores. The per capita net state domestic product at current prices for 2003–04 was Rs 57,621.

Minerals and industry: Chandigarh has about fifteen medium and large-scale industrial units. These units mainly manufacture steel and wooden furniture, antibiotics, electric metres, electronic components and equipment, machine tools, soaps and detergents, biomedical equipment, tractor parts, cement pipes and tiles, washing machines, sports goods, plastic goods etc. These units employ close to 30,000 people. There are also about twenty major exporting units. The mineral wealth is negligible.

Agriculture: The agricultural produce in Chandigarh includes crops like wheat, maize and rice. Fruits like lemon, litchi, mango, orange, guava, pear, plum, grape and peach are also cultivated.

Power: In order to meet its power requirement, Chandigarh gets power from Central generation projects and neighbouring states.

Education

Educational institutes: Punjab University, Post-graduate Institute of Medical Education and Research, The Government Medical College , Punjab Engineering College, Chandigarh College of Architecture, The Government College of Art, Chandigarh College of Engineering and Polytechnic (The Central Polytechnic College). The Government Polytechnic for Women, Industrial Training Institute, The Government Central Crafts Institute for Women and the Food Craft Institute.

Tourism

Major tourist attractions: Government Museum and Art Gallery, Museum of the Evolution of Life, International Dolls Museum, Punjab Kala Kendra, The Rock Garden, Sukhna Lake, Zakir Rose Garden, Leisure Valley.

Airports: Chandigarh.

National Parks: There are no national parks. The Sukhna Lake Wildlife Sanctuary was established in 1986 and has an area of 25.42 sq. km.

Administration

Legislature: Chandigarh has no legislature; instead, it is administered by an administrator appointed by the President of India (under the provisions of Article 239 of the Constitution). The parliament is directly responsible for legislating for Chandigarh, and administrative control of the Union territory rests with the Union ministry of home affairs. Regarding policy matters concerning Chandigarh, the ministry receives advice from a committee constituted by the Union home minister.

Judiciary: The High Court of Punjab and Haryana is at Chandigarh. The chief justice is D.K. Jain.

Districts:

District	Area (sq. km)	Population	Headquarters	Urban Agglomerations
Chandigarh	114	900,635	Chandigarh	Chandigarh

Dadra and Nagar Haveli

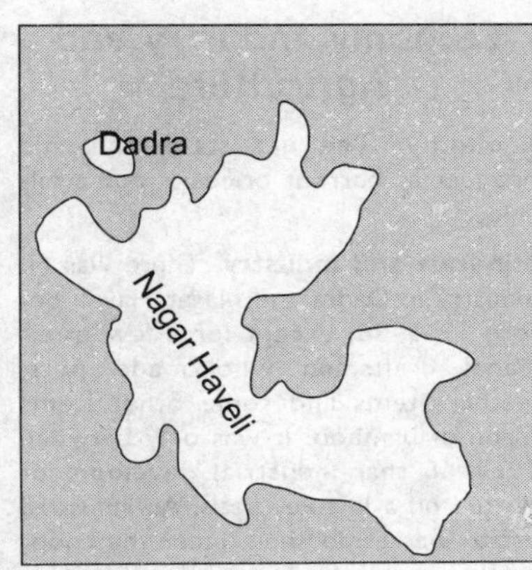

Key Statistics

Capital: Silvassa.
Area: 491 sq. km.
Population: Total: 220,490, Male: 121,666, Female: 98,824.
Population density: 449 per sq. km.
Sex ratio: 812 females per 1000 males.
Principal languages: Gujarati, Hindi, Konkani.
Literacy rates: Total: 57.6%, Male: 71.2%, Female: 40.2%.

Government

Administrator: Rajani Kant Verma.

Geography

Physical characteristics: Reaching elevations of about 305m in the northeast and east near the Western Ghats, the territory of Dadra and Nagar Haveli is hilly and undulating. The lowland areas are generally restricted to the central plains.

Neighbouring States and Union territories:
States: Maharashtra, Gujarat.

Union territories: Daman and Diu.

Major rivers: The Damanganga is the only navigable river in Dadra and Nagar Haveli. It flows through the territory towards Daman in the north-west.

Climate: From November to March, the climate is very pleasant in Dadra and Nagar Haveli. The region otherwise experiences hot summers with the average maximum temperature in May approaching 34°C. Most of the rainfall takes place between June and September, averaging about 3,000mm annually.

Flora and Fauna:

Flora: Around 40 per cent of the total geographical area spread over fifty-eight villages is covered with forests. Teak, khair, sisam, sadra and mahara constitute the main vegetation of the territory, of which teak and khair are the most predominant. Teak is the main source of timber, whereas a forest-based industry producing 'katha' from khair wood helps the local economy.

History

The recorded history of Dadra and Nagar Haveli starts from the medieval period. A Rajput invader became the ruler of a small state called Ramnagar (which included Nagar Haveli in its territory) in AD 1262, by defeating the Koli chieftains of the area. The region continued to remain under Rajput rule till the mid-eighteenth century, when it was conquered by the Marathas. In 1783, Nagar Haveli was ceded to the Portuguese, as compensation for a Portuguese vessel that the Maratha navy had destroyed. In 1785, Dadra was also acquired by the Portuguese. After the independence of India, Goan nationalists tried to break away from Portuguese control, and their first success was the possession of Dadra on 21 July 1954. Two weeks later, they also captured Nagar Haveli, and a pro-Indian administration was formed in Dadra and Nagar Haveli. On 1 June 1961, the administration requested accession to the Indian Union, and the government of India that had already acknowledged their induction to the union from the day of liberation, made it official on 11 August 1961.

Culture

The Dhol dance (incorporating aerobatics and rhythm), the Gheria dance of the Dubla tribe, the Mask dance or Bhavada, the Bohada mask dance performed by the Koknas and the human pyramid formations by the Tur dancers are some of the prominent dance forms.

Fairs and festivals: The Union territory of Dadra and Nagar Haveli normally celebrates all festivals of Hindus, Muslims and Christians, while the tribal communities celebrate their own festivals. The Dhodia and Varli tribes celebrate Diwaso, while the Dhodia tribe also celebrates Raksha Bandhan. The 'Gram Devi' and 'Khali Puja' are celebrated by all tribes before and after harvest respectively.

Economy, Industry and Agriculture

Economy: The net state domestic product at current prices is not available.

Minerals and industry: There was no industry in Dadra and Nagar Haveli before 1965–66, except for a few traditional craftsmen who made pots, leather items and some other items made of bamboo. It was only between 1967–68 that industrial development started on a low-key basis. An industrial estate was established under the cooperative sector by Dan Udyog Sahakari Sangh Ltd, after which three Government Industrial Estates were developed at Masat, Silvassa and Khadoli. As on March 2003, there were 1617 industries in the region including cottage, village and small scale industries, and 406 medium scale industries in engineering, textiles, electronics, pharmaceuticals and plastics.

Agriculture: Dadra and Nagar Haveli is mainly rural, with 79 per cent of its population consisting of tribals. There are about 22,850 hectares of area under cultivation. Paddy, small millets, pulses and ragi are the main crops, and the agricultural production is mainly dependent on rain, and mostly on a single crop system. Other than the main crops, additional crops like wheat, jowar, tuvr, sugar cane and oilseeds are also cultivated. Among vegetables, cauliflower, brinjal, tomato, and cabbage are grown. The tribals have been given exclusive rights for collection of minor forest produce for free, since they depend mainly on forests.

Power: The Central sector power generating stations located in the western region handle the power requirement of the territory.

Education

Educational institutes: Lions English School, Prabhat Scholar's Academy.

Tourism

Major tourist attractions: Khanvel; The Tribal Cultural Museum, Silvassa; Vanganga Lake.

Airports: None.

National Parks: There are no National Parks in Dadra and Nagar Haveli, and there is only one wildlife sanctuary—the Dadra and Nagar Haveli Wildlife Sanctuary. It has an area of 92.16 sq. km and is located in the Dadra and Nagar Haveli district.

Administration

Legislature: An administrator, appointed by the Government of India, heads the Union territory.

Judiciary: Dadra and Nagar Haveli comes under the jurisdiction of the Bombay High Court. The chief justice of the Bombay High Court is Dalveer Bhandari.

Districts: There is only one district, which is Dadra and Nagar Haveli.

District	Area (sq. km)	Population	Headquarters	Urban Agglomerations
Dadra and Nagar Haveli	491	220,490	Silvassa	–

Daman and Diu

Key Statistics

Capital: Daman.
Area: 112 sq. km.
Population: Total: 158,204, Male: 92,512, Female: 65,692
Population density: 1411 per sq. km.
Sex ratio: 710 females per 1000 males.
Principal languages: Gujarati, Hindi, Marathi.
Literacy rates: Total: 78.2%, Male: 86.8%, Female: 65.6%.

Government

Administrator: Arun Mathur.

Geography

Physical characteristics: Daman is situated on an alluvial coastal plain, even though headlands and low pla-

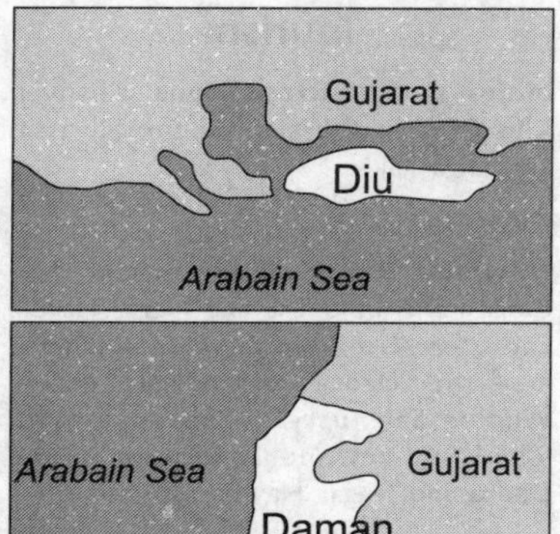

teaus are created in the area due to outcrops of basalt. The area surrounding the town of Daman is traversed by the river Damanganga which flows through the territory. A marshy creek separates the island of Diu from the Kathiawar peninsula in Gujarat, though the territory of Diu also encompasses a small part of the mainland. The island is about 11 km long and 2 km wide.

Neighbouring States and Union territories:
States: Gujarat, Maharashtra.

Union territories: Dadra and Nagar Haveli.

Major rivers: Damanganga, Kalai and Kolak.

Climate: In Daman, the average daily maximum temperatures range from 29°C in January to 34°C in May, which is quite similar to that of Diu. However, Daman receives more rainfall than Diu; it averages 2,000mm annually in Daman whereas Diu has an annual rainfall of about 585mm. The rainfall is mainly received between the months of June and September.

Flora and Fauna:
Flora: The flora of the island mainly consists of vegetation ranging from fuliflora, tortolis, acasias, palm trees (locally referred to as hokka), casuarina, equistifolia, procofis, and several groves of coconut palms.

Fauna: The island has different varieties of birds, including koels, doves, blue rock pigeons, parrots, crows and sparrows, making it a bird watchers' delight. A large number of migratory birds fly into the island from August and stay on until February, which constitutes a major attraction. The inland and the coastal waters are rich in fishes, especially hilsa, Bombay duck, shark, dara, prawns, and the popular pomfret.

History

The town of Daman possibly gets its name from the Damanganga river, whereas Diu is derived from the Sanskrit word dvipa, which means island. Daman, in the thirteenth century, formed part of the state of Ramnagar, which then became a tributary of the sultans of Gujarat. Diu was taken over by the sultan of Gujarat in the fifteenth century, which until then had been ruled over by many dynasties of Kathiawar (Saurashtra). Both Daman and Diu were acquired by the Portuguese in order to control the trade of the Indian Ocean. The Portuguese in 1535 signed a treaty with Bahadur Shah of Gujarat in order to build a fort at Diu. Towards the middle of the 1550s, all Gujarati ships entering and leaving the Gulf of Khambhat (Cambay) ports were required to pay Portuguese duties at Diu. Daman was renowned for its shipbuilding yards and docks, and was conquered by the Portuguese in 1559. Daman and Diu were subject to the governor-general of Goa as part of the Portuguese province Estado da India (state of India). The Portugese ruled them for more than four centuries, and they remained as outposts of Portuguese overseas territory until December 1961, when 'Operation Vijay' was launched by India restoring Daman and Diu to India to make them an integral part of the country. It initially became part of the erstwhile Union territory of Goa, Daman and Diu, but became a separate Union territory once statehood was given to Goa on 30 May 1987.

Culture

Dance and music are a part of the daily life of the people of Daman. Different Portuguese dances are still widely prevalent and performed, and they reflect the distinct fusion of tribal, urban, European and Indian cultures.

Fairs and festivals: Some of the important festivals in Daman and Diu are Holi, Diwali, Bhai Duj, Raksha Bandhan, Id-ul-Fitr, Navratri, Moharram, Id-ul-Zuha, Carnival, Feast of St. Francis Xavier, Good Friday and Easter.

Economy, Industry and Agriculture

Economy: The net state domestic product at current prices is not available.

Minerals and industry: Daman and Diu has 2,707 small and medium-scale industries. Omnibus Industrial Development Corporation at Daman has developed two industrial areas. The other industrial areas are Kadaiya, Bhimpore, Kanchigam and Dabhel.

Agriculture: The important crops of Daman include rice, ragi (finger millet), beans and pulses (legumes); however, Diu only has 20 per cent of cultivated land area, and crops such as wheat and bajra (pearl millet) are more suited to the dry climate.

Power: The Central sector power stations in the western region have granted power allocation to the Union territory of Daman and Diu, with which all villages have been electrified.

Education

Educational institute: Daman Government Arts College.

Tourism

Major tourist attractions: Fort of Moti Daman, Jampore Beach, Kadaiya Lake Garden.

Airports: Daman, Diu.

National Parks: Though there are no National Parks here, it has a wildlife sanctuary—Fudam Wildlife Sanctuary (area 2.18 sq. km in Diu).

Administration

Legislature: Daman and Diu does not have a legislative assembly. They are each organized as administrative districts and the Government of India appoints an administrator to govern these districts.

Judiciary: The Union Territory of Daman and Diu is under the jurisdiction of the Bombay High Court. The chief justice is Dalveer Bhandari.

Districts:

District	Area (sq. km)	Population	Headquarters	Urban Agglomerations
Daman	72	113,949	Daman	–
Diu	40	44,110	Diu	–

Lakshadweep

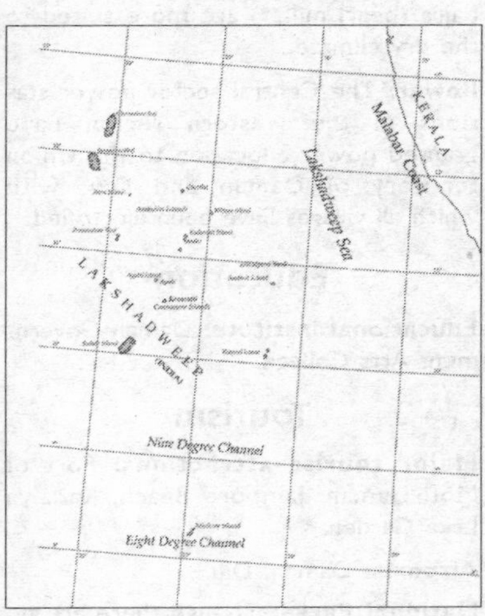

Key Statistics

Capital: Kavaratti.
Area: 32 sq. km.
Population: Total: 60,650, Male: 31,131, Female: 29,519.
Population density: 1,894 per sq. km.
Sex ratio: 948 females per 1000 males.
Principal languages: Malayalam, Tamil, Hindi.
Literacy rates: Total: 86.7%, Male: 92.5%, Female: 80.5%.

Government

Administrator: Parimal Rai. He assumed charge on 22 November 2004.

Geography

Physical characteristics: Lakshadweep is an archipelago of twelve atolls, three reefs and five submerged banks. It lies scattered over 45,000 sq. km of the Indian Ocean. There are twenty-seven coral islands—India's only coral islands. In all, there are ten inhabited islands, seventeen uninhabited islands with attached islets, four newly formed islets and five submerged reefs. The easternmost island lies about 300 km off the western coast of Kerala. Lakshadweep has a lagoon area of about 4,200 sq. km and territorial waters of 20,000 sq. km. Only ten of the islands are inhabited. The ten inhabited islands are Andrott, Amini, Agatti, Bitra, Chetlat, Kadmath, Kalpeni, Kavaratti, Kiltan and Minicoy. Bitra is the smallest of all, with a nominal population. The main islands are Kavaratti, Minicoy and Amini.

The Amindivis are the northernmost islands of the group and Minicoy Island the southernmost. The eastern sides of the islands are higher and hence more suitable for human habitation. The low-lying lagoons on the western sides protect the islanders from the south-west monsoon. None of the islands exceed 1.5 km in width. They have sandy soils, derived from corals.

Neighbouring States and Union territories: None. The Union Territory lies in the Indian Ocean with no land borders. However, Kerala is the closest state. Kochi in Kerala is the usual point of origin for scheduled ships and aircraft travelling to the state.

Major rivers: There are no major rivers.

Climate: Lakshadweep has a tropical climate. Summer temperatures range between 22°C and 35°C while winter temperature varies between 20°C and 32°C. The monsoon season is between October and November. Normal rainfall is around 1,600mm in the Minicoy group of islands and 1,500mm in the Amindivi group of islands.

Flora and Fauna:

Flora: Coconut is the only crop of economic importance in the Union territory. Different varieties of coconut found in Lakshadweep include Laccadive micro, Laccadive ordinary and green dwarf. Banana, vazha, breadfruit, chakka, colocassia, chambu, drumstick moringakkai and wild almond grow extensively in Lakshadweep. It is also home to shrub jungle plants like kanni, chavok, punna and cheerani. Two different varieties of sea grass are seen adjacent to the beaches. These prevent sea erosion and movement of the beach sediments.

Fauna: The seas around Lakshadweep are rich in marine life. Sharks, tuna, flying fish, devil ray, bonito, octopus, sail fish, turtles, sea cucumber and snapper are found here. Colourful coral fish such as butterfly fish, parrotfish and surgeonfish are also found in plenty. Oceanic birds are also found in Lakshadweep. These include tharathasi and karifetu. Other species of birds found in Lakshadweep include seagull, tern, teal, heron and water heron. Money cowry is widely found in the shallow lagoons and reefs. The hermit crab is commonly found.

History

It is commonly believed that Cheraman Perumal, the last king of Kerala, set up the first settlement on what is today Lakshadweep, after he was shipwrecked. However, there are historical records to show that a Muslim saint named Ubaidullah was shipwrecked around the seventh century and it was he who converted the inhabitants to Islam.

Control over the islands remained with the Hindu ruler of Chirakkal for some years, after which it passed on to the Muslim rulers of Arakkal, in Cannanore, around the middle of the sixteenth century. The oppressive nature of the Arakkal rule resulted in the islanders seeking refuge with Tipu Sultan in 1783. Tipu Sultan was on friendly terms with the Beebi of Arakkal and the Amini islands passed into his control. After Tipu Sultan's defeat at the battle of Seringapattam in 1799, the British East India Company annexed the islands and administered them from Mangalore.

In 1847, a severe cyclone hit the island of Andrott. When the raja of Chirakkal found it difficult to pay for the damages, the East India Company granted a loan. The raja was however unable to repay the loan or the mounting interest and in 1854 all the remaining islands were handed over to the British, who administered the islands till India became independent in 1947. Till 1956, the islands were a part of the erstwhile Madras state. On 1 November 1956, the islands became a Union territory of the Indian Union. The headquarters of the administration was shifted from Kozhikode/Calicut in Kerala to Kavaratti Island in March 1964. Between 1956 and 1973, the territory was called Laccadive, Minicoy, and Amindivi Islands. In 1973, it was renamed Lakshadweep.

Culture

Most of the people on Lakshadweep are Muslims with a small number of Hindus. The commonly spoken languages include Mahl, similar to old Sinhalese. The Hindu society is characterized by the matrilineal system of kinship and a rigid caste system. The folklore and customs are largely derived from the sea. Kiltan Island has a rich tradition of folk dances, namely kolkali and parichakali. Other dance forms of the Union territory include Lava dance, Ulakamut, Bhandiya, Kottuvili, Oppana, Duff and Attam. Opana is a well-known form of music performed at marriages. The Union territory is noted for carpentry and woodcarving. A variety of handicrafts are also made out of material like tortoise-shell, coconut shell, coconut fibre and corals. However, picking of corals from their natural habitat is a punishable offence.

Fairs and festivals: Id-ul-Fitr, Bakrid, Muharram, Id-e-Milad-un-Nabi and Dussehra are important festivals of Lakshadweep.

Economy, Industry and Agriculture

Economy: Figures not available.

Minerals and industry: The two most important industries of the state revolve around the coconut plant and fishes. Extraction of coconut fibre and its conversion into fibre products is a main industry of Lakshadweep. There are many fibre factories, coir production-cum-demonstration centres and fibre curling units in different islands. Fishing is the other important industrial activity. The huge potential that Lakshadweep possesses in fishing has resulted in the setting up of boat-building yards, fish-processing factories and the adoption of mechanized fishing boats. Tourism is also a major industry. Two handicaraft training centres were established at Kavaratti and Kalpeni in 1973 and 1979 respectively. A hosiery factory was established in 1967 at Kalpeni.

Agriculture: Agriculture is the most important component of the economy of Lakshadweep. The key products are coconut and coir. Coconut is the Union territory's only major crop.

Power: Lakshadweep gets most of its power supply from diesel generating sets. There are a few solar power plants while wind power plants are also planned for the Union territory.

Education

There are no universities or major institutes of higher education in the Union territory.

Tourism

Major tourist attractions: Lighthouse, Minicoy; Ujra Mosque, Kavaratti; Hazrat Ubaidullah, Andrott; Buddhist archaeological remains, Andrott; Water Sport Institute, Kadmat.

Airports: Agatti.

National Parks: None.

Administration

Legislature: The President of India appoints an administrator to govern the territory.

Judiciary: Lakshadweep is under the jurisdiction of the High Court of Kerala. The acting chief justice is K.S. Radhakrishnan.

Districts:

District	Area (sq. km)	Population	Headquarters	Urban Agglomerations
Lakshadweep	32	60,650	Kavaratti	–

Pondicherry

Key Statistics

Capital: Pondicherry.
Area: 492 sq. km.
Population: Total: 974,345, Male: 486,961, Female: 487,384.
Population density: 2029 per sq. km.
Sex ratio: 1001 females per 1000 males.
Principal languages: Tamil, Malayalam, Telugu.
Literacy rates: Total: 81.2%, Male: 88.6%, Female: 73.9%.

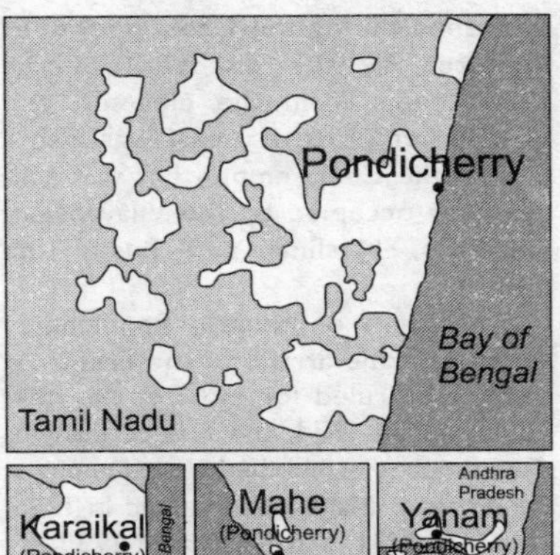

Government

Lieutenant Governor: Lt. Gen. (Retd) M.M. Lakhera was sworn in on 3 June 2004.

Chief Minister: Thiru N. Rangasamy. He was sworn in on 27 October 2001.

Geography

Physical characteristics: The Union territory of Pondicherry has four constituent parts: Pondicherry, Karaikal, Mahe and Yanam. Podicherry and Karaikal are bordering Tamil Nadu, Mahe is situated on the Malabar Coast surrounded by the state of Kerala and Yanam is surrounded by the East Godavari district of Andhra Pradesh.

A canal divides the town of Pondicherry into two parts. The main streets run parallel to one another. The port of Pondicherry does not have a harbour and ships are anchored at some distance offshore. The Pondicherry area has about 300 villages.

Karaikal lies on Coromandel Coast, about 300km south of Chennai, at a distance of about 135km from Pondicherry town. It is located near the mouth of the river Arasalar, in the Kaveri delta. The Nagappattinam and Thiruvarur districts of Tamil Nadu surround Karaikal.

Mahe consists of two parts. The town of Mahe lies on the left bank of the river Mahe near its mouth while the area called Naluthrara is on the right bank and consists of the villages of Chambara, Chalakara, Palour, and Pandaquel. Mahe town is situated 647km away from Pondicherry town, between Badagara and Thalassery.

The town of Yanam lies at the spot where the river Koringa (Atreya) branches off from Gauthami into two parts, about 870km from Pondicherry town.

Neighbouring States and Union territories:

1. Karaikal
   States: Tamil Nadu.
2. Mahe
   States: Kerala.
3. Pondicherry
   States: Tamil Nadu.
4. Yanam
   States: Andhra Pradesh.

Major rivers: Arasalar (Karaikal), Mahe (Mahe), Koringa and Gauthami (Yanam).

Climate: Pondicherry has a hot and humid climate for most of the year. Temperature varies between 26°C and 38°C. It is mostly dry. The short monsoon season is between July and September. The months of May and June can be very humid. The summer is between March and July, when temperatures can touch 40°C and higher, mainly in May and June. On the west coast (Mahe), the monsoon season lasts between July and October. The winter usually starts in November, but sometime in mid-October, which is also when the north-east monsoon brings some rainfall. Temperatures remain in the region of 30°C.

Flora and Fauna:

Flora: The flora of Pondicherry can be listed under seven categories. These are: hydrophytes (aquatic plants), halophytes (plants that grow in salty soil), plants on sand dunes, plants on sandstones, avenue trees, hedge plants and ornamental plants.

Hydrophytes or aquatic plants found in Pondicherry include the lotus, akasathamarai and vetiver. Halophytes found here include muttaikkorai, sattaranai, thakkali, thumbai, kanavalai, mayil kondai pul, karisalankanni, tutti and gilugilupai. Plants on sand dunes occurring in Pondicherry include woody plants like casuarina and eucalyptus. They grow along the sea coast. This category of plants also includes some herbs. The vegetative landscape of Pondicherry comprises mostly tall palms.

Pondicherry also possesses a limited variety of mangrove species, mainly in the estuaries and the riverine sides of Ariyankuppam river and Malattar. A mangrove patch is also present in Thengaithittu and Murthikuppam.

Another striking feature of the flora of Pondicherry is the sacred groves. Pondicherry does not have natural forest cover. However, there are patches of sacred groves. These may be termed as natural islands of vegetation that are maintained and preserved for centuries for a religious purpose. Such groves are usually looked after by the local communities. The distribution of species varies from grove to grove. Pondicherry is also home to some tropical dry evergreen species and some medicinal plants.

Fauna: The marine biodiversity of the Union territory include mackerel, shrimps, sardines, perches, ribbonfish and flying fish.

History

Remains of an ancient port town have been excavated at Arikamedu, 6 km from Pondicherry town. There are evidences here to suggest that it had trade connections with Rome and Greece around the period between 100 BC and AD 100. Pondicherry flourished during the Chola period, as indicated by the discovery of the Chola coins from the eleventh and twelfth centuries. Karaikal was also a part of the Chola empire but was successively occupied by the Vijayanagar, Marathas, Muslims and finally the French.

The history of modern Pondicherry starts with the arrival of the French in 1673, who ruled for most of the next 281 years. In 1674, the French East India Company established a settlement at Pondicherry. Mahe was founded in 1725, Yanam in 1731, and Karaikal in 1739.

Mahe was the site of prolonged conflict between the British and French troops in the eighteenth and nineteenth centuries. In 1726, the French captured the town. Later however, it was added several times to the British Madras Presidency. It was finally restored to the French in 1817.

Yanam was also a part of the Chola empire but came under Muslim occupation in the sixteenth century. In the seventeenth and eighteenth centuries it was the scene of conflict between Muslim, British, and French troops. When much of the coastal plain region that includes Yanam was incorporated into the Madras Presidency in 1765, Yanam remained a French enclave.

At the time of Independence in 1947, the French restored Pondicherry, Mahe, Karaikal and Yanam to the Union of India. De facto transfer of these four French possessions to the Union of India took place on 1 November 1954 while de jure transfer took place on 28 May 1956. The instruments of ratification were signed on 16 August 1962.

Politics

With India becoming independent in August 1947, the citizens of French India hoisted the Indian national flag all over the French settlements. The Jaipur session of the Indian National

Congress passed a resolution for the peaceful merger of Pondicherry with India. The Indo-French agreement of June 1948 was signed and the French gave freedom to the French Indian population to choose their political status by a referendum. While Chandannagar (another French colony) merged with India on the basis of referendum, Pondicherry could not enjoy that facility because of a different system and practice of elections. As per the understanding reached between the Government of India and France, the question of the merger of Pondicherry with the Indian Union was referred to the elected representatives of the people for decision in a secret ballot on 18 October 1954. 170 out of 178 elected representatives favoured the merger. This was the de facto transfer of power, which took place on 1 November 1954, while the de jure transfer took place on 16 August 1962. As the people aspired for a popular government, the parliament enacted the Government of Union Territories Act, 1963 which came into force on 1 July 1963, and the pattern of government prevailing in the rest of the country was introduced in Pondicherry, subject to certain limitations. The Congress has consistently won the elections in Pondicherry ever since the former French enclave became a part of the Indian Union. In the twelve elections held between 1962 and 1999, the Congress won nine times, the All India Anna Dravida Munnetra Kazhagam (AIADMK) twice and the DMK once.

Culture

There is a strong French influence in Pondicherry even today. Pondicherry was home to the famous poets, Subramania Bharathi and Bharathidasan. Pondicherry is also famous for the Aurobindo Ashram and Auroville. Pondicherry is well known for its handmade paper, the use of dried flowers on stationery items, aromatic candles and candles with pressed-in dried flowers. Incense sticks made at the ashram and in Auroville are also famous.

Fairs and festivals: Festivals of Pondicherry are unique in the sense that the French influence still remains in its festivals and celebrations. The mask festival, Masquerade, is held in March–April. During this festival, the inhabitants wear costumes and masks and dance down the streets to accompanying music. On the eve of Bastille Day (14 July), retired soldiers parade in the streets singing the French and Indian national anthems. The Maasi Magam Festival is celebrated during the full moon period around mid-March. In Yanam, Vishnu Festival is celebrated in March. In March–April (first week after Easter), the Villianur Lourdes Festival is held. The Chitrai Kalai Vizha summer festival is held in April. The Villianur Temple Car Festival is usually celebrated around the middle of May but its exact date depends on the appearance of the full moon. During the Mangani Festival Karaikal experiences a month-long period of festivity that accompanies a feast dedicated to Karaikal Ammaiyar. The Virampattinam Car Festival takes place in August while the Fete de Pondicherry coincides with the Indian Independence Day. Other festivals celebrated in the Union territory are St. Theresa Festival in Mahe and Isai Vizha, both celebrated in October.

Economy, Industry and Agriculture

Economy: The net state domestic product at current prices (new series) in 2003–04 (provisional) was Rs 5,209 crores. The per capita state domestic product at current prices in 2003–04 (provisional) was Rs 50,936.

Minerals and industry: The significant industrial products of the Union territory include food products, cotton products, wood products, paper products, leather, rubber, plastic products, chemical and chemical products, non-metallic mineral products, metal products and machinery products. There are seven industrial estates in Pondicherry.

Agriculture: Around 35 per cent of the population is dependent on agriculture. Paddy is the most important crop in the territory, followed by pulses. Coconut, spices, condiments and areca nut are grown in Mahe while Yanam grows spices, chilli, pulses and groundnut.

Power: Pondicherry draws its power requirements from the southern grid. A gas-based power plant is being established at Karaikal.

Education

Educational institutes: Pondicherry University is at Pondicherry, Ecole Français d' Extrème Orient Institute for Indology, French Institute, Jawaharlal Institute of Post-graduate Medical Education and Research (JIPMER), Pondicherry Institute of Linguistics and Culture, Vinayaka Mission Medical College (Karaikal).

Tourism

Major tourist attractions:

1. Pondicherry: Auroville and Shri Aurobindo Ashram, Pondicherry Museum, botanical garden, Sri Gokilambal Thirukameswarar Temple, Mansion of Ananda Rangapillai, Eglise De Sacre Coeur De Jesus.

2. Karaikal: Lord Darbaraneswara Temple, Karaikal Ammaiyar Temple, Jadaayupureeswar Temple, Dargah of Mastan Syed Dawood, Our Lady Angel's Church.

3. Mahe: Tagore Park, St. Theresa's Church, Puthalam, Othenan's Fort, St George Fort, Sree Krishna Temple, Choodikotta.

4. Yanam: Annavaram, Draksharamam, Padagaya Temple.

Airports: None.

National Parks: None.

Administration

Legislature: Pondicherry has a thirty-seat legislative assembly of which five seats are reserved for SCs. The tenure of the current house expires on 8 June 2006. The present party position is as under:

Name of Party	Seats
Indian National Congress	10
Dravida Munnetra Khazagam	7
Pudhucherry Munnetra Congress	3
All India Anna Dravida Munnetra Khazagam	3
Communist Party of India	1
Pattali Makkal Katchi	2
Marumalarchi Dravida Munnetra Kazhagam	1
Independent	3
Total	**30**

Judiciary: Pondicherry falls under the jurisdiction of the Madras High Court. The chief justice is Thiru Markandey Katju.

Districts:

District	Area (sq. km)	Population	Headquarters	Urban Agglomerations
Karaikal	161.0	31,362	Karaikal	–
Mahe	9.0	36,823	Mahe	–
Pondicherry	290.0	735,004	Pondicherry	Pondicherry
Yanam	20.0	170,640	Yanam	–

States at a Glance

State	Capital	Governor	Chief Minister
Andhra Pradesh	Hyderabad	Rameshwar Thakur	Y.S. Rajasekhar Reddy
Arunachal Pradesh	Itanagar	S.K. Singh	Gegong Apang
Assam	Dispur	Lt Gen. (Retd) Ajai Singh	Tarun Gogoi
Bihar	Patna	Ramkrishnan Suryabhan Gavai	Nitish Kumar
Chhattisgarh	Raipur	Lt Gen (Retd) K.M. Seth	Raman Singh
Goa	Panaji	S.C. Jamir	Pratapsingh Rane
Gujarat	Gandhinagar	Nawal Krishna Sharma	Narendra Modi
Haryana	Chandigarh	A.R. Kidwai	Bhupinder Singh Hooda
Himachal Pradesh	Shimla	Vishnu Sadashiv Kokje	Virbhadra Singh
Jammu and Kashmir	Srinagar/Jammu	Lt Gen (Retd) S.K. Sinha	Ghulam Nabi Azad
Jharkhand	Ranchi	Syed Sibtey Razi	Arjun Munda
Karnataka	Bangalore	T.N. Chaturvedi	H.D. Kumaraswamy
Kerala	Thiruvananthapuram	R.L. Bhatia	V.S. Achuthanandan
Madhya Pradesh	Bhopal	Balram Jakhar	Shivraj Chouhan
Maharashtra	Mumbai	S.M. Krishna	Vilasrao Deshmukh
Manipur	Imphal	Shivinder Singh Sidhu	Okram Ibobi Singh
Meghalaya	Shillong	Mundakkal Matthew Jacob	J. Dringwell Rymbai
Mizoram	Aizawl	Amolak Rattan Kohli	Pu Zoramthanga
Nagaland	Kohima	Shyamal Datta	Neiphi-u Rio
Orissa	Bhubaneswar	Rameshwar Thakur	Naveen Patnaik
Punjab	Chandigarh	Gen (Retd) S.F. Rodrigues	Capt Amarinder Singh
Rajasthan	Jaipur	Pratibha Patil	Vasundhara Raje Scindia
Sikkim	Gangtok	V. Rama Rao	Pawan Kumar Chamling
Tamil Nadu	Chennai	Surjeet Singh Barnala	Kalaignar Muthuvel Karunanidhi

State	Capital	Governor	Chief Minister
Tripura	Agartala	Dinesh Nandan Sahaya	Manik Sarkar
Uttaranchal	Dehradun	Sudarshan Agarwal	N.D. Tiwari
Uttar Pradesh	Lucknow	T.V. Rajeswar	Mulayam Singh Yadav
West Bengal	Kolkata	Gopalkrishna Gandhi	Buddhadeb Bhattacharya
National Capital Territory		**Lt Governor**	**Chief Minister**
Delhi	Delhi	Banwari Lal Joshi	Sheila Dikshit
Union Territory		**Lt Governor/Administrator**	
Andaman and Nicobar	Port Blair	(acting Lt Governor) Lt Gen. (Retd) Madan Mohan Lakhera	
Chandigarh	Chandigarh	Gen. (Retd) S.F. Rodrigues	
Dadra and Nagar Haveli	Silvassa	Rajani Kant Verma	
Daman and Diu	Daman	Arun Mathur	
Lakshadweep	Kavaratti	Parimal Rai	
Pondicherry	Pondicherry	Lt Gen. (Retd) M.M. Lakhera	Thiru N. Rangasamy

The World

All the 192 countries that are members of the UN appear here in alphabetical order. There are detailed write-ups for the more significant countries, and all of India's neighbours, while the other nations appear in brief profiles. Historical, economic, political and demographic parameters of every country is part of this section. All dominions and dependencies appear under the respective countries.

Afghanistan

History

Alexander the Great used Afghanistan as the gateway to India in the fourth century BC. Islamic conquerors arrived in the seventh century AD, while Genghis Khan and Tamerlane reached in the thirteenth and fourteenth centuries.

Three Anglo-Afghan Wars were fought in the nineteenth and early twentieth centuries. In 1893, UK denoted the Durand Line as the unofficial boundary between British India and Afghanistan.

In 1919, Afghanistan became independent. In 1926 Emir Amanullah established the Afghan monarchy and proclaimed himself king. He tried to introduce social reforms in the country but this led to opposition from conservative sections of the country. In 1929, Amanullah fled the country after civil unrest erupted over his reforms.

In 1953, General Mohammed Daud became the new prime minister. He contacted the Soviet Union for economic and military assistance and also introduced social reforms that included the abolition of purdah. But in 1963, Prime Minister Daud was forced to resign. In 1964, constitutional monarchy was established in the country.

In 1973, Mohammed Daud seized power in a coup and declared Afghanistan a republic. In 1978, the leftist People's Democratic Party ousted and killed him. However, the party's Khalq and Parcham factions began fighting amongst themselves. This led to a purge or exile of almost all the Parcham leaders. Meanwhile, conservative Islamic and ethnic leaders who had earlier objected to social changes began an armed revolt.

In 1979, a power struggle between leftist leaders Hafizullah Amin and Nur Mohammed Taraki in Kabul resulted in victory for Amin. However revolts in the countryside continued and the Afghan army faced collapse. In December 1979, the Soviet Union sent in its troops to remove Amin from power. Amin was deposed and executed. Babrak Karmal, leader of the party's Parcham faction, was installed as ruler, backed by Soviet troops.

Before long, the Soviet invasion reached a dead end as the local mujahideens put up a fierce resistance. Although the invading force of about 100,000 Soviet troops controlled the cities, larger towns, and major garrisons, the mujahideens enjoyed relative freedom all over the countryside. Even the formidable Soviet war machine could not crush their uprising. Meanwhile, the USA provided money and sophisticated equipment to the Afghans and their allies in the region to fight the Soviets. But perhaps the greatest victims of the war were the millions of Afghans who were displaced in the war and became refugees in Pakistan and Iran. In 1988, USA, USSR, Pakistan, and Afghanistan signed an agreement that resulted in the complete withdrawal of Soviet troops in 1989.

In April 1992, Afghan rebel groups stormed Kabul and overthrew the communist president, Mohammad Najibullah. In 1993, the different mujahideen groups agreed on the formation of a government with the ethnic Tajik, Burhanuddin Rabbani, proclaimed president. However, factional rivalry continued through 1994. It was around this point of time that the Taliban, led by a former mujahideen commander named Mullah Mohammad Omar, emerged as a major challenge to the Rabbani government.

In 1996, the Taliban seized control of Kabul and introduced a strict puritan version of Islam. The new regime banned women from working outside their homes, introduced Islamic punishments that included stoning to death and amputations. Rabbani fled the capital to join the anti-Taliban Northern Alliance led by Ahmad Shah Masood. Soon, the Talibans extended their control over all parts of Afghanistan except for a small part that the Northern Alliance held. Soon after occupying Kabul, the Taliban dragged former President Najibullah and his brother from the UN compound and killed them.

In 1997, Pakistan and Saudi Arabia recognized the Taliban as the legitimate rulers of Afghanistan even though most other countries continued to recognize Rabbani as the head of state. Meanwhile, the USA launched missile strikes at suspected bases of al-Qaeda leader Osama bin Laden, who was hiding in Afghanistan. In 1999, the UN imposed financial sanctions and an air embargo to force Afghanistan to hand over Osama bin Laden for trial. The sanctions were toughened in 2001. In March 2001, the Taliban destroyed giant Buddha statues in Bamiyan even as international organizations tried to save them. In May, the Taliban authorities ordered members of religious minorities to wear tags identifying themselves as non-Muslims. It also asked Hindu women to veil themselves. In September, Northern Alliance leader Ahmad Shah Masood was killed while giving a press briefing.

In October 2001, soon after the 9/11 attacks, USA and UK launched air-strikes against Afghanistan when the Taliban refused to hand over Osama bin Laden. These air strikes were followed by ground attacks by US special operations forces allied with Northern Alliance fighters. These operations succeeded in driving the Taliban out of power by December. However, neither Mullah Mohammad Omar nor Osama bin Laden could be found.

On 5 December 2001, various Afghan groups meeting in the German city of Bonn agreed on an interim government pending general elections. On 22 December, Pashtun royalist Hamid Karzai was sworn in as head of a thirty-member interim power-sharing government.

In January 2002, the first contingent of foreign peacekeepers arrived in the country. In April, former Afghan king Zahir Shah returned but assured the country that he would not stake claim to the throne. In September, President Karzai escaped an assassination attempt in his hometown Kandahar.

In June 2003, fresh clashes erupted between Taliban fighters and government forces in Kandahar province. In August 2003, NATO assumed its first-ever operational commitment outside Europe when it took control of security in Kabul. In January 2004, the Loya Jirga (grand council) adopted a new constitution that contained a strong emphasis on presidential power. On 9 October 2004, Hamid Karzai became the first democratically elected president of Afghanistan. The National Assembly was inaugurated on 19 December 2005.

Geography

Location: Southern Asia, north and west of Pakistan, east of Iran.

Area: 647,500 sq. km.

Terrain: Mostly rugged mountains with plains in the north and south-west.

Natural resources: Natural gas, petroleum, coal, copper, chromite, talc, barites, sulphur, lead, zinc, iron ore, salt, precious and semiprecious stones.

Climate: The climate varies from arid to semi-arid. It has cold winters and hot summers.

People

Population: 31,056,997 (July 2006 est.).

Population growth rate: 2.67% (2006 est.).

Sex ratio: 1.05 male(s)/female (2006 est.).

Religions: Sunni Muslim 80%, Shi'a Muslim 19%, Others 1%.

Languages: Pashtu (official) 35%, Afghan Persian or Dari (official) 50%, Turkic languages (primarily Uzbek and Turkmen) 11%, 30 minor languages (primarily Balochi and Pashai) 4%, much bilingualism.

Literacy rate: Total 36%, Male 51%, Female 21% (1999 est.).

Infant mortality rate: 163.07 deaths/ 1,000 live births (2005 est).

Life expectancy: Total 42.9 years, Male 42.71 years, Female 43.1 years (2005 est.).

Government

Capital: Kabul.

Government type: Islamic republic.

Independence: 19 August 1919 (from UK control over Afghan foreign affairs).

Legal system: According to the Bonn Agreement, a judicial commission will rebuild the country's justice system in accordance with Islamic principles, international standards, the rule of law, and Afghan legal traditions. According to the new constitution, no law should be 'contrary to Islam'; the state is obliged to create a prosperous and progressive society based on social justice, protection of human dignity, protection of human rights, and realization of democracy, and to ensure national unity and equality among all ethnic groups and tribes; the state shall abide by the UN charter, international treaties, international conventions that Afghanistan signed, and the Universal Declaration of Human Rights.

Executive branch:

Chief of state: President of the Islamic Republic of Afghanistan, Hamid Karzai (since 7 December 2004). The president is both chief of state and head of government. Former King Zahir Shah holds the honorific 'Father of the Country', and presides symbolically over certain occasions, but lacks any governing authority. The honorific is not hereditary.

Economy

Currency: Afghani.

Economy—overview:
Afghanistan's economic outlook has improved significantly, since the fall of the Taliban regime in 2001, because of the infusion of over $4 billion in international assistance, recovery of the agricultural sector and growth of the service sector, and the reestablishment of market institutions. Real GDP growth is estimated to have slowed last fiscal year primarily because adverse weather conditions cut agricultural production, but is expected to rebound over 2005–06 because of foreign donor reconstruction and service sector growth. Despite the progress of the past few years, Afghanistan remains extremely poor, landlocked, and highly dependent on foreign aid, farming, and trade with neighbouring countries. It will probably take the remainder of the decade and continuing donor aid and attention to significantly raise Afghanistan's living standards from its current status, among the lowest in the world. Much of the population continues to suffer from shortages of housing, clean water, electricity, medical care, and jobs, but the Afghan government and international donors remain committed to improving access to these basic necessities by prioritizing infrastructure development, education, housing development, job programmes and economic reform over the next year. Growing political stability and continued international commitment to Afghan reconstruction is creating an optimistic outlook for continuing improvements in the Afghan economy in 2006. Expanding poppy cultivation and a growing opium trade may account for one-third of GDP and looms as one of Kabul's most serious policy challenges.

GDP: Purchasing power parity—$21.5 billion (2004 est.).

GDP—real growth rate: 8% (2005 est.).

GDP—per capita: Purchasing power parity—$800 (2004 est.).

Inflation rate: 16.3% (2005 est.).

Population below poverty line: 53% (2003).

Exports: $471 million (this figure does not include illicit exports) (2005 est.)—Fruits, nuts, carpets, wool, cotton, hides and pelts, precious and semi-precious gems.

Imports: $3.87 billion (2005 est.)—Capital goods, food, textiles, petroleum products.

External debt: $8 billion in bilateral debt plus $500 million in debt to multilateral development banks (2004).

Transport and Communications

Railways: 24.6 km.

Roads: 34,789 km.

Telephones: 33,100 (2002).

Mobile cellular: 15,000 (2002).

Internet users: 1,000 (2002).

Internet country code: .af

Albania

History

The Byzantine empire ruled Albania from 535 to 1204. Thereafter, the Ottoman Turks ruled the country for about 400 years.

In 1912, Albania became independent from the Ottoman empire. Italy invaded Albania just before World War II.

After World War II, Albanian Communist Party leader Enver Hoxha was installed as the country's leader. In 1948, the Soviet Union began supplying aid and assistance to Albania. In 1955, Albania was one of the founding members of the Warsaw Pact. However, in 1961, the Soviet Union broke off diplomatic ties with Albania over an ideological difference and Albania allied itself with China.

In 1967, Albania declared itself the world's first atheist state. In 1968, Albania withdrew from the Warsaw Pact over the invasion of Czechoslovakia.

Following the collapse of communist regimes all over eastern Europe in 1990, thousands of Albanians attempted to flee through Western embassies. They seized ships at Albanian ports and sailed illegally to Italy.

Geography

Location: South-eastern Europe, bordering the Adriatic Sea and Ionian Sea, between Greece and Serbia and Montenegro.

Area: 28,748 sq. km.

Terrain: Mostly mountains and hills; small plains along coast.

Natural resources: Petroleum, natural gas, coal, bauxite, chromite, copper, iron ore, nickel, salt, timber, hydropower.

Climate: Albania has a mild temperate climate with cool, cloudy, wet winters and hot, clear, dry summers. The interior is cooler and wetter.

People

Population: 3,581,655 (July 2006 est.).

Population growth rate: 0.52% (2006 est.).

Sex ratio: 1.04 male(s)/female (2006 est.).

Religions: Muslim 70%, Albanian Orthodox 20%, Roman Catholic 10%.

Languages: Albanian (official—Tosk is the official dialect), Greek.

Literacy rate: Total 86.5%, Male 93.3%, Female 79.5% (2003 est.).

Infant mortality rate: 21.52 deaths/1,000 live births (2005 est.).

Life expectancy: Total 77.24 years, Male 74.6 years, Female 80.15 years (2005 est.).

Government

Capital: Tirana.

Government type: Emerging democracy.

Independence: 28 November 1912 (from Ottoman Empire).

Legal system: Has a civil law system.

Executive branch:
Chief of state: President of the Republic Alfred Moisiu (since 24 July 2002).

Head of government: Prime Minister Sali Berisha (since 10 September 2005).

Economy

Currency: Lek.

Economy—overview
In the 2005 general elections, the Democratic Party and its allies won a decisive victory on pledges of reducing crime and corruption, promoting economic growth, and decreasing the size of government. Although Albania's economy continues to grow, the country is still one of the poorest in Europe, hampered by a large informal economy and an inadequate energy and transportation infrastructure. Albania has played a largely helpful role in managing inter-ethnic tensions in south-eastern Europe, and is continuing to work towards joining NATO and the EU.

GDP: Purchasing power parity—$18.05 billion (2005 est.). Note: Albania has a large grey economy that may be as large as 50 per cent of official GDP.

GDP—real growth rate: 5.5% (2005 est.).

GDP—per capita: Purchasing power parity—$4,900 (2005 est.).

Inflation rate: 2.5% (2005).

Population below poverty line: 25% (2004 est.).

Unemployment rate: 14.4% officially; may exceed 30% (2004 est.).

Exports: $708.8 million f.o.b. (2005 est.)—Textiles and footwear, asphalt, metals and metallic ores, crude oil, vegetables, fruits, tobacco.

Imports: $2.473 billion f.o.b. (2005 est.)—Machinery and equipment, foodstuff, textiles, chemicals.

External debt: $1.41 billion (2003).

Transport and Communications

Railways: 447 km.

Roads: 18,000 km.

Telephones: 255,000 (2003).

Mobile cellular: 1,100,000 (2003).

Internet users: 75,000 (2005).

Internet country code: .al

Algeria

History

Phoenicians settled in the coastal areas of Algeria in the first millennium BC. It later became a part of the Roman empire and then, in the sixteenth century, became a part of the Ottoman empire. In 1830, the French occupied Algeria and in 1848, it became a part of France. Around 250,000 people were killed in the Algerian War of Independence. Algeria gained independence in 1962.

The country witnessed serious rioting and demonstrations in the 1980s, due to the country's worsening economic condition. In 1991, the first ever parliamentary elections were held in Algeria and the fundamentalist Islamic party, the Front Islamique du Salut (FIS), emerged the largest party. The country's military leadership promptly

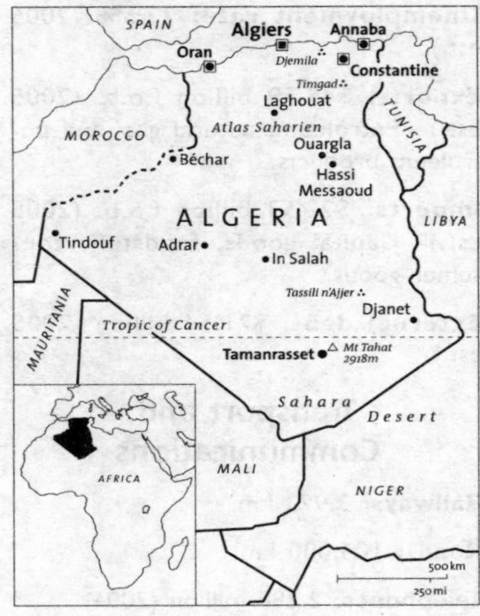

called off the general elections and a five-member Higher State Council, with Mohamed Boudiaf as the head, took control of the country. This plunged the country into a violent civil war. It has been estimated that nearly 100,000 people have been killed in the conflict that has been noted for its brutality and violence. In December 1991, the Islamic Salvation Front won the first round of the country's first multi-party elections. The military then cancelled the second round, forced the then-president Bendjedid to resign, and banned the Islamic Salvation Front. The ensuing conflict engulfed Algeria in the violent Algerian Civil War. More than 100,000 people were killed, often in unprovoked massacres of civilians. After 1998, the war waned, and by 2002 the main guerrilla groups had either been destroyed or surrendered, taking advantage of an amnesty programme, though sporadic fighting continued in some areas. Elections resumed in 1995, and in 1999, after a series of short-term leaders representing the military, Abdelaziz Bouteflika, the current president, was elected. The issue of Berber language and identity increased in significance, particularly after the extensive Kabyle protests of 2001 and the near-total boycott of local elections in Kabylie; the government responded with concessions including the naming of Tamazight (Berber) as a national language and teaching it in schools.

Geography

Location: Northern Africa, bordering the Mediterranean Sea, between Morocco and Tunisia.

Area: 2,381,740 sq. km.

Terrain: Mostly high plateau and desert; some mountains; narrow, discontinuous coastal plain.

Natural resources: Petroleum, natural gas, iron ore, phosphates, uranium, lead, zinc.

Climate: The climate of Algeria varies from arid to semi-arid. During the summers, a hot dust/sand-laden wind named sirocco blows over the region.

People

Population: 32,930,091 (July 2006 est.).

Population growth rate: 1.22% (2006 est.).

Sex ratio: 1.02 male(s)/female (2006 est.).

Religions: Sunni Muslim (state religion) 99%, Christian and Jewish 1%.

Languages: Tamazight (official), Arabic (official), French, Berber dialects.

Literacy rate: Total 70%, Male 78.8%, Female 61% (2003 est.).

Infant mortality rate: 29.87 deaths/1,000 live births (2006 est.).

Life expectancy: Total 3.26 years, Male 71.68 years, Female 74.92 years (2006 est.).

Government

Capital: Algiers.

Government type: Republic.

Independence: 5 July 1962 (from France).

Legal system: Socialist, based on French and Islamic law.

Executive branch:

Chief of state: President Abdelaziz Bouteflika (since 28 April 1999).

Head of government: Prime Minister Ahmed Ouyahia (since 9 May 2003).

Economy

Currency: Algerian dinar.

GDP: Purchasing power parity—$237 billion (2005 est.).

GDP—real growth rate: 7.1% (2005 est.).

GDP—per capita: Purchasing power parity—$7,300 (2005 est.).

Inflation rate: 4.7% (2005 est.).

Population below poverty line: 23% (1999 est.).

Unemployment rate: 22.5% (2005 est.).

Exports: $49.59 billion f.o.b. (2005 est.)—Petroleum, natural gas, and petroleum products.

Imports: $22.53 billion f.o.b. (2005 est.)—Capital goods, foodstuff, consumer goods.

External debt: $21.54 billion (2005 est.).

Transport and Communications

Railways: 3,973 km.

Roads: 104,000 km.

Telephones: 2.288 million (2004).

Mobile cellular: 4,682,700 (2004).

Inernet users: 4,682,700 (2004).

Internet country code: .dz

Andorra

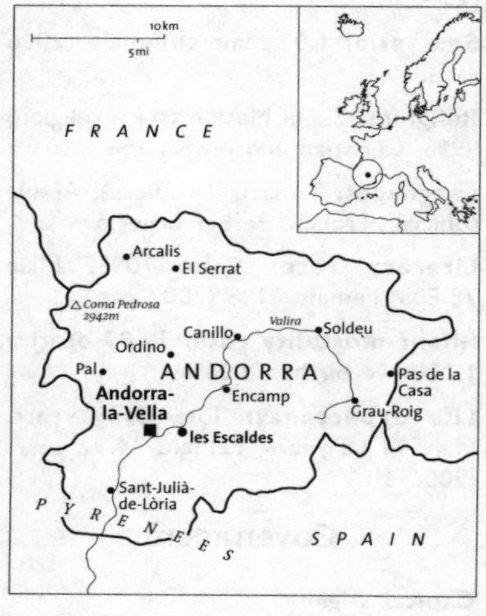

Geography

Location: South-western Europe, between France and Spain.

Area: 468 sq. km.

Natural resources: Hydropower, mineral water, timber, iron ore, lead.

Climate: Andorra has snowy, cold winters and warm, dry summers.

People

Population: 71,201 (July 2006 est.).

Population growth rate: 0.89% (2006 est.).

Sex ratio: 1.08 male(s)/female (2006 est.).

Religions: Roman Catholic (predominant).

Languages: Catalan (official), French, Castilian, Portuguese.

Literacy rate: 100%.

Infant mortality rate: 4.04 deaths/ 1,000 live births (2006 est.).

Life expectancy: Total 83.51 years, Male 80.61 years, Female 86.61 years (2006 est.).

Government

Capital: Andorra la Vella.

Government type: Parliamentary democracy (since March 1993) that retains as its chiefs of state a co-principality; the two princes are the President of France and the bishop of Seo de Urgel, Spain, who are represented locally by co-princes' representatives.

Independence: 1278 (was formed under the joint suzerainty of the French count of Foix and the Spanish bishop of Urgel).

Legal system: Based on French and Spanish civil codes.

Executive branch:
Chief of state: French co-prince Jacques Chirac (since 17 May 1995), represented by Philippe Massoni (since 26 July 2002); Spanish co-prince Bishop Joan Enric Vives i Sicilia (since 12 May 2003), represented by Nemesi Marquesi Oste.

Head of government: Executive Council President Albert Pintat Santolania (since 27 May 2005).

Economy

Currency: Euro.

GDP: Purchasing power parity—$1.84 billion (2004 est.).

GDP—real growth rate: 4% (2004 est.).

GDP—per capita: Purchasing power parity—$24,000 (2004 est.).

Inflation rate: 3.4% (2004).

Exports: $145 million f.o.b. (2004)—Tobacco products, furniture.

Imports: $1.077 billion (1998)—Consumer goods, food, electricity.

Transport and Communications

Roads: 269 km.

Telephones: 35,000 (2001).

Mobile cellular: 51,900 (2003).

Internet users: 11,000 (2003).

Internet country code: .ad

Angola

History

People speaking the Khoisan language are believed to have been the original inhabitants of the area that is today Angola. Bantu-speaking people migrated to this region in large numbers after 1000 and emerged as the dominant group.

The Portuguese first arrived in the region in the 1480s and the present-day capital city of Luanda was founded in 1575. Soon, it emerged as an important point on the European trade route with India and South-east Asia. It also acted as a key source of slaves for the Portuguese colony of Brazil.

It was in the 1950s that the nationalist movement developed in Angola and the guerrilla war started. The socialist guerrilla independence movement, the

Popular Liberation Movement of Angola (Movimento Popular de Libertacao de Angola, MPLA) originated in 1956 while the National Front for the Liberation of Angola (Frente Nacional de Libertacao de Angola, FNLA) was founded in 1957. Jonas Savimbi set up the National Union for the Total Independence of Angola (Uniao Nacional para a Independencia Total de Angola, UNITA) in 1966.

Angola gained independence in November 1975 when Portugal withdrew from the country without formally handing power to any one organization. A power struggle emerged between MPLA, backed by Cuba, and the FNLA–UNITA combine, backed by South Africa and the USA. The MPLA, which controlled Luanda, proclaimed itself as the government of independent Angola. On the other hand, UNITA and the FNLA set up a rival government in Huambo.

In 1994, the two warring factions signed a peace deal, the Lusaka Protocol peace accord. In 1996, Jose Eduardo dos Santos (MPLA) and Jonas Savimbi (UNITA) agreed to form a unified government; but the experiment did not work out.

In February 2002, Jonas Savimbi was killed by government troops. Following this, in April 2002, the Angolan government and UNITA signed a ceasefire agreement.

Angola, like many sub-Saharan nations, is subject to periodic outbreaks of infectious diseases. In April 2005, Angola was in the midst of an outbreak of the Marburg virus which was rapidly becoming the worst outbreak of a haemorrhagic fever in recorded history, with over 237 deaths recorded out of 261 reported cases, and having spread to seven out of the eighteen provinces as of 19 April 2005.

Geography

Location: Southern Africa, bordering the South Atlantic Ocean, between Namibia and the Democratic Republic of the Congo.

Area: 1,246,700 sq. km.

Terrain: Narrow coastal plain; rises abruptly to vast interior plateau.

Natural resources: Petroleum, diamonds, iron ore, phosphates, copper, feldspar, gold, bauxite, uranium.

Climate: The climate of Angola is semi-arid in the south and along the coast. The northern part of the country has a cool, dry season from May to October and a hot, rainy season from November to April.

People

Population: 12,127,071 (July 2006 est.).

Population growth rate: 2.45% (2006 est.).

Sex ratio: 1.02 male(s)/female (2006 est.).

Religions: Indigenous beliefs 47%, Roman Catholic 38%, Protestant 15% (1998 est.).

Languages: Portuguese (official), Bantu and other African languages.

Literacy rate: Total 42%, Male 56%, Female 28% (1998 est.).

Infant mortality rate: 185.36 deaths/ 1,000 live births (2006 est.).

Life expectancy: Total 38.62 years, Male 37.47 years, Female 39.83 years (2006 est.).

Government

Capital: Luanda.

Government type: Republic, multi-party democracy with a strong presidential system.

Independence: 11 November 1975 (from Portugal).

Legal system: Based on Portuguese civil law system and customary law; modified to accommodate political pluralism and increased use of free markets.

Executive branch:
Chief of state: President Jose Eduardo Dos Santos (since 21 September 1979). The president is both the chief of state and head of government.

Economy

Currency: Kwanza.

GDP: Purchasing power parity—$27.66 billion (2005 est.).

GDP—real growth rate: 14.1% (2005 est.).

GDP—per capita: Purchasing power parity—$2,500 (2005 est.).

Inflation rate (consumer prices): 17.7% (2005 est.).

Population below poverty line: 70% (2003 est.).

Unemployment rate: Extensive unemployment and underemployment affecting more than half the population (2001 est.).

Exports: $26.8 billion f.o.b. (2005 est.)—Crude oil, diamonds, refined petroleum products, gas, coffee, sisal, fish and fish products, timber, cotton.

Imports: $8.165 billion f.o.b. (2005 est.)—Machinery and electrical equipment, vehicles and spare parts; medicines, food, textiles, military goods.

External debt: $9.879 billion (2005 est.).

Transport and Communications

Railways: 2,761 km.

Roads: 51,429 km.

Telephones: 96,300 (2003).

Mobile cellular: 940,000 (2004).

Internet users: 172,000 (2005).

Internet country code: .ao

Antigua and Barbuda

History

English settlers colonized Antigua in 1632. Barbuda was first colonized in 1678. In 1958, Antigua and Barbuda, then part of the Leeward Islands territory, joined the West Indies Federation. In November 1981, Antigua and Barbuda attained full independence.

Geography

Location: Caribbean, islands between the Caribbean Sea and the North Atlantic Ocean, east-south-east of Puerto Rico.

Area: 443 sq. km (Antigua 280 sq. km, Barbuda 161 sq. km).

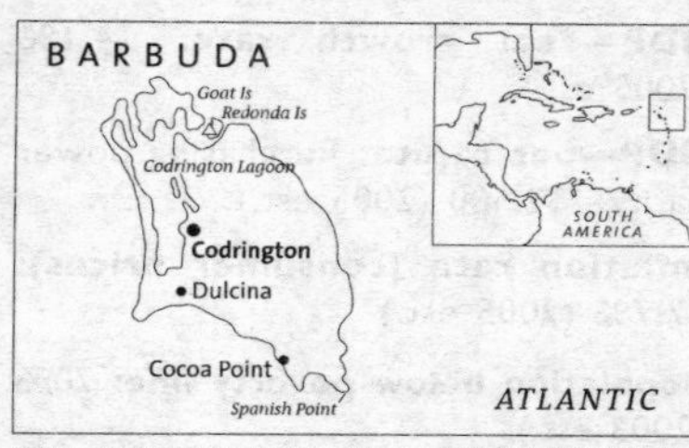

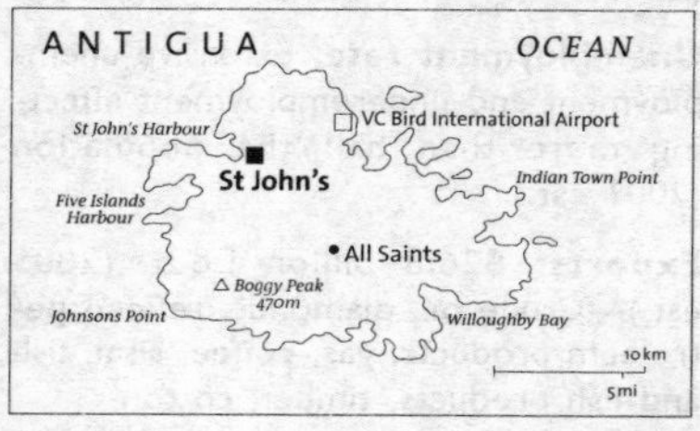

Natural resources: Negligible.

Climate: Antigua and Barbuda has a pleasant tropical climate.

People

Population: 69,108 (July 2006 est.).

Population growth rate: 0.55% (2006 est.).

Sex ratio: 1 male(s)/female (2006 est.).

Religions: Christian (predominantly Anglican with other Protestant, and some Roman Catholic).

Languages: English (official), local dialects.

Literacy rate: Total 85.8%, Male NA, Female NA (2003 est.).

Infant mortality rate: 18.86 deaths/1,000 live births (2006 est.).

Life expectancy: Total 72.16 years, Male 69.78 years, Female 74.66 years (2006 est.).

Government

Capital: Saint John's.

Government type: Constitutional monarchy with UK-style parliament.

Independence: 1 November 1981 (from UK).

Legal system: Based on English common law.

Executive branch:

Chief of state: Queen Elizabeth II (since 6 February 1952), represented by Governor General James B. Carlisle (since 1993).

Head of government: Baldwin Spencer (since 2004).

Economy

Currency: East Caribbean dollar.

GDP: Purchasing power parity—$750 million (2002 est.).

GDP—real growth rate: 3% (2002 est.).

GDP—per capita: Purchasing power parity—$11,000 (2002 est.).

Inflation rate: 0.4% (2000 est.).

Exports: $214 million (2004)—Petroleum products, manufactured products, machinery and transport equipment, food and live animals.

Imports: $735 million (2004 est.)—Food and live animals, machinery and transport equipment, manufactures, chemicals, oil.

External debt: $231 million (1999).

Transport and Communications

Railways: 77 km.

Roads: 1,165 km.

Telephones: 38,000 (2002).

Mobile cellular: 38,200 (2002).

Internet users: 10,000 (2002).

Internet country code: .ag

Argentina

History

Prior to the arrival of the Europeans, indigenous people inhabited the area that is today Argentina. The north-western part of the country was a part of the Inca empire.

In 1535, Spain sent an expedition led by Pedro de Mendoza to settle Argentina. Although Mendoza met with initial success and even founded Santa María del Buen Aire, which became Buenos Aires in 1536, lack of food doomed the expedition. In 1776, Spain created the viceroyalty of the Río de la Plata that consisted of modern-day Argentina, Uruguay, Paraguay, and southern Bolivia. Its capital was at Buenos Aires.

Between 1865 and 1870, Argentina, Brazil and Uruguay joined together to fight Latin America's bloodiest conflict, the War of the Triple Alliance, against Paraguay. It resulted in a humiliating defeat for Paraguay.

In 1881, Argentina and Chile agreed on their border along the Andes mountains. Subsequently, Argentina gained exclusive rights to the Atlantic Ocean coast while Chile obtained the Pacific Ocean waters.

Argentina declared itself a neutral nation at the outbreak of World War II. However, in 1943, a military regime came to power. One of its key leaders was Colonel Juan Peron. Subsequently, in 1944, Argentina severed diplomatic relations with Japan and Germany and declared war on them in 1945. In 1946, Peron was elected the country's new President. His second wife, Eva Duarte de Peron (popularly called Evita), was put in unofficial charge of the department of social welfare. She was responsible for generous wage increases to the workers that helped her obtain considerable support for her husband. Juan Peron was overthrown in 1955, returned to power in 1973, but died the following year. His third wife and vice-president, Isabel, succeeded him as Argentina's next President.

In 1975, Argentina's inflation touched 300 per cent. In 1976, a military junta led by General Jorge Videla seized power. The new regime dissolved the parliament and initiated the so-called 'Dirty War' in which thousands of opponents of the regime disappeared.

In 1981, General Leopoldo Galtieri became the new head of the military regime. In April 1982, Argentine forces occupied the British territory of Falkland Islands that lay off its coast. This sparked off the Falklands Islands War and UK regained possession of the islands in June 1982. Defeat in the war cost Galtieri his job and General Reynaldo Bignone replaced him.

Civilian rule returned to Argentina in 1983 with Raul Alfonsin as President. Inflation levels touched 900 per cent. In

1989, Carlos Menem was elected President. He introduced an economic austerity programme. However, this, along with the introduction of a new currency in 1992, could not prevent the economy from going into a recession in 1998. In November 2002, Argentina defaulted on an $800 million debt repayment to the World Bank, after it failed to re-secure IMF aid. In September 2003, Argentina and the IMF reached an arrangement whereby Argentina would only pay interest on its loans.

Geography

Location: Southern South America, bordering the South Atlantic Ocean, between Chile and Uruguay.

Area: 2,766,890 sq. km.

Terrain: Argentina has the plains of the Pampas in the northern half, the plateau of Patagonia in the south and the Andes mountains along the western border.

Natural resources: Lead, zinc, tin, copper, iron ore, manganese, petroleum, uranium, and the agricultural produce of the fertile plains of the Pampas.

Climate: The climate of Argentina is mostly temperate. However, the climate in the south-east is arid and in the south-west it is sub-antarctic.

People

Population: 39,921,833 (July 2006 est.).

Population growth rate: 0.96% (2006 est.).

Sex ratio: 0.97 male(s)/female (2006 est.).

Religions: Nominally Roman Catholic 92%, Protestant 2%, Jewish 2%, others 4%.

Languages: Spanish (official), English, Italian, German, French.

Literacy rate: Total 97.1%, Male 97.1%, Female 97.1% (2003 est.).

Infant mortality rate: 14.73 deaths/1,000 live births (2006 est.).

Life expectancy: Total 76.12 years, Male 72.38 years, Female 80.05 years (2006 est.).

Government

Capital: Buenos Aires.

Government type: Republic.

Independence: 9 July 1816 (from Spain).

Legal system: Mixture of US and west European legal systems.

Executive branch:

Chief of state: President Nestor Kirchner (since 25 May 2003). The president is both the chief of state and head of government.

Economy

Currency: Argentine peso.

Economy—overview:
Argentina is rich in natural resources, and has a diversified industrial base, a well-educated population and a well-developed export-oriented agricultural sector. In the last ten years, Argentina has suffered from chronic economic problems of high levels of external debt, runaway inflation, budget deficits and capital flight. The economic situation worsened in 2001 and government attempts at salvaging the economy proved inadequate. The peso's parity with the dollar was abandoned in January 2002, when the peso was devalued. The currency was subsequently floated in February that year. Soon after, the exchange rate plummeted and inflation rose sharply. The economy stabilized by mid-2002.

By 2003, a recovery was under way, and the International Monetary Fund agreed to a vital new loan. In 2005, the country restructured its massive debt, offering creditors new bonds for old, defaulted ones. But with poverty still rife, many Argentines still await the benefits of economic upturn.

GDP: Purchasing power parity—$537.2 billion (2005 est.).

GDP—real growth rate: 8.2% (2005 est.).

GDP—per capita: Purchasing power parity—$13,600 (2005 est.).

Inflation rate: 12.3% (2005 est.).

Population below poverty line: 38.5% (June 2005).

Unemployment rate: 11.1% (September 2005).

Exports: $40 billion f.o.b. (2005 est.)—Edible oils, fuels and energy, cereals, food, motor vehicles.

Imports: $28.8 billion f.o.b. (2005 est.)—Machinery and equipment, motor vehicles, chemicals, metal manufactures, plastics.

External debt: $119 billion (2005 est.).

Transport and Communications

Railways: 34,091 km.

Roads: 229,144 km.

Telephones: 8.7 million (2004).

Mobile cellular: 13,512,400 (2004).

Internet users: 4.1 million (2002).

Internet country code: .ar

Armenia

History

Armenia is one of the oldest civilizations in the world. It was the first country to officially adopt Christianity as its religion, around 300 AD.

The most notorious of the foreign powers to have ruled over Armenia were the Ottoman Turks. They massacred thousands of Armenians in 1894 and 1896 when they showed signs of growing nationalism. In 1915, in the middle of World War I, the Ottomans ordered the deportation of the Armenian population to the deserts of the Middle East. It is estimated that between 600,000 and 1.5 million Armenians were either murdered or died of starvation.

Following Turkish defeat in World War I, Armenia declared its independence in May 1918. However, the Soviet Army annexed the nation in 1920. In 1936, Armenia became a Soviet republic. Armenia declared its independence from a collapsing Soviet Union in September 1991.

Geography

Location: South-western Asia, east of Turkey.

Area: 29,800 sq. km.

Terrain: The Armenian Highland region is mountainous. There is little forestland but the rivers are fast-flowing.

Natural resources: Gold, copper, molybdenum, zinc, alumina.

Climate: Armenia has a highland climate with hot summers and cold winters.

People

Population: 2,976,372 (July 2006 est.).

Population growth rate: –0.19% (2006 est.).

Sex ratio: 0.9 male(s)/female (2006 est.).

Religions: Armenian Apostolic 94%, other Christian 4%, Yezidi (Zoroastrian/animist) 2%.

Languages: Armenian 96%, Russian 2%, others 2%.

Literacy rate: Total 98.6%, Male 99.4%, Female 98% (2003 est.).

Infant mortality rate: 22.47 deaths/1,000 live births (2005 est.).

Life expectancy: Total 71.84 years, Male 68.25 years, Female 76.02 years (2006 est.).

Government

Capital: Yerevan.

Government type: Republic.

Independence: 21 September 1991 (from the Soviet Union).

Legal system: Based on civil law system.

Executive branch:

Chief of state: President Robert Kocharian (since 30 March 1998).

Head of government: Prime Minister Andranik Markaryan (since 12 May 2000).

Economy

Economy—overview

Armenia had developed a modern industrial sector when it was a part of the Soviet Union. It used to exchange manufactured products and equipment for raw material. Since the collapse of the Soviet Union in 1991, Armenia has taken up small-scale agriculture, as against the large collective farms of the Soviet era. The process of privatization of industry has begun.

By May 1994, when a ceasefire took hold, Armenian forces held not only Nagorno-Karabakh but also a significant portion of Azerbaijan proper. The economies of both sides have been hurt by their inability to make substantial progress towards a peaceful resolution. Turkey imposed an economic blockade on Armenia and closed the common border because of the Armenian occupation of Nagorno-Karabakh and surrounding areas.

In 1994, the Armenian government launched an ambitious IMF-sponsored economic liberalization programme that resulted in positive growth rates in 1995–2005. Armenia joined the WTO in January 2003. The government made some improvements in tax and customs administration in 2005, but anti-corruption measures will be more difficult to implement. Investment in the construction and industrial sectors is expected to continue in 2006 and will help to ensure an annual average real GDP growth of about 7.5 per cent. In the 2006 Index of Economic Freedom, Armenia ranked twenty-seventh best, tied with Japan and ahead of countries like Norway, Spain, Portugal and Italy. However, Armenia ranked very low on property rights, worse than countries like Botswana, Trinidad and Tobago.

Currency: Dram.

GDP: Purchasing power parity—$13.46 billion (2005 est.).

GDP—real growth rate: 13.9% (2005 est.).

GDP—per capita: Purchasing power parity—$4,500 (2005 est.).

Inflation rate: –0.2% (2005 est.).

Population below poverty line: 50% (2002 est.).

Unemployment rate: 31.6% (2004 est.).

Exports: $800 million f.o.b. (2005 est.)—Diamonds, mineral products, foodstuff, energy.

Imports: $1.5 billion f.o.b. (2005 est.)—Natural gas, petroleum, tobacco products, foodstuff, diamonds.

External debt: $1.819 billion (September 2005).

Transport and Communications

Railways: 845 km in common carrier service; does not include industrial lines.

Roads: 7,633 km.

Telephones: 582,500 (2004).

Mobile cellular: 203,300 (2004).

Internet users: 150,000 (2003).

Internet country code: .am

Australia

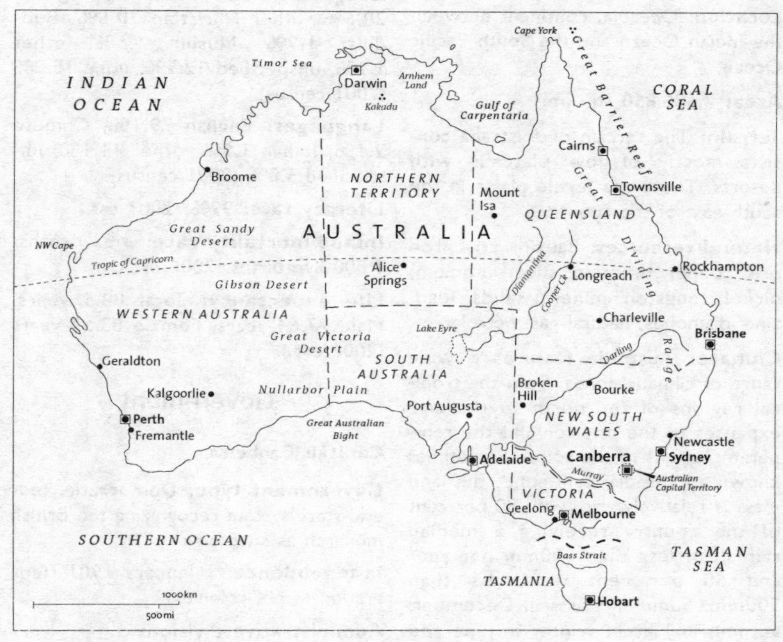

History

It is believed that the native aborigines arrived in Australia some 40,000–60,000 years ago. Europeans arrived on the scene in the seventeenth century. The first large-scale expedition was that of 1770 led by James Cook. The proliferation of Europeans in Australia had devastating effects on the local aborigine population.

The independence of the thirteen American colonies led the British to start colonizing Australia. In 1788, British Navy captain Arthur Phillip founded a penal settlement at Sydney when he arrived with a fleet of eleven vessels carrying nearly 800 convicts.

In 1901, the federation of Australia was achieved but the country remains under British sovereignty.

Geography

Location: Oceania, continent between the Indian Ocean and the South Pacific Ocean.

Area: 7,686,850 sq. km.

Terrain: The terrain of Australia consists mostly of low plateaus with deserts. There are fertile plains in the south-east of the country.

Natural resources: Bauxite, coal, iron ore, copper, tin, gold, silver, uranium, nickel, tungsten, mineral sands, lead, zinc, diamonds, natural gas, petroleum.

Climate: Australia features a wide range of climatic zones, from the tropical regions of the north to the arid expanses of the interior and the temperate regions of the south. Sometimes known as 'the dry continent', the land mass is relatively arid, with 80 per cent of the country receiving a median rainfall of less than 600mm per year and 50 per cent with less than 300mm. Summer starts in December, autumn in March, winter in June and spring in September. Seasonal fluctuations can be large, with temperatures ranging from above 50°C to well below zero. Although the climate is mostly of the continental type, the insular nature of the land mass results in modifications to the general continental pattern.

Long-term concerns include pollution, particularly depletion of the ozone layer, and management and conservation of coastal areas, especially the Great Barrier Reef.

People

Population: 20,264,082 (July 2006 est.).

Population growth rate: 0.85% (2006 est.).

Sex ratio: 0.99 male(s)/female (2006 est.).

Ethnic groups: Caucasian 92%, Asian 7%, aboriginal and others 1%.

Religions: Catholic 26.4%, Anglican 20.5%, other Christian 20.5%, Buddhist 1.9%, Muslim 1.5%, other 1.2%, unspecified 12.7%, none 15.3% (2001 census).

Languages: English 79.1%, Chinese 2.1%, Italian 1.9%, other 11.1%, unspecified 5.8% (2001 census).

Literacy rate: 99% (2003 est.).

Infant mortality rate: 4.63 deaths/1,000 live births (2006 est.).

Life expectancy: Total 80.5 years, Male 77.64 years, Female 83.52 years (2006 est.).

Government

Capital: Canberra.

Government type: Democratic, federal state system recognizing the British monarch as sovereign.

Independence: 1 January 1901 (federation of UK colonies).

Administrative divisions:

Six states and two territories*:

Australian Capital Territory*, New South Wales, Northern Territory*, Queensland, South Australia, Tasmania, Victoria, and Western Australia.

Legal system: Based on English common law.

Executive branch:
Chief of state: Queen of Australia Elizabeth II (since 6 February 1952), represented by Governor General Maj. Gen. (Retd.) Michael Jeffrey (since 11 August 2003).

Head of government: Prime Minister John Winston Howard (since 11 March 1996); Deputy Prime Minister Mark Vaile (since 6 July 2005).

Elections and election results: Elections to the Senate were last held on 9 October 2004 and the next elections will be held by June 2008. Elections to the House of Representatives were last held on 9 October 2004 and will be next held by November 2007.

Economy

Currency: Australian dollar.

Economy—overview:
Australia has a Western-style capitalist economy and a per capita GDP on par with the top four West European economies. The country's rising output in the domestic economy has been a major factor in combating the global slump. Its emphasis on reforms is also a contributory reason behind the economy's strength. It was one of the OECD's fastest-growing economies during the 1990s, a performance due in large part to economic reforms adopted in the 1980s.

The impact of drought, weak foreign demand, and strong import demand pushed the trade deficit up from $8 billion in 2002, to $18 billion in 2003, $13 billion in 2004, and $16 billion in 2005. Housing prices probably peaked in 2005, diminishing the prospect that interest rates would be raised to prevent a speculative bubble. Conservative fiscal policies have kept Australia's budget in surplus from 2002 to 2005.

GDP: Purchasing power parity—640.1 billion (2005 est.).

GDP—real growth rate: 2.5% (2005 est.).

GDP—per capita: Purchasing power parity—$31,900 (2005 est.).

Inflation rate: 2.3% (2004 est.).

Unemployment rate: 5.2% (2005).

Exports: $103 billion (2005 est.)—Coal, gold, meat, wool, alumina, iron ore, wheat, machinery and transport equipment.

Imports: $119.6 billion (2005 est.)—Machinery and transport equipment, computers and office machines, telecommunication equipment and parts; crude oil and petroleum products.

External debt: $509.6 billion (30 June 2005 est.).

Transport and Communications

Railways: 54,439 km (3,859 km electrified).

Roads: 811,603 km.

Telephones: 11.66 million (2004).

Mobile cellular: 16.48 million (2004).

Internet users: 9,472,000 (2003).

Internet country code: .au

Austria

History

In the fifth century, sustained Hun and eastern German attacks destroyed the Roman provincial defence network on the Danube. Several Germanic tribes like the Goths, Rugii, Heruli and Langobardi settled in the Austrian lands. Charlemagne, who later became the Holy Roman Emperor, conquered the area in about 788. From the thirteenth century, the House of Hapsburg, also called the House of Austria, ruled over Austria till World War I.

The Congress of Vienna of 1814–15 that took place at the end of the Napoleonic Wars, reorganized Europe and changed the political landscape of the continent. Austria emerged as one of the major gainers. This helped turn the country into a dominant power in Europe. Between 1867 and 1918, the Hapsburg empire that emerged from the constitutional compromise, or Ausgleich, of 1867 was known as Austria–Hungary, or the Austro-Hungarian empire.

The assassination of Archduke Francis Ferdinand of Austria in 1914 triggered off World War I. During the War, Austria fought alongside Germany, Bulgaria and the Ottoman Empire as one of the Central Powers. The war ended in ruin for Austria–Hungary and the empire collapsed.

In July 1934, the imprisonment of some Nazis led to an attempted Nazi coup and the assassination of Chancellor Dollfuss. In 1936, Austria acknowledged itself to be a 'German state'. In 1938 came the Anschluss, or the political union of Austria with Germany. This came about when Hitler annexed the country.

In 1945, Soviet troops liberated Vienna from German occupation and Austria came under occupation by British, French, Soviet and US forces. In 1955, Austria signed a treaty with France, UK, USA and USSR to establish an independent and 'permanently neutral' Austria. The country also joined the UN the same year.

In 1986, former UN Secretary General Kurt Waldheim was elected Austrian President. In 1995, Austria joined the European Union.

Geography

Location: Central Europe, north of Italy and Slovenia.

Area: 83,870 sq. km.

Terrain: The terrain of Austria is mostly mountainous in the west and south and mostly flat or gently sloping along the eastern and northern margins.

Natural resources: Oil, coal, lignite, timber, iron ore, copper, zinc, antimony, magnesite, tungsten, graphite, salt, hydropower.

Climate: Austria has a continental temperate climate. The winters are cold with frequent rain. There is some snowfall in the lowlands and in the mountains.

People

Population: 8,192,880 (July 2006 est.).

Population growth rate: 0.09% (2006 est.).

Sex ratio: 0.95 male(s)/female (2006 est.).

Religions: Roman Catholic 74%, Protestant 5%, Muslim 4%, others 17%.

Languages: German (official nationwide), Slovene (official in Carinthia), Croatian Hungarian (both official in Burgenland).

Literacy rate: 98% (2004 est.).

Infant mortality rate: 4.6 deaths/1,000 live births (2006 est.).

Life expectancy: Total 79.07 years, Male 76.17 years, Female 82.11 years (2006 est.).

Government

Capital: Vienna.

Government type: Federal republic.

Independence: 1156 (from Bavaria).

Legal system: Civil law system with Roman law origin; judicial review of legislative acts by the constitutional court; separate administrative and civil/penal supreme courts.

Executive branch:

Chief of state: President Heinz Fischer (since 8 July 2004).

Head of government: Chancellor Wolfgang Schuessel (since 4 February 2000).

Economy

Currency: Euro.

Economy—overview:

Austria has a prosperous, well-developed market economy, a high standard of living and has close relations with other EU economies, mainly Germany. There has been a strong inflow of foreign investors drawn by Austria's EU membership. Austria entered the Economic and Monetary Union in 1999.

GDP: Purchasing power parity—$267.6 billion (2005 est.).

GDP—real growth rate: 1.9% (2005 est.).

GDP—per capita: Purchasing power parity—$32,900 (2005 est.).

Inflation rate: 2.3% (2005 est.).

Population below poverty line: 5.9% (2004).

Unemployment rate: 5.1% (2005 est.).

Exports: $122.5 billion f.o.b. (2005 est.)—Machinery and equipment, motor vehicles and parts, paper and paperboard, metal goods, chemicals, iron and steel; textiles, foodstuff.

Imports: $118.8 billion f.o.b. (2005 est.)—Machinery and equipment, motor vehicles, chemicals, metal goods, oil and oil products; foodstuff.

External debt: $510.6 billion (June 2005 est.).

Transport and Communications

Railways: 6,021 km (3,552 km electrified).

Roads: 133,718 km.

Telephones: 3.791 million (2004).

Mobile cellular: 7.99 million (2004).

Internet users: 3.73 million (2003).

Internet country code: .at

Azerbaijan

History

Nomadic Turkic tribes, Kurds, Iranian-speakers and the Caucasian Albanians lived in eastern Transcaucasia in ancient and medieval times. Following Arab incursions in the seventh century, local rulers called shahanshah set up an Islamic form of regime. In the early sixteenth century, Azerbaijan's Caucasian Muslims became Shiite Muslims.

In 1828, the Treaty of Turkmanchay between Russia and Persia divided Azerbaijan into a Soviet Azerbaijan (which is the present-day nation of Azerbaijan) and a southern region of Azerbaijan that is today a part of Iran. In 1918, following the Bolshevik Revolution in Russia, Azerbaijan declared its independence. However, in 1920, the Red Army invaded the country and declared it to be a Soviet Socialist Republic. In 1936, Azerbaijan became a full-fledged republic of the Soviet Union.

Since 1988, Azerbaijan has been involved in a territorial dispute with neighbouring Armenia over the enclave of Nagorno-Karabakh. The majority of the population of Nagorno-Karabakh is Armenian Christian by faith who want to become a part of Armenia or a separate independent nation. A ceasefire was reached in 1994, but the issue remains unresolved. In 2001, the Presidents of Armenia and Azerbaijan met peace negotiators from France, Russia and USA to work out a solution. In August 1991, Azerbaijan declared its independence from the disintegrating Soviet Union.

Geography

Location: South-western Asia, bordering the Caspian Sea, between Iran and Russia, with a small European portion north of the Caucasus range.

Area: 86,600 sq. km. This includes the area of exclave of Naxcivan Autonomous Republic and the Nagorno–Karabakh region.

Terrain: Azerbaijan consists of the large, flat Kur–Araz Ovaligi or Kura–Araks Lowland, much of which lies below sea level, the Great Caucasus mountains in the north and Qarabag Yaylasi or Karabakh Upland in the west. Baku lies on Abseron Yasaqligi or Apsheron Peninsula that projects into the Caspian Sea.

Natural resources: Petroleum, natural gas, iron ore, nonferrous metals, alumina.

Climate: The climate of Azerbaijan is of the dry semi-arid steppe type.

People

Population: 7,961,619 (July 2006 est.).

Population growth rate: 0.66% (2006 est.).

Sex ratio: 0.94 male(s)/female (2006 est.).

Religions: Muslim 93.4%, Russian Orthodox 2.5%, Armenian Orthodox 2.3%, others 1.8% (1995 est.).

Languages: Azerbaijani (Azeri) 89%, Russian 3%, Armenian 2%, others 6% (1995 est.).

Literacy rate: Total 98.8%, Male 99.5%, Female 98.2% (2003 est.).

Infant mortality rate: 79 deaths/ 1,000 live births (2006 est.).

Life expectancy: Total 63.85 years, Male 59.78 years, Female 68.13 years (2006 est.).

Government

Capital: Baku (Baki).

Government type: Republic.

Independence: 30 August 1991 (from the Soviet Union).

Legal system: Based on civil law system.

Executive branch:
Chief of state: President Ilham Aliyev (since 31 October 2003).
Head of government: Prime Minister Artur Rasizade (since 4 November 2003).

Economy

Currency: Azerbaijani manat.

Economy—overview:
Azerbaijan's biggest export is petroleum and the negotiation of production-sharing arrangements with foreign firms have so far resulted in the commitment of $60 billion to long-term development of oilfields. Azerbaijan suffers from problems that other former Soviet republics have faced in making the switch to a market economy. However, the country's sizable energy resources are a major help to its long-term prospects. Azerbaijan has also started on a process of economic reform.

GDP: Purchasing power parity—$37.92 billion (2005 est.).

GDP—real growth rate: 10.4% (2005 est.).

GDP—per capita: Purchasing power parity—$4,800 (2005 est.).

Inflation rate: 4.6% (2004 est.).

Population below poverty line: 49% (2002 est.).

Unemployment rate: 1.2% (official rate) (2005 est.).

Exports: $6.117 billion f.o.b. (2005 est.)—oil and gas 90%, machinery, cotton, foodstuff.

Imports: $4.656 billion f.o.b. (2005 est.)—Machinery and equipment, oil products, foodstuff, metals, chemicals.

External debt: $2.253 billion (2005 est.).

Transport and Communications

Railways: 2,957 km.

Roads: 27,016 km.

Telephones: 923,800 (2002).

Mobile cellular: 870,000 (2002).

Internet users: 408,000 (2005).

Internet country code: .az

The Bahamas

History

The present-day Bahamian island of San Salvador was the first New World land that Christopher Columbus landed on in October 1492. British settlements on the islands first appeared in the seventeenth century.

Between 1717 and 1964, Bahamas remained a British Crown colony. In 1964, it was granted self-government. In June 1973, it became an independent country.

Geography

Location: Caribbean chain of islands in the North Atlantic Ocean, south-east of the US state of Florida, north-east of Cuba.

Area: 13,940 sq. km.

Natural resources: Salt, aragonite, timber, arable land.

Climate: The Bahamas has a tropical marine climate that is moderated by the influence of the warm waters of the Gulf Stream.

Hurricane Frances, one of the worst ever for the islands, struck the Bahamas in 2004. The northern Bahamas were subsequently hit by the less potent Hurricane Jeanne, also in 2004.

People

Population: 303,770 (2006 est.).

Population growth rate: 0.64% (2006 est.).

Sex ratio: 0.96 male(s)/female (2006 est.).

Religions: Baptist 35.4%, Anglican 15.1%, Roman Catholic 13.5%, Pentecostal 8.1%, Church of God 4.8%, Methodist 4.2%, other Christian 15.2%, none or unspecified 2.9%, other 0.8% (2000 census).

Languages: English (official), Creole (among Haitian immigrants).

Literacy rate: Total 95.6%, Male 94.7%, Female 96.5% (2003 est.).

Infant mortality rate: 24.68 deaths/1,000 live births (2006 est.).

Life expectancy: Total 65.6 years, Male 62.24 years, Female 69.03 years (2006 est.).

Government

Capital: Nassau.

Government type: Constitutional parliamentary democracy.

Independence: 10 July 1973 (from the UK).

Legal system: Based on English common law.

Executive branch:
Chief of state: Queen Elizabeth II (since 6 February 1952), represented by Governor-General Ivy Dumont (since May 2002).

Head of government: Prime Minister Perry Christie (since 3 May 2002).

Economy

Currency: Bahamian dollar (BSD).

GDP: Purchasing power parity—$6.098 billion (2005 est.).

GDP—real growth rate: 3.5% (2005 est.).

GDP—per capita: Purchasing power parity—$20,200 (2005 est.).

Inflation rate: 1.2% (2004 est.).

Unemployment rate: 10.2% (2005 est.).

Exports: $469.3 million (2004 est.)—fish and crawfish; rum, salt, chemicals; fruits and vegetables.

Imports: $1.82 billion (2004 est.)—Machinery and transport equipment, manufactures, chemicals, mineral fuels; food and live animals.

External debt: $342.6 million (2004).

Transport and Communications

Railways: None.

Roads: 2,693 km.

Telephones: 139,900 (2004).

Mobile cellular: 186,000 (2004).

Internet users: 93,000 (2005).

Internet country code: .bs

Bahrain

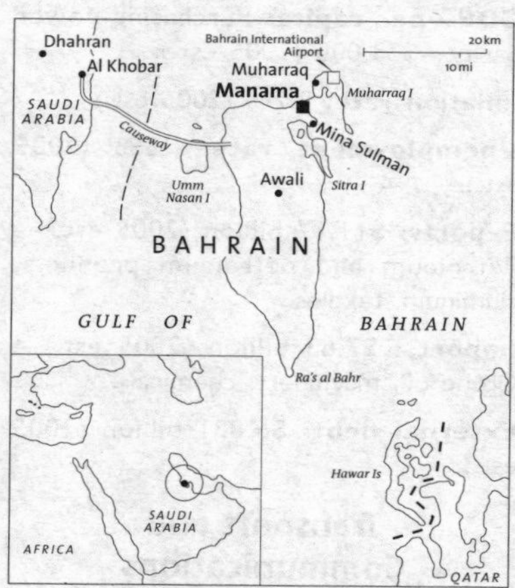

History

Persians ruled the islands of Bahrain in the fourth century AD and then returned to claim Bahrain again in 1602 after Arab and Portuguese rule. Ahmad ibn al-Khalifah took over in 1783. The al-Khalifahs remain the ruling family in Bahrain.

In 1820, Bahrain became a British protectorate and became fully independent in 1971. In 1975, the Emir, Sheikh Isa Bin-Salman Al Khalifah, dissolved the assembly and started ruling by decree.

Bahrain has been a key ally of the US, serving as an airbase during the Persian Gulf War in 1991. It is also the base of the US Navy's Fifth Fleet.

Geography

Location: Middle East, archipelago in the Persian Gulf, east of Saudi Arabia.

Area: 665 sq. km.

Terrain: Bahrain is mostly a low desert plain that rises gently to a low central escarpment.

Natural resources: Oil, natural gas, fish, pearls.

Climate: Bahrain has an arid climate with mild winters and hot, humid summers.

People

Population: 698,585. This includes 235,108 non-nationals (July 2006 est.).

Population growth rate: 1.45% (2006 est.).

Sex ratio: 1.26 male(s)/female (2006 est.).

Religions: Muslim (Shi'a and Sunni) 81.2%, Christian 9%, other 9.8%, (2001 census).

Languages: Arabic, English, Farsi, Urdu.

Literacy rate: Total 89.1%, Male 91.9%, Female 85% (2003 est.).

Infant mortality rate: 16.8 deaths/1,000 live births (2006 est.).

Life expectancy: Total 74.45 years, Male 71.97 years, Female 77 years (2006 est.).

Government

Capital: Manama.

Government type: Constitutional hereditary monarchy.

Independence: 15 August 1971 (from the UK).

Legal system: Based on Islamic law and English common law.

Executive branch:
Chief of state: King Hamad bin Isa Al Khalifa (since 6 March 1999); heir apparent Crown Prince Salman bin Hamad (the monarch's son).

Head of government: Prime Minister Khalifa bin Salman Al Khalifa (since 1971).

Economy

Currency: Bahraini dinar.

Economy—overview:
60 per cent of export receipts, 60 per cent of government revenues and 30 per cent of GDP of Bahrain come from petroleum production and refining. The country has well- developed communication and transport facilities, which has attracted many multinational firms with business interests in the Persian Gulf region.

On 11–12 November 2005, Bahrain hosted the Forum for the Future, bringing together leaders from the Middle East and G8 countries to discuss political and economic reform in the region. According to the 2006 Index of Economic Freedom published by the Heritage Foundation/*Wall Street Journal*, Bahrain has the freest economy in the Middle East, and is the twenty-fifth freest in the world.

GDP: Purchasing power parity—$15.83 billion (2005 est.).

GDP—real growth rate: 5.9% (2005 est.).

GDP—per capita: Purchasing power parity—$23,000 (2005 est.).

Inflation rate: 2.7% (2005 est.).

Unemployment rate: 15% (2005 est.).

Exports: $11.17 billion (2005 est.)—Petroleum and petroleum products, aluminum, textiles.

Imports: $7.83 billion (2005 est.)—Crude oil, machinery, chemicals.

External debt: $6.831 billion (2005 est.).

Transport and Communications

Railways: None.

Roads: 3,498 km.

Telephones: 191,600 (2004).

Mobile cellular: 649,800 (2004).

Internet users: 152,700 (2005).

Internet country code: .bh

Bangladesh

History

The earliest reference to the region that is today West Bengal and Bangladesh was to a kingdom called Vanga or Banga. In 1576 Bengal became a part of the Mughal empire and

majority of East Bengalis converted to Islam. With the decline and subsequent fall of the Mughals, the suba, or dominion, of Bengal became semi-independent. In 1608, the capital was moved from Rajmahal to Dhaka and in 1704 to Murshidabad. It was during this period that the English East India Company established its base at Calcutta.

At the time of partition in 1947, the two predominantly Islamic regions of the Indian subcontinent were made into one Islamic country—Pakistan. What is today Bangladesh was then known as East Pakistan. Inspite of sharing a common religion, all other characteristics of these two regions were vastly different.

Tension between East and West Pakistan developed because of their widespread disparities. Soon, in East Pakistan, the Awami League, a political party founded by Sheikh Mujibur Rahman, sought independence from West Pakistan. The Awami League swept the elections of December 1970, winning 167 of the 169 seats allotted to East Pakistan in the National Assembly (out of a total of 313 seats). This gave the League an overall majority. On the other hand, in West Pakistan, the Pakistan People's Party, led by Zulfikar Ali Bhutto, won eighty-one of 144 seats.

President Yahya Khan of Pakistan carried out negotiations in March 1971 even though military forces continued to reach East Pakistan in large numbers from West Pakistan. On 25 March, the army launched a massive attack in East Pakistan inflicting heavy casualties that included many students. Mujib himself was arrested and flown to West Pakistan. Most other leaders of the Awami League set up a government-in-exile in Calcutta and declared East Pakistan as an independent state named Bangladesh. In the vicious conflict that followed, around ten million people, mainly Hindus, fled to India. When the situation assumed alarming proportions, Indian military forces invaded the territory of East Pakistan on 3 December 1971. The Pakistani military surrendered on 16 December. Mujib was released from jail and returned to assume leadership of the newly born Bangladesh government in January 1972.

After its independence, Bangladesh passed through successive phases of martial law, military coups and political assassinations. President Zia-ur-Rahman was assassinated in 1981 and Abdus Sattar assumed power. The following year, General Ershad seized power in a military coup. In 1990, General Ershad was ousted from power and lost the elections that followed in 1991. Democracy was re-established in the country and Begum Khaleda Zia, the widow of President Zia, became Prime Minister. Soon afterwards, General Ershad was imprisoned on charges of corruption and possession of illegal arms. The Constitution was altered, making the president a largely ceremonial designation and vesting primary executive power in the prime minister's office. A general election was held in 1996, but a boycott by opposition parties reduced its credibility. The re-elected Khaleda Zia subsequently resigned and a caretaker government under Muhammad Habibur Rahman was appointed. A coalition government headed by Sheikh Hasina Wazed of the Awami League (Sheikh Mujib's daughter) was voted into power in a second set of elections held in the same year. In October 2001 the Bangladesh Nationalist Party won the parliamentary elections and Khaleda Zia returned to power.

Two radical Islamist parties, Jagrata Muslim Janata Bangladesh (JMJB) and Jama'atul Mujahideen Bangladesh (JMB), were banned in February 2005. Since then a series of bomb attacks have been blamed on them, and hundreds of their suspected members have been detained in numerous security operations. The first recorded case of a suicide bomb attack in Bangladesh took place in November 2005.

Geography

Location: Southern Asia, bordering the Bay of Bengal, between Myanmar and India.

Area: 144,000 sq. km.

Terrain: Mostly flat alluvial plain; hilly in south-east.

Natural resources: Natural gas, arable land, timber, coal.

Climate: Bangladesh has a tropical climate with a mild winter from November to February and a hot, humid summer from March to June. The humid, warm rainy monsoon season is from June to October.

People

Population: 147,365,352 (July 2006 est.).

Population growth rate: 2.09% (2006 est.).

Sex ratio: 1.05 male(s)/female (2006 est.).

Religions: Muslim 83%, Hindu 16%, others 1% (1998).

Languages: Bangla (official, also known as Bengali), English.

Literacy rate: Total 43.1%, Male 53.9%, Female 31.8% (2003 est.).

Infant mortality rate: 60.83 deaths/ 1,000 live births (2006 est.).

Life expectancy: Total 62.46 years, Male 62.47 years, Female 62.45 years (2006 est.).

Government

Capital: Dhaka.

Government type: Parliamentary democracy.

Independence: 16 December 1971 (from Pakistan). 26 March 1971 is the date of independence from Pakistan while 16 December 1971 is known as Victory Day and commemorates the official creation of the state of Bangladesh.

Legal system: Based on English Common Law.

Executive branch:

Chief of state: President Tajuddin Ahmed (since 6 September 2002).

Head of government: Prime Minister Khaleda Zia of the Bangladesh Nationalist Party (since 10 October 2001).

Elections: The National Parliament elects the president for a five-year term. The election scheduled for 16 September 2002 was not held, as Tajuddin Ahmed was the only presidential candidate. He was sworn in on 6 September 2002 (the next election will be held by 2007). After the legislative elections, the leader of the party that wins the majority is usually appointed prime minister by the president.

Legislative branch:

There is a unicameral National Parliament or Jatiya Sangsad of 300 seats. Members are elected by popular vote from single territorial constituencies and they serve five-year terms.

Elections: Last held on 1 October 2001 (next elections are to be held before October 2006).
Note: the election of October 2001 brought a majority BNP government aligned with three other smaller parties—Jamaat-i-Islami, Islami Oikya Jote, and Jatiya Party (Naziur).

Economy

Currency: Taka (BDT).

Economy—overview:
Sustained domestic and international efforts to improve the economic situation of Bangladesh has succeeded little in delivering tangible improvements to this poor and densely populated nation. As much as half of the country's GDP is generated through the service sector. The agriculture sector accounts for the employment of nearly two-thirds of Bangladeshis. Rice is the single most important product. There are various major constraints to growth. These include frequent natural calamities such as cyclones and floods, inefficient public sector enterprises, underdeveloped ports, a rapidly growing labour force in excess of agricultural requirement. Other reasons include delays in exploiting energy resources such as natural gas, insufficient power supplies, and slow implementation of economic reforms.

GDP: Purchasing power parity—$304.3 billion (2005 est.).

GDP—real growth rate: 5.7% (2005 est.).

GDP—per capita: Purchasing power parity—$2,100 (2005 est.).

Inflation rate: 6.7% (2005 est.).

Population below poverty line: 45% (2004 est.).

Unemployment rate: 2.5% (includes underemployment) (2005 est.).

Exports: $9.372 billion (2005 est.).

Imports: $12.97 billion (2005 est.).

External debt: $21.25 billion (2005 est.).

Transport and Communications

Railways: 2,706 km.

Roads: 239,226 km.

Telephones: 831,000 (2004).

Mobile cellular: 2,781,600 (2004).

Internet users: 300,000 (2005).

Internet country code: .bd

Barbados

History

It s believed that Arawak Indians were the first inhabitants of the island of Barbados. The Portuguese were the first Europeans to visit the island but the British were the first to set up a colony there, in 1627. The initial cotton and tobacco plantations that were started on the island soon gave way to more profitable sugar plantations. African slaves were brought in to work on the plantations and soon they accounted for 90 per cent of the population on the island. Later on, Barbados became the administrative headquarters of the Windward Islands but became a separate colony in 1885. UK granted it independence in 1966.

Geography

Location: Caribbean island in the North Atlantic Ocean, north-east of Venezuela.

Area: 431 sq. km.

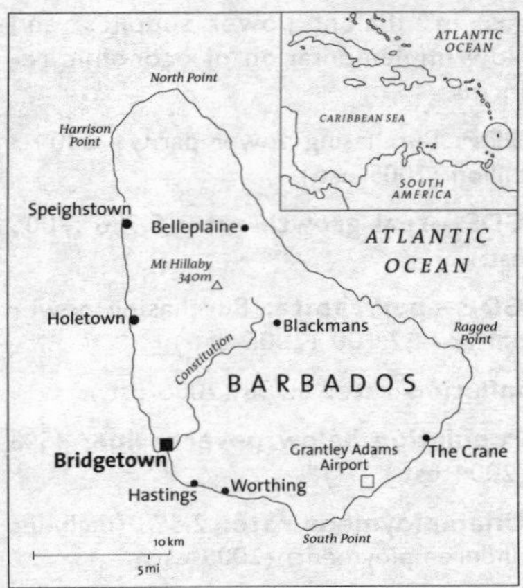

Natural resources: Petroleum, fish, natural gas.

Climate: Barbados has a tropical climate with a rainy season between June and October.

People

Population: 279,912 (July 2006 est.).

Population growth rate: 0.37% (2006 est.).

Sex ratio: 0.94 male(s)/female (2006 est.).

Religions: Protestant 67% (Anglican 40%, Pentecostal 8%, Methodist 7%, others 12%), Roman Catholic 4%, none 17%, others 12%.

Languages: English.

Literacy rate: Total 99.7%, Male 99.7%, Female 99.7% (2002 est.).

Infant mortality rate: 11.77 deaths/1,000 live births (2006 est.).

Life expectancy: Total 72.79 years, Male 70.79 years, Female 74.82 years (2006 est.).

Government

Capital: Bridgetown.

Government type: Parliamentary democracy; independent sovereign state within the Commonwealth.

Independence: 30 November 1966 (from the UK).

Legal system: English common law; no judicial review of legislative acts.

Executive branch:

Chief of state: Queen Elizabeth II (since 6 February 1952), represented by Governor-General Sir Clifford Straughn Husbands (since 1 June 1996).

Head of government: Prime Minister Owen Seymour Arthur (since 6 September 1994).

Economy

Currency: Barbadian dollar.

GDP: Purchasing power parity—$4.745 billion (2005 est.).

GDP—real growth rate: 4.1% (2005 est.).

GDP—per capita: Purchasing power parity—$17,000 (2005 est.).

Inflation rate: –0.5% (2004 est.).

Unemployment rate: 10.7% (2003 est.).

Exports: $209 million (2004 est.)—Sugar and molasses, rum, other foods and beverages, chemicals, electrical components.

Imports: $1.476 billion (2004 est.)—Consumer goods, machinery, foodstuff, construction materials, chemicals, fuel, electrical components.

External debt: $668 million (2003).

Transport and Communications

Railways: None.

Roads: 1,600 km.

Telephones: 135,700 (2004).

Mobile cellular: 200,100 (2004).

Internet users: 150,000 (2005).

Internet country code: .bb

Belarus

In 1991, Belarus declared its independence from the collapsing Soviet Union.

As of 2005, there appears to be a movement in Belarus towards uniting with Russia. In November 2005, a draft constitution was sent to both Vladimir Putin and Lukashenko for approval. However, it is unlikely that such a step will be taken with Lukashenko in power, as Lukashenko would probably insist on sharing presidential powers with Putin on a federal level—something akin to the governor of the American state of Texas being on par with the President of the United States. This move, along with others, is part of the 1996 plan created by Lukashenko and former Russian President Boris Yeltsin to create a union between two nations.

History

In the fifth century AD, eastern Slavic tribes colonized Belarus, also known as Byelorussia or White Russia in historical times. The territory became a part of the Grand Duchy of Lithuania and later, in 1569, it was integrated with Poland. As a result of the repeated partitions of Poland, Belarus became a part of Russia.

In the aftermath of World War I, Belarus proclaimed its independence in 1918. But soon after, the Soviet Red Army invaded Belarus and in 1919, the Belarusian Soviet Socialist Republic was proclaimed.

The 1930s saw the execution of hundreds of thousands in Belarus as a result of the Stalinist purges. More than a million people were killed during the German invasion of Belarus in 1941 and the capital city, Minsk, was severely damaged. The Soviet Army finally drove the Germans out in 1944.

In 1986, Belarus was heavily affected by the fallout of the nuclear explosion at Chernobyl in neighbouring Ukraine.

Geography

Location: Eastern Europe, east of Poland.

Area: 207,600 sq. km.

Terrain: Generally flat terrain with extensive marshlands.

Natural resources: Forests, peat deposits, small quantities of oil and natural gas, granite, dolomitic limestone, marl, chalk, sand, gravel, clay.

Climate: Belarus has cold winters, cool and moist summers. Its climate is of a transitional type, between continental and maritime climates.

People

Population: 10,293,011 (July 2006 est.).

Population growth rate: –0.06% (2006 est.).

Sex ratio: 0.88 male(s)/female (2006 est.).

Religions: Eastern Orthodox 80%, others (including Roman Catholic, Protestant, Jewish, and Muslim) 20% (1997 est.).

Languages: Belarusian, Russian.

Literacy rate: Total 99.6%, Male 99.8%, Female 99.5% (2003 est.).

Infant mortality rate: 13 deaths/ 1,000 live births (2006 est.).

Life expectancy: Total 69.08 years, Male 63.47 years, Female 74.98 years (2006 est.).

Government

Capital: Minsk.

Government type: Republic.

Independence: 25 August 1991 (from the Soviet Union).

Legal system: Based on civil law system.

Executive branch:
Chief of state: President Aleksandr Lukashenko (since 20 July 1994).

Head of government: Prime Minister Sergei Sidorsky (since 19 December 2003).

Economy

Currency: Belarusian ruble.

Economy—overview:
Belarus remains heavily dependent on Russian gas to meet its energy needs. Although Russia, in the beginning of 2006, increased the price of gas supplied to several republics of the former Soviet Union, the tariff remained the same for Belarus as it was in 2005.

GDP: Purchasing power parity—$70.68 billion (2005 est.)

GDP—real growth rate: 8% (2005 est.).

GDP—per capita: Purchasing power parity—$6,900 (2005 est.).

Inflation rate: 8% (2005 est.).

Population below poverty line: 27.1% (2003 est.).

Unemployment rate: 2% officially registered unemployed; large number of underemployed workers (2004).

Exports: $16.14 billion f.o.b. (2005 est.)—Machinery and equipment, mineral products, chemicals, metals; textiles, foodstuff.

Imports: $16.94 billion f.o.b. (2005 est.)—Mineral products, machinery and equipment, chemicals, foodstuff, metals.

External debt: $4.662 billion (30 June 2005 est.).

Transport and Communications

Railways: 5,512 km. (2004)

Roads: 93,055 km.

Telephones: 3,284,300 (2005).

Mobile cellular: 4.098 million (2005).

Internet users: 20,973 (2005).

Internet country code: .by

Belgium

History

Roman ruler Julius Caesar occupied the area that is today Belgium in the period between 57–50 BC. In the sixteenth century, it became a part of the Holy Roman Empire. In 1555, the Low Countries (a region consisting of present-day Belgium, the Netherlands and Luxembourg) was united with Spain. The Treaty of Utrecht of 1713 gave the control of this region to Austria. Later on, France annexed the re-

gion. After the ouster of Napoleon, the Congress of Vienna (1814–15) gave Belgium to the Netherlands. But in 1830, Belgians rebelled against Dutch rule and declared their independence.

During World War II, Germany invaded Belgium and held the king, Leopold III, as prisoner. Allied forces liberated Belgium from German occupation in 1944. King Leopold III attempted to return to the throne in 1950 but social unrest forced him to abdicate in favour of his son, Baudouin. In the 1960s, Belgium granted independence to its African colonies.

The headquarters of both the European Union and North Atlantic Treaty Organization (NATO) are at the Belgian capital city, Brussels. It is also one of the homes of the European parliament.

Geography

Location: Western Europe, bordering the North Sea, between France and the Netherlands.

Area: 30,528 sq. km.

Terrain: Belgium has flat coastal plains in the north-west, rolling hills in the central part of the country and mountains of the Ardennes Forest in the south-east.

Natural resources: Coal, natural gas, construction materials, silica sand, carbonates.

Climate: Belgium has a temperate climate with mild winters and cool summers.

People

Population: 10,379,067 (July 2006 est.).

Population growth rate: 0.13% (2006 est.).

Sex ratio: 0.96 male(s)/female (2006 est.).

Religions: Roman Catholic 75%, Protestant and others 25%.

Languages: Dutch (official) 60%, French (official) 40%, German (official) less than 1%, legally bilingual (Dutch and French).

Literacy rate: Total 99%, Male 99%, Female 99% (2003).

Infant mortality rate: 4.62 deaths/1,000 live births (2006 est.).

Life expectancy: Total 78.77 years, Male 75.59 years, Female 82.09 years (2006 est.).

Government

Capital: Brussels.

Government type: Federal parliamentary democracy under a constitutional monarch.

Independence: 4 October 1830 (date on which a provisional government declared independence from the Netherlands).

Legal system: Civil law system influenced by English constitutional theory; judicial review of legislative acts.

Executive branch:
Chief of state: King Albert II (since 9 August 1993).

Head of government: Prime Minister Guy Verhofstadt (since 13 July 1999).

Economy

Currency: Euro.

Economy—overview:
Belgium has a modern private enterprise-based economy. The country enjoys a central geographic location, well-developed transport network and a diversified industrial and commercial base. However, a major drawback is the lack of natural resources. Almost three-quarters of Belgium's trade is with other EU countries. Public debt is about 100 per cent of GDP.

GDP: Purchasing power parity—$325 billion (2005 est.).

GDP—real growth rate: 1.5% (2005 est.).

GDP—per capita: Purchasing power parity—$31,400 (2005 est.).

Inflation rate: 1.9% (2004 est.).

Population below poverty line: 4% (1989 est.).

Unemployment rate: 8.4% (2005 est.).

Exports: $269.6 billion f.o.b. (2005 est.)—Machinery and equipment, chemicals, diamonds, metals and metal products, foodstuff.

Imports: $264.5 billion f.o.b. (2005 est.)—Machinery and equipment, chemicals, diamonds, pharmaceuticals, foodstuff, transportation equipment, oil products.

External debt: $980.1 billion (June 2005 est.).

Transport and Communications

Railways: 3,521 km.

Roads: 149,757 km.

Telephones: 4.801 million (2004).

Mobile cellular: 9,131,700 (2004).

Internet users: 5.1 million (2005).

Internet country code: .be

Belize

History

The Mayan civilization flourished till about 1200 in the area that is today Belize. A few shipwrecked British sailors began the first recorded European settlement in 1638. In 1840, it officially became the Colony of British Honduras. In January 1964, it was granted full internal self-government. In 1981, the country was granted full independence.

Throughout Belize's history, Guatemala has claimed ownership of all or part of the territory. This claim is occasionally reflected in maps showing Belize as Guatemala's eastern-most province. As of 2005, the border dispute with Guatemala remains unresolved and quite contentious; at various times the issue has involved mediation assistance from the United Kingdom and the CARICOM heads of government. Since independence, a British garrison has been retained in Belize at the request of the Belizean government. Notably, both Guatemala and Belize are participating in the confidence-building measures, including the Guatemala-Belize Language Exchange Project

Geography

Location: Middle America, bordering the Caribbean Sea, between Guatemala and Mexico.

Area: 22,966 sq. km.

Natural resources: Arable land potential, timber, fish, hydropower.

Climate: Belize has a hot and humid tropical climate.

People

Population: 287,730 (July 2006 est.).

Population growth rate: 2.31% (2006 est.).

Sex ratio: 1.03 male(s)/female (2006 est.).

Religions: Roman Catholic 49.6%, Protestant 27%, none 9.4%, others 14%.

Languages: English (official), Spanish, Mayan, Garifuna (Carib), Creole.

Literacy rate: 94.1% (2003 est.).

Infant mortality rate: 24.89 deaths/1,000 live births (2006 est.).

Life expectancy: Total 68.3 years, Male 66.43 years, Female 70.26 years (2006 est.).

Government

Capital: Belmopan.

Government type: Parliamentary democracy.

Independence: 21 September 1981 (from the UK).

Legal system: English law.

Executive branch:

Chief of state: Queen Elizabeth II (since 6 February 1952), represented by Governor-General Sir Colville Young Sr (since 17 November 1993).

Head of government: Prime Minister Said Wilbert Musa (since 28 August 1998).

Economy

Currency: Belizean dollar.

GDP: Purchasing power parity—$1.778 billion (2004 est.).

GDP—real growth rate: 3.8% (2005 est.).

GDP—per capita: Purchasing power parity—$6,800 (2005 est.).

Inflation rate: 3% (2005 est.).

Population below poverty line: 33% (1999 est.).

Unemployment rate: 12.9% (2003 est.).

Exports: $349.9 million f.o.b. (2005 est.)—Sugar, banana, citrus, clothing, fish products, molasses, wood.

Imports: $622.4 million c.i.f. (2005 est.)—Machinery and transport equipment, manufactured goods; fuels, chemicals, pharmaceuticals; food, beverages, tobacco.

External debt: $1.362 billion (2004 est.).

Transport and Communications

Railways: None.

Roads: 2,872 km.

Telephones: 33,700 (2004).

Mobile cellular: 91,700 (2004).

Internet users: 30,000 (2002).

Internet country code: .bz

Benin

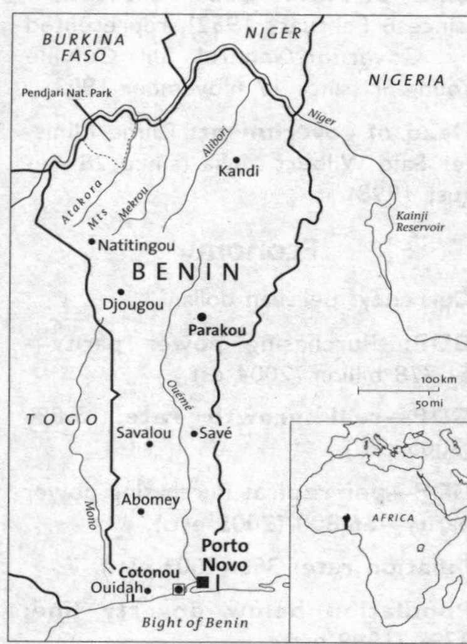

History

The Abomey kingdom of Dahomey was formed in 1625. France annexed Dahomey in 1893 and incorporated it into French West Africa in 1904. It attained independence in 1960 and Hubert Maga became the country's first President. In 1963 a coup led by the army's Chief of Staff, Colonel Christophe Soglo, deposed President Maga.

In 1975, Dahomey was renamed the People's Republic of Benin and the Parti de la Revolution Populaire du Benin (PRPB) was created as the country's only political party. In 1991, Nicephore Soglo defeated Kerekou in the first multi-candidate presidential elections. Kerekou returned to power in 1996 and was re-elected in 2001.

Geography

Location: Western Africa, bordering the Bight of Benin, between Nigeria and Togo.

Area: 112,620 sq. km.

Natural resources: Offshore oil deposits, limestone, marble, timber.

Climate: Benin has a tropical climate.

People

Population: 7,862,944 (July 2006 est.).

Population growth rate: 2.73% (2006 est.).

Sex ratio: 0.98 male(s)/female (2006 est.).

Religions: Indigenous beliefs 50%, Christian 30%, Muslim 20%.

Languages: French (official), Fon and Yoruba, tribal languages.

Literacy rate: Total 33.6%, Male 46.4%, Female 22.6% (2002).

Infant mortality rate: 79.56 deaths/1,000 live births (2006 est.).

Life expectancy: Total 53.04 years, Male 51.9 years, Female 54.22 years (2006 est.).

Government

Capital: Porto Novo (official capital). Cotonou (seat of government).

Government type: Republic under multiparty democratic rule.

Independence: 1 August 1960 (from France).

Legal system: Based on French civil law and customary law.

Executive branch:

Chief of state: President Yayi Boni (since 6 April 2006). The president is both the chief of state and head of government.

Economy

Currency: Communaute Financiere Africaine franc (CFA Franc).

GDP: Purchasing power parity—$8.553 billion (2005 est.).

GDP—real growth rate: 4.5% (2005 est.).

GDP—per capita: Purchasing power parity—$1,200 (2005 est.).

Inflation rate: 3.2% (2005 est.).

Population below poverty line: 33% (2001 est.).

Exports: $826.9 million f.o.b. (2005 est.)—Cotton, crude oil, palm products, cocoa.

Imports: $1.043 million f.o.b. (2005 est.)—Foodstuffs, capital goods, petroleum products.

External debt: $1.6 billion (2000).

Transport and Communications

Railways: 578 km.

Roads: 6,787 km.

Telephones: 72,800 (2004).

Mobile cellular: 75,100 (2005).

Internet users: 70,000 (2003).

Internet country code: .bj

Bhutan

History

The name Bhutan is believed to be derived from the Sanskrit 'bhotant' which means 'the end of Tibet', or from 'Bhu-uttan', meaning 'high land'. Historically, the Bhutanese refer to their country as Druk Yul or the 'land of the thunder dragon'. A Tibetan lama named Shabdrung Ngawang Namgyal arrived in Bhutan in 1616. He introduced the present dual system of religious and secular government. He also created the system of Dzongs in Bhutan. He unified the country and established himself as the supreme leader with civil power vested in a high officer known as the Druk Desi. Religious affairs were charged to another leader, the Je Khenpo who is the chief abbot of Bhutan.

Civil wars plagued Bhutan in the two centuries following Shabdrung's death. This meant that the regional Penlops or governors gained more and more power. This ended with the election of the Penlop of Trongsa, Ugyen Wangchuck, as the first king of Bhutan in 1907.

In 1865, British troops invaded the area. In 1910, Bhutan allowed its foreign affairs to be taken care of by the UK. In 1949, it entered into the Treaty of Friendship and Cooperation with India.

In early 2005, a new constitution was presented, and will be put up for ratification by a referendum before being implementd. In December 2005, King Jigme Singye Wangchuck announced that he would step down as king of Bhutan in 2008 and would be succeeded by his son, the crown prince Jigme Khesar Namgyel Wangchuck. A group comprising ethnic Nepalese claiming to be Bhutanese exiles, have criticized the constitution saying that the king was trying to overshadow the refugee problem in the country by introducing 'limited democracy'.

Geography

Location: Southern Asia, between China and India.

Area: 47,000 sq. km.

Terrain: Mostly mountainous with some fertile valleys and savanna.

Natural resources: Timber, hydropower, gypsum, dolomite, limestone, calcium carbide.

Climate: Bhutan's climate varies from tropical in the southern plains to cool winters and hot summers in the central valleys and severe winters and cool summers in the Himalayas.

People

Population: 672,425 (Population and Housing Census of Bhutan 2005 est.). Other estimates as high as 2,279,000.

Population growth rate: 1.3% (2005 est.).

Sex ratio: 1.11 male(s)/female (2005 est.).

Religions: Lamaistic Buddhist 75%, Indian- and Nepalese-influenced Hinduism 25%.

Languages: Dzongkha (official); Bhotes speak various Tibetan dialects; Nepalese speak various Nepalese dialects.

Literacy rate: Total 47%, Male 60%, Female 34% (2003 est.).

Infant mortality rate: 98.41 deaths/ 1,000 live births (2006 est.).

Life expectancy: Total 54.78 years, Male 55.02 years, Female 54.53 years (2006 est.).

Government

Capital: Thimphu.

Government type: Monarchy. There is a special treaty relationship with India.

Independence: 8 August 1949 (from the UK).

Legal system: Based on Indian law and English Common Law.

Executive branch:
Chief of state: King Jigme Singye Wangchuck (since 24 July 1972).

Head of government: Chairman of the council of ministers Sangay Ngedup (since 5 September 2005).

Legislative branch:
There is a unicameral National Assembly or Tshogdu with 150 seats of which 105 are elected from village constituencies, ten represent religious bodies and thirty-five are designated by the monarch to represent government and other secular interests. The members serve three-year terms.

Economy

Currency: Ngultrum.

Economy—overview:
Bhutan has one of the world's smallest and least developed economies. Agriculture and forestry are the main sources of livelihood for more than 90 per cent of the population. Agriculture consists largely of subsistence farming and animal husbandry. The mountainous terrain makes it tough to set up and develop roads and other forms of infrastructure. The country has close ties with India. There are strong trade (India is its single biggest source of imports and the biggest destination for its exports) and monetary links (the Ngultrum is treated at par with the Indian rupee and is also legal tender in Bhutan). It also depends heavily on India's financial assistance. Some of Bhutan's five-year plans have been financed by India. The industrial sector is

technologically underdeveloped and most of the production is of the small sector cottage industry type. Bhutan's resources include its hydropower potential and its attraction as a tourism destination.

GDP: Purchasing power parity—$2.9 billion (2003 est.).

GDP—real growth rate: 5.3% (2003 est.).

GDP—per capita: Purchasing power parity—$1,400 (2003 est.).

Inflation rate: 3% (2002 est.).

Exports: $154 million f.o.b. (2000 est.).

Imports: $196 million c.i.f. (2000 est.).

External debt: $ 245 million (2000).

Transport and Communications

Railways: None.

Roads: 8,050 km.

Telephones: 30,300 (2004).

Mobile cellular: 22,000 (2005).

Internet users: 15,000 (2003).

Internet country code: .bt

Bolivia

History

The area that comprises modern-day Bolivia was once a part of the Inca empire. In 1824, Venezuelan statesman Simon Bolivar, from whom Bolivia takes its name, liberated the country from Spanish rule and in 1825, Bolivia gained its independence with Simon Bolivar as its president. In the later part of the nineteenth century, Bolivia lost great expanses of territory to its neighbouring countries.

Bolivia witnessed numerous coups and internal conflicts in the 1950s and 1960s. In 1967, USA helped the Bolivian government suppress a peasant uprising led by Ernesto 'Che' Guevara, who was killed after being betrayed by peasants. A string of military rulers followed till 1983, when the military junta handed over power to a civilian administration led by Siles Zuazo.

The 2005 Bolivian presidential election was held on 18 December 2005. The two main candidates were Juan Evo Morales Ayma of the Movement Toward Socialism (MAS) party, and Jorge Quiroga, leader of the Democratic and Social Power (PODEMOS) party and former of the Acción Democrática Nacionalista (ADN) party. Morales won the election with 54 per cent of the votes, an absolute majority. He was sworn in on 22 January 2006 for a five-year term. For the first time since the Spanish conquest in the early 1500s, Bolivia, a nation with a majority indigenous population, has an indigenous leader, and Morales has stated that the 500 years of colonialism are now over.

Geography

Location: Central South America, south-west of Brazil.

Area: 1,098,580 sq. km.

Terrain: The lofty Andes mountains and a highland plateau (Altiplano), along with lower hills and the lowland plains of the Amazon Basin.

Natural resources: Tin, natural gas, petroleum, zinc, tungsten, antimony, silver, iron, lead, gold, timber, hydropower.

Climate: Bolivia's climate varies from humid and tropical to cold and semi-arid.

People

Population: 8,989,046 (July 2006 est.).

Population growth rate: 1.45% (2006 est.).

Sex ratio: 0.98 male(s)/female (2006 est.).

Religions: Roman Catholic 95%, Protestant (Evangelical Methodist).

Languages: Spanish (official), Quechua (official), Aymara (official).

Literacy rate: Total 87.2%, Male 93.1%, Female 81.6% (2003 est.).

Infant mortality rate: 51.77 deaths/1,000 live births (2006 est.).

Life expectancy: Total 65.84 years, Male 63.21 years, Female 68.61 years (2006 est.).

Government

Capital: La Paz (seat of government). Sucre (legal capital and seat of judiciary).

Government type: Republic.

Independence: 6 August 1825 (from Spain).

Legal system: Based on Spanish law and Napoleonic code.

Executive branch:

Chief of state: President Eduardo Rodrigrez Veltzé (since 9 June 2005). The president is both the chief of state and head of government: Vice-president (vacant).

Economy

Currency: Boliviano.

GDP: Purchasing power parity—$25.95 billion (2005 est.).

GDP—real growth rate: 4% (2005 est.).

GDP—per capita: Purchasing power parity—$2,900 (2005 est.).

Inflation rate: 4.9% (2005 est.).

Population below poverty line: 64% (2004 est.).

Unemployment rate: 8% in urban areas; there is widespread underemployment (2005 est.).

Exports: $2.371 billion f.o.b. (2005 est.)—Soybeans, natural gas, zinc, gold, wood (2000).

Imports: $1.845 billion f.o.b. (2005 est.)—Capital goods, raw materials and semi-manufactures, chemicals, petroleum, food.

External debt: $6.43 billion (2005 est.).

Transport and Communications

Railways: 3,519 km.

Roads: 60,762 km.

Telephones: 625,400 (2004).

Mobile cellular: 1,800,800 (2004).

Internet users: 350,000 (2005).

Internet country code: .bo

Bosnia and Herzegovina

History

The Romans annexed the area that is today Bosnia and Herzegovina in the second and first centuries BC. The Slavs started settling in the region in the seventh century. In 1463, the Ottoman Turks conquered Bosnia. The Congress of Berlin that followed the Russo- Turkish War of 1877–8 gave Austria–Hungary the mandate to govern Bosnia and Herzegovina.

On 28 June 1914, a Bosnian Serb student named Gavrilo Princip assassinated the Austrian Archduke Franz Ferdinand in Sarajevo. This triggered off World War I. By the time the War ended, the kingdom of Austria–Hungary had collapsed and Bosnia and Herzegovina became a part of the kingdom of Serbs, Croats and Slovenes in 1918. The country was renamed Yugoslavia in 1929.

Following the collapse of communism elsewhere in Europe in the 1990s, Bosnia and Herzegovina declared its independence from Yugoslavia in 1992. However, the state was beset by grave problems from the very start. While Muslim nationalists wanted a centralized independent state of Bosnia, the Croats wanted to join an independent Croatian state while Serb nationalists wanted to remain within the Belgrade-dominated remains of Yugoslavia. In the 1992 referendum on independence, Croat and Muslim nationalists formed a tactical alliance and outvoted Serbs, enraging the latter. A bloody civil war erupted and the Bosnian Serbs gained control over half of the country by August 1992.

In August and September 1995, NATO carried out air strikes against Serb positions. This enabled Muslims and Croats to retake substantial chunks of territory from the Serbs. Soon afterwards, the Dayton Peace Accord was signed. This led to the formation of two entities—one Muslim–Croat federation and a Serb entity (Republika Srpska) within the greater state of Bosnia and Herzegovina.

Geography

Location: South-eastern Europe, bordering the Adriatic Sea and Croatia.

Area: 51,129 sq. km.

Terrain: Mountains and valleys.

Natural resources: Coal, iron ore, bauxite, copper, lead, zinc, chromite, cobalt, manganese, nickel, clay, gypsum, salt, sand, forests, hydropower.

Climate: Bosnia and Herzegovina has hot summers and cold winters.

People

Population: 4,498,976 (July 2006 est.).

Population growth rate: 1.35% (2006 est.).

Sex ratio: 0.97 male(s)/female (2006 est.).

Religions: Muslim 40%, Orthodox 31%, Roman Catholic 15%, others 14%.

Languages: Bosnian, Croatian, Serbian.

Infant mortality rate: 9.82 deaths/ 1,000 live births (2006 est.).

Life expectancy: Total 78 years, Male 74.39 years, Female 81.88 years (2006 est.).

Government

Capital: Sarajevo.

Government type: Federal democratic republic.

Independence: 1 March 1992 (from Yugoslavia; date on which referendum for independence was completed); 3 March 1992 (date on which independence was declared).

Legal system: Based on civil law system.

Executive branch:

Chief of state: The presidency rotates between a Serb, a Bosnian Muslim and a Croat. Each member holds office for eight months. Chairman of the presidency: Ivo Miro Jovic (since 28 June 2005; presidency member since 9 May 2005; Croat; note: Dragan Covic was sacked by High Representative Paddy Ashdown on 29 Mar 2005). The other members of the three-member rotating (every eight months) presidency are Borislav Paravac (since 10 April 2003; Serb); and Sulejman Tihic (since 5 October 2002; Bosnian Muslim).

Head of government: Prime Minister Adnan Terzic (since 20 December 2002).

Economy

Currency: Marka.

GDP: Purchasing power parity—$22.89 billion note: Bosnia has a large informal sector that could also be as much as much as 50 per cent of official GDP (2005 est.).

GDP—real growth rate: 5.3% (2005 est.).

GDP—per capita: Purchasing power parity—$6,800 (2005 est.).

Inflation rate: 1.4% (2005 est.).

Population below poverty line: 25% (2004 est.).

Unemployment rate: 44% (2004 est.).

Exports: $2.7 billion f.o.b. (2005 est.)—Metals, clothing, wood products.

Imports: $6.8 billion f.o.b. (2005 est.)—Machinery and equipment, chemicals, fuels, foodstuff.

External debt: $3.1 billion (2005 est.).

Transport and Communications

Railways: 1,021 km (795 km electrified).

Roads: 21,846 km.

Telephones: 928,000 (2004).

Mobile cellular: 1,050,000 (2003).

Internet users: 225,000 (2005).

Internet country code: .ba

Botswana

History

In 1885, UK established a protectorate named Bechuanaland, which they expanded in 1890. In 1966, UK granted it full independence. It became the Republic of Botswana with Seretse Khama as president.

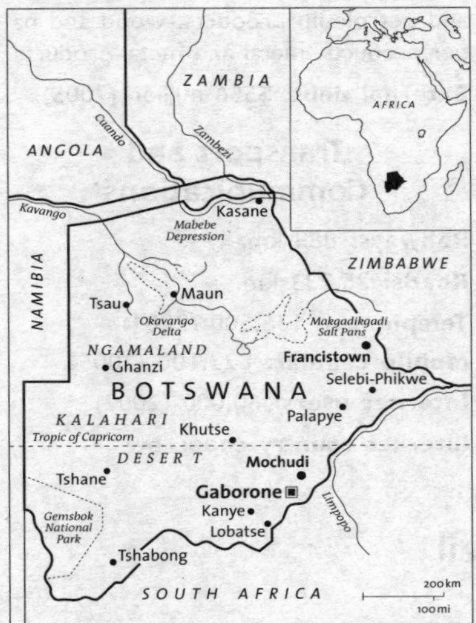

In 2000, faced with one of the world's worst AIDS incidence rates, President Mogae announced that AIDS drugs would be made available for free from 2001.

Geography

Location: Southern Africa, north of South Africa.

Area: 600,370 sq. km.

Terrain: Predominantly flat to gently rolling tableland. The Kalahari desert lies in the south-west.

Natural resources: Diamonds, copper, nickel, salt, soda ash, potash, coal, iron ore, silver.

Climate: Botswana has a semi-arid climate with warm winters and hot summers.

People

Population: 1,639,833 (July 2005 est.).

Population growth rate: –0.04% (2006 est.).

Sex ratio: 0.96 male(s)/female (2006 est.).

Religions: Christian 71.6%, Badimo 6%, other 1.4%, unspecified 0.4%, none 20.6% (2001 census).

Languages: English (official) 2.1%, Setswana 78.2%, Kalanga 7.9%, Sekgalagadi 2.8%, other 8.6%, unspecified 0.4% (2001 census).

Literacy rate: Total 79.8%, Male 76.9%, Female 82.4% (2003 est.).

Infant mortality rate: 53.7 deaths/1,000 live births (2006 est.).

Life expectancy: Total 33.74 years, Male 33.9 years, Female 33.56 years (2006 est.).

Government

Capital: Gaborone.

Government type: Parliamentary republic.

Independence: 30 September 1966 (from UK).

Legal system: Based on Roman–Dutch law and local customary law.

Executive branch:

Chief of state: President Festus Mogae (since 1 April 1998) and Vice-President Seretse Ian Khama (since 13 July 1998). The president is both the chief of state and head of government.

Economy

Currency: Pula.

Economy—overview:

The Central Bank devalued the pula by 7.5 per cent in February 2004 in a bid to maintain export competitiveness against the real appreciation of the pula. There was a further 12 per cent devaluation in May 2005 and the policy of a 'crawling peg' was adopted.

GDP: Purchasing power parity—$17.24 billion (2005 est.).

GDP—real growth rate: 4.5% (2005 est.).

GDP—per capita: Purchasing power parity—$10,500 (2005 est.).

Inflation rate: 8.3% (2005 est.).

Population below poverty line: 30.3% (2003 est.).

Unemployment rate: 23.8% (2004 est.).

Exports: $3.68 billion f.o.b. (2005 est.)—Diamond, copper, nickel, soda ash, meat, textiles.

Imports: $3.37 billion f.o.b. (2005 est.)—Foodstuff, machinery, electrical goods, transport equipment, textiles, fuel and petroleum products, wood and paper products, metal and metal products.

External debt: $556 million (2005).

Transport and Communications

Railways: 888 km.

Roads: 25,233 km.

Telephones: 136,500 (2004).

Mobile cellular: 823,100 (2005).

Internet users: 60,000 (2002).

Internet country code: .bw

Brazil

History

Archaeological evidence shows that the region that is today called Brazil has been inhabited since at least 9000 BC. The indigenous Indians who inhabited the coastal region at the time of first contact with Europeans is believed to have numbered between two million and six million.

In 1500, Portuguese explorer Pedro Alvares Cabral reached the area while on a voyage to India. Portugal initially called its new territory Vera Cruz, but later renamed it Brazil because of the large amounts of brazilwood, source of a valuable dye, that was found there. Before long, Brazil also became an important sugar-producing region for Portugal.

In 1789, Jose Joaquim da Silva Xavier, popularly known as Tiradentes, led the first rebellion against the Portuguese. The Portuguese authorities suppressed the rebellion and executed Tiradentes. In 1807, when Napoleon invaded Portugal, the Portuguese prince regent Dom Joao took refuge in Brazil. On 16 December 1815, he designated the Portuguese territories as the United Kingdom of Portugal, Brazil, and the Algarves. This had the effect of granting Brazil equality with Portugal. In 1822, Dom Joao's son, Dom Pedro, proclaimed the independence of Brazil. On 1 December, he was crowned emperor of Brazil. In 1889, the monarchy was overthrown and a federal republic established in Brazil. Brazil had already begun to rise as a coffee-producing giant and by 1902, it was producing over 60 per cent of the world's total coffee.

A revolt in 1930 saw Getulio Vargas taking charge as the head of a provisional revolutionary government. In 1937, Vargas led a coup and began ruling as a dictator. This was also the start of the welfare state in Brazil.

In 1960, the capital city was moved to Brasilia. From the 1980s, an economic crisis loomed over Brazil, and by 1991, inflation touched 1500 per cent.

Geography

Location: Eastern South America, bordering the Atlantic Ocean.

Area: 8,511,965 sq. km.

Terrain: The terrain of Brazil is mostly flat with rolling lowlands in the north, a narrow coastal belt, some plains, hills, and mountains.

Natural resources: Bauxite, gold, iron ore, manganese, nickel, phosphates, platinum, tin, uranium, petroleum, hydropower, timber.

Climate: The climate of Brazil is mostly tropical but temperate in the south.

People

Population: 188,078,227 (July 2006 est.).

Population growth rate: 1.04% (2006 est.).

Sex ratio: 0.98 male(s)/female (2006 est.).

Religions: Roman Catholic (nominal) 73.6%, Protestant 15.4%, Spiritualist 1.3%, Bantu/Voodoo 0.3%, other 1.8%, unspecified 0.2%, none 7.4%, (2000 census).

Languages: Portuguese (official), Spanish, English, French.

Literacy rate: Total 86.4%, Male 86.1%, Female 86.6% (2003 est.).

Infant mortality rate: 28.6 deaths/1,000 live births (2006 est.).

Life expectancy: Total 71.97 years, Male 68.02 years, Female 76.12 years (2006 est.).

Government

Capital: Brasilia.

Government type: Federative republic.

Independence: 7 September 1822 (from Portugal).

Legal system: Based on Roman codes.

Executive branch:

Chief of state: President Luiz Inacio 'Lula' Da Silva (since 1 January 2003). Vice-President Jose Alencar (since 1 January 2003). The president is both the chief of state and head of government.

Economy

Currency: Real.

Economy—overview:

The Brazilian economy is the largest of all South American economies. It has large and well-developed agricultural, service, mining and manufacturing sectors. Between 2001 and 2003, the economy successfully withstood a number of external and internal crises. Nevertheless, the economy is not without its fair share of problems, the most significant ones being debt related.

GDP: Purchasing power parity—$1.556 trillion (2005 est.).

GDP—real growth rate: 2.4% (2005 est.).

GDP—per capita: Purchasing power parity—$8,400 (2005 est.).

Inflation rate: 5.7% (2005 est.).

Population below poverty line: 22% (1998 est.).

Unemployment rate: 9.9% (2005 est.).

Exports: $115.1 billion f.o.b. (2005 est.)—Transport equipment, iron ore, soybeans, footwear, coffee, automobiles.

Imports: $78.02 billion f.o.b. (2005 est.)—Machinery, electrical and transport equipment, chemical products, oil.

External debt: $211.4 billion (2005).

Transport and Communications

Railways: 29,412 km.

Roads: 1,724,929 km.

Telephones: 42,382,200 (2004).

Mobile cellular: 65.605 million (2004).

Internet users: 14,300,000 (2002).

Internet country code: .br

Brunei

History

In the sixth century AD, Brunei enjoyed trade relations with China. Later, it came under Hindu influence by means of its connections with the Majapahit kingdom in Java. The power of Brunei started to decline towards the end of the sixteenth century when internal conflict affected the country. This decline con tinued through the nineteenth century. In 1841, Sarawak passed to the English. Later, it lost the island of Labuan in Brunei Bay and Sabah in present-day eastern East Malaysia. Petroleum was first produced in 1929.

In 1888, Brunei became a British protectorate. During World War II, the Japanese occupied Brunei between 1941–5. The British returned to power after the World War was over.

Geography

Location: South-eastern Asia, bordering the South China Sea and Malaysia.

Area: 5,770 sq. km.

Terrain: Brunei consists mostly of flat coastal plain that rises to mountains in the east.

Natural resources: Petroleum, natural gas, timber.

Climate: Brunei has a tropical hot, humid and rainy climate.

People

Population: 379,444 (July 2006 est.).

Population growth rate: 1.87% (2006 est.).

Sex ratio: 1.09 male(s)/female (2006 est.).

Religions: Muslim (official) 67%, Buddhist 13%, Christian 10%, indigenous beliefs and others 10%.

Languages: Malay (official), English, Chinese.

Literacy rate: Total 93.9%, Male 96.3%, Female 91.4% (2005 est.).

Infant mortality rate: 12.25 deaths/1,000 live births (2006 est.).

Life expectancy: Total 75.01 years, Male 72.57 years, Female 77.59 years (2006 est.).

Government

Capital: Bandar Seri Begawan.

Government type: Constitutional sultanate.

Independence: 1 January 1984 (from UK).

Legal system: Based on English common law; for Muslims, Islamic Shari'a law supersedes civil law in a number of areas.

Executive branch:
Chief of state: Sultan and Prime Minister Sir Hassanal Bolkiah (since 5 October 1967). The monarch is both the chief of state and head of government.

Since 1962, the sultan has ruled the country by decree. In a rare move towards political reform, an appointed parliament was revived in 2004. The constitution provides for an expanded house with up to fifteen elected MPs. However, no date has been set for elections.

In September 2004, the sultan reopened Brunei's parliament, twenty years after it was suspended. Observers saw the move as a tentative step towards giving some political power to the country's citizens.

Economy

Currency: Bruneian dollar.

Economy—overview:
Brunei has a small and wealthy economy. Crude oil and natural gas production account for almost 50 per cent of GDP. Per capita GDP is much higher than most other Third World countries and Brunei earns a lot of income from overseas investments. The government provides for all medical services and subsidizes rice and housing.

GDP: Purchasing power parity—$6.842 billion (2003 est.).

GDP—real growth rate: 3.2% (2003 est.).

GDP—per capita: Purchasing power parity—$23,600 (2003 est.).

Inflation rate: 0.3% (2003 est.).

Unemployment rate: 3.2% (2002 est.).

Exports: $4.514 billion f.o.b. (2004 est.)—Crude oil, natural gas, refined products.

Imports: $1.641 billion c.i.f. (2004 est.)—Machinery and transport equipment, manufactured goods, food, chemicals.

External debt: None.

Transport and Communications

Railways: 13 km (private line).

Roads: 1,150 km.

Telephones: 90,000 (2002).

Mobile cellular: 137,000 (2002).

Internet users: 35,000 (2002).

Internet country code: .bn

Bulgaria

History

Thracians lived in the country that is today Bulgaria from around 3500 BC. Thereafter, the Roman empire annexed the lands and by about the first century AD, it was a part of the empire. After the fall of the Roman empire, nu-

merous tribes invaded the area, the most important of which were the Bulgars.

The Ottoman Turks conquered Bulgaria in 1836. The Russians forced Turkey to grant Bulgaria independence following the Russo-Turkish War of 1877–8.

Bulgaria fought numerous wars in the first half of the twentieth century in the hope of gaining territory, mainly Macedonia, but most of these ended in failure. In 1944, the Soviet army invaded German-occupied Bulgaria. In 1946, a referendum abolished the monarchy and declared a republic. The Communist Party won the ensuing election and Georgi Dimitrov was elected prime minister. Bulgaria joined NATO on 29 March 2004 and is set to join the European Union at the earliest on 1 January 2007 after signing the Treaty of Accession on 25 April 2005.

Geography

Location: South-eastern Europe, bordering the Black Sea, between Romania and Turkey.

Area: 110,910 sq. km.

Terrain: Mostly mountains. There are lowlands in the north and the south-east.

Natural resources: Bauxite, copper, lead, zinc, coal, timber, arable land.

Climate: Bulgaria has a temperate climate with cold, damp winters and hot, dry summers.

People

Population: 7,385,367 (July 2006 est.).

Population growth rate: –0.86% (2006 est.).

Sex ratio: 0.93 male(s)/female (2006 est.).

Religions: Bulgarian Orthodox 82.6%, Muslim 12.2%, Roman Catholic 1.7%, Jewish 0.1%, Protestant, Gregorian–Armenian, and others 3.4% (1998).

Languages: Bulgarian, secondary languages closely correspond to ethnic breakdown.

Literacy rate: Total 98.6%, Male 99.1%, Female 98.2% (2003 est.).

Infant mortality rate: 19.85 deaths/1,000 live births (2006 est.).

Life expectancy: Total 72.3 years, Male 68.68 years, Female 76.13 years (2006 est.).

Government

Capital: Sofia.

Government type: Parliamentary democracy.

Independence: 3 March 1878 (from the Ottoman empire).

Legal system: Civil law and criminal law based on Roman law.

Executive branch:

Chief of state: President Georgi Parvanov (since 22 January 2002); Vice-President Angel Marin (since 22 January 2002).

Head of government: Prime Minister Sergei Stanishev (since 16 August 2005).

Economy

Currency: Lev.

GDP: Purchasing power parity—$71.54 billion (2005 est.).

GDP—real growth rate: 5.5% (2005 est.).

GDP—per capita: Purchasing power parity—$9,600 (2005 est.).

Inflation rate: 6.1% (2004 est.).

Population below poverty line: 13.4% (2002 est.).

Unemployment rate: 11.5% (2005 est.).

Exports: $11.67 billion f.o.b. (2005 est.)—Clothing, footwear, iron and steel, machinery and equipment, fuels.

Imports: $15.9 billion f.o.b. (2005 est.)—Fuels, minerals, and raw materials; machinery and equipment; metals and ores; chemicals and plastics; food, textiles.

External debt: $15.46 billion (2005 est.).

Transport and Communications

Railways: 4,294 km.

Roads: 102,016 km.

Telephones: 2,726,800 (2004).

Mobile cellular: 4,729,700 (2004).

Internet users: 630,000 (2002).

Internet country code: .bg

Burkina Faso

History

In 1947, Upper Volta was established as a separate territory within French West Africa. In 1960, it became independent.

In the first thirty years after independence, Upper Volta saw one coup after another. In 1984, the country was renamed as Burkina Faso. The country has one of the highest infection rates of HIV in the region.

Geography

Location: Western Africa, north of Ghana.

Area: 274,200 sq. km.

Natural resources: Manganese, limestone, marble; small deposits of gold, antimony, copper, nickel, bauxite, lead, phosphates, zinc, silver.

Climate: Burkina Faso has a tropical climate with warm, dry winters and hot, wet summers.

People

Population: 13,902,972 (July 2006 est.).

Population growth rate: 3% (2006 est.).

Sex ratio: 0.99 male(s)/female (2006 est.).

Religions: Indigenous beliefs 40%, Muslim 50%, Christian (mainly Roman Catholic) 10%.

Languages: French (official), native African languages belonging to Sudanic family.

Literacy rate: Total 26.6%, Male 36.9%, Female 16.6% (2003 est.). Note: Burkina Faso is the most illiterate country in Africa.

Infant mortality rate: 91.35 deaths/1,000 live births (2006 est.).

Life expectancy: Total 48.85 years, Male 47.33 years, Female 50.42 years (2006 est.).

Government

Capital: Ouagadougou.

Government type: Parliamentary republic.

Independence: 5 August 1960 (from France).

Legal system: Based on French civil law system and customary law.

Executive branch:
Chief of state: President Blaise Compaore (since 15 October 1987).

The president is elected by popular vote for a five-year term. In April 2000, the constitution was amended, reducing the presidential term from seven to five years, enforceable as of 2005 and allowing the president to be reelected only once. The prime minister is appointed by the president with the consent of the legislature.

Elections were last held on 13 November 2005; the next is to be held in 2010. Blaise Compaore, a former military leader, won a third successive term in the presidential elections in November 2005 (per cent of popular vote: Blaise Compaora 80.3 per cent, Benewende Stanislas Sankara 4.9 per cent). Poll officials said he had taken more than 80 per cent of the vote. He was one of twelve candidates

Elections and election results: President elected by popular vote for a five-year term; election last held 13 November 2005 (next to be held in 2010); in April 2000, the constitution was amended reducing the presidential term from seven to five years, enforceable as of 2005, and allowing the president to be re-elected only once; prime minister appointed by the president with the consent of the legislature.

Blaise Compaore reelected president; per cent of popular vote—Blaise Compaore 80.3 per cent, Benewende Stanislas Sankara 4.9 per cent. Blaise Campaore, a former military leader, won a third successive term in presidential elections in November 2005. Poll officials said he had taken more than 80 per cent of the vote. He was one of twelve candidates

Head of government: Prime Minister Ernest Paramanga Yonli (since 6 November 2000).

Economy

Currency: Communaute Financiere Africaine franc.

GDP: Purchasing power parity—$16.95 billion (2005 est.).

GDP—real growth rate: 4.5% (2005 est.).

GDP—per capita: Purchasing power parity—$1,300 (2005 est.).

Inflation rate: 3% (2005 est.).

Population below poverty line: 45% (2003 est.).

Exports: $395 million f.o.b. (2005 est.)—Cotton, livestock, gold.

Imports: $992 million f.o.b. (2005 est.)—Capital goods, foodstuff, petroleum.

External debt: $1.85 billion (2003).

Transport and Communications

Railways: 622 km.

Roads: 12,506 km.

Telephones: 81,400 (2004).

Mobile cellular: 572,000 (2005).

Internet users: 48,000 (2003).

Internet country code: .bf

Burundi

History

In 1890, the Tutsi kingdom of Urundi and neighbouring Ruanda (present-day Rwanda) was incorporated into German East Africa. In 1923, Belgium was granted League of Nations mandate to administer Ruanda–Urundi. In 1962, Urundi was separated from Ruanda–Urundi, and granted independence as Burundi, a monarchy under King Mwambutsa IV. The next four decades saw constant coups, massacres and assassinations, mostly along ethnic lines.

In October 2001, talks brokered by Nelson Mandela led to a transitional government in Burundi. Hutu and Tutsi leaders were meant to share power. However, the main Hutu rebel groups refused to sign ceasefire and fighting intensified. Fighting continued into 2004.

Geography

Location: Central Africa, east of the Democratic Republic of the Congo.

Area: 27,830 sq. km.

Natural resources: Nickel, uranium, rare earth oxides, peat, cobalt, copper, platinum (not yet exploited), vanadium, arable land, hydropower.

Climate: Burundi has an equatorial climate.

People

Population: 8,090,068 (July 2006 est.).

Population growth rate: 3.7% (2006 est.).

Sex ratio: 0.99 male(s)/female (2006 est.).

Religions: Christian 67% (Roman Catholic 62%, Protestant 5%), indigenous beliefs 23%, Muslim 10%.

Languages: Kirundi (official), French (official), Swahili (along Lake Tanganyika and in the Bujumbura area).

Literacy rate: Total 51.6%, Male 58.5%, Female 45.2% (2003 est.).

Infant mortality rate: 63.13 deaths/1,000 live births (2006 est.).

Life expectancy: Total 50.81 years, Male 50.07 years, Female 51.58 years (2006 est.).

Government

Capital: Bujumbura.

Government type: Republic.

Independence: 1 July 1962 (from UN trusteeship under Belgian administration).

Legal system: Based on German and Belgian civil codes and customary law.

Executive branch:
Chief of state: President Domitien Pierre Nkurunziza (since 26 August 2005).

Head of government: President Pierre Nkurunziza (since 26 August 2005).

Economy

Currency: Burundi franc.

GDP: Purchasing power parity—$5.654 billion (2005 est.).

GDP—real growth rate: 1.1% (2005 est.).

GDP—per capita: Purchasing power parity—$700 (2005 est.).

Inflation rate: 14% (2005 est.).

Population below poverty line: 68% (2002 est.).

Exports: $52 million f.o.b. (2005 est.)—Coffee, tea, sugar, cotton, hides.

Imports: $200 million f.o.b. (2005 est.).

External debt: $1.2 billion (2003).

Transport and Communications

Railways: None.

Roads: 14,480 km.

Telephones: 23,900 (2003).

Mobile cellular: 153,000 (2005).

Internet users: 25,000 (2005).

Internet country code: .bi

Cambodia

History

In the first century AD, Chinese and Indian pilgrims and traders stopped on the coast of present-day Cambodia. A kingdom which Chinese writers called Funan existed in south Cambodia at this point of time.

The region that is today Cambodia came under the rule of the Hindu Khmers in around 600. It was during Khmer rule that the famous Angkor Wat and Angkor Thom temple complexes were constructed. The period of the Khmer rule from the ninth to the fifteenth centuries is considered as the classical era of Cambodian history.

France colonized the region in 1863 and joined together Cambodia, Laos and Vietnam into one protectorate called French Indochina. In 1941, Norodom Sihanouk came to power on the ceremonial throne of Cambodia. In 1953, France granted Cambodia independence. In 1955, Norodom Sihanouk abdicated the throne to his parents but remained as the head of government.

In March 1970, Gen. Lon Nol overthrew Sihanouk while he was away on foreign tours. In 1975, Lon Nol was himself overthrown by Pol Pot, leader of the Khmer Rouge forces. This was the starting point of one of the most gruesome periods of modern world history. Millions of Cambodians were killed by state-sponsored terrorism or due to forced labour. The country was renamed Kampuchea.

In January 1979, Vietnamese forces removed Pol Pot from power. Pol Pot,

along with tens of thousands of Khmer Rouge fighters, withdrew into the hills of western Cambodia. They joined forces with pro-Sihanouk forces to launch a guerilla movement aimed at overthrowing the pro-Vietnam government that had been installed in the country. In 1993, a deal was worked out whereby power would be shared by pro-Vietnamese leader Hun Sen and Sihanouk's son, Prince Ranariddh. The two of them would be co-prime ministers.

Elections in July 2003 were relatively peaceful, but it took one year of negotiations between contending political parties before a coalition government was formed.

Geography

Location: South-eastern Asia, bordering the Gulf of Thailand, between Thailand, Vietnam and Laos.

Area: 181,040 sq. km.

Terrain: The terrain of Cambodia is mostly made up of low, flat plains with mountains in the south-west and north.

Natural resources: Timber, gemstones, some iron ore, manganese, phosphates, hydropower potential.

Climate: Cambodia has a tropical climate. The monsoon season is from May to November while the dry season is from December to April.

People

Population: 13,881,427 (July 2006 est.).

Population growth rate: 1.78% (2006 est.).

Sex ratio: 0.95 male(s)/female (2006 est.).

Religions: Theravada Buddhist 95%, others 5%.

Languages: Khmer (official) 95%, French, English.

Literacy rate: Total 73.6%, Male 84.7%, Female 64.1% (2004 est.)

Infant mortality rate: 68.78 deaths/1,000 live births (2006 est.).

Life expectancy: Total 59.29 years, Male 57.35 years, Female 61.32 years (2006 est.).

Government

Capital: Phnom Penh.

Government type: Multiparty democracy under a constitutional monarchy.

Independence: 9 November 1953 (from France).

Legal system: Primarily a civil law mixture of French-influenced codes from the United Nations Transitional Authority in Cambodia (UNTAC) period, royal decrees, and acts of the legislature.

Executive branch:

Chief of state: King Norodom Sihamoni (since November 2004).

Head of government: Prime Minister Hun Sen (since 30 November 1998).

Economy

Currency: Riel.

Economy—overview: The long-term development of the Cambodian economy after years of strife and conflict remains a formidable task. Its infrastructure is undeveloped, its population lacking in technical skills and higher education. Foreign investment and foreign aid suffer due to the lack of confidence in the country.

GDP: Purchasing power parity—$30.65 billion (2005 est.).

GDP—real growth rate: 6% (2005 est.).

GDP—per capita: Purchasing power parity—$2,200 (2005 est.).

Inflation rate: 4.3% (2005 est.).

Population below poverty line: 40% (2004 est.).

Unemployment rate: 2.5% (2000 est.).

Exports: $2.663 billion f.o.b. (2005 est.)—Timber, garments, rubber, rice, fish.

Imports: $3.538 billion f.o.b. (2005 est.)—Petroleum products, cigarettes, gold, construction materials, machinery, motor vehicles.

External debt: $800 million (2003 est.).

Transport and Communications

Railways: 602 km.

Roads: 12,323 km.

Telephones: 36,400 (2003).

Mobile cellular: 498,000 (2003).

Internet users: 41,000 (2005).

Internet country code: .kh

Cameroon

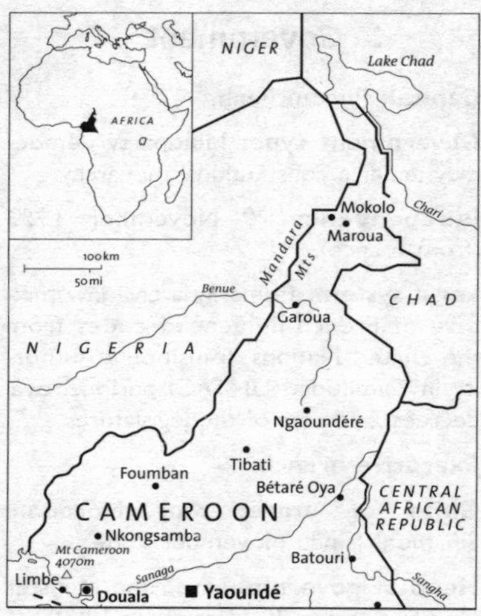

History

The Portuguese and the Dutch were among the first European powers to colonize Cameroon. In 1919, the London Declaration divided Cameroon into a British administrative zone (20 per cent of the land) and a French zone (80 per cent). In 1922, the League of Nations granted a mandate to the UK and France for their respective administrative zones.

In 1958, French Cameroon was granted self-government with Ahmadou Ahidjo as prime minister. Following a UN-sponsored referendum in 1961, one part of the British-administered Cameroon, Southern Cameroon, joined the Republic of Cameroon to become the Federal Republic of Cameroons. The other part, Northern Cameroon, joined Nigeria. In 1972, a national referendum was held and subsequently Cameroon became a unitary state. It was renamed the United Republic of Cameroon.

Geography

Location: Western Africa, bordering the Bight of Biafra, between Equatorial Guinea and Nigeria.

Area: 475,440 sq. km.

Terrain: Diverse, with coastal plain in the south-west, dissected plateau in the centre, mountains in the west, and plains in the north.

Natural resources: Petroleum, bauxite, iron ore, timber, hydropower.

Climate: The climate of Cameroon is tropical along the coast but semi-arid and hot in the northern part of the country.

People

Population: 17,340,702 (July 2006 est.).

Population growth rate: 2.04% (2006 est.).

Sex ratio: 1.01 male(s)/female (2006 est.).

Religions: Indigenous beliefs 40%, Christian 40%, Muslim 20%.

Languages: English (official), French (official), 24 major African language groups.

Literacy rate: Total 79%, Male 84.7%, Female 73.4% (2003 est.).

Infant mortality rate: 63.52 deaths/ 1,000 live births (2006 est.).

Life expectancy: Total 51.16 years, Male 50.98 years, Female 51.39 years (2006 est.). Note: Estimates for this country explicitly take into account the effects of the high mortality due to AIDS which result in lower life expectancy, higher infant mortality and death rates, lower population and growth rates, and changes in the distribution of population by age and sex than would otherwise be expected.

Government

Capital: Yaounde.

Government type: Unitary republic; multiparty presidential regime.

Independence: 1 January 1960 (from French-administered UN trusteeship).

Legal system: Based on French civil law system, with Common Law influence.

Executive branch:

Chief of state: President Paul Biya (since 6 November 1982).

Head of government: Prime Minister Ephraim Inoni (since 8 December 2004).

Economy

Currency: Communaute Financiere Africaine franc.

GDP: Purchasing power parity—$40.83 billion (2005 est.).

GDP—real growth rate: 2.8% (2005 est.).

GDP—per capita: Purchasing power parity—$2,400 (2005 est.).

Inflation rate: 1.5% (2005 est.).

Population below poverty line: 48% (2000 est.).

Unemployment rate: 30% (2001 est.).

Exports: $3.236 billion f.o.b. (2005 est.)—Crude oil and petroleum products, lumber, cocoa beans, aluminium, coffee, cotton.

Imports: $2.514 billion f.o.b. (2005 est.)—Machinery, electrical equipment, transport equipment, fuel, food.

External debt: $8.46 billion (2004 est.).

Transport and Communications

Railways: 1,008 km.

Roads: 80,932 km.

Telephones: 110,900 (2002).

Mobile cellular: 2.259 (2005).

Internet users: 60,000 (2002).

Internet country code: .cm

Canada

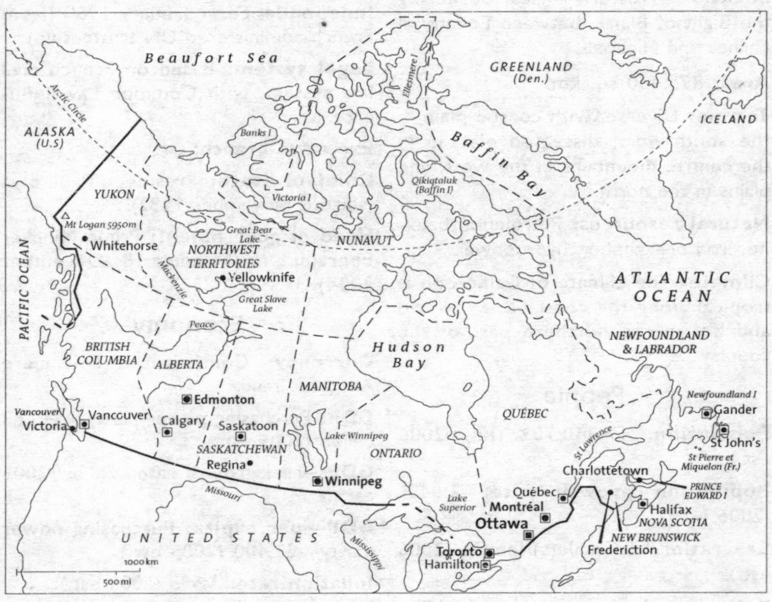

History

The first inhabitants of what is today Canada were people like the Inuits (Eskimos). It is thought that the Norse explorer Leif Eriksson reached either Labrador or Nova Scotia in 1000. In 1534, Jacques Cartier took and claimed Canada for France. It soon came to be called New France. The British responded to the French inroads into Canada by setting up the British Hudson's Bay Company in 1670. The main reasons behind French and British interest in Canada were the prospects in fisheries and the fur trade.

Soon the rivalries took a serious course and in 1713, the French lost Hudson Bay, Nova Scotia and Newfoundland. The British added to their conquests during the Seven Year's War (1756–63). Ultimately, the French took leave of the North American mainland.

In 1849, the UK recognized Canada's right to self-government. The British North American Act of 1867 created the dominion of Canada by confederating Upper and Lower Canada, New Brunswick and Nova Scotia. In 1869, Canada purchased the vast lands in the Middle West. This led to the formation of the states of Manitoba (in 1870), Alberta and Saskatchewan (both in 1905).

The Statute of Westminister of 1931 recognized the equal status of UK and its dominions including Canada. Hence, Canada was recognized as a partner nation of UK, which was not subordinate in any form to UK and only associated by the common allegiance to the Crown.

Geography

Location: Northern North America, bordering the North Atlantic Ocean on the east, North Pacific Ocean on the west, and the Arctic Ocean on the north, north of the USA.

Area: 9,984,670 sq. km.

Terrain: Canada consists mostly of plains with mountains in the west and lowlands in the south-east.

Natural resources: Iron ore, nickel, zinc, copper, gold, lead, molybdenum, potash, diamonds, silver, fish, timber, wildlife, coal, petroleum, natural gas, hydropower.

Climate: The climate of Canada varies from temperate in the south to subarctic and arctic in the north.

People

Population: 33,098,932 (July 2006 est.).

Population growth rate: 0.88% (2006 est.).

Sex ratio: 0.98 male(s)/female (2006 est.).

Religions: Roman Catholic 42.6%, Protestant 23.3% (including United Church 9.5%, Anglican 6.8%, Baptist 2.4%, Lutheran 2%), other Christian 4.4%, Muslim 1.9%, other and unspecified 11.8%, none 16% (2001 census).

Languages: English 59.3% (official), French 23.2% (official), others 17.5%.

Literacy rate: Total 99%, Male 99%, Female 99% (2003 est.).

Infant mortality rate: 4.69 deaths/1,000 live births (2006 est.).

Life expectancy: Total 80.22 years, Male 76.86 years, Female 83.74 years (2006 est.).

Government

Capital: Ottawa.

Government type: A constitutional monarchy that is also a parliamentary democracy and a federation.

Independence: 1 July 1867 (from UK).

Legal system: Based on English common law, except in Quebec, where civil law system based on French law prevails.

Executive branch:

Chief of state: Queen Elizabeth II (since 6 February 1952), represented by Governor General Michaëlle Jean (since 27 September 2005).

Head of government: Prime Minister Stepher Harper (since 6 Feb 2006);

Legislative branch:

Canada has a bicameral parliament or parlement that consists of the Senate or Senat (the Governor General appoints the members with the advice of the prime minister and they serve until reaching seventy-five years of age; the normal limit is 105 senators) and the House of Commons or Chambre des Communes (301 seats; members elected by direct, popular vote to serve for up to five-year terms).

Elections and election results: Elections to the House of Commons were last held in 2006.

Twelve years of Liberal government ended when incumbent prime minister Paul Martin was defeated by Stephen Harper's opposition Conservatives in elections on 23 January 2006.

Elections: House of Commons—last held 23 January 2006 (next to be held in 2011). Election results: House of Commons (per cent of vote by party)—Conservative Party 36.3%, Liberal Party 30.2%, New Democratic Party 17.5%, Bloc Quebecois 10.5%, Greens 4.5%, other 1%; party-wise seats—Conservative Party 124, Liberal Party 103, New Democratic Party 29, Bloc Quebecois 51, other 1.

Economy

Currency: Canadian dollar.

Economy—overview:

Canada has an affluent, high-tech in-

Population growth rate: 0.64% (2006 est.).

Sex ratio: 0.95 male(s)/female (2006 est.).

Religions: Roman Catholic (infused with indigenous beliefs); Protestant (mostly Church of the Nazarene).

Languages: Portuguese, Crioulo (a mixture of Portuguese and West African words).

Literacy rate: Total 76.6%, Male 85.8%, Female 69.2% (2003 est.).

Infant mortality rate: 46.52 deaths/1,000 live births (2006 est.).

Life expectancy: Total 70.73 years, Male 67.41 years, Female 74.15 years (2006 est.).

Government

Capital: Praia.

Government type: Republic.

Independence: 5 July 1975 (from Portugal).

Legal system: Derived from the legal system of Portugal.

Executive branch:
Chief of state: President Pedro de Verona Rodrigues Pires (since 22 March 2001). Incumbent leader Pedro Pires won the presidential elections in February 2006, gaining 51 per cent of the vote and narrowly defeating his rival, Carlos Veiga. The pair has been Cape Verde's dominant political personalities since independence in 1975. Poverty, unemployment and the state of the economy were key issues in the 2006 poll.

Head of government: Prime Minister Jose Maria Pereira Neves (since 1 February 2001).

Economy

Currency: Cape Verdean escudo.

GDP: Purchasing power parity—$2.99 billion (2005 est.).

GDP—real growth rate: 5.5% (2005 est.).

GDP—per capita: Purchasing power parity—$6,200 (2005 est.).

Inflation rate: 1.8% (2005 est.).

Population below poverty line: 30% (2000).

Unemployment rate: 21% (2000 est.).

Exports: $73.35 million f.o.b. (2005 est.)—Fuel, shoes, garments, fish, hides.

Imports: $500 million f.o.b. (2005 est.)—Foodstuff, industrial products, transport equipment, fuels.

External debt: $325 million (2002).

Transport and Communications

Railways: None.

Roads: 1,350 km.

Telephones: 73,400 (2005).

Mobile cellular: 81,700 (2005).

Internet users: 25,000 (2005).

Internet country code: .cv

Central African Republic

History

France occupied the region that is today Central African Republic in the 1880s and in 1894 it set up the colony of Ubanghi Shari. In 1960, the Central African Republic became independent.

Geography

Location: Central Africa, north of the Democratic Republic of the Congo.

Area: 622,984 sq. km.

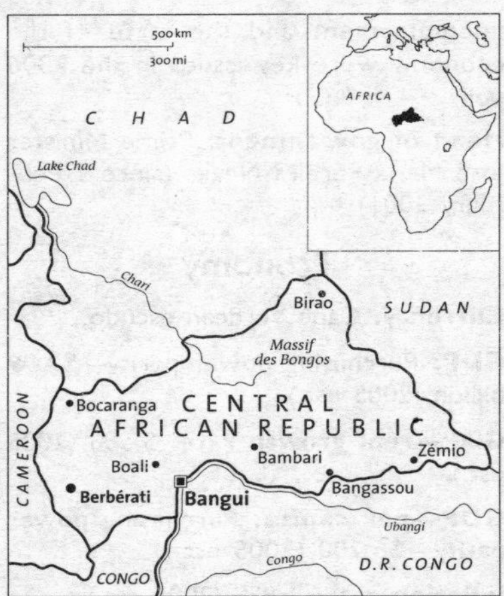

Terrain: Flat to rolling plateau; scattered hills in the north-east and south-west.

Natural resources: Diamond, uranium, timber, gold, oil, hydropower.

Climate: Central African Republic has a tropical climate with hot, dry winters and mild to hot, wet summers.

People

Population: 4,303,356 (July 2006 est.).

Population growth rate: 1.53% (2006 est.).

Sex ratio: 0.98 male(s)/female (2006 est.).

Religions: Indigenous beliefs 35%, Protestant 25%, Roman Catholic 25% (animistic beliefs and practices strongly influence the Christians), Muslim 15%.

Languages: French (official), Sangho (lingua franca and national language), tribal languages.

Literacy rate: Total 51%, Male 63.3%, Female 39.9% (2003 est.).

Infant mortality rate: 85.63 deaths/1,000 live births (2006 est.).

Life expectancy: Total 43.54 years, Male 43.46 years, Female 43.62 years (2006 est.).

Government

Capital: Bangui.

Government type: Republic.

Independence: 13 August 1960 (from France).

Legal system: Based on French law.

Executive branch:
Chief of state: President Francois Bozize (since 15 March 2003). This former coup leader took more than 64 per cent of the vote in the second round of presidential elections in May 2005, ending two years of military rule. His rival was Martin Ziguele, a former prime minister. Francois Bozize first took power in a 2003 coup.

The newly elected president called for national unity. He had pledged in his campaign to bring security to the coup-prone country.

Head of government: Prime Minister Elie Dote (since 13 June 2005). Note: Celestin Gaombalet resigned 11 June 2005.

Economy

Currency: Communaute Financiere Africaine franc.

GDP: Purchasing power parity—$4.784 billion (2005 est.).

GDP—real growth rate: 2.2% (2005 est.).

GDP—per capita: Purchasing power parity—$1,110 (2005 est.).

Inflation rate: 3.6% (2001 est.).

Unemployment rate: 8% (2001 est.).

Exports: $131 million f.o.b. (2004 est.)—Diamond, timber, cotton, coffee, tobacco.

Imports: $203 million f.o.b. (2004 est.)—Food, textiles, petroleum products, machinery, electrical equipment, motor vehicles, chemicals, pharmaceuticals.

External debt: $1.06 billion (2002 est.).

Transport and Communications

Railways: None.

Roads: 23,810 km.

Telephones: 10,000 (2004).

Mobile cellular: 60,000 (2004).

Internet users: 9,000 (2005).

Internet country code: .cf

Chad

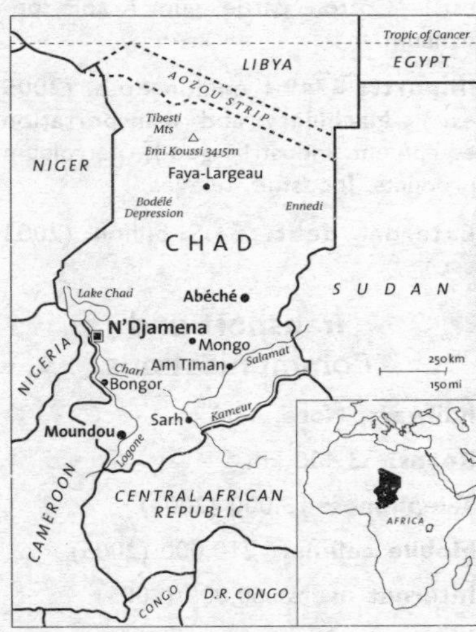

History

Berbers began arriving in the area around Lake Chad in the eighth century AD. The onset of Islam happened around 1085. By 1913, France completed its conquest of Chad. In 1960, Chad became independent with Francois Ngarta Tombalbaye as President.

Chad, part of France's African holdings until 1960, endured three decades of civil warfare as well as invasions by Libya before a semblance of peace was finally restored in 1990. The government eventually drafted a democratic constitution, and held flawed presidential elections in 1996 and 2001. In 1998, a rebellion broke out in northern Chad; there are sporadic eruptions despite several peace agreements between the government and the rebels. In 2005 new rebel groups emerged in western Sudan and have made probing attacks into eastern Chad. Power remains in the hands of an ethnic minority. In June 2005, President Idriss Deby held a referendum, successfully removing constitutional term limits.

Geography

Location: Central Africa, south of Libya.

Area: 1.284 million sq. km.

Terrain: Broad, arid plains in the centre, desert in the north, mountains in the north-west, lowlands in the south.

Natural resources: Petroleum, uranium, natron, kaolin, fish.

Climate: The climate of Chad is tropical in the south and arid in the north.

People

Population: 9,944,201 (July 2006 est.).

Population growth rate: 2.93% (2006 est.).

Sex ratio: 0.96 male(s)/female (2006 est.).

Religions: Muslim 51%, Christian 35%, animist 7%, others 7%.

Languages: French (official), Arabic (official), Sara (in south), more than 120 different languages and dialects.

Literacy rate: Total 47.5%, Male 56%, Female 39.3% (2003 est.).

Infant mortality rate: 91.45 deaths/1,000 live births (2006 est.).

Life expectancy: Total 47.52 years, Male 45.88 years, Female 49.21 years (2006 est.).

Government

Capital: N'Djamena.

Government type: Republic.

Independence: 11 August 1960 (from France).

Legal system: Based on French civil law system and Chadian customary law.

Executive branch:
Chief of state: President Lt Gen. Idriss Deby (since 4 December 1990).

Head of government: Prime Minister Pascal Yoadimnadji (since 3 February 2005).

Economy

Currency: Communaute Financiere Africaine franc.

GDP: Purchasing power parity—$14.79 billion (2005 est.).

GDP—real growth rate: 6% (2005 est.).

GDP—per capita: Purchasing power parity—$1,500 (2005 est.).

Inflation rate: 5.5% (2005 est.).

Population below poverty line: 80% (2001 est.).

Exports: $3.016 billion f.o.b. (2005 est.)—Cotton, cattle, gum Arabic, petroleum.

Imports: $749.1 million f.o.b. (2005 est.)—Machinery and transportation equipment, industrial goods, petroleum products, foodstuff, textiles.

External debt: $1.5 billion (2003 est.).

Transport and Communications

Railways: None.

Roads: 33,400 km.

Telephones: 13,000 (2004).

Mobile cellular: 210,000 (2005).

Internet users: 60,000 (2005).

Internet country code: .td

Chile

History

There were at least 500,000 natives living in the region that is today Chile when Spanish conquest of the area began in the middle of the sixteenth century. The most significant of these were the Araucanian Indian group. They put up a strong resistance to the Spanish right up to the 1880s.

In the sixteenth century, numerous English and Dutch pirates and adventurers raided the Chilean coast in search of easy wealth. In 1810, a junta of locally elected leaders in Santiago proclaimed autonomy for Chile. In 1818, Chile became independent with Bernardo O' Higgins as the supreme director.

In 1970, Salvador Allende became the world's first democratically elected Marxist president and initiated an extensive programme of nationalization and social reform. However, a US-

sponsored coup toppled Allende in 1973 and installed General Augusto Pinochet as the country's new dictator. After Pinochet lost a referendum on whether he should remain in power in 1988, Patricio Aylwin was elected Chile's new president in 1989–90. Although Pinochet stepped down as head of state in 1990, he remained commander-in-chief of the army.

Geography

Location: Southern South America, bordering the South Pacific Ocean, Argentina, Bolivia and Peru.

Area: 756,950 sq. km. This includes Easter Island (Isla de Pascua) and Isla Sala y Gomez.

Terrain: The terrain of Chile consists of low coastal mountains, a fertile central valley and the Andes mountains in the east.

Natural resources: Copper, timber, iron ore, nitrates, precious metals, molybdenum, hydropower.

Climate: Chile is mostly temperate.

People

Population: 16,134,219 (July 2006 est.).

Population growth rate: 0.94% (2006 est.).

Sex ratio: 0.98 male(s)/female (2006 est.).

Religions: Roman Catholic 89%, Protestant 11%, Jewish.

Languages: Spanish.

Literacy rate: Total 96.2%, Male 96.4%, Female 96.1% (2003 est.).

Infant mortality rate: 8.58 deaths/1,000 live births (2006 est.).

Life expectancy: Total 76.77 years, Male 73.49 years, Female 80.21 years (2006 est.).

Government

Capital: Santiago.

Government type: Republic.

Independence: 18 September 1810 (from Spain).

Legal system: Based on Code of 1857 derived from Spanish law and subsequent codes influenced by French and Austrian law.

Executive branch:
Chief of state: President Michelle Bachelet Jeria (since 11 March 2006). The president is both the chief of state and head of government.

Economy

Currency: Chilean peso.

Economy—overview:
Chile has a strong market-oriented economy, one of the most robust in South America. It enjoys a reputation for strong financial institutions and good policy. Nevertheless, Chile experienced a recession in 1999, partly due to se-

vere drought. Chile also suffers from chronic unemployment.

Chile has also signed a free trade agreement with USA that became effective on 1 January 2004. It also signed a free trade agreement with China in November 2005. Record-high copper prices strengthened the peso to a five-and-a-half-year high, as of December 2005, and will boost GDP in 2006.

GDP: Purchasing power parity—$187.1 billion (2005 est.).

GDP—real growth rate: 6% (2005 est.).

GDP—per capita: Purchasing power parity—$11,300 (2005 est.).

Inflation rate: 3.2% (2005 est.).

Population below poverty line: 18.2% (2005 est.).

Unemployment rate: 8% (2005 est.).

Exports: $38.03 billion f.o.b. (2005 est.)—Copper, fish, fruits, paper and pulp, chemicals, wine.

Imports: $30.09 billion f.o.b. (2005 est.)—Consumer goods, chemicals, motor vehicles, fuels, electrical machinery, heavy industrial machinery, food.

External debt: $44.8 billion (2005 est.).

Transport and Communications

Railways: 6,585 km.

Roads: 79,605 km.

Telephone: 3,318,300 (2004).

Mobile cellular: 9,566,600 (2004).

Internet users: 5.6 million (2004).

Internet country code: .cl

China

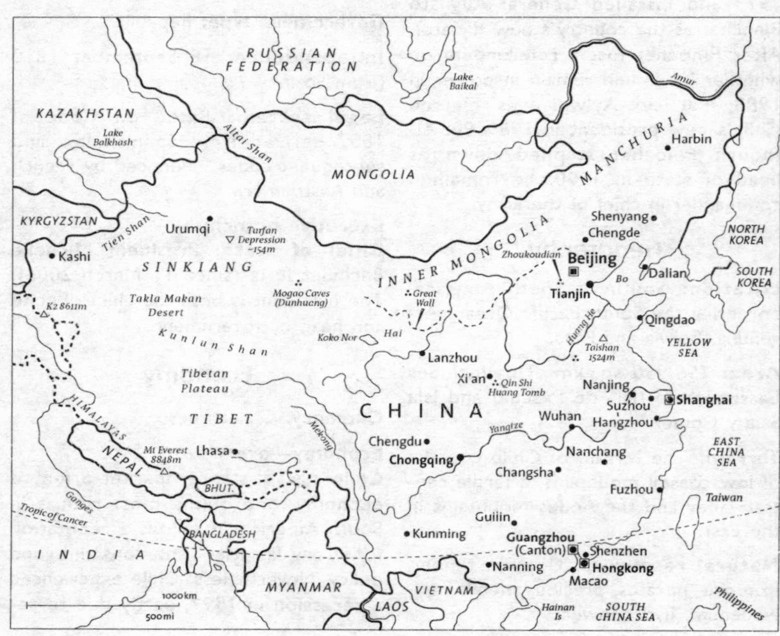

History

The recorded history of China goes back nearly 4,000 years, although archeologists have traced the beginnings of human civilization in China to an even earlier time.

According to Chinese tradition, the Xia dynasty (2070–1600 BC) was the first Chinese dynasty to rule a state. The Shang dynasty (1600–1046 BC) overthrew the Xia dynasty. The Western Zhou dynasty (1046–771 BC) succeeded the Shang dynasty and was followed by the Eastern Zhou dynasty which is divided into two eras. The first of these two eras was the Spring and Autumn era that lasted between 770 and 476 BC while the Warring States era lasted between 475 and 221 BC.

Next came the Qin dynasty (221–207 BC) The first emperor of the Qin dynasty, Qin Shi Huang (259–210 BC) founded the first centralized, unified, multi-ethnic feudal state in Chinese history. He is also credited with the construction of the Great Wall of China, which stretches for 5,000 km in northern China.

A peasant uprising overthrew the Qin dynasty and led to the founding of the Han dynasty in 206 BC. After the Han dynasty came the Three Kingdoms Period (AD 220–65), the Jin dynasty (265–420), the Southern and Northern dynasties (420–589), and the Sui dynasty (581–618).

The Tang dynasty followed the Sui dynasty. During the Tang dynasty, a successful government and administration system based on the Sui model was developed. Besides, it was a period of great cultural and artistic activity in the country. It is widely regarded as a golden period of Chinese history.

A period of almost continual warfare followed the demise of the Tang dynasty. This was the period of Five dynasties and Ten States. The Song dynasty ruled over China between 960–1279.

In 1206, the famous Genghis Khan established the Mongolian Khanate. In 1271, his grandson, Kublai Khan, founded the Yuan dynasty (1271–1368) after conquering the Central Plains. He founded a united country that also included Xinjiang, Tibet and Yunnan. It was during the Song-Yuan period, that the Chinese developed on their inventions—paper, printing, the compass and gunpowder and introduced them to the rest of the world.

Next came the Ming dynasty (1368–1644) and the last Chinese royal dynasty, the Qing dynasty (1644–1911). The rapid decline of the Qing dynasty in the nineteenth century encouraged British nationals to import large quantities of opium into China. The Qing government's imposition of a ban on opium trafficking in China led to the Opium War with UK in the 1840. It culminated in the signing of the Treaty of Nanking, which in many ways was an act of capitulation by the Chinese government to foreign forces on its own soil.

The Revolution of 1911, led by Dr Sun Yat-sen, overthrew the 200-odd-year-old Qing dynasty. It ended more than 2,000 years of feudal monarchy and established the Republic of China (1912–49).

The unequal terms and conditions imposed on China following World War I precipitated the 4th May Movement of 1919. In 1921, twelve communist delegates representing different parts of the Chinese nation, including Mao Zedong, held the First National Congress in Shanghai to found the Communist Party of China.

The years to follow witnessed the Chinese people, led by the Communist Party of China, fight the Northern Expeditionary War (1924–7), the War of Agrarian Revolution (1927–37), the War of Resistance against Japan (1937–45) and the War of Liberation (1945–9). Although the Communist Party succeeded in defeating the Kuomintang and the Japanese, another civil war erupted soon after the anti-Japanese war. The three-year war finally overthrew the Kuomintang government in 1949. On 1 October 1949, the People's Republic of China (PRC) was officially founded.

In October 1950, Chinese forces invaded eastern Tibet. In 1951, Tibet and China signed a treaty that guaranteed Tibetan autonomy and religion but also allowed the setting up of Chinese civil and military offices at Lhasa, the Tibetan capital. When a popular rebellion erupted at Lhasa in March 1959, the Dalai Lama escaped to India, along with many of his aides. In 1962, China and India were involved in a brief border war. In 1979, China instituted a policy of 'reform and opening to the outside world', which aimed to modernize both the political and economic machinery of China. During 3–4 June 1989, the Chinese government used military forces including tanks and armed soldiers to suppress a dramatic series of pro-democracy student demonstrations resulting in the loss of hundreds of lives. In 1997, UK handed its colony of Hong Kong back to China. The Portuguese handover of Macao followed in 1999.

Geography

Location: Eastern Asia, bordering the East China Sea, Korea Bay, Yellow Sea, and South China Sea, between North Korea and Vietnam.

Area: Total: 9,596,960 sq. km.

Terrain: The terrain of China consists mostly of mountains and high plateaus. There are deserts in the west, and plains, deltas and hills in the east.

Natural resources: Coal, iron ore, petroleum, natural gas, mercury, tin, tungsten, antimony, manganese, molybdenum, vanadium, magnetite, aluminum, lead, zinc, uranium, hydropower potential.

Climate: The vast expanse of China means that the country's climate is extremely diverse. China has a tropical climate in the south but is subarctic in the north.

People

Population: 1,313,973,713 (July 2006 est.).

Population growth rate: 0.59% (2006 est.).

Sex ratio: 1.06 male(s)/female (2006 est.).

Religions: Officially atheist; unofficially: Daoist (Taoist), Buddhist, Muslim, Christian (2002 est.).

Languages: Standard Chinese or Mandarin (Putonghua, based on the Beijing dialect), Yue (Cantonese), Wu (Shanghaiese), Minbei (Fuzhou), Minnan (Hokkien-Taiwanese), Xiang, Gan, Hakka dialects, minority languages.

Literacy rate: Total 90.9%, Male 95.1%, Female 86.5% (2002 est.).

Infant mortality rate: 23.12 deaths/1,000 live births (2006 est.).

Life expectancy: Total 72.58 years, Male 70.89 years, Female 74.46 years (2006 est.).

Government

Capital: Beijing.

Government type: Communist state.

Independence: 221 BC (unification under the Qin or Ch'in Dynasty 221 BC; Qing or Ch'ing Dynasty replaced by the Republic on 12 February 1912; People's Republic established 1 October 1949).

Administrative divisions: Twenty-three provinces (sheng), five autonomous regions* (zizhiqu), four municipalities** (shi), two Special Administrative Regions (SARs)***. 1. Anhui 2. Beijing** 3. Chongqing** 4. Fujian 5. Gansu 6. Guangdong 7. Guangxi* 8. Guizhou 9. Hainan 10. Hebei 11. Heilongjiang 12. Henan 13. Hong Kong*** 14. Hubei 15. Hunan 16. Jiangsu 17. Jiangxi 18. Jilin 19. Liaoning 20. Macao*** 21. Nei Mongol* 22. Ningxia* 23. Qinghai 24. Shaanxi 25. Shandong 26. Shanghai** 27. Shanxi 28. Sichuan 29. Tianjin** 30. Xinjiang* 31. Xizang* (Tibet) 32. Yunnan 33. Zhejiang. China considers Taiwan its twenty-third province.

Legal system: China's legal system is a complex combination of custom and statute, largely criminal law. China's legal system is based on civil law system, derived from Soviet and continental civil code legal principles; legislature retains power to interpret statutes; constitution ambiguous on judicial review of legislation; has not accepted compulsory ICJ jurisdiction rudimentary civil code in effect since 1 January 1987; new legal codes in effect since 1 January 1980.

Executive branch:
Chief of state: President Hu Jintao (since 15 March 2003) and Vice-President Zeng Qinghong (since 15 March 2003).

Head of government: Premier Wen Jiabao (since 16 March 2003).

Elections and election results: The National People's Congress elects the president and the vice-president for five-year terms. The last elections were held during 15–17 March 2003 and the next are scheduled for mid-March 2008. The president nominates the premier, and then it is to be confirmed by the National People's Congress.

Legislative branch:
China has a unicameral National People's Congress or Quanguo Renmin Daibiao Dahui (2,985 seats; members elected by municipal, regional, and provincial people's congresses to serve five-year terms).

Elections and election results: Last elections were held in December 2002– February 2003 and the next are scheduled for 2007–8.

Economy

Currency: Yuan, also referred to as the Renminbi.

Economy—overview:
Measured on a purchasing power parity (PPP) basis, China in 2005 stood as the second-largest economy in the world after the US, although in per capita terms the country is still lower-middle income and 150 million Chinese fall below international poverty lines. Economic development has generally been more rapid in coastal provinces than in the interior and there are large disparities in per capita incomes between regions. The government has struggled to (a) sustain adequate job growth for tens of millions of workers laid off from state-owned enterprises, migrants, and new entrants to the work force; (b) reduce corruption and other economic crimes; and (c) contain environmental damage and social strife related to the economy's rapid transformation. Between 100 to 150 million surplus rural workers are adrift between the villages and the cities, many subsisting on part-time, low-paying jobs. One demographic consequence of the 'one-child policy' is that China is now one of the most rapidly aging countries in the world. Another long-term threat to growth is the deterioration in the environment, notably air pollution, soil erosion, and the steady fall of the water table especially in the north. China continues to lose arable land because of erosion and economic development.

China has benefited from a huge expansion in computer Internet use, with more than 100 million users at the end of 2005. Foreign investment remains a strong element in China's remarkable expansion in world trade and has been an important factor in the growth of urban jobs. On 21 July 2005 China revalued its currency by 2.1 per cent against the US dollar and moved to an exchange rate system that references a basket of currencies. Reports of shortages of electric power in the summer of 2005 in southern China receded by September–October and did not have a substantial impact on China's economy. More power generating capacity is scheduled to come on line in 2006 as large scale investments are completed. The Central Committee of the Chinese Communist Party in October 2005 approved the draft Eleventh Five-Year Plan and the National People's Congress is expected to give final approval in March 2006. The plan calls for a 20 per cent reduction in energy consumption per unit of GDP by 2010 and an estimated 45 per cent increase in GDP by 2010. The plan states that conserving resources and protecting the environment are basic goals but it lacks details on the policies and reforms necessary to achieve these goals.

GDP: Purchasing power parity—$8.859 trillion (2005 est.).

GDP—real growth rate: 9.9% (official data) (2005 est.).

GDP—per capita: Purchasing power parity—$6,800 (2005 est.).

Inflation rate: 1.9% (2005 est.).

Population below poverty line: 10% (2001 est.).

Unemployment rate: 4.2% official registered unemployment in urban areas in 2004; substantial unemployment and underemployment in rural areas; an official Chinese journal estimated overall unemployment (including rural areas) for 2003 at 20 per cent (2004).

Exports: $752.2 billion f.o.b. (2005 est.)—Machinery and equipment; textiles and clothing, footwear, toys and sporting goods; mineral fuels.

Imports: $631.8 billion f.o.b. (2005 est.)—Machinery and equipment, mineral fuels, plastics, iron and steel, chemicals.

External debt: $242 billion (2005 est.).

Transport and Communications

Railways: 71,898 km.

Roads: 1,809,829 km.

Telephones: 311.756 million (2004).

Mobile celluler: 334.824 million (2004).

Internet users: 111 million (2005).

Internet country code: .cn

Colombia

History

At the time of the Spanish conquest in the sixteenth century, native people speaking the Chibcha language were the most important of the local inhabitants of the area that is today Colombia.

In 1819, the South American liberator and statesman Simon Bolivar defeated the Spanish and formed the Republic of Gran Colombia, consisting of Colombia, Ecuador, Panama and Venezuela. However, Gran Colombia disintegrated in 1829–30 when Venezuela and Ecuador left. This led to the formation of the state of Nueva Granada consisting of present-day Colombia and Panama. But even Nueva Granada collapsed with the War of the Thousand

Days of 1899–1903 in which some 120,000 people perished. Colombia was rocked by a civil war again in 1948–57 when an estimated 250,000–300,000 were killed.

In 1978, the government started its campaign against the Colombian drug traffickers. Colombia's role as a key supplier in the international drug market gained significance following the major crackdown launched in Mexico in 1975. Before long, Colombia had become the source of almost 70 per cent of the marijuana being imported into USA. As the volume of trafficking grew, it also gave rise to two major Mafia-like organizations. These were the so-called drug cartels—the Medellin cartel, led by Pablo Escobar, and the Cali cartel. In July 2000, President Andres Pastrana launched Plan Colombia. It succeeded in obtaining nearly US$1 billion in the form of military aid from USA, in order to fight drug trafficking and rebels who protected the traffickers.

Geography

Location: Northern South America, bordering the Caribbean Sea, between Panama and Venezuela, and bordering the North Pacific Ocean, between Ecuador and Panama.

Area: 1,138,910 sq. km. This includes Isla de Malpelo, Roncador Cay, Serrana Bank, and Serranilla Bank.

Terrain: Flat coastal lowlands, central highlands, high Andes mountains, eastern lowland plains.

Natural resources: Petroleum, natural gas, coal, iron ore, nickel, gold, copper, emeralds, hydropower.

Climate: The climate of Colombia is tropical along coast and the eastern plains but cooler in the highlands.

People

Population: 43,593,035 (July 2006 est.).

Population growth rate: 1.46% (2006 est.).

Sex ratio: 0.96 male(s)/female (2006 est.).

Religions: Roman Catholic 90%.

Languages: Spanish.

Literacy rate: Total 92.5%, Male 92.4%, Female 92.6% (2003 est.).

Infant mortality rate: 20.35 deaths/1,000 live births (2006 est.).

Life expectancy: Total 71.99 years, Male 68.15 years, Female 75.96 years (2006 est.).

Government

Capital: Bogota.

Government type: Republic; executive branch dominates government structure.

Independence: 20 July 1810 (from Spain).

Legal system: Based on Spanish law; a new criminal code modelled after US procedures was enacted into law is 2004 and is gradually being implemented; judicial review of executive and legislative acts; accept compulsory ICJ jurisdiction, with reservations.

Executive branch:
Chief of state: President Alvaro Uribe Velez (since 7 August 2002). Vice-President Francisco Santos (since 7 August 2002). The President is both the chief of state and head of government.

Economy

Currency: Colombian peso.

Economy—overview:
Serious internal conflict is one of the main factors that hamper the Colombian economy. Other significant factors affecting the economy are austerity measures, weak domestic and foreign demand, high unemployment and an uncertain future for two of Colombia's leading exports—oil and coffee. The Colombian government's reform measures, economic policy and democratic security strategy have inspired confidence in the economy.

GDP: Purchasing power parity—$337.5 billion (2005 est.).

GDP—real growth rate: 5.1% (2005 est.).

GDP—per capita: Purchasing power parity—$7,900 (2005 est.).

Inflation rate: 5% (2005 est.).

Population below poverty line: 49.2% (2005).

Unemployment rate: 10.2% (2005 est.).

Exports: $19.3 billion f.o.b. (2005 est.)—Petroleum, coffee, coal, apparel, banana, cut flowers.

Imports: $18 billion f.o.b. (2005 est.)—Industrial equipment, transportation equipment, consumer goods, chemicals, paper products, fuels, electricity.

External debt: $37.06 billion (2005 est.).

Transport and Communications

Railways: 3,304 km.

Roads: 112,998 km.

Telephones: 7.767 million (2004).

Mobile cellular: 10,400,600 (2004).

Internet users: 3,585,688 (2004).

Internet country code: .co

Comoros

History

In 1886, Comoros became a French protectorate. In 1961, it gained autonomy. In 1974, three of the islands forming the colony of Comoros voted for independence in a referendum. In 1886, Comoros became a French protectorate. In 1961, it gained autonomy. In 1974, three of the islands forming the colony of Comoros voted for independence in a referendum. On 6 July 1975, the Comorian parliament passed a resolution declaring independence.

Unstable Comoros has endured nineteen coups or attempted coups since gaining independence from France in 1975. In 1997, the islands of Anjouan and Moheli declared their independence from Comoros. In 1999, military chief Col Azali seized power. He pledged to resolve the secessionist crisis through a confederal arrangement named the

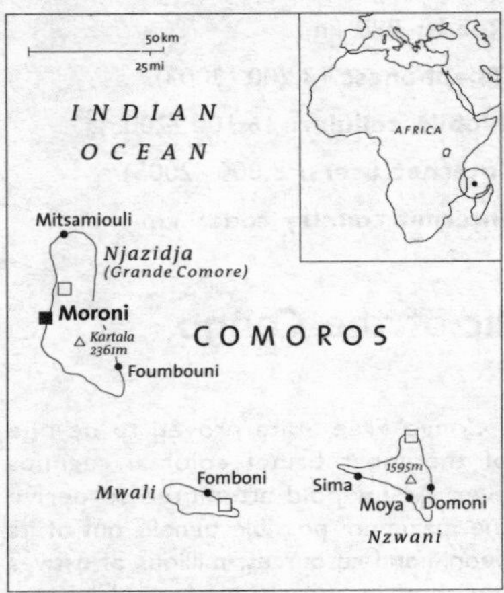

2000 Fomboni Accord. In December 2001, voters approved a new constitution and presidential elections took place in the spring of 2002. Each island in the archipelago elected its own president and a new union president took office in May of 2002.

Geography

Location: Southern Africa, group of islands at the northern mouth of the Mozambique Channel.

Area: 2,170 sq. km.

Natural resources: Negligible.

Climate: Tropical marine climate.

People

Population: 690,948 (July 2006 est.).

Population growth rate: 2.87% (2006 est.).

Sex ratio: 0.99 male(s)/female (2006 est.).

Religions: Sunni Muslim 98%, Roman Catholic 2%.

Languages: Arabic (official), French (official), Shikomoro (a blend of Swahili and Arabic).

Literacy rate: Total 56.5%, Male 63.6%, Female 49.3% (2003 est.).

Infant mortality rate: 72.85 deaths/1,000 live births (2006 est.).

Life expectancy: Total 62.33 years, Male 60 years, Female 64.72 years (2006 est.).

Government

Capital: Moroni.

Government type: Independent republic.

Independence: 6 July 1975 (from France).

Legal system: French and Sharia (Islamic) law in a new consolidated code.

Executive branch:

Chief of state: President Azali Assoumani (since 26 May 2002). The president is both the chief of state and the head of government.

Economy

Currency: Comoran franc.

GDP: Purchasing power parity—$441 million (2002 est.).

GDP—real growth rate: 3% (2005 est.).

GDP—per capita: Purchasing power parity—$600 (2005 est.).

Inflation rate: 3.5% (2001 est.).

Population below poverty line: 60% (2002 est.).

Unemployment rate: 20% (1996 est.).

Exports: $34 million f.o.b. (2004 est.)—Vanilla, ylang-ylang, cloves, perfume oil, copra.

Imports: $115 million f.o.b. (2004 est.)—Rice and other foodstuff, consumer goods; petroleum products, cement, transport equipment.

External debt: $232 million (2000 est.).

Transport and Communications

Railways: None.

Roads: 880 km.

Telephones: 13,200 (2003).

Mobile cellular: 16,100 (2005).

Internet users: 8,000 (2005).

Internet country code: .km

Democratic Republic of the Congo

History

In the 1200s, the Kongo empire included parts of modern-day Democratic Republic of the Congo. The first Europeans arrived in the fifteenth century. In the sixteenth and seventeenth centuries, British, French, Dutch and Portuguese merchants carried out slave trade in the region.

Under the commission of the Belgian King Leopold II, British–American explorer Henry Morton Stanley sailed along the Congo river in 1877 and facilitated further exploration of the hinterlands. He also concluded treaties with local chiefs that later enabled Leopold II to obtain personal rights to the lands. In 1885, the Belgian king announced the creation of the Congo Free State with himself as the sovereign.

Congo Free State proved to be one of the most brutal colonial regimes ever. As Leopold attempted to derive the maximum possible benefit out of its people and resources, millions of natives perished in starvation, forced labour, torture and outright killings.

In June 1960, Belgian Congo became independent with Joseph Kasavubu as president and Patrice Lumumba as prime minister. Lumumba was murdered in January 1961. In 1965, commander-in-chief of the armed forces, Joseph Mobutu seized power in a coup.

In 1971, Joseph Mobutu embarked on a campaign of renaming. He renamed the country Zaire, Katanga province Shaba and the river Congo river Zaire. In 1973–4, he nationalized the foreign-owned firms in the country and drove out European investors. While the country's economic condition declined, Mobutu is believed to have amassed a huge personal fortune. In 1990–1, he finally ended his dictatorial rule and agreed to a multiparty system. Mobutu was finally ousted from power in May 1997 when the rebels (with Rwandan help) captured the capital Kinshasa.

In January 2001, President Laurent Kabila was shot dead by a bodyguard. His son, Joseph Kabila became the new president. In October 2002, Kabila negotiated the withdrawal of Rwandan forces occupying eastern Congo. In December 2002, the Pretoria Accord was signed by warring parties to end fighting. A transitional government was set up is July 2003. Joseph Kabila remains president and four vice-presidents represent the former government, former rebel group and the political opposition.

Geography

Location: Central Africa, north-east of Angola.

Area: 2,345,410 sq. km.

Terrain: A vast central basin that is actually a low-lying plateau. There are mountains in the east.

Natural resources: Cobalt, copper, cadmium, petroleum, industrial and gem diamonds, gold, silver, zinc, manganese, tin, germanium, uranium, radium, bauxite, iron ore, coal, hydropower, timber.

Climate: Generally tropical climate. It is hot and humid in the equatorial river basin, cooler and wetter in the eastern highlands, cooler and drier in the southern highlands.

People

Population: 60,085,804 (2005 est.).

Population growth rate: 2.98% (2005 est.).

Sex ratio: 0.98 male(s)/female (2005 est.).

Religions: Roman Catholic 50%, Protestant 20%, Kimbanguist 10%, Muslim 10%, other syncretic sects and indigenous beliefs 10%.

Languages: French (official), Lingala (a lingua franca trade language), Kingwana (a dialect of Kiswahili or Swahili), Kikongo, Tshiluba.

Literacy rate: Total 65.5%, Male 76.2%, Female 55.1% (2003 est.).

Infant mortality rate: 92.87 deaths/1,000 live births (2005 est.).

Life expectancy: Total 49.35 years, Male 47.29 years, Female 51.47 years (2005 est.).

Government

Capital: Kinshasa.

Government type: Dictatorship.

Independence: 30 June 1960 (from Belgium).

Legal system: Based on Belgian Civil Law system and tribal law.

Executive branch:
Chief of state: President Joseph Kabila (since 26 January 2001). The president is both the chief of state and head of government.

Economy

Currency: Congolese franc.

GDP: Purchasing power parity—$42.74 billion (2004 est.).

GDP—real growth rate: 7.5% (2004 est.).

GDP—per capita: Purchasing power parity—$700 (2004 est.).

Inflation rate: 14% (2003 est.).

Exports: $1.417 billion f.o.b. (2002 est.)—Diamond, copper, crude oil, coffee, cobalt.

Imports: $933 million f.o.b. (2002 est.)—Foodstuff, mining and other machinery, transport equipment, fuels.

External debt: $11.6 billion (2000 est.).

Transport and Communications

Railways: 5,138 km.

Roads: 157,000 km (including 30 km of expressways) (1999 est.).

Telephones: 10,000 (2002).

Mobile cellular: 1,000,000 (2003).

Internet users: 50,000 (2002).

Internet country code: .cd

Republic of the Congo

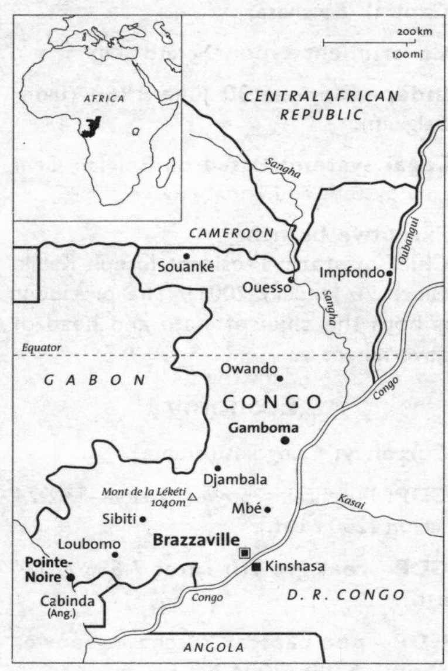

History

In 1880, French explorer Pierre Savorgnan de Brazza negotiated an agreement with the Bateke ethnic group that led to the setting up of a French protectorate over the north bank of the Congo river. This new entity was initially called French Congo and later Middle Congo. In 1958, Congo gained autonomy and in 1960 it became independent with Fulbert Youlou as president.

A quarter century of experimentation with Marxism was abandoned in 1990 and a democratically elected government took office in 1992. A brief civil war in 1997 restored former Marxist President Denis Sassou-Nguesso, but ushered in a period of ethnic and political unrest.

Geography

Location: Western Africa, bordering the South Atlantic Ocean, between Angola and Gabon.

Area: 342,000 sq. km.

Terrain: A central plateau, coastal plain, southern basin, and northern basin.

Natural resources: Petroleum, timber, potash, lead, zinc, uranium, copper, phosphates, natural gas, hydropower.

Climate: Tropical climate with a rainy season between March and June and a dry season from June to October.

People

Population: 62,660,551 (July 2006 est.).

Population growth rate: 3.07% (2006 est.).

Sex ratio: 0.99 male(s)/female (2006 est.).

Religions: Christian 50%, animist 48%, Muslim 2%.

Languages: French (official), Lingala and Monokutuba (lingua franca trade languages), many local languages and dialects (of which Kikongo is the most widespread).

Literacy rate: Total 88.62%, Male 89.6%, Female 78.4% (2006 est.).

Infant mortality rate: 88.62 deaths/1,000 live births (2006 est.).

Life expectancy: Total 51.46 years, Male 50.01 years, Female 52.94 years (2006 est.).

Government

Capital: Brazzaville.

Government type: Republic.

Independence: 15 August 1960 (from France).

Legal system: Based on French civil law system and customary law.

Executive branch:
Chief of state: President Denis Sassou-Nguesso (since 25 October 1997). The president is both the chief of state and head of government.

Economy

Currency: Communaute Financiere Africaine franc.

GDP: Purchasing power parity—$40.67 billion (2005 est.).

GDP—real growth rate: 6.5% (2005 est.).

GDP—per capita: Purchasing power parity--$700 (2005 est.).

Inflation rate: 2% (2005 est.).

Exports: $2.09 billion f.o.b. (2005 est.)—Petroleum, lumber, plywood, sugar, cocoa, coffee, diamond.

Imports: $806.5 million f.o.b. (2005 est.)—Capital equipment, construction materials, foodstuff.

External debt: $5 billion (2000 est.).

Transport and Communications

Railways: 894 km.

Roads: 12,800 km.

Telephones: 10,000 (2002).

Mobile cellular: 2.6 million (2005).

Internet users: 50,000 (2002).

Internet country code: .cd

Costa Rica

History

When Christopher Columbus visited the lands in 1502, native Indian tribes inhabited the area. The Spanish conquest began in 1563. In 1821, Costa Rica attained independence, but for two years it formed a part of the short-lived Mexican empire. In 1848, Costa Rica became a republic.

Geography

Location: Middle America, bordering both the Caribbean Sea and the North Pacific Ocean, between Nicaragua and Panama.

Area: 51,100 sq. km (this includes Isla del Coco).

Natural resources: Hydropower.

Climate: Tropical; cooler in the highlands.

People

Population: 4,075,261 (July 2006 est.).

Population growth rate: 1.45% (2006 est.).

Sex ratio: 1.02 male(s)/female (2006 est.).

Religions: Roman Catholic 76.3%, Evangelical 13.7%, Jehovah's Witnesses 1.3%, other Protestant 0.7%, others 4.8%, none 3.2%.

Languages: Spanish (official), English.

Literacy rate: Total 96%, Male 95.9%, Female 96.1% (2003 est.).

Infant mortality rate: 9.7 deaths/ 1,000 live births (2006 est.).

Life expectancy: Total 77.02 years, Male 74.43 years, Female 79.74 years (2006 est.).

Government

Capital: San Jose.

Government type: Democratic republic.

Independence: 15 September 1821 (from Spain).

Legal system: Based on Spanish civil law system; judicial review of legislative acts in the Supreme Court; has accepted compulsory ICJ jurisdiction.

Executive branch:
Chief of state: President Oscar Arias Sanchez (since 8 May 2006). The president is both the chief of state and head of government.

Elections: President and vice-presidents elected on the same ticket by popular vote for a single four-year term; election last held 5 February 2006 (next to be held February 2010).

Election results: Oscar Arias Sanchez elected president; per cent of vote—Oscar Arias Sanchez (PLN) 40.9%, Otto Soliz (PAC) 39.8%, Otto Guevara Guth (PML) 8%, Ricardo Toledo (PUSC) 3%. Note: official results pending the resolution of election challenges.

Economy

Currency: Costa Rican colon.

GDP: Purchasing power parity—$44.68 billion (2005 est.).

GDP—real growth rate: 4% (2005 est.).

GDP—per capita: Purchasing power parity—$11,100 (2005 est.).

Inflation rate: 13.8% (2005 est.).

Population below poverty line: 18% (2004 est.).

Unemployment rate: 6.6% (2005 est.).

Exports: $7.005 billion (2005 est.)—Coffee, banana, sugar, pineapple, textiles, electronic components, medical equipment.

Imports: $9.69 billion (2005 est.)—Raw materials, consumer goods, capital equipment, petroleum.

External debt: $3.633 billion (30 June 2005 est.).

Transport and Communications

Railways: 278 km.

Roads: 35,889 km.

Telephones: 1,343,200 (2004).

Mobile cellular: 923,100 (2004).

Internet users: 1 million (2005).

Internet country code: .cr

Cote d'Ivoire

History

In 1842, France established a protectorate over Ivory Coast and in 1893, made it a colony. In 1960, Cote d'Ivoire became independent under President Felix Houphouet-Boigny.

Geography

Location: Western Africa, bordering the North Atlantic Ocean, between Ghana and Liberia.

Area: 322,460 sq. km.

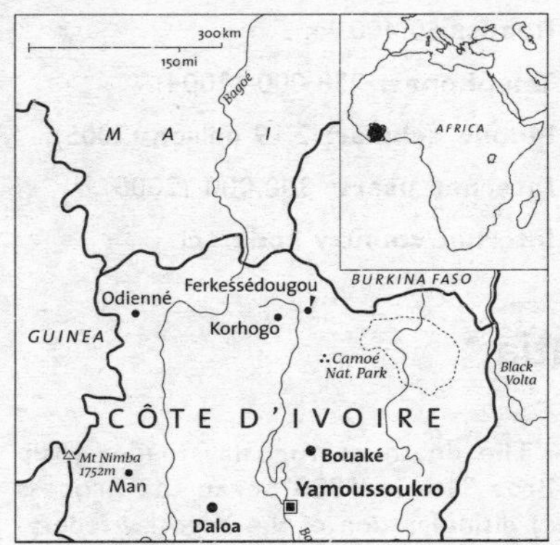

Terrain: Consists mostly of flat to undulating plains. There are mountains in the north-west.

Natural resources: Petroleum, natural gas, diamonds, manganese, iron ore, cobalt, bauxite, copper, hydropower.

Climate: Tropical along the coast and semiarid in the far north.

People

Population: 17,654,843 (July 2006 est.).

Population growth rate: 2.03% (2006 est.).

Sex ratio: 1 male(s)/female (2006 est.).

Religions: Christian 20–30%, Muslim 35–40%, indigenous 25–40% (2001). The majority of foreigners (migratory workers) are Muslim (70%) and Christian (20%).

Languages: French (official), 60 native dialects with Dioula the most widely spoken.

Literacy rate: Total 50.9%, Male 57.9%, Female 43.6% (2003 est.).

Infant mortality rate: 89.11 deaths/1,000 live births (2006 est.).

Life expectancy: Total 48.82 years, Male 46.24 years, Female 51.48 years (2006 est.).

Government

Capital: Yamoussoukro. (Even though Yamoussoukro has been the official capital since 1983, Abidjan still remains the commercial and administrative centre.)

Government type: Republic; multiparty presidential regine (established 1960).

Independence: 7 August 1960 (from France).

Legal system: Based on French civil law system and customary law; judicial review in the Constitutional Chamber of the Supreme Court; has not accepted compulsory ICJ jurisdiction.

Executive branch:

Chief of state: President Laurent Gbagbo (since 26 October 2000).

Head of government: Transitional Prime Minister Charles Konan Banny (since 7 December 2005).

Economy

Currency: Communaute Financiere Africaine franc.

GDP: Purchasing power parity—$28.52 billion (2005 est.).

GDP—real growth rate: –1% (2005 est.).

GDP—per capita: Purchasing power parity—$1,600 (2005 est.).

Inflation rate: 1.4% (2004 est.).

Population below poverty line: 37% (1995).

Unemployment rate: 13% in urban areas (1998).

Exports: $6.49 billion f.o.b. (2005 est.)—Cocoa, coffee, timber, petroleum, cotton, banana, pineapple, palm oil, fish.

Imports: $4.759 billion f.o.b. (2005 est.)—Fuel, capital equipment, foodstuffs.

External debt: $13.26 billion (2005 est.).

Transport and Communications

Railways: 660 km.

Roads: 50,400 km.

Telephones: 238,000 (2004).

Mobile cellular: 2.19 million (2005).

Internet users: 300,000 (2005).

Internet country code: .ci

Croatia

History

Croats settled the area that is today Croatia in the seventh century. In 925, Croats defeated the Byzantine and Frank invaders and set up their own independent kingdom. Civil war erupted in 1089 and led to the Hungarian conquest in 1091. In 1102, Croat tribal chiefs and Hungary signed a pact that caused the political union of Croatia with Hungary under the Hungarian monarch.

During World War II, Germany occupied Yugoslavia and installed a puppet regime in Croatia. The fascist puppet government under Ante Pavelic sought to create a Catholic, all-Croat republic and killed hundreds of thousands of Serbs and Jews.

The death of Yugoslav leader Josip Broz Tito in 1980 began the process of disintegration of the Yugoslav federation. The collapse of communism in the 1990s accelerated the process. In 1990, the first free elections in Croatia in more than fifty years were held.

In 1991, Croatia declared its independence from Yugoslavia. This led the Croatian Serbs in the eastern part of the country to expel Croats with the help of the Yugoslav army. A three-month-long Serbian siege of the eastern Croatian town of Vukovar resulted in a near-complete destruction of the city. When Serb forces captured the city in November 1991, they unleashed brutality on its inhabitants.

In 1992, Franjo Tudjman was elected Croatian president. The UN negotiated a ceasefire and set up four protected areas in Croatia, with 14,000 UN troops separating the Croats and Serbs to prevent hostilities. Under UN supervision, the last Serb-held enclave in eastern Slavonia was returned to Croatia in 1998.

Geography

Location: South-eastern Europe, bordering the Adriatic Sea, between Bosnia–Herzegovina and Slovenia.

Area: 56,542 sq. km.

Terrain: Geographically diverse terrain with flat plains along the border with Hungary, low mountains and highlands near the Adriatic coastline and some islands.

Natural resources: Oil, some coal, bauxite, iron ore, calcium, gypsum, natural asphalt, silica, mica, clays, salt, hydropower.

Climate: Mediterranean and continental climate.

People

Population: 4,494,749 (July 2006 est.).

Population growth rate: –0.03% (2006 est.).

Sex ratio: 0.93 male(s)/female (2006 est.).

Religions: Roman Catholic 87.8%, Orthodox 4.4%, Muslim 1.3%, Protestant 0.3%, others and unknown 6.2% (2001).

Languages: Croatian 96%, others 4% (including Italian, Hungarian, Czech, Slovak, and German).

Literacy rate: Total 98.5%, Male 99.4%, Female 97.8% (2003 est.).

Infant mortality rate: 6.72 deaths/1,000 live births (2006 est.).

Life expectancy: Total 74.68 years, Male 71.03 years, Female 78.53 years (2006 est.).

Government

Capital: Zagreb.

Government type: Presidential/parliamentary democracy.

Independence: 25 June 1991 (from Yugoslavia).

Legal system: Based on civil law system.

Executive branch:

Chief of state: President Stjepan (Stipe) Mesic (since 18 February 2000).

Head of government: Prime Minister Ivo Sanader (since 9 December 2003).

Economy

Currency: Kuna.

GDP: Purchasing power parity—$55.76 billion (2005 est.).

GDP—real growth rate: 4% (2005 est.).

GDP—per capita: Purchasing power parity—$11,600 (2005 est.).

Inflation rate: 2.5% (2004 est.).

Population below poverty line: 11% (2003).

Unemployment rate: 18.7% is the official rate; labour force Surveys india cate unemployment around 14% (December 2004 est.).

Exports: $10.3 billion f.o.b. (2005 est.)—Transport equipment, textiles, chemicals, foodstuff, fuels.

Imports: $18.93 billion f.o.b. (2005 est.)—Machinery, transport and electrical equipment, chemicals, fuels and lubricants, foodstuff.

External debt: $29.28 billion (30 June 2005 est.).

Transport and Communications

Railways: 2,726 km (2003).

Roads: 28,588 km (2002).

Telephones: 1,887,600 (2004).

Mobile cellular: 2,553,000 (2003).

Internet users: 1,014,000 (2003).

Internet country code: .hr

Cuba

History

Arawak Indians inhabited Cuba when Christopher Columbus arrived in 1492. The first Spanish settlements came up in 1511, under the leadership of Diego de Velazquez. Between 1763 and 1860, Cuba's population increased from less than 150,000 to more than 1.3 million with slaves making up the biggest share of the increase. In the nineteenth century, the Cuban sugar industry underwent rapid expansion and at one point Cuba produced nearly one-third of the world's sugar.

The first war of independence raged between 1868 and 1878. As the economic and political situation in the colony worsened, the second War of Independence, led by the poet Jose Marti, broke out in 1895. In 1898, an explosion took place on board the US battleship *Maine* in Havana harbour. The United States declared war on Spain in April 1898. In August, Spain signed a peace treaty ending all hostilities with USA and ceding Cuba.

Cuba became independent in 1902 with Tomas Estrada Palma as its president. However, under the Platt Amendment of 1901, USA had the right to oversee Cuba's international commitments, economy, and internal affairs. It also allowed the USA to establish a naval station at Guantánamo Bay.

In 1940, after a succession of puppet rulers, Fulgencio Batista became the president. In 1953, Fidel Castro launched an unsuccessful attempt to dethrone the Batista regime. He returned in 1956 and launched a guerilla campaign, aided by Ernesto 'Che' Guevara. Batista fled the country on New Year's Day 1959.

In 1960, the Cuban government nationalized all US businesses in Cuba, leading USA to break off diplomatic ties with Havana. In April 1961, USA sponsored an unsuccessful invasion attempt by Cuban exiles at the Bay of Pigs in south central Cuba. This, along with a US trade embargo and numerous US attempts to exterminate Fidel Castro prompted Cuba to drift towards the Soviet Union. Ultimately, Castro proclaimed Cuba a communist state.

In October 1962, a major confrontation brought the United States and the Soviet Union to the brink of nuclear war. The issue was the presence of Soviet nuclear-armed missiles in Cuba.

Geography

Location: Caribbean island between the Caribbean Sea and the North Atlantic Ocean.

Area: 110,860 sq. km.

Terrain: Mostly flat to rolling plains, with rugged hills and mountains in the south-east.

Natural resources: Cobalt, nickel, iron ore, copper, manganese, salt, timber, silica, petroleum, arable land.

Climate: Tropical climate moderated by trade winds.

People

Population: 11,382,820 (July 2006 est.).

Population growth rate: 0.31% (2006 est.).

Sex ratio: 0.99 male(s)/female (2006 est.).

Religions: Nominally 85% Roman Catholic before Castro assumed power; Protestants, Jehovah's Witnesses, Jews, and Santeria are also represented.

Languages: Spanish.

Literacy rate: Total 97%, Male 97.2%, Female 96.9% (2003 est.).

Infant mortality rate: 6.22 deaths/1,000 live births (2006 est.).

Life expectancy: Total 77.41 years, Male 75.11 years, Female 79.85 years (2006 est.).

Government

Capital: Havana.

Government type: Communist state.

Independence: 20 May 1902 (from Spain 10 December 1898; administered by the US from 1898 to 1902).

Legal system: Based on Spanish and American law, with large elements of communist legal theory.

Executive branch:
Chief of state: President of the Council of State and President of the Council of Ministers Fidel Castro Ruz (he served as prime minister from February 1959 to 24 February 1976 when the office was abolished; he has been president since 2 December 1976). The president is both the chief of state and head of government.

Economy

Currency: Cuban peso.

Economy—overview:
In general, the standard of living of the average Cuban is at a lower level than it was before the economic depression of the early 1990s. This was caused largely by the loss of Soviet aid following the collapse of the Soviet Union. The Cuban government has undertaken limited reforms in recent years to improve efficiency and solve numerous problems such as shortages of food, consumer goods and services. One unique feature of the economy is the contrast between efficient export zones and the inefficient domestic sector.

GDP: Purchasing power parity—$39.17 billion (2004 est.).

GDP—real growth rate: 8% (2005 est.).

GDP—per capita: Purchasing power parity—$3,500 (2005 est.).

Inflation rate: 4.2% (2005 est.).

Unemployment rate: 1.9% (2005 est.).

Exports: $2.388 billion f.o.b. (2005 est.)—Sugar, nickel, tobacco, fish, medical products, citrus, coffee.

Imports: $6.916 billion f.o.b. (2005 est.)—Petroleum, food, machinery and equipment, chemicals.

External debt: $13.1 billion (in convertible currency); another $15 billion–$20 billion owed to Russia (2005 est.).

Transport and Communications

Railways: 4,226 km.

Roads: 60,858 km.

Telephones: 768,200 (2004).

Mobile cellular: 75,800 (2004).

Internet users: 150,000 (2005).

Internet country code: .cu

Cyprus

History

Cyprus was the centre of Phoenician and Greek colonies in ancient times. In 1571, the island passed into Turkish hands and subsequently, a large Turkish colony was built on the island. UK annexed the island during World War I and in 1925, declared it to be a Crown colony. in August 1960, the island became an independent nation.

In 1974, a Greece-sponsored coup toppled Cypriot President Archbishop Makarios. Five days later, Turkey sent in troops with the objective of protecting the Turkish Cypriot community in the country. This invasion had the effect of partitioning the island into a Turkish Cypriot northern part and a Greek Cypriot part in the south. Meanwhile, the coup failed and the Greek military junta that had propped it up also collapsed. Archbishop Makarios returned to take up the presidency in December 1974. He offered self-government to the Turkish Cypriots but refused to transfer populations or partition the country.

In view of the impending Cypriot entry into European Union, twin referendums were held in the Greek and Turkish Cypriot areas on 24 April 2004. This was a last-minute attempt to achieve united EU entry. However, while the Greek part of the island endorsed the plan, Turkish Cypriots rejected it overwhelmingly. On 1 May 2004, Cyprus, but only the Greek part of it, joined the EU.

Geography

Location: Middle East, island in the Mediterranean Sea, south of Turkey.

Area: 9,250 sq. km (of which 3,355 sq. km is in the Turkish Cypriot area).

Natural resources: Copper, pyrites, asbestos, gypsum, timber, salt, marble, clay earth pigment.

Climate: Temperate Mediterranean climate with hot, dry summers and cool winters.

People

Population: 784,301 (July 2006 est.).

Population growth rate: 0.53% (2006 est.).

Sex ratio: 1 male(s)/female (2006 est.).

Religions: Greek Orthodox 78%, Muslim 18%, Maronite, Armenian Apostolic, and others 4%.

Languages: Greek, Turkish, English.

Literacy rate: Total 97.6%, Male 98.9%, Female 96.3% (2003 est.).

Infant mortality rate: 7.04 deaths/1,000 live births (2006 est.).

Life expectancy: Total 77.82 years, Male 75.44 years, Female 80.31 years (2006 est.).

Government

Capital: Nicosia.

Government type: Republic.

Independence: 16 August 1960 (from UK). The Turkish Cypriot area proclaimed self-rule on 13 February 1975.

Legal system: Based on common law, with civil law modifications.

Executive branch:

Chief of state: President Tassos Papadopoulos (since 1 March 2003). The president is both the chief of state and head of government.

Economy

Currency: Cypriot pound.

GDP: Republic of Cyprus: Purchasing power parity—$16.85 billion—(2005 est.); North Cyprus: Purchasing power parity—$4.54 billion (2005 est.).

GDP—real growth rate: Republic of Cyprus: 3.7% (2005 est.); North Cyprus: 10.6% (2004 est.).

GDP—per capita: Purchasing power parity—Republic of Cyprus: $21,600 (2005 est.); North Cyprus: $7.135 (2004 est.).

Inflation rate: Republic of Cyprus: 2.3% (2005 est.); North Cyprus: 9.1% (2004 est.).

Exports: Republic of Cyprus: $1.237 billion f.o.b.; North Cyprus: $49.3 million f.o.b. (2005 est.)—Citrus, potato, pharmaceuticals, cement, clothing and cigarettes.

Imports: Republic of Cyprus: $5.552 billion f.o.b. North Cyprus: 415.2 million f.o.b. (2005 est.)—Consumer goods, petroleum and lubricants, intermediate goods, machinery, transport equipment.

External debt: Republic of Cyprus: $7.803 billion f.o.b.; North Cyprus: NA (2005 est.)

Transport and Communications

Railways: None.

Roads: Total 14,110 km (Republic of Cyprus: 11,760; North Cyprus: 2,350 km).

Telephones: Republic of Cyprus: 418,400 (2004); North Cyprus: 86,228 (2002).

Mobile cellular: Republic of Cyprus: 640,500 (2004); North Cyprus: 143,178 (2002).

Internet users: 298,000 (2005).

Internet country code: .cy

Czech Republic

History

Celtic, then Germanic and finally Slavic tribes settled in the lands that is today the Czech Republic. The Czechs founded the kingdom of Bohemia and the Premyslide dynasty that ruled Bohemia and Moravia from the tenth to the sixteenth centuries. After spending years under German domination, the Hussite movement founded by reformer Jan Hus rekindled Czech nationalism in the fifteenth and sixteenth centuries. A Czech rebellion in 1618 led to the Thirty Years War (1618–48). As a result of defeat in the War, the Czechs had to submit to Austrian domination for the next 300 years. It was only after the collapse of the Austro-Hungarian empire at the end of World War I that the Czechs gained freedom again.

The union of the Czech territories with Slovakia was announced in Prague in November 1918, leading to the creation of the Republic of Czechoslovakia

with Thomas Masaryk as President. In March 1939, Germany occupied Czechoslovakia and made it a German protectorate. The country was freed from German occupation in 1945.

In 1960, Czechoslovakia became the Czechoslovak Socialist Republic under a new constitution. In January 1968, the new Communist Party leader Alexander Dubcek launched a programme of liberalizing reforms known as 'Prague Spring'. In August 1968, Soviet-led Warsaw Pact troops invaded Czechoslovakia. The troops took Dubcek to Moscow and forced him to terminate the reforms he had initiated. In April 1969, Gustav Husak replaced Dubcek as the new Communist Party leader. In 1975, he took over as the new president. In 1977, a group of dissidents that included playwright Vaclav Havel published 'Charter 77'. It called for the restoration of civil and political rights in the country.

The country was rocked by mass demonstrations and protests in 1988 that continued into 1989. In November 1989, the leadership of the Communist Party resigned. In December, a new government took power. Vaclav Havel became the new president, Marian Calfa the new prime minister. Alexander Dubcek was elected chairman of Federal Assembly.

On 1 January 1993, Czechoslovakia split into two independent countries, the Czech Republic and Slovakia. Vaclav Havel was elected president of the new country while Vaclav Klaus became the prime minister.

Geography

Location: Central Europe, south-east of Germany.

Area: 78,866 sq. km.

Terrain: Bohemia in the western part of the country consists of rolling plains, hills, and plateaus surrounded by low mountains. In the eastern part of the country, Moravia consists of very hilly terrain.

Natural resources: Hard coal, soft coal, kaolin, clay, graphite, timber.

Climate: Temperate climate with cool summers and cold, cloudy and humid winters.

People

Population: 10,235,455 (July 2006 est.).

Population growth rate: –0.06% (2006 est.).

Sex ratio: 0.95 male(s)/female (2006 est.).

Religions: Roman Catholic 26.8%, Protestant 2.1%, other 3.3%, Unspecified 8.8%, Unaffiliated 59% (2001 census).

Languages: Czech.

Literacy rate: 99.9%, Male 99%, Female 99% (2003 est.).

Infant mortality rate: 3.89 deaths/1,000 live births (2006 est.).

Life expectancy: Total 76.22 years, Male 72.94 years, Female 79.69 years (2006 est.).

Government

Capital: Prague.

Government type: Parliamentary democracy.

Independence: 1 January 1993 (date on which Czechoslovakia split into the Czech Republic and Slovakia).

Legal system: Civil law system based on Austro-Hungarian codes.

Executive branch:
Chief of state: President Vaclav Klaus (since 7 March 2003).

Head of government: Prime Minister Jiri Paroubek (since 25 April 2005).

Economy

Currency: Czech koruna.

GDP: Purchasing power parity—$199.4 billion (2005 est.).

GDP—real growth rate: 6% (2005 est.).

GDP—per capita: Purchasing power parity—$19,500 (2005 est.).

Inflation rate: 2% (2005 est.).

Unemployment rate: 9.1% (2005 est.).

Exports: $78.37 billion f.o.b. (2005 est.)—Machinery and transport equipment, intermediate manufactures, chemicals, raw materials and fuel (2000).

Imports: $76.59 billion f.o.b. (2005 est.)—Machinery and transport equipment, intermediate manufactures, raw materials and fuels, chemicals (2000).

External debt: $43.2 billion (30 June 2005 est.).

Transport and Communications

Railways: 9,543 km.

Roads: 127,672 km.

Telephones: 3,427,000 (2004).

Mobile cellular: 10,782,600 (2004).

Internet users: 2.7 million (2003).

Internet country code: .cz

Denmark

History

The initial settlers of the country were nomadic hunters and fishermen who developed into an agrarian community. Towards the end of the eighth century, the Danish were among the Vikings who raided the British Isles and other parts of western Europe. A unified kingdom of Denmark first came about in the tenth century. This was also the time when Christianity was introduced to the country.

In 1849, Denmark became a constitutional monarchy with a bicameral parliament. In 1944, the Danish territory of Iceland declared its independence from Denmark. In 1953, a significant change was made to the constitution. Subsequently, the parliament was turned into a unicameral one. Also in 1953, Greenland became an integral part of Denmark.

Geography

Location: Northern Europe, bordering the Baltic Sea and the North Sea, on a peninsula north of Germany (Jutland); Denmark also includes two major islands—Sjaelland and Fyn.

Area: 43,094 sq. km.

Terrain: Low and flat to gently rolling plains.

Natural resources: Petroleum, natural gas, fish, salt, limestone, chalk, stone, gravel and sand.

Climate: Humid and overcast temperate climate. The country experiences mild and windy winter and cool summer.

People

Population: 5,450,661 (July 2006 est.).

Population growth rate: 0.33% (2006 est.).

Sex ratio: 0.98 male(s)/female (2006 est.).

Religions: Evangelical Lutheran 95%, other Protestant and Roman Catholic 3%, Muslim 2%.

Languages: Danish, Faroese, Greenlandic (an Inuit dialect), German; English is the predominant second language.

Literacy rate: Total 99%, Male 99%, Female 99% (2003).

Infant mortality rate: 4.51 deaths/1,000 live births (2006 est.).

Life expectancy: Total 77.79 years, Male 75.49 years, Female 80.22 years (2006 est.).

Government

Capital: Copenhagen.

Government type: Constitutional monarchy.

Independence: Denmark was first organized as a unified state in the 10th century. In 1849, Denmark became a constitutional monarchy.

Legal system: Civil law system; judicial review of legislative acts.

Executive branch:

Chief of state: Queen Margrethe II (since 14 January 1972); Heir Apparent Crown Prince Frederik.

Head of government: Prime Minister Anders Fogh Rasmussen (since 27 November 2001).

Economy

Currency: Danish Krone.

Economy—overview:
Denmark has a modern market economy with well-developed and technologically advanced agricultural and industrial sectors. Notable features of the Danish economy include high living standards, a stable currency, high level of dependence on foreign trade and government welfare measures. The country is also a net exporter of food and energy and also has a balance of payments surplus. Denmark has decided not to join twelve other EU members in the euro. The Danish krone is pegged to the euro.

GDP: Purchasing power parity—$188.1 billion (2005 est.).

GDP—real growth rate: 3.4% (2006 est.).

GDP—per capita: Purchasing power parity—$34,600 (2005 est.).

Inflation rate: 1.9% (2005 est.).

Unemployment rate: 5.5% (2005).

Exports: $84.95 billion f.o.b. (2005 est.)—Machinery and instruments, meat and meat products, dairy products, fish, chemicals, furniture, ships, windmills.

Imports: $74.69 billion f.o.b. (2005 est.)—Machinery and equipment, raw materials and semi-manufactures for industry, chemicals, grain and foodstuff, consumer goods.

External debt: $352.9 billion (30 June 2005).

Transport and Communications

Railways: 2,628 km.

Roads: 71,847 km.

Telephones: 3,487,800 (2004).

Mobile cellular: 5.168 million (2004).

Internet users: 3,762,500 (2005).

Internet country code: .dk

Djibouti

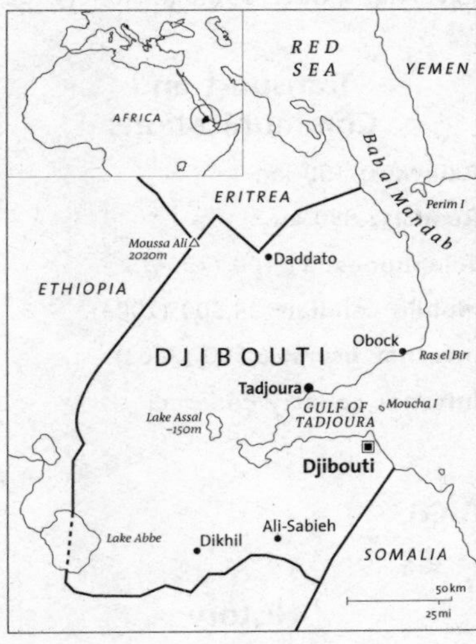

History

Immigrants from Arabia arrived in the region in the third century BC. The present-day Afars, one of the two most important ethnic groups of Djibouti, are the descendants of these immigrants. The Somali Issas, the other most important ethnic group, came later on. Islam was introduced to the region in 825 AD.

France came to control Djibouti in the nineteenth century by means of treaties with the local rulers. In 1888, France established the colony of Somaliland in the region and in 1892 Djibouti became the capital of this colony. In 1977, the French Territory of the Afars and the Issas became independent as Djibouti.

Geography

Location: Eastern Africa, bordering the Gulf of Aden and the Red Sea, between Eritrea and Somalia.

Area: 23,000 sq. km.

Natural resources: Geothermal areas.

Climate: Dry and torrid desert climate.

People

Population: 486,530 (July 2006 est.).

Population growth rate: 2.02% (2006 est.).

Sex ratio: 1.05 male(s)/female (2006 est.).

Religions: Muslim 94%, Christian 6%.

Languages: French (official), Arabic (official), Somali, Afar.

Literacy rate: Total 67.9%, Male 78%, Female 58.4% (2003 est.).

Infant mortality rate: 102.44 deaths/1,000 live births (2006 est.).

Life expectancy: Total 43.17 years, Male 41.86 years, Female 44.52 years (2006 est.).

Government

Capital: Djibouti.

Government type: Republic.

Independence: 27 June 1977 (from France).

Legal system: Based on French civil law system, traditional practices, and Islamic law.

Executive branch:
Chief of state: President Ismail Omar Guelleh (since 8 May 1999).

Head of government: Prime Minister Dileita Mohamed Dileita (since 4 March 2001).

Economy

Currency: Djiboutian franc.

GDP: Purchasing power parity—$619 million (2002 est.).

GDP—real growth rate: 3.5% (2002 est.).

GDP—per capita: Purchasing power parity—$1,300 (2002 est.).

Inflation rate: 2% (2002 est.).

Population below poverty line: 50% (2001 est.).

Unemployment rate: 50% (2004 est.).

Exports: $250 million f.o.b. (2004 est.)—Re-exports, hides and skins, coffee.

Imports: $987 million f.o.b. (2004 est.)—Foods, beverages, transport equipment, chemicals, petroleum products.

External debt: $366 million (2002 est.).

Transport and Communications

Railways: 100 km.

Roads: 2,890 km.

Telephones: 11,100 (2004).

Mobile cellular: 34,500 (2004).

Internet users: 6,500 (2003).

Internet country code: .dj

Dominica

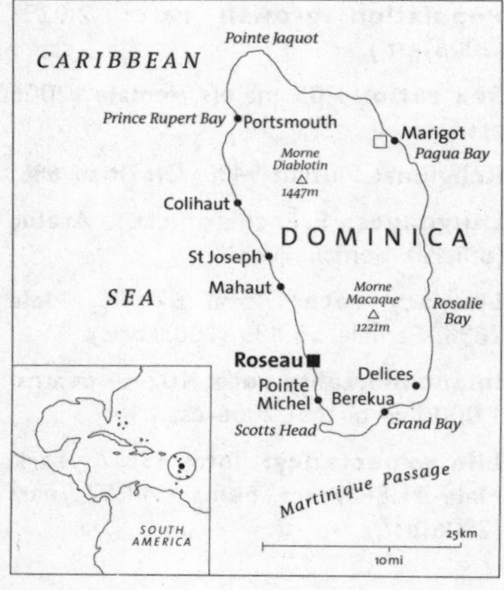

History

Christopher Columbus gave the island its present name. The French were the first to colonize the island in 1632. Between 1748 and 1805, the control of Dominica shifted repeatedly between France and UK. Initially administered as part of the Leeward Islands, Dominica became a separate colony in 1771. The 1967 Constitution granted the island full self-governance in internal affairs.

Geography

Location: Caribbean island between the Caribbean Sea and the North Atlantic Ocean.

Area: 754 sq. km.

Natural resources: Timber, hydropower, arable land.

Climate: Tropical, moderated by north-east trade winds; heavy rainfall.

People

Population: 68,910 (July 2006 est.).

Population growth rate: –0.8% (2006 est.).

Sex ratio: 1.01 male(s)/female (2006 est.).

Religions: Roman Catholic 77%, Protestant 15%, none 2%, others 6%.

Languages: English (official), French patois.

Literacy rate: Total 94% (2003 est.).

Infant mortality rate: 13.71 deaths/1,000 live births (2006 est.).

Life expectancy: Total 74.87 years, Male 71.95 years, Female 77.93 years (2006 est.).

Government

Capital: Roseau.

Government type: Parliamentary democracy; republic within the Commonwealth.

Independence: 3 November 1978 (from UK).

Legal system: Based on English common law.

Executive branch:

Chief of state: President Nicholas Liverpool (since 10 November 2003).

Head of government: Prime Minister Roosevelt Skerrit (since 8 January 2004).

Economy

Currency: East Caribbean dollar.

GDP: Purchasing power parity—$384 million (2003 est.).

GDP—real growth rate: –1% (2003 est.).

GDP—per capita: Purchasing power parity—$5,500 (2003 est.).

Inflation rate: 1% (2001 est.).

Population below poverty line: 30% (2002 est.).

Unemployment rate: 23% (2000 est.).

Exports: $74 million f.o.b. (2004 est.)—Banana, soap, bay oil, vegetables, grapefruit, orange.

Imports: $234 million f.o.b. (2004 est.)—Manufactured goods, machinery and equipment, food, chemicals.

External debt: $161.5 million (2001).

Transport and Communications

Railways: None.

Roads: 780 km.

Telephones: 21,000 (2004).

Mobile cellular: 41,800 (2004).

Internet users: 18,500 (2005).

Internet country code: .dm

Dominican Republic

History

Christopher Columbus explored the island on which Dominican Republic is situated in 1492. He named the island La Espanola and his son Diego was its first viceroy. In 1697, the eastern part of the island that later became the country of Haiti was given away to France. In 1809, the eastern two-

thirds of the island was given back to Spain. In 1821, this part declared its independence. Haitian troops invaded it within weeks of independence and occupied it till 1844. In 1916, chaos and disorder in the island nation prompted the US to send in troops who remained on the island till 1934.

Geography

Location: Caribbean, eastern two-thirds of the island of Hispaniola, between the Caribbean Sea and the North Atlantic Ocean, east of Haiti.

Area: 48,730 sq. km.

Natural resources: Nickel, bauxite, gold, silver.

Climate: Tropical maritime climate with little seasonal temperature variation.

People

Population: 9,183,984 (July 2006 est.).

Population growth rate: 1.47% (2006 est.).

Sex ratio: 1.03 male(s)/female (2006 est.).

Religions: Roman Catholic 95%.

Languages: Spanish.

Literacy rate: Total 84.7%, Male 84.6%, Female 84.8% (2003 est.).

Infant mortality rate: 28.25 deaths/1,000 live births (2006 est.).

Life expectancy: Total 71.73 years, Male 70.21 years, Female 73.33 years (2006 est.).

Government

Capital: Santo Domingo.

Government type: Representative democracy.

Independence: 27 February 1844 (from Haiti).

Legal system: Based on French civil codes.

Executive branch:

Chief of state: President Leonel Fernandez Reyna (since 16 August 2004). Vice-President Rafael Albuquerque de Castro (since 16 August 2004). The president is both the chief of state and head of government.

Economy

Currency: Dominican peso.

GDP: Purchasing power parity—$63.73 billion (2005 est.).

GDP—real growth rate: 9.3% (2005 est.).

GDP—per capita: Purchasing power parity—$7,000 (2005 est.).

Inflation rate: 4.3% (2005 est.).

Population below poverty line: 25%.

Unemployment rate: 17% (2005 est.).

Exports: $5.818 billion f.o.b. (2005 est.)—Ferro-nickel, sugar, gold, silver, coffee, cocoa, tobacco, meats, consumer goods.

Imports: $9.747 billion f.o.b. (2005 est.)—Foodstuff, petroleum, cotton and fabrics, chemicals and pharmaceuticals.

External debt: $7.907 billion (2005 est.).

Transport and Communications

Railways: 517 km.

Roads: 12,600 km.

Telephones: 936,200 (2004).

Mobile cellular: 2,534,100 (2004).

Internet users: 800,000 (2005).

Internet country code: .do

East Timor

History

The Portuguese settled on Timor in 1520, while the Spanish reached in 1522. The Portuguese remained in control of the East Timor province until 1975. The Democratic Republic of East Timor was formed in 1975. However, independence proved to be shortlived. Indonesian forces invaded and occupied the territory and declared it to be an integral part of Indonesia. In 1999, Indonesia bowed to mounting international pressure and allowed a referendum to ascertain the future of East Timor. The majority vote in favour of independence led to East Timor finally gaining independence in 2002.

Geography

Location: South-eastern Asia, northwest of Australia in the Lesser Sunda Islands at the eastern end of the Indonesian archipelago.

Area: 15,007 sq. km.

Natural resources: Gold, petroleum, natural gas, manganese, marble.

Terrain: Mountainous terrain.

Climate: Hot and humid tropical climte with distinct rainy and dry seasons.

People

Population: 1,062,777 (July 2006 est.).

Poplation growth rate: 2.08% (2006 est.).

Sex ratio: 1.04 male(s)/female (2006 est.).

Religions: Roman Catholic 90%, Musim 4%, Protestant 3%, Hindu 0.5%, Buddhist, Animist.

Languages: Tetum (official), Portuguese (official), Indonesian, English.

Literacy rate: 58.6% (2002).

Infant mortality rate: 45.89 deaths/1,000 live births (2006 est.).

Life expectancy: Total 66.26 years, Male 63.96 years, Female 68.67 years (2006 est.).

Government

Capital: Dili.

Government type: Republic.

Independence: 20 May 2002 (official date of international recognition of East Timor's independence from Indonesia).

Legal system: UN-drafted legal system based on Indonesian law.

Executive branch:

Chief of state: President Jose Alexander Gusmao, also referred to as Xanana Gusmao (since 20 May 2002). The president plays a largely symbolic role but has the power to veto legislation.

Head of government: Prime Minister Mari Bin Amude Alkatiri (since 20 May 2002).

Economy

Currency: US dollar.

Economy—overview:
In 1999, almost 70 per cent of East Timor's economic infrastructure was destroyed as a result of the freedom struggle. Since then, however, the country has been the site of a huge international reconstruction programme. Nevertheless, East Timor still faces a substantial task of reconstruction, administration and further development, such as that of the petroleum resources that are believed to lie in its waters.

GDP: Purchasing power parity—$370 million (2004 est.).

GDP—real growth rate: 1% (2004 est.).

GDP—per capita: Purchasing power parity—$400 (2004 est.).

Population below poverty line: 42% (2003 est.).

Unemployment rate: 50% (including underemployment) (1992 est.).

Exports: $10 million (2005 est.)—Coffee, sandalwood, marble.

Imports: $202 million (2004 est.)—Food.

Transport and Communications

Railways: None.

Roads: 5,500 km (2005).

Internet country code .tp

Ecuador

History

Indigenous tribes ruled the area that is now Ecuador till the Incas conquered the lands in the fifteenth century. In the sixteenth century, the Spanish conquistadors vanquished the Incas and added it to the viceroyalty of Peru. In 1822, Ecuador established its independence from Spain and became a part of independent Gran Colombia, which also included modern-day Colombia, Panama and Venezuela. In 1830, Ecuador seceded from Gran Colombia. In 1942, Ecuador handed over around 200,000 square kilometres of disputed territory to Peru.

Geography

Location: Western South America, bordering the Pacific Ocean at the Equator, between Colombia and Peru.

Area: 283,560 sq. km. This includes Galapagos Islands.

Terrain: Central plain, inter-Andean central highlands, and flat and rolling eastern jungle.

Natural resources: Petroleum, fish, timber, hydropower.

Climate: Tropical climate along the

coast and in the Amazonian jungle lowlands, but becomes cooler inland at higher altitudes.

People

Population: 13,547,510 (July 2006 est.).

Population growth rate: 5% (2006 est.).

Sex ratio: 1.02 male(s)/female (2006 est.).

Religions: Roman Catholic 95%.

Languages: Spanish (official), Amerindian languages (especially Quechua).

Literacy rate: Total 92.5%, Male 94%, Female 91% (2003 est.).

Infant mortality rate: 22.87 deaths/ 1,000 live births (2006 est.).

Life expectancy: Total 76.42 years, Male 73.55 years, Female 79.43 years (2006 est.).

Government

Capital: Quito.

Government type: Republic.

Independence: 24 May 1822 (from Spain).

Legal system: Based on civil law system.

Executive branch:
Chief of state: President Alfredo Palacio (since 20 April 2005); Vice-President Nicanor Alejandro (since 5 May 2005). The president is both the chief of state and head of government.

Economy

Currency: US dollar.

GDP: Purchasing power parity—$56.9 billion (2005 est.).

GDP—real growth rate: 3.9% (2005 est.).

GDP—per capita: Purchasing power parity—$4,300 (2005 est.).

Inflation rate: 3.1% (2005 est.).

Population below poverty line: 41% (2006 est.).

Unemployment rate: 9.7% (2005 est.).

Exports: $9.224 billion (2005 est.)—Petroleum, banana, shrimp, coffee, cocoa, cut flower, fish.

Imports: $8.436 billion (2005 est.)—Machinery and equipment, chemicals, raw materials, fuels; consumer goods.

External debt: $18.29 billion (November 2005 est.).

Transport and Communications

Railways: 966 km.

Roads: 43,197 km.

Telephones: 1,612,300 (2004).

Mobile cellular: 3,544,200 (2004).

Internet users: 624,600 (2005).

Internet country code: .ec

Egypt

History

Egypt is a cradle of human civilization. Settlement in the Nile Valley began around 7000 BC. Successive dynasties in Egypt ruled over a country that boasted of flourishing trade, prosperity and the unprecedented development of culture and traditions. Egypt's golden age coincided with the eighteenth and nineteenth dynasties, between the sixteenth to thirteenth centuries BC. This

was the age of the pharaohs, of hieroglyphics, and the pyramids. Their construction in around 2500 BC remains one of the greatest engineering achievements of all times.

In 669 BC, Assyrians from Mesopotamia conquered Egypt and established their rule over the country. In 525 BC came the Persian conquest. In 332 BC, Alexander the Great of Macedonia conquered Egypt and founded the city of Alexandria. In 31 BC, the Roman empire claimed Egypt following the death of Queen Cleopatra and Roman leader Octavian's defeat of her forces.

In AD 642, Arabs conquered Egypt. Between 1250 and 1517, the Mamluks/ Mamelukes, or the slave soldiers, ruled the country.

In 1517, Egypt was absorbed into the Turkish Ottoman Empire. Between 1798 and 1801, Napoleon's forces occupied the country. However, in 1801, the British and the Turks drove the French out of Egypt and the country was restored to the Ottoman empire.

The construction of the Suez Canal between 1859–69 was another turning point in the history of Egypt. In 1882, British troops seized control of Egypt and in 1914 it became a British protectorate. In 1922, Egypt gained independence and Fu'ad I became the king of Egypt.

On 14 May 1948, the proclamation of the State of Israel was made in Tel Aviv. The following day, armies from five Arab nations including Egypt invaded Israel but were beaten back. The subsequent armistices defined Israel's territorial limits. However, Egypt retained the Gaza Strip.

In 1952, Gamal Abdel Nasser led the Free Officers' Movement in a coup. This resulted in the installation of Muhammad Naguib as president and prime minister of Egypt. In June 1953, Naguib declared Egypt a republic and abolished the monarchy. In 1954, Gamal Abdel Nasser became the prime minister. In 1956, he became the new President.

On 26 July 1956, an international crisis erupted when President Nasser nationalized the Suez Canal to finance Egypt's construction of the Aswan High Dam. UK and France feared closure of the canal and the halting of petroleum shipments from the Persian Gulf region. In October, UK, France and Israel invaded Egypt. On 22 December, the UN evacuated British and French troops. This incident, now referred to as the Suez Crisis, proved to be a victory for Egypt and President Nasser.

President Nasser passed away in September 1970 and was succeeded by his Vice-President Anwar al-Sadat. In 1971, Egypt signed a Treaty of Friendship with the Soviet Union. The same year, the Aswan High Dam was completed, ushering in a new era for Egyptian irrigation, agriculture and industry.

On 6 October 1973, the Jewish holy day of Yom Kippur, Egypt and Syria attacked Israel, starting what is now called the Yom Kippur War. Israel and Egypt signed a ceasefire agreement in November and peace agreements on 18 January 1974.

In June 1975, the Suez Canal was reopened for the first time since the 1967 war. In 1977, Egypt became the first Arab country to recognize Israel when its president, Anwar Sadat, flew to Israel and even addressed its parliament. In September 1978, Egypt and Israel signed the Camp David accords. On 6 October 1981, opponents of the peace dialogue with Israel assassinated Anwar Sadat. A national referendum approved Hosni Mubarak as the new President of Egypt.

Geography

Location: Northern Africa, bordering the Mediterranean Sea, between Libya and the Gaza Strip, and the Red Sea north of Sudan, and includes the Asian Sinai Peninsula.

Area: 1,001,450 sq. km.

Terrain: Mostly a vast desert plateau that is interrupted by the Nile Valley and Delta.

Natural resources: Petroleum, natural gas, iron ore, phosphates, manganese, limestone, gypsum, talc, asbestos, lead, zinc.

Climate: Desert climate with hot, dry summers and moderate winters.

People

Population: 78,887,007 (July 2006 est.).

Population growth rate: 1.75% (2006 est.).

Sex ratio: 1.02 male(s)/female (2006 est.).

Religions: Muslim (mostly Sunni) 94%, Coptic Christian and others 6%.

Languages: Arabic (official), English and French widely understood by educated classes.

Literacy rate: Total 57.7%, Male 68.3%, Female 46.9% (2003 est.)

Infant mortality rate: 31.33 deaths/1,000 live births (2006 est.).

Life expectancy: Total 76 years, Male 68.77 years, Female 73.93 years (2006 est.).

Government

Capital: Cairo.

Government type: Republic.

Independence: 28 February 1922 (from UK).

Legal system: Based on English common law, Islamic law, and Napoleonic codes.

Executive branch:

Chief of state: President Mohammed Hosni Mubarak (since 14 October 1981).

Head of government: Prime Minister Ahmed Nazif (since July 2004).

Economy

Currency: Egyptian pound.

Economy—overview:

Although the government proposed new privatization and reform measures in late 2003 and early 2004, there has been a lack of any substantial economic reform since the mid 1990s. This is reflected in the limited foreign direct investment in Egypt and low annual GDP growth. The government is apprehensive of possible negative public reaction to reforms.

GDP: Purchasing power parity—$303.5 billion (2005 est.).

GDP—real growth rate: 4.9% (2005 est.).

GDP—per capita: Purchasing power parity—$3,900 (2005 est.).

Inflation rate: 4.3% (2005 est.).

Population below poverty line: 20% (2005 est.).

Unemployment rate: 10% (2005 est.).

Exports: $14.33 billion f.o.b. (2005 est.) —Crude oil and petroleum products, cotton, textiles, metal products, chemicals.

Imports: $24.1 billion f.o.b. (2005 est.)—Machinery and equipment, foodstuff, chemicals, wood products, fuels.

External debt: $28.95 billion (2005 est.).

Transport and Communications

Railways: 5,063 km.

Roads: 64,000 km.

Telephones: 10.4 million (2005).

Mobile cellular: 14,045,134 (2005).

Internet users: 5,000,000 (2005).

Internet country code: .eg

El Salvador

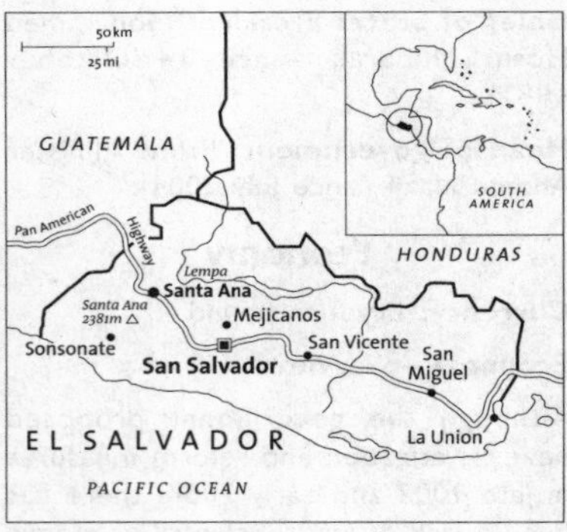

History

It is believed that the Pipil Indians who were descendants of the Aztecs migrated to the area in the eleventh century. The Spanish arrived in the 1520s. In 1821, El Salvador declared its independence from Spain. Between 1931 and 1979, a succession of military dictators ruled El Salvador.

Geography

Location: Middle America, bordering the North Pacific Ocean, between Guatemala and Honduras.

Area: 21,040 sq. km.

Natural resources: Hydropower, geothermal power, petroleum, arable land.

Climate: Coastal El Salvador has a tropical climate while the uplands have a temperate climate.

People

Population: 6,822,378 (July 2006 est.).

Population growth rate: 1.72% (2006 est.).

Sex ratio: 0.95 male(s)/female (2006 est.).

Religions: Roman Catholic 83%.

Languages: Spanish, Nahua (among some Amerindians).

Literacy rate: Total 80.2%, Male 82.8%, Female 77.7% (2003 est.).

Infant mortality rate: 24.39 deaths/ 1,000 live births (2006 est.).

Life expectancy: Total 71.49 years, Male 67.88 years, Female 75.28 years (2006 est.).

Government

Capital: San Salvador.

Government type: Republic.

Independence: 15 September 1821 (from Spain).

Legal system: Based on civil and Roman law, with traces of common law.

Executive branch:

Chief of state: President Elias Antonio

Saca Gonzalez (since 1 June 2004); Vice-President Ana Vilma De Escobar (since 1 June 2004). The president is both the chief of state and head of government.

Economy

Currency: US dollar.

GDP: Purchasing power parity—$31.24 billion (2005 est.).

GDP—real growth rate: 2.8% (2005 est.).

GDP—per capita: Purchasing power parity—$4,700 (2005 est.).

Inflation rate: 4.7% (2005 est.).

Population below poverty line: 36.1% (2004 est.).

Unemployment rate: 6.5% (2004 est.).

Exports: $3.586 billion (2005 est.)—Offshore assembly exports, coffee, sugar, shrimp, textiles, chemicals, electricity.

Imports: $6.678 billion (2005 est.)—Raw materials, consumer goods, capital goods, fuels, foodstuff, petroleum, electricity.

External debt: $8.273 billion (2005 est.).

Transport and Communications

Railways: 283 km.

Roads: 10,029 km.

Telephones: 887,800 (2004).

Mobile cellular: 1,832,600 (2004).

Internet users: 587,500 (2005).

Internet country code: .sv

Equatorial Guinea

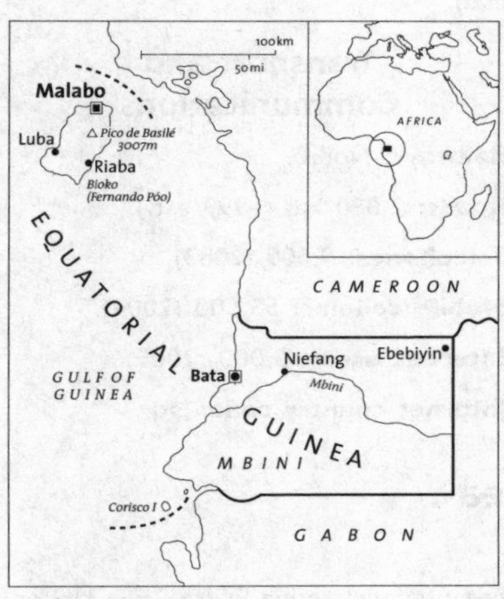

History

Pygmies were the original inhabitants of the mainland part of the country. Fang and Bubi people, the two most important ethnic groups today, migrated to the region in the seventeenth century. The Portuguese arrived in the fifteenth century. In 1477, Portugal ceded the island of Fernando Po (present-day Bioko) to Spain.

In 1968, Spanish Guinea became independent as the Republic of Equatorial Guinea. In 1996, oil and natural gas was struck in Equatorial Guinea. Today, the country is a key producer of petroleum in Africa.

Geography

Location: Western Africa, bordering the Bight of Biafra, between Cameroon and Gabon.

Area: 28,051 sq. km.

Natural resources: Oil, petroleum, timber, small unexploited deposits of gold, manganese, uranium, titanium, iron ore.

Climate: Hot and humid tropical climate.

People

Population: 540,109 (July 2006 est.).

Population growth rate: 2.05% (2006 est.).

Sex ratio: 0.96 male(s)/female (2006 est.).

Religions: Nominally Christian and predominantly Roman Catholic, pagan practices.

Languages: Spanish (official), French (official), pidgin English, Fang, Bubi, Ibo.

Literacy rate: Total 85.7%, Male 93.3%, Female 78.4% (2003 est.).

Infant mortality rate: 89.21 deaths/1,000 live births (2006 est.).

Life expectancy: Total 49.54 years, Male 48 years, Female 51.13 years (2006 est.).

Government

Capital: Malabo.

Government type: Republic.

Independence: 12 October 1968 (from Spain).

Legal system: Based on Spanish civil law and tribal custom.

Executive branch:
Chief of state: President Brig. Gen. (Ret.) Teodoro Obiang Nguema Mbasogo (since 3 August 1979).

Head of government: Miguel Abia Biteo Boriko (from June 2004).

Economy

Currency: Communaute Financiere Africaine franc.

GDP: Purchasing power parity—$25.69 billion (2005 est.).

GDP—real growth rate: 18.6% (2005 est.).

GDP—per capita: Purchasing power parity—$50,200 (2005 est.).

Inflation rate: 5% (2005 est.).

Unemployment rate: 30% (1998 est.).

Exports: $6.727 billion f.o.b. (2005 est.)—Petroleum, methanol, timber, cocoa.

Imports: $1.864 billion f.o.b. (2005 est.)—Petroleum sector equipment, other equipment.

External debt: $248 million (2000 est.).

Transport and Communications

Railways: None.

Roads: 2,880 km (1999 est.).

Telephones: 9,600 (2003).

Mobile cellular: 55,500 (2004).

Internet users: 5,000 (2005).

Internet country code: .gq

Eritrea

History

Between AD 300–600, Eritrea was a part of the Ethiopian kingdom of Aksum. In the 1500s the Ottoman empire annexed Eritrea. In 1941, the UK occupied Eritrea and in 1949, it began administering Eritrea as a United Nations Trust Territory. In 1962 Ethiopia annexed Eritrea. In 1993, Eritreans voted almost unanimously for independence in a referendum. Eritrea became independent in June 1993. In 1999, border skirmishes with Ethiopia devel-

oped into a full-fledged war. In June 2000, the two countries signed a ceasefire agreement and later, in December, a peace agreement.

Geography

Location: Eastern Africa, bordering the Red Sea, between Djibouti and Sudan.

Area: 121,320 sq. km.

Natural resources: Gold, potash, zinc, copper, salt, possibly oil and natural gas, fish.

Climate: Hot climate in the dry desert strip along the Red Sea coast. The central highlands are cooler and wetter.

People

Population: 4,786,994 (July 2006 est.).

Population growth rate: 2.47% (2006 est.).

Sex ratio: 0.99 male(s)/female (2006 est.).

Religions: Muslim, Coptic Christian, Roman Catholic, Protestant.

Languages: Afar, Arabic, Tigre and Kunama, Tigrinya, other Cushitic languages.

Literacy rate: Total 58.6%, Male 69.9%, Female 47.6% (2003 est.).

Infant mortality rate: 46.3 deaths/1,000 live births (2006 est.).

Life expectancy: Total 59.03 years, Male 57.44 years, Female 60.66 years (2006 est.).

Government

Capital: Asmara (formerly Asmera).

Government type: Transitional government.

Independence: 24 May 1993 (from Ethiopia).

Legal system: Primarily based on the Ethiopian legal code of 1957, with revisions.

Executive branch:

Chief of state: President Isaias Asewerki (since 8 June 1993). The president is the chief of state, head of government and the head of the State Council and National Assembly.

Economy

Currency: Nakfa.

GDP: Purchasing power parity—$4.471 billion (2005 est.).

GDP—real growth rate: 2% (2005 est.).

GDP—per capita: Purchasing power parity—$1,000 (2005 est.).

Inflation rate: 15% (2005 est.).

Population below poverty line: 50% (2004 est.).

Exports: $33.58 million f.o.b. (2005 est.)—Livestock, sorghum, textiles, food, small manufactures.

Imports: $676 million f.o.b. (2005 est.)—Machinery, petroleum products, food, manufactured goods.

External debt: $311 million (2000 est.).

Transport and Communications

Railways: 306 km.

Roads: 4,010 km.

Telephones: 39,300 (2004).

Mobile cellular: 20,000 (2004).

Internet users: 50,000 (2005).

Internet country code: .er

Estonia

History

In the fourteenth century, the Danes controlled the northern part of Estonia while the Teutonic Knights of Germany possessed the southern part of the country. In 1346, the Danes sold the part of Estonia in their control to the Teutonic Knights. The Teutonics now came to control all of Estonia, which they transformed into serfdom. In 1526, the Swedes came to control Estonia. In 1721, the Russians gained control of Estonia from Sweden. In 1918, Estonia proclaimed its independence. But in 1940, it was back under Soviet rule. Finally, in August 1991, Estonia gained independence. Estonia joined both NATO and the EU in the spring of 2004.

Geography

Location: Eastern Europe, bordering the Baltic Sea and Gulf of Finland, between Latvia and Russia.

Area: 45,226 sq. km. This includes the area of 1,520 islands in the Baltic Sea.

Natural resources: Oil shale, peat, phosphorite, clay, limestone, sand, dolomite, arable land, sea mud.

Climate: Maritime climate with wet and moderate winters and cool summers.

People

Population: 1,324,333 (July 2006 est.).

Population growth rate: –0.64% (2006 est.)

Sex ratio: 0.84 male(s)/female (2006 est.).

Religions: Evangelical Lutheran, Russian Orthodox, Estonian Orthodox, Baptist, Methodist, Seventh-Day Adventist, Roman Catholic, Pentecostal, Word of Life, Jewish.

Languages: Estonian (official), Russian, Ukrainian, Finnish, others.

Literacy rate: Total 99.8%, Male 99.8%, Female 99.8% (2003 est.).

Infant mortality rate: 7.73 deaths/ 1,000 live births (2006 est.).

Life expectancy: Total 72.04 years, Male 66.58 years, Female 77.83 years (2006 est.).

Government

Capital: Tallinn.

Government type: Parliamentary republic.

Independence: 20 August 1991 (from Soviet Union).

Legal system: Based on civil law system.

Executive branch:

Chief of state: President Arnold Ruutel (since 8 October 2001).

Head of government: Prime Minister Andrus Ansip (since 12 April 2005).

Economy

Currency: Estonian kroon.

GDP: Purchasing power parity—$22.29 billion (2005 est.).

GDP—real growth rate: 9.6% (2005 est.).

GDP—per capita: Purchasing power parity—$16,700 (2005 est.).

Inflation rate: 4% (2005 est.).

Unemployment rate: 9.2% (2005 est.).

Exports: $7.439 billion f.o.b. (2005 est.)—Machinery and equipment 33%, wood and paper 15%, textiles 14%, food products 8%, furniture 7%, metals, chemical products.

Imports: $9.189 billion f.o.b. (2005 est.)—Machinery and equipment 33.5%, chemical products 11.6%, textiles 10.3%, foodstuff 9.4%, transportation equipment 8.9%.

External debt: $10.09 billion (2005 est.).

Transport and Communications

Railways: 958 km (2003).

Roads: 56,849 km (2003).

Telephones: 444,000 (2004).

Mobile cellular: 1,255,700 (2004).

Internet users: 670,000 (2005).

Internet country code: .ee

Ethiopia

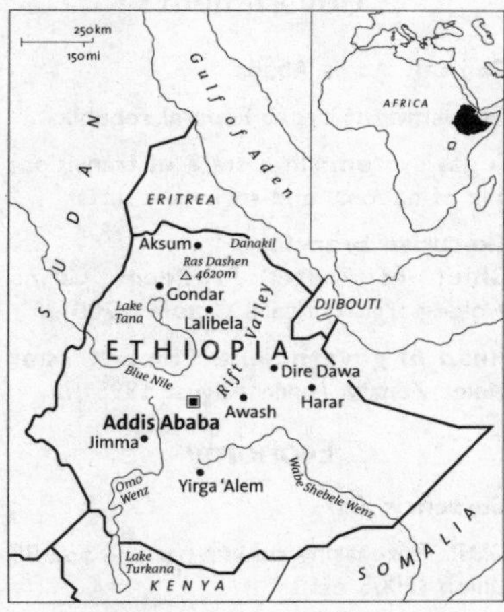

History

Some of the oldest human remains found on earth have been discovered in Ethiopia. Ethiopia was originally called Abyssinia. The Solomonic dynasty that once ruled the country claims its descent from the son of King Solomon and Queen Sheba.

In the seventh century BC, Ge'ez-speaking people established the kingdom of Da'amat in the northern parts of the country. Then in the second century AD, Semitic people originating from the Arabian Peninsula established the kingdom of Axum (Aksum).

In 1530–1, Muslim leader Ahmad Gran conquered most of Ethiopia. In 1868, a British expeditionary force defeated Emperor Tewodros II and he committed suicide to avoid capture. In 1889, the king of Shoa became Emperor Menelik II. He signed a bilateral friendship treaty at Wuchale with Italy.

In 1895, Italy invaded Ethiopia. But in 1896, the Ethiopians defeated the Italian forces in a battle fought at Adwa. The Ethiopians subsequently annulled the treaty of Wuchale.

In 1936, Italians invaded Ethiopia once again. They captured Addis Ababa, causing Haile Selassie to flee the country. The king of Italy was crowned emperor of Ethiopia. Italy combined Ethiopia with Eritrea and Italian Somaliland to form Italian East Africa. In 1941, British and Commonwealth troops in association with the Ethiopian resistance, the Arbegnoch, defeated the Italians and restored Haile Selassie to his throne.

In 1952, United Nations federated Eritrea with Ethiopia and in 1962 Haile Selassie annexed Eritrea and turned it into an Ethiopian province. In 1973–4 an estimated 200,000 people died in Wallo province as a result of famine. In September 1974, Haile Selassie was deposed in a military coup and General Teferi Benti became the head of state. The Constitution was dissolved and Ethiopia was declared a socialist state under the rule of a Provisional Military Administrative Council, also known as the Derg. In 1975, Haile Selassie passed away under mysterious circumstances while in custody. Benti himself was killed in 1977.

In the late 1990s, border clashes between Ethiopia and Eritrea developed into full-scale warfare. In June 2000, the two countries signed a ceasefire agreement and later in December, a peace agreement.

Geography

Location: Eastern Africa, west of Somalia.

Area: 1,127,127 sq. km.

Terrain: High flat plateau with a central mountain range.

Natural resources: Gold, platinum, copper, potash, natural gas, hydropower.

Climate: Tropical monsoon climate with wide variation caused by topograpy.

People

Population: 74,777,981 (July 2006 est.).

Population growth rate: 2.31% (2006 est.).

Sex ratio: 1 male(s)/female (2006 est.).

Religions: Muslim 45%–50%, Ethiopian Orthodox 35%–40%, animist 12%, others 3%–8%.

Languages: Amharic, Tigrinya, Oromigna, Guaragigna, Somali, Arabic, other local languages, English.

Literacy rate: Total 42.7%, Male 50.3%, Female 35.1% (2003 est.).

Infant mortality rate: 93.62 deaths/1,000 live births (2006 est.).

Life expectancy: Total 49.03 years, Male 47.86 years, Female 50.24 years (2006 est.).

Government

Capital: Addis Ababa.

Government type: Federal republic.

Legal system: In a state of transition; mix of national and regional courts.

Executive branch:
Chief of state: President Girma Woldegiorgis (since 8 October 2001).

Head of government: Prime Minister Meles Zenawi (since August 1995).

Economy

Currency: Birr.

GDP: Purchasing power parity—$62.88 billion (2005 est.).

GDP—real growth rate: 8.9% (2005 est.).

GDP—per capita: Purchasing power parity—$900 (2005 est.).

Inflation rate: 6% (2005 est.).

Population below poverty line: 50% (2004 est.).

Exports: $612 million f.o.b. (2005 est.)—Coffee, gold, leather products, live animals, oilseeds.

Imports: $2.722 billion f.o.b. (2005 est.)—Food and live animals, petroleum and petroleum products, chemicals, machinery, motor vehicles, cereals, textiles.

External debt: $2.9 billion (2001 est.).

Transport and Communications

Railways: 681 km.

Roads: 33,856 km.

Telephones: 435,000 (2003).

Mobile cellular: 178,000 (2004).

Internet users: 113,000 (2005).

Internet country code: .et

Fiji

History

The first Europeans to see the islands were the Dutch Abel Janzsoon Tasman (in 1643) and the British Captain James Cook (in 1774). Foreign interest in the islands grew due to the availability of sandalwood and sea cucumber. Fiji became a British Crown colony on 10 October 1874. In order to promote its own policies and to foster the economic development of the colony, the government encouraged Indian migrants to take up permanent residency on the islands. Fiji achieved independence on 10 October 1970.

Geography

Location: Oceania, island group in the South Pacific Ocean, about two-thirds of the way from Hawaii to New Zealand.

Area: 18,270 sq. km.

Terrain: Mostly mountainous terrain. The mountains are of volcanic origin.

Natural resources: Timber, fish, gold, copper, hydropower.

Climate: Tropical marine climate with slight seasonal temperature variation.

People

Population 905,949 (July 2006 est.).

Population growth rate: 1.4% (2006 est.).

Sex ratio: 1.01 male(s)/female (2006 est.).

Religions: Christian 52% (Methodist 37%, Roman Catholic 9%), Hindu 38%, Muslim 8%, others 2%.

Languages: English (official), Fijian, Hindustani.

Literacy rate: Total 93.7%, Male 95.5%, Female 91.9% (2003 est.).

Infant mortality rate: 12.3 deaths/ 1,000 live births (2006 est.).

Life expectancy: Total 69.82 years, Male 67.32 years, Female 72.45 years (2006 est.).

Government

Capital: Suva.

Government type: Republic.

Independence: 10 October 1970 (from UK).

Legal system: Based on the British system.

Executive branch:

Chief of state: President Ratu Josefa Iloilovatu Uluivuda (since 2000); Vice-President Jope Seniloli (since 2000).

Head of government: Prime Minister Laisenia Qarase (since 10 September 2000).

Economy

Currency: Fijian dollar.

Economy—overview:

Fiji has forest, mineral and fish resources and is one of the most developed of the Pacific island economies. However, there is a large subsistence sector. Sugar exports and tourism industry are the major sources of foreign exchange. Sugar processing constitutes one-third of country's industrial activity.

GDP: Purchasing power parity—$5.38 billion (2005 est.).

GDP—real growth rate: 1.7% (2005 est.).

GDP—per capita: Purcnasing power parity—$6,000 (2005 est.).

Inflation rate: 1.6% (2004 est.).

Population below poverty line: 25.5% (1990–1).

Unemployment rate: 7.6% (1999).

Exports: $862 million f.o.b. (2004)—Sugar, garments, gold, timber, fish, molasses, coconut oil.

Imports: $1.235 billion c.i.f. (2004)—Manufactured goods, machinery and transport equipment, petroleum products, food, chemicals.

External debt: $188.1 million (2001).

Transport and Communications

Railways: 597 km.

Roads: 3,440 km.

Telephones: 102,000 (2003).

Mobile cellular: 109,900 (2003).

Internet users: 55,000 (2003).

Internet country code: .fj

Finland

History

The first inhabitants of the area that is today Finland were the Sami people, also called Lapp. Later, Finnish-speaking people arrived in the region in the first millennium BC and drove the Samis northwards to the Arctic regions. In the eleventh century, repeated Finnish attacks on Swedish lands led to the Swedish conquest of Finland. In 1808, Russia invaded Sweden and the following year, Sweden handed over Finland to the Russians.

Finland declared its independence from Russia following the 1917 Revolution. In 1919, Finland became a republic.

During World War II, by the terms of the Treaty of Moscow of 1940, Finland surrendered a large part of south-eastern Finland to the Soviet Union. In 1944, the Soviet Red Army invaded the country. Finland had to hand over even more land to the Soviet Union and also

had to pay hundreds of millions of dollars in war reparations. In 1995, Finland became a member state of the European Union.

Geography

Location: Northern Europe, bordering the Baltic Sea, Gulf of Bothnia, and Gulf of Finland, between Sweden and Russia.

Area: 338,145 sq. km.

Terrain: Mostly low, flat to rolling plains interspersed with lakes and low hills.

Natural resources: Timber, iron ore, copper, lead, zinc, chromite, nickel, gold, silver, limestone.

Climate: Cold temperate climate.

People

Population: 5,231,372 (July 2006 est.).

Population growth rate: 0.14% (2006 est.).

Sex ratio: 0.96 male(s)/female (2006 est.).

Religions: Lutheran National Church 84.2%, Greek Orthodox in Finland 1.1%, other Christian 1.1%, other 0.1%, none 13.5% (2003).

Languages: Finnish 93.4% (official), Swedish 5.9% (official), small Sami- and Russian-speaking minorities.

Literacy rate: 100% (2000 est.).

Infant mortality rate: 3.55 deaths/ 1,000 live births (2006 est.).

Life expectancy: Total 78.5 years, Male 74.99 years, Female 82.17 years (2006 est.).

Government

Capital: Helsinki.

Government type: Republic.

Independence: 6 December 1917 (from Russia).

Legal system: Civil law system based on Swedish law.

Executive branch:

Chief of state: President Tarja Halonen (since 1 March 2000).

Head of government: Prime Minister Matti Vanhanen (since 24 June 2003) and Deputy Prime Minister Antti Kalliomaki (since 17 April 2003).

Economy

Currency: Euro.

Economy—overview:

Finland has a highly industrialized, largely free-market economy. The key economic sectors are manufacturing (such as telecommunications, electronics, wood, metals and engineering). One major success story in the manufacturing sector is that of Nokia. In 2000, Nokia accounted for 4% of Finland's GDP, nearly 30% of exports and 1% of jobs. Exports account for one-third of Finland's GDP. Other than timber and some minerals, Finland has to depend on imported raw materials, energy and components for producing manufactured products. Finland was one of the 12 countries joining the European Economic and Monetary Union (EMU).

GDP: Purchasing power parity—$161.5 billion (2005 est.).

GDP—real growth rate: 2.2% (2005 est.).

GDP—per capita: Purchasing power parity—$30,900 (2005 est.).

Inflation rate: 1.2% (2005 est.).

Unemployment rate: 7.9% (2005 est.).

Exports: $67.88 billion f.o.b. (2005 est.)—Machinery and equipment, chemicals, metals, timber, paper, pulp.

Imports: $56.45 billion f.o.b. (2005 est.)—Foodstuff, petroleum and petroleum products, chemicals, transport equipment, iron and steel, machinery, textile yarn and fabrics, grains.

External debt: $211.7 billion (30 June 2005).

Transport and Communications

Railways: 5,851 km.

Road: 78,168 km.

Telephones: 2.368 million (2004).

Mobile cellular: 4.988 million (2004).

Internet users: 3.286 million (2005).

Internet country code: .fi

France

History

Archaeological evidence shows that the area that is today France has been inhabited almost continuously since Paleolithic times. Around 1200 BC, the Celts (later called Gauls) migrated into the area. The Romans referred to the area as Transalpine Gaul. Roman emperor Augustus divided the country into four administrative provinces.

Between 751 and 987, the Carolingian dynasty ruled the territory. The greatest Carolingian ruler was Charlemagne, who later became the Holy Roman Emperor. In 843, the Treaty of Verdun divided the territories roughly corresponding with France, Germany and Italy among the three grandsons of Charlemagne. Consequently, Charles the Bald received what was then called Francia Occidentalis. France subsequently passed under the rule of the Capetian dynasty.

The House of Valois ruled France from 1328 to 1589. Between 1337 and 1453, France and England fought each other in the Hundred Years War that resulted in the return of British-held land to France. The House of Bourbon followed the Valois dynasty.

The Bourbons ruled France from 1589 to the 1790s and from 1814 to 1830. The Bourbon–Orleans dynasty ruled for eighteen years from 1830 to 1848.

Louis XIV, also called the Sun King, ruled from 1643 to 1715. His reign is widely regarded as a brilliant period of French history. Louis XIV extended France's eastern borders by defeating the Hapsburgs. He also fought the War of the Spanish Succession (1701–14) in which he took on a formidable European coalition but succeeded in securing the Spanish throne for his grandson.

In 1789, the French Revolution, also called the Revolution of 1789, swept the country and plunged it into a period of uncertainty and violence. On 14 July 1789, a mob of Parisians seized the Bastille prison, regarded as a symbol of royal tyranny and despotism. On 4 August 1789, the National Constituent Assembly decreed the abolition of the feudal regime. On 26 August, it introduced the Declaration of the Rights of Man and of the Citizen. On 20 September 1792, the National Convention was set up. It proclaimed the abolition of the monarchy and the establishment of the republic. On 19 January 1793, Louis XVI was condemned to death by 380 votes against 310. He was guillotined in Paris on 21 January 1793. Marie-Antoinette, his queen consort, was executed in October that year.

The period of the French Revolution from 5 September 1793, to 27 July 1794 is referred to as the 'Reign of Terror'. Faced with the dual problem of foreign war (with Austria) and civil war, the Revolutionary government decreed terror as the law of the day. It decided to take harsh measures against those suspected of being enemies of the revolution. A wave of executions swept through Paris. The Committee of Public Safety, of which Maximilien Robespierre was the most prominent member, held virtual dictatorial control over the French government. It is now estimated that at least 300,000 suspects were arrested during the Reign of Terror, of which 17,000 were officially executed. Many died in prison, often without a trial.

Soon after the fall of Robespierre, and a crucial victory over Austria in the ongoing war, the government terminated its strict economic and social laws, even abandoning the aim of economic equality. The reactions that followed these moves ultimately led a young French general to defeat the royalists and seize power in Paris. His name was Napoleon Bonaparte.

From 1799 to 1804, Napoleon served as the First Consul. Then, in 1804 he crowned himself emperor of France in the presence of the Pope. Napoleon is widely regarded as one of the most influential personalities of Western history. Considered to be a brilliant military strategist, he also brought about the Napoleonic Code, which not only became the civil law of France but was also used as the starting point of civil-law codes in countries around the world.

Under Napolean's leadership, France was elevated to a position of dominance in Europe; its only major rival for European domination was the UK. Napoleon's ambitions of invading UK were dealt a deathblow on 21 October 1805 when a fleet of thirty-three ships under Admiral Pierre de Villeneuve was defeated by a British fleet of twenty-seven ships under Admiral Horatio Nelson, west of Cape Trafalgar, Spain. Napoleon's invasion of Russia in 1812 also ended in disaster. The warfare, shortage of supplies and the fierce cold of the Russian winter claimed 500,000 men. It also cost Napoleon his confidence and crucially, his allies.

A new coalition was formed in 1813 and the invasion of France was under way early in 1814. On 6 April, Napoleon abdicated. He was exiled to the island of Elba. In March 1815, he returned to France and formed a new army. However, the comeback proved to be shortlived and Napoleon suffered his final defeat at Waterloo in June 1815. Napoleon abdicated for the second time, on 22 June. The Bourbon monarchy was restored with Louis XVIII. Napoleon was imprisoned and exiled to the island of Saint Helena from October 1815. He passed away there, on 5 May 1821.

In 1848, the Second Republic was established with a nephew of Napoleon, Louis Napoleon, at its head. In 1852, he declared the Second Empire and took to the throne as Napoleon III. His abdication following defeat in the Franco-Prussian War (1870–1) led to the formation of the Third Republic.

World War I saw massive casualties in the trench warfare that took place in the northern parts of France. By the end of the war, nearly 1.3 million Frenchmen had been killed and more than twice that number wounded or crippled. The landmark peace document, the Treaty of Versailles, was signed at the end of the War.

Germany occupied France during World War II. General Charles de Gaulle, undersecretary of war, established a government-in-exile (Free French) in London and later in Algiers, Algeria. A sustained French Resistance campaign and the setting up of a subservient Vichy regime that owed allegiance to Nazi Germany characterized the German occupation of France. The Allied invasion of western Europe began on 6 June 1944 from Normandy in northern France. This was the famous D-Day of World War II and led to the liberation of France. Charles de Gaulle returned to set up a provisional government.

The provisional government lasted till 1947, when the Fourth Republic was established. In the Fifth Republic, Charles de Gaulle returned as President and served till 1969.

The First Indo-China War ended in French defeat in Vietnam in 1954. This led to French evacuation from the country. Algeria gained independence from France in 1962. Meanwhile, in 1956, French colonial rule came to an end in Morocco and Tunisia.

Geography

Location: Western Europe, bordering the Mediterranean Sea, between Italy and Spain; bordering the Bay of Biscay and English Channel, between Belgium and Spain, south-east of the UK.

Area: 547,030 sq. km (includes only metropolitan France; excludes the overseas administrative divisions).

Terrain: Mostly flat plains or gently rolling hills in the north and west. Rest of the country is mountainous, with the Pyrenees in the south and the Alps in the east.

Natural resources: Coal, iron ore, bauxite, zinc, uranium, antimony, arsenic, potash, feldspar, fluorspar, gypsum, timber, fish.

Climate: Generally cool winters and mild summers. The Mediterranean areas have mild winters and hot summers.

People

Population: 60,876,136 (July 2006 est.).

Population growth rate: 0.35% (2006 est.).

Sex ratio: 0.95 male(s)/female (2006 est.).

Religions: Roman Catholic 83–88%, Protestant 2%, Jewish 1%, Muslim 5–10%, unaffiliated 4%.

Languages: French 100%, Provencal, Breton, Alsatian, Corsican, Catalan, Basque, Flemish.

Literacy rate: Total 99%, Male 99%, Female 99% (1980 est.).

Infant mortality rate: 4.21 deaths/ 1,000 live births (2006 est.).

Life expectancy: Total 79.73 years, Male 76.1 years, Female 83.54 years (2006 est.).

Government

Capital: Paris.

Government type: Republic.

Independence: AD 486 (unification under Clovis).

Legal system: Civil law system with indigenous concepts; review of administrative but not legislative acts.

Executive branch:
Chief of state: President Jacques Chirac (since 17 May 1995).

Head of government: Prime Minister Dominique Villepin (since 31 May 2005).

Elections and election results: The president is elected by popular vote for a five-year term. The election was last held on 21 April and 5 May 2002 and the next election is scheduled for April 2007 (first round) and May 2007 (second round). A majority of the National Assembly nominates the prime minister.

Legislative branch:
France has a bicameral parliament or Parlement that consists of the Senate or Senat and the National Assembly or Assemblee Nationale. The Senate has 331 seats. An electoral college indirectly elects members to serve nine-year terms by thirds every three years. In the period leading up to 2010, 25 new seats will be added to the Senate to make a total of 346 seats—326 for metropolitan France and overseas departments, two for New Caledonia, two for Mayotte, one for Saint-Pierre and Miquelon, three for overseas territories, and twelve for French nationals abroad. An electoral college will indirectly elect members to serve six-year terms, with one half of the seats being renewed every three years. The National Assembly has 577 seats. Members are elected by popular vote under a single-member majoritarian system to serve five-year terms.

Elections and election results: Senate elections were last held on 26 September 2004.

National Assembly elections were last held during 8–16 June 2002 and the next elections are scheduled for not later than June 2007.

Economy

Currency: Euro.

Economy—overview:
France has a prosperous, modern economy undergoing transition from one that included widespread government ownership and control to a market-driven one. The list of large organizations that have been partially or fully privatized in recent times include Air France, Renault, and France Telecom. Income taxes have been lowered and measures introduced to boost employment. The country suffers from the problems of high cost of labour and the problems posed by the 35-hour workweek and restrictions on retrenchments. Efforts have also been initiated for pension reforms.

GDP: Purchasing power parity—$1.816 trillion (2005 est.).

GDP—real growth rate: 1.4% (2005 est.).

GDP—per capita: Purchasing power parity—$29,900 (2005 est.).

Inflation rate: 1.9% (2005 est.).

Population below poverty line: 6.5% (2000).

Unemployment rate: 10% (2005 est.).

Exports: $443.4 billion f.o.b. (2005 est.)—machinery and transportation equipment, aircraft, plastics, chemicals, pharmaceutical products, iron and steel, beverages.

Imports: $473.3 billion f.o.b. (2005 est.)—machinery and equipment, vehicles, crude oil, aircraft, plastics, chemicals.

External debt: $2.826 trillion (30 June 2005 est.).

Transport and Communications

Railways: 29,519 km.

Roads: 893,100 km.

Telephones: 33,870,200 (2004).

Mobile cellular: 44,551,800 (2004).

Internet users: 26,214,174 (2005).

Internet country code: .fr

Gabon

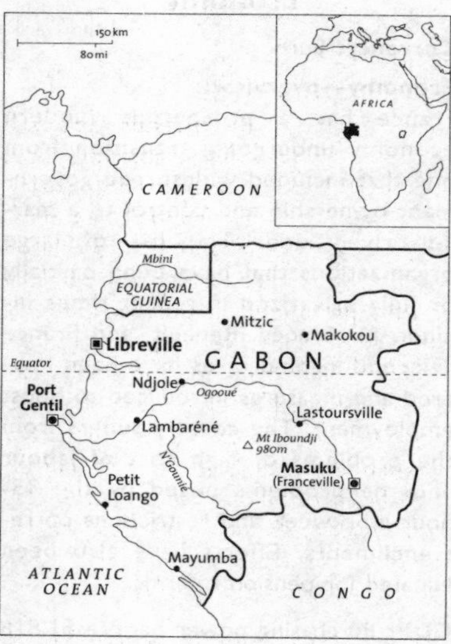

History

The Portuguese were the first Europeans to arrive in the area in 1470. The Dutch arrived in 1593 and the French in 1630. In 1839, a local Mpongwe ruler signed away the sovereignty of the land to the French. In 1910, Gabon became a part of French Equatorial Africa. It gained independence in 1960.

Geography

Location: Western Africa, bordering the Atlantic Ocean at the Equator, between the Republic of the Congo and Equatorial Guinea.

Area: 267,667 sq. km.

Terrain: Narrow coastal plain with a hilly interior and savanna in the east and the north.

Natural resources: Petroleum, manganese, uranium, gold, timber, iron ore, hydropower.

Climate: Hot and humid tropical climate.

People

Population: 1,424,906 (July 2006 est.).

Population growth rate: 2.13% (2006 est.).

Sex ratio: 0.99 male(s)/female (2006 est.).

Religions: Christian 55%–75%, animist, Muslim less than 1%.

Languages: French (official), Fang, Myene, Nzebi, Bapounou/Eschira, Bandjabi.

Literacy rate: Total 63.2%, Male 73.7%, Female 53.3% (1995 est.).

Infant mortality rate: 54.51 deaths/1,000 live births (2006 est.).

Life expectancy: Total 54.49 years, Male 53.21 years, Female 55.81 years (2006 est.).

Government

Capital: Libreville.

Government type: Republic.

Independence: 17 August 1960 (from France).

Legal system: Based on French civil law system and customary law.

Executive branch:
Chief of state: President El Hadj Omar Bongo (since 2 December 1967).

Head of government: Prime Minister Jean Eyeghe Ndong (since 20 January 2006).

Economy

Currency: Communaute Financiere Africaine franc.

GDP: Purchasing power parity—$9.535 billion (2005 est.).

GDP—real growth rate: 2.1% (2005 est.).

GDP—per capita: Purchasing power parity—$6,800 (2005 est.).

Inflation rate: 1.5% (2005 est.).

Unemployment rate: 21% (1997 est.).

Exports: $5.813 billion f.o.b. (2005 est.)—crude oil 77%, timber, manganese, uranium (2001).

Imports: $1.533 billion f.o.b. (2005 est.)—machinery and equipment, foodstuff, chemicals, construction materials.

External debt: $3.857 billion (2005 est.).

Transport and Communications

Railways: 814 km.

Roads: 32,333 km.

Telephones: 38,700 (2004).

Mobile cellular: 489,400 (2004).

Internet users: 40,000 (2005).

Internet country code: .ga

The Gambia

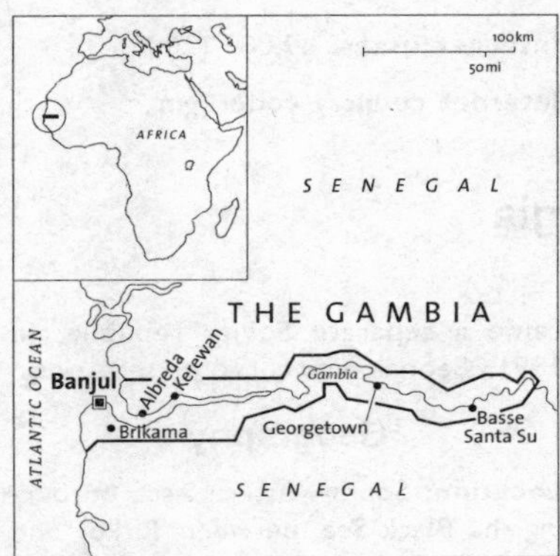

History

The present-day boundaries of the Gambia were demarcated by an agreement between Britain and France in 1889. In 1894, the Gambia became a British protectorate. In 1965, the Gambia became an independent country within the Commonwealth. In 1970, the Gambia became a republic.

Geography

Location: Western Africa, bordering the North Atlantic Ocean and Senegal.

Area: 11,300 sq. km.

Natural resources: Fish.

Climate: Tropical climate with a hot, rainy season from June to November and a cooler, dry season from November to May.

People

Population: 1,641,564 (July 2006 est.).

Population growth rate: 2.84% (2006 est.).

Sex ratio: 1 male(s)/female (2006 est.).

Religions: Muslim 90%, Christian 9%, indigenous beliefs 1%.

Languages: English (official), Mandinka, Wolof, Fula, other indigenous vernaculars.

Literacy rate: Total 40.1%, Male 47.8%, Female 32.8% (2003 est.).

Infant mortality rate: 71.58 deaths/ 1,000 live births (2006 est.).

Life expectancy: Total 54.14 years, Male 52.3 years, Female 56.03 years (2006 est.).

Government

Capital: Banjul.

Government type: Republic under multiparty democratic rule.

Independence: 18 February 1965 (from UK).

Legal system: Based on a composite of English common law, Koranic law, and customary law.

Executive branch:

Chief of state: President Yahya A.J.J. Jammeh (since 18 October 1996). The president is both the chief of state and head of government.

Economy

Currency: Dalasi.

GDP: Purchasing power parity—$3.024 billion (2005 est.).

GDP—real growth rate: 5.5% (2005 est.).

GDP—per capita: Purchasing power parity—$1,900 (2005 est.).

Inflation rate: 8.8% (2004 est.).

Exports: $140.3 million f.o.b. (2005 est.)—peanut products, fish, cotton lint, palm kernels, re-exports.

Imports: $197 million f.o.b. (2005 est.)—foodstuff, manufactures, fuel, machinery and transport equipment.

External debt: $628.8 million (2003 est.).

Transport and Communications

Railways: None.

Roads: 3,742 km.

Telephones: 38,400 (2002).

Mobile cellular: 175,000 (2004).

Internet users: 49,000 (2005).

Internet country code: .gm

Georgia

History

In around 4 BC, Georgia became a kingdom. In the later part of the twelfth century, the kingdom enlarged to include the whole of Transcaucasia. In the thirteenth century, Mongols swept across the country and annihilated much of its population. In the eighteenth century, Georgia came under Russian control. Georgia declared its independence in 1918. In 1936, it became a separate Soviet republic. In 1991, Georgia announced its secession.

Geography

Location: South-western Asia, bordering the Black Sea, between Turkey and Russia.

Area: 69,700 sq. km.

Terrain: Mostly mountainous.

Natural resources: Forests, hydropower, manganese deposits, iron ore,

copper, coal and oil deposits, coastal climate and soils.

Climate: Georgia has a warm and pleasant climate. The climate on the Black Sea coast resembles that of the Mediterranean region of Europe.

People

Population: 4,661,473 (July 2006 est.).

Population growth rate: –0.34% (2006 est.).

Sex ratio: 0.91 male(s)/female (2006 est.).

Religions: Orthodox Christian 83.9%, Armenian-Gregorian 3.9%, Catholic 0.8%, Muslim 9.9%, other 0.8%, none 0.7% (2002 census).

Languages: Georgian 71% (official), Russian 9%, Armenian 7%, Azeri 6%, others 7%.

Literacy rate: Total 100%, Male 100%, Female 100% (2004 est.).

Infant mortality rate: 17.97 deaths/1,000 live births (2006 est.).

Life expectancy: Total 76.09 years, Male 72.8 years, Female 79.87 years (2006 est.).

Government

Capital: T'bilisi.

Government type: Republic.

Independence: 9 April 1991 (from Soviet Union).

Legal system: Based on civil law system.

Executive branch:

Chief of state: President Mikhail Saakashvili (since 25 January 2004); the president is both the chief of state and head of government.

Economy

Currency: Lari.

Economy—overview:

The bulk of Georgia's economic activities are in the form of agricultural production, mining of manganese and copper ores and the output of a small industrial sector. Georgia possesses substantial hydropower resources but has to import most of its energy, such as oil products and natural gas. The economy has suffered severe damage due to prolonged local conflict but Georgia has made good economic gains since 1995. This has been largely possible due to the help of the IMF and World Bank.

Georgia also suffers from energy shortages; it privatized the T'bilisi electricity distribution network in 1998, but payment collection rates remain low, both in T'bilisi and throughout the region. The country is pinning its hopes for long-term growth on its role as a transit state for pipelines and trade. The construction on the Baku-T'bilisi-Ceyhan oil pipeline and the Baku-T'bilisi-Erzerum gas pipeline have brought much-needed investment and job opportunities. Nevertheless, high energy prices in 2006 will compound the pressure on the country's inefficient energy sector. Restructuring the sector and finding energy supply alternatives to Russia remains a major challenge.

GDP: Purchasing power parity—$15.56 billion (2005 est.).

GDP—real growth rate: 7% (2005 est.).

GDP—per capita: Purchasing power parity—$3,300 (2005 est.).

Inflation rate: 8% (2005 est.).

Population below poverty line: 54% (2001 est.).

Unemployment rate: 12.6% (2004 est.).

Exports: $1.4 billion (2005 est.)—scrap metal, machinery, chemicals, fuel re-exports, citrus fruits, tea, wine.

Imports: $2.5 billion (2005 est.)—fuels, machinery and parts, transport equipment, grain and other foods, pharmaceuticals.

External debt: $2.04 billion (2004).

Transport and Communications

Railways: 1,612 km.

Roads: 20,247 km.

Telephones: 683,200 (2004).

Mobile cellular: 840,600 (2004).

Internet users: 175,600 (2005).

Internet country code: .ge

Germany

History

It is believed that the Celts were the first inhabitants of the area that is today Germany. German tribes arrived in the area later. At the Battle of Teutoburg Forest in AD 9 German forces under Arminius defeated the Romans and wiped out three Roman legions. By the fourth century two powerful Germanic confederations had developed. These were the Alemanni on the Rhine and the Goths on the Danube. The arrival of nomadic non-German horsemen from the east pushed Germanic people into the Roman empire. Meanwhile, the westward movement of the Huns put the frontiers of the Roman empire under increasing pressure. The death of Hun leader Attila, in 453, followed by the final demise of the remains of the Roman empire, put Germany in a position of dominance in Europe. Gradually, a number of German states arose all over the continent.

However, the states lacked political unity although some of them shared languages, customs and traditions. Before long, the Franks and the Ostrogoths clashed as both of them sought to expand their domination over Europe. Over time, the Franks emerged dominant.

Between 476 and 750, the Merovingians were the dominant Frankish dynasty. The Carolingian dynasty succeeded the Merovingians. The most famous Carolingian ruler was Charlemagne. At one point of time, he united in one single state almost all the Christian territories of western Europe. In 800, Pope Leo crowned him emperor of western Europe. Frankish and German kings ruled the empire for ten centuries, right upto 1806.

In the mid-nineteenth century, Prussia became a formidable force under Fredrick the Great. In 1867, the German states north of the Main river joined together in a union named North German Confederation. The Prussians were the dominant force in the Confederation. The 1860s also saw the rise of Otto von Bismarck. He became the prime minister of Prussia in 1862. He also led Prussia to successive victories in wars against Austria, Denmark and France. These wars had the effect of creating a united Germany. The German empire was founded on 18 January 1871, the date on which King Wilhelm I of Prussia was proclaimed emperor of Germany at Versailles. Bismarck became the chancellor. In 1890, the new emperor, Wilhelm II, sought and obtained Bismarck's resignation as chancellor. Wilhelm II steered Germany on the 'New Course' policy. The foreign policy that he adopted led to the isolation of Germany in the global theatre.

On 28 June 1914, a Bosnian Serb named Gavrilo Princip assassinated Archduke Francis Ferdinand, heir presumptive to the Austrian throne, and his wife Sophie in Sarajevo. Austria–Hungary declared war on Serbia on 28 July. Russia responded by ordering a mobilization of its forces. On 1 August, Germany declared war against Russia and subsequently on France and Belgium. This brought a new country into the war, as the UK was committed to defend Belgium. It declared war against Germany on 4 August.

World War I ended in 1918 with the defeat of the Central Powers, including the German empire. The armistice that Germany had to sign as a result of the defeat meant the loss of its colonies to other European powers, surrender of land to its neighbours and the payment of substantial war reparations to the victors.

Soon after the end of the war, the empire collapsed. A moderate state called the Weimar Republic was formed. The 1920s proved to be a dark period in German history. The economy was in a state of ruin, crippled by the war, a currency crisis, and the enormous burden of war reparations.

In 1920–21, Adolf Hitler became the leader of the National Socialist (Nazi) Party. On 30 January 1933, he became the chancellor. Following the death of President Paul von Hindenburg in 1934, he assumed the twin titles of Führer and chancellor. This also gave him the supreme command of the armed forces. Once at the helm of affairs in Germany, Hitler set up a strict totalitarian state. He fanned the population's suppressed pride in their fatherland by announcing his intentions of abrogating the Treaty of Versailles, territorial expansion of the country, reconstruction of the Reich's armed forces and restoration of the nation's wounded pride. On 30 June 1934, Hitler and his trusted SS forces carried out a bloody elimination of political rivals within the Nazi party itself. This is now known as the Night of the Long Knives.

Hitler then set about implementing his grandiose plans. He withdrew Germany from the League of Nations in October 1933. In January 1934, he signed a non-aggression treaty with Poland. In June 1935, he negotiated a naval treaty with UK that recognized

Germany's right to a powerful navy once again. In March 1936, he used the excuse of a treaty between France and the Soviet Union to move into Rhineland. By 1937, Germany had linked up with Italy and Japan. The Third Reich had restored Germany to European dominance.

In 1936, Austria acknowledged itself to be a 'German state'. In 1938 came the Anschluss, or the political union of Austria with Germany. Hitler's next territorial demand was Czechoslovakia, which he took in 1939. He then forced Lithuania to give up some of its territories on the border with Prussia. On 1 September 1939, Germany invaded Poland. Two days later, UK and France declared war on Germany. World War II had started.

During the War, the Nazi government and its Axis collaborators carried out a systematic state-sponsored killing of six million Jewish people. The Germans called this 'the final solution to the Jewish question'. This is now referred to as the Holocaust. The Nazis set up 'ghettoes' of Jewish populations all across its new territorial acquisitions in Europe. Disease, hunger and malnutrition raged through the ghettoes and helped the Nazis eliminate the Jews without firing a single shot. When German forces moved into Russian territories, the Nazis set up special mobile killing units to murder Jews, Soviet commissars, and gypsies.

The War ended with German defeat and the division of the country into distinct occupation zones. In 1949, Germany was divided into West Germany and East Germany. The western zone that USA, France, and UK controlled became Federal Republic of Germany (West Germany). The Soviet zone became East Germany, or the communist German Democratic Republic. Konrad Adenauer became West Germany's first chancellor while Walter Ulbricht led East Germany. The city of Berlin became a divided city. In 1955, West Germany joined NATO while East Germany joined the Soviet Union-led Warsaw Pact.

On the evening of 9 November 1989, the communist authorities of East Germany announced new travel regulations. The government planned to issue official permissions for direct travel to the West. However, the general population misunderstood the announcement as a decision to open the Berlin Wall. Within hours, huge crowds had built up at the checkpoints, demanding to be allowed into West Berlin. The confused and uninformed border guards allowed them through. A night of euphoria and revelry followed as tens of thousands of East Germans swarmed into the free West and celebrated their new-found freedom with the West Berliners.

The opening of the Berlin wall proved to be the beginning of the end for East Germany and its communist regime. As the demonstrations grew in intensity, the Communist Party appointed a new reform-minded leader who promised free, multiparty elections. The communists suffered a crushing defeat in the March 1990 elections. In July, a monetary union of the two Germanys was achieved under the West German currency.

In July 1990, West German Chancellor Helmut Kohl struck a deal with Soviet leader Mikhail Gorbachev whereby Gorbachev dropped his objections to a unified Germany within NATO in return for a big West German financial aid to the Soviet Union. In 1991, Berlin was named as the capital of the united country.

Geography

Location: Central Europe, bordering the Baltic Sea and the North Sea, between the Netherlands and Poland, south of Denmark.

Area: 357,021 sq. km.

Terrain: The Bavarian Alps in the south, lowlands in the north, and uplands in the central part.

Natural resources: Coal, lignite, natural gas, iron ore, copper, nickel, uranium, potash, salt, construction materials, timber, arable land.

People

Population: 82,422,299 (July 2006 est.).

Population growth rate: –0.02% (2006 est.).

Sex ratio: 0.96 male(s)/female (2006 est.).

Religions: Protestant 34%, Roman Catholic 34%, Muslim 3.7%, unaffiliated or others 28.3%.

Languages: German.

Literacy rate: 99% (2003 est.).

Infant mortality rate: 4.12 deaths/1,000 live births (2006 est.).

Life expectancy: Total 78.8 years, Male 75.81 years, Female 81.96 years (2006 est.).

Government

Capital: Berlin.

Government type: Federal republic.

Independence: 3 October 1990 (date of unification of West Germany and East Germany).

Executive branch:

Chief of state: Horst Koehler (elected in May 2004; sworn in in July 2004).

Head of government: Chancellor Angela Merkel (since 22 November 2005).

Elections and election results: A Federal Convention that includes all members of the Federal Assembly and an equal number of delegates elected by the state parliaments elect the president for a five-year term. The election was last held on 23 May 2004. The chancellor is elected by an absolute majority of the Federal Assembly for a four-year term. The election was last held on 22 November 2005 and the next election is scheduled for November 2009.

Legislative branch:

Germany has a bicameral parliament or Parlament that consists of the Federal Assembly or Bundestag and the Federal Council or Bundesrat. The Federal Assembly has 603 seats. Members are elected by popular vote under a system combining direct and proportional representation. A party must win 5 per cent of the national vote or three direct mandates to gain representation. Members serve four-year terms. The Federal Council or Bundesrat has sixty-nine votes. State governments are directly represented by votes and each state has three to six votes depending on population and is required to vote as a block.

Elections and election results:

There are no elections to the Federal Council. The chancellor is elected by an absolute majority of the Federal Assembly for a four-year term. The last election was held on 22 November 2005; the next election is scheduled for November 2009. Horst Koehler was elected president; he received 604 votes of the Federal Convention against 589 for Gesine Schwan. Angela Merkel was elected chancellor; vote by Federal Assembly: 397 to 202, with twelve abstentions.

Economy

Currency: Euro.

Economy—overview:

The prosperous and technologically advanced German economy is among the five largest economies of the world, no mean feat considering the situation of the country at the end of World War II and almost half a century of fractured existence as two separate countries. However, Germany today is one of the slowest growing economies in the entire Euro zone with slim chances of a rapid turnaround. One of the major challenges facing the country today is the ongoing process of integration and modernization of the erstwhile East German economy. Other constraints include the country's aging population, high unemployment levels, and social security expenditure in excess of contributions from the working population. Germany's labour market suffers from structural rigidities, such as strict regulations on retrenchment and the determination of wages on a national basis. However, Germany has initiated corporate restructuring and structural reforms.

GDP: Purchasing power parity—$2.504 trillion (2005 est.).

GDP—real growth rate: 0.9% (2005 est.).

GDP—per capita: Purchasing power parity—$30,400 (2005 est.).

Inflation rate: 2% (2005 est.).

Population below poverty line: NA.

Unemployment rate: 11.6% (2005 est.).

Exports: $1.016 trillion f.o.b. (2005 est.)—machinery, vehicles, chemicals, metals and manufactures, foodstuff, textiles.

Imports: $801 trillion f.o.b. (2005 est.)—machinery, vehicles, chemicals, foodstuffs, textiles, metals.

External debt: $3.626 trillion (30 June 2005 est.).

Transport and Communications

Railways: 46,142 km (20,100 km electrified).

Roads: 231,581 km (including 12,037 km of expressway) (2003).

Telephones: 54.574 million (2004).

Mobile celluler: 71.3 million (2004).

Internet users: 48,722,055 (2005).

Internet country code: .de

Ghana

History

The Portuguese arrived in the Gold Coast area of Ghana in the fifteenth century. Later came the English, the Dutch and the Swedes. In 1874, UK proclaimed the coastal area of Ghana as a Crown colony. In March 1957, Ghana became the first among the African colonies to gain independence. In 1960, it became a republic.

Geography

Location: Western Africa, bordering the Gulf of Guinea, between Cote d'Ivoire and Togo.

Area: 239,460 sq. km.

Terrain: Mostly low plains with a dissected plateau in the south central area.

Natural resources: Gold, timber, industrial diamonds, bauxite, manganese, fish, rubber, hydropower.

Climate: Tropical climate.

People

Population: 22,409,572 (July 2006 est.).

Population growth rate: 2.07% (2006 est.).

Sex ratio: 1 male(s)/female (2006 est.).

Religions: Christian 63%, Muslim 16%, indigenous beliefs 21%.

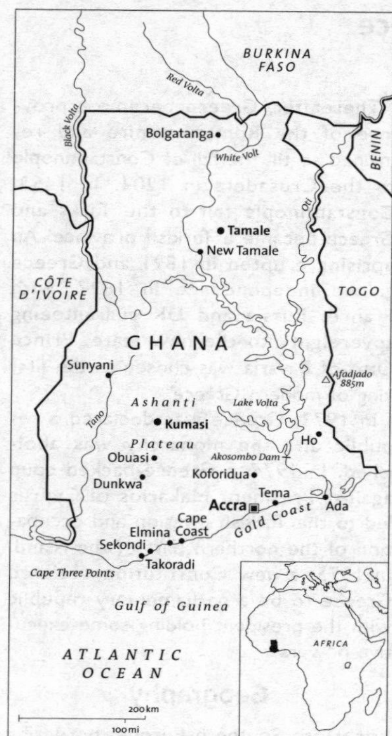

Languages: English (official), African languages (including Akan, Moshi-Dagomba, Ewe, and Ga).

Literacy rate: Total 74.8%, Male 82.7%, Female 67.1% (2003 est.).

Infant mortality rate: 55.02 deaths/ 1,000 live births (2006 est.).

Life expectancy: Total 58.87 years, Male 58.07 years, Female 59.69 years (2006 est.).

Government

Capital: Accra.

Government type: Constitutional democracy.

Independence: 6 March 1957 (from UK).

Legal system: Based on English common law and customary law.

Executive branch:

Chief of state: President John Agyekum Kufuor (since 7 January 2001); Vice-President Alhaji Aliu Mahama (since 7 January 2001). The president is both the chief of state and head of government.

Economy

Currency: Cedi.

GDP: Purchasing power parity—$54.45 billion (2005 est.).

GDP—real growth rate: 4.3% (2005 est.).

GDP—per capita: Purchasing power parity—$2,500 (2005 est.).

Inflation rate: 15% (2005 est.).

Population below poverty line: 31.4% (1992 est.).

Unemployment rate: 20% (1997 est.).

Exports: $2.911 billion f.o.b. (2005 est.)—gold, cocoa, timber, tuna, bauxite, aluminum, manganese ore, diamond.

Imports: $4.273 billion f.o.b. (2005 est.)—capital equipment, petroleum, foodstuff.

External debt: $7.084 billion (2005 est.).

Transport and Communications

Railways: 953 km.

Roads: 47,787 km.

Telephones: 313,300 (2004).

Mobile cellular: 1.695 million (2004).

Internet users: 368,000 (2005).

Internet country code: .gh

Greece

History

Advanced and prosperous civilizations flourished in the area of the Aegean Sea between 7000–3000 BC (Stone Age) and about 3000–1000 BC (Bronze Age). These were among the earliest advanced civilizations in Europe.

The period starting from around 1200 BC and upto the death of Alexander the Great (in 323 BC) is the period of the ancient Greek civilization. This was a period of great political, scientific, philosophical and artistic achievements and left a significant mark on Western civilization. Between 431 and 404 BC, the two leading city states in ancient Greece, Athens and Sparta, fought each other in what is now called the Peloponnesian War. The consequent weakening of the nation resulted in its conquest by Phillip II of Macedon. His son was the famous Alexander the Great, widely regarded as one of the greatest conquerors of all times.

Thereafter, Greece became a province of the Roman empire and remained so till the fall of Constantinople to the Crusaders in 1204. In 1453, Constantinople fell to the Turks and Greece became a Turkish province. An uprising erupted in 1821 and Greece gained independence in 1827, with France, Russia and UK guaranteeing sovereignty to the new state. Prince Otto of Bavaria was chosen as the first king of modern Greece.

In 1973, Greece was declared a republic and the monarchy was abolished. In 1974, a Greece-backed coup against President Makarios of Cyprus led to the Turkish invasion and occupation of the northern part of the island. In 1975, a new Constitution declared Greece to be a parliamentary republic with the president holding some executive powers.

Geography

Location: Southern Europe, bordering the Aegean Sea, Ionian Sea, and the Mediterranean Sea, between Albania and Turkey.

Area: 131,940 sq. km.

Terrain: Mostly mountanious with ranges extending into the sea as peninsulas or chain of islands.

Natural resources: Lignite, petroleum, iron ore, bauxite, lead, zinc, nickel, magnesite, marble, salt, hydropower potential.

Climate: Greece has a temperate climate with mild, wet winters and hot, dry summers.

People

Population: 10,688,058 (July 2006 est.).

Population growth rate: 0.18% (2006 est.).

Sex ratio: 0.96 male(s)/female (2006 est.).

Religions: Greek Orthodox (Christian) 98%, Muslim 1.3%, others 0.7%.

Languages: Greek 99% (official), English, French.

Literacy rate: Total 97.5%, Male 98.6%, Female 96.5% (2003 est.).

Infant mortality rate: 5.43 deaths/1,000 live births (2006 est.).

Life expectancy: Total 79.24 years, Male 76.72 years, Female 81.91 years (2006 est.).

Government

Capital: Athens.

Government type: Parliamentary republic.

Independence: 1829 (from the Ottoman Empire).

Legal system: Based on codified Roman law with a judiciary divided into civil, criminal, and administrative courts.

Executive branch:

Chief of state: President Karolos Papoulias (since 12 March 2005).

Head of government: Prime Minister Konstandinos Karamanlis (since March 2004).

Economy

Currency: Euro.

GDP: Purchasing power parity—$236.8 billion (2005 est.).

GDP—real growth rate: 3.7% (2005 est.).

GDP—per capita: Purchasing power parity—$22,200 (2005 est.).

Inflation rate: 3.8% (2005 est.).

Unemployment rate: 10.8% (2005 est.).

Exports: $18.54 billion f.o.b. (2005 est.)—food and beverages, manufactured goods, petroleum products, chemicals, textiles.

Imports: $48.2 billion f.o.b. (2005 est.)—machinery, transport equipment, fuels, chemicals.

External debt: $75.1 billion (2005 est.).

Transport and Communications

Railways: 2,571 km (764 km electrified).

Roads: 116,470 km.

Telephones: 6,348,800 (2004).

Mobile cellular: 9,305,700 (2004).

Internet users: 3.8 million (2005).

Internet country code: .gr

Grenada

History

The first inhabitants of Grenada were Arawak Indians who were later succeeded by Carib Indians. Although Christopher Columbus arrived in 1498, the Caribs continued to dominate the area for another 150 years. The French seized control in 1672 and held on to power till 1762 when the British arrived on the scene and invaded the territory. In 1833, the black slaves of the country were freed. Between 1885 and 1958, Grenada was the headquarters of the British Windward Islands territory. In 1967, it became a self-governing state in association with UK and finally gained independence in 1974. Grenada was seized by a Marxist military council on 19 October 1983. Six days later the island was invaded by US forces and those of six other Carib-

bean nations, which quickly captured the ringleaders and their hundreds of Cuban advisers. Free elections were re-instituted the following year.

Geography

Location: Caribbean, island between the Caribbean Sea and Atlantic Ocean, north of Trinidad and Tobago.

Area: 344 sq. km.

Natural resources: Timber, tropical fruit, deepwater harbours.

Climate: Tropical climate tempered by the north-east trade winds.

People

Population: 89,703 (July 2006 est.).

Population growth rate: 0.26% (2006 est.).

Sex ratio: 1.08 male(s)/female (2006 est.).

Religions: Roman Catholic 53%, Anglican 13.8%, Protestant 33.2%.

Languages: English (official), French patois.

Literacy rate: Total 96%, Male NA, Female NA (2003 est.).

Infant mortality rate: 14.27 deaths/1,000 live births (2006 est.).

Life expectancy: Total 64.87 years, Male 63.06 years, Female 66.68 years (2006 est.).

Government

Capital: Saint George's.

Independence: 7 February 1974 (from UK).

Legal system: Based on English common law.

Executive branch:

Chief of state: Queen Elizabeth II (since 6 February 1952), represented by Governor General Daniel Williams (since 9 August 1996).

Head of government: Prime Minister Keith Mitchell (since 22 June 1995).

Economy

Currency: East Caribbean dollar.

GDP: Purchasing power parity—$440 million (2002 est.).

GDP—real growth rate: 2.5% (2002 est.).

GDP—per capita: Purchasing power parity—$5,000 (2002 est.).

Inflation rate: 2.8% (2001 est.).

Population below poverty line: 32% (2000).

Unemployment rate: 12.5% (2000 est.).

Exports: $40 million (2004 est.)—bananas, cocoa, nutmeg, fruit and vegetables, clothing, mace.

Imports: $276 million (2004 est.)—food, manufactures, machinery, chemicals, fuel.

External debt: $196 million (2000).

Transport and Communications

Railways: None.

Roads: 1,127 (1999) km.

Telephones: 32,700 (2004).

Mobile cellular: 43,300 (2004).

Internet users: 8,000 (2005).

Internet country code: .gd

Guatemala

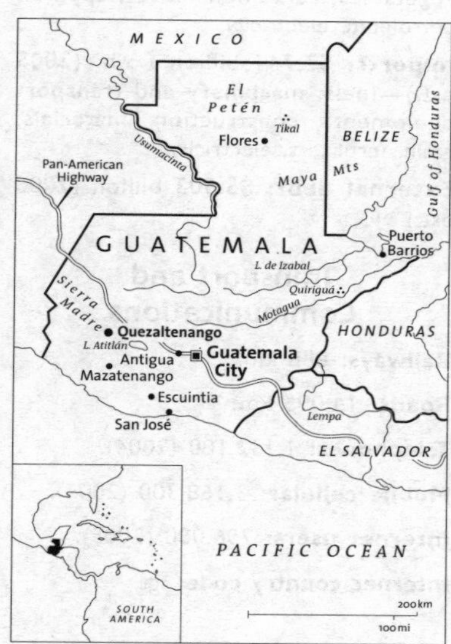

History

In ancient times, Guatemala was part of the Mayan civilization. The Spanish conquered the territories in the 1520s. Along with other Central American colonies, Guatemala declared independence from Spain in 1821 and became a part of the Mexican empire that lasted till 1823. Thereafter, Guatemala became the political centre of the United Provinces of Central America. After the collapse of this union, Guatemala became an independent republic led by successive dictators. In 1960, the country lapsed into a thirty-six-year civil war between the government and leftist forces which resulted in the loss of hundreds of thousands of lives. A peace agreement was finally signed in 1996.

Geography

Location: Middle America, bordering the North Pacific Ocean, between El Salvador and Mexico, and bordering the Gulf of Honduras (Caribbean Sea) between Honduras and Belize.

Area: 108,890 sq. km.

Terrain: Mostly mountainous with a narrow coastal plain and a rolling limestone plateau.

Natural resources: Petroleum, nickel, rare woods, fish, chicle, hydropower.

Climate: Tropical climate. The lowlands are hot and humid while the highlands are cooler.

People

Population: 12,293,545 (July 2006 est.).

Population growth rate: 2.27% (2006 est.).

Sex ratio: 0.99 male(s)/female (2006 est.).

Religions: Roman Catholic, Protestant, indigenous Mayan beliefs.

Languages: Spanish 60%, Amerindian languages 40% (23 officially recognized Amerindian languages, including Quiche, Cakchiquel, Kekchi, Mam, Garifuna and Xinca).

Literacy rate: Total 70.6%, Male 78%, Female 63.3% (2003 est.).

Infant mortality rate: 30.94 deaths/ 1,000 live births (2006 est.).

Life expectancy: Total 69.38 years, Male 67.65 years, Female 71.18 years (2006 est.).

Government

Capital: Guatemala City.

Government type: Constitutional democratic republic.

Independence: 15 September 1821 (from Spain).

Legal system: Civil law system; judicial review of legislative acts.

Executive branch:
Chief of state: President Oscar Berger (since 2004). The president is both the chief of state and head of government.

Economy

Currency: Quetzal, US dollar, others allowed.

GDP: Purchasing power parity—$56.86 billion (2005 est.).

GDP—real growth rate: 3.2% (2005 est.).

GDP—per capita: Purchasing power parity—$4,700 (2005 est.).

Inflation rate: 9.1% (2004 est.).

Population below poverty line: 75% (2004 est.).

Unemployment rate: 7.5% (2003 est.).

Exports: $3.94 billion f.o.b. (2005 est.)—coffee, sugar, banana, fruits and vegetables, cardamom, meat, apparel, petroleum, electricity.

Imports: $7.744 billion f.o.b. (2005 est.)—fuels, machinery and transport equipment, construction materials, grain, fertilizers, electricity.

External debt: $5.503 billion (2005 est.).

Transport and Communications

Railways: 886 km.

Roads: 14,095 km.

Telephones: 1,132,100 (2004).

Mobile cellular: 3,168,300 (2004).

Internet users: 756,000 (2005).

Internet country code: .gt

Guinea

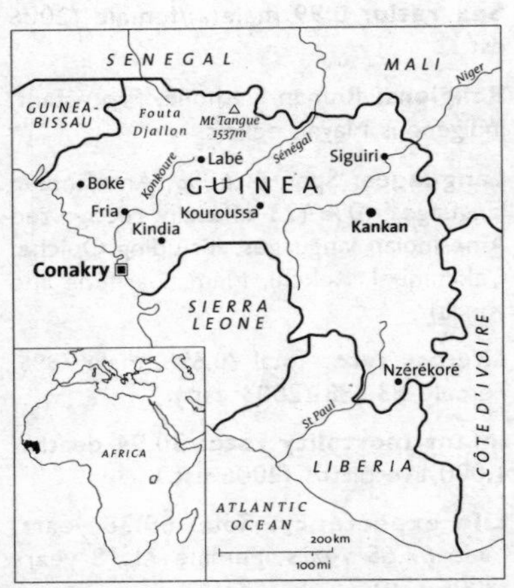

History

In the nineteenth century, France made Guinea a protectorate and then a colony. In October 1958, Guinea became independent.

Geography

Location: Western Africa, bordering the North Atlantic Ocean, between Guinea-Bissau and Sierra Leone.

Area: 245,857 sq. km.

Terrain: Generally flat coastal plain with a hilly interior.

Natural resources: Bauxite, iron ore, diamonds, gold, uranium, hydropower, fish.

Climate: Generally hot and humid climate.

People

Population: 9,690,222 (July 2006 est.).

Population growth rate: 2.63% (2006 est.).

Sex ratio: 1 male(s)/female (2006 est.).

Religions: Muslim 85%, Christian 8%, indigenous beliefs 7%.

Languages: French (official), each ethnic group has its own language.

Literacy rate: Total 35.9%, Male 49.9%, Female 21.9% (1995 est.).

Infant mortality rate: 90 deaths/ 1,000 live births (2006 est.).

Life expectancy: Total 49.5 years, Male 48.34 years, Female 50.7 years (2006 est.).

Government

Capital: Conakry.

Government type: Republic.

Independence: 2 October 1958 (from France).

Legal system: Guinea's legal codes are currently undergoing revision. They are based on French civil law system, customary law, and decree.

Executive branch:

Chief of state: President Lansana Conte (head of military government since 5 April 1984, president since 19 December 1993).

Head of government: Prime Minister Cellou Dalein Diallo (since 4 December 2004).

Economy

Currency: Guinean franc.

GDP: Purchasing power parity—$18.99 billion (2005 est.).

GDP—real growth rate: 2% (2005 est.).

GDP—per capita: Purchasing power parity—$2,000 (2005 est.).

Inflation rate: 25% (2005 est.).

Population below poverty line: 40% (2003 est.).

Exports: $612.1 million f.o.b. (2005 est.)—bauxite, alumina, gold, diamond, coffee, fish, agricultural products.

Imports: $680 million f.o.b. (2005 est.)—petroleum products, metals, machinery, transport equipment, textiles, grain and other foodstuff.

External debt: $3.46 billion (2003 est.).

Transport and Communications

Railways: 837 km.

Roads: 44,348 km.

Telephones: 26,200 (2003).

Mobile cellular: 111,500 (2003).

Internet users: 46,000 (2005).

Internet country code: .gn

Guinea-Bissau

History

The area that is today Guinea-Bissau was once the Gabu kingdom, part of a greater Mali empire. The Portuguese were the first Europeans to arrive, in the fifteenth century. In 1974, Portugal granted Guinea-Bissau independence with Amilcar Cabral's brother Luis Cabral as president.

Geography

Location: Western Africa, bordering the North Atlantic Ocean, between Guinea and Senegal.

Area: 36,120 sq. km.

Natural resources: Fish, timber, phosphates, bauxite, deposits of petroleum (unexploited).

Climate: Generally hot and humid tropical climate.

People

Population: 1,442,029 (July 2006 est.).

Population growth rate: 2.07% (2006 est.).

Sex ratio: 0.94 male(s)/female (2006 est.).

Religions: Indigenous beliefs 50%, Muslim 45%, Christian 5%.

Languages: Portuguese (official), Crioulo, African languages.

Literacy rate: Total 42.4%, Male 58.1%, Female 27.4% (2003 est.).

Infant mortality rate: 105.21 deaths/ 1,000 live births (2006 est.).

Life expectancy: Total 46.87 years, Male 45.05 years, Female 48.75 years (2006 est.).

Government

Capital: Bissau.

Government type: Republic.

Independence: 24 September 1973—date of unilateral declaration of independence by Guinea-Bissau.

Executive branch:

Chief of state: President Joao Bernardo 'Niro' Vieira (since 1 October 2005).

Head of government: Prime Minister Aristides Gomes (since 2 November 2005).

Economy

Currency: Communaute Financiere Africaine franc.

GDP: Purchasing power parity—$1.185 billion (2005 est.).

GDP—real growth rate: 2.3% (2005 est.).

GDP—per capita: Purchasing power parity—$800 (2005 est.).

Inflation rate: 4% (2002 est.).

Exports: $116 million f.o.b. (2004 est.)—cashew nuts, shrimp, peanuts, palm kernels, sawn lumber.

Imports: $176 million f.o.b. (2004 est.)—foodstuff, machinery and transport equipment, petroleum products.

External debt: $941.5 million (2000 est.).

Transport and Communications

Railways: None.

Roads: 4,400 km

Telephones: 10,600 (2003).

Mobile cellular: 1,300 (2003).

Internet users: 26,000 (2005).

Internet country code: .gw

Guyana

History

Christopher Columbus sighted Guyana during one of his voyages in 1498. In the sixteenth and seventeenth centuries, the English, the French and the Dutch had all established colonies. In 1831, it was formed into the colony of British Guiana. When slavery was abolished in 1834, a large number of indentured labourers from the East Indies were imported to meet the labour shortage. In 1961, UK granted the colony full autonomy. Guyana attained independence in 1966.

Geography

Location: Northern South America, bordering the North Atlantic Ocean, between Surinam and Venezuela.

Area: 214,970 sq. km.

Terrain: Mostly rolling highlands. There is also a low coastal plain and a savanna in the south.

Natural resources: Bauxite, gold, diamonds, hardwood timber, shrimp, fish.

Climate: Hot and humid tropical climate moderated by north-east trade winds.

People

Population: 767,245 (July 2006 est.).

Population growth rate: 0.25% (2006 est.).

Sex ratio: 1.01 male(s)/female (2006 est.).

Religions: Christian 50%, Hindu 35%, Muslim 10%, others 5%.

Languages: English, Amerindian dialects, Creole, Hindi, Urdu.

Literacy rate: Total 98.8%, Male 99.1%, Female 98.5% (2003 est.).

Infant mortality rate: 32.19 deaths/1,000 live births (2006 est.).

Life expectancy: Total 65.86 years, Male 63.21 years, Female 68.65 years (2006 est.).

Government

Capital: Georgetown.

Government type: Republic within the Commonwealth.

Independence: 26 May 1966 (from UK).

Legal system: Based on English common law with certain admixtures of Roman–Dutch law.

Executive branch:

Chief of state: President Bharrat Jagdeo (since 11 August 1999).

Head of government: Prime Minister Samuel Hinds (since December 1997).

Economy

Currency: Guyanese dollar.

GDP: Purchasing power parity—$3.549 billion (2005 est.).

GDP—real growth rate: –2.5% (2005 est.).

GDP—per capita: Purchasing power parity—$4,600 (2005 est.).

Inflation rate: 5.5% (2005 est.).

Unemployment rate: 9.1% (2000).

Exports: $587.2 million f.o.b. (2005 est.)—sugar, gold, bauxite, rice, shrimp, molasses, rum, timber.

Imports: $681.6 million c.i.f. (2005 est.)—manufactures, machinery, petroleum, food.

External debt: $1.2 billion (2004 est.).

Transport and Communications

Railways: 187 km (entirely dedicated to ore transport).

Roads: 7,970 km.

Telephones: 102,700 (2004).

Mobile cellular: 104,600 (2005).

Internet users: 145,000 (2005).

Internet country code: .gy

Haiti

History

Arawak Indians were the original inhabitants of the island on which Haiti lies. In 1492, Christopher Columbus landed on the island and named it Hispaniola, or Little Spain. In 1697, Spain ceded the western part of Hispaniola to France, and this became the colony of Saint-Dominique. In 1791, the 480,000-strong slave population of the colony rose in rebellion against the colonial rulers. This resulted in the declaration of independence by Pierre-Dominique Toussant l'Ouverture, the leader of the slave uprising. Ultimately in 1804, the colony gained independence as Haiti, under its new leader, Jean-Jacques Dessalines.

After a succession of regimes and rulers, a physician named François Duvalier (or 'Papa Doc' Duvalier) became the president in September 1957. He promised political and economic power to the black masses. Violence, a shrinking economy, international isolation, vanishing US aid and continuing tension with Dominican Republic marked his regime. In July 1958, there was an unsuccessful attempt to overthrow Duvalier. This prompted him to set up a paramilitary group. This was the infamous Tontons Macoutes that terrorized the Haitian population during Duvalier's regime and effectively turned the country into a police state. In 1964 Duvalier engineered his election as 'President for life'.

In 1971, Duvalier passed away and was succeeded by his nineteenth-year-old son, Jean-Claude Duvalier, or 'Baby Doc' who also declared himself 'President for life'. His reign lasted till 1986 when he fled the country under mounting discontent.

In 1990, the former priest Jean-Bertrand Aristide was elected the president of Haiti. In 1991, a coup led by Brigadier-General Raoul Cedras ousted Aristide and led to sanctions by the US. In 1995, Aristide supporters won parliamentary elections and Rene Preval was installed as the new president of Haiti. Aristide returned as the president of Haiti in 2000. In 2004, Arisitide went into exile after an uprising against his regime intensified and rebel forces took one town after another and even reached the capital, Port-au-Prince. Boniface Alexandre, the Supreme Court chief justice became the interim president.

Geography

Location: Caribbean, western one-third of the island of Hispaniola, between the Caribbean Sea and the North Atlantic Ocean, west of the Dominican Republic.

Area: 27,750 sq. km.

Natural resources: Bauxite, copper, calcium carbonate, gold, marble, hydropower.

Climate: Haiti has a tropical climate but is semi-arid in the part where mountains in the east cut off trade winds.

People

Population: 8,308,504 (July 2006 est.).

Population growth rate: 2.3% (2006 est.).

Sex ratio: 0.97 male(s)/female (2006 est.).

Religions: Roman Catholic 80%, Protestant 16% (Baptist 10%, Pentecostal 4%, Adventist 1%, others 1%), none 1%, others 3% (1982). Roughly half of the population also practises Voodoo.

Languages: French (official), Creole (official).

Literacy rate: Total 52.9%, Male 54.8%, Female 51.2% (2003 est.).

Infant mortality rate: 71.65 deaths/1,000 live births (2006 est.).

Life expectancy: Total 53.23 years (2006 est.).

Government

Capital: Port-au-Prince.

Government type: Elected government.

Independence: 1 January 1804 (from France).

Legal system: Based on Roman civil law system.

Executive branch:

Chief of state: President Rene Preval (since 14 May 2006).

Head of government: Prime Minister Jacques Edouard Alexis (since 30 May 2006).

Economy

Currency: Gourde.

GDP: Purchasing power parity—$14.15 billion (2005 est.).

GDP—real growth rate: 2% (2005 est.).

GDP—per capita: Purchasing power parity—$1,700 (2005 est.).

Inflation rate: 22% (2004 est.).

Population below poverty line: 80% (2003 est.).

Unemployment rate: Widespread unemployment and underemployment; More than two-thirds of the labour force do not have formal jobs (2002 est.).

Exports: $390.7 million f.o.b. (2005 est.)—manufactures, coffee, oils, cocoa.

Imports: $1.471 billion c.i.f. (2005 est.)—food, manufactured goods, machinery and transport equipment, fuels, raw materials.

External debt: $1.3 billion (2005 est.).

Transport and Communications

Railways: None.

Roads: 4,160 km.

Telephones: 140,000 (2004).

Mobile cellular: 400,000 (2004).

Internet users: 500,000 (2005).

Internet country code: .ht

Honduras

History

In 1502, Christopher Columbus explored Honduras. It became a Spanish colony, although British elements briefly controlled the Mosquito Coast region. Honduras declared its independence from Spain in 1821.

After two-and-a-half decades of mostly military rule, a freely elected civilian government came to power in 1982. During the 1980s, Honduras proved a haven for anti-Sandinista contras fighting the Marxist Nicaraguan government and an ally to Salvadorean government forces fighting leftist guerrillas.

The country was devastated by Hurricane Mitch in 1998, which killed about 5,600 people and caused approximately $2 billion in damage.

Geography

Location: Middle America, bordering the Caribbean Sea, between Guatemala and Nicaragua.

Area: 112,090 sq. km.

Terrain: Mostly mountainous in the interior with narrow coastal plains.

Natural resources: Timber, gold, silver, copper, lead, zinc, iron ore, antimony, coal, fish, hydropower.

Climate: Subtropical in lowlands but temperate in the mountainous region.

People

Population: 7,326,496 (July 2005 est.).

Population growth rate: 2.16% (2006 est.).

Sex ratio: 1.01 male(s)/female (2006 est.).

Religions: Roman Catholic 97%, Protestant minority.

Languages: Spanish, Amerindian dialects.

Literacy rate: Total 76.2%, Male 76.1%, Female 76.3% (2003 est.).

Infant mortality rate: 25.82 deaths/1,000 live births (2006 est.).

Life expectancy: Total 69.33 years, Male 67.75 years, Female 70.98 years (2006 est.).

Government

Capital: Tegucigalpa.

Government type: Democratic constitutional republic.

Independence: 15 September 1821 (from Spain).

Legal system: Has its origins in Roman and Spanish civil law with increasing influence of English common law; recent judicial reforms have included the replacement of Napoleonic legal codes with the oral adversarial system.

Executive branch:
Chief of state: President Manuel Zelaya Rozales (since 27 January 2006). The president is both the chief of state and head of government.

Economy

Currency: Lempira.

GDP: Purchasing power parity—$20.59 billion (2005 est.).

GDP—real growth rate: 4.2% (2005 est.).

GDP—per capita: Purchasing power parity—$2,900 (2005 est.).

Inflation rate (consumer prices): 9.2% (2005 est.).

Population below poverty line: 53% (1993 est.).

Unemployment rate: 28% (2005 est.).

Exports: $1.726 billion f.o.b. (2005 est.)—coffee, banana, shrimp, lobster, meat, zinc, lumber (2000).

Imports: $4.161 billion f.o.b. (2005 est.)—machinery and transport equipment, industrial raw materials, chemical products, fuels, foodstuff (2000).

External debt: $4.675 billion (2005 est.).

Transport and Communications

Railways: 699 km.

Roads: 13,603 km.

Telephones: 390,100 (2004).

Mobile cellular: 707,200 (2004).

Internet users: 223,000 (2005).

Internet country code: .hn

Hungary

History

The area that is today Hungary was once a part of the Roman empire. The Magyars conquered all of Hungary in 896 and set up a kingdom. In 1241, a Mongol invasion wiped out almost half of the country's population. During the rule of Louis I the Great (1342–82), the Hungarian empire reached the Baltic, the Black and the Mediterranean Seas. In 1389, war broke out between Hungary and the Turks. In the sixteenth century, Hungary accepted Hapsburg rule to avoid Turk subjugation. The dual monarchy of Austria–Hungary was formed in 1867.

During World War II, Hungary allied with Germany and took part in the 1941 German invasion of Russia. In 1945, Soviet forces drove the Germans out of Hungary. In 1946, the parliament abolished the monarchy and set up a republic. The communists seized control in 1948. The country was turned into a one-party state, modelled on the Soviet Union.

In 1989, Hungarian communists in power voluntarily dismantled the one-

party state and turned the country into a multiparty state. In 1999, Hungary joined NATO and in 2004 it became a member state of the EU.

Geography

Location: Central Europe, north-west of Romania.

Area: 93,030 sq. km.

Terrain: Mostly flat to rolling plains. There are hills and low mountains on the border with Slovakia.

Natural resources: Bauxite, coal, natural gas, fertile soils, arable land.

Climate: Temperate climate with cold, cloudy and humid winters and warm summers.

People

Population: 9,981,334 (July 2006 est.).

Population growth rate: –0.25% (2006 est.).

Sex ratio: 0.91 male(s)/female (2006 est.).

Religions: Roman Catholic 51.9%, Calvinist 15.9%, Lutheran 3%, Greek Catholic 2.6%, other Christian 1%, others or unspecified 11.1%, unaffiliated 14.5% (2001 census).

Languages: Hungarian 93.6%, other or unspecified 6.4% (2001 census).

Literacy rate: Total 99.4%, Male 99.5%, Female 99.3% (2003 est.).

Infant mortality rate: 8.39 deaths/1,000 live births (2006 est.).

Life expectancy: Total 72.66 years, Male 68.45 years, Female 77.14 years (2006 est.).

Government

Capital: Budapest.

Government type: Parliamentary democracy.

Independence: 1001 (date of unification by King Stephen I).

Legal system: Rule of law based on Western model.

Executive branch:

Chief of state: Laszlo Solyom (since 5 August 2005).

Head of government: Prime Minister Ferner Gyurcsany (since 29 September 2004).

Economy

Currency: Forint.

Economy—overview:
Since the fall of communism, the Hungarian economy has been transformed from a centrally planned to a market economy. The country has recorded strong economic growth in recent years with the private sector accounting for more than 80 per cent of GDP. In 2000, Hungarian sovereign debt was upgraded to the second-highest rating among all the central European economies making the transition to market economies.

GDP: Purchasing power parity—$162.6 billion (2005 est.).

GDP—real growth rate: 4.1% (2005 est.).

GDP—per capita: Purchasing power parity—$16,300 (2005 est.).

Inflation rate: 3.7% (2005 est.).

Population below poverty line: 8.6% (1993 est.).

Unemployment rate: 7.1% (2005 est.).

Exports: $61.75 billion f.o.b. (2005 est.)—machinery and equipment, other manufactures, food products, raw materials, fuels and electricity (2001).

Imports: $64.83 billion f.o.b. (2005 est.)—machinery and equipment 51.6%, other manufactures 35.3%, fuels and electricity 8.2%, food products 2.9%, raw materials 2.0% (2001).

External debt: $76.23 billion (30 June 2005 est.).

Transport and Communications

Railways: 7,937 km.

Roads: 159,568 km.

Telephones: 3,577,300 (2004).

Mobile cellular: 8,727,200 (2004).

Internet users: 3.05 million (2005).

Internet country code: .hu

Iceland

History

The first human settlers of the island of Iceland were Irish monks who left when the first Norse people arrived in the ninth century. In 930, a constitution was drawn up and a form of democratic system was initiated. Iceland was the world's oldest democracy and had the world's oldest functioning legislative assembly, the Althing, set up in 930. In 1000, Iceland adopted Christianity. During 1262–4, Iceland came under Norwegian rule and recognized the king of Norway as their monarch. Later, it came under Danish control through the Kalmar union of 1397 that brought the kingdoms of Norway, Sweden, and Denmark together under a single monarch. This union lasted until 1523.

During 1402–4 and again between 1494–5, Iceland was hit by plague epidemics that wiped out half the population each time. In 1602, Denmark assumed a monopoly on all Icelandic trade. This monopoly remained in force for the next 200 years.

In 1904, Iceland attained home rule. In 1918, it achieved full self-government under the Danish crown, with Denmark retaining control only over foreign affairs. In 1944, following a referendum, the republic of Iceland was proclaimed on 17 June.

Geography

Location: Northern Europe, island between the Greenland Sea and the

North Atlantic Ocean, north-west of the British Isles.

Area: 103,000 sq. km.

Terrain: Consists mostly of a plateau along with scattered mountain peaks and ice hills. The coast is deeply broken by bays and fjords.

Natural resources: Fish, hydropower, geothermal power, diatomite .

Climate: Temperate climate that is moderated by the North Atlantic Current. The country has mild, windy winters and damp, cool summers.

People

Population: 299,388 (July 2006 est.).

Population growth rate: 0.87% (2006 est.).

Sex ratio: 1 male(s)/female (2006 est.).

Religions: Lutheran Church of Iceland 85.5%, Reykjavik Free Church 2.1%, Roman Catholic Church 2%, Hafnarfjorour Free Church 1.5%, other Christian 2.7%, other or unspecified 3.8%, unaffiliated 2.4% (2004).

Languages: Icelandic, English, Nordic languages, German is widely spoken.

Literacy rate: 99.9% (1997 est.).

Infant mortality rate: 3.29 deaths/1,000 live births (2006 est.).

Life expectancy: Total 80.31 years, Male 78.23 years, Female 82.48 years (2006 est.).

Government

Capital: Reykjavik.

Government type: Constitutional republic.

Independence: 17 June 1944 (from Denmark).

Legal system: Civil law system based on Danish law.

Executive branch:

Chief of state: President Olafur Ragnar Grimsson (since 1 August 1996).

Head of government: Prime Minister Geir H. Haarde (since 7 June 2006).

Economy

Currency: Icelandic krona.

GDP: Purchasing power parity—$10.57 billion (2005 est.).

GDP—real growth rate: 5.7% (2005 est.).

GDP—per capita: Purchasing power parity—$35,600 (2005 est.).

Inflation rate: 4.1% (2005 est.).

Unemployment rate: 2.1% (2005 est.).

Exports: $3.215 billion f.o.b. (2005 est.)—fish and fish products 70%, animal products, aluminium, diatomite, ferrosilicon.

Imports: $4.582 billion (2005 est.)—machinery and equipment, petroleum products; foodstuff, textiles.

External debt: $3.073 billion (2002).

Transport and Communications

Railways: None.

Roads: 13,004 km.

Telephones: 190,500 (2004).

Mobile cellular: 290,100 (2004).

Internet users: 225,000 (2004).

Internet country code: .is

India

History

The history of India is the story of a civilization that despite much internal strife and frequent invasions has retained its identity for five thousand years. The first known permanent settlements appeared 9,000 years ago and developed into the Indus Valley Civilization, which peaked between 2600 BC and 1900 BC.

After the gradual decline of the Indus Valley Civilization, the Vedic civilization followed. The earliest literary source that sheds light on India's past is the *Rig Veda*, composed between 1500 BC and 1000 BC. Though warriors and conquerors, the Aryans lived alongside Indus, introducing them to the caste system and establishing the basis of the Indian religions. The Aryans inhabited the northern regions for about 700 years, and then moved further south and east when they developed iron tools and weapons. They eventually settled in the Ganges valley and built large kingdoms throughout much of northern India.

In the sixth century BC the kingdom of Magadha—one of the sixteen Mahajanapadas—had established paramountcy over other kingdoms of the Ganges valley. This was the time when Buddhism and Jainism emerged as popular movements to pose a serious challenge to Brahmanic orthodoxy.

Alexander the Great's invasion took place between 327 BC and 325 BC. Soon after Alexander's invasion, Chandragupta founded the Mauryan empire. Under the Mauryan king Ashoka, this empire extended all over India except the extreme south. Ashoka contributed greatly to India's cultural landscape. The empire began to disintegrate under weak successors. Pushyamitra Shunga, a Brahmin general usurped the throne after slaying the last Mauryan king and presided over a loosely federal polity.

From 180 BC, a series of invasions from Central Asia followed, with the successive establishment in the northern Indian subcontinent of the Indo-Greek, Indo-Scythian and Indo-Parthian kingdoms, and finally the Kushan empire. From the third century onwards the Gupta dynasty oversaw the period referred to as India's 'Golden Age'. The rule of Harshavardhana from AD 606 to 647 was the only consolidated rule in India after the Guptas in the first millennium AD. The dominions of Harsha disintegrated into a multiplicity of warring petty states and principalities following his death. This anarchic state of affairs prevailed throughout India until the beginning of the eleventh century.

In the south, several dynasties including the Chalukyas, Cheras, Cholas, Pallavas, and Pandyas prevailed during different periods. Science, art, literature, mathematics, astronomy, engineering, religion and philosophy flourished under the patronage of these kings.

The first Muslim victories in Indian territory had taken place in the seventh century, but it was not until the eleventh century that the full-scale Islamic invasion began, headed by Mahmud of Ghazni. The Mongol invasion of Genghis Khan followed in 1219 and in 1397 Timur Lang's hordes poured in.

The Slave dynasty served as the first sultans of Delhi in India from 1206 to 1290. From 1290 to 1526, the rule of the Khalji, Tughlaq, Sayyid and Lodi dynasties of the Delhi Sultanate followed. In 1526, the Mughal empire was established by Babur under who India once again achieved a large measure of political unity.

Akbar was the greatest sovereign of the Mughal empire. The Mughal empire attained its peak of cultural splendour under the rule of Shah Jahan. His reign (1628–58) coincided with the golden age of Indian Saracenic architecture, best exemplified by the Taj Mahal.

Shah Jahan was driven from the throne in 1658 by his son Aurangzeb. In the half century following the death of Aurangzeb, the Mughal empire ceased to exist as an effective state. From the eleventh to the fifteenth centuries, southern India was dominated by Hindu Chola and Vijayanagar dynasties.

Meanwhile, from the fifteenth century onwards, the struggle between European powers for dominance in Indian affairs had begun. With Vasco da Gama's discovery of the ocean route around the Cape of Good Hope, Portugal, Holland and France began a race for the rich Indian and Spice Islands trade. England, France, the Netherlands and Denmark floated East India companies. During the late sixteenth and seventeenth centuries, these companies competed with each other fiercely.

By the last quarter of the eighteenth century, the English had vanquished all others and established themselves as the dominant power in India. The military campaigns of Robert Clive and the administrative enterprise of Warren Hastings (1772–1785) contributed significantly to this achievement. Once the British had consolidated their power through annexation of territories, commercial exploitation of the natural resources and native labour became ruthless. Bitterness at the annexations and confiscations, together with religious and racial hatred and resentment at the rapid westernizing policies of the white rulers, caused discontent and riots. Having crushed the rebellion of 1857, popularly known as the Sepoy Mutiny, the East India Company finally ceded its control over India to the British Crown in 1858.

By the end of the nineteenth century the first nationalist aspirations of India had begun to be revealed, expressing themselves in riots and rebellions fermented by the Congress party, which was founded in 1885. In the late nineteenth century, with the appointment of Indian councilors to advise the British viceroy and the establishment of provincial councils with Indian members, the first steps were taken towards self-government in British India.

Discontent with British rule became intense during the early twentieth century. The British instituted a programme of power-sharing, but Congress leaders like Motilal Nehru and Sarojini Naidu in the 1920s and Subhash Chandra Bose, Vallabhbhai Patel and Jawaharlal Nehru in the 1930s saw these reforms as instruments for continuing British control indefinitely. They organized movements of non-cooperation and civil disobedience from 1920 onwards. The government tried to suppress these mass movements brutally. A violent example was the Jallianwallah Bagh massacre of 1919.

A prolonged struggle for independence, the Indian independence movement, followed, led by Mahatma Gandhi, regarded officially as the father of modern India. The culmination of this path-breaking struggle was reached on 15 August 1947 when India gained full independence from British rule, later becoming a republic on 26 January 1950. British India was divided into two independent nations; India with Nehru as prime minister and Pakistan with Muhammad Ali Jinnah as governorgeneral.

Nehru governed India until his death in 1964. Indira Gandhi was the prime minister from 1966 to 1977 and again from 1980 to 1984. In 1975, beset with deepening political and economic problems, Mrs Gandhi declared a state of emergency and suspended many civil liberties. On 31 October 1984, Mrs Gandhi was assassinated and her son Rajiv Gandhi was chosen by the Congress (I) to take her place.

India's unresolved border disputes escalated into a brief war with China in 1962, and with Pakistan in 1947, 1965 and 1971, and a border altercation in the state of Kashmir (the Kargil conflict) in 1999. In 1998, India became one of the handful of countries in the world to attain full nuclear capability.

Significant economic reforms, beginning in 1991 and initiated by the present prime minister Dr Manmohan Singh, have transformed India into one of the fastest growing economies in the world.

Geography

Location: Southern Asia, bordering the Arabian Sea and the Bay of Bengal, between Myanmar and Pakistan.

Area: 3,300,000 sq. km.

Terrain: The terrain of India consists of the Himalayas in the north, the Deccan Plateau in the central and southern parts, the Gangetic plains, the coastal plains along the east and west coast, the mountains of the Eastern and Western Ghats, and the Thar desert in the west.

Natural resources: Coal, iron ore, manganese, mica, bauxite, titanium ore, chromite, natural gas, diamonds, petroleum, limestone, arable land.

Climate: India has a tropical climate with relatively high temperatures and dry winters. The Himalayas function as a meteorological barrier for the country. The monsoons play a very important role in the Indian climate.

People

Population: Total: 1,095,351,995 (2006 census); Scheduled Caste: 166,635,700; Scheduled Tribe: 84,326,240.

Population growth rate: 1.38% (2006 est.).

Population density: 324 persons per sq km (2001 census).

Sex ratio: 1.06 male(s)/female (2006 census).

Religions: Hindu, Muslim, Christian, Sikh, Buddhist, Jain, Parsi.

Languages: 18 languages recognized by the Indian Constitution. These are: Assamese, Bengali, Gujarati, Hindi, Kannada, Kashmiri, Konkani, Malayalam, Manipuri, Marathi, Nepali, Oriya, Punjabi, Sanskrit, Sindhi, Tamil, Telugu, Urdu. Hindi is the official language and the main link language.

Literacy rate: Total: 64.8%, Male: 75.3%, Female: 53.7% (2000 est.).

Infant mortality rate: 54.63 deaths/1000 live births (2006 est.).

Life expectancy: Total: 64.71 years, Male: 63.9 years, Female: 65.57 years (2006 est).

Ethnic groups: Indo-Aryan 72%, Dravidian 25%, Mongoloid and other 3% (2000 est.).

Government

Capital: New Delhi.

Government type: Federal republic.

Independence: 15 August 1947 (from UK).

Administrative divisions: 28 states, 6 union territories* and 1 National Capital Territory (NCT) **.

1. Andaman and Nicobar Islands*
2. Andhra Pradesh
3. Arunachal Pradesh
4. Assam
5. Bihar
6. Chandigarh*
7. Chhattisgarh
8. Dadra and Nagar Haveli*
9. Daman and Diu*
10. Delhi**
11. Goa
12. Gujarat
13. Haryana
14. Himachal Pradesh
15. Jammu and Kashmir
16. Jharkhand
17. Karnataka
18. Kerala
19. Lakshadweep*
20. Madhya Pradesh
21. Maharashtra
22. Manipur
23. Meghalaya
24. Mizoram
25. Nagaland
26. Orissa
27. Pondicherry*
28. Punjab
29. Rajasthan
30. Sikkim
31. Tamil Nadu
32. Tripura
33. Uttaranchal
34. Uttar Pradesh
35. West Bengal

Constitution: 26 January 1950.

Legal system: Based on English common law with limited judicial review of legislative acts.

Executive branch:

Chief of state: President Dr Avul Pakir Jainulabdeen Abdul Kalam (since 25 July 2002). Vice-President Bhairon Singh Sekhawat (since 16 August 2002).

Head of government: Prime Minister Dr Manmohan Singh (since 22 May 2004).

Legislative branch: India has a bicameral parliament or Sansad that consists of the Council of States or Rajya Sabha and the People's Assembly or Lok Sabha. The Rajya Sabha consists of not more than 250 members. The number of members elected by each state is roughly in proportion to their population. At present, there are 233 members of the Rajya Sabha who have been elected by the Vidhan Sabhas. Besides these, there are twelve members nominated by the President as representatives of literature, science, art and social services. Rajya Sabha members serve for six years. The elections are held in a staggered manner with one-third of the assembly being elected every two years. The Lok Sabha has 545 seats of which 543 are elected by popular vote and two appointed by the President. All members serve five-year terms.

Election and election results: Elections to the Lok Sabha were last held in May 2004. A United Progressive Alliance (UPA) government, headed by the Congress and including left parties, came to power, winning 278 seats.

Judicial branch: Supreme Court (the President appoints the judges and they remain in office until they reach the age of sixty-five).

Economy

Currency: Rupee.

GDP—purchasing power parity: \$3.611 trillion (2005 est.).

GDP—real growth rate: 7.6% (2005 est.).

GDP—per capita purchasing power parity: $3,300 (2005 est.).

Inflation rate: 4.6% (2005 est.).

Population below poverty line: 25% (2002 est.).

Unemployment rate: 9.9% (2005).

Exports: $76.23 billion f.o.b. (2005 est.)—Textile goods, gems and jewelry, engineering goods, chemicals, leather manufactures.

Imports: $113.1 billion f.o.b. (2005 est.)—Crude oil, machinery, gems, fertilizer, chemicals.

External debt: $119.7 billion (2005 est.).

Transportation and Communication

Railways: 109,221 km.

Roads: 3,300,000 km. (National Highways: 52,010 km.)

Telephones: 67.285 million (2005 est.).

Mobile cellular: 69,193,321 (2006 est.).

Internet users: 50.6 million (2005 est.).

Internet country code: in

Indonesia

History

In the first and second centuries AD, the islands of Indonesia came under Hindu influence. Muslims arrived in the thirteenth century. The Portuguese reached the islands in the sixteenth century but the Dutch drove them out by 1595. The latter established ports in Java with the objective of controlling the region's spice trade. The British took possession of the islands following Dutch defeat at the hands of the French in 1811 but returned them to the Dutch in 1816. In 1922, Indonesia became an integral part of the Netherlands, as Dutch East Indies.

During World War II, Japan occupied Indonesia with the aim of gaining control over its petroleum resources. When the war ended, Indonesia declared its independence under nationalist leaders like Sukarno and Mohammed Hatta.

In September 1965, Sukarno was implicated in a coup in which six top army generals were abducted, tortured and killed. On 11 March 1966, Sukarno handed over emergency powers to General Suharto. He later became president of Indonesia.

In 1997, Indonesia was one of the worst hit in the Asian economic crisis. The economic downturn soon turned into a political crisis when anti-government protests and riots flared up across Indonesia. It ultimately forced Suharto to step down and hand over power to his vice-president, Bacharuddin Jusuf Habibie.

In 1999, the first ever free parliamentary elections were held in Indonesia. Abdurrahman Wahid, also called Gus Dur, became the new Indonesian president, in a stunning upset, defeating the popular Megawati Sukarnoputri, daughter of Sukarno. In the same year ethnic violence broke out in Maluku and other parts of Indonesia, while the province of East Timor voted for independence in a UN-sponsored referendum. This resulted in brutal violence unleashed by pro-Indonesian militia. In July 2001, the Indonesian parliament removed Wahid and appointed Megawati Sukarnoputri as the new president. In October 2004, Susilo B. Yudhoyouo became the new president after elections.

Geography

Location: South-eastern Asia, archipelago between the Indian Ocean and the Pacific Ocean.

Area: 1,919,440 sq. km.

Terrain: The islands of Indonesia consists mostly of coastal lowlands but the larger islands have mountains in the interiors.

Natural resources: Petroleum, tin, natural gas, nickel, timber, bauxite, copper, fertile soils, coal, gold, silver.

Climate: Hot and humid tropical climate which is more moderate in the highlands.

People

Population: 245,452,739 (July 2006 est.).

Population growth rate: 1.41% (2006 est.).

Sex ratio: 1 male(s)/female (2006 est.).

Religions: Muslim 88%, Protestant 5%, Roman Catholic 3%, Hindu 2%, Buddhist 1%, others 1% (1998).

Languages: Bahasa Indonesia (official), English, Dutch, local dialects (most widely spoken is Javanese).

Literacy rate: Total 87.9%, Male 92.5%, Female 83.4% (2002 est.).

Infant mortality rate: 34.39 deaths/1,000 live births (2006 est.).

Life expectancy: Total 69.87 years, Male 67.42 years, Female 72.45 years (2006 est.).

Government

Capital: Jakarta.

Government type: Republic.

Independence: 17 August 1945 (date of proclamation of independence); 27 December 1949 (date on which Indonesia became legally independent from the Netherlands).

Legal system: Based on Roman–Dutch law, modified by indigenous concepts and by new criminal procedure codes.

Executive branch:
Chief of state: President Susilo B. Yudhoyono (since 20 October 2004). The president is both the chief of state and head of government.

Economy

Currency: Indonesian rupiah.

Economy—overview:
Indonesia suffers from a multitude of internal problems that pose serious hurdles to economic development in

the country. Internal reform and adoption of measures to boost investor confidence are two of the measures that would be beneficial to the economy.

GDP: Purchasing power parity—$865.6 billion (2005 est.).

GDP—real growth rate: 5.6% (2005 est.).

GDP—per capita: Purchasing power parity—$3,600 (2005 est.).

Inflation rate: 10.4% (2005 est.).

Population below poverty line: 16.7% (2004).

Unemployment rate: 10.9% (2005 est.).

Exports: $83.64 billion f.o.b. (2005 est.)—oil and gas, electrical appliances, plywood, textiles, rubber.

Imports: $62.02 billion f.o.b. (2005 est.)—machinery and equipment; chemicals, fuels, foodstuff.

External debt: $131 billion (2005 est.).

Transport and Communications

Railways: 6,458 km.

Roads: 368,360 km.

Telephones: 9.99 million (2004).

Mobile cellular: 30 million (2004).

Internet users: 18 million (2005).

Internet country code: .id

Iran

History

The Medes and Persians held sway over the region that we today call Iran till about 500 BC. The Persian ruler Cyrus the Great overthrew the Medes and began ruling as the head of the Persian or Achaemenid empire. In around 331 BC, Alexander the Great took Persia. Thereafter, a succession of powers controlled Persia at different points of time. The Mongols invaded the area in the twelfth century and the Safavid dynasty ruled from the sixteenth to the eighteenth century. It was during the reign of the Safavids that Shiite Islam became the dominant religion. After the Safavids, came the Qajar dynasty. They ruled from 1794 to 1925.

In late February 1921, the military commander Reza Khan seized power. In 1925 the Iranian parliament deposed the monarch, who was away undergoing prolonged treatment in Europe. The parliament elected Reza Khan as the Shah of Persia. He founded the Pahlavi dynasty and assumed the name of Reza Shah Pahlavi. In 1935, Persia changed its name to Iran.

In 1941, the Soviet Union and Great Britain occupied Iran, apprehensive of the pro-German tendencies of the Shah. Mohammad Reza Shah Pahlavi replaced his father as the Shah of Iran on 16 September 1941. In the 1960s, the Shah initiated a campaign of modernization and westernization of Iran and launched the 'White Revolution'. However, his authoritarian rule sparked off widespread civil unrest in the late 1970s. In January 1979, the Shah, along with his family, were exiled out of Iran. In February that year, the Islamic fundamentalist leader, Ayatollah Ruhollah Khomeini, returned to Iran at the end of fourteen years of exile. On 1 April 1979, the Islamic Republic of Iran was proclaimed following a referendum.

On 4 November 1979, revolutionaries forced their way into the US embassy in Tehran and took fifty-two Americans as hostage. USA retaliated by imposing an economic boycott, severing diplomatic relations and ordering the deportation of Iranian students studying in USA.

On 22 September 1980, Iraq invaded Iran in a culmination of a dispute over Iranian oilfields. This was the start of the Iran–Iraq War. In August 1988, Iran accepted a UN-mediated ceasefire that it had previously rejected.

In May 1997, reformist politician Mohammad Khatami won the presidential election by a landslide, beating the dominant conservatives. In July 1999, pro-democracy students at Tehran University held a mass demonstration. Conservatives and hardliners regained control of the Iranian parliament in legislative elections held in February and May 2004.

Geography

Location: Middle East, bordering the Gulf of Oman, the Persian Gulf, and the Caspian Sea, between Iraq and Pakistan.

Area: 1.648 million sq. km.

Terrain: Rugged terrain with a mountainous rim, high central basin with deserts and mountains. The coasts have small, discontinuous plains.

Natural resources: Petroleum, natural gas, coal, chromium, copper, iron ore, lead, manganese, zinc, sulphur.

Climate: Mostly arid or semi-arid but the Caspian coast has subtropical climate.

People

Population: 68,688,433 (July 2006 est.).

Population growth rate: 1.1% (2006 est.).

Sex ratio: 1.04 male(s)/female (2006 est.).

Religions: Shi'a Muslim 89%, Sunni Muslim 10%, Zoroastrian, Jewish, Christian, and Baha'i 1%.

Languages: Persian and Persian dialects 58%, Turkic and Turkic dialects 26%, Kurdish 9%, Luri 2%, Balochi 1%, Arabic 1%, Turkish 1%, others 2%.

Literacy rate: Total 79.4%, Male 85.6%, Female 73% (2003 est.).

Infant mortality rate: 40.3 deaths/ 1,000 live births (2006 est.).

Life expectancy: Total 70.26 years, Male 68.86 years, Female 71.74 years (2006 est.).

Government

Capital: Tehran.

Government type: Theocratic republic.

Independence: 1 April 1979 (proclamation of Islamic Republic of Iran).

Legal system: The constitution codifies Islamic principles of government.

Executive branch:

Chief of state: Supreme Leader Ayatollah Ali Hoseini-Khamenei (since 4 June 1989).

Head of government: President Mahmud Ahmadi-Nejad (since 3 August 2005); First Vice-President Parviz Davudi (since 11 September 2005).

Economy

Currency: Iranian rial.

Economy—overview:
Iran has a centrally planned economy with the state owning oil and other large enterprises. Although President Khatami has continued with the market reform measures started by his predecessor, Akbar Hashemi Rafsanjani, and also announced plans to diversify Iran's oil-reliant economy, his own political future is in serious doubt following the heavy defeat suffered by the reformist alliance at the 2004 parliamentary elections.

GDP: Purchasing power parity—$561.6 billion (2005 est.).

GDP—real growth rate: 6.1% (2005 est.).

GDP—per capita: Purchasing power parity—$8,300 (2005 est.).

Inflation rate: 16% (2005 est.).

Population below poverty line: 40% (2002 est.).

Unemployment rate: 11.2% (2004 est.).

Exports: $55.42 billion f.o.b. (2004 est.)—petroleum 85%, carpets, fruits and nuts, iron and steel, chemicals.

Imports: $42.5 billion f.o.b. (2004 est.)—industrial raw materials and intermediate goods, capital goods, foodstuff and other consumer goods, technical services, military supplies.

External debt: $16.94 billion (2005 est.).

Transport and Communications

Railways: 178,152 km.

Roads: 167,157 km.

Telephones: 14,571,100 (2003).

Mobile cellular: 4.3 million (2004).

Internet users: 7.5 million (2005 est.).

Internet country code: .ir

Iraq

History

In ancient times, the area that is today Iraq was called Mesopotamia, the 'land between the rivers'. This was due to its location between the Tigris and the Euphrates rivers. Mesopotamia was home to one of the first advanced civilizations on the face of the earth. After 2000 BC, the area became the home of the Babylonian and Assyrian empires. Cyrus the Great of Persia conquered Mesopotamia in 538 BC while Alexander the Great claimed Mesopotamia in 331 BC. The Arabs conquered the country between AD 637–40 and set up the capital of the caliphate in Baghdad.

Mongols plundered the country with much brutality in 1258. In the sixteenth, seventeenth and eighteenth centuries, the country became the subject of Turkish–Persian rivalry. Turkish suzerainty imposed in 1638 gave way to direct Turkish rule in 1831.

The UK occupied most parts of Mesopotamia during World War I and received a mandate for the country in 1920. The UK renamed the country Mesopotamia and in 1922 recognized a kingdom that was formed under Faysal, son of the Sharif of Mecca, who was crowned Iraq's first king in August 1921.

In October 1932, Iraq gained independence. However, the UK occupied the country once again during World War II. On 14 July 1958, a military coup deposed the monarchy and declared a republic with Abd-al-Karim Qasim as the prime minister.

In 1972, Iraq and the Soviet Union signed a fifteen-year Treaty of Friendship and Cooperation. The same year, the Iraqi government nationalized the Iraq Petroleum Company. In 1979, Saddam Hussein took over as the new president.

The Iran–Iraq war started on 4 September 1980 when Iran started shelling Iraqi border towns. On 22 September 1980, Iraq invaded Iran in a dispute over possessing the Iranian oilfields. In August 1988 Iran accepted a UN-mediated ceasefire that it had previously rejected.

On 2 August 1990, Iraq invaded Kuwait. This attracted UN condemnation. The United Nations Security Council (UNSC) Resolution 660 called for a full withdrawal of Iraqi forces from Kuwait. On 6 August, UNSC imposed economic sanctions on Iraq. On 8 August, Iraq announced the merger of Iraq and Kuwait. On 29 November, UNSC authorized the states cooperating with Kuwait to use all necessary means to uphold UNSC Resolution 660. The Gulf War started on 16–17 January 1991, when coalition forces began Operation Desert Storm with air attacks on Iraq. The ground operations started on 24 February 1991 and culminated in the liberation of Kuwait on 27 February. On 3 March, Iraq accepted the terms of a ceasefire.

On 15 October 1995 Saddam Hussein won a referendum that allowed him to remain president for another seven years. On 31 August 1996 Iraqi forces launched an offensive into the northern no-fly zone and captured the Kurdish city of Irbil.

In December 1998, USA and UK launched 'Operation Desert Fox', a bombing campaign to destroy Iraq's nuclear, chemical and biological weapons. In February 2001, USA and UK carried out bombing raids to eliminate Iraq's air defence network even though there was little international support in favour of such an attack.

In September 2002, US President George W. Bush called upon world leaders at a UN General Assembly session to deal with what he called 'grave and gathering danger' posed by Iraq. The same month, British Prime Minister Tony Blair released a dossier on the weapons capabilities of Iraq. On 17 March 2003, UK's ambassador to the UN declared that the diplomatic process on Iraq was over. Soon afterwards, arms inspectors left the country and President George W. Bush gave Saddam Hussein and his sons an ultimatum to leave the country within forty-eight hours or face war. On the expiry of the ultimatum, on 20 March, American missiles bombarded targets in Baghdad. US and British ground troops entered Iraq from the south in the following days. On 9 April, US forces advanced into central Baghdad. In the following days Kurdish fighters and US forces gained control of the northern cities of Kirkuk and Mosul.

In October 2003, the UN Security Council approved an amended US resolution on Iraq that bestowed legitimacy on the US-led administration in Iraq. The big break that the coalition forces were looking for in Iraq finally came on 14 December 2003, when Saddam Hussein was captured in Tikrit. On 1 July 2004, Saddam Hussein appeared in an Iraqi court for the first time. He was brought to the court in handcuffs and chains to stand trial on charges of war crimes and genocide. He remained defiant, describing President Bush as the 'real criminal', defending Iraq's 1990 invasion of Kuwait. He said he was still the Iraqi President and rejected the court's jurisdiction. The Coalition Provisional Authority transferred sovereignty to the Iraqi Interim Government (IG) in June 2004. Iraqis voted on 30 January 2005 to elect a 275-member Transitional National Assembly and voted on 15 December 2005 to elect a 275-member Council of Representatives that will finalize a permanent constitution.

Geography

Location: Middle East, bordering the Persian Gulf, between Iran and Kuwait.

Area: 437,072 sq. km.

Terrain: Broad plains with marshlands along the Iranian border in the south.

Natural resources: Petroleum, natural gas, phosphates, sulphur.

Climate: Desert climate with winters that range from mild to cool. The summers are dry, hot, and cloudless.

People

Population: 26,783,383 (July 2006 est.).

Population growth rate: 2.66% (2006 est.).

Sex ratio: 1.02 male(s)/female (2006 est.).

Religions: Muslim 97% (Shi'a 60%–65%, Sunni 32%–37%), Christian and others 3%.

Languages: Arabic, Kurdish, Assyrian, Armenian.

Literacy rate: Total 40.4%, Male 55.9%, Female 24.4% (2003 est.).

Infant mortality rate: 69.01 deaths/1,000 live births (2006 est.).

Life expectancy: Total 69.01 years, Male 67.76 years, Female 70.31 years (2006 est.).

Government

Capital: Baghdad.

Government type: None. The Iraqi interim government was appointed on 1 June 2004.

Independence: 3 October 1932 (from League of Nations mandate under British administration).

Legal system: Based on civil and Islamic law under the Iraqi interim government and Transitional Administrative Law.

Executive branch:

Chief of state: Iraqi transitional government President Jalal Tolabani (since 6 April 2005); Deputy Presidents Abil Abd al-Mahdi and Ghazi al-Ujayal al-Yown (since 6 April 2005). The president and deputy presidents comprise the Presidency Council.

Head of government: Prime Minister Nuri al-Maliki (since 20 May 2006); Deputy Prime Ministers Rowsach Shaways, Ahmad Chaelabi and Abid al-Mutlaq al-jabbvm (since May 2005).

Elections: Held 15 December 2005 to elect a 275-member Council of Representatives.

Economy

Currency: New Iraqi dinar.

Economy—overview:

The oil sector dominates Iraq's economy and has traditionally contributed about 95 per cent of the country's foreign exchange earnings. Iraq faced severe financial problems in the 1980s due to heavy cost of waging war on Iran and the damage caused to the oil export facilities by the ongoing war. This forced the government to impose austerity measures. The government had to borrow heavily and reschedule foreign debt payments. The economic losses because of the war are estimated at around $100 billion. The end of the war in 1988 was followed by a gradual restoration of the infrastructure and the resumption of oil exports. But before the country could recover from this war fully, Iraq occupied Kuwait in August 1990. The consequent international economic sanctions and international military action severely affected the Iraqi economy. Legitimate oil exports ground to a halt following the imposition of a trade embargo on Iraq. Meanwhile the government pursued a policy of utilizing resources to support the military, security forces and important supporters of the regime. This had an adverse effect on the economy. The start of the UN's oil-for-food programme in December 1996 helped improve the situation. Under this programme, Iraq was allowed to export limited amounts of oil in exchange for essential commodities like food and medicine, and some supplies to rebuild the country's infrastructure. In December 1999, the UN Security Council authorized Iraq to export as much oil as it was necessary in order to meet humanitarian needs. The military actions of 2003 have caused the shutdown of much of the central economic administrative system. The country's infrastructure is undergoing extensive rebuilding and production is creeping back towards pre-war levels. A joint UN and World Bank study released in 2003 put Iraq's key reconstruction needs through 2007 at $55 billion. In October 2003, international donors pledged assistance worth more than $33 billion.

GDP: Purchasing power parity—$94.1 billion (2005 est.).

GDP—real growth rate: –3% (2005 est.).

GDP—per capita: Purchasing power parity—$3,400 (2005 est.).

Inflation rate: 40% (2005 est.).

Exports: $17.78 billion f.o.b. (2004 est.)—crude oil.

Imports: $19.57 billion f.o.b. (2004 est.)—food, medicine, manufactures.

External debt: $82.1 billion (2005 est.).

Transport and Communications

Railways: 2,200 km.

Roads: 45,550 km.

Telephones: 1,034,200 (2004).

Mobile cellular: 574,000 (2004).

Internet users: 36,000 (2005).

Internet country code: .iq

Ireland

History

In the twelfth century, the Vatican handed all of Ireland as a papal fief to the English Crown. However, it was only in the seventeenth century that the British achieved total control over the Irish.

The Act of Union of 1801 made Great Britain and Ireland into the 'United Kingdom of Great Britain and Ireland'. The Irish economy declined

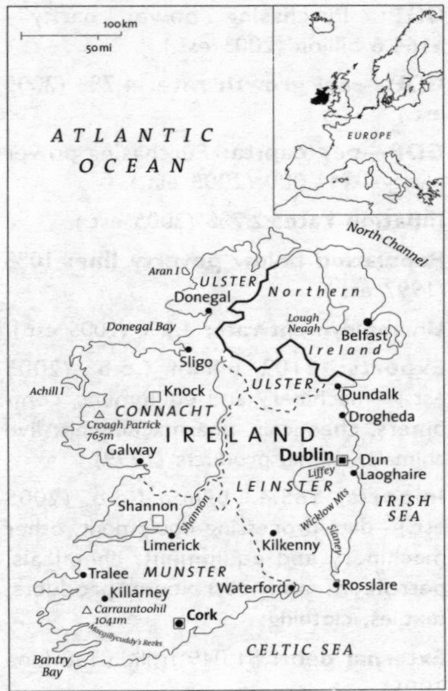

steadily in the following decades. The Irish Potato Famine, also called the Great Irish Famine, struck the nation in the 1840s when the potato crop failed for successive years. Nearly two million people migrated to North America.

In 1916, Irish Nationalists launched a rebellion against British rule. It is referred to as the Easter Rising or the Easter Rebellion and began on Easter Monday, 24 April 1916, in Dublin. The British crushed the rebellion and executed its leaders. However, the Easter Rising proved to be the beginning of the end of British rule over Ireland.

In 1919, the Sinn Fein (meaning 'Ourselves Alone') nationalist movement set up an assembly in Dublin. This proclaimed Irish independence. At the same time, the Irish Republican Army (IRA) launched a guerrilla campaign against British forces.

On Easter Monday 1949, the anniversary of the 1916 uprising, Eire became the Republic of Ireland (Ireland excluding Northern Ireland). Northern Ireland remains part of UK even today. Soon afterwards, Ireland withdrew from the British Commonwealth.

Geography

Location: Western Europe, occupying five-sixths of the island of Ireland in the North Atlantic Ocean, west of Great Britain.

Area: 70,280 sq. km.

Terrain: Mostly level to rolling interior plain surrounded by rugged hills and low mountains. There are sea cliffs on the west coast.

Natural resources: Natural gas, peat, copper, lead, zinc, silver, barite, gypsum, limestone, dolomite.

Climate: Temperate maritime climate that is modified by the North Atlantic current. The country has mild winters and cool summers.

People

Population: 4,062,235 (July 2006 est.).

Population growth rate: 1.15% (2006 est.).

Sex ratio: 0.99 male(s)/female (2006 est.).

Religions: Roman Catholic 88.4%, Church of Ireland 3%, other Christian 1.6%, other 1.5%, unspecified 2%, none 3.5% (2002 census).

Languages: English is the language generally used while Irish (Gaelic) is spoken in areas located along the western coast.

Literacy rate: 99% (2003 est.).

Infant mortality rate: 5.31 deaths/ 1,000 live births (2006 est.).

Life expectancy: Total 77.73 years, Male 75.11 years, Female 80.52 years (2006 est.).

Government

Capital: Dublin.

Government type: Unitary multiparty republic with two legislative houses.

Independence: 6 December 1921 (from UK).

Legal system: Based on English common law, substantially modified by indigenous concepts.

Executive branch:

Chief of state: President Mary McAleese (since 11 November 1997).

Head of government: Prime Minister Bertie Ahern (since 26 June 1997).

Economy

Currency: Euro.

Economy—overview:
The Irish economy is a small, modern economy with a high degree of reliance on trade. Industry accounts for over 40 per cent of GDP, about 80 per cent of exports and almost 30 per cent of employment. Exports are a key driver for Ireland's growth. Increased levels of construction activity, consumer spending and business investment have also boosted the economy in recent times. Ireland was one of the eleven countries that launched the euro currency system in January 1999.

GDP: Purchasing power parity—$164.6 billion (2005 est.).

GDP—real growth rate: 4.7% (2005 est.).

GDP—per capita: Purchasing power parity—$41,000 (2005 est.).

Inflation rate: 2.7% (2005 est.).

Population below poverty line: 10% (1997 est.).

Unemployment rate: 4.2% (2005 est.).

Exports: $102 billion f.o.b. (2005 est.)—machinery and equipment, computers, chemicals, pharmaceuticals; live animals, animal products (1999).

Imports: $65.47 billion f.o.b. (2005 est.)—data-processing equipment, other machinery and equipment, chemicals, petroleum and petroleum products, textiles, clothing.

External debt: $1.049 trillion (30 June 2005).

Transport and Communications

Railways: 3,312 km.
Roads: 95,736 km.

Telephones: 2,019,100 (2004).
Mobile cellular: 3.78 million (2004).
Internet users: 2.06 million (2005).
Internet country code: .ie

Israel

History

In 1896, Austrian journalist Theodor Herzl proposed in his pamphlet 'Der Judenstaat' or 'The Jewish State' that a world council of nations should settle the Jewish question. By 1903, around 25,000 Zionist immigrants arrived in the area that is today Israel. Another 40,000 immigrants arrived in the period between 1904 and 1914. About half a million Arab residents already lived in the area that was then a part of the Turkish Ottoman empire. In 1917, the British Foreign Secretary Arthur Balfour promised 'the establishment in Palestine of a national home for the Jewish people', in a letter to Baron Rothschild, a leading Zionist. However, in May 1939, the British government changed

its policy and recommended a limit of 75,000 further immigrants and suggested a stop to immigration by 1944. Needless to say, Zionists condemned this new policy. Meanwhile, hundreds of thousands of Jews immigrated to British Mandate Palestine.

On 14 May 1948, the proclamation of the State of Israel was made in Tel Aviv. The following day, armies from five Arab nations, Egypt, Jordan, Iraq, Lebanon and Syria invaded Israel only to be beaten back. The armistices that followed helped define Israel's territorial limits mostly along the frontier of the earlier British Mandate Palestine. However, Egypt retained the Gaza Strip while Jordan kept the area around East Jerusalem and the territory now known as the West Bank.

In October 1956, Israel invaded the Sinai Peninsula. In five days the Israeli army captured Gaza, Rafah and Al-'Arish. The Israeli forces took thousands of prisoners and occupied most of the peninsula east of the Suez Canal.

In January 1964, Arab governments voted to create a body called the Palestine Liberation Organization (PLO). Its military force, the Palestine Liberation Army, was formed in 1968.

In 1967, rising tensions between Israel and its Arab neighbours boiled over and resulted in six days of warfare, starting on 5 June 1967 and ending on 11 June. This was the Six Day War. Israel seized Gaza and the Sinai from Egypt, the Golan Heights from Syria, and evicted Jordanian forces from the West Bank and East Jerusalem. In a stunning move, Israel eliminated Egypt's powerful air force on the first day of fighting by destroying its aircraft while they were still on the ground.

On 6 October 1973, which was the Jewish holy day of Yom Kippur, Egypt and Syria attacked Israel. This was the Yom Kippur War. Israel and Egypt signed a ceasefire agreement in November and peace agreements on 18 January 1974.

In the 1970s, Palestinians targeted Israelis all across the world. One of the most high-profile attacks was at the Munich Olympic Games in 1972 when Palestine attackers killed 11 Israeli athletes. In 1974, PLO Chairman Yasser Arafat made a dramatic first appearance at the United Nations.

In 1977, Egypt became the first Arab country to recognize Israel when its President Anwar Sadat flew to Israel and even addressed its Parliament. In September 1978, Egypt and Israel signed the Camp David accords. The Egyptian move attracted widespread criticism from other Arab countries. In 1981, opponents of the peace dialogue with Israel assassinated Anwar Sadat.

The peace process received a boost with the election of the left-wing Labour government in June 1992 with Yitzhak Rabin as prime minister. It culminated with the 'Declaration of Principles' and a historic handshake between Rabin and Yasser Arafat on the lawns of the White House in Washington DC. The 1994 Nobel Prize for

Peace was jointly awarded to Yasser Arafat, Yitzhak Rabin and Shimon Peres. On 24 September 1995, the so-called Oslo II agreement was signed in Egypt. The agreement divided the West Bank into three zones, one zone under full Palestinian control, one under joint Israeli–Palestinian control and the third under Israeli control. On 4 November, a Jewish religious extremist, assassinated Israeli Prime Minister Yitzhak Rabin at a peace rally. Shimon Peres succeeded him as the Israeli prime minister. In May 1996, he lost the elections. In his place came Binyamin Netanyahu, a vocal critic of the peace process. In May 1999, Netanyahu lost the elections. The new prime minister Ehud Barak vowed to solve the conflict within one year. His tenure saw rising violence and a faltering peace process and ended with his resignation in 2001. The electorate swept Ariel Sharon into power, with an eye on a tougher approach to the Palestinian problem.

Geography

Location: Middle East, bordering the Mediterranean Sea, between Egypt and Lebanon.

Area: 20,770 sq. km.

Terrain: The Negev Desert in the south, a low coastal plain and central mountains.

Natural resources: Timber, potash, copper ore, natural gas, phosphate rock, magnesium bromide, clays, sand.

Climate: Temperate climate but hot and dry in the southern and eastern desert areas.

People

Population: 6,352,117 (July 2006 est.). This includes about 20,000 Israeli settlers in the Israeli-occupied Golan Heights, about 187,000 in the West Bank, more than 5,000 in the Gaza Strip, and fewer than 177,000 in East Jerusalem.

Population growth rate: 1.18% (2006 est.).

Sex ratio: 0.99 male(s)/female (2006 est.).

Religions: Jewish 76.5%, Muslim 15.9% (mostly Sunni Muslim), Arab Christian 1.7%, other Christian 0.4%, Druze 1.6%, unspecified 3.9 (2003 est.).

Languages: Hebrew (official), Arabic is used officially for the Arab minority, English is the most commonly used foreign language.

Literacy rate: Total 95.4%, Male 97.3%, Female 93.6% (2003 est.).

Infant mortality rate: 6.89 deaths/1,000 live births (2006 est.).

Life expectancy: Total 79.46 years, Male 77.33 years, Female 81.7 years (2006 est.).

Government

Capital: Jerusalem.

Government type: Parliamentary democracy.

Independence: 14 May 1948 (from League of Nations mandate under British administration).

Legal system: Mixture of English common law, British mandate regulations, and, in personal matters, Jewish, Christian, and Muslim legal systems.

Executive branch:

Chief of state: President Moshe Katsav (since 31 July 2000).

Head of government: Prime Minister (Acting) Ehud Olmert (since May 2006).

Economy

Currency: New Israeli shekel.

Economy—overview:

Israel has a technologically advanced market economy. The country suffers from limited natural resources. Yet it has developed its agricultural and industrial sectors over the last two decades. USA is the creditor of almost half of the government's external debt. It is also the major source of economic and military aid. Israel's economy grew at a fast pace in the early 1990s, thanks partly to the emigration of Jewish immigrants from the former Soviet Union during 1989–99 and the opening of new markets at the end of the Cold War. However, the violent Israeli–Palestinian conflict is a major drawback for the growth and development of the Israeli economy.

GDP: Purchasing power parity—$154.5 billion (2005 est.).

GDP—real growth rate: 5.2% (2005 est.).

GDP—per capita: Purchasing power parity—$24,600 (2005 est.).

Inflation rate: 1.3% (2005 est.).

Population below poverty line: 21% (2005 est.).

Unemployment rate: 8.9% (2005 est.).

Exports: $40.14 billion f.o.b. (2005 est.)—machinery and equipment, software, cut diamonds, agricultural products, chemicals, textiles and apparel.

Imports: $43.19 billion f.o.b. (2005 est.)—raw materials, military equipment, investment goods, rough diamonds, fuels, grain, consumer goods.

External debt: $73.87 billion (30 June 2005 est.).

Transport and Communications

Railways: 17, 237 km.

Roads: 16,903 km.

Telephones: 3 million (2004).

Mobile cellular: 7,222 million (2004).

Internet users: 3,200,000 (2005).

Internet country code: .il

Italy

History

Between the ninth and third–fourth centuries BC, the Etruscan civilization dominated the area that is modern-day Italy. The Romans followed the Etruscans and were in turn driven out by the Barbarian invasions of the fourth and fifth centuries AD.

Between the fifteenth and eighteenth centuries, France, the Holy Roman empire, Spain and even Austria ruled the region. However, this could not stop Italy from becoming the nerve centre of European culture, mainly during the Renaissance period.

When Napoleonic rule came to an end in 1815, Italy was in the form of a collection of smaller independent states. The process of unification of peninsular

Italy was completed by 1870 when Papal Rome was added to the kingdom. Italy was finally one nation under a constitutional monarchy.

In October 1922, the fascist leader Benito Amilcare Andrea Mussolini, or Il Duce (which is Italian for 'The Leader') became the youngest prime minister of Italy. During World War II, Italy joined forces with Germany to form the Axis powers. It proved to be the undoing of both nations. By the time World War II ended, both dictators lay dead, their countries in ruins. In 1946, Italy declared itself a republic.

Geography

Location: Italy lies in southern Europe. It is a peninsula that extends into the central Mediterranean Sea, northeast of Tunisia.

Area: 301,230 sq. km (including Sardinia and Sicily).

Terrain: Mostly rugged and mountainous with some plains and coastal lowlands.

Natural resources: Mercury, potash, marble, sulphur, natural gas and crude oil reserves, fish, coal, and arable land.

Climate: Predominantly Mediterranean climate. However, the climate is of the Alpine type in the far north and hot and dry in the south.

People

Population: 58,133,509 (July 2006 est.).

Population growth rate: 0.04% (2006 est.).

Sex ratio: 0.96 male(s)/female (2006 est.).

Religions: Predominately Roman Catholic with mature Protestant and Jewish communities and a growing Muslim immigrant community.

Languages: Italian (official), German, French, Slovene.

Literacy rate: Total 98.6%, Male 99%, Female 98.3% (2003 est.).

Infant mortality rate: 5.83 deaths/ 1,000 live births (2006 est.).

Life expectancy: Total 79.81 years, Male 76.88 years, Female 82.94 years (2006 est.).

Government

Capital: Rome.

Government type: Republic.

Independence: 17 March 1861 (Kingdom of Italy proclaimed; Italy was not finally unified until 1870).

Legal system: Based on civil law system.

Executive branch:
Chief of state: President Giorgio Napolitano (since 17 May 2006).

Head of government: Prime Minister (referred to in Italy as the president of the Council of Ministers) Romano Prodi Silvio Berlusconi (since 17 May 2006).

Elections and election results: The president is elected by an electoral college consisting of both houses of parliament and fifty-eight regional representatives for a seven-year term (no term limits); election last held 10 May 2006 (next to be held May 2013); prime minister appointed by the president and confirmed by parliament. Giorgio Napolitano elected president on the fourth round of voting; electoral college vote: 543.

Economy

Currency: Euro.

Economy—overview:
Italy has a diversified industrial economy and its per capita output is roughly the same as France and the UK. A striking feature of Italy's capitalistic economy is that it is divided into a developed industrial north and a less developed, welfare-dependent agricul-

ture-dependent south with 20 per cent unemployment. Italy imports most of the raw materials and 75 per cent of the energy needed by its industries. Recently, Italy has pursued a tight fiscal policy in order to meet the requirements of the Economic and Monetary Unions. It has also benefited from lower interest and inflation rates. However, Italy has been sluggish on implementing much-needed structural reforms. These would have included reducing the high tax burden and overhauling of the rigid labour market and over-generous pension system.

GDP: Purchasing power parity—$1.689 trillion (2005 est.).

GDP—real growth rate: 0.1% (2005 est.).

GDP—per capita: Purchasing power parity—$29,200 (2005 est.).

Inflation rate: 1.9% (2005 est.).

Unemployment rate: 7.9% (2005 est.).

Exports: $371.9 billion f.o.b. (2005 est.).

Imports: $369.2 billion f.o.b. (2005 est.).

External debt: $1.682 trillion (30 June 2005 est.).

Transport and Communications

Railways: 19,319 km.

Roads: 479,688 km.

Telephones: 25.957 million (2004).

Mobile cellular: 62.75 million (2004).

Internet users: 28,870,000 (2005).

Internet country code: .it

Jamaica

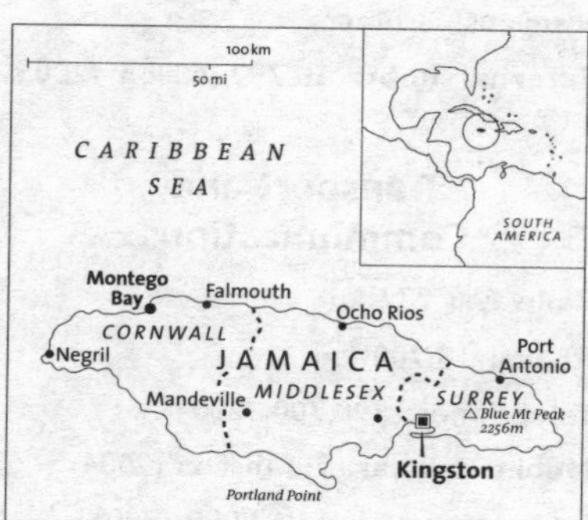

History

At the time of arrival of Christopher Columbus in 1494, Arawak Indians inhabited the island of Jamaica. It remained a Spanish possession till 1655 when the British gained control. Black slaves were imported to work in the sugar plantations. The abolition of the slave trade in 1807, coupled with the global slump in sugar prices caused a depression in Jamaica that eventually led to an uprising in the island in 1865. In 1866, Jamaica became a Crown colony. In 1958, Jamaica played a leading role in the formation of the West Indian Federation. In 1962, Jamaica declared independence following a referendum.

Geography

Location: Caribbean, island in the Caribbean Sea, south of Cuba.

Area: 10,991 sq. km.

Natural resources: Bauxite, gypsum, limestone.

Climate: Hot and humid tropical climate. The interiors have temperate climate.

People

Population: 2,758,124 (July 2006 est.).

Population growth rate: 0.8% (2006 est.).

Sex ratio: .98 male(s)/female (2006 est.).

Religions: Protestant 61.3% (Church of God 21.2%, Baptist 8.8%, Anglican 5.5%, Seventh-Day Adventist 9%, Pentecostal 7.6%, Methodist 2.7%, United Church 2.7%, Brethren 1.1%, Jehovah's Witness 1.6%, Moravian 1.1%), Roman Catholic 4%, other including some spiritual cults 34.7%.

Languages: English, patois English.

Literacy rate: Total 87.9%, Male 84.1%, Female 91.6% (2003 est.).

Infant mortality rate: 15.98 deaths/ 1,000 live births (2006 est.).

Life expectancy: Total 73.24 years, Male 71.54 years, Female 75.03 years (2006 est.).

Government

Capital: Kingston.

Government type: Constitutional parliamentary democracy.

Independence: 6 August 1962 (from UK).

Legal system: Based on English common law.

Executive branch:
Chief of state: Queen Elizabeth II (since 6 February 1952), represented by Governor General Kenneth O. Hall (since 15 February 2006).

Head of government: Prime Minister Portia Simpson Mller (since 30 March 2006).

Economy

Currency: Jamaican dollar.

GDP: Purchasing power parity—$12.17 billion (2005 est.).

GDP—real growth rate: 1.5% (2005 est.).

GDP—per capita: Purchasing power parity—$4,400 (2005 est.).

Inflation rate: 14.9% (2005 est.).

Population below poverty line: 19.1% (2003 est.).

Unemployment rate: 11.5% (2005 est.).

Exports: $1.608 billion f.o.b. (2005 est.)—alumina, bauxite, sugar, banana, rum.

Imports: $4.093 billion f.o.b. (2005 est.)—machinery and transport equipment, construction materials, fuel, food, chemicals, fertilizers.

External debt: $6.792 billion (2005 est.).

Transport and Communications

Railways: 272 km.

Roads: 18,700 km.

Telephones: 390,700 (2004).

Mobile cellular: 2.2 million (2004).

Internet users: 1,067,000 (2005).

Internet country code: .jm

Japan

History

The first unified Japanese state came about under the Yamato clan in the fourth–fifth centuries AD, which is also the time when Buddhism reached Japan via Korea. In 1192, Minamoto Yoritomo established the first shogunate in Japan.

The first contact with Europe occurred in 1542 when an off-course Portuguese ship arrived in Japan. This was followed by traders from Portugal and other European countries. The Tokugawa shogunate (1603–1867) imposed a policy of isolation that prohibited all trade ties with the West, except one Dutch trading post. The shogun system was abolished when Emperor Meiji came to the throne in 1868. Under Emperor Meiji, Japan initiated a process of rapid modernization and westernisation. A constitution was adopted, a parliamentary form of government took office and an imperial army was raised through conscription. Before long, Japan sought to expand its boundaries. This led to wars, first with China (1894–5) and then with Russia (1904–5). It annexed Korea in 1910 and Manchuria (now part of China) in 1931.

During World War II, Japan hastened the entry of USA into the war when it attacked its naval base at Pearl Harbour (7 December 1941). The War ended with the surrender of Japan, following the nuclear attacks on Hiroshima and Nagasaki in August 1945.

In 1947, Japan adopted a new constitution. It embarked on a process of rebuilding of the nation from the ravages of the War that had left it in ruins. The decades to follow witnessed unprecedented growth that soon propelled Japan to become the world's second largest economy. In 2005, Japan began a two-year term as a non-permanent member of the UN security Council

Geography

Location: Eastern Asia, island chain between the North Pacific Ocean and the Sea of Japan, east of the Korean Peninsula.

Area: 377,835 sq. km.

Terrain: Mostly rugged and mountainous. Consequently, the plains and valleys are densely populated.

Natural resources: Japan has negligible mineral resources but high in fish resources.

Climate: Varies from tropical in the south to cool temperate in the north.

People

Population: 127,463,611 (July 2006 est.).

Population growth rate: 0.02% (2006 est.).

Sex ratio: 0.95 male(s)/female (2006 est.).

Religions: Percentage of population observing both Shinto and Buddhism—84%, others 16% (including Christian 0.7%).

Languages: Japanese.

Literacy rate: 99% (2002 est.).

Infant mortality rate: 3.24 deaths/ 1,000 live births (2006 est.).

Life expectancy: Total 81.25 years, Male 77.96 years, Female 84.7 years (2006 est.).

Government

Capital: Tokyo.

Government type: Constitutional monarchy with a parliamentary government.

Independence: 660 BC, which is the traditional date of founding by Emperor Jimmu.

Legal system: Modelled after European civil law system with English–American influence.

Executive branch:
Chief of state: Emperor Akihito (since 7 January 1989).

Head of government: Prime Minister Junichiro Koizumi (since 26 April 2001).

Legislative branch:
Japan has a bicameral parliament. The Diet or the Kokkai consists of the House of Councillors or Sangi-in and the House of Representatives or Shugi-in. The House of Councillors has 247 seats. Members are elected for six-year terms, a half being elected every three years. One hundred forty-nine member are elected from members of multi-seat constituencies and ninety-eight are elected by proportional representation.

The House of Representatives has 480 seats. Members are elected for four-year terms—300 from single-seat constituencies and 180 by proportional representation in eleven regional blocs.

Elections to the House of Councillors were last held on 29 July 2001. Elections to the House of Representatives were last held on 9 November 2003.

House of Councillors

LDP	115
DPJ	82
Komeito	24
JCP	9
SDP	5
Others	7

Distribution of seats as of October 2004 was:

LDP	114
DPJ	84
Komeito	24
JCP	9
SDP	5
Others	6

House of Representatives

Distribution of seats as of 13 November 2003 was:

LDP	244
DPJ	177
Komeito	34
JCP	9
SDP	6
Others	10

Economy

Currency: Yen.

Economy—overview:
In the years following the Second World War, Japan rapidly achieved economic prosperity and became one of the world's largest economies. This was largely due to strong cooperation between the government and the industry, development of high technology, a strong work ethic and a comparatively low defence allocation (around 1 per cent of GDP). For three decades, the country enjoyed high overall real economic growth. It averaged 10 per cent in the 1960s, 5 per cent in the 1970s and 4 per cent in the 1980s. The economic situation deteriorated in the 1990s, mainly after the recession of 1997, with growth averaging just 1.7 per cent.

One of the notable features of the Japanese economy is the interaction between manufacturers, suppliers, and distributors in closely knit groups called keiretsu. Another significant feature has been the guarantee of lifetime employment for much of the urban labour force. Even today, a large part of the work force remains with the same employer all their working life. The recession in the mid-1990s has however contributed to the gradual erosion of both features in the Japanese society.

Japan has very little of its own natural resources and the country's industry is heavily dependent on imported raw materials and fuels. The much smaller agricultural sector is highly subsidized and protected and crop yields are among the highest in the world. Although the country is self-sufficient in rice, Japan needs to import about 50 per cent of its requirements of other grain and fodder crops. Japan has one of the world's largest fishing fleets and accounts for nearly 15 per cent of the global catch.

The slump of the 1990s was largely due to the over-investment in the late 1980s and policies that intended to extract speculative excesses from the stock and real estate markets. Government efforts to rejuvenate the economy have met with little success. The slowing down of the US, European, and Asian economies during 2000–03 further hampered recovery.

In 2004 and 2005, growth improved and the lingering fears of deflation in prices and economic activity lessened.

Japan's huge government debt, which totals 170 per cent of GDP, and the aging population are two major long-run problems. A rise in taxes could be viewed as endangering the revival of growth. Internal conflict over the proper way to reform the financial system will continue as Japan Post's banking, insurance, and delivery services undergo privatization between 2007 and 2017.

One remarkable feature is the country's robotic workforce. Japan has 410,000 of the world's 720,000 working robots population.

GDP: Purchasing power parity—$4.018 trillion (2005 est.).

GDP—real growth rate: 2.7% (2005 est.).

GDP—per capita: Purchasing power parity—$31,500 (2005 est.).

Inflation rate: –0.2% (2005 est.).

Unemployment rate: 4.3% (2005).

Exports: $550.5 billion f.o.b. (2005 est.).

Imports: $451.8 billion f.o.b. (2005 est.).

External debt: $1.545 trillion (31 December 2004).

Transport and Communications

Railways: 23,577 km (16,519 km electrified).

Roads: 1,177,278 km.

Telephones: 58.788 million (2004).

Mobile cellular: 91,473,900 (2004).

Internet users: 86.3 million (2005).

Internet country code: .jp

Jordan

History

David and later Solomon incorporated parts of present-day Jordan into their kingdoms. Later, the Seleucids and the Arabs held sway. In the sixteenth century, Jordan became a part of the Turkish Ottoman empire.

In 1920, the area comprising Transjordan, as it was then called, became a part of the British mandate of Palestine. In 1927, Transjordan became an independent state under British mandate. In 1949, Jordan annexed the

West Bank territory. However, Israel snatched it back during the Six Day War of 1967. In 1994, Jordan signed a full peace agreement with Israel.

Geography

Location: Middle East, north-west of Saudi Arabia.

Area: 92,300 sq. km.

Terrain: Desert plateau in the east and highland area in the west. A great rift valley separates the east and west banks of the Jordan River.

Natural resources: Phosphates, potash, shale oil.

Climate: Mostly arid desert type.

People

Population: 5,906,760 (July 2006 est.).

Population growth rate: 2.49% (2006 est.).

Sex ratio: 1.1 male(s)/female (2006 est.).

Religions: Sunni Muslim 92%, Christian 6%, others 2% (2001 est.).

Languages: Arabic (official), English widely understood.

Literacy rate: Total 91.3%, Male 95.9%, Female 86.3% (2003 est.).

Infant mortality rate: 16.76 deaths/ 1,000 live births (2006 est.).

Life expectancy: Total 78.4 years, Male 75.9 years, Female 81.05 years (2006 est.).

Government

Capital: Amman.

Government type: Constitutional monarchy.

Independence: 25 May 1946 (from League of Nations mandate under British administration).

Legal system: Based on Islamic law and French codes.

Executive branch:

Chief of state: King Abdallah II (since 7 February 1999); Crown Prince Hamzah (half-brother of the monarch, born 29 March 1980).

Head of government: Prime Minister Marouf al-Bakhit (since 24 November 2005).

Economy

Currency: Jordanian dinar.

Economy—overview:

Jordan suffers from inadequate supplies of water and other natural resources like oil. The war in Iraq in 2003 hurt the Jordanian economy, as it was dependent on Iraq for discounted oil. Key among the problems that the Jordanian economy faces are poverty, debt and unemployment. The ascent of King Abdallah to the throne has also seen the institution of some amount of economic reforms.

GDP: Purchasing power parity—$26.8 billion (2005 est.).

GDP—real growth rate: 6.1% (2005

est.).

GDP—per capita: Purchasing power parity—$4,700 (2005 est.).

Inflation rate: 5% (2005 est.).

Population below poverty line: 30% (2001 est.).

Unemployment rate: 12.5% (2004 est.).

Exports: $4.226 billion f.o.b. (2005 est.)—phosphates, fertilizers, potash, agricultural products, manufactures, pharmaceuticals.

Imports: $8.681 billion f.o.b. (2005 est.)—crude oil, machinery, transport equipment, food, live animals, manufactures.

External debt: $8.273 billion (2005 est.).

Transport and Communications

Railways: 505 km.

Roads: 7,364 km (2003).

Telephones: 617,300 (2004).

Mobile cellular: 1,594,500 (2004).

Internet users: 600,000 (2005).

Internet country code: .jo

Kazakhstan

History

Turkic-speaking tribes and Mongols invaded and settled in what is now Kazakhstan between the first and eighth centuries AD. Arab invaders introduced Islam in the eighth century. It was in the late fifteenth century that the Kazakhs emerged as a distinct ethnic group with the formation of the Kazakh khanate.

In the eighteenth century, the Kazakhs formally joined Russia in order to gain protection from the invading Mongols. In 1920, Kazakhstan became an autonomous republic of the USSR.

In 1936, Kazakhstan became a full-fledged union republic of the USSR. In December 1991, Kazakhstan declared its independence from the collapsing Soviet Union.

Geography

Location: Central Asia, north-west of China; a small portion west of the Ural River in easternmost Europe.

Area: 2,717,300 sq. km.

Terrain: Kazakhstan extends from the Volga to the Altai Mountains and from the plains in western Siberia to oases and desert in Central Asia.

Natural resources: Petroleum, natural gas, coal, iron ore, manganese, chrome ore, nickel, cobalt, copper, molybdenum, lead, zinc, bauxite, gold, uranium.

Climate: Continental climate with cold winters and hot summers.

People

Population: 15,233,244 (July 2006 est.).

Population growth rate: 0.33% (2006 est.).

Sex ratio: 0.93 male(s)/female (2006 est.).

Religions: Muslim 47%, Russian Orthodox 44%, Protestant 2%, others 7%.

Languages: Kazakh (Qazaq, state language) 64.4%, Russian 95% (2001 est.).

Literacy rate: Total 98.4%, Male 99.1%, Female 97.7% (1999 est.).

Infant mortality rate: 28.3 deaths/1,000 live births (2005 est.).

Life expectancy: Total 66.89 years, Male 61.56 years, Female 72.52 years (2006 est.).

Government

Capital: Astana.

Government type: Republic.

Independence: 16 December 1991 (from the Soviet Union).

Legal system: Based on civil law system.

Executive branch:
Chief of state: President Nursultan A. Nazarbayev (chairman of the Supreme Soviet from 22 February 1990, elected president 1 December 1991).

Head of government: Prime Minister Daniyal Akhmetov (since 13 June 2003).

Economy

Currency: Tenge.

Economy—overview:
Kazakhstan has large reserves of fossil fuel as well as other minerals and metals, a large livestock population and it is a globally significant producer of grain. Kazakhstan's industrial sector rests on the extraction and processing of these natural resources and also on a growing machine-building sector specializing in construction equipment, tractors, agricultural machinery, and some defence items. A short-term contraction of the economy followed immediately after the collapse of the Soviet Union in December 1991. The Caspian Consortium pipeline started in 2001, from western Kazakhstan's Tengiz oilfield to the Black Sea. Kazakhstan's new industrial policy aims to diversify the economy by removing the over-reliance on the oil sector.

GDP: Purchasing power parity—$124.3 billion (2005 est.).

GDP—real growth rate: 9.2% (2005 est.).

GDP—per capita: Purchasing power parity—$8,200 (2005 est.).

Inflation rate: 7.4% (2005 est.).

Population below poverty line: 19% (2004 est.).

Unemployment rate: 7.6% (2005 est.).

Exports: $30.09 billion f.o.b. (2005 est.)—oil and oil products, ferrous metals, chemicals, machinery, grain, wool, meat, coal.

Imports: $17.51 billion f.o.b. (2005 est.)—machinery and equipment 41%, metal products 28%, foodstuff 8%.

External debt: $32.7 billion (2005 est.).

Transport and Communications

Railways: 13,700 km.

Roads: 258,029 km.

Telephones: 2.5 million (2004).

Mobile cellular: 2,758,900 (2004).

Internet users: 400,000 (2005).

Internet country code: .kz

Kenya

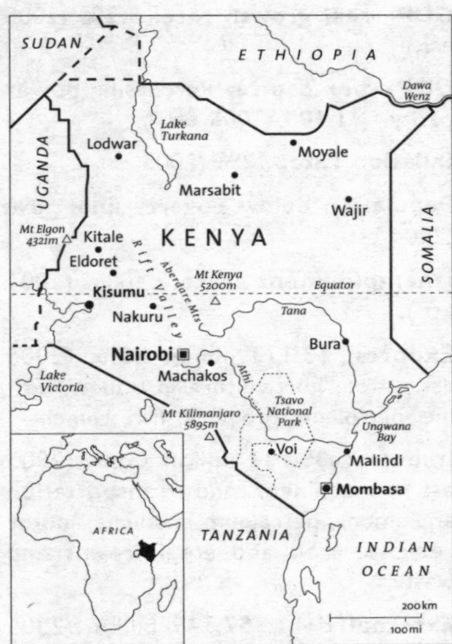

History

Evidence shows that Kenya was home to some of the earliest human settlements in the world. In the 1890s, Kenya became a part of the British East African Protectorate and in 1920 it became a British Crown colony. In 1944, the Kenyan African Union (KAU) was formed to campaign for African independence. In 1947, Jomo Kenyatta became a KAU leader. In 1952, a secret Kikuyu guerrilla group named Mau Mau began a violent campaign against white settlers. The following year, Kenyatta was charged with management of Mau Mau and jailed. The KAU was banned. In 1956, the government put down the Mau Mau rebellion but only after thousands were killed. In 1960, the Kenya African National Union (KANU) was formed. In 1961, Kenyatta took over the leadership of KANU. In 1963, Kenya became independent with Kenyatta as the prime minister. In 1964, Kenya became a republic with Kenyatta as the president.

Geography

Location: Eastern Africa, bordering the Indian Ocean, between Somalia and Tanzania.

Area: 582,650 sq. km.

Terrain: Low plains that rise to the central highlands bisected by the Great Rift Valley. There is a fertile plateau in the west.

Natural resources: Gold, limestone, soda ash, salt, rubies, fluorspar, garnets, wildlife, hydropower.

Climate: Varies from tropical along the coastal region to arid in the interiors.

People

Population: 34,707,817 (July 2006 est.).

Population growth rate: 2.57% (2006 est.).

Sex ratio: 1.01 male(s)/female (2006 est.).

Religions: Protestant 45%, Roman Catholic 33%, indigenous beliefs 10%, Muslim 10%, others 2%.

Languages: English (official), Kiswahili (official), several indigenous languages.

Literacy rate: Total 85.1%, Male 90.6%, Female 79.7% (2003 est.).

Infant mortality rate: 59.26 deaths/1,000 live births (2006 est.).

Life expectancy: Total 48.93 years, Male 49.78 years, Female 48.07 years (2006 est.).

Government

Capital: Nairobi.

Government type: Republic.

Independence: 12 December 1963 (from UK).

Legal system: Based on Kenyan statutory law, Kenyan and English common law, tribal law, and Islamic law.

Executive branch:
Chief of state: President Mwai Kibaki (since 30 December 2002) and Vice-President Moody Awori (since 25 September 2003). The president is both the chief of state and head of government.

Economy

Currency: Kenyan shilling.

Economy—overview:
Kenya is a regional centre for trade and finance in East Africa. Its economy has been hurt in recent times due to its reliance upon certain primary goods whose prices have remained low. In 1997, the IMF suspended Kenya's Enhanced Structural Adjustment Programme after the government failed to maintain reforms and curb corruption. A severe drought hit the country from 1999 to 2000, resulting in water and energy rationing and reduced agricultural output. The IMF resumed loans in 2000 to help Kenya through the drought period but stopped payments again in 2001 after the government failed to introduce suggested anti-corruption measures.

GDP: Purchasing power parity—$37.15 billion (2005 est.).

GDP—real growth rate: 5.2% (2005 est.).

GDP—per capita: Purchasing power parity—$1,100 (2005 est.).

Inflation rate: 12% (2005 est.).

Population below poverty line: 50% (2004 est.).

Unemployment rate: 40% (2001 est.).

Exports: $3.173 billion f.o.b. (2005 est.)—tea, horticultural products, coffee, petroleum products, fish, cement.

Imports: $5.126 billion f.o.b. (2005 est.)—machinery and transportation equipment, petroleum products, motor vehicles, iron and steel, resins and plastics.

External debt: $7.349 billion (2005 est.).

Transport and Communications

Railways: 2,778 km.

Roads: 63,942 km.

Telephones: 299,300 (2004).

Mobile cellular: 2,546,200 (2004).

Internet users: 1.5 million (2005).

Internet country code: .ke

Kiribati

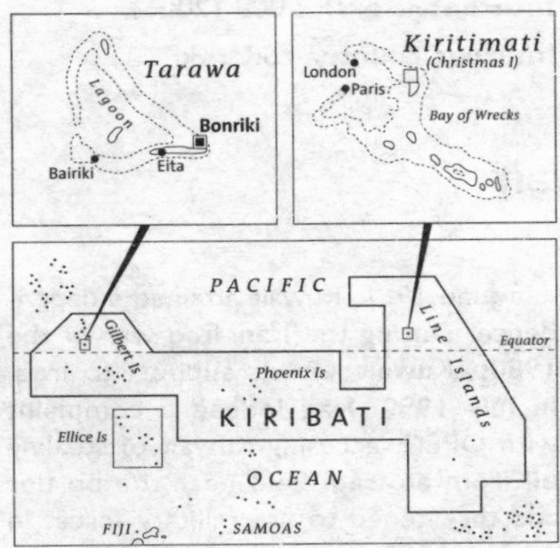

History

The islands comprising modern-day Kiribati were first settled in the first century AD. In 1892, the Gilbert Islands became a British protectorate while Banaba was annexed in 1900. These two were then joined with the Ellice Islands as the Gilbert and Ellice Islands Colony in 1916. The Gilbert Islands became independent as Kiribati in 1979.

Geography

Location: Oceania, group of thirty-three coral atolls in the Pacific Ocean, around the equator.

Area: 811 sq. km (this includes three island groups—Gilbert Islands, Line Islands, Phoenix Islands).

Natural resources: Phosphate (production discontinued in 1979).

Climate: Hot and humid tropical marine type of climate.

People

Population: 105,432 (July 2006 est.).

Population growth rate: 2.24% (2006 est.).

Sex ratio: 0.99 male(s)/female (2006 est.).

Religions: Roman Catholic 52%, Protestant (Congregational) 40%, some Seventh-day Adventist, Muslim, Baha'i, Latter-day Saints, and Church of God (1999).

Languages: I-Kiribati, English (official).

Infant mortality rate: 47.27 deaths/1,000 live births (2006 est.).

Life expectancy: Total 62.08 years, Male 59.06 years, Female 65.24 years (2006 est.).

Government

Capital: Tarawa.

Government type: Republic.

Independence: 12 July 1979 (from UK).

Executive branch:

Chief of state: President Anote Tong (since 10 July 2003). The president is both the chief of state and head of government.

Economy

Currency: Australian dollar.

GDP: Purchasing power parity—$79 million—supplemented by a nearly equal amount from external sources (2001 est.).

GDP—real growth rate: 1.5% (2001 est.).

GDP—per capita: Purchasing power parity—$800 (2001 est.).

Inflation rate: 2.5% (2001 est.).

Exports: $17 million f.o.b. (2004)—copra 62%, coconuts, seaweed, fish.

Imports: $62 million c.i.f. (2004)—foodstuff, machinery and equipment, miscellaneous manufactured goods, fuel.

External debt: $10 million (1999 est.).

Transport and Communications

Railways: None.

Roads: 670 km (1999 est.).

Telephones: 4,500 (2002).

Mobile cellular: 500 (2003).

Internet users: 2,000 (2003).

Internet country code: .ki

Kuwait

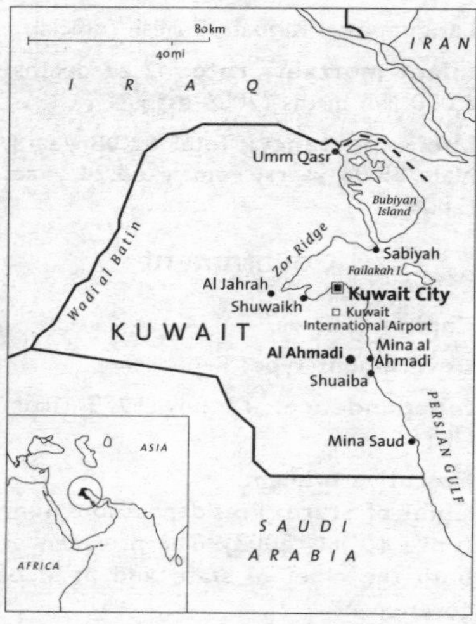

History

It is believed that an ancient civilization dating back to the third millennium BC flourished in Kuwait. The modern history of Kuwait starts in the eighteenth century, when a group of Arabs migrated to the area that is today Kuwait. They set up an oligarchic principality of merchants engaged in fishing, pearling and trade. In course of time, Al Sabah emerged as the dominant clan and, in 1756, they were formally established as rulers.

In 1899, Kuwait became a British protectorate. In 1937, oil reserves were discovered in Kuwait. After the end of World War II, the country transformed itself, based on its petroleum riches.

In June 1961, Kuwait attained independence. During the Iran–Iraq war of the 1980s, Kuwait lent its support to Iraq. In July 1990, Iraq lodged a complaint with OPEC, accusing Kuwait of stealing oil from an Iraqi field near the border and threatened to use military force. In August 1990, more than 100,000 Iraqi troops invaded and annexed Kuwait. A US-led and UN-backed military campaign was launched and by late February 1991, allied forces had reached Kuwait City. Retreating Iraqi forces carried out widespread looting, set fire to 742 of the country's 1,080 oil wells and allowed crude oil to flow into the desert and the sea. In 1993, the UN demarcated a new Kuwait–Iraq border.

Geography

Location: Middle East, bordering the Persian Gulf, between Iraq and Saudi Arabia.

Area: 17,820 sq. km.

Terrain: Flat to slightly undulating desert plain.

Natural resources: Petroleum, fish, shrimp, natural gas.

Climate: Dry desert type of climate with intensely hot summers and short, cool winters.

People

Population: 2,418,393. This includes 1,291,354 non-nationals (July 2006 est.).

Population growth rate: 3.52%. This rate reflects a return to pre-Gulf crisis immigration of expatriates (2006 est.).

Sex ratio: 1.52 male(s)/female (2006 est.).

Religions: Muslim 85% (Sunni 70%, Shi'a 30%), Christian, Hindu, Parsi, and others 15%.

Languages: Arabic (official), English widely spoken.

Literacy rate: Total 83.5%, Male 85.1%, Female 81.7% (2003 est.).

Infant mortality rate: 9.71 deaths/ 1,000 live births (2006 est.).

Life expectancy: Total 77.2 years, Male 76.13 years, Female 78.31 years (2006 est.).

Government

Capital: Kuwait City.

Government type: Nominal constitutional monarchy.

Independence: 19 June 1961 (from UK).

Legal system: Civil law system with Islamic law significant in personal matters.

Executive branch:
Chief of state: Amir Sabah al-Ahmad al-Jabir al-Sabah (since 29 January 2006); Crown Prince Nawaf al-Ahmad al-Sabah.

Head of government: Prime Minister Nasir al-Muhammad al-Ahmad al-Sabah (since 7 February 2006).

Economy

Currency: Kuwaiti dinar.

Economy—overview:
Kuwait is a small prosperous country with a relatively open economy and proven crude oil reserves of about 98 billion barrels. This is around 10 per cent of total world reserves. Nearly half of Kuwait's GDP, 95 per cent of export revenues and 80 per cent of government income comes from petroleum. It depends almost wholly on food imports, except for fish. About 75 per cent of drinking water is distilled from seawater or imported.

GDP: Purchasing power parity—$44.77 billion (2005 est.).

GDP—real growth rate: 4.8% (2005 est.).

GDP—per capita: Purchasing power parity—$19,200 (2005 est.).

Inflation rate: 3.5% (2005 est.).

Unemployment rate: 2.2% (2004 est.).

Exports: $44.43 billion f.o.b. (2005 est.)—oil and refined products, fertilizers.

Imports: $12.23 billion f.o.b. (2005 est.)—food, construction materials, vehicles and parts, clothing.

External debt: $14.93 billion (2005 est.).

Transport and Communications

Railways: None.

Roads: 4,450 km.

Telephones: 497,000 (2004).

Mobile cellular: 2 million (2004).

Internet users: 600,000 (2005).

Internet country code: .kw

Kyrgyzstan

History

In the eighth century, Arab invaders conquered large parts of Central Asia, including what is today Kyrgyzstan, and introduced Islam. By 1685, Kyrgyz people settled in the area that is now Kyrgyzstan. In 1758, Chinese Manchus

defeated the Oirat Mongols and the Kyrgyz people became nominal subjects of the Chinese empire. Early in the nineteenth century, the land passed into the jurisdiction of the Uzbek khanate of Kokand. In 1876, Russia conquered the khanate of Kokand and incorporated what is now Kyrgyzstan into the Russian empire. In 1926, the Kyrgyz Autonomous Region was upgraded to an Autonomous Soviet Socialist Republic. In 1991, Kirgizia was renamed Kyrgyzstan and declared its independence from the crumbling Soviet Union.

Geography

Location: Central Asia, west of China.

Area: 198,500 sq. km.

Terrain: Consists of the peaks of Tien Shan and its associated valleys and basins.

Natural resources: Hydropower, gold, rare earth metals, coal, oil, natural gas, nepheline, mercury, zinc, bismuth, lead.

Climate: Varies from dry continental to arctic in the Tien Shan areas. Ferghana Valley in the south-west has a subtropical climate while the northern foothill zone has a temperate climate.

People

Population: 5,213,898 (July 2006 est.).

Population growth rate: 1.32% (2006 est.).

Sex ratio: 0.96 male(s)/female (2006 est.).

Religions: Muslim 75%, Russian Orthodox 20%, others 5%.

Languages: Kyrgyz (official), Russian (official).

Literacy rate: Total 98.7%, Male 99.3%, Female 98.1% (1999 est.).

Infant mortality rate: 34.49 deaths/1,000 live births (2006 est.).

Life expectancy: Total 68.49 years, Male 64.48 years, Female 72.37 years (2006 est.).

Government

Capital: Bishkek.

Government type: Republic.

Independence: 31 August 1991 (from the Soviet Union).

Legal system: Based on civil law system.

Executive branch:
Chief of state: President Kurwanbek Bakiyev (since 14 August 2005); note: former President Askar Akayev resigned effective 11 April 2005 following widespread protests that forced him to free the country on 24 March 2005.

Head of government: Prime Minister Feliks Kulov (since 1 September 2005).

Economy

Currency: Kyrgyzstani som.

Economy—overview:
Kyrgyzstan was the first CIS country to be accepted into the World Trade Organization. Kyrgyzstan has a poor, largely agricultural economy, with cotton, tobacco, wool, and meat being the chief agricultural products. However, tobacco and cotton are significant export items. The country also exports gold, uranium, mercury, electricity, and natural gas. In recent times, Kyrgyzstan has implemented market reforms and land reform and the state has sold

most of its stock in enterprises. The drastic reduction in production immediately after the break-up of the Soviet Union in December 1991 was recovered by mid-1995 and was accompanied by an increase in exports. In partnership with international financial institutions, the government has undertaken a comprehensive medium-term poverty reduction and economic growth strategy.

GDP: Purchasing power parity—$10.65 billion (2005 est.).

GDP—real growth rate: 2% (2005 est.).

GDP—per capita: Purchasing power parity—$2,100 (2005 est.).

Inflation rate: 3.2% (2004 est.).

Population below poverty line: 40% (2004 est.).

Unemployment rate: 18% (2004 est.).

Exports: $759 million f.o.b. (2005 est.)—cotton, wool, meat, tobacco, hydropower, natural gas, gold, mercury, uranium, machinery, shoes.

Imports: $937.4 million f.o.b. (2005 est.)—oil and gas, foodstuff, machinery and equipment, chemicals.

External debt: $2.428 billion (31 December 2004 est.).

Transport and Communications

Railways: 470 km.

Roads: 18,500 km.

Telephones: 416,400 (2004).

Mobile cellular: 263,400 (2004).

Internet users: 263,000 (2005).

Internet country code: .kg

Laos

History

It was in the eighth century that the Lao people started migrating from southern China into the area that is today Laos. The first Laotian state, the Lan Xang kingdom, was founded in the fourteenth century. In 1893, Laos became a French protectorate. It was subsequently integrated into Indo-China. In March 1945 the Japanese took administrative control of Indo-China. In April 1945, the independence of Laos was proclaimed.

In the 1960s, USA carried out large-scale aerial bombardment of Laos in an attempt to destroy North Vietnamese safe havens and to eliminate the supply lines. It has been estimated that more bombs were dropped on Laos than were used through World War II. In

1973, a ceasefire agreement divided Laos between the communists and the royalists. In 1975, the Pathet Lao, renamed the Lao People's Front, seized power.

Geography

Location: South-eastern Asia, northeast of Thailand, west of Vietnam.

Area: 236,800 sq. km.

Terrain: Consists mostly of rugged mountains with some plains and plateaus.

Natural resources: Timber, hydropower, gypsum, tin, gold, gemstones.

Climate: Tropical monsoon type of climate with a rainy season from May to November and a dry season from December to April.

People

Population: 6,368,481 (July 2006 est.).

Population growth rate: 2.39% (2006 est.).

Sex ratio: 0.98 male(s)/female (2006 est.).

Religions: Buddhist 60%, animist and others 40%.

Languages: Lao (official), French, English, and various ethnic languages.

Literacy rate: Total 66.4%, Male 77.4%, Female 55.5% (2002 est.).

Infant mortality rate: 83.31 deaths/1,000 live births (2006 est.).

Life expectancy: Total 55.49 years, Male 53.45 years, Female 57.61 years (2006 est.).

Government

Capital: Vientiane.

Government type: Communist state.

Independence: 19 July 1949 (from France).

Legal system: The Laotian legal system is based on traditional customs, French legal norms and procedures, and socialist practice.

Executive branch:
Chief of state: President Lt Gen. Choummali Saignason (since 8 June 2006).

Head of government: Prime Minister Bouasone Bouphavanh (since 8 June 2006).

Elections and election results: The president and vice-president are elected by the National Assembly for five-year terms; election last held 8 June 2006 (next to be held in 2011); prime minister nominated by the president and elected by the National Assembly for a five-year term. Choummali Saignason was elected president; Boun-Gnanag Volachit elected vice-president; per cent of National Assembly vote: 100 per cent; Bouasone Bouphavanh elected prime minister; per cent of National Assembly vote: 97 per cent.

Economy

Currency: Kip.

Economy—overview:
Laos is one of the few remaining official Communist states. In 1986, it began decentralizing control over industries and encouraging private enterprise. The country has achieved a high growth rate ever since. The country suffers from inadequate infrastructure with no railways, limited availability of electricity, only a basic road network, and limited telecommunication networks. Subsistence agriculture accounts for nearly half of the country's GDP and 80 per cent of total employment.

GDP: Purchasing power parity—$12.13 billion (2005 est.).

GDP—real growth rate: 7.2% (2005 est.).

GDP—per capita: Purchasing power parity—$1,900 (2005 est.).

Inflation rate: 10% (2005 est.).

Population below poverty line: 34% (2002 est.).

Unemployment rate: 2.4% (1997 est.).

Exports: $379 million f.o.b. (2005 est.)—garments, wood products, coffee, electricity, tin.

Imports: $541 million f.o.b. (2005 est.)—machinery and equipment, vehicles, fuel, consumer goods.

External debt: $2.49 billion (2001).

Transport and Communications

Railways: None.

Roads: 32,620 km.

Telephones: 90,067 (2006).

Mobile cellular: 520,546 (2006).

Internet users: 20,900 (2005).

Internet country code: .la

Latvia

History

Baltic tribes originally inhabited the region that is today Latvia. Then the region came under the influence of German knights. The Russians controlled the affairs of Latvia for 200 years, till 1918. In 1918, Latvia declared its independence. But civil war ensued and ended in a peace treaty signed with the Soviet Union. In 1941, Germany invaded Latvia. In August 1991, Latvia declared full independence. Latvia joined both NATO and the EU in the spring of 2004.

Geography

Location: Eastern Europe, bordering the Baltic Sea, between Estonia and Lithuania.

Area: 64,589 sq. km.

Terrain: A low plain.

Natural resources: Peat, limestone, dolomite, amber, hydropower, wood, arable land.

Climate: Maritime climate with wet, moderate winters.

People

Population: 2,274,735 (July 2006 est.).

Population growth rate: –0.67% (2006 est.).

Sex ratio: 0.86 male(s)/female (2006 est.).

Religions: Lutheran, Roman Catholic, Russian Orthodox.

Languages: Latvian (official) 58.2%, Russian 37.5%, Lithuanian and other 4.3% (2000 census).

Literacy rate: 99.8% (2003 est.).

Infant mortality rate: 9.35 deaths/1,000 live births (2006 est.).

Life expectancy: Total 71.33 years, Male 66.08 years, Female 76.85 years (2006 est.).

Government

Capital: Riga.

Government type: Parliamentary democracy.

Independence: 21 August 1991 (from the Soviet Union).

Legal system: Based on civil law system.

Executive branch:

Chief of state: President Vaira Vike-Freiberga (since 8 July 1999).

Head of government: Prime Minister Aigars Kalvitis (since 2 December 2004).

Economy

Currency: Latvian lat.

GDP: Purchasing power parity—$30.29 billion (2005 est.).

GDP—real growth rate: 10.2% (2005 est.).

GDP—per capita: Purchasing power parity—$13,200 (2005 est.).

Inflation rate: 5.9% (2005 est.).

Unemployment rate: 8.8% (2005 est.).

Exports: $5.749 billion f.o.b. (2005 est.)—wood and wood products, machinery and equipment, metals, textiles, foodstuff.

Imports: $8.559 billion f.o.b. (2005 est.)—machinery and equipment, chemicals, fuels, vehicles.

External debt: $13.2 billion (30 June 2005 est.).

Transport and Communications

Railways: 2,303 km.

Roads: 69,919 km.

Telephones: 650,500 (2004).

Mobile cellular: 1,536,700 (2004).

Internet users: 810,000 (2005).

Internet country code: .lv

Lebanon

History

In about 3000 BC, the Phoenicians are believed to have arrived in the coastal areas of Lebanon. This area came to be called Phoenicia. Byblos is regarded as the first urban settlement in the area and has been dated to around 3050–2850 BC. A period of close contact with Egypt followed under the Amorites. However, Egypt lost its control over the area by the fourteenth century BC. This led to the emergence of a number of city states all over Phoenicia.

By the second millennium BC the Phoenicians had begun extending their influence along the eastern shores of the Mediterranean Sea by establishing a series of settlements. In the ninth century BC, Assyrians threatened the independence of Phoenicia. In 868 BC, Ashurnasirpal II reached the Mediterranean and forced the Phoenician cities to pay tribute. When the Babylonian King Nebuchadnezzar II marched against Phoenicia and besieged Tyre, the city resisted successfully for thirteen years but was finally taken.

In 538 BC, the control of Phoenicia passed from the Babylonians to their conquerors, the Persians. In 332 BC Tyre resisted a siege launched by Alexander the Great for eight months before Alexander finally captured the city. Most of the citizens were sold into slavery and Tyre lost its position as the dominant city of the region to Alexan-

dria. Phoenicia was eventually incorporated into the Roman province of Syria.

By the end of the eleventh century, Lebanon became a part of the crusaders' states. The northern part of the country became a part of Tripolis while the southern part of the country became a part of the kingdom of Jerusalem. Lebanon came under increasing French influence. At the end of World War I, Allied forces occupied Lebanon and placed it under a French military administration. In 1923, the League of Nations formally gave the mandate for Lebanon and Syria to France. In December 1943, France agreed to transfer power to the Lebanese government with effect from 1 January 1944.

In the 1960s, Palestine began using Lebanon as the base for their anti-Israeli activities. Civil war rocked Lebanon between 1975 and 1991. In June 1982, Israel launched a full-scale invasion of Lebanon, code-named 'Operation Peace for Galilee'. In July 1986, Syrian observers were stationed in Beirut to monitor a peace agreement. In 1991, the Syrian-backed Lebanese government started retaking territory from the militia in southern Lebanon. This signalled the beginning of the end of the civil war in Lebanon.

Geography

Location: Middle East, between Israel and Syria, bordering the Mediterranean Sea.

Area: 10,400 sq. km.

Terrain: Consists mostly of a narrow coastal plain. The El Beqaa or Bekaa Valley separates Lebanon and the Anti-Lebanon Mountains.

Natural resources: Limestone, iron ore, salt, water, arable land.

Climate: Mediterranean climate with mild to cool wet winters and hot, dry summers.

People

Population: 3,874,050 (July 2006 est.).

Population growth rate: 1.23% (2006 est.).

Sex ratio: 0.94 male(s)/female (2006 est.).

Religions: Muslim (Shi'a, Sunni, Druze, Isma'ilite, Alawite or Nusayri) 59.7%, Christian (Maronite Catholic, Greek Orthodox, Melkite Catholic, Armenian Orthodox, Syrian Catholic, Armenian Catholic, Syrian Orthodox, Roman Catholic, Chaldean, Assyrian, Copt, Protestant) 39%, other 1.3%.

Languages: Arabic (official), French, English, Armenian.

Literacy rate: Total 87.4%, Male 93.1%, Female 82.2% (2003 est.).

Infant mortality rate: 23.72 deaths/ 1,000 live births (2006 est.).

Life expectancy: Total 72.88 years, Male 70.41 years, Female 75.48 years (2006 est.).

Government

Capital: Beirut.

Government type: Republic.

Independence: 22 November 1943 (from League of Nations mandate under French administration).

Legal system: Combination of Ottoman law, Napoleonic code, canon law and civil law.

Executive branch:

Chief of state: President Emile Lahud (since 24 November 1998).

Head of government: Prime Minister Fuad Siniora (since 30 June 2005).

Economy

Currency: Lebanese pound.

Economy—overview:
Lebanon's economic infrastructure suffered much damage in the 1975–91 civil war that also reduced national output by half. The prevailing atmosphere of peace since then has enabled the Central government to resume tax collections and regain access to ports and government facilities. A financially sound banking system and a resilient manufacturing sector have helped economic recovery in recent years. In 1993, the government launched 'Horizon 2000', a $20 billion reconstruction programme. In the 1990s, annual inflation has dropped to almost nil from over 100 per cent at one point of time. Much of Lebanon's war-damaged infrastructure has been rebuilt. However, the economic battle is far from over. Most of the reconstruction was funded through heavy borrowing mostly from domestic banks. The government has initiated an economic austerity programme to cut down on government spending, increase revenue collection, and privatize state-held enterprises in a bid to reduce the mounting national debt. In November 2002, the government met with international donors at the Paris II Conference to seek bilateral assistance in restructuring its domestic debt at lower rates of interest.

GDP: Purchasing power parity—$23.69 billion (2005 est.).

GDP—real growth rate: 0.5% (2005 est.).

GDP—per capita: Purchasing power parity—$6,200 (2005 est.).

Inflation rate: 2.4% (2005 est.).

Population below poverty line: 28% (1999 est.).

Unemployment rate: 18% (1997 est.).

Exports: $1.782 billion f.o.b. (2005 est.)—jewellery, consumer goods, inorganic chemicals, fruit, tobacco, construction materials, paper, electric power machinery and switchgear, textile fibres.

Imports: $8.855 billion f.o.b. (2005 est.)—petroleum products, cars, medicinal products, clothing, tobacco, meat and live animals, consumer goods, textile fabrics.

External debt: $25.92 billion (2005 est.).

Transport and Communications

Railways: 401 km.

Roads: 7,300 km.

Telephones: 630,000 (2004).

Mobile cellular: 888,000 (2004).

Internet users: 600,000 (2005).

Internet country code: .lb

Lesotho

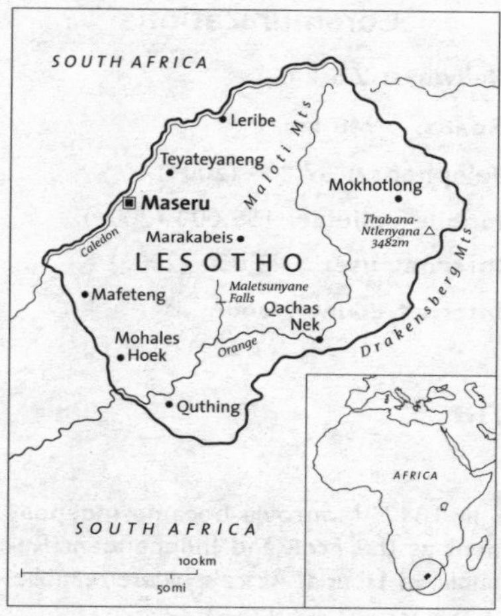

History

Native chief Moshoeshoe founded Basutoland, the forerunner of Lesotho, in the 1820s. In the 1860s, it became a British protectorate. Basutoland finally gained independence in 1966 as the kingdom of Lesotho, with Moshoeshoe II as king and Chief Leabua Jonathan as prime minister.

Geography

Location: Southern Africa, an enclave of South Africa.

Area: 30,355 sq. km.

Natural resources: Water, agricultural and grazing land, diamond and other minerals.

Climate: Temperate; cool to cold, dry winters; hot, wet summers.

People

Population: 2,022,331 (2006 est.).

Population growth rate: –0.46% (2006 est.).

Sex ratio: 0.95 male(s)/female (2006 est.).

Religions: Christian 80%, indigenous beliefs 20%.

Languages: Sesotho (South Sotho), English (official), Zulu, Xhosa.

Literacy rate: Total 84.8%, Male 74.5%, Female 94.5% (2003 est.).

Infant mortality rate: 87.24 deaths/1,000 live births (2006 est.).

Life expectancy: Total 34.4 years, Male 35.55 years, Female 33.21 years (2006 est.).

Government

Capital: Maseru.

Government type: Parliamentary constitutional monarchy.

Independence: 4 October 1966 (from UK).

Legal system: Based on English common law and Roman–Dutch law.

Executive branch:
Chief of state: King Letsie III (since 7 February 1996).

Head of government: Prime Minister Pakalitha Mosisili (since 23 May 1998).

Economy

Currency: Loti, South African rand.

GDP: Purchasing power parity—$5.124 billion (2005 est.).

GDP—real growth rate: 2% (2005 est.).

GDP—per capita: Purchasing power parity—$2,500 (2005 est.).

Inflation rate: 5.3% (2004 est.).

Population below poverty line: 49% (1999).

Unemployment rate: 45% (2002 est.).

Exports: $602.8 million f.o.b. (2005 est.)—manufactures 75% (clothing, footwear, road vehicles), wool and mohair, food and live animals (2000).

Imports: $1.166 million f.o.b. (2005 est.)—food, building materials, vehicles, machinery, medicines, petroleum products (2000).

External debt: $735 million (2002).

Transport and Communications

Railways: 2.6 km.

Roads: 5,940 km.

Telephones: 37,200 (2004).

Mobile cellular: 159,000 (2004).

Internet users: 43,000 (2005).

Internet country code: .ls

Liberia

History

It was the American Colonization Society's efforts of settling slaves freed in USA that led to the creation of Liberia in 1822. The society decided that the resettling of freed slaves in West Africa would be a viable solution to slavery. Some 12,000 slaves were subsequently taken to Liberia, initially called Monrovia.

In 1847, Monrovia became independent as the Free and Independent Republic of Liberia, Africa's oldest republic.

Geography

Location: Western Africa, bordering the North Atlantic Ocean, between Cote d'Ivoire and Sierra Leone.

Area: 111,370 sq. km.

Terrain: Mostly flat rolling coastal plain that rises in a rolling plateau and low mountains in the north-east.

Natural resources: Iron ore, timber, diamond, gold, hydropower.

Climate: Hot and humid tropical climate.

People

Population: 3,042,004 (July 2006 est.).

Population growth rate: 4.91% (2006 est.).

Sex ratio: 0.99 male(s)/female (2006 est.).

Religions: Indigenous beliefs 40%, Christian 40%, Muslim 20%.

Languages: English 20% (official), around 20 ethnic group languages.

Literacy rate: Total 57.5%, Male 73.3%, Female 41.6% (2003 est.).

Infant mortality rate: 155.76 deaths/ 1,000 live births (2006 est.).

Life expectancy: Total 39.65 years, Male 37.99 years, Female 41.35 years (2006 est.).

Government

Capital: Monrovia.

Government type: Republic.

Independence: 26 July 1847.

Legal system: Dual system of statutory law based on Anglo-American common law for the modern sector and customary law based on unwritten tribal practices for indigenous sector.

Executive branch:
Chief of state: President Ellen Johnson-Sirleaf (since 16 January 2006). The chairman is both the chief of state and head of government.

Economy

Currency: Liberian dollar.

GDP: Purchasing power parity—$2.755 billion (2005 est.).

GDP—real growth rate: 8% (2005 est.).

GDP—per capita: Purchasing power parity—$1000 (2005 est.).

Inflation rate: 15% (2003 est.).

Population below poverty line: 80%.

Unemployment rate: 85% (2003 est.).

Exports: $910 million f.o.b. (2004 est.)—rubber, timber, iron, diamond, cocoa, coffee.

Imports: $4.839 billion f.o.b. (2004 est.)—fuels, chemicals, machinery, transportation equipment, manufactures, foodstuff.

External debt: $3.2 billion (2005 est.).

Transport and Communications

Railways: 490 km.

Roads: 10,600 km.

Telephones: 7,000 (2001).

Mobile cellular: 2,000 (2001).

Internet users: 1,000 (2002).

Internet country code: .lr

Libya

History

In the seventh century BC, Phoenicians settled in Tripolitania in western Libya. In the fourth century BC, Greeks colonized Cyrenaica in the eastern part of the country. They gave it the name, Libya. In the sixth century AD, Libya became a part of the Byzantine empire. But in 643, Arabs under Amr Ibn al-As conquered Libya and spread Islam. In the sixteenth century, Libya became a part of the Ottoman empire. It joined together the three provinces of Tripolitania, Cyrenaica and Fezzan into a single regency in Tripoli. In 1911–12, Italy conquered Libya. In 1942, the Allied forces evicted Italians from Libya. They then divided the country amongst the French (who controlled Fezzan) and the British (who administered Cyrenaica and Tripolitania). In 1951, Libya became independent under King Idris al-Sanusi.

In 1969, Col. Muammar Abu Minyar al-Qadhafi deposed King Idris in a military coup. He subsequently pursued a pan-Arab agenda and tried to form mergers with several Arab countries. He also in-

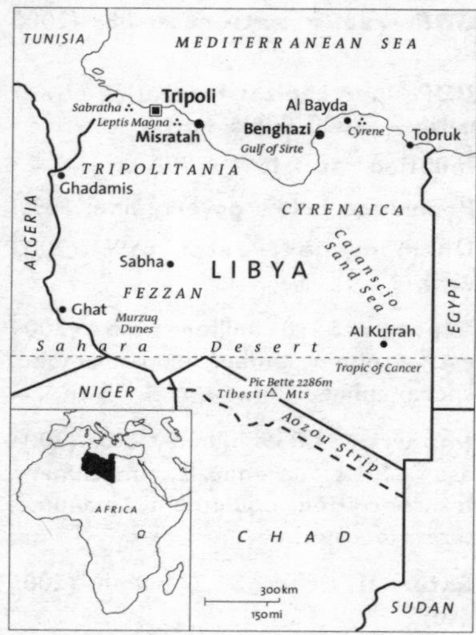

troduced state socialism and nationalized most of the country's economic activity, including the oil industry. In 1970, Libya ordered the closure of British and American airbases in the country.

In 1986, USA carried out air strikes against Libyan military facilities and residential areas in Tripoli and Benghazi, killing 101 people. Qadhafi's house was also attacked. USA justified the attacks by holding Libya responsible for the bombing of a Berlin discotheque that US military personnel frequented.

In 1992, UN imposed sanctions on Libya. This was in an attempt to force it to hand over two of its citizens suspected of involvement in the blowing up of a Pan Am airliner over the Scottish town of Lockerbie in December 1988. In August 2003, Libya signed a compensation deal worth $2.7 billion with lawyers representing families of Lockerbie bombing victims. Libya also formally took responsibility for the bombing in a letter to the UN Security Council. This led to the lifting of UN sanctions on Libya in September.

Geography

Location: Northern Africa, bordering the Mediterranean Sea, between Egypt and Tunisia.

Area: 1,759,540 sq. km.

Terrain: Mostly barren with flat to undulating plains, plateaus and depressions.

Natural resources: Petroleum, natural gas, gypsum.

Climate: Mediterranean type of climate along the coast and a dry extreme desert type of climate in the interiors.

People

Population: 5,900,754 including 166,510 non-nationals (July 2005 est.).

Population growth rate: 2.3% (2006 est.).

Sex ratio: 1.05 male(s)/female (2006 est.).

Religions: Sunni Muslim 97%.

Languages: Arabic, Italian, English.

Literacy rate: Total 82.6%, Male 92.4%, Female 72% (2003 est.).

Infant mortality rate: 23.71 deaths/1,000 live births (2006 est.).

Life expectancy: Total 76.69 years, Male 74.46 years, Female 79.02 years (2006 est.).

Government

Capital: Tripoli.

Government type: Military dictatorship.

Independence: 24 December 1951.

Legal system: Based on Italian civil law system and Islamic law.

Executive branch:
Chief of state: Revolutionary Leader Col. Muammar Abu Minyar al-Qadhafi (since 1 September 1969).

Head of government: Secretary of the General People's Committee (Prime Minister) al-Baghdadi Ali al-Mahmudi (since 5 March 2006).

Economy

Currency: Libyan dinar.

Economy—overview:
The Libyan economy is primarily dependent upon revenues from the oil sector. Almost all of Libya's export earnings and about one-quarter of GDP comes from the petroleum industry. Libya enjoys one of the highest per capita GDPs in Africa, thanks to its oil revenues and small population. However, very little of this income trickles down to the lower orders of society. The process of economic reforms gathered momentum after UN sanctions were lifted in September 2003.

GDP: Purchasing power parity—$65.79 billion (2005 est.).

GDP—real growth rate: 8.5% (2005 est.).

GDP—per capita: Purchasing power parity—$11,400 (2005 est.).

Inflation rate: –1% (2005 est.).

Unemployment rate: 30% (2004).

Exports: $30.79 billion f.o.b. (2005 est.) —crude oil, refined petroleum products.

Imports: $10.82 billion f.o.b. (2005 est.)—machinery, transport equipment, food, manufactured goods (1999).

External debt: $4.267 billion (2005 est.).

Transport and Communications

Railways: None.

Roads: 83,200 km.

Telephones: 750,000 (2003).

Mobile cellular: 100,000 (2003).

Internet users: 205,000 (2005).

Internet country code: .ly

Liechtenstein

History

The present-day principality of Liechtenstein was founded in 1719 by combining the two Holy Roman Empire lordships of Vaduz and Schellenburg. Between 1815 and 1866, Liechtenstein was a part of the German Confederation. Liechtenstein became fully independent in 1866.

Geography

Location: Central Europe, between Austria and Switzerland.

Area: 160 sq. km.

Natural resources: Hydroelectric potential, arable land.

Climate: Continental climate with cold, cloudy winters with frequent snow or rain and cool to moderately warm summers.

People

Population: 33,987 (July 2006 est.).

Population growth rate: 0.78% (2006 est.).

Sex ratio: 0.95 male(s)/female (2006 est.).

Religions: Roman Catholic 76.2%, Protestant 7%, unknown 10.6%, others 6.2% (June 2002).

Languages: German (official), Alemannic dialect.

Literacy rate: 100%.

Infant mortality rate: 4.64 deaths/1,000 live births (2006 est.).

Life expectancy: Total 79.68 years, Male 76.1 years, Female 83.28 years (2006 est.).

Government

Capital: Vaduz.

Government type: Hereditary constitutional monarchy on a democratic and parliamentary basis.

Independence: 23 January 1719 (Imperial Principality of Liechtenstein established); 12 June 1806 (independence from the Holy Roman Empire).

Legal system: Local civil and penal codes.

Executive branch:

Chief of state: Prince Hans Adam II (since 13 November 1989, assumed executive powers 26 August 1984); Heir Apparent Prince Alois, son of the monarch (born 11 June 1968).

Head of government: Head of Government Otmar Hasler (since 5 April 2001) and Deputy Head of Government Rita Kieber-Beck (since 5 April 2001).

Economy

Currency: Swiss franc.

GDP: Purchasing power parity—$825 million (1999 est.).

GDP—real growth rate: 11% (1999 est.).

GDP—per capita: Purchasing power parity—$25,000 (1999 est.).

Inflation rate: 1% (2001).

Unemployment rate: 1.3% (2002 est.).

Exports: $2.47 billion (1996)—small speciality machinery, connectors for audio and video, parts for motor vehicles, dental products, hardware, prepared foodstuff, electronic equipment, optical products.

Imports: $917.3 million (1996)—agricultural products, raw materials, machinery, metal goods, textiles, foodstuff, motor vehicles.

External debt: None.

Transport and Communications

Railways: 18.5 km.

Roads: 323 km.

Telephones: 19,900 (2002).

Mobile cellular: 11,400 (2002).

Internet users: 20,000 (2002).

Internet country code: .li

Lithuania

History

From the fourteenth to the sixteenth centuries, Lithuania and Poland was one of the strongest empires in the world and formed a confederation for about 200 years. Russians claimed Lithuania after the division of Poland in 1795. At the end of World War I, Lithuania took advantage of a weak Russia to declare its independence in 1918.

Independent between the two World Wars, Lithuania was annexed by the USSR in 1940. On 11 March 1990, Lithuania became the first of the Soviet republics to declare its independence, but Moscow did not recognize this proclamation until September 1991 (following the abortive coup in Moscow). The last Russian troops withdrew in 1993. Lithuania subsequently restructured its economy for integration into Western European institutions; it joined both NATO and the EU in the spring of 2004.

Geography

Location: Eastern Europe, bordering the Baltic Sea, between Latvia and Russia.

Area: 65,200 sq. km.

Terrain: Lowland with scattered small lakes.

Natural resources: Peat, arable land.

Climate: Transitional type of climate that lies between maritime and continental wet.

People

Population: 3,585,906 (July 2006 est.).

Population growth rate: –0.3% (2006 est.).

Sex ratio: 0.89 male(s)/female (2006 est.).

Religions: Roman Catholic (primarily), Lutheran, Russian Orthodox, Protestant, Evangelical Christian Baptist, Muslim, Jewish.

Languages: Lithuanian (official), Polish, Russian.

Literacy rate: 99.6% (2003 est.).

Infant mortality rate: 6.78 deaths/1,000 live births (2006 est.).

Life expectancy: Total 74.2 years, Male 69.2 years, Female 79.49 years (2006 est.).

Government

Capital: Vilnius.

Government type: Parliamentary democracy.

Independence: 11 March 1990—date of declaration of independence from Soviet Union.

Legal system: Based on civil law system; legislative acts can be appealed to the constitutional court.

Executive branch:

Chief of state: Prime Minister Gediminas Kirkias (since 4 July 2006).

Head of government: Prime Minister Gediminas Kirkilas (since 4 July 2006).

Economy

Currency: Litas.

GDP: Purchasing power parity—$49.21 billion (2005 est.).

GDP—real growth rate: 7.5% (2005 est.).

GDP—per capita: Purchasing power parity—$13,700 (2005 est.).

Inflation rate (consumer prices): 2.6% (2005 est.).

Unemployment rate: 5.3% (2005 est.).

Exports: $10.95 billion f.o.b. (2005 est.)—mineral products, textiles and clothing, machinery and equipment, chemicals, wood and wood products, foodstuff (2001).

Imports: $13.33 billion f.o.b. (2005 est.)—mineral products, machinery and equipment, transport equipment, chemicals, textiles and clothing, metals (2001).

External debt: $10.47 billion (31 December 2004 est.).

Transport and Communications

Railways: 1,998 km.

Roads: 78,893 km.

Telephones: 820,000 (2004).

Mobile cellular: 3,421,500 (2004).

Internet users: 968,000 (2005).

Internet country code: .lt

Luxembourg

History

Luxembourg became independent in 963, when Siegfried, Count de Ardennes, exchanged his lands for the Roman castle named Lucilinburhuc. This castle proved to be the birthplace of Luxembourg.

Geography

Location: Western Europe, between France and Germany.

Area: 2,586 sq. km.

Natural resources: Arable land.

Climate: Modified continental climate with mild winters and cool summers.

People

Population: 474,413 (July 2006 est.).

Population growth rate: 1.23% (2006 est.).

Sex ratio: 0.97 male(s)/female (2006 est.).

Religions: 87% Roman Catholic, 13% Protestants, Jews, and Muslims (2000).

Languages: Luxembourgish (national language), German (administrative language), French (administrative language).

Literacy rate: 100% (2000 est.).

Infant mortality rate: 4.74 deaths/ 1,000 live births (2006 est.).

Life expectancy: Total 78.89 years, Male 75.6 years, Female 82.38 years (2006 est.).

Government

Capital: Luxembourg.

Government type: Constitutional monarchy.

Independence: 1839 (from the Netherlands).

Legal system: Based on civil law system.

Executive branch:
Chief of state: Grand Duke Henri (since 7 October 2000); Heir Apparent Prince Guillaume (son of the monarch, born 11 November 1981).

Head of government: Prime Minister Jean-Claude Juncker (since 1 January 1995) and Vice Prime Minister Lydie Polfer (since 7 August 1999).

Economy

Currency: Euro.

GDP: Purchasing power parity—$30.74 billion (2005 est.).

GDP—real growth rate: 3.7% (2005 est.).

GDP—per capita: Purchasing power parity—$55,600 (2005 est.).

Inflation rate: 3.6% (2005 est.).

Unemployment rate: 4.9% (2005 est.).

Exports: $13.39 billion f.o.b. (2005)—machinery and equipment, steel products, chemicals, rubber products, glass.

Imports: $18.74 billion c.i.f. (2005)—minerals, metals, foodstuff, quality consumer goods.

Transport and Communications

Railways: 274 km.

Roads: 5,210 km.

Telephones: 360,100 (2003).

Mobile cellular: 539,000 (2003).

Internet users: 270,800 (2005).

Internet country code: .lu

Macedonia

History

Macedon gained prominence in the fourth century BC due to the conquests of Alexander the Great. Later, Macedonia became part of the Roman empire, the Byzantine empire and the Ottoman empire. The nineteenth century saw constant rivalry for the possession of Macedonia, for its economic wealth and strategic location.

In 1991, the country declared its independence even as ethnic Albanians within Macedonia demanded their own territory while Greece objected to the use of the name Macedonia, as one of its provinces had the same name.

Geography

Location: South-eastern Europe, north of Greece.

Area: 25,333 sq. km.

Terrain: Mountanious with deep basins and valleys.

Natural resources: Low-grade iron ore, copper, lead, zinc, chromite, manganese, nickel, tungsten, gold, silver, asbestos, gypsum, timber, arable land.

Climate: Warm, dry summers and autumns and relatively cold winters with heavy snowfall.

People

Population: 2,050,554 (July 2006 est.).

Population growth rate: 0.26% (2006 est.).

Sex ratio: 1 male(s)/female (2006 est.).

Religions: Macedonian Orthodox 32.4%, other Christian 0.27%, Muslim 16%, other and unspecified 50.5% (2002 census).

Languages: Macedonian 68%, Albanian 25%, Turkish 3%, Serbo-Croatian 2%, others 2%.

Infant mortality rate: 9.81 deaths/1,000 live births (2006 est.).

Life expectancy: Total 73.97 years, Male 71.51 years, Female 76.62 years (2006 est.).

Government

Capital: Skopje.

Government type: Parliamentary democracy.

Independence: 8 September 1991—date of signing of referendum by registered voters endorsing independence (from Yugoslavia).

Legal system: Based on civil law system.

Executive branch:
Chief of state: President Branko Crvenkovski (sworn in on 12 May 2004).

Head of government: Prime Minister Vlado Buckovski (since 17 December 2004).

Economy

Currency: Macedonian denar.

GDP: Purchasing power parity—$16.03 billion (2005 est.).

GDP—real growth rate: 3.7% (2005 est.).

GDP—per capita: Purchasing power parity—$7,800 (2005 est.).

Inflation rate: 0.5% (2005 est.).

Population below poverty line: 29.6% (2004 est.).

Unemployment rate: 38% (2005 est.).

Exports: $2.047 billion f.o.b. (2004 est.)—food, beverages, tobacco, iron and steel.

Imports: $3.196 billion f.o.b. (2005 est.)—machinery and equipment, chemicals, fuels, food products.

External debt: $2.207 billion (2005 est.).

Transport and Communications

Railways: 699 km.

Roads: 8,684 km.

Telephones: 525,000 (2003).

Mobile cellular: 830,000 (2005).

Internet users: 392,671 (2004).

Internet country code: .mk

Madagascar

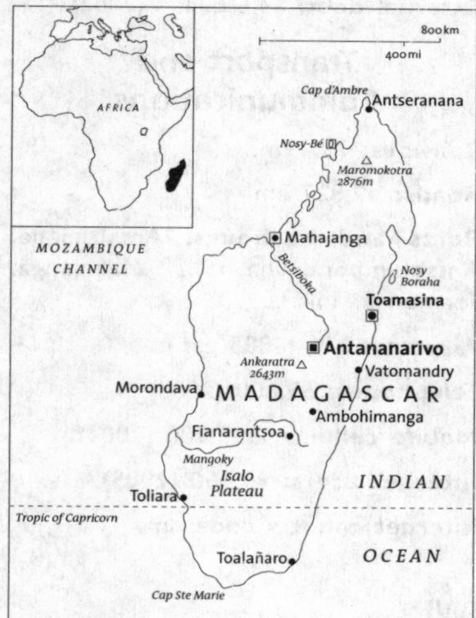

History

The first European known to have reach Madagascar was a Portuguese navigator named Diogo Dias, in 1500. The French soon followed.

In the early nineteenth century, a kingdom under Radama I took shape, uniting most of the island. The British allied with Radama I, giving him the title of king of Madagascar, and helped him against the French. In late nineteenth century, France succeeded in establishing a protectorate on the island. Madagascar gained independence in 1960 with Philibert Tsiranana as president.

Geography

Location: Southern Africa, island in the Indian Ocean, east of Mozambique.

Area: 587,040 sq. km.

Terrain: Narrow costal plain with a high plateau and mountains in the centre.

Natural resources: Graphite, chromite, coal, bauxite, salt, quartz, tar sands, semiprecious stones, mica, fish, hydropower.

Climate: Tropical along the coast, temperate further inland and arid in the south.

People

Population: 18,595,469 (July 2006 est.).

Population growth rate: 3.03% (2006 est.).

Sex ratio: 0.99 male(s)/female (2006 est.).

Religions: Indigenous beliefs 52%, Christian 41%, Muslim 7%.

Languages: French (official), Malagasy (official).

Literacy rate: Total 68.9%, Male 75.5%, Female 62.5% (2003 est.).

Infant mortality rate: 75.21 deaths/ live births (2006 est.).

Life expectancy: Total 57.34 years, Male 54.93 years, Female 59.82 years (2006 est.).

Government

Capital: Antananarivo.

Government type: Republic.

Independence: 26 June 1960 (from France).

Legal system: Based on French civil law system and traditional Malagasy law.

Executive branch:
Chief of state: President Marc Ravalomanana (since 6 May 2002).

Head of government: Prime Minister Jacques Sylla (since 27 May 2002).

Economy

Currency: Madagascar ariary.

GDP: Purchasing power parity—$16.36 billion (2005 est.).

GDP—real growth rate: 5.1% (2005 est.).

GDP—per capita: Purchasing power parity—$900 (2005 est.).

Inflation rate: 10.5% (2005 est.).

Population below poverty line: 50% (2004 est.).

Exports: $951 million f.o.b. (2005 est.)—coffee, vanilla, shellfish, sugar, cotton cloth, chromite, petroleum products.

Imports: $1.4 billion f.o.b. (2005 est.)—capital goods, petroleum, consumer goods, food.

External debt: $4.6 billion (2002).

Transport and Communications

Railways: 732 km.

Roads: 49,827 km.

Ports and harbours: Antsiranana, Antsohimbondrona, Mahajanga, Toamasina, Toliara.

Airports: 116 (2003 est.).

Telephones: 59,600 (2003).

Mobile cellular: 333,900 (2004).

Internet users: 90,000 (2005).

Internet country code: .mg

Malawi

History

David Livingstone was the first European to carry out in-depth exploration of the area in the nineteenth century. In 1884, Cecil Rhodes' British South African Company received a charter to develop the region. This brought the company into conflict with the Arab slave traders in the 1880s. In 1891 UK annexed the territory and established the Nyasaland Districts Protectorate. It was called the British Central Africa Protectorate from 1893 and Nyasaland from 1907. In 1964, Nyasaland gained independence as Malawi.

Geography

Location: Southern Africa, east of Zambia.

Area: 118,480 sq. km.

Terrain: Narrow elongated plateau with rolling plains, hills and some mountains.

Natural resources: Limestone, arable land, hydropower, uranium (unexploited), coal, and bauxite.

Climate: Subtropical climate with a rainy season from November to May and dry season from May to November.

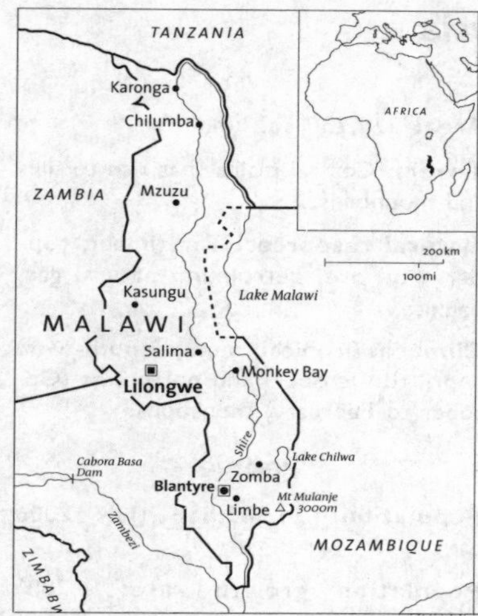

People

Population: 13,013,926 (2006 est.).

Population growth rate: 2.38% (2006 est.).

Sex ratio: 0.99 male(s)/female (2006 est.).

Religions: Christian 79.9%, Muslim 12.8%, other 3%, none 4.3% (1998 census).

Languages: Chichewa (official) 57.2%, Chinyanja 12.8%, Chiyao 10.1%, Chitumbuka 9.5%, Chisena 2.7%, Chilomwe 2.4%, Chitonga 1.7%, other 3.6% (1998 census).

Literacy rate: Total 62.7%, Male 76.1%, Female 49.8% (2003 est.).

Infant mortality rate: 94.37 deaths/1,000 live births (2006 est.).

Life expectancy: Total 41.7 years, Male 41.93 years, Female 41.45 years (2006 est.).

Government

Capital: Lilongwe.

Government type: Multiparty democracy.

Independence: 6 July 1964 (from UK).

Legal system: Based on English common law and customary law.

Executive branch:
Chief of state: President Bingu wa Mutharica (since 24 May 2004). The president is both the chief of state and head of government.

Economy

Currency: Malawian kwacha.

GDP: Purchasing power parity—$7.524 billion (2005 est.).

GDP—real growth rate: –3% (2005 est.).

GDP—per capita: Purchasing Power Parity—$600 (2005 est.).

Inflation rate: 15.4% (2005 est.).

Population below poverty line: 55% (2004 est.).

Exports: $364 million f.o.b. (2005 est.)—tobacco, tea, sugar, cotton, coffee, peanuts, wood products, apparel.

Imports: $645 million f.o.b. (2005 est.)—food, petroleum products, semi-manufactures, consumer goods, transportation equipment.

External debt: $3.284 billion (2005).

Transport and Communications

Railways: 797 km.

Roads: 28,400 km.

Telephones: 93,000 (2004).

Mobile cellular: 222,100 (2004).

Internet users: 46,100 (2003).

Internet country code: .mw

Malaysia

History

Malaya is believed to have been inhabitated for about 6000–8000 years. It is thought that there were small kingdoms in the region in the second and third centuries AD. It was at this point of time that Indian explorers first arrived in the area. Malacca, which was founded by Sumatran exiles around 1400, was taken by the Portuguese in 1511 and the Dutch in 1641.

The area subsequently came under British influence by 1867, when they founded the Straits Settlements which included Singapore, Malaya and Penang. In the nineteenth century, the Chinese began coming into this region. In 1941, the region was invaded by Japan.

In 1948, the British gave in to rising nationalism to form the semi-autonomous Federation of Malay. In 1957, Malay gained independence.

Geography

Location: South-eastern Asia, peninsula and northern one-third of the island of Borneo, bordering Indonesia and the South China Sea, south of Vietnam.

Area: 329,750 sq. km.

Terrain: Coastal plains that rise to hills and mountains.

Natural resources: Tin, timber, copper, iron ore, petroleum, natural gas, bauxite.

Climate: Tropical; annual south-west (April to October) and north-east (October to February) monsoons.

People

Population: 24,385,858 (July 2006 est.).

Population growth rate: 1.78% (2006 est.).

Sex ratio: 1.01 male(s)/female (2006 est.).

Religions: Muslim, Buddhist, Daoist, Hindu, Christian, Sikh. (In addition, Shamanism is practised in east Malaysia.)

Languages: Bahasa Melayu (official), English, Chinese dialects, Tamil, Telugu, Malayalam, Panjabi, Thai.

Literacy rate: Total 88.9%, Male 92.4%, Female 85.4% (2003 est.).

Infant mortality rate: 17.16 deaths/1,000 live births (2006 est.).

Life expectancy: Total 72.5 years, Male 69.8 years, Female 75.38 years (2006 est.).

Government

Capital: Kuala Lumpur.

Government type: Constitutional monarchy.

Independence: 31 August 1957 (from UK).

Legal system: Based on English common law.

Executive branch:
Chief of state: Paramount Ruler Tuanku Syed Sirajuddin ibni Almarhum Tuanku Syed Putra Jamalullail, the Raja of Perlis (since 12 December 2001).

Head of government: Prime Minister Abdullah bin Ahmad Badawi (since 31 October 2003).

Economy

Currency: Ringgit.

Economy—overview:
Malaysia is a middle-income country that transformed itself in the period between 1971 and the late 1990s from a producer of raw materials into an emerging multi-sector economy. In this period, growth was almost exclusively driven by exports, mainly of electronics. Consequently, the country was hard hit by the global economic downturn and the slump in the Information Technology (IT) sector in 2001. In 2001, GDP grew only by 0.5 per cent mainly due to an estimated 11 per cent fall in exports. However, a substantial fiscal stimulus package lessened the impact of the worst of the recession. The economy rebounded in 2002. It is unlikely that the country will experience a crisis similar to the one in 1997, thanks to its foreign exchange reserves and relatively small external debt. Nevertheless, the economy remains vulnerable to a prolonged slowdown in Japan and the US, which remain the top export destinations and key sources of foreign investment.

GDP: Purchasing power parity—$290.2 billion (2005 est.).

GDP—real growth rate: 5.3% (2005 est.).

GDP—per capita: Purchasing power parity—$12,100 (2005 est.).

Inflation rate: 2.9% (2005 est.).

Population below poverty line: 8% (1998 est.).

Unemployment rate: 3.6% (2005 est.).

Exports: $147.1 billion f.o.b. (2005 est.).

Imports: $118.7 billion f.o.b. (2005 est.).

External debt: $56.72 billion (30 June 2005 est.).

Transport and Communications

Railways: 1,890 km.

Roads: 65,877 km.

Telephones: 4,446,300 (2004).

Mobile cellular: 14,611,900 (2004).

Internet users: 10.04 million (2005).

Internet country code: .my

Maldives

History

In ancient times, Maldives was known as the source of cowrie shells that acted as a currency in parts of India, South Asia and the Middle East. Cowrie shells from Maldives have been found even at centres of the Indus Valley Civilization.

The first people likely to have settled down in the Maldives were members of south-west Indian fishing communities. Mentions of what is today Maldives can be found in some of the ancient chronicles of south India.

On 16 December 1887, the ruling monarch, Sultan Muinuddheen II, signed an agreement with the British governor

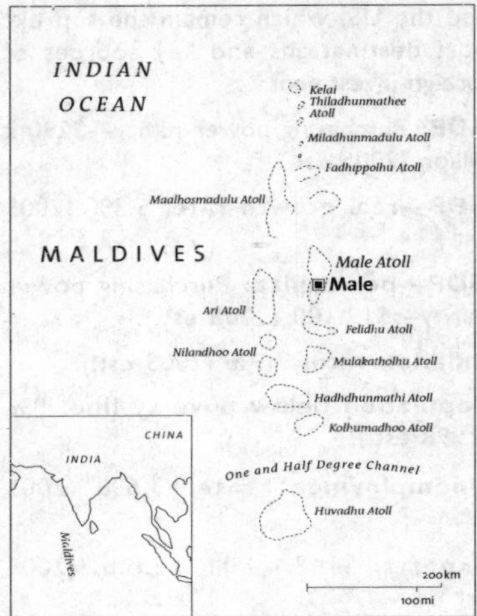

of Ceylon (now Sri Lanka). Under the terms of this agreement, Maldives became a British protectorate. On 26 July 1965, Maldives gained independence. On 11 November 1968, the sultanate was abolished and a republic was established.

Geography

Location: Southern Asia, group of atolls in the Indian Ocean, south-southwest of India.

Area: 300 sq. km.

Terrain: Flat, with white sandy beaches.

Natural resources: Fish.

Climate: Hot and humid tropical climate.

People

Population: 359,008 (July 2006 est.).

Population growth rate: 2.78% (2006 est.).

Sex ratio: 1.05 male(s)/female (2006 est.).

Religions: Sunni Muslim.

Languages: Maldivian Dhivehi (a dialect of Sinhala while the script is derived from Arabic), English spoken by most government officials.

Literacy rate: Total 97.2%, Male 97.1%, Female 97.3% (2003 est.).

Infant mortality rate: 54.89 deaths/1,000 live births (2006 est.).

Life expectancy: Total 64.41 years, Male 63.08 years, Female 65.8 years (2006 est.).

Government

Capital: Male.

Government type: Republic.

Independence: 26 July 1965 (from UK).

Legal system: Based on Islamic law with admixtures of English common law.

Executive branch:
Chief of state: President Maumoon Abdul Gayoom (since 11 November 1978). (The president is both the chief of state and head of government).

Economy

Currency: Rufiyaa.

Economy—overview:
Tourism is the largest industry of the country and accounts for 20 per cent of GDP and more than 60 per cent of its foreign exchange receipts. Import duties and tourism-related taxes contribute to over 90 per cent of the government's tax revenue.

Fishing is another key sector of the Maldivian economy. In 1989, the Maldivian government initiated an economic reform process. It lifted import quotas and allowed the private sector to export its products. It has allowed greater foreign investment. The country suffers from a shortage of cultivable land and domestic labour, which in turn imposes constraints on agriculture and manufacturing. Even basic commodities like food have to be imported. Industry consists mainly of boat building, garment production and handicrafts and accounts for about 18 per cent of GDP. One major future source of concern for the Maldivian authorities is the global warming and subsequent rise in sea levels. Maldives is a low-lying country with 80 per cent of the area lying at a height of one metre or less above sea level.

GDP: Purchasing power parity—$1.25 billion (2002 est.).

GDP—real growth rate: 2.3% (2002 est.).

GDP—per capita: Purchasing power parity—$3,900 (2002 est.).

Inflation rate: 1% (2002 est.).

Exports: $123 million f.o.b. (2004 est.).

Imports: $645 million f.o.b. (2004 est.).

External debt: $281 million (2003 est.).

Transport and Communications

Railways: None.

Roads: Not available.

Telephones: 31,500 (2004).

Mobile cellular: 113,200 (2004).

Internet users: 19,000 (2005).

Internet country code: .mv

Mali

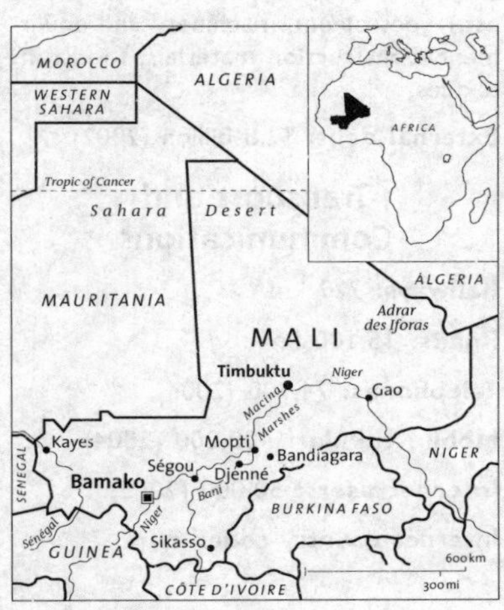

History

Human remains dating back to 5000 BC have been found in Mali. The region's gold deposits and trade in a variety of commodities resulted in the developing of trading centres like Timbuktu and Djenne-Jeno. It has also been on the trans-Saharan caravan routes from the first century AD.

Towards the end of the nineteenth century, the area came under French domination. In 1904, it became a French colony. In 1920, it was renamed French Sudan. In November 1958, the territory became an autonomous state within the French Community, with the name Sudanese Republic. In September 1960, the republic of Mali was proclaimed.

Geography

Location: Western Africa, bordering Algeria and Niger.

Area: 1,240,000 sq. km.

Terrain: Mostly flat or rolling northern plains covered by sand; savanna in the south and rugged hills in the north-east.

Natural resources: Gold, phosphates, kaolin, salt, limestone, uranium, hydropower; the country also has unexploited deposits of bauxite, iron ore, manganese, tin, and copper.

Climate: Subtropical to arid.

People

Population: 11,716,829 (July 2006 est.).

Population growth rate: 2.63% (2006 est.).

Sex ratio: 0.98 male(s)/female (2006 est.).

Religions: Muslim 90%, indigenous beliefs 9%, Christian 1%.

Languages: French (official), Bambara 80%, numerous African languages.

Literacy rate: Total 46.4%, Male 53.5%, Female 39.6% (2003 est.).

Infant mortality rate: 107.58 deaths/1,000 live births (2006 est.).

Life expectancy: Total 49 years, Male 47.05 years, Female 51.01 years (2006 est.).

Government

Capital: Bamako.

Government type: Republic.

Independence: 22 September 1960 (from France).

Legal system: Based on French civil law system and customary law.

Executive branch:

Chief of state: President Amadou Toumani Toure (since 8 June 2002).

Head of government: Prime Minister Ousmane Issoufi Maiga (since 30 April 2004).

Economy

Currency: Communaute Financiere Africaine franc.

GDP: Purchasing power parity—$13.56 billion (2005 est.).

GDP—real growth rate: 6% (2005 est.).

GDP—per capita: Purchasing power parity—$1,200 (2005 est.).

Inflation rate: 4.5% (2002 est.).

Population below poverty line: 64% (2001 est.).

Unemployment rate: 14.6% (2001 est.).

Exports: $323 million f.o.b. (2004 est.)—cotton, gold, livestock.

Imports: $1.858 billion f.o.b. (2004 est.)—petroleum, machinery and equipment, construction materials, foodstuff, textiles.

External debt: $2.8 billion (2002).

Transport and Communications

Railways: 729 km.

Roads: 15,100 km.

Telephones: 74,900 (2004).

Mobile cellular: 400,000 (2004).

Internet users: 50,000 (2005).

Internet country code: .ml

Malta

History

Malta passed through to the Arabs, Normans and a series of feudal rulers. In 1530, the Order of the Hospital of St. John of Jerusalem (the Knights Hospitalers), a religious and military order of the Roman Catholic Church, obtained control of the islands.

In the early nineteenth century, the Maltese people acknowledged British sovereignty. During World War II, the islands frustrated Axis invasion attempts and became one of the most heavily

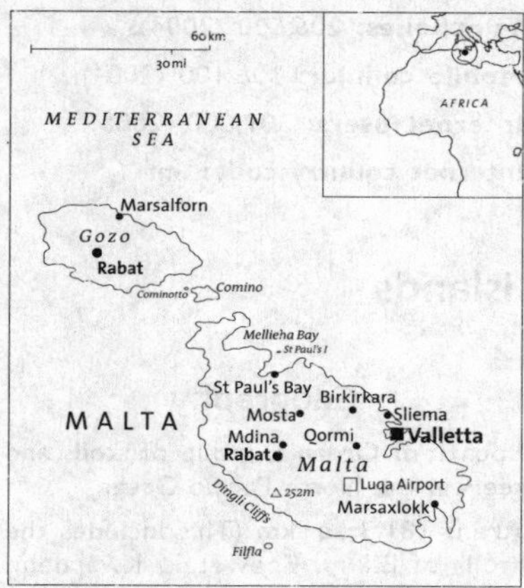

bombed targets during the War. UK rewarded the entire island with George Cross, its highest civilian decoration. Even today, the flag of Malta bears a representation of the medal of the George Cross.

Malta became an independent country within the Commonwealth on 21 September 1964 and a republic on 13 December 1974.

Malta became a member of the EU in May 2004.

Geography

Location: Southern Europe, islands in the Mediterranean Sea, south of Sicily (Italy).

Area: 316 sq. km.

Natural resources: Limestone, salt, arable land.

Climate: Mediterranean climate with mild, rainy winters and hot, dry summers.

People

Population: 400,214 (July 2006 est.).

Population growth rate: 0.42% (2006 est.).

Sex ratio: 0.99 male(s)/female (2006 est.).

Religions: Roman Catholic 98%.

Languages: Maltese (official), English (official).

Literacy rate: Total 92.8%, Male 92%, Female 93.6% (2003 est.).

Infant mortality rate: 3.86 deaths/1,000 live births (2006 est.).

Life expectancy: Total 79.01 years, Male 76.83 years, Female 81.31 years (2006 est).

Government

Capital: Valletta.

Government type: Republic.

Independence: 21 September 1964 (from UK).

Legal system: Based on English common law and Roman civil law.

Executive branch:
Chief of state: President Eddie Fenech Adami (since 4 April 2004).

Head of government: Prime Minister Lawrence Gonzi (since 23 March 2004).

Economy

Currency: Maltese lira.

GDP: Purchasing power parity—$7.926 billion (2005 est.).

GDP—real growth rate: 1% (2005 est.).

GDP—per capita: Purchasing power parity—$19,900 (2005 est.).

Inflation rate: 2.8% (2005 est.).

Unemployment rate: 7.8% (2005 est.).

Exports: $2.744 billion f.o.b. (2005 est.)—machinery and transport equipment, manufactures.

Imports: $3.859 billion f.o.b. (2005 est.)—machinery and transport equipment, manufactured and semi-manufactured goods, food, drink, and tobacco.

External debt: $188.8 million (2005).

Transport and Communications

Railways: None.

Roads: 2,222 km.

Telephones: 206,500 (2004).

Mobile cellular: 306,100 (2004).

Internet users: 301,000 (2005).

Internet country code: .mt

Marshall Islands

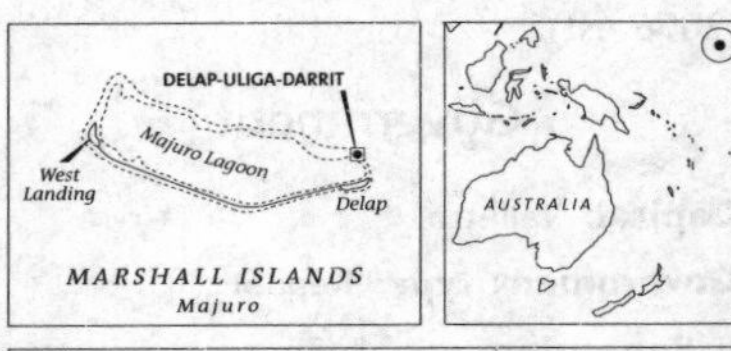

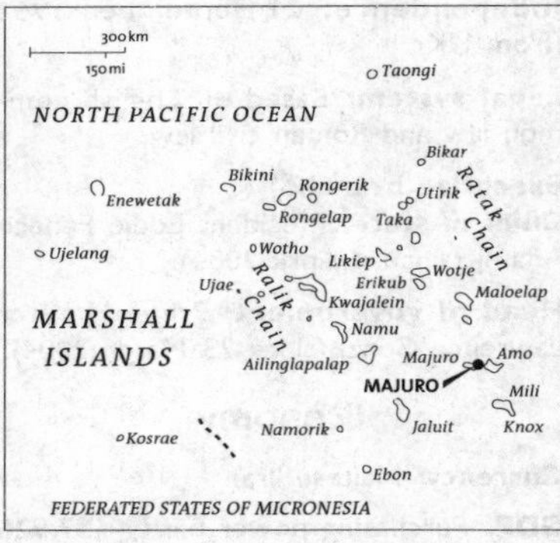

History

The Spanish explored the islands in the sixteenth century. In 1788, they were named after a British captain. In 1947, the United Nations placed the Marshall Islands, along with the Mariana and Caroline Islands, under a US Trust Territory. Between 1946 and 1958, the US carried out nuclear tests on the Bikini and Enewetak islands. In 1983, the US paid $183.7 million as damages for contamination of the islands due to nuclear testing. Another $3.8 million was paid later to the displaced islanders of Bikini. In 1986, Marshall Islands attained self-government after entering into a Compact of Free Association.

Geography

Location: Oceania, group of atolls and reefs in the North Pacific Ocean.

Area: 181.3 sq. km (This includes the atolls of Bikini, Enewetak, Kwajalein, Majuro, Rongelap, and Utirik).

Natural resources: Coconut products, marine products, deep seabed minerals.

Climate: Hot and humid climate.

People

Population: 60,422 (July 2006 est.).

Population growth rate: 2.25% (2006 est.).

Sex ratio: 1.04 male(s)/female (2006 est.).

Religions: Christian (mostly Protestant).

Languages: Marshallese 98.2%, other languages 1.8% (1999 census). English is widely spoken as a second language; both English and Marshallese are official languages. Two major Marshallese dialects are from the Malayo-Polynesian family, Japanese.

Literacy rate: Total 93.7%, Male 93.6%, Female 93.7% (1999).

Infant mortality rate: 28.43% (2006 est.).

Life expectancy: Total 70.31 years, Male 68.33 years, Female 72.39 years (2006 est.).

Government

Capital: Majuro.

Government type: Constitutional government in free association with the US.

Independence: 21 October 1986 (from the US-administered UN trusteeship).

Legal system: Based on adapted Trust Territory laws, acts of the legislature, municipal, common, and customary laws.

Executive branch:
Chief of state: President Kessai Hesa Note (since 5 January 2004). The president is both the chief of state and head of government.

Economy

Currency: US Dollar.

GDP: Purchasing power parity—$115 million (2001 est.).

GDP—real growth rate: 1% (2001 est.).

GDP—per capita: Purchasing power parity—$1,600 (2001 est.).

Inflation rate: 2% (2001 est.).

Exports: $9 million f.o.b. (2000)—copra cake, coconut oil, handicrafts, fish.

Imports: $54 million f.o.b. (2000)—foodstuff, machinery and equipment, fuels, beverages and tobacco.

External debt: $86.5 million (2000 est.).

Transport and Communications

Railways: None.

Roads: 64.5 km.

Telephones: 5,510 (2004).

Mobile cellular: 1,198 (2004).

Internet users: 2,000 (2005).

Internet country code: .mh

Mauritania

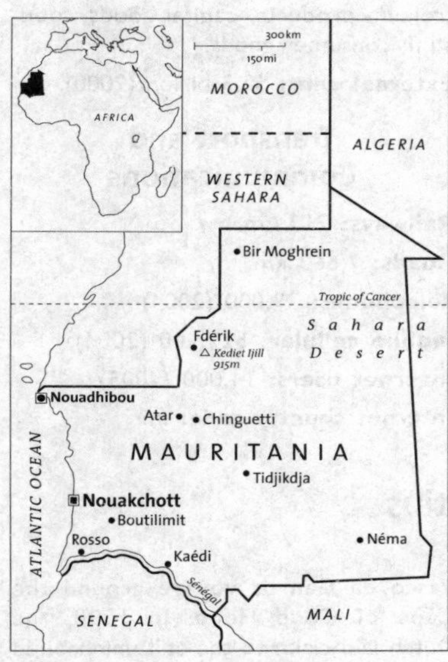

History

The earliest settlers of Mauritania were the sub-Saharan peoples and the Berbers. In the fifteenth century, Arab tribes reached Mauritania via a caravan route that linked the region with Morocco. This gave rise to a mixed Arab-Berber culture.

In 1904, Mauritania became a French colony. In 1920, it became a part of French West Africa and was administered from Senegal. Mauritania gained independence in November 1960.

Geography

Location: Northern Africa, bordering the North Atlantic Ocean, between Senegal and Western Sahara.

Area: 1,030,700 sq. km.

Terrain: Barren flat plains with some hills in the central part of the country.

Natural resources: Iron ore, gypsum, copper, phosphate, diamonds, gold, oil, fish.

Climate: Hot, dry, dusty desert climate.

People

Population: 3,177,388 (July 2006 est.).

Population growth rate: 2.88% (2006 est.).

Sex ratio: 0.98 male(s)/female (2006 est.).

Religions: Muslim 100%.

Languages: Hassaniya Arabic (official), Pulaar, Soninke, Wolof (official), French.

Literacy rate: Total 41.7%, Male 51.8%, Female 31.9% (2003 est.).

Infant mortality rate: 69.48 deaths/ 1,000 live births (2006 est.).

Life expectancy: Total 53.12 years, Male 50.88 years, Female 5.42 years (2006 est.).

Government

Capital: Nouakchott.

Government type: Republic.

Independence: 28 November 1960 (from France).

Legal system: A combination of Shari'a (Islamic law) and French civil law.

Executive branch:
Chief of state: President Col Ely Ould Mohamed Vall, whose Military Council for Justice and Democracy deposed longtime President Maaouya Ould Sid Ahmed Taya in a coup on 3 August 2005.
Head of government: Prime Minister Sidi Mohamed Ould Boubakar (since 6 August 2005).

Economy

Currency: Ouguiya.

GDP: Purchasing power parity—$6.891 billion (2005 est.).

GDP—real growth rate: 5.5% (2005 est.).

GDP—per capita: Purchasing power parity—$2,200 (2005 est.).

Inflation rate: 7% (2005 est.).

Population below poverty line: 40% (2004 est.).

Unemployment rate: 20% (2004 est.).

Exports: $784 million f.o.b. (2004)—iron ore, fish and fish products, gold.

Imports: $1.124 million f.o.b. (2004)—machinery and equipment, petroleum products, capital goods, foodstuff, consumer goods.

External debt: $2.5 billion (2000).

Transport and Communications

Railways: 717 km.

Roads: 7,660 km.

Telephones: 39,000 (2004).

Mobile cellular: 522,400 (2004).

Internet users: 14,000 (2005).

Internet country code: .mr

Mauritius

History

In 1498, Portuguese explorers chanced upon the island in the aftermath of Vasco da Gama's voyage around the Cape of Good Hope. In 1598, the Dutch laid claim to the still uninhabited island and renamed it after their head

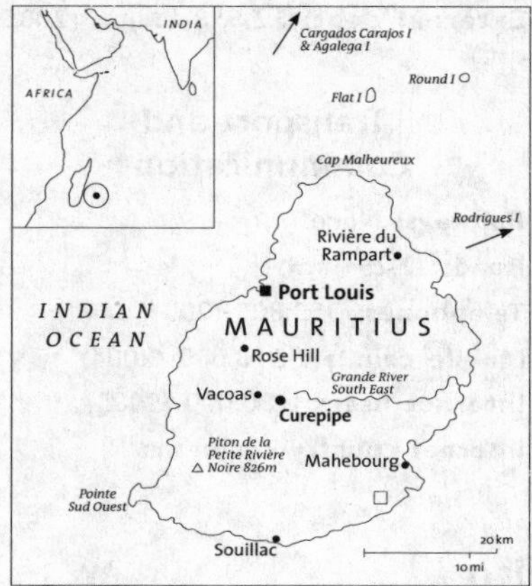

of state, Maurice, Prince of Orange.

In 1715, the French East India Company laid claim to Mauritius. They started settling the island from the 1720s and founded Port Louis as a staging ground for attacking the British in India. In 1834, the British abolished slavery. As a replacement for slavery, the British introduced the system of indentured labour. This led to the arrival of hundreds of thousands of workers from India.

In 1926, the first Indo-Mauritians were elected to government council. Internal self-government was introduced in 1957. Mauritius finally gained independence in March 1968.

Geography

Location: Southern Africa, island in the Indian Ocean, east of Madagascar.

Area: 2,040 sq. km (this includes Agalega Islands, Cargados Carajos Shoals [Saint Brandon], and Rodrigues).

Natural resources: Arable land, fish.

Climate: Tropical climate.

People

Population: 1,240,827 (July 2006 est.).

Population growth rate: 0.82% (2006 est.).

Sex ratio: 0.97 male(s)/female (2006 est.).

Religions: Hindu 48%, Roman Catholic 23.6%, other Christian 8.6%, Muslim 16.6%, other 2.5%, unspecified 0.3%, none 0.4%

Languages: Creole 80.5%, Bhojpuri 12.1%, French 3.4%, English (official; spoken by less than 1% of the population), other 3.7%, unspecified 0.3%.

Literacy rate: Total 85.6%, Male 88.6%, Female 82.7% (2003 est.).

Infant mortality rate: 15.03 deaths/1,000 live births (2005 est.).

Life expectancy: Total 72.63 years, Male 68.66 years, Female 76.66 years (2006 est.).

Government

Capital: Port Louis.

Government type: Parliamentary democracy.

Independence: 12 March 1968 (from UK).

Legal system: Based on French civil law system with aspects of English common law in some areas.

Executive branch:
Chief of state: President Sir Anerood Jugnauth (since 7 October 2003).

Head of government: Prime Minister Navinchandra Ramgoolam (since 5 July 2005).

Economy

Currency: Mauritian rupee.

GDP: Purchasing power parity—$16.09 billion (2005 est.).

GDP—real growth rate: 3% (2005 est.).

GDP—per capita: Purchasing power parity—$13,300 (2005 est.).

Inflation rate: 5.6% (2005 est.).

Population below poverty line: 10% (2001 est.).

Unemployment rate: 10.5% (2005 est).

Exports: $1.949 billion f.o.b. (2005 est.)—clothing and textiles, sugar, cut flowers, molasses.

Imports: $2.507 billion f.o.b. (2005 est.)—manufactured goods, capital equipment, foodstuff, petroleum products, chemicals.

External debt: $2.958 billion (2005 est.).

Transport and Communications

Railways: None.

Roads: 2,254 km.

Telephones: 353,800 (2004).

Mobile cellular: 510,000 (2004).

Internet users: 180,000 (2005).

Internet country code: .mu

Mexico

History

The region that comprises present-day Mexico has been the home of ancient civilizations such as the Olmec, Toltec, Mayan and Aztec. The Aztec empire was still expanding when the Spanish appeared on the scene in 1519. The empire finally came to an end with the conquest of the Aztec capital, Tenochtitlan, in 1521 by forces led by the Spanish explorer, Hernan Cortes. The Spanish conquered the remains of the Mayan civilization in the mid-sixteenth century and by 1681, Mexico had become a part of the viceroyalty of New Spain.

The first major revolt against the Spanish came in 1810 and independence was finally negotiated in 1821. In 1823, Mexico became a republic.

In 1845, Mexico lost Texas to the USA and following defeat in the Mexican War (1846–8) and the subsequent signing of the Treaty of Guadelupe Hidalgo, it had to give up vast stretches that today constitute western and south-western USA.

Geography

Location: Middle America, bordered with the Caribbean Sea and the Gulf of Mexico between Belize and the USA.

Area: 1,972,550 sq. km.

Terrain: High, rugged mountains, low coastal plains, high plateaus and even desert areas.

Natural resources: Mexico has deposits of petroleum, silver, copper, gold, lead, zinc, natural gas, timber.

Climate: Varies from tropical to desert.

People

Population: 107,449,525 (July 2006 est.).

Population growth rate: 1.16% (2006 est.).

Sex ratio: 0.96 male(s)/female (2006 est.).

Religions: Nominally Roman Catholic 89%, Protestant 6%, others 5%.

Languages: Spanish, various Mayan, Nahuatl, and other regional indigenous languages.

Literacy rate: 92.2% (2003 est.).

Infant mortality rate: 20.26 deaths/ 1,000 live births (2006 est.).

Life expectancy: Total 75.41 years, Male 72.63 years, Female 78.33 years (2006 est.).

Government

Capital: Mexico City.

Government type: Federal republic.

Independence: 16 September 1810, from Spain.

Legal system: Mixture of US constitutional theory and civil law system.

Executive branch:
Chief of state: President Vicente Fox Quesada (since 1 December 2000). The president is both the chief of state and head of government.

Economy

Currency: Mexican peso.

Economy—overview:
Mexico has a free market economy with a mixture of modern and obsolete industry and agriculture. There is an increasing level of domination of the private sector. Recent years have seen increased competition in key infrastructures like telecommunications, electricity, airports, seaports, railroads and natural gas distribution.

The economy is marked by a chronic unequal distribution of income. Ever since NAFTA was implemented in 1994, trade with the US and Canada has tripled. The economy registered a growth of 6.9 per cent in 2000, but real GDP decreased by 0.3 per cent in 2001. In 2002, there was only a nominal rise of 1 per cent. The main cause behind this downturn was the slowdown in the USA.

Mexico has implemented free trade agreements with Guatemala, Honduras, El Salvador, and the European Free Trade Area. This means that more than 90 per cent of the country's trade is now under free trade agreements. In 2001, foreign direct investment touched $25 billion although half of this came from one single case—Citigroup's acquisition of Mexico's second-largest bank, Banamex.

GDP: Purchasing power parity—$1.067 trillion (2005 est.).

GDP—real growth rate: 3% (2005 est.).

GDP—per capita: Purchasing power parity—$10,000 (2005 est.).

Inflation rate: 4.1% (2005 est.).

Population below poverty line: 40% (2003 est.).

Unemployment rate: 3.6% plus considerable underemployment, of perhaps 25% (2005 est.).

Exports: $213.7 billion f.o.b. (2005 est.).

Imports: $223.7 billion f.o.b. (2005 est.).

External debt: $174.3 billion (30 June 2005 est.).

Transport and Communications

Railways: 17,634 km.

Roads: 329,532 km.

Telephones: 18,073,200 (2004).

Mobile cellular: 38,451,100 (2004).

Internet users: 10,033,000 (2003).

Internet country code: .mx

Federated States of Micronesia

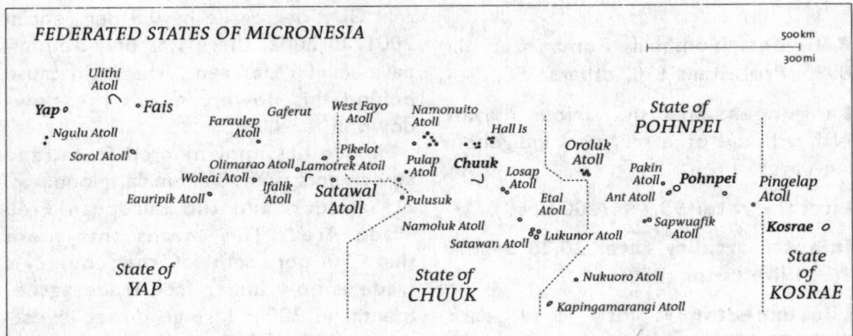

History

In the seventeenth century, Spain colonized the islands of present-day Micronesia that were originally inhabited by Polynesians and Micronesians. In April 1947, the United Nations created the Trust Territory of the Pacific Islands that placed the Caroline, Northern Mariana and Marshall Islands under US administration. In 1979, the Micronesian Federation attained self-governance and in 1983, the islands accepted the Compact of Free Association with the USA. It became independent in 1986 when the US government declared the Trust Territory agreements no longer effective. In 1991, the Micronesian Federation became a member of the United Nations.

Geography

Location: Island group in the North Pacific Ocean.

Area: 702 sq. km. This includes Pohnpei (Ponape), Chuuk (Truk) Islands, Yap Islands, and Kosrae (Kosaie).

Natural resources: Forests, marine products, deep-seabed minerals.

Climate: Tropical climate with heavy rainfall round the year mainly in the eastern islands.

People

Population: 108,004 (July 2006 est.).

Population growth rate: –0.11% (2006 est.).

Sex ratio: 1.05 male(s)/female (2005 est.).

Religions: Roman Catholic 50%, Protestant 47%.

Languages: English (official and common language), Kapingamarangi, Kosrean, Nukuoro, Pohnpeian, Trukese, Ulithian, Woleaian, Yapese.

Literacy rate: Total 89%, Male 91%, Female 88% (1980 est.).

Infant mortality rate: 29.16 deaths/1,000 live births (2006 est.).

Life expectancy: Total 70.05 years, Male 68.24 years, Female 71.95 years (2006 est.).

Government

Capital: Palikir.

Government type: Constitutional government in free association with the US.

Independence: 3 November 1986 (from the US-administered UN Trusteeship).

Legal system: Based on adapted Trust Territory laws, acts of the legislature, municipal, common, and customary laws.

Executive branch:
Chief of state: President Joseph J. Urusemal (since 11 May 2003); Vice-President Redley Killion. The president is both the chief of state and head of government.

Economy

Currency: US Dollar.

GDP: Purchasing power parity—$277 million.

GDP—real growth rate: 1% (2002 est.).

GDP—per capita: Purchasing power parity—$2,000 (2002 est.).

Inflation rate: 1% (2002 est.).

Population below poverty line: 26.7% (1999 est.).

Unemployment rate: 16% (1999 est.).

Exports: $22 million f.o.b. (2000 est.)—fish, garments, banana, black pepper.

Imports: $149 million f.o.b. (2000 est.)—food, manufactured goods, machinery and equipment, beverages.

External debt: $53.1 million (2003 est.).

Transport and Communications

Railways: None.

Roads: 240 km.

Telephones: 12,000 (2004).

Mobile cellular: 12,800 (2004).

Internet users: 12,000 (2005).

Internet country code: .fm

Moldova

History

The principality of Moldavia came under Ottoman Turk rule in the sixteenth century. Russia acquired Moldavian territory in 1791 and again in 1812. In 1918, Romania acquired the rest of the Moldavian territory that had remained with Turkey. In 1924, the Autonomous Soviet Socialist Republic of Moldavia was formed. In 1991, Moldavian Soviet Socialist Republic proclaimed its independence and changed its name to the Romanian spelling, Moldova.

The poorest nation in Europe, Moldova became the first former Soviet state to elect a Communist as its president in 2001.

Geography

Location: Eastern Europe, north-east of Romania.

Area: 33,843 sq. km.

Natural resources: Lignite, phosphorites, gypsum, arable land, limestone.

Climate: Moderate winters and warm summers.

People

Population: 4,466,706 (July 2006 est.).

Population growth rate: 0.28% (2006 est.).

Sex ratio: 0.91 male(s)/female (2006 est.).

Religions: Eastern Orthodox 98%, Jewish 1.5%, Baptist and others 0.5% (2000).

Languages: Moldovan (official), Russian, Gagauz (a Turkish dialect).

Literacy rate: Total 99.1%, Male 99.6%, Female 98.7% (2003 est.).

Infant mortality rate: 38.38 deaths/1,000 live births (2006 est.).

Life expectancy: Total 65.65 years, Male 61.61 years, Female 69.88 years (2006 est.).

Government

Capital: Chisinau.

Government type: Republic.

Independence: 27 August 1991 (from Soviet Union).

Legal system: Based on civil law system.

Executive branch:

Chief of state: President Vladimir Voronin (since 4 April 2001).

Head of government: Prime Minister Vasile Tarlev (since 15 April 2001).

Economy

Currency: Moldovan leu.

GDP: Purchasing power parity—$8.175 billion (2005 est.).

GDP—real growth rate: 7.1% (2005 est.).

GDP—per capita: Purchasing power parity—$1,800 (2005 est.).

Inflation rate: 12% (2005 est.).

Population below poverty line: 80% (2001 est.).

Unemployment rate: 8% (2002 est.).

Exports: $1.04 billion f.o.b. (2005 est.)—foodstuff, textiles, machinery.

Imports: $2.23 billion f.o.b. (2005 est.)—mineral products and fuel, machinery and equipment, chemicals, textiles (2000).

External debt: $1.926 billion (2005 est.).

Transport and Communications

Railways: 1,138 km.

Roads: 12,730 km.

Telephones: 863,400 (2004).

Mobile cellular: 787,000 (2004).

Internet users: 406,000 (2005).

Internet country code: .md

Monaco

History

In 1297 a member the Grimaldi family from the Italian city of Genoa, Francois Grimaldi, seized power in Monaco. Between 1524 and 1641, the Grimaldi family allied itself with Spain, and Monaco came under Spanish protection. In

1949, Prince Rainier III succeeded to the throne after the death of his grandfather, Louis II. In 1956, Prince Rainier married Hollywood actress Grace Kelly.

Geography

Location: Western Europe, bordering the Mediterranean Sea on the southern coast of France, near the border with Italy.

Area: 1.95 sq. km.

Terrain: Hilly, rugged and rocky terrain.

Natural resources: None.

Climate: Mediterranean climate.

People

Population: 32,543 (July 2006 est.).

Population growth rate: 0.4% (2006 est.).

Sex ratio: 0.91 male(s)/female (2006 est.).

Religions: Roman Catholic 90%.

Languages: French (official), English, Italian, Monegasque.

Literacy rate: 99%.

Infant mortality rate: 5.35 deaths/ 1,000 live births (2006 est.).

Life expectancy: Total 79.69 years, Male 75.85 years, Female 83.74 years (2006 est.).

Government

Capital: Monaco.

Government type: Constitutional monarchy.

Independence: 1419 (date on which the rule of the House of Grimaldi began in earnest).

Legal system: Based on French law.

Executive branch:
Chief of state: Prince Albert II (since 6 April 2005).

Head of government: Minister of State Jean-Paul Proust (since 1 June 2005).

Economy

Currency: Euro.

Economy—overview:
Monaco is a small prosperous nation famous for its high living standards, tourism industry and gambling. It is also a frequent destination for cruise ships, and a major construction project in 2001 installed a floating jetty to extend the pier used by cruise ships in the main harbour. In recent years, however, the country has initiated a process of diversification into services and small non-polluting industries. The state levies no income tax on residents of the principality and business taxes are low. These two factors have established Monaco as a tax haven not only for wealthy individuals but also for foreign companies. Although the banking system in Monaco is run by the French banking commission, the principality has strict laws that restrict the revealing of information to outsiders. This has led to accusations of money laundering in the country. A number of industrial sectors are state-owned monopolies. However, Monaco does not publish national income figures. This makes it difficult to generate economic data for the country.

GDP: Purchasing power parity—$870 million (2000 est.).

GDP—real growth rate: 0.9% (2000 est.).

GDP—per capita: Purchasing power parity—$27,000 (2000 est.).

Inflation rate: 1.9% (2000).

Unemployment rate: 22% (1999).

External debt: $18 billion (2000 est.).

Transport and Communications

Railways: 1.7 km.

Roads: 50 km.

Telephones: 33,700 (2002).

Mobile cellular: 19,300 (2002).

Internet users: 16,000 (2002).

Internet country code: .mc

Mongolia

History

Between the fourth and tenth centuries, Turkic-speaking people dominated the region. The famous Genghis Khan united the Mongols under one umbrella and also conquered large swathes of Central Asia.

Inner Mongolia became a part of China in 1644. With the fall of the Ch'ing dynasty, Mongols declared independence from China in 1911 and finally drove away the Chinese with Russian assistance in 1921.

Geography

Location: Northern Asia, between China and Russia.

Area: 1,564,116 sq. km.

Terrain: Vast semi-desert and desert plains, grassy steppes, mountains in the west and south-west; Gobi Desert in south-central.

Natural resources: Oil, coal, copper, molybdenum, tungsten, phosphates, tin, nickel, zinc, wolfram, fluorspar, gold, silver, iron, phosphate.

Climate: Desert.

People

Population: 2,832,224 (July 2006 est.).

Population growth rate: 1.46% (2006 est.).

Sex ratio: 1 male(s)/female (2006 est.).

Religions: Buddhist Lamaism 50%, Muslim (primarily in the south-west) 4%, Shamanist and Christian 6% (2006 est.).

Languages: Khalkha Mongol 90%, Turkic, Russian.

Literacy rate: Total 97.8%, Male 98%, Female 97.5% (2002 est.).

Infant mortality rate: 52.12 deaths/1,000 live births (2006 est.).

Life expectancy: Total 64.89 years, Male 62.64 years, Female 67.25 years (2006 est.).

Government

Capital: Ulaanbaatar.

Government type: Mixed parliamentary/presidential.

Independence: 11 July 1921 (from China).

Legal system: Mixture of Soviet, German, and US systems of law that combines aspects of a parliamentary system with some aspects of a presidential system.

Executive branch:
Chief of state: President Nambaryn Enkhbayar (since 24 June 2005).

Head of government: Prime Minister Miegombyn Enkhbold (since 25 January 2006).

Economy

Currency: Togrog/Tugrik.

Economy—overview:
Traditionally, economic activity in Mongolia has been based on agriculture and breeding of livestock. But the country also possesses large deposits of metals like copper, coal, molybdenum, tin, tungsten, and gold that account for a substantial portion of industrial production. At one point of time, Soviet Russian assistance accounted for as much as one-third of GDP. But this vanished almost overnight at the time of the disintegration of the USSR in 1990–1. The deep recession that Mongolia experienced as a result was compounded by the ruling party's reluctance to launch any major and meaningful economic reform. The later Democratic Coalition (DC) government initiated widespread liberalization and the opening up of the country's economy across various sectors. Economic growth hit a roadblock in 1996 due to a number of natural disasters and falling prices of copper and cashmere, but picked up during 1997–99. Mongolia was hit by a temporary Russian ban on exports of oil and oil products in August and September 1999. Mongolia joined the World Trade Organization (WTO) in 1997 and the international donor community pledged over $300 million per year at the Consultative Group Meeting held in Ulaanbaatar in June 1999. The country also suffers from a heavy burden of external debt. Real GDP growth in 2000–1 was held down by a number of factors, namely falling prices for Mongolia's primary sector exports, internal opposition to privatization, and adverse effects of weather on agriculture in early 2000 and 2001. In 2002, however, even though the country was hit by a drought, GDP rose by 4 per cent. This was followed by a 5 per cent rise in 2003. Russia claims Mongolia owes it $11 billion from the old Soviet period.

GDP: Purchasing power parity—$5.242 billion (2005 est.).

GDP—real growth rate: 6.2% official estimate (2005).

GDP—per capita: Purchasing power parity—$1,900 (2005 est.).

Inflation rate: 9.5% (2005 est.).

Population below poverty line: 36.1% (2004 est.).

Unemployment rate: 6.7% (2003).

Exports: $852 million f.o.b. (2004 est.).

Imports: $1.011 billion c.i.f. (2004 est.).

External debt: $1.36 billion (2004 est.).

Transport and Communications

Railways: 1,810 km.

Roads: 49,256 km.

Telephones: 142,300 (2004).

Mobile cellular: 404,400 (2004).

Internet users: 200,000 (2005).

Internet country code: .mn

Montenegro

History

From the sixteenth to nineteenth centuries, Montenegro became a theocratic state ruled by a series of bishop princes. In 1852, it was transformed into a secular principality. Montenegro was absorbed into the newly-formed Yugoslavia at the end of World War I.

After the conclusion of World War II, it became a constituent republic of the Socialist Federal Republic of Yugoslavia. When the latter dissolved in 1992, Montenegro federated with Serbia, first as the Federal Republic of Yugoslavia and, after 2003, in a looser union of Serbia and Montenegro. Following a three-year postponement, Montenegro held an independence referendum in the spring of 2006 under rules set by the EU. The vote for severing ties with Serbia exceeded the 55 per cent threshold, allowing Montenegro to formally declare its independence on 3 June 2006.

Geography

Location: Southeastern Europe, between the Adriatic Sea and Serbia.

Area: 13,812 sq km.

Terrain: Highly indented coastline with narrow coastal plain backed by rugged high limestone mountains and plateaus.

Natural resources: Bauxite, hydroelectricity.

Climate: Mediterranean climate, hot dry summers and autumns and relatively cold winters with heavy snowfalls inland.

People

Population: 630,548 (2004).

Population growth rate: 3.5% (2004).

Religions: Orthodox, Muslim, Roman Catholic

Languages: Serbian (Ijekavian dialect—official)

Government

Capital: Podgorica (administrative capital); Cetinje (capital city).

Government type: Republic.

Independence: 3 June 2006 (from Serbia and Montenegro); note: a referendum on independence was held 21 May 2006.

Legal system: based on civil law system.

Executive branch:

Chief of state: President Filip Vujanovic (since 11 May 2003).

Head of government: Prime Minister Milo Djukanovic (since 8 January 2003).

Economy

Currency: Euro.

Economy—overview:
The republic of Montenegro severed its economy from federal control and from Serbia during the Milosevic era and continues to maintain its own central bank, uses the euro instead of the Yugoslav dinar as official currency, collects customs tariffs, and manages its own budget. The dissolution of the loose political union between Serbia and Montenegro in 2006 led to separate membership in several international financial institutions, such as the IMF, World Bank, and the European Bank for Reconstruction and Development. Montenegro is pursuing its own membership in the World Trade Organization as well as negotiating a Stabilization and Association agreement with the

European Union in anticipation of eventual membership. Severe unemployment remains a key political and economic problem for this entire region. Montenegro has privatized its large aluminum complex, its dominant industry, as well as most of its financial sector, and has begun to attract foreign direct investment in the tourism sector.

GDP: Purchasing power parity—$2.412 billion (2005 est.).

GDP—per capita: Purchasing power parity—$3,800 (2005 est.).

Unemployment rate: 27.7% (2005).

Population below poverty line: 12.2% (2003).

Inflation rate: 3.4% (2004).

Exports: $171.3 million (2003).

Imports: $601.7 million (2003).

Transport and Communications

Telephones: 177,663 (2005).

Mobile cellular: 543,220 (2005).

Internet users: 50,000 (2004).

Internet country code: .cg.yu.

Railways: 250 km.

Roadways: 7,353 km.

Morocco

History

Since the second millennium BC, Morocco has been the home of the Berber people. The Arab invasion came around 685. In 1660, the Alawite dynasty came to power. This dynasty rules Morocco to this day. The European powers became interested in establishing colonies in Morocco in the nineteenth century. In 1904, France and Spain arrived at an agreement that divided Morocco into zones of French and Spanish control. In 1912, Morocco became a French protectorate under the Treaty of Fez. The French protectorate ended in 1956 after much unrest and nationalist activities.

Geography

Location: Northern Africa, bordering the North Atlantic Ocean and the Mediterranean Sea, between Algeria and Western Sahara.

Area: 446,550 sq. km.

Terrain: The northern coast and the interior are mountanious. There are extensive inter-montane valleys and bordering plateaus. There are also rich coastal plains.

Natural resources: Phosphates, iron ore, manganese, lead, zinc, fish, salt.

Climate: Mediterranean climate; more extreme in the interiors.

People

Population: 33,241,259 (July 2006 est.).

Population growth rate: 1.55% (2006 est.).

Sex ratio: 0.99 male(s)/female (2006 est.).

Religions: Muslim 98.7%, Christian 1.1%, Jewish 0.2%.

Languages: Arabic (official), Berber dialects, French.

Literacy rate: Total 51.7%, Male 64.1%, Female 39.4% (2003 est.).

Infant mortality rate: 40.24 deaths/1,000 live births (2006 est.).

Life expectancy: Total 70.94 years, Male 68.62 years, Female 73.37 years (2006 est.).

Government

Capital: Rabat.

Government type: Constitutional monarchy.

Independence: 2 March 1956 (from France).

Legal system: Based on Islamic law and French and Spanish civil law system.

Executive branch:

Chief of state: King Mohamed VI (since 30 July 1999).

Head of government: Prime Minister Driss Jettou (since 9 October 2002).

Economy

Currency: Moroccan dirham.

GDP: Purchasing power parity—$138.3 billion (2005 est.).

GDP—real growth rate: 1.8% (2005 est.).

GDP—per capita: Purchasing power parity—$4,200 (2005 est.).

Inflation rate: 2.1% (2005 est.).

Population below poverty line: 19% (2005 est.).

Unemployment rate: 10.5% (2005 est.).

Exports: $9.472 billion f.o.b. (2005 est.)—clothing, fish, inorganic chemicals, transistors, crude minerals, fertilizers, petroleum products, fruits, vegetables.

Imports: $18.15 billion f.o.b. (2005 est.)—crude petroleum, textile fabric, telecommunications equipment, wheat, gas and electricity, transistors, plastics.

External debt: $15.6 billion (2005 est.).

Transport and Communications

Railways: 1,907 km.

Roads: 57,694 km.

Telephones: 1,308,600 (2004).

Mobile cellular: 9,336,900 (2004).

Internet users: 3.5 million (2005).

Internet country code: .ma

Mozambique

History

Bantu-speaking tribes moved into the region that is today Mozambique in the third century AD. Arabs and Swahili people came later. Vasco da Gama explored the area in 1498 and the Portuguese colonized it in 1505. Till 1752, Mozambique was administered as part of the Portuguese territory of Goa.

In the eighteenth and nineteenth centuries, Mozambique became an important slave-trading centre. In 1878, Portugal leased large areas of the

colony to private organizations for commercial activity. In 1975, Mozambique became independent as a single-party state.

Geography

Location: South-eastern Africa, bordering the Mozambique Channel, between South Africa and Tanzania.

Area: 801,590 sq. km.

Terrain: Central lowlands with upland in the centre, high plateaus in the north-west, and mountains in the west.

Natural resources: Coal, titanium, natural gas, hydropower, tantalum, graphite.

Climate: Varies from tropical to subtropical.

People

Population: 19,686,505 (July 2006 est.).

Population growth rate: 1.38% (2006 est.).

Sex ratio: 0.97 male(s)/female (2006 est.).

Religions: Catholic 23.8%, Zionist Christian 17.5%, Muslim 17.8%, other 17.8%, none 23.1% (1997 census).

Languages: Emakhuwa 26.1%, Xichangana 11.3%, Portuguese 8.8% (official; spoken by 27% of population as a second language), Elomwe 7.6%, Cisena 6.8%, Echuwabo 5.8%, other Mozambican languages 32%, other foreign languages 0.3%, unspecified 1.3%

Literacy rate: Total 47.8%, Male 63.5%, Female 32.7% (2003 est.).

Infant mortality rate: 129.24 deaths/ 1,000 live births (2006 est.).

Life expectancy: Total 39.82 years, Male 39.53 years, Female 40.13 years (2006 est.).

Government

Capital: Maputo.

Government type: Republic.

Independence: 25 June 1975 (from Portugal).

Legal system: Based on Portuguese civil law system and customary law.

Executive branch:

Chief of state: President Arwando Guebuza (since 2 February 2005).

Head of government: Prime Minister Luisa Diogo (since 17 February 2004).

Economy

Currency: Metical.

GDP: Purchasing power parity—$26.03 billion (2005 est.).

GDP—real growth rate: 7% (2005 est.).

GDP—per capita: Purchasing power parity—$1,300 (2005 est.).

Inflation rate: 7.8% (2005 est.).

Population below poverty line: 70% (2001 est.).

Unemployment rate: 21% (1997 est.).

Exports: $1.69 billion f.o.b. (2005 est.)—aluminum, prawns, cashews, cotton, sugar, citrus, timber, bulk electricity.

Imports: $2.041 million f.o.b. (2005 est.)—machinery and equipment, vehicles, fuel, chemicals, metal products, foodstuff, textiles.

External debt: $966 million (2002 est.).

Transport and Communications

Railways: 3,123 km.

Roads: 30,400 km.

Telephones: 77,600 (2003).

Mobile cellular: 708,000 (2004).

Internet users: 138,000 (2005).

Internet country code: .mz

Myanmar

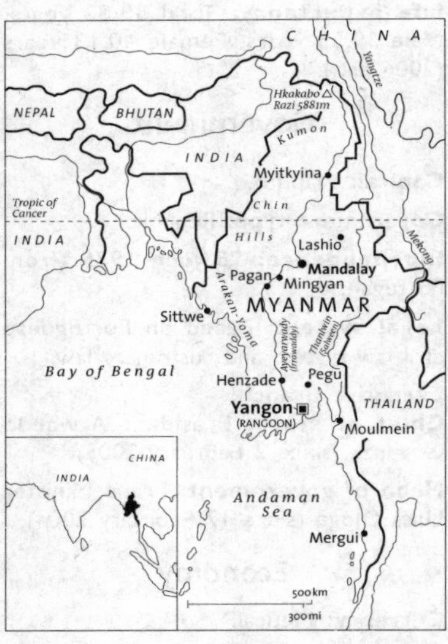

History

In the sixteenth–seventeenth centuries, the British, Portuguese and the Dutch carried out trade activities in the area. The modern-day state of Myanmar (then Burma) was founded in the eighteenth century but was annexed by the British in 1885. Thereafter it became a province of India. The Government of India Act of 1935 separated Burma from India. During World War II, Japan occupied the country.

Geography

Location: South-eastern Asia, bordering the Andaman Sea and the Bay of Bengal, between Bangladesh and Thailand.

Area: 678,500 sq. km.

Terrain: Central lowlands ringed by steep, rugged highlands.

Natural resources: Petroleum, timber, tin, antimony, zinc, copper, tungsten, lead, coal, some marble, limestone, precious stones, natural gas, hydropower.

Climate: Tropical monsoon type of climate.

People

Population: 47,382,633 (July 2006 est.).

Population growth rate: 0.81% (2006 est.).

Sex ratio: 0.97 male(s)/female (2006 est.).

Religions: Buddhist 89%, Christian 4% (Baptist 3%, Roman Catholic 1%), Muslim 4%, animist 1%, others 2%.

Languages: Burmese, minority ethnic groups have their own languages.

Literacy rate: Total 85.3%, Male 89.2%, Female 81.4% (2002).

Infant mortality rate: 61.85 deaths/1,000 live births (2006 est.).

Life expectancy: Total 60.97 years, Male 58.07 years, Female 64.03 years (2006 est.).

Government

Capital: Yangon.

Government type: Military regime.

Independence: 4 January 1948 (from UK).

Legal system: The country has not accepted compulsory ICJ jurisdiction.

Executive branch:
Chief of state: Chairman of the State Peace and Development Council Sr Gen. Than Shwe (since 23 April 1992). The chief of state is also the head of government.

Head of government: Prime Minister, Gen Soe Win (since 19 October 2004).

Economy

Currency: Kyat.

Economy—overview:
Although Myanmar is rich in natural resources, it remains one of the poorest countries in the world with widespread poverty. In the early 1990s, the military regime took steps to liberalize the economy. But those efforts have met with little success and were consequently stalled. The country has not been able to achieve monetary or fiscal stability. Its economy suffers from serious imbalances. There is a steep inflation rate and the official exchange rate overvalues the Burmese currency, the kyat, by more than 100 times the market rate. Most overseas development assistance stopped after the military regime suppressed the democracy movement in 1988 and ignored the results of the 1990 election.

GDP: Purchasing power parity—$78.74 billion (2005 est.).

GDP—real growth rate: 2.9% (2005 est.).

GDP—per capita: Purchasing power parity—$1,700 (2005 est.).

Inflation rate: 18% (2005 est.).

Population below poverty line: 25% (2000 est.).

Unemployment rate: 5% (2005 est.).

Exports: $3.111 billion f.o.b. (2005).

Imports: $3.454 billion f.o.b. (2005).

External debt: $6.967 billion (2005 est.).

Transport and Communications

Railways: 3,955 km.

Roads: 27,000 km (2005).

Telephones: 424,900 (2004 est.). Note: Myanmar has an adequate telephone network that meets requirements for local and inter-city as well as international service.

Mobile cellular: 92,500 (2004).

Internet users: 10,000 (2002).

Internet country code: .mm

Namibia

History

The Portuguese were the first Europeans to reach the area, in the late fifteenth century. In the late nineteenth century, the present international borders of Namibia were demarcated through German treaties with UK and Portugal. Subsequently, Germany annexed the territory as South West Af-

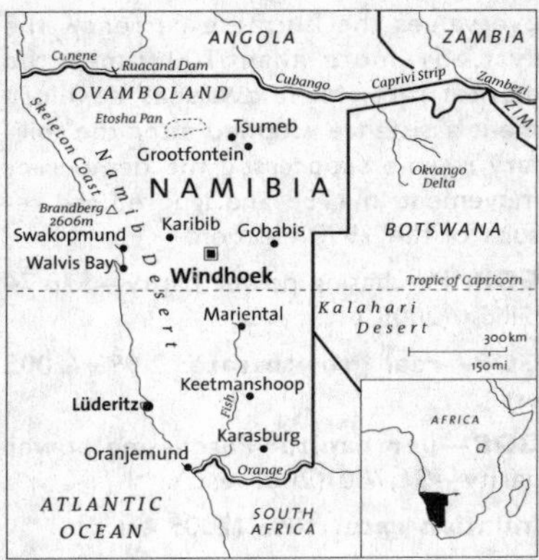

rica. The Germans responded to uprisings by native populations by using brutal and overwhelming force that decimated as much as 90 per cent of the Herero and Nama populations.

During World War I, South Africa invaded and captured South West Africa in 1914–15. In 1920, the League of Nations granted South Africa the mandate to govern South West Africa. In 1961, the UN General Assembly demanded the termination of South Africa's mandate over South West Africa and set its independence as an objective. In 1968, the UN General Assembly officially renamed South West Africa as Namibia. In March 1990, Namibia became independent.

Geography

Location: Southern Africa, bordering the South Atlantic Ocean, between Angola and South Africa.

Area: 825,418 sq. km.

Terrain: Deserts along the coast and in the east, the rest of the country is mostly a high plateau.

Natural resources: Diamonds, copper, uranium, gold, lead, tin, lithium, cadmium, zinc, salt, vanadium, natural gas, hydropower, fish.

Climate: Hot and dry desert climate.

People

Population: 2,044,147 (July 2006 est.).

Population growth rate: 0.59% (2006 est.).

Sex ratio: 1.01 male(s)/female (2006 est.).

Religions: Christian 80% to 90% (at least Lutheran), indigenous beliefs 10% to 20%.

Languages: English 7% (official), Afrikaans (it is the common language of most of the population including about 60% of the white population), German 32%, indigenous languages (Oshivambo, Herero, Nama).

Literacy rate: Total 84%, Male 84.4%, Female 83.7% (2003 est.).

Infant mortality rate: 48.1 deaths/1,000 live births (2006 est.).

Life expectancy: Total 43.39 years, Male 42.46 years, Female 42.29 years (2006 est.).

Government

Capital: Windhoek.

Government type: Republic.

Independence: 21 March 1990 (from South African mandate).

Legal system: Based on Roman–Dutch law and 1990 Constitution.

Executive branch:

Chief of state: President Hifikepunye Pohamba (since 21 March 2005).

Head of government: Prime Minister Nahas Angula (since 21 March 2005).

Economy

Currency: Namibian dollar.

GDP: Purchasing power parity—$14.23 billion (2005 est.).

GDP—real growth rate: 3.5% (2005 est.).

GDP—per capita: Purchasing power parity—$7,000 (2005 est.).

Inflation rate: 2.7% (2005 est.).

Population below poverty line: The UNDPs 2005 Human Development Report indicated that 34.9 per cent of the population live on $1 per day and 55.8 per cent live on $2 per day (2002 est.).

Unemployment rate: 35% (1998 est.).

Exports: $2.04 billion f.o.b. (2005 est.)—diamond, copper, gold, zinc, lead, uranium; cattle, processed fish, karakul skins.

Imports: $2.35 billion f.o.b. (2005 est.)—foodstuff, petroleum products and fuel, machinery and equipment, chemicals.

External debt: $1.164 billion (2005 est.).

Transport and Communications

Railways: 2,382 km.

Roads: 42,237 km (2002 est.).

Telephones: 127,900 (2004).

Mobile cellular: 286,100 (2004).

Internet users: 75,000 (2005).

Internet country code: .na

Nauru

History

Germany incorporated Nauru into its Marshall Islands protectorate in late 1888. During World War I, Australian forces occupied Nauru and evicted German nationals. In 1920, Nauru became a mandated territory within the League of Nations, with Australia, UK and New Zealand as the responsible authorities. On 31 January 1968, Nauru became independent.

Geography

Location: Island in the South Pacific Ocean, south of the Marshall Islands.

Area: 21 sq. km.

Natural resources: Phosphates, fish.

Climate: Tropical monsoonal type of climate.

People

Population: 13,287 (July 2006 est.).

Population growth rate: 1.81% (2006 est.).

Sex ratio: 1 male(s)/female (2006 est.).

Religions: Christian (two-thirds Protestant, one-third Roman Catholic).

Languages: Nauruan (official, a distinct Pacific Island language), English widely understood, spoken, and used for most government and commercial purposes.

Infant mortality rate: 9.78 deaths/1,000 live births (2006 est.).

Life expectancy: Total 63.08 years, Male 59.15 years, Female 66.84 years (2006 est.).

Government

Capital: Nauru has no official capital; the government offices are in Yaren district.

Government type: Republic.

Independence: 31 January 1968 (from the UN trusteeship administered by Australia, NZ, and UK).

Legal system: Acts of the Nauru Parliament and British common law.

Executive branch:
Chief of state: President Ludwig Scotty (since 26 October 2004). The president is both the chief of state and head of government.

Economy

Currency: Australian dollar.

GDP: Purchasing power parity—$60 million (2005 est.).

GDP—per capita: Purchasing power parity—$5,000 (2005 est.).

Inflation rate: –3.6% (1993).

Exports: $64,000 f.o.b. (2005 est.)—phosphates.

Imports: $20 million c.i.f. (2004 est.)—food, fuel, manufactures, building materials, machinery.

External debt: $33.3 million (2003).

Transport and Communications

Railways: 5 km.

Roads: 30 km.

Telephones: 1,900 (2002).

Mobile cellular: 1,500 (2002).

Internet users: 300 (2002).

Internet country code: .nr

Nepal

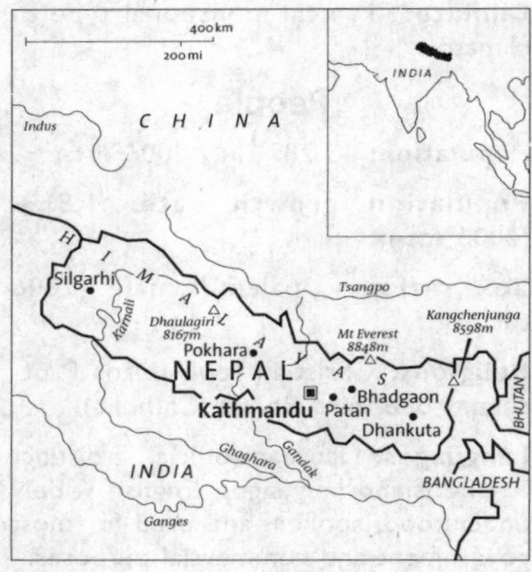

History

The first civilizations of Nepal were largely confined to the Kathmandu valley, due to its fertility. Nepal was also the birthplace of Gautama Buddha, founder of Buddhism.

The country assumed its current limits during the rule of the Malla kings (1200–1769). It was King Prithvi Narayan Shah who unified the region into one country in 1768. The UK recognized the independence of the country in 1923. Between 1846 and 1951, the Rana family ruled over Nepal as prime ministers. In 1951, however, the king assumed all powers and established a constitutional monarchy.

In 2001, the crown prince massacred ten members of the royal family, including the king and queen, and then took his own life. In October 2002, the new king dismissed the prime minister and his cabinet for 'incompetence' after they dissolved the parliament and were subsequently unable to hold elections because of the ongoing insurgency. While stopping short of reestablishing parliament, the king in June 2004 reinstated the most recently elected prime minister who formed a four-party coalition government. Citing dissatisfaction with the government's lack of progress in addressing the Maoist insurgency, the king, in February 2005, dissolved the government, declared a state of emergency, imprisoned party leaders, and assumed power.

Geography

Location: Southern Asia, between China and India.

Area: 140,800 sq. km.

Terrain: Terai or flat river plain of the Ganga in south, central hill region, rugged Himalayas in north.

Natural resources: Quartz, scenic beauty, timber, hydropower, small deposits of lignite, copper, cobalt, iron ore.

Climate: Varies from cool summers and severe winters in the north to subtropical summers and mild winters in the south.

People

Population: 28,287,147 (July 2005 est.).

Population growth rate: 2.17% (2006 est.).

Sex ratio: 1.06 male(s)/female (2006 est.).

Religions: Hindu 80.6%, Buddhist 10.7%, Muslim 4.2%, Kirant 3.6%, other 0.9% (2001 census). Note: Nepal is the only official Hindu state in the world.

Languages: Nepali (official; spoken by 90% of the population), about a dozen other languages and about 30 major dialects. Many in the government and in the world of business also speak English.

Literacy rate: Total 48.6%, Male 62.7%, Female 34.9% (2000–2004 est.).

Infant mortality rate: 65.32 deaths/ 1,000 live births (2006 est.).

Life expectancy: Total 60.18 years, Male 60.43 years, Female 59.91 years (2006 est.).

Government

Capital: Kathmandu.

Government type: Parliamentary democracy and constitutional monarchy.

Independence/date of formation: 1768 (when it was unified by Prithvi Narayan Shah).

Legal system: Based on Hindu legal concepts and English common law.

Executive branch:
Chief of state: King Gyanendra Bir Bikram Shah (succeeded the throne on 4 June 2001 following the death of his nephew, King Dipendra Bir Bikram Shah).

Head of government: Prime Minister Girija Prasad Koirala (since 30 April 2006); Deputy Prime Minister Khadga Prasad Oli (since 2 May 2006).

Election results: None. The monarch is hereditary; following legislative elections, the leader of the majority party or leader of a majority coalition is usually appointed prime minister by the monarch. (King Birendra Bir Bikram Shah Dev died in a shooting at the royal palace on 1 June 2001 that also claimed the lives of most of the royal family. King Birendra's son, Crown Prince Dipendra, is believed to have been responsible for the shootings. He also shot himself. Dipendra was crowned king immediately after the shootings. He died three days later and was succeeded by his uncle, the present king.)

Legislative branch:
Nepal has a bicameral parliament consisting of the National Council (sixty seats of which the House of Representatives appoints thirty-five, the king appoints ten, and an electoral college elects fifteen. One-third of the members are elected every two years to serve six-year terms) and the House of

Representatives (205 seats. Members are elected by popular vote to serve five-year terms.).

Economy

Currency: Nepalese rupee.

Economy—overview:
Nepal is one of the poorest and least developed countries in the world. As much as 42 per cent of its population lives below the poverty line. Agriculture is the most important component of the economy. It provides livelihood for more than 80 per cent of the population and accounts for 40 per cent of GDP. The most important forms of industrial activity include the processing of agricultural produce including jute, tobacco, sugar cane and grain. As much as 80 per cent of foreign exchange earnings in recent years have come from textile and carpet production. But this too has fallen in 2001–2 due to the overall slowdown in the world economy and attacks by Maoist insurgents on factory owners and workers. Tourism is another key source of foreign exchange. But this too suffered in the aftermath of 9/11 and the internal strife in Nepal on account of Maoist guerillas. Since 1991, the government has implemented economic reforms. These have taken the shape of reduction of business licences and registration requirements that aim to simplify investment in the country, reduction of subsidies, privatization of state industries, and trimming of the bureaucracy. Nepal has substantial potential in hydropower and tourism. Consequently, these areas have seen recent foreign investment interest. The small size of the economy, its remote landlocked geographic location, and its susceptibility to natural calamities hampers foreign trade and investment in other sectors.

GDP: Purchasing power parity—$39.9 billion (2005 est.).

GDP—real growth rate: 2.7% (2005 est.).

GDP—per capita: Purchasing power parity—$1,400 (2005 est.).

Inflation rate: 7.8% (October 2005 est.).

Population below poverty line: 31% (2003–2004).

Unemployment rate: 42% (2004 est.).

Exports: $822 million f.o.b., but does not include unrecorded border trade with India (2004 est.).

Imports: $2 billion f.o.b. (2004 est.).

External debt: $3.34 billion (March 2005 est.).

Transport and Communications

Railways: 59 km.

Roads: 15,905 km.

Telephones: 417,900 (2004).

Mobile cellular: 116,800 (2004).

Internet users: 175,000 (2005).

Internet country code: .np

The Netherlands

History

The Netherlands was a part of Charlemagne's empire in the eighth and ninth centuries. After passing through the control of Burgundy and the Hapsburgs, it came under Spanish rule in the sixteenth century. A revolt led by William of Orange broke out in 1568. The 1579 Union of Utrecht

agreement led to the unification of the northern provinces into the United Provinces of the Netherlands. Spain finally recognized Dutch independence in the seventeenth century.

In 1602, the Dutch East India Company was set up. By the seventeenth century, the Netherlands emerged as one of the key European colonial powers. The Thirty Years War reaffirmed the Netherlands as an independent nation. In 1688, the British Parliament invited William of Orange and his wife, Mary Stuart, to take up the English throne as William III and Mary II.

When World War II broke out in 1939, the Netherlands declared itself to be neutral. In spite of this, Nazi Germany invaded the country in 1940 while in Asia, Japan occupied Dutch East Indies. Following the invasion, the Dutch royal family fled to England. The Germans were driven out in 1945. In 1949, Dutch East Indies was granted independence and it became the Republic of Indonesia. In 1963, the Netherlands handed over its remaining Asian territory, New Guinea, to Indonesia.

The Netherlands was a founding member of NATO and the EEC (now the EU).

Geography

Location: Western Europe, bordering the North Sea, between Belgium and Germany.

Area: 41,526 sq. km.

Terrain: Mostly coastal lowlands and reclaimed land below sea level called polders. There are some hills in the south-eastern part of the country.

Natural resources: Natural gas, petroleum, peat, limestone, salt, sand and gravel, arable land.

Climate: Temperate marine type of climate with cool summers and mild winters.

People

Population: 16,491,461 (July 2006 est.).

Population growth rate: 0.49% (2006 est.).

Sex ratio: 0.98 male(s)/female (2006 est.).

Religions: Roman Catholic 31%, Protestant 21%, Muslim 4.4%, others 3.6%, unaffiliated 40%.

Languages: Dutch (official language), Frisian (official language).

Literacy rate: 99% (2000 est.).

Infant mortality: 4.96 deaths/1,000 live births (2006 est.).

Life expectancy: Total 78.96 years, Male 76.39 years, Female 81.67 years (2006 est.).

Government

Capital: Amsterdam; The Hague is the seat of government.

Government type: Constitutional monarchy.

Independence: 1579 (from Spain), (the year in which the Union of Utrecht was concluded, leading to the formation of the Netherlands.

Legal system: Civil law system incorporating French penal theory.

Executive branch:
Chief of state: Queen Beatrix (since 30 April 1980); Heir Apparent Willem-Alexander (born 27 April 1967), son of the monarch.

Head of government: Prime Minister Jan Peter Balkenende (since 22 July 2002).

Economy

Currency: Euro.

Economy—overview:
The prosperous open economy of the Netherlands is heavily reliant on foreign trade. Key features of the economy are moderate inflation and unemployment, a substantial current account surplus and stable industrial relations. It is also an important European transportation hub. Rotterdam is one of the world's busiest ports while Amsterdam's Schiphol Airport is among the busiest in the world. Besides a well-developed industrial sector, the country also has a highly mechanized agricultural sector that is a very important source of exports. The Netherlands was one of the eleven EU countries that launched the euro currency on 1 January 2002.

GDP: Purchasing power parity—$499.8 billion (2005 est.).

GDP—real growth rate: 1.1% (2005 est.).

GDP—per capita: Purchasing power parity—$30,500 (2005 est.).

Inflation rate: 1.7% (2005 est.).

Unemployment rate: 6.7% (2005 est.).

Exports: $365.1 billion f.o.b. (2005 est.)—machinery and equipment, chemicals, fuels; foodstuff.

Imports: $326.6 billion f.o.b. (2005 est.)—machinery and transport equipment, chemicals, fuels; foodstuff, clothing.

External Debt: $1.645 trillion (30 June 2005)

Transport and Communications

Railways: 2,808 km.

Roads: 116,500 km.

Telephones: 7.861 million (2004).

Mobile cellular: 14.8 million (2004).

Internet users: 10,806,328 (2004).

Internet country code: .nl

New Zealand

History

British explorer James Cook charted the main islands in 1769. In 1840, New Zealand became a British Crown colony. The landmark Treaty of Waitangi was signed in 1840 between the Maori tribes and the British. It provided for the recognition of Maori rights to territory in return for their acceptance of British rule. In 1893, New Zealand became the first country to give women the right to vote. In 1907, the Dominion of New Zealand was established.

Geography

Location: Oceania, islands in the South Pacific Ocean, southeast of Australia.

Area: 268,680 sq. km. (This includes Antipodes Islands, Auckland Islands, Bounty Islands, Campbell Island,

Chatham Islands, and Kermadec Islands.)

Terrain: Predominantly mountainous with some large coastal plains.

Natural resources: Natural gas, iron ore, sand, coal, timber, hydropower, gold, limestone.

Climate: Temperate climate with sharp regional contrasts.

People

Population: 4,076,140 (July 2006 est.).

Population growth rate: 0.99% (2006 est.).

Sex ratio: 0.99 male(s)/female (2006 est.).

Religions: Anglican 14.9%, Presbyterian 10.9%, Roman Catholic 12.4%, Methodist 2.9%, Pentecostal 1.7%, Baptist 1.3%, other Christian 9.4%, other 3.3%, unspecified 17.2%, none 26% (2001 census).

Languages: English (official), Maori (official).

Literacy rate: 99% (2003 est.).

Infant mortality rate: 5.76 deaths/1,000 live births (2006 est.).

Life expectancy: Total 78.81 years, Male 75.82 years, Female 81.93 years (2006 est.).

Government

Capital: Wellington.

Government type: Parliamentary democracy.

Independence: 26 September 1907 (from UK).

Legal system: Based on English law, with special land legislation and land courts for the Maori.

Executive branch:
Chief of state: Queen Elizabeth II (since 6 February 1952), represented by Governor General Dame Silvia Cartwright (since 4 April 2001).

Head of government: Prime Minister Helen Clark (since 10 December 1999) and Deputy Prime Minister Michael Cullen (since July 2002).

Economy

Currency: New Zealand dollar.

Economy—overview:
Major economic restructuring since 1984 has transformed New Zealand from an agrarian economy that was dependent on access to the British market to a more industrialized, globally competitive free market economy. Per capita incomes, although rising, have remained below the level of the four largest EU economies. The growth rate of the economy is heavily dependent on trade and the global economic slowdown and the slump in commodity prices have affected it.

GDP: Purchasing power parity—$101.8 billion (2005 est.).

GDP—real growth rate: 2.2% (2005 est.).

GDP—per capita: Purchasing power parity—$25,200 (2005 est.).

Inflation rate: 3% (2005 est.).

Unemployment rate: 4% (2005 est.).

Exports: $22.21 billion (2005 est.)—dairy products, meat, wood and wood products, fish, machinery.

Imports: $24.57 billion (2005 est.)—machinery and equipment, vehicles and aircraft, petroleum, electronics, textiles, plastics.

External debt: $57.67 billion (2005 est.).

Transport and Communications

Railways: 3,898 km.

Roads: 92,66 km.

Telephones: 1,800,500 (2004).

Mobile cellular: 3.027 (2004).

Internet users: 3.2 million (2005).

Internet country code: .nz

Nicaragua

History

The Spanish governed Nicaragua till its independence in 1821. The dictatorial Somoza dynasty ruled Nicaragua during 1936–79. Thereafter, the Sandinistas came to power. The US-backed Contra rebels opposed their regime in the 1980s.

Geography

Location: Middle America, bordering both the Caribbean Sea and the North Pacific Ocean, between Costa Rica and Honduras.

Area: 129,494 sq. km.

Terrain: Extensive plains along the Atlantic coast which rise to central interior mountains. The Pacific coastal plain is narrow and interruted by volcanoes.

Natural resources: Gold, silver, copper, tungsten, lead, zinc, timber, fish.

Climate: Tropical in the lowlands but cooler in the highlands.

People

Population: 5,570,129 (July 2006 est.).

Population growth rate: 1.89% (2006 est.).

Sex ratio: 1 male(s)/female (2006 est.).

Religions: Roman Catholic 72.9%, Evangelical 15.1%, Moravian 1.5%, Episcopal 0.1%, other 1.9%, none 8.5% (1995 census).

Languages: Spanish (official), English and indigenous languages on the Carribean coast.

Literacy rate: Total 67.5%, Male 67.2%, Female 67.8% (2003 est.).

Infant mortality rate: 28.11 deaths/1,000 live births (2006 est.).

Life expectancy: Total 70.63 years, Male 68.55 years, Female 72.81 years (2006 est.).

Government

Capital: Managua.

Government type: Republic.

Independence: 15 September 1821 (from Spain).

Legal system: Civil law system; Supreme court may review administrative acts.

Executive branch:
Chief of state: President Enrique Bolanos Geyer (since 10 January 2002); Vice-President Jose Rizo Castellon (since 10 January 2002). The president is both chief of state and head of government

Economy

Currency: Gold Cordoba.

GDP: Purchasing power parity—$16.09 billion (2005 est.).

GDP—real growth rate: 4% (2005 est.).

GDP—per capita: Purchasing power parity—$2,900 (2005 est.).

Inflation rate: 9.6% (2005 est.).

Population below poverty line: 50% (2001 est.).

Unemployment rate: 6.9% (plus 46.5% underemployment) (2005 est.).

Exports: $1.55 billion f.o.b. (2005 est.)—coffee, shrimp and lobster, cotton, tobacco, bananas, beef, sugar, gold.

Imports: $2.952 billion f.o.b. (2005 est.)—machinery and equipment, raw materials, petroleum products, consumer goods.

External debt: $5.144 billion (2005 est.).

Transport and Communications

Railways: 19,036 km.

Roads: 18,712 km.

Telephones: 214,500 (2004).

Mobile cellular: 738,600 (2004).

Internet users: 125,000 (2005).

Internet country code: .ni

Niger

History

In the 1890s, Niger became a part of French West Africa. In 1958, Niger became an autonomous republic of the French Community. In 1960, Niger became independent with Diori Haman as president.

Geography

Location: Western Africa, south-east of Algeria.

Area: 1,267,000 sq. km.

Terrain: Predominantly desert plains and sand dunes. There are plains in the south and hills in the north.

Natural resources: Uranium, coal, iron ore, tin, phosphates, gold, petroleum.

Climate: Hot, dry and dusty desert climate.

People

Population: 12,525,094 (July 2006 est.).

Population growth rate: 2.92% (2006 est.).

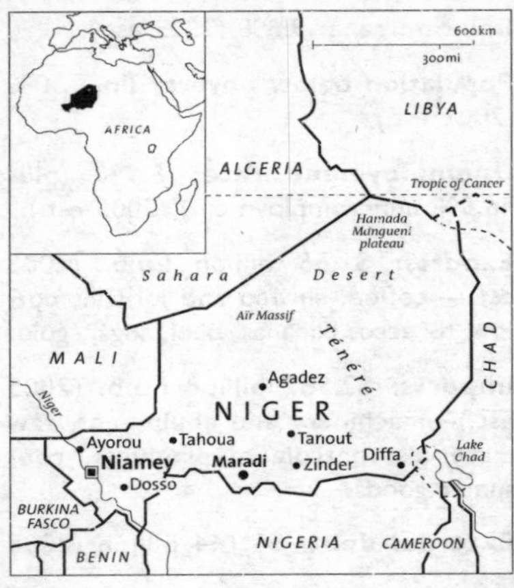

Sex ratio: 1.05 male(s)/female (2006 est.).

Religions: Muslim 80%, indigenous beliefs and Christian.

Languages: French (official), Hausa, Djerma.

Literacy rate: Total 17.6%, Male 25.8%, Female 9.7% (2003 est.).

Infant mortality rate: 118.25 deaths/1,000 live births (2006 est.).

Life expectancy: Total 43.76 years, Male 43.8 years, Female 43.73 years (2006 est.).

Government

Capital: Niamey.

Government type: Republic.

Independence: 3 August 1960 (from France).

Legal system: Based on French civil law system and customary law.

Executive branch:

Chief of state: President Tandja Mamadou (since 22 December 1999). The president is both chief of state and head of government.

Economy

Currency: Communaute Financiere Africaine franc.

GDP: Purchasing power parity—$11.28 billion (2005 est.).

GDP—real growth rate: 4.5% (2005 est.).

GDP—per capita: Purchasing power parity—$900 (2005 est.).

Inflation rate: 0.2% (2005 est.).

Population below poverty line: 63% (1993 est.).

Exports: $222 million f.o.b. (2004 est.)—uranium ore, livestock, cowpeas, onions.

Imports: $588 million f.o.b. (2004 est.)—foodstuff, machinery, vehicles and parts, petroleum, cereals.

External debt: $2.1 billion (2003 est.).

Transport and Communications

Railways: None.

Roads: 10,100 km.

Telephones: 24,100 (2004).

Mobile cellular: 148,300 (2004).

Internet users: 24,000 (2005).

Internet country code: .ne

Nigeria

History

Between the eleventh and the fourteenth centuries, the Kanem empire controlled the area. Islam was introduced in the thirteenth century. From the beginning of the nineteenth century and till 1851, the Fulani Empire con-

trolled the region. In 1851, UK took Lagos and by 1886, it expanded its authority over all of the territory, which it called the 'Colony and Protectorate of Nigeria'. It governed the territory by 'indirect rule' through local leaders. Nigeria gained independence in 1960.

Geography

Location: Western Africa, bordering the Gulf of Guinea, between Benin and Cameroon.

Area: 923,768 sq. km.

Terrain: Southern lowlands that merge into central hills and plateaus. There are mountains in the south-east, and plains in the north.

Natural resources: Natural gas, petroleum, tin, columbite, iron ore, coal, limestone, lead, zinc, arable land.

Climate: Equatorial climate in the southern part of the country, tropical climate in the central part and arid climate in the northern part.

People

Population: 131,859,731 (July 2006 est.).

Population growth rate: 2.38% (2006 est.).

Sex ratio: 1.02 male(s)/female (2006 est.).

Religions: Muslim 50%, Christian 40%, indigenous beliefs 10%.

Languages: English (official), Hausa, Yoruba, Igbo (Ibo), Fulani.

Literacy rate: Total 68%, Male 75.7%, Female 60.6% (2003 est.).

Infant mortality rate: 97.14 deaths/1,000 live births (2006 est.).

Life expectancy: Total 47.08 years, Male 46.52 years, Female 47.66 years (2006 est.).

Government

Capital: Abuja.

Government type: Federal republic.

Independence: 1 October 1960 (from UK).

Legal system: Based on English common law, Islamic Sharia law (only in some northern states), and traditional law.

Executive branch:

Chief of state: President Olusegun Obasanjo (since 29 May 1999). The president is both the chief of state and head of government.

Economy

Currency: Naira.

Economy—overview:

Nigeria possesses substantial petroleum resources. But years of political instability, poor macroeconomic management, corruption, and lack of infrastructure have negated the benefits of its mineral wealth. Nevertheless, the present civilian administration has initiated some reforms. Over the years, Nigeria has failed to diversify the economy away from its high degree of reliance on the oil sector that accounts for over 90 per cent of foreign exchange earnings, around 20 per cent of GDP, and over 60 per cent of budgetary revenues. The mostly subsistence agricultural sector has also failed to keep pace with Nigeria's rapid population growth. Consequently, the country that was once a net exporter of food is now forced to import food. In August 2000, Nigeria entered into an IMF stand-by agreement by which the country received a debt-restructuring deal from the Paris Club and a $1 billion credit from the IMF. However, both of these were subject to economic reforms. However, Nigeria pulled out of its IMF programme in April 2002, when it failed to meet both spending and exchange rate targets, thus making it ineligible for further debt waivers from the Paris Club. In 2003 the government began deregulating fuel prices, announced the privatization of the country's four oil refineries, and instituted the National Economic Empowerment Development Strategy, a domestically designed and run programme modelled on the.

GDP: Purchasing power parity—$174.1 billion (2005 est.).

GDP—real growth rate: 6.2% (2005 est.).

GDP—per capita: Purchasing power parity—$1,400 (2005 est.).

Inflation rate: 15.6% (2005 est.).

Population below poverty line: 60% (2000 est.).

Unemployment rate: 2.9% (2005 est.).

Exports: $52.16 billion f.o.b. (2005 est.)—petroleum and petroleum products 95%, cocoa, rubber.

Imports: $25.95 billion f.o.b. (2005 est.)—machinery, chemicals, transport equipment, manufactured goods, food and live animals.

External debt: $37.49 billion (2005 est.).

Transport and Communications

Railways: 3,557 km.

Roads: 194,394 km.

Telephones: 1,027,500 (2004).

Mobile cellular: 9,147,200 (2004).

Internet users: 1,769,700 (2005).

Internet country code: .ng

North Korea

History

It is believed that the ancient kingdom of Choson was founded in the third millennium BC. China annexed it in 108 BC. The Yi dynasty ruled it from 1392 to 1910 when Japan conquered all of Korea. Allied forces freed Korea from the Japanese in 1945. The part of the Korean peninsula north of the thirty eighth parallel was occupied by the Soviet Union while USA occupied the region to the south of this line of latitude. In 1946, North Korea's Communist party, the Korean Workers' Party, was inaugurated along with a Soviet-backed leadership that included Kim Il-sung, the future leader of the country. Independence came in 1948 with the withdrawal of Soviet troops and the proclamation of Democratic People's Republic of Korea. Kim Il-sung introduced the personal philosophy of Juche, or self-reliance, which became a guiding principle for North Korea's development. He served as premier from 1948 to 1972 and president and head of state from 1972 till his demise in 1994.

When South Korea declared its independence in 1950, North Korea

launched an invasion attempt that soon developed into the Korean War. It ended inconclusively with the signing of the Armistice in 1953. It is believed to have resulted in an estimated 4,000,000 casualties, including civilians.

Geography

Location: Eastern Asia, northern half of the Korean Peninsula bordering the Korea Bay and the Sea of Japan, between China and South Korea.

Area: 120,540 sq. km.

Terrain: Mostly hilly and mountainous with deep and narrow valleys. There are wide coastal plains in the west and broken ones in the east.

Natural resources: Coal, lead, tungsten, zinc, graphite, magnesite, iron ore, copper, gold, pyrites, salt, fluorspar, hydropower.

Climate: Temperate climate with rainfall concentrated in the summer.

People

Population: 23,113,019 (July 2006 est.).

Population growth rate: 0.84% (2006 est.).

Sex ratio: 0.94 male(s)/female (2006 est.).

Religions: Traditionally Buddhist and Confucianist, some Christian and syncretic Chondogyo (Religion of the Heavenly Way).

Languages: Korean.

Literacy rate: 99%.

Infant mortality rate: 23.29 deaths/1,000 live births (2006 est.).

Life expectancy: Total 71.65 years, Male 68.92 years, Female 74.51 years (2006 est.).

Government

Capital: Pyongyang.

Government type: Authoritarian socialist; one-man dictatorship.

Independence: 15 August 1945 (from Japan).

Legal system: Based on German civil law system with Japanese influences and communist legal theory.

Executive branch:
Chief of state: Kim Jong-il (since July 1994). The late leader Kim Il-sung is now referred to as the 'Eternal President' of the country.

Head of government: Premier Pak Pong-ju (since 3 September 2003).

Economy

Currency: Won.

Economy—overview:
North Korea has a strict centrally planned economy. Its industry suffers from under-investment and shortages that have resulted in decline in industrial output and power generation. North Korea has suffered from successive years of food shortages created by severe droughts, chronic shortages of inputs, inefficient collective farming and lack of cultivable land. The country managed to prevent mass starvation in recent years due to huge international food aid deliveries. By some estimates,

North Korea spends almost a third of its GDP on its armed forces. This eats up funds and resources that could otherwise have been used to develop other sectors. In recent times, the government has initiated some rationalization measures at earning hard currency, developing information technology industry and attracting foreign investments. However, it is still a far way off from full-fledged market reforms.

GDP: Purchasing power parity—$40 billion (2005 est.).

GDP—real growth rate: 1% (2005 est.).

GDP—per capita: Purchasing power parity—$1,700 (2005 est.).

Exports: $1.275 billion f.o.b. (2004 est.)—minerals, metallurgical products, manufactures (including armaments), textiles and fishery products.

Imports: $2.819 billion c.i.f. (2004 est.)—petroleum, coking coal, machinery and equipment, textiles, grain.

External debt: $12 billion (1996 est.).

Transport and Communications

Railways: 5,214 km.

Roads: 31,200 km.

Telephones: 980,000 (2003).

Internet country code: .kp

Norway

History

The oldest relics of human habitation in Norway date back to 9500 to 6000 BC. Between 3000 and 2500 BC new immigrants arrived in the eastern part of the country. These new settlers were predominantly farmers and herdsmen and they gradually replaced the original population of hunters and fishermen of the west coast.

Among the Norwegians were the Vikings or Norsemen, the group of seafaring warriors who raided and colonized large areas of Europe from the ninth to the eleventh century. In 1015, Olaf II Haraldsson became the first effective ruler of all of Norway and initiated the conversion of Norwegians to Christianity. Between 1442 and 1814, Danish kings ruled over Norway. In 1814, Sweden gained control of the country but granted a lot of autonomy to the Norwegians. In 1905, Norway arranged an amicable separation with Sweden and invited a Danish prince to take up the Norwegian throne.

Geography

Location: Northern Europe, bordering the North Sea and the North Atlantic Ocean, west of Sweden.

Area: 324,220 sq. km.

Terrain: Glaciated terrain consisting mostly of high plateaus and mountains broken by valleys. The coastline is deeply indented by fjords. The northern part of the country is arctic tundra.

Natural resources: Petroleum, natural gas, iron ore, copper, lead, zinc, titanium, pyrites, nickel, fish, timber, hydropower.

Climate: Temperate along the coastal areas but modified by the effect of the North Atlantic Current. The interiors are colder with increased precipitation.

People

Population: 4,610,820 (July 2006 est.).

Population growth rate: 0.38% (2006 est.).

Sex ratio: 0.98 male(s)/female (2006 est.).

Religions: Evangelical Lutheran (state church), other Protestant and Roman Catholic.

Languages: Bokmal Norwegian (official), Nynorsk Norwegian (official), Sami, Finnish.

Literacy rate: 100%.

Infant mortality rate: 3.67 deaths/ 1,000 live births (2006 est.).

Life expectancy: Total 79.54 years, Male 76.91 years, Female 82.31 years (2006 est.).

Government

Capital: Oslo.

Government type: Constitutional monarchy.

Independence: 7 June 1905 (date on which Norway declared the dissolution of its union with Sweden).

Legal system: Mixture of customary law, civil law system, and common law traditions.

Executive branch:

Chief of state: King Harald V (since 17 January 1991); Heir Apparent Crown Prince Haakon Magnus, son of the monarch (born 20 July 1973).

Head of government: Prime Minister Jens Stoltenberg (since 17 October 2005).

Economy

Currency: Norwegian krone.

Economy—overview:
Norway is a prosperous welfare state with a mixture of free market and government control over key sectors like petroleum. Norway boasts a rich collection of natural resources like petroleum, minerals, hydropower, forests and fish. Oil and gas makes up one-third of exports. In fact, Norway is among the top oil exporters. Norway has remained outside the EU. Norway has realized its heavy reliance on petroleum exports. Therefore, with an eye on the future when petroleum will possibly run out, Norway has been saving its current budget surpluses in a Government Petroleum Fund. This fund is invested abroad and is valued at more than $40 billion.

GDP: Purchasing power parity—$194.1 billion (2005 est.).

GDP—real growth rate: 3.9% (2005 est.).

GDP—per capita: Purchasing power parity—$42,300 (2005 est.).

Inflation rate: 2.1% (2005 est.).

Unemployment rate: 4.2% (2005 est.).

Exports: $111.2 billion f.o.b. (2005 est.)—petroleum and petroleum products, machinery and equipment, metals, chemicals, ships, fish.

Imports: $58.12 billion f.o.b. (2005 est.)—machinery and equipment, chemicals, metals, foodstuff.

External debt: $281 billion (Norway is a net external creditor) **(30 june 2005)**

Transport and Communications

Railways: 4,077 km.

Roads: 91,916 km.

Telephones: 2.228 million (2003).

Mobile cellular: 4,163,400 (2003).

Internet users: 3.14 million (2005).

Internet country code: .no

Oman

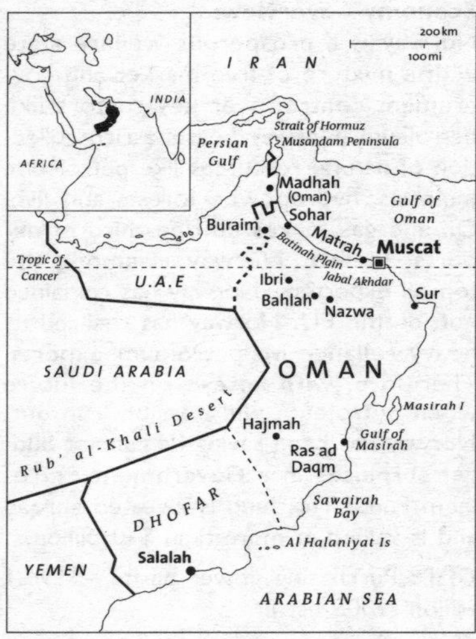

History

The Arab migrations into what is today Oman began in the ninth century BC. Conversion into Islam took place in the seventh century AD. The Ibadi Imams ruled the country till 1154, when a royal dynasty was set up. The Portuguese held sway over the coastal areas between 1507 and 1650. In 1650, they were expelled from the country. The Al Bu Said dynasty was founded in the mid-eighteenth century and still rules Oman. Oil was struck in 1964.

Geography

Location: Middle East, bordering the Arabian Sea, Gulf of Oman, and Persian Gulf, between Yemen and UAE.

Area: 212,460 sq. km.

Terrain: The central region is a desert plain while the north and south has rugged mountains.

Natural resources: Petroleum, natural gas, marble, limestone, copper, asbestos, chromium, gypsum.

Climate: Dry desert type of climate.

People

Population: 3,102,229 including 577,293 non-nationals (July 2006 est.).

Population growth rate: 3.28% (2006 est.).

Sex ratio: 1.25 male(s)/female (2006 est.).

Religions: Ibadhi Muslim 75%, Sunni Muslim, Shi'a Muslim, Hindu.

Languages: Arabic (official), English, Baluchi, Urdu, Indian dialects.

Literacy rate: Total 75.8%, Male 83.1%, Female 67.2% (2005 est.).

Infant mortality rate: 18.89 deaths/ 1,000 live births (2006 est.).

Life expectancy: Total 73.37 years, Male 71.14 years, Female 75.72 years (2006 est.).

Government

Capital: Muscat.

Government type: Monarchy.

Independence: 1650 (expulsion of the Portuguese).

Legal system: Based on English common law and Islamic law; ultimate appeal to the monarch.

Executive branch:
Chief of state: Sultan and Prime Minister Qaboos bin Said Al Said (since 23 July 1970); the monarch is both the chief of state and head of government.

Economy

Currency: Omani rial.

Economy—overview:
The recovery of oil prices improved Oman's economic performance in 2000. The country embarked on vari-

ous reform measures that have taken the shape of privatization of utilities, the development of a body of commercial law to facilitate foreign investment, and increased budgetary outlays. Oman joined the World Trade Organization (WTO) in November 2000. In 2001, GDP growth improved in spite of a global slowdown. But in 2002, it slumped back to 2.2 per cent. The government has been trying to replace expatriate workers with local workers in a bid to reduce unemployment. The government is also trying to develop Oman's gas resources. In 2005, Oman signed agreements with several foreign investors to boost oil reserves, build and operate a power plant, and develop a second mobile phone network in the country.

GDP: Purchasing power parity—$39.65 billion (2005 est.).

GDP—real growth rate: 4.3% (2005 est.).

GDP—per capita: Purchasing power parity—$13,200 (2005 est.).

Inflation rate: 0.4% (2005 est.).

Unemployment rate: 15% (2004 est.).

Exports: $19.01 billion f.o.b. (2005 est.).

Imports: $8.709 billion f.o.b. (2005 est.).

External debt: $4.586 billion (2005 est.).

Transport and Communications

Railways: None.

Roads: 34,965 km.

Telephones: 242,700 (2004).

Mobile cellular: 805,000 (2004).

Internet users: 245,000 (2005).

Internet country code: .om

Pakistan

History

Pakistan was home to the settlements of the Indus Valley Civilization. Later, the area was controlled by a succession of invading forces such as the Aryans, the Persians, the Greeks, the Turks and the Arabs.

Islam was introduced in 711 and by 1526, it had become a part of the Mughal empire. By 1857, the British had gained control of the region. At the time of India's independence in 1947, the region, along with what is today Bangladesh, was separated from India to form Pakistan, as a dominion within the Commonwealth in August 1947. Mohammed Ali Jinnah became the governor general and Liaquat Ali Khan the prime minister. The western part, now Pakistan, was then called West Pakistan. What is today Bangladesh formed the eastern part of the nascent nation and was then called East Pakistan. West Pakistan consisted of Sind, Baluchistan, North-west Frontier Province, along with a truncated part of Punjab. East Pakistan was formed by dividing Bengal. Full-fledged warfare between India and Pakistan followed in 1965 and 1971. The latter resulted in the formation of Bangladesh. Fighting over Kashmir broke out in May 1999, once again, in what is known as the Kargil War.

Geography

Location: Pakistan lies in southern Asia, bordering the Arabian Sea, between India on the east, Iran and Afghanistan on the west.

Area: 803,940 sq. km.

Terrain: The flat Indus plain lies in the east. There are mountains in the north and north-west while the Baluchistan plateau lies in the west.

Natural resources: Land, extensive natural gas reserves, limited petroleum, poor quality coal, iron ore, copper, salt, limestone.

Climate: Hot, dry desert type of climate in most parts of the country. The climate is of the temperate type in the north-west.

People

Population: 165,803,560 (July 2006 est.).

Population growth rate: 2.09% (2006 est.).

Sex ratio: 1.05 male(s)/female (2006 est.).

Religions: Muslim 97% (Sunni 77%, Shi'a 20%), Christian, Hindu, and others 3%.

Languages: Punjabi 48%, Sindhi 12%, Siraiki (a Punjabi variant) 10%, Pashto 8%, Urdu (official) 8%, Baluchi 3%, Hindko 2%, Brahui 1%, English (official and lingua franca of Pakistani elite and most government ministries), Burushaski, and others 8%.

Literacy rate: Total 48.7%, Male 61.7%, Female 35.2% (2004 est.).

Infant mortality rate: 70.45 deaths/1,000 live births (2006 est.).

Life expectancy: Total 63.39 years, Male 62.4 years, Female 64.44 years (2006 est.).

Government

Capital: Islamabad.

Government type: Federal republic.

Independence: 14 August 1947 (from UK).

Administrative divisions:

Four provinces, one territory*, and one capital territory**

1. Baluchistan 2. Federally Administered Tribal Areas* 3. Islamabad Capital Territory** 4. North-West Frontier Province 5. Punjab 6. Sindh.

Legal system: Based on English common law with provisions to accommodate Pakistan's status as an Islamic state.

Executive branch:

Chief of state: President Pervez Musharraf (since 20 June 2001).

Head of government: Prime Minister Shaukat Aziz (since 28 August 2004).

Elections and election results: The parliament elects the President for a five-year term. In a referendum held on 30 April 2002, Musharraf's presidency was extended by five more years (the next referendum is scheduled to be held in 2007).

The 10 October 2002 elections resulted in the election of Prime Minister Mir Zafarullah Khan Jamali. Shaukat Aziz replaced Jamali as prime minister in 2004.

Legislative branch:

Pakistan has a bicameral parliament or Majlis-E-Shoora. It consist of the Senate (it has 100 seats; members indirectly elected by provincial assemblies to serve four-year terms, and the National Assembly (it has 342 seats of which sixty seats represent women, ten seats represent minorities, members elected by popular vote to serve four-year terms).

Elections and election results: Senate last elections held 24 and 27 February 2003 (next to be held by February 2007); National Assembly—last elections held 10 October 2002 (next to be held by October 2006).

Economy

Currency: Pakistani rupee.

Economy—overview:
Pakistan is an underdeveloped country that suffers from low levels of foreign investment. The country's economic prospects continued to improve in 2002 thanks to substantial inflows of foreign assistance beginning in 2001. Foreign exchange reserves have grown to record levels. This is largely due to fast growth in worker remittances. Since 2000, the country has witnessed some economic reform.

GDP: Purchasing power parity—$393.4 billion (2005 est.).

GDP—real growth rate: 6.9% (2005 est.).

GDP—per capita: Purchasing power parity—$2,400 (2005 est.).

Inflation rate: 9.2% (2005 est.).

Population below poverty line: 32% (2001 est.).

Unemployment rate: 6.6% plus substantial underemployment (2005 est.).

Exports: $14.85 billion f.o.b. (2005 est.).

Imports: $21.26 billion f.o.b. (2005 est.).

External debt: $39.94 billion (2005 est.).

Transport and Communications

Railways: 8,163 km.

Roads: 254,410 km.

Telephones: 4,502,200 (2004).

Mobile cellular: 5,022,900 (2004).

Internet users: 7.5 million (2005).

Internet country code: .pk

Palau

History

It is believed that the original settlers of Palau came from modern-day Indonesia in around 2500 BC. In 1543, the Spanish explorer Ruy Lopez de Villalobos visited the islands. For 300 years till 1899, the islands remained in Spanish possession. During World War I, Japan occupied the islands. During World War II, the islands served as a key base for the Japanese but were later taken by the US. In 1992, Palau signed a Compact of Free Association that meant that the USA would provide economic assistance to the islands in return for the right to build military installations. In 1994, Palau became a sovereign nation.

Geography

Location: Oceania, group of islands in the North Pacific Ocean, southeast of the Philippines.

Area: 458 sq. km.

Natural resources: Forests, gold, marine products, deep-seabed minerals.

Climate: Hot and humid climate.

People

Population: 20,579 (July 2006 est.).

Population growth rate: 1.31% (2006 est.).

Sex ratio: 1.13 male(s)/female (2006 est.).

Religions: Christian, Modekngei religion (one-third of the population observes this religion, which is indigenous to Palau).

Languages: English and Palauan (official).

Literacy rate: Total 92%, Male 93%, Female 90% (1980 est.).

Infant mortality rate: 14.46 deaths/1,000 live births (2006 est.).

Life expectancy: Total 70.42 years, Male 67.26 years, Female 73.77 years (2006 est.).

Government

Capital: Koror. A new capital is being built about 20 km north-east of Koror.

Government type: Constitutional government in free association with the US.

Independence: 1 October 1994 (from the US-administered UN Trusteeship).

Legal system: Based on Trust Territory laws, acts of the legislature, municipal, common, and customary laws.

Executive branch:
Chief of state: President Tommy Esang Remengesau Jr (since 19 January 2001) and Vice-President Camsek Chin (since 1 January 2005). The president is both the chief of state and head of government.

Economy

Currency: US Dollar.

GDP: Purchasing power parity—$174 million.

GDP—real growth rate: 1% (2001 est.).

GDP—per capita: Purchasing power parity—$9,000 (2001 est.).

Inflation rate: 3.4% (2000 est.).

Exports: $18 million f.o.b. (2001 est.)—Shellfish, tuna, copra, garments.

Imports: $99 million f.o.b. (2001 est.).

External debt: None.

Transport and Communications

Railways: None.

Roads: 61 km.

Telephones: 6,700 (2002).

Mobile cellular: 1,000 (2002).

Internet country code: .pw

Panama

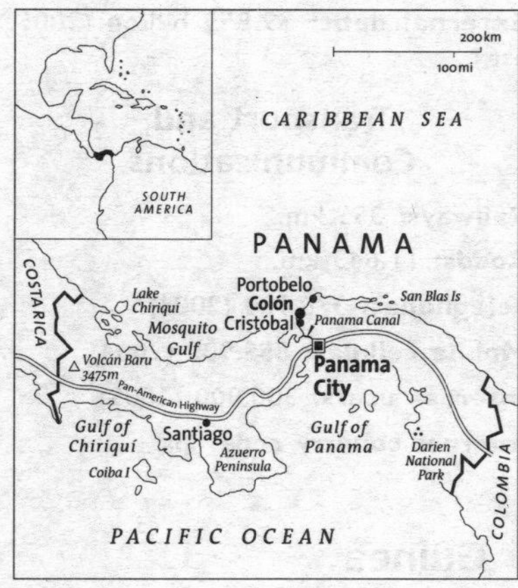

History

Panama was home to indigenous people when Spanish exploration started in the early 1500s. It declared its independence from Spain in 1821 but joined the confederacy of Gran Colombia. In 1903, it seceded from Colombia with US backing. The ceding of the Panama Canal Zone to USA followed soon after.

In 1988, US courts indicted Panamanian strongman General Manuel Noriega on drug charges. In 1989, the Panamanian Parliament named Noriega as the 'maximum leader'. He promptly announced a state of war between USA and Panama. In December that year, US forces seized the capital. Noriega surrendered in January 1990.

Geography

Location: Middle America, bordering both the Caribbean Sea and the North Pacific Ocean, between Colombia and Costa Rica.

Area: 78,200 sq. km.

Natural resources: Copper, mahogany forests, shrimp, hydropower.

Climate: Hot, humid, cloudy tropical maritime climate with a prolonged rainy season.

People

Population: 3,191,319 (July 2006 est.).

Population growth rate: 1.6% (2006 est.).

Sex ratio: 1.02 male(s)/female (2006 est.).

Religions: Roman Catholic 85%, Protestant 15%.

Languages: Spanish (official), English 14%.

Literacy rate: Total 92.6%, Male 93.2%, Female 91.9% (2003 est.).

Infant mortality rate: 16.37 deaths/1,000 live births (2006 est.)

Life expectancy: Total 75.22 years, Male 72.68 years, Female 77.87 years (2006 est.).

Government

Capital: Panama City.

Government type: Constitutional democracy.

Independence: 28 November 1821 (from Spain); 3 November 1903 (from Colombia).

Legal system: Based on civil law system.

Executive branch:
Chief of state: President Martin Torrijos Espino (since 1 September 2004). The president is both the chief of state and head of government.

Economy

Currency: Balboa, US dollar.

GDP: Purchasing power parity—$22.76 billion (2005 est.).

GDP—real growth rate: 6.4% (2005 est.).

GDP—per capita: Purchasing power parity—$7,200 (2005 est.).

Inflation rate: 2.5% (2005 est.).

Population below poverty line: 37% (1999 est.).

Unemployment rate: 8.7% (2005 est.).

Exports: $7.481 billion f.o.b. (Colon Free Zone) (2005 est.)—Banana, shrimp, sugar, coffee, clothing.

Imports: $8.734 billion f.o.b. (Colon Free Zone) (2005 est.)—Capital goods, crude oil, foodstuff, consumer goods, chemicals.

External debt: $9.859 billion (2005 est.).

Transport and Communications

Railways: 355 km.

Roads: 11,643 km.

Telephones: 376,100 (2004).

Mobile cellular: 855,900 (2004).

Internet users: 300,000 (2005).

Internet country code: .pa

Papua New Guinea

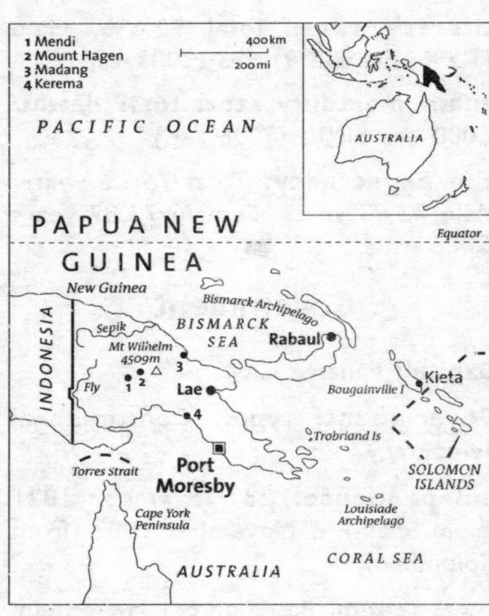

History

In 1906, the control of the British New Guinea territory was shifted to Australia. The name was changed to 'Territory of Papua'. In 1945, it became a United Nations trusteeship under Australian administration. The territories were combined under a new name, the Territory of Papua and New Guinea.

In 1951, partial home rule was granted while autonomy in internal affairs was granted nine years later. Full independence came in 1975.

Geography

Location: Oceania, group of islands including the eastern half of the island of New Guinea between the Coral Sea and the South Pacific Ocean, east of Indonesia.

Area: 462,840 sq. km.

Terrain: Mostly mountainous terrain with coastal lowlands and rolling foothills.

Natural resources: Gold, copper, silver, natural gas, timber, oil, fisheries.

Climate: Tropical climate.

People

Population: 5,670,544 (July 2006 est.).

Population growth rate: 2.21% (2006 est.).

Sex ratio: 1.05 male(s)/female (2006 est.).

Religions: Roman Catholic 22%, Lutheran 16%, Presbyterian/Methodist/London Missionary Society 8%, Anglican 5%, Evangelical Alliance 4%, Seventh-Day Adventist 1%, other Protestant 10%, indigenous beliefs 34%.

Languages: English spoken by 1–2%. Melanesian pidgin serves as the lingua franca, Motu spoken in Papua region. There are over 700 indigenous languages.

Literacy rate: Total 66%, Male 72.3%, Female 59.3% (2003 est.).

Infant mortality rate: 49.96 deaths/1,000 live births (2006 est.).

Life expectancy: Total 65.28 years, Male 63.08 years, Female 67.58 years (2006 est.).

Government

Capital: Port Moresby.

Government type: Constitutional monarchy with parliamentary democracy.

Independence: 16 September 1975 (from the Australian-administered UN trusteeship).

Legal system: Based on English common law.

Executive branch:

Chief of state: Queen Elizabeth II (since 6 February 1952), represented by Governor General Sir Paulius Matane (since 29 June 2004).

Head of government: Deputy prime minister vacant.

Economy

Currency: Kina.

Economy—overview:

Papua New Guinea is rich in natural resources, but exploitation is impeded by rugged terrain and the high cost of developing infrastructure. Eighty-five per cent of the population depends on subsistence agriculture for livelihood. Mineral deposits such as oil, copper and gold, constitute 72 per cent of export earnings.

GDP: Purchasing power parity—$14.37 billion (2005 est.).

GDP—real growth rate: 2.9% (2005 est.).

GDP—per capita: Purchasing power parity—$2,600 (2005 est.).

Inflation rate: 1.7% (2005 est.).

Population below poverty line: 37% (2002 est.).

Exports: $2.833 billion f.o.b. (2005 est.)—oil, gold, copper ore, logs, palm oil, coffee, cocoa, crayfish, prawns.

Imports: $1.651 billion f.o.b. (2005 est.)—machinery and transport equipment, manufactured goods, food, fuels, chemicals.

External debt: $1.978 billion (2005 est.).

Transport and Communications

Railways: None.

Roads: 19,600 km.

Telephones: 62,000 (2002).

Mobile cellular: 15,000 (2002).

Internet users: 170,000 (2005).

Internet country code: .pg

Paraguay

History

In 1776, Spain transferred Paraguay from the viceroyalty of Peru to the viceroyalty of La Plata with its capital at Buenos Aires in Argentina. In 1811, Paraguay became independent. Three

dictators ruled the newborn nation over the next half-century. The third of them, Francisco Solano López, led Paraguay to the bloodiest conflict in Latin American history. This was the War of the Triple Alliance, also called the Paraguayan War, in which Paraguay took on the allied forces of Argentina, Brazil, and Uruguay. The war not only resulted in a loss of territory but also a great loss of human life. Paraguay went back to war during 1932–5. This was the Chaco War and this time Paraguay won commercially important territory from Bolivia.

Geography

Location: Central South America, north-east of Argentina.

Area: 406,750 sq. km.

Terrain: Grassy plains and wooded hills east of Rio Paraguay; Gran Chaco region west of Rio Paraguay mostly low, marshy plain near the river; and dry forest and thorny scrub elsewhere.

Natural resources: Hydropower, timber, iron ore, manganese, limestone.

Climate: Varies from subtropical to temperate with substantial rainfall in the eastern parts but semi-arid in the far west.

People

Population: 6,506,464 (July 2006 est.).

Population growth rate: 2.45% (2006 est.).

Sex ratio: 1.01 male(s)/female (2006 est.).

Religions: Roman Catholic 90%, Mennonite, and other Protestant.

Languages: Spanish (official), Guarani (official).

Literacy rate: Total 94%, Male 94.9%, Female 93% (2003 est.).

Infant mortality rate: 24.78 deaths/1,000 live births (2006 est.).

Life expectancy: Total 75.1 years, Male 72.56 years, Female 77.78 years (2006 est.).

Government

Capital: Asuncion.

Government type: Constitutional republic.

Independence: 14 May 1811 (from Spain).

Legal system: Based on Argentine codes, Roman law, and French codes.

Executive branch:
Chief of state: President Nicanor Duarte Frutos (since 15 August 2003). Vice-President Luis Castiglioni (since 15 August 2003). The president is both the chief of state and head of government.

Economy

Currency: Guarani.

GDP: Purchasing power parity—$29.08 billion (2005 est.).

GDP—real growth rate: 2.7% (2005 est.).

GDP—per capita: Purchasing power parity—$4,900 (2005 est.).

Inflation rate: 7.5% (2005 est.).

Population below poverty line: 32% (2005 est.).

Unemployment rate: 16% (2005 est.).

Exports: $3.13 billion f.o.b. (2005 est.)—soybeans, animal feed, cotton, meat, edible oils, electricity.

Imports: $3.832 billion f.o.b. (2005 est.)—automobiles, consumer goods, tobacco, petroleum products, electrical machinery.

External debt: $3.535 billion (2005 est.).

Transport and Communications

Railways: 441 km.

Roads: 29,500 km.

Telephones: 280,800 (2003).

Mobile cellular: 1,770,300 (2003).

Internet users: 150,000 (2005).

Internet country code: .py

Peru

History

Cuzco in present-day Peru became the capital city of the Inca empire in the twelfth century. At the time of the Spanish conquest in the 1530s, the well-developed and prosperous Inca empire was in the midst of a civil war. After the fall of the Inca empire, its territories became a part of the viceroyalty of Peru with its capital in Lima. In 1780, the Spanish suppressed a rebellion led by Tupac Amaru, who claimed descent from the Inca rulers. In 1821, Peru gained independence from Spain.

Between 1945 and 1980, the Shining Path, or Sendero Luminoso, guerrillas began their armed rebellion against the Peruvian government. Their violent movement intensified through the 1980s. It is estimated that the Shining Path's activities killed around 30,000 people and greatly harmed the Peruvian economy in the last twenty years of the twentieth century.

Geography

Location: Western South America, bordering the South Pacific Ocean, between Chile and Ecuador.

Area: 1,285,220 sq. km.

Terrain: The Andes mountains in the centre (the sierra), a coastal plain in the west (the costa) and the lowland jungle of Amazon basin in the east (selva).

Natural resources: Copper, silver, gold, petroleum, timber, fish, iron ore, coal, phosphate, potash, hydropower, natural gas.

Climate: Ranges from tropical in the east to dry desert in the west. The climate of the Andes region varies between temperate to frigid.

People

Population: 28,302,603 (July 2006 est.).

Population growth rate: 1.32% (2006 est.).

Sex ratio: 1.01 male(s)/female (2006 est.).

Religions: Roman Catholic 81%, Seventh-Day Adventist 1.4%, other Christian 0.7%, other 0.6%, unspecified or none 16.3% (2003 est.)

Languages: Spanish (official), Quechua (official), Aymara, numerous minor Amazonian languages.

Literacy rate: Total 87.7%, Male 93.5%, Female 82.1% (2004 est.).

Infant mortality rate: 30.94 deaths/1,000 live births (2006 est.).

Life expectancy: Total 69.84 years, Male 68.05 years, Female 71.71 years (2006 est.).

Government

Capital: Lima.

Government type: Constitutional republic.

Independence: 28 July 1821 (from Spain).

Legal system: Based on civil law system.

Executive branch:
Chief of state: President Alejandro Toledo Manrique (since 28 July 2001). The president is both the chief of state and head of government.

Economy

Currency: Nuevo Sol (PEN).

Economy—overview: Peru has abundant mineral resources and rich fishing grounds. At the same time, lack of infrastructure hampers trade and investment while over-reliance on minerals exposes the economy to the dangers of fluctuations in global prices. The economy was one of the fastest growing in Latin America in 2002 and 2003. The Camisea natural gas pipeline project is scheduled to begin operations in 2004.

GDP: Purchasing power parity—$164.5 billion (2005 est.).

GDP—real growth rate: 6.7% (2005 est.).

GDP—per capita: Purchasing power parity—$5,900 (2005 est.).

Inflation rate: 1.6% (2005 est.).

Population below poverty line: 54% (2004 est.).

Unemployment rate: 8.7% in metropolitan Lima; widespread underemployment (2005 est.).

Exports: $15.95 billion f.o.b. (2005 est.)—fish and fish products, gold, copper, zinc, crude petroleum and by-products, lead, coffee, sugar, cotton.

Imports: $12.15 billion f.o.b. (2005 est.)—machinery, transport equipment, foodstuff, petroleum, iron and steel, chemicals, pharmaceuticals.

External debt: $30.18 billion (2005 est.).

Transport and Communications

Railways: 3,462 km.

Roads: 78,672 km.

Telephones: 2,049,800 (2004).

Mobile cellular: 4,092,600 (2004).

Internet users: 4.57 million (2005).

Internet country code: .pe

The Philippines

History

The Spanish colonization of the Philippines began with the arrival of Ferdinand Magellan in 1521. In 1898, the Philippines became a colony of the United States after the Spanish-American War. The United States brought widespread education to the islands. The Philippines achieved independence in 1946. Ferdinand Marcos, who became the President in 1965, declared martial law in 1972. This spell of martial law in the country lasted till 1981 and Marcos was ousted in 1986.

Geography

Location: South-eastern Asia, archipelago between the Philippine Sea and the South China Sea, east of Vietnam.

Area: 300,000 sq. km.

Terrain: Mostly mountainous with coastal lowlands.

Natural resources: Timber, nickel, cobalt, petroleum, silver, gold, salt, copper.

Climate: Hot and dry between March to May, rainy from June to October, and cold from November to February.

People

Population: 89,468,677 (July 2006 est.).

Population growth rate: 1.8% (2006 est.).

Sex ratio: 1 male(s)/female (2006 est.).

Religions: Roman Catholic 83%, Protestant 9%, Muslim 5%, Buddhist and others 3%.

Languages: Filipino (based on Tagalog) and English.

Literacy rate: Total 95.9%, Male 96%, Female 95.8% (2003 est.).

Infant mortality rate: 22.81 deaths/1,000 live births (2006 est.).

Life expectancy: Total 70.21 years, Male 67.32 years, Female 73.24 years (2006 est.).

Government

Capital: Manila.

Government type: Republic.

Independence: 12 June 1898 (from Spain); 4 July 1946 (from USA).

Legal system: Based on Spanish and Anglo-American law.

Executive branch:

Chief of state: President Gloria Macapagal-Arroyo (since 20 January 2001). The president is both the chief of state and head of government.

Economy

Currency: Philippine peso.

Economy—overview:

The Philippine economy is a combination of agriculture, light industry, and supporting services. In 1998, the economy faltered due largely to the Asian financial crisis and adverse weather conditions. Growth plummeted to 0.6 per cent in 1998 from 5 per cent in 1997. There was some recovery in the following years (about 3.3 per cent in 1999, 4.5 per cent in 2000, and 4.5 per cent in 2001). A growth of 4.4 per cent in 2002 was marred by a record budget deficit. The Philippines has a public sector debt of more than 100 per cent of GDP.

GDP: Purchasing power parity—$451.3 billion (2005 est.).

GDP—real growth rate: 5.1% (2005 est.).

GDP—per capita: Purchasing power parity—$5,100 (2005 est.).

Inflation rate: 7.9% (2005 est.).

Population below poverty line: 40% (2001 est.).

Unemployment rate: 12.2% (2005 est.).

Exports: $41.25 billion f.o.b. (2005 est.).

Imports: $42.66 billion f.o.b. (2005 est.).

External debt: $67.62 billion (2005 est.).

Transport and Communications

Railways: 897 km.

Roads: 202,124 km.

Telephones: 3,437,500 (2004).

Mobile cellular: 32,935,900 (2004).

Internet users: 7.82 million (2005).

Internet country code: .ph

Poland

History

In 966, Mieszko I of the Piast dynasty founded an entity known as Great Poland in the northern part of the present-day country. The tribes of southern Poland united to form Little Poland.The two entities joined together in 1047 under the reign of Casimir I, the Restorer. In 1386, Poland united with Lithuania by virtue of a royal marriage. This united state emerged to be a formidable force in Europe, mainly between the fourteenth and sixteenth centuries when it defeated the Russians, the Ottoman Turks and the Knights of the Teutonic Order.

However, the monarchy declined in the eighteenth century with disastrous consequences. The Russians, the Austrians and the Prussians divided the country thrice. Consequently, the state of Poland ceased to exist. However, the Poles continued their efforts to regain a national identity through the nineteenth century. Their efforts bore fruit in 1918 when the independent Polish state was created after the end of World War I.

In 1939, Germany invaded Poland. This was the starting point of World War II as UK declared war on Germany in reaction to the invasion, while the Soviet Union invaded the country from the east. During the War, Poland was the scene of some of the worst atrocities ever. Germans built concentration camps in Poland that included Auschwitz, Treblinka and Majdanek. Millions of Jews from all over Europe were rounded up at these camps and exterminated.

The Soviet Army finally took Warsaw in January 1945. The Germans were driven out of the country by March 1945. The post-war Potsdam Conference demarcated the borders of the country. In 1947, Poland became a Communist People's Republic.

In the 1980s, Lech Walesa emerged as the leader of the first independent labour union in a Soviet bloc country. In 1990, Walesa was elected president of Poland. He introduced various worker reforms and steered the country away from communism.

Geography

Location: Central Europe, east of Germany.

Area: 312,685 sq. km.

Terrain: Mostly flat plain; mountains along the southern border.

Natural resources: Coal, sulphur, copper, natural gas, silver, lead, salt, amber, arable land.

Climate: Temperate climate. The winters are cold, cloudy and moderately severe with frequent precipitation. The summers are mild with frequent showers and thundershowers.

People

Population: 38,536,869 (July 2006 est.).

Population growth rate: –0.05% (2006 est.).

Sex ratio: 0.94 male(s)/female (2006 est.).

Religions: Roman Catholic 89.8% (about 75% practicing), Eastern Orthodox 1.3%, Protestant 0.3%, and other 0.3% unspecified 8.3% (2002).

Languages: Polish.

Literacy rate: 99.8% (2003 est.).

Infant mortality rate: 7.22 deaths/1,000 live births (2006 est.).

Life expectancy: Total 74.97 years, Male 70.95 years, Female 79.23 years (2006 est.).

Government

Capital: Warsaw.

Government type: Republic.

Independence: 11 November 1918 (date on which an independent republic was proclaimed).

Legal system: Mixture of Continental (Napoleonic) civil law and holdover communist legal theory.

Executive branch:

Chief of state: President Lech Kaczynski (since 23 December 2005).

Head of government: Prime Minister Kazimierz Marcinkiewicz (since 31 October 2005); Deputy Prime Ministers Ludwik Dorn (since 23 November 2005) and Zyta Gilowska (since 7 Jannuary 2006).

Economy

Currency: Zloty.

GDP: Purchasing power parity—$514 billion (2005 est.).

GDP—real growth rate: 3.2% (2005 est.).

GDP—per capita: Purchasing power parity—$13,300 (2005 est.).

Inflation rate: 2.1% (2005 est.).

Population below poverty line: 17% (2003 est.).

Unemployment rate: 18.3% (2005 est.).

Exports: $92.72 billion f.o.b. (2005 est.)—machinery and transport equipment, intermediate manufactured goods, miscellaneous manufactured goods, food and live animals.

Imports: $95.67 billion f.o.b. (2005 est.)—machinery and transport equipment, intermediate manufactured goods, chemicals, miscellaneous manufactured goods.

External debt: $123.4 billion (2005 est.).

Transport and Communications

Railways: 23,852 km.

Roads: 423,997 km.

Telephones: 12,300,000 (2003).

Mobile cellular: 23,096,100 (2004).

Internet users: 10.6 million (2005).

Internet country code: .pl

Portugal

History

Portugal gained independence from Spain in 1143. The following centuries saw the rapid expansion of Portuguese rule all over the world. In 1488, Bartolomeu Dias reached the Cape of Good Hope, the southernmost tip of the African mainland. In 1498, Vasco da Gama reached India. By the middle of the sixteenth century, the Portuguese empire included Brazil, Indo-China, East and West Africa and Malaya.

Spain invaded Portugal in 1581 and held it for the next sixty years, triggering a marked decline in Portuguese trade and commerce. The Portuguese hold over its far-flung colonies also suffered. Its European rivals wasted no time in snatching one territory after another from Portuguese rule. By the time the Spanish occupation was over, the only significant overseas possessions left for Portugal was Brazil, Angola and Mozambique.

In 1908, King Carlos and his heir were both assassinated in Lisbon. His second, Manuel, took to the throne. But he was ousted in a revolution. A republic was proclaimed in 1910. In 1911, a new constitution separated the church from the state.

In 1974, a left-wing military coup installed broad democratic reforms. The following year, Portugal granted independence to all of its African colonies.

Portugal is a founding member of NATO and entered the EC (now the EU) in 1986.

Geography

Location: South-western Europe, bordering the North Atlantic Ocean, west of Spain.

Area: 92,391 sq. km (this includes Azores and Madeira Islands).

Terrain: Rolling plains in the south and a mountainous area north of the Tagus River.

Natural resources: Fish, forests (cork), iron ore, copper, zinc, tin, tungsten, silver, gold, uranium, marble, clay, gypsum, salt, arable land, hydropower.

Climate: Maritime temperate climate.

People

Population: 10,605,870 (July 2006 est.).

Population growth rate: 0.36% (2006 est.).

Sex ratio: 0.95 male(s)/female (2006 est.).

Religions: Roman Catholic 94%, Protestant.

Languages: Portuguese (official), Mirandese (official).

Literacy rate: Total 93.3%, Male 95.5%, Female 91.3% (2003 est.).

Infant mortality rate: 4.98 deaths/ 1,000 live births (2006 est.).

Life expectancy: Total 77.7 years, Male 74.43 years, Female 81.2 years (2006 est.).

Government

Capital: Lisbon.

Government type: Parliamentary democracy.

Independence: 1143 (independent republic proclaimed on 5 October 1910).

Legal system: Civil law system.

Executive branch:
Chief of state: President Anibal Cavaco Silva (since 9 March 2006).

Head of government: Prime Minister Jose Socrates (since 12 March 2005).

Economy

Currency: Euro.

Economy—overview:
Portugal has a well diversified service-based economy. It was one of the countries that started circulating the euro common currency on 1 January 2002. One of the major obstacles facing the country is its educational system.

GDP: Purchasing power parity—$204.4 billion (2005 est.).

GDP—real growth rate: 0.3% (2005 est.).

GDP—per capita: Purchasing power parity—$19,300 (2005 est.).

Inflation rate: 2.4% (2005 est.).

Unemployment rate: 7.3% (2005 est.).

Exports: $38.8 billion f.o.b. (2005 est.)—clothing and footwear, machinery, chemicals, cork and paper products, hides.

Imports: $60.35 billion f.o.b. (2005 est.)—machinery and transport equipment, chemicals, petroleum, textiles, agricultural products.

External debt: $298.7 billion (30 June 2005 est.).

Transport and Communications

Railways: 2,850 km.

Roads: 72,600 km.

Telephones: 4,238,300 (2004).

Mobile cellular: 10,362,100 (2004).

Internet users: 6.09 million (2004).

Internet country code: .pt

Qatar

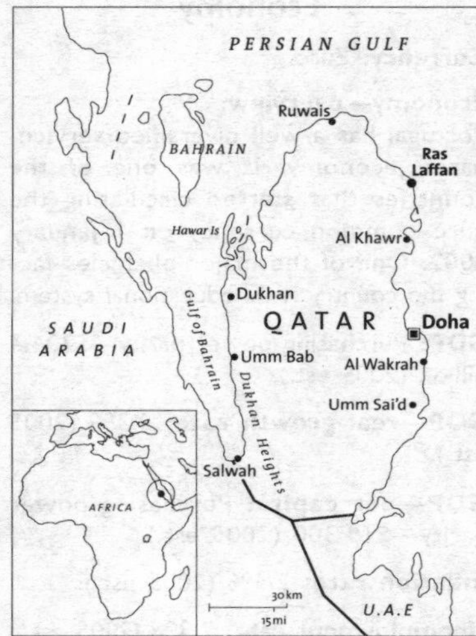

History

In 1783 the Âl Khalîfah family of Kuwait led the conquest of Bahrain, and installed themselves as the ruling family. They remained so in the twentieth century. In 1867 a dispute arose between the Âl Khalîfahs of Bahrain and Qatar over the town of Az-Zubârah which escalated into a major confrontation. It was at this point of time that UK signed a separate treaty with Qatar, whom it had viewed as a Bahraini dependency till then. Between 1916 and 1971, Qatar was a British protectorate. In 1971, it declared independence.

Geography

Location: Middle East, peninsula bordering the Persian Gulf and Saudi Arabia.

Area: 11,437 sq. km.

Terrain: Flat and barren desert covered with loose sand and gravel.

Natural resources: Petroleum, natural gas, fish.

Climate: Summer lasts from May to September when temperatures and humidity are both very high. The winter months are from December to February. These are milder with pleasant and cool evenings.

People

Population: 885,359 (July 2006 est.).

Population growth rate: 2.5% (2006 est.).

Sex ratio: 1.87 male(s)/female (2006 est.).

Religions: Muslim 95%.

Languages: Arabic (official), English commonly used as a second language.

Literacy rate: Total 89%, Male 89.1%, Female 88.6% (2004 est.).

Infant mortality rate: 18.04 deaths/1,000 live births (2006 est.).

Life expectancy: Total 73.9 years, Male 71.37 years, Female 76.57 years (2006 est.).

Government

Capital: Doha.

Government type: Traditional monarchy.

Independence: 3 September 1971 (from UK).

Legal system: There is a discretionary system of law controlled by the amir. Civil codes are being implemented. Islamic law dominates family and personal matters.

Executive branch:
Chief of state: Amir Hamad bin Khalifa Al Thani (since 27 June 1995).

Head of government: Prime Minister Abdallah bin Khalifa Al Thani, brother of the monarch (since 30 October 1996); Deputy Prime Minister Muhammad bin Khalifa Al Thani (since 20 January 1998).

Economy

Currency: Qatari rial.

Economy—overview:
Oil and gas account for more than 55 per cent of GDP, around 85 per cent of export earnings and 70 per cent of government revenues. Thanks to petroleum, Qatar has a per capita GDP that can be compared to that of the leading West European industrial countries. Qatar has proven oil reserves of 14.5 billion barrels. Qatar's proven reserves of natural gas exceed 17.9 trillion cubic metres, third largest in the world and about 5 per cent of the world total. Since 2000, Qatar has posted trade surpluses, mostly due to high oil prices and rising natural gas exports.

GDP: Purchasing power parity—$23.64 billion (2005 est.).

GDP—real growth rate: 8.8% (2005 est.).

GDP—per capita: Purchasing power parity—$27.400 (2005 est.).

Inflation rate: 7.8% (2005).

Unemployment rate: 2.7% (2001).

Exports: $24.9 billion f.o.b. (2005 est.).

Imports: $6.706 billion f.o.b. (2005 est.).

External debt: $20.63 billion (2005 est.).

Transport and Communications

Railways: None.

Roads: 1,230 km.

Telephones: 190,900 (2004).

Mobile cellular: 490,300 (2004).

Internet users: 165,000 (2005).

Internet country code: .qa

Romania

History

In May 1877, Romania proclaimed its independence from Turkey and in March 1881, the kingdom of Romania was proclaimed. The 1930s saw the rise of a fascist 'Iron Guard' movement in Romania. In 1938, King Carol II established a royal dictatorship in the country. During World War II, Romania joined the Axis powers and was part of the 1940 attack on Soviet Union. In August 1944, the Soviet Red Army invaded Romania. In 1945, a Soviet-backed government was installed in Romania. The Romanian People's Republic was proclaimed in December 1947.

In 1965, Nicolae Ceausescu became the new leader of the Communist Party. He not only promulgated a foreign policy independent from that of the Soviet Union but also denounced the Soviet invasion of Czechoslovakia in 1968. In 1975, USA granted Romania 'most favoured nation' status. However, Ceausescu's regime soon turned Romania into a police state.

Ceausescu and his wife were apprehended, given a trial and executed on Christmas Day, 1989. The opponents of communism set up the National Salvation Front to lead the country through this crucial phase. Ion Iliescu was chosen as the leader.

Geography

Location: South-eastern Europe, bordering the Black Sea, between Bulgaria and Ukraine.

Area: 237,500 sq. km.

Terrain: The country has the central Transylvanian Basin that is separated from the plains of Moldova on the east by the Caspainian mountains and from the Walachian Plain on the south by the Transylvanian Alps.

Natural resources: Petroleum (reserves declining), timber, natural gas, coal, iron ore, salt, arable land, hydropower.

Climate: Temperate climate. The winters are cold and cloudy with frequent snow and fog.

People

Population: 22,303,552 (July 2006 est.).

Population growth rate: –0.12% (2006 est.).

Sex ratio: 0.95 male(s)/female (2005 est.).

Religions: Eastern Orthodox (including all sub-denominations) 87%, Protestant 6.8%, Catholic 5.6%, others (mostly Muslim) 0.4%, unaffiliated 0.2% (2002).

Languages: Romanian (official), Hungarian, German.

Literacy rate: Total 98.4%, Male 99.1%, Female 97.7% (2003 est.).

Infant mortality rate: 25.5 deaths/1,000 live births (2006 est.).

Life expectancy: Total 71.63 years, Male 68.14 years, Female 75.34 years (2006 est.).

Government

Capital: Bucharest.

Government type: Republic.

Independence: 9 May 1877 (date of proclamation of independence from Turkey); 30 December 1947 (date on which republic was proclaimed).

Legal system: Based on the constitution of France's Fifth Republic.

Executive branch:
Chief of state: President Traian Basescu (since 20 December 2004).

Head of government: Prime Minister Calin Popescu Tariceanu (since 29 December 2004).

Economy

Currency: Leu.

GDP: Purchasing power parity—$183.6 billion (2005 est.).

GDP—real growth rate: 4.5% (2005 est.).

GDP—per capita: Purchasing power parity—$8,200 (2005 est.).

Inflation rate: 8.6% (2005).

Population below poverty line: 25% (2005).

Unemployment rate: 6.5% (2005).

Exports: $27.72 billion f.o.b. (2005 est.)—textiles and footwear, metals and metal products, machinery and equipment, minerals and fuels, chemicals, agricultural products.

Imports: $38.15 billion f.o.b. (2005 est.)—machinery and equipment, fuels and minerals, chemicals, textile and products, basic metals, agricultural products.

External debt: $29.47 billion (2005 est.).

Transport and Communications

Railways: 198,817 km (3,888 km electrified).

Roads: 198,755 km.

Telephones: 4,389,100 (2004).

Mobile cellular: 10,215,400 (2004).

Internet users: 4.5 million (2004).

Internet country code: .ro

Russia

History

According to tradition, the Viking Rurik reached Russia in 862 and established the first Russian dynasty. The various factions were united in the tenth and eleventh centuries.

Between 1552 and 1556, Ivan IV 'the Terrible' conquered the Tartar khanates of Kazan and Astrakhan and established Russian rule over the lower and middle Volga region. He was the first person to be proclaimed tsar of Russia (in 1547). His reign saw the completion of the establishment of a centrally administered Russian state and the creation of an empire that also included non-Slav states. He gained notoriety for his reign of terror against the hereditary nobility.

In the 1580s, the Cossacks began invading Siberia. In 1613, the National Council elected Michael Romanov as tsar. This started the Romanov dynasty that ruled Russia until the 1917 revolution. His grandson, Peter the Great, introduced far-reaching structural reforms in the government, creating a regular conscript army and navy, and subordinating the church to the crown.

From 1798–1814, Russia intervened in the Napoleonic wars in France. Napoleon's defeat in the 1812 invasion of Russia hastened his downfall. The Crimean War was fought between the Russians and the British, French, and Ottoman Turkish from 1853 to 1856. The 1856–64 Caucasian War completed the Russian annexation of the North Caucasus. The area of the present-day Central Asian republics was annexed between 1864–5.

In 1897, the Social Democratic Party was founded in Russia. In 1903, the party split into two factions—the Bolsheviks and the Mensheviks. In 1904–5, Russian expansion in Manchuria precipitated a war with Japan. Defeat in this war sparked the 1905 revolution that forced Tsar Nicholas II to grant a Constitution and establish a popularly elected constitutional body, the Duma.

The 1917 revolution had its roots in the riots that broke out in the city of Petrograd (now St. Petersburg) over food scarcity. Tsar Nicholas II was forced to abdicate bringing more than 300 years of Romanov rule to an end. The Bolsheviks were installed in power. The first head of government was the founder of the Bolshevik Russian Communist Party, Vladimir Ilich Ulyanov, better known as Lenin. Lenin served till his death in 1924. The death of Lenin in 1924 resulted in a power struggle within the Communist Party, between Joseph Stalin and Leon Trotsky. After being dismissed from the office of Commissar of War, Trotsky was exiled in 1929. In 1940, he was murdered in Mexico City.

Stalin consolidated his stranglehold on power through a series of purges that eliminated his rivals and dissenters. He finally assumed premiership in 1941. Stalin successfully led USSR in World War II, in which he linked up with the Allied forces alongside UK and USA.

The Union of Soviet Socialist Republics, USSR, was formed as a federation on 30 December 1922. At its height, USSR, or Soviet Union, was the world's largest country. It was one of the only two global superpowers. The country covered around 22,400,000 square kilometres, seven times the area of India and more than twice the size of the United States. The country occupied nearly one-sixth of the earth's land surface, covering eleven of the world's twenty-four time zones. It had the longest coastline and the longest frontiers of any country in the world.

Under the leadership of the Communist Party of the Soviet Union, USSR had an authoritarian and highly centralized political and economic system. The economic foundation of the USSR was described as 'Socialist ownership of the means of production, distribution, and exchange'. A series of five-year plans that set targets for all forms of production controlled the economy of the entire country.

In 1949, Soviet Union exploded its first atomic device. It followed this up with its first hydrogen bomb, exploded in 1953. In 1957, USSR launched the first-ever artificial earth satellite, Sputnik, to orbit the earth. In 1961, Soviet cosmonaut Yuri Gagarin accomplished the first manned orbital flight.

The emergence of two global giants, USSR and USA soon led to the development of a bipolar power structure in the world and heralded the Cold War. The Soviet cause was propagated through the installation of communist regimes in Eastern Europe, the formation of the Warsaw Pact, and the establishment of communist regimes in China, Cuba and North Korea. The Cold War reached a peak between 1948 and 1953. The death of Stalin in 1953 somewhat lulled the low-intensity conflict. But the tension resumed in the late 1950s and the early 1960s.

In October 1962, a major confrontation brought the United States and the Soviet Union to the brink of nuclear war. The issue was the presence of Soviet nuclear-armed missiles in Cuba. In May 1960, Soviet Premier Nikita

Khrushchev pledged to defend Cuba with Soviet weapons. In July 1962, USA realized that the Soviet Union had begun missile shipments to Cuba. In retaliation, USA placed Cuba under a naval blockade. Finally, on 28 October, the Soviet Union informed USA it was stopping work on its missile sites in Cuba and taking back its missiles from the island. In return, the United States pledged never to invade Cuba and also secretly promised to withdraw US nuclear missiles stationed in Turkey.

The prevailing atmosphere of peace between USSR and USA came to an end when Soviet troops invaded Afghanistan in December 1979. The Soviet aim was to protect the regime of pro-Soviet leader Babrak Karmal.

The USA provided money and sophisticated equipment to the Afghans and their allies in the region to fight the Soviets. In 1988 USA, USSR, Pakistan, and Afghanistan signed an agresement that resulted in the complete withdrawal of Soviet troops in 1989.

In 1985, Mikhail Gorbachev became the new general secretary of the Communist Party while Andrey Gromyko became the new president. Gorbachev promulgated the policies of openness (glasnost) and restructuring (perestroika). In 1988, Gorbachev took over as the new president.

In 1989, Soviet troops suppressed a nationalist riot in the republic of Georgia. The same year, the Lithuanian Communist Party declared its independence from the Soviet communist Party. In 1990, Soviet troops were sent to Azerbaijan following inter-ethnic killings. Gorbachev opposed the independence of the Baltic states and imposed sanctions on Lithuania. Meanwhile, communist leader Boris Yeltsin was elected the president of the Russian Soviet Federative Socialist Republic. He left the Soviet Communist Party soon afterwards.

In August 1991, senior communist party officials detained Gorbachev at his holiday villa in Crimea. The coup however came to an end within days when the coup leaders themselves were arrested. This set off a chain of events leading to the ultimate collapse of the USSR.

Boris Yeltsin banned the Soviet Communist Party in Russia and seized its assets. He also recognized the independence of the Baltic republics. When the republic of Ukraine declared its independence from the Union, other republics followed suit and announced their breaking away. In September 1991, the Congress of People's Deputies voted for the dissolution of the Soviet Union. On Christmas Day 1991, Mikhail Gorbachev resigned as the Soviet President. On 31 December 1999, President Boris Yeltsin unexpectedly announced his resignation and named Prime Minister Putin as the acting President.

Geography

Location: Northern Asia and northern Europe, bordering the Arctic Ocean, North Pacific Ocean and the Black Sea.

Area: 17,075,200 sq. km.

Terrain: Broad plains and low hills west of the Urals. Siberia has vast stretches of coniferous forest and tundra. There are uplands and mountains along the southern border regions.

Natural resources: Russia is one of the world's largest oil and natural gas producers. Other natural resources present in the country include coal, various minerals and timber.

Climate: The vast expanse of Russia means that climate varies from one part of the country to another. The country has a humid continental type of climate in most parts of European Russia. The climate of Siberia is of the sub-arctic type although the polar north has tundra climate. The winters vary from cool along the Black Sea coast to frigid in Siberia while summers vary from warm in the steppes to cool along Arctic coast.

People

Population: 142,893,540 (July 2006 est.).

Population growth rate: –0.37% (2006 est.).

Sex ratio: 0.86 male(s)/female (2006 est.).

Religions: Russian Orthodox, Muslim, others.

Languages: Russian, local languages.

Literacy rate: 99.6% (2003 est.).

Infant mortality rate: 15.13 deaths/1,000 live births (2006 est.).

Life expectancy: Total 67.08 years, Male 60.45 years, Female 74.14 years (2006 est.).

Government

Capital: Moscow.

Government type: Federation.

Independence: 24 August 1991 (from Soviet Union).

Legal system: Based on civil law system; judicial review of legislative acts.

Executive branch:

Chief of state: President Vladimir Vladimirovich Putin (acting president since 31 December 1999, president since 7 May 2000).

Head of government: Premier Mikhail Yefimovich Fradkov (since 5 March 2004).

Elections and election results: The president is elected by popular vote for a four-year term. The election was last held on 14 March 2004 and will be held next in March 2008. The president appoints the premier with the approval of the Duma.

Legislative branch:

Russia has a bicameral Federal Assembly or Federalnoye Sobraniye that consists of the Federation Council or Sovet Federatsii and the State Duma or Gosudarstvennaya Duma. The Federation Council has 178 seats. Members serve four-year terms. The State Duma has 450 seats 225 seats are elected by proportional representation from party lists winning at least 5 per cent of the vote. The remaining 225 seats are elected from single-member constituencies. Members are elected by direct, popular vote to serve four-year terms.

Elections and election results: State Duma elections were last held on 7 December 2003 and will be next held in December 2007.

Economy

Currency: Russian rouble (RUR).

Economy—overview:

The Russian economy has staged a recovery since the financial crisis of 1998. The year 2003 was its fifth straight year of growth and the country's average annual growth has been around 6.5 per cent. The main drivers of this growth were high oil prices and a relatively cheap ruble. Besides, the economy has also seen significant investment and consumer-driven demand since 2000. Russia's international financial position has also improved since the 1998 financial crisis. One noteworthy feature has been that its foreign debt has dropped from around 90 per cent of GDP to around 28 per cent. Its foreign reserves have grown from only $12 billion a few years back to around $80 billion, largely due to oil export earnings. All these factors, along with the government effort to carry out structural reforms have raised business and investor confidence in the country. However, the economy is not without flaws. Petroleum, metals, and timber make up more than 80 per cent of exports. This exposes the country to the potential dangers associated with world price swings. Another major problem facing the country is its outdated manufacturing sector, corruption, problematic banking system, and government intervention in the legal system. The recent controversy surrounding the arrest and trial of the head of one of Russia's largest oil companies has shaken foreign perception of the country.

GDP: Purchasing power parity—$1.589 trillion (2005 est.).

GDP—real growth rate: 6.4% (2005 est.).

GDP—per capita: Purchasing power parity—$11,100 (2005 est.).

Inflation rate: 11% (2005 est.).

Population below poverty line: 17.8% (January 2003 est.).

Unemployment rate: 7.6% plus considereable unemployment (2005 est.).

Exports: $245 billion (2005 est.)—petroleum and petroleum products, natural gas, metals, chemicals, military products, wood and wood products.

Imports: $125 billion (2005 est.)—machinery and equipment, consumer goods, medicines, meat, sugar, semi-finished metal products.

External debt: $230.3 billion (30 June 2005 est.).

Transport and Communications

Railways: 87,157 km.

Roads: 537,289 km.

Telephones: 39.616 million (2004).

Mobile cellular: 74.42 million (2004).

Internet users: 23.7 million (2005).

Internet country code: .ru

Rwanda

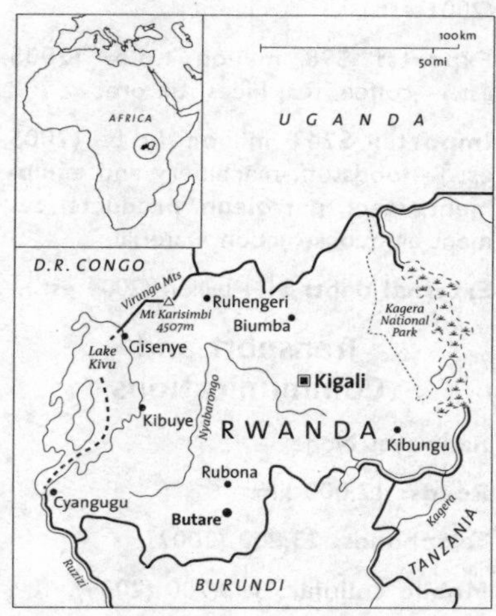

History

In 1890, Rwanda became a part of German East Africa. In 1916, Belgium occupied the territory. Subsequently, Belgium ruled the territory indirectly through Tutsi kings. In 1962, Rwanda became independent.

In 1988, around 50,000 Hutu refugees from Burundi escaped to Rwanda following ethnic violence there. In April 1994, the Rwandan and Burundian presidents were both killed when their plane was shot down. This was followed by the systematic massacre of Tutsis by Hutu militia. Around 800,000 Tutsis and moderate Hutus were killed in 100 days.

In December 2001, Rwanda adopted a new flag and national anthem. In June 2002, the International Court of Justice in the Hague began to consider a suit filed by Democratic Republic of the Congo against Rwanda and its allies for human rights abuse, genocide and armed aggression. Paul Kagame won landslide victories in presidential and parliamentary elections held in 2003. In 2004, a French report concluded that it was Paul Kagame who ordered the

1994 shooting down of the aircraft carrying the Rwandan and Burundian presidents.

Geography

Location: Central Africa, east of Democratic Republic of the Congo.

Area: 26,338 sq. km.

Natural resources: Gold, cassiterite (tin ore), wolframite (tungsten ore), methane, hydropower, arable land.

Climate: Temperate climate. There are two rainy seasons, one from February to April and the other from November to January.

People

Population: 8,648,248 (July 2006 est.).

Population growth rate: 2.43% (2006 est.).

Sex ratio: 0.99 male(s)/female (2006 est.).

Religions: Roman Catholic 56.5%, Protestant 26%, Adventist 11.1%, Muslim 4.6%, indigenous beliefs 0.1%, none 1.7%.

Languages: Kinyarwanda (official), French (official), English (official), Kiswahili (Swahili) used for commercial purpose.

Literacy rate: Total 70.4%, Male 76.3%, Female 64.7% (2003 est.).

Infant mortality rate: 89.61 deaths/1,000 live births (2005 est.).

Life expectancy: Total 47.3 years, Male 46.26 years, Female 48.38 years (2006 est.).

Government

Capital: Kigali.

Government type: Republic; presidential, multiparty system.

Independence: 1 July 1962 (from Belgium-administered UN trusteeship).

Legal system: Based on German and Belgian civil law systems and customary law.

Executive branch:

Chief of state: President Paul Kagame (since 22 April 2000).

Head of government: Prime Minister Bernard Makuza (since 8 March 2000).

Economy

Currency: Rwandan franc.

GDP: Purchasing power parity—$12.65 billion (2005 est.).

GDP—real growth rate: 5.2% (2005 est.).

GDP—per capita: Purchasing power parity—$1,500 (2005 est.).

Inflation rate: 8% (2005 est.).

Population below poverty line: 60% (2001 est.).

Exports: $98 million f.o.b. (2005 est.)—coffee, tea, hides, tin ore.

Imports: $243 million f.o.b. (2005 est.)—foodstuff, machinery and equipment, steel, petroleum products, cement and construction material.

External debt: $1.4 billion (2004 est.).

Transport and Communications

Railways: None.

Roads: 12,000 km.

Telephones: 23,200 (2002).

Mobile cellular: 138,700 (2004).

Internet users: 38,000 (2005).

Internet country code: .rw

Saint Kitts and Nevis

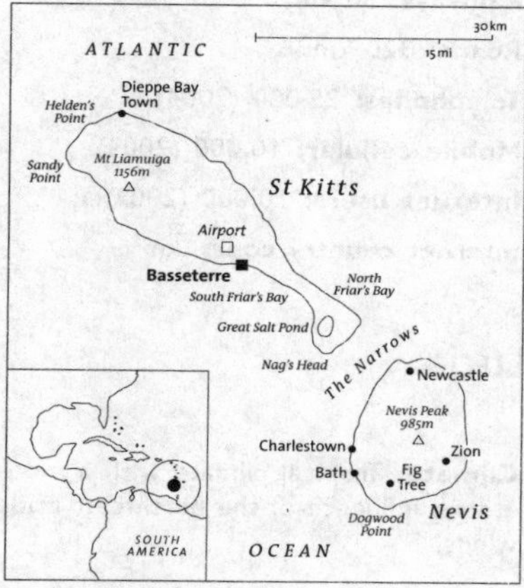

History

The British settled in St. Kitts (formerly St. Christopher) in 1623 and Nevis in 1628. The French arrived at St. Kitts in 1627 and this sparked off a conflict between the two European powers that ended with a decisive French defeat in 1782. In 1958, the islands became a part of the West Indian federation and remained so till its dissolution in 1962. St. Kitts and Nevis became independent in 1983.

Geography

Location: Caribbean islands in the Caribbean Sea, about one-third of the way from Puerto Rico to Trinidad and Tobago.

Area: 261 sq. km (Saint Kitts 168 sq. km; Nevis 93 sq. km).

Natural resources: Arable land.

Climate: Tropical climate with constant sea breezes. There is little seasonal temperature variation.

People

Population: 39,129 (July 2006 est.).

Population growth rate: 0.5% (2006 est.).

Sex ratio: 0.99 male(s)/female (2006 est.).

Religions: Anglican, other Protestant, Roman Catholic.

Languages: English.

Literacy rate: Total 97.8% (2003 est.).

Infant mortality rate: 14.12 deaths/1,000 live births (2006 est.).

Life expectancy: Total 72.4 years, Male 69.56 years, Female 75.42 years (2006 est.).

Government

Capital: Basseterre.

Government type: Constitutional monarchy with Westminster-style parliament.

Independence: 19 September 1983 (from UK).

Legal system: Based on English common law.

Executive branch:
Chief of state: Queen Elizabeth II (since 6 February 1952), represented by Governor General Cuthbert Montraville Sebastian (since 1 January 1996).

Head of government: Prime Minister Dr Denzil Douglas (since 6 July 1995) and Deputy Prime Minister Sam Condor (since 6 July 1995).

Economy

Currency: East Caribbean dollar.

GDP: Purchasing power parity—$339 million (2002 est.).

GDP—real growth rate: –1.9% (2002 est.).

GDP—per capita: Purchasing power parity—$8,800 (2002 est.).

Inflation rate: 1.7% (2001 est.).

Unemployment rate: 4.5% (1997).

Exports: $70 million (2004 est.)—machinery, food, electronics, beverages, tobacco.

Imports: $405 million (2004 est.)—machinery, manufactures, food, fuels.

External debt: $171 million (2001).

Transport and Communications

Railways: 50 km.

Roads: 320 km.

Telephones: 25,000 (2004).

Mobile cellular: 10,000 (2004).

Internet users: 10,000 (2002).

Internet country code: .kn

Saint Lucia

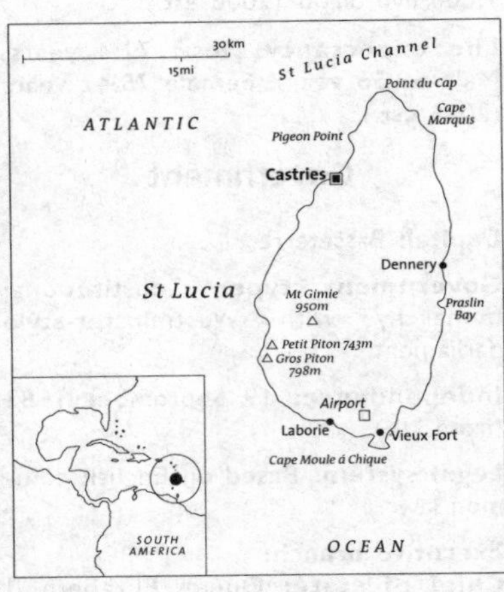

History

Saint Lucia became a British possession. In 1871, it became a part of the British territory of Windward Islands. In 1979, St. Lucia achieved independence.

Geography

Location: Caribbean, island between the Caribbean Sea and North Atlantic Ocean, north of Trinidad and Tobago.

Area: 616 sq. km.

Natural resources: Forests, sandy beaches, minerals (pumice), mineral springs, geothermal potential.

Climate: Tropical climate with a moderating influence of the north-east trade winds.

People

Population: 168,458 (July 2006 est.).

Population growth rate: 1.29% (2006 est.).

Sex ratio: 0.97 male(s)/female (2006 est.).

Religions: Roman Catholic 67.5%, Seventh Day Adventist 8.5% Pentecostal 5.7%, Anglican 2%, Evangelical 2%, other Christian 5.1%, Rastafarian 2.1%, other 1.1%, unspecified 1.5%, none 4.5%.

Languages: English (official), French patois.

Literacy rate: Total 90.1%, Male 89.5%, Female 90.6% (2001 est.).

Infant mortality rate: 13.17 deaths/1,000 live births (2006 est).

Life expectancy: Total 73.84 years, Male 70.29 years, Female 77.65 years (2006 est.).

Government

Capital: Castries.

Government type: Westminster-style parliamentary democracy.

Independence: 22 February 1979 (from UK).

Legal system: Based on English common law.

Executive branch:
Chief of state: Queen Elizabeth II (since 6 February 1952), represented by Governor General Dr Perlette Louisy (since September 1997).

Head of government: Prime Minister Kenneth Davis Anthony (since 24 May 1997) and Deputy Prime Minister Mario Michel (since 24 May 1997).

Economy

Currency: East Caribbean dollar.

GDP: Purchasing power parity—$866 million (2002 est.).

GDP—real growth rate: 3.3% (2002 est.).

GDP—per capita: Purchasing power parity—$5,400 (2002 est.).

Inflation rate: 3% (2001 est.).

Unemployment rate: 20% (2003 est.).

Exports: $82 million (2004 est.)—banana, clothing, cocoa, vegetables, fruits, coconut oil.

Imports: $410 million (2004 est.)—food 23%, manufactured goods 21%, machinery and transportation equipment 19%, chemicals, fuels.

External debt: $214 million (2000).

Transport and Communications

Railways: None.

Roads: 1,210 km.

Telephones: 51,100 (2002).

Mobile cellular: 93,000 (2004).

Internet users: 55,000 (2005).

Internet country code: .lc

Saint Vincent and the Grenadines

History

In 1763, the islands became a British colony. Between 1958 and 1962, the islands were part of the West Indies Federation. They finally gained independence in 1979.

Geography

Location: Caribbean, islands between the Caribbean Sea and North Atlantic Ocean, north of Trinidad and Tobago.

Area: 389 sq. km (Saint Vincent 344 sq. km).

Natural resources: Hydropower, cropland.

Climate: Tropical climate with little seasonal temperature variation.

People

Population: 117,848 (July 2006 est.).

Population growth rate: 0.26% (2006 est.).

Sex ratio: 1.04 male(s)/female (2006 est.).

Religions: Anglican 47%, Methodist 28%, Roman Catholic 13%, Hindu, Seventh-Day Adventist, other Protestant.

Languages: English, French patois.

Literacy rate: Total 96%, Male 96%, Female 96% (1970 est.).

Infant mortality rate: 14.4 deaths/1,000 live births (2006 est.).

Life expectancy: Total 73.85 years, Male 71.99 years, Female 75.77 years (2006 est.).

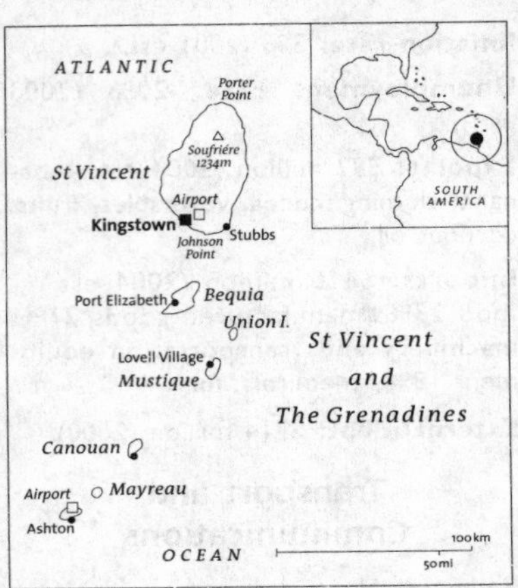

Government

Capital: Kingstown.

Government type: Parliamentary democracy; independent sovereign state within the Commonwealth.

Independence: 27 October 1979 (from UK).

Legal system: Based on English common law.

Executive branch:
Chief of state: Queen Elizabeth II (since 6 February 1952), represented by Governor General Sir Fredrick Nathaniel Ballantyne (since 2 September 2002).

Head of government: Prime Minister Ralph E. Gonsalves (since 29 March 2001).

Economy

Currency: East Caribbean dollar.

GDP: Purchasing power parity—$342 million (2002 est.).

GDP—real growth rate: 0.7% (2002 est.).

GDP—per capita: Purchasing power parity—$2,900 (2002 est.).

Inflation rate: –0.4% (2001 est.).

Unemployment rate: 15% (2001 est.).

Exports: $37 million (2004 est.).

Imports: $225 million (2004 est.).

External debt: $167.2 million (2000).

Transport and Communications

Railways: 829 km.

Roads: 1,829 km.

Telephones: 19,000 (2004).

Mobile cellular: 57,000 (2004).

Internet users: 8,000 (2005).

Internet country code: .vc

Samoa

History

USA, UK and Germany all contested for the islands till they were divided between USA and Germany in 1899. In 1914, New Zealand occupied Western Samoa. In 1962, it became independent and in 1997 the word 'Western' was dropped from the name.

Geography

Location: Oceania, group of islands in the South Pacific Ocean, north-east of Australia.

Area: 2,944 sq. km.

Natural resources: Hardwood forests, fish, hydropower.

Climate: Tropical climate with a rainy season between October to March and a dry season from May to October.

People

Population: 176,908 (July 2006 est.).

Population growth rate: –0.2% (2006 est.).

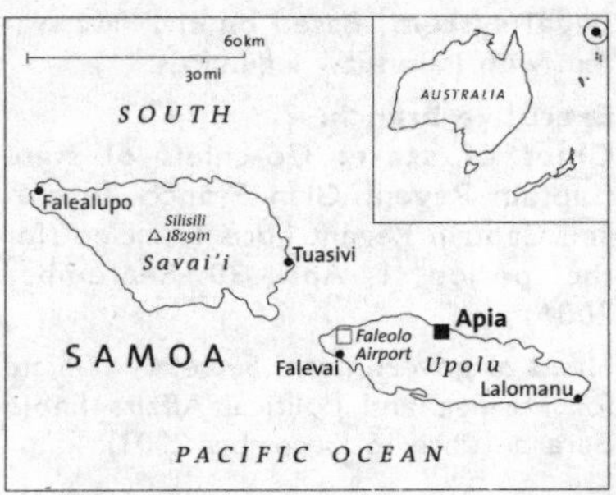

Sex ratio: 1.39 male(s)/female (2006 est.).

Religions: Christian 99.7%.

Languages: Samoan (Polynesian), English.

Literacy rate: 99.7% (2003 est.).

Infant mortality rate: 26.85 deaths/1,000 live births (2006 est.).

Life expectancy: Total 71 years, Male 68.2 years, Female 73.94 years (2006 est.).

Government

Capital: Apia.

Government type: Constitutional monarchy under native chief.

Independence: 1 January 1962 (from New Zealand-administered UN trusteeship).

Legal system: Based on English common law and local customs.

Executive branch:

Chief of state: Chief Tanumafili II Malietoa. (He was the co-chief of state from 1 January 1962 and became the sole chief of state from 5 April 1963.)

Head of government: Prime Minister Sailele Malielegaoi Tuila'epa (since 1996).

Economy

Currency: Tala.

GDP: Purchasing power parity—$1 billion (2002 est.).

GDP—real growth rate: 5% (2002 est.).

GDP—per capita: Purchasing power parity—$5,600 (2002 est.).

Inflation rate: 4% (2001 est.).

Exports: $94 million f.o.b. (2002)—fish, coconut oil and cream, copra, taro, automotive parts, garments, beer.

Imports: $285 million f.o.b. (2004)—machinery and equipment, industrial supplies, foodstuffs.

External debt: $197 million (2000).

Transport and Communications

Railways: None.

Roads: 790 km.

Telephones: 13,300 (2003).

Mobile cellular: 10,500 (2003).

Internet users: 6,000 (2004).

Internet country code: .ws

San Marino

History

According to tradition, a Christian stonemason named Marinus founded San Marino in AD 301. In 1463, the Pope awarded the towns of Fiorentino, Montegiardino and Serravalle to San Marino. The town of Faetano joined the republic in 1464. In 1631, the papacy recognized San Marino's independence. In 1862, San Marino signed a customs union and treaty of friendship and cooperation with Italy.

Geography

Location: Southern Europe, an enclave in central Italy.

Area: 61.2 sq. km.

Natural resources: Building stone.

Climate: Mediterranean climate with mild to cool winters and warm, sunny summers.

People

Population: 29,251 (July 2006 est.).

Population growth rate: 1.26% (2006 est.).

Sex ratio: 0.92 male(s)/female (2006 est.).

Religions: Roman Catholic.

Languages: Italian.

Literacy rate: Total 96%, Male 97%, Female 95% (1976 est.).

Infant mortality rate: 5.63 deaths/ 1,000 live births (2006 est.).

Life expectancy: Total 81.71 years, Male 78.23 years, Female 85.5 years (2006 est.).

Government

Capital: San Marino.

Government type: Republic.

Independence: 3 September 301 (date of foundation of the republic).

Legal system: Based on civil law system with Italian law influences.

Executive branch:

Chief of state: Co-chiefs of state Captain Regent Gian Franco Terenzi and Captain Regent Loris Francine (for the period 1 April–30 September 2006).

Head of government: Secretary of State for Foreign and Political Affairs Fabio Berardi (since 15 December 2003).

Economy

Currency: Euro.

GDP: Purchasing power parity—$940 million (2001 est.).

GDP—real growth rate: 7.5% (2001 est.).

GDP—per capita: Purchasing power parity—$34,600 (2001 est.).

Inflation rate: 3.3% (2001).

Unemployment rate: 2.6% (2001).

Transport and Communications

Railways: None.

Roads: 104 km (2003).

Telephones: 20,600 (2002).

Mobile cellular: 16,800 (2002).

Internet users: 14,300 (2002).

Internet country code: .sm

Sao Tome and Principe

History

The Portuguese explored the uninhabited islands in the fifteenth century and colonized them in the sixteenth century. In the seventeenth century, Sao Tome and Principe emerged as one of the world's leading sugar producers. Later, coffee and cocoa cultivation was started. In 1908, Sao Tome and Principe was the world's largest producer of cocoa.

In 1951, Sao Tome and Principe became an overseas province of Portugal. In July 1975, Sao Tome and Principe became independent.

Geography

Location: Western Africa, islands in the

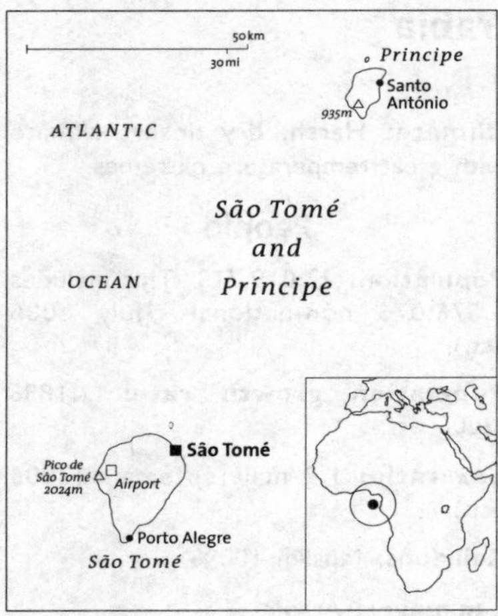

Gulf of Guinea, straddling the equator, west of Gabon.

Area: 1,001 sq. km.

Natural resources: Fish, hydropower.

Climate: Hot and humid tropical climate.

People

Population: 193,413 (July 2006 est.).

Population growth rate: 3.15% (2006 est.).

Sex ratio: 0.98 male/female (2006 est.).

Religions: Christian 80% (Roman Catholic, Evangelical Protestant, Seventh-Day Adventist).

Languages: Portuguese (official).

Literacy rate: Total 79.3%, Male 85%, Female 62% (1991 est.).

Infant mortality rate: 41.83 deaths/1,000 live births (2006 est.).

Life expectancy: Total 67.31 years, Male 65.73 years, Female 68.95 years (2006 est.).

Government

Capital: Sao Tome.

Government type: Republic.

Independence: 12 July 1975 (from Portugal).

Legal system: Based on Portuguese legal system and customary law.

Executive branch:
Chief of state: President Fradique de Menezes (since 3 September 2001).

Head of government: Prime Minister Tome Vera Cruz (since 21 April 2006).

Economy

Currency: Dobra.

GDP: Purchasing power parity—$214 million (2003 est.).

GDP—real growth rate: 6% (2004 est.).

GDP—per capita: Purchasing power parity—$1,200 (2003 est.).

Inflation rate: 15.1% (2005 est.).

Exports: $8 million f.o.b. (2005 est.)—cocoa, copra, coffee, palm oil.

Imports: $38 million f.o.b. (2005 est.)—machinery and electrical equipment, food products, petroleum products.

External debt: $318 million (2002).

Transport and Communications

Railways: None.

Roads: 320 km.

Telephones: 7,000 (2003).

Mobile cellular: 4,800 (2003).

Internet users: 20,000 (2005).

Internet country code: .st

Saudi Arabia

History

In 622, Prophet Mohammed founded Islam in Medina. In medieval times, there were numerous conflicts between various rulers for the control of the Arabian peninsula. The Ottomans gained control in 1517. Between 1915 and 1927, the British held the lands of what is today Saudi Arabia. In 1927, they recognized the sovereignty of the kingdoms of Hejaz and Najd. These two kingdoms were united to form the kingdom of Saudi Arabia in 1932.

Geography

Location: Middle East, bordering the Persian Gulf and the Red Sea, north of Yemen.

Area: 1,960,582 sq. km.

Terrain: Sandy desert with vast uninhabited stretches.

Natural resources: Petroleum, natural gas, iron ore, gold, copper.

Climate: Harsh, dry desert climate with great temperature extremes.

People

Population: 27,019,713. This includes 5,576,076 non-nationals (July 2006 est.).

Population growth rate: 2.18% (2006 est.).

Sex ratio: 1.2 male(s)/female (2006 est.).

Religions: Muslim 100%.

Languages: Arabic.

Literacy rate: Total 78.8%, Male 84.7%, Female 70.8% (2003 est.).

Infant mortality rate: 12.81 deaths/1,000 live births (2006 est.).

Life expectancy: Total 75.67 years, Male 73.66 years, Female 77.78 years (2006 est.).

Government

Capital: Riyadh.

Government type: Monarchy.

Independence: 23 September 1932 (unification of the kingdom).

Legal system: Based on Islamic law.

Executive branch:

Chief of state: King and Prime Minister Abdallah bin Abd al-Aziz Al Saud (since 1 August 2005); heir apparent Crown Prince Sultan bin Abd al-Aziz Al Saud (half-brother to the monarch, born 5 January 1928). The monarch is both the chief of state and head of government.

Economy

Currency: Saudi riyal.

Economy—overview:

Saudi Arabia has an oil-based economy with strong governmental controls over major economic activities. Saudi Arabia has the largest reserves of petroleum in the world (26 per cent of the proved reserves), ranks as the largest exporter of petroleum, and plays a leading role in OPEC. The petroleum sector accounts for roughly 75 per cent of budget revenues, 45 per cent of GDP, and 90 per cent of export earnings. About 25 per cent of GDP comes from the private sector. Roughly four million foreign workers play an important role in the Saudi economy, for example, in the oil and service sectors. The government in 1999 announced plans to begin privatizing the electricity companies, which follows the ongoing privatization of the telecommunications company. The government is supporting private sector growth to lessen the kingdom's dependence on oil and increase employment opportunities for the swelling Saudi population. Priorities for government spending in the short term include additional funds for the water and sewage systems and for education. Water shortages and rapid population growth constrain the government's efforts to increase self-sufficiency in agricultural products.

GDP: Purchasing power parity—$338 billion (2005 est.).

GDP—real growth rate: 6.1% (2005 est.).

GDP—per capita: Purchasing power parity—$12,800 (2005 est.).

Inflation rate: 0.6% (2005 est.).

Unemployment rate: 25% (2004 est.).

Exports: $165 billion f.o.b. (2005 est.); 90% of this is in the form of petroleum and petroleum products.

Imports: $44.39 billion f.o.b. (2005 est.).

External debt: $34.55 billion (2005 est.).

Transport and Communications

Railways: 1,392 km.

Roads: 152,044 km.

Telephones: 3,695,100 (2004).

Mobile cellular: 9,175,800 (2004).

Internet users: 2.54 million (2005).

Internet country code: .sa

Senegal

History

In the 1440s, Portuguese traders reached the estuary of the Senegal river. The Dutch set up a slave-trading centre on the island of Goree in the sixteenth century. The French set up their first settlement in the seventeenth century. During the Seven Year's War of 1756–63, UK took over French settlements in Senegal and formed the colony of Senegambia. France regained its territories during American Revolutionary War of 1775–83.

In 1895, Senegal became a part of French West Africa. In June 1960, Senegal became independent as part of Mali Federation. In August 1960, Senegal withdrew from the Mali Federation and became a separate republic with Leopold Senghor as president. In 1982, Senegal and the Gambia formed a confederation named Senegambia. The confederation was dissolved in 1989.

Geography

Location: Western Africa, bordering

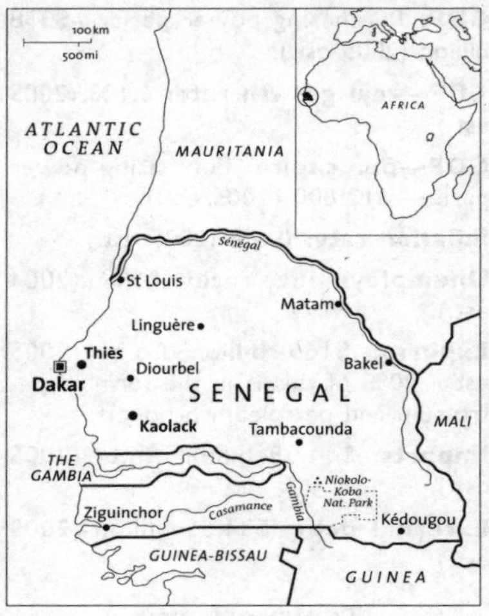

the North Atlantic Ocean, between Guinea-Bissau and Mauritania.

Area: 196,190 sq. km.

Terrain: Low rolling plains rising to foothills in the south-west.

Natural resources: Fish, phosphates, iron ore.

Climate: Hot and humid tropical climate.

People

Population: 11,987,121 (July 2006 est.).

Population growth rate: 2.34% (2006 est.).

Sex ratio: 1 male(s)/female (2006 est.).

Religions: Muslim 94%, indigenous beliefs 1%, Christian 5% (mostly Roman Catholic).

Languages: French (official), Wolof, Pulaar, Jola, Mandinka.

Literacy rate: Total 40.2%, Male 50%, Female 30.7% (2003 est.).

Infant mortality rate: 52.94 deaths/1,000 live births (2006 est.).

Life expectancy: Total 59.25 years, Male 57.7 years, Female 60.85 years (2006 est.).

Government

Capital: Dakar.

Government type: Republic under multiparty democratic rule.

Independence: 4 April 1960 (from France).

Legal system: Based on French civil law system.

Executive branch:

Chief of state: President Abdoulaye Wade (since 1 April 2000).

Head of government: Prime Minister Macky Sall (since 21 April 2004).

Economy

Currency: Communaute Financiere Africaine franc.

GDP: Purchasing power parity—$23.53 billion (2005 est.).

GDP—real growth rate: 6.1% (2005 est.).

GDP—per capita: Purchasing power parity—$1,800 (2005 est.).

Inflation rate: 1.7% (2005 est.).

Population below poverty line: 54% (2001 est.).

Unemployment rate: 48% (2001 est.).

Exports: $1.526 billion f.o.b. (2005 est.)—fish, groundnut (peanut), petroleum products, phosphates, cotton.

Imports: $2.405 billion f.o.b. (2005 est.)—foods and beverages, capital goods, fuels.

External debt: $3.476 billion (2004 est.).

Transport and Communications

Railways: 906 km.

Roads: 13,576 km.

Telephones: 244,900 (2004).

Mobile cellular: 1,121,300 (2004).

Internet users: 482,000 (2005).

Internet country code: .sn

Serbia

History

The Kingdom of Serbs, Croats, and Slovenes was formed in 1918. The name of the kingdom was changed to Yugoslavia in 1929. Occupation by Nazi Germany in 1941 was resisted by various paramilitary bands that fought each other as well as the invaders. The group headed by Josip Tito took full control of Yugoslavia upon German expulsion in 1945. Although Communist, his new government and its successors, after his death in 1980, managed to steer their own path between the Warsaw Pact nations and the West for the next four and a half decades. In the early 1990s, Yugoslavia began to unravel along ethnic lines: Slovenia, Croatia, Macedonia, and Bosnia and Herzegovina became independent states in 1992. The remaining republics of Serbia and Montenegro declared a new Federal Republic of Yugoslavia in April 1992 and, under President Slobodan Milosevic, Serbia led various military intervention efforts to unite ethnic Serbs in neighbouring republics into a 'Greater Serbia'. These actions led to Yugoslavia being ousted from the UN in 1992, but Serbia continued its campaign until signing the Dayton Peace Accords in 1995. In 1998-99, massive expulsions by FRY forces and Serb paramilitaries of ethnic Albanians living in Kosovo provoked an international response, including the NATO bombing of Belgrade and the stationing of a NATO-led force in Kosovo. In 2000, in the Federal elections, Vojislav Kostunica became president. In 2001, the country's suspension from the UN was lifted, and it was once more accepted into UN organizations under the name of the Federal Republic of Yugoslavia. Kosovo has been governed by the UN Interim Administration Mission in Kosovo (UNMIK) since June 1999, under the authority of UN Security Council Resolution 1244, pending a determination by the international community of its future status. In 2002, the Serbian and Montenegrin components of Yugoslavia began negotiations to forge a looser relationship. In February 2003 lawmakers restructured the country into a loose federation of two republics called Serbia and Montenegro. The Constitutional Charter of Serbia and Montenegro included a provision that allowed either republic to hold a referendum after three years that would allow for their independence from the state union. In the spring of 2006, Montenegro took advantage of the provision to undertake a successful independence vote enabling it to secede on 3 June. On 5 June, Serbia declared that it was the successor state to the union of Serbia and Montenegro.

Geography

Location: Southeastern Europe, between Macedonia and Hungary.

Area: 88,361 sq km.

Terrain: Extremely varied; to the north, rich fertile plains; to the east, limestone ranges and basins; to the southeast, ancient mountains and hills.

Natural resources: Oil, gas, coal, iron ore, copper, lead, zinc, antimony, chromite, nickel, gold, silver, magnesium, pyrite, limestone, marble, salt, arable land.

Climate: In the north, continental climate (cold winters and hot, humid summers with well distributed rainfall); in other parts, continental and Mediterranean climate (hot, dry summers and autumns and relatively cold winters with heavy snowfall).

People

Population: 9,396,411 (2002 census).

Life expectancy at birth: Total: 74 years, Male: 71 years, Female: 76 years.

Religions: Serbian Orthodox, Muslim, Roman Catholic, Protestant.

Languages: Serbian (official nationwide); Romanian, Hungarian, Slovak, and Croatian (all official in Vojvodina); Albanian (official in Kosovo).

Literacy: Total: 96.4%, Male: 98.9%, Female: 94.1% (2002 est.).

Government

Capital: Belgrade.

Government type: Republic.

Independence: 5 June 2006 (from Serbia and Montenegro).

Legal system: Based on civil law system

Executive branch:

Chief of state: President Boris Tadic (since 11 July 2004).

Head of government: Prime Minister Vojislav Kostunica (since 3 March 2004).

Elections: president elected by direct vote for a five-year term (eligible for a second term); election last held 27 June 2004 (next to be held June 2009); prime minister elected by the Assembly.

Economy

Currency: New Yugoslav dinar (YUM); note—in Kosovo both the euro and the Yugoslav dinar are legal.

Economy—overview:
Milosevic-era mismanagement of the economy, an extended period of economic sanctions, and the damage to Yugoslavia's infrastructure and industry during the NATO air strikes in 1999 left the economy only half the size it was in 1990. After the ousting of former Federal Yugoslav President Milosevic in October 2000, the Democratic Opposition of Serbia (DOS) coalition government implemented stabilization measures and embarked on a market reform programme. After renewing its membership in the IMF in December 2000, a downsized Yugoslavia continued to reintegrate into the international community by rejoining the World Bank (IBRD) and the European Bank for Reconstruction and Development (EBRD). A World Bank–European Commission sponsored Donors' Conference held in June 2001 raised $1.3 billion for economic restructuring. An agreement rescheduling the country's $4.5 billion Paris Club government debts was concluded in November 2001—it wrote off 66 per cent of the debt and the London Club of private creditors forgave $1.7 billion of debt, just over half the total owed, in July 2004. Belgrade has made only minimal progress in restructuring and privatizing its holdings in major sectors of the economy, including the energy and telecommunications sectors. Serbia has made halting progress towards eventual EU membership and is currently pursuing a Stabilization and Association Agreement with Brussels. It is also pursuing membership in the World Trade Organization. Unemployment remains an ongoing political and economic problem. The republic of Montenegro severed its economy from Serbia during the Milosevic era; therefore, the formal separation of Serbia and Montenegro in June 2006 had little real impact on either economy. Kosovo's economy con-

tinues to transition to a market-based system, and is largely dependent on the international community and the diaspora for financial and technical assistance. The euro and the Yugoslav dinar are both accepted currencies in Kosovo. While maintaining ultimate oversight, UNMIK continues to work with the EU and Kosovo's local provisional government to accelerate economic growth, lower unemployment, and attract foreign investment to help Kosovo integrate into regional economic structures. The complexity of Serbia and Kosovo's political and legal relationships has created uncertainty over property rights and hindered the privatization of state-owned assets located in Kosovo. The majority of Kosovo's population lives in rural towns outside of Kosovo's largest city Pristina and inefficient, near-subsistence farming is common.

Note: Economic data for Serbia currently reflects information for the former Serbia and Montenegro.

GDP: Purchasing power parity—$41.15 billion for Serbia (including Kosovo) (2005 est.).

GDP—real growth rate: 5.9% for Serbia alone (excluding Kosovo) (2005 est.).

GDP—per capita: Purchasing power parity—$4,400 for Serbia (including Kosovo) (2005).

Unemployment rate: 31.6% 2005).

Population below poverty line: 30% (1999 est.).

Inflation rate: 15.5% (2005).

Exports: $4.553 billion (2005).

Imports: $10.58 billion (2005).

External debt: $15.43 billion (2005 est.).

Transport and Communications

Railways: 4,135 km.

Roads: 37,937 km.

Telephones: 2,685,400 (2004).

Mobile cellular: 4,729,600 (2004).

Internet users: 1.4 million (2006).

Internet country code: .yu.

Seychelles

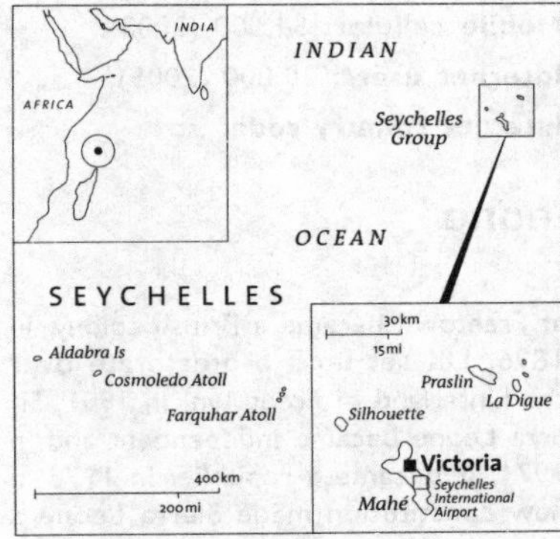

History

In 1903 the Seychelles became a British Crown colony. Self-government was granted in 1975. Seychelles finally gained independence in 1976.

Geography

Location: Eastern Africa, group of islands in the Indian Ocean, north-east of Madagascar.

Area: 455 sq. km.

Terrain: The Mahe group is granitic, with a narrow coastal strip. Others are coral, flat, elevated reefs.

Natural resources: Fish, copra, cinnamon trees.

Climate: Humid tropical marine climate.

People

Population: 81,541 (July 2006 est.).

Population growth rate: 0.43% (2006 est.).

Sex ratio: 0.93 male(s)/female (2006 est.).

Religions: Roman Catholic 86.6%, Anglican 6.8%, other Christian 2.5%, others 4.1%.

Languages: English (official) 4.9%, Creole 91.8%, other 3.1%, unspecified 0.2% (2002 census).

Literacy rate: Total 91.9%, Male 91.4%, Female 92.3% (2003 est.).

Infant mortality rate: 15.14 deaths/1,000 live births (2006 est.).

Life expectancy: Total 72.08 years, Male 66.69 years, Female 77.63 years (2006 est.).

Government

Capital: Victoria.

Government type: Republic.

Independence: 29 June 1976 (from UK).

Legal system: Based on English common law, French civil law, and customary law.

Executive branch:
Chief of state: President James Michel (since 14 April 2004). The president is both the chief of state and head of government.

Economy

Currency: Seychelles rupee.

GDP: Purchasing power parity—$626 million (2002 est.).

GDP—real growth rate: –3% (2005 est.).

GDP—per capita: Purchasing power parity—$7,800 (2002 est.).

Inflation rate: 4.4% (2005 est.).

Exports: $312.1 million f.o.b. (2005 est.)—canned tuna, frozen fish, cinnamon bark, copra, petroleum products (re-exports).

Imports: $459.9 million f.o.b. (2005 est.)—machinery and equipment, foodstuff, petroleum products, chemicals.

External debt: $276.8 million (2005 est.).

Transport and Communications

Railways: 280 km.

Roads: 280 km.

Telephones: 21,200 (2004).

Mobile cellular: 54,500 (2003).

Internet users: 20,000 (2005).

Internet country code: .sc

Sierra Leone

History

The first Europeans to reach the region were the Portuguese, who gave it the name Sierra Leone. In 1787, British abolitionists and philanthropists established a settlement in Freetown for former slaves. In 1808, this settlement at Freetown became a British colony. In 1896, UK set up a protectorate over the hinterland of Freetown. In 1961, Sierra Leone became independent and in 1971, it became a republic. In 1978, a new constitution made Sierra Leone a one-party state with the All People's Congress as the only legal party.

Geography

Location: Western Africa, bordering the North Atlantic Ocean, between Guinea and Liberia.

Area: 71,740 sq. km.

Natural resources: Diamonds, titanium ore, bauxite, iron ore, gold, chromite.

Climate: Hot and humid tropical.

People

Population: 6,005,250 (July 2006 est.).

Population growth rate: 2.3% (2006 est.).

Sex ratio: 0.94 male(s)/female (2006 est.).

Religions: Muslim 60%, indigenous beliefs 30%, Christian 10%.

Languages: English (official), Mende, Temne, Krio.

Literacy rate: Total 29.6%, Male 39.8%, Female 20.5% (2000 est.).

Infant mortality rate: 160.39 deaths/1,000 live births (2006 est.).

Life expectancy: Total 40.22 years, Male 38.05 years, Female 42.46 years (2006 est.).

Government

Capital: Freetown.

Government type: Constitutional democracy.

Independence: 27 April 1961 (from UK).

Legal system: Based on English law and customary laws indigenous to local tribes.

Executive branch:

Chief of state: President Ahmad Tejan Kabbah (since 29 March 1996, reinstated 10 March 1998). The president is both the chief of state and head of government.

Economy

Currency: Leone.

GDP: Purchasing power parity—$4.921 billion (2005 est.).

GDP—real growth rate: 6.3% (2005 est.).

GDP—per capita: Purchasing power parity—$800 (2005 est.).

Inflation rate: 1% (2002 est.).

Population below poverty line: 68% (1989 est.).

Exports: $185 million f.o.b. (2004 est.)—diamond, rutile, cocoa, coffee, fish (1999).

Imports: $531 million f.o.b. (2004 est.)—foodstuff, machinery and equipment, fuels and lubricants, chemicals (1995).

External debt: $1.61 billion (2003 est.).

Transport and Communications

Railways: 84 km.

Roads: 11,330 km.

Telephones: 24,000 (2002).

Mobile cellular: 113,200 (2003).

Internet users: 2,005 (2005).

Internet country code: .sl

Singapore

History

The earliest known mention of Singapore is in a third century Chinese account that described Singapore as 'Pu-luo-chung' ('island at the end of a peninsula'). Fishermen and pirates originally inhabited Singapore and till the fourteenth century, it served as an outpost of the Sumatran empire of Shrivijaya. In the fourteenth century, it passed to Java and Siam and in the fifteenth century it became a part of the Malacca empire. The Portuguese in the sixteenth and the Dutch in the seventeenth century controlled the area. Then in 1819, the area was passed on to the British East India Company. It became a part of the Straits Settlements and the hub of British colonial activity in the region.

During World War II, during 1942–5, the Japanese occupied the islands. It became a British Crown colony once again in 1946 but achieved full internal self-governance in 1959. In 1963, Singapore became a part of the Federation of Malaysia along with Malaya, Sabah and Sarawak. In 1965, Singapore withdrew from the federation to become an independent state.

Geography

Location: South-eastern Asia, islands between Malaysia and Indonesia.

Area: 692.7 sq. km.

Terrain: Lowland with a gently undulating central plateau that contains a water catchment area and a nature preserve.

Natural resources: Fish, deepwater ports.

Climate: Warm and humid climate.

People

Population: 4,492,150 (July 2006 est.).

Population growth rate: 1.42% (2006 est.).

Sex ratio: 0.96 male(s)/female (2006 est.).

Religions: Buddhist (Chinese), Muslim (Malays), Christian, Hindu, Sikh, Taoist, Confucianist.

Languages: Chinese (official), Malay (official and national), Tamil (official), English (official).

Literacy rate: Total 93.2%, Male 96.7%, Female 89.7% (2003 est.).

Infant mortality rate: 2.29 deaths/1,000 live births (2006 est.).

Life expectancy: Total 81.71 years, Male 79.13 years, Female 84.49 years (2006 est.).

Government

Capital: Singapore.

Government type: Parliamentary republic.

Independence: 9 August 1965 (from Malaysian Federation).

Legal system: Based on English common law.

Executive branch:
Chief of state: President Sellapan Rama Nathan (since 1 September 1999).

Head of government: Prime Minister Lee Hsien Loong (since 2004).

Economy

Currency: Singapore dollar.

Economy—overview:
Singapore is a highly developed free market economy marked by an open and corruption-free environment and stable prices. It also has one of the highest per capita GDPs in the world. The economy relies heavily on exports, mainly in the sphere of electronics and manufacturing. In 2001–2, the global recession and the slump in the technology sector hit Singapore's economy hard.

GDP: Purchasing power parity—$124.3 billion (2005 est.).

GDP—real growth rate: 6.4% (2005 est.).

GDP—per capita: Purchasing power parity—$28,100 (2005 est.).

Inflation rate: 1% (2005 est.).

Unemployment rate: 3.3% (2005 est.).

Exports: $204.8 billion f.o.b. (2005 est.).

Imports: $188.3 billion (2005 est.).

External debt: $24.67 billion (2005 est.).

Transport and Communications

Railways: 131 km (2003).

Roads: 3,165 km.

Telephones: 1,847,800 (2005).

Mobile cellular: 4,256,800 (2005).

Internet users: 2,421,800 (2005).

Internet country code: .sg

Slovakia

History

Slavic Slovaks settled in the region that is present-day Slovakia in the sixth century. The Moravian empire united the Slovaks in the ninth century. Germans and Magyars conquered Moravia in 907 and the Slovaks went under Hungarian rule that lasted till the collapse of the Hapsburg empire in 1918. The Slovaks then joined Bohemia, Moravia and a part of Silesia to form the new country of Czechoslovakia.

Political reforms in Czechoslovakia began with the fall of communism in the 1990s and the election of Vaclav Havel as president of Czechoslovakia in 1989. Talks on the future of Czechoslovakia began in 1991. Finally, it was decided the two republics should separate and become two fully independent nations. The republic of Slovakia came into existence on 1 January 1993.

Slovakia joined both NATO and the EU in the spring of 2004.

Geography

Location: Central Europe, south of Poland.

Area: 48,845 sq. km.

Terrain: Rugged mountains in the central and northern parts and lowlands in the south.

Natural resources: Brown coal and lignite, iron ore, copper and manganese ore, salt, arable land.

Climate: Temperate climate with cool summers and cold, cloudy, and humid winters.

People

Population: 5,439,448 (July 2006 est.).

Population growth rate: 0.15% (2006 est.).

Sex ratio: 0.94 male(s)/female (2006 est.).

Religions: Roman Catholic 68.9%, Protestant 10.8%, Greek Catholic 4.1%, other or unspecified 3.2%, none 13% (2001 census).

Languages: Slovak (official), Hungarian.

Literacy: Total population 99.6%, Male 99.7%, Female 99.6% (2001 est.).

Infant mortality rate: 7.26 deaths/1,000 live births (2006 est.).

Life expectancy: Total 74.73 years, Male 70.76 years, Female 78.89 years (2006 est.).

Government

Capital: Bratislava.

Government type: Parliamentary democracy.

Independence: 1 January 1993 (date on which Czechoslovakia split into the Czech Republic and Slovakia).

Legal system: Civil law system based on Austro-Hungarian codes.

Executive branch:

Chief of state: President Ivan Gasparovic (since 15 June 2004).

Head of government: Prime Minister Robert Fico (since 4 July 2006).

Economy

Currency: Slovak koruna.

GDP: Purchasing power parity—$87.32 billion (2005 est.).

GDP—real growth rate: 5.5% (2005 est.).

GDP—per capita: Purchasing power parity—$16,100 (2005 est.).

Inflation rate: 2.7% (2005 est.).

Unemployment rate: 11.4% (2005 est.).

Exports: $32.39 billion f.o.b. (2005 est.)—machinery and transport equipment, intermediate manufactured goods, miscellaneous manufactured goods, chemicals (1999).

Imports: $34.48 billion f.o.b. (2005 est.)—machinery and transport equipment, intermediate manufactured goods, fuels, chemicals, miscellaneous manufactured goods (1999).

External debt: $26.54 billion (2005 est.).

Transport and Communications

Railways: 3,661 km.

Roads: 42,993 km.

Telephones: 1,250,400 (2004).

Mobile cellular: 4,275,200 (2004).

Internet users: 2.276 million (2005).

Internet country code: .sk

Slovenia

History

The Slovene group of Slavic people settled in the area in the sixth century AD. In the seventh century, they set up the Slavic state of Samu. This state was allied with the Avars who dominated the Hungarian plains till Charlemagne defeated them in the late eighth century. In 1867, Slovenia became a part of the Austro-Hungarian kingdom. Following the defeat of the Austro-Hungarian kingdom in World War I, Slovenia declared its independence. In 1918, it joined Serbia, Montenegro and Croatia to form a new nation, later renamed Yugoslavia.

In the 1991, the Slovenia declared its independence. In the spring of 2004, Slovenia acceded to both NATO and the EU.

Geography

Location: Central Europe, eastern Alps bordering the Adriatic Sea, between Austria and Croatia.

Area: 20,273 sq. km.

Terrain: A short coastal strip on the Adriatic, an alpine region adjacent to Italy and Austria, and valleys with numerous rivers to the east.

Natural resources: Lignite, coal, lead, zinc, mercury, uranium, silver, hydropower, forests.

Climate: Mediterranean climate in the coastal area. The plateaus and eastern valleys have continental climate with mild to hot summers and cold winters.

People

Population: 2,010,347 (July 2006 est.).

Population growth rate: –0.05% (2006 est.).

Sex ratio: 0.95 male(s)/female (2006 est.).

Religions: Catholic 57.8%, Orthodox 2.3%, other Christian 0.9%, Muslim 2.4%, unaffiliated 3.5%, other or unspecified 23%, none 10.1% (2002 census).

Languages: Slovenian 92%, Serbo-Croatian 6.2%, other 1.8%.

Literacy rate: 99.7% (2003 est.).

Infant mortality rate: 4.4 deaths/ 1,000 live births (2006 est.).

Life expectancy: Total 76.33 years, Male 72.63 years, Female 80.29 years (2006 est.).

Government

Capital: Ljubljana.

Government type: Parliamentary democratic republic.

Independence: 25 June 1991 (from Yugoslavia).

Legal system: Based on civil law system.

Executive branch:

Chief of state: President Janez Drnovsek (since 22 December 2002).

Head of government: Prime Minister Janez Jansa (since 9 November 2004).

Economy

Currency: Tolar.

GDP: Purchasing power parity—$43.36 billion (2005 est.).

GDP—real growth rate: 3.9% (2005 est.).

GDP—per capita: Purchasing power parity—$21,600 (2005 est.).

Inflation rate: 2.4% (2005 est.).

Unemployment rate: 9.8% (2005 est.).

Exports: $18.53 billion f.o.b. (2005 est.)—manufactured goods, machinery and transport equipment, chemicals, food.

Imports: $19.62 billion f.o.b. (2005 est.)—machinery and transport equipment, manufactured goods, chemicals, fuels and lubricants, food.

External debt: $22.91 billion (2005 est.).

Transport and Communications

Railways: 1,201 km.

Roads: 38,400 km.

Telephones: 812,300 (2003).

Mobile cellular: 1,739,100 (2003).

Internet users: 950,000 (2005).

Internet country code: .si

Solomon Islands

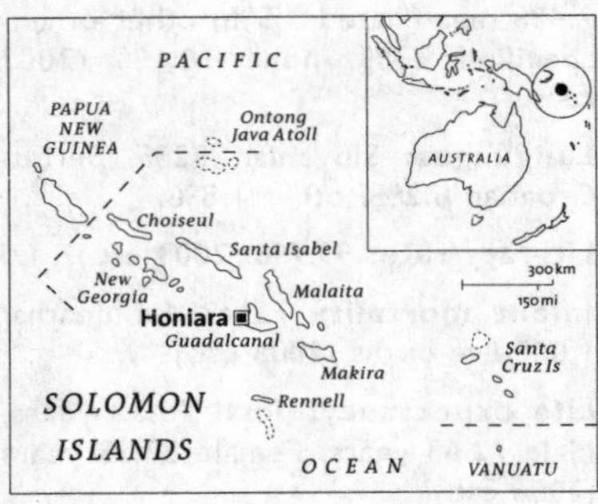

History

In 1893, the islands became a British protectorate. Japanese occupation of the islands during World War II sparked off bitter fighting with the Allies. In 1975, the islands attained self-governance. In 1978 Solomon Islands became independent.

Geography

Location: Oceania, group of islands in the South Pacific Ocean, east of Papua New Guinea.

Area: 28,450 sq. km.

Natural resources: Fish, forests, gold, bauxite, phosphates, lead, zinc, nickel.

Climate: Tropical monsoon type of weather with few extremes of temperature.

People

Population: 552,438 (July 2006 est.).

Population growth rate: 2.61% (2006 est.).

Sex ratio: 1.03 male(s)/female (2006 est.).

Religions: Anglican 45%, Roman Catholic 18%, United (Methodist/Presbyterian) 12%, Baptist 9%, Seventh-Day Adventist 7%, other Protestant 5%, indigenous beliefs 4%.

Languages: Melanesian pidgin is lingua franca in much of the country; English is official but spoken by only 1–2% of the population. There are 120 indigenous languages.

Infant mortality rate: 20.63 deaths/1,000 live births (2006 est.).

Life expectancy: Total 72.91 years, Male 70.4 years, Female 75.55 years (2006 est.).

Government

Capital: Honiara.

Government type: Parliamentary democracy.

Independence: 7 July 1978 (from UK).

Legal system: English common law.

Executive branch:
Chief of state: Queen Elizabeth II (since 6 February 1952), represented by Governor General Naihaniel Waena (since 7 July 2004).

Head of government: Prime Minister Manasseh Sogavare (since 4 May 2006); note: Prime Minister Snyder Rini, elected on 18 April 2006 and sworn in on 20 April 2006, resigned on 26 April prior to a no-confidence vote in parliament; Sogavare elected on 4 May.

Economy

Currency: Solomon Islands dollar.

GDP: Purchasing power parity—$800 million (2002 est.).

GDP—real growth rate: 5.8% (2003 est.).

GDP—per capita: Purchasing power parity—$1,700 (2002 est.).

Inflation rate: 10% (2003 est.).

Exports: $171 million f.o.b. (2004 est.)—timber, fish, copra, palm oil, cocoa.

Imports: $159 million f.o.b. (2004 est.)—food, plant and equipment, manufactured goods, fuels, chemicals.

External debt: $180.4 million (2002 est.).

Transport and Communications

Railways: None.

Roads: 1,360 km.

Telephones: 6,200 (2003).

Mobile cellular: 1,500 (2003).

Internet users: 8,400 (2005).

Internet country code: .sb

Somalia

History

When UK occupied Aden (in present-day Yemen) in 1839, Somalia became its source of foodstuffs. By the 1920s, the area that is today Somalia was under the control of two protectorates, one British and one Italian. UK gained control over the entire territory after 1941. In 1950, Italy returned as the UN-appointed trustee of its former territory. In 1960, UK and Italy granted independence to its Somali territories, British Somaliland and Italian Somaliland, thus enabling the creation of the United Republic of Somalia in July 1960.

In 1991, numerous clans that had grown up all across the country and had some access to weapons set up their own domains. The most significant among these domains was Somaliland. The Somali National Movement (SNM) secured control of the former British Somaliland region in the

northern part of the country and declared an independent 'Somaliland Republic'. Even today, Somaliland has its own capital (Hargeisa), a working political system with its own president (Dahir Riyale Kahin), its government institutions, a security set-up and its own currency (Somaliland shilling). What it does not have, however, is the crucial international recognition of being a sovereign state separate from Somalia.

In December 1992, USA led a multinational force of more than 35,000 troops to Somalia. However, the international troops faced strong resistance. Fighting ravaged the food-growing regions, cutting off food supplies for the country's population. Mogadishu itself was devastated. This led to US withdrawal from the country. In 1995, even the UN retreated, having failed to restore peace and order.

In April 2002, warlords in the south-western part of the country unilaterally declared autonomy for six districts and formed the 'South-western Regional Government'. In October 2002, the transitional government signed a ceasefire with twenty-one warring factions in order to stop hostilities for the duration of the peace talks.

Geography

Location: Eastern Africa, bordering the Gulf of Aden and the Indian Ocean, east of Ethiopia.

Area: 637,657 sq. km.

Terrain: Mostly flat to undulationg plateau rising to hills in the north.

Natural resources: Uranium, iron ore, tin, gypsum, bauxite, copper, salt, natural gas, likely oil reserves. (Besides uranium, the reserves of the other minerals are largely unexploited.)

Climate: Desert type of climate.

People

Population: 8,863,338 (July 2006 est.).

Population growth rate: 2.85% (2006 est.).

Sex ratio: 1 male(s)/female (2006 est.).

Religions: Sunni Muslim.

Languages: Somali (official), Arabic, Italian, English.

Literacy rate: Total 37.8%, Male 49.7%, Female 25.8% (2001 est.).

Infant mortality rate: 114.89 deaths/1,000 live births (2006 est.).

Life expectancy: Total 48.47 years, Male 46.41 years, Female 50.28 years (2006 est.).

Government

Capital: Mogadishu.

Government type: No permanent national government; transitional, parliamentary national government. A new transitioned faceted government concessions of a 275–member parliament was established or October 2004. However, it is based in Kendra and has not established effective governance inside Somalia.

Independence: 1 July 1960 (from a merger of British Somaliland.

Legal system: No national system; Shari'a and secular courts exist in some parts of the country.

Executive branch:

Chief of state: Abdullahi Yusuf Ahmed (since 14 October 2004).

Head of government: Prime Minister Ali Mohammed Ghedi (since 24 December 2004).

Economy

Currency: Somali shilling.

GDP: Purchasing power parity—$4.809 billion (2005 est.).

GDP—real growth rate: 2.4% (2005 est.).

GDP—per capita: Purchasing power parity—$600 (2005 est.).

Exports: $241 million f.o.b. (2004 est.)—livestock, banana, hides, fish, charcoal, scrap metal.

Imports: $576 million f.o.b. (2004 est.)—manufactured products, petroleum products, foodstuff, construction materials, qat.

External debt: $3 billion (2001 est.).

Transport and Communications

Railways: None.

Roads: 22,100 km.

Telephones: 200,000 (2004 est.).

Mobile cellular: 500,000 (2004).

Internet users: 89,000 (2002).

Internet country code: .so

South Africa

History

In the 1480s, Portuguese navigator Bartholomeu Dias became the first European to travel round the southern tip of Africa. In 1497, Portuguese explorer Vasco da Gama landed on the Natal coast. In 1652, Jan van Riebeeck, who represented the Dutch East India Company, established the Cape Colony at Table Bay. However, in 1795, British forces seized Cape Colony from the Dutch. A powerful Zulu empire grew up in the region between 1816 and 1826. Between 1835 and 1840, the Boers (Africans of Dutch origin) founded Orange Free State and Transvaal.

In 1867, diamonds were discovered at Kimberley. Soon afterwards, UK annexed Transvaal. In 1879, the British defeated the Zulus in Natal. In 1880–1, the Boers rebelled against the British, resulting in the first Anglo-Boer War. In the mid-1880s, gold was discovered in the Transvaal and led to a gold rush. The second Anglo-Boer War began in 1899 when British troops gathered on the Transvaal border ignoring an ultimatum. Consequently, Transvaal and Orange Free State were made self-governing colonies of the British empire.

In 1910, the Union of South Africa was formed out of the former British colonies of the Cape and Natal, and the Boer republics of Transvaal, and Orange Free State. In 1912, the Native National Congress, later renamed the African National Congress (ANC), was founded. In 1948, the National Party came to power and implemented a policy of apartheid. This was a policy of segregation and political and economic discrimination against non-European groups living in the country.

The ANC responded to this move by launching its campaign of civil dis-

obedience under the leadership of Nelson Mandela. In 1956, Mandela was charged with high treason, along with 155 other activists. The government banned ANC. In 1961, South Africa was proclaimed a republic and left the Commonwealth. Mounting international pressure against the South African government led to the exclusion of South Africa from the Olympic Games. Meanwhile, ANC launched its military wing with Mandela as its head and embarked on a sabotage campaign.

In 1964, Nelson Mandela was arrested and charged with sabotage and attempt to overthrow the government. He was sentenced to life imprisonment.

In 1989, F.W. de Klerk replaced P.W. Botha as president. Soon afterwards, public facilities were desegregated and many ANC activists were freed from prison. In 1990, the ban on ANC was removed. Nelson Mandela was released after twenty-seven years in prison. In 1991, talks began between the ANC and the National Party on the formation of a new multiracial democracy for South Africa. Remaining apartheid laws were repealed, leading to the lifting of international sanctions. The 1993 Nobel Peace prize was awarded to Nelson Mandela and F.W. de Klerk.

In April 1994, the ANC won the country's first ever non-racial elections. Nelson Mandela became president. South Africa's Commonwealth membership was restored and the remaining international sanctions were lifted. In 1996, the Truth and Reconciliation Commission with Archbishop Desmond Tutu as its head began hearings on human rights violations committed by former government and liberation movements during the apartheid era. In 1998, the Truth and Reconciliation Commission released its report. It declared apartheid as a crime against humanity. The report also held the ANC accountable for human rights abuses. The ANC won the 1999 general elections. Nelson Mandela stepped down from power and handed the presidency to his vice-president, Thabo Mbeki.

Geography

Location: Southern Africa, at the southern tip of the continent of Africa.

Area: 1,219,912 sq. km.

Terrain: Vast interior plateau rimmed by rugged hills and a narrow coastal plain.

Natural resources: Gold, chromium, antimony, coal, iron ore, manganese, nickel, phosphates, tin, uranium, gemstones, diamond, platinum, copper, vanadium, salt, natural gas.

Climate: Mostly semi-arid but subtropical along the east coast.

People

Population: 44,187,637 (July 2006 est.).

Population growth rate: –0.4% (2006 est.).

Sex ratio: 0.95 male(s)/female (2006 est.).

Religions: Christian 68% (includes most whites and coloureds, about 60% of blacks and about 40% of Indians), Muslim 2%, Hindu 1.5% (60% of Indians), indigenous beliefs and animist 28.5%.

Languages: IsiZulu 23.8%, IsiXhosa 17.6%, Africaans 13.3%, Sepedi 9.4%, Enghsh 8.2%, Setwara 8.2%, Sesotho 7.9%, Xitsonga 4.4%, other 7.2% (2001 census).

Literacy rate: Total 86.4%, Male 87%, Female 85.7% (2003 est.).

Infant mortality rate: 60.66 deaths/ 1,000 live births (2006 est.).

Life expectancy: Total 42.73 years, Male 43.25 years, Female 42.19 years (2006 est.).

Government

Capital: Pretoria (Cape Town is the legislative centre and Bloemfontein the judicial centre).

Government type: Republic.

Independence: 31 May 1910 (from UK).

Legal system: Based on Roman–Dutch law and English common law.

Executive branch:
Chief of state: President Thabo Mbeki (since 16 June 1999). The president is both the chief of state and head of government.

Economy

Currency: Rand.

Economy—overview:
South Africa is an emerging market that enjoys numerous benefits. These include plenty of natural resources, well-developed service sectors, one of the largest stock exchanges in the world and a modern infrastructure. Nevertheless, it has been difficult to sustain a rate of growth high enough to make substantial dents in the country's unemployment problem. Besides, the country still suffers from the economic problems that continue from the apartheid era such as poverty and lack of economic empowerment among the backward sections. The country also suffers from high HIV/AIDS infection rates and crime rates, two significant detractors to foreign investment.

GDP: Purchasing power parity—$533.2 billion (2005 est.).

GDP—real growth rate: 4.9% (2005 est.).

GDP—per capita: Purchasing power parity—$12,000 (2005 est.).

Inflation rate: 4.6% (2005 est.).

Population below poverty line: 50% (2000 est.).

Unemployment rate: 25.2% (includes workers not looking for employment any longer) (2005 est.).

Exports: $50.91 billion f.o.b. (2005 est.)—gold, diamond, platinum, other metals and minerals, machinery and equipment (1998 est.).

Imports: $52.97 billion f.o.b. (2005 est.)—machinery and equipment, chemicals, petroleum products, scientific instruments, foodstuff (2000 est.).

External debt: $44.33 billion (30 June 2005 est.).

Transport and Communications

Railways: 22,298 km (includes a 2,228 km commuter rail system).

Roads: 362,099 km.

Telephones: 4.844 million (2003).

Mobile cellular: 19.5 million (2004).

Internet users: 3.6 million (2005).

Internet country code: .za

South Korea

History

It is believed that the ancient kingdom of Choson was founded in the third millennium BC. In 108 BC, China annexed the region. The Yi dynasty ruled it from 1392 to 1910. Japan conquered all of Korea in 1910. In 1945, Allied forces evicted the Japanese from Korea. The part of the Korean peninsula north of the thirty-eighth parallel was occupied by Soviet Union while USA occupied the region to the south of this line of latitude, present-day South Korea.

The Republic of Korea was proclaimed in 1948. South Korea declared its independence in 1950, prompting North Korea to launch an invasion attempt that soon developed into the Korean War. It ended with the signing of armistice in 1953. The war is believed to have claimed 4,000,000 casualties, including civilians.

A military coup took place in 1961, following which General Park Chung-hee took power. Martial law was imposed in 1972 and General Park increased his powers by changing the Constitution. In 1979 General Park was assassinated. General Chun Doo-hwan replaced him as the nation's leader. Martial law was declared again in 1980. In 1987, President Chun was removed from office by student unrest and mounting international pressure.

In 2000, a historic summit took place in the North Korean capital city, Pyongyang, between President Kim Dae-jung and the North Korean leader, Kim Jong-il. The summit resulted in North Korea stopping propaganda broadcasts against the South. It also saw the reopening of border liaison offices at the heavily fortified borders of the two countries. The same year, Kim Dae-jung was awarded the Nobel Peace Prize.

Geography

Location: Eastern Asia, southern half of the Korean Peninsula bordering the Sea of Japan and the Yellow Sea.

Area: 98,480 sq. km.

Terrain: Mostly hills and mountains. There are wide coastal plains in the west and south.

Natural resources: Coal, tungsten, graphite, molybdenum, lead, hydropower potential.

Climate: Temperate climate.

People

Population: 48,846,823 (July 2006 est.).

Population growth rate: 0.42% (2006 est.).

Sex ratio: 1.01 male(s)/female (2006 est.).

Religions: No affiliation 46%, Christian 26%, Buddhist 26%, Confucianist 1%, others 1%.

Languages: Korean, English.

Literacy rate: Total 98.1%, Male 99.3%, Female 97% (2003 est.).

Infant mortality rate: 6.16 deaths/ 1,000 live births (2006 est.).

Life expectancy: Total 77.04 years, Male 73.61 years, Female 80.75 years (2006 est.).

Government

Capital: Seoul.

Government type: Republic.

Independence: 15 August 1945 (from Japan).

Legal system: Combination of the elements of continental European civil law systems, Anglo-American law, and Chinese classical thought.

Executive branch:

Chief of state: President No Mu-hyun (Roh Moo-hyun) (since 25 February 2003). In March 2004, President Roh Moo-hyun was suspended after the parliament voted to impeach him over breach of election rules and for incompetence. However, in May 2004, a constitutional court overturned this parliamentary vote to impeach President Roh Moo-hyun. He was immediately reinstated.

Head of government: Prime Minister Han Myeong-sook (since 19 April 2006).

Economy

Currency: Won.

Economy—overview:

South Korea is one of the Four Tigers of East Asia that has achieved a high growth and has successfully emerged as a high-tech modern world economy. Thirty years ago, South Korea's GDP per capita was similar to those in the poorer African and Asian countries. The country achieved this success through the 1980s by means of close ties between government and the business enterprises and focused policy implementation. However, the Asian financial crisis of 1997–9 revealed the weaknesses in South Korea's economy such as its massive foreign borrowing and its flawed financial sector. In 2003, the six-day working week was shortened to five days.

GDP: Purchasing power parity—$695.3 billion (2005 est.).

GDP—real growth rate: 3.9% (2005 est.).

GDP—per capita: Purchasing power parity—$20,400 (2005 est.).

Inflation rate: 2.6% (2005 est.).

Population below poverty line: 15% (2003 est.).

Unemployment rate: 3.7% (2005 est.).

Exports: $288.2 billion f.o.b. (2005 est.)—electronic products, machinery and equipment, motor vehicles, steel, ships, textiles, clothing, footwear, fish.

Imports: $256 billion f.o.b. (2005 est.)—machinery, electronics and electronic equipment, oil, steel, transport equipment, textiles, organic chemicals, grains.

External debt: $188.4 billion (30 June 2005 est.).

Transport and Communications

Railways: 3,472 km.

Roads: 97,252 km.

Telephones: 26,595,100 (2004).

Mobile callular: 36,586,100 (2004).

Internet users: 33.9 million (2005).

Internet country code: .kr

Spain

History

Celts, Basques and Iberians were the original inhabitants of Spain. In 711, the Muslims under Tariq ibn Ziyad arrived from Africa and in a few years time, gained control of most of the Iberian peninsula. However, the reign of the Almohads saw the Christians regaining control of the Iberian peninsula.

The accession of Ferdinand II to the throne of Aragon in 1479 resulted in the union of Aragon (eastern Spain) and Castile (western Spain). Consequently, Spain emerged as one of the most powerful monarchies in Europe. The completion of the reconquest was followed by the establishment of Roman Catholicism as the state religion and the expulsion of Jews and Muslims, as a result of the Spanish Inquisition.

The sixteenth century was a period of Spanish exploration, conquest and colonization all over the world. In South America, the conquistadors wiped out the local Aztec, Inca and Mayan civilizations. Hernan Cortes led an expedition against Aztec Mexico and conquered the Aztec capital, Tenochtitlan, in 1521. The Pacific coastal regions were conquered between 1522 and 1524. In 1535, Spain established the viceroyalty of New Spain. It was charged with the governance of Spain's newly acquired territories in the New World.

In 1588, King Philip II of Spain sent a huge fleet of about 130 ships, around 8,000 sailors and an estimated 19,000 soldiers to invade England. This fleet is now referred to as the Spanish Armada. He planned to send in the Spanish army from present-day Belgium to coincide with the Armada's arrival on English shores. The consequent English defeat of the Armada not only saved England from Spanish invasion but also marked the simultaneous ascent of England and the decline of Spain as maritime powers.

On 1 October 1936, the Nationalist leader, General Franco, was named head of state and he set up a government in Burgos. Soon, foreign powers got embroiled in the Republican–Nationalist conflict. The Soviets directed Spanish communists to support the Republicans. The Mexican government also contributed to the Republican cause. Germany and Italy sent troops and vehicles to help the Nationalists. In August 1936, France, UK, the Soviet Union, Germany, and Italy signed a non-intervention agreement. General Francisco Franco served as the head of the government of Spain until 1973 and head of state until his death in 1975.

In 1959, an organization named Euzkadi Ta Askatasuna, meaning Basque Fatherland and Freedom, commonly referred to by its abbreviated form, ETA, was founded. The creation of an independent homeland in Spain's Basque region was declared to be its goal. In December 1973, Basque nationalists assassinated Prime Minister Admiral Luis Carrero Blanco in Madrid. Spain made the switch from dictatorship to monarchy in 1975 after General Franco passed away on 20 November. King Juan Carlos succeeded him as the head of state.

Geography

Location: South-western Europe, bordering the Bay of Biscay, Mediterranean Sea, North Atlantic Ocean, and Pyrenees Mountains, south-west of France.

Area: 504,782 sq. km.

Terrain: Large, flat to dissected plateau surrounded by rugged hills. The Pyrenees Mountains lie in the north of the country.

Natural resources: Coal, lignite, iron ore, copper, lead, zinc, uranium, tungsten, mercury, pyrite, magnesite, fluorspar, gypsum, sepiolite, kaolin, potash, hydropower, arable land.

Climate: Temperate climate with clear, hot summers in the interiors but more moderate and cloudy in the coastal parts.

People

Population: 40,397,842 (July 2006 est.).

Population growth rate: 0.13% (2006 est.).

Sex ratio: 0.96 male(s)/female (2006 est.).

Religions: Roman Catholic 94%, others 6%.

Languages: Castilian Spanish 74%, Catalan 17%, Galician 7%, Basque 2%.

Literacy rate: Total 97.9%, Male 98.7%, Female 97.2% (2003 est.).

Infant mortality rate: 4.37 deaths/ 1,000 live births (2006 est.).

Life expectancy: Total 79.65 years, Male 76.32 years, Female 83.2 years (2006 est.).

Government

Capital: Madrid.

Government type: Parliamentary monarchy.

Independence: 1492 (Date of seizure of Granada leading to the unification of several kingdoms. This is traditionally considered to be the creation of present-day Spain).

Legal system: Civil law system, with regional applications.

Executive branch:

Chief of state: King Juan Carlos I (since 22 November 1975). Heir Apparent Prince Felipe, son of the monarch, born 30 January 1968.

Head of government: President Jose Luis Rodriguez Zapatero (since 17 April 2004).

Economy

Currency: Euro.

Economy—overview:
Spain has a mixed capitalist economy. Spain was one of the countries that launched the European single currency (the euro) on 1 January 1999. The previous administration led by Jose Maria Aznar promoted a policy of economic deregulation, liberalization, and privatization, besides introducing tax reforms. One of the major problems facing the country is unemployment. Although unemployment levels fell steadily under the Aznar administration, it still remained high. The Spanish economy will also face challenges posed by its necessary adjustments required for integration to the monetary and economic policies of a united Europe.

GDP: Purchasing power parity—$1.029 billion (2005 est.).

GDP—real growth rate: 3.4% (2005 est.).

GDP—per capita: Purchasing power parity—$25,500 (2005 est.).

Inflation rate: 3.4% (2004 est.).

Unemployment rate: 10.1% (2005 est.).

Exports: $194.3 billion f.o.b. (2005 est.)—machinery, motor vehicles, foodstuffs.

Imports: $271.8 billion f.o.b. (2005 est.)—machinery and equipment, fuels, chemicals, semi-finished goods; foodstuff, consumer goods.

External debt: $1.249 trillion (30 June 2005 est.).

Transport and Communications

Railways: 14,781 km.

Roads: 666,292 km.

Telephones: 17,934,500 (2004).

Mobile cellular: 38,646,800 (2004).

Internet users: 17,142,198 (2005).

Internet country code: .es

Sri Lanka

History

The first human settlers of Sri Lanka are thought to be tribes of the proto-Australoid ethnic group similar to the pre-Dravidian hill tribes of southern India. The Indo-Aryans immigrated from India in about the fifth century BC and combined with the early settlers to develop into the Sinhalese. The Tamils are believed to be later immigrants from Dravidian India. The time period of their movement into Sri Lanka is believed to have spread out from the third century BC to about AD 1200. The Tamil component of the island's population increased when south Indians were brought to work in the plantations in the nineteenth century.

The period between the thirteenth and fifteenth centuries saw foreign invasions from India, Malaya and China. The country was then called Ceylon. The Portuguese arrived in 1505 and by 1619, they controlled most of the island. The Sinhalese acquired the help of the Dutch to help throw out the Portuguese from the island. In 1796, the Dutch East India Company handed over power to the British. In 1808, Ceylon became a Crown Colony.

In 1948, Ceylon became an independent country. It changed its name to Sri Lanka in 1972.

Geography

Location: Southern Asia, island in the Indian Ocean, south of India.

Area: 65,610 sq. km.

Terrain: Flat to rolling plains with mountains in the south-central interior region.

Natural resources: Limestone, graphite, mineral sands, gems, phosphates, clay, hydropower.

Climate: Tropical monsoon climate.

People

Population: 20,222,240 (July 2006 est.).

Population growth rate: 0.78% (2006 est.).

Sex ratio: 0.96 male(s)/female (2006 est.).

Religions: Buddhist 70%, Hindu 15%, Christian 8%, Muslim 7% (1999).

Languages: Sinhala (official and national language) 74%, Tamil (national language) 18%, others 8%.

Literacy rate: Total 92.3%, Male 94.8%, Female 90% (2003 est.).

Infant mortality rate: 13.97 deaths/ 1,000 live births (2006 est.).

Life expectancy: Total 73.41 years, Male 70.83 years, Female 76.12 years (2006 est.).

Government

Capital: Colombo. Sri Jayewardenepura Kotte is the legislative capital.

Government type: Republic.

Independence: 4 February 1948 (from UK).

Legal system: A mixture of English common law, Roman–Dutch, Muslim, Sinhalese and customary law.

Executive branch:

Chief of state: President Mahinda Rajapakse (since 19 November 2005); note: Ratnagiri Wickremanayake (since 21 November 2005) is the prime minister. The president is considered both the chief of state and head of government.

Election and election results: The president is elected by popular vote for a six-year term. The last elections were held 17 November 2005 (next to be held 2011).

Election results: Mahinda Rajapakse was elected president; per cent of vote; Mahinda Rajapakse 50.3%, Ranil Wickremesinghe 48.4%, other 1.3%.

Legislative branch:

Sri Lanka has a unicameral parliament of 225 seats and its members are elected by popular vote on the basis of a modified proportional representation system to serve six-year terms.

Election and election results:

The last election were held on 2 April 2004 and the next are due in 2010.

Economy

Currency: Sri Lankan rupee.

Economy—overview:

In 1977, Colombo gave up its import substitution trade policy for market-oriented policies and export-oriented trade. The key sectors now are food processing, textiles and apparel, food and beverages, telecommunications, and insurance and banking. GDP grew at an average annual rate of 5.5 per cent in the early 1990s but a drought and a worsening security situation caused growth to slump to 3.8 per cent in 1996. In the period 1997–2000, the economy rejuvenated with an average growth of 5.3 per cent. In 2001, however, the first contraction in the country's history took place (–1.4 per cent), due to a myriad of problems like the global slowdown, power shortages and budgetary problems. The prolonged civil conflict that plagued the country for many years was also a contributory reason. In 2002, however, growth rebounded to 3.2 per cent.

In late December 2004, a major tsunami took about 31,000 lives, left more than 6,300 missing and 443,000 displaced, and destroyed an estimated

$1.5 billion worth of property.

GDP: Purchasing power parity—$85.34 billion (2005 est.).

GDP—real growth rate: 5.6% (2005 est.).

GDP—per capita: Purchasing power parity—$4,300 (2005 est.).

Inflation rate: 11.2% (2005 est.).

Population below poverty line: 22% (1997 est.).

Unemployment rate: 8.4% (2005 est.).

Exports: $6.442 billion f.o.b. (2005 est.)—textiles and apparel, tea, diamond, coconut products, petroleum products.

Imports: $8.37 billion f.o.b. (2005 est.)—textiles, mineral products, petroleum, foodstuff, machinery and equipment.

External debt: $11.59 billion (2005 est.).

Transport and Communications

Railways: 1,449 km.

Roads: 97,287 km.

Telephones: 1,130,923 (2005).

Mobile cellular: 3,084,845 (2005).

Internet users: 280,000 (2005).

Internet country code: .lk

Sudan

History

An Egyptian and Nubian civilization named Kush grew and flourished in the region around present-day Sudan till AD 350. The arrival of Arabs and their subsequent domination over the region resulted in conversions to Islam. Between 1898 and 1955, the country was called Anglo-Egyptian Sudan. In 1953, UK and Egypt granted self-governance and in 1956, Sudan became independent. A succession of short-lived regimes ruled Sudan ever since it gained independence.

Geography

Location: Northern Africa, bordering the Red Sea, between Egypt and Eritrea.

Area: 2,505,810 sq. km.

Terrain: Generally flat, featureless plain; mountains in the far south, north-east and west; a desert dominates the south.

Natural resources: Petroleum, iron ore, copper, chromium ore, zinc, tungsten, mica, silver, gold, hydropower.

Climate: Tropical in the south, arid desert in the north.

People

Population: 41,236,378 (July 2006 est.).

Population growth rate: 2.55% (2006 est.).

Sex ratio: 1.02 male(s)/female (2006 est.).

Religions: Sunni Muslim 70% (in the north), indigenous beliefs 25%, Christian 5% (mostly in the south and in Khartoum).

Languages: Arabic (official), Nubian, Ta Bedawie, diverse dialects of Nilotic, Nilo-Hamitic, Sudanic languages, English.

Literacy rate: Total 61.1%, Male 71.8%, Female 50.5% (2003 est.).

Infant mortality rate: 61.05 deaths/1,000 live births (2006 est.).

Life expectancy: Total 58.92 years, Male 57.69 years, Female 60.21 years (2006 est.).

Government

Capital: Khartoum.

Government type: Coalition government run by an alliance of the National Congress Party (NCP) and the Sudan People's Liberation Movement (SPLM).

Independence: 1 January 1956 (from Egypt and UK).

Legal system: Based on English common law and Islamic law.

Executive branch:

Chief of state: President Lt Gen. Umar Hassan Ahmad al-Bashir (since 16 October 1993). The President is both the chief of state and head of government. Gen. al-Bashir assumed supreme executive power in 1989. He subsequently retained power through many transitional governments in the early and mid-1990s. He was popularly elected for the first time in March 1996.

Economy

Currency: Sudanese dinar.

GDP: Purchasing power parity—$85.45 billion (2005 est.).

GDP—real growth rate: 7% (2005 est.).

GDP—per capita: Purchasing power parity—$2,100 (2005 est.).

Inflation rate: 11% (2005 est.).

Unemployment rate: 18.7% (2002 est.)

Exports: $6.989 billion f.o.b. (2005 est.)—oil and petroleum products; cotton, sesame, livestock, groundnuts, gum arabic, sugar.

Imports: $5.028 billion f.o.b. (2005 est.)—foodstuff, manufactured goods, refinery and transport equipment, medicines and chemicals, textiles, wheat.

External debt: $18.15 billion (2005 est.).

Transport and Communications

Railways: 5,995 km.

Roads: 11,900 km.

Telephones: 1,028,900 (2004).

Mobile cellular: 1,048,600 (2004).

Internet users: 1.14 million (2005).

Internet country code: .sd

Suriname

History

A group of British planters set up the first permanent settlement of Europeans in Suriname in 1651. A Dutch fleet seized Suriname in 1667. The Netherlands held Suriname till its independence in 1975.

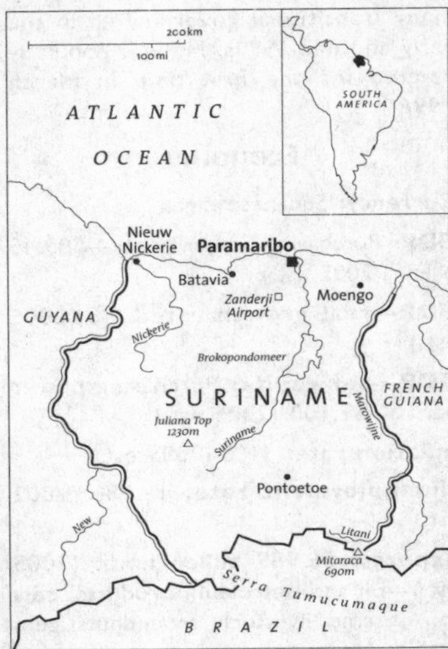

Geography

Location: Northern South America, bordering the North Atlantic Ocean, between French Guiana and Guyana.

Area: 163,270 sq. km.

Terrain: Mostly rolling hills; narrow coastal plain with swamps.

Natural resources: Timber, hydropower, fish, kaolin, shrimp, bauxite, gold, and small amounts of nickel, copper, platinum, iron ore.

Climate: Tropical climate.

People

Population: 439,117 (July 2006 est.).

Population growth rate: 0.2% (2006 est.).

Sex ratio: 1.04 male(s)/female (2006 est.).

Religions: Hindu 27.4%, Muslim 19.6%, Roman Catholic 22.8%, Protestant 25.2% (predominantly Moravian), indigenous beliefs 5%.

Languages: Dutch, English.

Literacy rate: Total 88%, Male 92.3%, Female 84.1% (2000 est.).

Infant mortality rate: 23.02 deaths/1,000 live births (2006 est.).

Life expectancy: Total 69.01 years, Male 66.66 years, Female 71.47 year (2006 est.).

Government

Capital: Paramaribo.

Government type: Constitutional democracy.

Independence: 25 November 1975 (from the Netherlands).

Legal system: Based on Dutch legal system incorporating French penal theory.

Executive branch:

Chief of state: President Runaldo Ronald Venetiaan (since 12 August 2000); Vice-President Jules Rattankoemar Ajodhia (since 12 August 2000). The president is both the chief of state and head of government.

Economy

Currency: Surinamese guilder.

GDP: Purchasing power parity—$2.818 billion (2005 est.).

GDP—real growth rate: 2% (2005 est.).

GDP—per capita: Purchasing power parity—$4,100 (2005 est.).

Inflation rate: 9.5% (2005 est.).

Population below poverty line: 70% (2002 est.).

Unemployment rate: 9.5% (2004).

Exports: $881 million f.o.b. (2004)—alumina, crude oil, lumber, shrimp and fish, rice, banana.

Imports: $750 million f.o.b. (2004)—capital equipment, petroleum, foodstuff, cotton, consumer goods.

External debt: $504.3 million (2005 est.).

Transport and Communications

Railways: 301 km (single-track).

Roads: 4,492 km.

Telephones: 81,300 (2004).

Mobile cellular: 212,800 (2004).

Internet users: 30,000 (2005).

Internet country code: .sr

Swaziland

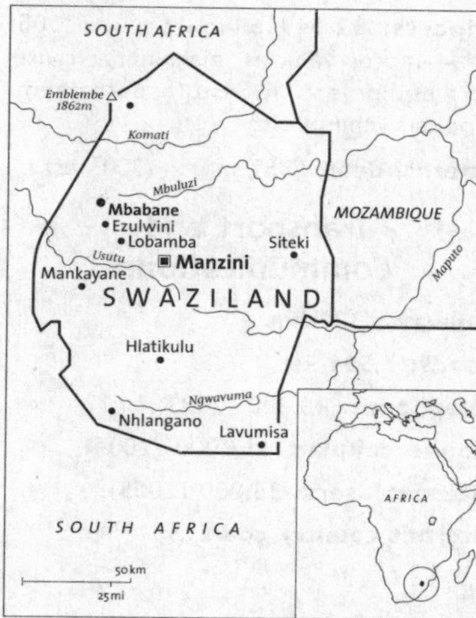

History

In the eighteenth century, a number of Bantu clans broke away from a bigger group in modern-day Mozambique and settled in the area that is today Swaziland. Prevailing tensions with the Zulu led their King Mswazi to appeal to the British for help in the 1840s. In 1881, the governments of UK and Transvaal assured the Swazi state of their independence. Between 1894 and 1899, Swaziland was a South African protectorate. In 1902, the control of the state was transferred to UK. Swaziland gained independence in 1968.

Geography

Location: Southern Africa, between Mozambique and South Africa.

Area: 17,363 sq. km.

Terrain: Mostly mountains and hills, with some moderately sloping plains.

Natural resources: Asbestos, coal, clay, cassiterite, hydropower, forests, small gold and diamond deposits, quarry stone, and talc.

Climate: Tropical.

People

Population: 1,136,334 (July 2006 est.).

Population growth rate: –0.23% (2006 est.).

Sex ratio: 0.95 male(s)/female (2006 est.).

Religions: Zionist (a combination of Christianity and indigenous ancestral worship) 40%, Roman Catholic 20%, Muslim 10%.

Languages: English (official, government business conducted in English), Siswati (official).

Literacy rate: Total 81.6%, Male 82.6%, Female 80.8% (2003 est.).

Infant mortality rate: 71.85 deaths/ 1,000 live births (2006 est.).

Life expectancy: Total 32.62 years, Male 32.1 years, Female 33.17 years (2006 est.).

Government

Capital: Mbabane; Lobamba is the royal and legislative capital.

Government type: Monarchy.

Independence: 6 September 1968 (from UK).

Legal system: Based on South African Roman–Dutch law in statutory courts and Swazi traditional law and custom in traditional courts.

Executive branch:
Chief of state: King Mswati III (since 25 April 1986).

Head of government: Prime Minister Absolom Themba Dlamini (since 14 November 2003).

Economy

Currency: Lilangeni.

GDP: Purchasing power parity—$5.685 billion (2005 est.).

GDP—real growth rate: 1.8% (2005 est.).

GDP—per capita: Purchasing power parity—$5,000 (2005 est.).

Inflation rate: 4% (2005 est.).

Population below poverty line: 69% (2005).

Unemployment rate: 40% (2005 est.).

Exports: $1.991 billion f.o.b. (2005 est.)—soft drink concentrates, sugar, wood pulp, cotton yarn, refrigerators, citrus and canned fruit.

Imports: $2.149 billion f.o.b. (2005 est.)—motor vehicles, machinery, transport equipment, foodstuff, petroleum products, chemicals.

External debt: $357 million (2003 est.).

Transport and Communications

Railways: 301 km.

Roads: 3,594 km.

Telephones: 46,200 (2003).

Mobile cellular: 113,000 (2004).

Internet users: 36,000 (2005).

Internet country code: .sz

Sweden

History

The Kalmar Union of 1397 united Sweden with Norway and Denmark, with Denmark as the dominant state. However, this union failed and led to bitter conflict between the Swedes and the Danes. In 1520, the Danish king Christian II conquered Sweden and subsequently ordered the mass execution of Swedish nobles. This massacre is referred to as the Stockholm Bloodbath.

In June 1523 Gustav Vasa was elected king. Under his leadership, Sweden broke away from Danish domination. Sweden played a key role in the Thirty Year's War (1618–48) and the 1648 Treaty of Westphalia gave Sweden substantial territories.

Geography

Location: Northern Europe, bordering the Baltic Sea, Gulf of Bothnia, Kattegat, and Skagerrak, between Finland and Norway.

Area: 449,964 sq. km.

Terrain: Mostly flat or in the form of gently rolling lowlands. There are mountains in the western part of the country.

Natural resources: Iron ore, copper, lead, zinc, gold, silver, tungsten, ura-

nium, arsenic, feldspar, timber, hydropower.

Climate: Temperate in the south and subarctic in the north.

People

Population: 9,016,596 (July 2006 est.).

Population growth rate: 0.16% (2006 est.).

Sex ratio: 0.98 male(s)/female (2006 est.).

Religions: Lutheran 87%, Roman Catholic, Orthodox, Baptist, Muslim, Jewish, Buddhist.

Languages: Swedish, Sami, Finnish.

Literacy rate: 99% (2003 est.).

Infant mortality rate: 2.76 deaths/ 1,000 live births (2006 est.).

Life expectancy: Total 80.51 years, Male 78.29 years, Female 82.87 years (2006 est.).

Government

Capital: Stockholm.

Government type: Constitutional monarchy.

Independence: 6 June 1523 (date on which Gustav Vasa was elected king).

Legal system: Civil law system influenced by customary law.

Executive branch:
Chief of state: King Carl XVI Gustaf (since 19 September 1973); Heir Apparent Princess Victoria Ingrid Alice Desiree, daughter of the monarch (born 14 July 1977).

Head of government: Prime Minister Goran Persson (since 21 March 1996).

Economy

Currency: Swedish krona.

Economy—overview:
The Swedish economy is a combination of high-tech capitalism and an extensive welfare system that has led to a high standard of living. Sweden enjoys very good infrastructure, a skilled labour force, resources like hydropower, iron ore and timber. However, the Swedish economy is heavily reliant on foreign trade. On 14 September 2003, Swedish voters voted against an entry into the euro system.

GDP: Purchasing power parity—$268 billion (2005 est.).

GDP—real growth rate: 2.7% (2005 est.).

GDP—per capita: Purchasing power parity—$29,800 (2005 est.).

Inflation rate: 0.5% (2005 est.).

Unemployment rate: 6% (2005 est.).

Exports: $126.6 billion f.o.b. (2005 est.)—machinery, motor vehicles, paper products, pulp and wood, iron and steel products, chemicals.

Imports: $104.4 billion f.o.b. (2005 est.)—machinery, petroleum and petroleum products, chemicals, motor vehicles, iron and steel; foodstuff, clothing.

External debt: $516.1 billion (30 June 2005).

Transport and Communications

Railways: 11,481 km.

Roads: 429,981 km.

Telephones: 6.447 million (2004).

Mobile cellular: 9.775 million (2004).

Internet users: 6.8 million (2005).

Internet country code: .se

Switzerland

History

Switzerland was known as Helvetia in ancient times. It later became a league of cantons in the Holy Roman Empire. The 1648 Treaty of Westphalia gave the country independence from the Holy Roman Empire. In 1798, French revolutionary troops occupied the country and proclaimed the Helvetic republic. However, in 1803, Napoleon restored the old federal government. In the nineteenth century, the French-speaking and Italian-speaking citizens of Switzerland gained political equality.

In 1920, Switzerland joined the League of Nations and subsequently Geneva became the League's headquarters. Even today, the European headquarters of the United Nations are in Geneva. In both World Wars, Switzerland remained neutral.

Geography

Location: Central Europe, east of France, north of Italy.

Area: 41,290 sq. km.

Terrain: Mostly mountainous with the Alps in the south and the Jura in the north-west. There is a central plateau of rolling hills, plains, and large lakes.

Natural resources: Hydropower potential, timber, salt.

Climate: Temperate climate that varies with altitude.

People

Population: 7,523,934 (July 2006 est.).

Population growth rate: 0.43% (2006 est.).

Sex ratio: 0.97 male(s)/female (2006 est.).

Religions: Roman Catholic 41.8%, Protestant 35.3%, Orthodox 1.8%, other Christian 0.4%, Muslim 4.3%, unspecified 4.3%, other 1%, none 11.1% (2000 census).

Languages: German (official) 63.7%, French (official) 19.2%, Italian (official) 7.6%, Romansch (official) 0.6%, others 8.9%.

Literacy rate: 99% (2003 est.).

Infant mortality rate: 4.34 deaths/ 1,000 live births (2006 est.).

Life expectancy: Total 80.51 years, Male 77.69 years, Female 83.48 years (2006 est.).

Government

Capital: Bern.

Government type: Federal republic.

Independence: 1 August 1291 (Founding of the Swiss Confederation).

Legal system: Civil law system influenced by customary law.

Executive branch:
Chief of state: President Moritz Leuenberger (since 8 January 2006); Vice-President Micheline Calmy-Rey (since 8 January 2006). The president is both the chief of state and head of government.

Economy

Currency: Swiss franc.

Economy—overview:
The Swiss economy is a prosperous and stable market economy. The characteristics of the economy are a highly skilled labour force, low unemployment and a high per capita GDP. Switzerland is the chosen destination for investors seeking a safe haven due to its secretive banking services.

GDP: Purchasing power parity—$241.8 billion (2005 est.).

GDP—real growth rate: 1.8% (2005 est.).

GDP—per capita: Purchasing power parity—$32,300 (2005 est.).

Inflation rate: 1.2% (2005 est.).

Exports: $148.6 billion f.o.b. (2005 est.)—machinery, chemicals, metals, watches, agricultural products.

Imports: $135 billion f.o.b. (2005 est.)—machinery, chemicals, vehicles, metals, agricultural products, textiles.

External debt: $856 billion (30 June 2005).

Transport and Communications

Railways: 4,527 km.

Roads: 71,220 km.

Telephones: 5,262,600 (2004).

Mobile cellular: 6.275 million (2004).

Internet users: 4,944,438 (2005).

Internet country code: .ch

Syria

History

From the third century BC onwards, the area that is today Syria has been under control of the Sumerians, Assyrians, Babylonians, Egyptians, Hittites, Akkadians and Amorites. In the sixth century BC, it became a part of the Persian Achaemenian dynasty that in turn passed to Alexander the Great in 330 BC. It later formed parts of the Roman empire, Byzantine empire and the Ottoman empire. UK invaded Syria during World War I and it became a French mandate after the War. Syria achieved independence in 1946. Between 1958 and 1961, it united with Egypt to form the United Arab Republic.

Geography

Location: Middle East, bordering the Mediterranean Sea, between Lebanon and Turkey.

Area: 185,180 sq. km (This includes 1,295 sq. km of Israeli-occupied territory).

Terrain: Primarily semi-arid and desert plateau; narrow coastal plain; mountains in the west.

Natural resources: Petroleum, phosphates, chrome and manganese ores, asphalt, iron ore, rock salt, marble, gypsum, hydropower.

Climate: Mostly desert with hot, dry, sunny summers from June to August and mild, rainy winters from December to February along the coast.

People

Population: 18,881,361 (July 2006 est.) Besides this, about 40,000 people live in the Israeli-occupied Golan Heights, including above 20,000 Arabs and over 20,000 Israeli settlers.

Population growth rate: 2.3% (2006 est.).

Sex ratio: 1.05 male(s)/female (2006 est.).

Religions: Sunni Muslim 74%, Alawite, Druze, and other Muslim sects 16%, Christian (various sects) 10%, Jewish.

Languages: Arabic (official); Kurdish, Armenian, Aramaic, Circassian widely understood; French, English also understood.

Literacy rate: Total 76.9%, Male 89.7%, Female 64% (2003 est.).

Infant mortality rate: 28.61 deaths/ 1,000 live births (2006 est.).

Life expectancy: Total 70.32 years, Male 69.01 years, Female 71.7 years (2006 est.).

Government

Capital: Damascus.

Government type: Republic under military regime since March 1963.

Independence: 17 April 1946 (from League of Nations mandate under French administration).

Legal system: Based on Islamic law and civil law system; special religious courts.

Executive branch:
Chief of state: President Bashar al-Aasad (since 17 July 2000).

Head of government: Prime Minister Muhammad Naji al-Utri (since 10 September 2003).

Economy

Currency: Syrian pound.

Economy—overview:
Syria's slow economic growth rate, slower than its average annual population growth rate, has caused a persistent decline in its per capita GDP. External factors like the Israeli–Palestinian conflict, international war on terrorism, and the war between the US-led coalition and Iraq is likely to drive real annual GDP growth to healthier levels.

GDP: Purchasing power parity—$72.33 billion (2005 est.).

GDP—real growth rate: 4.5% (2005 est.).

GDP—per capita: Purchasing power parity—$3,900 (2005 est.).

Inflation rate: 2.6% (2005 est.).

Population below poverty line: 20% (2004 est.).

Unemployment rate: 12.3% (2004 est.).

Exports: $6.344 billion f.o.b. (2005 est.)—crude oil , petroleum products, fruits and vegetables, cotton fibre, clothing, meat and live animals.

Imports: $5.973 billion f.o.b. (2005 est.)—machinery and transport equipment, food and livestock, metal and metal products, chemicals and chemical products.

External debt: $8.59 billion (2004 est.); note: excludes military debt and debt to Russia.

Transport and Communications

Railways: 2,711 km.

Roads: 91,795 km.

Telephones: 2.66 million (2004).

Mobile cellular: 2.345 million (2004).

Internet users: 800,000 (2005).

Internet country code: .sy

Tajikistan

History

The Persians settled in the area in the sixth century BC. The region later formed parts of the empires of Persians and Alexander the Great. Uzbeks controlled the area in the fifteenth–nineteenth centuries AD. The Russians annexed much of the region in the 1860s and in 1924 it became an autonomous republic administered by the Uzbek Republic. Tajikistan gained the status of a republic in 1929. In 1991, it gained independence after the disintegration of the Soviet Union.

Geography

Location: Central Asia, west of China.

Area: 143,100 sq. km.

Terrain: The Pamir and Alay Mountains dominate the landscape. The Western Fergana Valley lies to the north, while the Kofarnihon and Vakhsh Valleys feature in the south-west.

Natural resources: Hydropower, some petroleum, uranium, mercury, brown coal, lead, zinc, antimony, tungsten, silver, gold.

Climate: Mid-latitude continental with hot summers and mild winters; semi-arid to arctic in the Pamir Mountains.

People

Population: 7,320,815 (July 2006 est.).

Population growth rate: 2.19% (2006 est.).

Sex ratio: 0.99 male(s)/female (2006 est.).

Religions: Sunni Muslim 85%, Shi'a Muslim 5%.

Languages: Tajik (official), Russian widely used in government and business.

Literacy rate: 99.4% (2003 est.).

Infant mortality rate: 106.49 deaths/1,000 live births (2006 est.).

Life expectancy: Total 64.94 years, Male 62.03 years, Female 68 years (2006 est.).

Government

Capital: Dushanbe.

Government type: Republic.

Independence: 9 September 1991 (from Soviet Union).

Legal system: Based on civil law system. There is no judicial review of legislative acts.

Executive branch:
Chief of state: President Emomali Rahmonov (since 6 November 1994).

Head of government: Prime Minister Oqil Oqilov (since 20 January 1999).

Economy

Currency: Somoni.

Economy—overview:
As little as 8 per cent to 10 per cent of the land area is arable and cotton is the most important crop. There is a small amount of a variety of mineral resources in Tajikistan. These include silver, gold, uranium, and tungsten. Industrial activity is meagre. Tajikistan has the lowest per capita GDP among the fifteen former Soviet republics. The civil war that raged in the country during 1992–7 caused further damage to the already weak infrastructure and caused industrial and agricultural production to plummet.

GDP: Purchasing power parity—$8.73 billion (2005 est.).

GDP—real growth rate: 8% (2005 est.).

GDP—per capita: Purchasing power parity—$1,200 (2005 est.).

Inflation rate: 8% (2005 est.).

Population below poverty line: 60% (2004 est.).

Unemployment rate: 12% (2004 est.).

Exports: $950 million f.o.b. (2005 est.)—aluminum, electricity, cotton, fruits, vegetable oil, textiles.

Imports: $1.25 billion f.o.b. (2005 est.)—electricity, petroleum products, aluminum oxide, machinery and equipment, foodstuff.

External debt: $888 million (2004 est.).

Transport and Communications

Railways: 482 km.

Roads: 27,767 km (2000).

Telephones: 245,200 (2004).

Mobile cellular: 47,600 (2003).

Internet users: 5,000 (2005).

Internet country code: .tj

Tanzania

History

Portuguese explorers reached the coastal regions of Tanzania in 1500 and held some influence till the seventeenth century when the sultan of Oman took over. In 1885, Tanganyika, along with what are today Rwanda and Burundi,

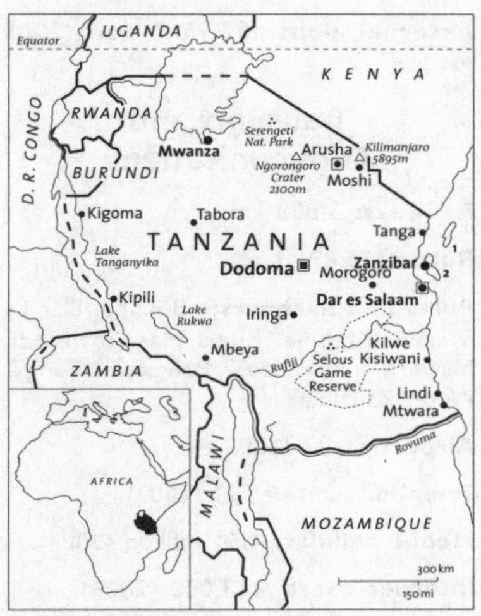

was formed into the colony of German East Africa. After World War I, UK administered the territory, first under a League of Nations mandate and then as a UN trust territory.

In 1961, Tanganyika became independent with Julius Nyerere as prime minister. The following year, it became a republic. In 1964, the Afro-Shirazi Party ousted the Sultanate of Zanzibar in a left-wing revolution. Tanganyika and Zanzibar then merged together to form United Republic of Tanganyika and Zanzibar. In October 1964, it was renamed as United Republic of Tanzania.

Geography

Location: Eastern Africa, bordering the Indian Ocean, between Kenya and Mozambique.

Area: 945,087 sq. km. (This includes the islands of Mafia, Pemba, and Zanzibar.)

Terrain: Plains along the coast, a central plateau and highlands in the north and in the south.

Natural resources: Hydropower, tin, phosphates, iron ore, coal, diamond, gemstones, gold, natural gas, nickel.

Climate: Tropical climate along the coast and temperate climate in the highlands.

People

Population: 37,445,392 (July 2006 est.).

Population growth rate: 1.83% (2006 est.).

Sex ratio: 0.98 male(s)/female (2006 est.).

Religions: Mainland—Christian 30%, Muslim 35%, indigenous beliefs 35%. Zanzibar—99% Muslim.

Languages: Kiswahili or Swahili (official), Kiunguju (name for Swahili in Zanzibar), English, Arabic, many local languages.

Literacy rate: Total 78.2%, Male 85.9%, Female 70.7% (2003 est.).

Infant mortality rate: 96.48 deaths/1,000 live births (2006 est.).

Life expectancy: Total 45.64 years, Male 44.93 years, Female 46.37 years (2006 est.).

Government

Capital: Dar es Salaam; legislative offices have been transferred to Dodoma, the planned new national capital.

Government type: Republic.

Independence: 26 April 1964 (date on which Tanganyika united with Zanzibar to form the United Republic of Tanganyika and Zanzibar, renamed United Republic of Tanzania on 29 October 1964).

Legal system: Based on English common law.

Executive branch:
Chief of state: President Jakaya Kikwete (since 21 December 2005). The president is both chief of state and head of government.

Economy

Currency: Tanzanian shilling.

GDP: Purchasing power parity—$27.07 billion (2005 est.).

GDP—real growth rate: 0% (2005 est.).

GDP—per capita: Purchasing power parity—$700 (2005 est.).

Inflation rate: 4% (2005 est.).

Population below poverty line: 36% (2002 est.).

Exports: $1.581 billion f.o.b. (2005 est.)—gold, coffee, cashew nuts, manufactures, cotton.

Imports: $2.391 billion f.o.b. (2005 est.)—consumer goods, machinery and transportation equipment, industrial raw materials, crude oil.

External debt: $7.95 billion (2005 est.).

Transport and Communications

Railways: 3,690 km.

Roads: 78,891 km

Ports and harbours: Bukoba, Dar es Salaam, Kigoma, Kilwa Masoko, Lindi, Mtwara, Mwanza, Pangani, Tanga, Wete, Zanzibar.

Airports: 123 (2003 est.).

Telephones: 149,100 (2003).

Mobile cellular: 1.64 million (2004).

Internet users: 333,000 (2005).

Internet country code: .tz

Thailand

History

What is today Thailand was part of the Mon and Khmer kingdoms from the ninth century AD. Around the tenth century AD, Thai-speaking people migrated into the region from China. Later, in the thirteenth century, two distinct kingdoms emerged in the region. The Sukhothai kingdom emerged around 1220 AD, while the Chiang Mai was founded in 1296. In 1350, the kingdom of Ayutthaya replaced the Sukhothai kingdom. In 1767, the Burmese destroyed the kingdom of Ayutthaya. In 1782, the Chakri dynasty came to power. The dynasty shifted the capital to Bangkok and expanded the kingdom into the Malay peninsula and Laos and Cambodia. In 1856, the name Siam was adopted.

When Western powers extended their influence in the South-east Asian region in the nineteenth century, Siam was the only kingdom that avoided colonization. In 1932, the country became a constitutional monarchy subsequent to a military coup. In 1939, the present name of Thailand was adopted.

Geography

Location: South-eastern Asia, bordering the Andaman Sea and the Gulf of Thailand, south-east of Myanmar.

Area: 514,000 sq. km.

Terrain: The central area is a plain, the Khorat Plateau lies in the east and there are mountains in the other regions.

Natural resources: Tin, natural gas, tungsten, tantalum, timber, rubber, lead, fish, gypsum, lignite, fluorite, arable land.

Climate: Tropical climate. The rainy, warm, cloudy south-west monsoon season is from mid-May to September

while the dry, cool north-east monsoon season is from November to mid-March.

People

Population: 64,631,595 (July 2006 est.).

Population growth rate: 68% (2006 est.).

Sex ratio: 0.98 male(s)/female (2006 est.).

Religions: Buddhist 95%, Muslim 3.8%, Christian 0.5%, Hindu 0.1%, others 0.6%.

Languages: Thai, English (secondary language of the elite), ethnic and regional dialects.

Literacy rate: Total 92.6%, Male 94.9%, Female 90.5% (2002 est.).

Infant mortality rate: 19.49 deaths/1,000 live births (2006 est.).

Life expectancy: Total 72.25 years, Male 69.95 years, Female 74.68 years (2006 est.).

Government

Capital: Bangkok.

Government type: Constitutional monarchy.

Independence: 1238 (traditional founding date).

Legal system: Based on civil law system, with influences of common law.

Executive branch:
Chief of state: King Bhumibol Adulyadej (since 9 June 1946).

Head of government: Prime Minister Thaksin Shinawatra (since 9 February 2001).

Economy

Currency: Baht.

Economy—overview:
Thailand has a free enterprise economy that is open to foreign investment. Between 1985 and 1995, Thailand enjoyed a very high growth rate averaging almost 9 per cent annually. But this also increased speculative pressure on Thailand's currency, the baht. All this precipitated the 1997 crisis that revealed financial sector weaknesses and led the government to float the baht. Strong exports helped Thailand stage a recovery. The economy grew by 4.2 per cent in 1999 and 4.4 per cent in 2000 but growth slumped to 1.4 per cent in 2001. GDP grew by 5.2 per cent in 2002. In late December 2004, a major tsunami caused massive destruction of property in the southern provinces of Krabi, Phangnga, and Phuket. Growth slowed to 4.6 per cent in 2005. The downturn can be attributed to high oil prices, weaker demand from Western markets, severe drought in rural regions, tsunami-related declines in tourism, and lower consumer confidence. On the positive side, the Thai economy performed well, beginning in the third quarter of 2005. Ex-

port-oriented manufacturing—in particular automobile production—and farm output are driving these gains.

GDP: Purchasing power parity—$560.7 billion (2005 est.).

GDP—real growth rate: 4.5% (2005 est.).

GDP—per capita: Purchasing power parity—$8,300 (2005 est.).

Inflation rate: 4.8% (2005 est.).

Population below poverty line: 10% (2004 est.).

Unemployment rate: 1.4% (2005 est.).

Exports: $105.8 billion f.o.b. (2005 est.)—computers, seafood, clothing, transistors, rice (2000).

Imports: $107 billion f.o.b. (2005 est.)—fuels, capital goods, intermediate goods and raw materials, consumer goods.

External debt: $50.63 billion (30 June 2005 est.).

Transport and Communications

Railways: 4,071 km.

Roads: 57,403 km.

Telephones: 6.797 million (2004).

Mobile cellular: 26,500,000 (2005).

Internet users: 8.42 million (2005).

Internet country code: .th

Togo

History

In 1884, Germany set up the protectorate of Togoland. In 1914, British and French forces seized Togoland. In 1922, the League of Nations granted mandates to UK to administer the western part of Togoland and to France to rule the eastern part. In 1956, the British-held part of Togoland was included into Gold Coast that later became Ghana. In 1960, the French-administered part of Togoland became independent as Togo.

Geography

Location: Western Africa, bordering the Bight of Benin, between Benin and Ghana.

Area: 56,785 sq. km.

Terrain: Gently rolling savanna in the north, central hills, a southern plateau and a low coastal plain with extensive lagoons and marshes.

Natural resources: Phosphates, limestone, marble, arable land.

Climate: Tropical climate. Hot and humid in the south and semi-arid in the north.

People

Population: 5,548,702 (July 2006 est.).

Population growth rate: 2.72% (2006 est.).

Sex ratio: 0.96 male(s)/female (2006 est.).

Religions: Indigenous beliefs 51%, Christian 29%, Muslim 20%.

Languages: French (official and the language of commerce), Ewe and Mina (the two major African languages in the south), Kabye/Kabiye, Dagomba (the two major African languages in the north).

Literacy rate: Total 60.9%, Male 75.4%, Female 46.9% (2003 est.).

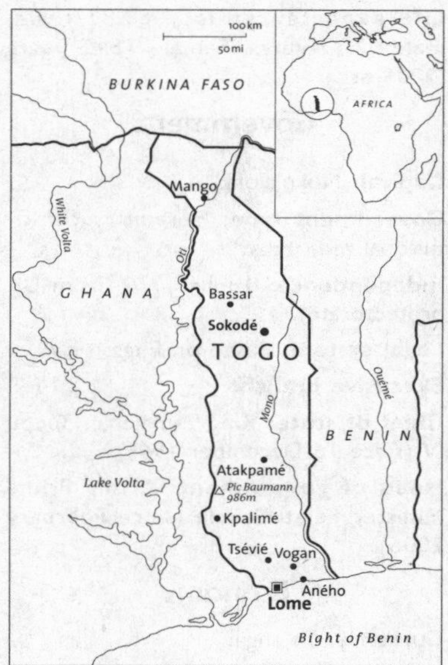

Infant mortality rate: 60.63 deaths/ 1,000 live births (2006 est.).

Life expectancy: Total 57.42 years, Male 55.41 years, Female 59.49 years (2006 est.).

Government

Capital: Lome.

Government type: Republic under transition to multiparty democratic rule.

Independence: 27 April 1960 (from French-administered UN trusteeship).

Legal system: French-based court system.

Executive branch:

Chief of state: President Faure Gnassingbe (since 6 Feburary 2005).

Head of government: Prime Minister Edem Kodjo (since 8 June 2005).

Economy

Currency: Communaute Financiere Africaine franc.

GDP: Purchasing power parity—$965 billion (2005 est.).

GDP—real growth rate: 1% (2005 est.).

GDP—per capita: Purchasing power parity—$1,700 (2005 est.).

Inflation rate: 5.5% (2005 est.).

Population below poverty line: 32% (1989 est.).

Exports: $768 million f.o.b. (2005 est.)—re-exports, cotton, phosphates, coffee, cocoa.

Imports: $1.047 million f.o.b. (2005 est.)—machinery and equipment, foodstuff, petroleum products.

External debt: $2 billion (2005).

Transport and Communications

Railways: 568 km.

Roads: 7,520 km.

Telephones: 60,600 (2003).

Mobile cellular: 220,000 (2003).

Internet users: 221,000 (2005).

Internet country code: .tg

Tonga

History

Polynesians were the original settlers of Tonga. The Dutch arrived in 1616 while the British explorer James Cook came here in 1773 and 1777. Taufa'ahau Tupou founded the present ruling dynasty in 1831 and took the

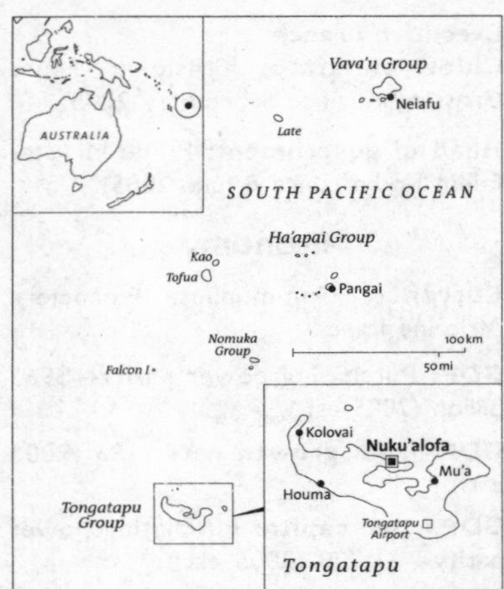

name George I. In 1900, his grandson George II signed a treaty of friendship with UK following which the kingdom became a British protectorate. In 1959, the treaty was revised but in 1970, Tonga became independent.

Geography

Location: Oceania, archipelago in the South Pacific Ocean.

Area: 748 sq. km.

Natural resources: Fish, fertile soil.

Climate: Tropical climate modified by trade winds.

People

Population: 114,689 (July 2006 est.).

Population growth rate: 2.01% (2006 est.).

Sex ratio: 0.99 male(s)/female (2006 est.).

Religions: Christian.

Languages: Tongan, English.

Literacy rate: Total 98.5%, Male 98.4%, Female 98.7% (1996 est.).

Infant mortality rate: 12.3 deaths/1,000 live births (2006 est.).

Life expectancy: Total 69.82 years, Male 67.32 years, Female 72.45 years (2006 est.).

Government

Capital: Nuku'alofa.

Government type: Hereditary constitutional monarchy.

Independence: 4 June 1970 (from UK protectorate).

Legal system: Based on English law.

Executive branch:

Chief of state: King Taufa'ahau Tupou IV (since 16 December 1965).

Head of government: Acting Prime Minister Feleti Sevele (since February 2006).

Economy

Currency: Pa'anga.

GDP: Purchasing power parity—$244 million (2004 est.).

GDP—real growth rate: 1.4% (FY 2003–04 est.).

GDP—per capita: Purchasing power parity—$2,300 (2002 est.).

Inflation rate: 10.3% (2002 est.).

Unemployment rate: 13% (FY 2003–04 est.).

Exports: $34 million f.o.b. (2004 est.)—squash, fish, vanilla beans, root crops.

Imports: $122 million f.o.b. (2004 est.)—foodstuff, machinery and transport equipment, fuels, chemicals.

External debt: $63.4 million (2001).

Transport and Communications

Railways: None.

Roads: 680 km.

Telephones: 11,200 (2002).

Mobile cellular: 9,000 (2004).

Internet users: 3,000 (2004).

Internet country code: .to

Trinidad and Tobago

History

When Christopher Columbus explored the two islands in 1498, Arawak Indians lived on Trinidad while Carib Indians lived on Tobago. The islands remained a Spanish possession till 1802 when they went into British possession. Thousands of indentured labourers were imported from India between 1845 and 1917. In 1889, the islands were united as one colony.

Limited self-government was granted in 1925. Between 1958 and 1962, the islands were a part of the West Indies Federation. In 1962, Trinidad and Tobago became independent. In 1976, the country became a republic.

Geography

Location: Caribbean islands between the Caribbean Sea and the North Atlantic Ocean, north-east of Venezuela.

Area: 5,128 sq. km.

Natural resources: Petroleum, natural gas, asphalt.

Climate: Tropical climate with a rainy season from June to December.

People

Population: 1,065,842 (July 2006 est.).

Population growth rate: –0.87% (2006 est.).

Sex ratio: 1.07 male(s)/female (2006 est.).

Religions: Roman Catholic 29.4%, Hindu 23.8%, Anglican 10.9%, Muslim 5.8%, Presbyterian 3.4%, others 26.7%.

Languages: English (official), Hindi, French, Spanish, Chinese.

Literacy rate: Total 98.6%, Male 99.1%, Female 98% (2003 est.).

Infant mortality rate: 25.05 deaths/1,000 live births (2006 est.).

Life expectancy: Total 66.76 years, Male 65.71 years, Female 67.86 years (2006 est.).

Government

Capital: Port-of-Spain.

Government type: Parliamentary democracy.

Independence: 31 August 1962 (from UK).

Legal system: Based on English common law.

Executive branch:
Chief of state: President George Maxwell Richards (since 17 March 2003).

Head of government: Prime Minister Patrick Manning (since 24 December 2001).

Economy

Currency: Trinidad and Tobago dollar.

GDP: Purchasing power parity—$18.01 billion (2005 est.).

GDP—real growth rate: 7% (2005 est.).

GDP—per capita: Purchasing power parity—$16,700 (2005 est.).

Inflation rate: 6.8% (2005 est.).

Population below poverty line: 21% (1992 est.).

Unemployment rate: 8% (2005 est.).

Exports: $9.161 billion f.o.b. (2005 est.)—petroleum and petroleum products, chemicals, steel products, fertilizer, sugar, cocoa, coffee, citrus, flowers.

Imports: $6.011 billion f.o.b. (2005 est.)—machinery, transportation equipment, manufactured goods, food, live animals.

External debt: $2.986 billion (2005 est.).

Transport and Communications

Railways: None.

Roads: 8,320 km.

Telephones: 321,300 (2004).

Mobile cellular: 321,300 (2004).

Internet users: 160,000 (2005).

Internet country code: .tt

Tunisia

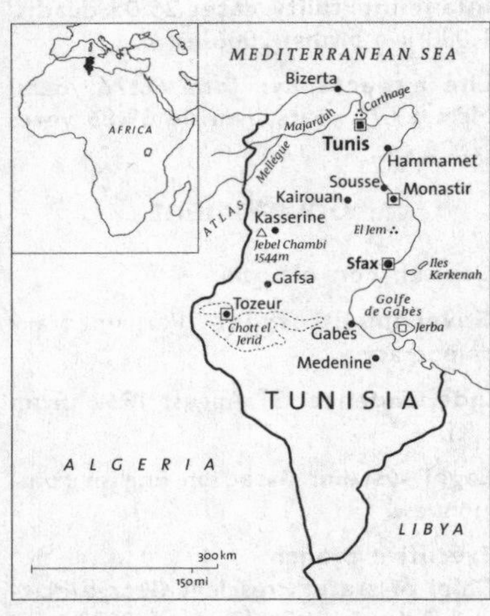

History

In the twelfth century BC, Phoenicians established settlements along the North African coast in the area that is today Tunisia. These included the city of Carthage, near present-day Tunis. However, the three Punic Wars between Carthage and Rome led to the destruction of Carthage. In the 1600s, Tunisia became a part of the Turkish Ottoman empire. In 1881, French troops occupied the capital city, Tunis. Thereafter, France took control of Tunisia's economic and foreign affairs. Tunisia formally became a French protectorate in 1883. In 1956, Tunisia became independent. In 1957, the monarchy was abolished and Tunisia became a republic.

Geography

Location: Northern Africa, bordering the Mediterranean Sea, between Algeria and Libya.

Area: 163,610 sq. km.

Terrain: Mountains in the north and a hot, dry central plain; the semi-arid region in the south merges into the Sahara.

Natural resources: Petroleum, phosphates, iron ore, lead, zinc, salt.

Climate: Temperate climate in the north and desert climate in the south.

People

Population: 10,175,014 (July 2006 est.).

Population growth rate: 0.99% (2006 est.).

Sex ratio: 1.02 male(s)/female (2006 est.).

Religions: Muslim 98%, Christian 1%, Jewish and others 1%.

Languages: Arabic (official and one of the languages of commerce), French (commerce).

Literacy rate: Total 74.3%, Male 83.4%, Female 65.3% (2004 est.).

Infant mortality rate: 23.84 deaths/1,000 live births (2006 est.).

Life expectancy: Total 75.12 years, Male 73.4 years, Female 76.96 years (2006 est.).

Government

Capital: Tunis.

Government type: Republic.

Independence: 20 March 1956 (from France).

Legal system: Based on French civil law system and Islamic law.

Executive branch:
Chief of state: President Zine El Abidine Ben Ali (since 7 November 1987).

Head of government: Prime Minister Mohamed Ghannouchi (since 17 November 1999).

Economy

Currency: Tunisian dinar.

GDP: Purchasing power parity—$83.54 billion (2005 est.).

GDP—real growth rate: 4.3% (2005 est.).

GDP—per capita: Purchasing power parity—$8,300 (2005 est.).

Inflation rate: 3.2% (2005 est.).

Population below poverty line: 7.4% (2005 est.).

Unemployment rate: 13.5% (2005 est.).

Exports: $10.3 billion f.o.b. (2005 est.)—textiles, mechanical goods, phosphates and chemicals, agricultural products, hydrocarbons.

Imports: $12.86 billion f.o.b. (2005 est.)—textiles, machinery and equipment, hydrocarbons, chemicals, food.

External debt: $18.91 billion (30 June 2005 est.).

Transport and Communications

Railways: 2,152 km.

Roads: 18,997 km.

Telephones: 1,203,500 (2004).

Mobile cellular: 3,563 million (2004).

Internet users: 835,000 (2005 est.).

Internet country code: .tn

Turkey

History

In 1900 BC and thereafter, the Hittite empire occupied the Asian part of the area that is today known as Turkey. In the sixth century BC, the Persian empire annexed the area. The Roman empire followed. Emperor Constantine declared Constantinople, now Istanbul, the capital of the Eastern Roman empire. After the Romans came the Byzantine empire, and in the thirteenth century AD came the Ottoman Empire. The Ottomans stamped their supremacy over the area for 600 years thereafter. At its height, the Ottoman empire included large

parts of south-eastern Europe, Syria, Israel, Iraq and most of the Arabian Peninsula in Asia and Egypt and North Africa till Algeria in the west. The empire came to an end in 1922, succeeded by the Turkish republic and a host of smaller states in south-eastern Europe and the Middle East.

The revolt of the Young Turks took place in 1909. Following this, the Sultan allowed for a Constitution and a liberal government. Furthermore, the country lost territory in the aftermath of World War I, consequent to its alliance with Germany.

The republic of Turkey was declared in 1923 under the leadership of Kemal Ataturk and in 1924 the caliphate was abolished.

Geography

Location: Turkey straddles south-eastern Europe and south-western Asia. The portion of Turkey that lies west of the Bosporus is geographically a part of Europe. The country borders the Black Sea between Bulgaria and Georgia and the Aegean Sea and the Mediterranean Sea, between Greece and Syria.

Area: 780,580 sq. km.

Terrain: Turkey has a high central plateau (Anatolia), a narrow coastal plain and a number of mountain ranges.

Natural resources: Antimony, copper, borate, coal, chromium, mercury, sulphur, iron ore, arable land, hydropower.

Climate: Temperate climate with hot, dry summers and mild, wet winters.

People

Population: 70,413,958 (July 2006 est.).

Population growth rate: 1.06% (2006 est.).

Sex ratio: 1.02 male(s)/female (2006 est.).

Religions: Muslim 99.8% (mostly Sunni), other 0.2% (mostly Christians and Jews).

Languages: Turkish (official), Kurdish, Arabic, Armenian, Greek.

Literacy rate: Total 86.5%, Male 94.3%, Female 78.7% (2003 est.).

Infant mortality rate: 39.69 deaths/1,000 live births (2006 est.).

Life expectancy: Total 72.62 years, Male 70.18 years, Female 75.18 years (2006 est.).

Government

Capital: Ankara.

Government type: Republican parliamentary democracy.

Independence: 29 October 1923 (successor state to the Ottoman Empire).

Legal system: Derived from various European continental legal systems.

Executive branch:

Chief of state: President Ahmet Necdet Sezer (since 16 May 2000).

Head of government: Prime Minister Recep Tayyip Erdogan (14 March 2003).

Economy

Currency: Turkish lira.

Economy—overview:
Turkey's economy is a combination of modern industry and commerce and a traditional agriculture sector. While the country has a dynamic private sector, the state continues to play a major role in industry, transport, banking and communication. The dominated by the private sector textiles and clothing industry is not only the country's largest industry but also the single largest source of exports. Lately, the Turkish economy has suffered erratic growth and imbalances. Turkey has recorded real GNP growth in excess of 6 per cent in many years but this has been offset by sharp declines in output in 1994, 1999 and 2001. The public sector fiscal deficit has consistently exceeded 10 per cent of GDP, thanks to interest payments. This has exceeded 50 per cent of central government spending. In 2003, the country recorded an inflation rate of 26 per cent, a low figure in recent times. The bleak scenario because of these factors means that foreign investment the country has been low. In 2000–1, the Turkish economy faced a crisis created by a growing trade deficit and weaknesses in the banking sector. This led to the floating of the lira, worsening recession.

The economy is turning around with the implementation of economic reforms, and 2004 GDP growth reached 9 per cent. Inflation fell to 7.7 per cent in 2005—a thirty-year low. Despite these strong economic gains in 2002–05, which were largely due to renewed investor interest in emerging markets, IMF backing and tighter fiscal policy, the economy is still burdened by a high current account deficit and high debt.

GDP: Purchasing power parity—$572 billion (2005 est.).

GDP—real growth rate: 5.6% (2005 est.).

GDP—per capita: Purchasing power parity—$8,200 (2005 est.).

Inflation rate: 7.7% (2005 est.).

Unemployment rate: 10% (plus underemployment of 4.0%) (2005 est.).

Exports: $72.49 billion f.o.b. (2005 est.)—finished textiles, foodstuff, textiles, metal manufactures, transport equipment.

Imports: $101.2 billion c.i.f. (2005 est.).

External debt: $161.8 billion (30 June 2005 est.).

Transport and Communications

Railways: 8,697 km.

Roads: 354,421 km.

Telephones: 19,125,200 (2004).

Mobile cellular: 34,707,500 (2004).

Internet users: 5.5 million (2003).

Internet country code: .tr

Turkmenistan

History

The area that is today Turkmenistan was a part of the Parthian empire between the mid-third century BC and fourth century AD. Turkmens are believed to have arrived in the region in the eleventh century. The Russian advance into Turkmenistan came in the 1860s and the 1870s. Turkmenistan was later carved out of Turkistan Autonomous Soviet Socialist Republic. In 1925, it became an independent Soviet Socialist Republic. In 1991, Turkmenistan proclaimed its independence from the Union of Soviet Socialist Republic (USSR).

Geography

Location: Central Asia, bordering the Caspian Sea, between Iran and Kazakhstan.

Area: 488,100 sq. km.

Terrain: Largely flat, partly rolling, sandy desert with dunes that rise to form mountains in the south. There are low mountains along the border with Iran. The Caspian Sea lies to the west.

Natural resources: Petroleum, natural gas, coal, sulphur, salt.

Climate: Subtropical desert.

People

Population: 5,042,920 (July 2006 est.).

Population growth rate: 1.83% (2006 est.).

Sex ratio: 0.98 male(s)/female (2006 est.).

Ethnic groups: Turkmen 77%, Uzbek 9.2%, Russian 6.7%, Kazakh 2%, others 5.1%.

Religions: Muslim 89%, Eastern Orthodox 9%, unknown 2%.

Languages: Turkmen 72%, Russian 12%, Uzbek 9%, others 7%.

Literacy rate: Total 98.8%, Male 99.3%, Female 98.3% (1999 est.).

Infant mortality rate: 72.56 deaths/1,000 live births (2006 est.).

Life expectancy: Total 61.83 years, Male 58.43 years, Female 65.41 years (2006 est.).

Government

Capital: Ashgabat.

Government type: Republic.

Independence: 27 October 1991 (from the Soviet Union).

Legal system: Based on civil law system.

Executive branch:

Chief of state: President and Chairman of the Cabinet of Ministers Saparmurat Niyazov (since 27 October 1990). The president is both the chief of state and head of government.

Economy

Currency: Turkmen manat.

Economy—overview:

Turkmenistan's economic statistics are veiled in much secrecy and subject to error margins. Turkmenistan is mostly a desert. The country also has large gas and oil resources. Intensive agriculture is carried out in irrigated oases. Cotton occupies almost half of its irrigated land. Payment obligations arising out of short-term debts and distribution constraints faced by its petroleum and natural gas resources hurt the Turkmen economy. Nevertheless, there was a sizable rise in exports in 2003 along with an increase in GDP. This was mainly due to a smart recovery staged by the agriculture sector, industrial growth and rising international prices for petroleum and natural gas.

GDP: Purchasing power parity—$39.54 billion (2005 est.).

GDP—real growth rate: 4% (IMF, 2005 est.).

GDP—per capita: Purchasing power parity—$8,000 (2005 est.).

Inflation rate: 10% (2005 est.).

Unemployment rate: 60% (2004 est.).

Population below poverty line: 58% (2003 est.).

Exports: $4.7 billion f.o.b. (2005 est.)—gas, oil, cotton fibre, textiles.

Imports: $4.175 billion f.o.b. (2005 est.)—machinery and equipment, foodstuff.

External debt: $2.4 billion to $5 billion (2001 est.).

Transport and Communications

Railways: 2,440 km.

Roads: 24,000 km.

Telephones: 376,100 (2003).

Mobile cellular: 52,000 (2004).

Internet users: 36,000 (2005).

Internet country code: .tm

Tuvalu

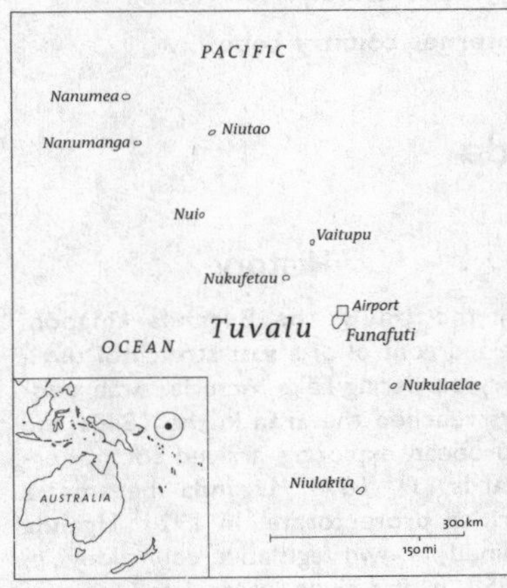

History

Tuvalu was formerly known as Ellice Islands. In 1892, the islands became a British protectorate and in 1915–16 the UK annexed them as part of the colony of the Gilbert and Ellice Islands. In 1975, the Ellice Islands were separated from the Gilbert Islands, renamed as Tuvalu and given home rule. Full independence was granted in 1978.

Geography

Location: Oceania, island group consisting of nine coral atolls in the South Pacific Ocean.

Area: 26 sq. km.

Natural resources: Fish.

Climate: Tropical climate.

People

Population: 11,810 (July 2006 est.).

Population growth rate: 1.51% (2006 est.).

Sex ratio: 0.95 male(s)/female (2006 est.).

Religions: Church of Tuvalu (Congregationalist) 97%, Seventh-Day Adventist 1.4%, Baha'i 1%, others 0.6%.

Languages: Tuvaluan, English, Samoan, Kiribati (on the island of Nui).

Infant mortality rate: 19.47 deaths/1,000 live births (2006 est.)

Life expectancy: Total 68.32 years, Male 66.08 years, Female 70.66 years (2006 est.).

Government

Capital: Funafuti.

Government type: Constitutional monarchy with a parliamentary democracy.

Independence: 1 October 1978 (from UK).

Executive branch:
Chief of state: Queen Elizabeth II (since 6 February 1952), represented by Governor General Filoimea Telito (since 15 April 2005).

Head of government: Prime Minister Maatia Toafa (since 11 October 2004).

Economy

Currency: Australian dollar; there is also a Tuvaluan dollar.

GDP: Purchasing power parity—$12.2 million (2000 est.).

GDP—real growth rate: 3% (2000 est.).

GDP—per capita: Purchasing power parity—$1,100 (2000 est.).

Inflation rate: 5% (2000 est.).

Exports: $1 million f.o.b. (2004)—copra, fish.

Imports: $31 million c.i.f. (2004)—food, animals, mineral fuels, machinery, manufactured goods.

Transport and Communications

Railways: None.

Roads: 8 km.

Telephones: 700 (2002).

Internet users: 1,300 (2002).

Internet country code: .tv

Uganda

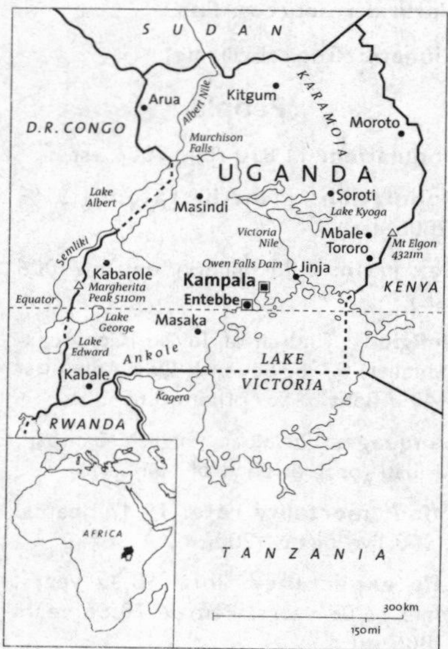

History

By the 1800s, the Buganda kingdom gained control of a vast stretch of territory bordering Lake Victoria. Arab traders reached the area in the 1840s and European explorers arrived soon afterwards. In 1894, Uganda became a British protectorate. In 1921, Uganda gained its own legislative council and in 1958, it was given internal self-government. In 1962, Uganda became independent with Milton Obote as prime minister. In 1963, Uganda became a republic with Sir Edward Mutesa, the king of Buganda, as the first president. In 1966, Milton Obote seized control of the government from President Mutesa.

In 1971, General Idi Amin seized power from President Milton Obote. Amin ruled directly with hardly any delegation of power. His expulsion of all Asians from Uganda in 1972 led to a breakdown of Uganda's economy. A Muslim himself, Amin reversed Uganda's friendly relations with Israel and built up new links with Libya and the Palestinians.

Some 100,000 to 300,000 Ugandans were allegedly tortured or murdered during Amin's presidency. Amin's downfall came about when, in 1978, he invaded Tanzania to annex its Kagera region. Tanzania responded in 1979 by invading Uganda. This had the effect of unifying the various anti-Amin forces under the Uganda National Liberation Front. Amin fled the country, first to Libya and finally to Saudi Arabia, where he passed away in August 2003.

Geography

Location: Eastern Africa, west of Kenya.

Area: 236,040 sq. km.

Terrain: Plateau with a rim of mountains.

Natural resources: Copper, cobalt, hydropower, limestone, salt, arable land.

Climate: Generally rainy tropical climate with two dry seasons from December to February and June to August.

People

Population: 28,195,754 (July 2006 est.).

Population growth rate: 3.37% (2006 est.).

Sex ratio: 1 male(s)/female (2006 est.).

Religions: Roman Catholic 33%, Protestant 33%, Muslim 16%, indigenous beliefs 18%.

Languages: English (official national language), Ganda or Luganda (most widely used of the Niger–Congo languages), other Niger–Congo languages, Nilo-Saharan languages, Swahili, Arabic.

Literacy rate: Total 69.9%, Male 79.5%, Female 60.4% (2003 est.).

Infant mortality rate: 66.15 deaths/ 1,000 live births (2006 est.).

Life expectancy: Total 52.67 years, Male 51.68 years, Female 53.69 years (2006 est.).

Government

Capital: Kampala.

Government type: Republic.

Independence: 9 October 1962 (from UK).

Legal system: In 1995, the government restored the legal system to one based on English common law and customary law.

Executive branch:

Chief of state: President Lt Gen. Yoweri Kaguta Museveni (since he seized power on 26 January 1986). The president is both chief of state and head of government.

Economy

Currency: Ugandan shilling.

GDP: Purchasing power parity—$48.73 billion (2005 est.).

GDP—real growth rate: 4% (2005 est.).

GDP—per capita: Purchasing power parity—$1,800 (2005 est.).

Inflation rate: 9.7% (2005 est.).

Population below poverty line: 35% (2001 est.).

Exports: $768 million f.o.b. (2005 est.)—coffee, fish and fish products, tea, gold, cotton, flowers, horticultural products.

Imports: $1.608 billion f.o.b. (2005 est.)—capital equipment, vehicles, petroleum, medical supplies, cereals.

External debt: $4.949 billion (2005 est.).

Transport and Communications

Railways: 1,241 km.

Roads: 70,746 km.

Telephones: 71,600 (2004).

Mobile cellular: 1.165 million (2004).

Internet users: 200,000 (2005).

Internet country code: .ug

Ukraine

History

A major state emerged in the area from the ninth century onwards. This is referred to as the Kievan Rus. Kiev became a major political and cultural centre in the tenth century. A Mongol invasion that culminated with the sack of Kiev in 1240 ended the glory days.

In the fifteenth century, a new martial society called the Cossacks emerged in the southern steppe frontier region of Ukraine. Although the Polish government availed of their services as an effective fighting force, the Cossacks eventually rose in revolt. The Polish authorities subdued them, but only after much difficulty.

In 1645, Ukraine requested protection against the Polish from Moscow. The treaty they signed recognized the suzerainty of Moscow and led to the annexation of Kiev. The state of Ukraine was subsequently absorbed into the Russian empire.

Ukraine took advantage of the confusion resulting from the Russian Revolution and in January 1918, it declared independence from the empire. In 1920, the Soviets gained control of Ukraine once again. The 1930s saw large-scale death and deportations, as the Stalinist regime implemented its policies of collectivization and purges. More suffering was to follow when Nazi Germany occupied the country during World War II while Stalin deported some 200,000 Crimean Tatars to Siberia and Central Asia following accusations of collaboration with Nazi Germany.

The worst nuclear accident in history took place on the morning of 26 April 1986 at the Chernobyl nuclear power station in Ukraine. It was later estimated that five million people were exposed to radiation in Ukraine, Belarus and Russia.

In 1991, Ukraine declared its independence following an attempted coup in Moscow.

Geography

Location: Eastern Europe, bordering the Black Sea, between Poland, Romania, and Moldova in the west and Russia in the east.

Area: 603,700 sq. km.

Terrain: Mostly fertile plains (steppes) and plateaus. Carpathian Mountains in the west, and the Crimean Peninsula in the south.

Natural resources: Iron ore, coal, manganese, natural gas, oil, salt, sulphur, graphite, titanium, magnesium, kaolin, nickel, mercury, timber, arable land.

Climate: Temperate continental climate.

People

Population: 46,710,816 (July 2006 est.).

Population growth rate: –0.6% (2006 est.).

Sex ratio: 0.86 male(s)/female (2006 est.).

Religions: Ukrainian Orthodox, Moscow Patriarchate, Kiev Patriarchate, Ukrainian Autocephalous Orthodox, Ukrainian Catholic (Uniate), Protestant, Jewish.

Languages: Ukrainian, Russian, Romanian, Polish, Hungarian.

Literacy rate: 99.7% (2003 est.).

Infant mortality rate: 9.9 deaths/1,000 live births (2006 est.).

Life expectancy: Total 69.98 years, Male 64.71 years, Female 75.59 years (2006 est.).

Government

Capital: Kiev (Kyyiv).

Government type: Republic.

Independence: 24 August 1991 (from the Soviet Union).

Legal system: Based on civil law system; judicial review of legislative acts.

Executive branch:

Chief of state: President Viktor A. Yushchenko (since 23 January 2005).

Head of government: Prime Minister Yuriy Yekhanurov (since 22 September 2005).

Economy

Currency: Hryvnia.

GDP: Purchasing power parity—$340.4 billion (2005 est.).

GDP—real growth rate: 2.4% (2005 est.).

GDP—per capita: Purchasing power parity—$7,200 (2005 est.).

Inflation rate: 13.9% (2005 est.).

Population below poverty line: 29% (2003 est.).

Unemployment rate: 2.9% officially registered; large number of unregistered or underemployed workers; the International Labour Organization calculates the Ukraine's real unemployment level is around 9-10% (2005 est.).

Exports: $38.22 billion (2005 est.)—ferrous and nonferrous metals, fuel and petroleum products, chemicals, machinery and transport equipment, food products.

Imports: $37.18 billion (2005 est.)—energy, machinery and equipment, chemicals.

External debt: $33.93 billion (30 June 2005 est.).

Transport and Communications

Railways: 22,473 km.

Roads: 169,679 km.

Telephones: 10,833,300 (2002).

Mobile cellular: 4,200,000 (2002).

Internet users: 3.8 million (2003).

Internet country code: .ua

United Arab Emirates

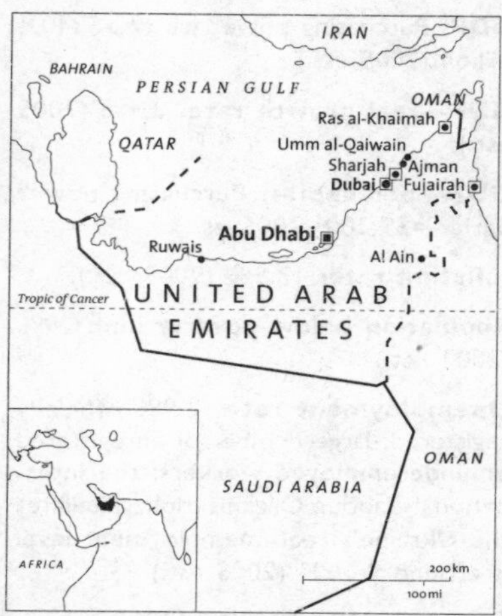

History

Initially, seafaring people inhabited the area that is today United Arab Emirates. Later, a sect called the Carmathians formed a powerful sheikhdom in the area. Following the disintegration of this sheikhdom, the people resorted to piracy. When they provoked Muscat and Oman, the British intervened and enforced peace. This area along the coast of the eastern Arabian peninsula came to be known as the Trucial Coast.

Although the British came to administer the region from 1853, each of the constituent states had full internal control. In 1960, the states formed the Trucial States Council. This was followed by the formation of the six-member federation. Bahrain and Oman opted out while Ra's-al-Khaymah joined in 1972.

Geography

Location: Middle East, bordering the Gulf of Oman and the Persian Gulf, between Oman and Saudi Arabia.

Area: 82,880 sq. km.

Terrain: Flat, barren coastal plain that merges into the sand dunes of a desert wasteland. Mountains lie in the east.

Natural resources: Petroleum, natural gas.

Climate: Desert climate but the eastern mountains are cooler.

People

Population: 2,602,713 including an estimated 1,606,079 non-nationals (July 2006 est.).

Population growth rate: 1.52% (2006 est.).

Sex ratio: 1.43 male(s)/female (2006 est.).

Religions: Muslim 96% (Shi'a 16%), Christian, Hindu, and others 4%.

Languages: Arabic (official), Persian, English, Hindi, Urdu.

Literacy rate: Total 77.9%, Male 76.1%, Female 81.7% (2003 est.).

Infant mortality rate: 14.09 deaths/ 1,000 live births (2006 est.).

Life expectancy: Total 75.4 years, Male 72.92 years, Female 78.08 years (2006 est.).

Government

Capital: Abu Dhabi.

Government type: Federation.

Independence: 2 December 1971 (from UK).

Legal system: A federal court system.

Executive branch:

Chief of state: President Sheikh Khalifa bin Zayed al-Nahyan (since November 2004).

Head of government: Prime Minister Muhammad bin Rashid al-Maktum (since 5 January 2006).

Economy

Currency: Dirham.

Economy—overview:
The country has an open economy. The country boasts of a high per capita income and substantial annual trade surplus. The country's prosperity is based on oil and gas output that accounts for about 33 per cent of GDP. At the present levels of production, the country's oil and gas reserves should last for more than 100 years.

GDP: Purchasing power parity—$111.3 billion (2005 est.).

GDP—real growth rate: 6.7% (2005 est.).

GDP—per capita: Purchasing power parity—$43,400 (2005 est.).

Inflation rate: 4.5% (2005 est.).

Unemployment rate: 2.4% (2001).

Exports: $103.1 billion f.o.b. (2005 est.)—crude oil, natural gas, re-exports, dried fish, dates.

Imports: $60.15 billion f.o.b. (2005 est.)—machinery and transport equipment, food, chemicals.

External debt: $30.21 billion (2005 est.).

Transport and Communications

Railways: None.

Roads: 1,088 km.

Telephones: 1,187,700 (2004).

Mobile cellular: 3,683,100 (2004).

Internet users: 1,384,800 (2005).

Internet country code: .ae

United Kingdom

History

Romans invaded UK in the first century BC. The Roman withdrawal in the fifth century AD led to a series of invasions by Scandinavians and people from the Low Countries. Several large Anglo-Saxon kingdoms were established all over the country. In 1066, a succession dispute led to the Norman Conquest when William of Normandy (William the Conqueror) invaded the country and defeated the Saxon king, Harold II at the Battle of Hastings. This led to the establishment of French law and traditions in the country.

The rule of the Plantagenets saw an increasing degree of centralization of powers in the crown and the removal of much of the powers of the nobles. However, in 1215, King John was forced to sign the Magna Carta that awarded civil rights to the common people.

In 1284, England and Wales joined together in a union. This was formalized in 1536 through an Act of Union.

Edward III's claim to the French throne led to the Hundred Years War between 1338 and 1453 and the subsequent loss of most large British territories in France. In the fourteenth century, the Black Death plague epidemic swept UK, along with other parts of Europe. This reduced the British population by almost one-third.

The War of the Roses took place between 1455 and 1485. It arose from the struggle for the throne between the House of York and the House of Lancaster and ended in victory for Henry Tudor (later Henry VII). The reign of Henry VIII saw the breaking

away of the Church of England from the Roman Catholic Church.

The reign of Elizabeth I between 1558 and 1603 is referred to as the Elizabethan Age, and saw the emergence of England as a major European power in politics, trade and commerce, and the arts. This period also saw the development of a more moderate Church of England. In 1588, the Spanish sent a huge fleet, the Spanish Armada to invade England. But the invasion failed and resulted in the rise of UK as a maritime power.

In 1642, a civil war erupted between Charles I and the parliament. It resulted in the defeat and execution of Charles I in 1649. Between 1649 and 1653, a Council of States led the country. Oliver Cromwell, who led the parliamentarians in the civil war, ruled the country as 'lord protector' of England, Scotland, and Ireland from 1653 to 1658. Oliver Cromwell's death was followed by the restoration of the monarchy. Charles II became the new Stuart king in 1660. His brother, James I succeeded him but was ousted in the Revolution of 1688. During the reign of Queen Anne, England fought in the War of Spanish Succession.

In 1707, England and Scotland was joined together in an Act of the Union. The sixteenth and seventeenth centuries also saw the emergence of the British empire all over the world. The empire continued to grow thorough the eighteenth and nineteenth centuries.

The country fought with France in the Napoleonic Wars of the eighteenth century. It ended with French defeat at the Battle of Waterloo in 1815.

Queen Victoria ruled as the queen of the United Kingdom of Great Britain and Ireland from 1837 to 1901 and as the Empress of India from 1876–1901. The Victorian era saw the emergence of a strong democratic system of government and the gradual transformation of the British monarchy to a largely ceremonial function.

In 1920, the British Parliament passed the Government of Ireland Act that established one parliament for the six counties of Northern Ireland and another for the rest of Ireland. In 1921, the Anglo-Irish Treaty established the Irish Free State as an independent dominion of the British Crown with full internal self-government. However, the Free State was separated from Northern Ireland that remains part of the United Kingdom even today.

The United Kingdom emerged victorious in both World War I and World War II. Coalition governments were formed for much of the two World Wars. The resignation of Prime Minister Neville Chamberlain in 1950 led to the formation of a coalition government headed by Sir Winston Churchill. He served as the prime minister from 1940–5 and again from 1951–5. He is widely regarded as UK's greatest prime minister.

Edward VIII succeeded to the throne in January 1936. However, he abdicated the throne in December 1936, in order to marry a divorcee, Wallis Simpson. The throne passed on to his brother who became George VI. On 6 February 1952, King George VI's daughter, Elizabeth Alexandra Mary was coronated as Queen Elizabeth II.

In 1973, UK joined the European Economic Community. In 1979, Margaret Thatcher became the country's first woman prime minister. In 1981, she began a programme of privatization of state-run industries.

In 1982, the UK fought Argentina in the Falklands War. It ended in British victory and the surrender of Argentine forces on the Falklands Islands.

In 1992, the separation between Princess Diana and Prince Charles, heir to the British throne, was announced. In May 1997, the Labour Party won a landslide election victory under its new leader, Tony Blair.

In 2003–4, the Blair government was hit by the controversy over the Iraq invasion. The prime minister was accused of misleading the country by exaggerating the threat that Iraq really posed and its arsenal of weapons of mass destruction. It later emerged that the dossier that the prime minister's office compiled to convince the Parliament was based on inaccurate intelligence. The prime minister, the defence secretary and other government officials and aides, senior BBC officials and journalists had to testify at an inquiry into the death of Dr David Kelly, a government scientist who had first revealed to the press that the government had probably exaggerated claims regarding Iraqi weapons.

Geography

Location: Group of islands in Western Europe, including the northern one-sixth of the island of Ireland, between the North Atlantic Ocean and the North Sea, north-west of France.

Area: 244,820 sq. km.

Terrain: Consists largely of rugged hills and low mountains. There are plains in the east and the south-east.

Natural resources: Coal, petroleum, natural gas, iron ore, lead, zinc, gold, tin, limestone, salt, clay, chalk, gypsum, potash, silica sand, slate, arable land.

Climate: Temperate climate moderated by prevailing south-west winds over the North Atlantic Current.

People

Population: 60,809,153 (July 2006 est.).

Population growth rate: 0.28% (2006 est.).

Sex ratio: 0.98 male(s)/female (2006 est.).

Religions: Anglican and Roman Catholic (around 40 million), Muslim (around 1.5 million), Presbyterian (around 800,000), Methodist 760,000, Sikh (around 500,000), Hindu (around 500,000), Jew (around 350,000).

Languages: English, Welsh, Scottish form of Gaelic.

Literacy rate: 99% (2003 est.).

Infant mortality rate: 5.08 deaths/1,000 live births (2006 est.).

Life expectancy: Total 78.54 years, Male 76.09 years, Female 81.13 years (2006 est.).

Government

Capital: London.

Government type: Constitutional monarchy.

Independence: 1284 (date of union between England and Wales, formalized in 1536 through an Act of Union); 1707 (date of joining together of England and Scotland as Great Britain through an Act of Union); 1801 (date of legislative union of Great Britain and

Ireland implemented with the adoption of the name The United Kingdom of Great Britain and Ireland).

Constitution: UK has no written constitution. Instead, there are statutes and common law and practice.

Legal system: Common law tradition with early Roman and modern continental influences.

Executive branch:
Chief of state: Queen Elizabeth II (since 6 February 1952). Heir Apparent Prince Charles (son of the queen; born 14 November 1948).

Head of government: Prime Minister Anthony (Tony) Blair (since 2 May 1997).

Legislative branch:
UK has a bicameral parliament. The parliament has two chambers. The House of Commons has 646 members, elected for a five year term in single-seat constituencies. The House of Lords has 675 members, 557 life peers and 118 hereditary members (June 2001).

Elections and election results: In the House of Lords, elections are held only when vacancies in the hereditary peerage arise. The last such election was held in 1999 to determine the 92 hereditary peers. Elections to the House of Commons were last held on 5 May 2005.

Economy

Currency: British pound.

Economy—overview:
The British economy is among the largest in Europe. UK and its capital city of London is one of the most important trading and financial centres of the world. The country boasts of an efficient and highly mechanized agricultural sector, substantial mineral resources, and a well-developed services sector. It has one of the strongest economies in the world with low inflation, interest rates, and unemployment. However, the British population remains opposed to joining the European Economic and Monetary Union (EMU) and the euro common currency.

GDP: Purchasing power parity—$1.83 trillion (2005 est.).

GDP—real growth rate: 1.8% (2005 est.).

GDP—per capita: Purchasing power parity—$30,300 (2005 est.).

Inflation rate: 2.2% (2005 est.).

Population below poverty line: 17% (2002 est.).

Unemployment rate: 4.7% (2005 est.).

Exports: $372.7 billion f.o.b. (2005 est.)—manufactured goods, fuels, chemicals, food, beverages, tobacco.

Imports: $483.7 billion f.o.b. (2005 est.)—manufactured goods, machinery, fuels, foodstuff.

External debt: $7.107 billion (30 June 2005).

Transport and Communications

Railways: 17,274 km.

Roads: 387,674 km.

Telephones: 32.943 million (2005).

Mobile cellular: 61.091 million (2004).

Internet users: 37.8 million (2005).

Internet country code: .uk

United States of America

History

Christopher Columbus never set foot on the mainland United States. However, the first European explorations of the continental United States were staged from the Spanish bases that Columbus had helped establish in the region.

In 1585, Walter Raleigh established the first British colony in North America. The settlement was later abandoned. It was finally in 1607 that English settlers succeeded when they set up Jamestown in present-day Virginia. In 1620, the Pilgrim Fathers, a group of European settlers, set up Plymouth Colony, near present-day Cape Cod.

In 1609, the Dutch East India Company hired Henry Hudson to explore the area around what is today New York City and the Hudson river. In 1624, the Dutch purchased the island of Manhattan from local Indians for the reported price of $24. They renamed it New Amsterdam. The new diseases the Europeans brought with them and their desire for land posed a serious challenge to the native population. The initial cordial relations soon gave way to conflict, war and, almost always, further loss of land.

Meanwhile, in the seventeenth and eighteenth centuries, Europeans imported hundreds of thousands of Africans and sold them into slavery to work on cotton and tobacco plantations. British imperialist designs on the New World received a boost in 1763 when it gained control of territory up to the Mississippi river, following victory over France in the Seven Years War. Thereafter, the British government decided to raise the costs of administering and protecting its North American colonies from the colony itself. It therefore set out to impose new taxes. This led to widespread opposition and hatred to British rule. Dissent soon gave way to fighting between the British and Americans in 1775. The following year, the thirteen North American colonies declared their independence from Britain. The document that announced this separation is the famous Declaration of Independence. In 1789, George Washington, who had served as the commander in chief of the American forces during the War of Independence, was elected the first president of USA.

In 1860, the anti-slavery Republican Party candidate Abraham Lincoln was elected President. The eleven pro-slavery southern states reacted by breaking away from the Union and forming the Confederate States of America under the leadership of Jefferson Davis. This was the flash point for the US Civil War. The Confederate forces surrendered in April 1965. Within a week, Abraham Lincoln was assassinated.

In 1898, USA gained territory when it received Puerto Rico, Guam, the Philippines and Cuba following the Spanish–American war. The same year, it annexed Hawaii. In 1920, the US government banned the manufacture and sale of alcoholic liquors. This was the Prohibition era and it lasted till 1933.

In 1929, USA, along with the rest of North America, Europe and other industrialized economies plunged into the Great Depression. It was triggered by the Wall Street stock market crash of 1929 and resulted in the unemployment of 13 million people.

In 1932, Franklin D. Roosevelt was elected as the new US president. He launched the 'New Deal' recovery programme that aimed to restore the economy. He also lifted the ban on sale of alcohol.

In 1941, Japanese war planes attacked a US military base at Pearl Harbour in Hawaii. This led the US to declare war on Japan. Soon thereafter, Germany declared war on US. USA's entry into World War II on a massive scale eventually led to the defeat of the Axis powers led by Germany, Japan and Italy. In 1945, USA became the first, and so far only country, to use nuclear weapons in war when it dropped two atomic bombs on the Japanese cities of Hiroshima and Nagasaki. It caused horrendous casualties and led to the surrender of Japan.

The post-World War II years saw the polarization of the world into a pro-USA block and a pro-Soviet Union block. This marked the start of the Cold War, that only ended with the collapse of the Soviet Union in the 1990s. In 1950–3, USA played a leading role in the Korean War.

The 1950s were marked by the campaign of civil disobedience to secure civil rights for Americans of African descent. In 1960, Democratic Party candidate John F. Kennedy was elected US President. The following year, USA organized and sponsored the unsuccessful Bay of Pigs invasion of Cuba by Cuban exiles. In 1962, USA and USSR came to the brink of nuclear war following the Cuban missile crisis.

In 1963, President John F. Kennedy was assassinated. Between 1955 and 1975, USA fought the prolonged and unsuccessful Vietnam War along with South Vietnam to prevent the communists of North Vietnam from uniting South Vietnam with North Vietnam.

On 11 September 2001, four US passenger aircraft were hijacked and crashed into the World Trade Center in New York, the US Defence Department headquarters and the Pentagon, in Washington DC. More than 3,000 people were estimated killed. This led USA to declare its 'War on Terror'. In October 2001, USA lead a military campaign in Afghanistan to defeat the Taliban regime and find Osama bin

Laden, who was suspected of masterminding the 9/11 attacks.

Geography

Location: North America, bordering both the North Atlantic Ocean and the North Pacific Ocean, between Canada and Mexico.

Area: 9,631,418 sq. km.

Terrain: Mountains in the west, hills and low mountains in the east, a vast central plain, mountains and broad river valleys in Alaska. Hawaii has a rugged, volcanic topography.

Natural resources: Coal, copper, lead, molybdenum, phosphates, uranium, bauxite, gold, iron, mercury, nickel, potash, silver, tungsten, zinc, petroleum, natural gas, timber.

Climate: Mostly temperate, tropical in Hawaii and Florida, arctic in Alaska, semi-arid in the Great Plains west of the Mississippi River and arid in the Great Basin of the south-west.

People

Population: 298,444,215 (July 2006 est.).

Population growth rate: 0.91% (2006 est.).

Sex ratio: 0.97 male(s)/female (2006 est.).

Religions: Protestant 52%, Roman Catholic 24%, Mormon 2%, Jewish 1%, Muslim 1%, other 10%, none 10% (2002 est.).

Languages: English, Spanish (spoken by a sizable minority).

Literacy rate: 99% (2003 est.).

Infant mortality rate: 6.43 deaths/ 1,000 live births (2006 est.).

Life expectancy: Total 77.85 years, Male 75.02 years, Female 80.82 years (2006 est.).

Government

Capital: Washington DC.

Government type: Constitution-based federal republic.

Independence: 4 July 1776 (from Great Britain).

Legal system: Based on English common law; judicial review of legislative acts.

Executive branch:

Chief of state: President George W. Bush (since 20 January 2001) and Vice-President Richard B. Cheney (since 20 January 2001). Both re-elected in November 2004. The president is both the chief of state and head of government.

Elections and election results: President and vice-president are elected on the same ticket by a college of representatives who are elected directly from each state. The president and vice-president serve four-year terms. The last elections were held on 2 November 2004.

Legislative branch:

USA has a bicameral Congress. It consists of the Senate that has 100 seats, one-third of which are renewed every two years. Two members are elected from each state by popular vote to serve six-year terms. The other chamber is the House of Representatives that has 435 seats. Members are directly elected by popular vote to serve two-year terms.

Elections and Election Results: Elections to the Senate were last held in November 2004. Elections to the House of Representatives were last held in November 2004.

Economy

Currency: US dollar.

Economy—overview:
The US has the largest and the most

technologically powerful economy in the world, with a per capita GDP of over $40,000.

The rise in GDP in 2004 and 2005 was under girded by substantial gains in labour productivity. The economy suffered from a sharp increase in energy prices in mid-2005, but by late in the year those prices dropped back to earlier levels. Hurricane Katrina caused extensive damage in the Gulf Coast region, but had a small impact on overall GDP growth for the year. Long-term problems include inadequate investment in economic infrastructure, rapidly rising medical and pension costs of an aging population, sizable trade and budget deficits, and stagnation of family income in the lower economic groups.

GDP: Purchasing power parity—$36 trillion (2005 est.).

GDP—real growth rate: 3.5% (2005 est.).

GDP—per capita: Purchasing power parity—$41,800 (2005 est.).

Inflation rate: 3.2% (2005).

Population below poverty line: 12% (2004 est.).

Unemployment rate: 5.1% (2005 est.).

Exports: $927.5 billion f.o.b. (2005 est.)—capital goods, automobiles, industrial supplies and raw materials, consumer goods, agricultural products.

Imports: $1.727 trillion f.o.b. (2005 est.)—crude oil and refined petroleum products, machinery, automobiles, consumer goods, industrial raw materials, food and beverages.

External debt: $8.837 trillion (30 June 2005 est.).

Transport and Communications

Railways: 227,736 km.

Roads: 6,407,637 km.

Telephones: 181,599,900 (2003).

Mobile cellular: 194,479,364 (2005).

Internet users: 203,824,428 (2005).

Internet country code: .us

Uruguay

History

European explorers arrived in the area in the sixteenth century. These included Ferdinand Magellan who came in 1520 and Sebastian Cabot who came in 1526. In 1726, the Spanish founded the city of Montevideo and took control of Uruguay from the Portuguese. In 1776, Uruguay became a part of the viceroyalty of La Plata, with its capital at Buenos Aires, Argentina. In 1808, Uruguay rebelled against the viceroyalty of La Plata after Napoleon Bonaparte overthrew the Spanish monarchy in Europe.

The early part of the nineteenth century saw a struggle between Argentina and Brazil to control Banda Oriental, as Uruguay was then known. Uruguay became independent in 1825 with Argentine assistance and in 1828 it became a republic. During 1838–65, the country was hit by a civil war between the 'Whites' and 'Colorados' or 'Reds'. During 1865–70, Uruguay joined Argentina and Brazil in the War of the Triple Alliance, also called the Paraguayan War. It ended with the decimation of Paraguay. In 1903, Uruguay set up a welfare state under the leadership of Jose Batiley Ordonez who served as

the country's president between 1903–7 and 1911–15.

A Marxist urban guerrilla movement called the Tupamaros began in the early 1960s and lasted till 1975. In 1973, the armed forces overthrew the civilian government. This initiated a period of brutal repression during which Uruguay came to be known as 'the torture chamber of Latin America' and was believed to have the largest number of political prisoners per capita in the world. A civilian government returned in 1985 with Julio Maria Sanguinetti as the president.

Geography

Location: South America, bordering the South Atlantic Ocean, between Argentina and Brazil.

Area: 176,220 sq. km.

Terrain: Rolling plains and low hills, and a fertile coastal lowland.

Natural resources: Arable land, hydropower, minor minerals, fisheries.

Climate: Warm temperate climate.

People

Population: 3,431,932 (July 2006 est.).

Population growth rate: 0.46% (2006 est.).

Sex ratio: 0.95 male(s)/female (2006 est.).

Religions: Roman Catholic 66%, Protestant 2%, Jewish 1%, non-professing or others 31%.

Languages: Spanish, Portunol or Brazilero.

Literacy rate: Total 98%, Male 97.6%, Female 98.4% (2003 est.).

Infant mortality rate: 11.61 deaths/1,000 live births (2006 est.).

Life expectancy: Total 76.33 years, Male 73.12 years, Female 79.65 years (2006 est.).

Government

Capital: Montevideo.

Government type: Constitutional republic.

Independence: 25 August 1825 (from Brazil).

Legal system: Based on Spanish civil law system.

Executive branch:
Chief of state: President Tabare Vazquez (since 1 March 2005) and Vice-President Rodoifo Nin Noua (since 1 March 2005). The president is both the chief of state and head of government.

Economy

Currency: Uruguayan peso.

GDP: Purchasing power parity—$32.96 billion (2005 est.).

GDP—real growth rate: 6.5% (2005 est.).

GDP—per capita: Purchasing power parity—$9,600 (2005 est.).

Inflation rate: 4.9% (2005 est.).

Population below poverty line: 22% of households (2004).

Unemployment rate: 12.5% (2005 est.).

Exports: $3.55 billion f.o.b. (2005 est.)—meat, rice, leather products, wool, vehicles, dairy products.

Imports: $3.54 billion f.o.b. (2005 est.)—machinery, chemicals, road vehicles, crude petroleum.

External debt: $11.22 billion (June 2005 est.).

Transport and Communications

Railways: 2,073 km.

Roads: 77,732 km (2004).

Telephones: 1 million (2004).

Mobile cellular: 652,000 (2002).

Internet users: 680,000 (2005).

Internet country code: .uy

Uzbekistan

History

The land that is today Uzbekistan formed parts of the Persian empire and Tamerlane's empire. The area remained under the control of the successors of Tamerlane till the Uzbeks invaded it in the sixteenth century and merged it with neighbouring areas. However, upon their downfall, the territory fragmented into smaller units. In the nineteenth century, the Russians invaded the region.

In 1924, the area was formed into the Uzbek Republic and in 1925 the Uzbekistan Soviet Socialist Republic was formed. In June 1990, Uzbekistan issued its own laws and in December 1991, it declared its independence.

Geography

Location: Central Asia, north of Afghanistan.

Area: 447,400 sq. km.

Terrain: Mostly flat or rolling sandy desert with sand dunes. There are also broad, flat irrigated river valleys.

Natural resources: Natural gas, petroleum, coal, gold, uranium, silver, copper, lead and zinc, tungsten, molybdenum.

Climate: Mostly of the mid-latitude desert type with long and hot summers and mild winters.

People

Population: 27,307,134 (July 2006 est.).

Population growth rate: 1.7% (2006 est.).

Sex ratio: 0.98 male(s)/female (2006 est.).

Religions: Muslim 88% (mostly Sunnis), Eastern Orthodox 9%, others 3%.

Languages: Uzbek 74.3%, Russian 14.2%, Tajik 4.4%, others 7.1%.

Literacy rate: 99.3% (2003 est.).

Infant mortality rate: 69.99 deaths/ 1,000 live births (2006 est.).

Life expectancy: Total 64.58 years, Male 61.19 years, Female 68.14 years (2006 est.).

Government

Capital: Tashkent (Toshkent).

Government type: Republic with an authoritarian presidential rule. There is very little power outside the executive branch.

Independence: 1 September 1991 (from Soviet Union).

Legal system: An evolution of Soviet civil law.

Executive branch:

Chief of state: President Islom Karimov (since 24 March 1990).

Head of government: Prime Minister Shavkat Mirziyayev (since 11 December 2003).

Economy

Currency (code): Uzbekistani soum.

Economy—overview:

Uzbekistan is one of the world's largest cotton exporters and also a significant producer of gold and oil. Besides, it is a key producer of chemicals and machinery in the region. After independence, the government attempted to retain its Soviet-type economy with subsidies and strict controls on production and prices. The adverse conditions generated by the Asian and Russian financial crises by promoting import substitute industrialization and by monitoring and tightening export and currency controls.

GDP: Purchasing power parity—$48.24 billion (2005 est.).

GDP—real growth rate: 7.1% (2005 est.).

GDP—per capita: Purchasing power parity—$1,800 (2005 est.).

Inflation rate: 7.1% (2005 est.).

Population below poverty line: 28% (2004 est.).

Unemployment rate: 0.7% officially; 20% underemployment (2005 est.).

Exports: $5 billion f.o.b. (2005 est.)—cotton 41.5%, gold 9.6%, energy products 9.6%, mineral fertilizers, ferrous metals, textiles, food products, automobiles (1998 est.).

Imports: $3.8 billion f.o.b. (2005 est.)—machinery and equipment 49.8%, foodstuff 16.4%, chemicals, metals (1998 est.).

External debt: $5.184 billion (2005 est.).

Transport and Communications

Railways: 3,950 km.

Roads: 81,600 km.

Telephones: 1,717,100 (2003).

Mobile cellular: 544,100 (2004).

Internet users: 880,000 (2005).

Internet country code: .uz

Vanuatu

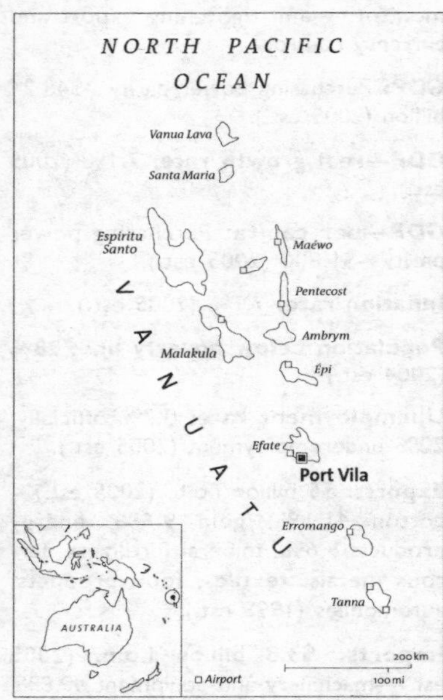

History

In 1606, the Portuguese Pedro Fernandes de Queiros sighted the islands while in 1774, the British explorer James Cook charted them. It was Cook who named the archipelago New Hebrides. A joint Anglo-French government ruled the islands from 1906. During World War II, the islands served as a major base for the Allied forces. In 1980, the islands were granted independence as Vanuatu.

Geography

Location: Oceania, group of islands in the South Pacific Ocean, north-east of Queensland, Australia.

Area: 12,200 sq. km.

Terrain: Mountainous islands of volcanic origins.

Natural resources: Manganese, hardwood forests, fish.

Climate: Tropical climate moderated by south-east trade winds.

People

Population: 208,869 (July 2006 est.).

Population growth rate: 1.49% (2006 est.).

Sex ratio: 1.05 male(s)/female (2006 est.).

Religions: Presbyterian 36.7%, Anglican 15%, Roman Catholic 15%, indigenous beliefs 7.6%, Seventh-Day Adventist 6.2%, Church of Christ 3.8%, others 15.7%.

Languages: Local languages (more than 100) 72.6%, pidgin (known as Bislama or Bichelama) 23.1%, English 1.9%, French 1.4%, other 0.3%, unspecified 0.7% (1999 census).

Literacy rate: Total 53%, Male 57%, Female 48% (1979 est.).

Infant mortality rate: 53.8 deaths/1,000 live births (2006 est.).

Life expectancy: Total 62.85 years, Male 61.34 years, Female 64.44 years (2006 est.).

Government

Capital: Port-Vila.

Government type: Parliamentary republic.

Independence: 30 July 1980 (from France and UK).

Legal system: Unified system created from former dual French and British systems.

Executive branch:
Chief of state: President Kalkot Matas Kelekele (since 16 August 2004).

Head of government: Prime Minister Ham Lini (since 11 December 2004).

Economy

Currency: Vatu.

GDP: Purchasing power parity—$580 million (2003 est.).

GDP—real growth rate: –1.1% (2003 est.).

GDP—per capita: Purchasing power parity—$2,900 (2003 est.).

Inflation rate: 3.1% (2003 est.).

Exports: $205 million f.o.b. (2004)—copra, beef, cocoa, timber, kava, coffee.

Imports: $233 million c.i.f. (2004).

External debt: $83.7 million (2002 est.).

Transport and Communications

Railways: None.

Roads: 1,070 km.

Telephones: 6,800 (2004).

Mobile cellular: 10,500 (2004).

Internet users: 7,500 (2004).

Internet country code: .vu

Vatican City

History

The Vatican City state is the sole surviving remnant of the Papal states that, at one point of time, occupied thousands of square kilometres in Italy. During the Risorgimento (the nineteenth century movement for Italian unification), most of the area of the Papal States were absorbed into Italy. The Lateran Treaty of 1929 set up an independent state of Vatican City.

Geography

Location: Southern Europe, an enclave of Rome (Italy).

Area: 0.44 sq. km.

Natural resources: None.

Climate: Temperate climate.

People

Population: 932 (July 2006 est.).

Population growth rate: 0.01% (2006 est.).

Religions: Roman Catholic.

Languages: Italian, Latin, French, various other languages.

Literacy rate: 100%.

Government

Capital: Vatican City.

Government type: Ecclesiastical.

Independence: 11 February 1929.

Legal system: Based on Code of Canon Law and its revised forms.

Executive branch:

Chief of state: Pope Benedict XVI (since 19 April 2005).

Head of government: Secretary of State Cardinal Angelo Sodano (since 2 December 1990).

Economy

Currency: Euro.

Economy—overview:

The Vatican City has a unique, non-commercial economy that is supported financially by an annual contribution from Roman Catholic dioceses all over the world, by special collections (known as Peter's Pence), museum admission fees, sale of postage stamps, medals, coins, and tourist mementos, sale of publications, investments and real estate income also account for a sizable portion of revenue.

Transport and Communications

Railways: 0.86 km.

Roads: City streets.

Telephones: 5,120 (2005)

Internet country code: .va

Venezuela

History

Spanish colonization of the area began in the 1520s. Napoleon's invasion of Spain encouraged Venezuelans to declare their independence in 1810.

Venezuela was part of the republic of Gran Colombia that was proclaimed on 17 December 1819, with Simon Bolivar as president. However, Venezuela seceded from Gran Colombia in 1829 and became an independent republic with its capital at Caracas.

For almost a century between 1830 and 1935, a series of warlord-like leaders, locally referred to as caudillos, ruled over Venezuela. This period, marked by repeated internal strife, ended with the death of dictator Juan Vicente Gomez in 1935.

Meanwhile, towards 1928, Venezuela emerged as the world's second largest producer of petroleum and the leading petroleum exporter. The Venezuelan economy experienced a boom in the 1970s due to high global oil prices.

Geography

Location: Northern South America, bordering the Caribbean Sea and the North Atlantic Ocean, between Colombia and Guyana.

Area: 912,050 sq. km.

Terrain: The Andes Mountains and Maracaibo Lowlands in the north-west, a central plain (llanos) and the Guiana Highlands in the south-east.

Natural resources: Petroleum, natural gas, iron ore, gold, bauxite, other minerals, hydropower, diamonds.

Climate: Hot and humid tropical that is more moderate in the highlands.

People

Population: 25,730,435 (July 2006 est.).

Population growth rate: 1.38% (2006 est.).

Sex ratio: 1.02 male(s)/female (2006 est.).

Religions: Nominally Roman Catholic 96%, Protestant 2%, others 2%.

Languages: Spanish (official), numerous indigenous dialects.

Literacy rate: Total 93.4%, Male 93.8%, Female 93.1% (2003 est.).

Infant mortality rate: 21.54 deaths/ 1,000 live births (2006 est.).

Life expectancy: Total 74.54 years, Male 71.49 years, Female 77.81 years (2006 est.).

Government

Capital: Caracas.

Government type: Federal republic.

Independence: 5 July 1811 (from Spain).

Legal system: Based on organic laws.

Executive branch:
Chief of state: President Hugo Chavez Frias (since 3 February 1999). Vice-President Jose Vicente Rangel (since 28 April 2002). The president is both the chief of state and head of government.

Economy

Currency: Bolivar.

Economy—overview:
Venezuela's petroleum sector accounts for around one-third of the country's GDP, over half of the government's operating revenues and around 80% of export earnings. However, internal instability, followed by a two-month national oil strike between December 2002 and February 2003 seriously damaged the Venezuelan economy.

GDP: Purchasing power parity—$153.7 billion (2005 est.).

GDP—real growth rate: 9.3% (2005 est.).

GDP—per capita: Purchasing power parity—$6,100 (2005 est.).

Inflation rate: 15.7% (2005 est.).

Population below poverty line: 47% (1998 est.).

Unemployment rate: 12.3% (2005 est.).

Exports: $52.73 billion f.o.b. (2005 est.)—petroleum, bauxite and aluminum, steel, chemicais, agricultural products, basic manufactures.

Imports: $24.63 billion f.o.b. (2005 est.)—raw materials, machinery and equipment, transport equipment, construction materials.

External debt: $39.79 billion (2005 est.).

Transport and Communications

Railways: 682 km.

Roads: 96,155 km.

Telephones: 3,346,500 (2004).

Mobile cellular: 8.421 million (2004).

Internet users: 3.04 million (2005).

Internet country code: .ve

Vietnam

History

In the early seventeenth century, the area that is today Vietnam was divided into two parts. While the northern part was called Tonkin, the southern part was called Cochin China. In 1802, the two parts were unified under a single dynasty.

The French gained control of Saigon (now Ho Chi Minh City) in 1859. Soon

after, they came to control much of the remaining area of the country and ruled it till World War II. During 1940–5, the Japanese controlled Vietnam and declared the country independent. The French opposed this and this led to the first Indochina War. The French evacuated Vietnam after defeat at Dien Bien Phu in 1954.

The defeat of the French led to the division of the nation into North Vietnam (Democratic Republic of Vietnam, under Ho Chi Minh) and South Vietnam (Republic of Vietnam, under emperor Bao Dai). In 1955, Bao Dai's premier Ngo Dinh Diem deposed him and established a strong authoritarian rule with US backing.

Ngo Dinh Diem refused to hold a combined north–south election in 1956. His decision met with US approval. Consequently, North Vietnam decided to use military force as the means of unification of the South with the North. This led to the Vietnam War that raged on till 1975.

On 30 April 1975, the remains of the South Vietnamese government surrendered unconditionally to North Vietnamese forces that promptly occupied Saigon. On 2 July 1976, the country was officially united as the Socialist Republic of Vietnam with Hanoi as its capital.

Geography

Location: Vietnam lies in South-eastern Asia, bordering the Gulf of Thailand, Gulf of Tonkin and South China Sea, alongside China, Laos and Cambodia.

Area: 329,560 sq. km.

Terrain: Low and flat delta in the south and north of the country. There are highlands in the central part while the hilly mountainous region lies in the north and north-west.

Natural resources: Phosphates, coal, manganese, bauxite, chromate, offshore oil and gas deposits, forests, hydropower.

Climate: Tropical in the south, monsoon type in the north.

People

Population: 84,402,966 (July 2006 est.).

Population growth rate: 1.02% (2005 est.).

Sex ratio: 0.98 male(s)/female (2006 est.).

Religions: Buddhist, Hoa Hao, Cao Dai, Christian (predominantly Roman Catholic, some Protestant), indigenous beliefs, Muslim.

Languages: Vietnamese (official), English, French, Chinese, and Khmer; mountain area languages (Mon-Khmer and Malayo-Polynesian).

Literacy rate: Total 94%, Male 95.8%, Female 92.3% (2003 est.).

Infant mortality rate: 25.14 deaths/1,000 live births (2006 est.).

Life expectancy: Total 70.85 years,

Male 68.05 years, Female 73.85 years (2006 est.).

Government

Capital: Hanoi.

Government type: Communist state.

Independence: 2 September 1945 (from France).

Legal system: Based on Communist legal theory and French civil law system.

Executive branch:
Chief of state: President Nguyen Minh Triet (since 27 June 2006).

Head of government: Prime Minister Nguyen Tan Dung (since 27 June 2006).

Elections: president elected by the National Assembly from among its members for five-year term; election last held 27 June 2006; prime minister appointed by the president from among the members of the National Assembly; deputy prime ministers appointed by the prime minister; appointment of prime minister and deputy prime ministers confirmed by National Assembly.

Election results: Nguyen Minh Triet elected president; percent of National Assembly vote—94%; Nguyen Tan Dung elected prime minister; per cent of National Assembly vote— 92%.

Economy

Currency: Dong.

Economy—overview:
Vietnam has a centrally planned economy that was dealt a blow by the collapse of the Soviet Union as it was provided with substantial assistance from it. During 1993–7, growth averaged around 9 per cent per year. The 1997 Asian financial crisis revealed the flaws in the Vietnamese economy. GDP growth of 8.5 per cent in 1997 shrank to 6 per in 1998 and 5 per cent in 1999 but then rose to 6 per cent–7 per cent during 2000–2. Many of Vietnam's domestic industries such as coal, cement, steel, and paper are reported to suffer from large stockpiles of inventory.

Vietnam became a member of the WTO in 2005. Among other benefits, accession allows Vietnam to take advantage of the phase out of the Agreement on Textiles and Clothing, which eliminated quotas on textiles and clothing for WTO partners on 1 January 2005.

GDP: Purchasing power parity—$232.2 billion (2005 est.).

GDP—real growth rate: 8.4% (2005 est.).

GDP—per capita: Purchasing power parity—$2,800 (2005 est.).

Inflation rate: 8.4% (2005 est.).

Population below poverty line: 19.5% (2004 est.).

Unemployment rate: 2.4% (2005 est.).

Exports: $32.23 billion f.o.b. (2005 est.)—crude oil, marine products, rice, coffee, rubber, tea, garments, shoes.

Imports: $36.88 billion f.o.b. (2005 est.)—machinery and equipment, petroleum products, fertilizer, steel products, raw cotton, grain, cement, motorcycles.

External debt: $19.17 billion (2005 est.).

Transport and Communications

Railways: 2,600 km.

Roads: 222,179 km (2004).

Telephones: 10,124,900 (2004).

Mobile cellular: 4.96 million (2004).

Internet users: 5.87 million (2005).

Internet country code: .vn

Yemen

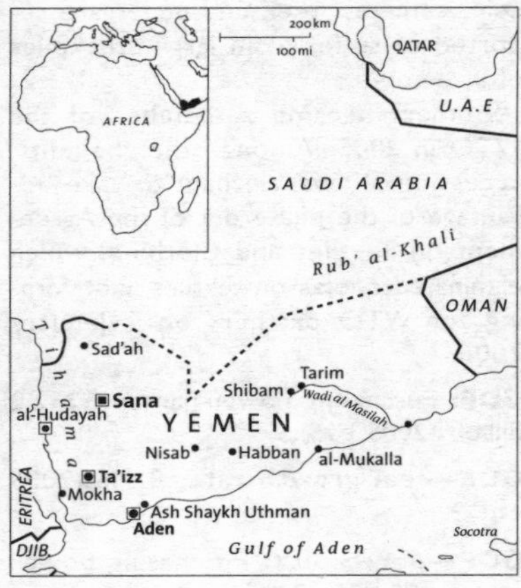

History

Ancient Yemen was centred on the port of Aden and was an important centre of trade in myrrh and frankincense. Romans invaded Yemen in the first century AD and the Persians and Ethiopians did so in the sixth century. In 628, the people of the area converted to Islam and in the tenth century, it came under the control of the Rassite dynasty of the Zaidi sect. The Ottoman Turks ruled over the area from 1538 until their decline in 1918.

Imams ruled the northern part of Yemen till a pro-Egyptian coup took place in 1962. A Yemen Arab Republic was declared. Meanwhile, in the south, the strategically located port of Aden came under the control of the British. By 1937, it came to be called Aden Protectorate. The Nationalist's Liberation Front fought against the British and this led to the formation of the People's Republic of Southern Yemen in 1967. In 1979, it became the only Marxist state of the Arab world. On 22 March 1990, the two countries, pro-West Yemen and Marxist Yemen Arab Republic, united after 300 years of separation.

Geography

Location: Middle East, bordering the Arabian Sea, Gulf of Aden, and Red Sea, between Oman and Saudi Arabia.

Area: 527,970 sq. km.

Terrain: Narrow coastal plain with flat-topped hills and rugged mountains. There are also dissected upland desert plains.

Natural resources: Petroleum, fish, rock salt, marble, small deposits of coal, gold, lead, nickel, copper, and fertile soil.

Climate: Mostly desert type of climate.

People

Population: 21,456,188 (July 2006 est.).

Population growth rate: 3.46% (2006 est.).

Sex ratio: 1.04 male(s)/female (2006 est.).

Religions: Muslim including Shaf'i (Sunni) and Zaiydi (Shi'a), small numbers of Jew, Christian, and Hindu.

Literacy rate: Total 50.2%, Male 70.5%, Female 30% (2003 est.).

Infant mortality rate: 59.88 deaths/ 1,000 live births (2006 est.).

Life expectancy: Total 62.12 years, Male 60.23 years, Female 64.11 years (2006 est.).

Government

Capital: Sana'a.

Government type: Republic.

Independence: 22 May 1990. The merger of the Yemen Arab Republic and the Marxist-dominated People's Democratic Republic of Yemen created the Republic of Yemen.

Legal system: Based on Islamic law, Turkish law, English Common Law, and local tribal customary law.

Executive branch:
Chief of state: President Field Marshall Ali Abdallah Salih (since 22 May 1990, the former President of North Yemen. He assumed office following the merger of North and South Yemen). Vice-President Maj. Gen. Abd al-Rab Mansur al-Hadi (since 3 October 1994).

Head of government: Prime Minister Abd al-Qadir Ba Jamal (since 4 April 2001).

Economy

Currency: Yemeni rial.

Economy—overview:
Yemen reported strong growth in the mid-1990s largely due to oil production, but periodic fluctuations in oil prices have harmed the economy. Yemen has started out on an IMF-supported structural adjustment programme meant to modernize and streamline the economy. This has led to significant foreign debt relief and restructuring. In July 2005, a reduction in famel subidic sparked riots in which over twenty Yemenis were killed and hundreds were injured.

GDP: Purchasing power parity—$19.37 billion (2005 est.).

GDP—real growth rate: 2.4% (2005 est.).

GDP—per capita: Purchasing power parity—$900 (2005 est.).

Inflation rate: 9.6% (2005 est.).

Unemployment rate: 35% (2003 est.).

Exports: $6.387 billion f.o.b. (2005 est.)—crude oil, coffee, dried and salted fish.

Imports: $4.19 billion f.o.b. (2005 est.)—food and live animals, machinery and equipment, chemicals.

External debt: $5.689 billion (2005 est.).

Transport and Communications

Railways: None.

Roads: 65,144 km (2004).

Telephones: 798,100 (2004).

Mobile cellular: 1.072 million (2004).

Internet users: 220,000 (2005).

Internet country code: .ye

Zambia

History

In the twelfth century, Shona people arrived in the area and established the empire of the Mwene Mutapa. In the sixteenth century, people from the Luba and Lunda empires of present-day Democratic Republic of Congo arrived to set up small kingdoms. Portuguese explorers arrived in the late eighteenth century. British missionary David Livingstone came in 1851. In 1889, UK established control over the area (as Northern Rhodesia). It administered the area through a system of indirect rule that left power in the hands of local rulers. The Federation of Rhodesia and Nyasaland was created in 1953. It consisted of Northern Rhodesia, Southern Rhodesia (now Zimbabwe) and Nyasaland (now Malawi). The Federation was dissolved in 1963. Zambia gained independence in 1964 with Kenneth Kaunda as President. In the 1970s, Zambian support for the independence struggle in Rhodesia proved to be crucial to the creation of an independent Zimbabwe.

Geography

Location: Southern Africa, east of Angola.

Area: 752,614 sq. km.

Terrain: High plateau with some hills and mountains.

Natural resources: Copper, cobalt, zinc, lead, coal, emerald, gold, silver, uranium, hydropower.

Climate: Tropical climate with a rainy season from October to April.

People

Population: 11,502,010 (July 2006 est.).

Population growth rate: 2.11% (2006 est.).

Sex ratio: 0.99 male(s)/female (2006 est.).

Religions: Christian 50%–75%, Muslim and Hindu 24%–49%, indigenous beliefs 1%.

Languages: English (official), Bemba, Kaonda, Lozi, Lunda, Luvale, Nyanja, Tonga, about 70 other indigenous languages.

Literacy rate: Total 80.6%, Male 86.8%, Female 74.8% (2003 est.).

Infant mortality rate: 86.84 deaths/1,000 live births (2006 est.).

Life expectancy: Total 40.03 years, Male 39.76 years, Female 40.31 years (2006 est.).

Government

Capital: Lusaka.

Government type: Republic.

Independence: 24 October 1964 (from UK).

Legal system: Based on English common law and customary law.

Executive branch:
Chief of state: President Levy Mwanawasa (since 2 January 2002); Vice-President Nevers Mumba (since May 2003). The president is both the chief of state and head of government.

Economy

Currency: Zambian kwacha.

GDP: Purchasing power parity—$10.59 billion (2005 est.).

GDP—real growth rate: 5.1% (2005 est.).

GDP—per capita: Purchasing power parity—$900 (2005 est.).

Inflation rate: 19% (2005 est.).

Population below poverty line: 86% (1993).

Unemployment rate: 50% (2000 est.).

Exports: $1.947 billion f.o.b. (2005 est.)—copper, cobalt, electricity, tobacco, flowers, cotton.

Imports: $1.934 billion f.o.b. (2005 est.)—machinery, transportation equipment, petroleum products, electricity, fertilizer, foodstuff, clothing.

External debt: $5.866 billion (2005 est.).

Transport and Communications

Railways: 2,173 km.

Roads: 91,440 km.

Telephones: 88,400 (2003).

Mobile cellular: 300,000 (2004).

Internet users: 68,200 (2003).

Internet country code: .zm

Zimbabwe

History

Europeans arrived in the region in the nineteenth century. In 1889, Cecil Rhodes's British South Africa Company obtained a British mandate to colonize part of the region that subsequently became Southern Rhodesia. In 1922, British South Africa Company administration came to an end and the white minority opted for self-government. Meanwhile, black opposition to colonial rule grew and led to the emergence of two nationalist groups in the 1960s. These were the Zimbabwe African People's Union (ZAPU) and the Zimbabwe African National Union (ZANU).

In 1953, UK established the Central African Federation, consisting of Southern Rhodesia (Zimbabwe), Northern Rhodesia (Zambia) and Nyasaland (Malawi). However, the Federation disintegrated in 1963 when Zambia and Malawi became independent.

In 1964, Ian Smith of the Rhodesian Front (RF) became the prime minister. The following year, Smith unilaterally declared independence under white minority rule. This caused widespread international outrage and led to the imposition of economic sanctions. It also triggered guerrilla warfare against white rule that intensified in 1972 as the rival ZANU and ZAPU forces launched operations out of Zambia and Mozambique.

In 1979, British-brokered all-party talks in London led to a peace agreement and a new Constitution that guaranteed minority rights. In 1980, pro-independence leader Robert Mugabe and his ZANU party won Brit-

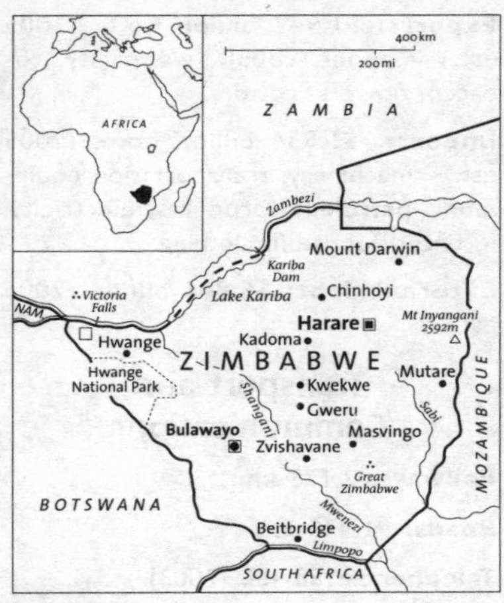

ish-supervised independence elections. Mugabe became prime minister. Zimbabwe finally gained independence on 18 April 1980.

Geography

Location: Southern Africa, between South Africa and Zambia.

Area: 390,580 sq. km.

Terrain: High plateau, with mountains in the east.

Natural resources: Coal, chromium ore, asbestos, gold, nickel, copper, iron ore, vanadium, lithium, tin, platinum group metals.

Climate: Tropical climate.

People

Population: 12,236,805 (July 2006 est.).

Population growth rate: 0.62% (2006 est.).

Sex ratio: 1 male(s)/female (2006 est.).

Religions: Syncretic (partly Christian, partly indigenous beliefs) 50%, Christian 25%, indigenous beliefs 24%, Muslim and others 1%.

Languages: English (official), Shona, Sindebele (the language of the Ndebele, sometimes called Ndebele), and many tribal dialects.

Literacy rate: Total 90.7%, Male 94.2%, Female 87.2% (2003 est.).

Infant mortality rate: 51.71 deaths/ 1,000 live births (2006 est.).

Life expectancy: Total 39.29 years, Male 40.39 years, Female 38.16 years (2006 est.).

Government

Capital: Harare.

Government type: Parliamentary democracy.

Independence: 18 April 1980 (from UK).

Legal system: Mixture of Roman–Dutch and English common law.

Executive branch:

Chief of state: Executive President Robert Gabriel Mugabe (since 31 December 1987). The president is both the chief of state and head of government.

Economy

Currency: Zimbabwean dollar.

GDP: Purchasing power parity—$28.37 billion (2005 est.).

GDP—real growth rate: –7% (2005 est.).

GDP—per capita: Purchasing power parity—$2,300 (2005 est.).

Inflation rate: 585% (2005 est.).

Population below poverty line: 80% (2004 est.).

Unemployment rate: 80% (2005 est.).

Exports: $1.644 billion f.o.b. (2005 est.)—tobacco, gold, ferro alloys, textiles/clothing.

Imports: $2.059 billion f.o.b. (2005 est.)—machinery and transport equipment, other manufactures, chemicals, fuels.

External debt: $5.17 billion (2005 est.).

Transport and Communications

Railways: 3,077 km.

Roads: 97,440 km.

Telephones: 317,000 (2004).

Mobile cellular: 423,600 (2004).

Internet users: 82,000 (2005).

Internet country code: .zw

Overseas Territories

Despite the rapid process of decolonization since World War II, around 10 million people in fifty-nine territories around the world continue to live under the protection of Australia, China, Denmark, France, the Netherlands, Norway, New Zealand, the UK, or the USA. These territories are administered in a wide variety of ways.

Australia

Australia's overseas territories have not been an issue since Papua New Guinea became independent in 1975. Consequently there is no overriding policy towards them. Norfolk Island is inhabited by descendants of the *HMS Bounty* mutineers and more recent Australian migrants.

Ashmore & Cartier Islands

(Indian Ocean)

Status: External territory

Claimed: 1978

Area: 5.2 sq km

These uninhabited islands came under Australian authority in 1931.

Christmas Island

(Indian Ocean)

Status: External territory

Claimed: 1958

Capital: Flying Fish Cove

Population: 1,275

Area: 134.6 sq km

Named in 1643 for the day of its discovery.

Cocos Islands

(Indian Ocean)

Status: External territory

Claimed: 1955

Capital: West Island

Population: 647

Area: 14.24 sq km

There are twenty-seven coral islands in the group.

Coral Sea Islands

(South Pacific)

Status: External territory

Claimed: 1969

Population: 3 (meteorologists)

Area: Less than 3 sq km

Uninhabited except for a small meteorological staff on the Willis Islets.

Heard & McDonald Islands

(Indian Ocean)

Status: External territory

Claimed: 1947

Area: 417 sq km

These uninhabited, barren, sub-Antarctic islands were transferred from the UK to Australia in 1947.

Norfolk Island

(South Pacific)

Status: External territory

Claimed: 1913

Capital: Kingston

Population: 2,665

Area: 34.4 sq km

In 1856, the island was resettled by Pitcairn Islanders, descendants of the *Bounty* mutineers and their Tahitian companions.

China

Hong Kong

(South China Sea)

Status: Special administrative region

Claimed: 1997

Capital: Hong Kong

Population: 6,940,432

Area: 1,092 sq km

Occupied by the UK in 1841, Hong Kong was formally ceded by China the following year; various adjacent lands were added later in the nineteenth century. Pursuant to an agreement signed by China and the UK on 19 December 1984, Hong Kong became the Hong Kong Special Administrative Region (SAR) of China on 1 July 1997. In this agreement, China has promised that, under its 'one country, two systems' formula, China's socialist economic system will not be imposed on Hong Kong and that Hong Kong will enjoy a high degree of autonomy in all matters except foreign and defense affairs for the next fifty years.

Macau

(South China Sea)

Status: Special administrative region

Claimed: 1999

Capital: Macau

Population: 477,850

Area: 18 sq km

Colonized by the Portuguese in the sixteenth century, Macau was the first European settlement in the Far East. Pursuant to an agreement signed by China and Portugal on 13 April 1987, Macau became the Macau Special Administrative Region (SAR) of China on 20 December 1999. In this agreement, China has promised that, under its 'one country, two systems' formula, China's socialist economic system will not be imposed on Hong Kong and that Hong Kong will enjoy a high degree of autonomy in all matters except foreign and defense affairs for the next fifty years.

Denmark

The Faeroe Islands have been under Danish administration since Queen Margrethe I of Denmark inherited Norway in 1380. The Home Rule Act of 1948 gave the Faeroese control over all their internal affairs. Greenland first came under Danish rule in 1380. Today, Denmark remains responsible for the island's foreign affairs and defence.

Faeroe Islands

(North Atlantic)

Status: External territory

Claimed: 1380

Capital: Torshavn

Population: 48,065

Area: 1,399 sq km

Strong sense of national identity. Voted against Denmark joining the EC in 1973. Economy based on fishing, agriculture, Danish subsidies.

Greenland

(North Atlantic)

Status: External territory

Claimed: 1380

Capital: Nuuk

Population: 55,385

Area: 2,175,516 sq km

World's largest island. Much of the land is permanently ice-covered. Self-governing since 1979. Left the EU in 1985. Population is a mixture of Inuit and European in origin.

France

France has developed economic ties with its Territories d'Outre-Mer, thereby stressing interdependence over independence. Overseas departements, officially part of France, have their own governments. Territorial collectivites and overseas territoires have varying degrees of autonomy.

Clipperton Island

(East Pacific)

Status: Dependency of French Polynesia

Clawed: 1930

Area: 7 sq km

This isolated island was named for John Clipperton, a pirate who made it his hideout early in the eighteenth century.

French Guiana

(South America)

Status: Overseas department

Claimed: 1817

Capital: Cayenne

Population: 133,376

Area: 90,996 sq km

The last colony in South America. Population is largely African and indigenous Indian. European Space Agency rocket launch facility.

French Polynesia

(South Pacific)

Status: Overseas territory

Claimed: 1843

Capital: Papeete

Population: 210,333

Area: 4,165 sq km

Most People live on Tahiti. Economy dependent on tourism and French military. Recent calls for autonomy.

Guadeloupe

(Caribbean)

Status: Overseas department

Claimed: 1635

Capital: Basse-Tere

Population: 422,114

Area: 1,780 sq km

Prospers from a strong infrastructure, plus French and EU aid. Indigenous population demands more autonomy.

Martinique
(Caribbean)

Status: Overseas department

Claimed: 1635

Capital: Fort-de-France

Population: 387,656

Area: 1,100 sq km

Population largely of African origin. High living standards resulting from tourism and French subsidies.

Mayotte
(Indian Ocean)

Status: Territorial collectivity

Claimed: 1843

Capital: Mamoudzou

Population: 89,938

Area: 374 sq km

Mayotte was ceded to France along with the other islands of the Comoros group in 1843. It was the only island in the archipelago that voted in 1974 to retain its link with France and forego independence.

New Caledonia
(South Pacific)

Status: Overseas territory

Claimed: 1853

Capital: Noumea

Population: 178,056

Area: 19,103 sq km

Tensions between Francophile expatriates and indigenous population over wealth inequalities and independence. Large nickel deposits.

Reunion
(Indian Ocean)

Status: Overseas department

Claimed: 1638

Capital: Saint-Denis

Population: 639,629

Area: 2,512 sq km

Wealth disparities between white and black communities. Ethnic tensions erupted into rioting in 1991. Large French military base.

Saint Pierre & Miquelon
(North America)

Status: Territorial collectivity

Claimed: 1604

Capital: Saint Pierre

Population: 6,652

Area: 242 sq km

The sole remaining vestige of France's once-vast North American possessions.

Wallis & Futuna
(Pacific)

Status: Overseas territory

Claimed: 1842

Capital: Mata-Utu

Population: 14,175

Area: 274 sq km

In 1959, the inhabitants of the islands voted to become a French overseas territory.

The Netherlands

The country's two remaining territories were formerly part of the Dutch West Indies. Both are now self-governing, but the Netherlands remains responsible for their defence.

Aruba

(Caribbean)

Status: Autonomous part of the Netherlands

Claimed: 1643

Capital: Oranjestad

Population: 62,365

Area: 194 sq km

In 1990, Aruba requested and received from the Netherlands cancellation of the agreement to automatically give independence to the island in 1996.

Netherlands Antilles

(Caribbean)

Status: Autonomous part of the Netherlands

Claimed: 1816

Capital: Willemstad

Population: 191,311

Area: 800 sq km

Economy based on tourism, oil refining and offshore finance. Living standards are high. Political instability and allegations of drug trafficking on smaller islands.

New Zealand

New Zealand's government has no desire to retain any overseas territories. However, the economic weakness of Tokelau, Niue and the Cook Islands has forced it to remain responsible for their foreign policy and defence.

Cook Islands

(South Pacific)

Status: Associated territory

Claimed: 1901

Capital: Avarua

Population: 18,903

Area: 293 sq km

Named after Captain Cook, who sighted them in 1770.

Niue

(South Pacific)

Status: Associated territory

Claimed: 1901

Capital: Alofi

Population: 1,977

Area: 264 sq km

One of the world's largest coral islands.

Tokelau

(South Pacific)

Status: Department territory

Claimed: 1926

Population: 1,544

Area: 10.4 sq km

Originally settled by Polynesian emigrants, transferred by the British to New Zealand in 1925.

Norway

In 1920, forty-one nations signed the Spitsbergen treaty recognizing Norwegian sovereignty over Svalbard. There is a NATO base on Jan Mayen. Bouvet Island is a nature reserve.

Bouvet Island
(South Atlantic)

Status: Dependency

Claimed: 1928

Area: 58 sq km

This uninhabited volcanic island is almost entirely covered by glaciers.

Jan Mayen
(North Atlantic)

Status: Dependency

Claimed: 1929

Area: 381 sq km

The northernmost active volcano on earth.

Svalbard
(Arctic Ocean)

Status: Dependency

Claimed: 1920

Capital: Longyearbyen

Population: 3,209

Area: 62,906 sq km

In accordance with the 1920 Spitsbergen Treaty, nationals of the treaty powers have equal rights to exploit Svalbard's coal deposits, subject to Norwegian regulation. The only companies still mining are Russian and Norwegian.

United Kingdom

The UK has the largest number of overseas territories. Locally governed by a mixture of elected representatives and appointed officials, they all enjoy a large measure of internal self-government, but certain powers, such as foreign affairs and defence, are reserved for governors of the British Crown.

Anguilla
(Caribbean)

Status: Dependent territory

Claimed: 1650

Capital: The Valley

Population: 8,960

Area: 96 sq km

In 1980, became a separate British dependency, splitting from Saint Kitts and Nevis.

Ascension
(Atlantic)

Status: Dependency of St. Helena

Claimed: 1673

Population: 1,099

Area: 88 sq km

A critical refuelling point in the air-bridge from the UK to the South Atlantic.

Bermuda
(North Atlantic)

Status: Crown colony

Claimed: 1612

Capital: Hamilton

Population: 60,686

Area: 53 sq km

Britain's oldest colony. Bermuda was first settled in 1609 by shipwrecked English colonists headed for Virginia. Tourism to the island to escape North American winters first developed in Victorian times. Tourism continues to be important to the island's economy, although international business has overtaken it in recent years. Bermuda has developed into a highly successful offshore financial centre. People are of African or European descent. 74 per cent voted against independence in 1995. Has one of the world's highest per capita incomes.

British Indian Ocean Territory

(Indian Ocean)

Status: Dependent territory

Claimed: 1814

Capital: Diego Garcia

Population: 3,400

Area: 60 sq km

Diego Garcia contains a joint UK–US naval support facility. All of the remaining islands are uninhabited.

British Virgin Islands

(Caribbean)

Status: Dependent territory

Claimed: 1672

Capital: Road Town

Population: 16,644

Area: 153 sq km

The economy is closely tied to the larger and more populous US Virgin Islands to the west.

Cayman Islands

(Caribbean)

Status: Dependent territory

Claimed: 1670

Capital: George Town

Population: 25,355

Area: 259 sq km

Colonized from Jamaica by the British during the nineteenth century.

Falkland Islands

(South Atlantic)

Status: Dependent territory

Claimed: 1832

Capital: Stanley

Population: 2,121

Area: 12,173 sq km

The UK asserted its claim to the islands by establishing a naval garrison there in 1832. Argentina invaded the islands on 2 April 1982. The British responded with an expeditionary force that landed seven weeks later and after fierce fighting forced Argentine surrender on 14 June 1982. British sovereignty is still not recognized by Argentina. Economy based on sheep farming, sale of fishing licenses. Large oil reserves have been discovered.

Gibraltar

(South-west Europe)

Status: Crown colony

Claimed: 1713

Capital: Gibraltar

Population: 28,074

Area: 6.5 sq km

Disputes over sovereignty between UK and Spain. The colony has traditionally survived on military and marine revenues, but cuts in defence spending by the UK have led to the development of an offshore banking industry.

Guernsey

(Channel Island)

Status: Crown dependency

Claimed: 1066

Capital: St Peter Port

Population: 58,867

Area: 65 sq km

The only British soil occupied by German troops in World War II.

Isle of Man

(British Isles)

Status: Crown dependency

Claimed: 1765

Capital: Douglas

Population: 69,788

Area: 572 sq km

Part of the Norwegian kingdom of the Hebrides until the thirteenth century; came under the British Crown in 1765.

Jersey

(Channel Islands)

Status: Crown dependency

Claimed: 1066

Capital: St. Helier

Population: 82,809

Area: 116 sq km

Jersey and the other Channel Islands represent the last remnants of the medieval Dukedom of Normandy that held sway in both France and England.

Montserrat

(Caribbean)

Status: Dependent territory

Claimed: 1632

Capital: Plymouth

Population: 11,852

Area: 102 sq km

Much of the island was devastated by the eruption of the Soufriere Hills Volcano in 1995.

Pitcairn Islands

(South Pacific)

Status: Dependent territory

Claimed: 1887

Capital: Adamstown

Population: 52

Area: 3.5 sq km

Settled in 1790 by the *Bounty* mutineers and their Tahitian companions.

St. Helena

(Atlantic)

Status: Dependent territory

Claimed: 1673

Capital: Jamestown

Population: 6,720

Area: 122 sq km

The place of Napoleon Bonaparte's exile.

South Georgia & The Sandwich Islands

(South Atlantic)

Status: Dependent territory

Claimed: 1775

Population: No permanent residents

Area: 3,592 sq km

Located about 1,000 km east of the Falkland Ismands.

Tristan Da Cunha

(South Atlantic)

Status: Dependency of St Helena

Claimed: 1612

Population: 297

Area: 98 sq km

Gough and Inaccessible Islands have been designated World Heritage Sites.

Turks & Caicos Islands

(Caribbean)

Status: Dependent territory

Claimed: 1766

Capital: Cockburn Town

Population: 12,350

Area: 430 sq km

Became a British overseas territory after Bahamas' independence.

United States of America

US Commonwealth territories are self-governing incorporated territories that are an integral part of the USA. Unincorporated territories have varying degrees of autonomy.

American Samoa

(South Pacific)

Status: Unincorporated territory

Claimed: 1900

Capital: Pago Pago

Population: 50,923

Area: 195 sq km

Strategic location in the South Pacific.

Baker & Howland Islands

(South Pacific)

Status: Unincorporated territory

Claimed: 1856

Area: 1.4 sq km

Part of the Pacific Remote Islands National Wildlife Refuge Complex.

Guam

(West Pacific)

Status: Unincorporated territory

Claimed: 1898

Capital: Agana

Population: 133,152

Area: 549 sq km

The military installation on the island is one of the most strategically important US bases in the Pacific.

Jarvis Island

(Pacific)

Status: Unincorporated territory

Claimed: 1856

Area: 4.5 sq km

Part of the Pacific Remote Islands National Wildlife Refuge Complex.

Johnston Atoll

(Pacific)

Status: Unincorporated territory

Claimed: 1858

Population: 1,375

Area: 2.8 sq km

Part of the Pacific Remote Islands National Wildlife Refuge Complex.

Kingman Reef

(Pacific)

Status: Administered territory

Claimed: 1856

Area: 1 sq km

Part of the Pacific Remote Islands National Wildlife Refuge Complex.

Midway Islands

(Pacific)

Status: Administered territory

Claimed: 1867

Population: 453

Area: 5.2 sq km

Part of the Pacific Remote Islands National Wildlife Refuge Complex.

Navassa Island

(Caribbean)

Status: Unincorporated territory

Claimed: 1856

Area: 5.2 sq km

This uninhabited island was claimed by the US in 1857 for its guano.

Northern Mariana Island

(Pacific)

Status: Commonwealth territory

Claimed: 1947

Capital: Saipan

Population: 48,581

Area: 457 sq km

Under US administration as part of the UN Trust Territory of the Pacific.

Palmyra Atoll

(Pacific)

Status: Unincorporated territory

Claimed: 1898

Area: 12 sq km

Part of the Pacific Remote Islands National Wildlife Refuge Complex.

Puerto Rico

(Caribbean)

Status: Commonwealth territory

Claimed: 1898

Capital: San Juan

Population: 3.6 million

Area: 8,959 sq km

Populated for centuries by aboriginal peoples, the island was claimed by the Spanish Crown in 1493 following Colombus's second voyage to the Americas. In 1898, after 400 years of colonial rule that saw the indigenous population nearly exterminated and African slave labour introduced, Puerto Rico was ceded to the USA as a result of the Spanish–American War. Puerto Ricans were granted US citizenship in 1917. Popularly-elected governors have served since 1948. In 1952, a constitution was enacted providing for internal self government. In plebiscites held in 1967, 1993, and 1998, voters chose not to alter the existing political status.

Virgin Islands

(Caribbean)

Status: Unincorporated territory

Claimed: 1917

Capital: Charlotte Amalie

Population: 101,809

Area: 355 sq km

Important location along the Anegada Passage.

Wake Island

(Pacific)

Status: Unincorporated territory

Claimed: 1898

Population: 302

Area: 6.5 sq km

Access to the atoll is restricted to official government business.

FLAGS OF THE WORLD

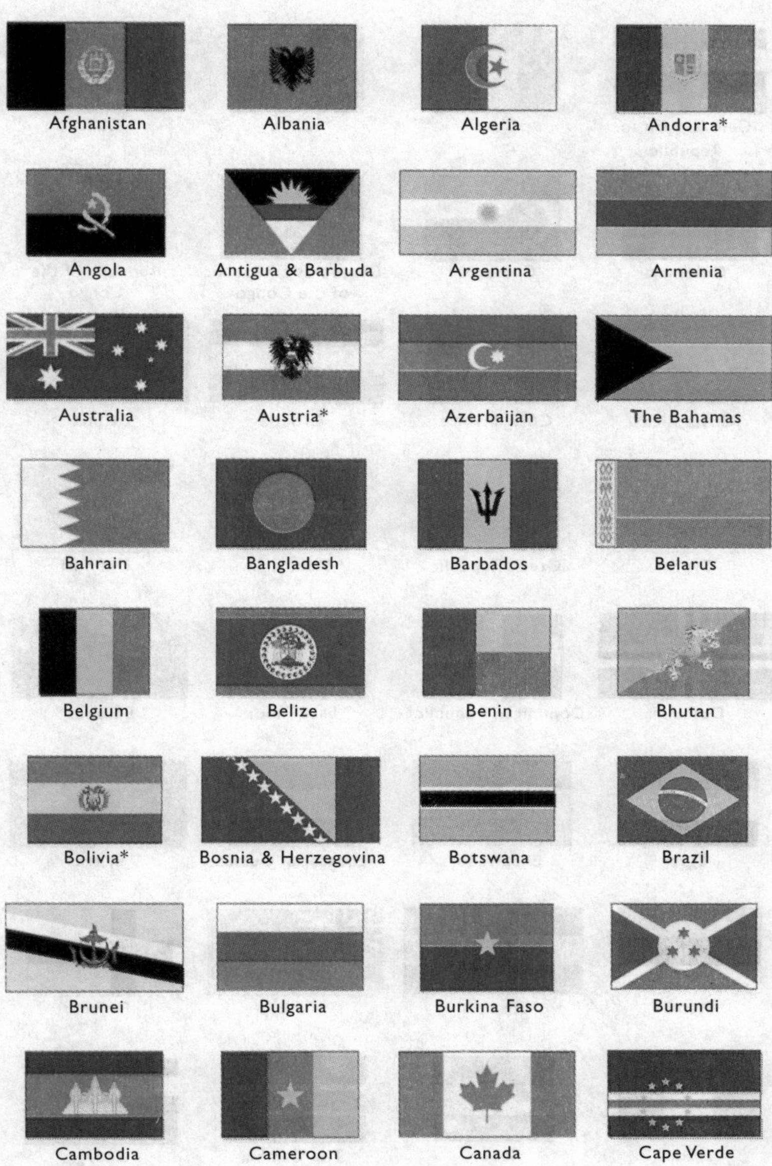

Afghanistan | Albania | Algeria | Andorra*
Angola | Antigua & Barbuda | Argentina | Armenia
Australia | Austria* | Azerbaijan | The Bahamas
Bahrain | Bangladesh | Barbados | Belarus
Belgium | Belize | Benin | Bhutan
Bolivia* | Bosnia & Herzegovina | Botswana | Brazil
Brunei | Bulgaria | Burkina Faso | Burundi
Cambodia | Cameroon | Canada | Cape Verde

Civil flags are shown except where marked thus (*); in these cases, government flags are shown in order to illustrate emblems. Both styles are official national flags.

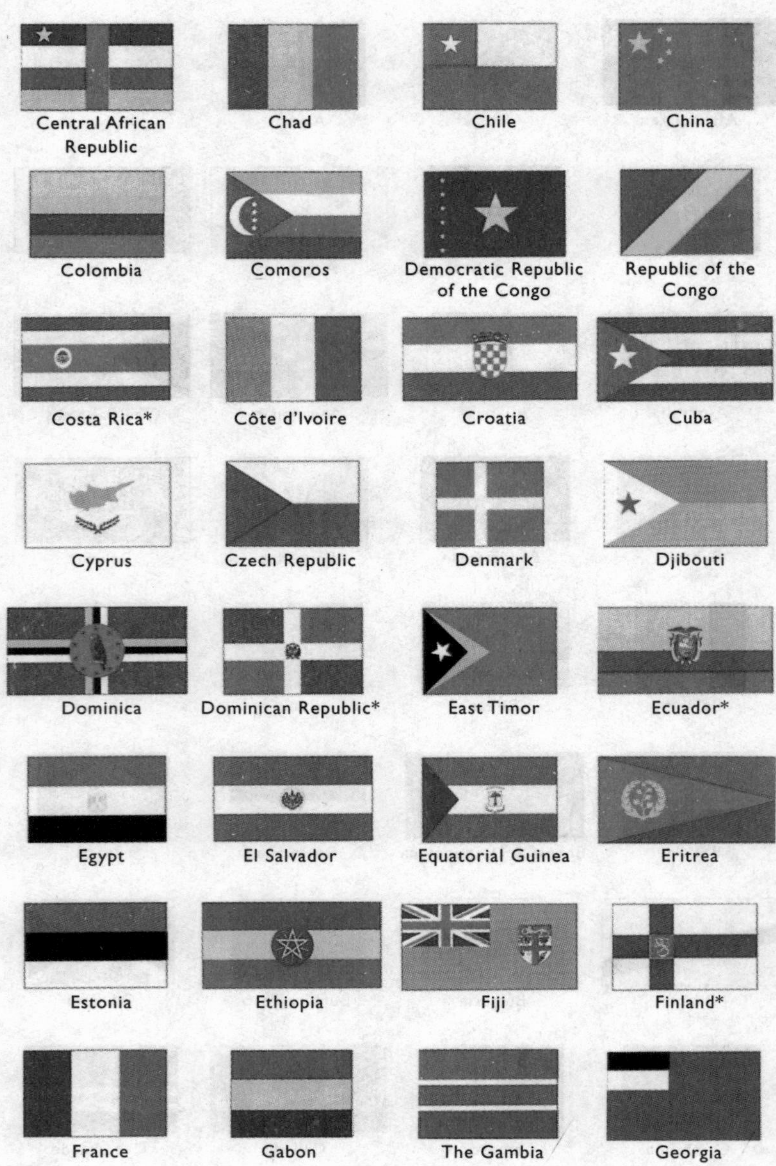

Civil flags are shown except where marked thus (*); in these cases, government flags are shown in order to illustrate emblems. Both styles are official national flags.

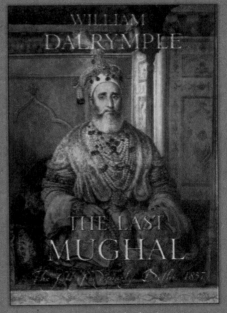

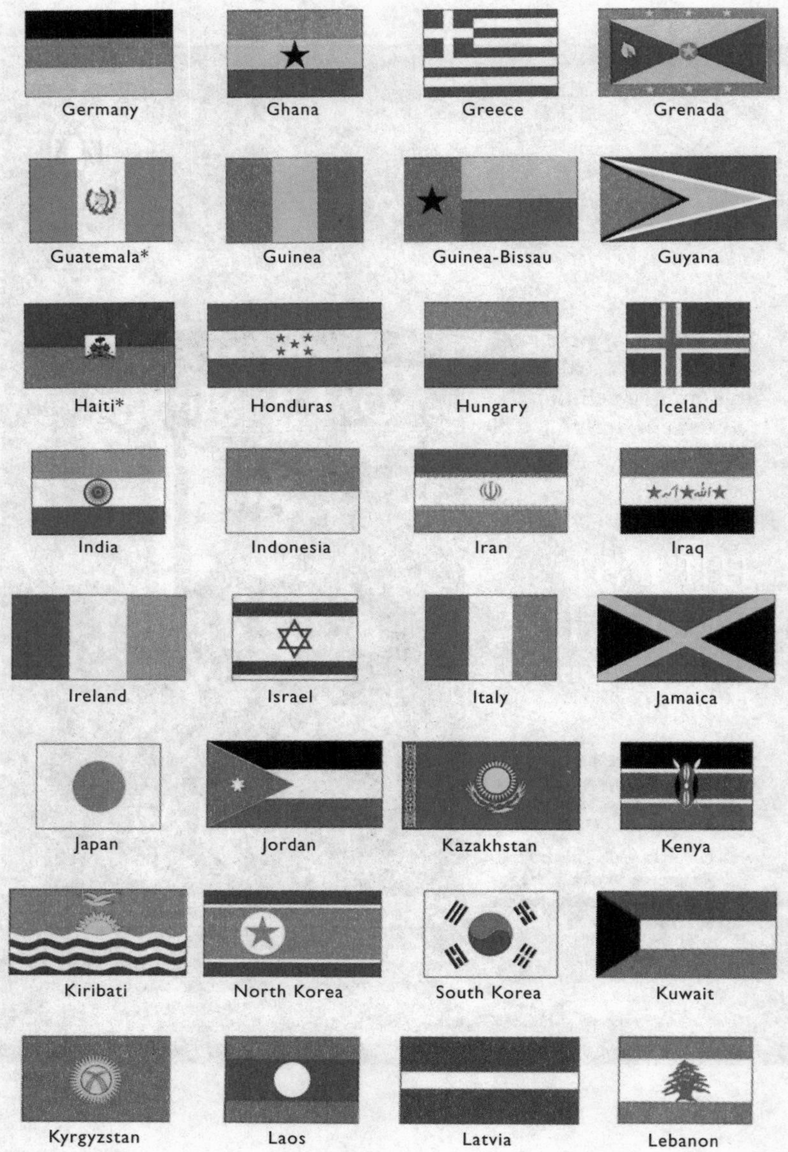

Civil flags are shown except where marked thus (*); in these cases, government flags are shown in order to illustrate emblems. Both styles are official national flags.

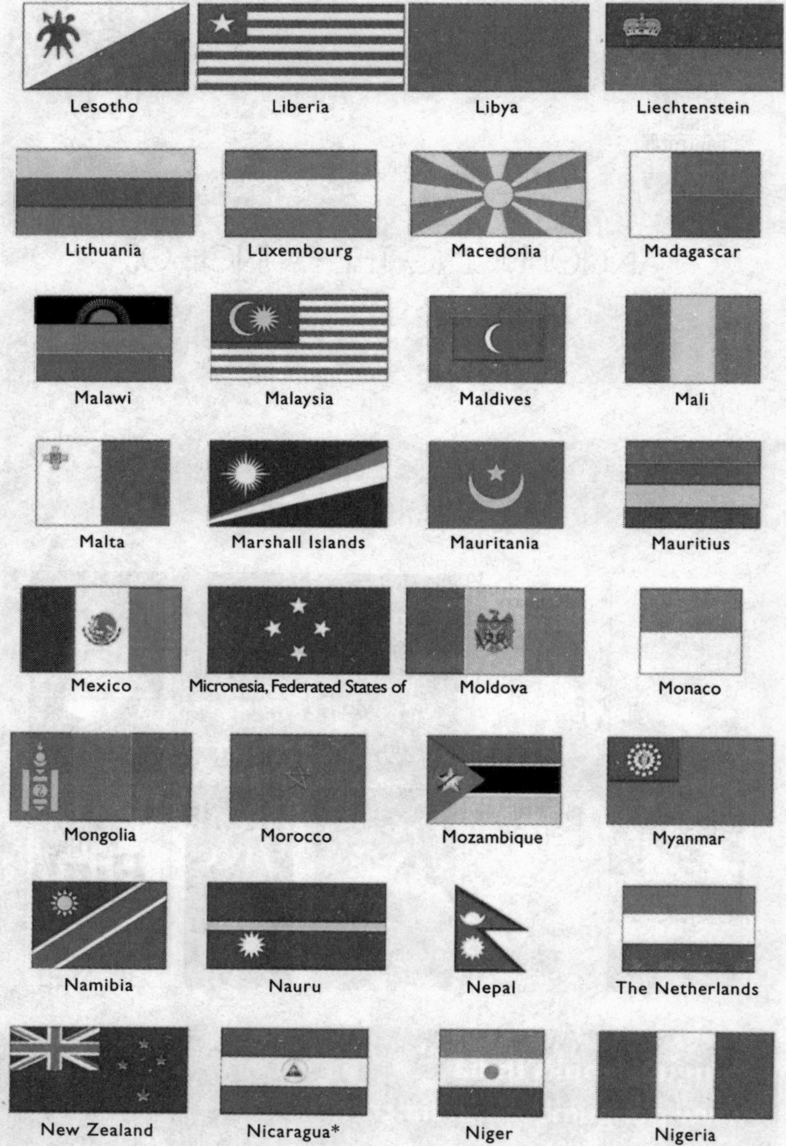

Lesotho | Liberia | Libya | Liechtenstein
Lithuania | Luxembourg | Macedonia | Madagascar
Malawi | Malaysia | Maldives | Mali
Malta | Marshall Islands | Mauritania | Mauritius
Mexico | Micronesia, Federated States of | Moldova | Monaco
Mongolia | Morocco | Mozambique | Myanmar
Namibia | Nauru | Nepal | The Netherlands
New Zealand | Nicaragua* | Niger | Nigeria

Civil flags are shown except where marked thus (*); in these cases, government flags are shown in order to illustrate emblems. Both styles are official national flags.

Flags of the World

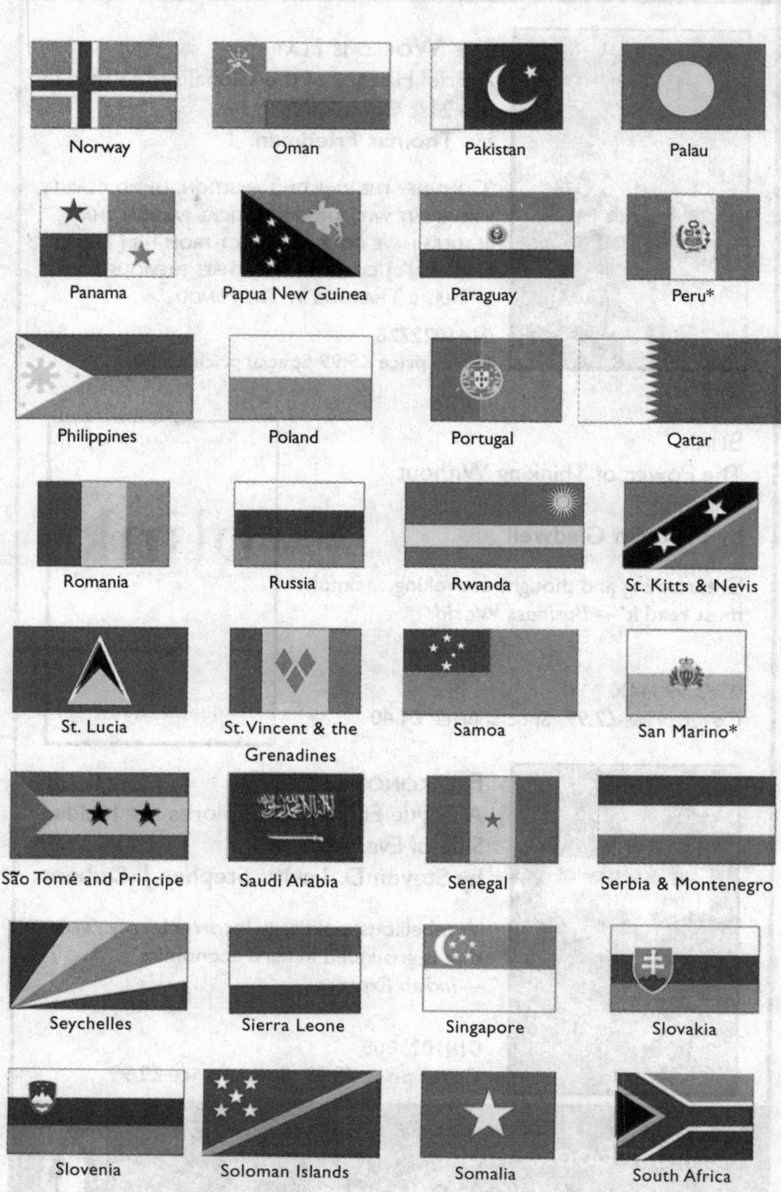

Civil flags are shown except where marked thus (*); in these cases, government flags are shown in order to illustrate emblems. Both styles are official national flags.

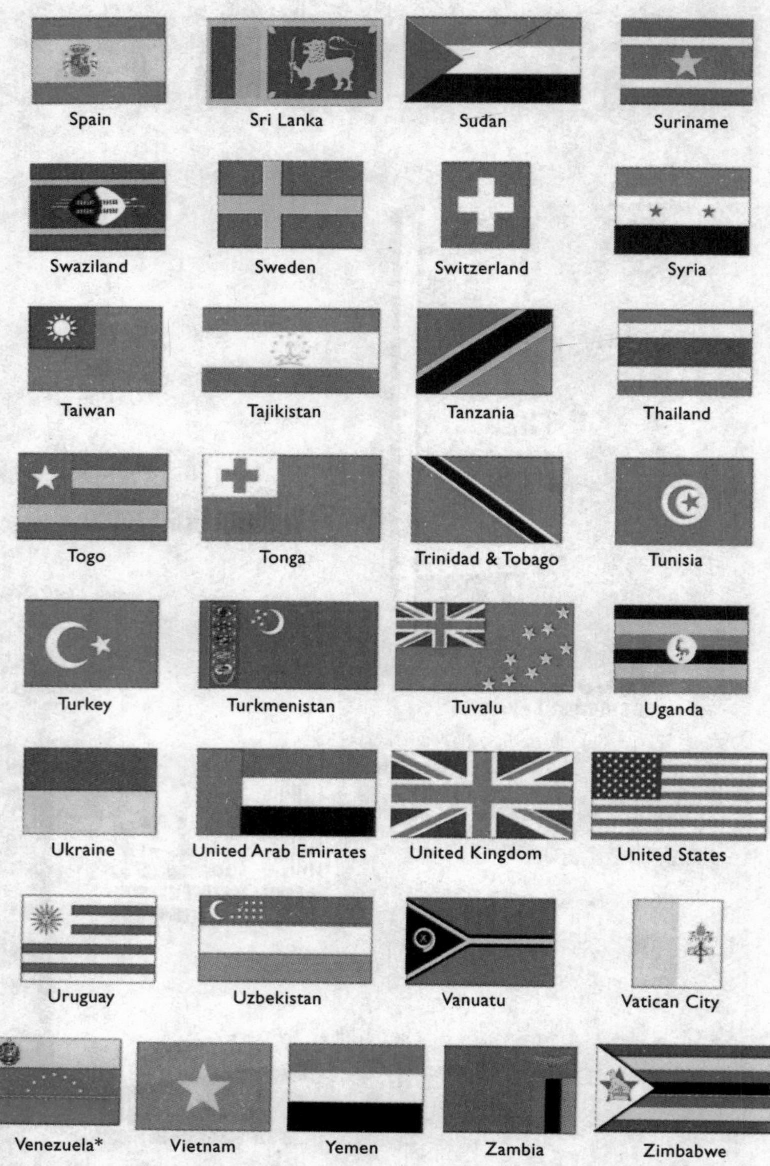

Civil flags are shown except where marked thus (*); in these cases, government flags are shown in order to illustrate emblems. Both styles are official national flags.

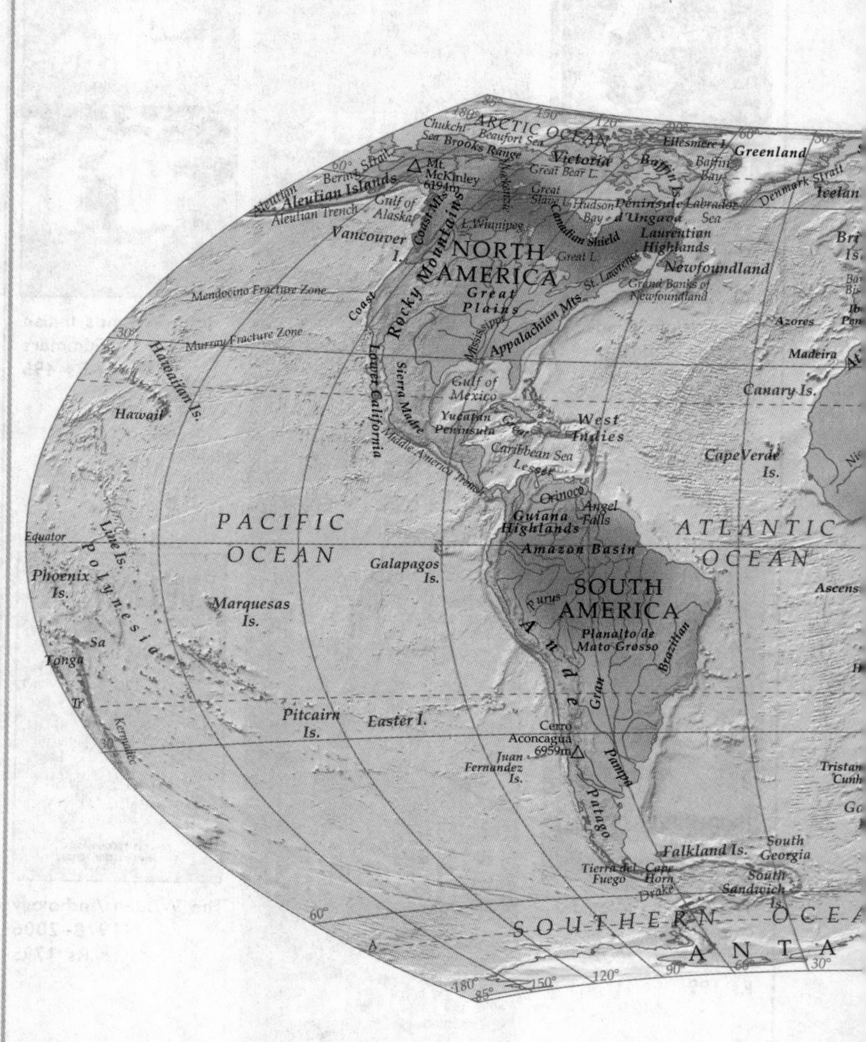
ARCTIC OCEAN
Chukchi Sea
Beaufort Sea
Brooks Range
Victoria
Great Bear L.
Baffin Is.
Baffin Bay
Ellesmere I.
Greenland
Denmark Strait
Bering Strait
Mt. McKinley 6194m
Aleutian Islands
Aleutian Trench
Gulf of Alaska
Coast Mts
Great Slave L.
Hudson Bay
Peninsule d'Ungava
Labrador Sea
Canadian Shield
L. Winnipeg
Laurentian Highlands
Vancouver I.
NORTH AMERICA
Rocky Mountains
Great L.
St. Lawrence
Newfoundland
Grand Banks of Newfoundland
Mendocino Fracture Zone
Coast
Great Plains
Mississippi
Appalachian Mts.
Azores
Murray Fracture Zone
Madeira
Hawaiian Is.
Lower California
Sierra Madre
Gulf of Mexico
Canary Is.
Hawaii
Yucatan Peninsula
West Indies
Middle America Trench
Caribbean Sea
CapeVerde Is.
Orinoco
Angel Falls
PACIFIC OCEAN
Guiana Highlands
ATLANTIC OCEAN
Equator
Line Is.
Amazon Basin
Galapagos Is.
Phoenix Is.
Polynesia
SOUTH AMERICA
Purus
Marquesas Is.
Andes
Planalto de Mato Grosso
Brazilian
Tonga
Gran
Pitcairn Is.
Easter I.
Cerro Aconcagua 6959m
Juan Fernandez Is.
Pampa
Patago
Falkland Is.
South Georgia
Tierra del Fuego
Cape Horn
Drake
South Sandwich Is.
SOUTHERN OCEAN
ANTA
180°
150°
120°
90°
60°
30°

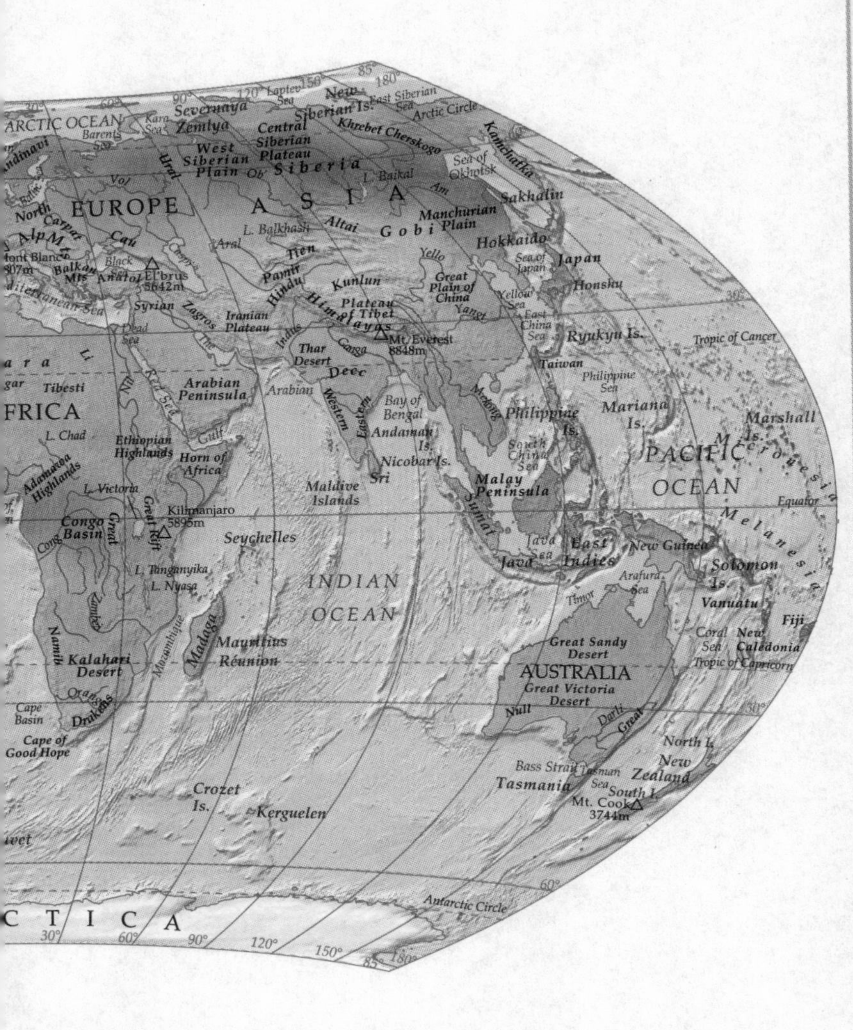

ARCTIC OCEAN
Barents Sea
Kara Sea
Severnaya Zemlya
Laptev Sea
New Siberian Is.
East Siberian Sea
Arctic Circle
Central Siberian Plateau
West Siberian Plain
Khrebet Cherskogo
Kamchatka
Sea of Okhotsk
Ural
Ob
Siberia
L. Baikal
EUROPE
ASIA
Sakhalin
North
Carpat
Alp
Mont Blanc
Manchurian Plain
Altai
L. Balkhash
Gobi
Hokkaido
Cau
Black Sea
Aral
Tien
Sea of Japan
Japan
Balkan Mts
Anatol
El'brus 5642m
Pamir
Hindu
Kunlun
Yello
Great Plain of China
Honshu
Yellow Sea
Himalayas
Plateau of Tibet
Syrian
Zagros
Iranian Plateau
Yangt
East China Sea
Ryukyu Is.
Dead Sea
Indus
Mt. Everest 8848m
Tropic of Cancer
Thar Desert
Ganga
Taiwan
Tibesti
Nil
Red Sea
Arabian Peninsula
Arabian
Deec
Philippine Sea
Bay of Bengal
Mekong
Philippine Is.
Mariana Is.
Marshall Is.
L. Chad
Ethiopian Highlands
Gulf
Western
Eastern
Andaman Is.
South China Sea
Micronesia
PACIFIC OCEAN
Adamawa Highlands
Horn of Africa
Nicobar Is.
Sri
Malay Peninsula
L. Victoria
Maldive Islands
Equator
Congo Basin
Great Rift
Kilimanjaro 5895m
Sumat
Melanesia
Seychelles
Java Sea
East Indies
New Guinea
Java
Solomon Is.
L. Tanganyika
L. Nyasa
INDIAN OCEAN
Arafura Sea
Timor
Vanuatu
Namib
Mozambique
Madaga
Mauritius
Réunion
Great Sandy Desert
Coral Sea
New Caledonia
Fiji
Kalahari Desert
Tropic of Capricorn
AUSTRALIA
Great Victoria Desert
Orange
Cape Basin
Drakens
Null
Darli
Great
Cape of Good Hope
North I.
New Zealand
Bass Strait
Tasman Sea
Tasmania
South I.
Crozet Is.
Kerguelen
Mt. Cook 3744m
Antarctic Circle
30°
60°
90°
120°
150°
180°
85°

THE NATIONS OF THE WORLD

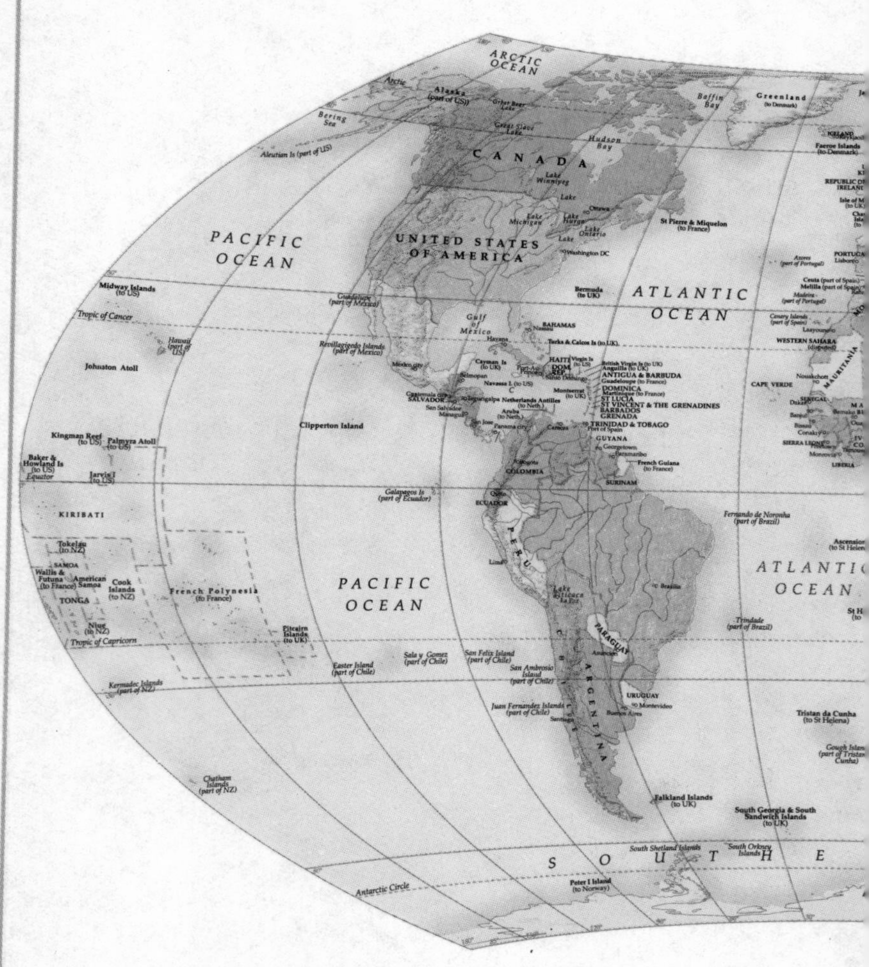

ARCTIC OCEAN
Alaska (part of US)
Bering Sea
Aleutian Is (part of US)
Great Bear Lake
Great Slave Lake
Hudson Bay
Baffin Bay
Greenland (to Denmark)
CANADA
Lake Winnipeg
Lake Michigan
Lake Huron
Lake Ontario
Ottawa
St Pierre & Miquelon (to France)
PACIFIC OCEAN
UNITED STATES OF AMERICA
Washington DC
Midway Islands (to US)
Tropic of Cancer
Guadalupe (part of Mexico)
Bermuda (to UK)
ATLANTIC OCEAN
Gulf of Mexico
BAHAMAS
Havana
Turks & Caicos Is (to UK)
Revillagigedo Islands (part of Mexico)
Hawaii (part of US)
Johnston Atoll
Mexico city
Cayman Is (to UK)
HAITI
DOM. REP.
ANTIGUA & BARBUDA
Guadeloupe (to France)
DOMINICA
Martinique (to France)
ST LUCIA
ST VINCENT & THE GRENADINES
BARBADOS
GRENADA
TRINIDAD & TOBAGO
Port of Spain
Navassa I. (to US)
Montserrat (to UK)
Netherlands Antilles (to Neth.)
Aruba (to Neth.)
Clipperton Island
Kingman Reef (to US)
Palmyra Atoll (to US)
Baker & Howland Is (to US)
Equator
Jarvis I (to US)
GUYANA
Georgetown
Paramaribo
French Guiana (to France)
SURINAM
COLOMBIA
Galapagos Is (part of Ecuador)
Quito
ECUADOR
KIRIBATI
Fernando de Noronha (part of Brazil)
Tokelau (to NZ)
SAMOA
Wallis & Futuna (to France)
American Samoa
Cook Islands (to NZ)
TONGA
Niue (to NZ)
French Polynesia (to France)
PACIFIC OCEAN
PERU
Lima
Brasilia
ATLANTIC OCEAN
Tropic of Capricorn
Pitcairn Islands (to UK)
PARAGUAY
Trindade (part of Brazil)
Easter Island (part of Chile)
Sala y Gomez (part of Chile)
San Felix Island (part of Chile)
San Ambrosio Island (part of Chile)
Kermadec Islands (part of NZ)
URUGUAY
Montevideo
Buenos Aires
ARGENTINA
Juan Fernandez Islands (part of Chile)
Santiago
Tristan da Cunha (to St Helena)
Chatham Islands (part of NZ)
Falkland Islands (to UK)
South Georgia & South Sandwich Islands (to UK)
South Shetland Islands
South Orkney Islands
S O U T H E
Antarctic Circle
Peter I Island (to Norway)
CAPE VERDE
WESTERN SAHARA (disputed)
Canary Islands (part of Spain)
Madeira (part of Portugal)
Azores (part of Portugal)
Faeroe Islands (to Denmark)

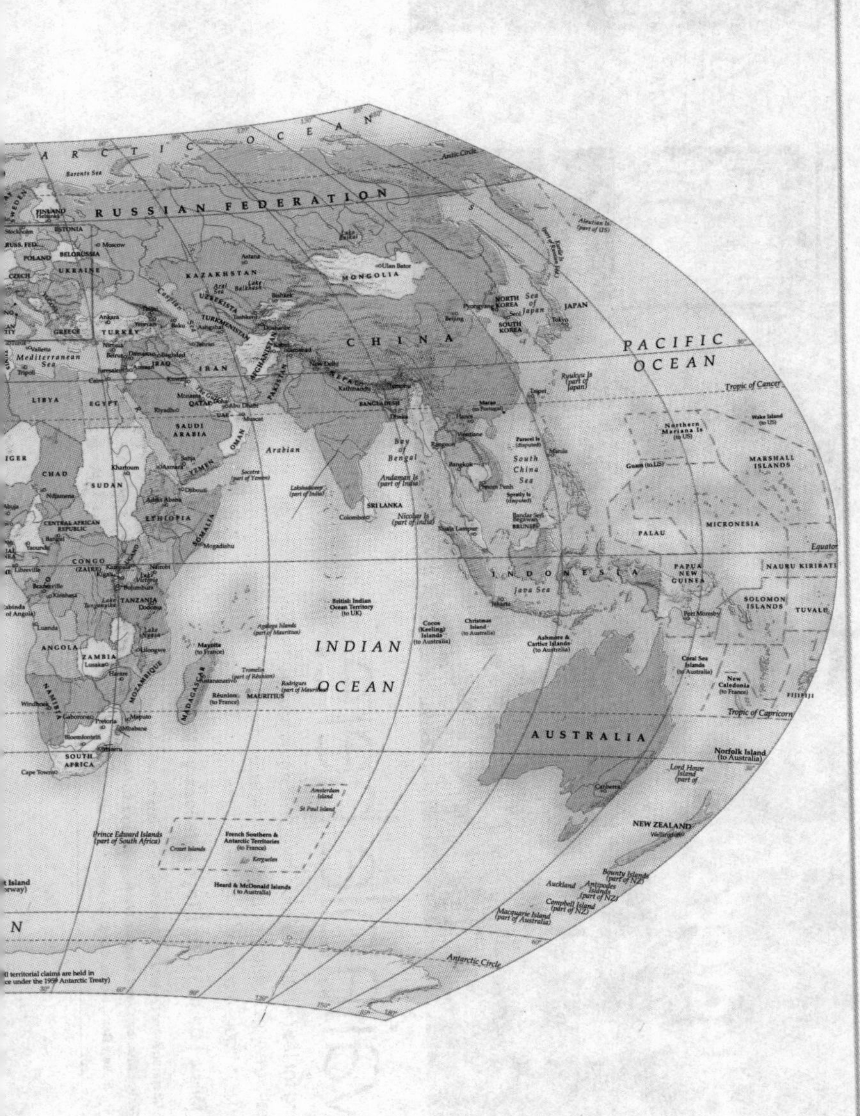
ARCTIC OCEAN
RUSSIAN FEDERATION
KAZAKHSTAN
MONGOLIA
CHINA
JAPAN
NORTH KOREA
SOUTH KOREA
Sea of Japan
PACIFIC OCEAN
Tropic of Cancer
IRAN
AFGHANISTAN
PAKISTAN
TURKEY
GREECE
UKRAINE
POLAND
ESTONIA
BELORUSSIA
Mediterranean Sea
LIBYA
EGYPT
SAUDI ARABIA
OMAN
YEMEN
CHAD
SUDAN
ETHIOPIA
SOMALIA
CENTRAL AFRICAN REPUBLIC
CONGO (ZAIRE)
TANZANIA
ANGOLA
ZAMBIA
MOZAMBIQUE
NAMIBIA
SOUTH AFRICA
MADAGASCAR
MAURITIUS
Arabian Sea
Bay of Bengal
SRI LANKA
BANGLADESH
South China Sea
INDIAN OCEAN
INDONESIA
Java Sea
PAPUA NEW GUINEA
SOLOMON ISLANDS
TUVALU
NAURU
KIRIBATI
MARSHALL ISLANDS
MICRONESIA
PALAU
Equator
AUSTRALIA
Tropic of Capricorn
NEW ZEALAND
Norfolk Island (to Australia)
Antarctic Circle
French Southern & Antarctic Territories (to France)
Heard & McDonald Islands (to Australia)
Prince Edward Islands (part of South Africa)
British Indian Ocean Territory (to UK)
Cocos (Keeling) Islands (to Australia)
Christmas Island (to Australia)
Ashmore & Cartier Islands (to Australia)
Coral Sea Islands (to Australia)
New Caledonia (to France)
Guam (to US)
Northern Mariana Is (to US)
Wake Island (to US)
Andaman Is (part of India)
Nicobar Is (part of India)
Lakshadweep (part of India)
Socotra (part of Yemen)
Mayotte (to France)
Réunion (to France)
Ryukyu Is (part of Japan)
Aleutian Is (part of US)
Macquarie Island (part of Australia)
Campbell Island (part of NZ)
Bounty Islands (part of NZ)
Antipodes Islands (part of NZ)
SCALE BAR
0 km 2000 4000
0 miles 2000 4000
Wagner VII Projection

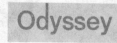

Politics

Government

India has a parliamentary form of government with its foundations in the principle of universal adult franchise. The sovereignty of the country rests with the people of India and the executive authority is responsible to the elected representatives of the people in the Parliament for all its decisions and actions. The Parliament of India has two houses: the Rajya Sabha, or the Council of States and the Lok Sabha, the House of the People.

The Rajya Sabha consists of not more than 250 members, of whom the President of India nominates twelve and the rest are elected. It is not subject to dissolution and one-third of its members retire at the end of every second year. The elections to Rajya Sabha are indirect, with the members of the Legislative Assembly of each state electing its members in accordance with the system of proportional representation by means of a single transferable vote. The Vice-President of India presides over the Rajya Sabha.

The Lok Sabha consists of 545 members. Of these, 530 are directly elected from the twenty-eight states and thirteen from the six Union territories and the National Capital territory of Delhi. Two members are nominated by the President to represent the Anglo-Indian community. Unless dissolved sooner, the term of the House is five years from the date appointed for its first meeting. The Lok Sabha elects its own presiding officer, the Speaker.

The President of India is the head of State and the commander-in-chief of the armed forces. He is elected by an electoral college comprising both Rajya Sabha and Lok Sabha members, as well as the legislatures of the constituent states. The President holds office for five years and can be re-elected. The members of both houses of Parliament jointly elect the Vice-President.

The President does not normally exercise any constitutional powers on his own initiative. These are exercised by the council of ministers, headed by the prime minister, who is responsible to the popularly elected Parliament. The President appoints the person enjoying majority support in the Lok Sabha as the prime minister. The former then appoints other ministers on the advice of the prime minister. The cabinet appointed by the President can remain in office only as long as it enjoys majority support in the Parliament.

The judiciary: The judiciary is independent of the executive. It is viewed as the guardian and interpreter of the Constitution. The Supreme Court is the highest judicial tribunal positioned at the top of a single unified system for the whole country. Each state has its own high court. A uniform code of civil and criminal laws applies to the whole country.

The states: The states have their own legislative assemblies and in some cases, a second legislative council. All members of the legislative assemblies are elected on the principle of universal adult franchise. The governor, appointed by the President, is the head of the state. All twenty-eight states, the Union territory of Pondicherry and NCT of Delhi have state assemblies with a cabinet headed by the chief minister responsible to the elected state legislature.

Presidents of India

Name	Tenure
Dr Rajendra Prasad (1884–1963)	26 January 1950–13 May 1962
Dr Sarvepalli Radhakrishnan (1888–1975)	13 May 1962–13 May 1967
Dr Zakir Husain (1897–1969)	13 May 1967–3 May 1969
Varahagiri Venkatagiri (1884–1980)	3 May 1969–20 July 1969 (Acting)
Justice Mohammad Hidayatullah (1905–1992)	20 July 1969–24 August 1969 (Acting)
Varahagiri Venkatagiri (1884–1980)	24 August 1969–24 August 1974
Fakhruddin Ali Ahmed (1905–77)	24 August 1974–11 February 1977
B.D. Jatti (1913–2002)	11 February 1977–25 July 1977 (Acting)
Neelam Sanjiva Reddy (1913–96)	25 July 1977–25 July 1982
Giani Zail Singh (1916–94)	25 July 1982–25 July 1987
R. Venkataraman (b. 1910)	25 July 1987–25 July 1992
Dr Shanker Dayal Sharma (1918–99)	25 July 1992–25 July 1997
K.R. Narayanan (1920–2005)	25 July 1997–25 July 2002
Dr A.P.J. Abdul Kalam (b. 1931)	25 July 2002–till date

Vice-Presidents of India

Name	Tenure
Dr Sarvepalli Radhakrishnan (1888–1975)	1952–62
Dr Zakir Husain (1897–1969)	1962–67
Varahagiri Venkatagiri (1884–1980)	1967–69
Gopal Swarup Pathak (1896–1982)	1969–74
B.D. Jatti (1913–2002)	1974–79
Justice Mohammad Hidayatullah (1905–92)	1979–84
R. Venkataraman (b. 1910)	1984–87
Dr Shanker Dayal Sharma (1918–99)	1987–92
K.R. Narayanan (1920–2005)	1992–97
Krishan Kant (1927–2002)	1997–2002
Bhairon Singh Shekhawat (b. 1923)	2002–till date

Prime Ministers of India

Name	Tenure
Jawaharlal Nehru (1889–1964)	15 August 1947-27 May 1964
Gulzari Lal Nanda (1898–1997)	27 May 1964–9 June 1964 (Acting)
Lal Bahadur Shastri (1904–66)	9 June 1964–11 January 1966
Gulzari Lal Nanda (1898–1997)	11 January 1966–24 January 1966 (Acting)
Indira Gandhi (1917–84)	24 January1966–24 March 1977
Morarji Desai (1896–1995)	24 March 1977–28 July 1979

Charan Singh (1902–87)	28 July 1979–14 January 1980
Indira Gandhi (1917–84)	14 January 1980–31 October 1984
Rajiv Gandhi (1944–91)	31 October 1984–1 December 1989
Vishwanath Pratap Singh (b. 1931)	2 December 1989–10 November 1990
Chandra Shekhar (b. 1927)	10 November 1990–21 June 1991
P.V. Narasimha Rao (1921–2004)	21 June 1991–16 May 1996
Atal Bihari Vajpayee (b. 1926)	16 May 1996–1 June 1996
H.D. Deve Gowda (b. 1933)	1 June 1996–21 April 1997
I.K. Gujral (b. 1933)	21 April 1998–18 March 1998
Atal Bihari Vajpayee (b. 1926)	19 March 1998–22 May 2004
Manmohan Singh(b. 1932)	22 May 2004–till date

Chief Justices of India

Name	Tenure
Harilal J. Kania	26 January 1950–6 November 1951
M. Patanjali Sastri	7 November 1951–3 January 1954
Mehar Chand Mahajan	4 January 1954–22 December 1954
B.K. Mukherjea	23 December 1954–31 January 1956
S.R. Das	1 February 1956–30 September 1959
Bhuvaneshwar Prasad Sinha	1 October 1959–31 January 1964
P.B. Gajendragadkar	1 February 1964–15 March 1966
A.K. Sarkar	16 March 1966–29 June 1966
K. Subba Rao	30 June 1966–11 April 1967
K.N. Wanchoo	12 April 1967–24 February 1968
M. Hidayatullah	25 February 1968–16 December 1970
J.C. Shah	17 December 1970–21 January 1971
S.M. Sikri	22 January 1971–25 April 1973
A.N. Ray	26 April 1973–27 January 1977
M.H. Beg	28 January 1977–21 February 1978
Y.V. Chandrachud	22 February 1978–11 July 1985
Prafullachandra Natvarlal Bhagwati	12 July 1985–20 December 1986
R.S. Pathak	21 December 1986–18 June 1989
E.S. Venkataramiah	19 June 1989–17 December 1989
S. Mukharjee	18 December 1989–25 September 1990
Ranganath Mishra	26 September 1990–24 November 1991
K.N. Singh	25 November 1991–12 December 1991
M.H. Kania	13 December 1991–17 November 1992
L.M. Sharma	18 November 1992–11 February 1993
M.N. Venkatachaliah	12 February 1993–24 October 1994
A.M. Ahmadi	25 October 1994–24 March 1997
J.S. Verma	25 March 1997–17 January 1998
M.M. Punchhi	18 January 1998–9 October 1998
A.S. Anand	10 October 1998–till date
S.P. Bharucha	1 November 2001–5 May 2002
B.N. Kirpal	6 May 2002–7 November 2002
G.B. Pattanaiak	8 November 2002–18 December 2002
V.N. Khare	19 December 2002–2 May 2004
S. Rajendra Babu	2 May 2004–1 June 2004
Ramesh Chandra Lahoti	1 June 2004–1 November 2005
Yogesh Kumar Sabharwal	1 November 2005–till date

The Constitution of India

Introduction

The Constitution of India is one of the world's longest written constitutions with 395 articles and twelve schedules. It was passed on 26 November 1949 by the Constituent Assembly and became fully applicable from 26 January 1950.

The Constitution of India draws from Western legal traditions in the way that it outlines the principles of liberal democracy. It provides for a bicameral parliament (a lower house and an upper house) along the lines of the British parliamentary pattern. It contains the Fundamental Rights, similar to the Bill of Rights contained in the United States Constitution. It also provides for a Supreme Court, as in the US Constitution.

India has a federal system, in which the residual powers of legislation are vested in the central government. This is similar to the Canadian set-up. The Constitution also contains detailed lists (the state list, the union list and the concurrent list), dividing powers between the central and state governments, similar to Australia. It contains a set of Directive Principles of State Policy. This is similar to the Irish Constitution.

The Constitution has the provision for the addition of Schedules by means of amendments. At present, the Constitution has twelve schedules. The assent of at least two-thirds of the Lok Sabha and the Rajya Sabha is needed to review the Constitution.

The Indian Constitution has been frequently amended. The first amendment was passed after only a year of the adoption of the Constitution, and it came into force on 18 June 1951. The most recent amendment, the Ninety-second Amendment, came into force on 1 July 2004. Most parts of the Constitution can be amended after a quorum of more than half of the members of each house in the Parliament passes an amendment with a two-thirds majority vote. However, articles relating to the distribution of legislative authority between the central and state governments must also be approved by 50 per cent of the state legislatures.

Preamble

WE, THE PEOPLE OF INDIA, having solemnly resolved to constitute India into a SOVEREIGN, SOCIALIST, SECULAR, DEMOCRATIC, REPUBLIC and to secure to all its citizens:

JUSTICE, social, economic and political;

LIBERTY of thought, expression, belief, faith and worship;

EQUALITY of status and of opportunity; and to promote among them all

FRATERNITY assuring the dignity of the individual and the unity and integrity of the nation;

IN OUR CONSTITUENT ASSEMBLY this twenty-sixth day of November 1949, do HEREBY ADOPT, ENACT AND GIVE TO OURSELVES THIS CONSTITUTION.

Schedules

FIRST SCHEDULE

I. The States

II. The Union Territories

SECOND SCHEDULE

Part A

Provisions as to the President and the Governors of States

Part B

(Repealed)

Part C

Provisions as to the Speaker and the Deputy Speaker of the House of the People and the Chairman and the Deputy Chairman of the Council of States and the Speaker and the Deputy Speaker of the Legislative Assembly and the Chairman and the Deputy Chairman of the Legislative Council of a State.

Parts of the Constitution

Part I	
The Union and its Territory	Articles 1–4
Part II	
Citizenship	Articles 5–11
Part III	
Fundamental Rights	Articles 12–35
Part IV	
Directive Principles of State Policy	Articles 36–51
Part IVA	
Fundamental Duties	Article 51A
Part V	
The Union	Articles 52–151
Part VI	
The States	Articles 152–237
Part VII	
The States in Part B of the First Schedule	Article 238
Part VIII	
The Union Territories	Articles 239–243
Part IX	
Panchayats	Articles 243–243O
Part IXA	
Municipalities	Articles 243P–243ZG
Part X	
The Scheduled and Tribal Areas	Articles 244–244A
Part XI	
Relations Between the Union and the States	Articles 245–263
Part XII	
Finance, Property, Contracts and Suits	Articles 264–300A
Part XIII	
Trade, Commerce and Intercourse within the Territory of India	Articles 301–307
Part XIV	
Services Under the Union and the States	Articles 308–323
Part XIVA	
Tribunals	Articles 323A–323B
Part XV	
Elections	Articles 324–329A
Part XVI	
Special Provisions Relating to Certain Classes	Articles 330–342
Part XVII	
Official Language	Articles 343–351
Part XVIII	
Emergency Provisions	Articles 352–360
Part XIX	
Miscellaneous	Articles 361–367
Part XX	
Amendment of the Constitution	Article 368
Part XXI	
Temporary, Transitional and Special Provisions	Articles 369–392
Part XXII	
Short title, Commencement, Authoritative text in Hindi and Repeals	Articles 393–395

Part D

Provisions as to the Judges of the Supreme Court and of the High Courts.

Part E

Provisions as to the Comptroller and Auditor-General of India.

THIRD SCHEDULE

Forms of Oaths or Affirmations.

FOURTH SCHEDULE

Allocation of Seats in the Council of States.

FIFTH SCHEDULE

Provision as to the Administration and Control of Scheduled Areas and Scheduled Tribes.

Part A

General.

Part B

Administration and Control of Scheduled Areas and Scheduled Tribes.

Part C

Scheduled Areas.

Part D

Amendment of the Schedule.

SIXTH SCHEDULE

Provisions as to the Administration of Tribal Areas in the States of Assam, Meghalaya, Tripura and Mizoram.

SEVENTH SCHEDULE

List I: Union List.

List II: State List.

List III: Concurrent List.

EIGHTH SCHEDULE

Languages.

NINTH SCHEDULE

Validation of certain Acts and Regulations.

TENTH SCHEDULE

Provisions as to disqualification on ground of defection.

ELEVENTH SCHEDULE

Powers, authority and responsibilities of Panchayats.

TWELFTH SCHEDULE

Powers, authority and responsibilities of Municipalities, etc.

Appendix

APPENDIX I

The Constitution (Application to Jammu and Kashmir) Order, 1954.

APPENDIX II

Re-statement with, reference to the present text of the Constitution, of the exceptions and modifications subject to which the Constitution applies to the State of Jammu and Kashmir.

APPENDIX III

Extracts from the Constitution (Forty-fourth Amendment) Act, 1978.

Speakers of the Lok Sabha

The Indian Parliament had its first communist Speaker in Somnath Chatterjee in 2004. The office of the Speaker occupies a pivotal position in India's parliamentary democracy. In the Warrant of Precedence, the Speaker comes after only the President, the Vice-President and the prime minister. Through the guidelines laid down by the Constitution, the Rules of Procedure and Conduct of Business in Lok Sabha and through established practices and conventions, adequate powers are vested in the office of the Speaker to enable him to ensure the smooth conduct of parliamentary proceedings and protect the independence and impartiality of the office. One of the first acts of a newly constituted House is to elect the Speaker. Usually, a member belonging to the ruling party is elected the Speaker. It has been the practice through the years that the ruling party nominates its candidate after informal consultations with the leaders of other opposition parties and groups in the Lok Sabha. This convention ensures that once elected, the Speaker enjoys the respect of all sections of the House. The Constitution of India provides that the Speaker's salary and allowances are to be charged to the Consolidated Fund of India. The Speaker holds office from the date of his election until immediately before the first meeting of the Lok Sabha after the dissolution of the one to which he was elected. He is eligible for re-election. The Speaker does not vacate his office on the dissolution of the Lok Sabha, unless he ceases to be a member of the House.

However, the Speaker may, at any time, resign from office by writing under his hand to the Deputy Speaker. The Speaker can be removed from office only on a resolution of the House passed by a majority of all members of the House.

List of Speakers

G.V. Mavalankar
(15 May 1952–27 February 1956)
M.A. Ayyangar
(8 March 1956–10 May 1957)
(11 May 1957–16 April 1962)
Sardar Hukam Singh
(17 April 1962–16 March 1967)
N. Sanjiva Reddy
(17 March 1967–19 July 1969)
G.S. Dhillon
(8 August 1969–17 March 1971)
(22 March 1971–1 December 1975)
Bali Ram Bhagat
(15 January 1976–25 March 1977)
N. Sanjiva Reddy
(26 March 1977–13 July 1977)
K.S. Hegde
(21 July 1977–21 January 1980)
Balram Jakhar
(22 January 1980–15 January 1985)
(16 January 1985–18 December 1989)
Rabi Ray
(19 December 1989–9 July 1991)
Shivraj V. Patil
(10 July 1991–22 May 1996)
P.A. Sangma
(25 March 1996–23 March 1998)
G.M.C. Balyogi
(24 March 1998–19 October 1999)
(22 October 1999–3 March 2002, died in office)
Manohar Joshi
(10 May 2002–2 June 2004)
Somnath Chatterjee
(4 June 2004–till date)

List of Union Council of Ministers (as on 1 November 2006)

Cabinet Ministers

1. Dr Manmohan Singh	Prime Minister and also in-charge of the ministries/departments not specifically allocated to the charge of any minister, viz.: (i) Ministry of Personnel, Public Grievances and Pensions; (ii) Ministry of Planning; (iii) Department of Atomic Energy: (iv) Department of Space
2. Pranab Mukherjee	Minister of External Affairs
3. Arjun Singh	Minister of Human Resource Development
4. Sharad Pawar	Minister of Agriculture and Minister of Consumer Affairs, Food and Public Distribution
5. Lalu Prasad Yadav	Minister of Railways
6. Shivraj V. Patil	Minister of Home Affairs
7. A.K. Antony	Minister of Defence
8. A.R. Antulay	Minister of Minority Affairs
9. Sushilkumar Shinde	Minister of Power
10. Ram Vilas Paswan	Minister of Chemicals and Fertilizers and Minister of Steel
11. S. Jaipal Reddy	Minister of Urban Development

12. Sis Ram Ola	Minister of Mines
13. P. Chidambaram	Minister of Finance
14. Mahavir Prasad	Minister of Small Scale Industries and Minister of Agro and Rural Industries
15. P.R. Kyndiah	Minister of Tribal Affairs
16. T.R. Baalu	Minister of Shipping, Road Transport and Highways
17. Shankersinh Vaghela	Minister of Textiles
18. Vayalar Ravi	Minister of Overseas Indian Affairs
19. Kamal Nath	Minister of Commerce and Industry
20. H.R. Bhardwaj	Minister of Law and Justice
21. Santosh Mohan Dev	Minister of Heavy Industries and Public Enterprises
22. Prof. Saif-ud-din Soz	Minister of Water Resources
23. Raghuvansh Prasad Singh	Minister of Rural Development
24. Priyaranjan Dasmunsi	Minister of Parliamentary Affairs and Minister of Information and Broadcasting
25. Mani Shankar Aiyar	Minister of Panchayati Raj, Minister of Youth Affairs and Sports and Minister of Development of North-Eastern Region
26. Meira Kumar	Minister of Social Justice and Empowerment
27. Murli Deora	Minister of Petroleum and Natural Gas
28. Ambika Soni	Minister of Tourism and Minister of Culture
29. Shibu Soren	Minister of Coal
30. A. Raja	Minister of Environment and Forests
31. Dayanidhi Maran	Minister of Communications and Information Technology
32. Dr Anbumani Ramdoss	Minister of Health and Family Welfare
33. Kapil Sibal	Minister of Science and Technology and Minister of Earth Sciences
34. Prem Chand Gupta	Minister of Company Affairs

Ministers of State (Independent Charge)

1. Oscar Fernandes	Minister of State (Independent Charge) of the Ministry of Labour and Employment
2. Renuka Chowdhury	Minister of State (Independent Charge) of the Ministry of Women and Child Development
3. Subodh Kant Sahay	Minister of State (Independent Charge) of the Ministry of Food Processing Industries
4. Vilas Muttemwar	Minister of State (Independent Charge) of the Ministry of Non-Conventional Energy Sources
5. Selja Kumari	Minister of State (Independent Charge) of the Ministry of Housing and Urban Poverty Alleviation
6. Praful Patel	Minister of State (Independent Charge) of the Ministry of Civil Aviation

7. G.K.Vasan	Minister of State (Independent Charge) of the Minister of Statistics and Programme Implementation

Ministers of State

1. E. Ahammed	Minister of State in the Ministry of External Affairs
2. Suresh Pachouri	Minister of State in the Ministry of Personnel, Public Grievances and Pensions and Minister of State in the Ministry of Parliamentary Affairs
3. B.K. Handique	Minister of State in the Ministry of Chemicals and Fertilizers and Minister of State in the Ministry of Parliamentary Affairs
4. Panabaka Lakshmi	Minister of State in the Ministry of Health and Family Welfare
5. Dr Dasari Narayan Rao	Minister of State in the Ministry of Coal
6. Dr Shakeel Ahmad	Minister of State in the Ministry of Communications and Information Technology
7. Rao Inderjit Singh	Minister of State in the Ministry of Defence
8. Naranbhai Rathwa	Minister of State in the Ministry of Railways
9. K.H. Muniappa	Minister of State in the Ministry of Shipping, Road Transport and Highways
10. M.V. Rajasekharan	Minister of State in the Ministry of Planning
11. Kantilal Bhuria	Minister of State in the Ministry of Agriculture and Minister of State in the Ministry of Consumer Affairs, Food and Public Distribution
12. Manikrao Gavit	Minister of State in the Ministry of Home Affairs
13. Shriprakash Jaiswal	Minister of State in the Ministry of Home Affairs
14. Prithviraj Chavan	Minister of State in the Prime Minister's Office
15. Taslimuddin	Minister of State in the Ministry of Agriculture and Minister of State in the Ministry of Consumer Affairs, Food and Public Distribution
16. Suryakanta Patil	Minister of State in the Ministry of Rural Development and Minister of State in the Ministry of Parliamentary Affairs
17. Md Ali Ashraf Fatmi	Minister of State in the Ministry of Human Resource Development
18. R. Velu	Minister of State in the Ministry of Railways
19. S.S. Palanimanickam	Minister of State in the Ministry of Finance

20. S. Regupathy	Minister of State in the Ministry of Home Affairs
21. K. Venkatapathy	Minister of State in the Ministry of Law and Justice
22. Subbulakshmi Jagadeesan	Minister of State in the Ministry of Social Justice and Empowerment
23. E.V.K.S. Elangovan	Minister of State in the Ministry of Textiles
24. Kanti Singh	Minister of State in the Department of Heavy Industry, Ministry of Heavy Industries and Public Enterprises
25. Namo Narain Meena	Minister of State in the Ministry of Environment and Forests
26. Dr Akhilesh Prasad Singh	Minister of State in the Ministry of Agriculture and Minister of State in the Ministry of Consumer Affairs Food and Public Distribution
27. Pawan Kumar Bansal	Minister of State in the Ministry of Finance
28. Anand Sharma	Minister of State in the Ministry of External Affairs
29. Ajay Maken	Minister of State in the Ministry of Urban Development
30. Dinsha J. Patel	Minister of State in the Ministry of Petroleum and Natural Gas
31. M.M. Pallam Raju	Minister of State in the Ministry of Defence
32. Dr T. Subbarami Reddy	Minister of State in the Ministry of Mines
33. Dr Akhilesh Das	Minister of State in the Ministry of Steel
34. Ashwani Kumar	Minister of State in the Department of Industrial Policy and Promotion, Ministry of Commerce and Industry
35. Jairam Ramesh	Minister of State in the Department of Commerce, Ministry of Commerce and Industry
36. Chandra Sekhar Sahu	Minister of State in the Ministry of Rural Development
37. D. Purandeswari	Minister of State in the Ministry of Human Resource Development
38. M.H. Ambareesh	Minister of State in the Ministry of Information and Broadcasting
39. Jaiprakash Narayan Yadav	Minister of State in the Ministry of Water Resources

Ministers for Home Affairs

Jawaharlal Nehru (1950)
Chakravarti Rajagopalachari (1950–51)
Kailash Nath Katju (1951–55)
Govind Ballabh Pant (1955–61)
Gulzari Lal Nanda (1963–66)
Indira Gandhi (1966)
Yeshwantrao Balwantrao Chavan (1966–70)
Indira Gandhi (1970–73)
Uma Shankar Dikshit (1973–74)

Kasu Brahamananda Reddy (1974–77)
Morarji Ranchhodji Desai (1978–79)
H.M. Patel (1979)
Ramasamy Venkataraman (1979–82)
Prakash Chand Sethi (1982–84)
P. V. Narasimha Rao (1984)
Shakarrao Bhaorao Chavan (1984–86)
P. V. Narasimha Rao (1986)
Ghulam Nabi Azad (1986)
Buta Singh (1986–89)
Shankarrao Bhaorao Chavan (1991–96)
Murli Manohar Joshi (1996)
H.D. Deve Gowda (1996)
Indrajit Gupta (1996–98)
L.K. Advani (1998–2004)
Shivraj Patil (2004–till date)

Defence Ministers

Baldev Singh (1947–52)
N. Gopalaswami Ayyangar (1952–53)
Jawaharlal Nehru (1953–55)
Kailash Nath Katju (1955–57)
Jawaharlal Nehru (1957–57)
V.K. Krishna Menon (1957–62)
Jawaharlal Nehru (1962–62)
Y.B. Chavan (1962–66)
Sardar Swaran Singh (1974–75)
Indira Gandhi (1975–75)
Bansi Lal (1975–77)
Jagjivan Ram (1977–79)
C. Subramanium (1979–80)
Indira Gandhi (1980–82)
R. Venkataraman (1982–84)
S.B. Chavan (1984)
P.V. Narasimha Rao (1984–85)
Rajiv Gandhi (1985–87)
V.P. Singh (1987)
K.C. Pant (1987–89)
V.P. Singh (1989–90)
Chandra Shekhar (1990–91)
P.V. Narasimha Rao (1991–91)
Sharad Pawar (1991–93)
P.V. Narasimha Rao (1993–96)
Pramod Mahajan (1996)
Mulayam Singh Yadav (1996–98)
George Fernandes (1998–2001)
Jaswant Singh (2001)
George Fernandes (2001–04)
Pranab Mukherjee (2004–06)
A.K. Antony (2006–till date)

Finance Ministers

R.K. Shanmukham Chetty (1947–49)
John Mathai (1949–51)
C.D. Deshmukh (1951–57)
T.T. Krishnamachari (1957–58)
Jawaharlal Nehru (1958–59)
Morarji Desai (1959–64)
T.T. Krishnamachari (1964–66)
Sachindra Chowdhury (1966–67)
Morarji Desai (1967–70)
Indira Gandhi (1970–71)
Y.B. Chavan (1971–75)
C. Subramaniam (1975–77)
H.M. Patel (1977–78)
Charan Singh (1979–80)
R. Venkataraman (1980–82)
Pranab Mukherjee (1982–85)
V.P. Singh (1985–87)
N.D. Tiwari (1988–89)
S.B. Chavan (1989–90)
Madhu Dandavate (1990–91)
Yashwant Sinha (Vote on Account) (1991–92)
Manmohan Singh (1991–96)
P. Chidambaram (1996–98)
Yashwant Sinha (1998–2002)
Jaswant Singh (2002–04)
P. Chidambaram (2004–till date)

Ministers for External Affairs

Jawaharlal Nehru (1947–64)
Gulzari Lal Nanda (1964)
Swaran Singh (1964–66)
Mahomedali Currin Chagla (1966–67)
Indira Gandhi (1967–67)
Dinesh Singh (1969–70)
Swaran Singh (1970–74)
Yeshwantrao Balwantrao Chavan (1974–77)
Atal Behari Vajpayee (1977–79)
P.V. Narasimha Rao (1980–84)
Rajiv Gandhi (1984–85)
Bali Ram Bhagat (1985–86)
P. Shiv Shankar (1986)
Narayan Datt Tiwari (1986–87)
Rajiv Gandhi (1987–88)
P.V. Narasimha Rao (1988–89)
Inder Kumar Gujral (1989–90)
Vidya Charan Shukla (1990–91)

Madhavsinh Solanki (1991–92)
P.V. Narasimha Rao (1992–93)
Dinesh Singh (1993–95)
Pranab Kumar Mukherjee (1995–96)
Sikander Bakht (1996)
Inder Kumar Gujral (1996–97)
Atal Behari Vajpayee (1997–98)
Jaswant Singh (1998–2002)
Yashwant Sinha (2002–04)
Natwar Singh (2004–05)
Dr Manmohan Singh (2005–06)
Pranab Kumar Mukherjee (2006–till date)

Table of Precedence

1. President
2. Vice-President
3. Prime Minister
4. Governors of states (within their respective states)
5. Former Presidents

5A. Deputy Prime Minister

6. Chief Justice of India
   Speaker of Lok Sabha
7. Cabinet Ministers of the Union
   Chief Ministers of states (within their respective states)
   Deputy Chairman, Planning Commission
   Former Prime Ministers
   Leaders of Opposition in Rajya Sabha and Lok Sabha

7A. Holders of Bharat Ratna decoration

8. Ambassadors Extraordinary and Plenipotentiary and High Commissioners of Commonwealth countries accredited to India
   Chief Ministers of states (outside their respective states)
   Governors of states (outside their respective states)
9. Judges of Supreme Court

9A. Chief Election Commissioner
   Comptroller and Auditor General of India

10. Deputy Chairman, Rajya Sabha
    Deputy Chief Ministers of States
    Deputy Speaker, Lok Sabha
    Members of the Planning Commission
    Ministers of State of the Union and any other Minister in the Ministry of Defence for defence matters
11. Attorney General of India
    Cabinet Secretary
    Lieutenant Governors (within their respective Union Territories)
12. Chiefs of Staff holding the rank of full General or equivalent rank
13. Envoys Extraordinary and Ministers Plenipotentiary accredited to India
14. Chairmen and Speakers of state Legislatures within their respective states
    Chief Justices of High Courts within their respective jurisdictions
15. Cabinet Ministers in states within their respective states
    Chief Ministers of Union territories and Chief Executive Councilor, Delhi, within their respective Union territories
    Deputy Ministers of the Union
16. Officiating Chiefs of Staff holding the rank of Lieutenant General or equivalent rank
17. Chairman, Central Administrative Tribunal
    Chairman, Minorities Commissi-on
    Chairman, Scheduled Castes and Scheduled Tribes Commission
    Chairman, Union Public Service Commission
    Chief Justices of High Courts outside their respective jurisdictions
    Puisne Judges of High Courts within their respective jurisdictions
18. Cabinet Ministers in states outside their respective states
    Chairmen and Speakers of state Legislatures outside their respective states
    Chairman, Monopolies and Restrictive Trade Practices Commission

Deputy Chairman and Deputy Speakers of state Legislatures within their respective states
Ministers of State in states within their respective states
Ministers of Union territories and Executive Councilors, Delhi, within their respective Union territories
Speakers of Legislative Assemblies in Union territories and Chairman of Delhi Metropolitan Council within their respective Union territories

19. Chief Commissioners of Union territories not having Councils of Ministers, within their respective Union territories
Deputy Ministers in states within their respective states
Deputy Speakers of Legislative Assemblies in Union territories and Deputy Chairman of metropolitan Council Delhi, within their respective Union territories
20. Deputy Chairmen and Deputy Speakers of state legislatures, outside their respective states
Ministers of state in states outside their respective states
Puisne Judges of High Courts outside their respective jurisdictions
21. Members of Parliament
22. Deputy Ministers in state outside their respective states
23. Army Commanders/Vice-Chief of the Army Staff or equivalent in other services
Chief Secretaries to state governments within their respective states
Commissioner for Linguistic Minorities
Commissioner for Scheduled Castes and Scheduled Tribes
Members, Minorities Commission
Members, Scheduled Castes and Scheduled Tribes Commission
Officers of the rank of full General or equivalent rank
Secretaries to the Government of India (including officers holding this office ex-officio)
Secretary, Minorities Commission
Secretary, Scheduled Castes and Scheduled Tribes Commission
Secretary to the President
Secretary to the Prime Minister
Secretary, Rajya Sabha/Lok Sabha
Solicitor General
Vice-Chairman, Central Administrative Tribunal
24. Officers of the rank of Lieutenant General or equivalent rank
25. Additional Secretaries to the Government of India
Additional Solicitor General
Advocate Generals of states
Chairman, Tariff Commission
Charge d' Affairs and Acting High Commissioners a pied and ad interim
Chief Ministers of Union territories and Chief Executive Councillor, Delhi, outside their respective Union territories
Chief Secretaries of state governments outside their respective states
Deputy Comptroller and Auditor General
Deputy Speakers of Legislative Assemblies in Union territories and Deputy Chairman, Delhi Metropolitan Council, outside their respective Union territories
Director, Central Bureau of Investigation
Director General, Border Security Force
Director General, Central Reserve Police
Director, Intelligence Bureau
Lieutenant Governor outside their respective Union territories
Members, Central Administrative Tribunal
Members, Monopolies and Restrictive Trade Practices Commission
Members, Union Public Service Commission

Ministers of Union territories and Executive Councillors, Delhi, outside their respective Union territories
Principal Staff Officers of the Armed Forces of the rank of major General or equivalent rank
Speakers of Legislative Assemblies in Union territories and Chairman of Delhi, Metropolitan Council, outside their respective Union territories

26. Joint Secretaries to the Government of India and officers of equivalent rank
Officers of the rank of Major-General or equivalent rank

Party Position in Lok Sabha in 2006

S.No.	Name of Party	Members	Leader
1.	Indian National Congress (INC)	146	Pranab Mukherjee
2.	Bharatiya Janata Party (BJP)	128	L.K. Advani
3.	Communist Party of India (Marxist) (CPI(M))	42	Basudeb Acharia
4.	Samajwadi Party (SP)	38	Prof. Ram Gopal Yadav
5.	Rashtriya Janata Dal (RJD)	23	Lalu Prasad
6.	Dravida Munnetra Kazhagam (DMK)	16	C. Kuppusami
7.	Bahujan Samaj Party (BSP)	15	Rajesh Verma
8.	Shiv Sena (SS)	12	Anant Geete
9.	Biju Janata Dal (BJD)	11	Braja Kishore Tripathy
10.	Communist Party of India (CPI)	10	Gurudas Dasgupta
11.	Nationalist Congress Party (NCP)	10	–
12.	Shiromani Akali Dal (SAD)	8	Sukhdev Singh Dhindsa
13.	Janata Dal (United) (JD(U))	7	Prabhunath Singh
14.	Pattali Makkal Katchi (PMK)	6	Prof. M. Ramadass
15.	Telangana Rashtra Samithi (TRS)	5	K. Chandrashekar Rao
16.	Jharkhand Mukti Morcha (JMM)	5	–
17.	Independent (Ind.)	5	–
18.	Telugu Desam Party (TDP)	4	K. Yerrannaidu
19.	Lok Jan Shakti Party (LJSP)	4	Ram Vilas Paswan
20.	Marumalarchi Dravida Munnetra Kazhagam (MDMK)	4	L. Ganesan
21.	Rashtriya Lok Dal (RLD)	3	–
22.	Revolutionary Socialist Party (RSP)	3	Joachim Baxla
23.	Janata Dal (Secular) (JD(S))	3	M.P. Veerendra Kumar
24.	Kerala Congress (KEC)	2	P.C. Thomas
25.	Jammu and Kashmir National Conference (J&KNC)	2	–
26.	All-India Forward Bloc (FBL)	2	–
27.	Asom Gana Parishad (AGP)	2	Dr Arun Kumar Sarma
28.	All-India Majlis-E-Ittehadul Muslimmen (AIMIM)	1	Shri Asaduddin Owaisi
29.	All-India Trinamool Congress (AITC)	1	Mamata Banerjee

30.	Bharatiya Navshakti Party (BNP)	1	Delkar Mohanbhai Sanjibhai
31.	Jammu and Kashmir Peoples Democratic Party (J&KPDP)	1	Mehbooba Mufti
32.	Sikkim Democratic Front (SDF)	1	Nakul Das Rai
33.	Samajwadi Janata Party (Rashtriya) (SJP(R))	1	Chandra Shekhar
34.	Republican Party of India (A) (RPI(A))	1	Athawale Ramdas Bandu
35.	National Loktantrik Party (NLP)	1	Baleshwar Yadav
36.	Nagaland Peoples Front (NPF)	1	W. Wangyuh
37.	Muslim League Kerala State Committee (MLKSC)	1	E. Ahmed
38.	Mizo National Front (MNF)	1	Vanlalzawma
	Vacant	18	
	Total Members:	545	

Political Parties in India

Akhil Bharatiya Loktantrik Congress (ABLC)
All-India Anna Dravida Munnetra Kazhagam (AIADMK)
All-India Forward Bloc (AIFB)
All-India Majlis-(e)-Ittehadul Muslimeen (AIMEIM)
All-India Trinamool Congress (AITC)
Asom Gana Parishad (AGP)
Bahujan Samaj Party (BSP)
Bhartiya Janata Party (BJP)
Bhartiya Navshakti Party (BNP)
Bharipa Bahujan Mahasangh (BBM)
Biju Janata Dal (BJD)
Communist Party of India (CPI)
Communist Party of India (Marxist) (CPI[M])
Communist Party of India (ML) Liberation (CPI [ML] L)
Dravida Munnetra Kazhagam (DMK)
Haryana Vikas Party (HVP)
Himachal Vikas Congress (HVC)
Indian Federal Democratic Party (IFDP)
Indian National Congress (INC)
Indian National Lok Dal (INLD)
Jammu & Kashmir National Conference (J&KNC)
Janata Dal (JP) (JD [JP])
Janata Dal (Secular) (JD [S])
Janata Dal (United) (JD[U])
Jharkhand Mukti Morcha (JMM)
Kerala Congress (KC)
Lok Dal (Secular) (LD [S])
Lok Jan Shakti Party (LJSP)
Marumalarchi Dravida Munnetra Kazhagam (MDMK)
Mizo National Front (MNF)
Muslim League (ML)
Nagaland Peoples Front (NPF)
Nationalist Congress Party (NCP)
Pattali Makkal Katchi (PMK)
Peasants and Workers Party of India (PWP)
Peoples Democratic Party (PDP)
Rashtriya Janata Dal (RJD)
Rashtriya Janata Dal (Democratic) (RJD [D])
Rashtriya Lok Dal (RLD)
Republican Party of India (A) (RPI [A])
Revolutionary Socialist Party (RSP)
Samajwadi Janata Party (Rashtriya) (SJP [R])
Samajwadi Party (SJP)
Samata Party (SP)
Shiromani Akali Dal (SAD)
Shiromani Akali Dal (SS Mann) (SAD [M])
Shiv Sena (SS)
Sikkim Democratic Front (SDF)
Swatantra Bharat Paksh (SBP)
Telangana Rashtra Samiti (TRS)
Telugu Desam Party (TDP)

National Parties

Name	Symbol
1. Bharatiya Janata Party	Lotus
2. Bahujan Samaj Party	Elephant
3. Communist Party of India	Ears of Corn and Sickle
4. Communist Party of India (Marxist)	Hammer Sickle and Star
5. Indian National Congress	Hand
6. Nationalist Congress Party	Clock

Assembly Elections 2005-06

Assam: After the May 2006 elections in Assam, Tarun Gogoi was sworn in for his second consecutive term as the chief minister, heading Assam's first coalition government led by the Congress. The Hagrama faction of the Bodoland People's Progressive Front, NCP and Independents support the government.

Party Positions

Name of the Party	Seats
Indian National Congress	53
Bharatiya Janata Party	10
Communist Party of India (Marxist)	2
Nationalist Congress Party	1
Communist Party of India	1
Asom Gana Parishad	24
Assam United Democratic Front	10
Asom Gana Parishad Pragtisheel	1
Autonomous State Demand Committee	1
Loko Sanmilon	1
Independent	22
Total	**126**

Bihar: In November 2005, the fifteen-year uninterrupted reign of Rashtriya Janata Dal (RJD) in Bihar came to an end with the Janata Dal (United)–Bharatiya Janata Party alliance securing 142 seats in the 243-member state assembly. In the February 2005 elections, the JD (U) had bagged fifty-five seats, the BJP thirty-seven, the RJD seventy-five, the LJP twenty-nine and the Congress ten. Despite several attempts, government formation was not possible because Ram Vilas Paswan of the LJP refused to align with either the RJD or the BJP. The Assembly was kept in suspended animation and dissolved in May.

Party Position

Party	Seats
Janata Dal (U)	88
Bharatiya Janata Party	55
Rashtriya Janata Dal	54
Communist Party of India	3
Communist Party of India-Marxist	1
Indian National Congress	9
Lok Jan Shakti Party	10
Communist Party of India (ML)(L)	5
Samajwadi Party	2
Nationalist Congress Party	1
Bahujan Samaj Party	4
Independents	10
Total	**243**

Kerala: In the May 2006 Assembly Elections a CPI (M)-led Left Democratic Front beat the incumbent Congress-led United Democratic Front by a margin of fifty-six seats.

Party Positions

Name of the Party	Seats
Communist Party of India (Marxist)	60
Indian National Congress	25
Communist Party of India	17
Nationalist Congress Party	1
Muslim League Kerala State Committee	7
Kerala Congress (M)	7

Name of the Party	Seats
Janata Dal (Secular)	5
Kerala Congress	4
Revolutionary Socialist Party	3
Janadhipathya Samrakshana Samithi	1
Democratic Indira Congress (Karunakaran)	1
Indian National League	1
Kerala Congress (B)	1
Congress (Secular)	1
Kerala Congress Secular	1
Independent	5
Total	140

Pondicherry: In the 2006 Assembly elections in Pondicherry the Congress-led alliance won twenty-one out of thirty seats.

Party positions

Name of the Party	Seats
Indian National Congress	10
Communist Party of India	1
Dravida Munnetra Kazhagam	7
All-India Anna Dravida Munnetra Kazhagam	3
Pattali Makkal Katchi	2
Marumalarchi Dravida Munnetra Kazhagam	1
Pudhucherry Munnetra Congress	3
Independent	3
Total	30

Tamil Nadu: In the Assembly Elections held in May 2006, Tamil Nadu voters, for the first time since 1967, turned in a poll decision that necessitated a coalition government. The ruling party AIADMK was voted out of power, with the DMK-led alliance regaining power after losing out in the previous elections with only thirty-seven seats. DMK chief, M. Karunanidhi, who led the DMK-led Democratic Progressive Alliance to victory, became the chief minister for the fifth time, heading a minority government with the DMK's allies—Congress, PMK and the Left parties—extending support from outside.

Party Positions

Name of the Party	Seats
Indian National Congress	34
Communist Party of India (Marxist)	9
Communist Party of India	6
Dravida Munnetra Kazhagam	96
All-India Anna Dravida Munnetra Kazhagam	61
Pattali Makkal Katchi	18
Marumalarchi Dravida Munnetra Kazhagam	6
Viduthalai Chiruthaigal Katch	2
Desiya Murpokku Dravida Kazhagam	1
Independent	1
Total	234

West Bengal: The CPI(M)-led Left Front won the 2006 West Bengal Assembly Elections for a historic seventh term.

Party Positions

Name of the Party	Seats
Communist Party of India (Marxist)	176
Indian National Congress	21
Communist Party of India	8
All-India Trinamool Congress	30
All-India Forward Bloc	23
Revolutionary Socialist Party	20
Rashtriya Janata Dal	1
West Bengal Socialist Party	4
Gorkha National Liberation Front	3
Jharkhand Party	1
Democratic Socialist Party	1
Independent	6
Total	294

Chief Election Commissioners of India

Name	Tenure
Sukumar Sen	21 March 1950–19 December 1958
K.V.K. Sundaram	20 December 1958–30 September 1967
S.P. Sen Verma	1 October 1967–30 September 1972
Dr Nagendra Singh	1 October 1972–6 February 1973
T. Swaminathan	7 February 1973–17 June 1977
S.L. Shakdhar	18 June 1977–17 June 1982
R.K. Trivedi	18 June 1982–31 December 1985
R.V.S. Peri Sastri	1 January 1986–15 November 1990
Smt V.S. Rama Devi	15 November 1990–12 December 1990
T.N. Seshan	12 December 1990–11 December 1996
M.S. Gill	12 December 1996–13 June 2001
J.M. Lyngdoh	13 June 2001–7 February 2004
T.S. Krishnamurthy	8 February 2004–15 May 2005
B.B. Tandon	16 May 2005–29 June 2006
N. Gopalaswami	29 June 2006–till date

Number of Assembly Seats in States and UTs

Name	Number of Seats
State	
Andhra Pradesh	295
Arunachal Pradesh	60
Assam	126
Bihar	243
Chhattisgarh	90
Goa	40
Gujarat	182
Haryana	90
Himachal Pradesh	68
Jammu and Kashmir	87
Jharkhand	81
Karnataka	225
Kerala	140
Madhya Pradesh	230
Maharashtra	288
Manipur	60
Meghalaya	60
Mizoram	40
Nagaland	60
Orissa	147
Punjab	117
Rajasthan	200
Sikkim	32
Tamil Nadu	234
Tripura	60
Uttaranchal	70
Uttar Pradesh	403
West Bengal	294

National Capital Territory

Delhi	70

Union Territory

Andaman and Nicobar	
Chandigarh	
Dadra and Nagar Haveli	
Daman and Diu	
Pondicherry	30

Number of Lok Sabha Seats in States and UTs

Name	Number of Seats
State	
Andhra Pradesh	42
Arunachal Pradesh	2
Assam	14
Bihar	40
Chhattisgarh	11
Goa	2
Gujarat	26
Haryana	9
Himachal Pradesh	4
Jammu and Kashmir	6
Jharkhand	14
Karnataka	28
Kerala	19
Madhya Pradesh	29
Maharashtra	47
Manipur	2
Meghalaya	2
Mizoram	1
Nagaland	1
Orissa	21
Punjab	13
Rajasthan	25
Sikkim	1
Tamil Nadu	39
Tripura	2
Uttar Pradesh	80
Uttaranchal	5
West Bengal	42
National Capital Territory	
Delhi	7

Union Territories	
Andaman and Nicobar	1
Chandigarh	1
Dadra and Nagar Haveli	1
Daman and Diu	1
Lakshadweep	1
Pondicherry	1
Others	
Nominated Members	2
Total	**542**

Number of Rajya Sabha Seats in States and UTs

Name	Number of Seats
State	
Andhra Pradesh	18
Arunachal Pradesh	1
Assam	7
Bihar	16
Chhattisgarh	5
Goa	1
Gujarat	11
Haryana	5
Himachal Pradesh	3
Jammu and Kashmir	4
Jharkhand	6
Karnataka	12
Kerala	9
Madhya Pradesh	11
Maharashtra	19
Manipur	1
Meghalaya	1
Mizoram	1
Nagaland	1
Orissa	10
Punjab	7
Rajasthan	10
Sikkim	1
Tamil Nadu	18
Tripura	1
Uttaranchal	3
Uttar Pradesh	31
West Bengal	16
National Capital Territory	
Delhi	3

Union Territories

Pondicherry	1

Others

Nominated members	12
Total	**245**

The Armed Forces

Army

The Indian Army has about 1 million personnel and thirty-four divisions. In 2002, it was estimated to have about 980,000 active troops, along with an Army Reserve consisting of 300,000 first-line troops (those within five years of full-time service) and another 500,000 second-line troops (subject to recall to service until fifty years of age). The Territorial Army has about 40,000 first-line troops and 160,000 second-line troops. The army is headquartered in New Delhi and is under the direction of the chief of the army staff, who is always a full general.

The army consists of a number of arms and services like Armoured Corps, Regiment of Artillery, Corps of Engineers, Corps of Signals, and Mechanized Infantry, among many others. It also has its own Military Nursing Service, Army Medical Corps, and Army Dental Corps. The army also has its own Recruiting Organization, Record Offices, Depots, Boys Establishments and Selection Centres and training institutions. These units are organized in twelve corps-level formations.

As of early 2002, the Indian Army was estimated to have between 3,300 and 4,900 tanks. Some estimates put the number of tanks in storage at 1,500. Such high figures of vehicles in storage make it difficult to estimate India's armoured vehicle inventory. The Indian Army operates indigenously manufactured Vijayanta tanks as well as T-55, T-72, T-72M1 and PT-76 tanks. The army plans to phase out the Vijayanta and T-55 tanks by 2010 and replace them with upgraded T-72M1s and T-90 tanks. The new Russian T-90 tanks (re-christened Bhishma) are being inducted into the army. The army has also ordered 124 models of the indigenously developed Arjun main battle tank. The army possesses sizeable artillery forces, with estimates placing the army's towed artillery capabilities at over 4,000 pieces. The army also has self-propelled artillery and field guns, howitzers, multi-barrel rocket launchers like the indigenous Pinaka and surface-to-air missiles.

Navy

The Indian Navy is one of the largest navies in the world. It is a three-dimensional force equipped with sophisticated missile-capable warships, aircraft carriers, advanced submarines and aircraft. A large number of the warships are of indigenous design and have been constructed in Indian shipyards. The navy also possesses modern dockyard facilities with state-of-the-art technology. At present, the navy has two major naval bases at Mumbai and Visakhapatnam. The naval headquarters is in New Delhi and is under the command of the chief of naval staff who is a full admiral.

In 1994, the total strength of the navy was estimated to be 54,000, including 5,000 naval aviation personnel and 1,000 marines. The navy currently operates one aircraft carrier (INS Viraat), over forty surface combatants, and more than a dozen submarines. However, the navy faces the challenges of an ageing fleet and a slow rate of replacement of ships and aircraft.

India also has a coast guard service, organized along the lines of the US Coast Guard. Besides the aircraft carrier, the navy also has cruisers, destroyers, frigates, minesweepers, survey ships, store carriers, tankers, and submarines. It also has shore establishments like training institutions, dockyard, storage deposits and other technical and administrative establishments. The navy also has a separate Aviation Wing consisting of Naval Air Stations and a Fleet Requirement Unit. The Indian Navy is under the command of the Chief of Naval Staff (CNS), located in New Delhi. It consists of two fleets, each commanded by a Rear Admiral. The Eastern Fleet is primarily based in Visakhapatnam on the Bay of Bengal. The Western Fleet is primarily based in Mumbai on the Arabian Sea.

In addition to the principal naval commands, there are three large subcommands under the direct charge of flag officers. These are:

1. Naval Aviation and Goa Area (in Goa)
2. Submarines (in Visakhapatnam), and
3. 'Fortress' in the Andaman and Nicobar Islands (Port Blair).

The navy has recently made a number of significant acquisitions. These include the Russian aircraft carrier Admiral Gorshkov (along with MiG-29K fighter jets that will operate out of the ship). The vessel is currently undergoing retrofitting in Russia and is expected to be ready by 2008-9. It has been reported that India has entered into an agreement with Russia for the lease-purchase of Russian Akula-class nuclear-powered submarines (SSNs). The first submarine would reportedly be delivered by 2005. However, both Indian and Russian authorities have refused to comment on these reports. Other recent significant acquisitions include the Talwar-class frigate, *INS Tabar* and the stealth frigate *INS Satpura*. Construction projects that are either underway or planned include the indigenous aircraft carrier, the 'Air Defence Ship', French Scorpene submarines and more stealth frigates.

Air Force

The Indian Air Force is one of the world's largest air forces with over 600 combat aircraft and more than 500 transports and helicopters. In 1994, it was estimated to have 110,000 personnel. The air force is headquartered in New Delhi and is headed by the chief of air staff, an air chief marshal.

The air force operates a wide variety of aircraft, support equipment, weapon systems, communication and detection systems. The aircraft in the air force inventory include air superiority fighters like the MiG-29 and MiG-23 aircraft, multi-role combat aircraft like the Sukhoi SU-30 and Mirage 2000 aircraft, tactical strike fighter aircraft like MiG-27, strategic reconnaissance aircraft like MiG-25, multirole fighter and ground attack aircraft like MiG-21, and deep penetration strike aircraft like Jaguar. It also uses older generation aircraft like Hunter and Canberra (tactical bomber and interdictor) but in ancillary roles. The transport fleet of the air force consists of aircraft like Ilyushin IL-76, Antonov AN-32 and AVRO and Dornier 228 aircraft. The air force also has Boeing 737 aircraft that are used for VIP transport. The helicopter fleet consists of Cheetah and Chetak helicopters, Mi-17 and Mi-26 helicopters as well as attack helicopters like Mi-25 and Mi-35. Newly inducted aircraft include IL-78 mid-air refueling tanker aircraft and the indigenous Dhruv Advanced Light Helicopter. India also intends to acquire more Mirage 2000-5 aircraft. The indigenous Light Combat Aircraft is undergoing development. India has also entered into a deal with UK for 66 Hawk Advanced Jet Trainer aircraft and for the Israeli Phalcon AWACS system.

Indian Missiles

The Defense Research and Development Laboratory (DRDL) is India's premier missile facility. India's ministry of defence initially constituted the Special Weapons Development Team in 1958 to undertake the development of first-generation anti-tank missiles. In 1961, the group was expanded to form the DRDL. In the 1970s, the DRDL undertook two additional projects. The first, Project Valiant, involved the development of a long-range ballistic missile. The second, Project Devil, was aimed at reverse engineering the Soviet SA-2 surface-to-air missile. Both projects were considered failures and came to be viewed by India's armed services and the government as competence-building exercises. Project Valiant was terminated in 1974; Project Devil ended in 1980. However, during the period 1972-80, the DRDL developed the infrastructure and facilities to undertake the design and development of missiles. The Indian government revived the missile programme during the 1980s under the rubric of the Integrated Guided Missile Development Programme (IGMDP). The IGMDP was launched in 1983 with the objective of developing five missile systems simultaneously. These included:

- Trishul
- Akash
- Nag
- Prithvi
- Agni-I

In the 1990s, the missile programme was expanded to include the development of:

- Agni II
- Surya
- Dhanush
- Sagarika
- Astra

List of Indians Missiles (Operational)

Name	Type	Range	First Test Fired From
Prithvi-I	Short Range Ballistic Missile	150 km	Sriharikota (1988)
Prithvi-II	Short Range Ballistic Missile	250 km	Balasore (1996)
Prithvi-III	Short Range Ballistic Missile	350–600 km	Balasore (2004)
Agni-I	Strategic Ballistic Missile	850 km	Chandipur (1992)
Agni-II	Strategic Ballistic Missile	3300 km	Balasore (1999)
Agni-III	Strategic Ballistic Missile	5500 km	Balasore (2006)
Akash	Medium Range Surface-to-Air Missile	60 km	Balasore (1990)
Trishul	Short Range Surface-to-Air Missile	12 km	Balasore (1983)
Nag	Anti-Tank Guided Missile	6 km	Balasore (1990)
Astra	Beyond Visual Range Air-to-Air Missile	80 km	Balasore (2003)

Chiefs of Armed Forces

Commanders-in-Chief

Gen. Sir Roy Bucher (1948–49)
Gen. K.M. Cariappa (1949–53)
Gen. Maharaj Rajendra Singhji (1953–55)

Chiefs of Army Staff

Gen. Maharaj Rajendra Singhji (1955–55)
Gen. S.M. Srinagesh (1955–57)
Gen. K.S. Thimayya, (1957–61)
Gen. P.N. Thapar (1961–62)
Gen. J.N. Chaudhuri (1962–66)
Gen P. K. Kumaramangalam (1966–69)
Gen. S.H.E.J. Manekshaw (1969–72)
Field Marshal S.H.E.J. Manekshaw (1972–73)
Gen. G.G. Bewoor (1973–75)
Gen. TN. Raina (1975–78)
Gen. O.P. Malhotra (1978–81)
Gen. K.V Krishna Rao (1981–83)
Gen. A.S. Vaidya (1983–86)
Gen. K. Sundarjee (1986–88)

Gen. V.N. Sharma (1988–90)
Gen. S.F. Rodrigues (1990–93)
Gen. B.C. Joshi (1993–94)
Gen. Shankar Roy Choudhury (1994–97)
Gen. V.P. Malik (1997–2000)
Gen. S. Padmanashan (2000–02)
Gen. N.C. Vij (2003–05)
Gen. J.J. Singh (2005–till date)

Chiefs of Naval Staff

Vice-Admiral R.D. Katari (1958–62)
Vice-Admiral B.S. Soman (1962–66)
Admiral A.K. Chatterjee (1966–70)
Admiral S.M. Nanda (1970–73)
Admiral S.N. Kohli (1973–76)
Admiral J.L. Cursetji (1976–79)
Admiral R.L. Pereira (1979–82)
Admiral O.S. Dawson (1982–84)
Admiral R.H. Tahiliani (1984–87)
Admiral J.G. Nadkarni (1987–90)
Admiral L. Ramdas (1990–92)
Admiral V.S. Shekhawat (1992–96)
Admiral Vishnu Bhagwat (1996–99)
Admiral Sushil Kumar (1999–2001)
Admiral Madhvendra Singh (2001–04)
Admiral Arun Prakash (2004–till date)

Chiefs of Air Staff

Air Marshal Sir Thomas Emhirst (1947–50)
Air Marshal Sir R.L.Chapman (1950–51)
Air Marshal Sir Gerald Gibbs (1951–54)
Air Marshal S. Mukherjee (1954–60)
Air Marshal A.M. Engineer (1960–64)
Air Chief Marshal Arjan Singh (1964–69)
Air Chief Marshal P.C. Lal (1969—73)
Air Chief Marshal O.P. Mehra (1973–76)
Air Chief Marshal H. Moolgaonkar (1976–78)
Air Chief Marshal I.H. Latif (1978–81)
Air Chief Marshal Dilbagh Singh (1981–84)
Air Chief Marshal L.K. Katre (1984–85)
Air Chief Marshal D.A. La Fontaine (1985–88)
Air Chief Marshal S.K. Mehra (1988–91)
Air Chief Marshal N.C. Suri (1991–93)
Air Chief Marshal S.K. Kaul (1993–95)
Air Chief Marshal Satish Kr Sateen (1995–98)
Air Chief Marshal A.Y. Tipnis (1999–2001)
Air Chief Marshal S. Krishnaswamy (2001–05)
Air Chief Marshal S.P Tyagi (2005–till date)

Political News–India

Raj Thackeray Quits Shiv Sena

On 18 December 2005, Raj Thackeray, nephew of Bal Thackeray, quit the Shiv Sena. On 27 November, Raj Thackeray resigned as Shiv Sena leader and president of the Bharatiya Vidyarthi Sena, the party's youth wing. Raj Thackeray founded his own party Maharashtra Navnirman Sena on 9 March 2006 in Mumbai.

BJP Suspends Uma Bharati

Uma Bharti was suspended from the primary membership of the Bharatiya Janata Party (BJP) by the party's parliamentary board, which met at the BJP headquarters in New Delhi in November 2005. She was suspended for 'her conduct and statements' regarding leadership change in Madhya Pradesh. She was suspended earlier from the party in November 2004 when she allegedly dared the then-BJP president L.K. Advani to take action against her at a meeting of party's central office-bearers. A month later the suspension was revoked when she apologized.

Operation Duryodhana

A sting operation, codenamed Operation Duryodhana, on a private TV channel, allegedly unearthed eleven MPs accepting cash for asking questions in Parliament. Spread over eight months, Operation Duryodhana logged more than fifty-six video and seventy audio tapes, besides recording more than 900 phone calls. Posing as representatives of a fictitious lobbying organization 'North Indian Small Manufacturers Association', two journalists allegedly unearthed the nexus between MPs and their middlemen and succeeded in having MPs, across party lines, submit more than sixty questions in Parliament's rigorous question balloting system. As a result, many MPs were suspended from their respective legislature wings.

Lal Krishna Advani Resigns as BJP President

Lal Krishna Advani resigned as Bharatiya Janata Party president on 31 December 2005 and formally declared that his successor would be Rajnath Singh. The new chief took charge at the BJP headquarters in New Delhi on 2 January 2006. Following a visit to Pakistan in 2005, Advani came under pressure from hardliners who were angered by comments he made about Pakistan's founder, Mohammed Ali Jinnah.

Buta Singh Quits

Bihar governor, Buta Singh, sent in his resignation to President A.P.J. Abdul Kalam on 26 January 2006 after hoisting the national flag and taking the salute at the Republic Day parade in Patna. This followed the Supreme Court's strictures against him on the dissolution of the Bihar Assembly. The Supreme Court held him guilty of misleading the Cabinet that the fractured verdict of the February 2005 Assembly poll had prevented any party or group from staking claim to form a government.

Samajwadi Party Suspends Raj Babbar

The parliamentary board of Samajwadi Party suspended Raj Babbar on 7 February 2006 for anti-party activities after the actor-turned-politician criticized party general secretary Amar Singh and demanded his removal. He accused Amar Singh of promoting 'broker culture' and 'maligning' the socialist moorings of the party.

Bharatiya Janata Party Suspends Madan Lal Khurana

BJP president Rajnath Singh, in consultation with senior party leaders, suspended former Delhi chief minister Madan Lal Khurana from the primary membership on 19 March 2006. The suspension came in the wake of Khurana's announcement at a press conference that he was going to join the 'Janadesh rally' being organized by expelled BJP leader and former Madhya Pradesh chief minister, Uma Bharti, in Delhi on 21 March.

Madhu Koda sworn in as new Jharkhand Chief Minister

On September 2006, Madhu Koda, an Independent, was sworn in as the new Jharkhand chief minister. This marked the end of a fortnight-long political crisis that saw the fall of the BJP-led coalition ahead of a trust vote. Three others, Kamlesh Singh of NCP and Independent MLAs Enos Ekka and Harinarain Rai who along with Koda moved against the Arjun Munda-led NDA government, were sworn in as ministers. Koda has the support of forty-two legislators in a house of eighty-two members. This was the state's fifth swearing-in in less than six years of its existence. Arjun Munda was chief minister twice. Babulal Marandi was the first chief minister and Shibu Soren headed the government for a short duration of nine days.

Political News–World

Angela Merkel is Elected the First Chancellor of Germany

Angela Merkel, leader of the Christian Democrats (CDU), was elected as Germany's eighth leader since World War II, by a coalition of the CDU/CSU and SPD delegates in the Federal Assembly (Bundestag). She succeeded Gerhard Schroeder, the two-term chancellor and a critic of US policy in Iraq. Merkel is the first female Chancellor of Germany. She has set a goal of returning Germany within ten years to being one the top three countries in Europe for economic growth and slashing the 11 per cent unemployment rate during her four-year term.

General Election of Iraqi National Assembly

Following the ratification of the Constitution of Iraq on 15 October 2005, a general election was held on 15 December to elect a permanent 275-member Iraqi National Assembly. The Independent Electoral Commission of Iraq released uncertified results on 20 January 2006. Iraq's most powerful Shiite Muslim alliance, led by religious parties, won the most seats but not a clear majority in the nation's first constitutional parliament. Of 275 seats in the Council of Representatives, the United Iraqi Alliance won 128 seats, while the Kurdish bloc of candidates was second with fifty-three seats. The tallies suggest that more Sunnis took part in the December vote after boycotting earlier elections.

Silvio Berlusconi Resigns as PM of Italy

On 2 May 2006 Silvio Berlusconi formally resigned as prime minister of Italy, paving the way for Romano Prodi to form a new government of the centre-left. The centre-right leader handed in his notice to President Carlo Azeglio Ciampi. In office for five years, Berlusconi served longer than any other Italian prime minister in the past fifty years. However, his popularity suffered as Italy's economy stagnated, the rate of inflation crept up and unemployment hovered around 10 per cent. Romano Prodi has promised a review of government finance, better tax collection and the re-introduction of inheritance tax on the country's wealthiest people.

Kuwait Holds Parliamentary Election, the Country's first with Universal Suffrage

Kuwait held a parliamentary election on 29 June 2006. The voters selected the fifty members of the country's National Assembly. For the first time, universal suffrage was in force, and all Kuwaiti citizens at least twenty-one years of age were allowed to participate. It is estimated that there are around 340,000 people eligible to vote in Kuwait. Total turnout was 66.4 per cent. Though 57 per cent of eligible Kuwaiti women registered to vote, turnout was a mere 35 per cent. There were no parties, but thirty-six of the fifty elected candidates were described as reformers. Women failed to win any seats in their first attempt to compete in parliamentary elections. The opposition, a loose alliance of reformists, liberals and Islamists, made gains, winning nearly two-thirds of the seats.

Elections in the Democratic Republic of Congo

The Democratic Republic of Congo held its first presidential and legislative multi-party elections in forty years on 30 July 2006. It was the first fully-democratic poll since independence from Belgium in 1960. But no clear winner emerged; Joseph Kabila and his opposition rival, Jean-Pierre Bemba, will contest a run-off vote in October 2006. Presently, Joseph Kabila heads an interim government, formed in June 2003, which includes members of former rebel groups, opposition politicians and Kabila loyalists.

Islamic Republic of Afghanistan Becomes Member of SAARC

On 13 November 2005, the thirteenth SAARC Summit in Dhaka issued a declaration to admit the Islamic republic of Afghanistan as a member, and to accord observer status to China and Japan. Afghanistan has become the eighth member of the South Asian Association for Regional Cooperation (SAARC), launched in Dhaka in 1985 with founding members Bangladesh, Bhutan, India, the Maldives, Nepal, Pakistan and Sri Lanka. The nations also agreed to organize development funds under a single financial institution with a permanent secretariat that would cover all SAARC programmes ranging from social, to infrastructure, to economic ones. On 2 August 2006, foreign ministers of SAARC countries decided to include the US, South Korea and the EU as observers at future SAARC summits.

UK's Terrorism Act 2006 Comes into Force

The Terrorism Act 2006, which came into force in UK in April 2006, made it illegal to glorify terrorism and distribute terrorist publications. The Act states that groups or organizations can be banned for these offences and covers anyone who gives or receives training on terrorism. The act also designates nuclear sites as areas where trespass can become a terrorist offence. The bill was introduced after the 7 July 2005 bomb attacks in London. However, Liberal Democrat and Conservative MPs voted against the Terrorism Bill, saying existing legislation already covered the glorification offence.

Thailand Crisis

On 19 September 2006, the Royal Thai Army staged a coup against the government of Prime Minister Thaksin Shinawatra. The coup, which was Thailand's first in fifteen years, followed a year-long political crisis involving Thaksin and political opponents and occurred less than a month before elections were scheduled to be held, on 15 October. The military postponed the upcoming elections, suspended the Constitution, dissolved Parliament, banned protests and all political activities, suppressed and censored media outlets, declared martial law, and arrested Cabinet members. The coup was bloodless, with no casualties reported. Gen Sonthi Boonyaratglin, leader of the Administrative Reform Council, told foreign diplomats that a civilian government and prime minister would be appointed to run the country within two weeks. The Constitution would be amended for a rapid return to democracy through a national election in a year's time. On 3 October, Gen. Surayud Chulanont became the new prime minister of Thiland.

Shinzo Abe Japan's New Prime Minister

In September 2006, Nationalist Shinzo Abe became the new prime minister of Japan. He got 339 votes out of 475 counted in the lower house, and 136 ballots out of 240 in the upper house. He started his political career as his father's secretary in 1982 and debuted in Japanese political circles in 1993, winning a House of Representatives seat by running in a constituency in Yamaguchi Prefecture. He was appointed deputy chief Cabinet secretary in the second Cabinet of Prime Minister Yoshiro Mori in 2000. He pledged to cut government spending, double foreign investment in the country, revise the pacifist constitution and end the debate over the nation's military.

Tony Blair Announces His Stepping Down

Tony Blair recently announced that he would step down as prime minister of UK within the next twelve months. He also apologized for Labour's conduct in recent days. The next general election will be held by 2010 at the latest. When Blair steps aside, Labour members will vote for a new leader. If Chancellor Gordon Brown is selected, as is expected, he will automatically become prime minister as the head of the largest party in Parliament. Although he has effectively been the second-ranking official in the country for more than nine years, Brown's supporters want him to have enough time to prove his command of the top job before facing David Cameron, leader of the Conservative Party, in the general election.

2006 Nobel Peace Prize Goes to Muhammad Yunus and Grameen Bank

On 13 October 2006, the 2006 Nobel Prize for Peace was awarded to Muhammad Yunus and Grameen Bank of Bangladesh for developing micro-credit as an instrument in the struggle against poverty. The Nobel Committee commended Yunus and Grameen Bank 'for their efforts to create economic and social development from below'.

Muhammad Yunus has shown himself to be a leader who has managed to translate visions into practical action for the benefit of millions of people, not only in Bangladesh, but also in many other countries. Loans to poor people without any financial security had appeared to be an impossible idea. From modest beginnings three decades ago, Yunus has, first and foremost through Grameen Bank, developed micro-credit into an ever more important instrument in the struggle against poverty. Grameen Bank has been a source of ideas and models for the many institutions in the field of micro-credit that have sprung up around the world. Yunus and Grameen Bank have shown that even the poorest of the poor can work to bring about their own development.

Micro-credit has proved to be an important liberating force in societies where women in particular have to struggle against repressive social and economic conditions. Economic growth and political democracy cannot achieve their full potential unless the female half of humanity participates on an equal footing with the male.

Yunus's long-term vision is to eliminate poverty in the world. That vision cannot be realized by means of micro-credit alone. But Muhammad Yunus and Grameen Bank have shown that, in the continuing efforts to achieve it, micro-credit must play a major part.

Economy

Indian Economy

The Indian economy has witnessed significant growth in recent years, with a new industrial resurgence, increased investment, modest inflation in spite of spiralling global crude prices, rapid growth in exports and imports with a widening current account deficit, the laying of some institutional foundations for faster development of physical infrastructure, progress in fiscal consolidation, and the launching of the National Rural Employment Guarantee (NREG) Scheme for inclusive growth and social security. Solid macro-economic fundamentals and optimistic future prospects have boosted the government's confidence to introduce further reforms and liberalization. This confidence is reflected in the further reduction of peak custom duties to bring them in line with the rates in south-east Asian countries, raising the ceiling on foreign investments in core sectors, passing of a new law on SEZs, with flexible labour laws, all of which are aimed at giving a big push to exports and foreign direct investment inflows into the country. In a robust demonstration of its nascent strengths, the Indian economy, after growing at 8.5 per cent and 7.5 per cent in the two previous years, is projected to grow at 8.1 per cent in the current year. The growth of Gross Domestic Product (GDP) at constant prices in excess of 8.0 per cent has been achieved by the economy in only five years of recorded history, two of which were in the last three years. According to the national income data released by the Central Statistical Organization (CSO) on 7 February 2006, the advance estimate (AE) for growth of GDP at factor cost at constant (1999-2000) prices in 2005-06, at 8.1 per cent, was up 0.6 percentage points over the 7.5 per cent growth recorded in 2004-05.The growth trend for the last three years appears to indicate the beginning of a new phase of cyclical upswing in the economy from 2003-04. The initial momentum to this new phase of expansion, in 2003-04, was provided by agriculture. After a somewhat subdued impetus from the farm sector in 2004-05, there is a moderate recovery in agricultural growth in 2005-06. This is partly because of a change in the rainfall pattern from erratic to a near-normal distribution. India has the distinction of consistent returns from the equities. Indian equities are highest across emerging Asia for the fiscal year (April 2005-March 2006). The returns from Indian equity markets have been far ahead of other emerging markets such as Mexico (52 per cent), Brazil (43 per cent) or Gulf Co-operation Council (GCC) economies, such as Kuwait (26 per cent). The bellwether BSE Sensex crossed the 12,000 mark on 20 April 2006. The number of initial public offerings (IPOs) per year, on the rise since 2002, increased from 26 to 55 between 2004 and 2005. According to Asian Development Bank, India faces two key policy challenges as the economy undergoes a structural transformation. First, it must continue consolidating its fiscal position. It will have to do so while ensuring both adequate hard infrastructure improvements to support industrial and high-skill services development, and public investment to advance rural productivity and human development. Second, it needs to improve the investment environment by lowering the cost of doing business.

Key Features of the Union Budget 2006-07

Implementation of the National Common Minimum Programme Mandate

- National Rural Employment Guarantee Scheme launched; in the current year, Rs11,700 crore to be spent to create rural employment.
- Investment rate increased from 25.3 per cent in 2002-03 to 30.1 per cent in 2004-05.

Bharat Nirman

- Against Rs 12,160 crore in the current year, Rs 18,696 crore will be provided in 2006-07 for the programme, increase of 54 per cent

North-Eastern Region (NER)

- In addition 10 per cent of the Plan budget of each ministry/department will be allocated for schemes and programmes in the North-Eastern Region (NER); for the flagship programmes allocation of Rs 4,870 crore in 2006-07; total allocation for NER is Rs.12,041 crore.

Sarva Siksha Abhiyan

- Outlay will increase from Rs 7,156 crore to Rs 10,041 crore in 2006-07; 500,000 additional classrooms will be constructed and 150,000 more teachers to be appointed; Rs 8,746 crore will be transferred to the Prarambhik Siksha Kosh from revenues through education cess.

Mid-day Meal Scheme

- Allocation will be enhanced from Rs 3,010 crore to Rs 4,813 crore.

Drinking Water and Sanitation

- 56,270 habitations and 140,000 schools will be covered in the current year; non-recurring and provision for Rajiv Gandhi National Drinking Water Mission will be increased from Rs 3,645 crore to Rs 4,680 crore.

National Rural Employment Guarantee Scheme

- Allocation of Rs 14,300 crore for rural employment in 2006-07 with Rs 11,300 crore under NREG Act and Rs 3000 crore under SGRY will be provided.

National Social Assistance Programme

- Old-age pension to destitutes above the age of sixty-five years will increase from Rs 75 per month to Rs 200 per month; Rs 1,430 crore provided for 2006-07.

Minorities

- Corpus of Maulana Azad Educational Foundation will be doubled to Rs 200 crore; Rs 16.47 crore will be contributed to strengthen equity base of National Minorities Development and Finance Corporation.

Investment

The government will provide equity support of Rs 16,901 crore and loans of Rs 2,789 crore to Central PSEs (including Railways).

Agriculture

- **Irrigation:** Outlay of Rs 4,500 crore under AIBP in 2005-06, grant component of Rs 1,680 crore; Command Area Development Programme will be revamped to allow participatory irrigation management through water users' associations; 20,000 water bodies with a command area of 1.47 million hectares identified in the first phase for repair, renovation and restoration; estimated cost Rs 4,481 crore.

- **Credit:** Farm credit increased to Rs 125,309 crore in 2004-05; expected to cross target of Rs 141,500 crore for 2005-06; to increase to Rs 175,000 crore in 2006-07 with addition of 50 lakh farmers; banks asked to open a separate window for self-help groups or joint-liability groups of tenant farmers; a one-time relief to be granted to farmers who have availed of crop loan from scheduled commercial banks.
- With effect from Kharif 2006-07 farmers will receive short-term credit at 7 per cent, with an upper limit of Rs 300,000 on the principal amount; subvention for this to be given to NABARD.
- National Agricultural Insurance Scheme to continue.
- A Special Purpose Tea Fund will be setup, expected contribution of Rs 100 crore in 2006-07.
- Central Institute of Horticulture will be established in Nagaland; National Fisheries Development Board will be constituted.

Manufacturing

- Five industries with employment opportunities identified in the manufacturing sector, these include textiles, food processing, petroleum, chemicals and petro-chemicals, leather and automobiles; in services, tourism and software can offer large number of jobs.
- Manufacturing Competitiveness Programme, including promotion of ICT, mini tool rooms, design clinics and marketing support for SMEs; implementation will be in the PPP model.
- **Textiles:** Allocation for Technology Upgradation Fund (TUF) enhanced from Rs 435 crore to Rs 535 crore; Rs 189 crore will be provided for Scheme for Integrated Textiles Parks (SITP), Jute Technology Mission will be launched; a National Jute Board to be established.
- **Handlooms:** Cluster Development approach will continue with 100 clusters to be added at a cost of Rs 50 crore in 2006-07; yarn depots will be established; a 'handloom' mark will be launched; scheme will be introduced to provide interest subsidy on term loans; provision for the handloom sector will be increased from Rs 195 crore to Rs 241 crore.
- **Food Processing Industry:** Food processing will be a priority sector for bank credit; NABARD will create a refinancing window with a corpus of Rs 1,000 crore, especially for agro-processing infrastructure and market development; National Institute of Food Technology Entrepreneurship and Management will be setup; Paddy Processing Research Centre, Thanjavur, will be developed into a national-level institute.
- **Petroleum, Chemicals and Petro-chemicals:** A task force set up to facilitate development of large PC&P Investment Regions; three such Investment Regions will be developed in 2006-07.
- **Small and Medium Enterprises:** 180 items identified for dereservation; corpus of Credit Guarantee Fund will be raised from Rs 1,132 crore to Rs 2,500 crore in five years; Credit Guarantee Trust for Small Industries

will be advised to reduce guarantee fee from 2.5 per cent to 1.5 per cent for all loans; insurance cover will be extended to 30,000 borrowers.

Services Sector

- **Tourism:** Development of fifteen tourist destinations and circuits will be taken up; fifty villages with core competency in handicrafts, handlooms and culture, close to existing destinations and circuits, will be identified and developed; Plan allocation increased from Rs 786 crore to Rs 830 crore.
- **Foreign Trade:** Share in world exports is targeted to be doubled by 2008-09.

Infrastructure

- **Telecommunication:** Will reach 250 million connections by December 2007, provision of Rs 1,500 crore for Universal Services Obligation Fund in 2006-07; more than 50 million rural connections will be rolled out in three years.
- **Power:** Five ultra mega power projects of 4,000 MW each will be awarded before 31 December 2006; to create an enabling and empowered framework to carry out reforms an Empowered Committee of Chief Ministers and Power Ministers will be setup 10,000 village s in 2005-06 and 40,000 more villages in 2006-07 will be electrified.
- **Coal:** Reserves of 20 billion tons will be de-blocked for power projects; definition of captive consumption will be amended to allow mining by producers with firm supply contracts with steel, cement and power companies; capacity of Central Mines Planning and Development Institute Limited to drill in order to prove reserves will be expanded.
- **Petroleum:** under NELP VI., fifty-five blocks and area of 355,000 sq. km offered; investment of Rs 22,000 crore expected in the refinery sector in the next few years.
- **Road Transport:** Budget support for NHDP enhanced from Rs 9,320 crore to Rs 9,945 crore in 2006-07; special accelerated road development programme for the north-eastern region at an estimated cost of Rs 4,618 crore approved with allocation of Rs 550 crore in 2006-07; 1,000 km of access-controlled expressways will be developed on the Design, Build, Finance and Operate (DBFO) model.
- **Maritime Development:** National Maritime Development Programme (NMDP) approved; work is in progress in 101 projects covering inland waterways, shipping and ports, including deepening of channels in Kandla, JNPT and Paradip; plan allocation for Department of Shipping increased by 37 per cent to Rs 735 crore; study to identify a suitable location for a new deep draft port in West Bengal will be carried out; National Institute of Port Management, Chennai, renamed National Maritime Academy, will be upgraded into a Central University with regional campuses at Mumbai, Kolkata and Visakhapatnam.
- India Infrastructure Finance Company Limited incorporated.

Financial Sector

- **Banking, Insurance and Pensions:** Net capital support to banking sector, standing at Rs 22,808 crore, will be restructured to facilitate increased access of banks to additional resources for lending to the productive sectors; Bill on insurance will be introduced in 2006-07.

- **Capital Market:** Limit on FII investment in government securities will be increased from $ 1.75 billion to $ 2 billion and the limit on FII investment in corporate debt from $ 0.5 billion to $ 1.5 billion; ceiling on aggregate investment by mutual funds in overseas instruments will be raised from $ 1 billion to $ 2 billion with removal of requirement of 10 per cent reciprocal share holding; limited number of qualified Indian mutual funds will be allowed to invest, cumulatively up to $ 1 billion, in overseas exchange traded funds; an investor protection fund will be set up under the aegis of SEBI.

Other Proposals

- **Research and Development:** National Agricultural Innovation Project for research at frontiers of agricultural science will be launched in July 2006; National S&T Entrepreneurship Board has set up Technology business Incubators, enabling concessions to be provided to incubate entrepreneurs.
- **Skills Development:** Rs 97 crore allocated for upgradation of ITIs; Skills Development Initiative (SDI) taken up through a PPP scheme with initial provision of Rs 10 crore.
- **Jammu and Kashmir:** State Plan for 2006-07 fixed at Rs 2,300 crore; additionally Rs 848 crore provided for the J&K Reconstruction Plan, including Rs 230 crore for the Baglihar Project; special central Plan assistance of Rs 1,300 crore provided for reforms in the power sector.
- **Defence Expenditure:** Increased to Rs 89,000 crore including Rs 37,458 crore for capital expenditure.
- **e-Governance:** National e-Governance Plan will be approved shortly; twenty-five projects, in mission mode, to be launched in 2006-07.
- **Celebrating History and Heritage:** Rs 10 crore allocated for celebration of 150th anniversary of the First War of Indian Independence; National Gandhi Museum, Rajghat and the Kasturba Gandhi National Memorial Fund, Indore will be given Rs 5 crore each;
- Rs 5 crore for safeguarding of old art forms and oral traditions.

Fiscal Consolidation

- **Twelfth Finance Commission:** Rs 94,402 crore will be released as the states' share in gross tax revenues in current year compared to Rs 78,595 crore in 2004-05; grants-in-aid to states are Rs 25,134 crore in RE 2005-06 against Rs 12,081 crore in 2004-05.

Indirect Taxes

Customs

- Peak rate for non-agricultural products reduced from 15 per cent to 12.5 per cent; duty on alloy steel and primary and secondary non-ferrous metals reduced from 10 per cent to 7.5 per cent; this will also be the rate of duty for ferro alloys; on steel melting scrap raised to 5 per cent and brought on part on par with primary steel;
- Duty on mineral products reduced to 5 per cent, with a few exceptions.
- Duty on ores and concentrates reduced from 5 per cent to 2 per cent.
- Duty on refractories and on a number of materials for manufacture of refractories reduced to 7.5 per cent.
- Duty will be reduced on basic inorganic chemicals from 15 per cent to 10 per cent; on basic cy-

clic and acyclic hydrocarbons and their derivatives to 5 per cent; on catalysts from 10 per cent to 7.5 per cent.

- Duty will be reduced on major bulk plastics like PVC, LDPE and PP from 10 per cent to 5 per cent; on naptha for plastics to nil; on styrene, EDC and VCM which are raw materials for plastics to 2 per cent.
- Reduction of customs duty on 10 anti-AIDS and fourteen anti-cancer drugs to 5 per cent; on certain life saving drugs, kits and equipment from 15 per cent to 5 per cent; these drugs also exempt from excise duty and CVD.
- Duty on packaging machines will be reduced from 15 per cent to 5 per cent.
- Concessional project rate of 10 per cent will be extended to pipeline projects for transportation of natural gas, crude petroleum and petroleum products.
- CVD of 4 per cent will be imposed on all imports with a few exceptions; full credit will be allowed to manufacturers of excisable goods.
- Customs duty on vanaspati will be increased to 80 per cent.
- Rates on clearances by EOUs to the Domestic Tariff Area (DTA) adjusted at 50 per cent of basic customs duty plus excise duty on like goods.
- Reduction of excise duty on all man-made fibre yarn and filament yarn from 16 per cent to 8 per cent; import duty on all man-made fibres and yarns from 15 per cent to 10 per cent; import duty on raw materials such as DMT, PTA and MEG from 15 per cent to 10 per cent; import duty on paraxylene to 2 per cent.

Excise

- With the intention to converge all rates at the CENVAT rate at 16 per cent; duty on aerated drinks and small cars will be reduced to 16 per cent.
- 8 per cent duty will be imposed on packaged software sold over the counter; customized software and software packages downloaded from the Internet will be exempted; DVD Drives, Flash Drives and Combo Drives will be fully exempted from excise duty.
- Condensed milk, ice cream, preparations of meat, fish and poultry, pectins, pasta and yeast will be fully exempted; duty on ready-to-eat packaged foods and instant food mixes, like dosa and idli mixes, will be reduced from 16 per cent to 8 per cent.
- Vegetable tanning extracts, namely, quebracho and chestnut will be exempted from duty; duty on footwear with a retail sale price between Rs 250 and Rs 750 will be reduced from 16 per cent to 8 per cent.
- Concessional rate of 8 per cent will be extended to all LPG stoves.
- Duty on compact fluorescent lamps will be reduced from 16 per cent to 8 per cent.
- Glassware will attract duty of 16 per cent on par with ceramic ware and plastic ware.
- Excise duty on specified printing, writing and packing paper will be reduced from 16 per cent to 12 per cent.
- Cess under the Oil Industries Development Act will be increased from Rs 1,800 per metric ton to Rs 2,500 per MT.
- Duty of 16 per cent will be levied on set-top boxes with reduction in customs duty from 15 per cent to nil.
- Increase in excise duty on cigarettes by about 5 per cent.
- Excise and customs tariff exemptions that are end-use based or have outlived their utility or need

certification or give rise to disputes being rescinded; exemption for the SSI sector will remain.

Service tax .

- New services will cover including ATM operations, maintenance and management; registrars, share transfer agents and bankers to an issue; sale of space or time, other than in the print media, for advertisements; sponsorship of events, other than sports events, by companies; international air travel excluding economy-class passengers; container services on rail, excluding the railway freight charges; business support services; auctioneering; recovery agents; ship management services; travel on cruise ships; and public relations management services.
- Coverage of certain services now subject to service tax will be expanded.
- Leasing and hire-purchase will be treated on par with loan transactions, interest and installment of principal amount will be abated in calculating value of the service.
- Proposal to set 1 April 2010 as the date for introducing national-level Goods and Service Tax (GST); service tax rate increased from 10 per cent to 12 per cent as another step towards converge between service tax rate and the CENVAT rate; net impact likely to be very small in view of credit available for service tax or excise duty payable.

Direct Taxes

- No change in rates of personal income tax or corporate income tax; no new taxes are being imposed.
- One-by-six scheme will stand abolished.
- Marginal revision in certain tax rates in the quest for equity-Minimum Alternate Tax (MAT) rate increased from 7.5 per cent of book profits to 10 per cent which is only one-third of the normal rate; long-term capital gains arising out of securities included in calculating book profits; period to take credit for MAT increased from five years to seven years.
- Increase of 25 per cent, across the board, on all rates of STT.
- Section 80IA of the Income Tax Act applies to infrastructure facilities; terminal date for developing an industrial park extended from 31 March 2006 to 31 March 2009; for the power sector, the date extended to 31 March 2010.
- Investments in fixed deposits in scheduled banks for a term of not less than five years included in section 80C of the Income tax Act; limit of Rs 10,000 in respect of contribution to certain pension funds removed in section 80CCC subject to overall ceiling of Rs 100,000.
- Definition of open-ended equity-oriented schemes of mutual funds in the Income tax Act aligned with the definition adopted by SEBI; open-ended equity-oriented schemes and close-ended equity oriented schemes will be treated on par for exemption from dividend.
- Exemption under section 10(23G) removed.
- Primary Agricultural Credit Societies and Primary Cooperative Agricultural and Rural Development Banks to continue will be exempted from tax under section 80P of the Income Tax Act; all other cooperative banks excluded from the scope of that section.
- Scope of section 54EC restricted to two institutions, viz., NHAI and REC; for NABARD, SIDBI and NHB, which are banks, route

of zero coupon bonds to raise low cost funds already opened; if needed, appropriate support will be provided to these institutions to enable them to access resources to fulfill their mandate effectively; benefit of section 54ED withdrawn with effect from 1 Apri 2006.

- Anonymous or pseudonymous donations to wholly charitable institutions will be taxed at the highest marginal rate; such donations to partly religious and partly charitable institutions/trusts will be taxed only if the donation is specifically for an educational or medical purpose; such donations to wholly religious institutions and religious trusts not to be covered by the new provision.
- Constituency allowances of members of state legislatures will be treated at par with constituency allowance received by members of Parliament.
- Permanent Account Number (PAN) is the critical element in capturing incomes and expenditures; scrutiny of Annual Information Returns (AIR) on high-value transactions reveals that 60 per cent of the transactions are without quoting PAN; hence proposal to take power to issue PAN suo motu in certain cases and to direct persons to apply for PAN in certain cases; in due course, more transactions to be notified for which quoting of PAN to be mandatory, a few more transactions to be prescribed to be reported in AIRs.
- Banking Cash Transaction Tax (BCTT) will continue for some more time until the AIR system is able to capture all significant financial transactions.
- Changes proposed for Fringe Benefit Tax:
  a. Value benefit in the form of 'tour and travel' at 5 per cent instead of 20 per cent;
  b. Value benefit in the form of 'hospitality' and 'use of hotel boarding and lodging facilities', in case of airline companies and shipping industry, at 5 per cent instead of 20 per cent;
  c. Exclude expenses on free samples of medicines and of medical equipment distributed to doctors;
  d. Exclude expenses incurred on brand ambassador and celebrity endorsement;
  e. Prescribe a threshold of Rs 100,000 under section 115WB(1) (c) so that only a contribution by an employer to an approved superannuation fund in excess of Rs 100,000 per year per employee to attract FBT. Under section 80C there is already exemption up to Rs 100,000 for contribution by an employee to an approved superannuation fund.
- Modernizing Tax Administration: The Departments of Income Tax and Customs and Central Excise will undergo Business Process Reengineering (BPR); nationwide networks to connect 745 income tax offices in 510 cities and 550 customs and central excise offices in 245 cities, creating national databases; national data centres, data warehousing facilities and disaster recovery sites being set up; jurisdiction-free filing of returns, e-payments of customs and excise duties will be possible; both departments will have fully computerized networks by end 2006.
- A statement on revenue foregone, (tax expenditure statement), capturing the departures from the normal tax regime introduced.
- VAT and CST: In order to moderate the price, LPG (domestic) included in the list of declared goods' under the CST Act.

Railway Budget 2006-07

Review of Performance in 2005-06

- Growth in freight loading and revenues is 10 per cent and over 18 per cent respectively.
- Loading target increased from 635 mt to 668 mt and freight revenue target increased from Rs 33,480 crore to Rs 36,490 crore.
- Tenth Plan targets of 624 mt and 396 billion ton km will be surpassed one year in advance.
- Passenger Earnings, Other Coaching Earnings and Sundry Other Earnings increased by 7per cent, 19 per cent and 56 per cent respectively over previous year.
- Gross Traffic Revenues expected to be Rs 54,600 crore and are 16 per cent higher than the previous year.
- Ordinary Working Expenses will increase by Rs 1,200 crore.
- Likely operating ratio 86.6 per cent; with changes in accounting practice relating to lease charges, the operating ratio will be 83.7 per cent.

Measures to Improve Freight Business

- Reduction in unit cost of freight traffic due to increase in loading capacity of wagons and some other measures.
- Additional loading of 4 to 8 ton per wagon adds 100 mt to loading capacity with resultant revenue generation of Rs 5000 crore.
- 25 ton axle load trains will run on two routes for the first time in the Indian subcontinent as a pilot project.
- Validity of brake power certificate for CC rakes increased from 6000 to 7500 km.
- Preferential Traffic Schedule modified and freight booked for distances beyond 800 km will be given priority within the class.
- Wagon manufacture will increase by about 25 per cent.
- Production of electric locomotives will increase by 17 per cent and diesel locomotives by 5 per cent.

Reduction of Losses in Passenger Business

- 'Increase volumes-reduce unit costs' strategy will be adopted in the passenger business.
- Cut down losses in the coaching services by about Rs 1000 crore in the coming year and by 50 per cent in the next three years by increasing the number of coaches and occupancy of trains, reducing travel time and reducing losses in the catering and parcel segments.
- All-India timetable will be reworked de-novo, by using computerized simulation techniques.
- Over 200 mail/express trains will be made super-fast.
- Journey time of a majority of the Shatabdis, Rajdhanis and of certain Mail/Express trains likely to reduce.
- The number of coaches in about 190 popular passenger carrying trains will be increased up to twenty-four coaches enabling Railways to earn Rs 200 crore additionally every year.
- Platform lengths at 200 stations will be increased at a cost of Rs 60 crore.
- Upgradation of lower-class passengers to higher class without any additional payment introduced on all Rajdhanis and mail/express trains.

Reduction in Losses in Parcel and Catering Business

- Policy of leasing out pantry cars and catering units at large stations through open bids will continue.
- Capacity utilization of parcel business will be improved.

- Leasing policy of brake and parcel vans liberalized.
- Open tenders will be invited, graded reduction of reserve price where response inadequate.
- Parcels can be loaded and unloaded at all stations where the halt is five minutes or more and the leaseholders can themselves prepare the loading manifest.
- Assistant Guards' cabins could also be leased out to the lease holders of brake van and parcel van, apart from the courier companies.
- 150 kg ceiling for booking luggage in the brake vans removed.
- Luggage portion of brake vans of ordinary passenger trains will be converted to second-class compartments.

2006 Declared the Year of Passenger Service with a Smile

Strategies to Shrink Queues at Booking Counters

- Charges leviable on issue of e-tickets reduced.
- i-ticket and e-ticket can also be bought through Rail Travel Service Agents.
- 800 more UTS centres will be opened.
- 200 automatic ticket-vending machines in Mumbai suburban area will be installed.
- 'Jansadharan Ticket Booking Scheme' formulated to make available pre-paid.
- Under the 'Gramin Ticket Booking Service', agencies being given at roadside stations to unemployed rural youth for issuing tickets.

Improvement in Passenger Amenities

- All 'A' and 'B' category stations will be made model stations.
- Help of architects will be taken in all divisions to make station buildings more beautiful, comfortable and with modern look.
- Modern facilities such as ATM, cyber cafes, etc., will be provided at all major stations.
- Pilot project started to upgrade retiring rooms, waiting rooms, station buildings, lavatories, etc., under public–private partnership schemes at a few stations, will be expanded further.

Modern Facilities in Passenger Trains

- Four popular trains will be provided with world-class passenger amenities and interiors.
- IRCTC will award license through open bidding to provide all on-board services.

Railway Safety

- Over-age tracks and bridges and track circuiting work on all stations on A, B and C routes will be completed by March 2007.
- Balance works under SRSF will be completed by March 2008.
- Number of consequential accidents comes down from 473 in 2001 to 234 in 2004-05.

Staff Welfare

- Increase in contribution to the Staff Benefit Fund for the next year—nearly nine-fold.
- 100 community halls will be constructed.
- While away from headquarter, food will be made available to running staff during duty hours at nominal rates.
- Quality shoes, socks, gloves, uniforms, necessary implements to all gangmen/keymen.

Improvement in Medical Facilities

- New super-specialty cardiology and nephrology hospital will be constructed at Patna.

Concessions

- 50 per cent concession in second-class fares to farmers and milk producers for travel to institutes of national level in other parts of the country for the purpose of training/learning better agricultural practices and dairy farming announced earlier extended to Sleeper Class.
- 50 per cent concession in second-class and sleeper-class fares to persons who have lost their limbs in accidents or due to any other causes, for travel to institutes of national level, for transplantation of artificial limbs along with one attendant.

Passenger Services

- The Thar Express between India and Pakistan inaugurated.

New Trains, Extension of Trains and Increase in Frequency

New Trains: 55 pairs
Extension of services: 37 pairs
Increase in frequency: 12 pairs
Re-routing of trains: 2 pairs

Construction of Freight Corridor

Dedicated Multimodal High Axle Load Freight Corridor with computerized control on Western and Eastern routes will be constructed at an estimated cost of Rs 22,000 crores.

Annual Plan 2006-2007

- The largest ever plan outlay of Rs 23,475 crore, consisting of:

a. Rs 7,511 crore of support from the general exchequer.
b. Rs 10,794 crore through internally generated resources.
c. Rs 5,170 crore through extra budgetary resources (Rs 4170 cr through market borrowing by IRFC, Rs 500 crore to be raised by RVNL and balance Rs 500 crore through Wagon Investment Scheme).

- Outlay for road related safety works: Rs 711 crore.
- The thrust of the Annual Plan is on early completion of throughput enhancement works, safety, development and expansion of the network.
- The outlay on safety related planheads, is Rs 2,922 crore for Track Renewals, Rs 590 crore for Bridges and Rs 1,518 crore for Signalling and Telecommunications, Rs 436 crore for construction of ROBs/RUBs and Rs 275 crore for manning of unmanned level crossings.

Budget Estimates 2006-07

- Freight loading target at 726 million ton and freight output at 479 btkm.
- Revenues in freight, passenger, other coaching and sundry other earning segments will be Rs 40,320 crore, Rs 16,800 crore, Rs 1400 crore and Rs 1308 crore, respectively.
- Gross Traffic Receipts (GTR) will be Rs 59,978 crore.
- Ordinary Working Expenses will be Rs 38,300 crore.
- Appropriation to Pension Fund and DRF will be Rs 7790 crore and Rs 4307 crore respectively.
- Internal generation before dividend will be Rs 14,293 crore.
- Operating ratio expected will be 84.3 per cent in 2006-07.

Freight Services

- No across-the-board increase in freight rates.
- Rationalization of goods tariff will continue further.
- Number of commodity groups will be reduced from 80 to 28.
- Highest class lowered to 220, freight rates of diesel and petrol less by 8 per cent.
- Over the next three years, the highest class will be lowered be-

low 200 and rates for the highest classification to be made less than double that of the lowest classification (except rates of some light commodities).

Schemes Announced

- Dynamic Pricing Policy for freight introduced during the current year will be also extended to passenger for peak and non-peak seasons, premium and non-premium services, and for busy and non-busy routes.
- Non-peak season incremental freight discount scheme launched.
- Discounts up to 30 per cent during non-peak season and 20 per cent non-peak season in the peak season with certain conditions on incremental freight in the empty flow direction.

Passenger Services

- No increase in passenger fares.
- Passenger tariff structure rationalized so that the fares of AC first and AC second class will be 11.5 times and 6.5 times the second-class fare, respectively. Reduction in AC-I fare by 18 per cent and AC-II fare by 10 per cent.
- Fully air-conditioned Garib Rath will run on a pilot project basis initially with four pairs of services, fares about 25 per cent lower than present AC-III tier fares.
- Renewal period of Monthly Season Tickets increased from three days to ten days and the super-fast charges applicable on MSTs and QSTs reduced to one-fourth of the current levels.
- Tariff fixation mechanism for military traffic will be rationalized and simplified.

The Planning Commisssion

The Planning Commission was set up by a resolution of the Government of India in March 1950, with Prime Minister Jawaharlal Nehru as the chairman. It was charged with the responsibility of assessing the resources of the country, augmenting deficient resources, formulating plans for the most effective and balanced utilization of resources and determining priorities. The prime minister is the chairman of the Planning Commission which works under the overall guidance of the National Development Council. The deputy chairman and the full-time members of the Commission, as a composite body, provide advice and guidance to the subject divisions for the formulation of five-year plans, annual plans, state plans, monitoring plan programmes, projects and schemes.

The First Five-Year Plan (1951-56) gave the highest priority to agriculture, including irrigation and power projects. The Second Five-Year Plan (1956-57 to 1960-61) laid emphasis on industrialization, particularly the development of the public sector. The Third Five-Year Plan (1961-62 to 1965-66) aimed at increasing the national income. India's national income or Gross National Product grew at an average rate of about 4 per cent per annum between 1951 and 1965. Due to two successive years of drought, devaluation of the currency, a general rise in prices and the erosion of resources, long-term planning had to be temporarily abandoned and there were three annual plans between 1966 to 1969 before the Fourth Five-Year Plan began in April 1969. It laid emphasis on improving the conditions of the less privileged through the provision of employment and education. The Fifth Plan (1974–79) concentrated on reining inflation and achieving stability in the economic situation. The Janata Party-led government terminated the Fifth Plan in its fourth year in March 1978. The foremost objective of the Sixth Plan (1980–85) was the removal of poverty. The first three years of the Seventh Five-Year Plan (1986–90) saw severe drought conditions, despite which foodgrain production grew by 3.2 per cent. Policies were aimed at rapid growth in food-grain production, higher employment levels and so on. Due to the political situation at the Centre, the Eighth Plan could not take off in 1990 and was launched in 1992 after the initiation of structural adjustment policies.

The years 1990-91 and 1991-92 were treated as annual plans. For the first eight Plans, concentration was on a growing public sector but since the launch of the Ninth Plan in 1997, the emphasis on the public sector has become less pronounced and the current thinking on planning in the country, in general, is that it should increasingly be of an indicative nature. A growth rate of 7 per cent in GDP was targeted for the Ninth Plan, with a current account deficit of 2.4 per cent of GDP and savings rate of 26.2 per cent of GDP.

The Tenth Plan is currently underway. The Tenth Five-Year Plan (2002–07) aims at harnessing the benefits of growth to improve the quality of life of the people. The acceleration in the growth trajectory of the Indian economy achieved in the second year (2003-04) of the Tenth Five-Year Plan, measuring an annual growth rate of 8.2 per cent in Gross Domestic Product (GDP), reassures India's growth potential. There is evidence of industrial revival and upswing in the investment climate as reflected in the growth performance of the economy in the first two quarters of the current year. The economy is expected to achieve an overall growth rate of 6.5 per cent, which signifies a continuing upturn of the economy.

The commitment to maintain the growth rate at 7-8 per cent annually on a sustainable basis has been reiterated by the National Common Minimum Programme (NCMP) of the United Progressive Alliance (UPA) government. Other economic agenda included in the NCMP are (i) providing universal access to quality basic education and health; (ii) generating gainful employment in agriculture, manufacturing and services, and promoting investment; (iii) assuring 100 days' employment to the breadwinner in each family at the minimum wage; (iv) focussing on agriculture and infrastructure; (v) accelerating fiscal consolidation and reform; and (vi) ensuring higher and more efficient fiscal devolution.

Targets for the Tenth Plan and Beyond

- Reduction of poverty ratio by 5 percentage points by 2007 and by 15 percentage points by 2012;
- Providing gainful and high-quality employment to add to the labour force over the Tenth Plan period;
- All children in school by 2003; all children to complete five years of schooling by 2007;
- Reduction in gender gaps in literacy and wage rates by at least 50 per cent by 2007;
- Reduction in the decadal rate of population growth between 2001 and 2011 to 16.2 per cent;
- Increase in literacy rates to 75 per cent within the Plan period;
- Reduction of Infant Mortality Rate (IMR) to 45 per 1000 live births by 2007 and to 28 by 2012;
- Reduction of Maternal Mortality Ratio (MMR) to 2 per 1000 live births by 2007 and to 1 by 2012;
- Increase in forest and tree cover to 25 per cent by 2007 and 33 per cent by 2012;
- All villages to have sustained access to potable drinking water within the Plan period;
- Cleaning of all major polluted rivers by 2007 and other notified stretches by 2012.

Macroeconomic Parameters for the Tenth Plan—A Comparison

	Base-Line	Target
Average GDP growth rate (% p.a.)	6.5	8.0
Gross Investment Rate (% of GDP mp)	27.8	32.6
Implicit ICOR	4.28	4.08
Current Account Deficit	1.5	2.8
Gross Domestic Savings, of which:	26.3	29.8
Public sector (of which)	2.4	4.6
Government	–0.6	1.7
Public enterprises	3.0	2.9
Private corporate sector	4.9	5.8
Household sector	19.0	19.4

Target Growth Scenario—Fiscal Parameters of the Central Government

(percentage of GDP)

	Ninth Plan	Tenth Plan
1. Revenue receipts	9.1	10.2
2. Revenue expenditure	12.5	10.7
3. Revenue deficit	3.4	0.5
4. Total expenditure	15.4	14.0
(a) Plan expenditure	3.9	4.5
(b) Non-plan expenditure	11.5	9.5
5. Non-debt capital Receipts	0.8	1.2
6. Fiscal deficit	5.0	2.6

Central Government Capital Receipts

(*Rs million*)

	2005-06 Budget Estimates	2005-06 Revised Estimates	2006-07 Budget Estimates
A. Non-debt Receipts			
1. Recoveries of loans & advances*	12000	11700	8000
2. Miscellaneous capital receipts	–	2356	3840
Total	12000	14056	11840
B. Debt Receipts to finance Fiscal Deficit			
3. Market Loans	103836	100373	113778
4. Short term borrowings	6455	8526	–110
5. External Assistance (Net)	9656	7514	8324
6. Securities issued against Small Savings	3010	1350	3010
7. State Provident Funds (Net)	5000	5500	6000
8. Other Receipts (Net)	20047	7875	17684
9. Draw-down of Cash Balance	3140	15037	–
Total	151144	146175	148686
Total Capital Receipts (A+B)	163144	160231	160526
Total Receipts	**514344**	**508705**	**563991**
Receipts under MSS (Net)	15019	–36981	46000
*excludes recoveries of short-term loans and advances from states and loans to Government servants, etc.	1525	1530	1530

Central Government Revenue Receipts

(Rs million)

	2005-06 Budget Estimates	2005-06 Revised Estimates	2006-07 Budget Estimates
1. Tax Revenue			
Gross Tax Revenue	370025	370141	442153
Union Excise duties	121533	112000	119000
Customs	53182	64215	77066
Corporation tax	110573	103573	133010
Income tax	66239	66239	77409
Service tax	17500	23000	34500
Taxes of the Union Territories	733	849	903
Other taxes and duties	265	265	265
Less-NCCD transferred to the National Calamity, Contingency Fund	1600	1600	1500
Less States' Share	94959	94402	113448
Net Tax Revenue	273466	274139	327205
2. Non-Tax Revenue			
Interest receipts	25500	21245	19263
Dividend and profits	23500	25481	27500
External grants	3218	3019	2616
Other non-tax revenue	24787	23837	26071
Receipts of Union Territories	729	753	810
Total Non-Tax Revenue	77734	74335	76260
Total Revenue Receipts	**351200**	**348474**	**403465**

Central Government Expenditures

(Rs million)

	2005-06 Budget Estimates	2005-06 Revised Estimates	2006-07 Budget Estimates
1. Non-Plan Expenditure			
A. Revenue Expenditure			
1. Interest Payments	133945	130032	139823
2. Defence	48625	48625	51542
3. Subsidies	47432	46874	46213
4. Grants to State and U.T. Governments	33953	30390	35361
5. Pensions	19542	20232	21312
6. Police	12237	12593	13682
7. Assistance to States from National Calamity Contingency Fund	1500	3062	1500
8. Economic Services (Agriculture, Industry, Power, Transport, Communications, Science & Technology, etc.)	13413	13655	12862
9. Other General Services (Organs of State, tax collection, external affairs, etc.)	9028	9524	10270

(Rs million)

	2005-06 Budget Estimates	2005-06 Revised Estimates	2006-07 Budget Estimates
10. Social Services (Education, Health, Broadcasting, etc.)	7522	9282	8546
11. Postal Deficit	1417	1113	1342
12. Expenditure of Union Territories without Legislature	2322	2316	2101
13. Amount met from National Calamity Contingency Fund	–1500	–2825	–1500
14. Grants to Foreign Governments	1094	1269	1376
Total Revenue Non-Plan Expenditure	330530	326142	344430
B. Capital Expenditure			
1. Defence	34375	33075	37458
2. Other Non-Plan Capital Outlay	4460	3635	7853
3. Loans to Public Enterprises	1258	2017	1480
4. Loans to State and U.T. Governments	100	99	100
5. Loans to Foreign Governments	256	174	158
6. Others	–132	–228	–216
Total Capital Non-Plan Expenditure	40317	38772	46833
Total Non-Plan Expenditure	370847	364914	391263
2. Plan Expenditure			
A. Revenue Expenditure			
1. Central Plan	83370	82836	107469
2. Central Assistance for State & Union Territory Plans	32612	31317	36293
State Plan	31687	30345	34690
Union Territory Plan	925	972	1403
Total Revenue Plan Expenditure	115982	114153	143762
B. Capital Expenditure			
1. Central Plan	27015	24417	23815
2. Central Assistance for State & Union Territory Plans	500	5221	5151
State Plan	55	4729	4072
Union Territory Plan	445	492	1079
Total Capital Plan Expenditure	27515	29638	28966
Total-Plan Expenditure	143497	143791	172728
Total Budget Support for Central Plan	110385	107253	131284
Total Central Assistance for State & UT Plans	33112	36538	41444
Total Expenditure	**514344**	**508705**	**563991**
Debt Servicing			
1. Repayment of debt	247984	222658	249196
2. Total Interest Payments	133945	130032	139823
3. Total debt servicing (1+2)	381929	352690	389019
4. Revenue Receipts	351200	348474	403465
5. Percentage of 2 to 4	38.1%	37.3%	34.7%

Rupee Exchange Rates

Year	Euro Average	US Dollar Average	Pound Sterling Average	Japanese Yen Average
2000-01	59.5459	45.6844	67.5522	41.4052
2001-02	60.2150	47.6919	68.3189	38.1790
2002-03	64.1257	48.3953	74.8193	39.7363
2003-04	65.6876	45.9516	77.7389	40.7077
2004-05	66.9282	44.9315	82.8644	41.8046

FIIs

Based on purchasing power parity, India is the fifth largest economy in the world (ranking above France, Italy, the United Kingdom, and Russia) and has the third largest GDP in the entire continent of Asia. It is also the second largest among emergin{ nations. India, for the European investors, is believed to be a good investment despite political uncertainty, bureaucratic hassles, shortages of power and infrastructural deficiencies. India presents a vast potential for overseas investment and is actively encouraging the entrance of foreign players into the market.

Foreign Investment Inflows

Year	Direct investment		Portfolio investment		Total	
	Rs crore	US $ million	Rs crore	US $ million	Rs crore	US $ million
1990-91	174	97	11	6	185	103
1991-92	316	129	10	4	326	133
1992-93	965	315	748	244	1713	559
1993-94	1838	586	11188	3567	13026	4153
1994-95	4126	1314	12007	3824	16133	5138
1995-96	7172	2144	9192	2748	16364	4892
1996-97	10015	2821	11758	3312	21773	6133
1997-98	13220	3557	6696	1828	19916	5385
1998-99	10358	2462	–257	–61	10101	2401
1999-00	9338	2155	13112	3026	22450	5181
2000-01	18406	4029	12609	2760	31015	6789
2001-02	29235	6130	9639	2021	38874	8151
2002-03	24367	5035	4738	979	29105	6014
2003-04	21473	4673	52279	11377	73752	16050
2004-05P	24870	5535	40029	8909	64899	14444

P: Provisional.

Negative (–) sign indicates outflow.

India's Exports and Imports

A Secretary heads the department of commerce in the ministry of commerce and industry, Government of India. The department is responsible for the country's external trade and all matters connected with it, such as commercial relations with other countries, state trading, export promotional measures and the development and regulation of certain export-oriented industries and commodities. It formulates policies in the sphere of foreign trade, in particular, the import and export policy of the country. Foreign trade has played a crucial role in India's economic growth. India's total external trade in the year 1950-51 stood at Rs 1,214 crores. It reached Rs 537,433 crores during 2002-03.

After witnessing an impressive growth since 2002-03, export growth continued to maintain momentum during the year 2004-05. According to provisional data available for April-January 2004-05, exports stood at Rs 274,313 crore (US$60,754 million) as against Rs 222,864 crore (US$48,390 million) in the corresponding period of last year, recording a growth of 23.1 per cent in rupee terms and 25.6 per cent in dollar terms. Imports also witnessed a robust growth of 32.1 per cent, having increased to Rs 376,815 crore (US$83,442 million) from Rs 285,327 crore (US$61,938 million) during April-January 2004-05. The trade deficit during April-January 2004–05 is estimated to have widened to Rs 102,502 crore ($22,687 million) from Rs 62,463 crore ($13,548 million) during the corresponding period of the previous year.

Exports, Commodity-wise 2004-05
(Values in Rs lakhs)

No.	Commodity	2003-04	2004-05	% Growth
1.	Live Animals	2,062.88	2,413.92	17.02
2.	Meat	169,389.76	171,972.33	1.52
3.	Fish	568,095.28	569,271.00	0.21
4.	Dairy Produce	40,970.83	67,718.01	65.28
5.	Products of Animal Origin	17,243.51	15,875.32	–7.93
6.	Plants, Bulbs, Roots	25,046.74	21,270.21	–15.08
7.	Edible Vegetables	151,001.19	163,406.92	8.22
8.	Fruit and Nuts	254,668.75	321,169.61	26.11
9.	Coffee, Tea and Spices	329,157.48	358,188.08	8.82
10.	Cereals	695,668.07	893,361.89	28.42
11.	Milling Products	47,172.60	19,442.84	–58.78
12.	Oil Seeds	205,240.77	163,119.94	–20.52
13.	Vegetable Saps and Extracts	111,339.64	143,662.86	29.03
14.	Other Vegetable Products	8,839.22	10,156.18	14.90
15.	Animal or Vegetable Fats and Oils	98,386.01	146,950.50	49.36
16.	Preparations of Meat	40,986.47	49,361.28	20.43
17.	Sugars and Sugar Confectionery	133,057.68	24,682.07	–81.45

No.	Commodity	2003-04	2004-05	% Growth
18.	Cocoa and Cocoa Preparations	1,947.83	2,869.01	47.29
19.	Preparations of Cereals	31,292.41	38,224.57	22.15
20.	Preparations of Vegetables	39,480.11	41,810.59	5.90
21.	Miscellaneous Edible Preparations	62,808.46	58,899.79	–6.22
22.	Beverages and Spirits	12,507.03	13,692.72	9.48
23.	Residues from Food Industries	340,033.40	317,242.42	–6.70
24.	Tobacco	109,647.06	124,210.19	13.28
25.	Salt, etc.	286,872.64	359,548.97	25.33
26.	Ores, Slag and Ash	600,684.11	1,600,843.27	166.50
27.	Mineral Fuels	1,715,981.04	3,122,063.45	81.94
28.	Inorganic Chemicals	194,875.30	273,003.81	40.09
29.	Organic Chemicals	1,297,459.39	1,555,700.67	19.90
30.	Pharmaceutical Products	744,452.62	884,179.41	18.77
31.	Fertilizers	3,331.31	5,811.60	74.45
32.	Tanning or Dyeing Extracts	311,159.73	287,452.28	–7.62
33.	Essential Oils	145,929.32	127,144.76	–12.87
34.	Soap	30,338.49	30,207.24	–0.43
35.	Albuminoidal Substances	32,375.70	44,307.96	36.86
36.	Explosives; Pyrotechnic Products	7,164.08	10,670.32	48.94
37.	Photographic Goods	10,604.50	12,932.34	21.95
38.	Miscellaneous Chemical Products	264,344.25	305,070.69	15.41
39.	Plastic	613,692.90	915,167.50	49.12
40.	Rubber	306,051.61	327,369.81	6.97
41.	Raw Hides	256,833.01	266,017.01	3.58
42.	Articles of Leather	459,453.16	468,098.92	1.88
43.	Furskins and Artificial Fur	162.93	252.52	54.98
44.	Wood	27,603.26	35,816.47	29.75
45.	Cork	303.98	454.60	49.55
46.	Straw and Wickerwork	1,089.96	1,217.47	11.70
47.	Pulp of Wood	383.29	630.18	64.41
48.	Paper and Paperboard	124,370.55	145,188.17	16.74
49.	Printed Books and Newspapers	43,161.00	51,054.60	18.29
50.	Silk	156,617.96	159,119.12	1.60
51.	Wool	26,399.06	30,493.97	15.51
52.	Cotton	1,133,049.60	950,866.67	–16.08
53.	Vegetable Textile Fibres	62,393.08	76,148.75	22.05
54.	Man-made Filaments	399,480.13	426,520.14	6.77
55.	Man-made Staple Fibres	331,249.41	337,970.13	2.03
56.	Wadding, Felt and Nonwovens	26,739.82	22,830.56	–14.62
57.	Carpets	337,368.47	349,335.95	3.55
58.	Special Woven Fabrics	51,077.16	49,676.71	–2.74
59.	Coated or Laminated Textile Fabrics	30,570.49	29,888.43	–2.23
60.	Knitted Fabrics	23,729.73	18,615.97	–21.55
61.	Clothing Accessories	1,241,489.84	1,121,048.24	–9.70
62.	Clothing Accessories, not Knitted or Crocheted	1,627,305.72	1,665,511.44	2.35

No.	Commodity	2003-04	2004-05	% Growth
63.	Made up Textile Articles	746,771.41	826,077.52	10.62
64.	Footwear	352,776.25	385,092.93	9.16
65.	Headgear	3,352.70	2,445.34	–27.06
66.	Umbrellas, Walking-sticks, etc.	534.50	594.85	11.29
67.	Articles Made of Feathers or Down	32,893.88	35,254.05	7.18
68.	Articles of Stone, Plaster, Cement	195,240.99	178,316.35	–8.67
69.	Ceramic Products	49,070.53	42,208.30	–13.98
70.	Glass and Glassware	96,499.51	93,525.22	–3.08
71.	Natural or Cultured Pearls, Precious or Semiprecious Stones	4,945,106.24	6,471,432.54	30.87
72.	Iron and Steel	1,190,681.96	1,831,803.86	53.84
73.	Articles of Iron or Steel	703,040.93	994,172.65	41.41
74.	Copper and Articles Thereof	262,418.34	416,722.87	58.80
75.	Nickel and Articles Thereof	3,173.45	3,458.71	8.99
76.	Aluminium and Articles Thereof	186,062.96	229,490.07	23.34
77.	Lead and Articles Thereof	1,880.34	3,971.44	111.21
78.	Zinc and Articles Thereof	14,220.78	14,665.73	3.13
79.	Tin and Articles Thereof	5,067.22	3,711.39	–26.76
80.	Other Base Metals	4,449.66	5,561.83	24.99
81.	Tools and Implements	136,761.06	160,356.91	17.25
82.	Miscellaneous Articles of Base Metal	79,348.64	75,589.45	–4.74
83.	Nuclear Reactors, Boilers, Machinery	1,151,714.64	1,418,727.60	23.18
84.	Electrical Machinery Parts	872,641.45	889,486.45	1.93
85.	Railway Locomotives	8,506.19	8,984.18	5.62
86.	Vehicles other than Stock Railway Rolling	801,348.94	1,067,103.63	33.16
87.	Aircraft, Spacecraft, and Parts Thereof	37,271.83	21,950.80	–41.11
88.	Ships and Boats	51,685.47	132,140.85	155.66
89.	Optical and Photographic Instruments	214,683.23	258,278.06	20.31
90.	Clocks and Watches	34,657.28	29,448.22	–15.03
91.	Musical Instruments	3,489.54	3,731.56	6.94
92.	Arms and Ammunition	1,545.32	784.50	–49.23
93.	Furniture	68,409.78	114,674.78	67.63
94.	Toys, Games and Sports Requisites	41,463.68	44,340.72	6.94
95.	Miscellaneous Manufactured Articles	68,348.47	61,532.61	–9.97
96.	Works of Art	227,521.18	164,004.49	–27.92
97.	Project Goods	39,151.72	33,113.18	–15.42
98.	Miscellaneous Goods	282,692.65	357,959.51	26.62
	India's Total Exports	**29,336,674.00**	**36,187,916.00**	**23.35**

Imports, Commodity-wise 2004-05

(Values in Rs lakhs)

No.	Commodity	2003-04	2004-05	% Growth
1.	Live Animals	344.57	416.40	20.84
2.	Meat	16.94	130.54	670.61
3.	Fish	5,171.93	6,375.72	23.28
4.	Dairy Produce	13,307.41	6,628.26	–50.19
5.	Products of Animal Origin	5,015.30	4,674.69	–6.79
6.	Plants, Bulbs, Roots	900.89	1,119.36	24.25
7.	Edible Vegetables	262,217.44	197,514.50	–24.68
8.	Fruit and Nuts	217,492.97	283,316.88	30.26
9.	Coffee, Tea and Spices	52,122.39	61,862.36	18.69
10.	Cereals	238.93	613.05	156.58
11.	Milling Products	2,841.94	3,667.82	29.06
12.	Oil Seeds	21,294.37	24,590.15	15.48
13.	Vegetable Saps and Extracts	15,737.24	20,374.43	29.47
14.	Other Vegetable Products	788.11	1,086.30	37.84
15.	Animal or Vegetable Fats and Oils	1,186,859.00	1,117,977.70	–5.80
16.	Preparations of Meat	199.51	364.08	82.49
17.	Sugars and Sugar Confectionery	14,550.38	130,747.88	798.59
18.	Cocoa and Cocoa Preparations	6,121.17	9,209.42	50.45
19.	Preparations of Cereals	8,560.33	10,866.87	26.94
20.	Preparations of Vegetables	7,850.65	8,050.15	2.54
21.	Miscellaneous Edible Preparations	6,645.41	7,293.14	9.75
22.	Beverages and Spirits	13,771.43	75,328.65	446.99
23.	Residues From Food Industries	34,850.41	35,547.55	2.00
24.	Tobacco	5,693.67	10,823.86	90.10
25.	Salt, etc.	184,977.68	244,911.99	32.40
26.	Ores, Slag and Ash	232,738.96	447,838.96	92.42
27.	Mineral Fuels	10,431,108.05	15,472,682.87	48.33
28.	Inorganic Chemicals	591,625.57	732,612.80	23.83
29.	Organic Chemicals	1,436,301.41	1,822,792.63	26.91
30.	Pharmaceutical Products	114,987.72	126,732.93	10.21
31.	Fertilizers	231,394.39	415,662.19	79.63
32.	Tanning or Dyeing Extracts	161,697.37	181,953.68	12.53
33.	Essential Oils	45,564.98	57,166.97	25.46
34.	Soap	60,862.51	63,563.15	4.44
35.	Albuminoidal Substances	26,810.97	31,036.36	15.76
36.	Explosives; Pyrotechnic Products	1,315.49	2,282.62	73.52
37.	Photographic Goods	111,194.05	101,908.89	–8.35
38.	Miscellaneous Chemical Products	336,205.29	391,606.29	16.48
39.	Plastic	568,527.64	720,311.05	26.70
40.	Rubber	224,757.69	295,827.79	31.62
41.	Raw Hides	105,178.37	119,121.15	13.26
42.	Articles of Leather	6,109.74	8,864.97	45.10
43.	Furskins and Artificial Fur	1,097.49	1,103.51	0.55
44.	Wood	332,538.22	401,481.30	20.73
45.	Cork	843.23	917.95	8.86
46.	Straw and Wickerwork	183.66	202.36	10.18

No.	Commodity	2003-04	2004-05	% Growth
47.	Pulp of Wood	188,004.27	213,555.39	13.59
48.	Paper and Paperboard	296,184.83	307,798.53	3.92
49.	Printed Books and Newspapers	135,556.28	161,704.13	19.29
50.	Silk	117,336.71	138,137.53	17.73
51.	Wool	110,241.75	104,376.20	–5.32
52.	Cotton	222,291.12	194,651.43	–12.43
53.	Vegetable Textile Fibres	30,036.23	29,026.53	–3.36
54.	Man-made Filaments	154,724.30	172,179.40	11.28
55.	Man-made Staple Fibres	63,323.43	72,853.54	15.05
56.	Wadding, Felt and Nonwovens	23,676.21	26,550.43	12.14
57.	Carpets	8,632.89	11,580.23	34.14
58.	Special Woven Fabrics	24,929.34	28,194.02	13.10
59.	Coated or Laminated Textile Fabrics	81,994.93	111,190.44	35.61
60.	Knitted or Fabrics	20,667.12	25,984.36	25.73
61.	Clothing Accessories	5,017.03	4,678.65	–6.74
62.	Clothing Accessories, not Knitted or Crocheted	12,765.05	9,767.51	–23.48
63.	Made up Textile Articles	51,027.16	37,431.11	–26.64
64.	Footwear	17,143.81	23,647.93	37.94
65.	Headgear	373.08	513.67	37.68
66.	Umbrellas, Walking-sticks, etc.	1,410.44	2,679.44	89.97
67.	Articles Made of Feathers or Down	776.19	1,014.16	30.66
68.	Articles of Stone, Plaster, Cement	35,180.13	46,918.98	33.37
69.	Ceramic Products	49,000.61	76,483.41	56.09
70.	Glass and Glassware	74,242.03	94,110.45	26.76
71.	Natural or Cultured Pearls, Precious or Semiprecious Stones	6,504,450.69	9,246,522.36	42.16
72.	Iron and Steel	815,531.09	1,465,561.90	79.71
73.	Articles of Iron or Steel	295,118.73	384,669.81	30.34
74.	Copper and Articles Thereof	151,399.89	230,981.20	52.56
75.	Nickel and Articles Thereof	104,996.46	118,448.78	12.81
76.	Aluminium and Articles Thereof	172,153.65	206,460.61	19.93
77.	Lead and Articles Thereof	45,069.68	69,134.21	53.39
78.	Zinc and Articles Thereof	63,594.76	68,301.34	7.40
79.	Tin and Articles Thereof	9,770.92	16,110.73	64.88
80.	Other Base Metals	35,296.42	37,504.75	6.26
81.	Tools and Implements	67,934.99	97,078.26	42.90
82.	Miscellaneous Articles of Base Metal	33,164.53	47,191.16	42.29
83.	Nuclear Reactors, Boilers, Machinery	3,185,745.86	4,188,061.60	31.46
84.	Electrical Machinery Parts	3,016,567.61	3,930,844.20	30.31
85.	Railway Locomotives	51,100.34	52,732.13	3.19
86.	Vehicles other Than Stock Railway Rolling	259,451.41	364,217.04	40.38

No.	Commodity	2003-04	2004-05	% Growth
87.	Aircraft, Spacecraft, and Parts Thereof	537,148.72	711,467.85	32.45
88.	Ships and Boats	636,329.13	791,382.54	24.37
89.	Optical and Photographic Instruments	714,302.78	880,462.34	23.26
90.	Clocks and Watches	19,272.41	23,218.88	20.48
91.	Musical Instruments	1,918.27	2,981.63	55.43
92.	Arms and Ammunition	1,499.91	1,293.46	–13.76
93.	Furniture	49,079.77	71,226.65	45.12
94.	Toys, Games and Sports Requisites	22,869.61	28,732.56	25.64
95.	Miscellaneous Manufactured Articles	44,088.94	48,942.63	11.01
96.	Works of Art	619.96	417.24	–32.70
97.	Project Goods	184,807.46	265,539.64	43.68
98.	Miscellaneous Goods	74,334.00	149,491.08	101.11
	India's Total Imports	**35,910,764.00**	**49,053,168.00**	**36.6**

Agriculture

India has made great progress in agriculture in terms of growth in output, yield and area under crops since Independence. It has gone through a green revolution, white revolution, yellow revolution and blue revolution. Today, India is the largest producer of milk, fruit, cashew nut, coconut and tea in the world, the second largest producer of wheat, vegetables, sugar and fish and the third largest producer of tobacco and rice. The per capita availability of foodgrain has risen in the country from 350 gm in 1951 to about 500 gm per day now, of milk from less than 125 gm to 210 gm per day and of eggs from 5 to 30 per annum despite the increase in population from 35 crores to 95 crores. However, India would have been in an even better position both in terms of agricultural output and economic development, had our planners given the required importance to development in the early years after Independence. Even today, Indian farmers are able to obtain only 15 per cent of their requirements of agricultural credit from banks. The various state seed corporations are able to produce only 10 per cent of the seeds required by our farmers. Only 23-30 per cent of the farmers are able to derive any benefits of extension services provided by various government agencies and every year about 20 per cent of the crop is lost due to mishandling, spillage, floods, droughts and pests and diseases. In fruits and vegetables, the loss is around 30 per cent. The farm sector in India offers numerous opportunities for investment. Its 350-million strong urban middle class with its changing food habits poses a huge market for agricultural products and processed food. The relatively low-cost but skilled workforce can be effectively utilized to set up large, low-cost production bases for domestic and export markets. The national policy aims at increasing the level of food processing from the present 2 per cent to 10 per cent by 2010 and 25 per cent by 2025. Though foreign direct investment is not directly allowed in agriculture, ample opportunities exist in related sectors. The fiscal budgets for 2004-05 and 2005-06 contain the most recent articulation of the government's strategy to give an impetus to the farm sector. Some of the highlights of the policy package are:

- The government has abolished licensing for almost all food and agro-processing industries, except for a few items such as beer, potable alcohol and wines, cane sugar, hydrogenated animal fats, oils etc. and items reserved for exclusive manufacturing in the small scale industries (SSIs).
- Automatic investment approval, including foreign technology agreements within specified norms, up to 100 per cent foreign equity or 100 per cent for NRIs and overseas corporate bodies is allowed for most of the food processing sector.

Recently India was forced to import wheat for the first time in six years. India grows one wheat crop a year, which is sown in the winter months and harvested from April. It currently grows wheat over 26.5 million hectares. The country produces about 70 million tonnes of wheat to feed its billion plus people. This year the government has so far contracted imports of 5.5 million tonnes of wheat from costly world markets to augment government stocks and rein in prices. It has also allowed private trade to import wheat at zero duty. There's very little wheat available even in the international market and this has put government food programmes in jeopardy. The country is now hoping to import more than 1.5 million tonnes of wheat from the international market. All major wheat-producing countries such as Egypt, China and Pakistan are now importing it. Also, for the last ten years, domestic production has remained static at around 70 million tonnes, while prices have risen from Rs 750 per quintal last year to Rs 900 per quintal.

Foodgrains Production

(Million tonnes)

Crop/Year	2001-02	2002-03	2003-04	2004-05	2005-06$
Rice	93.3	71.8	88.3	85.3	73.8
Wheat	72.8	65.8	72.1	72.0	–
Coarse Cereals	33.4	26.1	38.1	33.9	26.4
Pulses	13.4	11.1	14.9	13.4	5.0
Foodgrains					
(i) *Kharif*	112.1	87.2	116.9	103.3	105.3
(ii) *Rabi*	100.8	87.6	96.6	101.3	–
Total (i)+(ii)	212.9	174.8	213.5	204.6	–

Commercial Crops Production

(Million tonnes)

Crop/Year	2001-02	2002-03	2003-04	2004-05@	2005-06$
Groundnut	7.0	4.1	8.2	7.0	5.9
Rapeseed & Mustard	5.1	3.9	6.2	8.4	–
Soyabean	6.0	4.7	7.9	7.5	6.6
Other Oilseeds	2.6	2.1	3.0	3.2	2.1
Total nine oilseeds	20.7	14.8	25.3	26.1	14.6
Cotton*	10.0	8.6	13.9	17.0	15.9
Jute & Mesta**	11.7	11.3	11.2	10.5	10.1
Sugarcane	297.2	287.4	237.3	232.3	257.7

*Million bales of 170 kg each. **Million bales of 180 kg each.
@4th advance estimates $1st advance estimates (kharif only).

Annual Average Growth Rate (At Constant Prices)

Five Year Plan	Overall GDP Growth Rate	Agriculture & Allied Sectors
Seventh Plan (1985-90)	6.0	3.2
Annual Plan (1990-92)	3.4	1.3
Eighth Plan (1992-97)	6.7	4.7
Ninth Plan (1997-2002)	5.5	2.1
Tenth Plan (2002-07)		
2002-03	3.8	–6.9
2003-04(P)	8.5	10.0
2004-05(Q)	7.5	0.7
2005-06(A)	8.1	2.3

P: Provisional, Q: Quick estimates, A: Advance estimates

Note: Growth rates prior to 2001 based on 1993-94 prices and from 2000-01 onwards based on new series at 1999-2000 prices.

Irrigation

Under the Irrigation Component of Bharat Nirman, the target for the creation of additional irrigation potential of 1 crore hectares in four years (2005-06 to 2008-09) is planned to be met largely through expeditious completion of identified ongoing major and medium irrigation projects. There is a definite gap between irrigation potential created and the potential utilized. Under Bharat Nirman it is planned to restore and utilize irrigation potential of 10 lakh hectares through the implementation of extension, renovation and modernization of schemes along with command area development and water management practices. There are considerable areas in the country with unutilized ground-water resources. Irrigation potential of 28 lakh hectares is planned to be created through ground-water development. The remaining target for creating an irrigation potential of 10 lakh hectares is planned to be created by way of minor irrigation schemes, using surface flow.

Ten lakh hectares of irrigation potential is also planned by way of repair, renovation and restoration of water bodies and extension, renovation and modernization of minor irrigation schemes.

Statewise Ultimate Irrigation Potential from Major, Medium and Minor Irrigation

(in Thousand Hectares)

State Name	Ultimate Irrigation Potential (UIP)				
	Major and Medium Irrigation	Minor Irrigation			Total (UIP)
		Surface Water	Ground Water	Total (M.I)	
Andhra Pradesh	5000	2300	3960	6260	11260
Arunachal Pradesh	0	150	18	168	168
Assam	970	1000	900	1900	2870
Bihar	6500	1900	4947	6847	13347

Goa	62	25	29	54	116
Gujarat	3000	347	2756	3103	6103
Haryana	3000	50	4462	1512	4512
Himachal Pradesh	50	235	68	303	353
Jammu and Kashmir	250	400	708	1108	1358
Karnataka	2500	900	2574	3474	5974
Kerala	1000	800	879	1679	2679
Madhya Pradesh	6000	2200	9732	11932	17932
Maharashtra	4100	1200	3652	4852	8952
Manipur	135	100	369	469	604
Meghalaya	20	85	63	148	168
Mizoram	0	70	–	70	70
Nagaland	10	75	–	75	85
Orissa	3600	1000	4203	5203	8803
Punjab	3000	50	2917	2967	5967
Rajasthan	2750	600	1778	2378	5128
Sikkim	20	50	–	50	70
Tamil Nadu	1500	1200	2832	4032	5532
Tripura	100	100	81	181	281
Uttar Pradesh	12500	1200	16799	17999	30499
West Bengal	2300	1300	3318	4618	6918
Total States	58367	17337	64045	81382	139749
Total Uts	98	41	5	46	144
Grand Total	**58465**	**17378**	**64050**	**81428**	**139893**

Irrigated Area under Different Crops

(Million hectares)

	1990-91	1999-2000 (P)	2000-01 (P)	2001-02 (P)	2002-03 (P)
Rice	19.4	24.5	23.9	24.5	21.6
	(45.5)	(54.0)	(53.3)	(54.4)	(51.7)
Jowar	0.8	0.8	0.8	0.8	0.8
	(5.6)	(7.8)	(8.0)	(8.0)	(8.6)
Bajra	0.5	0.7	0.8	0.8	0.7
	(5.1)	(7.7)	(8.0)	(6.2)	(9.1)
Maize	1.2	1.5	1.5	1.3	1.3
	(19.7)	(21.2)	(22.1)	(19.4)	(19.4)
Wheat	19.5	24.2	22.6	23.1	22.2
	(81.1)	(87.7)	(87.6)	(87.8)	(88.1)
Barley	0.5	0.4	0.5	0.5	0.4
	(54.5)	(57.1)	(62.5)	(71.4)	(57.1)
Total Cereals	42.3	52.4	50.3	50.9	47.1
	(41.0)	(50.8)	(49.6)	(50.1)	(49.9)
Total Pulses	2.6	2.9	2.6	3.1	3.0
	(10.5)	(13.1)	(12.3)	(13.4)	(14.1)
Total Foodgrains	44.9	55.3	52.9	54.1	50.1
	(35.1)	(44.2)	(43.1)	(43.4)	(43.3)
Oilseeds	5.8	6.7	5.7	6.1	5.4
	(22.9)	(25.0)	(22.5)	(24.2)	(22.6)

Cotton	2.5	3.1	2.8	3.1	2.5
	(32.9)	(34.4)	(32.6)	(34.1)	(32.5)
Sugarcane	3.4	4.1	4.2	4.3	4.3
	(86.9)	(91.1)	(91.3)	(91.5)	(91.5)

(P) Provisional

Notes: 1. Figures in parentheses represent percentage of irrigated area to total area under the crop. 2. Irrigated area under oilseeds denotes the area under groundnut, rapeseed and mustard, linseed, sesame and others.

Coal Reserves

The ministry of coal is responsible for determining policies and strategies related to exploration and development of coal and lignite reserves, sanctioning important projects of high value and for deciding all related issues. India has a long history of commercial coal mining covering nearly 220 years, starting from 1774 by M/s Sumner and Heatly of the East India Company in the Raniganj Coalfield along the western bank of Damodar river. However, for about a century the growth of Indian coal mining remained slow for lack of demand. The introduction of steam locomotives in 1853 put it on the rise. Within a short span, production rose to an annual average of 1 million tonnes (mt) and India could produce 6.12 mts per year by 1900 and 18 mts per year by 1920. The production got a sudden boost from the First World War but went through a slump in the early thirties. It again reached a level of 29 mts by 1942 and 30 mts by 1946. Unscientific mining practices adopted by some of the mine owners and poor working conditions for labourers in some of the private coal mines became matters of concern for the government. For these reasons, the Central government took a decision to nationalize private coal mines. The nationalization was done in two phases, the first with the coking coal mines in 1971-72 and then with the non-coking coal mines in 1973. Fifty-five per cent of the country's energy consumption is met by coal. The country's industrial heritage was built upon indigenous coal. Commercial primary energy consumption in India has grown by about 700 per cent in the last four decades. The current per capita commercial primary energy consumption in India is about 350 kgoe/year (kilogram of oil equivalent per year) that is well below that of developed countries. Driven by the rising population, expanding economy and a quest for improved quality of life, energy usage in India is expected to rise to around 450 kgoe/year in 2010. Considering the limited reserve potentiality of petroleum and natural gas, eco-conservation restriction on hydel projects and geo-political perceptions of nuclear power, coal will continue to occupy centre-stage in India's energy scenario.

Inventory of Coal Reserves of India

As a result of exploration carried out down to a depth of 1200m by the GSI and other agencies, a cumulative total of 245.69 billion tonnes of coal resources have been estimated in the country as on 1 January 2004.

The state-wise distribution of coal resources and its categorization are as follows:

Statewise Resources of Indian Coal

State	Coal Resources in Million Tonnes			
	Proved	Indicated	Inferred	Total
Andhra Pradesh	8263	6079	2584	16926
Arunachal Pradesh	31	40	19	90
Assam	279	27	34	340
Bihar	0	0	160	160
Chhattisgarh	9373	26191	4411	39975
Jharkhand	35417	30439	6348	72204
Madhya Pradesh	7513	8815	2904	19232
Maharashtra	4653	2309	1620	8582
Meghalaya	117	41	301	459
Nagaland	4	1	15	20
Orissa	15161	30976	14847	60984
Uttar Pradesh	766	296	0	1062
West Bengal	11383	11876	4554	27813
Total	**92960**	**117090**	**37797**	**247847**

The Power Sector

The Indian power sector was one of the first sectors in which private participation was allowed in the early 1990s. At first, the focus was on private sector investments in power generation projects but the government later allowed private organizations to invest in distribution and transmission projects as well. As on March 2002, India had around 104,000 MW of installed power generating capacity. As much as 80 per cent of this installed capacity comes from thermal power plants while hydroelectric plants account for about 16 per cent. Nuclear plants account for the remaining installed capacity. Non-conventional energy sources contribute only a relatively small percentage. There are a large number of private power projects either at the planning stages or under construction. The Central Electricity Authority (CEA) has granted Techno-Economic Clearances (TECs) to over fifty private power projects that account for a total of around 30,000 MW. India needs substantial addition of power generation capacities, given its economic growth targets. According to Planning Commission estimates, India needs to add around 47,000 MW of power generation facilities in the near future, requiring an investment of around US$ 73 billion.

The Overall Generation (Thermal + Nuclear + Hydro) in Public Utilities in the Country over Years

Year	Generation (billion units)
2000-01	499.5
2001-02	515.3
2002-03	531.4
2003-04	558.3
2004-05	587.4
2005-06 (up to Feb. 06)	562.7

The Power Supply Position from 2000-01 Onwards

Year	Energy Requirement/ (MU)	Energy Availability/ (MU)	Energy Shortage/ (MU)	Energy Shortage (%)
2000-01	507216	467400	39816	7.8
2001-02	522537	483350	39187	7.5
2002-03	545983	497890	48093	8.8
2003-04	559264	519398	39866	7.1
2004-05	591373	548115	43258	7.3
2005-06 (up to Dec. 05)	466109	430408	35701	7.7

Peak Demand

Year	Peak Demand (MW)	Peak Met (MW)	Peak Shortage (MW)	Peak Shortage (%)
2000-01	78037	67880	10157	13.0
2001-02	78441	69189	9252	11.8
2002-03	81492	71547	9945	12.2
2003-04	84574	75066	9508	11.2
2004-05	87906	77652	10254	11.7
2005-06 (up to Dec.05)	90119	80631	9488	10.5

The Petroleum Industry

India ranks sixth in the world in terms of petroleum demand and is projected to replace South Korea and emerge as the fourth-largest consumer of energy, after the United States, China and Japan, by 2010. Since India is dependent on imports for its petroleum requirements, energy security has become a major government concern. In recent years this has taken the form of trying to get a stake in oil and gas fields from Myanmar to central Asia and Africa. However, the major thrust still lies in searching for hydrocarbons in onshore and offshore blocks in India. Recent gas finds are making oil majors take notice of the potential in prospective basins. The import of petroleum products was 8.83 million tonnes (mt) in 2004-05 and 7.32 mt in April-November 2005. Against this, exports of petroleum products were 18.21 mt in 2004-05 and 12.68 mt during the period April-November 2005. Refining capacity has increased from 118.37 mt per annum (mtpa) as on 1April 2003, to 127.37 mtpa as on 1 October 2005. The targeted capacity by the end of the Tenth Five Year Plan is 141.70 mtpa. To meet its demand, India is investing heavily in oil fields abroad. India's state-owned oil firms already have stakes in oil and gas fields in Russia, Sudan, Iraq, Libya, Egypt, Qatar, Ivory Coast, Australia, Vietnam and Myanmar.

Production of Crude Oil and Natural Gas

	Item	2002-03	2003-04	2004-05	2005-06 (Apr-Dec)
1.	Crude Oil Production ('000 Tonnes)				
(a)	Onshore:				
	Gujarat	6042	6131	6189	4665
	Assam/Nagaland	4660	4592	4701	3399
	Arunachal Pradesh	74	77	83	78
	Tamil Nadu	395	375	391	294
	Andhra Pradesh	300	281	227	154
	Total (a)	11471	11456	11591	8590
	of which Oil	2951	3002	3196	2465
	ONGC	8445	8380	8321	6055
	JVC/Private	75	74	74	70
(b)	Offshore:				
	ONGC	17560	17677	18164	12163
	JVC/Private	4013	4240	4226	3288
	Total (b)	21573	21917	22390	15451
	Grand Total (a+b)	33044	33373	33981	24041
2.	Natural Gas Production (Million Cubic Metres)				
(a)	Onshore:				
	Gujarat	3531	3517	3711	2750
	Assam/Nagaland	2047	2204	2248	1824
	Arunachal Pradesh	36	44	40	32
	Tripura	446	508	496	368
	Tamil Nadu	466	605	678	654
	Andhra Pradesh	2038	1927	1707	1255
	Rajasthan	162	168	213	174
	Total (a)	8726	8973	9093	7057
	of which Oil	1744	1887	2009	1708
	ONGC	5871	5779	5657	4175
	JVC/Private	1111	1307	1427	1174
(b)	Offshore:				
	ONGC	18367	17805	17313	12717
	JVC/Private	4296	5184	5357	4323
	Total (b)	22663	22989	22670	17040

Iron and Steel

The history of iron and steel in India in nearly 4,000 years old. The first steel ingots were rolled in TISCO in 1911. This was followed in 1936 by the establishment of the Mysore Iron and Steel Works, later renamed Visveswaraya Iron and Steel Works. In 1939, Indian Iron and Steel Company (IISCO), now a subsidiary of Steel Authority of India Limited (SAIL), was started. At the time of Independence, India possessed a small but viable steel industry with an annual capacity of 1.3 million tonnes. In 1951, India produced 1.1 million tonnes of finished steel. In the era of planned economy, iron and steel, a core and basic sector, received due attention of the government and with foreign assistance and indigenous resources, many new steel plants were set up. Until the 1990s, the iron and steel sector was by and large the exclusive preserve of only the public sector, the sole exception being TISCO. The new economic policy announced in 1991 was a significant milestone which brought about a sea change in the Indian iron and steel industry. The structure of the steel industry changed with the advent of major steel producers in the private sector with world-class technologies and capacities. Many all-India financial institutions came forward to support private initiatives and by sanctioning financial assistance, nineteen steel projects involving an investment of about Rs 30,000 crore created an additional capacity of 13 million tonnes (mt) per annum. Today India is the tenth largest steel producer in the world, producing 27.82 million tonnes of finished steel a year. The industry represents nearly Rs 9,000 crore of capital and directly provides employment to over 0.5 million people. The world's largest producer of steel is China (107 mt), followed by Japan (104 mt) and USA (97 mt). India's present per capita consumption of crude steel is only 24 kg which is very low compared to developed and developing countries–422 kg in USA, 417 kg in Germany, 109 kg in Russia and 87 kg in China. Our consumption is less than one-fifth of the world average, i.e., 12 kg. The Government of India has taken a number of steps to boost the per capita consumption of steel in the country.

Last Three Years' Import of Finished (Carbon) Steel

Year	Qty (in million tonnes)
2001-02	1.271
2002-03	1.510
2003-04	1.540
2004-05	2.109
2005-06 (prov.)	3.765
2006-07 (April–July, 2006) (prov. estimate)	0.850

Exports of Finished Carbon Steel and Pig Iron During the Last Four Years and the Current Year

(in million tonnes)

	Finished (Carbon) Steel	Pig Iron
2002-03	4.506	0.629
2003-04	4.835	0.518
2004-05	4.381	0.393
2005-06 (prov.)	4.350	0.300
2006-07 (April–July 06) (prov. estimate)	1.600	0.091

Last Four Years' Production of Pig Iron and Finished (Carbon) Steel

(in million tonnes)

Category	2002-03	2003-04	2004-05	2005-06 (prov.)	2006-07 (April-July 06) (Prov. Estimated)
Pig Iron	5.285	3.764	3.856	3.228	1.355
Finished Carbon Steel	33.671	36.957	40.055	42.636	14.300

The Textile Industry

The Indian textile industry is one of the largest and most important sectors in the economy in terms of output, foreign exchange earnings and employment in India. It contributes 20 per cent of industrial production, 9 per cent of excise collections, 18 per cent of employment in the industrial sector, nearly 20 per cent to the country's total export earnings and 4 per cent to the GDP. According to a study by CRISIL, the Indian textile and apparel industry can achieve a potential size of US$ 85 billion by 2010, with a domestic market size of US$ 45 billion and nearly 60 per cent of exports comprising garments. India has a natural competitive advantage in terms of a strong and large multi-fibre base, abundant, cheap, skilled labour, and presence across the entire value chain of the industry ranging from spinning, weaving, and made-ups to manufacturers of garments. India's textile industry comprises mostly small-scale, non-integrated spinning, weaving, finishing and apparel-making enterprises. During 2004-05, production of fabrics touched a peak of 45,378 million sq. m. In the year 2005-06 up to November, production of fabrics registered a further growth of 9 per cent over the corresponding period of the previous year. In keeping with the trend of textile companies increasing capacity and adding new manufacturing units, the last week of 2005 saw a substantial number of firms, both new and existing, queuing up to file an intent to manufacture document with the Department of Industrial Policy and Promotion (DIPP). Out of 161 companies that have filed Industrial Entrepreneur Memoranda (IEM) in the last week of December, textile firms accounted for more than a quarter of all new applications.

Growth and Investment in Textiles During 2005-06 (April-March)

- All India Index of Industrial Production (IIP) registered an increase of 8.0 per cent during 2005-06 as against the corresponding period of last year, the index of production for the textile group of industries showed a surge in the entire sector. There was a significant increase in respect of textile products (16.4 per cent) and cotton textiles (8.5 per cent). However, marginal increase in jute and other vegetable fibre textiles (0.5 per cent) and wool, silk and manmade fibre textiles (0.2 per cent) was witnessed.
- Spun yarn production increased by 5.1 per cent due to increase in cotton yarn and manmade filament yarn production.
- Cloth production was more by 8.2 per cent. The hosiery sector recorded the highest growth (13.1 per cent) followed by handloom (8.5 per cent) and powerloom (7.0 per cent).

- The share of textile sector in FDI was 1.02 per cent (in terms of amount) during this period as against 4.29 per cent in the corresponding period last year.
- The share in the number of Letters of Intent (LOI)/Direct Industrial Licenses (DIL) was 32.59 per cent and the share in investment was 27.71 per cent.

The Pharmaceutical Industry

The Indian pharmaceutical industry, now a $ 4 billion industry, in addition to over $ 3.1 billion exports, has made tremendous progress in terms of infrastructure development, technology base and range of products. The industry produces bulk drugs belonging to all major therapeutic groups requiring complicated manufacturing processes and has also developed excellent Good Manufacturing Practices (GMP)-compliant facilities for the production of different dosage forms. The strength of the industry lies in developing cost-effective technologies in the shortest possible time for drug intermediates and bulk actives without compromising on quality. Many Indian companies maintain highest standards in purity, stability and international 'SHE' requirements, viz. safety, health and environmental protection, in production and supply of bulk drugs to even innovator companies. Along with Brazil and PR China, India has carved a niche for itself by being a top generic pharma player. In 2002, over 20,000 registered drug manufacturers in India sold $9 billion worth of formulations and bulk drugs. Eighty-five per cent of these formulations were sold in India while over 60 per cent of the bulk drugs were exported, mostly to the US and Russia. Most of the players in the market are small-to-medium enterprises; 250 of the largest companies control 70 per cent of the Indian market. In terms of the global market, India currently holds a modest 1-2 per cent share, but it has been growing at approximately 10 per cent per year. India gained its foothold on the global scene with its innovatively-engineered generic drugs and active pharmaceutical ingredients (API), and it is now seeking to become a major player in outsourced clinical research as well as contract manufacturing and research. There are seventy-four US FDA-approved manufacturing facilities in India, more than in any other country outside the US and in 2005, almost 20 per cent of all Abbreviated New Drug Applications (ANDA) to the FDA are expected to be filed by Indian companies. As it expands its core business, the industry is being forced to adapt its business model to recent changes in the operating environment. The first and most significant change was the 1 January 2005 enactment of an amendment to India's patent law that reinstated product patents for the first time since 1972. Unlike in other countries, the divide between biotechnology and pharmaceuticals remains fairly defined in India. Biotech here still plays the role of pharma's little sister, but many outsiders have high expectations for the future. India accounted for 2 per cent of the $41 billion global biotech market and in 2003 was ranked third in the Asia-Pacific region and eleventh in the world in number of biotechs. In 2004-05, the Indian biotech industry saw its revenues grow 37 per cent to $1.1 billion. The Indian biotech market is dominated by biopharmaceuticals; 75 per cent of 2004-05 revenues came from biopharmaceuticals which saw 30 per cent growth last year. Of the revenues from biopharmaceuticals, vaccines led the way, comprising 47 per cent of sales. Biologics and large-molecule drugs tend to be more expensive than small-molecule drugs, and India hopes to sweep the market in biogenerics and contract manufacturing as drugs go off patent and Indian companies upgrade their manufacturing capabilities.

Major Pharmaceutical Companies

- Ranbaxy Laboratories
- Dr Reddy's Laboratories
- Cipla
- Nicolas Piramal India
- Aurobindo Pharma
- GlaxoSmithKline
- Lupin Laboratories
- Sun Pharmaceutical Industries
- Cadila Healthcare
- Wockhardt
- Biocon

The Telecom Industry

In 1999, the Government of India authored a National Telecom Policy 1999 (NTP-1999), which acknowledged that access to telecommunications is of utmost importance for the achievement of the country's social and economic goals. Availability of affordable and effective communication for citizens was the core vision and goal of this telecom policy. Since the announcement of the policy, the government has undertaken various concrete steps to achieve the policy objectives. The number of mobile phones (including 20.8 million WLL (M)) as on 31 January 2006, was about 83 million, which is over 63 per cent of the total number of phones in the country. Over 32 million new telephones were added during April-January of the current financial year, with five million additions occurring in January alone, taking the total number of phones in the country to 130.8 million as on 31 January 2006. Tele-density has increased from 8.8 per cent in January 2005 to 11.7 per cent at the end of January 2006. According to the Telecom Regulatory Authority of India (TRAI's) quarterly performance indicators, Internet user base has grown 15 per cent from September 2004 to September 2005, with private operators accounting for 2.6 million users. The gross subscriber base of the fixed and mobile services together reached 113.07 million at the end of the quarter July-September 2005, from 104.22 million as on June 2005, registering an increase of 8.49 per cent during the quarter. Under the Bharat Nirman Yojana, a total 66,822 villages are to be provided with village public telephones (VPT) by November 2007. The growth statistics of the sector combined with the government's decision to increase the foreign direct investment cap in the sector to 74 per cent is generating interest among global investors. India, one of the fastest growing countries in telecom manufacturing in the world, is expected to attract another US$ 855 million as foreign investment over the next two years. During the period August 1991 to January 2004, 926 proposals of Foreign Direct Investment (FDI) of Rs 57,260.14 crore were approved and the actual inflow of FDI during the above period was Rs 9872.5 crore. In terms of approval of FDI, the telecom sector is second largest after the power and oil refinery sector.

Yearly FDI Inflow into Indian Telecom Industry

(Rs million)

Year	FDI Inflow
1993	20.6
1994	140.2
1995	2,067.4
1996	7,648.3
1997	12,451.9
1998	17,756.4

1999	2,126.7
2000	2,885.8
2001	39,709.0
2002	10,815.0
2003	3,014.0
2004	874.2
Total	**99,509.4**

The IT Industry

Over the past decade, the information technology (IT) industry has become one of the fastest-growing industries in India, propelled by exports (the industry accounted for more than a quarter of India's services exports in 2004-05). The key segments that have contributed significantly (96 per cent of total) to the industry's exports include software and services (IT services) and IT-enabled services (ITES), i.e., business services. Over a period of time, India has established itself as a preferred global sourcing base in these segments and they are expected to continue to fuel growth in the future. These segments have evolved into a sophisticated model of operations. Indian IT and ITES companies have created global delivery models (onsite-near shore-offshore), entered into long-term engagements with customers, expanded their portfolio of services offerings, built scale, extended service propositions beyond cost savings to quality and innovation, evolved their pricing models and have tried to find sustainable solutions to various issues such as risk management, human capital attraction and retention and cost management. India has emerged as the fastest growing and the fourth-largest IT market in the Asia-Pacific. The industry (exports and domestic combined) is expected to touch Rs 247,000 crore (US$ 53.2 billion) by 2008 compared to Rs 87,000 crore (US$ 18.7 billion) in 2003, thus growing at a CAGR of 23.1 per cent. Exports of the Indian software and services sector was Rs 78,230 crore (US$ 17.2 billion) in 2004-05, up 34 per cent from Rs 58,240 crore (US$ 12.8 billion) in 2003-04. The total direct employment in the Indian IT-ITES sector is estimated to have grown by over a million, from 284,000 in FY 1999-2000 to a projected 1,287,000 in the current fiscal (2005-06). In addition to the nearly 1.3 million-strong workforce employed directly in the industry, Indian IT-ITES is estimated to have helped create an additional 3 million job opportunities through indirect and induced employment. Indirect employment includes expenditure on vendors including telecom, power, construction, facility management, IT, transportation, catering and other services. Induced employment is driven by consumption expenditure of employees on food, clothing, utilities, recreation, health and other services.

India-based Service Providers

Category	No. of players	Share of India's total IT/BPO export revenues	Performance
Tier I Players	3–4	45% of IT Services 4–5% of BPO	Revenues greater than US$ 1 billion
Tier II IT Players	7–10	25% of IT Services 4–5% of BPO	Revenues US$ 100 million-US$ 1 billion
Offshore operations of Global IT majors	20–30	10–15% of IT Services 10–15% of BPO	Revenues US$ 10 million-US$ 500 million

Pure play BPO providers	40–50	20% of BPO	Revenues US$ 10 million-US$ 200 million (Excluding top provider with US$ 500 million)
Captive BPO units	150	50% of BPO	Revenues US$ 25 million-US$ 150 million (top 10 units)
Emerging players	>3000	10–15% of IT Services 5% of BPO	Revenues less than US$ 100 million (IT) Revenues less than US$ 10 million (BPO)

The ITES/BPO Industry

IT-Enabled Services (ITES) or BPO (Business Process Outsourcing), as it is better known, holds tremendous potential for India. The public perceives ITES in India as almost synonymous with call centres, but it encompasses much more. The term comprises the outsourcing of such processes that can be enabled with information technology and covers areas as diverse as finance, HR (human resource), administration, healthcare, telecommunication, manufacturing, etc. These services are usually delivered to remote areas through the medium of telecom and Internet and implies the transfer of ownership and management of the process from the customer to the service provider. India, with its large English-speaking graduate workforce and low wage levels, has emerged as an attractive destination for ITES.

IT-Enabled Services has been the key driver of growth for the Indian IT industry. The ITES–BPO sector in India grew at over 46 per cent from US$ 2.5 billion in 2002-03 to touch US$ 3.6 billion in 2003-04. Indian ITES–BPO exports have grown to US$ 6.3 billion in FY 2005-06, recording a growth of 37 per cent. It is expected to grow to US$ 8-8.5 billion in FY 2006-07. Net employment in the ITES–BPO segment has grown by approximately 100,000 in FY 2005-06, taking the total direct employment within this segment to 415,000.

IT Industry—Sector-wise Break-up

(US$ billion)

	FY 2004	FY 2005	FY 2006E
IT Services	10.4	13.5	17.5
—*Exports*	7.3	10	13.2
—*Domestic*	3.1	3.5	4.3
ITES-BPO	3.4	5.2	7.2
—*Exports*	3.1	4.6	6.3
—*Domestic*	0.3	0.6	0.9
Engineering Services and R&D, Software Products	2.9	3.9	4.8
—*Exports*	2.5	3.1	3.9
—*Domestic*	0.4	0.7	0.9
Total Software and Services Revenues	16.7	22.6	29.5
Of which, exports are	12.9	17.7	23.4
Hardware	5	5.9	6.9
Total IT Industry (including Hardware)	21.6	28.4	36.3

Stock Exchanges of India

The Indian Securities Market originated in 1875, when twenty-two brokers established the Bombay Stock Exchange (BSE) under a banyan tree. Presently, there are two national level exchanges in India—the Bombay Stock Exchange (BSE) and National Stock Exchange (NSE), along with twenty-one regional exchanges. There are around 9,400 broking outfits, with about 9,600 companies listed on the exchanges. The market capitalization is close to US$ 125.5 billion.

The Securities and Exchange Board of India (SEBI) is the statutory body, operating within the legal framework of Securities and Exchange Board of India Act, 1992. It exercises its powers under the Securities and Exchange Board of India Act, 1992; the Securities Contract (Regulation) Act, 1956; the Depositories Act, 1996; and also the delegated powers under the Companies Act, 1956.

The headquarters of SEBI are located in Mumbai. It has three regional offices—at Chennai, New Delhi and Kolkata. Its board is its main decision-making body, headed by the chairman and comprising five other members.

List of Stock Exchanges in India

North Zone

Uttar Pradesh Stock Exchange Assoc. Ltd, Kanpur
Ludhiana Stock Exchange Assoc. Ltd
Delhi Stock Exchange Assoc. Ltd
Jaipur Stock Exchange Ltd

East Zone

Bhubaneswar Stock Exchange Assoc Ltd
Calcutta Stock Exchange Assoc Ltd
Gauhati Stock Exchange Ltd
Magadh Stock Exchange Association, Patna

West Zone

The Stock Exchange, Ahmedabad
Vadodara Stock Exchange Ltd
Madhya Pradesh Stock Exchange Ltd, Indore
The Stock Exchange, Mumbai
OTC Exchange of India, Mumbai
National Stock Exchange of India Ltd, Mumbai
Pune Stock Exchange Ltd
Saurashtra Kutch Stock Exchange Ltd, Rajkot
Inter-connected Stock Exchange of India, Mumbai

South Zone

Bangalore Stock Exchange Ltd
Madras Stock Exchange Ltd
Cochin Stock Exchange Ltd
Coimbatore Stock Exchange
Hyderabad Stock Exchange Ltd
Mangalore Stock Exchange Ltd

The Sensex

The BSE Sensex or Bombay Stock Exchange Sensitive Index is a value-weighted index comprising thirty stocks with the base April 1979=100. It consists of the thirty largest and most actively traded stocks, representative of various sectors, on the Bombay Stock Exchange. These companies account for around one-fifth of the market capitalization of the BSE. At irregular intervals, the Bombay Stock Exchange (BSE) authorities review and modify its composition to make sure it reflects current market conditions.

The constituents of the BSE Sensex as on 31 March 2006 are as follows:

- Associated Cement Ltd
- Bajaj Auto Ltd
- Bharat Heavy Electricals Ltd
- Bharti Tele Ventures Ltd
- Cipla Ltd
- Dr Reddy's Laboratories Ltd
- Grasim Industries Ltd
- Gujarat Ambuja Cements Ltd
- HDFC
- HDFC Bank Ltd
- Hero Honda Motors Ltd
- Hindalco Industries Ltd
- Hindustan Lever Ltd

- ICICI Bank Ltd
- Infosys Technologies Ltd
- ITC Ltd
- Larsen and Toubro Ltd
- Maruti Udyog Ltd
- National Thermal Power Corporation Ltd
- ONGC Ltd
- Ranbaxy Laboratories Ltd
- Reliance Communications Ltd
- Reliance Industries Ltd
- Reliance Energy Ltd
- Satyam Computer Services Ltd
- State Bank of India
- Tata Consultancy Services Ltd
- Tata Motors
- Tata Steel
- Wipro Ltd

History of Replacement of Scrips in the Sensex

Date	Outgoing Scrips	Replaced by
01.01.1986	Bombay Burmah	Voltas
	Asian Cables	Peico
	Crompton Greaves	Premier Auto.
	Scinda	G.E. Shipping
03.08.1992	Zenith Ltd	Bharat Forge
19.08.1996	Ballarpur Inds.	Arvind Mills
	Bharat Forge	Bajaj Auto
	Bombay Dyeing	BHEL
	Ceat Tyres	BSES
	Century Text.	Colgate
	GSFC	Guj. Amb. Cement
	Hind. Motors	HPCL
	Indian Organic	ICICI
	Indian Rayon	IDBI
	Kirloskar Cummins	IPCL
	Mukand Iron	MTNL
	Philips	Ranbaxy Lab.
	Premier Auto	State Bank of India
	Siemens	Steel Authority of India
	Voltas	Tata Chem
16.11.1998	Arvind Mills	Castrol
	GE Shipping	Infosys Technologies
	IPCL	NIIT Ltd
	Steel Authority of India	Novartis
10.04.2000	IDBI	Dr Reddy's Laboratories
	Indian Hotels	Reliance Petroleum
	Tata Chem	Satyam Computers
	Tata Power	Zee Telefilms
08.01.2001	Novartis	Cipla Ltd
07.01.2002	NIIT Ltd	HCL Technologies
	Mahindra & Mahindra	Hero Honda Motors Ltd
31.05.2002	ICICI Ltd	ICICI Bank Ltd
10.10.2002	Reliance Petroleum Ltd	HDFC Ltd
10.11.2003	Castrol India Ltd	Bharti-Tele-Ventures Ltd
	Colgate Palomive (India) Ltd	HDFC Bank Ltd
	Glaxo Smithkline Pharma. Ltd	ONGC Ltd
	HCL Technologies Ltd	Tata Power Company Ltd

	Nestle (India) Ltd	Wipro Ltd
19.05.2004	Larsen & Toubro Ltd	Maruti Udyog Ltd
27.09.2004	Mahanagar Telephone Nigam Ltd	Larsen & Toubro Ltd
06.06.2005	Hindustan Petroleum Corp Ltd	NTPC
	Zee Telefilms Ltd	Tata Consultancy Services Ltd
12.06.2006	Tata Power	Reliance Communications Ltd

Insurance Industry in India

In India, the insurance business is divided into four categories. These are:

1. Life Insurance
2. Fire Insurance
3. Marine Insurance
4. Miscellaneous Insurance

While life insurers transact life insurance business, general insurers transact the business regarding the other forms of insurance. Insurance is a federal subject in India. The business of life insurance in India in its present form began in 1818 with the setting up of the Oriental Life Insurance Company in Calcutta. The first general insurance company set up in India was the Triton Insurance Company Ltd in 1850 in Calcutta. The primary legislations dealing with insurance business in India are the Insurance Act, 1938, and the Insurance Regulatory and Development Authority Act, 1999.

State Insurers

Life insurer

1. Life Insurance Corporation of India (LIC)

General insurers and reinsurers

2. General Insurance Corporation of India (GIC)

Private insurers

Life Insurers

1. Bajaj Allianz Life Insurance Company Ltd
2. Birla Sun Life Insurance Co. Ltd
3. HDFC Standard Life Insurance Co. Ltd
4. ICICI Prudential Life Insurance Co. Ltd
5. ING Vysya Life Insurance Company Pvt. Ltd
6. Life Insurance Corporation of India
7. Max New York Life Insurance Co. Ltd
8. Met Life India Insurance Company Pvt. Ltd
9. Kotak Mahindra Old Mutual Life Insurance Limited
10. SBI Life Insurance Co. Ltd
11. Tata AIG Life Insurance Company Limited
12. Reliance Life Insurance Company Limited.
13. Aviva Life Insurance Co. India Pvt. Ltd
14. Sahara India Life Insurance Co. Ltd
15. Shriram Life Insurance Co. Ltd
16. Bharti AXA Life Insurance Company Ltd

Non-life insurers

1. Bajaj Allianz General Insurance Co. Ltd
2. ICICI Lombard General Insurance Co. Ltd
3. IFFCO Tokio General Insurance Co. Ltd
4. National Insurance Co. Ltd
5. The New India Assurance Co. Ltd
6. The Oriental Insurance Co. Ltd
7. Reliance General Insurance Co. Ltd

8. Royal Sundaram Alliance Insurance Co. Ltd
9. Tata AIG General Insurance Co. Ltd
10. United India Insurance Co. Ltd
11. Cholamandalam MS General Insurance Co. Ltd
12. HDFC-Chubb General Insurance Co. Ltd
13. Export Credit Guarantee Corporation Ltd
14. Agriculture Insurance Co. of India Ltd
15. Star Health and Allied Insurance Company Ltd

Banking

Although different forms of banking, mainly in the form of money lending, existed in India since ancient times, banking in the form we know today began only around 100 years ago. The earliest such institutions under the British regime were agency houses that carried on banking business beside their trading activities. However, most of these agency houses were closed down between 1929–32. In 1919, the three presidency banks (Bank of Bengal, Bank of Bombay, and Bank of Madras) were amalgamated into the Imperial Bank of India. Later, in 1955, the Imperial Bank of India became the Tate Bank of India. Oudh Commercial Bank, founded in 1881, was the first bank of limited liability to be managed by Indians. The Swadeshi movement that began in 1906 inspired the formation of the number of commercial banks. The Banking Companies (Inspection Ordinance) and the Banking Companies (Restriction of Branches) Act were passed in January and February 1946 respectively. The Banking Companies Act was passed in February 1949. It was later renamed the Banking Regulation Act. On 19 July 1969, the government issued an ordinance, acquiring the ownership and control of fourteen major banks in the country, with deposits above Rs 50 crore each. The aim was to bring commercial banks to the mainstream of economic development with definite social obligations and objectives. On 15 April 1980, six more commercial banks were nationalized. The government laid down the objectives of the public-sector banking system on 21 July 1969. A high-level committee was set up on 14 August 1991 to examine all aspects relating to the structure, organization, functions and procedures of the financial system, in view of the changing economic scenario of the country. Based on the recommendations of his committee, headed by the chairman, M. Narsimham, a comprehensive reform of the banking system was introduced in 1992-93. The objective of this reform programme was to ensure that the balance sheets of banks reflected their real financial health. Another important measure of the reforms process was the introduction of capital adequacy norms in line with international standards. The setting up of new private sector banks was not allowed in the post-nationalization era. However, this was allowed in 1993. The aim was to introduce greater competition that in turn would lead to higher productivity and efficiency. In December 1997, the Government of India set up a high-level committee under the chairmanship of M. Narasimham to review the implementation of financial system reforms as initiated in the post-liberalization era and to plan the reforms necessary in the future. The committee submitted its report to the government in April 1998. To meet the challenges of going global, the Indian banking sector is implementing internationally followed prudential accounting norms for the classification of assets, income recognition and loan-loss provisioning. The scope of disclosure and transparency has also been raised in accordance with international practices. India has complied with almost all the Core Principles of Effective Banking Supervision of the Basel Committee. Some Indian banks also present their accounts as per the US GAAP.

The Indian banking industry is currently in a transitional phase. On the one hand, the public sector banks, which are the mainstay of the Indian banking system, are in the process of consolidating their position by capitalizing on the strength of their huge networks and customer bases. On the other, the private sector banks are venturing into a whole new game of mergers and acquisitions to expand their bases. Net domestic credit in the banking system has witnessed a steady increase of 17.5 per cent from US$ 445 billion on 21 January 2005 to US$ 523 billion on 20 January 2006. The growth in net domestic credit during the current financial year up to 20 January 2006 was 14.4 per cent. Nationalized banks were the largest contributors to total bank credit at 47.8 per cent as of September 2005. While foreign banks' contribution to total bank credit was low at 6.7 per cent, the contribution of the State Bank of India and its associates accounted for 23.8 per cent of the total bank credit. Credit extended by other SCBs stood at 18.9 per cent. Indian banks, particularly private banks, are riding high on the retail business. ICICI Bank and HDFC Bank have witnessed over 70 per cent year-on-year growth in retail loan assets in the second quarter of 2005-06. Annual revenues in the domestic retail banking market are expected to more than double to US$ 16.5 billion by 2010 from about US$ 6.4 billion at present, says a McKinsey study. Foreign banks are working on expanding their bases in the country. The ministry of finance and the Reserve Bank of India have agreed to allow foreign banks to open twenty branches a year as against twelve now. India has managed to achieve an impressive rate of savings, with the World Bank estimating a share of financial assets in GDP of 173 per cent, compared with 104 per cent in Mexico, 112 per cent in Indonesia and 157 per cent in Brazil.

Nationalized Banks

1. Allahabad Bank
2. Andhra Bank
3. Bank of Baroda
4. Bank of India
5. Bank of Maharashtra
6. Canara Bank
7. Central Bank of India
8. Corporation Bank
9. Dena Bank
10. Indian Bank
11. Indian Overseas Bank
12. Oriental Bank of Commerce
13. Punjab and Sind Bank
14. Punjab National Bank
15. Syndicate Bank
16. Union Bank of India
17. United Bank of India
18. United Commercial Bank
19. Vijaya Bank

State Bank of India and its Associate Banks

1. State Bank of India
2. State Bank of Bikaner and Jaipur
3. State Bank of Hyderabad
4. State Bank of Indore
5. State Bank of Mysore
6. State Bank of Patiala
7. State Bank of Saurashtra
8. State Bank of Travancore

Private Indian Banks

1. Bank of Rajasthan Ltd
2. Bharat Overseas Bank Ltd
3. Catholic Syrian Bank Ltd
4. Federal Bank Ltd
5. Dhanalakshmi Bank Ltd
6. Jammu & Kashmir Bank Ltd
7. Karnataka Bank Ltd
8. Karur Vysya Bank Ltd
9. City Union Bank Ltd
10. Lakshmi Vilas Bank Ltd
11. Nainital Bank Ltd

12. Ratnakar Bank Ltd
13. Sangli Bank Ltd
14. South Indian Bank Ltd
15. Tamilnad Mercantile Bank Ltd
16. United Western Bank Ltd
17. ING Vysya Bank Ltd
18. Lord Krishna Bank Ltd
19. ICICI Bank Ltd
20. UTI Bank Ltd
21. IndusInd Bank Ltd
22. Yes Bank Ltd
23. SBI Commercial and International Bank Ltd
24. Ganesh Bank of Kurundwad Ltd
25. Centurion Bank of Punjab
26. HDFC Bank Ltd
27. Development Credit Bank Ltd
28. Kotak Mahindra Bank Ltd
29. Industrial Development Bank of India Ltd

Private Foreign Banks

1. ABN AMRO Bank N.V.
2. Abu Dhabi Commercial Bank Ltd
3. American Express Bank Ltd
5. Bank of Bahrain & Kuwait BSC
6. Mashreq Bank PSC
7. Bank of Nova Scotia
8. Bank of Tokyo Mitsubishi UFJ Ltd
9. Citibank N.A.
10. Deutsche Bank
11. Hongkong and Shanghai Banking Corporation Ltd
12. Societe Generale
13. Sonali Bank
14. BNP Paribas
15. Barclays Bank p.l.c.
16. DBS Bank Ltd
17. Bank Internasional Indonesia
18. Arab Bangladesh Bank Ltd
19. Standard Chartered Bank
20. State Bank of Mauritius Ltd
21. Bank of Ceylon
22. Cho Hung Bank
23. Chinatrust Commercial Bank Ltd
24. Krung Thai Bank plc.
25. Antwerp Diamond Bank N.V.
26. JP Morgan Chase Bank
27. Mizuho Corporate Bank Ltd
28. Oman International Bank SAOG
29. Calyon Bank

State Co-operative Banks

1. The Andaman and Nicobar State Co-operative Bank Ltd
2. The Andhra Pradesh State Co-operative Bank Ltd
3. The Arunachal Pradesh State co-operative Apex Bank Ltd
4. The Assam Co-operative Apex Bank Ltd
5. The Bihar State Co-operative Bank Ltd
6. The Chandigarh State Co-operative Bank Ltd
7. The Delhi State Co-operative Bank Ltd
8. The Goa State Co-operative Bank Ltd
9. The Gujarat State Co-operative Bank Ltd
10. The Haryana State Co-operative Apex Bank Ltd
11. The Himachal Pradesh State Co-operative Bank Ltd
12. The Jammu and Kashmir State Co-operative Bank Ltd
13. The Karnataka State Co-operative Apex Bank Ltd
14. The Kerala State Co-operative Bank Ltd
15. The Madhya Pradesh Rajya Sahakari Bank Maryadit
16. The Maharashtra State Co-operative Bank Ltd
17. The Manipur State Co-operative Bank Ltd
18. The Meghalaya Co-operative Apex Bank Ltd
19. The Mizoram Co-operative Apex Bank Ltd
20. The Nagaland State Co-operative Bank Ltd
21. The Orissa State Co-operative Bank Ltd
22. The Pondicherry State Co-operative Bank Ltd
23. The Punjab State Co-operative Bank Ltd
24. The Rajasthan State Co-operative Bank Ltd
25. The Sikkim State Co-operative Bank Ltd

26. The Tamil Nadu State Apex Co-operative Bank Ltd
27. The Tripura State Co-operative Bank Ltd
28. The Uttar Pradesh Co-operative Bank Ltd
29. The West Bengal State Co-operative Bank Ltd
30. The Chhattisgarh RajyaSahakari Bank Maryadit
31. The Uttaranchal Rajya Sahakari Bank Ltd

Mutual Funds

A mutual fund is a form of collective investment that pools money from many investors and invests the money in stocks, bonds, short-term money market instruments, and/or other securities. In a mutual fund, the fund manager trades the fund's underlying securities, realizing capital gains or loss, and collects the dividend or interest income. The investment proceeds are then passed along to the individual investors.

Types of Mutual Fund Schemes

By Structure

- Open-Ended Schemes
- Close-Ended Schemes
- Interval Schemes

By Investment Objectives

- Growth Schemes
- Income Schemes
- Balanced Schemes
- Money Market Schemes

Other Schemes

- Tax Saving Schemes
- Special Schemes
- Index Schemes
- Sector Specific Schemes

The mutual fund industry in India came into being in 1963 with the setting up of the Unit Trust of India (UTI). In 1987, Public Sector Banks and Insurance Companies opened their own mutual funds, thus starting the second phase in the growth of the mutual funds industry. By the end of 1988, the industry's total assets under management (AUM) reached Rs 67 billion. The industry registered a major milestone in 1993 when the first private sector player, the erstwhile Kothari Pioneer Mutual Fund (now merged with Franklin Templeton), was set up. Since then, several international players have also entered the fray. The industry has also witnessed a spate of mergers and acquisitions, the most recent ones being the acquisition of Alliance Mutual by Birla Sun Life, GIC Mutual by Canbank Mutual, and Sun F&C by Principal Mutual. While the Indian mutual fund industry has grown in size by about 320 per cent from March 1993 (Rs 470 billion) to December 2004 (Rs 1505 billion) in terms of AUM, the AUM of the sector excluding UTI has grown over eight times from Rs152 billion in March 1999 to Rs1295 billion as at December 2004. The latest phase in the industry's evolution began with the bifurcation of UTI. The Indian mutual fund industry has grown by about 4.2 times from 1993 (Rs 470 billion) to 2005 (Rs 1992 billion) in terms of AUM. The private sector was allowed entry to set up asset management companies in 1993. There was a brief period of five years during which asset growth was slow. The AUM for the mutual fund industry started to grow rapidly after 1998. Between 1998 and 2005 the AUM of the sector excluding UTI grew by over fifteen times, from Rs 114 billion in 1998 to Rs1738 billion as at 2005. Though India is a minor player in the global mutual funds industry, its AUM as a proportion of the global AUM has steadily increased, doubling from 1999 levels. The mutual fund industry assets were estimated over Rs 287,000 crore in July 2006, and in just a period of one month, the figure has risen to Rs 306,000 crore. The industry thus has recorded a growth of nearly 8 per cent.

Assets Under Management as on 31 August 2006 Category and Type-wise

(in crore Rs)

	Open End	Close End	Total	% of Total
Income	36,515	30,786	67,301	22
Growth	87,139	7,954	95,093	31
Balanced	6,778	888	7,667	2
Liquid/Money Market	128,102	–	128,102	42
Gilt	2,239	–	2,239	1
Equity Linked Savings Schemes	5,354	1,352	6,706	2
Total	266,127	40,980	307,107	100

VAT

The Value-Added Tax (VAT) is based on the value addition to goods. VAT was introduced in Europe in the 1970s. In India, a VAT system has been introduced by the Government of India for about ten years in respect of Central excise duties. Under the VAT system, covering about 550 goods, there are only two basic VAT rates of 4 per cent and 12.5 per cent, plus a specific category of tax-exempted goods and a special VAT rate of 1 per cent only for gold and silver ornaments, etc. Under the 4-per cent VAT rate category, there are the largest number of goods (about 270), common for all the states, comprising items of basic necessities such as medicines and drugs, all agricultural and industrial inputs, capital goods and declared goods. The schedule of commodities is attached to the VAT bill of every state. The remaining commodities, common for all the states, fall under the general VAT rate of 12.5 per cent.

States and Union Territories Which Have Implemented VAT

- Maharashtra — 1 April 2005
- Orissa — 1 April 2005
- Jharkhand — 1 April 2006
- Haryana — 1 April 2003
- Uttaranchal — 1 October 2005
- Himachal Pradesh — 1 April 2005
- Punjab — 1April 2005
- Andhra Pradesh — 1April 2005
- Karnataka — 1 April 2005
- Tamil Nadu — Not implemented till 31 March 2006
- Kerala — 1 April 2005
- Gujarat — 1 April 2006
- Rajasthan — 1 April 2006
- Madhya Pradesh — 1 April 2006
- Chhattisgarh — 1 April 2006
- Goa — 1 April 2005
- West Bengal — 1 April 2005
- Uttar Pradesh — Not implemented till 31 March 2006
- Assam — 1 May 2005
- Jammu and Kashmir — 2 April 2005

• Meghalaya	1 May 2005
• Manipur	1 July 2005
• Arunachal Pradesh	1 April 2005
• Tripura	1 April 2005
• Mizoram	1 April 2005
• Nagaland	28 June 2005
• Delhi	1 April 2005
• Andaman and Nicobar	Does not have a sales tax system
• Lakshadweep	Does not have a sales tax system
• Chandigarh	15 December 2005
• Pondicherry	Not implemented
• Daman and Diu	1 April 2005
• Dadra and Nagar	1 April 2005

Economy News

The Union Cabinet Gives its Nod for Setting up the Sixth Pay Commission

The revision of wages of 3.3 million central government employees by the Sixth Pay Commission was cleared by the Cabinet on 20 July 2006—a decision that would put an additional burden of at least Rs 20,000 crore on the exchequer annually. The three-member Sixth Pay Commission has been given eighteen months to submit its recommendations. The Commission, which will have two members apart from the chairman, with the rank of minister of state rank, would also examine the need and quantum to sanction interim relief to the employees.

Foreign Direct Investment (FDI) in Telecom Increased from 49 to 74 per cent

In October 2005, the Union Cabinet announced the increasing of the limit of foreign direct investment (FDI) in telecom from 49 to 74 per cent. At the industry level, the decision would facilitate the inflow of much-needed capital since the telecom business is growing at more than 30 per cent annually, especially the mobile sector which has doubled in size over the last two years. The 74 per cent holding would include all foreign investments made directly or indirectly by foreign institutional investors, non-resident Indians, foreign currency convertible bonds, depositary receipts and convertible preference shares. Indian citizens or an Indian company will hold the remaining 26 per cent equity.

Narayan Murthy Resigns as Chairman of BIAL

On 20 October 2006, former Infosys chairman and chief mentor N.R. Narayan Murthy resigned as chairman of Bangalore International Airport Ltd (BIAL), following remarks made by former Prime Minister H.D. Deve Gowda, questioning his contribution in the past five years to the idea of the Greenfield Airport coming up at Devanahalli.

Prime Minister Launches Bharat Nirman Initiative

In December 2005, Prime Minister Dr Manmohan Singh launched the Rs 174,000 crore Bharat Nirman initiative aimed at developing the rural infrastructure including water supply, power, housing and roads. Under the initiative, 10 million hectares of unirrigated land will be irrigated. All villages whose population is 1,000 or more, and 500 or more in hilly areas, will be connected with roads. Twenty-five million houses will be given electricity connections. More than 6 million houses will be built in villages. The remaining

74,000 habitations, which do not have access to safe drinking water, will be provided these facilities. Each and every village will have at least one telephone connection.

Finance Minister Launches Electronic Remittance Gateway 'Insta Remit' for Overseas Indians

On 7 January 2006, on the first day of the fourth Pravasi Bharatiya Divas, the Union finance minister P. Chidambaram launched an easy-to-use electronic remittance gateway, 'insta remit', for overseas Indians, developed by the ministry of overseas Indians affairs in partnership with the UTI Bank. The gateway enables Non-Resident Indians (NRis) and People of Indian Origin (PIO) to send money to 14,500 Real Time Global Settlements (RTGS) across the country instantly.

India and US Sign a Protocol on Co-operation in the $950 million FutureGen Project

On 3 April 2006, India and the US signed a protocol on co-operation in the $950 million FutureGen project, for building and operating the first coal-fired emission-free power plant. The project is a public–private initiative, targeted at building a plant with 275 MW capacity. The agreement was signed in the presence of Union power minister Sushil Kumar Shinde and Jeffery D. Jarret, who is the assistant secretary in the US department of energy. The project, which would also have the participation of Indian companies, is expected to be commissioned by 2012.

Five BJP-ruled States Switch to VAT Regime

On 1 April 2006, five Bharatiya Janata Party-ruled states (Chhattisgarh, Gujarat, Jharkhand, Madhya Pradesh and Rajasthan) switched over to the value-added tax (VAT) regime from the sales tax system, taking the number of states who have opted for the new system to twenty-seven. Traders would be able to recover VAT on raw materials and intermediate goods. Small businesses with turnovers of up to Rs 5 lakh are exempt from the new tax, which has two main slabs of 4 per cent and 12.5 per cent. The five states, along with Tamil Nadu and Uttar Pradesh, had earlier refused to implement the new tax, citing protests by traders and the absence of a clear-cut roadmap for the abolition of central sales tax (CST).

Cabinet Approves the Implementation of the Bangalore Metro Rail Project

On 27 April 2006, the Union Cabinet gave its approval for implementation of the Bangalore Metro Rail Project by the Bangalore Metro Rail Corporation Ltd, covering a length of 33 km. The project was estimated to cost Rs 6,395 crore, including an escalation at the rate of five per cent per annum in the costs during the five years it would take to complete the construction work.

Prime Minister Launches Quality Mark for Handloom Products

On 28 June 2006 Prime Minister Manmohan Singh launched a quality mark for handloom products on the lines of the Wool mark and the Silk mark that would help buyers distinguish between genuine items diligently crafted by artisans and the poor imitations mass-produced by power-looms. The creation of handloom mark was entrusted to the National Institute of Design, Ahmedabad. The form of the logo has been derived from the interlocking of the warp and the weft. The Mumbai-based Textiles Committee, a statutory body under the Ministry of Textiles, has been engaged as the Implementation Agency for the implementation of the Handloom Mark scheme across the country.

Saudi Arabia Becomes a Member of the World Trade Organization

Saudi Arabia formally joined the World Trade Organization (WTO), becoming its 149th member, just two days ahead of a key WTO summit in Hong Kong. It was admitted by the WTO's member governments on 11 November 2005, following twelve years of intense negotiations. As a result of its negotiations to join the WTO, the kingdom has committed itself to further liberalize its trade regime and speed up its integration in the world economy, while offering a transparent and predictable environment for trade and foreign investment in accordance with WTO rules.

Ministry for Petroleum and Natural Gas Announces Bio-diesel Policy

The government issued a directive in October 2005 that from 1 January 2006, the public sector oil marketing companies (OMCs) will purchase bio-diesel (B100) at Rs 25 a litre for blending with diesel (HSD) to the extent of 20 per cent in phases. Unveiling the new bio-diesel purchase, the government announced that to start with, 5 per cent of bio-diesel, a non-edible oil extracted from 'Jatropha' and 'Pongamia', would be mixed with diesel during trial runs. At a later stage, in phases, the B100 blending with diesel is to be increased to 20 per cent.

The Union Cabinet Approves the Setting Up of the National Investment Fund (NIF)

On 3 November 2005, the Union Cabinet approved the setting up of the National Investment Fund (NIF) and making it operational so as to clear the decks for ploughing of 75 per cent of its income—derived through the disinvestment proceeds of Central public sector enterprises (CPSEs)—for funding social sector projects. It was decided that from 1 April 2006, realization from disinvestments of public sector enterprises (PSEs) would be appropriated from the Consolidated Fund of India and the NIF will be created.

26 per cent FDI in TV Channels

The government allowed foreign direct investment (FDI) up to 26 per cent to include investment by foreign institutional investors in uplinking of television channels in the news and current affairs category. Earlier, the provision for 26 per cent foreign equity in this sector did not include the participation of FIIs.

The National Rural Employment Guarantee Act Launched

In February 2006, Prime Minister Manmohan Singh launched the National Rural Employment Guarantee Act (NREGA) for creating new rural infrastructure, improving road connectivity, school buildings and water supply to villages. The Act guarantees 100 days of wage employment in a year to every rural household in 200 districts across the country.

Edmund S. Phelps Awarded 2006 Nobel Prize for Economics

On 9 October 2006, the Sveriges Riksbank Prize in Economic Sciences in Memory of Alfred Nobel was awarded to Edmund S. Phelps of the USA 'for his analysis of intertemporal tradeoffs in macroeconomic policy'.

Sensex Records New High

On 13 October 2006, the BSE Sensex hit a new all-time high of 12,690. The Sensex recorded the new high in 111 sessions. The previous all-time high, recorded on 11 May, was 12,671. It took the Sensex only eighty-six sessions to reach the new high from its low of 8,799 recorded on 14 June. Banking, FMCG, IT and metal sectors led the Sensex rally, with a gain of 153 points on the morning of the 13th.

Science

The Universe

The Solar System

The Solar System is the stellar system comprising the Sun and the retinue of celestial objects gravitationally bound to it: the eight planets, their 162 known moons, three currently identified dwarf planets and their four known moons, and thousands of small bodies. This last category includes asteroids, meteoroids, comets, and interplanetary dust. In order of their distances from the Sun, the planets are Mercury, Venus, Earth, Mars, Jupiter, Saturn, Uranus, and Neptune. From 1930 to 2006, Pluto, one of the largest known Kuiper belt objects, was considered the Solar System's ninth planet. However, in 2006 the International Astronomical Union (IAU) created an official definition of the term 'planet'. Under this definition, Pluto is reclassified as a dwarf planet, and there are eight planets in the Solar System. In addition to Pluto, the IAU currently recognizes two other dwarf planets: Ceres, the largest asteroid, and Eris, which lies beyond the Kuiper belt in a region called the scattered disc. Of the known dwarf planets, only Ceres has no moons.

Classical Planets

Mercury

Criteria	**Value**
Mass (10^{24}kg)	0.33
Diameter (km)	4879
Density (kg/m^3)	5427
Gravity (m/s^2)	3.7
Escape Velocity (km/s)	4.3
Rotation Period (hours)	1407.6
Length of Day (hours)	4222.6
Distance from Sun (10^6 km)	57.9
Perihelion (10^6 km)	46
Aphelion (10^6 km)	69.8
Orbital Period (days)	88
Orbital Velocity (km/s)	47.9
Orbital Inclination (degrees)	7
Orbital Eccentricity	0.205
Axial Tilt (degrees)	0.01
Mean Temperature (C)	167
Surface Pressure (bars)	0
Number of Moons	0
Ring System?	No
Global Magnetic Field?	Yes

Venus

Criteria	**Value**
Mass (10^{24}kg)	4.87
Diameter (km)	12,104
Density (kg/m^3)	5,243
Gravity (m/s^2)	8.9
Escape Velocity (km/s)	10.4
Rotation Period (hours)	-5832.5
Length of Day (hours)	2802
Distance from Sun (10^6 km)	108.2
Perihelion (10^6 km)	107.5
Aphelion (10^6 km)	108.9
Orbital Period (days)	224.7
Orbital Velocity (km/s)	35
Orbital Inclination (degrees)	3.4
Orbital Eccentricity	0.007
Axial Tilt (degrees)	177.4
Mean Temperature (C)	464
Surface Pressure (bars)	92
Number of Moons	0
Ring System?	No
Global Magnetic Field?	No

Earth

Criteria	Value
Mass (10^{24}kg)	5.97
Diameter (km)	12,756
Density (kg/m^3)	5515
Gravity (m/s^2)	9.8
Escape Velocity (km/s)	11.2
Rotation Period (hours)	23.9
Length of Day (hours)	24
Distance from Sun (10^6 km)	149.6
Perihelion (10^6 km)	147.1
Aphelion (10^6 km)	152.1
Orbital Period (days)	365.2
Orbital Velocity (km/s)	29.8
Orbital Inclination (degrees)	0
Orbital Eccentricity	0.017
Axial Tilt (degrees)	23.5
Mean Temperature (C)	15
Surface Pressure (bars)	1
Number of Moons	1
Ring System?	No
Global Magnetic Field?	Yes

Mars

Criteria	Value
Mass (10^{24}kg)	0.642
Diameter (km)	6794
Density (kg/m^3)	3933
Gravity (m/s^2)	3.7
Escape Velocity (km/s)	5
Rotation Period (hours)	24.6
Length of Day (hours)	24.7
Distance from Sun (10^6 km)	227.9
Perihelion (10^6 km)	206.6
Aphelion (10^6 km)	249.2
Orbital Period (days)	687
Orbital Velocity (km/s)	24.1
Orbital Inclination (degrees)	1.9
Orbital Eccentricity	0.094
Axial Tilt (degrees)	25.2
Mean Temperature (C)	-65
Surface Pressure (bars)	0.01
Number of Moons	2
Ring System?	No
Global Magnetic Field?	No

Jupiter

Criteria	Value
Mass (10^{24}kg)	1899
Diameter (km)	142,984
Density (kg/m^3)	1326
Gravity (m/s^2)	23.1
Escape Velocity (km/s)	59.5
Rotation Period (hours)	9.9
Length of Day (hours)	9.9
Distance from Sun (10^6 km)	778.6
Perihelion (10^6 km)	740.5
Aphelion (10^6 km)	816.6
Orbital Period (days)	4331
Orbital Velocity (km/s)	13.1
Orbital Inclination (degrees)	1.3
Orbital Eccentricity	0.049
Axial Tilt (degrees)	3.1
Mean Temperature (C)	-110
Surface Pressure (bars)	Unknown
Number of Moons	63
Ring System?	Yes
Global Magnetic Field?	Yes

Saturn

Criteria	Value
Mass (10^{24}kg)	568
Diameter (km)	120,536
Density (kg/m^3)	687
Gravity (m/s^2)	9
Escape Velocity (km/s)	35.5
Rotation Period (hours)	10.7
Length of Day (hours)	10.7
Distance from Sun (10^6 km)	1433.5
Perihelion (10^6 km)	1352.6
Aphelion (10^6 km)	1514.5
Orbital Period (days)	10,747
Orbital Velocity (km/s)	9.7
Orbital Inclination (degrees)	2.5
Orbital Eccentricity	0.057
Axial Tilt (degrees)	26.7
Mean Temperature (C)	-140
Surface Pressure (bars)	Unknown
Number of Moons	56
Ring System?	Yes
Global Magnetic Field?	Yes

Uranus

Criteria	Value
Mass (10^{24}kg)	86.8
Diameter (km)	51,118
Density (kg/m^3)	1270
Gravity (m/s^2)	8.7
Escape Velocity (km/s)	21.3

Rotation Period (hours)	-17.2
Length of Day (hours)	17.2
Distance from Sun (10^6 km)	2872.5
Perihelion (10^6 km)	2741.3
Aphelion (10^6 km)	3003.6
Orbital Period (days)	30,589
Orbital Velocity (km/s)	6.8
Orbital Inclination (degrees)	0.8
Orbital Eccentricity	0.046
Axial Tilt (degrees)	97.8
Mean Temperature (C)	-195
Surface Pressure (bars)	Unknown
Number of Moons	27
Ring System?	Yes
Global Magnetic Field?	Yes

Neptune

Criteria	Value
Mass (10^{24}kg)	102
Diameter (km)	49,528
Density (kg/m^3)	1638
Gravity (m/s^2)	11
Escape Velocity (km/s)	23.5
Rotation Period (hours)	16.1
Length of Day (hours)	16.1
Distance from Sun (10^6 km)	4495.1
Perihelion (10^6 km)	4444.5
Aphelion (10^6 km)	4545.7
Orbital Period (days)	59,800
Orbital Velocity (km/s)	5.4
Orbital Inclination (degrees)	1.8
Orbital Eccentricity	0.011
Axial Tilt (degrees)	28.3
Mean Temperature (C)	-200
Surface Pressure (bars)	Unknown
Number of Moons	13
Ring System?	Yes
Global Magnetic Field?	Yes

Dwarf Planets

Name	Ceres	Pluto	Eris
Diameter	975×909 km	2306 ± 20 km	2400 ± 100 km
Mass in kg	9.5×10^{20} kg	$\sim 1.305 \times 10^{22}$ kg	$\sim 1.5 \times 10^{22}$ kg *(est.)*
Mean equatorial radius	0.0738	0.18	0.19
in km	471	1,148.07	~1,200
Volume	0.00042	0.005	0.007
Orbital radius (AU)	2.5-2.9	29.66-49.30	37.77-97.56
Orbital period (in sidereal Years)	4.599	248.09	557
Number of natural satellites	0	3	1

Glossary

Mass (10^{24}kg or 10^{21}tons): This is the mass of the planet in septillion (1 followed by 24 zeros) kilograms or sextillion (1 followed by 21 zeros) tons. Strictly speaking tons are measures of weight, not mass, but are used here to represent the mass of one ton of material under Earth gravity.

Diameter (km or miles): The diameter of the planet at the equator, the distance through the center of the planet from one point on the equator to the opposite side, in kilometers or miles.

Density (kg/m^3 or lbs/ft^3): The average density (mass divided by volume) of the whole planet (not including the atmosphere for the terrestrial planets) in kilograms per cubic meter or pounds per cubic foot.

Gravity (m/s^2 or ft/s^2): The gravitational acceleration on the surface at the equator in meters per second squared or feet per second squared, including the effects of rotation. For the gas giant planets the gravity is given at the 1 bar pressure level in the atmosphere. The gravity on Earth is designated as 1 'G', so the Earth ratio fact sheets gives the gravity of the other planets in Gs.

Escape Velocity (km/s): Initial velocity, in kilometres per second or miles per second, needed at the surface (at the 1 bar pressure level for the gas giants) to escape the body's gravitational pull, ignoring atmospheric drag.

Rotation Period (hours): This is the time it takes for the planet to complete one rotation relative to the fixed background stars (not relative to the Sun) in hours. Negative numbers indicate retrograde (backwards relative to the Earth) rotation.

Length of Day (hours): The average time in hours for the Sun to move from the noon position in the sky at a point on the equator back to the same position.

Distance from Sun (10^6 km or 10^6 miles): This is the average distance from the planet to the Sun in millions of kilometres or millions of miles, also known as the semi-major axis. All planets have orbits which are elliptical, not perfectly circular, so there is a point in the orbit at which the planet is closest to the Sun, the perihelion, and a point furthest from the Sun, the aphelion. The average distance from the Sun is midway between these two values. The average distance from the Earth to the Sun is defined as 1 Astronomical Unit (AU), so the ratio table gives this distance in AU.

- For the Moon, the average distance from the Earth is given.

Perihelion, Aphelion (10^6 km or 10^6 miles): The closest and furthest points in a planet's orbit about the Sun, see 'Distance from Sun' above.

- For the Moon, the closest and furthest points to Earth are given, known as the perigee and apogee respectively.

Orbital Period (days): This is the time in Earth days for a planet to orbit the Sun from one vernal equinox to the next. Also known as the tropical orbit period, this is equal to a year on Earth.

- For the Moon, the sidereal orbit period, the time to orbit once relative to the fixed background stars, is given. The time from full Moon to full Moon, or synodic period, is 29.53 days.

Orbital Velocity (km/s or miles/s): The average velocity or speed of the planet as it orbits the Sun, in kilometres per second or miles per second.

Orbital Inclination (degrees): The angle in degrees at which a planet orbits around the Sun is tilted relative to the ecliptic plane. The ecliptic plane is defined as the plane containing the Earth's orbit, so the Earth's inclination is 0.

Orbital Eccentricity: This is a measure of how far a planet's orbit about the Sun (or the Moon's orbit about the Earth) is from being circular. The larger the eccentricity, the more elongated is the orbit, an eccentricity of 0 means the orbit is a perfect circle. There are no units for eccentricity.

Axial Tilt (degrees): The angle in degrees the axis of a planet (the imaginary line running through the centre of the planet from the north to south poles) is tilted relative to a line perpendicular to the planet's orbit around the Sun.

- Venus rotates in a retrograde direction, opposite the other planets, so the tilt is almost 180 degrees, it is considered to be spinning with its 'top', or north pole pointing 'downward' (southward). Uranus rotates almost on its side relative to the orbit. The ratios with Earth refer to the axis without reference to north or south.

Mean Temperature (C or F): This is the average temperature over the whole planet's surface (or for the gas giants at the one bar level) in degrees C (Celsius or Centigrade) or degrees F (Fahrenheit). For Mercury and the

Moon, for example, this is an average over the sunlit (very hot) and dark (very cold) hemispheres and so is not representative of any given region on the planet, and most of the surface is quite different from this average value. As with the Earth, there will tend to be variations in temperature from the equator to the poles, from the day to night sides, and seasonal changes on most of the planets.

Surface Pressure (bars or atmospheres): This is the atmospheric pressure (the weight of the atmosphere per unit area) at the surface of the planet in bars or atmospheres.

- The surfaces of Jupiter, Saturn, Uranus, and Neptune are deep in the atmosphere and the location and pressures are not known.

Number of Moons This gives the number of IAU officially confirmed moons orbiting a planet. New moons are still being discovered.

Ring System? This tells whether a planet has a set of rings around it, Saturn being the most obvious example.

Global Magnetic Field? This tells whether the planet has a measurable large-scale magnetic field. Mars and the Moon have localized regional magnetic fields but no global field.

More on the Solar System

The Moon is the Earth's sole natural satellite. It takes 1.3 seconds for the Moon's light to reach us. The Moon, however, has no light of its own, but merely reflects the rays of the Sun. It takes exactly 27 days, 7 hours and 43 minutes to complete one lunar revolution of the Earth. Neil Armstrong and Edwin Aldrin were the first two men to set foot on the Moon on 21 July 1969, having reached there in the spacecraft *Apollo XI*.

Other significant features of the solar system are **Asteroids**, which are thought to be debris from the formation of the inner planets. There is a large 'asteroid belt' that lies between Mars and Jupiter. When asteroids enter the atmosphere of the Earth, they burn up due to friction and are known as meteors or meteorites.

Comets are occasional visitors to the solar system. They are relatively small extraterrestrial bodies consisting of a frozen mass that travels around the Sun in a highly elliptical orbit. Some important comets include Hailey's Comet, named after its discoverer Edmund Hailey. It is believed to orbit the Sun every seventy-six years. Comet Smith-Tuttle has been in the news as it is thought to be headed straight for Earth, with an impact date set at 17 August 2116. In case of impact, the comet would have the destructive power of a 20 million megaton bomb, or 1.6 million Hiroshima bombs. Comet Shoemaker-Levy 9 broke up into twenty-one fragments before hitting Jupiter in 1994, a rare celestial event that was widely observed by astronomers worldwide.

Main Planetary Satellites

	Year Discovered	Distance from Planet (km)	(mi)	Diameter (km)	(mi)
Earth					
Moon	–	384,000	238,000	3,476	2,155
Mars					
Phobos	1877	937,800	582,700	27	17
Deimos	1877	2,346,000	1,458,000	15	9
Jupiter					
Metis	1979	128,000	79,000	40	25
Adrastea	1979	129,000	80,000	24	15
Amalthea	1892	181,000	112,000	270	168

Thebe	1979	222,000	138,000	100	60
Io	1610	422,000	262,000	3,650	2,260
Europa	1610	671,000	417,000	3,140	1,950
Ganymede	1610	1,070,000	665,000	5,260	3,270
Callisto	1610	1,883,000	1,170,000	4,800	3,000
Leda	1974	11,100,000	6,900,000	20	12
Himalia	1904	11,480,000	7,134,000	186	116
Lysithea	1938	11,720,000	7,293,000	36	22
Elara	1905	11,740,000	7,295,000	90	50
Ananke	1951	21,200,000	13,174,000	30	19
Carme	1938	22,600,000	14,044,000	40	25
Pasiphae	1908	23,500,000	14,603,000	50	30
Sinope	1914	23,700,000	14,727,000	36	22
Saturn					
Pan	1990	134,000	83,000	10	6
Atlas	1980	138,000	86,000	40	25
Prometheus	1980	139,000	86,000	100	60
Pandora	1980	142,000	88,000	100	60
Epimetheus	1980	151,000	94,000	140	90
Janus	1966	151,000	94,000	200	120
Mimas	1789	186,000	116,000	390	240
Enceladus	1789	238,000	148,000	500	310
Calypso	1980	295,000	183,000	30	19
Telesto	1980	295,000	183,000	30	19
Tethys	1684	295,000	183,000	1,060	660
Dione	1684	377,000	234,000	1,120	700
Helene	1980	377,000	234,000	15	9
Rhea	1672	527,000	327,000	1,530	950
Titan	1655	1,222,000	759,000	5,150	3,200
Hyperion	1848	1,481,000	920,000	480	300
Iapetus	1671	3,560,000	2,212,000	1,460	910
Phoebe	1898	12,950,000	8,047,060	220	137
Uranus					
Miranda	1948	130,000	81,000	480	300
Ariel	1851	191,000	119,000	1,160	720
Umbriel	1851	266,000	165,000	1,170	720
Titania	1787	436,000	271,000	1,580	980
Oberon	1787	583,000	362,000	1,524	947
Neptune					
Triton	1846	355,000	221,000	2,705	1,681
Nereid	1949	5,510,000	3,424,000	340	210
Pluto					
Charon	1978	19,600	12,200	1,200	745

Historic Comets

Name	First Seen	Period of Orbit (years)	Date of Last Perihelion[a] Passage
Arend-Road	1957	not known	8 Apr 57
Mrkos	1957	not known	1 Aug 57

Humason	1962	3000	14 May
Ikeya	1963	not known	21 Mar 63
Ikeya–Seki	1965	879.88	21 Oct 65
Tago–Sato–Kosaka	1969	420,000	21 Dec 69
Bennett	1970	1,680	20 Mar 70
Kohoutek	1973	75,000	28 Dec 73
Kobayashi–Berger–Milon	1975	not known	5 Sep 75
West	1976	500,000	25 Feb 76
Halley	240BC	76.1	9 Feb 86
Hale–Bopp	1995	6,580	1 Apr 97

[a] 'Perihelion' refers to the position of the close approach to the Sun of an object in an elliptical orbit.

Space Explorations

Humans have been looking up to the sky much before recorded history. However, since the middle of the twentieth century, exploring the skies have begun in earnest. Initially, it was a race to reach the moon between the US and the former USSR. Now, words such as Black Hole and time warp have become a part of the common man's lexicon. Here is a brief overview of what humans have been doing in space in the past five decades.

4 October 1957: The Soviet Union launches *Sputnik* I, becoming the first nation to successfully launch an artificial satellite.

31 January 1958: The United States launches its first artificial satellite, *Explorer I*.

3 November 1957: Laika, the first animal sent to space, travels into orbit on board *Sputnik II*.

1 October 1958: National Aeronautics and Space Administration (NASA) is christened as the successor to the National Advisory Committee for Aeronautics. The latter was responsible for researching the growing aeronautical industry since 1915. NASA was given the task of overseeing the civilian space program in USA.

2 January 1959: USSR launches *Luna 1*, which was meant to reach the Moon. Although *Luna 1* failed to reach the Moon, it became the first artificial object to escape Earth orbit.

14 September 1959: Soviet *Luna* 2 becomes the first artificial object to reach the Moon.

12 April 1961: Soviet cosmonaut Yuri Gagarin becomes the first man in space. This began the era of manned space flights.

5 May 1961: Alan Shepard becomes the first American in space when he completes a 15-minute sub-orbital flight. Nine months later, John Glenn becomes the first American man to orbit the Earth. USA's first manned flight programme Project Mercury was launched with Shepard and Glen.

25 May 1961: US President John F. Kennedy commits the US to landing an astronaut on the moon before the end of the decade. The Apollo Programme was announced.

16 June 1963: Valentina Tereshkova, the first woman to travel in space, was launched into space on board *Vostok 6*.

18 March 1965: *Voskhod* 2 cosmonaut Aleksey Leonov executes the first 'space walk'.

March 1966: Soviet *Venera 3* crash-lands on the Martian surface becoming the first spacecraft to strike another planet.

27 January 1967: Project Apollo suffers a setback when a fire in the *Apollo* command module kills three astronauts, holding up manned flights for nearly two years.

24 December 1968: *Apollo 8* circles the moon on Christmas Eve.

20 July 1969: Neil Armstrong and Edwin 'Buzz' Aldrin of the *Apollo 11* mission become the first humans to walk on the moon.

14 April 1970: The *Apollo 13* spacecraft loses its main power supply after an on board explosion on its way to the moon. However, the spacecraft and its astronauts are safely brought back to Earth.

19 April 1971: USSR launches the world's first space station, *Salyut 1*. However, it could not stay in space because of its low orbit. It was followed by *Salyut 2* (that disintegrated soon after launch). *Salyut 3* and *Salyut 5* were military space stations, while *Salyut 4* and *Salyut 6* were meant for civilian purposes.

14 May 1973: US launches its first space station, *Skylab*.

12 April 1981: The first space shuttle, *Columbia*, is launched from Kennedy Space Center with astronauts John Young and Robert Crippen at the helm. The space shuttle is a winged, re-usable manned spacecraft meant for scientific missions and for carrying payloads in its cargo bay.

28 January 1986: The space shuttle *Challenger* explodes within seconds of lift-off, killing all seven aboard. The dead included teacher Christa McAuliffe, the first private citizen chosen for space flight. This accident grounded the shuttle programme for many years.

20 February 1986: Russia launches the first part of the space station *Mir*.

15 November 1988: The first and only orbital launch of the Soviet space shuttle *Buran* takes place. It was an unmanned. The Soviet space shuttle programme was sanctioned in 1976 in response to the US shuttle programme. No further flights were carried out after the funding was cut following the collapse of the Soviet Union. Although construction of two more orbiters were started, the remained unfinished and were ultimately dismantled.

24 April 1990: NASA launches the Hubble Space Telescope.

21 August 1993: The first US mission to Mars since 1975, Mars *Observer*, disappears three days before its scheduled entry into orbit around Mars.

7 November 1996: USA launches Mars *Global Surveyor* that enters Martian orbit in 1998 and started mapping the planet.

4 July 1997: The US *Pathfinder* spacecraft lands on Mars. Its miniature rover vehicle named Sojourner explores the surface of the planet. The *Pathfinder* transmits back a huge amount of new data about Mars that includes colour images of the surface of the planet.

29 May 1999: The *Discovery* becomes the first shuttle to dock with the International Space Station (ISS).

23 July 1999: The space shuttle *Columbia* deploys the Chandra X-Ray Observatory. Air Force Colonel Eileen Collins becomes the first woman to command a shuttle mission.

14 February 2000: A probe named Near Earth Asteroid Rendezvous (NEAR) Shoemaker conducts the first long-term, close-up study of an asteroid, Eros.

23 March 2001: The abandoned Russian space station, *Mir*, re-enters the Earth's atmosphere and falls into the South Pacific Ocean. It had remained in orbit for over 14 years. The aging *Mir* was abandoned in 1999 due to a lack of funding from the Russian government.

27 April 2001: Dennis Tito, the first space tourist, blasts off on his trip to the International Space Station.

1 February 2003: The *Columbia* space shuttle explodes over Texas minutes before its scheduled landing in Florida. The seven-person crew that includes Kalpana Chawla and the first Israeli to go into space, are killed.

15 October 2003: China sends its first manned spacecraft into orbit, making it the third country to send a human into space. Yang Liwei, a thirty-

eight-year-old army lieutenant travels into space on board a spacecraft named *Shenzhou V*.

2 March 2004: Europe's Rosetta cometary probe is successfully launched into orbit around the Sun. Rosetta is the first probe ever designed to enter orbit around a comet's nucleus and release a landing craft onto its surface. It is scheduled to reach the comet 67P/ Churyumov-Gerasimenko in 2014 after three flybys of the Earth and one of Mars.

1 April 2004: NASA's Mars Exploration Rover Spirit finds hints of past water on Mars.

5 August 2004: The US Cassini spacecraft makes new discoveries around Saturn including a new radiation belt.

23 December 2004: Russia launches an unmanned cargo ship to the international space station.

15 April 2005: A Russian Soyuz-FG rocket lifts off at Baikonur, Kazakhstan, carrying three men to the international space station.

21 June 2005: A Russian Northern Fleet submarine launches the world's first solar-sail spacecraft, $4 million Cosmos 1, but the craft fails to reach orbit.

9 August 2005: *Discovery* and its crew of seven returns back to Earth ending a 14-day test of space shuttle safety.

1 October 2005: A Russian rocket launches the world's third space tourist, US millionaire scientist Gregory Olsen, and a US–Russian crew on a two-day trip to the international space station.

7 October 2005: Russia test-launches a collapsible mini-spacecraft, which is designed to carry cargo and even passengers from the international space station to Earth.

12 October 2005: A rocket carrying two Chinese astronauts is launched from a base in China's desert northwest Gansu province, returning the country's manned space programme to orbit two years after its history-making first flight.

30 March 2006: A Russian-American crew and Marcos Pontes, Brazil's first astronaut, lifts off in a Soyuz TMA-8 spacecraft to dock with the international space station.

4 July 2006: The US space shuttle *Discovery* is launched from the Kennedy Space Center in Cape Canaveral, Florida, with seven astronauts.

Space Shuttle

The US space shuttle is officially referred to as the 'Space Transportation System' (STS). At present, the Shuttle is the United States government's only manned launch vehicle currently in service. The Space Shuttle consists of three main components: the reusable Orbiter, an expendable external fuel tank and a pair of reusable solid-fuel booster rockets. The fuel tank and booster rockets are jettisoned during launch and only the Orbiter goes into orbit. The North American Rockwell company (now part of the Boeing Company) built the Space Shuttle orbiter. The Martin Marietta (now part of Lockheed Martin) company designed the external fuel tank and Morton Thiokol (now the Thiokol corporation) designed the solid rocket boosters. The Shuttle is the first orbital spacecraft designed for partial reusability. Its main functions are carriage of large payloads to various orbits, crew rotation for the International Space Station (ISS), and performance of servicing missions. The Shuttle has also been designed to recover satellites and other payloads from orbit and return them to Earth. Each Shuttle was designed for a projected lifespan of 100 launches or 10-years operational life. The Shuttle programme was launched on 5 January 1972, with an announcement from then US President Richard M. Nixon. The first orbiter to be built was named *Enterprise* and was rolled out on 17 September 1976. It later conducted a series of successful tests. However, the *Enterprise* never made a space flight. The first fully functional Shuttle Orbiter was the *Columbia*, which was delivered to Kennedy Space Center in March 1979. It was first launched on 12 April 1981—the 20th anniversary of Yuri Gagarin's space flight. *Challenger* was delivered in July 1982, *Discovery* was delivered in November 1983, and *Atlantis* was delivered in April 1985. Two Shuttles have been lost till date. *Challenger* was destroyed in an explosion during launch on 28 January 1986. *Columbia* was destroyed during reentry on 1 February 2003. All on board, including Kalpana Chawla perished in the accident.

Indian Space Research Centres

The Government of India set up its Space Commission and Department of Space (DOS) in June 1972. The Indian Space Research Organisation (ISRO) under DOS carries out India's space programme through its establishments located in different places in India. The primary objectives of the Indian space programme include development of satellites, launch vehicles, sounding rockets and related ground systems. Since its inception, the space programme has passed many milestones. ISRO enjoys co-operative arrangements with several countries and space agencies. ISRO also provides training to personnel from other countries while its hardware and services are commercially available through Antrix Corporation Ltd., which is the commercial arm of Department of Space (DOS). It was incorporated in September 1992 for the promotion and commercial exploration of products and services from the Indian Space Programme.

The various space centres of Department of Space are as follows:

Name	Place
Vikram Sarabhai Space Centre	Thiruvananthapuram
ISRO Satellite Centre	Bangalore
Satish Dhawan Space Centre	Hassan
Liquid Propulsion Systems Centre	Mahendragiri and Thiruvananthapuram
Space Applications Centre	Ahmedabad
Development and Educational Communication Unit	Ahmedabad
ISRO Telemetry, Tracking and Command Network	Bangalore and Lucknow
INSAT Master Control Facility	Hassan
ISRO Inertial Systems Unit	Thiruvananthapuram
National Remote Sensing Agency	Hyderabad
Regional Remote Sensing Service Centres	Bangalore, Kharagpur, Nagpur, Jodhpur and Dehradun
Physical Research Laboratory	Ahmedabad
National Mesosphere/ Stratosphere Troposphere Radar Facility	Tirupati

Indian Eyes in Space

Name	Date	Achievements
Aryabhatta	19.04.1975	First Indian satellite. Launched by Russian launch vehicle Intercosmos from USSR.
Bhaskara-I	07.06.1979	First experimental remote sensing satellite. Carried TV and Microwave

Name	Date	Achievements
		cameras. Launched by Russian launch vehicle Intercosmos from USSR.
Bhaskara-II	20.11.1981	Second experimental remote sensing satellite similar to Bhaskara-1. Launched by Russian launch vehicle Intercosmos from USSR.
Ariane Passenger Payload Experiment (APPLE)	19.06.1981	First experimental communication satellite. Launched by the European Ariane from French Guiana.
Rohini (RS-1)	18.07.1980	Used for measuring in-flight performance of second experimental launch of SLV-3 from India.
Rohini (RS-D1)	31.05.1981	Used for conducting some remote sensing technology studies. Launched by the first developmental launch of SLV-3 from India.
Rohini (RS-D2)	17.04.1983	Identical to RS-D1. Launched by the second developmental launch of SLV-3 from India.
Stretched Rohini Satellite Series (SROSS-C)	20.05.1992	Launched by third developmental flight of ASLV from India. Carried Gamma Ray astronomy and aeronomy payload.
Stretched Rohini Satellite Series (SROSS-C2)	04.05.1994	Launched by fourth developmental flight of ASLV from India. Identical to SROSS-C. Still in service.
Indian National Satellite (INSAT-1A)	10.04.1982	First operational multi-purpose communication and meteorology satellite procured from USA. Was operational for six months. Launched from USA
Indian National Satellite (INSAT-1B)	30.08.1983	Identical to INSAT-1A. Served for more than its design life of seven years. Launched from USA.
Indian National Satellite (INSAT-1C)	21.07.1988	Same as INSAT-1A. Served for one and a half years. Launched by European Ariane launch vehicle from French Guiana.
Indian National Satellite (INSAT-1D)	12.06.1990	Identical to INSAT-1A. Launched from USA. Still in service.
Indian National Satellite (INSAT-2A)	10.07.1992	First satellite in the second-generation Indian-built INSAT-2 series. Has enhanced capability than INSAT-1 series. Launched by European Ariane launch vehicle from French Guiana. Still in service.
Indian National Satellite (INSAT-2B)	23.07.1993	Second satellite in INSAT-2 series. Identical to INSAT-2A. Launched by European Ariane launch vehicle from French Guiana. Still in service.
Indian National	07.12.1995	Has additional capabilities such as mobile

Name	Date	Achievements
Satellite (INSAT-2C)		satellite service, business communication and television outreach beyond Indian boundaries. Launched by European launch vehicle from French Guiana. Still in service.
INSAT-2E	03.04.1999	Multipurpose communication and meteorological satellite launched by Ariane from French Guiana.
INSAT-3A	22.03.2000	The first satellite in the third generation INSAT-3 series, launched by Ariane from Kourou French Guyana.
INSAT-3B	24.01.2002	Successful launched by Ariane from Kourou French Guyana.
INSAT-3C	10.04.2003	Successfully launched by Ariane from Kourou French Guyana.
INSAT-3E	28.09.2003	Successfully launched by Ariane from Kourou French Guyana.
INSAT-4A	22.12.2005	Successfully launched by Ariane from Kourou French Guyana.
Indian Remote Sensing Satellite (IRS-1A)	17.03.1988	First operational remote sensing satellite. Launched from USSR.
Indian Remote Sensing Satellite (IRS-1B)	29.08.1991	Same as IRS-1A. Launched from USSR Still in service.
Indian Remote Sensing Satellite (IRS-P2)	15.10.1994	Carried remote sensing payload. Launched by second developmental flight of PSLV from India.
Indian Remote Sensing Satellite (IRS-1C)	28.12.1995	Carries advanced remote sensing cameras. Launched from former USSR. Still in service.
Indian Remote Sensing Satellite (IRS-P3)	21.03.1996	Carries remote sensing payload and an X-ray astronomy payload. Launched by third developmental flight of PSLV from India. Still in service.
Indian Remote Sensing Satellite (IRS-1D)	29.09.1997	Same as IRS-1C. Launched from India. Still in service.
INSAT-2E	03.04.1999	The last satellite in the multipurpose INSAT-2 series, launched by Ariane from Kourou French Guyana.
Indian Remote Sensing Satellite, IRS-P4 (OCEANSAT)	26.05.1999	Launched by Polar Satellite Launch Vehicle (PSLV-C2) along with Korean KITSAT-3 and German DLR-TUBSAT from Sriharikota.
GSLV-D1 with GSAT-1 on board	18.04.2001	The first developmental launch from Sriharikota.

Name	Date	Achievements
GSLV-D2 with GSAT-2 on board	08.05.2003	The Second developmental launch from Sriharikota.
GSLV (GSLV-F01)	20.09.2004	The first operational flight which successfully launched EDUSAT from SDSC SHAR, Sriharikota.
Polar Satellite Launch Vehicle, PSLV-C3	22.10.2001	Successfully launched three satellites — Technology Experiment Satellite (TES) of ISRO, BIRD of Germany and PROBA of Belgium-into their intended orbits.
Polar Satellite Launch Vehicle, PSLV-C4	12.09.2002	Successfully launched KALPANA-1 satel lite from Sriharikota.
Polar Satellite Launch Vehicle, PSLV-C5	17.10.2003	Successfully launched RESOURCESAT-1 (IRS-P6) satellite from Sriharikota.
Polar Satellite Launch Vehicle, PSLV-C6	05.05.2005	Successfully launched CARTOSAT-1 and HAMSAT satellites from Sriharikota.

(*Source*: ISRO)

Physics

Personal Computer Timeline

2006 marks the twenty-fifth anniversary of the personal computer.

1981: IBM introduces IBM PC, the standard model was sold for $2880. It used the Intel 8088 CPU running at 4.77 MHz, containing 29,000 transistors; MDA (Mono Display Adapter, text only) is introduced with IBM PC; The TCP/IP protocol is established.

1982: MIDI, Musical Instrument Digital Interface, is published by International MIDI Association (IMA). The MIDI standard allows computers to be connected to instruments like keyboards through a low-bandwidth (31250 bit/s) protocol; IBM launches the double-sided 320 KB floppy disk drives.

1983: IBM XT released, similar to the original IBM PC but with a hard drive. It had a 10 MB hard disk, 128 KB of RAM, one floppy drive, mono monitor and a printer, all for $5000; MS-DOS 2.0, PC-DOS 2.0 is introduced with the IBM XT; IBM releases the IBM PCjr; Domain Name System (DNS) introduced to the Internet, which then consisted of about 1000 hosts.

1984: Motorola releases the 68020 processor; IBM AT is released, featuring a 6 MHz 80286 processor; MS-DOS 3.0, PC-DOS 3.0 is released for the IBM AT, it supported larger hard disks as well as High Density (1.2 MB) 5¼" floppy disks.

1985: PostScript, a powerful page description language, is introduced by Adobe Systems; CD-ROM is invented by Phillips, produced in collaboration with Sony; Enhanced Graphics Adapter is released; Microsoft Windows is launched; LIM EMS standard, a memory paging scheme for PCs, is introduced by Lotus, Intel and Microsoft.

1987: Microsoft Windows 2 is released; Fractal Image Compression Algorithm is invented by English mathematician Michael F. Barnsley, allowing digital images to be compressed and stored using fractal codes rather than normal image data; Motorola releases the 68030 processor; PS/2 Systems introduced by IBM, the PS/2 Model 30 based on an 8086 processor and an old XT bus, Models 50 and 60 based on the 80286 processor and the Model 80 based on the 80386 processor. These used the 3½" floppy disks, storing 1.44 MB on each. VGA is released (designed for the PS/2) by IBM; The 8514/A is introduced by IBM. This is a graphics card that includes its own processor to speed up the drawing of common objects. The advantages includes a reduction in CPU workload; MS-DOS 3.3, PC-DOS 3.3 is released with the IBM PS/2. It enabled hard disk partitions, splitting a hard disk into two or more logical drives; OS/2 is launched by Microsoft and IBM.

1988: First optical chip developed, it uses light instead of electricity to increase processing speed; WORM (Write Once Read Many times)-disk is marketed for the first time by IBM; IBM PS/2 Model 30 286 is released, based on an 80286 processor.

1989: World Wide Web is invented by Tim Berners-Lee; 80486 DX is released by Intel. It contains the equivalent of about 1.2 million transistors. At the time of release the fastest version ran at 25 MHz and achieved up to 20 MIPS.

1990: Windows 3.0 version is introduced by Microsoft; MPC (Multimedia PC) Level 1 specification is published by a council of companies including Microsoft and Creative Labs. This specified the minimum standards for a Multimedia IBM PC.

1991: Linux is introduced.

1992: The PowerPC 601, developed by IBM, Motorola and Apple Computer, is released. This is the first generation of PowerPC processors; Windows 3.1 version is introduced by Microsoft.

1993: Commercial providers are allowed to sell internet connections to individuals; The Intel Pentium processor is released. At the time it was available in 60 and 66 MHz versions which achieved up to 100 MIPs, with over 3.1 million transistors; MPC Level 2 specification is introduced. This was designed to allow playback of a 15 frame video in a window 320x240 pixels; Windows NT 3.1 is released, which supports 32-bit programs.

1994: Netscape Navigator 1.0 is written as an alternative browser to NCSA Mosaic; Linus Torvalds releases version 1.0 of the Linux kernel.

1995: Intel releases the 133 MHz version of the Pentium processor; Windows 95 is launched by Microsoft; Pentium Pro is released. At introduction it achieved a clock speed of up to 200 MHz; JavaScript development is announced by Netscape.

1996: Netscape Navigator 2.0 is released, first browser to support JavaScript; The first public release of Opera, version 2.1 for Windows is released; Intel releases the 200 MHz version of the Pentium Processor.

1997: Intel releases its Pentium II processor (233, 266 and 300 MHz versions); Internet Explorer 4.0 is released.

1998: Microsoft releases Windows 98.

1999: Linux Kernel 2.2.0 is released. The number of people running Linux is estimated at over 10 million, making it not only an important operating system in the Unix world, but an increasingly important one in the PC world; AMD releases the Athlon 750 MHz version.

2000: Windows 2000 is launched, Microsoft's replacement for Windows 95/98 and Windows NT; Intel releases the Pentium IV.

2001: Linux kernel version 2.4.0 is released; Microsoft releases Windows XP, based on Windows 2000 and Windows NT kernel.

2002: United Linux is officially formed.

2004: Mozilla Firefox 1.0 is released.

2005: Microsoft announces its next consumer operating system, Windows Vista, to be released in early 2007.

Chemistry

Elements

Symbol	Element	Atomic no.	Weight
Ac	Actinium	89	[227.0278]
Ag	Silver	47	107.8682
Al	Aluminium	13	26.98154
Am	Americium	95	[243]
Ar	Argon	18	39.948
As	Arsenic	33	74.9216
At	Astatine	85	[210]
Au	Gold	79	196.9665
B	Boron	5	10.811
Ba	Barium	56	137.33
Be	Beryllium	4	9.01218
Bh	Bohrium	107	[262]
Bi	Bismuth	83	208.9804
Bk	Berkelium	97	[247]
Br	Bromine	35	79.904
C	Carbon	6	12.011
Ca	Calcium	20	40.078
Cd	Cadmium	48	112.41
Ce	Cerium	58	140.12
Cf	Californium	98	[252]
Cl	Chlorine	17	35.453
Cm	Curium	96	[247]
Co	Cobalt	27	58.9332
Cr	Chromium	24	51.9961
Cs	Caesium/Cesium	55	132.9054
Cu	Copper	29	63.546
Db	Dubnium	105	[262]
Dy	Dysprosium	66	162.50
Er	Erbium	68	167.26
Es	Einsteinium	99	[254]
Eu	Europium	63	151.96
F	Fluorine	9	18.998403
Fe	Iron	26	55.847
Fm	Fermium	100	[257]
Fr	Francium	87	[223]
Ga	Gallium	31	69.723
Gd	Gadolinium	64	157.25
Ge	Germanium	32	72.59
H	Hydrogen	1	1.00794
He	Helium	2	4.002602
Hf	Hafnium	72	178.49
Hg	Mercury	50	200.59
Ho	Holmium	67	164.9304
Hs	Hassium	108	[265]
I	Iodine	53	126.9045
In	Indium	49	114.82
Ir	Iridium	77	192.22
K	Potassium	19	39.0983

Symbol	Element	Atomic no.	Weight
Kr	Krypton	36	83.80
La	Lanthanum	57	138.9055
Li	Lithium	3	6.941
Lr	Lutetium	71	174.967
Lw	Lawrencium	103	[260]
Md	Mendelevium	101	[258]
Mg	Magnesium	12	24.305
Mn	Manganese	25	54.9380
Mo	Molybdenum	42	95.94
Mt	Meitnerium	109	[266]
N	Nitrogen	7	14.0067
Na	Sodium	11	22.98977
Nb	Niobium	41	92.9064
Nd	Neodymium	60	144.24
Ne	Neon	10	20.179
Ni	Nickel	28	58.69
No	Nobelium	102	[259]
Np	Neptunium	93	[237.0482]
O	Oxygen	8	15.9994
Os	Osmium	76	190.2
P	Phosphorus	15	30.97376
Pa	Protactinium	91	[231.0359]
Pb	Lead	82	207.2
Pd	Palladium	46	106.42
Pm	Promethium	61	[145]
Po	Polonium	84	[209]
Pr	Praseodymium	59	140.9077
Pt	Platinum	78	195.08
Pu	Plutonium	94	[244]
Ra	Radium	88	[226.0254]
Rb	Rubidium	37	95.4678
Re	Rhenium	75	186.207
Rf	Rutherfordium	104	[261]
Rh	Rhodium	45	102.9055
Rn	Radon	86	[222]
Ru	Ruthenium	44	101.77
S	Sulphur/sulfur	16	32.066
Sb	Antimony	51	121.75
Sc	Scandium	21	44.95591
Se	Selenium	34	78.96
Sg	Seaborgium	106	[263]
Si	Silicon	14	28.0855
Sm	Samarium	62	150.36
Su	Tin	50	118.69
Sr	Strontium	38	87.62
Ta	Tantalum	73	180.9479
Tb	Terbium	65	158.9254
Tc	Technetium	43	[98]
Te	Tellurium	52	127.60
Th	Thorium	90	232.0381
Ti	Titanium	22	47.98

Symbol	Element	Atomic no.	Weight
Tl	Thallium	81	204.383
Tm	Thulium	69	168.9342
U	Uranium	92	238.0289
Uub	Ununbium	112	[277]
Uun	Ununnilium	110	[269]
Uuu	Ununumium	111	[272]
V	Vanadium	23	50.9415
W	Tungsten	74	183.85
Xe	Xenon	54	131.29
Y	Yttrium	39	88.9059
Yb	Ytterbium	70	173.04
Zn	Zinc	30	65.38
Zr	Zirconium	40	91.224

Atomic weights are taken from the 1993 list of the International Union of Pure and Applied Chemistry. For radioactive elements, the mass number of the most stable isotope is given in square brackets.

Health

Growth of World Population

In early 2006, the world population reached 6.5 billion. In line with population projections, this figure continues to grow at rates that were unprecedented prior to the twentieth century. By some estimates, there are now one billion people in the world between the ages of fifteen and twenty-four. The UN has issued multiple projections of future world population, based on different assumptions. Over the last ten years, the UN has consistently revised these projections downward. Current projections by the UN's Population Division, based on the 2004 revision of the World Population Prospects database, are as follows:

Year	Population (billions)
2010	6.8
2020	7.6
2030	8.2
2040	8.7
2050	8.9

Asia accounts for over 60 per cent of the world population with almost 3.8 billion people. China and India alone comprise 20 per cent and 16 per cent respectively. Africa follows with 840 million people, 12 per cent of the world population. Europe's 710 million people make up 11 per cent of the world's population. North America is home to 514 million (8 per cent), South America to 371 million (5.3 per cent) and Oceania to roughly 60 million (.9 per cent).

Growth of World Population by Billion and Year

World Population	Year	Elapsed Year
1 billion	1805	indefinite
2 billion	1926	121
3 billion	1960	34
4 billion	1974	14
5 billion	1987	13
6 billion	1999	12

Communicable Diseases

Name	Cause	Transmission Period	Incubation
AIDS (Acquired Immune Deficiency Syndrome)	Human Immuno-deficiency Virus (HIV)	Sexual relations; sharing of syringes; blood transfusion	several years
Chickenpox (varicella)	Herpes zoster virus	Infected persons; articles contaminated by discharge from mucous membranes	10–21 days
Cholera	*Vibrio cholerae* bacterium	Contaminated water and seafood	a few hours–5 days
Common cold	Numerous viruses	Respiratory droplets of infected person	1–4 days
Diphtheria	*Corynebacterium diphtheriae* bacterium	Respiratory secretions and saliva of infected persons or carriers	2–6 days
Encephalitis	Viruses	Bite from infected mosquito	4–21 days
Gas gangrene	*Clostridium welchii* bacterium	Soil or soil-contaminated articles	1–4 days
Gonorrhoea	*Neisseria gonorrhoeae* bacterium	Urethral or vaginal secretions of infected person	3–8 days
Hepatitis A (infectious)	Hepatitis A virus	Contaminated food and water	15–50 days
Hepatitis B (serum type B)	Hepatitis B virus	Infected blood; parenteral injection	6 weeks–6 month
Infectious mononucleosis (US) Glandular fever (UK)	Epstein-Barr virus	Saliva; direct oral contact with infected person	2–6 weeks
Influenza	Numerous viruses (types A. B, C)	Direct contact; respiratory droplets, possibly airborne	1–4 days
Legionnaires' disease	*Legionella pneumophila* bacterium	Water droplets in contaminated hot-water systems, cooling towers, etc.	1–3 days
Leprosy	*Mycobacterium leprae* bacillus	Droplet infection (minimally contagious)	variable

Name	Cause	Transmission Period	Incubation
Malaria	*Plasmodium* protozoa	Bite from infected mosquito	6–37 days
Measles (rubeola)	Rubeola virus	Droplet infection	10–15 days
Meningitis	Various bacteria (bacterial meningitis) and viruses (viral meningitis)	Respiratory droplets	varies with caus ative agent
Mumps	Virus	Direct contact with infected persons; respiratory droplets and oral secretions	14–21 days
Paratyphoid fevers	*Salmonella* bacteria	Ingestion of contaminated food and water	1–14 days
Pneumonia	*Streptococcus pneumoniae* bacterium	Droplet infection	1–3 weeks
Poliomyelitis	Polio viruses	Direct contact with nasopharyngeal secretions of indicted persons; vomit	7–21 days
Rabies	Virus	Bite from rabid animal	10 days–6 months
Rubella (German measles)	Rubella virus	Direct contact or droplet spread of nasopharyngeal secretion	14–21 days
SARS (severe acute respiratory syndrome)	SARS–associated coronavirus	Direct contact with infected persons, or respiratory droplets	2–7 days
Scarlet fever	Group A haemolytic *Streptococcus* bacteria	Direct or indirect contact with infected persons, or droplet infection	1–5 days
Shingles	*See* chickenpox	*See* chickenpox	
Syphilis	*Treponema pallidum* bacterium	Sexual relations; contact with open lesions; blood transfusion	10–90 days
Tetanus (lockjaw)	*Clostridum tentani* bacillus	Animal faeces and soil	3–21 days
Tuberculosis	*Mycobacterium tuberculosis* bacillus	Droplet spread; ingestion from contaminated milk	variable
Typhoid fever	*Salmonella typhi* bacillus	Contaminated food and water	7–21 days
Whooping cough	*Bordetella pertussis* bacterium	Droplet spread	10–21 days
Yellow fever	Arbovirus	Bite from infected mosquito	3–6 days

Main Types of Vitamins

Vitamin	Chemical Name	Precursor	Main Symptom of Deficiency	Dietary Source
Fat-soluble vitamins				
A	Retinol	Beta-carotene	Xerophthalmia (eye disease)	Retinol: milk butter, cheese, egg yolk, liver, fatty fish Carotene: green vegetables, yellow and red fruits and vegetables, especially carrots
D	Cholecalciferol	UV-activated 7-dehydro-cholesterol	Rickets, osteomalacia	Fatty fish; margarine, some fortified milks
K	Phytomenadione		Haemorrhagic problems	Green leafy vegetables, liver
E	Tocopherols		Multiple effects	Vegetable oils
Water-soluble vitamins				
C	Ascorbic acid		Scurvy	Citrus fruits, potatoes, green leafy vegetables
B-vitamins				
B_1	Thiamine		Beri-beri	Seeds and grains: widely distributed
B_2	Riboflavin		Failure to thrive	Liver, milk; cheese, yeast
–	Nicotinic acid		Pellagra	Meat, fish, cereals, pulses
B_6	Pyridoxine		Dermatitis; neurological disorders	Cereals, liver, meat, fruits, leafy vegetables
B_{12}	Cyanocobalamin		Anaemia	Meat; milk; liver
–	Folic add		Anaemia	Liver, green vegetables
–	Pantothenic acid		Dermatitis	Widespread
–	Biotin		Dermatitis	Liver, kidney, yeast extracts

Main Trace Minerals

Mineral	Main Symptom of Deficiency	Dietary Source	Proportion of Total Body Weight (%)
Calcium	Rickets in children; osteoporosis in adults	Milk, butter, cheese, sardines, green leafy vegetables, citrus fruits	2.5
Chromium	Adult-onset diabetes	Brewer's yeast, black pepper, liver, wholemeal bread; beer	<0.01
Copper	Anaemia, Menkes syndrome	Green vegetables, fish, oysters, liver	<0.01
Fluorine	Tooth decay, possibly osteoporosis	Fluoridated drinking water, seafood, tea	<0.01
Iodine	Goitre; cretinism in new-born children	Seafood, salt-water fish, seaweed, iodized salt, table salt	<0.01
Iron	Anaemia	Liver, kidney, green leafy vegetables, egg yolk, dried fruit, potatoes, molasses	0.01
Magnesium	Irregular heartbeat, muscular weakness, insomnia	Green leafy vegetables (eaten raw), nuts, whole grains	0.07
Manganese	Not known in humans	Legumes, cereals, green leafy vegetables, tea	<0.01
Molybdenum	Not known in humans	Legumes, cereals, liver, kidney, some dark-green vegetables	<0.01
Phosphorus	Muscular weakness, bone pain, loss of appetite	Meat, poultry, fish, eggs, dried beans and peas, milk products	1.1
Potassium	Irregular heartbeat, muscular weakness, fatigue; kidney and lung failure	Fresh vegetables, meat, orange juice, bananas: bran	0.10
Selenium	Not known in humans	Seafood, cereals, meat, egg yolk, garlic	<0.01
Sodium	Impaired acid-base balance in body fluids (very rare)	Table salt; other naturally occurring salts	0.10
Zinc	Impaired wound healing, loss of appetite, impaired sexual development	Meat, whole grains, legumes, oysters, milk	<0.01

Inventions and Inventors

Invention	Year	Inventor	Note
Aeroplane	1903	Orville and Wilbur Wright (the Wright brothers)	A Brazillian named Alberto Santos-Dumont was the first person to achieve the first officially observed powered flight in Europe (1906). At that point of time, most of continental Europe was unaware of the 1903 feat of the Wright brothers and Santos-Dumont was widely credited as the inventor of the airplane. In 1991, a Brazilian government decree declared him the 'Father of Aviation'.
Aerosol can	1926	Erik Rotheim	The concept of an aerosol originated in the 1790s with the introduction of pressurized carbonated beverages in France. In 1837, a man named Perpigna invented a soda siphon incorporating a valve.
Air-conditioning	1911	Willis Carrier	Willis H. Carrier is regarded as the father of air-conditioning. However, a textile engineer named Stuart H. Cramer of Charlotte North Carolina used the term 'air-conditioning' in a patent claim filed for a device that added water vapour to air in textile plants to 'condition' the yarn and used the term in a convention of cotton manufacturers in May 1906.
Antibiotics	1928	Alexander Fleming	Louis Pasteur and Jules-Francois Joubert made the first demonstration of antibiotic effect in1887.
Antiseptic medicine	1865	Joseph Lister	Ignaz Philipp Semmelweis made the first introduction of antisepsis into medical practice in 1847. Joseph Lister first successfully used this new method in August 1865.
Aqualung	1943	Jacques-Yves Cousteau and Émile Gagnan	
Aspirin	1899	Felix Hoffmann	Hippocrates, the 'father of medicine', made the first use of salicyn, an active component of

Invention	Year	Inventor	Note
			Aspirin. In 1853, French chemist Charles Frederic Gerhardt was the first to synthesize the drug. Hoffmann rediscovered Gerhardt's formula.
Atomic theory	1808	John Dalton	Aristotle and Theophrastus credited Leucippus with having originated the theory of atomism.
Atomic structure	1911	Ernest Rutherford	The Rutherford atomic model has been alternatively called the nuclear atom, or the planetary model of the atom. Neils Bohr's atomic model, the Bohr atomic model, was created in 1913 and was the first that incorporated quantum theory.
Automobile	1769	Nicolas-Joseph Cugnot	In 1769 and 1770, Cugnot made two huge steam-powered tricycles that are today recognized as the first true automobiles. These were tractors intended for hauling artillery. Karl Benz ran his first three-wheeled car with an internal combustion engine in in 1885. He built his first four-wheeled car in 1890. Gottlieb Daimler and Wilhelm Maybach launched their first car also in 1885.
Bicycle	1818	Karl de Drais de Sauerbrun	
Bifocal lens	1760	Benjamin Franklin	
Bridges	1800	James Finley (Suspension, Iron chains)	Marc Séguin originated the wire-cable suspension bridge in 1825. Ithiel Town invented the lattice truss bridge in 1820.
Calculating machine (Analytical Engine)	1835	Charles Babbage	
Calculating machine (Digital calculator)	1642	Blaise Pascal	
Camera	1814	Joseph Nicéphore Niépce	
Camera (Polaroid)	1947	Edwin Herbert Land	
Chewing gum	1848	John Curtis	The ancient Mayans chewed chicle, the sap of the sapodilla tree. Thomas Adams invented a

Invention	Year	Inventor	Note
			chicle-based chewing gum in 1871.
Integrated circuit	1959	Jack Kilby and Robert Noyce	In the same year, 1959 Jack Kilby received a US patent for miniaturized electronic circuits and Robert Noyce received US patent #2,981,877 for a silicon-based integrated circuit. However, these were for two different types of integrated circuits.
Digital compact Disc (CD)	1965	James Russell	
Electric motor	1822	Michael Faraday	
Electromagnet	1823	William Sturgeon	
Frozen foods	1824	Clarence Birdseye	
Heart (artificial)	1957	Willem Kolff	
Helicopter	1939	Igor Sikorsky	Paul Cornu originated the first piloted helicopter in 1907. However, this design was not successful.
Hot-air balloon	1783	Joseph and Étienne Montgolfier	In 1709, a Brazillian named Padre Bartolomeu Lourenço de Gusmão presented a miniature balloon made of glued paper sections to King João V of Portugal and his court and ambassadors of other countries. However, inspite of experimental success, he could not attain much success with his aeronautical studies.
Laser	1960	Theodore Maiman	In 1958, Charles Townes and Arthur Schawlow theorized a visible laser, an invention that would use infrared and/or visible spectrum light.
Liquid crystal Displays (LCDs)	1970	James Fergason	
Lightning rod	1752	Benjamin Franklin	
Locomotive	1804	Richard Trevithick (Steam powered)	George Stephenson invented the first practical locomotive with a multiple-fire-tube boiler in 1829.
Lock (cylinder)	1861	Linus Yale	
Loom (Jacquard loom)	1804	Joseph-Marie Jacquard	
Machine gun	1884	Hiram Maxim (first satisfactory fully automatic machine gun)	Richard Gatling invented the multi-barrel machine gun in 1862.
Optical Telescope	1608	Hans Lippershey	In 1609, Galileo Galilei built his

Invention	Year	Inventor	Note
			first refracting telescope using a glass lens. He was also the first to use the telescope for astronomical purposes. In 1668, Sir Isaac Newton built a new type of telescope, the reflecting telescope, using mirrors. However, the first description of a practical reflecting telescope was made in 1663 by James Gregory.
Pen	1884	L.E. Waterman	Ball-point pens were invented by Lazlo Biro in 1944.
Plastics	1862	Alexander Parkes	In 1870, John W. Hyatt made the first plastic made of nitrocellulose, celluloid.
Polio vaccine	1914	Jonas Edward Salk	
Pressure cooker	1679	Denis Papin	
Radar	1904	Christian Hulsmeyer	British physicist Robert Watson-Watt made the first practical radar system in 1935.
Radio	1895	Guglielmo Marconi	Nikola Tesla had demonstrated a workable model of radio in 1893. In 1943, the US patent office granted him the patent for radio, overturning Marconi's claim.
Refrigerator	1748	William Cullen	American inventor Oliver Evans designed the first refrigeration machine in 1805. Jacob Perkins built a practical refrigerating machine in 1834.
Revolver	1835	Samuel Colt	
Rocket (liquid-fueled)	1926	Robert Goddard	
Safety pin	1849	Walter Hunt	
Sewing Machine	1790	Thomas Saint	The first American patent was issued to Elias Howe in 1846.
Star catalogue	1572	Tycho Brahe	First modern star catalogue.
Steam engine	1639	Thomas Savery	James Watt made his double-acting engine in 1782.
Steamship	1783	Marquis Claude de Jouffroy d'Abbans	
Stethoscope	1819	R.T.H. Laënnec	
Tape recorder	1898	Valdemar Poulsen	
Television	1884	Paul G. Nipkow	In 1925, Charles Jenkins and John L. Baird, both demonstrated the mechanical transmission of images over wire circuits.
Teflon	1938	Roy J. Plunkett	
Telegraph	1837	Samuel Morse	

Invention	Year	Inventor	Note
Telephone	1876	Alexander Graham Bell	
Thermometer	1593	Galileo Galilei	Daniel Gabriel Fahrenheit produced mercury thermometers in 1714. The first centigrade scale is attributed to Anders Celsius, who developed it in 1742.
Tyre (pneumatic)	1888	John Dunlop	
Transistor	1947	John Bardeen, Walter H. Brattain, and William B. Shockley	
Typewriter	1867	Christopher Latham Sholes	
Vacuum cleaner	1869	Ives McGaffey	Hubert Cecil Booth received a British patent for a vacuum cleaner in 1901.
World Wide Web	1989	Tim Berners-Lee	
Xerography	1938	Chester Carlson	
Zero	5th–6th century	Indian mathematicians	Indian mathematicians of the 5th and 6th centuries are credited with the origin of the base-10 number system complete with a symbol and a position for zero. However, the concept of zero appeared earlier, in the Mayan and Babylonian number systems. But these were faulty. In the Mayan case, their inconsistency in base notation made it virtually useless for computations. The Babylonians used it only between two numbers to indicate an empty position and never at the end of a number.
Zipper	1891	W.L. Judson	

Science News

Dogs Can Sniff Cancer Growth in Humans: US researchers in California reveal that dogs have an uncanny ability to sniff out lung and breast cancer in its early stages of development. Published in the journal *Integrative Cancer Therapies*, the study reveals evidence that a dog's extraordinary ability can distinguish people with both early and late stage lung and breast cancers from healthy control subjects. The study—led by Michael McCulloch of the Pine Street Foundation and Tadeusz Jezierski of the Polish Academy of Sciences—is the first to test whether dogs can detect cancers only by sniffing the exhaled breath of cancer patients.

Save Metals: A study by Yale researchers into the supply and usage of copper, zinc and other metals has determined that supplies of these resources—even if recycled—may fail to meet the needs of the global population. The study, appearing in the *Proceedings of the National Academy of Sciences*, found that all of the copper in ore, plus all of the copper currently in use, would be required to bring the world to the level of the developed nations for power transmission, construction and other services and products that depend on copper.

Ice Sheet Shrinking: NASA scientist Jay Zwally reported in the *Journal of Glaciology* findings on the changing ice cover of Greenland and Antarctica that tally with other recent studies indicating unprecedented thinning of the massive ice sheets. Zwally's survey, carried out using satellites and airborne mapping, confirms that climate warming is changing how much water remains locked in Earth's largest storehouses of ice and snow. Adding up the overall gains and loses of ice from the Greenland and Antarctic ice sheets, Zwally said there was a net loss of ice to the sea of around 20 billion tons.

Fat Isn't All That Bad: While fat does a good job of sequestering away junk such as PCB from the environment, it appears that it may do even *more* important work in keeping the body's *own* chemical cocktail in balance. Researchers at the University of California, Irvine (UCI), have found that fat droplets appear to regulate excess proteins in the body. Excess and misshapen proteins are the culprits in mad cow disease and are believed to be behind a number of other diseases. The new study, published in *Current Biology*, found that the fat keeps extra proteins out of the way until they are needed, so that they don't cause harm within the cell.

Looking for Partners: According to a new study published in the *Proceedings of the National Academy of Sciences*, the researchers, from China and the UK, say that cultures like China and India that favour male babies have bred an enormous surplus of men who will struggle to find sexual partners and will likely find themselves marginalized in society. The study states that over the next twenty years, there will be a 12 to 15 per cent excess of young men in parts of China and India.

Mass Suicide by Cancer Cells: A synthetic compound that can initiate suicide in cancer cells could become the future of anti-cancer therapies, say researchers in a paper published in *Nature Chemical Biology*. The new technique is tipped to be an effective way to introduce personalized cancer treatments. Scientists have found a synthetic compound—procaspase activating compound 1 (christened PAC-1)—which can restore communications to the cancer cell and trick them into committing suicide.

Snail Toxin for Nerve Disorders: University of Utah researchers reported in *The Journal of Biological Chemistry* that have found that a nerve toxin used by venomous sea snails can dock with nicotine receptors in the brain, which could lead to new treatments for certain mental illnesses and brain diseases. The toxin—called alpha conotoxin OmIA—was isolated from a cone snail known as *conus omaria*, whose natural habitat is the Pacific and Indian oceans. The toxin may enable scientists to more effectively develop medications for a wide range of disorders including Parkinson's disease, Alzheimer's disease, depression, nicotine addiction and perhaps even schizophrenia.

Nano-transistor: Computer engineers at the University of Rochester have designed a prototype nano-scale transistor that is radically different from any other type of semiconductor. Called the 'Ballistic Deflection Transistor' (BDT), the new device works by bouncing individual electrons off deflectors, something similar to a game of snooker played at the atomic scale at unimaginable speeds.

Stem Cell Controversy: On 3 August 2005, Hwang Woo-Suk, pioneer South Korean biomedical scientist, announced that his team of researchers had become the first team to successfully clone a dog. On 29 December 2005, it was announced that all eleven of Hwang's stem cell lines were fabricated. On 20 January 2006 Hwang maintained that two of his eleven forged stem cell lines had been maliciously switched for cells from regular, not cloned, embryos. He alleged that members of his research project have deceived him with false data.

X Prize For Decoding DNA: The X Prize Foundation, a nonprofit-education organization, is looking for a new adventure into human genes.The Santa Monica, California, foundation offered a $5 million to $20 million prize to the first team that completely decodes the DNA of 100 or more people in a matter of weeks. Such speedy gene sequencing would represent a technology breakthrough for medical research. Researchers say quick and affordable decoding of many people's DNA will accelerate the effort to understand the links between genes and diseases. The prize is the brainchild of J. Craig Venter, the biologist and former president of Celera Genomics Group.

John C. Mather and George F. Smoot Win 2006 Nobel Prize in Physics: On 3 October 2006, John C. Mather and George F. Smoot, both of the USA, were awarded the 2006 Nobel Prize in Physics 'for their discovery of the blackbody form and anisotropy of the cosmic microwave background radiation'.

Roger D. Kornberg Awarded 2006 Nobel Prize in Chemistry: On 4 October 2006, Roger D. Kornberg of the USA was awarded the 2006 Nobel Prize in Chemistry 'for his studies of the molecular basis of eukaryotic transcription'.

2006 Medicine Nobel Goes to Andrew Z. Fire and Craig C. Mello: On 2 October 2006, Andrew Z. Fire and Craig C. Mello, both of the USA, were awarded the 2006 Nobel Prize in Physiology or Medicine 'for their discovery of RNA interference-gene silencing by double-stranded RNA'.

Major Examinations

A. All India Entrance Examination for BE/B.Tech courses

Some of the notable institutions that offer four-year B.Tech courses to students after 10+2 with Physics, Chemistry, and Mathematics on the basis of the All India Entrance Examination for BE/B.Tech courses:

1. Indian Institutes of Technology
2. Banaras Hindu University
3. School of Mines, Dhanbad
4. Birla Institute of Technology, Ranchi
5. Birla Institute of Technology and Science, Pilani
6. University of Roorkee
7. Manipal Institute of Technology
8. Annamallai University, Faculty of Engineering and Technology.
9. Naval College of Engineering
10. National Dairy Institute, Karnal
11. Aligarh Muslim University

B. All India Pre-Medical/Pre-Dental Entrance Examination

Some of the notable institutions that give admission on the basis of the All India Pre-Medical/Pre-Dental Entrance Examination:

1. The Central Board of Secondary Education, New Delhi
2. All India Institute of Medical Sciences, New Delhi
3. The Armed Forces Medical College, Pune
4. Christian Medical College, Vellore
5. The Mahatma Gandhi Institute of Medical Science, Sevagram
6. Jawaharlal Nehru Medical College, Aligarh
7. Jawaharlal Institute of Post Graduation Medical Education and Research, Pondicherry
8. Banaras Hindu University
9. Kasturba Medical College, Mangalore
10. Medical College and Dental College, Pune

C. Joint Entrance Examination, the admission test conducted by Indian Institutes of Technology

List of the Indian Institutes of Technology that give admission on the basis of the Joint Entrance Examination:

1. Indian Institute of Technology, Powai, Mumbai
2. Indian Institute of Technology, Hauzkhas, New Delhi
3. Indian Institute of Technology, Guwahati, Assam
4. Indian Institute of Technology, Kanpur
5. Indian Institute of Technology, Kharagpur
6. Indian Institute of Technology, Chennai
7. Indian Institute of Technology, Roorkee

D. Some examinations conducted by Staff Selection Commission (SSC)

1. Combined Matric level Examination for recruitment to the posts of:

   a. Lower Division Clerks in Ministries/Departments, Attached and Subordinate offices of the

Govt. of India

b. Stenographer Grade 'D' in Ministries/Departments, Attached and Subordinate offices of the Govt. of India, and

c. Stenographer Grade 'C ' in Ministries/Departments, Attached and Subordinate offices of the Govt. of India

2. Combined Graduate level Examination for recruitment to the posts of:

   a. Assistants in Ministries/Departments, Attached and Subordinate office of the Govt. of India
   b. Inspectors of Central Excise and Customs
   c. Inspectors of Income Tax
   d. Preventive Officers in Customs
   e. Examiner in Customs
   f. Sub-Inspectors in Delhi Police and CBI
   g. Sub-Inspectors in BSF, CRPF, ITBP and CISF
   h. Divisional Accountant, Jr. Accountant, Auditor and UDCs in various offices of Govt. of India

3. Section Officer (Audit) in various offices under Comptroller and Auditor General of India
4. Section Officer (Commercial) in the offices under Comptroller and Auditor General of India
5. Investigator in National Sample Survey Organization, M/o Planning
6. Junior Hindi Translators

E. Some examinations conducted by Union Public Service Commission (UPSC)

1. Civil Services (Preliminary) Examination
2. Civil Services (Main) Examination
3. Indian Forest Service Examination
4. Engineering Services Examination
5. Geologist Examination
6. Special Class Railway Apprentices Examination
7. National Defence Academy and Naval Academy Examination
8. Combined Defence Services Examination
9. Combined Medical Services Examination
10. Indian Economic Service/Indian Statistical Service Examination
11. Section Officers/Stenographers (Grade-B/Grade-I) Limited Departmental Competitive Examination
12. Central Police Forces (Assistant Commandants) Examination

F. Defence Competitive Exams

1. Combined Defence Services Exam
2. National Defence Academy Exam
3. I.A.F. Airman (Technical Trades) Exam
4. I.A.F. Airman (Non-Technical Trades) Exam
5. I.A.F. Airman (Educational Instructors Trade) Exam
6. Indian Navy Sailors Matric Entry Recruitment Exam
7. Indian Navy Artificer Apprentices Exam
8. Indian Navy Dockyard Apprentices Exam
9. Indian Army Soldiers (Technical) Exam
10. Indian Army Soldiers Nursing Assistant's Exam
11. Indian Army Soldiers General Duty Exam
12. Indian Army Soldiers Clerks Exam

G. Insurance Competitive Exams

1. L.I.C/G.I.C Competitive Exams
2. L.I.C Officers' Exam
3. G.I.C Officers' Exam
4. L.I.C Development Officers' Exam
5. G.I.C Assistants Exam

H. SLET and NET

State Eligibility Test for Lectureship Eligibility (SLET)

States conducting SLET:

1. Maharashtra
2. Goa

3. Tamil Nadu (under consideration as on 14-07-2005)
4. Madhya Pradesh
5. Andhra Pradesh
6. Himachal Pradesh
7. Jammu & Kashmir
8. Rajasthan
9. West Bengal
10. NE-SLET (Which includes all North Eastern states and Sikkim)
11. Karnataka (Under consideration as on 14-07-2005)

It was resolved in the UGC's Commission Meeting that commencing from the SLET examinations scheduled in or after June 2002, SLET-qualified candidates will be eligible for appointment to the post of lecturer only in the universities/colleges belonging to the state from where they have passed the SLET examination. The status of SLET shall remain unchanged for SLET examinations conducted prior to 1 June 2002. In other words, candidates clearing SLET before June 2002 were eligible for appointment to the post of lecturer anywhere in India.

National Eligibility Test (NET)

The University Grants Commission (UGC) conducts the National Eligibility Test (NET) to determine eligibility for lectureship and to endow Junior Research Fellowships (JRF) for Indian nationals, with the object of ensuring minimum standards for entrants in the teaching profession and research field. The examination is conducted in Humanities (including languages), Social Sciences, Forensic Science, Environmental Sciences, Computer Science and Applications and Electronic Science. The Council of Scientific and Industrial Research (CSIR) conducts the UGC-CSIR NET for other Science subjects. These include Life Sciences, Physical Sciences, Chemical Sciences, Mathematical Sciences and Earth Atmospheric Ocean & Planetary Sciences and are held jointly with the UGC. The tests are conducted twice a year, usually in the months of June and December. For research candidates, the Junior Research Fellowship (JRF) is available for five years, subject to fulfilment of certain conditions. UGC has allocated a number of fellowships to universities for candidates who qualify the test for JRF. JRFs are awarded to meritorious candidates from among those who qualify in NET, provided they have opted for it at the time of application. The JRF test has been conducted since 1984. The Government of India, through a notification dated 22 July 1988, has entrusted the task of conducting the eligibility test for lectureship to UGC. Consequently, UGC conducted the first National Eligibility Test, common to both eligibility for Lectureship and Junior Research Fellowship in two parts, in December 1989 and in March 1990.

I. Admission Tests for Management Programmes

1. Common Admission Test (CAT)

List of institutions accepting CAT scores for admission:

1. IIM, Ahmedabad
2. IIM, Bangalore
3. IIM, Kolkata
4. IIM, Lucknow
5. IIM, Kozhikode
6. IIM, Indore
7. Management Development Institute, Gurgaon
8. National Institute of Industrial Engineering, Mumbai
9. S.P. Jain Institute of Management and Research, Mumbai
10. Mudra Institute of Communication, Ahmedabad
11. Institute of Management Technology, Ghaziabad
12. T.A. Pai Management Institute, Manipal
13. Indian Institute of Forest Management, Bhopal
14. Indian Institute of Social Welfare and Business Management, Kolkata

15. International Management Institute, New Delhi
16. K.J. Somaiya Institute of Management Studies and Research, Mumbai
17. Institute of Management Development and Research, Pune
18. Nirma Institute of Management, Ahmedabad
19. Principal L.N. Welingkar Institute of Management Development and Research, Mumbai
20. Institute for Financial Management and Research, Chennai
21. Fore School of Management, New Delhi
22. Indian Institute of Tourism and Travel Management, Gwalior
23. New Delhi Institute of Management, New Delhi
24. Institute for Integrated Learning in Management, New Delhi
25. National Institute of Management, Kolkata
26. Institute of Engineering and Management, Kolkata
27. Motilal Nehru National Institute of Technology, Allahabad
28. Globsyn Business School, Kolkata
29. International School of Business, Burhanpur
30. EMPI Business School, New Delhi
31. International Institute for Special Education, Lucknow
32. Alliance Business Academy, Bangalore
33. Kirloskar Institute of Advanced Management Studies, Devangere
34. Institute of Management Studies, Dehradun
35. Birla Institute of Technology, Ranchi
36. Institute of Management Studies, Ghaziabad
37. SDM Institute for Management Development, Mysore
38. Institute of Public Enterprise, Hyderabad
39. N.L. Dalmia Institute of Management Studies and Research, Mumbai
40. Ishan Institute of Management and Technology, New Delhi
41. Indian Institute of e-Business Management, Pune
42. Institute of Marketing and Management, New Delhi
43. NIILM Centre for Management Studies, New Delhi
44. Institute of Business Administration and Training, Bhubaneswar
45. DC School of Management and Technology, Idukki
46. National Insurance Academy, Pune
47. National Institute of Bank Management, Pune
48. Indian School of Mines, Dhanbad
49. Lal Bahadur Shastri Institute of Management, New Delhi
50. Indian Institute of Management Training, Pune
51. EMPI Institute of Advertising, Communication and Management, New Delhi
52. Aravali Institute of Management, Jodhpur
53. Amrita Institute of Management, Coimbatore
54. United Institute of Management, Allahabad,
55. College of Agri Business Management, Pantnagar
56. Hindustan Inst of Management and Computer, Agra
57. Department of Business Administration, Lucknow
58. Institute of Finance and International Management Bangalore, Karnataka
59. Thakur Institute of Management Studies and Research, Mumbai
60. Pailan College of Management and Technology, Kolkata
61. School of Management Sciences, Varanasi
62. Jaipuria Institute of Management, Lucknow
63. Management Education Centre, Kolkata

2. XLRI Aptitude Test (XAT)

List of institutions accepting XAT scores for admission:

1. Xavier Labour Relations Institute (XLRI), Jamshedpur
2. Xavier Institute of Management (XIM), Bhubaneswar
3. Bharathidasan Institute of Management, Trichy
4. Goa Institute of Management, Panjim
5. Principal L.N. Welingkar Institute of Management Development and Research, Mumbai
6. Institute of Technology and Management, Chennai
7. Loyola Institute of Business Administration, Chennai
8. International School of Business and Media, Pune
9. Akson Institute of Management Studies, Bangalore
10. Asia-Pacific Institute of Management, New Delhi
11. Institute for Technology and Management, Mumbai
12. Institute of Management and Information Science, Bhubaneswar
13. Xavier Institute of Social Service (XISS), Ranchi
14. Indira Group of Institutes, Pune
15. AICAR Business School, Mumbai

3. Institute of Rural Management, Anand (IRMA)

List of institutions accepting IRMA scores for admission:

1. Institute of Rural Management, Anand
2. Xavier Institute of Management (XIM), Bhubaneswar

4. Joint Management Entrance Test (JMET)

List of institutions accepting JMET scores for admission:

1. Shailesh Mehta School of Management, IIT Powai, Mumbai
2. Department of Management Studies, IIT Delhi
3. Vinod Gupta School of Management (IIT Kharagpur)
4. Department of Humanities and Social Sciences, IIT Madras
5. Department of Management Studies, IISc Bangalore
6. Department of Industrial and Management Engineering, IIT Kanpur
7. Department of Management Studies, IIT Roorkee

5. Indian Institute of Foreign Trade (IIFT)

List of institutions accepting IIFT test scores for admission:

1. Indian Institute of Foreign Trade, New Delhi
2. K.J. Somaiya Institute of Management Studies and Research, Mumbai
3. Geetam Institute of Foreign Studies, Visakhapatnam
4. Gandhi Institute of Technology and Management, Delhi

6. AIMS (Association of Indian Management Schools) Test for Management Admissions (ATMA)

Institutes accepting ATMA scores for admission:

1. Alliance Business Academy, Bangalore
2. Indian Business Academy, Bangalore
3. Institute of Business Management and Technology, Bangalore
4. MATS School of Business and MATS School of Information Technology, Bangalore
5. Bhubaneswar Institute of Management and Information Technology (BIMIT), Bhubaneswar
6. M.O.P Vaishnav College for Women (Madras University MBA), Chennai
7. SSN School of Management and Computer Applications, (SSN College of Engineering) (Anna University MBA), Chennai
8. Institute of Technology and Science, Ghaziabad
9. Integrated Academy of Management and Technology (INMANTEC), Ghaziabad
10. Jagan Institute of Management Studies, New Delhi

11. Shiva Institute of Management Studies, Ghaziabad
12. Institute of Marketing and Management Marketing, New Delhi
13. Education and Research Institute. New Delhi
14. Govindram Seksaria Institute of Management and Research, Indore
15. Prestige Institute of Management, Gwalior
16. Prestige Institute of Management and Research, Indore
17. Khandesh College Education Society's Institute of Management and Research, Jalgaon
18. B.P.H.E. Society's Institute of Management Studies, Career Development and Research, Ahmednagar
19. N.L. Dalmia Institute of Management Studies and Research, Mumbai
20. S.I.E.S College of Management Studies, Mumbai
21. Amrutvahini Institute of Management and Business Administration, Pune
22. Audyogik Shikshan Mandal's Institute of Business Management and Research, Pune
23. Apex Institute of Management, Pune
24. Indian Institute of Cost and Management Studies and Research, Pune
25. Indian Institute of Management Training (IIMT), Pune
26. Institute of International Business and Research, Pune
27. Indian Institute of Science and Management, Ranchi
28. Vasantraodada Patil Institute of Management Studies and Research, Sangli
29. Maharshi Karve Stree Shikshan Samstha's Smt. Hiraben Nanavati Insitute of Management and Research, Pune
30. Suryadatta Group of Institutes, Pune (Pune University)
31. Shri Shivaji Maratha Society's Institute of Management and Research, Pune (Pune University)
32. Bharati Vidyapeeth's Institute of Management and Rural Development Administration, Sangli
33. Bharati Vidyapeeth's Abhijit Kadam Institute of Management and Social Sciences, Solapur
34. Bharati Vidyapeeth's Institute of Management, Kolhapur
35. Bharati Vidyapeeth's Yashwantrao Mohite Institute of Management, Karad
36. Indo-American School of Business, Visakhapatnam
37. Indian Institute of Tourism and Travel Management, Gwalior
38. Institute of Business Management, Bangalore
39. Prestige Institute of Management, Dewas (Vikram University, Ujjain MBA)
40. SCMS—School of Technology and Management (Mahatma Gandhi University MBA)
41. SCMS—School of Communication and Management Studies, Management House, Cochin
42. Shikshana Prasaraka Mandali's Prin. N.G. Naralkar Institute of Career Development and Research, Pune
43. Dr. Vikhe Patil Foundation's Centre for Management Research and Development, Pune
44. Rajiv Gandhi Vocational Education Training College, Gwalior
45. Department of Business Administration, Awadesh Pratap Singh University, Rewa (Awadhesh Pratap Singh University MBA)
46. Institute of Business Management and Research, Bangalore
47. Institute of Business Management Research, Hubli
48. Sinhgad Institute of Management, Pune
49. Teerthanker Mahaveer Institute of Management and Technology,

Moradabad (U.P Technical University MBA)

50. University Institute of Management, Rani Durga University, Jabalpur
51. Bansilal Ramnath Agarwal Charitable Trust's Vishwakarma Institute of Management, Pune
52. NIILM University, New Delhi
53. Vidyasagar Institute of Management, Bhopal
54. Ambedkar Institute of Management Studies, Visakhapatnam
55. EMPI Business School, Chattarpur
56. Data Systems Research Foundation, Pune
57. Deen Dayal Upadhyaya Institute of Management and Higher Studies, Kanpur
58. Indian Institute of Tourism and Travel Management, Gwalior (MP Bhoj Open University, Bhopal MBA)
59. Technocrats Institute of Technology, Bhopal (Barkatullah University MBA)
60. Pioneer Institute of Professional Studies, Indore (Devi Ahilya Vishwavidyalaya MBA)
61. BVM College of Management Education, Gwalior (Jiwaji University MBA)
62. Medi-Caps Institute of Technology and Management, Indore (Devi Ahilya Vishwavidyalaya MBA)
63. Lakshmi Narain College of Technology, Bhopal
64. Pandit Jawaharlal Nehru Institute of Business Management, Vikram University, Ujjain (Vikram University MBA)
65. VNS Institute of Management, Bhopal (Barkatullah University MBA)
66. Samrat Ashok Technological Institute, Vidisha (Barkatullah University MBA)
67. Maharishi Centre Educational Excellence, Bhopal (Barkatullah University MBA)
68. Institute of Professional Education and Research (IPER), Bhopal (Barkatullah University MBA)
69. Bansal MBA College, Bhopal (Barkatullah University MBA)
70. Institute of Management Studies (IMS), Indore (Devi Ahilya Vishwavidyalaya MBA)
71. Anna University, Chennai
72. Department of Management Studies, Adhiyamaan College of Engineering, Hosur (Anna University MBA)
73. MEPCO Schlenk Engineering College, Dist. Virudhunagar (Anna University MBA)
74. Akson Academie, Bangalore (Bangalore University MBA)
75. Institute for Development and Research in Banking Technology (IDRBT), Hyderabad
76. M.O.P Vaishnav College for Women, Chennai (University of Madras MBA)
77. National Institute of Technology (Formerly Regional Engineering College), Tiruchirapalli
78. Symbiosis Institute of Business Management, Pune
79. L.N. Welingkar Institute of Management Development and Research, Mumbai
80. Bansilal Ramnath Agarwal Charitable Trust's Vishwakarma Institute of Management, Pune
81. Symbiosis Institute of Computer Studies and Research, Pune
82. Shri Shivaji Maratha Society's Institute of Management and Research, Pune (University of Pune MBA)
83. Department of Management Sciences, University of Pune, Pune (University of Pune MBA)
84. Thakur Institute of Management Studies and Research, Mumbai
85. Faculty of Management, International University for Human Transformation, Raipur
86. University Institute of Management, Rani Durgavati Vishwavidyalaya, Jabalpur

87. Mahatma Gandhichitrakoot Gramoday Vishwavidyalaya, Satna
88. Institute of Management, Jiwaji University, Gwalior
89. Faculty of Management Studies, Dr. Hari Singh Gour University, Sagar
90. Institute of Professional Studies, Indore
91. Department of Business Administration, Awadhesh Pratap Singh University, Rewa
92. Hindu Institute of Management, Sonepat (M.D. University, Rohtak MBA)
93. Crescent Institute of Management, Bhopal (Barkatullah University MBA)
94. IILM Institute for Higher Education, Gurgaon
95. IILM Institute for Higher Education, Lucknow
96. IILM Academy of Higher Learning, Greater Noida
97. Prestige Institute of Management, Gwalior (Jiwaji University MBA)
98. Prestige Institute of Management, Dewas (Vikram University, Ujjain MBA)
99. C.R. Institute of Management (C.R.I.M), University Teaching Department, Barkatullah University, Bhopal
100. Govindram Seksaria Institute of Management and Research, Indore (Devi Ahilya Vishwavidyalaya MBA)
101. Shri Vaishnav Institute of Management, Indore (Devi Ahilya Vishwavidyalaya MBA)
102. Mahakal Institute of Management, Ujjain (Vikram University MBA)
103. Institute of Business Management and Research, Indore (Devi Ahilya Vishwavidyalaya MBA)
104. Xavier Institute of Development Action and Studies (XIDAS), Jabalpur (Rani Durgavati Vishwavidyalaya MBA)
105. RKDF Institute of Management, Bhopal (Barkatullah University MBA)
106. Sri Satya Sai Institute of Management, Bhopal (Barkatullah University MBA)
107. Bhabha Management Research Institute, Bhopal (Barkatullah University MBA)

7. Under Graduate Aptitude Test (UGAT)

Institutes accepting UGAT score for admission to Bachelor Programmes:

1. University of Petroleum and Energy Studies, Dehradun/New Delhi
1. Amity Business School, Noida
2. Jagannath International Management School, New Delhi
4. International Management Centre, New Delhi
4. EMPI Business School, New Delhi
5. NIILM Centre for Management Studies, New Delhi
6. R.K. College of Systems and Management, New Delhi
7. Institute of Marketing and Management, New Delhi
8. AIM University, New Delhi
9. Apeejay Institute of Management and Information Technology, New Delhi
10. New Delhi Institute of Management, New Delhi
11. Delhi School of e-Learning, New Delhi
12. Jagan Institute of Management Studies, New Delhi
13. The Delhi School of Communication, New Delhi
14. S.G.S.S.—IIT New Delhi
15. Institute of Management Studies Noida
16. Army Institute of Management and Technology, Greater Noida
17. Ansal Institute of Technology, Gurgaon
18. Unique Institute of Management and Technology, Ghaziabad
19. Shiva Institute of Management Studies and Technology, Ghaziabad
20. NIMT Institute of Management and Technology, Ghaziabad

21. Mewar University, Ghaziabad
22. Integrated Academy of Management and Technology, Ghaziabad
23. BLS Institute of Education Ghaziabad
24. Jaipuria Institute of Management Ghaziabad
25. Institute of Environment and Management, Lucknow
26. Sherwood College of Management, Lucknow
27. Graduate School of Business and Administration, Greater Noida
28. Invertis Institute of Management Studies, Bareilly
29. Institute of Media, Management and Technology, Dehradun
30. Ram Institute of Hotel Management and Catering Technology, Dehradun
31. Institute of Technology and Management, Dehradun
32. Beehive College of Advance Studies, Dehradun
33. SD College of Management Studies, Muzzaffar Nagar
34. Amrapali Institute of Management and Computer Applications, Haldwani
35. NIMT Institute of Management and Technology, Jaipur
36. MES College of Arts and Commerce, Goa
37. Rosary College of Commerce and Arts, Goa
38. SVS College of Commerce and Management Studies, Goa
39. Suryadatta College of Management, Information Research and Technology Pune
40. IPS Academy, Indore
41. Christian Eminent Academy of Management, Professional Education and Research, Indore
42. International Institute of Foreign Trade and Research, Indore
43. MATS University, Raipur
44. IIAS International University, Bhilai
45. University of Technology and Science, Raipur
46. International University for Human Transformation, Raipur
47. Alliance Business Academy, Bangalore
48. Dayananda Sagar College of Management and Information Technology, Bangalore
49. T John College, Bangalore
50. Acharya Institute of Management and Sciences, Bangalore
51. Sri Bhagwan Mahaveer Jain College Bangalore
52. KLE Society, Belgaum
53. Rajarajan Academy of Higher Learning Ltd., Chennai
54. Annex College of Management Studies, Kolkata
55. International School of Business, Kolkata
56. Indian Institute of Hotel Management and Catering Bhubaneswar
57. Rourkela Institute of Management Studies, Rourkela
58. RJ School of Management Studies, Balasore
59. Durgapur Society of Management Science, Durgapur
60. RAI University

8. Management Aptitude Test

The Government of India has approved MAT as a National Entrance Test for admission to MBA and equivalent programmes. MAT is necessary for admission into the Post Graduate Diploma in Management (PGDM), Post Graduate Diploma in Information Technology & Management (PGDITM) and equivalent programmes offered by the All India Management Association (AIMA-CME) or other Management Institutes.

Participating Management Institutes / Universities (MAT of 4 December 2005).

Northern Region

1. Academy of Management Studies, Dehradun
2. AIMA-Centre for Management Education (PGDM), New Delhi

3. AIMA-Centre for Management Education (PGDITM), New Delhi
4. Amity Business School, Noida
5. Amrapali Institute of Management & Computer Applications, Haldwani
6. Apeejay Institute of Management & Information Technology, New Delhi
7. Apeejay School of Management, New Delhi
8. Asia Pacific Institute of Management, New Delhi
9. Asian School of Media Studies, Noida
10. Bhai Gurdas Institute of Management & Technolgy, Sangrur
11. Birla Institute of Management Technology, Greater Noida
12. BLS Institute of Education, Ghaziabad
13. BLS Institute of Management, Ghaziabad
14. Centre for Management Development, Modinagar
15. Centre for Management Technology, Greater Noida
16. Cosmic Business School, New Delhi
17. CT Institute of Management & IT, Jalandhar
18. DPC Institute of Management, New Delhi
19. Dr Gaur Hari Singhania Institute of Management & Research, Kanpur
20. EMPI Institutions, New Delhi
21. Fortune Institute of International Business, New Delhi
22. Global Institute of Management Technology, New Delhi
23. Graduate School of Business & Administration, Greater Noida
24. Guru Nanak Institute of Management, New Delhi
25. Gurukul Kangri Vishwavidyalaya, Haridwar
26. IBAT School of Management, Greater Noida
27. IILM Institute for Higher Education, Gurgaon
28. IIMR Pharma Business School, Delhi
29. IIMT Management College, Meerut
30. Indian Institute of Finance, New Delhi
31. Institute for Integrated Learning in Mgmt, New Delhi
32. Institute of Business Administration & Management, New Delhi
33. Institute of Environment & Management, Lucknow
34. Institute of Informatics & Management Sciences, Meerut
35. Institute of Management & Development, New Delhi
36. Institute of Management Education, Ghaziabad
37. Institute of Management Studies, Ghaziabad
38. Institute of Management Studies, Dehradun
39. Institute of Marketing & Mgmt, New Delhi
40. Institute of Productivity & Management, Meerut
41. Institute of Productivity & Management, Ghaziabad
42. Institute of Productivity & Management, Lucknow
43. Institute of Productivity & Management, Kanpur
44. Institute of Professional Excellence & Management, Ghaziabad
45. Institute of Technology & Science, Ghaziabad
46. Integrated Academy of Management & Technology, Ghaziabad
47. International Institute for Special Education, Lucknow
48. International Management Centre, New Delhi
49. Ishan Institute of Management & Technology, New Delhi
50. Jagan Instt of Management Studies, Delhi
51. Jagannath Institute of Management Sciences, New Delhi
52. Jaipuria Institute of Management, Ghaziabad

53. Jamia Hamdard, New Delhi
54. Landmark Foundation, Dehradun
55. Maharishi Institute of Management, Noida
56. Management Education & Research Institute, New Delhi
57. Master School of Management, Meerut
58. Motilal Rastogi School of Management, Lucknow
59. Netaji Subhash Institute of Management Sciences, New Delhi
60. New Delhi Institute of Management, New Delhi
61. NICE Management College, Meerut
62. NIILM School of Business, New Delhi
63. Nimbus Academy of Management, Dehradun
64. NIMT, Ghaziabad
65. NIMT, Greater Noida
66. Rai Business School, New Delhi
67. RIMT-Institute of Management & Computer Technology, Mandigobindgarh
68. Shiva Institute of Management Studies, Ghaziabad
69. Shri Guru Ram Rai Institute of Technology & Science, Dehradun
70. Skyline Business School, New Delhi
71. Sri Sringeri Sharda Institute of Management, New Delhi
72. SRM Institute of Management & Technology, Modinagar
73. Teerthankar Mahaveer Institute of Management & Technology, Moradabad
74. The Delhi School of Communication, New Delhi
75. Unique Institute of Management & Technology, Modinagar
76. University of Petroleum & Energy Studies, New Delhi

Western Region

1. AIMA-Centre for Management Education (PGDM), New Delhi
2. AIMA-Centre for Management Education (PGDITM), New Delhi
3. Asia Pacific Institute of Management, Jaipur
4. College of Commerce, Science & Information Technology, Pune
5. IBAT School of Management, Pune
6. Indian Institute of Education & Business Management, Chandigarh
7. Indian Institute of Management Training, Pune
8. Indian Institute of Rural Management, Jaipur
9. Institute of Business Management & Research, Pune
10. Institute of Health Management Research, Jaipur
11. Institute of Management & Computer Studies, Mumbai
12. Institute of Rural Management, Jodhpur
13. International Institute of Foreign Trade & Research, Indore
14. International School of Business Management, Jaipur
15. JK Institute of Technology & Management, Navi Mumbai
16. Maharishi Arvind Institute of Science & Management, Jaipur
17. MKM Indian Institute of Management, Jaipur
18. Mody Institute of Technology, Laxmangarh
19. NIMT, Kotputli
20. Rai Business School, Mumbai
21. Rai Business School, Pune
22. School of International Business & Management, Jaipur
23. Som-Lalit Institute of Management Studies, Ahmedabad
24. Suryadatta Group of Institutions, Pune

Eastern Region

1. Academy for Professional Excellence, Kolkata
2. Annex College of Management Studies, Kolkata
3. Arya School of Management & Information Technology, Bhubaneswar

4. Bengal College of Engineering & Technology, Durgapur
5. Bharatiya Vidya Bhavan, Kolkata
6. BRM Institute of Management & Information Technology, Bhubaneswar
7. CMCE College, Bokaro
8. Eastern Institute for Integrated Learning in Management, Kolkata
9. Eastern Institute of Management, Kolkata
10. Future Institute of Engineering & Management, Kolkata
11. Global Institute of Management, Bhubaneswar
12. Heritage Institute of Technology, Kolkata
13. IBAT School of Management, Bhubaneswar
14. Indian Institute of Business Management, Patna
15. Institute of Business Management, Kolkata
16. Institute of Management & Information Sciences, Bhubaneswar
17. Institute of Management Bhubaneswar, Bhubaneswar
18. Institute of Professional Studies & Research, Cuttack
19. Institute of Science & Management, Ranchi
20. International Institute of Management Sciences, Kolkata
21. Lalit Narayan Mishra College of Business Management, Muzaffarpur
22. North Eastern Regional Institute of Management, Guwahati
23. Rajdhani College of Engineering & Management, Bhubaneswar
24. Regional College of Management, Bhubaneswar
25. Rourkela Institute of Management Studies, Rourkela
26. Sairam College, Bhubaneswar
27. Sikkim Manipal Institute of Technology, Rangpo
28. Tezpur University, Tezpur
29. The University of Burdwan, Burdwan
30. Vaishali Institute of Business & Rural Management, Muzaffarpur
31. Xavier Institute of Social Service, Ranchi

Southern Region

1. Academy for Management Studies, Tirupati
2. Acharya Institute of Management & Sciences, Bangalore
3. Acharya Institute of Technology, Bangalore
4. Alliance Business Academy, Bangalore
5. Alliance International College, Coimbatore
6. Ambedkar Institute of Management Studies, Visakhapatnam
7. Asan Memorial Institute of Management, Chennai
8. Asia Pacific Institute of Management, Hyderabad
9. Balla Institute of Technology & Management, Visakhapatnam
10. Bangalore Institute of Management Studies, Bangalore
11. Bharatiya Vidya Bhavan, Bangalore
12. Bhavan-SIET Institute of Management, Bangalore
13. CBM College, Coimbatore
14. Christ College, Bangalore
15. CMR Group of Institutions, Bangalore
16. Coimbatore Institute of Management & Technology, Coimbatore
17. Dayananda Sagar Business School, Bangalore
18. DC School of Management & Technology, Kottayam
19. Farook Institute of Management Studies, Calicut
20. Fatima College, Madurai
21. Guru Nanak Institute of Management, Chennai
22. Guruvayurappan Institute of Management, Coimbatore
23. IBAT School of Management, Bangalore
24. Indian Institute of Plantation Management, Bangalore
25. Institute of Business Management & Research, Bangalore

26. Institute of Business Management & Technology, Bangalore
27. Institute of Finance & International Management, Bangalore
28. INTECH Institute of Business Management, Bangalore
29. Mar Athanasios College for Advanced Studies, Tiruvalla
30. MATS School of Business & IT, Bangalore
31. MES College of Engineering, Malappuram (Dist)
32. MP Birla Institute of Management, Bangalore
33. MS Ramaiah Institute of Management, Bangalore
34. NIILM Business School, Bangalore
35. Park's College, Coimbatore
36. PES Institute of Technolgy, Bangalore
37. R L Institute of Management Studies, Madurai
38. Rai Business School, Bangalore
39. Rai Business School, Chennai
40. Rajagiri School of Management, Kochi
41. Rajalakshmi Engineering College, Chennai
42. RJS Institute of Management Studies, Bangalore
43. SCMS School of Communication & Management Studies, Cochin
44. SCMS School of Technology & Management, Cochin
45. Sidvin School of Business Institute of Technology, Bangalore
46. Sir M Visvesvaraya Institute of Technology, Bangalore
47. Siva Sivani Institute of Management, Secunderabad
48. Sona School of Management, Salem
49. Sree Narayana Guru Institute of Science & Technology, North Paravur
50. Sree Narayana Gurukulam College of Engineering, Ernakulam
51. T John College, Bangalore
52. TKM Institute of Management, Kollam
53. Vael's Institute of Business Administration, Chennai

Exams for Education Abroad

Most institutes of higher education abroad assess the performance of students through certain tests before admitting her/his application for consideration. Different institutions have different requirements. These tests are prepared by professional testing organizations, like the US Educational Testing Service (ETS), that administers a wide array of tests including SAT, GRE, TOEFL and TSE. These tests are valid for admission to universities in USA, Canada, UK, and Australia, among others.

Notable exams for the purpose of gaining admission in educational institutes abroad:

1. Graduate Record Examinations (GRE)
2. Graduate Management Admission Test (GMAT)
3. The International English Language Testing System (IELTS)
4. Test of English as a Foreign Language (TOEFL)
5. Scholastic Aptitude Test (SAT)
6. Michigan English Language Assessment Battery (MELAB)
7. American College Testing Programme (ACT)

Indian Institutes of Management

After 1947, India focused on the development of science and technology education within the country. It soon became apparent that the country needed to train personnel to help grow and manage the talent pool of technologists and scientists. This led to the creation of the Indian Institutes of Management in the country. The Indian Institute of Management Calcutta was set up in 1961. It launched a two-year full time post graduate programme. The first batch of stu-

List of IIMs

	Name	Established in
1.	Indian Institute of Management, Ahmedabad	1961
2.	Indian Institute of Management, Calcutta	1961
3.	Indian Institute of Management, Bangalore	1973
4.	Indian Institute of Management, Lucknow	1984
5.	Indian Institute of Management, Kozhikode	1996
6.	Indian Institute of Management, Indore	1997

dents graduated in 1966. The institute was established in collaboration with Alfred P Sloan School of Management, Ford Foundation, the Government of India and the Government of West Bengal. The Indian businesses also played a major role in the setting up of IIM Calcutta.

Indian Institutes of Technology (IIT)

In 1946 a committee was set up by Jogendra Singh, member, Viceroy's Executive Council, Department of Education, Health and Agriculture to consider the setting up of Higher Technical Institutions for post World War II industrial development in India. The 22-member committee, headed by N.R. Sarkar, in its report recommended the establishment of four higher technical institutions in the Eastern, Western, Northern and Southern regions, on the lines of the Massachusetts Institute of Technology, USA, with a number of secondary institutions affiliated to it. The committee also suggested that the institutes would not only produce undergraduates but they should be engaged in research, producing research workers and technical teachers. They felt that the proportion of undergraduates and postgraduate students should be 2:1. With the recommendations of the Sarkar Committee in view, the first Indian Institute of Technology was set up in May 1950 at Kharagpur, in West Bengal. Since then six other institutes have come up in the country.

List of IITs

	Name	Established in
1.	Indian Institute of Technology, Kharagpur	1950
2.	Indian Institute of Technology, Bombay	1958
3.	Indian Institute of Technology, Madras	1959
4.	Indian Institute of Technology, Kanpur	1960
5.	Indian Institute of Technology, Delhi	1961
6.	Indian Institute of Technology, Guwahati	1994
7.	Indian Institute of Technology, Roorkee	2001

UPSC Programme of Examinations to be Held in the Year 2007

Ser No	Name of Examination	Date of Notification/ Last date for receipt of applications	Date of Commencement and its duration	Minimum academic qualifications prescribed	Age Limits	Remarks
1	Combined Medical Services Exam, 2007	26 Aug 2006 25 Sept 2006	21 Jan 2007 1 Day	MBBS Degree	Below 32 years as on 1.1.2007	Candidates appearing at the final MBBS Examination also eligible to compete subject to certain conditions. Selected candidates will be appointed only after they have completed compulsory rotating internship.
2	CDS Exam (I), 2007	23 Sept 2006 23 Oct 2006	18 Feb 2007 1 Day	i) For IMA & OTA:- Degree of a recognized university or equivalent ii) For Naval Academy:- B.Sc. (with Physics & Mathematics) or Bachelor of Engineering iii) For Air Force Academy:-Degree of a recognized University (with Physics and Mathematics at 10+2 level) or Bachelor of Engineering	19-24 years as on 1.1.2008 for IMA; 19–22 years as on 1.1.2008 for Naval Academy; 19–23 years as on 1.1.2008 for Air Force Academy; and 19–25 years as on 1.1.2008 for OTA	Candidates appearing at the degree or equivalent examination also eligible to compete subject to certain conditions.

3	NDA & NA Exam (I), 2007	14 Oct 2006 13 Nov 2006	22 Apr 2007 1 Day	i) For Army Wing of NDA:- 12th Class pass of the 10+2 pattern of School Education or equivalent examination conducted by a State Education Board or a University ii) For Air Force and Naval Wings of NDA and for 10+2 (Executive Branch) Course at Naval Academy: 12th Class pass of the 10+2 pattern of School Education or equivalent with Physics and Mathematics conducted by a State Education Board or a University	16-1/2 to 19 years as on 1.1.2008	Candidates appearing at the 12th Class under the 10+2 pattern of School Education or equivalent examination also eligible to compete subject to certain conditions.
4	Civil Services (Prel) Exam, 2007	18 Nov 2006 18 Dec 2006	20 May 2007 1 Day	A degree from a recognized university or equivalent	21–30 years as on 1.8.2007	Candidates appearing at the degree examination also eligible to compete subject to certain conditions.
5	Engineering Services Exam, 2007	06 Jan 2007 05 Feb 2007	09 Jun 2007 3 Days	A degree in Engineering from a recognized university or equivalent. M.Sc. Degree or its equivalent with Wireless Communications,	21–30 years as on 1.8.2007	Candidates appearing at Engineering Degree or equivalent also eligible to compete subject to certain conditions.

Ser No	Name of Examination	Date of Notification/ Last date for receipt of applications	Date of Commencement and its duration	Minimum academic qualifications prescribed	Age Limits	Remarks
				Electronics, Radio Physics or Radio Engineering as special subject acceptable for certain services/posts only		
6	IFS Exam, 2007	03 Feb 2007 05 Mar 2007	07 July 2007 10 Days	A Bachelor's degree with at least one of the subjects namely Animal Husbandry & Veterinary Science, Botany, Chemistry, Geology, Mathematics,Physics, Statistics and Zoology or a degree in Agriculture or Forestry or Engineering of a recognized University or equivalent	21–30 years as on 1.7.2007	Candidates appearing at degree examination (with prescribed subject) also eligible to compete subject to certain conditions.
7	SCRA Exam, 2007	17 Feb 2007 19 Mar 2007	22 July 2007 1 Day	Intermediate or Senior Secondary (12 years) Examination under 10+2 pattern of School Education or equivalent with Mathematics and at least one of the subjects	17–21 years as on 1.8.2007	Candidates appearing at the Intermediate/Senior Secondary (12 years) examination under 10+2 pattern of School Education/Ist year of the 3 years

				Physics and Chemistry as Subjects of the Examination in Ist or IInd Division		degree course or equivalent examination with the prescribed subjects also eligible subject to certain conditions.
8	NDA & NA Exam (II), 2007	17 Mar 2007 16 Apr 2007	19 Aug 2007 1 Day	i) For Army Wing of NDA:- 12th Class pass of the 10+2 pattern of School Education or equivalent examination conducted by a State Education Board or a University ii) For Air Force and Naval Wings of NDA and for 10+2 (Executive Branch) Course at Naval Academy: 12th Class pass of the 10+2 pattern of School Education or equivalent with Physics and Mathematics conducted by a State Education Board or a University	16½ to 19 years as on 1.7.2008	Candidates appearing at the 12th Class under the 10+2 pattern of School Education or equivalent examination also eligible to compete subject to certain conditions.
9	CDS Exam (II), 2007	21 Apr 2007 21 May 2007	16 Sep 2007 1 Day	i) For IMA & OTA:- Degree of a recognized university or equivalent ii) For Naval Academy:- B.Sc. (with Physics &	19–24 years as on 1.7.2008 for IMA; 19–22 years as on 1.7.2008 for	Candidates appearing at the degree or equivalent examination also eligible to compete subject to certain

Ser No	Name of Examination	Date of Notification/ Last date for receipt of applications	Date of Commencement and its duration	Minimum academic qualifications prescribed	Age Limits	Remarks
				Mathematics) or Bachelor of Engineering iii) For Air Force Academy:- Degree of a recognized University (with Physics and Mathematics at 10+2 level) or Bachelor of Engineering	Naval Academy; 19–23 years as on1.7.2008 for Air Force Academy; and 19–25 years as on 1.7.2008 for OTA	conditions.
10	Central Police Forces (AC) Exam 2007	05 May 2007 04 June 2007	07 Oct 2007 1 Day	A degree from a recognized University or equivalent	20–25 years as on 1.8.2007	Candidates appearing at the Degree or equivalent examination also eligible to compete subject to certain conditions.
11	Civil Services (Main) Exam, 2007	—	26 Oct 2007 21 Days	A degree from a recognized University or equivalent	21–30 years as on 1.8.2007	Only such of the candidates as are declared qualified on the results of Preliminary Examination are eligible to take the Main Examination.
12	IES/ISS Exam, 2007	09 Jun 2007 09 July 2007	01 Dec 2007 03 Days	A post-graduate degree in Economics/Applied Economics/Business	21–30 years as on 1.1.2007	Candidates appearing at the Post-graduate degree or equivalent

				Economics/ Econometrics for the IES and a Post-graduate degree in Statistics/Mathematical Statistics/Applied Statistics for the ISS, from a recognized University or equivalent		examination in the relevant disciplines also eligible to compete subject to certain conditions.
13	Geologists' Exam, 2007	16 Jun 2007 16 July 2007	08 Dec 2007 03 Days	Master's Degree in Geology or Applied Geology or Marine Geology from a recognized University or equivalent	21–32 years as on 1.1.2007	Candidates appearing at their Master's Degree or equivalent examination (with prescribed subjects) also eligible to compete subject to certain conditions.
14	SO/Steno (Gd B/Gd-I) Ltd Deptt Competitive Exam, 2007	23 Jun 2007 20 Aug 2007	26 Dec 2007 4 Days	–	–	Departmental Examination open to only certain categories of Government Servants.

Sports

Cricket 2007 World Cup

West Indies will host the 2007 Cricket World Cup from 11 March to 28 April 2007. Sixteen teams, divided into four groups of four each, will participate in this quadrangular tournament. The top two teams from each group will then compete in a 'Super 8' format, from which the semi-finalists will be decided. The teams, other than the ten Test-playing nations, who have qualified for this edition of the World Cup are Kenya, Bermuda, Canada, Ireland, Netherlands and Scotland.

World Cup Statistics

Highest Totals

Score	Match	Year
398-5 (50.0 ov)	Sri Lanka v Kenya at Kandy	1996
373-6 (50.0 ov)	India v Sri Lanka at Taunton	1999
360-4 (50.0 ov)	West Indies v Sri Lanka at Karachi	1987
359-2 (50.0 ov)	Australia v India at Johannesburg	2003
340-2 (50.0 ov)	Zimbabwe v Namibia at Harare	2003
338-5 (60.0 ov)	Pakistan v Sri Lanka at Swansea	1983
334-4 (60.0 ov)	England v India at Lord's	1975
333-9 (60.0 ov)	England v Sri Lanka at Taunton	1983
330-6 (60.0 ov)	Pakistan v Sri Lanka at Nottingham	1975
329-2 (50.0 ov)	India v Kenya at Bristol	1999

Lowest Totals

Score	Match	Year
36 (18.4 ov)	Canada v Sri Lanka at Paarl	2003
45 (40.3 ov)	Canada v England at Manchester	1979
45 (14.0 ov)	Namibia v Australia at Potchefstroom	2003
68 (31.3 ov)	Scotland v West Indies at Leicester	1999
74 (40.2 ov)	Pakistan v England at Adelaide	1992
84 (17.4 ov)	Namibia v Pakistan at Kimberley	2003
86 (37.2 ov)	Sri Lanka v West Indies at Manchester	1975
93 (36.2 ov)	England v Australia at Leeds	1975
93 (35.2 ov)	West Indies v Kenya at Poona	1996
94 (52.3 ov)	East Africa v England at Birmingham	1975

Top Scorers

Player	Team	Mat	Runs	HS	100s
*S.R. Tendulkar	Ind	33	1732	152	4
Javed Miandad	Pak	33	1083	103	1
P.A. de Silva	SL	35	1064	145	2

I.V.A. Richards	WI	23	1013	181	3
M.E Waugh	Aus	22	1004	130	4
*R.T. Ponting	Aus	28	998	140*	3
S.R Waugh	Aus	33	978	120*	1
A. Ranatunga	SL	30	969	88*	0
*B.C. Lara	WI	25	956	116	2
Saeed Anwar	Pak	21	915	113*	3

Top Wicket Takers

Player	Team	Mat	Wkts
Wasim Akram	Pak	38	55
*G.D. McGrath	Aus	28	45
J. Srinath	Ind	34	44
A.A. Donald	SA	25	38
*W.P.U.J.C. Vaas	SL	21	36
Imran Khan	Pak	28	34
*C.Z. Harris	NZ	28	32
*S.K. Warne	Aus	17	32
I.T. Botham	Eng	22	30
*M. Muralitharan	SL	21	30

*Indicates cricketers still playing

India's Performance in the World Cup

Year	Matches played	Won	Lost	Position
1975	3	1	2	Failed to qualify for semi final
1979	3	0	3	Failed to qualify for semi final
1983	8	6	2	Won
1987	7	5	2	Semi finalist
1992	8	2	5	Failed to qualify for semi final
1996	7	4	3	Semi finalist
1999	8	4	4	Qualified for the Super 6
2003	11	9	2	Finalist

ICC Champions Trophy Down the Years (Winners)

Year	Winner	Host
1998	South Africa	Bangladesh
2000	New Zealand	Kenya
2002	India/Sri Lanka	Sri Lanka
2004	West Indies	England

India's Overall Performance in ODIs

	P	W	L	T	NR
Overall	628	297	302	3	26
Home	211	116	89	1	5
Away	191	66	113	0	12
Neutral	226	115	100	2	9
1970s	13	2	11	0	0
1980s	155	69	80	0	6
1990s	257	122	120	3	12
2000s	203	104	91	0	8

India's Overall Performance in Tests

	P	W	L	T	D
Overall	400	88	129	1	182
Home	207	62	47	1	97
Away	193	26	82	0	85
1930s	7	0	5	0	2
1940s	13	0	6	0	7
1950s	44	6	17	0	21
1960s	52	9	21	0	22
1970s	64	17	19	0	28
1980s	81	11	21	1	48
1990s	69	18	20	0	31
2000s	70	27	20	0	23

Indian Wisden Cricketers of the Year

1897	K.S. Ranjitsinhji
1930	K.S. Duleepsinhji
1932	Nawab of Pataudi (Sr)
1933	C.K. Nayudu
1937	Vijay Merchant
1947	Vinoo Mankad
1968	Nawab of Pataudi (Jr)
1972	B.S. Chandrasekhar
1980	Sunil Gavaskar
1983	Kapil Dev
1984	Mohinder Amarnath
1987	Dilip Vengsarkar
1991	Mohd Azharuddin
1996	Anil Kumble
1997	Sachin Tendulkar
2000	Rahul Dravid
2002	V.V.S. Laxman

Top Ten Batsmen Tests

Name	Mat	I	NO	Runs	HS	Ave	100
B.C. Lara	128	227	6	11505	400*	52.05	32
A.R. Border	156	265	44	11174	205	50.56	27
S.R. Waugh	168	260	46	10927	200	51.06	32
S.R. Tendulkar	132	211	22	10469	248*	55.39	35
S.M. Gavaskar	125	214	16	10122	236*	51.12	34
R. Dravid	104	176	22	9049	270	58.75	23
G.A. Gooch	118	215	6	8900	333	42.58	20
Javed Miandad	124	189	21	8832	280*	52.57	23
R.T. Ponting	105	175	24	8792	257	58.22	31
I.V.A. Richards	121	182	12	8540	291	50.23	24

Top Five Scores (Team) in Tests

952-6d	Sri Lanka v India	Colombo (RPS)	1997
903-7d	England v Australia	The Oval	1938
849	England v West Indies	Kingston	1929/30
790-3d	West Indies v Pakistan	Kingston	1957/58
758-8d	Australia v West Indies	Kingston	1954/55

Top Five Scores (Individual) in Tests

400*	B.C. Lara	West Indies v England at St John's, 4th Test,	2003/04
380	M.L. Hayden	Australia v Zimbabwe at Perth, 1st Test,	2003/04
375	B.C. Lara	West Indies v England at St John's, 5th Test,	1993/94
374	D.P.M.D. Jayawardene	Sri Lanka v South Africa at Colombo (SSC), 1st Test,	2006
365*	G.S. Sobers	West Indies v Pakistan at Kingston, 3rd Test,	1957/58

Top Ten Bowlers Tests

	Mat	Wickets	Ave
S.K. Warne	140	685	25.25
M. Muralitharan	108	657	21.96
G.D. McGrath	119	542	21.55
A. Kumble	110	533	28.75
C.A. Walsh	132	519	24.44
N. Kapil Dev	131	434	29.64
R.J. Hadlee	86	431	22.29
Wasim Akram	104	414	23.62
C.E.L. Ambrose	98	405	20.99
S.M. Pollock	102	395	23.42

Top Ten Batsmen ODIs

Name	Mat	I	NO	Runs	HS	Ave	SR	100
S.R. Tendulkar	367	358	35	14370	186*	44.48	85.88	40
Inzamam-ul-Haq	367	341	51	11549	137*	39.82	74.63	10
S.T. Jayasuriya	364	354	15	11104	189	32.75	89.90	22
S.C. Ganguly	279	270	21	10123	183	40.65	73.79	22
B.C. Lara	275	267	29	9821	169	41.26	79.52	19
R. Dravid	297	276	35	9576	153	39.73	70.42	12
M. Azharuddin	334	308	54	9378	153*	36.92	73.99	7
R.T. Ponting	256	250	29	9293	164	42.04	79.32	20
P.A. de Silva	308	296	30	9284	145	34.90	81.13	11
Saeed Anwar	247	244	19	8823	194	39.21	80.66	20

Top Five Scores (Team) in ODIs

443-9 (50 overs)	Sri Lanka v Netherlands	Amstelveen	2006
438-9 (49.5 overs)	South Africa v Australia	Johannesburg	2005/06
434-4 (50 overs)	Australia v South Africa	Johannesburg	2005/06
418-5 (50 overs)	South Africa v Zimbabwe	Potchefstroom	2006/07
398-5 (50 overs)	Sri Lanka v Kenya	Kandy	1995/96

Top Five Scores (Individual) in ODIs

194	Saeed Anwar	Pakistan v India at Chennai,	1996/97
189*	I.V.A Richards	West Indies v England at Manchester,	1984
189	S.T. Jayasuriya	Sri Lanka v India at Sharjah,	2000/01
188*	G. Kirsten	South Africa v United Arab Emirates at Rawalpindi,	1995/96
186*	S.R. Tendulkar	India v New Zealand at Hyderabad,	1999/00

Top Ten Bowlers ODIs

Name	Mat	W	Ave	Best	5w
Wasim Akram	356	502	23.52	5-15	6
Waqar Younis	262	416	23.84	7-36	13
M. Muralitharan	276	416	23.28	7-30	8
W.P.U.J.C. Vaas	281	354	27.39	8-19	4
S.M. Pollock	261	349	24.39	6-35	4
G.D. McGrath	225	332	22.57	7-15	7
A. Kumble	264	329	30.76	6-12	2
J. Srinath	229	315	28.08	5-23	3
S.K. Warne	194	293	25.73	5-33	1
Saqlain Mushtaq	169	288	21.78	5-20	6

All cricket statistics updated till 1 October 2006

World Cup Football

On 21 May 1904, the Fédération Internationale de Football Association (FIFA) was founded in Paris by representatives of seven countries—Belgium, Denmark, France, Netherlands, Spain, Sweden and Switzerland. On 28 May 1928, the FIFA Congress in Amsterdam decided to stage a world championship of football and Uruguay was finally chosen as the host country in 1929. The original World Cup trophy bore Frenchman Jules Rimet's name since he proposed the tournament. In 1970, the trophy was awarded to Brazil permanently when it became the first country to win the world cup thrice and a new trophy called the 'FIFA World Cup' was put up for competition. The tournament was not held for twelve years, during the period of the Second World War. Though the tournament was held alternately in Europe and the Americas since 1958, it broke new ground when it was held in Japan and Korea in 2002. Since 1930, only seven teams have been able to win the trophy.

Germany hosted the Eighteenth FIFA World Cup, the quadrennial international association football world championship tournament, from 9 June to 9 July 2006. Italy won its fourth world championship, defeating France 5–3 in a penalty shootout after extra time finished in a 1–1 draw. Germany defeated Portugal 3–1 to finish third.

Teams representing 198 national football associations from six continents participated in the qualification process, that began in 2003, in which thirty-two teams qualified for the final tournament.

The 2006 FIFA World Cup was notable for the number of yellow and red cards given out, breaking the record set by the 1990 World Cup. 345 yellow cards and 28 red cards were shown, with the round of sixteen-match between Portugal and the Netherlands accounting for sixteen yellow cards and four red cards. In another interesting first, English referee Graham Poll showed three yellow cards to a Croatian player in their match against Australia. It was the first time this had happened in a World Cup match, as Poll had forgotten to send off the player after the latter's second booking.

List of World Cup Winners

Year	Host	Winner	Runner-up
1930	Uruguay	Uruguay	Argentina
1934	Italy	Italy	Czechoslovakia
1938	France	Italy	Hungary
1950	Brazil	Uruguay	Brazil
1954	Switzerland	West Germany	Hungary
1958	Sweden	Brazil	Sweden
1962	Chile	Brazil	Czechoslovakia
1966	England	England	West Germany
1970	Mexico	Brazil	Italy
1974	West Germany	West Germany	Netherlands
1978	Argentina	Argentina	Netherlands
1982	Spain	Italy	West Germany
1986	Mexico	Argentina	West Germany
1990	Italy	West Germany	Argentina
1994	United States	Brazil	Italy
1998	France	France	Brazil
2002	South Korea and Japan	Brazil	Germany
2006	Germany	Italy	France

The Golden Ball

The Adidas Golden Ball award is presented to the outstanding player at each FIFA World Cup finals, with a shortlist drawn up by the FIFA technical committee and the winner voted for by representatives of the media. Those who finish as runners-up in media voting receive the Adidas Silver Ball and Bronze Ball awards as the second and third best players in the tournament respectively. The 2006 World Cup was the first time that the top three players came from fewer than three countries, and the first time that the top three had played in the finals game, although several German players and one Portuguese player were shortlisted. It is also the first time since Gary Lineker in 1986 that the Golden Boot winner did not place in the top three, although Miroslav Klose was shortlisted. France captain Zinedine Zidane was named the best player of the 2006 World Cup despite his sending-off in the final. Zidane's winning performance means that the majority of Golden Ball recipients have now come from non-World Cup winning teams. Nonetheless, a player from the tournament winners has always been represented in the top three.

Golden Ball winners

1982: Paolo Rossi (Italy)
1986: Diego Maradona (Argentina)
1990: Salvatore Schillaci (Italy)
1994: Romario (Brazil)
1998: Ronaldo (Brazil)
2002: Oliver Kahn (Germany)
2006: Zinedine Zidane (France)

The Golden Boot

The Golden Boot (or Golden Shoe) is awarded to the top goal-scorer of the World Cup final tournament. The award was introduced at the 1982 World Cup for the first time.

World Cup		Top Goal-scorer	Goals
1930	Uruguay	Guillermo Stábile (Argentina)	8
1934	Italy	Edmund Conen (Germany)	
		OldøichNejedlý (Czechoslovakia)	
		Angelo Schiavio (Italy)	4
1938	France	Leônidas (Brazil)	8
1950	Brazil	Ademir (Brazil)	9
1954	Switzerland	Sándor Kocsis (Hungary)	11
1958	Sweden	Just Fontaine (France)	13
1962	Chile	Garrincha (Brazil)	
		Vavá (Brazil)	
		Leonel Sánchez (Chile)	
		Dra□en Jerkoviæ (Yugoslavia)	
		Valentin Ivanov (Soviet Union)	
		Flórián Albert (Hungary)	4
1966	England	Eusébio (Portugal)	9
1970	Mexico	Gerd Müller (West Germany)	10
1974	West Germany	Grzegorz Lato (Poland)	7
1978	Argentina	Mario Kempes (Argentina)	6
1982	Spain	Paolo Rossi (Italy)	6
1986	Mexico	Gary Lineker (England)	6
1990	Italy	Salvatore Schillaci (Italy)	6
1994	USA	Hristo Stoitchkov (Bulgaria)	
		Oleg Salenko (Russia)	6
1998	France	Davor Šuker (Croatia)	6
2002	Korea/Japan	Ronaldo (Brazil)	8
2006	Germany	Miroslav Klose (Germany)	5

UEFA European Championship

In 1956, the groundwork for an international competition among European teams began, and two years later the initial matches of the first European Nations' Cup (now known as the UEFA European Championship) got under way. The trophy is named after Frenchman Henri Delaunay who served as UEFA's first general secretary.

Greece were the surprise winners of the 2004 Euro Cup.

List of Winners

Year	Winner	Runner-up
1960	USSR	Yugoslavia
1964	Spain	USSR
1968	Italy	Yugoslavia
1972	West Germany	USSR
1976	Czechoslovakia	West Germany
1980	West Germany	Belgium
1984	France	Spain
1988	Netherlands	USSR
1992	Denmark	Germany
1996	Germany	Czech Republic
2000	France	Italy
2004	Greece	Portugal

Commonwealth Games

The Commonwealth Games were initially known as the British Empire Games (from 1930–1950). From 1954, their name was modified to 'British Empire and Commonwealth Games', the name being retained till 1962. From 1966 to 1974, they took on the title 'British Commonwealth Games' and from 1978 onwards they was finally renamed the 'Commonwealth Games'. In 1930, the first Commonwealth Games were held in Hamilton, Canada where 400 athletes from eleven countries took part. Since 1930, the Games have been conducted at four-year intervals excepting 1942 and 1946, because of World War II. The 2006 Commonwealth Game were held in Melbourne, Australia. Delhi will host the 2010 Commonwealth Games.

India's Performance at the Commonwealth Games

Year	Medals Won			
	Gold	Silver	Bronze	Total
1934	0	0	1	1
1938	0	0	0	0
1954	0	0	0	0
1958	2	1	0	3
1966	3	4	3	10
1970	5	3	4	12
1974	4	8	3	15
1978	5	4	6	15
1982	5	8	3	16
1990	13	8	11	32
1994	6	11	7	24
1998	7	10	8	25
2002	30	22	17	69
2006	22	17	11	50
Total Medals	**102**	**96**	**74**	**272**

Asian Games

The Asian Games, or the Asiad, is a multi-sport event held every four years for athletes from all over Asia. The games are regulated by the Olympic Council of Asia (OCA) under the supervision of the International Olympic Committee (IOC). In 1951, the first Asian Games was held in New Delhi. In the 1994 Asian Games, OCA admitted old Soviet republics Kazakhstan, Kyrgystan, Uzbekistan, Turkmenistan, and Tajikistan. Israel has however has been permanently excluded and asked to join European competitions.

The Fifteenth Asian Games will be held in Doha, Qatar from 27 November 2006 to 15 December 2006. Doha is the first city in its region and only the second in West Asia since Tehran in 1974 to host the games. 'Orry', a Qatari oryx, is the official mascot of the Doha Asian Games.

India's Performance in the Asian Games

Year	Venue	Gold	Silver	Bronze	Total
1951	New Delhi	15	16	21	52
1954	Manila	5	4	9	18
1958	Tokya	5	4	4	13
1962	Jakarta	10	13	11	34
1966	Bangkok	7	3	11	21
1970	Bangkok	6	9	10	25
1974	Tehran	4	12	12	28
1978	Bangkok	11	11	6	28
1982	New Delhi	13	19	25	57
1986	Seoul	5	9	23	37
1990	Beijing	1	8	14	23
1994	Hiroshima	4	3	15	22
1998	Bangkok	7	11	17	35
2002	Busan	11	12	13	36
	Total	**104**	**134**	**191**	**429**

Hockey World Cup

The concept for an international hockey competition at the world level originated in a joint proposal made by India and Pakistan at an FIH (International Hockey Federation) Council meeting on 30 March 1969. The proposal called for a tournament in between the Olympic years. Pakistan was chosen to host the inaugural World Cup in October 1971. However India and Pakistan were locked in a tense standoff over the situation in East Pakistan. The prevailing political situation resulted in the shifting of the site to the Spanish city of Barcelona. From 1978 onwards, the tournament has been held once in four years. India has won the tournament only once, in 1975.

Year	Host	Winner	Runner-up
1971	Spain	Pakistan	Spain
1973	The Netherlands	The Netherlands	India
1975	Malaysia	India	Pakistan
1978	Argentina	Pakistan	The Netherlands

1982	India	Pakistan	West Germany
1986	England	Australia	England
1990	Pakistan	The Netherlands	Pakistan
1994	Australia	Pakistan	The Netherlands
1998	The Netherlands	The Netherlands	Spain
2002	Malaysia	Germany	Australia
2006	Germany	Germany	Australia

Tennis

2006 Grand Slam Winners

Grand Slam	Men's winner	Women's winner
Australian Open	Roger Federer	Amelie Mauresmo
French Open	Rafael Nadal	Justin Henin-Hardenne
Wimbledon	Roger Federer	Amelie Mauresmo
US Open	Roger Federer	Maria Sharapova

Chess

FIDE, the world chess body, awards the title 'International Grandmaster'. It is a lifetime title.

Indian International Grandmasters

Name	Year
1. Viswanathan Anand	1987
2. Dibyendu Barua	1991
3. Praveen M. Thipsay	1997
4. Krishnan Sasikiran	2000
5. Abhijit Kunte	2000
6. P. Harikrishna	2001
7. R.B. Ramesh	2001
8. Koneru, Humpy	2002
9. Surya Shekhar Ganguly	2002
10. Sandipan, Chanda	2003
11. Tejas Bakre	2004
12. Magesh Chandran	2005
13. Neelotpal Das	2006
14. Parimarjan Negi	2006
15. Deepan Chakkravarthy	2006

Billiards

IBSF World Champions in Billiards (The Indian winners and runner-up)

(Point Format)

Year	Winner	Runner-Up
2005	Pankaj Advani	Geet Sethi
2002	-	Geet Sethi
2001	Geet Sethi	Ashok Shandilya
1997	-	Ashok Shandilya
1990	Manoj Kothari	Ashok Shandilya
1987	Geet Sethi	-
1985	Geet Sethi	-
1983	Michael Ferreira	Subhash Agrawal
1981	Michael Ferreira	-
1975	-	Michael Ferreira
1973	-	Satish Mohan
1969	-	Michael Ferreira

1964	Wilson Jones	-
1962	-	Wilson Jones
1958	Wilson Jones	-

(Frame Format)

Year	Winner	Runner-Up
2005	Pankaj Advani	Devendra Joshi
2003		Geet Sethi
2002	Ashok Shandilya	-

IBSF World Champions in Snooker (The Indian winners and runner-up)

Year	Winner	Runner-Up
2003	Pankaj Advani	-
1984	O.B. Agrawal	-

Rajiv Gandhi Khel Ratna Awards

In 1991–92, the Rajiv Gandhi Khel Ratna Award was instituted by the Indian Government. The award is given for the most outstanding and spectacular performance by a sportsperson or a team in a year. The award comprises a medal, a cash prize of Rs 5 lakhs and a scroll of honour.

List of Awardees

Year	Sports	Winner
2005–06	Billiards and Snooker	Pankaj Advani
2004–05	Shooting	Rajyavardhan Singh Rathore
2003–04	Athletics	Anju Bobby George
2002–03	Athletics	K.M. Beenamol
2002–03	Shooting	Anjali R. Bhagwat
2001–02	Shooting	Abhinav Bindra
2000–01	Badminton	Pullela Gopi Chand
1999–2000	Hockey	Dhanraj Pillay
1998–99	Athletics	Jyotirmoyee Sikdar
1997–98	Cricket	Sachin Tendulkar
1996–97	Tennis	Leander Peas
1996–97	Weightlifting	Kunjurani Devi
1995–96	Weightlifting	Karnam Malleshwari
1994–95	Yachting (Team Events)	Cdr Homi D. Motiwala and Lt Cdr P.K. Garg
1992 –93	Billiards	Geet Sethi
1991–92	Chess	Vishwanathan Anand

Arjuna Awards

Instituted in 1961, the Arjuna Awards are given in honour of outstanding performances in sports and games. The government has recently revised the scheme for the Arjuna Awards. According to revised guidelines, a sportsperson, in order to be eligible for this award, should not only perform consistently for the previous three years at the international level while excelling for the year in which the award is given, but also exhibit qualities of sportsmanship, leadership and discipline. The award consists of a statuette, a cash award of Rs 3 lakhs, a scroll of honour and a ceremonial dress.

From 2001, the award is only given in disciplines that fall under the following categories:

1. Olympic Games/Asian Games/Commonwealth Games/World Cup/World Championship Disciplines and Cricket
2. Indigenous games
3. Sports for the physically challenged

Arjuna Awards for 2005

Tarundeep Rai (Archery)
Dola Banerjee (Archery)
Manjit Kaur (Athletics)
Aparna Popat (Badminton)
Anuja Prakash Thakur (Billiards & Snooker)
Akhil Kumar (Boxing)
Surya Shekhar Ganguly (Chess)
Anju Jain (Cricket)
Viren Rasquinha (Hockey)
Ramesh Kumar (Kabaddi)
Gagan Narang (Shooting)
Shikha Tandon (Swimming)
Soumyadeep Roy (Table-tennis)
Sushil Kumar (Wrestling)
Rajinder Singh Rahelu (Physically handicapped)

Dronacharya Awards

Instituted in 1985, the Dronacharya Award honours reputed coaches who have successfully coached sportspersons and teams helping them accomplish outstanding results in international competitions. The recipient of this award is given a statuette of Guru Dronacharya, a cash prize of Rs 3 lakhs, a ceremonial dress, and a scroll of honour.

List of Awardees 2005–06

Captain M. Venu (Boxing)
Balwan Singh (Kabaddi)
Maha Singh Rao (Wzrestling)
Ismail Baig (Rowing)

Dhyan Chand Award for Lifetime Achievement

From 2002, a new Dhyan Chand Award for Lifetime Achievement in Sports and Games has been instituted, in order to honour sportsmen who, by their performances have contributed and continue to contribute to sports in India, even after retirement. The award consists of a cash prize of Rs 1.50 lakhs, a scroll of honour and a plaque. The awardees for 2005-06 are:

Uday K. Prabhu (Athletics)
Commander Nandy Singh (Hockey)
Harish Chandra M. Birajdar (Wrestling)

Domestic Championships

(This year's Ranji, Duleep, Irani, Challenger, Santosh, Federation, NFL winners)

Domestic competition	Sport	Winner
Ranji Trophy (Elite) for 2005/06	Cricket	Uttar Pradesh
Ranji Trophy (Plate) for 2005/06	Cricket	Saurashtra
Duleep Trophy for 2005/06	Cricket	West Zone
Irani Trophy for 2006/07	Cricket	Rest of India
Challenger Trophy for 2006/07	Cricket	India Blue and India Red jointly
Santosh Trophy for 2005	Football	Goa
Federation Cup for 2005	Football	Mahindra United
National Football League 2005/06	Football	Mahindra United

Sports News

Chess World Championship: VeselinTolpalov became the new world chess champion in October 2005, defeating Vishwanathan Anand, Peter Svider and eleven other contenders at the world chess championship at San Luis, Argentina. Topalov and Vladimir Kramnik agreed to play a world championship reunification match in September 2006 at Kalmyki with the winner being declared the world champion.

Sachin Tendulkar Breaks Sunil Gavaskar's Record of Test Centuries: Sachin Tendulkar became the world's highest Test century maker in December 2005 at the Ferozeshah Kotla against Sri Lanka surpassing Sunil Gavaskar's record of 34 hundreds.

Sharad Pawar Becomes the BCCI Chief: Union Agriculture Minister Sharad Pawar was elected president of the Board of Control for Cricket in India (BCCI) for 2005-06 at its seventy-sixth annual general meeting, defeating Ranbir Singh Mahendra by 20–11 votes. He was re-elected in 2006 for a further two years. Venkatpathy Raju replaced V.B. Chandrasekhar and Dilip Vengsarkar replaced Kiran More in the selection committee.

Tiger Woods Wins Two Grand Slams in 2006: In a year in which he lost his father Earl Woods, Tiger Woods won two Grand Slam titles consecutively (British Open and PGA Championship) to bring his tally of Grand Slam wins to twelve. He also missed the cut in a Grand Slam for the first time since 1996. Jack Nicklaus has the most number of Grand Slam wins with eighteen titles to his credit.

Roger Federer Wins Three Grand Slams in 2006: Roger Federer won three Grand Slams (Australian Open, Wimbledon, and US Open) in 2006, losing only the French Open final to Rafael Nadal. This was the second time in three years that he has accomplished the feat.

Saina Nehwal Wins Philippines Open: Sixteen-year-old badminton player Saina Nehwal won the Philippines Open in 2006 to become the first Indian female player to win a four-star badminton event. She also reached a world-ranking of 30 during the year.

Manavjit Singh and Abhinav Bindra Win the World Championship in Shooting: Abhinav Bindra became the first Indian shooter to win a World Championship gold at Zagreb in 2006. Dr Karni Singh's silver in 1962 was the best by an Indian in a World Championship meet before. Manavjit Singh Sandhu, who won another gold medal in Trap shooting in the same championship, was also ranked world number one during the year. Shooter Samaresh Jung was adjudged the best athlete of the 2006 Commonwealth Games, winning five gold medals, a silver and a bronze medal.

Floyd Landis and Justin Gatlin in Doping Scandal: Winner of the 2006 Tour de France, Floyd Landis, tested positive for performance-enhancing drugs. A hearing is scheduled for early 2007, failing which could result in his loss of the Tour de France title and a two-year ban. Former 100-metre world-record holder Justin Gatlin also tested positive and was banned for eight years from track and field events. This was his second such offence. Marion Jones also tested positive for performance-enhancing drugs but her B sample tested negative and she was cleared.

Martina Hingis Wins the 2006 Sunfeast Open in Kolkata; Sania Wins the Doubles Title: Martina Hingis won the 2006 Sunfeast Open singles title in Kolkata, defeating Olga Poutchkova in the final. She had earlier defeated Sania Mirza in the semi-final. Sania Mirza, along with Liezel Huber, won the doubles title. The same duo has also won the doubles title at Hyderabad earlier in the year. Sania reached a career high doubles ranking of 26 during the year.

Michael Schumacher Retires from Formula One: Seven-time world champion Michael Schumacher announced his retirement from Formula One after winning the Italian Grand Prix. According to the announcement, his last race would be the Brazilian Grand Prix on 22 October. Kimi Raikonen would replace him in the Ferrari team in 2007 and would be partnered by Felipe Massa.

Germany Win the Hockey World Cup; Sandeep Singh Injured in an Accident: The eleventh Hockey World Cup for men was held from 6 September to 17 September 2006 in Mönchengladbach, Germany. Germany won for the second time consecutively after beating Australia 4–3 while Spain emerged in the third place, defeating Korea. India finished at a dismal eleventh position. Before the tournament began, Indian penalty corner specialist Sandeep Singh was injured when he was accidentally shot inside a train by a Railway Protection Force jawan.

Leander Paes Wins the 2006 US Open Doubles Title/Mahesh Bhupathi Wins the 2006 Australian Open Mixed Doubles Title: In September 2006, Leander Paes and Martin Damm won the US Open doubles title, defeating Jonas Bjorkman and Max Mirnyi 6-7(5-7), 6-4, 6-3 in the final. Earlier, in January 2006, Mahesh Bhupathi and Martina Hingis won the Australian Open mixed doubles title defeating Elena Likhovtseva and Daniel Nestor 6-3, 6-3 in the final. It was Leander's seventh Grand Slam title (including mixed doubles) and Mahesh's tenth Grand Slam title (including doubles).

Ball Tampering Controversy: In September 2006, Pakistan captain Inzamam-ul-Haq was cleared of ball tampering charges by the International Cricket Council (ICC) but banned for four one-day matches for bringing the game into disrepute. The ban followed Pakistan's refusal to take the field after tea on the fourth day of the fourth Test against England at The Oval in August 2006 after it was penalized five runs for alleged ball tampering. England was awarded the match on a forfeit for the first time in the history of Test cricket and won the four Test series 3-0. Pakistan's protest followed a decision by umpires Darrell Hair and Billy Doctrove to change the ball and penalize Pakistan five runs for alleged ball tampering. Days after the match was called off, Darrel Hair was involved in further controversy when the ICC revealed that he had asked them for $500,000 in return for retiring from the elite umpires' panel.

South Africa Chase Down Record Australia Total in One-Day International: The one-day international (ODI) cricket match between South Africa and Australia, played on 12 March 2006 at New Wanderers Stadium, Johannesburg, broke many records. Australia, batting first after winning the toss scored 434 for 4 off their 50 overs, beating the previous record of 398-5 by Sri Lanka against Kenya in 1996. Ricky Ponting top scored with 164 runs off 105 balls. In reply, South Africa scored 438-9, winning by 1 wicket with one ball to spare. Herschelle Gibbs top scored for South Africa with 175 runs off 111 balls. South Africa's total of 438 runs was the highest ever runs scored in an ODI till it was overtaken by Sri Lanka, who scored 443-9 in 50 overs against the Netherlands later in the year.

India Hosts ICC Champions Trophy: India hosted cricket's second-most prestigious tournament, the ICC

Champions Trophy, from 7 October to 5 November 2006. The tournament comprised a total of twenty-one matches featuring the world's top ten one-day teams—Australia, South Afarica, Pakistan, Sri Lanka, India, New Zealand, England, West Indies, Bangladesh and Zimbabwe—divided between four venues: the Sawai Mansingh Stadium, Jaipur, the Punjab Cricket Association Stadium, Mohali, the Sardar Patel Gujarat Stadium, Ahmedabad and the Brabourne Stadium, Mumbai, which also hosted the final on 5 November.

India, Pakistan, Sri Lanka, Bangladesh to Host 2011 Cricket World Cup: On 30 April 2006, the ICC awarded the 2011 Cricket World Cup to Asia (India, Pakistan, Sri Lanka, Bangladesh), who won the bid to host the tournament over an Australia–New Zealand combine. The opening ceremony of the 2011 World Cup will be held in Dhaka while the final will be held at a new state-of-the-art stadium in New Delhi. The 2015 World Cup will be hosted by Australia and New Zealand while the 2019 tournament will be held in England.

Arts

Kiran Desai's *The Inheritance of Loss* Wins the Man Booker Prize 2006

On 10 October 2006, Kiran Desai's novel *The Inheritance of Loss* won the very prestigious Man Booker Prize for Fiction for 2006. Harvey McGrath, Chairman of the Man Group plc, presented Kiran Desai with a cheque for £ 50,000.

Kiran Desai is the first Indian-born writer to win the prestigious literary award since Arundhati Roy, whose *The God of Small Things* won in 1997. At thirty-five, Kiran Desai is also the youngest woman ever to win the Booker in its thirty-eight-year history.

Kiran Desai is the daughter of renowned writer Anita Desai, who has been shortlisted thrice for the Booker Prize, but has never won. *The Inheritance of Loss* is Kiran Desai's second novel after the internationally acclaimed *Hullabaloo in the Guava Orchard* (1998) which won the Betty Trask Prize. Eight years in the making, *The Inheritance of Loss* was published in January 2006.

The judging panel for the 2006 Man Booker Prize for Fiction was: Hermione Lee (Chair), biographer, academic and reviewer; Simon Armitage, poet and novelist; Candia McWilliam, award-winning novelist; critic Anthony Quinn; and actor Fiona Shaw.

The Inheritance of Loss was announced the winner from a shortlist comprising six books, including *The Secret River* by Kate Grenville, *Carry Me Down* by M.J. Hyland, *In the Country of Men* by Hisham Matar, *Mother's Milk* by Edward St Aubyn and *The Night Watch* by Sarah Waters.

The Inheritance of Loss is set in the northeastern Himalayas, where a rising insurgency challenges the old way of life. It is the story of an embittered old judge who lives in a crumbling, isolated house at the foot of Mount Kanchenjunga; his orphaned granddaughter Sai who comes to live with him; the cook who watches over Sai but whose thoughts are mostly with his son, Biju, hopscotching from one New York restaurant job to another; and Sai's new-sprung romance with her handsome Nepali tutor which is threatened by a Nepalese insurgency in the mountains. This majestic novel of a busy, grasping time—every moment holding out the possibility of hope or betrayal—illuminates the consequences of colonialism and global conflicts of religion, race, and nationalism.

The Man Booker Prize

The Man Booker Prize is one of the most prestigious awards in the world of literature. The award was set up in 1968 when publisher Tom Maschler, inspired by the French literary award Prix Goncourt, approached the Booker Brothers (who had a highly successful 'Authors' Division' publishing a lot of celebrated writers) and persuaded them to establish a literary prize. This resulted in the establishment of the Booker Prize.

The Man Booker Prize is awarded to the best full-length novel of the year, decided by a panel of judges. Only a novel written by a citizen of the Commonwealth or the Republic of Ireland is eligible for the award. The book must be a unified and substantial piece of work; neither a novella nor a book of short stories is eligible. Further, an English translation of a book written originally in another language is not eligible; neither is a self-published book. A book submitted on behalf of an author who was deceased at the date of publication is also not considered for selection. The award is sponsored by Man Group plc; hence it is called 'Man Booker Prize for Fiction'. The winner of the Booker Prize receives £ 50,000.

List of Winners

Year	Author	Country	Book
1969	P.H. Newby	United Kingdom	*Something to Answer For*
1970	Bernice Rubens	United Kingdom	*The Elected Member*
1971	V.S. Naipaul	United Kingdom	*In a Free State*
1972	John Berger	United Kingdom	*G*
1973	J.G. Farrell	United Kingdom	*The Siege of Krishnapur*
1974	Stanley Middleton	United Kingdom	*Holiday*
	Nadine Gordimer	South Africa	*The Conservationist*
1975	Ruth Prawer Jhabvala	United Kingdom	*Heat and Dust*
1976	David Storey	United Kingdom	*Saville Saville*
1977	Paul Scott	United Kingdom	*Staying On*
1978	Iris Murdoch	United Kingdom	*The Sea, The Sea*
1979	Penelope Fitzgerald	United Kingdom	*Offshore*
1980	William Golding	United Kingdom	*Rites of Passage*
1981	Salman Rushdie	United Kingdom	*Midnight's Children*
1982	Thomas Keneally	Australia	*Schindler's Ark*
1983	J.M. Coetzee	South Africa	*Life and Times of Michael K*
1984	Anita Brookner	United Kingdom	*Hotel du Lac*
1985	Keri Hulme	New Zealand	*The Bone People*
1986	Kingsley Amis	United Kingdom	*The Old Devils*
1987	Penelope Lively	United Kingdom	*Moon Tiger*
1988	Peter Carey	Australia	*Oscar and Lucinda*
1989	Kazuo Ishiguro	United Kingdom	*The Remains of the Day*
1990	A.S. Byatt	United Kingdom	*Possession*
1991	Ben Okri	United Kingdom	*The Famished Road*
1992	Michael Ondaatje	Canada	*The English Patient*
	Barry Unsworth	United Kingdom	*Sacred Hunger*
1993	Roddy Doyle	Ireland	*Paddy Clarke Ha Ha Ha*
1994	James Kelman	United Kingdom	*How Late It Was, How Late*
1995	Pat Barker	United Kingdom	*The Ghost Road*
1996	Graham Swift	United Kingdom	*Last Orders*
1997	Arundhati Roy	India	*The God of Small Things*
1998	Ian McEwan	United Kingdom	*Amsterdam*
1999	J.M. Coetzee	South Africa	*Disgrace*

2000	Margaret Atwood	Canada	*The Blind Assassin*
2001	Peter Carey	Australia	*True History of the Kelly Gang*
2002	Yann Martel	Canada	*Life of Pi*
2003	DBC Pierre	Australia	*Vernon God Little*
2004	Alan Holinghurst	United Kingdom	*The Line of Beauty*
2005	John Banville	Ireland	*The Sea*
2006	Kiran Desai	India	*The Inheritance of Loss*

Man Booker International Prize

Albanian novelist Ismail Kadaré became the first ever winner of the Man Booker International Prize on 2 June 2005. The Man Booker International Prize is unique in the world of literature in that it can be won by an author of any nationality, provided that his or her work is available in the English language. It will be awarded every second year.

Jnanpith Award

The Jnanpith Award is regarded as the highest literary award in India. It is awarded for the best creative literary writing by an Indian, in one of the languages included in the eighth schedule of the Indian Constitution. The award carries a bronze replica of Vagdevi, a citation and a cash prize of Rs 5 lakh. The Award was the brainchild of Rama Jain, and was instituted on 22 May 1961, though the first award was given in 1965. The award is given by an organization called 'Bharatiya Jnanpith', of which Rama Jain was the first president.

Jnanpith Laureates	Year
G. Shankara Kurup for his poems *Odakkuzhal* in Malayalam	1965
Tarashankar Bandopadhyaya for the novel *Ganadevta* in Bengali	1966
Dr K.V. Puttappa for *Sri Ramayana Darshanam* in Kannada	1967
Uma Shankar Joshi for *Nishitha* in Gujarati	1967
Sumitra Nandan Pant for *Chidambara* in Hindi	1968
Firaq Gorakpuri for *Gul-e-Naghma* in Urdu	1969
Vishwanath Satyanarayan for *Ramayana Kalpavrikshamu* in Telugu	1970
Bishnu Dey for *Smriti Satta Bhavishyat* in Bengali	1971
Ramdhari Singh Dinkar for *Urvashi* in Hindi	1972
Dattatreya Ramachandran Bendre for *Nakutanti* in Kannada	1973
Gopinath Mohanty for *Mattimatal* in Oriya	1973
Vishnu Sakaram Khandekar for *Yayati* in Marathi	1974
P.V. Akilandam for his novel *Chittirappavai* in Tamil	1975
Asha Purna Devi for *Pratham Pratisruti*, in Bengali	1976
K. Shivaram Karanth for *Mukajjiya Kanasugalu* in Kannada	1977
S.H.V. Ajneya for his novel *Kitni Navon men Kitni Bar* in Hindi	1978
Birendra Kumar Bhattacharya for his novel *Mrityunjay* in Assamese	1979
S.K. Pottekkatt for his novel *Oru Desattinte Katha* in Malayalam	1980
Amrita Pritam for her literary collection *Kagaz te Canvas* in Punjabi	1981

Mahadevi Varma (Hindi) 1982
Masti Venkatesh Ayengar (Kannada) 1983
Takazhi Sivashankar Pillai (Malayalam) 1984
Pannalal Patel (Gujarati) 1985
Sachidanand Rout Roy (Oriya) 1986
Vishnu Vaman Shirwadkar Kusumagraj (Marathi) 1987
Dr C. Narayanan Reddy (Telugu) 1988
Qurratulain Hyder (Urdu) 1989
V.K. Gokak (Kannada) 1990
Subhash Mukhopadhyay (Bengali) 1991
Naresh Mehta (Hindi) 1992
Sitakant Mahapatra (Oriya) 1993
U.R. Anantha Murthy (Kannada) 1994
M.T. Vasudevan Nair (Malayalam) 1995
Mahesweta Devi (Bengali) 1996
Ali Sardar Jafri (Urdu) 1997
Girish Karnad (Kannada) 1998
Nirmal Verma (Hindi) 1999
Gurdial Singh (Punjabi) 1999
Dr Indira Goswami (Assamese) 2000
Rajendra Keshavlal Shah (Gujarati) 2001
D. Jayakanthan (Tamil) 2002
Vinda Karandikar (Marathi) 2003

Note: From 1982, the award was given for overall contribution to literature. (The award for 2002 was awarded in 2005; in 2007 the winner for 2004 would be announced.)

The Sahitya Akademi Award

The Sahitya Akademi was formally launched by the Government of India on 12 March 1954 and later registered as a society on 7 January 1956. It was instituted in order to coordinate and encourage literary activities in all Indian languages, thereby contributing to the cultural unity of the country. According to the Government of India Resolution, the Akademi is a national organization set up in order to work for the development of Indian letters, thereby setting high literary standards. Since 1954, the Sahitya Akademi awards are given to books of outstanding literary merit published in any of the major Indian languages, as recognized by the Akademi. The award comprises a monetary component of Rs 40,000 along with a plaque. The Akademi gives twenty-two awards to literary works in the languages recognized by it. It also gives an equal number of awards to literary translations from and into the languages of India. All these awards are given after a year-long process of discussion, scrutiny and selection. The Akademi intends to award literary works that are a reflection of current tastes, and also contribute to the establishment of a distinct Indian sensibility.

The languages that the Akademi recognizes are: Assamese, Bengali, Dogri, English, Gujarati, Hindi, Kannada, Kashmiri, Konkani, Maithili, Malayalam, Manipuri, Marathi, Nepali, Oriya, Punjabi, Rajasthani, Sanskrit, Sindhi, Tamil, Telugu and Urdu.

The Sahitya Akademi awards for 2005 are as follows:

Language	Book	Author
Assamese	*Mouna Ounth Mukhar Hriday* (novel)	Yeshe Dorje Thongchi
Bengali	*Haspataley Lekha Kabiyaguchha* (poetry)	Binoy Mazumdar
Bodo	*Jiuni Mwgthang Bisombi Arw Aroj* (poetry)	Mangalsingh Hazowary
Dogri	*Dhaldi Dhuppe Da Sek* (short stories)	Krishan Sharma
Gujarati	*Akhand Zalar Vage* (poetry)	Suresh Dalal
Hindi	*Kyap* (novel)	Manohar Shyam Joshi
Kannada	*Teru* (novel)	Raghavendra Patil
Kashmiri	*Yath Miani Joye* (poetry)	Hamidi Kashmiri
Konkani	*Bhaangarsaall* (short stories)	N. Shivdas
Maithili	*Chanan Ghan Gachchiya* (poetry)	Vivekanand Thakur
Malayalam	*Jappana Pukayila* (short stories)	G.V. Kakkanadan
Manipuri	*Pangal Shonbi Eishe Adomgeeni* (short stories)	M. Nabakishore Singh
Marathi	*Bhijaki Vahi* (poetry)	Arun Kolatkar
Nepali	*Jeevan Goreto Ma* (novel)	Krishna Singh Moktan
Oriya	*Gopapura* (short stories)	Ramachandra Behera
Punjabi	*Agni-Kalas* (short stories)	Gurbachan Singh Bhullar
Rajasthani	*Kisturi Mirag* (short stories)	Chetan Swami
Sanskrit	*Sri-Bhargava-Raghaviyam* (epic)	Swami Rambhadrachaya
Santhali	*Bhabna* (poetry)	Jadumani Besra
Sindhi	*Andhero Roshan Thiye* (poetry)	Dholan 'Rahi'
Tamil	*Kalmaram* (novel)	G. Thilakavathi
Telugu	*Tana Margam* (short stories)	Abburi Chayadevi
Urdu	*Ret Per Khema* (memoirs)	Jabir Husain

Translation into English

Title of the Translation	Translator	Title of the Original (language/genre)	Author
The Last Wilderness	Pratik Kanjilal	*Antim Aranya* (Hindi/novel)	Nirmal Verma

Indian Cinema

In July 1896, the Lumiere Brothers screened a number of films using their new invention, the first commercially viable cinema projector, at Watson's Hotel in Mumbai. This is regarded as the first screening of motion pictures in India.

India's first indigenous feature film was Dadasaheb Phalke's *Raja Harishchandra*, released in 1913. Over the years, a number of awards have been instituted to give due recognition to achievements in the world of films and filmmaking. The Filmfare Awards is one of India's oldest national-level film awards.

National Film Awards

The National Film Awards was started on the recommendation of the Film Enquiry Committee as an annual event in 1954. Initially, only three awards were instituted—the President's Gold Medal for the best feature film and the best documentary and the Prime Minister's Silver Medal for the best children's film. The medallions were later changed to Swarna Kamal (Golden Lotus) and Rajat Kamal (Silver Lotus). Cash prizes were later added. Separate awards for artists and film technicians were introduced in 1968.

At the time of going to press, the National Film Awards for 2005 were still not announced.

Best Feature Film

Year	Film
1953	*Shyamchi Aai*
1954	*Mirza Ghalib*
1955	*Pather Panchali*
1956	*Kabuliwala*
1957	*Do Ankhen Barah Haath*
1958	*Sagar Sangame*
1959	*Apur Sansar*
1960	*Anuradha*
1961	*Bhagini Nivedita*
1962	*Dada Thakur*
1963	*Shehar Aur Sapna*
1964	*Charulata*
1965	*Chemmen*
1966	*Teesri Kasam*
1967	*Hatey Bazarey*
1968	*Goopy Gyne Bagha Byne*
1969	*Bhuvan Shome*
1970	*Samkskara*
1971	*Simabaddha*
1972	*Swayamvaram*
1973	*Nirmalayam*
1974	*Chorus*
1975	*Chomana Dudi*
1976	*Mrigayaa*
1977	*Ghattashraddha*
1978	*Ganadevata*
1979	*Ekdin Pratidin*
1980	*Akaler Sandhane*
1981	*Dakhal*
1982	*Chokh*
1983	*Adi Shankaracharya*
1984	*Damul*
1985	*Chidambaram*
1986	*Tabarana Kathe*
1987	*Halodhia Choraye Baodhan Khai*
1988	*Piravi*
1989	*Bagh Bahadur*
1990	*Marupakkam*
1991	*Agantuk*
1992	*Bhagwat Geeta*
1993	*Charachar*
1994	*Unishe April*
1995	*Kathapurushan*
1996	*Lal Darja*
1997	*Thai Saheba*
1998	*Samar*
1999	*Vaanaprastham*
2000	*Shantam*
2001	*Dweepa*
2002	*Mondo Meyer Upakhyan*
2003	*Shwaas*
2004	*Page 3*

Dada Saheb Phalke Award

The Dada Saheb Phalke Award was instituted in 1969, in honour of the late Shri Dada Saheb Phalke, in order to commemorate his contribution to the Indian film industry. The award is given to recognize an individual's lifetime contribution to Indian films. The award is decided by the Government of India and presented at the National Awards ceremony every year. The Dada Saheb Phalke Award consists of a cash prize of Rs 2 lakhs, a Swarna Kamal and a shawl.

Recipients of the Dada Saheb Phalke Award

1969	Devika Rani Roerich
1970	B.N. Sircar
1971	Prithviraj Kapoor
1972	Pankaj Mullick
1973	Sulochana (Ruby Myers)
1974	B.N. Reddi
1975	Dhiren Ganguly
1976	Kanan Devi

1977	Nitin Bose
1978	R.C. Boral
1979	Sohrab Modi
1980	P. Jairaj
1981	Naushad Ali
1982	L.V. Prasad
1983	Durga Khote
1984	Satyajit Ray
1985	V. Shantaram
1986	B. Nagi Reddy
1987	Raj Kapoor
1988	Ashok Kumar
1989	Lata Mangeshkar
1990	Akkineni Nageshwara Rao
1991	Balachandra Govind Pendharakar
1992	Dr Bhupen Hazarika
1993	Majrooh Sultanpuri
1994	Dilip Kumar
1995	Dr Rajkumar
1996	Shivaji Ganesan
1997	Kavi Pradeep
1998	B.R. Chopra
1999	Hrishikesh Mukherjee
2000	Asha Bhosle
2001	Yash Chopra
2002	Dev Anand
2003	Mrinal Sen
2004	Adoor Gopalkrishnan

Filmfare Awards

The Filmfare Awards were established to honour the best talents of the Hindi film industry and provide them with substantial encouragement. The winners of the awards are decided by the readers of the film magazine by polling their opinions.

The Metro Theatre in Mumbai hosted the first Filmfare Awards on 21 March 1954 with Hollywood actor Gregory Peck being the guest of honour. Only five awards were presented at the first ceremony—Best Film, Best Director, Best Male Performance, Best Female Performance and Best Music Director. Every award winner receives a trophy.

Filmfare Winners since 1995

Best Director (Popular Choice)

Year	Film	Director
1995	*Dilwale Dulhania Le Jayenge*	Aditya Chopra
1996	*Bandit Queen*	Shekhar Kapoor
1997	*Border*	J.P. Dutta
1998	*Kuch Kuch Hota Hai*	Karan Johar
1999	*Hum Dil De Chuke Sanam*	Sanjay Leela Bansali
2000	*Kaho Naa Pyaar Hai*	Rakesh Roshan
2001	*Lagaan*	Ashutosh Gowarikar
2002	*Devdas*	Sanjay Leela Bhansali
2003	*Koi Mil Gaya*	Rakesh Roshan
2004	*Hum Tum*	Kunal Kohli
2005	*Black*	Sanjay Leela Bhansali

Best Film (Popular Choice)

Year	Film
1995	*Dilwale Dulhania Le Jayenge*
1996	*Raja Hindustani*
1997	*Dil To Pagal Hai*
1998	*Kuch Kuch Hota Hai*
1999	*Hum Dil De Chuke Sanam*
2000	*Kaho Naa Pyaar Hai*
2001	*Lagaan*
2002	*Devdas*
2003	*Koi Mil Gaya*
2004	*Veer-Zaara*
2005	*Black*

Best Actor (Popular Choice)

Year	Film	Actor
1995	*Dilwale Dulhania Le Jayenge*	Shah Rukh Khan
1996	*Raja Hindustani*	Aamir Khan
1997	*Dil To Pagal Hai*	Shah Rukh Khan
1998	*Kuch Kuch Hota Hai*	Shah Rukh Khan
1999	*Vaastav*	Sunjay Dutt
2000	*Kaho Naa Pyar Hai*	Hrithik Roshan
2001	*Lagaan*	Aamir Khan
2002	*Devdas*	Shah Rukh Khan
2003	*Koi Mil Gaya*	Hrithik Roshan
2004	*Swades*	Shah Rukh Khan
2005	*Black*	Amitabh Bachchan

Best Actress (Popular Choice)

Year	Film	Actress
1995	*Dilwale Dulhania Le Jayenge*	Kajol
1996	*Raja Hindustani*	Karisma Kapoor
1997	*Dil To Pagal Hai*	Madhuri Dixit
1998	*Kuch Kuch Hota Hai*	Kajol
1999	*Hum Dil De Chuke Sanam*	Aishwarya Rai
2000	*Fiza*	Karisma Kapoor
2001	*Kabhie Khushi Kabhie Gham*	Kajol
2002	*Devdas*	Aishwarya Rai
2003	*Kal Ho Na Ho*	Preity Zinta
2004	*Hum Tum*	Rani Mukherji
2005	*Black*	Rani Mukherji

Bollywood: Top Grossing Films of All Time

1950s

Rank	Film Name	Inflation Adjusted All-India Net
1.	*Mother India*	Rs 1,087,595,050
2.	*Naya Daur*	Rs 640,816,340
3.	*Awaara*	Rs 636,486,434
4.	*Do Bigha Zameen*	Rs 578,421,039
5.	*Pyaasa*	Rs 576,734,709

1960s

Rank	Film Name	Inflation Adjusted All-India Net
1.	*Mughal-E-Azam*	Rs 893,306,421
2.	*Aradhana*	Rs 867,238,106
3.	*Sangam*	Rs 754,807,653
4.	*Ganga Jamuna*	Rs 682,608,642
5.	*Do Raaste*	Rs 672,857,146

1970s

Rank	Film Name	Inflation Adjusted All-India Net
1.	*Sholay*	Rs 1,963,500,000
2.	*Muqaddar Ka Sikandar*	Rs 872,222,239

3.	*Bobby*	Rs 779,432,590
4.	*Amar Akbar Anthony*	Rs 772,797,929
5.	*Dharam Veer*	Rs 691,450,780

1980s

Rank	Film Name	Inflation Adjusted All-India Net
1.	*Coolie*	Rs 631,888,533
2.	*Naseeb*	Rs 588,014,974
3.	*Qurbani*	Rs 532,203,366
4.	*Shaan*	Rs 518,898,279
5.	*Laawaris*	Rs 499,812,735

1990s

Rank	Film Name	Inflation Adjusted All-India Net
1.	*Hum Aapke Hai Kaun*	Rs 1,132,211,563
2.	*Dilwale Dulhaniya Le Jayenge*	Rs 855,119,824
3.	*Raja Hindustani*	Rs 706,500,020
4.	*Kuch Kuch Hota Hai*	Rs 550,082,443
5.	*Karan Arjun*	Rs 547,276,680

Bollywood: Top-Grossing Films for 2005

Rank	Film	Net Gross
1.	*No Entry*	448,400,000
2.	*Bunty Aur Babli*	346,200,000
3.	*Mangal Pandey*	293,200,000
4.	*Maine Pyaar Kyun Kiya*	269,400,000
5.	*Garam Masala*	269,100,000

International Cinema

Today the Academy Awards, better known as the Oscars, are the most well-known film industry awards in the world and is often considered to be the pinnacle of achievement in the world of films.

Oscars

The Academy of Motion Pictures Arts and Sciences gives the Academy Awards. The first awards were handed out on 16 May 1929 at a ceremony during a banquet held in the Blossom Room of the Hollywood Roosevelt Hotel. The awardees were given what is officially named the Academy Award of Merit; the statuette is better known by a nickname, Oscar. The first Oscar went to Emil Jannings, who was named best actor for his roles in *The Last Command* and *The Way of All Flesh*. In 1929, fifteen Oscars were awarded. All voting for the Academy Awards is conducted by secret ballot and tabulated by the international auditing firm of PricewaterhouseCoopers.

Oscar Winners since 2000

Best Actor

Year	Actor	Film
2000	Russell Crowe	*Gladiator*
2001	Denzel Washington	*Training Day*

2002	Adrien Brody	*The Pianist*
2003	Sean Penn	*Mystic River*
2004	Jamie Foxx	*Ray*
2005	Philip Seymour Hoffman	*Capote*

Best Actress

Year	Actor	Film
2000	Julia Roberts	*Erin Brockovich*
2001	Halle Berry	*Monster's Ball*
2002	Nicole Kidman	*The Hours*
2003	Charlize Theron	*Monster*
2004	Hilary Swank	*Million Dollar Baby*
2005	Reese Witherspoon	*Walk the Line*

Best Direction

Year	Director	Film
2000	Steven Soderbergh	*Traffic*
2001	Ron Howard	*A Beautiful Mind*
2002	Roman Polanski	*The Pianist*
2003	Peter Jackson	*The Lord of the Rings: The Return of the King*
2004	Clint Eastwood	*Million Dollar Baby*
2005	Ang Lee	*Brokeback Mountain*

Best Picture

Year	Film	Producer
2000	*Gladiator*	Douglas Wick, David Franzoni and Branko Lustig
2001	*A Beautiful Mind*	Brian Grazer and Ron Howard
2002	*Chicago*	Martin Richards
2003	*The Lord of the Rings: The Return of the King*	Barrie M. Osborne, Peter Jackson and Fran Walsh
2004	*Million Dollar Baby*	Clint Eastwood, Albert S. Ruddy and Tom Rosenberg
2005	*Crash*	Paul Haggis and Cathy Schulman

Hollywood: All Time Top Grossing Films

Rank	Title	Worldwide Box Office
1.	*Titanic* (1997)	$1,835,300,000
2.	*The Lord of the Rings: The Return of the King* (2003)	$1,129,219,252
3.	*Pirates of the Caribbean: Dead Man's Chest* (2006)	$1,051,331,126
4.	*Harry Potter and the Sorcerer's Stone* (2001)	$968,657,891
5.	*Star Wars: Episode I - The Phantom Menace* (1999)	$922,379,000

6.	*The Lord of the Rings: The Two Towers* (2002)	$921,600,000
7.	*Jurassic Park* (1993)	$919,700,000
8.	*Harry Potter and the Goblet of Fire* (2005)	$892,194,397
9.	*Shrek 2* (2004)	$880,871,036
10.	*Harry Potter and the Chamber of Secrets* (2002)	$866,300,000

2005 Top Grossers

Rank	Title	Total Gross
1.	*Star Wars: Episode III—Revenge of the Sith*	$380,262,555
2.	*The Chronicles of Narnia: The Lion, the Witch and the Wardrobe*	$291,709,845
3.	*Harry Potter and the Goblet of Fire*	$289,994,397
4.	*War of the Worlds*	$234,280,354
5.	*King Kong*	$218,051,260

Note: All figures are approximate and subject to change with time.

Arts News

Orhan Pamuk Wins 2006 Literature Nobel

On 12 October, the 2006 Nobel Prize in Literature was awarded to Turkish writer Orhan Pamuk 'who in the quest for the melancholic soul of his native city has discovered new symbols for the clash and interlacing of cultures'.

Orhan Pamuk, described as 'one of the freshest, most original voices in contemporary fiction', writes in Turkish. Five of his novels including *The White Castle*, *The Black Book* and *The New Life* are available in English. In 2003 he won the International IMPAC Award for *My Name Is Red*, and his latest novel, published in translation in 2004, was *Snow*, which *The Times* described as 'a novel of profound relevance to the present moment'. His most recent book is the memoir *Istanbul*, described by Jan Morris as 'an irresistibly seductive book'.

Orhan Pamuk was born 7 June 1952 in Istanbul into a prosperous, secular middle-class family. Growing up, Pamuk was set on becoming a painter. He graduated from Robert College, then studied architecture at Istanbul Technical University and journalism at Istanbul University. He spent the years 1985-88 in the United States where he was a visiting researcher at Columbia University in New York and for a short period attached to the University of Iowa. He now lives in Istanbul.

Pamuk has said that growing up, he experienced a shift from a traditional Ottoman family environment to a more Western-oriented lifestyle. According to the author, the major theme of *My Name is Red* is the relationship between East and West, describing the different views on the artist's relation to his work in both cultures. *Istanbul: Memories and the City* interweaves recollections of sthe writer's upbringing with a portrayal of Istanbul's literary and cultural history. In Pamuk's latest novel *Snow*, the novel becomes a tale of love and poetic creativity just as it knowledgeably describes the political and religious conflicts that characterize Turkish society of our day.

In his home country, Pamuk has a reputation as a social commentator even though he sees himself as principally a fiction writer with no political agenda. He was the first author in the Muslim world to publicly condemn the fatwa against Salman Rushdie. He took a stand for his Turkish colleague Yasar Kemal when Kemal was put on trial in 1995. Pamuk himself was charged after having mentioned, in a Swiss newspaper, that 30,000 Kurds and one million Armenians were killed in Turkey. The charge aroused widespread international protest. It has subsequently been dropped.

Black Sweeps Filmfare Awards

Sanjay Leela Bhansali's film *Black*, about a deaf, mute and blind woman and her relationship with her teacher, swept the 2005 Filmfare Awards, picking up the Best Film award, the Best Director award for Sanjay Leela Bhansali, the Best Actor award for Amitabh Bachchan and the Best Actress award for Rani Mukherji. It was also tipped to win the National Film Awards (which had not been announced at the time of going to press) for Best Film and Best Actor.

Rang De Basanti is India's Official Entry at the Oscars

Rakyesh Omprakash Mehra's critically acclaimed hit *Rang De Basanti*, starring Aamir Khan, has been chosen as India's official entry in the Best Foreigh Language Film category at the Oscars for 2006. *Rang De Basanti* is also likely to be entered in several individual categories at the Oscars. Another very popular and critically acclaimed film, *Lage Raho Munnabhai*, will compete in several individual categories at this year's Oscars. Meanwhile, Deepa Mehta's controversial film *Water*, set in India, has been chosen as Canada's entry for the Oscars.

General Knowledge

Nobel Prize

The Nobel Prize is the first international award given annually since 1901 for achievements in physics, chemistry, medicine, literature and peace. The prize consists of a medal, a personal diploma, and a prize amount. In 1968, the Sveriges Riksbank (Bank of Sweden) instituted the prize in Economic Sciences in memory of Alfred Nobel, founder of the Nobel Prize. The festival day of the Nobel Foundation is on 10 December, the death anniversary of the testator.

Winners of the Nobel Prize:

Economics

Year	Name	Country
2000	James J. Heckman	United States of America
	Daniel L. McFadden	United States of America
2001	George A. Akerlof	United States of America
	A. Michael Spence	United States of America
	Joseph E. Stiglitz	United States of America
2002	Daniel Kahneman	United States of America
	Vernon L. Smith	United States of America
2003	Robert F. Engle	United States of America
	Clive W.J. Granger	United Kingdom
2004	Finn E. Kydland	United States of America
	Edward C. Prescot	United States of America
2005	Robert J. Aumann	Israel/United States of America
	Thomas C. Schelling	United States of America
2006	Edmund S. Phelps	United States of America

Medicine

Year	Name	Country
2000	Arvid Carlsson	Sweden
	Paul Greengard	United States of America
	Eric R. Kandel	United States of America
2001	Leland H. Hartwell	United States of America
	Tim Hunt	United Kingdom
	Sir Paul Nurse	United Kingdom
2002	Sydney Brenner	United Kingdom
	H. Robert Horvitz	United States of America
	John E. Sulston	United Kingdom,
2003	Paul C. Lauterbur	United States of America
	Sir Peter Mansfield	United Kingdom

2004	Richard Axel	United States of America
	Linda B. Buck	United States of America
2005	Barry J. Marshall	Australia
	J. Robin Warren	Australia
2006	Andrew Z. Fire	United States of America
	Craig C. Mello	United States of America

Peace

Year	Name	Country
2000	Kim Dae-jung	South Korea
2001	United Nations	United States of America
	Kofi Annan	Ghana
2002	Jimmy Carter	United States of America
2003	Shirin Ebadi	Iran
2004	Wangari Muta Maathai	Kenya
2005	International Atomic Energy Agency	Austria
	Mohamed El Baradei	Egypt
2006	Muhammad Yunus	Bangladesh
	Grameen Bank	Bangladesh

Chemistry

Year	Name	Country
2000	Alan Heeger	United States of America
	Alan G. MacDiarmid	United States of America
	Hideki Shirakawa	Japan
2001	William S. Knowles	United States of America
	Ryoji Noyori	Japan
	K. Barry Sharpless	United States of America
2002	John B. Fenn	United States of America
	Koichi Tanaka	Japan
	Kurt Wüthrich	Switzerland
2003	Peter Agre	United States of America
	Roderick MacKinnon	United States of America
2004	Aaron Ciechanover	Israel
	Avram Hershko	Israel
	Irwin Rose	United States of America
2005	Yves Chauvin	France
	Robert H. Grubbs	United States of America
	Richard R. Schrock	United States of America
2006	Roger D. Kornberg	United States of America

Physics

Year	Name	Country
2000	Zhores I. Alferov	Russia
	Herbert Kroemer	Germany
	Jack S. Kilby	United States of America
2001	Eric A. Cornell	United States of America
	Wolfgang Ketterle	Germany
	Carl E. Wieman	United States of America
2002	Raymond Davis Jr.	United States of America
	Masatoshi Koshiba	Japan
	Riccardo Giacconi	United States of America

2003	Alexei A. Abrikosov	Russia
	Vitaly L. Ginzburg	Russia
	Anthony J. Leggett	United Kingdom
2004	David J. Gross	United States of America
	H. David Politzer	United States of America
	Frank Wilczek	United States of America
2005	Roy J. Glauber	United States of America
	John L. Hall	United States of America
	Theodor W. Hänsch	Germany
2006	John C. Mather	United States of America
	George F. Smoot	United States of America

Literature

Year	Name	Country
2000	Gao Xingjian	France
2001	V.S. Naipaul	United Kingdom
2002	Imre Kertesz	Hungary
2003	J.M. Coetzee	South Africa
2004	Elfriede Jelinek	Austria
2005	Harold Pinter	United Kingdom
2006	Orhan Pamuk	Turkey

Bharat Ratna

The Bharat Ratna is India's highest civilian honour. It is generally conferred on 23 January each year for rendering outstanding services to the world community. The award was instituted by the President of India on 2 January 1954. The Bharat Ratna medallion is made of bronze and shaped like a pipal leaf. The ribbon is white. A replica of the sun with radiating rays can be seen on the obverse of the medallion with the words 'Bharat Ratna' inscribed beneath it. Our national emblem (the lion capital of Sarnath) is embossed on the reverse with the national motto 'Satyameva Jayate' (Only truth shall prevail). The award can also be granted posthumously. The awards are produced at the Kolkata Mint.

Bharat Ratna Recipients

Person	Year
Dr Sarvepali Radhakrishnan (1888–1975)	1954
Chakravarti Rajagopalachari (1878–1972)	1954
Dr Chandrasekhar Venkat Raman (1888–1970)	1954
Dr Bhagwan Das (1869–1958)	1955
Dr Mokshagundam Visvesvaraya (1861–1962)	1955
Jawaharlal Nehru (1889–1964)	1955
Govind Ballabh Pant (1887–1961)	1957
Dr Dhondo Keshave Karve (1858–1962)	1958
Dr Bidhan Chandra Roy (1882–1962)	1961
Purushottam Das Tandon (1882–1962)	1961
Dr Rajendra Prasad (1884–1963)	1962
Dr Zakir Husain (1897–1969)	1963
Dr Pandurang Vaman Kane (1880–1972)	1963

Lal Bahadur Shastri (posthumous) (1904–66)	1966
Indira Gandhi (1917–84)	1971
Varahagiri Venkatagiri (1894–80)	1975
Kumaraswami Kamraj (posthumous) (1903–75)	1976
Mary Taresa Bojaxhiu (Mother Teresa) (1910–97)	1980
Acharya Vinobha Bhave (posthumous) (1895–1982)	1983
Khan Abdul Ghaffar Khan (1890–1988)	1987
Marudu Gopalan Ramachandran (posthumous) (1917–87)	1988
Dr Bhim Rao Ramji Ambedkar (posthumous) (1891–1956)	1990
Dr Nelson Rolihlahla Mandela (b. 1918)	1990
Rajiv Gandhi (Posthumous) (1944–91)	1991
Sardar Vallabhbhai Patel (posthumous) (1875–1950)	1991
Morarji Ranchhodji Desai (1896–1995)	1991
Maulana Abul Kala Azad (1888–1958)	1992
Jehangir Ratanji Dadabhai Tata (1904–93)	1992
Satyajit Ray (1922–92)	1992
A.P.J. Abdul Kalam (b. 1931)	1997
Gulzarilal Nanda (1898–98)	1997
Aruna Asaf Ali (posthumous) (1909–96)	1997
M.S. Subbulakshmi (1916–2004)	1998
C. Subramaniam (1910–2000)	1998
Jayaprakash Narayan (posthumous) (1902–79)	1999
Ravi Shankar (b. 1920)	1999
Amartya Sen (b. 1933)	1999
Gopinath Bordoloi (posthumous) (1927–50)	1999
Lata Mangeshkar (b. 1929)	2001
Bismillah Khan (1916–2006)	2001

Note: From 2002–06, no one has been conferred the Bharat Ratna

Param Vir Chakra

Param Vir Chakra is India's highest gallantry award. It is awarded for the highest degree of valour in presence of the enemy. Officers and other enlisted personnel of all the military branches of India are eligible for this award. The award was established on 26 January 1950 by the President of India, with effect from 15 August 1947. The Param Vir Chakra medal was designed by Savitri Khanolankar, whose son-in-law, Major Somnath Sharma, coincidentally became the first recipient of the award. The medal symbolizes Rishi Dadhichi who donated his thigh bones to make Indra's weapon 'Vajra'. It has a radius of 1-3/8 inch and is made of bronze. The words 'Param Vir Chakra' are written on it in English and Hindi. A purple ribbon, 32 mm long, holds the medal. The award is India's post-Independence equivalent of the Victoria Cross.

Param Vir Chakra Recipients

	Name	Regiment	Year	Operation
1.	Major Somnath Sharma (posthumously)	Kumaon Regiment	Nov. 1947	Kashmir Operations 1947–48
2.	Lance Naik Karham Singh M.M.	I Sikh Regiment	Oct. 1948	Kashmir Operations 1947–48

3. 2nd Lt Rama Raghobe Rane	Corps of Engineers	Apr. 1948	Kashmir Operations 1947–48
4. Naik Jadu Nath Singh (posthumously)	1 Rajput Regiment	Feb. 1948	Kashmir Operations 1947–48
5. Company Hav. Major Piru Singh (posthumously)	6 Rajputana Rifles	Jul. 1948	Kashmir Operations 1947–48
6. Capt. Gurbachan Singh Salaria (posthumously)	3/1 Gurkha Rifles	Dec. 1961	Congo
7. Major Dhan Singh Thapa	1/8 Gurkha Rifles	Oct. 1962	Ladakh
8. Sub. Joginder Singh (posthumously)	1 Sikh Regiment	Oct. 1962	Northeast Frontier Agency
9. Major Shaitan Singh (posthumously)	Kumaon Regiment	Nov. 1962	Ladakh
10. Comp. Hav. Major Abdul Hamid (posthumously)	4 Grenadiers	Sept. 1965	Operation against Pakistan
11. Lt-Col Ardeshir Burzorji Tarapore (posthumously)	17 Poona Horse	Sept. 1965	Operation against Pakistan
12. Lance Naik Albert Ekka (posthumously)	14 Guards	Dec. 1971	Indo–Pakistan conflict
13. Flying Offr Nirmal Jit Singh Sekhon (posthumously)	Indian Air Force	Dec. 1971	Indo–Pakistan conflict
14. Lt Arun Khetarpal (posthumously)	17 Poona Horse	Dec. 1971	Indo–Pakistan conflict
15. Major Hoshiar Singh	Grenadiers	Dec. 1971	Indo–Pakistan conflict
16. Naib Sub. Bana Singh	8 J & K Light Infantry	Jun. 1987	Operations in Siachen Glacier
17. Major Ramaswamy Parmeshwaran (posthumously)	8 Mahar Regiment	Nov. 1987	IPKF Operations in Sri Lanka
18. Capt. Vikram Batra (posthumously)	13 J & K Rifles	Jul. 1999	Operation Vijay in Kargil
19. Lt Manoj Kumar Pandey (posthumously)	1/11 Gorkha Rifles	Jul. 1999	Operation Vijay in Kargil
20. Grenadier Yogendra Singh Yadav	18 Grenadiers	Jul. 1999	Operation Vijay in Kargil
21. Rifleman Sanjay Kumar	13 J & K Rifles	Jul. 1999	Operation Vijay in Kargil

Padma Awardees 2006

Padma Vibhushan

Adoor Gopalakrishnan
C.R. Krishnaswamy Rao
Charles Correa
Mahasveta Devi
Nirmala Deshpande
Norman E. Borlaug
Obaid Siddiqui
Prakash Narain Tandon
Justice V.N. Khare

Padma Bhushan

A.K. Hangal
Ustad Abdul Halim Jaffer Khan
Deepak Parekh
Devaki Jain
Dinesh Nandini Dalmia

Dusan Zbavitel
Ganga Prasad Birla
Ustad Ghulam Mustafa Khan
Gregory Maximovich Bongard-Levin
Late Dr Gunter Kruger
Hira Lall Sibal
Jaiveer Agarwal
Air Commodore Jasjit Singh
K.G. Subramanyam
Kamleshwar Prasad Saxena
Kewal Kishan Talwar
Konidala Chiranjeevi
Kunnath Puthiyaveetil Padmanabhan Nambiar
Lokesh Chandra
Madhav Gadgil
Moolamattom Varkey Pylee
N.S. Ramaswamy
Nandan M. Nilekani
Late P. Leela
P.P. Rao
P.S. Appu
Ramakanta Rath
S. Ramadorai
Ustad Sabri Khan
Sai Paranjpye
Shanno Khurana
Shashi Bhushan
Tarun Das
V. Shanta
Vijay Shankar Vyas
Vijaypat Singhania

Padma Shri

Sheikh Abdul Rahman Bin Abdullah Al-Mahmoud
Ajeet Cour
Anil Prakash Joshi
Aribam Shyam Sharma
Bahadur Singh
Bhuvaraghan Planiappan
Billy Arjan Singh
Bonbehari Vishnu Nimbkar
Devappagowda Chinnaiah
Fatma Rafiq Zakaria
Gayatri Sankaran
Ghanashyam Mishra
Hakim Syed Zillur Rehman
Harbhajan Singh Rissam
Swami Hari Govind Maharaj
Harsh Kumar Gupta
Ilena Citaristi
J.N. Chaudhry
Kamal Kumar Sethi
Kanaka Srinivasan
Kashmiri Lal Zakir
Kavungal Chatunni Panicker
Laltluangliana Khiangte
Lothar Lutze
Madhumita Bisht
Madhup Mudgal
Mangte Chungneijang Mary Kom
Mehmood Dhaulpuri
Mehmooda Ali Shah
Melhupra Vero
Mohan Kameswaran
Mohan Singh Gunjyal
Mrinal Pande
Narendra Kumar
P.S. Bedi
Pankaj Udhas
Prasad Sawkar
R. Balasubramanian
Rajendra Kumar Saboo
Ustad Rashid Khan
Sania Mirza
Sanjeev Bagai
Seyed Ehtesham Hasnain
Shahnaz Husain
Shobana Chandrakumar
Shree Lal Joshi
Guru Shyama Charan Pati
Sitanshu Yashaschandra
Sucheta Dalal
Sudha Murthy
Sudha Varghese
Sugathakumari
Suresh Krishna
Surinder Kaur
Suwalal Chhaganmal Bafna
Swaminathan Sivaram
Tehemton Erach
Tsering Landol
Upendra Kaul
Vasundhra Komkali
Yashodhar Mathpal

Ramon Magsaysay Award

Conceived by John D. Rockefeller III in April 1957, the trustees of the Rockefeller Brothers Fund, based in New York City, established the Ramon Magsaysay Award to commemorate President of the Philippines, Ramon Magsaysay, and to perpetuate his example of integrity in government and pragmatic idealism within a democratic society. The award is given to any person living in Asia without regard to race, gender, or religion. However, heads of State and heads of government (and their spouses) are not eligible during their terms of office. Each September, the Foundation solicits award nominations. Awards themselves are determined following evaluation by the Foundation's president and board of trustees. Presentation ceremonies are held in Manila on 31 August. The annual award is given in six categories:

1. Government Service; 2. Public Service; 3. Community Leadership; 4. Journalism, Literature, And Creative Communication Arts; 5. Peace and International Understanding; and 6. Emergent Leadership

Over the years many Indians have featured on list of awardees for their distinguished services. They are:

Government Service

Name	Year
1. Chintaman Deshmukh	1959
2. Kiran Bedi	1994
3. Tiruneilai Seshan	1996
4. James Michael Lyngdoh	2003

Public Service

Name	Year
1. Jayaprakash Narayan	1965
2. M.S. Subbulakshmi	1974
3. Manibhai Desai	1982
4. Murlidhar Amte	1985
5. Lakshmi Chand Jain	1989
6. Banoo Jehangir Coyaji	1993
7. Mahesh Chander Mehta	1997
8. V. Shanta	2005

Community Leadership

Name	Year
1. Vinoba Bhave	1958
2. Dara Khurody	1963
3. Verghese Kurien	1963
4. Tribhuvandas K. Patel	1963
5. Kamladevi Chattopadhyay	1966
6. Moncompu Sambasivan Swaminathan	1971
7. Ela Ramesh Bhatt	1977
8. Mabelle Arole	1979
9. Rajanikant S. Arole	1979
10. Pramod Karan Sethi	1981
11. Chandi Prasad Bhatt	1982
12. Pandurang Athavale	1996
13. Aruna Roy	2000
14. Rajendra Singh	2001
15. Shantha Sinha	2003

Journalism, Literature, and Creative Communication Arts

Name	Year
1. Amitabha Chowdhury	1961
2. Satyajit Ray	1967
3. B. George Verghese	1975
4. Sombhu Mitra	1976
5. Gour Kishore Ghosh	1981
6. Arun Shourie	1982
7. Rasipuram K. Laxman	1984
8. K.V. Subbanna	1991
9. Ravi Shankar	1992
10. Mahasweta Devi	1997

Peace and International Understanding

Name	Year
1. Mother Teresa	1962
2. Welthy Fisher	1964
3. Henning Holck Larsen	1976
4. Jockin Arputham	2000
5. Laxminarayan Ramdas	2004

Emergent Leadership

Name	Year
1. Sandeep Pandey	2002
2. Arvind Kejriwal	2006

United Nations

Secretary-General of the UN

The activities of the United Nations are coordinated and administered by the Secretariat, which is headed by the UN Secretary-General. On the recommendation of the Security Council, the General Assembly appoints the Secretary-General whose selection can be vetoed by any of the five permanent members in the Security Council.

The Secretary-General and his staff carry out functions entrusted by the General Assembly, Security Council, the Trusteeship Council and the Economic and Social Council. He is the chief administrative officer at all the meetings of these organs, and submits an annual report to the General Assembly on the work of the UN. The Secretary-General may also bring to the notice of the Security Council any issue that he considers to be a threat to international peace and security.

The Secretary-General is the most authoritative and visible figure of the UN in international affairs. He is regarded as the chief spokesman for the UN, and his headquarters are located at the UN building in New York City.

The UN Security Council will elect a new Secretary-General who would assume office on 1 January 2007. South Korea's foreign minister Ban Ki-Moon is designated to be the new Secretary-General.

List of Secretaries-General of the United Nations

1. Trygve Lie (Norway) (1946–1952), 2. Dag Hammarskjöld (Sweden) (1953–1961), 3. U. Thant (Myanmar) (1961–1971), 4. Kurt Waldheim (Austria) (1972–1981), 5. Javier de Perez de Cuellar (Peru) (1982–1991), 6. Boutros Boutros-Ghali (Egypt) (1992–1996), 7. Kofi Annan (Ghana) (1997–present).

Non-Aligned Movement (NAM)

The Non-Aligned Movement traces its origins in 1955 when heads of States of twenty-nine African and Asian countries met at Bandung, Indonesia, to discuss common concerns, including colonialism and Western influence. In 1961, the criteria for NAM membership were set up which stated that the member countries of NAM could not be involved in defence pacts or alliances with the major world powers. This was done to distance NAM from the Soviet and Western power blocks and prevent its members from becoming pawns in the Cold War.

Member States of NAM

1. Afghanistan, 2. Algeria, 3. Angola, 4. Bahamas, 5. Bahrain, 6. Bangladesh, 7. Barbados, 8. Belarus, 9. Belize, 10. Benin, 11. Bhutan, 12. Bolivia, 13. Botswana, 14. Brunei, 15. Burkina Faso, 16. Burundi, 17. Cambodia, 18. Cameroon, 19. Cape Verde, 20. Central African Republic, 21. Chad, 22. Chile, 23. Colombia, 24. Comoros, 25. Congo, 26. Cote d'Ivoire, 27. Cuba, 28. Democratic People's Rep of Korea (North Korea), 29. Democratic Republic of the Congo, 30. Dominican Republic, 31. Djibouti, 32. Ecuador, 33. Egypt, 34. Equatorial Guinea, 35. Eritrea, 36. Ethiopia, 37. Gabon, 38. Gambia, 39. Ghana, 40. Grenada, 41. Guatemala, 42. Guinea, 43. Guinea-Bissau, 44. Guyana, 45. Honduras, 46. India, 47. Indonesia, 48. Iran, 49. Iraq, 50. Jamaica, 51. Jordan, 52. Kenya, 53. Kuwait, 54. Laos, 55. Lebanon, 56. Lesotho, 57. Liberia, 58. Libya, 59. Madagascar, 60. Malawi, 61. Malaysia, 62. Maldives, 63. Mali, 64. Mauritania, 65. Mauritius, 66. Mongolia, 67. Morocco, 68. Mozambique, 69. Myanmar, 70. Namibia, 71. Nepal, 72. Nicaragua, 73. Niger, 74. Nigeria, 75. Oman, 76. Pakistan, 77. Palestine, 78. Panama, 79. Papua New Guinea, 80. Peru, 81. Philippines, 82. Qatar, 83. Rwanda, 84. Saint Lucia, 85. Saint Vincent and the Grenadines, 86. Sao Tome and Principe, 87. Saudi Arabia, 88. Senegal, 89. Seychelles, 90. Sierra

Leone, 91. Singapore, 92. Somalia, 93. South Africa, 94. Sri Lanka, 95. Sudan, 96. Suriname, 97. Swaziland, 98. Syria, 99. Thailand, 100. Timor Leste (East Timor), 101. Togo, 102. Trinidad and Tobago, 103. Tunisia, 104. Turkmenistan, 105. Uganda, 106. United Arab Emirates, 107. Tanzania, 108. Uzbekistan, 109. Vanuatu, 110. Venezuela, 111. Vietnam, 112. Yemen, 113. Zambia, 114. Zimbabwe

List of NAM Summits

First Conference—Belgrade, 1–6 September 1961
Second Conference—Cairo, 5–10 October 1964
Third Conference—Lusaka, 8–10 September 1970
Fourth Conference—Algiers, 5–9 September 1973
Fifth Conference—Colombo, 16–19 August 1976
Sixth Conference—Havana, 3–9 September 1979
Seventh Conference—New Delhi, 7–12 March 1983
Eighth Conference—Harare, 1–6 September 1986
Ninth Conference—Belgrade, 4–7 September 1989
Tenth Conference—Jakarta, 1–7 September 1992
Eleventh Conference—Cartagena de Indias, 18–20 October 1995
Twelfth Conference—Durban, 2–3 September 1998
Thirteenth Conference—Kuala Lumpur, 20–25 February 2003
Fourteenth Conference—Havana, 11–16 September 2006

G8

The Group of Eight (G8) Members

- Canada
- France
- Germany
- Italy
- Japan
- Russia
- United Kingdom
- United States of America

G6/7/8 Summits

1st (1975)—France
2nd (1976)—United States
3rd (1977)—United Kingdom
4th (1978)—Germany
5th (1979)—Japan
6th (1980)—Italy
7th (1981)—Canada
8th (1982)—France
9th (1983)—United States
10th (1984)—United Kingdom
11th (1985)—Germany
12th (1986)—Japan
13th (1987)—Italy
14th (1988)—Canada
15th (1989)—France
16th (1990)—United States
17th (1991)—United Kingdom
18th (1992)—Germany
19th (1993)—Japan
20th (1994)—Italy
21st (1995–1996)—Canada Russia (Special summit on nuclear security)
22nd (1996)—France
23rd (1997)—United States
24th (1998)—United Kingdom
25th (1999)—Germany
26th (2000)—Japan
27th (2001)—Italy
28th (2002)—Canada
29th (2003)—France
30th (2004)—United States
31st (2005)—United Kingdom
32nd (15–17 July 2006)—Russia

Future G8 Summits

33rd (2007)—Germany
34th (2008)—Japan
35th (2009)—Italy
36th (2010)—Canada
37th (2011)—France
38th (2012)—United States

European Union (EU)

List of Member States

1.Austria, 2.Belgium, 3. Cyprus, 4. Czech Republic, 5. Denmark, 6. Estonia, 7. Finland, 8. France, 9. Germany, 10. Greece, 11. Hungary, 12. Ireland, 13. Italy, 14. Latvia, 15. Lithuania, 16. Luxembourg, 17. Malta, 18. Poland, 19. Portugal, 20. Slovakia, 21. Slovenia, 22. Spain, 23. Sweden, 24. The Netherlands, 25. United Kingdom

Candidate Countries

1. Bulgaria, 2. Croatia, 3. Former Yugoslav Republic of Macedonia, 4. Romania, 5. Turkey

North Atlantic Treaty Organization (NATO)

NATO or the North Atlantic Treaty Organization is an alliance committed to fulfilling the initiatives and goals of the North Atlantic Treaty signed on 4 April 1949. It consists of twenty-six member countries from Europe and North America.

The fundamental role of NATO is to protect the security and freedom of its member countries by military and political means. It also plays an important role in peacekeeping and crisis management.

Members

1.Belgium, 2. Bulgaria, 3. Canada, 4.Czech Republic, 5. Denmark, 6.Estonia, 7. France, 8. Germany, 9.Greece, !0. Hungary, 11. Iceland, 12. Italy, !3. Latvia, 14. Lithuania, 15. Luxembourg, 16. The Netherlands, 17, Norway, 18. Poland, 19. Portugal, 20. Romania, 21. Slovakia, 22. Slovenia 23. Spain, 24. Turkey, 25. United Kingdom, 26. United States

Association of South-East Asian Nations (ASEAN)

On 8 August 1967, ASEAN or The Association of South-East Asian Nations was established in Bangkok by five countries—Philippines, Thailand, Malaysia, Singapore, and Indonesia. Later, five other countries joined the organization—Brunei (on 8 January 1984), Vietnam (on 28 July 1995), Laos and Myanmar (both on 23 July 1997), and Cambodia (on 30 April 1999).

Members

1. Brunei, 2. Cambodia, 3. Indonesia, 4. Laos, 5. Malaysia, 6. Myanmar, 7. Philippines, 8. Singapore, 9. Thailand, 10. Vietnam

Arab League

Members

1. Algeria, 2. Bahrain, 3. Comoros, 4. Djibouti, 5. Egypt, 6. Iraq, 7. Jordan, 8. Kuwait, 9. Lebanon, 10. Libya, 11. Mauritania, 12. Morocco, 13. Oman, 14. Palestine, 15. Qatar, 16. Saudi Arabia, 17. Somalia, 18. Sudan, 19. Syria, 20. Tunisia, 21.United Arab Emirates, 22.Yemen

International Monetary Fund

The International Monetary Fund (IMF) was conceived in July 1944 at an international conference held at Bretton Woods, New Hampshire, USA, when delegates from forty-four governments agreed on a framework for economic cooperation designed to avoid a repetition of the disastrous economic policies that had contributed to the Great Depression of the 1930s. It is accountable to its member countries. The day-to-day work of the IMF is carried out by an Executive Board, representing the 184 members of the IMF, and an internationally recruited staff under the leadership of a Managing Director and three Deputy Managing Directors—each member of this management team being drawn from a different region of the world. IMF's resources come mainly from the quota (or capital) subscriptions that countries pay when they join the IMF, or following periodic reviews in which quotas are increased. Countries pay 25 per cent of their quota subscriptions in Special Drawing Rights or major currencies, such as US dollars or Japanese yen. Quotas determine not only a country's subscription payments, but also the amount of financing that it can receive from the IMF, and its share in SDR allocations. Quotas also are the main determinant of the voting power of countries in the IMF. It works for global prosperity by promoting:

- Balanced expansion of world trade,
- Stability of exchange rates,
- Avoidance of competitive devaluations, and
- Orderly correction of balance of payments problems.

UNDP

The United Nations Development Programme (UNDP) was formed in 1965 to combine the Expanded Programme of Technical Assistance and the United Nations Special Fund. Since 1990, the UNDP has annually published the Human Development Report, based on the Human Development Index. UNDP is also one of several Implementing Agencies for the Global Environment Facility (GEF). UNDP helps developing countries attract and use aid effectively. It encourages the protection of human rights and the empowerment of women. The annual Human Development Report, commissioned by UNDP, focuses the global debate on key development issues, providing new measurement tools, innovative analysis and often controversial policy proposals. The Global Report's analytical framework and inclusive approach carry over into regional, national and local Human Development Reports, also supported by UNDP. In each country office, the UNDP Resident Representative normally also serves as the Resident Coordinator of development activities for the United Nations system as a whole. Through such coordination, UNDP seeks to ensure the most effective use of UN and international aid resources. World leaders have agreed to achieve the Millennium Development Goals, including the overarching goal of cutting poverty in half by 2015. In 2004 UNDP's total income reached $4 billion. The largest single donor was the United States, contributing $243 million in regular and other resources, followed closely by the United Kingdom, which contributed $233 million to UNDP. Japan, the Netherlands, Norway and Sweden each contributed more than $100 million.

The World Bank

The World Bank is one of the United Nations' specialized agencies, and is made up of 184 member countries. These countries are jointly responsible for how the organization is financed and how its money is spent. The Bank came into formal existence on 27 December 1945 following international ratification of the Bretton Woods agreements. Along with the rest of the development community, the World Bank centres its efforts on reaching the Millennium Development Goals, agreed to by UN members in 2000 and aimed at sustainable poverty reduction. The 'World Bank' is the name that has come to be used for the International Bank for Reconstruction and Development (IBRD) and the International Development Association (IDA). These organizations provide low-interest loans, interest-free credit, and grants to developing countries. Some 10,000 professionals from nearly every country in the world work in the World Bank's Washington DC headquarters or in its 109 country offices. In addition to IBRD and IDA, three other organizations make up the World Bank Group. The International Finance Corporation (IFC) promotes private sector investment by supporting high-risk sectors and countries. The Multilateral Investment Guarantee Agency (MIGA) provides political risk insurance (guarantees) to investors in and lenders to developing countries, and the International Centre for Settlement of Investment Disputes (ICSID) settles investment disputes between foreign investors and their host countries. Among numerous other global partnerships, the World Bank has put supporting the fight against HIV/AIDS at the top of its agenda. It is the world's largest long-term financer of HIV/AIDS programmes. Current Bank commitments for HIV/AIDS amount to more than $1.3 billion, with half of that for sub-Saharan Africa. The Bank is currently involved in more than 1,800 projects in virtually every sector and developing country. These are as diverse as providing microcredit in Bosnia and Herzegovina and raising AIDS awareness in communities in Guinea, supporting education of girls in Bangladesh and improving health care delivery in Mexico, helping East Timor rebuild upon independence or India to rebuild Gujarat after a devastating earthquake. In 2004 it provided $20.1 billion for 245 projects in developing countries worldwide.

World Trade Organization

The World Trade Organization (WTO) is the only global international organization dealing with the rules of trade between nations. WTO headquarters are located in Geneva, Switzerland. Pascal Lamy is the current Director-General. As of December 2005, there are 149 members in the organization with the latest to join being Saudi Arabia. All WTO members are required to grant one another most favoured nation status, such that trade concessions granted by a WTO member to another country must be granted to all WTO members. The past fifty years have seen an exceptional growth in world trade. Merchandise exports grew on average by 6 per cent annually. Total trade in 2000 was twenty-two times the level of 1950. GATT and the WTO have helped to create a strong and prosperous trading system contributing to unprecedented growth. The system was developed through a series of trade negotiations, or rounds, held under GATT. While most international organizations operate on a one country, one vote or even a weighted voting basis, many WTO decisions, such as adopting agreements, are officially determined by consensus of all member states. Unlike most other international organizations, the WTO has significant power to enforce its decisions through the authorization of trade sanctions against members that fail to comply with its decisions. Member states can bring disputes to the WTO's Dispute Settlement Body if they believe another member has breached WTO rules. A Dispute Settlement Panel, usually made up of three trade officials, hears disputes. The panels meet in secret and are not required to alert national parliaments that their laws have been challenged by another country.

Geography

Continents

Name	Area *(km²)*	% of total
Africa	30,970,000	20.2
Antarctica	15,500,000	9.3
Asia	44,493,000	29.6
Oceania	8,945,000	6.0
Europe	10,245,000	6.8
North America	24,454,000	16.3
South America	17,838,000	11.9

Oceans

Name	Area (km²)	% of total	Average depth (m)
Arctic	13,986,000	3	1,330
Atlantic	82,217,000	24	3,700
Indian	73,426,000	20	3,900
Pacific	181,300,000	46	4,300

Highest Mountains

Name	Height (m)	(ft)	Location
Everest	8,850	29,030	China–Nepal
K2	8,610	28,250	Kashmir–Jammu
Kanchenjunga	8,590	28,170	India–Nepal
Lhotse	8,500	27,890	China–Nepal
Kanchenjunga S. Peak	8,470	27,800	India–Nepal
Makalu I	8,470	27,800	China–Nepal
Kanchenjunga W. Peak	8,420	27,620	India–Nepal
Llotse E Peak	8,380	27,500	China–Nepal
Dhaulagiri	8,170	26,810	Nepal
Cho Oyu	8,150	26,750	China–Nepal
Manaslu	8,130	26,660	Nepal
Nanga Parbat	8,130	26,660	Kashmir–Jammu
Annapurna I	8,080	26,500	Nepal
Gasherbrum I	8,070	26,470	Kashmir–Jammu
Broad–highest	8,050	26,400	Kashmir–Jammu
Gasherbrum II	8,030	26,360	Kashmir--Jammu
Gosainthan	8,010	26,290	China
Broad–middle	8,000	26,250	Kashmir–Jammu
Gasherbrum III	7,950	26,090	Kashmir-Jammu
Annapurna II	7,940	26,040	Nepal
Nanda Devi	7,820	25,660	India

Largest Seas

Name	Area (km²)	(sq mi)
Coral Sea	4,791,000	1,850,200
Arabian Sea	3,863,000	1,492,000
S. China (Nan) Sea	3,685,000	1,423,000
Mediterranean Sea	2,516,000	971,000
Caribbean Sea	2,516,000	971,000
Bering Sea	2,304,000	890,000
Bay of Bengal	2,172,000	839,000
Sea of Okhotsk	1,590,000	614,000
Gulf of Mexico	1,543,000	596,000
Gulf of Guinea	1,533,000	592,000

Largest Lakes

	Lake	Country	Area (sq. km)
1.	Caspian Sea	Azerbaijan, Iran, Kazakhstan, Russian Federation, Turkmenistan	436,000
2.	Superior	Canada, United States of America	82,100
3.	Victoria	Kenya, Tanzania, Uganda	68,870
4.	Huron	Canada, United States of America	59,600
5.	Michigan	United States of America	57,800
6.	Tanganyika	Burundi, Congo (Democratic Republic), Tanzania, Zambia	32,600
7.	Baikal	Russian Federation	31,500
8.	Great Bear Lake	Canada	31,000
9.	Malawi	Malawi, Mozambique, Tanzania	29,500
10.	Great Slave	Canada	27,000
11.	Erie	Canada, United States of America	25,700
12.	Winnipeg	Canada	24,500
13.	Ontario	Canada, United States of America	18,960
14.	Balkhash	Kazakhstan	17,580
15.	Aral Sea	Kazakhstan, Uzbekistan	17,158
16.	Ladoga	Russian Federation	16,400
17.	Maracaibo	Venezuela	13,010
18.	Tonle Sap	Cambodia	13,000
19.	Agassiz	Canada, United States of America	11,911
20.	Patos	Brazil	10,140

Longest Rivers of the World

	Name	Outflow	Length in kilometres
1.	Nile	Mediterranean Sea	6,650
2.	Amazon-Ucayali-Apurimac	South Atlantic Ocean	6,400
3.	Yangtze	East China Sea	6,300
4.	Mississippi-Missouri- Red Rock	Gulf of Mexico	5,971
5.	Yenisey-Baikal-Selenga	Kara Sea	5,540
6.	Huang Ho	Gulf of Chihli	5,464
7.	Ob-Irtysh	Gulf of Ob	5,410
8.	Parana	Río de la Plata	4,880
9.	Congo South	Atlantic Ocean	4,700
10.	Amur-Argun	Sea of Okhotsk	4,444

Ten Largest Islands of the World (Excluding Continents)

	Name	Area	Location
1.	Greenland	822,700 sq. miles	North Atlantic Ocean
2.	New Guinea	309,000 sq. miles	Papua New Guinea–Indonesia
3.	Borneo	283,400 sq. miles	Indonesia–Malaysia–Brunei
4.	Madagascar	226,658 sq. miles	Indian Ocean

5.	Baffin Island	195,928 sq. miles	Northwest Territories, Canada
6.	Sumatra	167,600 sq. miles	Indonesia
7.	Honshu	87,805 sq. miles	Japan
8.	Victoria Island	83,897 sq. miles	Northwest Territories, Canada
9.	Great Britain	83,698 sq. miles	United Kingdom
10.	Ellesmere Island	75,767 sq. miles	Northwest Territories, Canada

Largest Deserts

Name/location	Area (km²)	(sq. mi)
Sahara, N. Africa	8,600,000	3,320,000
Arabian, S.W. Asia	2,330,000	900,000
Gobi. Mongolia and N.E. China	1,166,000	450,000
Patagonian, Argentina	673,000	260,000
Great Basin, S.W. USA	492,000	190,000
Chihuahuan, Mexico	450,000	175,000
Great Victoria, N.W. Australia	450,000	175,000
Great Victoria, S.W. Australia	235,000	125,000
Sonoran, S.W. USA	310,000	120,000
Kyzyl–Kum, Kazakhstan/Uzbekistan	300,000	115,000
Takla Makan, N. China	270,000	105,000
Kalahari., S.W. Africa	260,000	100,000

Deepest Caves

Name/location	Depth (m)	(ft)
Jean Bernard, France	1,494	4,900
Snezhnaya, Russia	1,340	4,397
Puertas de Illamina, Spain	1,338	4,390
Pierre–Saint–Martin, France	1,321	4,334
Sistema Huautla, Mexico	1,240	4,067

Some Famous Volcanoes of the World

Name	Location	Elevation (ft.)
Guallatiri	Chile	19,876
Cotopaxi	Ecuador	19,347
Kilimanjaro	Tanzania	19,340
El Misti	Peru	19,101
Citlaltépetl	Mexico	18,406
Popocatépetl	Mexico	17,930
Klyuchevskaya	Russia	15,584
Mauna Kea	Hawaii	13,796
Mauna Loa	Hawaii	13,678
Fuji	Japan	12,388
Etna	Italy	10,902
St Helens	United States of America	8,360
Vesuvius	Italy	4,198
Stromboli	Italy	3,038

Ten Largest Countries

S.No.	Country	Area (sq. km.)
1.	Russia	17,075,200
2.	Canada	9,984,670
3.	United States	9,631,420
4.	China	9,596,960
5.	Brazil	8,511,965
6.	Australia	7,686,850
7.	India	3,287,590
8.	Argentina	2,766,890
9.	Kazakhstan	2,717,300
10.	Sudan	2,505,810

Ten Most Populous Countries

S.No	Country	Population (July 2006)
1.	China	1,313,973,13
2.	India	1,095,351,995
3.	USA	298,444,215
4.	Indonesia	245,452,739
5.	Brazil	188,078,277
6.	Pakistan	165,803,560
7.	Bangladesh	147,365,352
8.	Russia	142,893,540
9.	Nigeria	131,859,731
10.	Japan	127,463,611
11.	Mexico	107,449,525

Countries with Highest GDPs

S.No.	Countries	GDP (Purchasing power parity in $ billion, 2005)
1.	USA	12,360
2.	China	8,859
3.	Japan	4,018
4.	India	3,611
5.	Germany	2,504
6.	UK	1,830
7.	France	1,816
8.	Italy	1,698
9.	Russia	1,589
10.	Brazil	1,556

Most Populous Cities of the World

Rank	City	Population	Year
1.	Mumbai, India	11,914,398	2001
2.	Shanghai, China	10,996,500	2003
3.	Sao Paulo, Brazil	10,677,019	2003
4.	Seoul, South Korea	10,207,296	2002

5.	Moscow, Russia	10,101,500	2001
6.	Delhi, India	9,817,439	2001
7.	Karachi, Pakistan	9,339,023	1998
8.	Istanbul, Turkey	8,831,805	2000
9.	Beijing, China	8,689,000	2001
10.	Mexico City, Mexico	8,591,309	2000
11.	Jakarta, Indonesia	8,389,443	2000
12.	Tokyo, Japan	8,340,000	2003
13.	New York, US	8,085,742	2003

World's Most Populous Urban Agglomerations (2005)

Rank	Name	Est. Population
1.	Tokyo, Japan	35,327,000
2.	Mexico City, Mexico	19,013,000
3.	New York-Newark, US	18,498,000
4.	Mumbai, India	18,336,000
5.	Sao Paulo, Brazil	18,333,000
6.	Delhi, India	15,334,000
7.	Kolkata, India	14,299,000
8.	Buenos Aires, Argentina	13,349,000
9.	Jakarta, Indonesia	13,194,000
10.	Shanghai, China	12,665,000
11.	Dhaka, Bangladesh	12,560,000
12.	Los Angeles-Long Beach-Santa Ana, US	12,146,000
13.	Karachi, Pakistan	11,819,000
14.	Rio de Janeiro, Brazil	11,469,000
15.	Osaka-Kobe, Japan	11,286,000
16.	Cairo, Egypt	11,146,000
17.	Lagos, Nigeria	11,135,000
18.	Beijing, China	10,849,000
19.	Metro Manila, Philippines	10,677,000
20.	Moscow, Russia	10,672,000

World's Largest Subways Systems (by Ridership)

City	Date System Completed	Number of Riders (Year)	Length (Km)
Moscow	1935	3.2 bil (1997)	340
Tokyo	1927	2.6 bil (1997/98)	281+
Seoul	1974	1.4 bil (1993)	278+
Mexico City	1969	1.4 bil(1996)	202
New York City	1904	1.3 bil (2001)	371
Paris	1900	1.2 bil (1998)	211
Osaka	1933	957 mil (1997)	114
London	1863	866 mil (1999)	415
Hong Kong	1979	790 mil (1999)	82
St Petersburg	1955	721 mil (1996)	110

World's Twenty-five Busiest Airports by Passengers and Cargo (2004)

S. No.	Airport	Total Passengers
1.	Atlanta, Hartsfied (ATL)	83,578,906
2.	Chicago, O'Hare (ORD)	75,373,888
3.	London, Heathrow (LHR)	67,343,960
4.	Tokyo, Haneda (HND)	62,320,968
5.	Los Angeles (LAX)	60,710,830
6.	Dallas/Ft. Worth (DFW)	59,412,217
7.	Frankfurt-Main (FRA)	51,098,271
8.	Paris, Charles de Gaulle (CDG)	50,860,561
9.	Amsterdam, Schiphol (AMS)	42,541,180
10.	Denver (DEN)	42,393,693
11.	Las Vegas (LAS)	41,436,571
12.	Phoenix, Sky Harbor (PHX)	39,493,519
13.	Madrid (MAD)	38,525,899
14.	Bangkok (BKK)	37,960,169
15.	New York (JFK)	37,362,010
16.	Minneapolis/St. Paul (MSP)	36748,577
17.	Hong Kong (HKG)	36,713,000
18.	Houston (IAH)	36,490,828
19.	Detroit (DTW)	35,199,307
20.	Beijing (PEK)	34,883,190
21.	San Francisco (SFO)	33,497,084
22.	Newark (EWR)	31,847,280
23.	London, Gatwick (LGW)	31,461,523
24.	Orlando (MCO)	31,110,852
25.	Tokyo, Narita (NRT)	31,106,264

Tallest Buildings of the World

	Building	City	Height	Floors	Year
1.	Taipei 101	Taipei	509 m	101	2004
2.	Petronas Tower 1	Kuala Lumpur	452 m	88	1998
3.	Petronas Tower 2	Kuala Lumpur	452 m	88	1998
4.	Sears Tower	Chicago	442 m	108	1974
5.	Jin Mao Tower	Shanghai	421 m	88	1998
6.	Two International Finance Center	Hong Kong	415 m	88	2003
7.	CITIC Plaza	Guangzhou	391 m	80	1997
8.	Shun Hing Square	Shenzhen	384 m	69	1996
9.	Empire State Building	New York City	381 m	102	1931
10.	Central Plaza	Hong Kong	374 m	78	1992

Notable Civil Engineering Projects (in progress or completed as of December 2004)

Name	Location		Year of Completion	Notes
Airports		**terminal area (sq m)**		
Suvarnabhumi	Near Bangkok, Thailand	563,000	2006	To replace Don Muang
Barajas International Airport (new Terminal 4)	North-east of Madrid, Spain	470,000	2005	New terminal in leading airport for Europe–Latin America flights
Changi International (new Terminal 3)	Eastern Singapore	430,000	2006	New terminal in Asia's 4th largest airport
Toronto Pearson International (new Terminal 1)	Toronto, ON, Canada	340,000	2004	Opened 6 Apr 2004; new terminal at Canada's busiest airport
Baiyun ('White Cloud') International (replacement)	Near Guangzhou, China	305,000	2004	Opened 5 Aug 2004; main hub airport of south China (excluding Hong Kong)
Ben-Gurion International (new Terminal 3)	South-east of Tel Aviv, Israel	223,000	2004	Opened 2 Nov 2004; new international terminal at the Middle East's busiest airport
Central Japan International	Artificial island off Nagoya, Japan	220,000	2005	To be Japan's 3rd largest airport
Dallas/Fort Worth International (new Terminal D)	Irving, TX	195,000	2005	New international terminal
Heathrow (new Terminal 5)	South-west of London	70,000	2008	Biggest construction project in the UK from 2002

Bridges		length (main span; m)		
Hangzhou Bay	Near Jiaxing, China–near Cixi, China	2,600	2009	To be world's longest transoceanic bridge/causeway; begun 2003
I-95 (Woodrow Wilson #2)	Alexandria VA–Maryland suburbs of Washington DC	1,829 each	2005–08	2 Bascule spans forming higher inverted V shape for ships; begun 2000
Nancha (1 bridge of 2-section Runyang)	Zhenjiang, China (across the Yangtze)	1,490	2005	To be world's third longest suspension bridge
Sutong	Nantong, China (100 km from Yangtze mouth)	1,088	2008	To be world's longest cable-stayed bridge
Stonecutters	Tsing Yi-Sha Tin, Hong Kong, China	1,018	2008	To be world's 2nd longest cable-stayed bridge
Tacoma Narrows (#3)	The Narrows of Puget Sound, Tacoma WA	853	2008	Built over collapsed Tacoma Narrows #1; longest US suspension bridge since 1964
Rion–Antirion	Near Patrai, Greece (across Gulf of Corinth)	560	2004	Opened 8 Aug 2004; 2nd longest all-span cable-stayed (2,252 m)
(New) Cooper River	Charleston–Mt. Pleasant SC	471	2005	To be longest cable-stayed bridge in North America
Millau Viaduct	Tarn Gorge, west of Millau, France	342	2004	Opened 14 Dec 2004; world's highest (270 m) bridge; longest all-span cable-stayed (2,460 m) bridge
Shibanpe	Chongqing, China (across the Yangtze)	330	2005	To be world's longest pre-stressed-concrete box girder bridge

Name	Location		Year of Completion	Notes
Buildings		**height (m)**		
Burj ('Tower')	Dubai Dubai, United Arab Emirates	805	2008	To be the world's tallest building
Taipei 101 (Taipei Financial Centre)	Taipei, Taiwan	508	2003	Declared world's tallest building 15 Apr 2004; opened in stages from November 2003
Shanghai World Financial Centre	Shanghai, China	492	2007	Begun 1997, resumed 2003; to be the world's 2nd tallest building
Union Square Phase 7	Hong Kong	474	2007	Begun 2002; 16-building complex
Federation Tower A	Moscow, Russia	340	2007	To be tallest building in Europe
Eureka Tower	Melbourne, Australia	300	2005	To be the 2nd tallest residential building in the world
Dams and Hydrologic Projects		**crest length (m)**		
Three Gorges (3rd of 3 phases)	West of Yichang, China	1,983	2009	To create world's largest reservoir (620 km long) beginning 2003 and 1/9th of national total generated power
Sardar Sarovar (Narmada) Project	Narmada river, Madhya Pradesh, India	1,210	2007	Largest dam of controversial 30-dam project; drinking water for Gujarat
Bakun Dam	Balui river, Sarawak, Borneo, Malaysia	740	2007	Will bring hydroelectricity to peninsular Malaysia via world's longest submarine cable
Caruachi (3rd of 5-dam Lower Caroní Development scheme)	Caroní river, northern Bolívar, Venezuela	360	2003–06	Hydroelectric generation began 28 Feb 2003
Belo Monte	Xingù river, Pará, Brazil	?	2008	To be 3rd largest dam in the world in terms of electricity output

Tucuruí (upgrade)	Tocantins river, eastern Pará, Brazil		2005	Generating capacity to be doubled; 1st Brazilian Amazon dam (1984)
Project Moses (flood-protection plan)	Venice, Italy	—	2010	79 submerged gates in 3 lagoon openings will rise in flood conditions
Highways		**length (km)**		
Golden Quadrilateral superhighway	Mumbai–Chennai–Kolkata–Delhi, India	5,846	2005–07	Upgrade to 4 lanes; Mumbai–Delhi (2005), Delhi–Kolkata (2007)
Trans-Siberian highway (final stage)	Khabarovsk–Chita, Russia	2,165	2004	Opened 26 Feb 2004; last link in 10,000-km Moscow–Vladivostok highway
Highway 1	Kabul–Kandahar–Herat, Afghanistan	1,048	2005	Final, 566-km Kandahar–Herat section to open in September
Egnatia Motorway	Igoumenitsa–Kipi, Greece	680	2006	First Greek highway at inter-national standards; 76 tunnels, 1,650 bridges
Croatian Motorway	Zagreb–Split, Croatia	380	2005	Mountainous terrain with unstable slopes, caves, and unexploded ordnance
Land Reclamation		**area (sq km)**		
Palm Jumeirah and Palm Jebel Ali islands	In the Persian Gulf, near Dubai, UAE	20–40	2006–09	Date-palm-tree-shaped islands ('two 17 fronds + trunk' and one 41fronds + trunk); ultraexclusive
Railways (heavy)		**length (km)**		
Trans-Kazakhstan	Dostyq (Druzhba), Kazakhstan–Gorgan, Iran	3,943	2008	China to Europe link, bypassing Russia and Uzbekistan; 3,083 km in Kazakhstan
Qinghai–Tibet	China: Golmud, Qinghai–Lhasa, Tibet	1,142	2007	World's highest railway (5,072m at summit); 86% above 4,000 m

Name	Location		Year of Completion	Notes
Xi'an–Nanjing	China: Xi'an, Shaanxi–Nanjing, Jiangsu	1,129	2007	For economic growth in interior; 954-km Xi'an-Hefei section finished 2003
Ferronorte (extension to Rondonópolis)	Alto Araguaia–Rondonópolis, Brazil	270	2007	For agricultural exports from Mato Grosso (Brazil interior)
Bothnia Line (Botniabanan)	Nyland–Umeå, Sweden	190	2010	Along north Swedish coast; difficult terrain with 25 km of tunnels
Railways (high speed)		**length (km)**		
Spanish high speed (second line)	Madrid, Spain–France (via Barcelona)	719	2009	To reach Barcelona in 2007?; Madrid–Lleida corridor opened 11 Oct 2003
Korea Train Express (KTX)	Seoul–Pusan, South Korea	412	2008	Will connect largest and 2nd largest cities; to Taegu as of 1 Apr 2004
Taiwan high speed	Hsi-chih–Tso-ying,	345	2005	Links Taiwan's 2 largest cities Taiwan (Taipei and Kao-hsiung) along west coast
Eastern France high speed	Eastern outskirts of Paris–near Metz, France	300	2007	106-km extension to Strasbourg in planning stage
Italian high speed (second line)	Rome–Naples, Italy	205	2005	Entire Turin–Naples high-speed routes (844 km) to be completed 2009?
Channel Tunnel Rail Link	Near Folkestone, England–central London	109	2007	74-km section (Folkestone–north Kent) opened 16 Sep 2003
Subways/metros/light rails		**length (km)**		
Shanghai Metro	Shanghai, China	99.9	2005-06	Length of 4 lines under construction in late 2004
Barcelona Metro (Line 9)	Airport–northeast Barcelona, Spain	47	2008	Connects to other metro lines and future high-speed rail

Guangzhou (Canton) Metro (Line 3)	Guangzhou, China (north-south line)	36.1	2006	15-line system planned; 83 km in 4 lines under construction in 2004
Shenzhen Metro (phase 1; Lines 1 and 4)	Shenzhen, China (adjacent to Hong Kong)	21.8	2004	Phase 1 of both lines began operation 28 Dec 2004
Delhi Metro (Line 1)	Delhi, India	21.3	2004	Opened 31 Mar 2004; 30.2 km of lines 2 and 3 to in open 2005
Copenhagen Metro (last extension)	Copenhagen, Denmark	21	2007	Connects city centre to airport
Bangkok Blue Line	North-south line in central Bangkok, Thailand	20	2004	Opened to the public 3 Jul 2004; Thailand's first underground system
Hiawatha Light Rail	Downtown Minneapolis –Bloomington MN	19.3	2004	Opened 4 Dec 2004
Las Vegas Monorail	Las Vegas NV (east side of the Strip)	6.1	2004	Opened 14 Jul 2004, temp. closure 8 Sep–23 Dec 2004; 5-km extension by 2007?
Tunnels		**length (m)**		
Apennine Range tunnels (9)	Bologna–Florence, Italy (high-speed railway)	73,400	2008	Longest tunnel (Vaglia, 18.6 km); tunnels to cover 93% of railway
Lötschberg #2	Frutigen–Raron, Switzerland	34,577	2007	To be world's 3rd longest rail tunnel; France–Italy link
Guadarrama	50 km north-northwest of Madrid, Spain	28,377	2007	To be world's 4th longest rail tunnel; Valladolid high-speed link
Södra Länken ('Southern Link')	Part of Stockholm, Sweden, ring road	16,600	2004	Opened 24 Oct 2004; complex of underground interchanges
Hsüeh-shan ('Snow Mountain')	Near Taipei, Taiwan	12,900	2005	Breakthrough 16 Sep 2004; world's 4th longest road tunnel
East and West tunnels of A86 ring road	Western outskirts of Paris, France	10,000/ 7,500	2007	Two tunnels under Versailles and nearby protected woodlands

1 m=3.28 ft; 1 km=0.62 mi

India

Height of Some Important Indian Mountain Peaks

S.No.	Peak Height	From Sea Level in Metres
1.	K2	8,611 in Pak-occupied territory
2.	Kanchenjunga	8,598
3.	Nanga Parbat	8,126
4.	Gasher Brum	8,068 in Pak-occupied territory
5.	Broad Peak	8,047 in Pak-occupied territory
6.	Disteghil Sar	7,885 in Pak-occupied territory
7.	Masher Brum East	7,821
8.	Nanda Devi	7,817
9.	Masher Brum West	7,806 in Pak-occupied territory
10.	Rakaposhi	7,788 in Pak-occupied territory
11.	Kamet	7,756
12.	Saser Kangri	7,672
13.	Skyang Kangri	7,544 in Pak-occupied territory
14.	Sia Kangri	7,422 in Pak-occupied territory
15.	Chaukhamba (Badrinath)	7,138
16.	Trisul West	7,138
17.	Nunkun	7,135
18.	Pauhunri	7,128
19.	Kangto	7,090
20.	Dunagiri	7,066

The Main Rivers of India

Name	Length (km)	Originates from	Flows into	Passes through
Ganga	2,507	Gaumukh	Bay of Bengal	Uttar Pradesh, Bihar and West Bengal
Yamuna	1,370	Yamunotri	Ganga	Delhi, Haryana and Uttar Pradesh
Brahmaputra	2,850	Chemayung-Dung glacier	Bay of Bengal	North Eastern states of India
Kaveri	765	Hills of Coorg, Karnataka	Bay of Bengal	Karnataka and Tamil Nadu
Godavari	1,465	Trimbakeshwar near Nasik Hills in Maharashtra	Bay of Bengal	South-easterly direction, through Maharashtra and Andhra Pradesh
Krishna	900	Near Mahabaleshwar in Maharashtra	Bay of Bengal	Maharashtra, Karnataka and Andhra Pradesh
Narmada	1,300	Amarkantak hill in Madhya Pradesh	Arabian Sea	Madhya Pradesh, Maharashtra and Gujarat
Tapti	724	Pachmarhi, Madhya Pradesh	Arabian Sea	Madhya Pradesh and Gujarat

Gomti	805	Himalaya range of Nepal	Ganga	Uttar Pradesh
Mahanadi	860	Satpura range	Bay of Bengal	Chhattisgarh, Jharkhand and Orissa

India's Dams

Major Pre-Independence Dams

Projects	Year
Tajewala Barrage	1873
Grand Anicut	1889
Bhandardara Dam	1926
Mettur Dam	1934

Major Post-Independence Dams

Projects	Year
Hirakud	1957
Tungabhadra	1958
Matatila	1958
Kota Barrage	1960
Gandhi Sagar	1960
Bhakra	1963
Jawahar Sagar	1973
Farakka Barrage	1974
Nagarjuna Sagar	1974
Paithan	1976
Dehar Power House	1977
Ghataprabha	1979
Mahi Bajaj Sagar	1985
Salal Projects	1987
Chamera	1994

Major Indian Ports

Along India's 5,560-km coastline there are twelve major ports and 184 minor/ intermediate ports. The ports at Kolkata, Mumbai, Chennai and Mormugao are more than 100 years old, while Kochi and Visakhapatnam ports are over sixty years old. The ports at Kandla, New Mangalore, Tuticorin, Paradip and Haldia were developed after Independence and the Jawaharlal Nehru Port Trust at Mumbai was commissioned in 1989. Major ports handle about 75 per cent of the country's port traffic.

Ports

1. Kolkata Port Trust, 15, Strand Road, Kolkata
2. Haldia Dock Complex, Jawahar Tower, Haldia Township, Haldia, Midnapore
3. Paradip Port Trust, P.O. Paradip Port,Distt. Jagatsingpur, Orissa
4. Visakhapatnam Port Trust, Visakhapatnam
5. Chennai Port Trust, Rajaji Salai, Chennai
6. Tuticorin Port Trust, Barathi Nagar, Tuticorin
7. Cochin Port Trust, Willingdon Island, Cochin
8. New Mangalore Port Trust, Panambur, Mangalore, D.K. District, Karnataka
9. Mormugao Port Trust, Headland, Sada, Goa
10. Mumbai Port Trust, Shoorji Vallabhdas Marg, Mumbai
11. Jawaharlal Nehru Port Trust, Sheva, Tal. Uran, New Mumbai
12. Kandla Port Trust, Post Box No. 50, Gandhidham (Kutch)
13. Ennore Port Limited, New No. 15 (Old 8), Kasturirangan Road, Alwarpet, Chennai

Indian Railways

The first railway train in India ran between Bombay (now Mumbai) and Thane on 16 April 1853, carrying 400 people in fourteen carriages. Presently, India has the largest railway system in Asia and the second largest in the world under a single management. It is also the fourth largest on the basis of route kilometrage. In India, 13,000 trains run every day on 63,000 route kilometres of track. 1.3 crore passengers travel daily and about 14 lakh metric tonnes of goods are transported all over the country.

Indian Railways–Facts at a Glance

Track Kilometres

Gauge	Route (km)	Running Track (km)	Total Track (km)
Broad Gauge (1,676 mm)	41,971	59,070	81,121
Metre Gauge (1,000 mm)	17,044	17,974	22,201
Narrow Gauge (762 mm/ 610 mm)	3,710	3,710	4,038
Total	**62,725**	**80,754**	**107,360**

1.	Route Length (km)	62,725
2.	Electrified Track (km)	13.018
3.	Stations	6,984
4.	Locomotives	
	Steam	85
	Diesel	4,363
	Electric	2,519
5.	Passenger Carriages	39,257
6.	Freight Cars	272,127
7.	Traffic Volume (Annual)	
	Passenger (million)	4,368
	Freight (million tonne)	429.3
8.	Employees	15,84,000

Indian Railways' Zones and Their Divisions with Heaquarters

S.No.	Name of the Zone	Headquarter	Divisions
1.	Central Railway	Mumbai	Bhusawal, Nagpur, Mumbai (CST)*, Solapur*, Pune ^
2.	Eastern Railway	Kolkata	Malda, Howarh, Sealdah, Asansol
3.	Northern Railway	New Delhi	Ambala, Ferozepur, Lucknow, Moradabad, Delhi
4.	North Eastern Railway	Gorakhpur	Lucknow, Varanasi, Izatnagar*
5.	Northeast Frontier Railway	Guwahati	Katihar, Lumding, Tinsukhia, Alipurduar*, Rangiya ^
6.	Southern Railway	Chennai	Chennai, Madurai, Palghat, Trichy, Trivandrum
7.	South Central Railway	Secunderabad	Secunderabad*, Hyderabad*, Guntakal*, Vijaywada*, Guntur ^, Nanded ^
8.	South Eastern Railway	Kolkata	Kharagpur, Chakradharpur*, Adra*, Ranchi ^
9.	Western Railway	Mumbai	Bhavnagar, Mumbai Central, Ratlam*, Rajkot*, Vadodara*, Ahmedabad ^
10.	East Central Railway	Hajipur**	Danapur, Dhanbad, Sonepur, Mughalsarai, Samastipur

11.	East Coast Railway	Bhubaneswar ^	Khurda Road, Waltair, Sambalpur
12.	North Central Railway	Allahabad ^	Allahabad*, Jhansi*, Agra ^
13.	North Western Railway	Jaipur**	Bikaner*, Jodhpur, Jaipur*, Ajmer*
14.	South East Central Railway	Bilaspur ^	Nagpur, Bilaspur*, Raipur ^
15.	South Western Railway	Hubli ^	Bangalore, Mysore, Hubli*
16.	West Central Railway	Jabalpur ^	Jabalpur, Bhopal, Kota*

*: Reorganized Divisions w.e.f 1.4.2003
**: New Zones operationalized on 1.10.2002
^: New Zones/Divisions operationalized on 1.4.2003

Road Network in India

With a total length of approximately 3.3 million kilometres, India has the second largest road network in the world. Roads have played a vital role in transportation and also enhancing trade. The government has taken initiatives to improve and strengthen the network of national highways, state highways and roads in major districts and rural areas.

Indian Road Network	Length (in km)
National Highways	58,112*
State Highways	137,119
Major District Roads	470,000
Village and Other Roads	2,650,000
Total Length	3,315,231

*National Highways are less than 2% of network but carry 40% of total traffic

Airlines Operating in India

List of Scheduled Indian Domestic/ International Airlines:

1. Air-India
2. Air Deccan
3. Air Sahara
4. Go Air
5. Indian
6. Indigo Airlines
7. Jagson Airlines
8. Jet Airways
9. Kingfisher Airlines
10. Paramount Airlines
11. SpiceJet Airlines

Subscriber Trunk Dialing Services

The Subscriber Trunk Dialing (STD) service started in India in 1960. It is presently available in more than 19,500 stations across the country, in all the district headquarters and in more than 97 per cent of the sub-divisional headquarters. In 1976, the International Subscriber Dialing Services or ISD was started between Mumbai and London, and is now available throughout India to almost every other country in the world.

STD Codes

Abohar	01634
Agartala	0381
Agra	0562
Ahmedabad	079
Ahmednagar	0241
Aizawl	03832
Ajmer	0145
Akola	0724
Alappuza	0477
Aligarh	0571
Allahabad	0532
Alwar	01442
Alwaye	04854
Ambala	0171
Amritsar	0183
Anand (V.V. Nagar)	02692
Asansol	0341
Aurangabad	02432
Bangalore	080

Bareilly	0581
Baroda	0265
Belgaum	0831
Bellary	08392
Bharatpur	05644
Bhatinda	0164
Bhavnagar	0278
Bhiwani	01664
Bhillai	0788
Bhopal	0755
Bhubaneshwar	0674
Bhuj	02832
Bikaner	0151
Bilaspur	07752
Bokaro	06542
Bongaigaon	03664
Burdwan	0342
Burnpur	03448
Chandigarh	0172
Chennai	044
Chikamagalur	08262
Chinglepet	04114
Chittor	08572
Coimbatore	0422
Coochbehar	03582
Coonoor	04264
Cudappah	08562
Cuttack	0671
Darbhanga	06272
Darjeeling	0354
Davangiri	08192
Dehra Dun	0135
Delhi	011
Dhanbad	0326
Dharwar	0836
Dibrugarh	0373
Dimapur	03862
Dindigul	0451
Dispur	0361
Durgapur	0343
Dwarka	02892
Ernakulam	0484
Erode	0424
Etah	05742
Faizabad	0527
Ferozepur	01632
Gandhinagar	02712
Gangtok	03592
Gaya	0631
Godhra	02672
Gorakhpur	0551
Guntur	0863

Gurgaon	0124
Guwahati	0361
Gwalior	0751
Haldia	03224
Hapur	0122
Hardwar	0133
Hissar	01662
Hubli	0836
Hyderabad	040
Imphal	03852
Indore	0731
Itanagar	03781
Jabalpur	0761
Jaipur	0141
Jaisalmer	02992
Jalandhar	0181
Jalgaon	0257
Jalpaiguri	03561
Jammu	0191
Jamnagar	0288
Jamshedpur	0657
Jhansi	0517
Jodhpur	0291
Jorhat	0376
Junagadh	0285
Kakinada	0884
Kalimpong	03552
Kalol	02764
Kalpakkam	04117
Kanchipuram	04112
Kannur	03222
Kanpur	0512
Kanyakumari	04653
Karimnagar	08722
Karnal	0184
Kavarathy	04866
Kharagpur	0495
Kochi	0484
Kozhikode	0497
Kodaikanal	04542
Kohima	03866
Kolar	08152
Kollam	0474
Kolhapur	0231
Kolkata	033
Kota	0744
Kottayam	0481
Kurnool	08518
Lucknow	0522
Ludhiana	0161
Machilipatnam	08672
Madikeri	08272

Madurai	0452
Mahabalipuram	04113
Malda	03512
Mangalore	0824
Mathura	0565
Meerut	0121
Minicoy Islands	048672
Modi Nagar	01232
Moradabad	0591
Mumbai	022
Mussoorie	0135632
Muzaffarnagar	0131
Muzaffarpur	0621
Mysore	0821
Nagpur	0712
Nainital	05942
Nasik	0253
Nellore	0861
Neyveli	04148
Ooty	0423
Palakkad	0491
Panipat	01742
Panjim	0832
Pathankot	0186
Patiala	0175
Patna	0612
Pilibhit	05882
Pondicherry	0413
Porbandar	0286
Port Blair	03192
Pune	020
Puri	06752
Raibareilly	0535
Raipur	0771
Rajahmundry	0883
Rajapalayam	04563
Rajkot	0281
Ranchi	0651
Rewari	01274
Rohtak	01262
Roorkee	01332
Rourkela	0661
Sagar	07582
Saharanpur	0132
Salem	0427
Samastipur	06274
Sangrur	01672
Shillong	0364
Shimla	0177
Silchar	03842
Siliguri	0353
Sirsa	01666
Sivakasi	04560
Solapur	0217
Sonepat	01264
Srinagar	0194
Surat	0261
Thanjavur	04362
Thiruvananthapuram	0471
Tinsukia	0374
Tiruchirapalli	0431
Tirunelveli	0462
Tirupati	08574
Trissur	0487
Tumkur	08167
Tuticorin	0461
Udaipur	0294
Udipi	08252
Ujjain	0734
Unnao	0515
Varanasi	0542
Vellore	0416
Vijayawada	0866
Vishakhapatnam	0891
Warangal	08712
Wardha	07152
Yamunanagar	01732

PIN Codes

The Postal Index Number Code system was introduced in India by the Postal Department on 15 August 1972. Under the scheme, every post office (head or sub) that delivered mails was allotted an individual six-digit Postal Index Number (PIN) code number. PIN Code digits from left to right progressively pinpoint and locate the geographical position of the Post Office and have a definite role.

The first two digits of the PIN indicate as below:

First Two Digits of PIN	Circle
11	Delhi
12 and 13	Haryana
14 to 16	Punjab
17	Himachal Pradesh
18 to 19	Jammu and Kashmir
20 to 28	Uttar Pradesh
30 to 34	Rajasthan

36 to 39	Gujarat
40 to 44	Maharastra
45 to 49	Madhya Pradesh
50 to 53	Andhra Pradesh
56 to 59	Karnataka
60 to 64	Tamil Nadu
67 to 69	Kerala
70 to 74	West Bengal
75 to 77	Orissa
78	Assam
79	North-Eastern
80 to 85	Bihar

Weights and Measures

The name International System of Units (SI) was adopted at the Eleventh General Conference on Weights and Measures. Following an international inquiry by the Bureau of Weights and Measures, which began in 1948, the Tenth General Conference on Weights and Measures (1954) approved the introduction of the 'ampere', the 'kelvin' and the 'candela' as base units for electric current, thermodynamic temperature and luminous intensity respectively. At the Fourteenth General Conference on Weights and Measures in 1971 the current version of the SI was completed by adding 'mole' as base unit for amount of substance, bringing the total number of base units to seven.

Quantity	Unit	Symbol	Definition
Length	Meter	m	The metre is the length of the path traveled by light in vacuum during a time interval of 1/299,792,458 of a second
Mass	Kilogram	kg	The kilogram is the unit of mass; it is equal to the mass of the international prototype of the kilogram
Time	Second	s	The second is the duration of 9,192,631,770 periods of the radiation corresponding to the transition between the two hyperfine levels of the ground state of the caesium 133 atom
Electric Current	Ampere	A	The ampere is that constant current which, if maintained in two straight parallel conductors of infinite length, of negligible circular cross-section, and placed 1 m apart in vacuum, would produce between these conductors a force equal to 2×10^{-7} newton per metre of length
Thermodynamic temperature	Kelvin	K	The kelvin, unit of thermodynamic temperature, is the fraction 1/273.16 of the thermodynamic temperature of the triple point of water

Amount of substance	Mole	mol	The mole is the amount of substance of a system which contains as many elementary entities as there are atoms in 0.012 kilogram of carbon 12
Luminous intensity	Candela	cd	The candela is the luminous intensity, in a given direction, of a source that emits monochromatic radiation of frequency 540 x 10^{12} hertz and that has a radiant intensity in that direction of 1/683 watt per steradian

Derived units

Derived units are units that may be expressed in terms of base units by means of the mathematical symbols of multiplication and division. Certain derived units have been given special names and symbols, and these special names and symbols may themselves be used in combination with those for base and other derived units to express the units of other quantities.

SI Derived Units Expressed in Terms of Base Units

Derived quantity	SI derived unit Name	Symbol
Area	square metre	m^2
Volume	cubic metre	m^3
Speed, Velocity	metre per second	m/s
Acceleration	metre per second squared	m/s^2
Wavenumber	reciprocal metre	m^{-1}
Density, Mass density	kilogram per cubic metre	kg/m^3
Specific volume	cubic metre per kilogram	m^3/kg
Current density	ampere per square metre	A/m^2
Magnetic field strength	ampere per metre	A/m
Concentration (of amount of substance)	mole per cubic metre	mol/m^3
Luminance	candela per square metre	cd/m^2
Refractive index	(the number) one	1[(a)]

SI Derived Units with Special Names and Symbols

Derived quantity	SI derived unit Name	Symbol	Expressed in terms of other SI units	Expressed in terms of SI base units
Plane angle	radian[(a)]	rad	-	$m \cdot m^{-1} = 1$[(b)]
Solid angle	steradian[(a)]	sr[(c)]	-	$m^2 \cdot m^{-2} = 1$[(b)]
Frequency	hertz	Hz	-	s^{-1}
Force	newton	N	-	$m \cdot kg \cdot s^{-2}$
Pressure, Stress	pascal	Pa	N/m^2	$m^{-1} \cdot kg \cdot s^{-2}$

Energy, Work, Quantity of heat	joule	J	N · m	$m^2 \cdot kg \cdot s^{-2}$
Power, Radiant flux	watt	W	J/s	$m^2 \cdot kg \cdot s^{-3}$
Electric charge, Quantity of electricity	coulomb	C	-	s · A
Electric potential difference, Electromotive force	volt	V	W/A	$m^2 \cdot kg \cdot s^{-3} \cdot A^{-1}$
Capacitance	farad	F	C/V	$m^{-2} \cdot kg^{-1} \cdot s^4 \cdot A^2$
Electric resistance	ohm	Ω	V/A	$m^2 \cdot kg \cdot s^{-3} \cdot A^{-2}$
Electric conductance	siemens	S	A/V	$m^{-2} \cdot kg^{-1} \cdot s^3 \cdot A^2$
Magnetic flux	weber	Wb	V · s	$m^2 \cdot kg \cdot s^{-2} \cdot A^{-1}$
Magnetic flux density	tesla	T	Wb/m²	$kg \cdot s^{-2} \cdot A^{-1}$
Inductance	henry	H	Wb/A	$m^2 \cdot kg \cdot s^{-2} \cdot A^{-2}$
Celsius temperature	degree Celsius[(d)]	°C	-	K
Luminous flux	lumen	lm	cd · sr[(c)]	$m^2 \cdot m^{-2} \cdot cd = cd$
Illuminance	lux	lx	lm/m²	$m^2 \cdot m^{-4} \cdot cd = m^{-2} \cdot cd$
Activity (referred to a radionuclide)	becquerel	Bq	-	s^{-1}
Absorbed dose, specific energy (imparted), kerma	gray	Gy	J/kg	$m^2 \cdot s^{-2}$
Dose equivalent, ambient dose equivalent, directional dose equivalent, personal dose equivalent, organ equivalent dose	sievert	Sv	J/kg	$m^2 \cdot s^{-2}$
Catalytic activity	katal	kat	-	$s^{-1} \cdot mol$

[(a)] The radian and steradian may be used with advantage in expressions for derived units to distinguish between quantities of different nature but the same dimension.

[(b)] In practice, the symbols rad and sr are used where appropriate, but the derived unit '1' is generally omitted in combination with a numerical value.

[(c)] In photometry, the name steradian and the symbol sr are usually retained in expressions for units.

[(d)] This unit may be used in combination with SI prefixes, e.g. millidegree Celsius, m°C.

SI Derived Units Whose Names and Symbols Include SI Derived Units with Special Names and Symbols

Derived quantity	SI derived unit Name	Symbol	Expressed in terms of SI base units
Dynamic viscosity	pascal second	Pa · s	$m^{-1} \cdot kg \cdot s^{-1}$
Moment of force	newton metre	N · m	$m^2 \cdot kg \cdot s^{-2}$
Surface tension	newton per metre	N/m	$kg \cdot s^{-2}$

Angular velocity	radian per second	rad/s	$m \cdot m^{-1} \cdot s^{-1} = s^{-1}$
Angular acceleration	radian per second squared	rad/s^2	$m \cdot m^{-1} \cdot s^{-2} = s^{-2}$
Heat flux density, Irradiance	watt per square metre	W/m^2	$kg \cdot s^{-3}$
Heat capacity, Entropy	joule per kelvin	J/K	$m^2 \cdot kg \cdot s^{-2} \cdot K^{-1}$
Specific heat capacity, Specific entropy	joule per kilogram kelvin	J/(kg·K)	$m^2 \cdot s^{-2} \cdot K^{-1}$
Specific energy	joule per kilogram	J/kg	$m^2 \cdot s^{-2}$
Thermal conductivity	watt per metre kelvin	W/(m·K)	$m \cdot kg \cdot s^{-3} \cdot K^{-1}$
Energy density	joule per cubic metre	J/m^3	$m^{-1} \cdot kg \cdot s^{-2}$
Electric field strength	volt per metre	V/m	$m \cdot kg \cdot s^{-3} \cdot A^{-1}$
Electric charge density	coulomb per cubic metre	C/m^3	$m^{-3} \cdot s \cdot A$
Electric flux density	coulomb per square metre	C/m^2	$m^{-2} \cdot s \cdot A$
Permittivity	farad per metre	F/m	$m^{-3} \cdot kg^{-1} \cdot s^4 \cdot A^2$
Permeability	henry per metre	H/m	$m \cdot kg \cdot s^{-2} \cdot A^{-2}$
Molar energy	joule per mole	J/mol	$m^2 \cdot kg \cdot s^{-2} \cdot mol^{-1}$
Molar entropy, molar heat capacity	joule per mole kelvin	J/(mol · K)	$m^2 \cdot kg \cdot s^{-2} \cdot K^{-1} \cdot mol^{-1}$
Exposure (x and y rays)	coulomb per kilogram	C/kg	$kg^{-1} \cdot s \cdot A$
Absorbed dose rate	gray per second	Gy/s	$m^2 \cdot s^{-3}$
Radiant intensity	watt per steradian	W/sr	$m^4 \cdot m^{-2} \cdot kg \cdot s^{-3} = m^2 \cdot kg \cdot s^{-3}$
Radiance	watt per square metre steradian	$W/(m^2 \cdot sr)$	$m^2 \cdot m^{-2} \cdot kg \cdot s^{-3} = kg \cdot s^{-3}$
Catalytic (activity) concentration	katal per cubic metre	kat/m^3	$m^{-3} \cdot s^{-1} \cdot mol$

General Knowledge Quiz

Decades: 1947–1956

1. Where in Delhi was the National Museum founded in 1949?
2. In which year was the Supreme Court of India inaugurated?
3. Who was appointed India's first chief election commissioner in 1950?
4. Whose autobiography *Autobiography of an Unknown Indian* was published in 1951?
5. In 1955, which company became the first company to market liquid petroleum gas for home use in India?
6. Which bank was nationalized and named State Bank of India in 1955?
7. 15 August 1948, the first anniversary of India's Independence, was commemorated by issuing postage stamps in four denominations, viz., 1½ as., 3½ as., 12as and Rs 10 depicting whom?
8. In 1952, under the conductorship of which musician did All India Radio set up the national orchestra?
9. In which year were independent India's first general elections based on adult franchise contested by seventy-four parties?
10. In 1952, in which city was the first International Film Festival of India held?

Decades: 1957–1966

1. In 1965, which port was inaugurated as a free trade zone?
2. In 1965, who was awarded the first Jnanpith Award for his collection of poems entitled *Odakkuzhal*?
3. Who was crowned Miss World on 18 November 1966?
4. In 1962, in which city of India was the second largest planetarium of the world built?
5. In 1961, India's first financial daily was launched. What is the name of the newspaper?
6. In 1960, which state was divided into Gujarat and Maharashtra?
7. In which year was the metric system of weights introduced?
8. In 1958, in which city was the Institute of Tibetology inaugurated?
9. Which film of Satyajit Ray received the National Award for best feature film of 1964?
10. In which year was the second census of independent India conducted?

Decades: 1967–1976

1. In 1972, the tiger replaced which animal as the national animal?
2. In 1976, who became the first woman to be awarded the Jnanpith for her novel *Pratham Pratisruti*?
3. What is the name of the first Indian-made sounding rocket launched into space on 20 November 1967?
4. Who shared, with Marshall Nirenberg and Robert Holley, the Nobel Prize for Medicine and Physiology in 1968 for interpreting the genetic code?
5. In 1969, who became the first recipient of the Dada Saheb Phalke Award for contribution to Indian cinema?
6. In 1970, which state became the first state to achieve electrification of all its villages?
7. In 1972, who launched the Self-Employed Women's Association (SEWA) in Gujarat?
8. Which noted Carnatic singer, received the 1974 Ramon Magsaysay Award for public service?
9. In 1979, which disease was eradicated from India?
10. In 1976, which two words were added to the Preamble of the In-

dian Constitution by the Forty-second Amendment?

Decades: 1977–1986

1. Which party gained absolute majority in Lok Sabha in 1977?
2. In 1977, which external affairs minister addressed for the first time the United Nations General Assembly in Hindi?
3. Which para-military force was set up in 1978 to guard India's territorial waters?
4. Who was awarded the Nobel Peace Prize in 1979?
5. In 1981, which work of Salman Rushdie won the Booker Prize?
6. In 1982, with which company did Maruti Udyog sign an agreement for the manufacture of small cars?
7. In 1983, for costume design in which film did Bhanu Athaiya win an Oscar?
8. In 1984, which cartoonist got the Ramon Magsaysay Award for journalism, literature and creative communication arts?
9. Which multi-sport event did India boycott in protest against British policy on South Africa in 1986?
10. In 1982, who was elected the seventh President of India?

Decades: 1987–1996

1. To rescue the President of which country from an attempted coup was Operation Cactus launched in 1988 by the Indian Air Force ?
2. Which work of Salman Rushdie was banned in India in 1988?
3. In 1989, who became the first woman judge of the Supreme Court of India?
4. In 1987, who became the first non-Indian to receive the Bharat Ratna award?
5. In 1991, which channel became the first satellite channel to be available in India?
6. In 1993, which state became the first state to set up a Women's commission?
7. In 1994, who won the Grammy Award, in the world music category?
8. In 1992 on which industrialist was the Bharat Ratna conferred?
9. Which train, capable of a speed of upto 140 kilometres an hour, was introduced in 1989?
10. In 1993, which Indian did UN Secretary-General Boutros Boutros-Ghali nominate as prosecutor of International War Crimes Court for former Yugoslavia?

States and Union Territories

1. In India, which was the first state to institute a Human Rights Commission of its own?
2. In which state at the Eaglenest Wildlife Sanctuary was the Bugun Liocichla, scientifically known as *Liocichla bugunorum*, a kind of babbler, discovered in May 2006?
3. Which union territory became part of India on 16 August 1962?
4. Which high court has largest jurisdiction in terms of states?
5. Which state was the first Indian state to ban plastic?
6. After Kerala, which north-eastern state has the second highest literacy of 88.49 per cent?
7. In terms of the number of electorate, which is the smallest Lok Sabha constituency in India?
8. Which state has the highest number of airports?
9. Which Union territory's principal language is Bengali?
10. In 1982, in which state assembly polls were the Electronic Voting Machines (EVMs) first used?
11. In post-Independent India, which became the first state to be organized on a linguistic basis on 1 October 1953?

12. On 2 October 1959, at Nagaur in which state was the first panchayat samiti inaugurated by Jawaharlal Nehru?
13. Which state is ranked first in hydro-electricity generation with a national market share of over 11 per cent?
14. Which state with 76,429 square km of forest cover has the maximum forest cover amongst all states and Union territories?
15. In which state was Indian Navy's first helicopter squadron commissioned in 1969?
16. Which airport at a height of 3,256 m is the highest non-military airport?
17. In 1995, who became the second woman chief minister of Uttar Pradesh?
18. According to the 2001 census, which state has the largest population?
19. The Assembly of which state has a six-year tenure?
20. In which state is the Keibul Lamjao National Park, the only floating park in the world, located?
21. Which was an independent state ruled by the Chogyal monarchy until 1975?
22. According to the 2001 census, which state has the lowest population density?
23. Which was the first state to set up Greenfield operational special economic zone (SEZ) in India?
24. Who was sworn in as the first chief minister of Chhattisgarh in November in 2003?
25. Who has been the chief minister of Chhattisgarh since 8 December 2003?
26. Which is the only state to have more teachers working than the sanctioned posts?
27. Following the loss of two assembly seats in by-elections, Keshubhai Patel resigned and handed over power to whom in 2001, in Gujarat?
28. Which present state capital remained the capital of Assam till January 1972?
29. Which actress turned politician has been the chief minister of Tamil Nadu thrice?
30. Which is the only Indian state to have its own constitution?
31. In which city was the National Sports Museum established in 1972?
32. After the Partition of India in 1947, the Punjab Education Department functioned from a camp office set up in the Metropole Hotel of which city?
33. Which Union territory was liberated in 1954 from Portuguese rule?
34. Which state has recorded the highest increase in the literacy rate among the states/Union territories of India?
35. On 2 August 1954, Vishwanath Lawande became the administrator of which union territory?
36. In 1969, which former chief minister of Jharkhand founded the Sonat Santahl Samaj?
37. On 18 November 2006, who was sworn in as the chief minister of Jharkhand?
38. The chief minister of which union territory is Thiru. N. Rangasamy?
39. In 2005, the Government of India made which state the permanent venue for International Film Festival of India (IFFI)?
40. Currently, apart from West Bengal and Kerala, in which other state does the CPI(M)-led Left Front run the government?
41. What is the official language of Tripura?
42. In which country was a five-point cease-fire agreement signed between the Government of India

and the National Socialist Council of Nagaland (Isaak-Muivah) on 14 June 2001?

43. Which state was created as an autonomous state within the state of Assam on 2 April 1970?
44. Which princely state was merged in the Indian Union on 15 October 1949?
45. Which mountainous region became the twenty-third state of the Indian Union in February 1987?
46. On 10 September 1967, the Nagaland government chose which language as the medium of instruction?
47. Which former chief minister of an Indian state was honoured by the Indonesia government as 'Bhumiputra'?
48. In the 1970s, which non-ferrous mineral deposit, estimated at 1.05 crore tonnes were discovered in Koraput, Kalahandi and Sambalpur districts of Orissa?
49. In 2003, the state legislative assembly of Himachal Pradesh was won by which political party?
50. With which present state of India were Kangra and most of the other hill areas of Punjab merged on 1 November 1966?
51. In which state was the first Cyber Crime Police Station set up on 30 August 2001?
52. Which is the largest coffee-producing state and accounts for about 56 per cent of India's total coffee output?
53. In 2006, the National Forest Survey has rated which city as the greenest city in India with a green cover of 35.7 per cent?
54. Which Tamil film actor was the chief minister of Tamil Nadu from 1977 until his death on 24 December 1987?
55. Which union territory was administered jointly with Goa from 1962 to 1987?
56. Till 1961, Daman and Diu was the colony of which European country?
57. Which former chief minister of Haryana is the son of Chaudhari Devi Lal, a former deputy prime minister of India?
58. According to 2001 census, the sex ratio in which state is 861 men for 1,000 women, the lowest among the states in India?
59. In which Indian state were eight new districts, three sub-divisions and fourteen tehsils created in July 2006?
60. In Andaman and Nicobar Islands on 12 November 1982, the post of chief commissioner was elevated to the rank of what?
61. In 2002, which Indian state was declared the world's first 'baby-friendly state' by the World Health Organization and the United Nations International Children's Fund?
62. Which famous garden in Chandigarh was first opened to the public in 1976?
63. In 2000, how many administrative districts of Bihar were separated to form the state of Jharkhand?
64. Which political party, led by Ram Vilas Paswan, was formed in the year 2000?
65. Which state ranks first nationwide in coal-based thermal electricity as well as nuclear electricity generation with national market shares of over 13 per cent and 17 per cent respectively?
66. On 2 July 2004, what was nominated as a World Heritage Site by the World Heritage Committee of UNESCO?
67. In 2000, in which state did the Bharatiya Janata Party come to power under the leadership of Nityanand Swamy?
68. Which city serves as the provisional capital of Uttaranchal since its founding in 2000?

69. Which high court had jurisdiction over the state of Himachal Pradesh till 1971?
70. Which high court has jurisdiction over the state of Goa?

Neighbouring Countries

1. Which neighbouring country of India gained independence on 4 February 1948?
2. Which flower was declared the national flower of Sri Lanka on 26 February 1986?
3. Who was elected Prime Minister of Bangladesh for the third time in October 2001?
4. On 7 December 2004, who became Afghanistan's first popularly elected President?
5. In which neighbouring country of India are 17 per cent seats reserved for women in Senate, National Assembly and Provincial Assemblies?
6. On 10 January 1966, Lal Bahadur Shastri and which President of Pakistan signed the Tashkent Accord for peaceful settlement of relations between India and Pakistan after the 1965 war?
7. On 16 October 1964, which country conducted its first nuclear explosion in Lop Nor?
8. Which Asian country was the last nation in the world to introduce television in 1999?
9. What is the name of the unit of currency adopted by Bhutan in 1974?
10. The mechanization of the traditional fishing boat called Dhoni in 1974 was a major milestone in the development of the fisheries industry of which country?
11. According to the 2001 census, in which country do Hindus constitute 80.6 per cent of the population?
12. In November 2001, which country joined the World Trade Organization, ending a decades-long struggle to gain free access to international markets?
13. In 1991, who was awarded the Nobel Peace Prize for her peaceful non-violent struggle for democracy and human rights?
14. From 1961 to 1971, which Asian diplomat was the Secretary-General of the United Nations?
15. Which Asian country's official English name was changed in 1989?
16. In which country was the Fifth SAARC Conference on Cooperation in Police Matters held on 9 May 2006?
17. In which country did the Grand Assembly adopt a new Constitution to provide for a strong presidency in January 2004?
18. In January 1954, the Constituent Assembly of Pakistan declared Urdu and which other language as official languages of Pakistan?
19. In 1996, which novel by Michael Ondaatje was made into a film with the same title by director Anthony Minghella?
20. Who was elected Sri Lanka's first female president in 1994?
21. Which political party was established to campaign for East Pakistan's autonomy from West Pakistan in 1949?
22. In Pakistan, in the first general elections, which party secured an absolute majority in the National Assembly?
23. Which Pakistani scientist received the Nobel Prize in Physics in 1979?
24. In 1997, in which country was a parliamentary act was passed to reserve three seats (out of twelve) in every union for female candidates?
25. Formed in the early 1970s by Vellupillai Prabhakaran, which guerrilla organization seeks to establish an independent Tamil

state, Eelam, in northern and eastern Sri Lanka?

26. In 1994, India and which neighbouring country of India signed agreements restoring banking relations severed in 1964?
27. On 9 October 2004, which neighbouring country of India held its first national democratic presidential election?
28. Which country has had the largest refugee repatriation in the world in the last thirty years?
29. Rahyithunge' Majlis is the main legislative body of which country?
30. Dong Fang Hóng I was the first successful space satellite of which country?
31. Who became Nepal's first elected premier in 1991 and began his fourth and most recent term in 2000?
32. In 1953, who along with Edmund Hillary became the first climber to reach the summit of Mount Everest?
33. In 1991, which party won the first democratic elections in Nepal?
34. In August 2005, which neighbouring country of India tested its first nuclear-capable cruise missile?
35. Which religion was given primary place as Sri Lanka's religion in 1972?
36. Which neighbouring country, a co-founder of the Non-Aligned Movement (NAM), withdrew from NAM in 1979?
37. In which year was the Maldivian unit of currency 'rufiyaa' introduced?
38. In 2000, who became the first Chinese-born author to win the Nobel prize for Literature?
39. Which former British colony was transferred to the People's Republic of China at midnight on 1 July 1997?
40. Who became the first Chinese to win the Best Director Award at Cannes film Festival in 1997?
41. Which country, sharing its border with India, has been a member of Mekong Ganga Cooperation (MGC) since its inception in November 2000?
42. The Constitution of which neighbouring country of India was written in 1972 and has undergone thirteen amendments?
43. If you were visiting the Royal Chitwan National Park, in which country would you be?
44. Which political party in China was founded in 1921?
45. Who stepped down as chairman of the Central Military Commission of China in 1989?
46. The national flower of which neighbouring country is the blue poppy?
47. In terms of area, which Asian country is the largest country with only one time zone?
48. CL is the international vehicle license plate code for which neighbouring country of India?

Politics

1. In India, who headed the first Communist government that came to power through democratic means in Kerala on 5 April 1957?
2. In terms of number of members which state has the largest Vidhan Sabha with 403 members?
3. Which Indian ministry has started a quarterly newsletter called *Janjatiya Jagran* in both Hindi and English?
4. The capital of which state comes administratively under Papumpare district?
5. Who was the first person born after independence to become the Speaker of Lok Sabha?

6. Which party's electoral symbol is the same as that of George W. Bush's Republican party—the elephant?
7. Who is the youngest member of Parliament in the fourteenth Lok Sabha?
8. Who nominates the members of the Rajya Sabha?
9. Which bill can be introduced only in the Lok Sabha?
10. Who was the chairman of the Drafting Committee of the Constituent Assembly?
11. In terms of the number of electorate, which is the smallest Lok Sabha constituency in India?
12. In the fourteenth Lok Sabha, who is the leader of the House?
13. In India, who supervises the election work in a state?
14. Which vice-president of India became Rajasthan's first non-Congress chief minister in 1977?
15. Which finance minister, who later became the prime minister has presented the most budgets?
16. Who has been the only woman finance minister of India?
17. Which former prime minister is the father of the present chief minister of Karnataka?
18. Whose birth anniversary is celebrated as a day of goodwill and friendship and is marked as Sadbhavana Diwas?
19. Which former Indian Prime Minister coined the slogan 'Jai Jawan, Jai Kisan'?
20. To whom are the state governors responsible for their actions?
21. Under Article 352 of the Indian Constitution, which Fundamental Right cannot be suspended even during an Emergency?
22. Which act makes it obligatory for all public authorities to disseminate information and help those seeking information with the necessary documents?
23. Who was first person to become prime minister of India with two successive mandates?
24. The Constitution (Twenty-first Amendment) Act included which language in the Eighth Schedule of the Indian constitution in 1967?
25. Article 164 of the Indian Constitution provides for a separate minister in charge of tribal welfare in which three states?
26. Which building was the residence of the first governor general of independent India?
27. What is a list of all eligible citizens who are entitled to cast their vote in an election called?
28. Who has been the longest-serving chairman of Rajya Sabha?
29. During which two prime ministers' tenures have three motions of no-confidence been moved?
30. In 1953, who was elected President of the eighth session of the UN General Assembly?
31. In 1970, Indira Gandhi inaugurated which autonomous hill state?
32. In 1982, which party did N. T. Rama Rao form in Andhra Pradesh?
33. Which is the only Union territory to have a legislative assembly?
34. Recognising it as a terrorist organization, which Assamese party did the Government of India ban under the Unlawful Activities (Prevention) Act in 1990?
35. In 1969, which poltical party was formed under the leadership of Charu Majumdar?
36. Which party amended its Constitution in February 2003 enabling the party president to hold the post for a lifetime?
37. Who is the present general secretary of the CPI(M)?
38. Who is the only parliamentarian to have been elected from four states?

39. The first chief minister of which state is Gopinath Bordoloi?
40. Who was independent India's first education minister?
41. Who was sworn in as the fifth chief minister of Jharkhand on 18 September 2006?
42. Which Congress Lok Sabha member of Parliament is the maharaja of Gwalior?
43. The conch shell is the symbol of which state party of Orissa?
44. Who was the president of the BJP until year-end 2005?
45. Who is the constitutional head of the executive of the Indian Union?
46. Which President served as vice-chancellor of Andhra University?
47. Since 1982, Hasim Abdul Halim has been the Speaker of the legislative assembly of which state?
48. Who on 21 June 1948 was the only Indian to have been appointed governor-general of India?
49. The qualifying age for membership of which house of Indian Parliament is twenty-five years?
50. Kuppahalli Sitaramayya Sudarshan is the present sarsanghachalak or the appointed leader of which organization?

Business

1. Which finance minister presented independent India's first budget in 1947?
2. To produce telephone instruments, the Indian Telephone Industries was established in which city in 1948?
3. ESSO Standard Refining Company Ltd was merged with Lube India to form which public sector company?
4. Which bank acted as the central currency authority and banker to the government of Pakistan till 1948?
5. Which was the first ship that was built in India and was used for overseas cargo service between India and Europe?
6. In 1948 Air-India inaugurated its international operations with a weekly service from Mumbai to which European city?
7. What was represented for the first time in the new coins of independent India issued in 1950 ?
8. Shahpoorji Pallonji Mistry financed which film to help his friend and director K. Asif in 1960?
9. Which finance minister presented the first budget in the first elected Parliament in 1952?
10. In 1953 which company tied up with US-based Otis to manufacture elevators in India?
11. A part of the Indian operation of which company was taken over by the Tatas in 1954 and named Voltas?
12. In 1954 which company started to manufacture commercial vehicles in collaboration with Daimler Benz of West Germany?
13. What was formed in a joint initiative undertaken by fourteen of India's Regional Stock Exchanges (RSEs) to consolidate the regional stock markets for more efficient trading?
14. Which hotel in Delhi became the country's first five-star deluxe hotel in 1956?
15. In which year did the Indian Coinage Act introduce decimal coinage in India?
16. Which communication giant was the first to cross one million and five million customer marks in India?
17. Which company traces its roots to the old coffee houses of Italy and opened its first outlet in New Delhi in 2000?
18. Who was the first person to feature in the commemorative coins launched in 1964?

19. The first Rs 10 coin was introduced to commemorate whose birth centenary?
20. In 1970, the National Dairy Development Board initiated which operation to increase the availability of milk and milk products?
21. India's first offshore oil well was inaugurated in which place in 1974?
22. What new feature was introduced for the first time in Indian television in 1976?
23. Who has joined hands with the Archaeological Survey of India to preserve and upgrade facilities at the Taj Mahal complex in Agra?
24. Which organization built India's first indigenous aircraft carrier in 2005?
25. In 1988 who created an aviation record by flying his single-engine aircraft from London to Ahmedabad in twenty-one days?
26. What is the name of the nodal agency to undertake multimedia advertising and publicity of policies and programmes of the Government of India?
27. In 1998, who became the first industrialist to be appointed as a public nominee on the governing board of the Securities and Exchange Board of India (SEBI) by the finance ministry?
28. Dr Bindeshwar Pathak is the founder of which famous movement?
29. Who is the lifelong chairman of Institute of Rural Management, Anand?
30. The *Economist* called which institution as the most selective business school in the world?
31. Set up in 1927, which is the largest and oldest apex business organization of Indian business?
32. Which company launched 'Sagar Sammriddhi', the biggest deep-water exploration campaign ever undertaken by a single operator, anywhere in the world?
33. Which Indian business great bought a ship called Dufferin where Indians could train to become marine officers?
34. Avahan is the India AIDS initiative of which foundation?
35. Who is the first Indian finance minister to present an Outcome Budget?
36. With which particular type of product you can associate the 'Bromark' logo?
37. Which Indian management guru's last published book is *A Bias for Action*?
38. In 1991, the Government of India launched an eco-labelling scheme to increase consumer awareness. What is it known as?
39. Who was the first prime minister to serve as the finance minister of India?
40. Which famous economist who has produced pioneering studies of gender inequality, always takes care to write 'her' rather than 'him' when referring to an abstract person?
41. Which was the first Indian company to ring the Nasdaq opening bell from India, by remote control?
42. In 1991, the interim and final budgets were presented for the first time by two ministers of two different political parties. If Manmohan Singh was one of them, who was the other?
43. Confederation of Indian Industries' Trade Fair Division organizes world class international fairs under which name?
44. Only two princely states actually issued paper currency in India. If Jammu and Kashmir was one what was the other?

45. In 1912, which Indian company pioneered the eight-hour day, long before the principle had been accepted in the United States or Europe?
46. Which Indian prime minister released the first Maruti for sale?
47. Indian Railwys have several freight rate scales for parcel traffic. If Scale P represents Premium Parcel Service and Scale S represent Standard Parcel Service then what does Scale R represent?
48. Which company launched India's first private sector basic telephone network in Madhya Pradesh in 1998?
49. Which industry contributes about 31 per cent the to GDP of India?
50. Which ruler first minted the rupee, a silver coin, weighing 179 gm?

Science

1. In which Indian state is the Vikram Sarabhai Space Centre (VSSC) located?
2. Which organization has begun the development of a mission to the moon, named Chandrayaan-1?
3. What is the significance of celebrating National Science Day on 28 February every year in India?
4. Which medium-range surface-to-air missile operates in conjunction with the Rajendra surveillance and engagement radar?
5. The applied research unit of which company is known as SETLabs?
6. Who founded the Indian Statistical Institute in 1931 and also contributed prominently to newly independent India's five-year plans?
7. Who made a significant contribution as Project Director to develop India's first indigenous Satellite Launch Vehicle (SLV-III) at ISRO?
8. With support from Homi Bhabha, who set up the first Rocket Launching station (TERLS) in India at Thumba?
9. Who is the originator of the database search algorithm used in quantum computing?
10. The actual name of which space centre was Sriharikota Range?
11. Who established Navdanya, a movement for biodiversity conservation and farmers' rights?
12. What was invented by orthopedic surgeon Dr Pramod Karan Sethi in collaboration with an artisan named Ram Chandra in 1968?
13. In 2003, METSAT or Meteorological Satellite was renamed after whom?
14. Who co-discovered S-duality and proposed a successful explanation of open string tachyon condensation?
15. Which is India's short-range surface-to-air missile designed to counter a low-level attack?
16. Who played a key role in the design and construction of the 100 MW Dhruva reactor in which several new technologies were deployed on a large scale for the first time?
17. Who was the director of Bhabha Atomic Research Centre (BARC) when India carried out its first nuclear test in Pokhran in 1974?
18. Whose work on conformal gravity theory with Sir Fred Hoyle demonstrated that a synthesis can be achieved between Albert Einstein's theory of relativity and Mach's principle?
19. The telescope that is responsible for the detection of Jupiter's satellite Ganymede and rings around planet Uranus is named after whom?
20. Who currently spearheads a movement called Mission 2007:

Every Village a Knowledge Centre, in India?

21. Which Indian is one of the founders of loop quantum gravity and has a set of variables (that represent an unusual way to rewrite the metric on the three-dimensional spatial slices) named after him?
22. Who, along with his colleagues, carried out the first successful heart transplantation in India?
23. After which Indian scientist is a sub-atomic particle with integral spin, called boson, named?
24. What was the name of the first research reactor that was commissioned in BARC in 1956?
25. In 1970, which organization did the Government of India establish to monitor the quality of Ayurveda, Unani and Siddha drugs?
26. For treating which disease did WHO recommend Directly Observed Treatment, Short Course (DOTS) strategy, launched formally in India in 1997?
27. Which experimental satellite for earth observations was launched on 7 June 1979?
28. Which is India's largest research reactor and primary source of weapons-grade plutonium?
29. Who was appointed the first chairman of the Atomic Energy Commission, set up in 1948?
30. Which is India's third generation 'fire and forget' anti-tank missile that uses Imaging Infra-Red (IIR) guidance with day and night capability?

The Arts

1. In 1959, who began her career as an actress in Satyajit Ray's film *Apur Sansar* (The World of Apu)?
2. In 2006, which actress auctioned a painting titled *Ibaadat* for Rs 25 lakhs to raise money for Imran Khan's cancer hospital?
3. Which famous award, instituted in 1961, is given for the best creative literary writing by any Indian citizen in any of the languages included in the VIII Schedule of the Indian Constitution?
4. Which actress has received the coveted National Film Award for Best Actress five times?
5. In 1967 who won the Golden Bear at the International Film Festival at Berlin for his documentary *Through the Eyes of a Painter*?
6. *The Namesake*, published in 2003, is the first novel of which author?
7. Which Indian novelist played a village girl in the 1985 award-winning film *Massey Sahib*?
8. In 2005, whose painting *Kali* was sold for Rs 10 million (approximately US $ 230,000) at Saffronart's online auction?
9. On which classical dancer did Satyajit Ray direct a documentary called *Bala* in 1976?
10. In 1971, who became the first person of Indian origin to win a Booker Prize for his book *In a Free State*?
11. Who is best known for his daily one-panel comic 'pocket cartoon' series *You Said It*, which began in 1951?
12. Which Punjabi writer's novel *Pinjar* was made into a Hindi film in 2003?
13. In 2004 the US Library of Congress appointed which Indian historian as the first holder of the Kluge Chair in Countries and Cultures of the South?
14. In 1988, who became the youngest percussionist to ever be awarded the title of Padma Shri?
15. Pandit Birju Maharaj is the current head of which gharana of kathak dance in India?

16. In 1985, Prime Minister Rajiv Gandhi appointed which Indian architect as the chairman of the National Commission on Urbanization?
17. Which exponent of Hindustani music invented the mohan veena, a stringed musical instrument?
18. *My Music, My Life* is the autobiography of which famous Indian?
19. Which Indian literary organization offers the Anand Coomarswamy and Premchand fellowships?
20. In 2004, which Indian actor was awarded an honorary OBE for his contribution to the British film industry?
21. Who designed the building of the Belgium embassy in New Delhi?
22. Whose dance performance *Kalpana* took four years to be completed and later became a model for dance spectaculars?
23. Which was the first Indian cinemascope film?
24. What was the name of Aamir Khan's fictional village in the film *Lagaan*?
25. Which museum, opened in 1951, displays Mir Yousuf Ali Khan's collection?
26. Which director made *Swayamvaram*, his first full-length feature film in 1972?
27. Which statutory autonomous body was established on 23 November 1997, following a demand that government-owned broadcasters in India should be given autonomy like those in many other countries?
28. Which Indian co-composed the opening music for the Atlanta Olympics?
29. Which organization was established by the Government of India in the year 1954 by the former Union minister of education, Dr Abul Kalam Azad for development and promotion of visual and plastic arts in India?
30. Who was the first tabla player to give solo concerts?
31. Who became the first non-French artist to be awarded the Prix de la Critique in 1956 for his painting *The Village*?
32. In 1959 which Guru Dutt film became the first black and white film to be shot in cinemascope?
33. Which Indian literary figure acted in two films, *In Which Annie Gives it Those Ones* and *Massey Sahib*?
34. In 1964 who painted the *Words and Symbol* series, using geometric shapes as in tantric symbolsm?
35. Which film of 2005 is an adaptation of the 1914 Bengali novella written by Sarat Chandra Chattopadhyay?
36. The International Dolls Museum was set up in which Indian city in 1965?
37. Which famous singer made her debut in the film *Chunariya* (1948)?
38. Which famous Indian singer acted in the film *Meera* directed by Ellis R. Dungan?
39. Which Marathi poet was popularly known as Kavi Girish?
40. About the life of which musician did Gautam Ghose direct *Sange Meel Se Mulaqat* a documentary film in 1989?
41. In 1979, which film became the first Indian short film to be nominated for an Oscar?
42. In 1979 who created his *Mother Teresa* series of paintings?
43. Which playback singer, for the second time, was nominated for the prestigious Grammy Awards 2005?
44. In 1982, who drew *Double Talk* in the *Sunday Observer* and thus became India's first published woman cartoonist?

45. Which was the first full-length feature film to be released in Sanskrit in 1982?
46. Which famous singer composed music for the Marathi film *Ram Ram Pahuna*, under the name Anandghan?
47. Vikram Seth's *The Golden Gate* was published in 1988. What is special about it?
48. Who became the first Indian to be conferred the Legion d' Honneur, France's highest civilian award, in Calcutta in 1989?
49. Lata Mangeshkar use to call which famous vocalist Tapaswini?
50. Who was honoured with the Chevalier of Artists award by the French government in 1995 in recognition of his contribution to Indian cinema?
51. Who teamed up with singer Asha Bhonsle to record *Legacy*, a selection of traditional Hindustani classical compositions, in 1996?
52. Who was honoured with Japan's highest arts award, the Praemium Imperiale, in 1997 for his lifelong contribution to music?
53. In 1997 who won the Arthur C. Clarke Prize for his novel *The Calcutta Chromosome*?
54. Which poet and Dada Saheb Phalke awardee wrote the nationalist song *Ae Mere Watan ke Logon*?
55. Who won the first-ever Golden Camera Award at the Cannes Film Festival for his film *Marana Simhasanam* (Throne of Death)?
56. Which 1993 novel was the century's longest novel in English with 1,349 pages and approximately 500,000 words?
57. Who was the first Indian to be on the Oscar's jury?
58. Which place in Hyderabad boasts of the world's largest integrated film production complex?
59. Who was the first actor to be nominated to the Rajya Sabha in 1952?
60. Who was selected by the United Producers' Talent Contest and made his film debut in Chetan Anand's *Aakhri Khat* in 1966?
61. Sanjay Leela Bhansali named which film after his favourite colour?
62. For the battle sequence of which film were 2,000 camels, 4,000 horses and 8,000 troops of the Jaipur regiment of the Indian Army used?
63. Which is the oldest among the contemporary classical dance forms of India?
64. Which film won the award for the best film in the first Filmfare awards function?
65. According to the *Guinness Book of World Records*, which sitarist has the longest international career?
66. What is the claim to fame of the 1985 film *Shiva Ka Insaaf*, starring Jackie Shroff and Poonam Dhillon?
67. In Tirupati, which famous singer received the title of 'Asthaan Sangeet Vidwaan Sarloo' (court musician of the shrine)?
68. Rasipuram Krishnaswami Ayyar Narayanaswami became R.K. Narayan at whose suggestion?
69. Which recepient of the Prix de France de la Jeune Peinture and the Havana Biennale Award was appointed Curator of Rashtrapati Bhavan in New Delhi in 1972?
70. Whose stort story *Shatranj Ke Khilari* was made into a film by Satyajit Ray in 1977?

Cricket

1. When Narendra Hirwani got 16 wickets on his Test debut, six of them were stumped. Who was the wicketkeeper?
2. Which ground has hosted the most number of Test matches in India?

3. Which city has hosted the most number of Test matches in India?
4. Who was the first Indian to score a triple century in first-class cricket?
5. Among Indian players, who holds the record of scoring the slowest Test century?
6. After Sachin Tendulkar, who is the youngest Indian to play a Test match?
7. In December 1994, who was appointed as the sheriff of Mumbai?
8. Which cricket tournament in India was named after a long-time treasurer and then the president of BCCI?
9. Who is the first Indian captain to lead India in more than 10 Test wins?
10. Who is the first New Zealander to play 250 ODIs?
11. Which Indian batsman scored three successive Test centuries at Lord's?
12. From whom did Azharuddin take over as India's captain for the first time?
13. Which Indian cricketer played in the infamous 'Bodyline' series?
14. Before Virender Sehwag, who held the record of the highest Test score by an Indian?
15. With whom did Pankaj Roy put on a world record 413 runs for the opening wicket partnership against New Zealand in 1955-56?
16. Whose record did Sachin Tendulkar overtake when he became the most capped player for India?
17. Who is the only captain to lead India to 21 Test wins?
18. Who is the only Indian to take more than 500 Test wickets?
19. Among Indian wicketkeepers, who has taken the most catches?
20. Who has taken most number of wickets for India in cricket World Cup?

Sports

1. Who was independent India's first individual Olympic medallist to have created history in 1952 Helsinki Olympic Games in wrestling?
2. In which city was the first Afro–Asian Games held in 2003?
3. Which team won the inaugural National Football League in 1996-97?
4. Who is the only Indian player to score a hat-trick in the Olympics, against Australia, in 1956?
5. Who became the first Indian to reach the final of the All-England Badminton Championships in 1947?
6. Who won the first of his twelve national billiards title in 1950?
7. Sachin Nag became India's first gold medallist in the Asian games in 1952. In which event did he win the gold?
8. India became the first Asian country to reach the semi-finals of the Olympic football tournament in which year?
9. The team comprising Major Kishen Singh, Kumar Bijay Singh, Rao Raja Himmat Singh and Maharaja Sawai Mansingh won which title in France in 1957?
10. Mihir Sen and Arati Saha became the first Indian man and woman to achieve which feat in 1958 and 1959 respectively?
11. Who became the first Indian to win the men's singles title at the London Lawn Tennis Championship tournament in 1959?
12. In 1960, who became the first hockey player in the world to play in four successive Olympic games in Rome?
13. Manuel Aaron became the first Indian to secure which title in 1961?
14. Who was the captain of the In-

dian footbal team that won the gold in the Jakarta Asian games in 1962?

15. Who led the first-ever Indian expedition that scaled Mt Everest in 1965?
16. Who was declared the World professional Wrestling Champion in 1968?
17. In 1974, India refused to play the final round of the Davis Cup against which country?
18. In 1977, who won the first of her sixteen consecutive national squash titles?
19. In 1982, who won the badminton gold at the Brisbane Commonwealth games?
20. In which year did India win its last Olympic hockey gold medal?
21. The 1982 Asian Games were held chiefly in New Delhi but some of the events were also conducted in which two other cities?
22. In 1984, who became the youngest Indian chess player to secure an International Master norm?
23. In 1984, who beame the first Indian to climb Mount Everest without oxygen?
24. Who set an Olympic hockey record by scoring 16 goals in Moscow in 1980?
25. Who completed his badminton Grand Slam by winning the All-England Badminton Championship in 1980?
26. In 1958, who became the first Indian to win a world individual title in any event?
27. In 1985, who won the Arthur Walker Trophy and claimed the World Amateur Billiards Championship on debut, thereby becoming the youngest-ever champion?
28. In 1987, who swam across the English Channel recording the fastest time ever by an Asian?
29. Which sport of Indian origin was introduced in the 1990 Beijing Asian Games?
30. Who became India's second chess Grand Master in 1991?
31. In 1992, who equalled the world record for the 30 m event in the China International Archery tournament?
32. In 1994, who became the world's second-youngest (aged 12 years) girl to swim across the English Channel?
33. In 1998, who broke Milkha Singh's thirty-eight year old national record in the 400m sprint?
34. The Olympic torch came to India for the first time enroute which city in 1964?
35. In 1992, who became the first woman to captain the Indian team in the Olympics?
36. Vishwanathan Anand is the only non-Russian to win which award after Bobby Fischer?
37. Which club won forty-two consecutive matches in 1994 season to record the longest sequence of wins in Indian football history?
38. Who is the only Indian to have won the Arjuna Award (1976), Dronacharya Award (1998) and the Padma Shri (1983) for sustained excellence in sport?
39. In 1997, Mahesh Bhupati became the first Indian to win a Grand Slam doubles tournament. Who was his partner?
40. In which Asian Games did India win its first-ever gold medal in tennis by winning the team title?
41. Which team did India defeat when they won the 1975 Hockey World Cup at Kuala Lumpur?
42. Who is the first non-American to win the US National under-16 title?
43. The All-India Tennis Association has instituted which award for the Indian coaches for their outstanding services to Indian tennis?

44. Who is the first Asian to receive the UNESCO Pierre Coubertin Award?
45. Who was the first woman from India to play the LPGA Tour?
46. Who was the first Indian to achieve a WGM norm?
47. In which Olympics did India win its only hockey silver medal?
48. On 12 February 2005, who became the first Indian woman to win a WTA singles title?
49. Who was the captain of the Indian Hockey team that won its first ever Olympic gold medal at the 1928 Games in Amsterdam?
50. Who is the first Arjuna awardee in Boxing?

General

1. By which organization was the Rajiv Gandhi National Quality Award instituted in 1991, with a view to encouraging lindian manufacturing and service organizations to strive for excellence?
2. The team headed by Dr Wilbur Schramm, the well-known authority on communication, drew up the blueprint of which educational organization in India?
3. Established in 1991 in Bihar, which is the only designated protected area for Gangetic river dolphin, an endangered species?
4. How many students are selected from India every year to receive the Rhodes scholarship which enables them to study in Oxford University?
5. For the first time after 1908, which train, also the world's oldest working steam engine, rolled out on 1 February 1997 to make a trip from Delhi to Alwar?
6. In 2006, which award has been conferred on Mohan Sundara Rajan from Bangalore, Karnataka, for writing popular science books and articles, science fiction and columns in newspapers?
7. The National Institute of Fashion Technology is an autonomous body functioning under the aegis of which ministry?
8. In which year were the Mountain Railways of India inscripted into the World heritage List of UNESCO?
9. Name the luxury train which is a joint venture of the Department of Tourism, Government of india, Rajasthan Tourism Development Corporation and Indian Railways and explores the Bikaner, Shekhawati regions of Rajasthan?
10. On 21 September 1992, with which other organization was an agreement to implement the First Phase of National AIDS Control Programme signed?
11. The recruitments for services in the post of Assisstant Divisional Medical Officers in the railway are done by the UPSC through which examinations?
12. Prime Minister Manmohan Singh flagged off a bus service connecting the Pakistani city of Muzaffarabad to which Indian city for the first time in fifty-seven years, on 7 April 2005?
13. The analgesic drug Diclofenac was identified as the most probable cause of the decline of which bird population when an investigation was initiated in the issue in 2000?
14. Who conducts the TOEFL examinations?
15. The Deccan Odyssey Train Service which startred in 2004, was a joint venture of Indian Railway, Maharashtra Tourism Development Corporation and which group of hotels?
16. The Delhi Transport Corporation started a bus service from Delhi to which Pakistani city on 11 July 2003?

17. A generous grant from New Zealand under which plan made it possible to lay the foundation stone of the All India Institute of Medical Sciences (AIIMS) in 1952?
18. The Government of India started the National Leprosy Control Programme in 1955, based on which form of treatment, through vertical units, implementing survey education and treatment activities?
19. The Indian Space Research Organization executes its programmes under which Department of the Indian Government set up in June 1972?
20. The National Institute of Fashion Technology has seven professionally managed centres across the country. Six of them are in Mumbai, Kolkata, Hyderabad, Chennai, Bangalore and New Delhi. Where is the seventh?
21. The ministry of tribal affairs was constituted in October of 1999, by the bifurcation of which ministry?
22. The GRE Subject Tests gauge undergraduate achievement in how many specific fields of study?
23. The Sardar Sarovar River Valley Project in Maharashtra is being constructed on which river?
24. When IIMC began functioning on 17 August 1965, under which ministry of India was it designated as a department?
25. The Catholic Bishops' Conference of India set up which institution in 1969 to develop scholarship and professionalism in media?
26. The Universal Immunization Programme, started in 1985 to provide universal coverage to infants and pregnant women with immunization against identified vaccine-preventable diseases, was expanded and strengthened in 1992-93 into which project?
27. On the recommendations of the B. C. Roy Committee, the remnants of the Indian Army Medical Corps was amalgamated into one unit to create what?
28. What is the department of AYUSH under the ministry of health and family welfare under the Government of India?
29. Which test conducted by ETS measures verbal reasoning, quantitative reasoning, critical thinking, and analytical writing skills that have been acquired over a long period of time and that are not related to any specific field of study?
30. What is the name of the Apex institute under the National Programme for Control of Bindness and Eye Awareness, at the tertiary level of Opthalmic Care?
31. What was the 'Ecole de Medicine de Pondicherry' renamed as on 13 July 1964?
32. What is the name of the award that can be conferred on a host of Bodies and individuals for their outstanding achievements in promoting the Official Language Policy of the government?
33. What is the name of the central nodal agency of the Government of India for the control and prevention of vector-borne diseases?
34. What is the name of the centrally sponsored scheme launched in 1992 which provides financial and technical support to major elephant-bearing states in the country?
35. What is the name of the project in Uttar Pradesh, which is a major initiative taken for reorienting and revitalizing the family planning services in the state?
36. Which Institute was established on 30 April 1928, as a profes-

sional body of Banks and Financial Institutions licensed under the provisions of Section 26 of the Indian Companies Act 1913?

37. What is the name of the Tiger Reserve in Madhya Pradesh with the year of notification as 1999-2000?
38. What is the name of the train to Lahore in Pakistan which starts from Attari?
39. The National Eligibility Test (NET) is conducted by National Educational Testing Bureau of University Grants Commission (UGC) in Humanities (including languages), Social Sciences, Forensic Science, Environmental Sciences, Computer Science and Application and which other field?
40. Which award is given for best reporting on women in Panchayati Raj?
41. Who administers the Programmes offered by the National Institute of Fashion Technology?
42. Which award is given to an institution which has done commendable work to promote education among educationally backward minorities?
43. Which award was instituted in 1965 and awarded for 2003 to the Prime Minister of Singapore Goh Chok Tong?
44. Which award, first given in 2003, is given by the Ministry of Environment and Forests for significant contribution in the field of Wildlife Protection, which is recognized as having shown exemplary courage or valour or having done exemplary work for protection of wildlife in the country?
45. Who is the president of the Indian Council of Forestry Research and Education (ICFRE) in Dehradun?
46. Which award, into its twenty-first edition, was conferred, for 2005, on lyricist Javed Akhtar and is to be given out on 31 October 2006 by Sonia Gandhi?
47. Which dam in India has the distinction of being the highest concrete gravity dam in Asia and the second highest in the world?
48. Which department under the ministry of environment and forests deals with all work relating to the Vienna Convention for the Protection of the Ozone Layer and the Montreal Protocol for the phasing out of Ozone Depleting Substances?
49. Birla Institute of Technology and Science (BITS) are at present are located at Pilani, Goa and Dubai. Where is the new BITS campus coming up?
50. The name Indian Institute of Technology was adopted before the formal inauguration of the first IIT by whom?
51. Which establishment was started by the Atomic Energy Commission on 3 January 1954, and renamed by Prime Minister Indira Gandhi as the Bhabha Atomic Research Centre on 12 January 1967 as fitting tribute to Dr Homi Bhabha?
52. Which Indian Institute of Technology began functioning in the borrowed building of Harcourt Butler Technological Institute in 1959?
53. Which Indian organization was created on 1 September 1956, with the objective of spreading life insurance more widely and in particular to the rural areas with a view to reach all insurable people in the country?
54. For general candidates what is the restriction on number of attempts for appearing in the Civil Service examinations?
55. Which luxury train, rated as one of the ten best in the world, made its inaugural trip on 26

January 1982, as a unique holiday concept hauled by a steam engine?

56. Where was the first Indian Institute of Technology set up in India in 1950?
57. Which organization in India has the motto 'Industry Impartiality Integrity'?
58. Which project has been constructed primarily with a view to preserve and maintain Kolkata port and is also the largest of its kind in India?
59. When was the National Defence Academy formally inaugurated?
60. Which project, initiated in November 1999 by the ministry of environment and forests in collaboration with the United Nations Development Programme, is being implemented in ten coastal states with special emphasis in Orissa?

Answers

Decades: 1947–1956

1. Rashtrapati Bhavan premises
2. 1950
3. Sukumar Sen
4. Nirad C. Chaudhuri
5. Bharat Petroleum
6. Imperial Bank
7. Mahatma Gandhi
8. Ravi Shankar
9. 1951
10. Mumbai

Decades: 1957–1966

1. Kandla port
2. G. Sankara Kurup
3. Reita Faria
4. Kolkata (then Calcutta)
5. *Economic Times*
6. Bombay State
7. 1958
8. Gangtok
9. *Charulata*
10. 1961

Decades: 1967–1976

1. Lion
2. Ashapurna Devi
3. Rohini (RH-75)
4. Dr Hargovind Khurana
5. Devika Rani Roerich
6. Haryana
7. Ela Bhatt
8. M.S. Subbulakshmi
9. Smallpox
10. Socialist and Secular

Decades: 1977–1986

1. Janata Party
2. Atal Bihari Vajpayee
3. The Indian Coast Guard
4. Mother Teresa
5. *Midnight's Children*
6. Suzuki Motor Company
7. *Gandhi*
8. R.K. Laxman
9. Edinburgh Commonwealth Games
10. Gaini Zail Singh

Decades: 1987–1996

1. Maldives
2. *The Satanic Verses*
3. Meera Sahib Fatima Beevi
4. Khan Abdul Ghaffar Khan
5. CNN
6. Maharashtra
7. Vishwa Mohan Bhatt
8. J.R.D. Tata
9. New Delhi–Bhopal Shatabdi Express
10. Soli Jehangir Sorabjee

States and Union Territories

1. West Bengal
2. Arunachal Pradesh
3. Pondicherry
4. Guwahati High Court

5. Sikkim
6. Mizoram
7. Lakshadweep
8. Gujarat
9. Andaman and Nicobar Islands
10. Kerala
11. State of Andhra
12. Rajasthan
13. Andhra Pradesh
14. Madhya Pradesh
15. Goa
16. Leh airport
17. Mayawati
18. Uttar Pradesh
19. Jammu and Kashmir
20. Manipur
21. Sikkim
22. Arunachal Pradesh
23. Madhya Pradesh
24. Shri Ajit Kumar Jogi
25. Dr Raman Singh
26. Assam
27. Narendra Modi
28. Shillong
29. J. Jayalalithaa
30. Jammu and Kashmir
31. Patiala
32. Simla
33. Dadra and Nagar Haveli
34. Rajasthan
35. Dadra and Nagar Haveli
36. Shibu Soren
37. Madu Koda
38. Pondicherry
39. Goa
40. Tripura
41. Bengali
42. Thailand
43. Meghalaya
44. Manipur
45. Mizoram
46. English
47. Biju Patnaik
48. Bauxite
49. Indian National Congress
50. Himachal Pradesh
51. Karnataka
52. Karnataka
53. Chandigarh
54. MGR—M.G. Ramachandran
55. Daman and Diu
56. Portugal
57. Om Prakash Chautala
58. Haryana
59. Jammu and Kashmir
60. Lt Governor
61. Kerala
62. The Rock Garden
63. Eighteen
64. Lok Jan Shakti Party
65. Maharashtra
66. Chhatrapati Shivaji Terminus
67. Uttaranchal
68. Dehradun
69. Delhi High Court
70. Bombay High Court

Neighbouring Countries

1. Sri Lanka
2. Nil Mahanel (Botanical name—*Nympheae Stelleta*)
3. Begum Khaleda Zia
4. Hamid Karzai
5. Pakistan
6. Ayub Khan
7. China
8. Bhutan
9. Ngultrum (Nu)
10. Maldives
11. Nepal
12. People's Republic of China
13. Aung San Suu Kyi
14. U. Thant
15. Myanmar
16. Bangladesh
17. Afghanistan
18. Bengali
19. *The English Patient*
20. Chandrika Kumaratunga
21. Awami League
22. Awami League
23. Professor Abdus Salam
24. Bangladesh
25. Liberation Tigers of Tamil Eelam

26. People's Republic of China
27. Afghanistan
28. Afghanistan
29. Maldives
30. People's Republic of China
31. G.P. Koirala
32. Nepal's Sherpa Tenzing Norgay
33. Nepali Congress Party
34. Pakistan
35. Buddhism
36. Myanmar
37. 1981
38. Gao Xingjian
39. Hong Kong
40. Kar Wai Wong
41. Myanmar
42. Bangladesh
43. Nepal
44. The Communist Party of China
45. Deng Xiaoping
46. Bhutan
47. China
48. Sri Lanka

Politics

1. E.M.S. Namboodiripad
2. Uttar Pradesh
3. Ministry of tribal affairs
4. Arunachal Pradesh
5. G.M.C. Balayogi
6. Bahujan Samaj Party
7. Sachin Pilot
8. President
9. Money Bill
10. B.R. Ambedkar
11. Lakshadweep
12. Pranab Mukherjee
13. The Chief Electoral Officer (CEO)
14. Bhairon Singh Shekhawat
15. Morarji Desai
16. Indira Gandhi
17. H.D. Devegowda
18. Rajiv Gandhi
19. Lal Bahadur Shastri
20. The President
21. Protection of Life and Personal Liberty
22. Right to Information Act
23. Jawaharlal Nehru
24. Sindhi
25. Bihar, Orissa and Madhya Pradesh
26. Rashtrapati Bhawan
27. Electoral roll
28. Dr S. Radhakrishnan
29. Lal Bahadur Shastri and P. V. Narasimha Rao
30. Vijaya Lakshmi Pandit
31. Meghalaya
32. Telugu Desam Party
33. Pondicherry
34. United Liberation Front of Assam (ULFA)
35. Communist Party Marxist–Leninist
36. Rashtriya Janata Dal
37. Prakash Karat
38. Atal Bihari Vajpayee
39. Assam
40. Abul Kalam Azad
41. Madhu Koda
42. Jyotiraditya Scindia
43. Biju Janata Dal
44. L.K. Advani
45. The President
46. S. Radhakrishnan
47. West Bengal
48. C. Rajagopalachari
49. Lok Sabha
50. Rashtriya Swayamsevak Sangh

Business

1. R.K. Shanmukham Chetty
2. Bangalore
3. HPCL
4. The Reserve Bank of India
5. S.S. *Jala Usha*
6. London
7. The Lion Capital
8. *Mughal-e-Azam*
9. C.D. Deshmukh
10. Mahindra and Mahindra
11. Volkart Brothers
12. Telco
13. The Inter-connected Stock Exchange of India Ltd (ISE)
14. Ashoka Hotel

15. 1957
16. Airtel
17. Barista
18. Jawaharlal Nehru
19. Mahatma Gandhi
20. Operation Flood
21. Gulf of Cambay
22. Commercial advertisements
23. The Taj Group of Hotels
24. Cochin Shipyard Limited
25. Vijaypat Singhania
26. The Directorate of Audio Visual Publicity
27. Kumar Mangalam Birla
28. Sulabh Sanitation Movement
29. Dr Vergese Kurien
30. IIM, Ahmedabad
31. FICCI
32. ONGC
33. Walchand Hirachand
34. Bill and Melinda Gates Foundation
35. P. Chidambaram
36. Broiler Chicken, it is the All-India Broiler Farmers Marketing Cooperative's logo
37. Sumantra Ghoshal
38. Ecomark
39. Jawaharlal Nehru
40. Amartya Sen
41. Infosys
42. Yashwant Sinha
43. Made in India
44. Hyderabad
45. Tata Steel
46. Indira Gandhi
47. Rajdhani Parcel Service
48. Bharati Telenet
49. Agriculture
50. Sher Shah Suri

Science

1. Kerala
2. Indian Space Research Organization (ISRO)
3. The day on which Sir C.V. Raman discovered what came to be called the Raman effect
4. Akash
5. Infosys Technologies Ltd
6. P.C. Mahalanobis
7. A.P.J. Abdul Kalam
8. Vikram Sarabhai
9. Lov Grover
10. The Satish Dhawan Space Centre (SDSC)
11. Vandana Shiva
12. Jaipur Foot
13. Kalpana Chawla
14. Ashok Sen
15. Trishul
16. Anil Kakodkar
17. Raja Ramanna
18. J.V. Narlikar
19. Vainu Bappu
20. M.S. Swaminathan
21. Abhay Ashtekar
22. Dr S. Venugopal
23. Satyendra Nath Bose
24. Apsara
25. Pharmaceutical Laboratory of Indian Medicine (PLIM)
26. Tuberculosis
27. Bhaskara-I
28. Dhruva reactor
29. Dr Homi Jehangir Bhabha
30. Nag

The Arts

1. Sharmila Tagore
2. Sushmita Sen
3. Jnanpith Award
4. Shabana Azmi
5. M.F. Husain
6. Jhumpa Lahiri
7. Arundhati Roy
8. Tyeb Mehta
9. Balasaraswathi
10. V.S. Naipaul
11. R.K. Laxman
12. Amrita Pritam
13. Romila Thapar
14. Zakir Hussain
15. Lucknow
16. Charles Correa
17. Pandit Vishwa Mohan Bhatt
18. Ravi Shankar

19. Sahitya Akademi
20. Om Puri
21. Satish Gujral
22. Uday Shankar
23. *Kagaz ke Phool*
24. Champaner
25. Salar Jung Museum
26. Adoor Gopalakrishnan
27. Prasar Bharati
28. Ustad Zakir Hussain
29. Lalit Kala Academy
30. Alla Rakha Khan
31. S.H. Raza
32. *Kagaz Ke Phool*
33. Arundhati Roy
34. K.C.S. Paniker
35. *Parineeta*
36. Delhi
37. Asha Bhosle
38. M.S. Subbulakshmi
39. Shanker Keshav Kanetkar
40. Ustad Bismillah Khan
41. *Encounter With Faces*
42. M.F. Hussain
43. Asha Bhonsle
44. Manjula Padmanabhan
45. *Adi Sankaracharya*
46. Lata Mangeshkar
47. It's a novel in verse
48. Satyajit Ray
49. M.S. Subbulakshmi
50. Sivaji Ganeshan
51. Ali Akbar Khan
52. Ravi Shankar
53. Amitav Ghosh
54. Kavi Pradip
55. Murali Nayar
56. *A Suitable Boy*
57. Bhanu Athaiya
58. Ramoji Film City
59. Prithviraj Kapoor
60. Rajesh Khanna
61. *Black*
62. *Mughal-e-Azam*
63. Bharatanatyam
64. *Do Bigha Zameen*
65. Ravi Shankar
66. First Hindi 3-D film
67. Lata Mangeshkar
68. Graham Greene
69. Jogen Choudhury
70. Munshi Premchand

Cricket

1. Kiran More
2. Eden Gardens
3. Mumbai
4. Vijay Hazare
5. Sanjay Manjrekar
6. Piyush Chawla
7. Sunil Gavaskar
8. Zal Irani Cup
9. M. Azharuddin
10. Chris Harris
11. Dilip Vengsarkar
12. Krishnamachary Srikkanth
13. Iftikar Ali Khan Pataudi (Pataudi Sr)
14. V.V.S. Laxman
15. Vinoo Mankad
16. Kapil Dev
17. Sourav Ganguly
18. Anil Kumble
19. Syed Kirmani
20. Javagal Srinath

Sports

1. Kashava Yadav
2. Hyderabad
3. JCT Mills
4. Neville D'Souza
5. Prakash Nath
6. Wilson Jones
7. 100m freestyle in swimming
8. 1956
9. World Cup Polo
10. Swim the English Channel
11. Ramanathan Krishnan
12. Leslie Claudius
13. International Master (Chess)
14. Chuni Goswami
15. Commander M.S. Kohli
16. Dara Singh
17. South Africa

18. Bhuvaneshwari Kumari
19. Syed Modi
20. 1980, Moscow
21. Bombay and Jaipur
22. Vishwanathan Anand
23. Phu Dorjee
24. Surinder Singh Sodhi
25. Prakash Padukone
26. Wilson Jones
27. Geet Sethi
28. Anita Sood
29. Kabaddi
30. Dibyendu Barua
31. Limba Ram
32. Rupali Ramdas Repale
33. Paramjit Singh
34. Tokyo
35. Shiny Wilson
36. Chess Oscar
37. Mohun Bagan
38. Bahadur Shah (Shotput)
39. Rika Hiraki
40. Hiroshima, 1994
41. Pakistan
42. Ramesh Krishnan
43. Dilip Bose Award
44. Vijay Amritraj
45. Simi Mehra
46. Bhagyashree Thipsey
47. Rome 1960
48. Sania Mirza
49. Jaipal Singh
50. Buddy D'souza

General

1. Bureau of Indian Standards
2. The Indian Institute of Mass Communication
3. Vikramshila Gangetic Dolphin Sanctuary
4. Six
5. The Fairy Queen
6. National Award for Outstanding Efforts in Science Communication through Books and Magazines
7. Ministry of textiles, Government of India
8. 1999
9. Heritage on Wheels
10. The World Bank
11. The Combined Medical Services Examination
12. Srinagar
13. Vulture
14. Educational Testing Service
15. The Taj Group of Hotels
16. Lahore
17. Colombo Plan
18. Dapsone domiciliary Treatment
19. Department of Space
20. Gandhinagar
21. Ministry of Social Justice and Empowerment
22. Eight
23. Narmada
24. Ministry of Information and Broadcasting, Government of India.
25. Xavier Institute of Communications
26. Child Survival and Safe Motherhood Project
27. The Armed Forces Medical College
28. The Depatment of Ayurveda, Yoga and Naturopathy, Unani, Siddha and Homoeopathy
29. GRE or Graduate Record Examinations General Tests.
30. Dr R. P. Centre in the All India Institute of Medical Sciences, New Delhi
31. Jawaharlal Institute of Post-graduate Medical Education and Research (JIPMER)
32. Indira Gandhi Rajbhasha Awards
33. Directorate of National Vector Borne Disease Control Programme
34. Project Elephant (PE)
35. The Innovations in Family Planning Services
36. Indian Institute of Banking and Finance
37. Bori, Satpura Panchmarhi

38. Samjhauta Express
39. Electronic Science
40. Sarojini Naidu Award
41. Academic Standards Committee
42. Maulana Abul Kalam Azad Literacy Award
43. Jawaharlal Nehru Award for International Understanding
44. The Amrita Devi Bishnoi Wildlife Protection Award
45. The minister of environment and forests.
46. Indira Gandhi Award for National Integration
47. The Bhakra dam, across the river Sutlej
48. The Ozone Cell Directorate
49. Hyderabad
50. Maulana Abul Kalam Azad
51. Atomic Energy Establishment, Trombay (AEET)
52. IIT Kanpur
53. The Life Insurance Corporation of India
54. Four
55. Palace on Wheels
56. Hijli, Kharagpur, in Eastern India
57. The Central Bureau of Investigation (CBI)
58. The Farakka Barrage Project
59. 16 January 1955
60. Sea Turtle Conservation Project

Index